THE GUINNESS
WHO'S WHO OF

COUNTRY MUSIC

General Editor: Colin Larkin

Introduction by Peter Doggett

GUINNESS PUBLISHING

Dedicated to Clarence White and Gram Parsons

First published in 1993 by
GUINNESS PUBLISHING LTD
33 London Road, Enfield, Middlesex EN2 6DJ, England

GUINNESS is a registered trademark of Guinness Publishing Ltd

British Library Cataloguing-in-Publication data
A catalogue record for this book is available from the British Library

ISBN 0-85112-726-6

Conceived, designed, edited and produced by
SQUARE ONE BOOKS LTD
Iron Bridge House, 3 Bridge Approach, Chalk Farm, London NW1 8BD
Editor and Designer: Colin Larkin
Picture Editors: Colin Larkin and John Martland
Editorial and production assistant: Susan Pipe
Special thanks to
Peter Doggett, Hugh T. Wilson, Spencer Leigh, John Tobler,
David Japp, John Reiss, David Roberts, Sarah Silvé, John Eley and Guy at L&S
Logo concept: Darren Perry

This book has been produced on Apple Macintosh computers
using Quark Xpress and Microsoft Word
Image set by L & S Communications Ltd

Printed and bound in Great Britain by The Bath Press

EDITORS NOTE

The Guinness Who's Who Of Country Music forms a part of the multi-volume Guinness Encyclopedia Of Popular Music. A further 16 specialist single volumes are planned in the near future.

Also available:
The Guinness Who's Who Of Indie And New Wave Music.
The Guinness Who's Who Of Heavy Metal.
The Guinness Who's Who Of Sixties Music.
The Guinness Who's Who Of Jazz.
The Guinness Who's Who Of Seventies Music.
The Guinnness Who's Who Of Blues.

Country music is presently enjoying an unprecedented boom. The phenomenal success of Garth Brooks and to a lesser degree Billy Ray Cyrus has opened up the country frontier to many more listeners, particularly amongst the under 30s. The boom started in recent years with the broad appeal of artists such as Clint Black, Mary-Chapin Carpenter and Joe Ely. They were bracketed as 'new country', (effectively post Sweetheart Of The Rodeo). That influential album by the Byrds in 1968 made country music acceptable to a much wider and younger audience. Gram Parsons' involvement with the band led to him becoming as important a figure in the genre, as Hank Williams had been three decades earlier.
After great debate, we decided not to include bands like the Byrds, the Eagles and Poco. They rightfully appear in other volumes in the series, but we felt that they are primarily known as rock bands. Similarly the Nitty Gritty Dirt Band and Alabama are included because they have maintained a purer country

path. Further discussion on this subject is welcomed by the editor under the subject of: When is a country/rock band not a country band? It may be that the consensus argues that the Flying Burrito Brothers should be in. I will happily bow to that suggestion. In selecting entries for this single volume we have attempted to include as many artists as space would allow. Further suggestions and additions for the next edition will be considered by writing to the Editor.

In the preparation of this work contributions were received from Spencer Leigh, Hugh T. Wilson, Peter Doggett, Colin Larkin, Johnny Rogan, John Tobler, Dave Laing, Jeff Tamarkin, Alan Clayson and Brian Hogg. Spencer Leigh and Hugh T. Wilson were responsible for the majority of the entries.

Photographic acknowledgements: All the photographs in this volume were supplied by Tony Gale of Pictorial Press except for those on pages 25, 31, 52, 59, 79, 117, 120, 129, 141, 168, 202, 207, 251, 253, 263, 269, 298, 299, 368 and 472 which were supplied by Lynda Morrison and John Tobler.

I would like to thank, in addition to Spencer and Hugh, Peter Doggett for looking over the final text and writing the introduction under such pressure. His years as an Editor have taught him all about deadlines. To John Martland who joined us at a very difficult time and added great enthusiasm to the project.
To Susan Pipe for her now familiar super-efficiency in putting it all together at the end. To John Reiss, David Japp and the legendary

4

Freddy for making the working environment
that much more secure. To Mark Cohen,
always the vital link in the chain. To David
Roberts, Sallie Collins and Sarah Silvé for
their production work and for Donald
McFarlan's receptive eardrum. Finally to
Laura, Ben, Tom, Dan and Goldie, who can
begin to see light at the end of a previously
endless tunnel and no longer have to listen to
cheatin' songs.

Colin Larkin, February 1993

INTRODUCTION

'What Is Soul?' asked Ben E. King in a 1967 hit, and it's a question that could be asked of every musical genre. Everyone has their own private vision of what makes up country, but although most of them overlap, few of them are identical.

Like the nation which spawned it, country music is broad and deep. It can encompass the hillbilly laments of Hank Williams; the mellifluous tones of Jim Reeves; the feminism of k.d. lang; the cowboy ballads of Gene Autry; the mountain music of Bill Monroe; the energetic pop of Garth Brooks; the outlaw imagery of Waylon Jennings; the traditional Irish songs of Daniel O'Donnell; the honky-tonk anthems of Lefty Frizzell; even the affectionate mimicry of the Rolling Stones. All those artists have performed music they would class as country; but many of them - the Stones, Brooks, lang, O'Donnell, even Reeves - have been attacked by purists of varying opinions for perverting the soul of *real* country music.

This tension between purity and miscegenation is as strong as any similar argument along racial lines. There have been periods when sections of the industry have been accused of selling out their principles, and the basic country sound, to the money-men of Hollywood, New York, or anywhere else where the sound of cascading dollar bills means more than a fiddle or a steel guitar.

In the mid-70s, artists like John Denver and Olivia Newton-John scooped up prestigious awards for records that bore no resemblance to the tradition of Hank Williams or George Jones. Some established performers were so horrified that they formed a breakaway organisation to challenge the establishment's desire to modernise the country industry. But that was a storm in a teacup compared to the *Urban Cowboy* disaster of the early 80s. The film, which starred John Travolta, catapulted country into the mainstream, but at the expense of everything that its traditional performers valued. It provoked a run on western-style clothing and cowboy hats, but saw country's traditional instruments buried beneath saccharin Hollywood pop arrangements. The inclusion of such blatantly non-country performers as Joe Walsh and Boz Scaggs on the soundtrack highlighted the extent of the betrayal.

More recently, the same debate has raged again, thanks to the achievements of Garth Brooks. Garth was raised on a mix of AOR stadium rock, singer-songwriters and honky-tonk country, and those influences have been blended into a crossover style that has made country the most vital commercial force in American music. As usual, the purists are appalled, while the stars rake in the money. It's an argument that won't be settled for years: at the time of writing, country is perched precariously between transforming America in its own image, and sacrificing its soul to Hollywood, one more time. By the mid-to-late 90s, we'll know whether Garth Brooks was John the Baptist, or the devil in disguise.

Despite its claims to a tradition stretching back over the centuries, the modern genre of country music is a comparatively recent invention. In 1944, *Billboard* magazine made its first attempt to sample the tastes of white people in the southern states by introducing a new chart - the Most Played Juke Box Folk

Records. Apart from a brief flirtation with 'hillbilly' in 1946/47, they retained the folk reference until the end of the decade, when it finally gave way to 'country & western'. That's what outsiders still call the music in Britain - though in the USA the 'western' was dropped as early as 1962, when the *Billboard* chart began to list the Hot Country Singles. Mention 'country & western' in the States, and you'll be regarded like a Japanese soldier marooned on a Pacific island who hasn't heard that World War II is over.

The difficulty in finding a title, and a definition, for country music stems from its confused origins. What we know as country wasn't one distinct form, but a cross-pollination of several - mostly rooted in the southern USA, it's true, but also tapping influences from California and Mexico.

It's become a cliché to call country the white man's blues - the sound of people trapped on the land or shunted into a big city ghetto. As with every generalisation, there's an element of truth here, not least because country and blues were linked more closely in the south than purists of either style often care to acknowledge. But the image of an entire under-class of American whites sharing a common musical voice is inaccurate, no matter how tempting it sounds.

The roots of country are more tangled than that. You can take musical fundamentalism too far and trace every style back to the Garden of Eden; but it's certainly true that one vital strand of modern country music came from the original emigrants from the British Isles. They carried traditional folk songs across the Atlantic - sagas passed down the generations, celebrations of the seasons, moral tales about sex, death and religion. In parts of the south, notably the Kentucky mountains, these folk songs survived almost unchanged into the 20th century. Performed with accompaniment from stringed instruments, this heritage of music led to what we know today as bluegrass - itself a refinement of the string band tradition you which can be traced right across the south.

Despite the stereotyped portrayal of all southern whites as rednecks, eager to form local chapters of the Ku Klux Klan, there was far more integration between black and white

music in the States than might be imagined. Like the blues, pre-country music moved from the land into the town. There it found an audience, and the gradual transformation from community singing to commercial entertainment altered the nature of the music.

In the 20th century, certainly, mainstream country music has always been oriented towards a paying audience - which puts paid to any romantic delusions of 'authenticity'. While strands of what became country music - like the white gospel tradition and mountain music - retained their isolation from the marketplace, the forerunners of today's country stars were every bit as concerned about their public reception as the superstars of the 90s.

Hence was born the enduring vision of country as something which would unite a community. Whereas rock stars continually highlight the gap between them and their audience, country performers can never forget that they are their fans' representatives in heaven. It's commercial suicide for country singers to ignore their fans: they can show off their wealth - in fact, it's expected of them - but they must never let slip that they feel superior to their audience. That mixture of humility and pride is essential to the country image, and it carries over to the music, keeping its spontaneity and excitement within acceptable boundaries. Sinners are forgiven for their drinking, adultery or inability to turn up for the show on time, but arrogance is a mortal sin.

Arrogance doesn't seem to have troubled the 19th century originators of American 'folk' or 'country'. While the mountain music tradition of string bands kept the British and Irish tunes alive, fiddlers held good-natured 'contests' to determine who was the most dextrous, and vocalists shared harmonies on gospel material reworked from ancient hymns. The banjo crossed over from black music to white in the 1860s, followed 30 years later by the guitar, again transplanted from blues performers.

Musicians had always been part of the medicine shows which crossed the south, offering entertainment, salvation and physical transformation to their audiences. Musicians like Fiddlin' John Carson came from this background, while another pioneering figure, Vernon Dalhart, introduced the Tin Pan Alley pop of New York to the traditional sound.

By the early 20s, the primitive recording industry was ready to tackle 'folk' performers. Eck Robertson's 'Sally Goodin'/'Arkansas Traveller' has claims to being the first country record; a year later, Ralph Peer of OKeh Records reluctantly cut a disc with Fiddlin' John Carson, whose voice he described as 'pluperfect awful'. But the record sold, and by 1927 Peer had travelled to Bristol, on the Tennessee/Virginia border, unearthing local talent for Victor Records.

The 'Bristol Sessions', as they're known, marked the recording debut of two acts who inspired much of what followed - the gospel-flavoured Carter Family, a vocal trio who created a country music dynasty which is continued today by Johnny Cash, Rosanne Cash and Carlene Carter; and the Singing Brakeman, Jimmie Rodgers, who mixed blues, jazz, cowboy songs, pop and folk, and became one of the Fathers of country music. Of course, he thought he was a pop singer, but that's another story. Just as the Carters' harmonies and repertoire still inspire acoustic groups today, so Rodgers' blend of styles, and his swagger as a performer, set the mould for later country stars.

The great depression of the late 20s and early 30s crushed the market for records, leaving radio as the most important influence on the fledgling country scene. The *Grand Ole Opry* wasn't the first or (originally) the most popular of the radio showcases for 'folk' performers, but it proved the most durable, and has rewritten country history in its wake. DeFord Bailey became the first black country star in the 30s; gradually, the *Opry* shed its string bands and took on solo performers, and by the end of the decade the time was ripe for Roy Acuff to take the *Opry* stage, where he remained a regular until 1992.

Other traditions also flourished. The slide guitar - one more gift from the blues scene - appeared in the late 20s, and soon metamorphosed into the dobro, widening the instrumental palette. In the early 30s, the Delmores inaugurated the tradition of 'brother' acts, opening the path for the Louvins, the Monroes, the Wilburns and the Everlys to follow. And Woody Guthrie's songs of American history and working life overcame all genre boundaries to invest country with a taste for social commentary.

The southern States weren't the only originators of what was now called 'hillbilly' or - at last - 'country' music. In California, Hollywood produced western movies which immortalised the singing cowboy. Real cowboys sang around the campfire, but only to their horses and cows. Film cowboys like Gene Autry, Roy Rogers and Tex Ritter sang to movie audiences around the world. Ironically, the film songs bore little relation to real cowboy tunes, coming instead from Tin Pan Alley music factories. But the image stuck, and helped contribute the 'western' to 'country & western' - at least in British eyes.

In the States, meanwhile, the 'western' came from western swing, a dazzling blend of dixieland jazz, polkas and Texas country music. Bob Wills And His Texas Playboys were the pioneers here, though their style rubbed off on generations of Texas performers, and survives intact with Asleep At The Wheel.

A thousand miles away, Bill Monroe was conceiving bluegrass - taking the old string band songs, building precise vocal harmony arrangements around them, and playing them on the fiddle, the banjo and the mandolin, with the guitar in support. The music he created in the 40s, originally with sidemen like Lester Flatt and Earl Scruggs, has since become an industry. It's been updated (as 'newgrass') and sometimes assimilated into the country mainstream (by Ricky Skaggs, in particular) but in its natural state, it remains effectively unchanged.

The biggest shift in country between 1945 and 1960 was the sweeping popularity of honky-tonk music - a term taken from bars in Texas towns, which were regarded lovingly as hotbeds of beer, lust and fistfights. Forced to use electric instruments to be heard above the drunken babble of the customers, the original honky-tonk performers fashioned a raw and ready sound that took bar-room life as its subject. Ernest Tubb exposed honky-tonk to the outside world, while artists like Merle Travis and Little Jimmy Dickens also carried the good news. But it took Hank Williams and Lefty Frizzell, two of country's greatest innovators and imbibers, to transform the honky-tonk sound into an art-form.

Forty years after his death, Williams is still regarded as the one most important figure in the history of country music. He drank, took drugs, womanised, and wrote (often with uncredited help) 20 or so of the most frequently recorded songs of the post-war era. Pop artists in New York covered Hank's hits, while scores of performers used his self-destructive career as a roadmap. When he died on New Year's Day 1953, prematurely aged by years of one-night-stands, he'd marked out the course for every subsequent generation to follow.

Lefty Frizzell, another premature casualty, took over Hank's mantle, before he too was supplanted by Webb Pierce, Ray Price and eventually George Jones. George dabbled with rockabilly under a pseudonym before returning to the strict path of honky-tonk righteousness, and it's *de rigeur* for every Nashville star to bow at the mention of his name. His mournful vocalising and remarkable phrasing could be classed as 'soul' under any other banner but country.

The drunken path of honky-tonk was interrupted in the mid-50s by the upstart rock 'n' roll - though its country cousin was rockabilly, which added a frenetic backbeat to a blend of honky-tonk, western swing and even a little bluegrass. At first, the country establishment took rockabilly on board as another shortlived dance craze, like the one which had seen Hank Snow record 'Rhumba Boogie' back in 1951. Then it came to be seen as more of a threat, and for more than a decade anyone with rock 'n' roll pretensions was treated with grave suspicion by the country audience. It was only in the late 60s that rockabilly pioneers like Carl Perkins, Jerry Lee Lewis and even Elvis Presley were recognised as country gentlemen at heart.

While rock 'n' roll briefly overturned the music scene, country indulged a brief flirtation with 'Americana' thanks to historical songs by the likes of Johnny Horton and Jimmy Driftwood, and then took a decisive

step towards the middle-of-the-road. Maybe they were ashamed of their music's hillbilly origins, but in the early 60s a group of country stars, headed by producer/guitarist Chet Atkins, inaugurated the 'Nashville Sound', which entailed bringing the trappings of pop - lush vocal choirs and strings - to mainstream country. The 'Nashville Sound' revolutionised the industry, producing hundreds of immaculately produced but ultimately staid hits between 1960 and the mid-70s, by which time the style had become known as 'countrypolitan'. Patsy Cline, Jim Reeves and many others thrived during this period, but increasingly the acoustic roots of the music were forgotten.

There was some dissent, notably from Bakersfield, California, which spawned a troupe of ragged-but-right performers led by Buck Owens and Merle Haggard. Much more than the 'Nashville Sound', Bakersfield country inspired the birth of yet another hybrid, country-rock, which began with the Everly Brothers, was revived by Gram Parsons with the International Submarine Band, and then became an industry in itself, centred in Los Angeles, in the early 70s.

Country-rock was frowned upon in Nashville, but one of its leading lights, Emmylou Harris, was later instrumental in restoring country to its roots. While Nashville kept one eye firmly on the pop market in the 70s and early 80s, Harris and her proteges, who included Ricky Skaggs and Vince Gill, kept the veteran styles alive.

But her efforts to bring the rowdiness back into country music paled alongside the so-called Outlaws, a manufactured movement which nonetheless caught the moment perfectly. Led by Waylon Jennings and Willie Nelson, the Outlaws thought of themselves as rebels fighting to break out of the straitjacket of the 'Nashville Sound'. Though the outlaw tag soon became a cliché - Jennings even wrote a song about it, 'Don't You Think This Outlaw Bit's Done Got Out Of Hand' - it did succeed in broadening the scope of what could be heard on country radio. And its influence on the Texas singer-songwriter scene continues to this day.

After *Urban Cowboy*, the rebels were marginalised once more. It took Emmylou

Harris, Ricky Skaggs and John Anderson to restore country to its roots. After all that, the stage was set for Randy Travis - described as the 'first of the New Traditionalists' - to set in motion what has come to be known in Britain as 'New Country'.

As usual, the blanket description masked an array of styles. Alongside Travis's subtle ballads and honky-tonk emerged such diverse performers as Texas songwriter Nanci Griffith, Canadian rockabilly k.d. lang, the Bakersfield revivalist Dwight Yoakam and, after 1988, a new generation spearheaded by Alan Jackson, Clint Black and Garth Brooks. With an increasingly frantic turnover of stars, the first of the new country acts began to suffer in the 90s, as the likes of Billy Ray Cyrus and Travis Tritt swept them aside.

The centre of country music in 1993 is Nashville, as it has been since the mid-50s. From the mesh of tree-lined streets known as Music Row come the major-label releases that are now broadcast across America - not just on radio, but also via two cable television channels, The Nashville Network (which mixes concerts, talk shows and features on southern life) and Country Music Television, which broadcasts video clips 24 hours a day, not just in the USA but also across Europe.

With country stars now required to be actors as well as musicians, there's an obvious danger that the genre will subside into a branch of the television industry, preferring bland good looks to anything more distinctive or dangerous. The video channels gobble up new artists and require the major labels to produce fresh names on a weekly basis; promising performers now rarely survive beyond their debut album if it doesn't make the charts. Video has widened country's audience around the world, but perhaps only at the expense of the music.

Thankfully, Nashville's traditional role as the bastion of the songwriter remains intact, while the flourishing acoustic roots scene, which incorporates bluegrass, folk, cajun and western swing, is keeping the heritage of country music alive. In commercial terms, country has never been more successful. One battle has already been won; the next, to preserve the intrinsic qualities of southern roots music, is just beginning.

Peter Doggett

A

Acuff, Roy

b. Roy Claxton Acuff, 15 September 1903, Maynardsville, Tennessee, USA, d. 23 November 1992. The third of five children born to Neill and Ida Acuff, he learned to play the harmonica and Jew's harp as a child and was involved with music from an early age. His father played the fiddle, his mother the piano and guitar and Roy sang with his siblings. School did not appeal to him in the early years and although he showed some interest in poetry and verse and excelled at sports, he was frequently in trouble. In 1919, the family relocated to Knoxville suburb, Fountain City and he attended Central High School. He sang in the school Glee Club and performed many acting roles, including appearing in Shakespearean plays. He graduated, probably in 1924, although he was still playing a leading part in the school's sporting activities in 1925, even though he was small for basketball and baseball. After leaving school he developed a reputation as a fighter. These fracas caused his parents concern and sometimes landed him in court. Roy auditioned unsuccessfully for a stage show in Chicago and did a few jobs locally in Knoxville. In 1929, the family moved to the Knoxville suburb of Arlington and he played semi-professional baseball. He seemed set to join the New York Yankees. However, during the summer of 1929, he suffered severe sunburn and collapsed. He also had a nervous breakdown that resulted in him being bedridden for most of 1930. During these long months, he learned to play his father's fiddle and listened to the records of early country artists.

In 1931, he began to appear on the streets, where he first learned to play the yo-yo that he later featured in his stage show. Realizing that a baseball career was impossible, he turned to country music later stating 'Everything was dark, until I found the fiddle. If it had not come along I don't know what I would have become'. In 1932, he toured with Dr Hauer's Medicine Show, where he fiddled and took part in skits (sometimes in blackface or as an old woman) and jokes that were designed to encourage the watchers to buy Mocoton Tonic, 'the cure for everything'. Encouraged by his success, he began to play with other musicians in the Knoxville area. He also appeared with his

brother Claude (always called Spot) and Red Jones as the Three Rolling Stones. In 1934, he appeared on radio with Jess Easterday, Clell Summey and Bob Wright as the Tennessee Crackerjacks on WROL Knoxville before moving to WNOX, where six days a week they presented *Mid-Day Merry-Go-Round*. In 1935, they became Roy Acuff and the Crazy Tennesseans and the same year he began to sing a song called 'The Great Speckled Bird', which he had first heard sung by Charles Swain and his group, the Black Shirts. (The title came from the Bible and though several people later claimed ownership of the song, the original six verses were written by Reverend Guy Smith and set to a traditional English melody very similar to 'I'm Thinking Tonight Of My Blue Eyes'.) He made his first recordings in Chicago for ARC Records in October 1936, under the direction of William Calloway, who it seems had been looking for someone to record that song. They recorded 20 sides in all and Acuff later commented 'He wanted "The Bird", he didn't want me'. Two songs, 'When Lulu's Gone' and 'Doin' It The Old Fashioned Way', were self-penned numbers of a somewhat risque nature and were released as being by the Bang Boys, when Acuff refused to let the company use his name on them.

Further recordings were made in 1937, after which Acuff stopped recording because he felt that Calloway and ARC were not treating him right. Acuff made a somewhat inauspicious debut on the *Grand Ole Opry* in October 1937, playing two fiddle tunes and attempting a crooning version of 'The Bird'. A return visit in February 1938, although hardly sensational, evoked such interest with the listeners that WSM offered him radio spots and concert appearances with the Delmore Brothers. He again sang 'The Bird', and Clell Summey made history by playing a dobro on the *Opry* for the first time. Harry Stone, the WSM manager, suggested that the monicker Crazy Tennesseans were not complimentary to the state and since they came from the Smoky Mountains they should use that name. Accordingly when they appeared a week later it was as Roy Acuff and The Smoky Mountain Boys. In 1938, ARC became part of Columbia and Acuff was persuaded by Art Satherley to sign a recording contract with that company. A single release of the Carter Family song 'Wabash Cannonball' became one of the most popular records of the year and went on to win him a gold disc. In 1939 he toured all over the USA while various changes occurred in his band. He recorded in Dallas in April 1940 and the following month travelled to Hollywood, where he appeared with his band in the Republic Pictures film *Grand Ole Opry*. During the making of the film he was suffering from appendicitis and had to be strapped up during filming. On completion he underwent surgery in Nashville and only missed one *Opry* show, being back the following Saturday singing 'The Bird'. His and the band's popularity grew with many members establishing their own reputation, especially Pete Kirby who, as Bashful Brother Oswald, provided excellent dobro playing and harmony vocals. It was estimated that Acuff earned in excess of $200,000 in 1942.

He became great friends with Fred Rose, who at the time had a daily piano programme on WSM, and in 1943, the two men founded the Acuff-Rose Publication Company to give protection to songwriters and performers. Acuff-Rose was the first country music publishing house in the States and played a major part in the development of Nashville becoming Music City USA. In later years, when asked if he and Fred Rose had ever imagined that their creation would turn out to be such a tremendous success, Acuff replied 'Not at all. I only thought possibly it might do good. But I never had any idea it would turn out like this, grow this big. At the time Fred and I were like two blind pigs scratching for an acorn.' Rose, who wrote the Sophie Tucker hit 'Red Hot Mama', initially did not like country music but changed his mind after standing in the wings of the *Opry* one night and watching Acuff sing 'Don't Make Me Go To Bed And I'll Be Good'. The 40s established Acuff as a major figure in country music and he was much in demand for appearances. After twice declining the invitation, in 1944 and 1946, he was even persuaded to run for state governor in 1948. He stood as a Republican and though failing to be elected, he polled more votes than any previous Republican candidate in Tennessee. He later said 'I could have won, if I had run as a Democrat, been a puppet and made campaign promises'. He took defeat with no regrets stating 'As a Governor I would have been just another politician. As a singer I can be Roy Acuff'. He made further film appearances in *Hi Neighbor* (1942), *O' My Darling Clementine* (1943) (not to be confused with the later Henry Fonda film *'Oh My Darling Clementine'*), *Cowboy Canteen* (1944), *Sing Neighbor Sing* (1944), *Night Train To Memphis* (1946), *Smoky Mountain Melody* (1948) and *Home In San Antone* (1948). Acuff resisted any further attempts to lure him back into films. He reckoned 'Give me radio every time, if you get scared you can hang on the mike. In the movies there's nothing to hold you up.'

In 1949, he figured prominently on the *Opry's* first overseas tour when he visited Europe with other major stars including Hank Williams. He had great success with recordings of such songs as 'Wreck On The Highway' and 'Fireball Mail' and enjoyed US country and pop chart success in 1944 with 'The Prodigal Son' and 'I'll Forgive You But I Can't Forget'. Other Top 10 country hits in the 40s included 'Jole Blon' and 'Waltz Of The Wind'. During World War II, he had success with his recording of 'Cowards Over Pearl Harbour' and his fame was such that Japanese troops are reported to have yelled 'To hell with Roosevelt; to hell with Babe Ruth; to hell with Roy Acuff' before making suicidal charges on the Pacific island of Okinawa. In 1947, he founded the Dunbar Cave Resort, a country music park near Clarksville, Tennessee, which soon proved to be an astute investment and with his wife's business ability and the Acuff-Rose interest, he soon acquired a considerable fortune. He maintained a very active schedule during the 50s and 60s, with concert appearances in the States, *Opry* shows and 18 overseas tours. He played at Burtonwood, England during a 1951 European tour and in 1953, toured Japan and Korea. A private tour of Australia in 1959, drew a review from a Sydney critic that stated 'First there was Mr. Acuff - a clear cut case of strangulation of the tonsils'. He parted from Columbia in 1952 and recorded for MGM, Decca and Capitol and although his records sold, he had few chart successes. He and Fred Rose formed Hickory records and Acuff had a Top 10 country chart hit in 1958 with 'Once More'. In 1962, the Country Music Association, grateful for his services to the music over the years, elected him to be the first living member of the Country Music Hall Of Fame. The plaque described him as the King Of Country Music. In July 1965, he was seriously injured in a 'wreck on the highway' but he soon recovered and was back at the *Opry*. He cancelled his personal concerts for the year but in early 1966 and 1967, he played in Vietnam and other Far East venues. Acuff cut back severely on his touring in the early 70s but still maintained a prominent role at the *Opry*. He was one of the many stars to record with the Nitty Gritty Dirt Band in 1972, when they recorded their triple album *Will The Circle Be Unbroken*, and continued to record in his own right, including the re-recording of some of his earlier numbers for different labels. In 1971, accompanied only by Charlie Collins on guitar, he recorded 20 fiddle tunes for an instrumental album but they remain unreleased.

Acuff became involved with the *Opry*land complex and figured prominently in the opening night ceremonies for the new *Opry* in 1974. He not only sang the 'Wabash Cannonball', but also endeavoured to teach President Nixon how to play with a yo-yo. The same year, at the age of 70, he claimed the record of being the oldest person to make the US country charts. He lost his record in 1980, when comedian George Burns, showed his aspirations to be a country singer at the tender age of 84 and charted with 'I Wish I Was Eighteen Again'. Acuff maintained his *Opry* connections throughout the 80s and remained a most respected member of the country music scene. In 1983, almost 80 years old, he returned to the Wembley Festival and once again proved to be one of the real successes of the event. He lived very close to the *Opry*, where he was the only member to have his own dressing-room and he was always referred to as Mr. Acuff by his fellow members. He continued to host and perform on the *Opry* until only a few weeks before his death in late 1992, aged 89. The simplicity of his songs with their tuneful melodies had been the secret of his success over the years. His recordings were never aimed at the charts; in the main they were either of a religious nature, about mother and/or home or train songs. They appealed to ordinary people and this is what led to his very considerable record sales over his long career. He had recorded duets with several artists including Kitty Wells ('Goodbye, Mr. Brown'), June Stearns ('Before I Met You'), Bill Anderson ('I Wonder If God Likes Country Music') and Boxcar Willie ('Fireball Mail'). Surprisingly, since 1955, he only had three singles released in the UK, plus the duet with Boxcar Willie. His last country chart hit was 'Old Time Sunshine Song', a modest number 97 in 1974.

In 1992, Acuff's health began to deteriorate, but whenever possible he maintained appearances on the *Opry*, even though he frequently had to resort to having a chair in the wings. At 6a.m. on 23 November, he died of congestive heart failure. He had left instructions that he did not wish his funeral to become something of a show business event as had happened with some other stars and in accordance with his wishes only the family and a few close friends were present when he was buried at 10a.m. that same day.

Albums: *Old Time Barn Dance* (1953, 10-inch album), *Songs Of The Smoky Mountains* (1954, 10-inch album), *Songs Of The Smoky Mountains* (1955), *The Great Speckled Bird* (1958), *Favorite Hymns* (1958), *Once More* (1961), *That Glory Bound Train* (1961), *Hymn Time* (1962), *Roy Acuff & His Smoky Mountain Boys* (1963), with the Jordanaires *Handclapping Gospel Songs* (1963), *Sings American Folk Songs* (1963), *Star Of The Grand Ole Opry* (1963), *The World Is His Stage* (1963), *The Great Roy Acuff* (1964), *Country Music Hall Of Fame* (1964), *The Voice Of Country Music* (1965), *The Great Roy Acuff* (1965), *Great Train Songs* (1965), *Roy Acuff (How Beautiful Heaven Must Be)* (1965), *Sacred Songs* (1965), *Sings Hank Williams* (1966), *Waiting For My Call To Glory* (1966), *Famous Opry Favorites* (1968), *Living Legend* (1968), *Roy Acuff Country* (1969), *Treasury Of Country Hits* (1969), *Roy Acuff Time* (1971), *Who Is Roy Acuff* (1973, double album), *Back In The Country* (1974), *Smoky Mountain Memories* (1975), *That's Country* (1975), *Greatest Hits Volume 1* (1978, double album), *Greatest Hits Volume 2* (1979, double album), *Country And Western Classics* (c.70s, three albums), *Sings Hank Williams* (1980), *Back In The Country* (1981), *Columbia Historic Edition* (1985), *Steamboat Whistle Blues 1936-1939* (1985), *Roy Acuff On Radio* (c.80s).

Further reading: *King Of Country Music: The Life Story Of Roy Acuff*, A.C Dunkleberger. *Roy Acuff The Smoky Mountain Boy*, Elizabeth Schlappi.

Acuff, Roy, Jnr.

b. Roy Neill Acuff, 25 July 1943, Nashville, Tennessee, USA. The son of Roy Acuff, he attended schools in Nashville and spent four years as a boarder at the Castle Heights Military School in Lebanon, Tennessee and finally graduated from Henderson High School in 1962. At times during his childhood, he saw little of his father owing to his touring commitments. A high school marriage failed but not before it produced Roy Neill Acuff Jnr. Initially showing little interest in music, he began to work in the offices at Acuff-Rose but in 1963, unbeknown to his father, he learned to sing and play the guitar. In 1965, he was given the opportunity to record for Columbia by Wesley Rose and a month later his father introduced him on the *Grand Ole Opry*. He played various venues in the USA and even toured US military bases in Germany. Occasionally he appeared with his father and in the early 70s, he sang backing vocals on some of his recordings. However, audiences made him nervous and he never enjoyed performing. He was much happier working behind the scenes and by the mid-70s, he had retired as a performer to become an executive of Acuff-Rose. During his brief recording career, he wrote and recorded several of his own songs including 'Back Down To Atlanta' and 'Street Singer'

Albums: *Roy Acuff Jnr* (1970), *California Lady* (1974).

Acuff-Rose Music

Founded in Nashville, Tennessee, USA 1942 by composer Fred Rose and *Grand Ole Opry* star Roy Acuff it was the first specialist country music publishing house. From 1945, the company was headed by Fred's son, Wesley Rose (b. 1918, Chicago, Illinois, USA, d. 26 April 1990, Nashville, Tennessee, USA). Its most significant signing was Hank Williams in 1946. His songs like 'Cold Cold Heart', 'I Can't Help It (If I'm Still In Love With You)' and 'Hey, Good Lookin'' were pop as well as country hits. 'Tennessee Waltz' (1950) was another crossover mega-hit. In 1952, the company set up its own record label, Hickory. Later Acuff-Rose writers included Marty Robbins, Don Gibson, Boudleaux and Felice Bryant, the Everly Brothers, Roy Orbison, Pee Wee King and John D. Loudermilk. Acuff and the Roses were all members of the Country Music Hall of Fame. Acuff-Rose had offices in 10 other countries. The catalogue was sold to *Opryland* in 1985 for $22 million.

Adkins, Wendel

Wendel Adkins was born in Kentucky around 1950 and raised in Fremont, Ohio. During his teens, he played organ in a rock band, but he preferred to be singing country music. He went to Nashville but poor management stifled his talent and his ambition. Adkins moved to Las Vegas and, because he was tall, good-looking and entertaining, he found a following in the casino hotels. His country act included impersonations of Willie Nelson and Johnny Cash, and he sounded like Waylon Jennings without trying. Ironically, it was Willie Nelson who discovered him and suggested that he moved from Las Vegas to Texas. He became associated with 'outlaw country' and he opened shows for both Nelson and David Allan Coe. His first album, *Sundowners*, was released on Motown's Hitsville label in 1977 and included a tribute to Nelson, 'Willie Didn't Win'. His second album was recorded live at one of Nelson's clubs, Whiskey River, and included the prophetic 'Luckenbach Ain't Never Gonna Be The Same'. During a residency at Gilley's, he recorded a live album, but although he was recording through the 80s, he never became a national country star. His

outspoken language on 'Rodeo Cowboys', the opening cut of *If That Ain't Country*, caught many disc jockeys out and may have lost him support.

Albums: *Sundowners* (1977), *Live At Whiskey River* (1982), *Live At Gilley's* (1983), *Cowboy Singer* (1984), *If That Ain't Country* (1985), *I Can't Let You Be A Memory* (1987).

Alabama

One of the biggest US country-rock acts of the 80s, the band's origins can be traced back to Fort Payne, Alabama. They were originally formed in 1969 as Wild Country by cousins Jeff Cook (b. 27 August 1949, Fort Payne, Alabama, USA; vocals/guitar), Randy Owen (b. 13 December 1949, Fort Payne, Alabama, USA; vocals/guitar), and Teddy Gentry (b. 22 January 1952, Fort Payne, Alabama, USA; bass/vocals). Their original drummer was the only non-relation and was soon rejected. After several misfires at the start of their career their big breakthrough came with a residency at a club in Myrtle Beach, South Carolina in 1973. Soon afterwards they turned professional. They recorded for several small labels in the 70s before they changed their name to Alabama in 1977. Their career blossomed with a sequence of hits in the country charts which followed the success of 'I Want To Be With You'. At this point they sought out a full-time drummer to fill out their sound and recruited Mark Herndon (b. 11 May 1955, Springfield, Massachusetts, USA). After 'My Home's In Alabama' reached the US Top 20 they signed to RCA Records in 1980 and found immediate success. A rich vein of country hits followed with 'Tennessee River' and 'Feels So Right'. Later singles like 'Love In The First Degree' also acquired crossover pop success. Of their five platinum albums during the 80s, the most successful was *40 Hour Week* which made US number 10. In 1986 they worked with Lionel Richie, but their recent work has seen them return to the C&W charts almost exclusively. Despite an increasingly formulaic sound, they remain a major live attraction, although their commercial profile has suffered from the rival attractions of younger bands like Diamond Rio and Sawyer Brown. However, their environmental anthem 'Pass It On Down' in 1990 confirmed that they are still capable of surprising their audience.

Albums: *Alabama* (1980), *My Home's In Alabama* (1980), *Feels So Right* (1981), *Mountain Music* (1982), *The Closer You Get* (1983), *Roll On* (1984), *40 Hour Week* (1985), *The Touch* (1986), *Just Us* (1987), *Southern Star* (1989), *Pass It On Down*

Alabama

(1990) *American Pride* (1992). Compilations: *Greatest Hits* (1986), *Greatest Hits Volume 2* (1991).

Allan, Johnnie

b. John Allan Guillot, 10 March 1938, Rayne, Louisiana, USA. Allan was raised in a sharecropping family, speaking both English and French. His great-uncle, Joe Falcon, made one of the first cajun records, 'Allons A Lafayette'. Since the age of 13, he has been playing rhythm guitar and steel guitar in local bands. In 1958 and as part of the Krazy Kats, Allan had regional hits with 'Lonely Days And Lonely Nights' and 'Angel Of Love'. Allan, who qualified as a teacher, divided his time between music and teaching in Lafayette. 'South To Louisiana', a regional version of Johnny Horton's 'North To Alaska', was a successful solo single. Allan made a single, 'Somewhere On Skid Row', with 'Promised Land' on the b-side, for Jin Records of Ville Patte, Louisiana. In 1972 Charlie Gillett, looking for releases for his new UK label, Oval, delighted in the fast and furious cajun treatment of Chuck Berry's song, and so 'Promised Land' became a UK single. Sadly, another cover version by Elvis Presley put paid to its chances. Allan is revered by the UK rock 'n' roll fraternity and has made successful appearances in the UK.
Albums: *Another Man's Woman* (c.70s), *Dedicated To You* (c.70s), *South To Louisiana* (c.70s), *Johnnie Allan And The Krazy Kats 1959-1960s* (1985), *Promised Land* (1995). Compilations: *Johnnie Allan Sings* (c.70s), *Johnnie Allan's Greatest Hits* (c.70s), *Portrait Of Johnnie Allan* (c.70s).

Allen, Deborah

b. Deborah Lynn Thurgood, 30 September 1953, Memphis, Tennessee, USA. A singer/songwriter, whose songs have proved major successes for other artists including 'Don't Worry 'Bout Me Baby' (Janie Fricke) and 'Can I See You Tonight?' (Tanya Tucker). Her own first US country chart success came in 1979 when she was working as a session singer. Thanks to the miracles of modern recording techniques and the thoughtfulness of RCA producer Bud Logan, she was chosen to superimpose her vocals over recordings made years earlier by Jim Reeves, a star then sadly dead for almost 15 years. The resulting 'duets' produced no less than three Top 10 US country hits, 'Don't Let Me Cross Over', 'Oh, How I Miss You Tonight' and 'Take Me In Your Arms And Hold Me'. Between 1980 and 1984, she had eight solo country singles including 'Baby I Lied' (a US country number 4 and US pop number 26) and 'I've Been Wrong Before' (a country number 2). She married songwriter Rafe Van Hoy, co-wrote songs with him and sang on the soundtrack of *The River Rat*.
Albums: *Trouble In Paradise* (1980), *Cheat The Night* (Mini-LP) (1983), *Let Me Be The First* (1984).

Allen, Jules Verne

b. 1 April 1883, Waxahachie, Ellis County, Texas, USA, d. 1945. Allen has strong claim to the title of being the original singing cowboy. By the time he was 10 years old, he was working as a ranch boy and over the years progressed to be a horse-wrangler, a rough-string rider and finally a top ranch hand, who also did occasional police work. He worked on some of the last big drives that herded cattle from the Mexican border to the railway stockyards of Montana but then enlisted in the army when America entered World War I. During earlier years he had played the guitar and sung for the entertainment of his fellow cowboys but on his military discharge, decided to try for a singing career. Around 1920, he became a western folk singer and sang of trail drives, round-ups and rodeos using many of the traditional ballads collected by such authorities as John Lomax, as well as songs he had written from personal experiences. Sometimes appearing as Longhorn Luke, he soon became popular on several radio stations including WFAA Dallas (where he first broadcast), WOAI San Antonio and WFI and KNX Los Angeles. Between April 1928 and April 1929, he recorded a total of 24 songs for RCA-Victor, all but four being of a cowboy nature and including such western classics as 'Home On The Range', 'The Chisholm Trail' and 'Little Joe The Wrangler'. His version of 'The Sante Fe Trail' was the first ever recorded. During the 30s, he continued with radio work, appearances at rodeos and other western events and was also a part-time police officer in the El Paso area. He never recorded again and little is known of his latter years except that he died in 1945.

Album: *Jules Allen, The Texas Cowboy* (1973).

Further reading: *Cowboy Lore*, Jules Verne Allen.

Allen, Rex

b. Rex Elvie Allen, 31 December 1922, Willcox, Arizona, USA. Country singer Allen was no imitation cowboy, as his family were homesteaders: a mountain lion was killed close to his home, his brother died from a rattlesnake bite, and the family lost everything in the drought of 1934. As Allen had ridden on the farm, he thought he could transfer to rodeos, but a fall from a Brahman bull directed his thoughts towards music. In 1945, he hosted *The National Barn Dance* for a radio station in Chicago and was able to afford an operation to correct his congenital squint. His first local hit was 'Take It Back And Change It For A Boy', and his early recordings found him yodelling, although he

subsequently kept his tone and pitch the same. Country singer Red Foley was not interested when he was asked to replace the popular singing cowboy, Roy Rogers, at Republic Studios, but he recommended the good looking, well-spoken Allen instead. Republic named him 'The Arizona Cowboy', which was the title of the first of his 19 film starring roles between 1950 and 1954, with the last, *The Phantom Stallion,* marking the end of the b-movie western. His son, country singer Rex Allen Jnr., said, 'He wanted to be the opposite of Roy Rogers. He rode a black horse, he didn't wear fringed shirts and he had his guns back-to-front. If he'd got involved in a real gunfight, he'd have been dead.' Allen's weatherbeaten sidekick was Slim Pickens, who was featured in *Dr. Strangelove* and *Pat Garrett And Billy The Kid* and made an album of narrations, *Slim Pickens* (1977), which included the outlandish 'The Fireman Cowboy', which they had written together. Television put paid to the sagebrush troubadours but Allen transferred to the new medium with 39 episodes of *Frontier Doctor.* Although Allen had a million-selling single, 'Crying In The Chapel' in 1953, later a hit for Elvis Presley, he did not record regularly and, in 1962, when he returned to the US charts, it was with a song he disliked; 'Don't Go Near The Indians'. His own suggestion, a new Willie Nelson song, 'Night Life', was vetoed. Allen's clear diction enabled him to narrate documentaries for Walt Disney and, in 1973 his voice was heard in the Hanna-Barbera cartoon, *Charlotte's Web.* He returned to Arizona and still makes a good living voicing commercials. Occasionally he joins his son on stage.

Albums: *Under Western Skies* (1956), *Mr. Cowboy* (1959), *Rex Allen Sings 16 Favourites* (1961), *The Faith Of A Man* (1962), *Rex Allen Sings And Tells Tales* (1962), *Rex Allen Sings Melodies Of The Plains* (1962), *Rex Allen* (1964), *Rex Allen Sings Western Ballads* (1965), *The Smooth Country Sound Of Rex Allen* (1968), *Golden Songs Of The Golden West* (1970), *The Touch Of God's Hand* (1970), *Favourite Songs* (1970), *Boney Kneed, Hairy Legged Cowboy Songs* (1978), *Rex Allen, The Hawaiian Cowboy* (1986).

Further reading: *The Arizona Cowboy*, Rex Allen.

Allen, Rex, Jnr.

b. Rex Elvie Allen Jnr., 23 August 1947, Chicago, Illinois, USA. School holidays were spent touring with his father, cowboy actor Rex Allen. He wrangled horses, played rodeo clown and sang 'That Little Boy Of Mine' with him. He recorded for several labels before having success with Warner Brothers in the US country charts with 'The Great Mail Robbery' in 1973, a tribute to his heritage 'Can You Hear Those Pioneers?' and his first Top 10 country record, 'Two Less Lonely People'. When he was invited to star in a modern-day western, he recorded an album, *Singing Cowboy*, including 'Last Of The Silver Screen Cowboys' with his father and Roy Rogers, but the film was never made. He often revived pop hits such as 'Crying In The Rain', 'Cat's In The Cradle' and 'The Air That I Breathe', but he is no longer a regular in the country charts. Allen is an energetic showman, scoring at the annual Wembley country music festival, but his career must, ultimately, be one of frustration.

Albums: *Another Goodbye Song* (1974), *Riding High* (1976), *Rex* (1977), *Brand New* (1978), *Me And My Broken Heart* (1979), *Oklahoma Rose* (1980), *Cat's In The Cradle* (1981), *Country Cowboy* (1982), *Singing Cowboy* (1982), *On The Move* (1985).

Allen, Rosalie

b. Julie Marlene Bedra, 27 June 1924, Old Forge, Pennsylvania, USA. Born of Polish immigrant stock, Allen was taught to play guitar and yodel by an elder brother as a child and moved to New York in her mid-teens where she found work on Denver Darling's *Swing Billies* radio programme. Between 1946 and 1953 she recorded for RCA, having chart successes in 1946 with her version of the Patsy Montana yodelling classic 'I Want To Be A Cowboy's Sweetheart' and 'Guitar Polka'. She also popularized 'He Taught Me How To Yodel', a female version of the Kenny Roberts novelty number 'She Taught Me To Yodel', a song that in 1962 became one of Frank Ifield's most popular stage numbers after being released as the b-side of his recording of 'Lovesick Blues'. She later joined Zeke Manners' show where she recorded duets with Elton Britt, including US country chart Top 10 hits with 'Beyond The Sunset' and 'Quicksilver' in 1950. In the early 50s she had her own television show, later opened a large record store in New Jersey and became New York's first hillbilly yodelling disc jockey on WOV. Her popularity made her one of the first female country stars. She eventually retired from the music business and moved to Alabama.

Albums: *Country & Western Hits* (1957), *Rosalie Allen & Elton Britt* (one side devoted to each) (1957), *Songs Of The Golden West* (1957), *Rosalie Allen* (1961), with Tex Fletcher *Rodeo* (c.60s), *Cowboy's Sweetheart* (1990).

Allen, Terry

b. 7 May 1943, Wichita, Kansas, USA. Sculptor, multi-media artist, songwriter, the gravel-voiced Allen remained an enigmatic figure during the 70s and 80s. Despite his living in California for many years, Allen is more often associated with the new country movement in Texas. Many listeners first became aware of him when his 'New Delhi Freight Train' was covered by Little Feat on *Time Loves A Hero*. Allen had already recorded *Juarez* (which Lowell George was at one point slated to produce) utilizing the talents of Peter Kaukonen and Greg Douglas; four of its songs were covered by Peter Rowan. Two of the album's finest songs surfaced several years later on Allen's *Bloodlines*. In the interim, he and his Panhandle Mystery Band produced the double *Lubbock (On Everything)* and *Smokin' The Dummy*, the latter containing a tribute to George. Allen next worked on the soundtrack to a German film, *Amerasia*, with a Thai group, and was said to be at work on a screenplay himself. His sardonic wit and strong feeling for his roots have led Allen to produce many memorable songs.

Albums: *Lubbock (On Everything)* (1979), *Bloodlines* (1983), *Amerasia* (1986), *Juarez* (1988), *Smokin' The Dummy* (1988).

Amazing Rhythm Aces

Formed in 1972, the Amazing Rhythm Aces were a US sextet consisting of Howard Russell Smith (guitar, vocals), Barry Burton (guitar, mandolin, dobro), Billy Earhart III (keyboards), Jeff Davis (bass) and Butch McDade (drums). Davis and McDade had previously backed singer Jesse Winchester. The group was a country/rock outfit which also incorporated elements of R&B and gospel into its sound. They recorded their debut, *Stacked Deck*, in Memphis in 1975, from which the single, 'Third Rate Romance', was culled. It reached the Top 20 on both the pop and country charts in the USA. The band later found success only in the country area, where its second single, 'Amazing Grace (Used To Be Her Favorite Song)' was a Top 10 entry. They disbanded in 1980. Smith went solo and Earhart joined Hank Williams Jnr.'s group, the Bama Band.

Albums: *Stacked Deck* (1975), *Too Stuffed To Jump* (1976), *Toucan Do It Too* (1977), *Burning The Ballroom Down* (1978), *The Amazing Rhythm Aces* (1978), *How The Hell Do You Spell Rhythum?* (1980).

Anderson, Bill

b. James William Anderson III, 1 November 1937,

Columbia, South Carolina, USA. Country performer Anderson learned the guitar when he was aged 12 and formed his own school band. He graduated in Journalism from the University of Georgia. He became a sportswriter and also worked for a radio station, an experience put into his song 'Country DJ'. In 1958 Ray Price won a gold disc when he recorded Anderson's 'City Lights'. Anderson's first hit as an artist was with 'That's What It's Like To Be Lonesome' in 1959. He followed this with 'The Tips Of My Fingers' (1960), a country success for Roy Clark and Eddy Arnold and a UK pop hit for Des O'Connor, and 'Po' Folks' (1961), which inspired the Po' Boys, the name of his band. His front man, Jimmy Gateley wrote Sonny James' country hit, 'The Minute You're Gone', a UK success for Cliff Richard. Anderson had his first US country number 1 in 1962 with 'Mama Sang A Sad Song' and the following year he made number 8 in the US pop charts with his half-spoken 'Still', which was successfully covered in the UK by both Karl Denver and Ken Dodd. Dodd also had success with '8 x 10' and always closed his stage show with 'Happiness'. Anderson also wrote several other successful songs including 'Once A Day' (the 1964 US country number 1 for Connie Smith, which launched her career), 'Happy Birthday To Me' (Hank Locklin), 'I Missed Me' (Jim Reeves), 'I've Enjoyed As Much Of This As I Can Stand' (Porter Wagoner), 'Five Little Fingers' (Frankie McBride), 'It Comes And Goes' (Burl Ives) and 'My Whole World Is Falling Down' (Brenda Lee). Anderson also wrote 'Face To The Wall' with Faron Young and 'When Two Worlds Collide' with Roger Miller, which they wrote by coming up with alternate lines on a car trip. Following his narration 'Golden Guitar', which was written by Curtis Leach, he was nicknamed Whispering Bill by the disc jockey Don Bowman, who also recorded a parody of 'Still'. Anderson says of his intimate and effusive style, 'I accepted a long time ago that a lot of people weren't going to like me. I'm glad some do.' During the Vietnam War, he recorded the patriotic 'Where Have All My Heroes Gone?' and says, 'There's a lot of me in my songs but that's not to say that they've got to be factual. Sometimes it's hard to make the truth rhyme.' For many years he worked and recorded with Jan Howard and they had a US country number 1 with 'For Loving You'. In 1972 her place was taken by Mary Lou Turner. He has also recorded with Roy Acuff ('I Wonder If God Loves Country Music') and, curiously, with David Allan Coe ('Get A Little Dirt

On Your Hands'). In the late 70s he established country disco with 'I Can't Wait Any Longer' and 'Double S', thus paving the way for T.G. Sheppard. During the 80s he was featured in US soap operas and hosted game shows, but his new career was set back in 1984 when he and his wife were involved in a car crash with a hit-and-run driver. Both recovered and Anderson has returned to working country venues.

Selected albums: *Bill Anderson Sings Country Heart Songs* (1961), *Still* (1963), *The Bill Anderson Showcase* (1964), *Bright Lights And Country Music* (1965), *From This Pen* (1965), *Bill Anderson Presents The Po' Boys* (1966), *I Love You Drops* (1966), *Get While The Gettin's Good* (1967), *The Po' Boys Pick Again* (1967), *I Can Do Nothing Alone* (1967), with Jan Howard *For Loving You* (1968), *Happy State Of Mind* (1969), *Wild Weekend* (1969), *Bill Anderson's Country Style* (1969), *My Life/But You Know I Love You* (1970), *Christmas* (1970), *Love Is A Sometimes Thing* (1971), with Howard *If It's All The Same To You* (1971), *Where Have All Our Heroes Gone?* (1971), *Always Remember* (1971), as Bill Anderson's Po' Boys *That Casual Country Feelin'* (1971), *Bill Anderson Sings For All The Lonely Women In The World* (1972), with Howard *Bill And Jan* (1972), *Just Plain Bill* (1972), with Howard *Singing His Praise* (1972), *Don't She Look Good* (1973), *Bill* (1973), *The Rich Sound Of Bill Anderson's Po' Boys* (1973), *Can I Come Home To You?* (1974), *Every Time I Turn The Radio On* (1974), with Mary Lou Turner *Sometimes* (1975), *Gentle On My Mind* (1975), *Live From London* (1975), *Peanuts And Diamonds And Other Jewels* (1976), *Scorpio* (1976), with Turner *Billy Boy And Mary Lou* (1977), *Love And Other Sad Stories* (1978), *Ladies Choice* (1978), *Whispering Bill Anderson* (1979), *On The Road With Bill Anderson* (1980), *Nashville Mirrors* (1980), *Bill Anderson Hosts Backstage At The Grand Ole Opry* (1982), *Southern Fried* (1983), *Yesterday Today And Tomorrow* (1984), *Bill Anderson Presents The Po' Folks Band* (1984), *A Place In The Country* (1986), *Yesteryear* (1990).

Further reading: *Whispering Bill*, Bill Anderson.

Anderson, John

b. 13 December 1954, Apopka, Florida, USA. As an adolescent, Anderson was playing the songs of British beat groups in his school band, but he then became infused with country music. He joined his sister, Donna, in Nashville in 1972 and they played together in clubs and bars. In 1974 he began recording for the Ace Of Hearts label but none of his singles ('Swoop Down Sweet Jesus', 'Losing

Again', 'A Heartbreak Ago') made any impression. He signed with Warner Brothers Records in 1977 and his first single was 'I Got A Feelin' (Somebody's Stealin')'. Although Anderson had several country hits ('My Pledge Of Love', 'Low Dog Blues', 'Your Lying Blue Eyes' and a perfect country theme, 'She Just Started Liking Cheating Songs'), he was not allowed to make an album until he was established. Some regard Anderson as continuing the tradition of Lefty Frizzell and George Jones, and he was delighted when his song, 'The Girl At The End Of The Bar', was covered by Jones. His revival of a poignant ballad, 'I Just Came Home To Count The Memories', originally a US country hit for Cal Smith, was given an identical arrangement to Elvis Costello's 'Good Year For The Roses'. As well as honky tonk ballads, he recorded the cheerful Billy Joe Shaver song, 'I'm Just An Old Chunk Of Coal (But I'm Gonna Be A Diamond Someday)', and his own uptempo 'Chicken Truck'. In 1982 he had his first US country number 1 with a song recommended to him by his sister, 'Wild And Blue'. Anderson and his frequent co-writer, Lionel Delmore, the son of Alton Delmore, wrote 'Swingin'', which sold 1.4 million and became the biggest-selling country single in Warners' history. Anderson, who plays lead guitar in his road band, called his instrument after the character in 'Swingin'', Charlotte. Anderson was one of country music's first video stars, but he fell out with both his record label and his management. He fared relatively poorly on MCA, although there was a spirited duet with Waylon Jennings, 'Somewhere Between Ragged And Right'. Mark Knopfler wrote and played guitar on a 1991 release, 'When It Comes To You'. That song appeared on *Seminole Wind*, a triumphant comeback album which restored Anderson to the top rank of his profession, spawning a succession of hit singles. Its title track, a lament for the loss of traditional Indian lands, was reminiscent of Robbie Robertson's best work with the Band in its portrayal of history and American landscape.

Albums: *John Anderson* (1980), *John Anderson 2* (1981), *I Just Came Home To Count The Memories* (1981), *Wild And Blue* (1982), *All The People Are Talking* (1983), *Eye Of The Hurricane* (1984), *Tokyo, Oklahoma* (1985), *Countryfied* (1986), *Blue Skies Again* (1988), *10* (1990), *Too Tough To Tame* (1990), *Seminole Wind* (1992).

Anderson, Liz

b. Elizabeth Jane Haaby, 13 March 1930, Pine Creek, near Roseau, Minnesota, USA. Anderson married country songwriter, Casey Anderson, in 1946, but worked as a secretary before turning to songwriting herself. She wrote 'Pick Of The Week' (Roy Drusky, 1964), '(My Friends Are Gonna Be) Strangers' (Merle Haggard, 1965), 'Guess My Eyes Were Bigger Than My Heart' (Conway Twitty, 1966), 'Just Between The Two Of Us' (Merle Haggard and Bonnie Owens, 1966) and 'I'm A Lonesome Fugitive' (Merle Haggard, 1967), which was written with her husband and established Haggard's rebellious image. She recorded on RCA from 1964-1970, and had country hits with 'Mama Spank', 'Tiny Tears', 'Husband Hunting' and, in 1972, recorded a country version of 'I'll Never Fall In Love Again' for Epic. 'The Game Of Triangles' was a musical tryst with Bobby Bare and Norma Jean. She wrote her daughter, Lynn Anderson's first country hit, 'Ride, Ride, Ride' in 1966, and they later made the US country charts with a duet, 'Mother May I'. Lynn recorded *Songs My Mother Wrote* and is still placing her mother's songs with contemporary artists. Liz and Casey remain in the music business and host a country show on cable television in Nashville.

Albums: *Liz Anderson Sings* (1967), *The Game Of Triangles* (with Bobby Bare and Norma Jean) (1967), *Cookin' Up Hits* (1967), *Favourites* (1968), *Like A Merry-Go-Round* (1968), *If The Creek Don't Rise* (1969), *The Liz Anderson Style* (1969), *Husband Hunting* (1970).

Anderson, Lynn

b. Lynn Rene Anderson, 26 September 1947, Grand Forks, North Dakota, USA. Anderson, the daughter of country songwriters, Casey and Liz Anderson, was raised in California. She started performing at the age of six, but her first successes were in horse shows. Her quarter horses amassed 700 trophies and she won major awards as a rider at shows all over California. In 1966, recording for the small Chart label, she had a US country entry with a song written by her mother, 'Ride, Ride, Ride', and then made the Top 10 with 'If I Kiss You, Will You Go Away?' and 'That's A No No'. She secured a residency on *The Lawrence Welk Show* and, in 1968, married songwriter, Glenn Sutton, who then produced her records. The combination of her stunning blonde hair and the irritatingly catchy Joe South song, 'Rose Garden' ('I beg your pardon, I never promised you a rose garden') helped her to Number 3 on both the USA and UK pop charts. It also topped the US country charts for

Lynn Anderson

five weeks. The album of the same name also went gold. Anderson regards 'Rose Garden' as perfect timing, 'We were coming out of the Vietnam years, and a lot of people were trying to recover. The song's message was that you can make something out of nothing.' Although she did not repeat her pop success, she had US country Number 1s with 'You're My Man', 'How Can I Unlove You?', 'Keep Me In Mind' and 'What A Man My Man Is'. She also scored with 'Top Of The World' and 'Wrap Your Love All Around Your Man'. Sutton and Anderson divorced in the mid-70s after she was promised more than a rose garden by Louisiana oil man Harold Stream III. During this marriage, she concentrated on horse riding and fund-raising activities, but, upon their separation in 1982, she returned to country music. She has had further country hits with 'You're Welcome To Tonight', a duet with Gary Morris, 'Fools For Each Other' with Ed Bruce, and 'Under The Boardwalk' with harmonies from Billy Joe Royal, but she is no longer recording albums prolifically.

Albums: *Ride, Ride, Ride* (1967), *Big Girls Don't Cry* (1968), *Promises, Promises* (1968), *Songs That Made Country Girls Famous* (1969), *At Home With Lynn Anderson* (1969), *With Love From Lynn* (1969), *I'm Alright* (1970), *No Love At All* (1970), *Stay There 'Til I Get There* (1970), *Uptown Country Girl* (1970), *Rose Garden* (1970), *Songs My Mother Wrote* (1970), *Lynn Anderson With Strings* (1971), *A Woman Lives For Love* (1971), *How Can I Unlove You?* (1971), *You're My Man* (1971), *The Christmas Album* (1971), *Cry* (1972), *Listen To A Country Song* (1972), *Keep Me In Mind* (1973), *Top Of The World* (1973), *Singing My Song* (1973), *What A Man My Man Is* (1974), *Smile For Me* (1974), *I've Never Loved Anyone More* (1975), *All The King's Horses* (1976), *Wrap Your Arms Around Your Man* (1977), *I Love What Love Is Doing To Me* (reissued in UK as *Angel In Your Arms*) (1977), *From The Inside* (1978), *Outlaw Is Just A State Of Mind* (1979), *Even Cowgirls Get The Blues* (1981), *Lynn Anderson Is Back* (1983), *What She Does Best* (1988), *Greatest Hits* (1992).

Anglin, Jack

b. 13 March 1916, on a farm near Columbia, Williamson County, Tennessee, USA, d. 7 March 1963. The youngest of seven children, he learned to play guitar as a child and at an early age was singing in a trio with his brothers, Jim and Van (aka Red). Jim wrote some songs and the three began to appear at local venues and radio as the Anglin Brothers. They briefly located in Athens, Alabama, where they became friendly with and influenced by the Delmore Brothers. Around 1930, they moved to Nashville. (c.1937, the Anglin Brothers recorded for ARC in Birmingham, Alabama). Jack worked at a local hosiery mill and here became acquainted with his future wife, Louise and through her, her brother Johnnie Wright. At the time Wright, his wife Muriel (Kitty Wells) and Louise were regulars on WSIX as Johnnie Wright And The Harmony Girls. The two men became friends and when, in 1939, the Anglin Brothers disbanded, Jack was soon performing with Wright as Johnnie Wright And The Happy Roving Cowboys with Jack Anglin. In 1940, they became Johnnie And Jack, who enjoyed much success as a vocal duo until Jack Anglin's career came to an untimely end in 1963. Driving alone to attend a memorial service for Patsy Cline not far from his home, he rounded a bend on New Due West Avenue in Madison at high speed, crashed and was instantly killed. No other vehicle was involved.

Albums as the Anglin Brothers: *The South's Favorite Trio (Early Harmony)* (c.1978).

Area Code 615

After Bob Dylan's 1969 *Nashville Skyline*, it became fashionable to record in Nashville. So, New York record producer, Elliot Mazer, went to Nashville and took four noted sessionmen into a studio to record some instrumentals – Kenneth Buttrey (drums), David Briggs (keyboards), Mac Gayden (guitar) and Norbert Putnam (bass). Mazer felt that the sessions needed more of a country feel so he then added Charlie McCoy (b. 28 March, 1941; harmonica), Wayne Moss (guitar), Ken Lauber (piano), Weldon Myrick (steel guitar), Buddy Spicher (fiddle), and Bobby Thompson (banjo). These leading session musicians began recording in their own right following interest generated by *Nashville Skyline*, on which McCoy and Buttery appeared. Area Code 615 was never intended as a permanent vehicle. The sessions came alive when Spicher and Thompson developed a bluegrass arrangement of 'Hey Jude', and the concept of recording familiar tunes with the lead instruments playing country and the rhythm rock 'n' roll was born. They named themselves Area Code 615 after the telephone code for Nashville. McCoy and Buttrey alone developed 'Stone Fox Chase', which became the theme for BBC television's long running rock programme *The Old Grey Whistle Test*. The musicians returned to individual session

work, although Moss, Gayden, Buttrey and occasionally McCoy worked as Barefoot Jerry.
Albums: *Area Code 615* (1969), *Trip In The Country* (1970)

Arnold, Eddy

b. Richard Edward Arnold, 15 May 1918, on a farm near Madisonville, Chester County, Tennessee, USA. Arnold's father and mother played fiddle and guitar respectively and he learned guitar as a child. His father died on his 11th birthday and Arnold left school prematurely to work on the farm. By the end of the year the bank foreclosed, and the farm was sold but the family stayed as sharecroppers. Deciding that such a thing would not happen to him again he turned his thoughts to music and began playing at local dances. In 1936, working with a fiddle-playing friend, Speedy McNatt, he made his debut on local radio WTJS Jackson and during the next few years played various venues including Memphis, Louisville and St. Louis. Between 1940 and 1943 he was a member of Pee Wee King's Golden West Cowboys, appearing with them on the *Grand Ole Opry* and touring with the *Opry's* travelling *Camel Caravan Show*. Late in 1943, as 'The Tennessee Plowboy', he launched his solo career playing six days a week on WSM. Signed by RCA Records he made his country chart debut in 1945 with 'Each Minute Seems A Million Years' and soon replaced Roy Acuff as country music's most popular and prolific singer. Between 1945 and 1955 he had 21 number 1 singles among his 68 US country chart hits. Sentimental ballads, incorporating the plaintive steel guitar work of Little Roy Wiggins, were the norm and many, such as the million sellers 'I'll Hold You In My Heart Till I Can Hold You In My Arms', 'Anytime', 'Bouquet Of Roses' and 'Just A Little Lovin' Will Go A Long Way', also became Top 30 US pop chart hits. Arguably his best remembered recording from this decade is 'Cattle Call'. During the late 40s he varied his image: although still retaining the nickname he became a country crooner wearing a tuxedo and bow tie. Colonel Tom Parker became his manager and was so successful with his promotion that Arnold was soon a nationally known star. Some of Parker's publicity stunts were unique for their time, such as the occasion when he travelled to a disc jockey convention in Nashville astride an elephant, bearing a cloth saying 'Never Forget Eddy Arnold'. Arnold began his solo *Opry* career as host of the *Ralston Purina* segment in 1946 but in 1948, due to

Parker's unacceptable demands on the WSM management for shares of gate receipts, he left, being replaced on the *Opry* roster by another country musician, George Morgan. In 1947, with the exception of Jimmy Wakely's recording of 'One Has My Heart', Arnold's recordings held the number 1 position in the country charts for the whole year. Arnold eventually tired of Parker's management and apparently sacked him; he has said it was because 'I am a very conservative man' but few believed that was the sole reason.

During the 50s he appeared on all major radio and television shows and became the first country singer to host his own network television show, *Eddy Arnold Time*. He also became one of the first country singers to play at Carnegie Hall and later appeared in concerts with major symphony orchestras. It is impossible to categorize his new style as either country or pure pop. Many of his early fans objected to it but the television and cabaret performances won him countless new fans from the wider audience and he easily maintained his popularity and chart successes. After 1954, his nickname no longer appeared on the records and he moved to MGM in 1972 but returned to RCA four years later. Between 1956 and 1983 he took his tally of US country chart hits to 145, his number 1 singles to 28 (and 92 of the entries had made the Top 10!). Again many recordings achieved crossover success including 'Tennessee Stud', 'What's He Doing In My World' and his biggest US pop hit 'Make The World Go Away', which reached number 6 in 1965 and the next year repeated it in the UK pop charts. Several of his albums have also achieved Top 10 status in the US album charts. He appeared in several films including starring in *Feudin' Rhythm* and *Hoedown* and even received a mention in *Jailhouse Rock*. He was elected to the Country Music Hall Of Fame in 1966 and by the 80s he had semi-retired to his home near Nashville. RCA have assessed that his record sales are in excess of 80 million – a figure bettered by pop stars, but exceeded only by Elvis Presley (who recorded seven of Arnold's songs) and Bing Crosby as comparable artists. His chart success, however, eclipses everybody and is unlikely ever to be beaten.

Albums: *Anytime* (1952), *All-Time Hits From The Hills* (1952), *All Time Favorites* (1953), *An American Institution (10th Anniversary Album)* (1954), *Chapel On The Hill* (1954), *Wanderin' With Eddy Arnold* (1955), *Anytime* (1955), *Chapel On The Hill* (1955), *All Time Favorites* (1955), *A Dozen Hits* (1956), *A Little On The Lonely Side* (1956), *When They Were*

Eddy Arnold

Young (1957), *My Darling, My Darling* (1957), *Praise Him, Praise Him (Fanny Crosby Hymns)* (1958), *Have Guitar, Will Travel* (reissued as *Eddy Arnold Goes Travelin'*) (1959), *Eddy Arnold* (1959), *Thereby Hangs A Tale* (1959), *Eddy Arnold Sings Them Again* (1960), *More Eddy Arnold* (1960), *You Gotta Have Love* (1960), *Christmas With Eddy Arnold* (1961), *Let's Make Memories Tonight* (1961), *One More Time* (1962), *Our Man Down South* (1963), *Country Songs I Love To Sing* (1963), *Faithfully Yours* (1963), *Cattle Call* (1963), *Pop Hits From The Country Side* (1964), *Eddy's Songs* (1964), with Needmore Creek Singers *Folk Song Book* (1964), *Sometimes I'm Happy, Sometimes I'm Blue* (1964), *The Easy Way* (1965), *I'm Throwing Rice (At The Girl I Love)* (1965), *My World* (1965), *Somebody Liked Me* (1966), *I Want To Go With You* (1966), *The Last Word In Lonesome* (1966), *Lonely Again* (1967), *Turn The World Around* (1967), *The Everloving World Of Eddy Arnold* (1968), *Romantic World Of Eddy Arnold* (1968), *Walkin' In Love Land* (1968), *Songs Of The Young World* (1969), *The Warmth Of Eddy Arnold* (1969), *The Glory Of Love* (1969), *This Is Eddy Arnold* (1970), *Standing Alone* (1970), *Love And Guitars* (1970), *Then You Can Tell Me Goodbye* (1971), *Welcome To My World* (1971), *Loving Her Was Easier* (1971), *Portrait Of My Woman* (1971), *Chained To A Memory* (1972), *Eddy Arnold (Sings For Housewives & Other Lovers)* (1972), *Lonely People* (1972), *I Love How You Love Me* (1973), *The World Of Eddy Arnold* (1973), *Christmas Greetings From Nashville* (1973), *So Many Ways/If The Whole World Stopped Lovin'* (1973), *Eddy Arnold Sings Love Songs* (1974), *I Wish That I Had Loved You Better* (1974), *Misty Blue* (1974), *She's Got Everything I Need* (1974), *Country Gold* (1975), *Pure Gold-Eddy Arnold* (1975), *The Wonderful World Of Eddy Arnold* (1975), *Eddy* (1976), *Eddy Arnold's World Of Hits* (1976), *I Need You All The Time* (1977), *Somebody Loves You* (1979), *Eddy Arnold's Best* (1979), *A Legend And His Lady* (1980), *Man For All Seasons* (1981), *Country Music - Eddy Arnold* (1981), *Don't Give Up On Me* (1982), *Close Enough To Love* (1983), *Eddy Arnold - A Legendary Performer* (1983). Further reading: *It's A Long Way From Chester County*, Eddy Arnold.

Ashworth, Ernie

b. Ernest Bert Ashworth, 15 December 1928, Huntsville, Alabama, USA. In his youth, the country singer-songwriter longed to be a star on the *Grand Ole Opry*. His first job was in the civil service, but he moved into radio in Huntsville in the late 40s and played in a local band, the Tune Twisters. Ashworth moved to Nashville in 1950 where he worked in radio and television. In 1955, as Billy Worth, he made his first recordings for MGM but he grew disillusioned and returned to Huntsville in 1957 where he worked in a missile factory. In 1960 Wesley Rose became his manager and secured a contract with US Decca Records. His first release, 'Each Moment Spent With You', reached number 4 in the US country charts. In 1962, after further country hits with 'You Can't Pick A Rose In December' and 'Forever Gone', he moved to Hickory Records and found success with 'Everybody But Me'. In 1963 his recording of John D. Loudermilk's 'Talk Back Trembling Lips' topped the US country charts, although it was a pop hit for Johnny Tillotson. In March 1964 Ashworth became a member of the *Opry* and remains a regular performer, now known as Ernie rather than Ernest. He was featured in the 1965 film, *The Farmer's Other Daughter*, and other successes included 'I Love To Dance With Annie' and 'The D.J. Cried'. Ashworth still tours but mostly he entertains tourists in Pigeon Forge, Tennessee.

Selected albums: *Talk Back Trembling Tips* (1963), *Hits Of Today And Tomorrow* (1964), *The Best Of Ernie Ashworth* (1968), *Ernest Ashworth Sings His Greatest Hits* (1976).

Asleep At The Wheel

Ray Benson (b. 16 March 1951, Philadelphia, Pennsylvania, USA; guitar/vocals), Christine O'Connell (b. 21 March 1953, Williamsport, Maryland, USA; vocals), Lucky Oceans (b. Reuben Gosfield, 22 April 1951, Philadelphia, Pennsylvania, USA; steel guitar), Floyd Domino (piano) and Leroy Preston (rhythm guitar/drums) formed the core of this protean western swing-styled unit. Although initially based in West Virginia, the group later moved to Austin, Texas where they found a more receptive audience in the wake of their infectious debut album. They scored a US Top 10 single in 1973 with 'The Letter That Johnny Walker Read' and won a Grammy for their version of Count Basie's 'One O'Clock Jump'. However, despite an undoubted in-concert appeal and an appearance in the rock film *Roadie*, the group's anachronistic style has hampered a more widespread success.

Albums: *Comin' Right At Ya* (1973), *Asleep At The Wheel* (1974), *Texas Gold* (1975), *Wheelin' And Dealin'* (1976), with various artists *Texas Country* (1976), *The Wheel* (1977), *Collision Course* (1978), *Served Live* (1979), *Framed* (1980), *Pasture Prime*

Asleep At The Wheel

(1985), *Jumpin' At The Woodside* (1986), *Ten* (1987), *Asleep At The Wheel* (1987), *Western Standard Time* (1988), *Greatest Hits - Live & Kickin'* (1992). Compilation: *The Very Best Of Asleep At The Wheel* (1987).

Atcher, Bob

b. James Robert Atcher, 11 May 1914, Hardin County, Kentucky, USA. Atcher was the son of a tobacco farmer and square dance fiddler. The family moved to the Red River Valley of North Dakota in 1918 and here Atcher developed his love for cowboy songs. In 1926 the family returned to Kentucky and Atcher was soon performing on local radio. By 1931, he had a repertoire of hundreds of songs and his shows were heard over a wide area. Bob Atcher And His Kentucky Mountain Minstrels included his brother Francis, and Loeta Applegate who was the first of several vocalists to be given the name of 'Bonnie Blue Eyes'. Atcher recorded for US Columbia Records from 1937-58. In 1939, his comic 'crying' version of the Carter Family's 'I'm Thinking Tonight Of My Blue Eyes', was successful. Atcher appeared in westerns, wore cowboy outfits and often appeared with his horse, Golden Storm. Atcher recorded many western songs and his version of 'You Are My Sunshine' was recorded before that of Jimmie Davis. He was a featured performer on WLS'

National Barn Dance for many years from 1948. His USA country hits include 'I Must Have Been Wrong', 'Signed, Sealed And Delivered', 'Tennessee Border' and 'Why Don't You Haul Off And Love Me?'. He also wrote 'Don't Rob Another Man's Castle' and 'Money, Marbles And Chalk'. In 1959 he became mayor of Schaumburg, Illinois and concentrated on politics for the next 16 years. In the mid-70s, he started performing with his family, often featuring gospel music.

Albums: *Bob Atcher's Early American Folk Songs* (1953, 10-inch album), *Songs Of The Saddle* (1954, 10-inch album), *Bob Atcher's Early American Folk Songs* (1955, 12-inch album), *Dean Of Cowboy Singers* (1964).

Atkins, Chet

b. Chester Burton Atkins, 20 June 1924, Luttrell, Tennessee, USA. Atkins is one of the most influential and prolific guitarists of the 20th century, as well as an important producer and an RCA Records executive. The son of a music teacher and brother of guitarist Jim Atkins (who played with Les Paul), Atkins began as a fiddler in the early 40s, with the Dixieland Swingers in Knoxville, Tennessee. He also played with artists including Bill Carlisle and Shorty Thompson. He moved to Cincinnati, Ohio in 1946 and his first recording session took place that year, for Jim

Chet Atkins

Bullet, and in 1947 Atkins was signed to RCA, recording 16 tracks on August 11, including a number of vocals. Atkins first performed at the Grand Ole Opry in Nashville in 1948, working with a band that included satirists Homer And Jethro. He toured with Maybelle Carter in 1949 and recorded as an accompanist with the Carter Family the following year. At that time he made a decision to concentrate on session work, encouraged and often hired by music publisher Fred Rose. Atkins recorded largely with MGM Records artists, such as Red Sovine and the Louvin Brothers, during this period, and most notably on 24 of Hank Williams' tracks for the label. He also recorded on several of the Everly Brothers' Cadence Records hits later in the 50s. In 1952 RCA executive Steve Sholes, who had signed Atkins for session work, gave him authority to build up the label's roster, and Atkins began a second career as a talent scout. By the mid-50s he was recording his own albums and producing 30 artists a year for RCA. Atkins' first album, Chet Atkins' Gallopin' Guitar, was issued in 1953, his discography eventually reaching to over 100 albums under his own name. Among the other artists with whom he worked at RCA were Elvis Presley, Jim Reeves, Don Gibson, Charley Pride, Waylon Jennings, Hank Snow, Jerry Reed, Perry Como and many others. He is generally regarded as the chief architect of the 'Nashville Sound'. His trademark guitar was a Grestch, which was later manufactured as the 'Chet Atkins Country Gentleman'. George Harrison endorsed this instrument, and this led to a huge increase in sales for the company during the 60s. During this decade Chet recorded the first of a series of guitar duet albums; including works with Snow, Reed, Merle Travis, Les Paul and Doc Watson. Atkins was named an RCA vice president in 1968 and remained in that position until 1979. In the early 80s he left RCA for Columbia Records and continued to record for that company into the 90s. He has won several Grammy awards and was elected to the Country Music Hall of Fame in 1973. Atkins' unique stature in the country music industry was encapsulated by the city's decision to name a street on 'Music Row' after him.
Selected albums: Chet Atkins' Gallopin' Guitar (1953), Chet Atkins In Three Dimensions (1956), Finger Style Guitar (1958), Mister Guitar (1959), Teensville (1959), Chet Atkins' Workshop (1960), Down Home (1961), The Best Of Chet Atkins (1963), with Hank Snow Reminiscing (1964), Chet Atkins Picks On The Beatles (1965), with Jerry Reed

Me And Jerry (1970), with Merle Travis The Atkins-Travis Traveling Show (1974), with Les Paul Chester And Lester (1975), with Floyd Cramer and Danny Davis Chet, Floyd And Danny (1977), Me And My Guitar (1977), with Les Paul Guitar Monsters (1978), The First Nashville Guitar Quartet (1979), The Best Of Chet On The Road...Live (1980), with Doc Watson Reflections (1980), with Lenny Breau Standard Brands (1981), Work It Out With Chet Atkins 1983), Stay Tuned (1985), Sails (1987), Chet Atkins, C.G.P. (1988), with Mark Knopfler Neck & Neck (1992), with Jerry Reed Sneakin' Around (1992). Compilations: Solid Gold Guitar (1982), Guitar Pickin' Man (1983), 20 Of The Best (1986), Best Of Chet Atkins And Friends (1987), The RCA Years (1992).

Auldridge, Mike

This highly respected dobro player has performed on a number of bluegrass and country albums, mostly with the Seldom Scene. Auldridge is the nephew of Ellsworth T. Cozzens, the Hawaiian steel guitarist who played on several Jimmie Rodgers records. Having started playing guitar at the age of 12, Auldridge progressed to banjo within a short space of time, and was almost 20 when he played dobro for the first time. In 1969, Auldridge joined Emerson and Waldron, but with Bill Emerson leaving to join the Country Gentlemen, Auldridge continued performing with Cliff Waldron, from Jolo, West Virginia. The act grew to become the New Shades Of Grass, a six-piece outfit. Waldron planned to tour extensively, not a popular move in the eyes of Auldridge, who left with group member Ben Eldridge. With John Duffey Eldridge (banjo), Tom Gray (bass), John Starling (guitar/vocals) they formed the Seldom Scene. They have made a number of fine bluegrass recordings and Auldridge continues to do session work for other artists.
Albums: Dobro (1974), Mike Auldridge (1976), Blues And Bluegrass (1977), An Old Dog (1978), with Jeff Newman Slidin' Smoke (1979), Eight String Swing (1988), Mike Auldrige And Old Dog (1989), Auldridge, Reid And Coleman High Time (1990).

Autry, Gene

b. Orvon Gene Autry, 29 September 1907, near Tioga, Texas, USA. The eldest of four children of Delbert Autry, a poor tenant farmer, who moved his family many times over the years, before eventually arriving at Ravia, Oklahoma. His grandfather, a Baptist minister, taught him to sing when he was a child so that he could perform in

Gene Autry

his church choir and at other local events. Autry also learned to ride at an early age and worked the fields with his father. He grew up listening to cowboy songs and received his first guitar at the age of 12. (Initially he studied the saxophone but chose the guitar so that he could sing as well.) He graduated from Ravia Community School in 1924 and after spending a few months with a Medicine Show, he found work as a telegraph operator for the Frisco Railroad in Chelsea, Oklahoma. He used to take his guitar to work and sing and one night was heard by the famous entertainer Will Rogers, who stopped to send a telegram. He suggested that Autry should look for a job in radio. After trying unsuccessfully to find work in New York, he returned to Oklahoma and began to appear on KVOO Tulsa as The Oklahoma Yodeling Cowboy. After hearing recordings of Jimmie Rodgers, he became something of a Rodgers clone as he tried to further his career. In 1929, he made his first RCA Victor recordings, 'My Dreaming Of You' and 'My Alabama Home', on which he was accompanied by Jimmy Long (a fellow telegrapher) and Frankie and Johnny Marvin. Further recordings followed for ARC Records under the direction of Art Satherly, some being released on various labels for chain store sales. It was because of releases on Conqueror for Sears that Autry found himself given the opportunity to join WLS in Chicago. In 1931, he became a featured artist on the *National Barn Dance*, as well as having his own *Conqueror Record Time*. Before long, Gene Autry 'Roundup' guitars and songbooks were being sold by Sears. Interestingly, WLS portrayed him as a singing cowboy even though, at this time, few of his songs were of that genre. Between 1931 and 1934, he was a hillbilly singer, who still at times sounded like Rodgers. In fact most experts later rated him the best of the Rodgers' impersonators. He began to include his own songs and such numbers as 'The Gangster's Warning' and 'My Old Pal Of Yesterday' became very popular.

Late in 1931, he recorded 'That Silver Haired Daddy Of Mine' as a duet with Jimmy Long, with whom he had co-written the song. The song eventually became Autry's first million selling record. By 1934, he was well known as a radio and recording personality. Having for some time been portrayed as a singing cowboy by the publicity departments of his record companies, he now took his first steps to make the publicity come true. He was given a small part in the Ken Maynard film *In Old Santa Fe* and soon after starred in a strange 12-episode western/science fiction serial called *The Phantom Empire*. In 1935, Republic Pictures signed him to a contract and *Tumbling Tumbleweeds* became his first starring western film. His previous singing cowboy image was now reality. He sang eight songs in the film including the title track, 'That Silver Haired Daddy' and 'Ridin' Down The Canyon'. Further films followed in quick succession and by 1940 Autry ranked fourth among all Hollywood money-making stars at the box office. In January 1940, Gene Autry's *Melody Ranch* radio show, sponsored by the Wrigley Gum Company, first appeared on CBS and soon became a national institution, running until 1956. Helped out by such artists as Pat Buttram, Johnny Bond and The Cass County Boys, Autry regularly righted wrongs, sang his hits and as a result of the programme, built himself a new home in the San Fernando Valley called Melody Ranch.

Quite apart from the radio shows and films, he toured extensively with his stage show. It featured roping, Indian dancers, comedy, fancy riding from Autry, smart horse tricks by Champion and music. By 1941, he was respected and famous all over the USA The little town of Berwyn, Oklahoma even changed its name to Gene Autry, Oklahoma. His songs such as 'Be Honest With Me', 'Back In The Saddle Again' (which became his signature tune), 'Your The Only Star In My Blue Heaven', 'Goodbye, Little Darlin' Goodbye' (later recorded by Johnny Cash) and many more became tremendously popular. In 1942, his income took a severe cut when he enlisted in the Air Force, being sworn-in live on a *Melody Ranch* programme. He spent some time working on recruitment but then became a pilot in Air Ferry Command and saw service in the Far East, India and North Africa. During this period, he co-wrote with Fred Rose his classic song, 'At Mail Call Today'. After his release from the services, he resumed his acting and recording career. Between 1944 and 1951, he registered 25 successive Top 10 country hits, including 'Here Comes Santa Claus' (later recorded by Elvis Presley), 'Rudolph, The Red-Nosed Reindeer', 'Peter Cottontail' and 'Frosty The Snow Man', which each sold one million copies. He also had Top 20 US pop chart success with 'Buttons And Bows'. He left Republic in 1947 and formed his own Flying A Productions, which produced his later films for release by Columbia. When he made his last b-western, *Last Of The Pony Riders*, in 1953 he had 89 feature films to his credit. Contrary to many beliefs, there never was a feud between Autry and his replacement at

Republic, Roy Rogers. It was purely something invented by Republic's publicity department.

During the 50s, he became very successful in business and purchased many radio and television stations. Between 1950 and 1956, he produced 91 episodes of *The Gene Autry Show* for CBS-TV. His company also produced many other television series, including *The Range Rider, The Adventures Of Champion* and *Annie Oakley*. His business interest became even more involved during the 60s, when apart from owning various radio and television companies, he became the owner of the California Angels major league baseball team. *Melody Ranch* reappeared as a television programme in the 60s and ran for seven years on Autry's KTLA station. It was syndicated to stations across the country and although Autry did not appear as a regular, he did make guest appearances. In 1986, Nashville Network decided to screen his Republic and Columbia b-westerns under the title of *Melody Ranch Theatre* with Autry himself doing opening and closing announcements. During his long career, Autry had three horses to fill the role of Champion. The original died in 1947. Champion III, who appeared in the Gene Autry television series and also as the star of the *Adventures Of Champion* television series, died in 1991 at the age of 42. There was also a personal appearance Champion and a pony known as Little Champ. During his career he regularly sported a custom made C.F. Martin guitar, with beautiful ornamental pearl inlay together with his name. Many artists over subsequent years have copied this guitar, having their own name inlaid into the fret board. Autry was elected to the Country Music Hall Of Fame in 1969 for his songwriting abilities as well as his singing and acting. In 1980, he was inducted into the Cowboy Hall Of Fame Of Great Westerners. At the time of his induction, he was described as 'one of the most famous men, not only in America but in the world'. Autry sold the final 10 acres of his Melody Ranch film set in 1991. The ranch, in Placerita Canyon, California, which was used for the making of such classic westerns as *High Noon* and the television series *Gunsmoke* is scheduled to become an historical feature. His last US country chart entry was 'Old Soldiers Never Die' in 1971. Judging by the popularity of his old films and his recordings, it is probably true to say that neither do old cowboys.

Selected albums: *Western Classics* (c.50s), *Western Classics Vol. 2* (c.50s), *Rusty The Rocking Horse & Bucky, The Bucking Bronco* (1955), *Little Johnny Pilgrim & Guffy The Goofy Gobbler* (1955), *Stampede* (1955), *The Story Of The Nativity* (1955), *Gene Autry & Champion Western Adventures* (1955), *Sings Peter Cottontail* (1955), *Merry Christmas with Gene Autry* (1955), *At The Rodeo* (1959), *Christmas With Gene Autry* (1958), *Greatest Hits* (1961), *Golden Hits* (1962), with Rosemary Clooney *Christmas Favorite* (1964), *Great Western Hits* (1965), *Melody Ranch* (1965), with Clooney and Art Carney *Sings Peter Cottontail (First Easter Record For Children)* (1965), *Gene Autry Sings* (1966), *Back In The Saddle Again* (1968), *Country Music Hall Of Fame* (1970), *Christmas Time* (1974), *Melody Ranch - A Radio Western Adventure* (1975), *Live From Madison Square Garden* (1976), *Christmas With Gene Autry* (1976), *Cowboy Hall Of Fame* (1976), *Favorites* (1976), *Classics* (1977), *Murray Hill Record Theatre Presents Gene Autry's Melody Ranch* (1977, 4 album set), *Melody Ranch (3 Shows)* (1977), *50th Anniversary Album* (1978), *Songs Of Faith* (1978), *Christmas Classics* (1978), *Back In The Saddle Again* (1980), *Columbia Historic Edition* (1982), *Sounds Like Jimmie Rodgers* (1985).

Further reading: *Back In The Saddle Again*, Gene Autry with Mickey Herskowitz. *The Gene Autry Book*, David Rothel.

Axton, Hoyt

b. 23 March 1938, Duncan, Oklahoma, USA. The son of Mae Axton (who wrote Elvis Presley's first hit, 'Heartbreak Hotel'). Hoyt began as a folk singer on the west coast. In 1962, he signed for Horizon Records for his first album, *The Balladeer*, which featured future Byrds leader Jim McGuinn on guitar. As the 60s unfolded, Axton expanded his repertoire to include blues and country, while also establishing himself as a songwriter of considerable talent. His first hit as a composer was the Kingston Trio's 'Greenback Dollar' and later in the decade he wrote Steppenwolf's famous drug song, 'The Pusher'. The victim of cocaine addiction for many years, he still managed to record a prolific number of albums, though it was as a composer that he enjoyed commercial success. Two major hits in the 70s, courtesy of Three Dog Night ('Joy To The World') and Ringo Starr ('No No Song') supplemented his income, while also maintaining his standing as a recording artist. Having overcome his drug dependency at the end of the decade, he appeared in the film *The Black Stallion*, formed his own record label Jeremiah, and continued touring on a regional basis. In 1991 he made an attempt to re-enter the recording market with the critically acclaimed *Spin Of The Wheel*.

Selected albums: *The Balladeer* (1962), *Thunder 'n'*

Hoyt Axton

Lightnin' (1963), *Saturday's Child* (1963), *Hoyt Axton Explodes* (1964), *Greenback Dollar* (1964), *Hoyt Axton Sings Bessie Smith* (1964), *My Way* (1964), *Mr Greenback Dollar Man* (1965), *My Griffin Is Gone* (1969), *Joy To The World* (1971), *Country Anthem* (1971), *Less Than A Song* (1973), *Life Machine* (1974), *Southbound* (1975), *Fearless* (1976), *Road Songs* (1977), *Snowblind Friend* (1977), *Free Sailin'* (1978), *A Rusty Old Halo* (1979), *Where Did The Money Go* (1980), *Everybody's Going On The Road* (1982), *Spin Of The Wheel* (1991).

B

Bailes Brothers

Homer Bailes, a carpenter and preacher, and his wife Nannie rented a small farm in Kanawha County, near Charleston, West Virginia, USA and in the face of abject poverty, they struggled to raise their four sons. They were Kyle (b. 7 May 1915), John (b. 24 June 1918, d. January 1990, Swainsboro, Georgia, USA), Walter Butler (b. 17 January 1920) and Homer (b. 8 May 1922). After her husband's death in 1925, Nannie took in washing to supplement the income and Kyle's schooling was curtailed as he found work to bring in some money. The boys had a guitar, which their mother managed to buy from a mail order catalogue. Nannie had children by a previous marriage and in the early 30s, their half-brother, Jennings Thomas, who worked as a rodeo rider and musician, arrived home and created sufficient interest in music for he and Kyle to sing together on local radio. A few years later, after crop failure, the family moved to Charleston, where Johnny found work to keep his two siblings at school but soon looked for a musical career. The boys sang together locally and appeared in churches as the Hymn Singers. Johnny worked for a time with a medicine show but he soon joined with Kyle and Walter on a regular radio programme on WCHS. In 1937, Johnnie Bailes and his close friend Red Sovine appeared as Smiley and Red the Singing Sailors and also became members of Jim Pike's Carolina Tar Heels. For a short time, in 1938, they played on WWVA Wheeling but returned to Charleston when Sovine married. In 1939, Johnnie formed a group known as the Happy Valley Folks, which included Skeets Williamson, his sister LaVerne (who became famous as Molly O'Day) and Little Jimmy Dickens, who was billed as the Singing Midget. They played regularly on WJLS Beckley and proved very popular. Walter and Kyle Bailes were playing with their group at WCHS and at WPAR but also soon moved to Beckley. Early in 1941, both groups disbanded and Johnnie and Walter appeared on WCHS as a duo, although on occasions they were joined by their brothers. They moved to WSAZ Huntington, where their popularity grew as a result of their radio show *Tri-State Jamboree,* so called because of the station's powerful transmissions that covered parts of Kentucky and Ohio as well as West Virginia. In 1943, their friendship with Roy Acuff led to their becoming members of the *Grand Ole Opry.* (Johnnie and Walter became the first West Virginians to star on the *Opry*). Kyle worked at various stations and after Homer's military service, both eventually joined their brothers in Nashville. Late in 1946, they recorded for King and about the same time, they left the *Opry* and moved to KWKH Shreveport. When the *Louisiana Hayride* commenced in 1948, they soon became firm favourites and had so many requests to play outside venues that a second group was formed, which contained Jimmie Osborne and Claude King. Their band, the West Virginia Home Folks, contained several noted instrumentalists, including steel guitarist Shot Jackson and mandolinist Clyde Baum. The four brothers recorded for Columbia in April 1947 and in July, Walter left to become a minister. Soon after Kyle also withdrew from playing but acted as manager and his place was taken by Tillman Franks. Johnnie and Homer had some disagreement and parted late in 1949, which led to them performing on different stations. After this the family continued to be involved with country and gospel music. In August 1952, Walter and Johnnie reunited at KCRT, Baytown, Texas, for a religious show in which Walter preached and Johnnie sang.

They also recorded together for King Records in 1953 and continued to work together until 1956, when Johnnie became a disc jockey in Georgia. During the 60s, Walter was in Birmingham and continued his work as an evangelist and sometimes sang with his wife, Kyle. She had worked throughout the 50s with Homer, then joined Walter in 1962 and together they performed with bluegrass gospel groups on occasions collaborating with Johnnie. Walter made many solo recordings and duets with Kyle, and in 1967 recorded an album with Homer. Late in 1972, Johnnie and Homer recorded an album for Starday. By the mid-70s, Kyle was involved with an air-conditioning business, Johnnie was the general manager of three radio stations owned by Webb Pierce. Homer, having entered the ministry, was the pastor of a church in Roanoke. Walter (sometimes referred to as the Chaplain of Music Row) continued to work as a gospel singer and evangelist and appeared and recorded with Frankie and Dorothy Jo Hope as the Walter Bailes Singers. The Bailes later promoted recordings on their own White Dove label. In the early 80s, Homer recorded two albums and in 1982, Kyle and Walter did a tour of Holland. Quite apart from their own recordings many other artists have also recorded songs written by the brothers. These include such noted country numbers as 'Give Mother My Crown' (Carl And Pearl Butler and Flatt And Scruggs), 'The Pale Horse And His Rider' (Hank Williams and Roy Acuff), 'Dust On The Bible' (Blue Sky Boys and Johnny And Jack and Kitty Wells), 'Whiskey Is The Devil' (Webb Pierce), 'Oh, So Many Years' (Everly Brothers and George Hamilton IV) and 'Will The Angels Have A Sweetheart' (Bill Clifton). Johnny Bailes died in January 1990 at Swainsboro, Georgia, USA.

Albums: as the Bailes Brothers (various combinations) *The Avenue Of Prayer* (1959), *I've Got My One Way Ticket* (1976), *Johnny And Homer* (1977), *Johnny And Homer Volume 2* (1977), *Johnny And Walter* (1978), *Gospel Reunion* (1978), *Family Reunion* (1983). Solo albums: Homer Bailes *Golden Treasures* (80s), *Tenderly He Watched* (80s). Walter Bailes *Bluegrass Gospel* (80s), *It Takes A Lot of Living To Learn* (80s).

Bailey, Deford

b. 1899, Carthage, Smith County, Tennessee, USA, d. 2 July 1982. Bailey suffered from infantile paralysis and although he recovered, he was left with a deformed back and only grew to 4 feet 10 inches. He learned guitar, fiddle, banjo and harmonica from his father and uncle, who were both noted musicians, and by the age of 14, was making a living from playing the harmonica. He moved to Nashville and, in 1925, he met Dr. Humphrey Bate, a respected harmonica player, who brought him to the attention of the *Grand Ole Opry*. Quite apart from being the *Opry*'s first black artist, Bailey was also its first solo star, although he only received $5 a performance. It was, however, difficult for him to play his self-termed 'black hillbilly' music to white audiences in the South. He recorded for the USA labels, Columbia, Brunswick and Victor during 1927-28 but he did not record after that. His best-known work is 'Pan American Blues', which is remembered for its train imitations, and he always appeared smartly dressed in a three-piece suit, matching hat and highly polished shoes. Bailey was dismissed by the *Opry* in 1941, allegedly for refusing to learn new tunes. Bailey, however, maintained that the real reason

was racial. He never forgave the *Opry* as he bitterly shined shoes for a living. He made a brief television appearance on a blues show in the 60s but he invariably rejected offers he received. There was no other black performer at the *Opry* until Charley Pride. In April 1982, Bailey made his last appearance at the *Opry*, playing 'Pan American Blues' on an old-timers show.

Selected album: *Harmonica Showcase* (1985).

Further reading: *Deford Bailey - A Black Star In Early Country Music*, David C. Morton and Charles K. Wolf.

Bailey, Razzy

b. Erastus Michael Bailey, 14 February 1939, Five Points, Alabama, USA. Razzy grew up on a small farm and his parents encouraged him to learn the guitar for their Saturday night singalongs. He cut his first record at the age of 10, formed his first band when he was 15 and spent nearly 20 years playing honky tonks in Georgia and Alabama. Among his singles were 'Stolen Moments', which was produced by Freddy Weller, and 'I Hate Hate' but commercial success eluded him. He recorded his own song, '9,999,999 Tears', with Freddy Weller and Billy Joe Royal on back-up vocals and production by Joe South. In 1976, Dickie Lee covered the song and made both the US country and pop charts. Razzy then started recording for the same label and in 1978 registered his first country Top 10 hit with 'What Time Do You Have To Be Back To Heaven?' In 1980, he topped the US country charts with a cheating song, 'Loving Up A Storm' and then, most unusually, he had three double-sided number 1s, 'I Keep Coming Back'/'True Life Country Music', 'Friends'/'Anywhere There's A Jukebox' and 'Midnight Hauler'/'Scratch My Back (And Whisper In My Ear)'. His last US country number 1 was with 'She Left Love All Over Me' in 1982. Bailey's records combine R&B with country music and his version of Wilson Pickett's 'In The Midnight Hour' was a country hit.

Albums: *If Love Had A Face* (1979), *Razzy Bailey* (1980), *Makin' Friends* (1981), *Feelin' Right* (1982), *A Little More Razz* (1982), *The Midnight Hour* (1984), *A Little Razzle Dazzle* (1984), *Arrival* (1985), *Cut From A Different Stone* (1985).

Baillie And The Boys

Michael Bonagura and Alan LeBoeuf merged their talents in the early 70s in a band called London Fog, and in 1973 they met Kathie Baillie, who was to marry Bonagura. They provided backing vocals for several pop acts including the Ramones and Talking Heads. In 1977, Alan LeBoeuf spent two years portraying Paul McCartney in the Broadway show, *Beatlemania*. In the 80s, they worked with country performer, Ed Bruce, and soon they were signed in their own right to make their own close harmony albums for RCA Records. They had US Top 10 country singles with 'Oh Heart', 'Wilder Days' and 'Long Shot'. LeBoeuf left in 1989 so they are now effectively Baillie And The Boy.

Albums: *Baillie And The Boys* (1987), *Turn The Tide* (1989), *The Lights Of Home* (1990).

Baker, Carroll

b. 4 March 1949, Bridgewater, Nova Scotia, Canada. Baker spent much of her childhood in the small fishing village of Port Medway, Nova Scotia. She was greatly influenced by her father, a well-known, old-time country fiddler, but did not share his dislike of rock 'n' roll. When she was 16-years-old, the family moved away from Toronto and she built up a reputation singing in local clubs. In 1970, she had a Canadian hit with her first record, 'Memories Of Home'. After several other successes, RCA Records, impressed that she was outselling their American country stars, guaranteed her world-wide distribution. Although Baker only ever had minor successes in the US country charts, she is known for her full-scale assault on Conway Twitty's 'I've Never Been This Far Before' and a maudlin narrative in which she assumed a child's voice, 'Portrait In The Window'. Her version of 'Me And Bobby McGee' successfully merged Kris Kristofferson and Janis Joplin's approaches. Audiences who saw her at the Wembley Country Festival in the UK or on tour with Slim Whitman were impressed by her powerful 'Why Me Lord?'. After a few years she realized that her main audience was in Canada. In 1985, she was among the featured artists on the Canadian charity single, 'Tears Are Not Enough' by Northern Lights, and in 1988 she recorded a passionate duet with Jack Scott, 'The Best Of Love'. She says, 'People in Nashville think that Canadians buy our records because 30% of the music played on the radio has to be made by Canadians. However, you can't make people buy records. They buy them 'cause they like them.'

Albums: *Carroll Baker* (1976), *Sweet Sensation* (1977), *If It Wasn't For You* (1978), *I'd Go Thru It All Over Again* (1979), *Hollywood Love* (1980), *All For The Love Of A Song* (1981), *20 Country Classics* (mid-80s), *A Step In The Right Direction* (1985), *Hymns Of Gold* (80s), *Heartbreak To Happiness*

(1986), *At Home In The Country* (1988).

Baker, Etta

b. 1913, Caldwell County, North Carolina, USA. From a black family that was proficient in blues, pop, hymns, rags, ballads, dance music and, through intermarriage, white country music, Etta Reid learned guitar, banjo, fiddle and piano, playing alongside her father, Boone Reid, and her elder sister Cora. She married 1936, when her husband, though himself a pianist, discouraged public performance. She was recorded in 1956, and her fluent, raggy guitar became something of a cult among urban folk revivalists, particularly on 'One Dime Blues'. (Her father and Cora's husband Lacey Phillips were also recorded, on banjo, in 1956.) Etta took up her career only after her husband had died. Baker resumed public performances and showed that she was still a magnificent guitarist and banjo player.

Albums: *Instrumental Music Of The Southern Appalachians* (1956), *Music From The Hills Of Caldwell County* (70s), *One Dime Blues* (1991).

Bandy, Moe

b. Marion Bandy, 12 February 1944, Meridian, Mississippi, USA. Bandy was nicknamed Moe by his father when a child in the hometown of the legendary Jimmie Rodgers, so it is perhaps not surprising that Bandy grew up to be a country singer. He later stated 'My grandfather worked on the railroads with Jimmie Rodgers. He was the boss of the railway yard in Meridian and Jimmie Rodgers worked for him. He said that he played his guitar all the time between work.' The Bandy family relocated to San Antonio, Texas, when the boy was six years old and he was educated there, graduating in 1962. His mother played piano and sang, Bandy was taught to play the guitar by his father but made little use of the ability until he was in his teens. His father's wish that he also play the fiddle never quite materialized. He made some appearances with his father's country band, the Mission City Playboys, but generally during his high school days he showed little interest in music but a great deal in rodeos. He tried bronco-busting and bull-riding and by the time he was 16, he was competing in rodeos all over Texas. In 1962, tired of the bruises and fractured bones, he began to look for a career in country music. He assembled a band that he called Moe And The Mavericks and found work playing small beer parlours, honky tonks and clubs over a wide area around San Antonio, Texas. When he was young he tried to sound like Hank Williams and George Jones - 'I even had my hair cut short like his'. Although work was plentiful the pay was poor and during the day he worked for his father as a sheet metal worker. This was to last for the next 12 years, during which time he made a few recordings for various small labels. In 1964, he had his first single, 'Lonely Lady', on the Satin label but it made little impression. He did manage to get his band a residency on a local television programme called *Country Corner* and in this capacity, he provided backing for several touring stars. In 1973, he went solo when record producer Ray Baker, who had listened to Bandy's demos the previous year, suggested he come to Nashville. Bandy managed to get a loan and recorded a song called 'I Just Started Hatin' Cheatin' Songs Today'. Initially released on Footprint Records with a limited pressing of 500 copies, it soon came to the attention of the Atlanta based GRC label. In March 1974, it entered the US country charts, eventually peaking at number 17. Other hits followed including 'It Was Always So Easy To Find An Unhappy Woman' and 'Don't Anyone Make Love At Home Anymore'. In 1975, a song written by his friend Lefty Frizzell and Whitey Shaffer, gave him a number 7 country hit which firmly established his reputation. 'Bandy The Rodeo Clown' was to become not only one of his own favourites but also one of his all time most popular recordings. (Shaffer was greatly amused by the way Bandy pronounced woman as 'wah-man' and began to send him songs with 'wah-man' in them). Bandy sang in a simple style that extracted the utmost from his songs of lost love, sadness and life. Although by no means a Hank Williams sound-a-like, he showed a very distinct influence in his method of putting across his honky tonk songs. He met with immediate success at Columbia with Paul Craft's 'Hank Williams, You Wrote My Life' and quickly added further hits including 'Here I Am Drunk Again'. Between 1977-79, he was a country chart regular with singles such as 'I'm Sorry For You, My Friend' (the song Hank had written for their mutual friend Lefty Frizzell), 'Cowboys Ain't Supposed To Cry', 'That's What Makes The Juke Box Play' and a duet with Janie Fricke 'It's A Cheatin' Situation'. In 1979, he achieved his first solo number 1 with 'I Cheated Me Right Out Of You'.

Also during 1979, as a result of touring together in Europe, Bandy joined forces with Joe Stampley and a single release of 'Just Good Ole Boys' became a number 1 country hit and led to a continuation of the partnership over the following years. The idea for the two singers to merge was hatched at the Hard Rock Cafe London during their appearance at the Wembley Festival. They thought that Moe and Joe sounded good together - like Waylon and Willie. It was not too surprising that they proved a successful double act. Between 1979-85, their further hits included 'Holding The Bag', 'Tell Ole I Ain't Here' and 'Hey Joe (Hey Moe)'. In 1984, they ran into copyright problems with their parody of pop singer Boy George called 'Where's The Dress', when they used the introduction of Culture Club's hit 'Karma Chameleon'. Referring to the matter later Moe said 'He didn't appreciate what we'd done and naturally he sued us. We paid him money, but I didn't like the way he spent it.' Apart from their single successes Moe and Joe recorded several albums together. During the 80s, Bandy maintained a steady line of solo successes including 'Yesterday Once More', 'Rodeo Romeo', 'She's Not Really Cheatin' (She's Just Gettin' Even)'and 'Till I'm Too Old To Die Young'. He also registered duet successes with Judy Bailey ('Following The Feeling') and Becky Hobbs ('Let's Get Over Them Together'). Over the years he maintained a touring schedule estimated to average between 250-300 days a year and he also made numerous network television shows. In later years he cut back considerably on his schedules. He was never a regular *Grand Ole Opry* member but has made guest appearances from time to time. He first appeared in Britain in 1978, when his hard-line pure country material made him a very popular artist with British country audiences. Bandy summed his music up when he said 'I really think my songs are about life. There's cheating, drinking and divorcing going on everywhere and that's what hardcore country music is all about'. He added: 'If I'd done all the things I sing about. I'd be dead'. Critics reviewing some of his later recordings wrote that it was strange that, at a time when more artists were actually recording his type of music, some of his recordings were spoiled by string and/or choir arrangements and suggested that an immediate return to his roots was needed.

Albums: *I Just Started Hatin' Cheatin' Songs Today* (1974), *It Was Always So Easy (To Find An Unhappy Woman)* (1975), *Bandy The Rodeo Clown* (1975), *Hank Williams, You Wrote My Life* (1976), *Here I Am Drunk Again* (1976), *I'm Sorry For You, My Friend* (1977), *Cowboys Ain't Supposed To Cry* (1977), *Love Is What Life's All About* (1978), *Soft Lights And Hard Country Music* (1978), *It's A*

Cheating Situation (1979), *One Of A Kind* (1979), with Joe Stampley *Just Good Ole Boys* (1979), *The Champ* (1980), *Following The Feeling* (1980), *Rodeo Romeo* (1981), with Stampley *Hey Moe, Hey Joe* (1981), *She's Not Really Cheatin' (She's Just Gettin' Even)* (1982), *20 Great Songs Of The American Cowboy* (1982), *Devoted To Your Memory* (1983), *I Still Love You The Same Ol' Way* (1983), *Sings The Songs Of Hank Williams* (1983), *Motel Matches* (1984), with Stampley *The Good Ole Boys Alive And Well* (1984), with Stampley *Live From Bad Bob's In Memphis* (1985), *Keeping It Country* (1986), *You Haven't Heard The Last Of Me* (1987), *No Regrets* (1988), *Many Mansions* (1989).

Bannon, R.C.

b. Daniel Shipley, 2 May 1945, Dallas, Texas, USA. Bannon sang in a church choir when young, and then worked numerous clubs in Texas in rock and soul bands. In 1968, whilst working as a disc jockey for a radio station in Seattle, he adopted the name of R.C. Bannon, based on the product RC Cola. In 1973 Bannon opened for Marty Robbins but the solo records he subsequently made for Capitol were not successful. He moved to Nashville in 1976 and secured a publishing contract with Warner Brothers Music. He wrote the US country hits, 'Only One Love In My Life' (a number 1 for Ronnie Milsap) and 'Women Get Lonely' (Charly McClain). His debut, *R.C.Bannon Arrives*, had sleeve notes by Robbins, and he had a US country chart entry with 'Somebody's Gonna Do It Tonight'. He married Louise Mandrell in February 1979 and their duets include 'Reunited', 'We Love Each Other' and 'Where There's Smoke, There's Fire'. He worked on arrangements for the US television series, *Barbara Mandrell And The Mandrell Sisters*, and wrote Barbara's 1983 US country number 1, 'One Of A Kind Pair Of Fools'.
Albums: *R.C. Bannon Arrives* (1978), with Louise Mandrell *Inseparable* (1979), with Louise Mandrell *Love Won't Let Us Go* (1980), with Louise Mandrell *Me And My R.C.* (1982), with Louise Mandrell *(You're My) Superwoman, (You're My) Incredible Man* (1982).

Barber, Glenn

b. Martin Glenn Barber, 2 February 1935, Hollis, Oklahoma, USA. The family soon moved to Pasadena, Texas and from an early age Barber showed an interest in country music. He first learned guitar but later was to become equally proficient on banjo, mandolin, steel guitar, dobro, bass and drums. He began to write songs and gained his first US *Billboard* country chart successes on the Sims and Starday labels in 1964. In 1968, he joined Hickory and immediately had a minor hit with his own song 'Don't Worry 'Bout The Mule'. This was followed by 'Kissed By The Rain, Warmed By The Sun' and 'She Cheats On Me', the latter also being recorded by Roy Orbison. During the 70s, he mustered 16 minor hits including his own version of 'Yes Ma'am, He Found Me In A Honky Tonk', a song later recorded by Leona Williams, and a version of Mickey Newbury's ballad 'Poison Red Berries'. In 1979, he had a minor hit with the then optimistically titled 'Everyone Wants To Disco'. When five years later it became an album track, he had discovered that they didn't and the song had been renamed 'Don't Take My Country Away'. In spite of his multi-instrumental talents and songwriting abilities, Barber has had no chart hits since 1980. Although busily recording in the early 80s, he now seems to have drifted from the music scene and turned his attentions to being a portrait painter.
Albums: *A New Star* (1970), *Glenn Barber* (1974), *First Love Feelings* (1983), *The Most Wanted Man From Tennessee* (1984), *Saturday's Heroes Are Gone* (1984).

Bare, Bobby

b. Robert Joseph Bare, 7 April 1935, Ironton, Ohio, USA. Bare was raised on a farm, his mother died when he was five, and his sister was adopted. As an adolescent, he dreamed of being Hank Williams: 'then Hank died and I didn't want to be like him no more.' Nevertheless, he started songwriting and secured an early morning radio spot, and later worked on television in Charleston, West Virginia. He moved to California and impressed Capitol Records, recording for them in 1955. After receiving his draft notice in 1958, he wrote a parody of Elvis Presley going into the army, 'All American Boy'. Returning to Ohio to join the army, he met his friend Bill Parsons and joined his recording session. He contributed 'All American Boy' with the intention that Parsons would learn it later. Parsons' name was put on the tape-box because Bare was still under contract to Capitol. The label's owner liked 'All American Boy'and released it under Parsons' name. The single climbed to number 2 on the US charts and made number 22 in the UK. The song resembles Shel Silverstein's, which was later recorded by Bare, but most of Bare's early songs were straight

Bobby Bare

country, being recorded by such contemporary stars as Wynn Stewart and Ferlin Husky. Bare resumed his own career on leaving the army, but the singles ('Lynchin'Party', 'Sailor Man', 'Lorena') made little impact. He wrote twist songs for Chubby Checker's film *Teenage Millionaire*, but Nashville songwriter Harlan Howard persuaded Chet Atkins to record him for RCA-Victor. A ballad, 'Shame On Me', made number 23 on the US pop charts and crossed over to the country market. Bare was travelling to Nashville to record the follow-up when he heard Billy Grammar's 'I Wanna Go Home' on the radio. He admired the story of the country boy going to the city ('By day I make the cars, By night I make the bars') so much that he immediately recorded the song as 'Detroit City'. Bare's record made number 16 on the US charts and won a Grammy.

He had his biggest US hit (number 10) with '500 Miles Away From Home'. His fourth pop hit (number 33) came with 'Miller's Cave'. Bare appeared in the 1964 film *A Distant Trumpet*, but he disliked being stuck in the Arizona desert and he was determined to move to Nashville, join the *Grand Ole Opry* and become a full-time country singer. He recorded prolifically, including an album of standards with Skeeter Davis, which featured a successful single, 'A Dear John Letter'. In 1966, Bare returned to his favourite theme (a country boy uneasy in the city) with the Tompall Glaser and Harlan Howard song, 'Streets Of Baltimore', which was arranged by Ray Stevens. It was followed by the equally realistic, Tom T. Hall's 'Margie's At The Lincoln Park Inn'. 'It's a great cheating song', says Bare, 'because you don't know if the guy is going to go back or not.' By this time, Bare was recording consistently strong material including an album about nostalgia, *A Bird Named Yesterday*, mostly written by Jack Clement. In 1970 Bare moved to Mercury and scored with two early Kris Kristofferson compositions, 'Come Sundown' and 'Please Don't Tell Me How The Story Ends'. Producer Jerry Kennedy's pared-down arrangements were ideal for his half-singing, half-talking style. Chet Atkins invited him back to RCA, where he moved on condition that he could produce his own records. He subsequently recruited songwriter Shel Silverstein to compose an album. The concept was simply one of stories, but *Lullabys, Legends And Lies*, released as a double-album in the USA and a single album in the UK with no loss in music, has become a classic country album. It included the cajun 'Marie Laveau', based on fact, which is his only US country number 1

and a concert favourite as Bare, arm outstretched, fist clenched, punches out the words. He had a US country hit with another track, 'Daddy What If', featuring his five-year-old son, Bobby Bare Jnr., who became the youngest person to have a chart record! 'The Winner', a witty song about the price of winning, had another 20 verses, which Bare omitted but which were subsequently published in *Playboy*. Another Silverstein-Bare collaboration, *Hard Time Hungrys*, dealt with social issues and included a sombre song about unemployment, 'Daddy's Been Around The House Too Long'. The success of his good-natured, family album, *Singin' In The Kitchen*, was marred by the death of his daughter, Cari, in 1976. Bare, never one to stand still, took chances by recording such strange, controversial material as 'Dropkick Me Jesus (Through The Goalposts Of Life)' and the expletive-driven 'Redneck Hippie Romance'. He returned to the mainstream with the superb *Bare* in 1978, which included laid-back ballads ('Too Many Nights Alone', 'Childhood Hero') and the hilarious 'Greasy Grit Gravy' with Waylon Jennings, Willie Nelson and Dr. Hook. His album, *Sleeper Wherever I Fall*, cost $100,000 to make, but Bare was lost in the varied arrangements and reverted to albums with small studio audiences. In 1979, Bare helped to establish Rosanne Cash's career by singing with her on 'No Memories Hangin' Round'. Bare's singles for Columbia included 'The Jogger' (in Silverstein's original version, the trucker beat Jesus!), 'Tequila Sheila', 'Gotta Get Rid Of This Band', 'When Hippies Get Older' and 'Numbers', inspired by the Dudley Moore film *10*. Bare has become more laconic and droopy-eyed with age but he continues to entertain audiences around the world. 'I like everything I record. I'm afraid that if I recorded something that I didn't like, it might be a big hit and I'd be stuck with it every night for the rest of my life. That's a real nightmare.'

Albums: *Detroit City* (1963), *500 Miles Away From Home* (1963), *The Travelling Bare* (1964), *Tender Years* (1965), with Skeeter Davis *Tunes For Two* (1965), *Constant Sorrow* (1965), *Talk Me Some Sense* (1966), *Streets Of Baltimore* (1966), *The Best Of Bobby Bare* (1966) *This I Believe* (1966), with Norma Jean and Liz Anderson *The Game Of Triangles* (1967), *A Bird Named Yesterday* (1967), with the Hillsiders *The English Countryside* (1967), *Folsom Prison Blues* (1968), *Lincoln Park Inn* (1969), with Davis *Your Husband, My Wife* aka *More Tunes For Two* (1970), *This Is Bare Country* (1970), *Where Have All The Seasons Gone?* (1971), *The Real Thing*

(1971), *I Need Some Good News Bad* (1971), *I'm A Long Way From Home* (1971), *What Am I Gonna Do?* (1972), *Memphis, Tennessee* (1973), *I Hate Carl ... (Take Me Down Easy* (1973), *Lullabys, Legends And Lies* (1974), as Bobby Bare and family *Singin' In The Kitchen* (1974), *Hard Time Hungrys* (1975), *Cowboys And Daddys* (1975), *The Winner And Other Losers* (1976), *Me And McDill* (1977), *Bare* (1978), *Sleeper Wherever I Fall* (1978), *Down And Dirty* (1980), *Drunk And Crazy* (1980), *As Is* (1981), *Ain't Got Nothin' To Lose* (1982), *Drinkin' From The Bottle, Singin' From The Heart* (1983). In 1987 Bear Family Records released a 3-CD set, *Bobby Bare - The Mercury Years, 1970-72*, with many previously unissued recordings.

Baxter, Andrew And Jim

b. Calhoun, Georgia, USA. A father and son duo, playing violin and guitar respectively, the Baxters recorded at four sessions between 1927-29. Their records offer a rare example of an older, more rural, black music tradition in Georgia. While some were blues, notably the gentle and melancholy 'KC Railroad Blues', others such as 'Georgia Stomp' were country dance tunes, similar in many ways to some of the white traditional music recorded around the same time. The latter even included spoken dance calls of the type more usually associated with white country music. Emphasizing this connection, Andrew, the elder of the two (who is said to have been half Cherokee Indian) made one record with the white old-time group the Georgia Yellow Hammers, at the 1927 session. Album: *The East Coast States, Vol. 2* (1968).

Begley, Philomena

b. 1946, Pomeroy, County Tyrone, Northern Ireland. Begley is the fourth child in a family of eight. Her father played accordion and her mother sang and, like many Irish performers, Philomena grew up with a love of country music. She worked in a hat factory and began singing part-time with the Old Cross Ceili Band, which, owing to the late 60s country boom in Ireland, became Country Flavour. In 1971 Philomena Begley and Country Flavour made the Irish Top 10 with 'Here Today, Gone Tomorrow', to be followed by 'Never Again'. In 1972 she formed her own band, the Ramblin' Men and had an Irish hit with 'Rambling Man'. Her subsequent Irish chart successes include 'Wait A Little Longer Please, Jesus', 'Blanket On The Ground' (number 5, while Billie Jo Spears reached number 11) and duets with Ray Lynam, 'You're The One I Can't Live Without' and 'My Elusive Dreams'. Begley has appeared on Nashville's *Grand Ole Opry* and has recorded at Porter Wagoner's studios. She is a favourite at London's Wembley Country Music Festivals and regularly tours the UK, both in her own right and as a support act to American performers. Despite her popularity as the Queen of Irish Country, Begley has no pretentions to stardom, happily living on the family farm with her husband and three children.

Albums: with Ray Lynam *The Two Of Us* (1973), *Meet The Queen Of Country Music* (1974), with Lynam *Together Again* (1975), *Philomena Begley Introduces Her Ramblin' Men* (1976), with Lynam *The Best Of Ray And Phil* (1976), *Queen Of The Silver Dollar* (1977), *Nashville Country* (1978), with Lynam *We Love To Sing* (1979), *Truck Drivin' Woman* (1979), *Fireside Country* (1980), *Philomena's Country* (1980), *Philomena* (1984), *Truckin' Queen* (1984), with Lynam *Simply Divine* (1985), *You're In My Heart* (1985), *More About Love* (1987), *Silver Anniversary Album* (1988), *Reflections* (1990), with Mick Flavin *In Harmony* (1991), *Country Queen for 30 Years* (1992).

Belew, Carl

b. Carl Robert Belew, 21 April 1931, Salina, Oklahoma, USA, d. November 1990. Belew left school at 15 and became a plumber, but he was set on being a musician. Marvin Rainwater arranged a recording session for Four Star Records in 1955 and then, in 1958, he wrote Johnnie And Jack's hit single, 'Stop The World (And Let Me Off)'. He also recorded rockabilly ('Cool Gator Shoes' and 'Folding Money') but eventually found success with his self-penned 'Lonely Street', a maudlin country ballad with a lyrical nod to 'Heartbreak Hotel'. It made the US Top 10 for Andy Williams and was subsequently recorded by Gene Vincent and Rex Allen Jnr. Another composition and country hit, 'Am I That Easy To Forget?', was a 1960 USA pop hit for Debbie Reynolds but he did not have UK success until Engelbert Humperdinck recorded it in 1968. The song, now a country standard, has also been recorded by Jim Reeves, Don Gibson, Leon Russell and, once again, Gene Vincent. Although Belew did not compose 'Crystal Chandelier' or 'Hello Out There' he garnered success with both songs. He did, however, write Eddy Arnold's US country number 1, 'What's He Doing In My World?'. Belew returned to the country charts in the 70s with 'All I Need Is You', a duet with Betty Jean Robinson, but ill-health dogged his later years. He died from cancer in

November 1990.

Albums: *Carl Belew* (1960), *Carl Belew* (1962), *Hello Out There* (1964), *Am I That Easy To Forget?* (1965), *Another Lonely Night* (1965), *Country Songs* (1966), *Lonely Street* (1967), *Twelve Shades Of Carl Belew* (1968), with Betty Jean Robinson *When My Baby Sings His Song* (1972), *Singing My Song* (1974).

Bellamy Brothers

Howard (b. 2 February 1946, Darby, Florida, USA) and David (b. 16 September 1950, Darby, Florida, USA) Bellamy became one of the top country acts of the 80s after beginning their career in pop and soul. The brothers' father played bluegrass music but David Bellamy's first professional job was as keyboardist with the soul band the Accidents in the mid-60s, backing artists including Percy Sledge. The brothers formed the band Jericho in 1968, but disbanded three years later. They then began writing songs for other artists, and David's 'Spiders And Snakes' was a Top 3 pop hit for Jim Stafford in 1973-74. The Bellamy Brothers signed to Warner Brothers Records the following year and in 1976 reached the top of the US charts and the UK Top 10 with 'Let Your Love Flow'. Although they continued to release albums and singles for the next few years, their days as a pop act were over. In 1979 the double-entendre-titled 'If I Said You Have A Beautiful Body Would You Hold It Against Me' became the first of 10 country number singles for the group. This became their biggest hit in the UK where it made the Top 3. By the late 80s, having transferred to Curb Records, the brothers still recorded Top 10 country singles on a regular basis, and enjoyed a strong following.

Albums: *Bellamy Brothers* (1976), *Plain And Fancy* (1977), *Beautiful Friends* (1978), *The Two And Only* (1979), *You Can Get Crazy* (1980), *Sons Of The Sun* (1980), *The Bellamy Brothers' Greatest Hits* (1982), *When We Were Boys* (1982), *Strong Weakness* (1983), *Restless* (1984), *Howard And David* (1986), *Bellamy Brothers' Greatest Hits Vol. 2* (1986), *Country Rap* (1987), *Crazy From The Heart* (1987), *Rebels Without A Clue* (1988), *Bellamy Brothers' Greatest Hits Vol. 3* (1989), *Rolling Thunder* (1990).

Bennett, Pinto

b. 20 May 1948, Mountain Home, Idaho, USA. Bennett grew up on a ranch and became immersed in the music of Hank Williams and Lefty Frizzell. From the 60s, he has been fusing honky tonk with more contemporary sounds and, although he is hardly a singer, he has developed a hard-rocking country style. In 1983, he tried his luck in Nashville with no success, but singer-songwriter Richard Dobson suggested that he followed his lead and contact the UK media. The new PT label offered him a contract and he secured performances in the UK's Wembley and Peterborough country music festivals. His *Pure Quill* album was highly acclaimed but Bennett - a huge, tattooed man with a handlebar moustache - is an unlikely star.

Albums: *Famous Motel Cowboy Songs* (1988), *Big In Winnemucca* (1988), *Pure Quill* (1989), *Ravages Of Time* (1992).

Black, Clint

b. 1962, Long Branch, New Jersey, USA. Black was born in New Jersey because his father was working there but the family soon headed back to Houston. Black was playing the harmonica at the age of 13 and the guitar at 15. He spent several years playing country music in Houston clubs, and his career took off when he met local musician, Hayden Nicholas. They wrote 'Straight From The Factory' as soon as they met and are now a songwriting partnership. Their demos impressed Bill Ham, the manager of Z.Z. Top, who quickly secured a deal with RCA Records. Most unusually, Black made number 1 on the US country chart with his first record, 'A Better Man', which he had written about a broken romance he had experienced. The title track from his album, *Killin' Time*, was also a number 1 record. The album was a multi-million seller and his second album, *Put Yourself In My Shoes*, is not far behind. It includes another number 1 single, 'Loving Blind'. In both vocal and songwriting ability, the obvious comparison is with Merle Haggard, and one that Black is happy to acknowledge. Managerial disputes halted his recording career after the release of *Put Yourself In My Shoes*, but Black's superstar status was affirmed in 1992 with the belated appearance of *The Hard Way*, which spawned a number 1 single ('We Tell Ourselves'), and showed heartening signs that Black was unwilling to rest on his artistic laurels.

In 1991, apart from a US country number 1 with 'Loving Blind', Black surprisingly duetted with Roy Rogers and the two made the charts with 'Hold On Partner'. His solo career continued in 1992, including Top 5 US country hits with 'We Tell Ourselves' and 'Burn One Down'.

Albums: *Killin' Time* (1989), *Put Yourself In My Shoes* (1990), *The Hard Way* (1992).

Clint Black

Blanchard, Jack, And Misty Morgan

b. 8 May 1942 and 23 May 1945 respectively, both in Buffalo, New York, USA, but moved to Ohio when children. Blanchard learned to play the saxophone and keyboards and found work with a small band; Morgan learned piano and organ as a child and initially worked clubs in the Cincinnati area. Their paths eventually crossed in the mid-60s when they met in Florida and soon after they married. They moved to Nashville, where Blanchard worked in songwriting, record production and as a newspaper cartoonist and in 1969 achieved a minor US country hit with 'Big Black Bird', one of Blanchard's songs. In 1970, his novelty song, 'Tennessee Birdwalk', reached number 1 in the US country and number 23 in the US pop charts. This was followed by further country and pop chart success with 'Humphrey The Camel' and country success with the Fortunes' 'You've Got Your Troubles'. Between 1970 and 1975, they had 12 more country hits on Mega or Epic including 'Somewhere In Virginia In The Rain' and 'The Legendary Chicken Fairy'. There were no further chart hits after 1975 and their careers have seemingly ended.

Albums: *Birds Of A Feather* (1970), *Two Sides Of Jack & Misty* (1972).

Blue Sky Boys

The Blue Sky Boys were Bill Bolick (b. 28 October 1917) and brother Earl (b. 16 November 1919, both near Hickory, North Carolina, USA). The fourth and fifth of the six children of religious parents, they learned many hymns and gospels songs as youngsters but no other member of the family played an instrument. Bill first learned banjo and guitar from a neighbour and passed on both his knowledge and the instruments to Earl. He was given a mandolin but, preferring the guitar, he showed no interest in it. Bill taught himself to play and adopted it as his main instrument and appeared as vocalist with a local group on WWNC Asheville in 1935 but soon after the brothers joined fiddler Homer Sherrill and appeared on radio as the Good Coffee Boys. Before long, they moved to WGST Atlanta, where they became the Blue Ridge Hillbillies. They first recorded for RCA Victor on 16 June 1936, where, for the first time, they became the Blue Sky Boys. They recorded 10 vocal duets with mandolin and guitar accompaniment, including their popular 'Sunny Side Of Life'. Further regular recordings followed and by the end of 1940, they had made almost 100 RCA recordings. Their quiet gentle harmonies, with Earl's melodic baritone and Bill's harmony tenor, also saw them much in demand for personal appearances, in spite of competition from other harmony groups, such as the Monroe Brothers and the Delmore Brothers. They popularized their versions of old songs such as 'Mary Of The Wild Moor' and 'The Knoxville Girl' and their records sold well. In 1938, they even had a British release on Regal Zonophone, although the label saw fit to bill them as The Alabama Barnstormers. Their career was suspended from 1941 to early 1946, when both saw military service overseas during World War II. They reformed at WGST; their harmonies were even better but they found ideas had changed and when they recorded in September 1946, they were reinforced by fiddle and bass. In May 1947, they recorded their classic 'Kentucky'. They accepted that modern acts were appearing but believing that they were solely old time artists, they resisted any attempts to change their style or their basic repertoire. They still toured but did not record again until 1949, when they made their version of the Louvin Brothers' 'Alabama'. After arguments with the label over what songs to record and their firm rejection of the suggestion that they use an electric guitar on the session, they made their final recordings for RCA in Nashville, in March 1950. In 1951, with differing ideas and tired of the attempts to modernise them, they not only retired but separated with Earl moving to Georgia and Bill to North Carolina. In 1962, Starday unsuccessfully tried to persuade them to make a comeback and released an album taken from earlier radio transcriptions. In 1963, Bill did persuade Earl to join him and they recorded two albums, *Together Again* and *Precious Moments*, for Starday Records. The former saw them with other musical backing, but the latter featured only a fiddle to complement their own mandolin and guitar.

They did make a few appearances at folk festivals and in 1965, Capitol recorded them singing their old time songs in concert at the UCLA Folk Festival in Los Angeles; the resultant album became a collector's item. Soon after, they retired again but in 1975, they again recorded in Nashville. The Blue Sky Boys were one of the finest of all the duet harmony groups and were a model for several later acts, including Jim And Jesse (McReynolds) and the Everly Brothers, who clearly show the Blue Sky Boys' influence on their album *Songs Our Daddy Taught Us*.

Albums: *A Treasury Of Rare Song Gems From The Past* (1962), *The Original & Great Blue Sky Boys*

(1963), *Together Again* (1963), *Precious Moments* (1963), *Presenting The Blue Sky Boys* (1966), *Bluegrass Mountain Music* (1974), *The Sunny Side Of Life* (1971), *The Blue Sky Boys* (1976, rec. 1963), *The Blue Sky Boys* (1976), *The Blue Sky Boys* (1976).

Boggs, Dock

b. Moran Lee Boggs, 7 February 1898, Norton, Virginia, USA, d. 1971. Boggs was known for his unusual banjo style which he learned from a black musician in Virginia. The technique involved a lower tuning of the banjo. Despite Boggs' interest in music, his devoutly religious wife frowned on him showing any real interest in music, so he continued playing as a hobby. Boggs had recorded briefly for Brunswick in 1927. He spent more than 40 years as a miner and turned again to music once he had retired. At the same time, there was growing demand for him to play at festivals and clubs. Boggs was 'discovered' by Mike Seeger on a field-collecting expedition at a time when Boggs had not played the banjo for some 25 years. He recorded mainly traditional and sentimental songs such as 'Pretty Polly' and 'Loving Nancy'. Between 1963 and 1966, Boggs recorded two albums for Folkways and one for Asch.
Compilations: *Dock Boggs, Vol.1/2 & Vols. 3/4* (c.1980).

Bogguss, Suzy

b. Suzy Kay Bogguss, 30 December 1956, Aledo, Illinois, USA. Bogguss grew up in a farming family which loved music but had diverse tastes: Bogguss's father favoured country music, her mother big bands and her brothers and sister, the 60s hits. She obtained a degree in art, but sang in clubs and coffee houses to earn extra money. She included country songs in her repertoire such as 'I Want To Be A Cowboy's Sweetheart' and 'Night Rider's Lament'. After five years of touring in a van, she secured a residency at a restaurant in Nashville. A tape she made in 1986 to sell at Dolly Parton's Dollywood impressed Capitol Records. Both 'I Don't Want To Set The World On Fire' and Merle Haggard's 'Somewhere Between' did reasonably well on the US country charts and her first album had an appealing mixture of old and new songs. Bogguss sang 'Happy Trails' with Michael Martin Murphey on his *Cowboy Songs* (1990), and she and Lee Greenwood had a US country hit with the duet, 'Hopelessly Yours'. Boggus has made a speciality of recording songs previously cut by Nanci Griffith, and sweetening

them just enough to win over the country audience. Her strategy paid off when she won the Horizon Award for the most promising artist at the 1992 CMA Awards ceremony.
Albums: *Somewhere Between* (1989), *Moment Of Truth* (1990), *Aces* (1991), *Voices In The Wind* (1992).

Bond, Johnny

b. Cyrus Whitfield Bond, 1 June 1915, Enville, Oklahoma, USA, d. 29 June 1978, Burbank, California, USA. Born into a poor farming family, Bond taught himself to play ukelele and guitar and played at local dances In 1934 he moved to Oklahoma and worked on radio, appearing as Cyrus Whitfield, Johnny Whitfield and then Johnny Bond. In 1937, he worked with Jimmy Wakely and Scotty Harrel as the Singing Cowboy Trio and then the Bell Boys. They appeared with Roy Rogers in the film, *Saga Of Death Valley*, and then became regulars on Gene Autry's radio series *Melody Ranch* as the Jimmy Wakely Trio. Bond wrote the standard 'Cimarron' in 1938 and toured, performed and made films with Autry after his own trio had broken up. He subsequently did the same for Tex Ritter by forming the Red River Valley Boys to back him. He also appeared in the western, *Duel In The Sun*, alongside Gregory Peck. During his 17 years with the US Columbia label, he wrote and recorded classics such as 'I Wonder Where You Are Tonight', 'Your Old Love Letters' and 'I'll Step Aside'. His novelty, 'Hot Rod Lincoln', for Autry's Republic label was subsequently revived by Commander Cody And His Lost Planet Airmen. With Starday Records, he scored with the humorous 'Ten Little Bottles' and its sequel, 'The Morning After'. Their success prompted Bond to record numerous other songs about drinking: see the album titles below. He wrote scripts for, and performed in, a revamped *Melody Ranch* from 1964-70. In failing health, he wrote *The Tex Ritter Story*, and a biography of Gene Autry which remains unpublished. In 1976 he made his only British tour and, following a heart attack, died in June 1978. His daughter manages his vast catalogue of hundreds of songs.
Albums: *That Wild, Wicked But Wonderful West* (1961), *Live It Up & Laugh It Up* (1962), *The Songs That Made Him Famous* (1963), *Johnny Bond's Best* (1964), *Hot Rod Lincoln* (1964), *Bottled In Bond* (1965), *Famous Hot Rodders I Have Known* (1965), *Ten Little Bottles* (1965), *Bottles Up* (1966), *The Branded Stock Of Johnny Bond* (1966), *The Man Who Comes Around* (1966), *Little Ole Wine Drinker Me*

(1967), *Ten Nights In A Barroom* (1967), *Drink Up And Go Home* (1968), *Something Old, New, Patriotic And Blue* (1970), *Three Sheets In The Wind* (1971), *Here Come The Elephants* (1971), *Sick, Sober And Sorry* (1971), *How I Love Them Old Songs* (1974), with the Willis Brothers *The Singing Cowboy Rides Again* (1977), *The Return Of The Singing Cowboy* (1977).

Further reading: *Reflections*, Johnny Bond, Los Angeles, 1976.

Boone, Debby

b. Deborah Anne Boone, 22 September 1956, Hackensack, New Jersey, USA. The third daughter of pop/country/gospel singer Pat Boone and wife Shirley and granddaughter of country star Red Foley. She worked with the Boone family from 1969 and sang with her sisters in a gospel quartet. In 1977, she went solo achieving a 10-week stay at number 1 in the US pop charts and sales in excess of four million with her Warner/Curb recording of the title song, (a gentle ballad), from the film *You Light Up My Life*. She won the Grammy for Best New Artist and the song won an Oscar for Best Original Song. The album of the same name eventually went platinum with sales of two million. The song also gave her her debut in the US country charts, where it peaked at number 4. The following year, she had Top 40 country hits with 'God Knows' and 'Baby I'm Yours' and in 1979, a number 11 with her version of 'My Heart Has A Mind Of Its Own' - a 1960 pop number 1 for Connie Francis. Her biggest country hit came in 1980, a number 1 with 'Are You On The Road To Loving Me Again'. She married Gabriel Ferrer, the son of actor José Ferrer and singer Rosemary Clooney. In the early 80s, after a few more minor hits, she decided to pursue an acting career. She felt that it was dishonest for her to seek further success as a country singer when it was not really her first choice of music.

Albums: With The Boone Girls *The Boone Girls* (c.70s), *First Class* (c.70s), *Heavenly Love* (1982); *You Light Up My Life* (1977), *Midstream* (1978), *Love Has No Reason* (1980).

Further reading: *Debby Boone*, Patricia Eldred.

Bowman, Don

b. 26 August 1937, Lubbock, Texas, USA. Bowman followed a childhood ambition by becoming a disc jockey, working initially at Lubbock and Littlefield at times with Waylon Jennings. The two men became friends and later wrote many songs together including 'Just To Satisfy You' and 'Anita You're Dreaming', which became hits for Waylon. Bowman's guitar playing (supposedly limited to three chords) led him to boast that he was the world's worst, which added to the comedy image he went on to build in establishing himself in the USA. He browbeat Chet Atkins into signing him to RCA in 1963 and he soon had US country chart success with 'Chit (sic) Atkins, Make Me A Star'. Further successes include 'Giddyup Do-Nut', 'Folsom Prison Blues #2', 'For Loving You' (a duet with Skeeter Davis) and finally in 1969 his version of of a song co-written with Jennings called 'Poor Ole Ugly Gladys Jones', which featured guest appearances by Jennings, Willie Nelson and Bobby Bare. He was voted CMA Comedian of the Year in 1967 and appeared in the films *Hillbillies In A Haunted House* (1967) and *Hillbillies In Las Vegas* (1968). His 1970 album *Whispering Country* was a tribute to Bill Anderson.

Albums: *Our Man In Trouble* (1964), *Fresh From The Funny Farm* (1965), *Funny Way To Make An Album* (1966), *From Mexico With Laughs* (1967), *Recorded Almost Live* (1967), *Funny Folk Flops* (1968), *Support Your Local Prison* (1969), *Whispering Country* (1970) *The All New Don Bowman* (1972), *Still Fighting Mental Health* (1979), *Willon And Waylee* (1979).

Boxcar Willie

b. Lecil Travis Martin, 1 September 1931, Sterratt, Dallas, USA. Boxcar Willie sings 'Daddy Was A Railroad Man' with pride and conviction as his father was a farmer and section hand on the railway, who sympathized with the hobos. Boxcar Willie's own love of trains is reflected in 'I Love The Sound Of A Whistle'. As a youngster, he ran away to ride the rails but he was always brought back to school. He developed an early love of country music and has recorded many songs associated with Jimmie Rodgers, Hank Williams and Lefty Frizzell as well as writing several tributes - 'Hank, You Still Make Me Cry', 'Hank And The Hobo' and 'Lefty Left Us Lonely'. Boxcar's first performances were as a straight country singer. He wrote a song called 'Boxcar Willie' and thereafter adopted that name. Although Marty Martin's first album was released in the late-50s, it was not until 1975 that he decided to create Boxcar Willie. The cover of the first Boxcar Willie album shows him in battered hat, striped bib overalls, crumpled jacket and worn-out shoes. It included 'The Lord Made A Hobo Out Of Me'. He subsequently became one of the biggest-selling country artists in the UK. His US albums were short on playing-time and the UK releases have tended to be more generous. The television-advertised, 20-track *King Of The Road* reached number 5 on the UK album charts. Boxcar Willie has been an enormous success at London's Wembley country music festivals, as is evidenced by his live album, which dates from 1982. Boxcar's noted 'Train Medley' is an express featuring seven songs and seven train-whistles in four minutes. His jokey name and love of train whistles led to wide public recognition although he has been mocked by country star, David Allan Coe. Boxcar Willie's duets have been diverse: he has recorded with Roy Acuff ('Fireball Mail', 'Streamline Cannonball'), Willie Nelson ('Song Of Songs', 'Boxcar's My Home') and Hank Williams Jnr ('Ramblin' In My Shoes'). Boxcar Willie's single of 'Good Hearted Woman' was recorded, partly in English, partly in German, with European country star, Gunter Gabriel. In 1981, at the age of 50, he won the Music City News award for Most Promising Male Vocalist! In 1982, he finally found success on the US country charts via a revival of Johnny Cash's 'Bad News', this time complete with train whistle, and he was made a member of the *Grand Ole Opry*. Amongst his subsequent entries are 'Country Music Nightmare', 'Not On The Bottom' and a duet of 'We Made Memories' with Penny DeHaven. In 1985 he recorded some tracks with Willie Nelson. He acted as a hobo in a jail scene in the film about Patsy Cline, *Sweet Dreams*. Boxcar Willie is the World Ambassador for the Hobo Foundation and he owns a travelling railway museum. While never a serious contender for country stardom in the USA, his persona and his belief (probably sincere) in old fashioned values have allowed him to retain major popularity in Europe, where he has been much more available than many bigger stars. He has apparently composed several hundred original songs, but is best known for versions of country classics like 'Wabash Cannonball', 'Wreck Of The Old 97', 'Kaw-Liga'. One of his best compositions, 'London Leaves', was written while he was travelling from Gatwick Airport to London, and, in interviews, he mentions his ambition is to raise the Titanic.

Albums: *Marty Martin Sings Country Music And Stuff Like That* (c.1958), *Boxcar Willie* (1976), *Daddy Was A Railroad Man* (1978), *Boxcar Willie Sings Hank Williams And Jimmie Rodgers* (1976), *King Of The Road* (1980), *Take Me Home* (1980), *Good Ol' Country Songs* (1982), *Last Train To Heaven* (1982), *Not The Man I Used To Be* (1983), *Live In Concert* (1984), *Boxcar Willie* (1985), *Falling In Love* (1988), *Jesus Makes House Calls* (1988), *The Spirit Of America* (1991), *Truck Driving Favourites* (1991). Compilations: *The Very Best Of Boxcar Willie* (1986) *The Boxcar Willie Collection* (1987), *Best Loved Favourites* (1989) *Best Loved Favourites, Vol. 2* (1990).

Boyd, Bill And Jim

Bill Boyd (b. 29 September 1910, d. 1977, Dallas, Texas, USA; vocals/guitar) and brother Jim (b. 28 September 1914, both on a ranch in Fannin County, Texas, USA; bass) first appeared on radio together in Greenville in 1926, before they moved to Dallas in 1929 and formed a band called Alexander's Daybreakers. In February 1932, Bill played guitar for Jimmie Rodgers's Dallas recordings of 'Roll Along Kentucky Moon' and 'Hobo's Meditation'. Shortly after with Jim, Art Davis and Walter Kirkes he formed the Cowboy Ramblers. Primarily a recording band, with members also playing in other groups at times, they first recorded for Bluebird in 1934, drawing their music from country, jazz and popular. Their most successful recording was a version of an old German instrumental march 'Under The Double Eagle', in which Boyd's guitar lead was complemented by Davis's blue sounding fiddle. The Cowboys increased later to a 10-piece western swing band, appeared in films, recorded extensively for Bluebird and were immensely popular in the Dallas area. Boyd, who should not be confused with cowboy actor William Boyd, hosted his own show on WRR Dallas for many years. He retired from the music business soon after making his last recordings in February 1950 and died in 1977. Jim appeared mainly with his brother as a member of the Cowboy Ramblers, although he was also a member of the Light Crust Doughboys (1938-39) and Men Of The West (1949-51). After his brother's death he continued to work in the Dallas area.

Albums: with Jim Boyd *Bill Boyd* (1943-1947 recordings).

Bradley, Owen

b. 21 October 1915, Westmoreland, Tennessee, USA. Bradley learned to play piano, guitar, harmonica and vibes and as a young man worked as a musician and arranger. He played in the famous dance band of Ted Weems, but between 1940 and 1958 he was the musical director and leader of the studio orchestra at WSM radio in Nashville. In 1947, he was also hired by Paul Cohen to work with him on record production for Decca (now MCA) in Nashville. Bradley's own recording career started on the Bullet label but in 1949, a Decca recording with his quintet of the Delmore Brother's 'Blues Stay Away From Me', became a Top 20 US country and pop hit - albeit his only chart entry. He enjoyed record production and in 1952, he and his brother Harold (b. 2 January 1926, Nashville, Tennessee, USA; he worked with Ernest Tubb and Eddy Arnold and later became a leading Nashville session musician) built their own recording studio (one of the first in Nashville), where initially they produced short documentary films. However, they also began to record singers such as Ernest Tubb and Kitty Wells. By 1956, they had moved to larger premises and had their famed Quonset hut studio on 16th Avenue South, Nashville. It was only a surplus army building but it contained superb recording equipment and facilities. It was here that Buddy Holly and Gene Vincent recorded some of their earliest sessions, although in the latter's case production was by Ken Nelson. Bradley also recorded several of the new country artists of the time, including Johnny Cash and Marty Robbins. The immediate area surrounding the old Quonset hut eventually became known as Music Row. It was here that, over the years, the recording industry of Nashville developed. When, in 1962, Columbia persuaded Bradley to sell the studios, they carefully built their new complex over and around hut, so as not to destroy the excellent acoustics of the building. His contract with Columbia prohibited him from opening another studio in the immediate area of Nashville for five years but in 1965, he found an old barn about 20 miles away and converted to the standards of the hut. This time it became known as Bradley's Barn and proved an extremely popular venue for Nashville musicians, as well as rock acts like the Beau Brummels who issued an LP entitled *Bradley's Barn*. Bradley and Chet Atkins were two of the leading record producers, who were mainly responsible for developing what came to be known as the Nashville Sound. Bradley (like Atkins) lessened the use of steel guitars and fiddles and instead gave his recordings a more pop-orientated treatment by the use of strings and backing vocals. He did, in fact, record both pop and country artists. He also appeared as a musician, not only on some of his Decca recording sessions but he actually played with Chet Atkins on Elvis Presley's RCA session, which saw the recording of 'Heartbreak Hotel'. Between 1958 and 1968, he was the country A&R director for Decca and was then promoted to be the label's vice president in

Nashville. During his years involved with record production, he worked with many major stars including Patsy Cline, Red Foley, Brenda Lee and Loretta Lynn. He proved popular with both the artists and with the management and as a reward for his services to the industry, he was elected to the *Country Music Hall Of Fame* in 1974. After retiring from MCA, he continued to work as a record producer - notably on k.d. lang's *Shadowland*, which reunited him with Brenda Lee and Loretta Lynn. (His son Jerry Bradley b. 30 January 1940 in Nashville, also a noted musician and producer, became head of RCA in Nashville in 1974).
Selected albums: *Christmas Time* (50s), *Strauss Waltzes* (50s), *Lazy River* (50s), *Singin' In The Rain* (50s), *Cherished Roses* (50s), *Bandstand Hop* (1958), *Big Guitar* (1959), *Paradise Island* (1960). Albums By Harold Bradley: *Bossa Nova Goes To Nashville* (1963), *Misty Guitar* (1964), *Guitar For Lovers Only* (1965).

Brady, Phil, And The Ranchers

b. 4 March 1939, Liverpool, England. Like many adolescents raised in the south of Liverpool, Brady learned about country music from the seamen returning from the USA. Encouraged by Hank Walters's Black Cat club, he formed his own band, the Ranchers in 1962, including Frank Peters on steel guitar, and they built a reputation in the north west despite the fierce opposition from beat music. They were featured on Decca's 1965 album, *Liverpool Goes Country*, and Brady recorded the first single, 'An American Sailor At The Cavern', for the Cavern Club's own label. Because the Cavern went into liquidation, most copies went to the Official Receiver, and it is the UK's most collectable British country single. Phil Brady And The Ranchers became nationally popular through the BBC programme, *Country Meets Folk*. He went to Nashville in 1968, played *Grand Ole Opry*, and recorded *Songs Of Nashville* on his return. They toured the UK with Buck Owens and Slim Whitman, and their instrumental, *A Little Bit Country*, was recorded at Joe Brown's studio with Brown on fiddle. Brady nearly had national success with the tear-jerking 'Little Rosa', which remains his most requested number, and other popular singles include 'The Exeter Bypass' and 'Let The Whole World Sing It With Me'. Brady, who has his own business in Rhyl, largely works in the north west but with the recession hitting clubs in 1990, he disbanded the Ranchers and began working solo, using backing tapes.

Albums: *Brady Country* (1968), *Songs Of Nashville* (1969), *No. 1 In The Country* (1970), with Jed Ford *On The Country Stage, Live From Gunton Hall* (1971), as the Ranchers *A Little Bit Country* (1973), reissued as *'Me And Bobbie McGee' And Other Favourites* in 1974), *Liverpool Sounds* (1977). Compilation: *Some Old Favourites* (80s).

Brasfield, Rod

b. Rodney Leon Brasfield, 2 August 1910, Smithville, near Tupelo, Mississippi, USA, d. 12 September 1958, Nashville, Tennessee, USA. In 1926, Brasfield left home and joined his brother Lawrence 'Boob' Brasfield, who was working with a touring tent show. Here he played bit parts and ran errands for the other members. After a while the brothers left the show and became a comedy act with Bisbee's Comedians, a more prestigious touring show. Rod acted as the straight man for his brother until one day when Lawrence was late, Rod found himself playing the main comedy act. He proved so successful that he never did anything but comedy again. He worked with the show until World War II, when he was called up for service in the US Army Air Corps. In 1943, owing to a back injury suffered when he was a child, he was given a medical discharge and immediately rejoined Bisbee. He was auditioned for the *Grand Ole Opry* and made his debut there in July 1944. In 1948, he replaced comedian Whitey Ford (Duke Of Paducah) on the NBC networked *Prince Albert Show*. Here his cross patter and rapport with Minnie Pearl saw them both become major stars of the *Opry*. The two comedians toured with the *Opry* road shows and visited Europe with Hank Williams, Marty Robbins and Little Jimmy Dickens. In 1955, Brasfield was a television regular appearing on the *Ozark Jubilee* as well as the sponsored *Opry* shows and worked with Red Foley, who acted as straight man for the two comedians. In 1956, he was hired by director Elia Kazan to play a serious role in his film *A Face In The Crowd*. He played opposite Andy Griffiths and his performance drew praise from the critics. It is generally accepted that on stage Brasfield never had a serious moment in his life but behind the scenes he suffered from a drink problem. Few serious interviews were obtained as he greatly disliked being questioned and on occasions when he had to talk to the media the answers were invariably of a humorous nature. Brasfield continued to work with Minnie Pearl and to play the *Opry* right up to his death. He suffered a heart attack in September 1958, in his caravan home in Nashville and was found to be dead on arrival at hospital. Rod Brasfield received country music's highest accolade in 1987, when he was inducted into the Country Music Hall Of Fame in Nashville.

Breen, Ann

b. Downpatrick, Co. Down, Northern Island. When in school, Breen first joined a pop band but she was leading Ann And The Country Band when only 16 years old. She played the cabaret circuit but kept a full-time sales job for seven years. A revival of 'Pal Of My Cradle Days' was a huge success in Ireland and a turntable hit in the UK, making the lower reaches of the chart. Breen recorded several other 'mother' songs including 'What A Friend We Have In Mother', 'Medals For Mothers' and 'A Mother's Love Is A Blessing'. By way of variety, she also recorded a father's song, 'In Your Heart'. Breen's albums mix Irish songs, American country songs, old-time songs and middle-of-the-road hits. An attempt at something different - the disco single, 'Domino' - was ill-advised. Breen's soft Irish brogue and likeable personality make her a popular concert attraction and she says, 'Most of the songs that I have recorded are not the real, sloppy wet songs but are sentimental songs that have been around for years and will be around for many more.'
Albums: *Country Songbird* (1981), reissued as *Pal Of My Cradle Days* in 1982, *Boy Of Mine* (1983), *You Always Hurt The One You Love* (1984), *This Album Is Just For You* (1985), *I'll Be Your Sweetheart* (1985), *If I Had My Life To Live Over* (1986), *The Ann Breen Collection* (1986), *Irish Style* (1987), *When I Grow Too Old To Dream* (1988), *An Evening With Ann Breen* (1991), *It's For My Dad* (1992).

Britt, Elton

b. James Britt Baker, 17 June 1913 (but over the years various other dates have been given), on a farm near Marshall, Arkansas, USA, d. 23 June 1972. His father was a champion fiddle player and his mother a noted singer. He learned to sing and play guitar and was performing in public at the age of 12. After hearing recordings by Riley Puckett and Jimmie Rodgers, he became very interested in yodelling and soon became proficient at the art. In 1929, he joined the Beverly Hillbillies (a vocal/instrumental group that should not to be confused with the 60s television series) and appeared with them on KMPC Hollywood. When the group split in 1933, Britt moved with Zeke Manners to New York, where (under various aliases) the pair performed and recorded for ARC.

Britt entered and won a yodelling competition organised by cowboy star Tom Mix, in spite of the challenge of leading exponents from Switzerland and Bavaria. The win saw Britt become known as the unofficial world yodelling champion. He made his first solo recordings for RCA Victor in 1937 but it was in 1942, that he scored his major success with his million-selling recording of 'There's A Star Spangled Banner Waving Somewhere'. In 1944, his recording of this patriotic war song saw Britt become the first country artist to be awarded an official Gold Disc. In 1946, he registered six Top 10 country hits including his smash hit 'Someday You'll Want Me To Want You' (a number 2 that charted for 18 weeks) and 'Detour' and achieved US Top 20 pop chart success with 'Wave To Me My Lady'. Further success with his popular 1948 recording of 'Chime Bells'. A yodelling classic, though generally attributed now to Britt and Bob Miller, it originated from the English vaudeville song 'Happy And Free Yodel', written and recorded years before by Harry Torrani. In 1949, Britt had a hit with George Morgan's song 'Candy Kisses' and also made several successful recordings with RCA's female yodelling star Rosalie Allen, including 'Beyond The Sunset' and 'Quicksilver'. In 1951, Britt toured Korea entertaining American troops and contacted a form of Asian fever which for a time prevented him making appearances and had a lasting effect on his career. During the late 50s and 60s, he made some television appearances and guested on the *Grand Ole Opry*. He made few recordings but did have some success with his yodelling version of 'The Skater's Waltz'. He was reunited with Zeke Manners when, in 1959, he recorded an album with Manner's band. A staunch admirer of Jimmie Rodgers, Britt who had made his first recordings three days after Rodgers died, somewhat ironically had a Rodgers connection to his own last recording when, on 6 October 1967, he recorded his own tribute song called 'The Jimmie Rodgers Blues'. Britt spent 22 years with RCA, later recording for Decca, ABC-Paramount and Ampar and apart from his own recordings, appeared as a guitarist on other artist's recordings. He also formed his own El-Tone Music publishing company. During his career he held the unique distinction for a country artist of having long running radio series on three major networks namely NBC, CBS and Mutual. He appeared in several b-western films including *Laramie*, *The Last Doggie* and *The Prodigal Son* and his love of the Old West saw him usually favour western-style dress at all times. He also possessed one of the largest collections of silver decorated saddles and guns. Early in his career, his dislike of cities saw him buy his own ranch in Maryland, where he raised cattle. Elton Britt, known affectionately by his many fans as the World's Highest Yodeller (proof of this may be heard on his own song 'Maybe I'll Cry Over You') died in June 1972, leaving a wife Janet and a son James Arlen Britt.

Albums: *Elton Britt Yodel Songs* (10-inch LP) (1954), *Yodel Songs* (1956), *Rosalie Allen & Elton Britt* (one side each) (1957), *The Wandering Cowboy* (1959), *Beyond The Sunset* (1960), *I Heard A Forest Praying* (1960), *The Singing Hills* (1965), *Something For Everyone* (1966), *Starring Elton Britt & Rosalie Allen* (1966), *When Evening Shadows Fall* (1968), *The Jimmie Rodgers Blues* (1969), *Sixteen Great Country Performances* (1971), *I Left My Heart In San Francisco* (1979).

Brooks, Garth

b. Troyal Garth Brooks, 7 February 1962, Yukon, Oklahoma, USA. Brooks' mother, country singer Colleen Carroll, appeared on *Ozark Mountain Jubilee* and recorded for Capitol Records. Brooks won an athletic scholarship in Oklahoma and entertained in clubs at night. He preferred music and soon was playing full-time. Whilst having a club residency, he learned over 350 songs. Working as a bouncer in Stillwater, he broke up a fight and hence met his future wife, Sandy. When he first married, he reminisced about his high school sweetheart and wondered if he had made a mistake. A few years later, he met her, realized that they had both changed, and wrote the song 'Unanswered Prayers'. Brooks signed with Capitol Records and was assigned to producer Allen Reynolds, known for his work with Don Williams. His first album, *Garth Brooks*, had an old-time, western swing and country feel and included a revival of a Jim Reeves success ('I Know One'), a western saga ('Cowboy Bill') and several new, love songs ('The Dance', 'If Tomorrow Never Comes' and his own 'Not Counting You'). Brooks's second album, *No Fences*, was even better, including his concert-stopping 'Friends In Low Places', and a revival of the Fleetwoods' 'Mr. Blue', both written by Dwayne Blackwell. The album sold nine million copies in the USA and Brooks has won numerous awards. His highly-successful UK debut in London in February 1991 included humorous impersonations of Julio Iglesias and Willie Nelson. Brooks' outstanding success in the Country Music Association's Awards in

Garth Brooks

October 1991 was followed by his album, *Ropin' The Wind*, selling four million copies in its first month of release and topping both the US pop and country charts. His version of a Billy Joel's 'Shameless', was a US country number 1, as also were his recordings of 'The Thunder Rolls', 'Two Of A Kind' and 'Working On A Full House'. Brooks chooses his songs carefully but he has yet to find the right duet song for him and his mother. He says, 'My mother has told me to take care of myself. In that way, I'll be around in 10 or 15 years and I can pay back the people who have invested time in me.' Brooks' survival as a commercial force seems in no doubt, but during 1992 rumours began to circulate that he was planning to quit the music business to concentrate on raising a family (his first daughter, named Taylor in honour of James Taylor, was born that spring). In the event, Brooks cancelled his touring engagements for the summer, but re-emerged before the end of the year with a Christmas record, *Beyond The Season*, and his follow-up to *Ropin' The Wind*, *The Chase*. Within four months, that album had sold five million copies, though critics noted that Brooks was moving subtly away from the honk-tonk style of his debut towards a 70s-orientated soft rock sound. Albums: *Garth Brooks* (1989), *No Fences* (1990), *Ropin' The Wind* (1991), *The Chase* (1992), *Beyond The Season* (1992).

Brown, Hylo

b. Frank Brown, 20 April 1922, River, Kentucky, USA. Brown began his long and distinguished career on WCMI Ashland, Kentucky in 1939. Over the years he has played with many of the top names including Bradley Kincaid and Bill Monroe and appeared at country music's most important venues. He acquired the nickname of 'Hylo' from his ability to sing in both tenor or bass voices and is also a fine guitarist. The full credit that he deserves has avoided him perhaps because he was born a few years too early. He possessed the ability to sing both bluegrass and ordinary country material equally well but the general opinion in his day was that one should either sing one or the other. Consequently he was never afforded the opportunity to demonstrate his full potential. It was not until years later that Ricky Skaggs convinced both record companies and the public that it was possible to sing both genres equally well. Between 1954 and 1960, Brown recorded for Capitol being especially remembered for the versions of his self-penned 'Lost To A Stranger' and his version of the Vagabonds', 'When It's Lamp Lighting Time In

The Valley'. In the early 60s, he recorded several albums for Starday and in the late 60s, a whole series for Rural Rhythm. Other albums have appeared and some 1960 Capitol recordings, with an overdub by the Jordanaires, were released for the first time by Bear Family in 1992.
Albums: *Hylo Brown* (1959), *Bluegrass Balladeer* (1961), *Bluegrass Goes To College* (1963), *Sing Me A Bluegrass Song* (1963), *Sings Bluegrass With A Five-String Banjo* (1963), *Meets The Lonesome Pine Fiddlers* (1963), *With The Lonesome Pine Fiddlers* (1963), *Hylo Brown* (1967), *Legends & Tall Tales* (1967), *Sings Country Gospel Songs* (1967), *Folk Songs Of America* (1967), *America's Favorite Balladeer* (1968), *Sings The Blues* (1968), *With The Blue Ridge Mountain Boys* (1968), *Sings His Bluegrass Hits* (1973), *Hylo Brown & His Timberliners Vol.1.* (1973), *Original Radio Recordings* (1976), *A Tribute To My Heroes* (1977), *Early Bluegrass* (1983), *Hylo Brown & The Timberliners 1954-60* (1992).

Brown, Jim Ed

b. Jim Edward Brown, 1 April 1934, Sparkman, Arkansas, USA. From the early 50s to 1967, Brown sang with sisters Maxine and Bonnie as the Browns but had solo successes in 1965 with 'I Heard From A Memory Last Night' and 'I'm Just A Country Boy', after his sisters had persuaded Chet Atkins to record him solo. When the trio disbanded in 1967, he a pursued a solo career. He appeared on the *Grand Ole Opry* and other top radio and television shows, actually hosting the Nashville Network *You Can Be A Star* Show and toured extensively. Between 1967 and 1981, recording for RCA, he registered a total of 46 US country chart entries. These included Top 10 hits with 'Pop A Top' (1967), 'Morning' (1970), 'Southern Loving' (1973) and 'It's That Time Of Night' (1974). In 1976, he began a successful association with Helen Cornelius. 'I Don't Want To Have To Marry You' was a country number 1 and the follow up 'Saying Hello, Saying I Love You, Saying Goodbye' a number 2. In 1977, they were voted Vocal Duo Of The Year by the Country Music Association. Further duet successes followed including, 'If The World Ran Out Of Love Tonight' (1978), 'Lying In Love With You' (1979) and 'Morning Comes Too Early' (1980). Some of his recordings were probably too pop-country for the traditionalists but, in 1979, they had a Top 10 country hit with their version of the Barbra Streisand/Neil Diamond number 1 pop hit 'You Don't Bring Me Flowers'. Their partnership ended in the early 80s, their last chart entry being

'Don't Bother To Knock'. Brown is still active in the music business but no longer a recording star.

Albums: *Alone With You* (1966), *Just Jim* (1967), *Gems By Jim* (1967), *Bottle Bottle* (1968), *Country's Best On Record* (1968), *Jim Ed Sings The Browns* (1968), *Remember Me* (1969), *This Is My Beat* (1969), *Just For You* (1970), *Going Up The Country* (1971), *Gentle On My Mind* (1971), *Morning* (1971), *Angel's Sunday* (1971), *She's Leaving* (1971), *Brown Is Blue* (1972), *Country Cream* (1972), *Evening* (1972), *Barrooms & Pop-A-Tops* (1973), *Hey Good Looking* (1973), *It's That Time Of Night* (1974). With Helen Cornelius: *I Don't Want To Have To Marry You* (1976), *Born Believer* (1977), *I'll Never Be Free* (1978), *You Don't Bring Me Flowers* (1979), *One Man One Woman* (1980).

Brown, T. Graham

b. Anthony Graham Brown, c.1954, Arabi, Georgia, USA. As much a southern R&B singer as a country vocalist/songwriter, Brown was at school in Athens, Georgia, with members of the B-52s. He earned extra cash singing cover versions in lounge bars, until he saw a television documentary on David Allen Coe, after which he formed Rio Diamond, an 'outlaw' band in 1976. By 1979, he was fronting T. Graham Brown's Rack Of Spam, a white soul band, singing Otis Redding material –

he later covered Redding's classic '(Sitting On) The Dock Of The Bay'. In 1982, he moved to Nashville, where he worked as a demo singer, recording songs for publishers who wanted famous artists to record their copyrighted material. A song he demoed as '1962' was later recorded by Randy Travis as '1982', but more lucrative was the use of his voice on jingles for products like Budweiser beer and McDonald hamburgers. Signed to a major label in 1985, he was known as T. Graham Brown to avoid confusion with the noted Nashville producer Tony Brown. His first album *I Tell It Like It Used To Be*, included two US country number 1 singles, 'Hell Or High Water' and 'Don't Go To Strangers', and he returned to the top again in 1988 with 'Darlene'. His albums were never huge hits, and an attempt to penetrate the European market in the late 80s was unsuccessful.

Albums: *I Tell It Like It Used To Be* (1986), *Brilliant Conversationalist* (1987), *Come As You Were* (1988), *Bumper To Bumper* (1990), *You Can't Take It With You* (1991).

Browns

Ella Maxine Brown (b. 27 April 1932, Sampti, Louisiana, USA), Jim Edward Brown (b. 1 April 1934, Sparkman, Arkansas, USA) and Bonnie Brown (b. 31 July 1937, Sparkman, Arkansas,

T. Graham Brown

USA). In 1953, greatly influenced by WSM broadcasts of the *Grand Ole Opry*, Maxine and her brother began singing as a duo. They first featured on *Barnyard Hayride* on KLRA Little Rock, before being signed to the *Louisiana Hayride* on KWKH Shreveport. They recorded some duet tracks for Fabor and in 1954 registered a Top 10 US country hit with their own song 'Looking Back To See'. (Jim Reeves actually played rhythm guitar on the recording.) In 1955, after being joined by sister Bonnie, they became a featureed act on Red Foley's *Ozark Jubilee* and their recording of 'Here Today And Gone Tomorrow' became their first country hit as a trio. In 1956, with help from Jim Reeves, they moved to RCA, where they immediately had a US country number 2 hit with their recording of the Louvin's 'I Take The Chance'. The following year they had major success with 'I Heard The Bluebirds Sing', but it was in 1959 that they scored their biggest hit with their million-selling recording of 'The Three Bells'. Based on a song called 'While The Angelus Was Ringing' and sometimes known as 'The Jimmy Brown Song' or 'Les Trois Cloches', the song was popularized in Europe by both Les Compagnons de la Chanson and Edith Piaf. The Browns recording topped both the US country and pop charts and even reached number 6 on the UK pop charts. Between 1959 and 1967, 12 further hits followed including 'Scarlet Ribbons', 'The Old Lamplighter', 'Then I'll Stop Loving You' and 'I'd Just Be Fool Enough'. In the early 60s, they appeared on all major television shows and toured extensively including trips to Europe and Japan, as well as running their own club in Pine Bluff, Arkansas. They joined the *Opry* in 1963 but ,in 1967, with Maxine and Bonnie wishing to spend more time with their families, they disbanded. In 1968, Maxine had a minor hit as a solo artist on the Chart label with 'Sugar Cane County' while Jim Ed continued his career as a solo artist with RCA.

Albums: *Jim Edward, Maxine & Bonnie Brown* (1957), *Sweet Sounds By The Browns* (1959), *Town & Country* (1960), *The Browns Sing Their Hits* (1960), *Our Favorite Folk Songs* (1961), *Songs From The Little Brown Church Hymnal* (1961), *Grand Ole Opry Favorites* (1964), *This Young Land* (1964), *I Heard The Bluebirds Sing* (1965), *Our Kind Of Country* (1966), *The Big Ones From The Country* (1967), *The Old Country Church* (1967), *A Harvest Of Country Songs* (1968). Maxine Brown solo: *Sugar Cane County* (1969).

Bryant, Boudleaux

b. Diadorius Boudleaux Bryant, 13 February 1920, Shellman, Georgia, USA, d. 30 June 1987. With his wife Felice Bryant, he formed one of the greatest songwriting teams in country music and pop history. From a musical family Boudleaux learned classical violin and piano from the age of five. During the early 30s his father organized a family band with Boudleaux and his four sisters and brothers, playing at county fairs in the mid-west. In 1937 Boudleaux moved to Atlanta, playing with the Atlanta Symphony Orchestra as well as jazz and country music groups. For several years he went on the road, playing in radio station bands in Detroit and Memphis before joining Hank Penny's Radio Cowboys which performed over the airwaves of WSB Atlanta.

In 1945 he met and married Felice Scudato and the pair began composing together. The earliest recordings of Bryant songs included the Three Sons' 'Give Me Some Sugar, Sugar Baby, And I'll Be Your Sweetie Pie' but the first break came when they sent 'Country Boy' to Nashville publisher Fred Rose of Acuff-Rose. When this became a hit for Jimmy Dickens, the duo moved to Nashville as staff writers for Acuff-Rose. Among their numerous successes in the 50s were 'Have A Good Time' (a pop success for Tony Bennett in 1952), 'Hey Joe' (recorded by Carl Smith and Frankie Laine in 1953) and the Eddy Arnold hits 'I've Been Thinking' and 'The Richest Man' (1955).

In 1957, Fred's son Wesley Rose commissioned the Bryants to switch to teenage material for the Everly Brothers. Beginning with 'Bye Bye Love', they supplied a stream of songs which were melodramatic vignettes of teen life. Several of them were composed by Boudleaux alone. These included the wistful 'All I Have To Do Is Dream', the tough and vengeful 'Bird Dog', 'Devoted To You' and 'Like Strangers'. At this time he wrote what has become his most-recorded song, 'Love Hurts'. This sorrowful, almost self-pitying ballad has been a favourite with the country-rock fraternity, through notable versions by Roy Orbison and Gram Parsons. There have also been less orthodox rock treatments by Jim Capaldi and Nazareth. From the early 60s, the Bryants returned to the country sphere, composing the country standard 'Rocky Top' as well as providing occasional hits for artists such as Sonny James ('Baltimore' 1964) and Roy Clark ('Come Live With Me' 1978). Shortly before Boudleaux's death in June 1987, the Bryants were inducted into the

Songwriters' Hall Of Fame.
Albums: *A Touch Of Bryant* (1978), *Surfin' On A New Wave* (1979).

Bryant, Felice

b. Felice Scaduto, 7 August 1925, Milwaukee, Wisconsin, USA. The lyricist of some of the Everly Brothers' biggest hits, Felice Bryant was a member of one of the most famous husband-and-wife songwriting teams in pop and country music. Recordings of their 750 published songs have sold over 300 million copies in versions by over 400 artists as diverse as Bob Dylan and Lawrence Welk. Of Italian extraction, Felice was already writing lyrics when she met Boudleaux Bryant while working as an elevator attendant in a Milwaukee hotel. A violinist with Hank Penny's band, Boudleaux had composed instrumental pieces and after their marriage in 1945 the duo began to write together. The success of 'Country Boy' for Jimmy Dickens led them to Nashville where they were the first full-time songwriters and pluggers. During the 50s, the Bryants' country hits were often covered by pop artists such as Al Martino, Frankie Laine and Tony Bennett. Then, in 1957, they switched to composing teenage pop material for the Everly Brothers. Felice and Boudleaux proved to have a sharp eye for the details of teen life and among the hits they supplied to the close-harmony duo were 'Bye Bye Love', 'Wake Up Little Susie', 'Problems', 'Poor Jenny' and 'Take A Message To Mary'. They also composed 'Raining In My Heart' (for Buddy Holly) and the witty 'Let's Think About Livin'' (Bob Luman).
After the rock 'n' roll era had subsided, the Bryants returned to the country scene, composing prolifically throughout the 60s and 70s in such genres as bluegrass and American Indian folk material. Their most enduring song from this period has been 'Rocky Top', a hymn of praise to the state of Tennessee. First recorded by the Osborne Brothers in 1969, it was adopted as a theme song by the University of Tennessee. In the late 70s, Felice and Boudleaux recorded their own compositions for the first time.
Albums: *A Touch Of Bryant* (1977), *Surfin' On A New Wave* (1979).

Buffett, Jimmy

b. 25 December 1946, Pascagoula, Mississippi, USA but raised in Mobile, Alabama. Country-rock singer Buffett describes his songs as '90 per cent autobiographical'. His records tell of wine, women, song and a love of sailing. He is 'the son of the son

of a sailor' and he tells of his grandfather's life in 'The Captain And The Kid'. His father was a naval architect, who often took Buffett on sailing trips. Buffett studied journalism at the University of Southern California, and described those years, and his urge to perform, in 'Migration'. Working as the Nashville correspondent for *Billboard* magazine, he built up the contacts which led to his first albums on Barnaby Records. The albums were not well produced and the best song was one he re-recorded, 'In The Shelter'. On a train journey, he and Jerry Jeff Walker wrote the poignant 'Railroad Lady', which has been recorded by Lefty Frizzell and Merle Haggard. Buffett settled in Key West and although initially involved in smuggling, he changed his ways when offered $25,000 to make an album for ABC Records. He went to Nashville, recorded *A White Sport Coat And A Pink Crustacean* for $10,000 and bought a boat with the remainder. The album included several story-songs about misdemeanours ('The Great Filling Station Holdup', 'Peanut Butter Conspiracy'), together with the lazy feel of 'He Went To Paris', which was recorded by Waylon Jennings. His humorous 'Why Don't We Get Drunk And Screw?' was written under the pseudonym of Marvin Gardens, who made imaginary appearances on Buffett's one-man concerts. Buffett's *Living And Dying In 3/4 Time*, included his US Top 30 hit, 'Come Monday'. Its ban in the UK by the BBC because of a reference to Hush Puppies shoes led to a shrewd Jonathan King cover, referring to tennis shoes instead. Buffett's 1974 album, *AIA*, was named after the access road to the beach in Florida and he commented, 'I never planned to make a whole series of albums about Key West. It was a natural process.' Buffett wrote the music for a film about cattle rustlers, *Rancho Deluxe*, scripted by Buffett's brother-in-law Tom McGuane. McGuane described Buffett's music as lying 'at the curious hinterland where Hank Williams and Xavier Cugat meet', and Buffett was the first person to consistently bring Caribbean rhythms to Nashville. (David Allan Coe, who recorded an attack on him called 'Jimmy Buffett', nevertheless copied his style.)
In 1975, Buffett formed the Coral Reefer Band and their first album together, *Havaa Daydreaming*, included a song about the boredom of touring, 'This Hotel Room'. Another title 'My Head Hurts, My Feet Stink And I Don't Love Jesus', was described by *Record World* as an album having 'something to offend everyone'. His next album, arguably his best, *Changes In Latitudes, Changes In*

Jimmy Buffett

Attitudes, included the million-selling single, 'Margaritaville'. A bitter verse about 'old men in tank tops' was initially omitted, but was included on Buffett's improbable concert album, *You Had To Be There*. Buffett made the US Top 10 albums with *Son Of A Son Of A Sailor*, which included the US pop hit, 'Cheeseburger In Paradise', a US pop hit, and 'Livingston Saturday Night', which was featured in the film *FM*. Buffett continued to record prolifically, moving over to contemporary rock sounds, but his songs began to lack sparkle. The best tracks on two of his albums were remakes of standards, 'Stars Fell On Alabama' and 'On A Slow Boat To China'. His *Hot Water* album included guest appearances by Rita Coolidge, the Neville Brothers, James Taylor and Steve Winwood, but it failed to restore him to the charts. In the UK, Buffett remains relatively unknown, perhaps through a reluctance to tour, but in the US he remains one of the ten biggest concert draws in the music industry. His songs continue to reflect his Key West lifestyle and to quote 'He Went To Paris', 'Some of it's tragic and some of it's magic, but I had a good life all the way.'

Albums: *Down To Earth* (1972), *High Cumberland Jubilee* (1972), *A White Sport Coat And A Pink Crustacean* (1973), *Living And Dying In 3/4 Time* (1974), *AIA* (1974), *Rancho DeLuxe* (1975, film soundtrack), *Havaa Daydreaming* (1976), *Changes In Latitudes, Changes In Attitudes* (1977), *Son Of A Son Of A Sailor* (1978), *You Had To Be There* (1978), *Volcano* (1979), *Coconut Telegraph* (1980), *Somewhere Over China* (1981), *One Particular Harbour* (1983), *Riddles In The Sand* (1984), *Last Mango In Paris* (1985), *Floridays* (1986), *Hot Water* (1988), *Off To See The Lizard* (1989), *Live Feeding Frenzy* (1991). Compilation: *Songs You Know By Heart - Greatest Hits* boxed set (1986).

Burgess, Wilma

b. Wilma Charlene Burgess, 11 June 1939, Orlando, Florida, USA. After high school, Burgess attended Stetson University, Orlando to study for a degree in physical education and had no thoughts of a career in music. She was initially only interested in pop music but a visit to an Eddy Arnold concert changed her mind. After graduation in 1960, she was persuaded by a friend to go to Nashville to sing some demos of his songs. Owen Bradley was impressed with her voice and promptly signed her to Decca. Between 1965-1969, primarily specializing in big ballads, she had Top 20 US country chart hits with 'Baby', 'Don't Touch Me', 'Misty Blue' and 'Tear Time'. In 1973, she left Decca and joined Shannon (owned by Jim Reeves Enterprises), where she managed some minor hits, including a Top 20 duet with Bud Logan (one time leader of Reeves's band, the Blue Boys) on 'Wake Me Into Love'. Her last chart hit was in 1975. She recorded for RCA until 1978 but little has been heard of her in recent years.

Albums: *Don't Touch Me* (1966), *Misty Blue* (1967), *Tear Time* (1967), *Tender Loving Country Sound* (1968), *Parting Is Such Sweet Sorrow* (1969), with Bud Logan *Walk Me Into Love* (1974).

Burnette, Dorsey

b. 28 December 1932, Memphis, Tennessee, USA, d. 19 August 1979. He was a member of a classic 50s rock 'n' roll act, a hit soloist act in the 60s and a country star in the 70s. He helped form the highly respected Johnny Burnette Trio, with younger brother Johnny in 1953. After appearing in the film *Rock, Rock, Rock* in 1956, Dorsey left the trio. He recorded with Johnny as The Texans (on Infinity and Jox) and wrote big hits for Ricky Nelson including, 'It's Late' and 'Waitin' In School'. As a soloist, he recorded for Abbott, Cee-Jam, and then Era, where he had his two biggest solo hits 'Tall Oak Tree' and 'Hey Little One' in 1960, both classics of their kind and both showcasing his deep rich country style voice. He then recorded without luck on Lama, Dot, Imperial, Reprise, Mel-O-Day, Condor, Liberty, Merri, Happy Tiger, Music Factory, Smash (where he re-recorded 'Tall Oak Tree'), Mercury and Hickory. In the 70s he had 15 Top 100 country hits (none making the Top 20) on Capitol, Melodyland, Calliope and Elektra, with whom he had only recently signed when he died of a heart attack on 19 August 1979. His son Billy Burnette is also a recording artist.

Burnette, Legendary Hank C.

b. Sven Ake Hogberg, Sweden. Burnette is a multi-instrumentalist who plays and sings all parts on his records, which he also engineers, arranges and produces. He re-creates the echo-laden rockabilly records of the late 50s and alternates between his compositions and familiar titles ('Peggy Sue', 'Boppin' The Blues', 'Red Cadillac And A Black Moustache'). His own wild instrumental, 'Spinning Rock Boogie', closely based on 'A Wonderful Time Up There', was a UK Top 30 hit in 1976.

Albums: *Don't Mess With My Ducktail* (1976),

Dorsey Burnette

Rockabilly Gasseroonie (1977), *Hot Licks And Fancy Tricks* (1979), *I've Got Rock* (1983).

Burton, James

b. 21 August 1939, Shreveport, Louisiana, USA. One of the most distinguished of rock and country-rock guitar players, Burton toured and recorded with Ricky Nelson, Elvis Presley and numerous other artists. His first recording was the highly influential 'Suzie Q' sung by Dale Hawkins in 1957. Burton also performed with country singer Bob Luman before moving to Los Angeles where he was hired to work with Nelson, then the latest teen sensation. For six years he toured and recorded with Nelson, perfecting a guitar sound known as 'chicken pickin''. This was achieved by dampening the strings for staccato sounding single-string riffs and solos. Among the best examples of this style are 'Hello Mary Lou', 'Never Be Anyone Else But You' and the more frantic, rockabilly-flavoured 'Believe What You Say'. During the late 60s and early 70s, Burton was much in demand as a session guitarist, working with Dale Hawkins on a comeback album as well as various artists including Buffalo Springfield, Judy Collins, John Phillips, Joni Mitchell, Michael Nesmith and Longbranch Pennywhistle, a group featuring future Eagles member Glenn Frey. Burton also played dobro on albums by P.F. Sloan and John Stewart. In addition, Burton's powerful rockabilly-influenced guitar work made a major contribution to the harsher country sound developed at this time by Merle Haggard. Burton made two albums of his own during these years, one in collaboration with steel guitarist Ralph Mooney.

During the 70s, Burton's work took him in contrasting directions. With pianist Glen D. Hardin (a former Crickets' member), he was a mainstay of Elvis Presley's touring and recording band from 1969-77, but he also played a leading role in the growing trend towards country/rock fusion. Burton's most significant performances in this vein came on the solo albums of ex-Byrds member Gram Parsons, *Grievous Angel* (1972) and *GP* (1973). After Parsons' death, Burton and Hardin toured with Emmylou Harris and backed her on several solo albums. More recently he has toured with Jerry Lee Lewis. As a session guitarist, Burton played on albums by Jesse Winchester, Ronnie Hawkins, Rodney Crowell, Phil from the Everly Brothers, J.J. Cale and Nicolette Larson.
Albums: with Ralph Mooney *Corn Pickin' And Slick Slidin'* (1969), *The Guitar Sound Of James Burton* (1971).

Bush, Johnny

b. John Bush Shin III, 17 February 1935, Houston, Texas, USA. Bush sang and played guitar as an adolescent. He moved to San Antonio, Texas in 1962 and was resident at the Texas Star Inn. He became a drummer and worked with Willie Nelson: at one stage Nelson was 'exclusively managed by Johnny Bush And The Hillbilly Playboys'. Nelson, and then Bush, moved to Ray Price's band but Bush had no luck in developing a solo career. He eventually became the leader of Willie Nelson's band, the Record Men, and had solo successes with 'You Ought To Hear Me Cry' and 'What A Way To Love' in 1967. Further US country hits followed with 'Undo The Right' and Marty Robbins' classic song 'You Gave Me A Mountain' before moving to RCA and the biggest single of .his career with Willie Nelson's 'Whiskey River'. He became known as the 'Country Caruso'. In 1975 Bush contracted cancer of the throat and it was thought that he may not sing again. In 1982 he and Willie Nelson reunited for a slow-paced album of vintage country songs although it included Paul Simon's 'Still Crazy After All These Years'. Bush is only able to sing for a few numbers at a time, but he still performs regularly.
Albums: *Sound Of A Heartache* (1968), *Undo The Right* (1968), *You Gave Me Mountain* (1969), *Bush Country* (1970), *Here's Johnny Bush* (1972), *Texas Dance Hall Girl* (1973), *Here Comes The World Again* (1973), *Whiskey River/There Stands The Glass* (1973), *Live From Texas* (1982), with Willie Nelson *Together Again* (1982).

Butler, Carl And Pearl

b. Carl Roberts Butler, 2 June 1927, Knoxville, Tennessee, USA, d. 4 September 1992, Franklin, Tennessee, USA. Butler was playing the guitar and singing at the age of 12 and writing songs and playing local clubs by the time he left high school. He saw military service in Europe and North Africa from 1944-46. After discharge, he formed the Lonesome Pine Boys and during the late 40s, was featured on radio stations in Knoxville and Raleigh. He made his debut on the *Grand Ole Opry* in 1948 and by the early 50s, was also appearing regularly on television in Knoxville. In 1951, his songwriting abilities received a boost when 'If Teardrops Were Pennies' became a Top 10 US country hit for Carl Smith (a feat to be repeated 22 years later by Porter Wagoner and Dolly Parton). He made his own recording debut with Capitol in 1951 but moved to Columbia in

James Burton

1953. He had minor success with such songs as 'Angel Band', 'River Of Tears' and his own version of 'If Teardrops Were Pennies'; he also ⁿⁱⁿⁿ ⁿⁿⁿₐ ₐ₋ₐₚₐₗ ₘₐₜₐᵣⁱₐₗ. During the 50s, with his powerful voice and honky-tonk style of music, he established a considerable reputation as a solo artist and in 1961, he gained his first US country chart hit with 'Honky Tonkitis'. However, in 1962, he decided to work as a duo with his wife. He had married Pearl Dee Jones (b. 20 September 1930, Nashville, Tennessee, USA, d. 3 March 1988) when he was just beginning his career, but she had previously only sung with Carl at family functions. The partnership immediately proved successful, when their recording of 'Don't Let Me Cross Over' which stayed at number 1 in the US country charts for 11 weeks. During the 60s, they appeared regularly on the Opry and had further Top 20 hits with 'Loving Arms', 'Too Late To Try Again' and 'I'm Hanging Up The Phone'. In 1967, they appeared in the film Second Fiddle To A Steel Guitar. The same year, as active members of the Salvation Army, they recorded their popular Avenue Of Prayer, gospel album, as a tribute to the Bailes Brothers. Carl Butler co-wrote some songs with Earl Scruggs, including 'Crying My Heart Out Over You'. It was initially a hit for Flatt And Scruggs in 1960 but became a number 1 country hit for Ricky Skaggs in 1982. Their last chart hit was in 1969, with 'We'll Sweep Out The Ashes In The Morning'. They recorded for Columbia until 1971 and then for Chart, CMH and Pedaca. Their sound was not technically harmony singing, since Carl's vocals were always totally dominant; Pearl merely sang in the background and never took solos. However, the public interest in their style and their recording successes undoubtedly led to the later appearances of male-female harmony duos including Wagoner-Parton and Twitty-Lynn. Butler was greatly influenced, as a boy, by Roy Acuff and this always showed in his emotional and loud singing style. He also became noted for his gaudy western-style Nudie costumes. They continued to tour during the 70s and 80s and made some appearances on the Opry and on the Midnight Jamboree from Ernest Tubb's Record Shop.

Pearl Butler died of thyroid complications in 1988. Carl began to restrict his appearances but did briefly sing with Nancy Anne. They cut a single but it failed and the partnership ended. Carl never recovered from the loss of Pearl and drifted into obscurity. He died at his home, on 4 September 1992, following a heart attack and was buried beside Pearl in the Williamson Memorial Gardens.

Fellow country stars George Jones, Carl Smith, Jack Greene, Marty Stuart and Ricky Skaggs were among the pallbearers for one of country music's greatest honky tonk singers.

Albums: as Carl Butler Don't Let Me Cross Over (1963), The Great Carl Butler Sings (1966), For The First Time (1971); as Carl And Pearl Butler Loving Arms (1964), The Old And The New (1965), Avenue Of Prayer (1967), Our Country World (1968), Honky Tonkin' (1969), Temptation Keeps Twistin' Her Arm (1972), Honky-Tonkitis (1980), Country We Love (1980).

Byrd, Jerry

b. 9 March 1920, Lima, Ohio, USA. One of country music's greatest steel guitarists, he first appeared on local radio in 1935. During the late 30s, he was featured on WLW Cincinnati's Mid-Western Hayride and the Renfro Valley Barn Dance. In 1945, after a spell in Detroit, he moved to Nashville and worked on the Grand Ole Opry, where he played with both Ernest Tubb and Red Foley and also recorded several songs including 'Lovesick Blues', 'Mansion On The Hill' and 'I'm So Lonesome I Could Cry' with Hank Williams. He rejoined WLW and the Mid-Western Hayride in 1948 but in 1951, returned to Nashville and worked with many artists including George Morgan. He first recorded as a solo artist for Mercury in 1949, and later for Decca, RCA and Monument. He wrote and recorded 'Steeling The Blues', 'Steeling The Chimes' and 'Byrd's Boogie'. Originally attracted to the instrument by Hawaiian guitarists such as Sol Hoopi, Byrd has been the influence for many of the modern steel guitar players. He always refused to play any steel guitar fitted with pedals, which he believed took away the instrument's real identity. Between 1964-1968, he led the band on Bobby Lord's television show. In the early 70s, after many years of playing and working there, he tired of the Nashville scene and retired to Hawaii, where he worked as as a steel guitar teacher.

Albums: On The Shores Of Waikiki (1951), Nani Hawaii (with Kuanna Islanders) (1953), Hawaiian Beach Party (1954), Guitar Magic (1954), Byrd's Expedition (1954), Hi-Fi Guitar (1958), Steel Guitar Favorites (1958), Byrd Of Paradise (1961), Memories Of Maria (1962), Blue Hawaiian Steel Guitar (1963), Man Of Steel (1964), Satin Strings Of Steel (1965), Admirable Byrd (1966), Potpourri (1966), Country Steel Guitar Greats (1966), Burnin' Sands, Pearly Shells And Steel Guitars (1967), Polynesian Suite (1969), Sound Hawaiian (1977).

C

Campbell, Archie

b. 7 November 1914, Bulls Gap, Greene County, Tennessee, USA, 29 August 1987. After graduating in 1936, Campbell, a singer, guitarist and comedian, gained his first radio experience on WNOX Knoxville, where he appeared on the *Tennessee Barn Dance* and *Mid-Day Merry-Go-Round*. In 1937, he moved to WDOD Chattanooga, where he remained until he joined the US Navy in 1941. After the war, he resumed his career and in 1952 he had his own television show on WATE Knoxville. In 1958, he joined the *Grand Ole Opry* where, changing both his image and style, he became a smartly dressed cigar-smoking performer on the 'Prince Albert' segment of the Opry. One of his gimmicks consisted of the telling of stories and changing the letters in the names around such as 'Rindercella' and 'The Bleeping Beauty'. He also performed serious numbers and had chart success with 'Trouble In Amen Corner' (which he wrote), 'The Men In My Little Girl's Life' and a duet with Lorene Mann entitled 'Dark End Of The Street'. In 1969 he moved to the syndicated *Hee-Haw* television show where he not only became a star of the series but also the chief script writer. He later became the host of the popular network television interview show *Yesteryear In Nashville*. During his career he recorded for RCA, Starday, Elektra and Chart. Away from country music, he was a poet, a sculptor and painter and an excellent golfer. Campbell died of a heart attack in Knoxville on 29 August 1987.

Albums: *Bedtime Stories For Adults* (1962), *Make Friends With Archie Campbell* (1962), *The Joker Is Wild* (1963), *The Cockfight & Other Tall Tales* (1966), *The Grand Ole Opry's Good Humor Man* (1966), *Have A Laugh On Me* (1966), *Kids, I Love 'Em* (1967), *The Golden Years* (1967), *The Many Talents Of Archie Campbell* (1968), with Junior Samples *Bull Session At Bull's Gap* (1968), with Lorene Mann *Archie & Lorene Tell It Like It Is* (1968), *Didn't He Shine* (1971), *Archie Campbell* (1976), *Live At Tupelo* (1977).

Campbell, Glen

b. Glen Travis Campbell, 22 April 1936, Delight, Arkansas, USA. Campbell hailed from a musical family and began his career with his uncle's Dick Bills Band in 1954 before forming Glen Campbell And The Western Wranglers, four years later. By the end of the 50s he had moved to Los Angeles, where he became a renowned session player and one of the finest guitarists in Hollywood. After briefly joining the Champs, he released a solo single, 'Too Late To Worry - Too Blue To Cry', which crept into the US Hot 100. Ever in demand, he took on the arduous task of replacing Brian Wilson on touring commitments with the Beach Boys. Campbell's period as a Beach Boy was short-lived and he soon returned to session work and recording, even enjoying a small hit with Buffy Sainte-Marie's 'The Universal Soldier'. By 1967, Capitol Records were pushing Campbell seriously as an artist in his own right. The breakthrough came with an accomplished version of John Hartford's 'Gentle On My Mind', which won a Grammy Award for Best Country 'n' Western Recording of 1967. Campbell's finest work was recorded during the late 60s, most notably a superb trilogy of hits written by Jim Webb. 'By The Time I Get To Phoenix', 'Wichita Lineman' and 'Galveston' were richly evocative compositions, full of yearning for towns in America that have seldom been celebrated in the annals of popular music. By this stage of his career, Campbell was actively pursuing television work and even starred with John Wayne in the film *True Grit* (1969). He recorded some duets with country singer Bobbie Gentry, including a revival of the Everly Brothers' 'All I Have To Do Is Dream', which proved a worldwide smash hit. Further hits followed, including 'Honey Come Back', 'It's Only Make Believe' and 'Dream Baby'. There was a second film appearance in *Norwood* (1970) and another duet album, this time with Anne Murray. Campbell's hit record output slowed somewhat in the early 70s, but by the mid-decade he found second wind and belatedly registered his first US number 1 single with 'Rhinestone Cowboy'. Two years later he repeated that feat with a version of Allan Touissant's 'Southern Nights'. Numerous hit compilations followed and Campbell found himself still in demand as a duettist with such artists as Rita Coolidge and Tanya Tucker. By the late 70s, he had become a C&W institution, regularly releasing albums, touring and appearing on television. In 1988, he returned to his young provider Jim Webb for the title track to *Still Within The Sound Of My Voice*. Campbell's career is most remarkable for its scope. A brilliant guitarist, star session player, temporary Beach Boy, class interpreter, television

Glen Campbell with Charley Pride

personality, strong vocalist, in–demand duettist and C&W idol, he has run the gamut of American music and never faltered.

Albums: *Too Late To Worry, Too Late To Cry* (1963), *The Astounding 12-String Guitar Of Glen Campbell* (1964), *The Big Bad Rock Guitar Of Glen Campbell* (1965), *Gentle On My Mind* (1967), *By The Time I Get To Phoenix* (1967), *Hey, Little One* (1968), *A New Place In The Sun* (1968), *Bobbie Gentry And Glen Campbell* (1968), *Wichita Lineman* (1968), *That Christmas Feeling* (1968), *Galveston* (1969), *Glen Campbell - Live* (1969), *Try A Little Kindness* (1970), *Oh Happy Day* (1970), *Norwood* (1970, film soundtrack), *The Glen Campbell Goodtime Album* (1970), *The Last Time I Saw Her* (1971), *Anne Murray/Glen Campbell* (1971), *Glen Travis Campbell* (1972), *I Knew Jesus (Before He Was A Star)* (1973), *Reunion (The Songs Of Jimmy Webb)* (1974), *Rhinestone Cowboy* (1975), *Bloodline* (1976), *Southern Nights* (1977), with the Royal Philharmonic Orchestra *Live At The Royal Festival Hall* (1978), *Basic* (1978), *Somethin' 'Bout You Baby I Like* (1980), *It's The World Gone Crazy* (1981), *Old Home Town* (1983), *Letter To Home* (1984), *Just A Matter Of Time* (1986), *No More Night* (1988), *Still Within The Sound Of My Voice* (1988), *Walkin' In The Sun* (1990), *Unconditional Love* (1991). Compilations: *Glen Campbell's Greatest Hits* (1971), *The Best Of Glen Campbell* (1976), *Twenty Golden Greats* (1987), *Country Boy* (1988).

Cargill, Henson

b. 5 February 1941, Oklahoma City, Oklahoma, USA. After studying law and working briefly as a deputy sheriff, Cargill moved to Nashville in 1967 to attempt a career as a country singer/songwriter. He signed to Monument Records, where his debut single became his biggest hit. With producer Fred F. Carter Jnr. he recorded 'Skip A Rope' which reached the US Top 30, as well as heading the country charts. Unusually for country music, this was a protest song, condemning parents who set a bad example for their children by evading income tax and practicing racial discrimination. The song was later recorded by soul singer Joe Tex. Cargill followed this with more orthodox hits like 'Row, Row, Row', 'None Of My Business' and 'Naked And Crying'. In the early 70s, he joined the newly formed Nashville arm of Atlantic Records, having success with 'Some Old California Memory'. He later moved back to Oklahoma and in 1980 made his last US country chart entry with 'Silence On The Line', released by Copper Mountain.

Albums: *Coming On Strong* (1968), *None Of My Business* (1969), *Henson Cargill Country* (1974).

Carlisles

Clifford Raymond Carlisle (b. 6 May 1904, near Mount Eden, Spencer County, Kentucky, USA, d. 2 April 1983, Lexington, Kentucky, USA) and William (Bill) Carlisle (b. 19 December 1908, Wakefield, Kentucky, USA). Born in a log cabin on a tobacco farm, Cliff Carlisle formed an early attraction to yodelling blues music and the Hawaiian guitar, which led to him becoming one of the best steel guitarists to play in country music. He is also considered a pioneer of the dobro and a fine yodeller and singer of most types of country songs, comedy and blues. During the 20s, he and singer/guitarist Wilbur Ball toured with vaudeville shows and in 1930 appeared on WHAS Louisville as the Lullaby Larkers. Due mainly to Carlisle's yodelling abilities they first recorded for Gennett Records in 1930, and, in June 1931, with Carlisle playing steel guitar, they accompanied Jimmie Rodgers on two recordings in Louisville. Between 1933 and 1936 Cliff also recorded several *risqué* ballads including his self-penned 'Mouse's Ear Blues', sometimes using for these a pseudonym such as Bob Clifford or Amos Greene. Bill Carlisle, who had joined his brother in the late 20s when they formed the Carlisles, also recorded as a solo artist in 1933, gaining success with his recording of 'Rattlesnake Daddy'. They toured extensively throughout the mid-west and for some years were based at Charlotte. Cliff's son Tommy first performed with them when he was three years old and later recorded as Sonny Boy Tommy, singing such songs as 'Lonely Little Orphan Child' and stayed with the group until he joined the US Army in the 40s. They signed with RCA-Victor in 1936 but during their years together recorded for most major record labels. Their song content changed during the next few years, even to including gospel material in lieu of the *risqué* numbers. In the late 40s, recordings on King Records of 'Rainbow At Midnight' and 'Tramp On The Street' made the US country charts before Cliff nominally retired in the early 50s. Bill, who acquired the nickname of 'Jumping' or 'Boundin' Bill' from his habit of leaping around when performing, formed a new Carlisles group. He soon established a reputation for humorous songs and attained major chart success with self-penned numbers such as 'Too Old To Cut The Mustard', 'Is Zat You, Myrtle?' and a country number 1, 'No Help Wanted'. In 1952, a duet recording of the first song was also a US Top 10 country hit for Ernest Tubb and Red Foley and a US pop hit for Bing Crosby and the Andrews Sisters. In 1953, the 'Carlisles' joined the *Grand Ole Opry* and when the band finally disbanded in the mid-60s, Bill stayed on, appearing at times with his children Billy and Sheila. His 1966 Hickory recording of 'What Kinda Deal Is This?' made number 4 on the US country charts. Cliff continued to write songs and in the 60s made some concert appearances and recordings with his brother and after a gap of 40 years, appeared with Wilbur Ball at the San Diego Folk Festival in 1971. Soon afterwards his health began to deteriorate and Cliff Carlisle died following a heart attack in April 1983. Bill continued to appear on the *Opry* and make public appearances.

Albums: by Cliff Carlisle *A Country Kind Of Songs & Hymns* (c.60s), *Cliff Carlisle, Volume 1* (1988), *Cliff Carlisle, Volume 2* (1988); Bill Carlisle *The Best Of Bill Carlisle* (1966), *Jumpin' Bill Carlisle* (1983); the Carlisle Family *Carlisle Family Album - Old Time Great Hymns featuring Bill & Cliff Carlisle* (1965); the Carlisles *On Stage With The Carlisles* (1958), *Fresh From The Country* (1959), *Maple On The Hill* (1964), *Busy Body Boogie* (1985).

Carpenter, Mary-Chapin

b. 21 January 1958, Princeton, New Jersey, USA. Her father was an executive for *Life* magazine, and she spent part of her early life living in Japan. She grew up with a love of contemporary pop hits although her mother's Woody Guthrie and Judy Collins records gave her some interest in country/folk music. She spent her time at home with her guitar and her father encouraged her to perform at a talent night. At university, she achieved a degree in American Civilization. By 1986, she was a local star, winning five Washington Area Music Awards without having made a record, after which she signed to a major label in Nashville with guitarist/producer John Jennings. She had felt she should have a conventional job, but she kept performing in bars, often having to sing current favourites. She realized that she was drinking too much, so she changed her habits and also resolved to only play in bars that would let her play original material. She also had recorded John Stewart's song, 'Runaway Train', for her first album, but Columbia decided that it would be better suited to Rosanne Cash, who took it to the top of the US country charts. Since then, she has made steady progress up the commercial ladder, attracting cover versions of her songs by such artists as Tony Rice and Joan Baez. A notable songwriter, she has also recorded cover versions, including 'Downtown Train' by Tom Waits - more recently a hit for Rod Stewart - on

Mary-Chapin Carpenter

Hometown Girl, and the stunning 'Quittin' Time', co-written by Robb Royer of Bread, on *State of The Heart*). Although she is regarded as a new star in country music, she has more in common with the folk singers of the early 70s. In 1991 she made the US country charts with a revival of Gene Vincent's light-hearted 'Right Now'. Her 1992 hit, the raunchy and self-mocking 'I Feel Lucky', preceded the release of another strong country album, *Come On, Come On*. Carpenter's complete acceptance by a country audience was sealed when she was voted the CMA's Female Vocalist of the Year that September.

Albums: *Home Town Girl* (1987), *State Of The Heart* (1989), *Shooting Straight In The Dark* (1990) *Come On, Come On* (1992).

Carson, Fiddlin' John

b. 23 March 1868, on a farm in the hills of Fannin County, Georgia, USA. (There have been suggestions of differing dates and places but none can be verified due to lack of old local records). It is likely that his forebears arrived from Ireland around 1780; probably some were fiddle players, who brought instruments with them. It is said that Carson first began to play the fiddle when he was about 11. He also rode as a jockey as a boy until he became too big and heavy. At one time he worked in a cotton mill, and there is little doubt that he was also occupied as a moonshiner. He regularly played the fiddle and eventually relocated to Atlanta, where he earned a living busking and playing at local functions including political rallies. Over the years he became such an expert fiddler that between 1914 and 1924 he was named Champion of Dixie on seven occasions. He became one of the first country artists to play on local radio when he appeared on WSB Atlanta in 1922. In 1923, Atlanta record store manager Polk Brockman, suggested to Ralph Peer of OKeh Records that he should record some local talent. When on 19 June 1923 Carson performed 'The Little Old Log Cabin In The Lane' and 'The Old Hen Cackled And The Rooster's Going To Crow', he was the first country artist that Peer recorded. Peer was unimpressed by Carson's vocal work, describing it as 'plu-perfect awful' and doubted the sales potential of the record. Initially, he pressed only 500 copies and was amazed when they quickly sold. When Carson realised how successfully his record sold he was heard to remark that he would have to quit making moonshine and start making records. Peer immediately arranged for Carson to make further recordings; between 1923 and 1931, often accompanied by the Virginia Reelers, who included his daughter Rose Lee Carson (Moonshine Kate), he recorded almost 150 tracks for OKeh. The material varied from country songs like 'Letter Edged In Black', traditional fiddle tunes such as 'Old Joe Clark' and popular ballads like 'Long Way To Tipperary' to the humorous 'Who Bit the Wart Off Grandma's Nose'. Carson made his final recordings (again accompanied by his daughter) for RCA Victor in Camden in February 1934. He continued to play at conventions and other functions and until a few days before his death, on 11 December 1949, he was working as a lift operator in the Capitol building in Atlanta, Georgia.

Albums: *The Old Hen Cackled And The Rooster's Going To Crow* (1976).

Further reading: *Fiddlin' Georgia Crazy; Fiddlin' John Carson, His Real World and the World of His Songs*, Gene Wiggins.

Carter, Carlene

b. Rebecca Carlene Smith, 26 September 1955, Nashville, Tennessee, USA. Carter is the daughter of country singers Carl Smith and June Carter and the grand-daughter of Maybelle Carter of the Carter Family. She learnt piano at six-years-old and guitar at ten, having lessons from Carl Perkins. Her parents divorced and, when she was 12, her mother married Johnny Cash. Carlene Carter herself first married when 16, and had a daughter Tiffany, but she and Joe Simpkins were divorced within two years. After college she joined her mother and stepfather on the road and was featured on Johnny Cash's strangely-titled family album, *The Junkie And The Juicehead Minus Me* in 1974. Carlene met Jack Routh, a writer for Cash's publishing company, and within three months they were married. They had a son, John Jackson Routh, but they separated in 1977. Carter brought her new boyfriend, Rodney Crowell, to the UK where she made an appealing, up-beat rock album with Graham Parker And The Rumour. Crowell's song 'Never Together But Close Sometimes' was almost a UK hit and her song, 'Easy From Now On', was recorded by Emmylou Harris. Carter had an assertive personality but she struggled with the dance tracks on her second album, *Two Sides To Every Woman*, which was made in New York. Appearing at a New York club, she introduced one of the songs, 'Swap-Meat Rag', with the words, 'If this song doesn't put the cunt back in country, nothing will.' Johnny Cash and June Carter, who were in the audience, were not amused, but

Carlene Carter

Carlene was awarded the 'Quote of the Year' by *Playboy* magazine. *Musical Shapes* was produced by her new husband Nick Lowe; the songs included her 'Appalachian Eyes' and a duet with Dave Edmunds, 'Baby Ride Easy'. Her 1981 album, *Blue Nun*, was also produced by Lowe and featured members of Rockpile and Squeeze. The album, with such titles as 'Do Me Lover' and 'Think Dirty', was an explicit celebration of sex, but just as she seemed to be rejecting her country roots, she joined her family on stage at the Wembley Country Music Festival for 'Will The Circle Be Unbroken?'. Carter, whose marriage to Lowe broke up, was prevented from calling her next album *Gold Miner's Daughter*, and settled for *C'est C Bon*. She was featured in *Too Drunk To Remember*, a short film shown at the London Film Festival, based on one of her songs. In 1985 she won acclaim for her role as one of the waitresses in the London cast of the country musical *Pump Boys And Dinettes*, which starred Paul Jones and Kiki Dee. In 1990 Carter, by making an album, *I Fell In Love*, aimed to please rather than alienate country fans. Produced by Howie Epstein, the musicians included Dave Edmunds, Kiki Dee, Albert Lee, Jim Keltner, and such songs as 'Me And Wildwood Rose' celebrated her country music heritage. Carter has the potential of a fine country songwriter and the song 'Guardian Angel', shows she has enough experiences to draw on.
Albums: *Carlene Carter* (1978), *Two Sides To Every Woman* (1979), *Musical Shapes* (1980), *Blue Nun* (1981), *C'est C Bon* (1983), *I Fell In Love* (1990), *Musical Shapes & Blue Nun* (1992).

Carter, Fred F., Jnr.

b. 31 December 1933, Winnsboro, Louisiana, USA. Carter has loved country music since a child and learned to play the guitar. Performing with local bands, he was signed by Conway Twitty in the late 50s. Carter played on numerous Nashville sessions during the 60s, putting his ability to improvise to good effect. He made a single for Monument, 'And You Wonder Why' in 1967. He played on records by Bob Dylan, Ronnie Hawkins, Waylon Jennings and, in particular, was featured on Simon And Garfunkel's 'The Boxer'. He ran both ABC Records' Nashville office and Nugget Records and produced *Cannons In The Rain* (John Stewart) and *American Son* (Levon Helm).

Carter, Wilf (Montana Slim)

b. 18 December 1904, Port Hilford, Nova Scotia, Canada. Carter's father, a travelling Baptist minister, was born in Switzerland and his mother in Aldershot, Hampshire, England. Rejecting his mother's wish to be a preacher, Wilf was working on a farm with a team of oxen and ploughing at the age of 13. After hearing a vaudeville artist called the Yodelling Fool, he was so impressed that he knew he had to seek a similar career. Soon afterwards he left home, living with tramps and hobos and working as a lumberjack and teamster before finding work as a cowboy. He learned to play the guitar and, writing most of his material, he was soon singing locally. In 1924, he joined the Canadian rodeo circuit, where he mixed competing with singing. Around 1926, he auditioned for a Calgary radio station and was told to 'stick to milking cows' but in 1930, after singing at the famed *Calgary Stampede*, he got his radio show. He also found employment with Canadian Pacific Railways, who used him as an entertainer on organized trail drives through the Rocky Mountains. They also sent him as a singer on their cruise ship S.S. Empress Of Britain to the West Indies. In December 1933, RCA-Victor in Montreal, noting the success of Jimmie Rodgers and his blue yodels in the States, decided to record Carter, who had become known as the Yodelling Cowboy. His first session produced his now classic 'Swiss Moonlight Lullaby' (written when he was a trail rider in Alberta) and a song about a real life murder hunt in 'The Capture Of Albert Johnson'. When he returned from the cruise, he found the record had been released and was proving popular. This launched a recording career that extended to the 80s and saw him record hundreds of his own songs. Many had a western influence such as 'Twilight On The Prairie'; some were event songs like 'The Life And Death Of John Dillinger'; others were nostalgic ballads of mother and home as witnessed in 'My Little Gray Haired Mother In The West'. Several referred to his rodeo days and many naturally featured his considerable talent for yodelling, including a speciality speed yodel, which he always referred to as his three-in-one. He worked on CFCN Calgary in 1933 but soon moved to New York, where he played on the CBS network. It was here in 1934 that he was first introduced as Montana Slim, probably to distinguish him from the Carter Family. He said he did not mind what they called him as long as they paid him, and, during his long career, he has become equally well known by both names. He was involved in a bad car crash in Montana in 1940, which kept him from touring and doing radio work for nine years, but did not prevent him recording. In 1949, accompanied by his two daughters, Sheila and Carol, he again toured especially in Canada. He went into semi-retirement in Florida in the 60s but continued to make appearances at special events such as the *Calgary Stampede*. He has been an influence to other artists, particularly Slim Whitman, who has sung several of Carter's songs, and had considerable success in Britain with 'Love Knot In My Lariat'. Wilf Carter (Montana Slim) was elected to the Nashville Songwriters Association International Hall Of Fame in 1971. He is one of the most prolific recording artists of his era; in addition to the USA and Canada (where some releases had differing liner notes and titles to accommodate both names) his records were regularly released in Britain and Australia. His popularity as a cowboy saw him elected to Calgary's Horseman's Hall Of Fame and there is a life-sized statue of him in the Canadian Wax Museum in Banff, Alberta. In recent years, he appears to have divided his time between his Florida and Arizona homes. He was nominated for the Country Music Hall Of Fame in 1982 and though unsuccessful then, he will no doubt be inducted one day.

Albums: *Montana Slim-Wilf Carter* i (1959), *I'm Ragged But I'm Right* (1959), *The Dynamite Trail* (1960), *Reminiscin' With Montana Slim* (1962), *By Request* (early 60s), *Wilf Carter As Montana Slim* (1964), *32 Wonderful Years* (1965), *Let's Go Back To The Bible* (mid-60s), *Nuggets Of The Golden West* (mid-60s), *Yodelling Memories* (mid-60s), *Christmas In Canada* (mid-60s), *Montana Slim/Wilf Carter* ii (1967), *God Bless Our Canada* (1967), *Waitin' For The Maple Leaves To Fall* (1967), *Calgary Horseman's Hall Of Fame* (mid-60s), *Balladeer Of The Golden West* (mid-60s), *Golden Memories* (late 60s), *If It Wasn't For The Farmer* (late 60s), *No Letter Today* (late 60s), *Old Prairie Melodies* (late 60s), *Sings Jimmie Rodgers* (1969), *Songs Of The Rail And Range* (early 70s), *How My Yodelling Days Began* (1970), *Hittin' The Track* (early 70s), *Sings Songs Of Australia* (early 70s), *Away Out There* (early 70s), *The Yodelling Swiss* (early 70s), *Walls Of Memory* (early 70s), *Bridle Hangin' On The Wall* (early 70s), *A Message From Home Sweet Home* (early 70s), *My Heartache's Your Happiness* (1972), *40th Anniversary* (1973), *Souvenir Album* (1974), *There Goes My Everything* (1975), *The First Five Sessions* (mid-70s), *The Sixth & Seventh Sessions* (mid-70s), *My Old Canadian Home* (mid-70s), *Have A Nice Day* (1977), *Songs I Love To Sing* (1977), *Walkin' The Streets Of Calgary* (1978), *I'm Happy Today* (1979), *Songs Of*

The Calgary Stampede (late 70s), *My Home On The Range* (1980), *Chinook Winds* (1981), *50 Golden Years* (1983), *Canadian Yodelling Cowboy* (1986), *The Days Of The Yodelling Cowboys Volume 3 Wilf Carter (Montana Slim)* (late 80s), *Montana Slim* (1987), *Whatever Happened To All Those Years?* (1988), *Reminiscin' With Wilf Carter* (1988).

Further reading: *The Yodelling Cowboy*, Wilf Carter.

Carter Family

The Carter Family have become known as country music's first family and are responsible for several songs such as 'The Wildwood Flower' and 'Keep On The Sunny Side' becoming country standards. The original three members of the Carter Family were Alvin Pleasant (A.P.) Delaney Carter (b. 15 April 1891, Maces Springs, Scott County, Virginia, USA), d. 7 November 1960, his wife Sara Dougherty (Carter) (b. 21 July 1898, Flat Woods, Coeburn, Wise County, Virginia, USA, d. 8 January 1979) and Sara's cousin, Maybelle Addington (Carter) (b. 10 May 1909, Copper Creek, Nickelsville, Scott County, Virginia, USA, d. 23 October 1978). A.P, also known as 'Doc' Carter began to play the fiddle as a boy and learned many old time songs from his mother. His father had been a fiddler but gave it up through religious beliefs when he married. As a young man, A.P. sang in a quartet with two uncles and his eldest sister in the local church. Initially, he worked on the railroad in Indiana but became homesick for his Clinch Mountain home in Virginia and in 1911, returned to his native area. He became interested in writing songs and found work travelling, selling fruit trees. One day in his travels, he met Sara, who legend says was playing the autoharp and singing 'Engine 143' and on 18 June 1915, they married. Sara had learned to play banjo, guitar and autoharp and, as a child, was regularly singing with Madge and Maybelle Addington and other friends in her local area. They made their home in Maces Springs where A.P. worked on varying jobs, including farming and gardening and began to appear singing and playing together at local church socials and other functions.

They auditioned for Brunswick, singing such songs as 'Log Cabin By The Sea' but when the record company suggested to A.P. that, performing as Fiddlin' Doc, he only record square dance fiddle songs he flatly refused because he felt it was against his mother and father's strong religious beliefs. After her marriage in 1926 to A.P.'s brother Ezra J. Carter, Maybelle (Addington) joined with her relatives and the trio began to entertain locally.

Carter Family

Like her new sister-in-law, Maybelle was equally competent on guitar, banjo and autoharp and was to become the main instrumentalist of the trio, as she developed her immediately identifiable style of picking out the melody on the bass strings and strumming a backing on the treble. (Maybelle may well have been influenced by black guitarist Leslie Riddles, who often accompanied A.P. when he went on his searching-for-songs trips). Sara, often playing chords on the autoharp, usually sang lead vocals, with A.P. providing bass and Maybelle alto harmonies. (Sara also yodelled on some of their recordings although this was probably more because of the instruction of the record company's producer than from her own free choice).

The Carter Family sound was something totally new. Vocals previously in the early folk and hillbilly music were usually of secondary importance to the instrumental work whereas the trio, with their simple harmonies, used their instruments to provide a musical accompaniment that never took precedent over their vocal work. In July 1927, their local newspaper informed that Ralph Peer of Victor Records was to audition local

artists in Bristol, Tennessee. In spite of the fact that Sara had three children (the youngest only seven-months-old) and that Maybelle was seven months pregnant with her first, they travelled the 25 miles to Bristol, where on 1 August, they made their first recordings. They recorded six tracks. Peer was impressed and the records proved sufficient sellers for Victor to give them a recording contract. Between 1928 and 1935, they recorded a many tracks for Victor, including the original versions of many of their classics such as 'Keep On The Sunny Side', 'Wildwood Flower', 'I'm Thinking Tonight Of My Blue Eyes', 'Homestead On The Farm' (aka 'I Wonder How The Old Folks Are At Home'), 'Jimmie Brown The Newsboy' and 'Wabash Cannonball'.

By the end of the 20s, the Carter Family were a very well known act. In 1931 in Louisville, Kentucky, they met and recorded with Jimmie Rodgers. It was at this session that Rodgers made his only valid duet recordings with a female vocalist when he recorded 'Why There's A Tear In My Eye' and 'The Wonderful City' with Sara Carter. (The latter song also being the only sacred number that Rodgers ever recorded). Combined recordings made at this time between the two acts comprised 'Jimmie Rodgers Visits The Carter Family' and 'The Carter Family And Jimmie Rodgers In Texas'. The former consisted of duets by Sara and Maybelle on 'My Clinch Mountain Home' and 'Little Darling Pal Of Mine' with Jimmie Rodgers and A.P both joining on a quartet version of 'Hot Time In The Old Town Tonight'. The latter featured Jimmie Rodgers with a solo version of 'Yodelling Cowboy' and Sara joining in with the vocal and yodel on 'T for Texas'. Both also included some talking by the two acts. The Carter Family managed to record, even though the families at times had moved apart. In 1929, A.P. relocated to Detroit to find work and at one time, Maybelle moved to Washington, DC. In 1932, Sara and A.P separated; they divorced a few years later, but the trio continued to record and perform together. (Later in 1939, Sara married A.P's cousin, Coy Bayes). In 1935 they left Victor and moved to ARC, where they re-recorded some of their popular earlier songs, though often using different arrangements, as well as recording new numbers. They signed to Decca in 1936 and later recorded for Columbia (formerly ARC). Their hitherto reluctance to perform outside of Virginia, Tennessee and North Carolina ended in 1938, when they accepted the opportunity to work on the powerful Border Radio stations XERA, XEG and XENT on the Mexican/Texas border at Del Rio and San Antonio. Here the Carter's children began to make appearances with the family; first, Sara's daughter Janette and Maybelle's daughter Anita, followed soon after by her sisters Helen and June.

Apart from their normal studio recordings, they recorded radio transcription discs at this time, which were used on various stations and helped to increase the Family's popularity. They remained in Texas until 1941, when they relocated to WBT Charlotte, North Carolina. In 14 October 1941, after rejoining Victor, the trio made their final recordings together; in 1943, while still at WBT, Sara decided to retire and the original Carter Family broke up. During their career, they recorded almost three hundred songs, never once varying from their traditional sound. A.P. claimed to have written many of them and the arguments still persist as to just how many were his own compositions and how many were traditional numbers that he had learned as a boy or found on his many song-searching trips. Sara Carter was undeniably a vocalist of great talent and could easily have become a successful solo artist. Maybelle Carter, apart from her instrumental abilities, was also a fine vocalist. A.P, who possessed a deep bass voice, was a very nervous man who suffered with palsy for many years. Some people believe this accounted for the tremolo on his voice at times and for the fact that he was often either late with his vocal, or failed to sing at all.

The influence of the Carter Family can be seen in the work of a great many artists and their songs have been recorded by the likes of Johnny Cash, Louvin Brothers, Emmylou Harris, Mac Wiseman, Flatt And Scruggs, Bill Monroe and Stonewall Jackson. They recorded the 'Wabash Cannonball' seven years before Roy Acuff began to sing it; this and many other Carter songs have become standards and have been recorded by many artists. Many of their numbers were beautifully descriptive of their native State, such as 'Mid The Green Fields Of Virginia', 'My Clinch Mountain Home' and 'My Little Home In Tennessee'. Several of Woody Guthrie's best known songs used Carter Family tunes including 'This Land Is Your Land' ('When The World's On Fire') and 'Reuben James' ('Wildwood Flower'). He also regularly performed 'It Takes A Worried Man', which the Carters sang as 'Worried Man Blues'. Other folk artists influenced by their music include Joan Baez, who recorded many of their songs such as 'Little Darling Pal Of Mine' and 'Will The Circle Be Unbroken'. After the break up of the original trio, Maybelle and her three daughters began to perform on the *Old Dominion Barn Dance* on WRVA Richmond. They appeared as Mother Maybelle and The Carter Sisters and were a popular act between 1943 and 1948. After spells at WNOX Knoxville and KWTO Springfield, they moved to WSM Nashville and joined the *Grand Ole Opry* in 1950, taking with them a young guitarist called Chet Atkins. During the 50s, Helen and Anita left to marry and pursue their own careers and June became a solo act. Maybelle remained a featured star of the *Opry* until 1967, when she was rejoined by Helen and Anita. In 1961, Maybelle even recorded an album of Carter Family songs with Flatt And Scruggs and in 1963, she appeared at the Newport Folk Festival. After June married singer Johnny Cash in 1968, Maybelle, Helen and Anita became regular members of the *Johnny Cash Show*. They had begun to make appearances with Cash the previous year. A.P retired to Maces Springs, where he opened a country store and lived with his daughter Gladys. Sara and her husband moved to Angel's Camp, California, where she withdrew from active participation in the music scene.

In 1952, seemingly at the request of her ex-husband, she was persuaded to record once more. Between 1952 and 1956, the A.P. Carter Family consisting of Sara, A.P. and their son and daughter Joe and Janette recorded almost 100 tracks for Acme Records. These included a 1956 recording made with Mrs. Jimmie Rodgers, which consisted of talk and a version of 'In The Sweet Bye And Bye'. Although these recordings never matched the work of the original trio, they did maintain traditional standards, whereas Maybelle and her daughters moved to a more modern country sound. In 1953, A.P. opened his 'Summer Park', in his beloved Clinch Mountains, near the home of Joe and Janette and held concerts, which featured such artists as the Stanley Brothers. A.P. Carter died at his home in Maces Springs on 7 November 1960. After A.P's death record companies began to release their material on album for the first time. In 1967 Sara was persuaded to appear with Maybelle at the Newport Folk Festival; the same year she and Maybelle, with Joe Carter taking his late father's bass part, recorded their classic *An Historic Reunion* album, which included their rather nostalgic 'Happiest Days Of All'. It was recorded in Nashville. The trio surprised the recording engineers by recording 12 tracks in just over four hours - an unusual event. It was the first time the two had recorded together for 25 years. (In 1991, Bear Family reissued these recordings, plus a version of 'No More Goodbyes' that had not been released by Columbia, on a compact disc that also contained a reissue of Mother Maybelle's 1966 album, *A Living Legend* and a further previously unissued recording of her instrumental 'Mama's Irish Jig'.)

In 1970, Sara and Maybelle were both present when the Original Carter Family became the first group ever to be elected to the *Country Music Hall Of Fame*. Their plaque included the words 'They are regarded by many as the epitome of country greatness and originators of a much copied style'. Maybelle Carter, a most respected member of the country music world, continued to perform until her death in Nashville on 23 October 1978. Sara Carter died in Lodi, California, after a long illness, on 8 January 1979. The Carter Family influenced other groups to repeat their sound notably the Phipps Family of Kentucky, who among their many albums recorded tributes to the Carters such as *Echoes Of The Carter Family* and *Most Requested Sacred Songs Of The Carter Family*. Further afield the Canadian Romaniuk Family also showed their ability to repeat the Carter Family sound with albums such as *Country Carter Style*.

Albums by the Original Carter Family: *The Famous Carter Family* (1961), *Great Original Recordings By The Carter Family* (1962), *The Original And Great Carter Family* (1962), *The Carter Family (Original Recordings)* (1963), *'Mid The Green Fields Of Virginia* (1963), *A Collection of Favorites (Folk, Country, Blues And Scared Songs)* (1963), *Keep On The Sunny Side* (1964), *Home Among The Hills* (1965), *More Favorites By The Carter Family* (1965), *Great Sacred Songs* (1966), *The Country Album* (1967), *Country Sounds Of The Original Carter Family* (1967), *Lonesome Pine Special* (1971), *More Golden Gems From The Original Carter Family* (1972), *The Carter Family On Border Radio* (1972), *My Old Cottage Home* (1973), *The Happiest Days Of All* (1974), *Famous Country Music Makers* (1974, UK release), *The Original Carter Family From 1936 Radio Transcripts* (1975), *Country's First Family* (1976), *Legendary Performers* (1978), *Carter Family In Texas Volumes 1 to 7* (late 70s), *Clinch Mountain Treasures* (1992). Albums by the A.P. Carter Family: *All Time Favorites* (mid-50s), *In Memory Of A.P. Carter (Keep On The Sunny Side)* (early 60s), *A.P. Carter's Clinch Mountain Ballads* (1970), *Their Last Recording (The Original A.P.Carter Family)* (1970). Albums by Sara and Maybelle Carter: *An Historic Reunion* (1967). Albums by Mother Maybelle with Anita, Helen and June: *The Carter Family Country Favorites* (mid-60s), *Travellin' Minstrel Band* (1972).

Further reading: *The Carter Family*, John Atkins, Bob Coltman, Alec Davidson, Kip Lornell.

Carver, Johnny

b. John David Carver, 20 November 1940, Jackson, Mississippi, USA. He started out in a family gospel group, formed his own band in high school and then took a band on the road around the USA. In 1965 he was the featured singer at the Palomino Club in Hollywood, which led to a contract with Imperial Records. His first country hits were with 'Your Lily White Hands', 'I Still Didn't Have The Sense To Go', 'Hold Me Tight' and 'Sweet Wine'. His songs were recorded by Ferlin Husky, Connie Smith and Roy Drusky. On ABC/Dot from 1973, he covered pop hits for the country market; 'Tie A Yellow Ribbon Round The Old Oak Tree', 'Afternoon Delight' and 'Living Next Door To Alice'. His last chart entry was in 1981 with 'S.O.S'.

Albums: *Real Country* (1967), *Leaving Again* (1968), *You're In Good Hands With Johnny Carver* (1968), *Sweet Wine/Hold Me Tight* (1969), *I Start Thinking*

About You (1973), *Tie A Yellow Ribbon Round The Old Oak Tree* (1973), *Don't Tell That Sweet Old Lady* (1974), *Double Exposure* (1974), *Lines, Circles and Triangles* (1974), *Strings* (1975), *Afternoon Delight* (1976).

Cash, Johnny

b. 26 February 1932, Kingsland, Arkansas, USA. Cash has traced his ancestry to 17th century Scotland and has admitted that he fabricated the much-publicized story that he was a quarter Cherokee. Cash's father, Ray, worked on sawmills and the railway; in 1936, the family was one of 600 chosen by the Federal Government to reclaim land by the Mississippi River, known as the Dyess Colony Scheme. Much of it was swampland and, in 1937, they were evacuated when the river overflowed. Cash recalled the circumstances in his 1959 country hit, 'Five Foot High And Risin''. Other songs stemming from his youth are 'Pickin' Time', 'Christmas As I Knew It' and 'Cisco Clifton's Filling Station'. Carl Perkins wrote 'Daddy Sang Bass' about Cash's family and the 'little brother' is Jack Cash, who was killed when he fell across an electric saw. Cash was posted to Germany as a radio-operator in the US Army. Many think the scar on his cheek is a knife wound but it is the result of a cyst being removed by a drunken doctor, whilst his hearing was permanently damaged by a German girl playfully sticking a pencil down his left ear. After his discharge, he settled in San Antonio with his bride, Vivian Liberto. One of their four children, Rosanne Cash, also became a country singer. Cash auditioned as a gospel singer for the owner of Sun Records in Memphis, Sam Phillips, who told him to return with something more commercial. Cash developed his 'boom chicka boom' sound with two friends: Luther Perkins, lead guitar and Marshall Grant, bass. Their first record, 'Hey Porter'/'Cry, Cry, Cry', credited to Johnny Cash And The Tennessee Two, was released in June 1955. Cash was irritated that Phillips had called him 'Johnny' as it sounded too young. 'Cry Cry Cry' made number 14 on the US country charts and was followed by 'Folsom Prison Blues', which Cash wrote after seeing a film, 'Inside The Walls Of Folsom Prison'. They played shows with Carl Perkins (no relation to Luther); Perkins' drummer, W.S. Holland, joined Cash in 1958 to make it the Tennessee Three. Cash encouraged Perkins to complete the writing of 'Blue Suede Shoes', while he finished 'I Walk The Line' at Carl's insistence; 'I got the idea from a Dale Carnegie course. It taught you to keep your eyes open for something good. I made a love song out of it. It was meant to be a slow, mournful ballad but I sped up the tempo until I didn't like it at all'. 'I Walk The Line' made number 17 on the US pop charts and was the title song for a 1970 film starring Gregory Peck. Among his other excellent Sun records are 'Home Of The Blues', which was the name of a Memphis record shop, 'Big River', 'Luther Played The Boogie', 'Give My Love To Rose' and 'There You Go', which topped the US country charts for five weeks. Producer Jack Clement added piano and vocal chorus. They scored further pop hits with the high school tale, 'Ballad Of A Teenage Queen' (number 14), 'Guess Things Happen That Way' (number 11) and 'The Ways Of A Woman In Love' (number 24). Whilst at Sun, Cash wrote 'You're My Baby' and 'Rock 'N' Roll Ruby' which were recorded by Roy Orbison and Warren Smith, respectively. Despite having his photograph taken with Elvis Presley, Jerry Lee Lewis and Carl Perkins, he did not take part in the 'million dollar session' but went shopping instead.

At a disc jockey's convention in Nashville in November 1957, Sun launched their first ever album release, *Johnny Cash With His Hot And Blue Guitar*, but Phillips was reluctant to record further LPs with Cash. This, and an unwillingness to increase his royalties, led to Cash joining Columbia in 1958. His cautionary tale about a gunfighter not listening to his mother, 'Don't Take Your Guns To Town', sold half a million copies and prompted a response from Charlie Rich, 'The Ballad Of Billy Joe', which was also recorded by Jerry Lee Lewis. Its b-side, 'I Still Miss Someone', is one of Cash's best compositions, and has been revived by Flatt And Scruggs, Crystal Gayle and Emmylou Harris. Cash took drugs to get through his schedule of 300 shows a year. His artistic integrity suffered and he regards *The Sound Of Johnny Cash* as his worst album. Nevertheless, he started on an inspiring series of concept albums about the working man (*Blood, Sweat And Tears*), cowboys (*Ballads Of The True West*) and the American Indian (*Bitter Tears*). The concepts are fascinating, the songs excellent, but the albums are bogged down with narration and self-righteousness, making Cash sound like a history teacher. His sympathy for a maligned American Indian, 'The Ballad Of Ira Hayes', led to threats from the Ku Klux Klan. Cash says, 'I didn't really care what condition I was in and it showed up on my recordings, but *Bitter Tears* was so important to me that I managed to get enough sleep to do it right.' For all his worthy causes, the

Johnny Cash

drugged-up country star was a troublemaker himself, although, despite press reports, he only ever spent three days in prison. His biggest misdemeanour was starting a forest fire for which he was fined $85,000. He wrecked hotel rooms and toyed with guns. He and his drinking buddy, country singer Carl Smith, rampaged through Smith's house and ruined his wife's Cadillac. Smith's marriage to June Carter of the Carter Family was nearing its end but few could have predicted Carter's next marriage. In 1963, Mexican brass was added to the ominous 'Ring Of Fire', written by Carter and Merle Kilgore, which again was a pop hit. Without Cash's support, Bob Dylan would have been dropped by Columbia, and Cash had his first British hit in 1965 with Dylan's 'It Ain't Me Babe'. Their off-beat duet, 'Girl From The North Country', was included on Dylan's *Nashville Skyline*, and the rest of their sessions have been widely bootlegged. Dylan also gave Cash an unreleased song, 'Wanted Man'. Cash said, 'I don't dance, tell jokes or wear my pants too tight, but I do know about a thousand songs.' With this in mind, he has turned his road show into a history of country music. In the 60s it featured Carl Perkins (who also played guitar for Cash after Luther Perkins' death in a fire), the Statler Brothers and the Carter Family. The highlight of Cash's act was 'Orange Blossom Special' played with two harmonicas. One night Cash proposed to June Carter on stage; she accepted and they were married in March 1968. Their successful duets include 'Jackson' and 'If I Were A Carpenter'.

In 1968 Columbia finally agreed to record one of Cash's prison concerts and the invigorating album, *Johnny Cash At Folsom Prison* is one of the most atmospheric of all live albums. It remains, arguably, Cash's best album - perhaps because it is history rather than being about history - and a contender for the best country record of all time. Cash explains, 'Prisoners are the greatest audience that an entertainer can perform for. We bring them a ray of sunshine and they're not ashamed to show their appreciation.' He included 'Graystone Chapel' written by an inmate, Glen Sherley, which he had been given by the Prison Chaplain. Sherley subsequently recorded an album with Cash's support, but he died in 1978. The Folsom Prison concert was followed by one at San Quentin, which was filmed for a television documentary. Shortly before that concert, Shel Silverstein gave Cash a poem, 'A Boy Named Sue'. Carl Perkins put chords to it and, without any rehearsals, the humorous song was recorded, giving Cash his only

Top 10 on the US pop charts and also made number 4 in the UK. Cash's popularity led to him hosting his own television series from 1969 71 but, despite notable guests such as Bob Dylan, the show was hampered by feeble jokes and middle-of-the road arrangements. Far better was the documentary, *Johnny Cash - The Man, His World, His Music*. Cash's catch-phrase 'Hello, I'm Johnny Cash' became so well-known that both Elvis Presley and the Kinks' Ray Davies sometimes opened with that remark. Cash championed Kris Kristofferson, wrote the liner notes for his first album, *Kristofferson*, and recorded several of his songs. 'To Beat The Devil' celebrated Cash overcoming drugs after many years, while 'The Loving Gift' was about the birth of Cash's son, John Carter Cash, who has since joined his stage show. Cash has often found strength and comfort in religion and he has recorded many spiritual albums. One of his most stirring performances is 'Were You There (When They Crucified My Lord)?' with the Carter Family. He made a documentary film and double-album *The Gospel Road* with Kristofferson, Larry Gatlin and the Statler Brothers, but, as he remarked, 'My record company would rather I'd be in prison than in church.' He justified himself commercially when 'A Thing Called Love', written by Jerry Reed, made with the Evangel Temple Choir, became one of his biggest selling UK records, reaching number 4 in 1972.

Cash is an imposing figure with his huge muscular frame, black hair, craggy face and deep bass voice. Unlike other country singers, he shuns lavish colours and in his song 'Man In Black' he explains that he wears black because of the injustice in the world. In truth, he started wearing black when he first appeared on the *Grand Ole Opry* because he felt that rhinestone suits detracted from the music. With little trouble, Cash could have been a major Hollywood star, particularly in westerns, and he acquitted himself well when the occasion arose. He made his debut in *Five Minutes To Live* in 1960 and his best role is opposite Kirk Douglas in the 1972 film *A Gunfight*, which was financed by Apache money, although religious principles prevented a scene with a naked actress. He was featured alongside Kris Kristofferson and Willie Nelson in a light-hearted remake of *Stagecoach* and starred in a television movie adaptation of his pool-hall song *The Baron*. Cash also gave a moving portrayal of a coalminer overcoming illiteracy in another television movie, *The Pride Of Jesse Hallam*. He recorded the theme for the US television series *The*

Rebel - Johnny Yuma and, amongst the previously unissued tracks released by Bear Family, is his submission for a James Bond theme, 'Thunderball'. By opening his own recording studios, House Of Cash, in 1972, he became even more prolific. His family joined him on the quirky *The Junkie And The Juicehead Minus Me* and his son-in-law J.W. Routh wrote several songs and performed with him on *The Rambler*. He has always followed writers and the inclusion of Nick Lowe, former husband of Carlene Carter, and Rodney Crowell, husband of Rosanne Cash, into his family increased his awareness. His recordings include the Rolling Stones' 'No Expectations', John Prine's 'Unwed Fathers', Guy Clark's 'The Last Gunfighter Ballad' and a touching portrayal of Bruce Springsteen's 'Highway Patrolman'. He showed his humour with 'Gone Girl', 'One Piece At A Time' and 'Chicken In Black'. He said, 'I record a song because I love it and let it become a part of me.' Cash moved to Mercury Records in 1986 and scored immediately with the whimsical 'The Night Hank Williams Came To Town'. He made an all-star album, *Water From The Wells Of Home* with Emmylou Harris, the Everly Brothers, Paul McCartney and many others. His 60s composition 'Tennessee Flat-Top Box' became a US country number 1 for daughter Rosanne in 1988. In the same year, various British modern folk artists recorded an album of his songs *'Til Things Are Brighter*, with proceeds going to an AIDS charity. Cash particularly enjoyed Sally Timms' waltz-time treatment of 'Cry, Cry, Cry'. On the crest of a revival, Cash has been hampered by pneumonia, heart surgery and a recurrence of drug problems. He has now returned to the stage, either touring with the Carter Family or as part of the Highwaymen with Kristofferson, Waylon Jennings and Nelson, whose concerts are more good-natured than their sombre albums. He is still passionate about what he believes in. 'A lot of people think of country singers as right-wing, redneck bigots,' he says, 'but I don't think I'm like that.'

Cash has made over 70 albums of original material, plus numerous guest appearances. His music reflects his love of America (a recent compilation was called *Patriot*), his compassion, his love of life, and, what is often lacking in country music, a sense of humour. His limited range is staggeringly good on the right songs, especially narrative ones. Like Bo Diddley's 'shave and a haircut' rhythm, he has developed his music around his 'boom chicka boom', and instilled enough variety to stave off boredom. His contribution to country music's history is inestimable and, as he says, 'They can get all the synthesizers they want, but nothing will ever take the place of the human heart'. His continuing popularity assured, Cash states he heeded the advice he was given during his one and only singing lesson, 'Never change your voice'.

Albums: *Johnny Cash With His Hot And Blue Guitar* (1957), *Johnny Cash Sings The Songs That Made Him Famous* (1958), *The Fabulous Johnny Cash* (1958), *Hymns By Johnny Cash* (1959), *Songs Of Our Soil* (1959), *Now There Was A Song* (1960), *Johnny Cash Sings Hank Williams And Other Favorite Tunes* (1960), *Ride This Train* (1960), *Hymns From The Heart* (1962), *The Sound Of Johnny Cash* (1962), *Blood, Sweat And Tears* (1963), *The Christmas Spirit* (1963), with the Carter Family *Keep On The Sunnyside* (1964), *I Walk The Line* (1964), *Bitter Tears (Ballads Of The American Indian)* (1964), *Orange Blossom Special* (1965), *Ballads Of The True West* (1965), *Mean As Hell* (1965), *The Sons Of Katie Elder* (1965, film soundtrack), *Ballads Of The True West, Volume 2* (1966), *Everybody Loves A Nut* (1966), *Happiness Is You* (1966), with June Carter *Carryin' On* (1967), *Old Golden Throat* (1968), *From Sea To Shining Sea* (1968), *Johnny Cash At Folsom Prison* (1968), *More Of Old Golden Throat* (1969), *The Holy Land* (1969), *Johnny Cash At San Quentin* (1969), *Get Rhythm* (1969, 50s Sun label recordings), *Showtime* (1969, 50s Sun label recordings), *Story Songs Of The Trains And Rivers* (1969, 50s Sun label recordings), *Hello I'm Johnny Cash* (1970), *The Singing Story Teller* (1970, 50s Sun label recordings), *The Johnny Cash Show* (1970), *I Walk The Line* (1970, film soundtrack), *Man In Black* (1971), *A Thing Called Love* (1972), *Christmas And The Cash Family* (1972), *America (A 200-Year Salute In Story And Song)* (1972), *The Gospel Road* (1973), *Any Old Wind That Blows* (1973), with June Carter *Johnny Cash And His Woman* (1973), *Inside A Swedish Prison* (1974), *The Junkie And The Juicehead Minus Me* (1974), *Ragged Old Flag* (1974), *John R. Cash* (1975), *Look At Them Beans* (1975), *The Johnny Cash Children's Album* (1975), *Destination Victoria Station* (1976), *Strawberry Cake* (1976), *One Piece At A Time* (1976), *The Last Gunfighter Ballad* (1977), *The Rambler* (1977), *Gone Girl* (1978), *The Unissued Johnny Cash* (1978), *I Would Like To See You Again* (1978), *Silver* (1979), *A Believer Sings The Truth* (1979), *Johnny And June* (1980), *Rockabilly Blues* (1980), *Tall Man* (1980), *The Baron* (1981), with Jerry Lee Lewis, Carl Perkins *The Survivors* (1982), *The Adventures Of Johnny Cash* (1982), *Johnny 99* (1983) *Rainbow*

(1985), with Kris Kristofferson, Waylon Jennings, Willie Nelson *Highwayman* (1985), with Jerry Lee Lewis, Roy Orbison, Carl Perkins *Homecoming* (1986), with Waylon Jennings *Heroes* (1986), *Believe In Him* (1986), *Johnny Cash Is Back In Town* (1987), *Classic Cash* (1988), *Water From The Wells Of Home* (1988), *Boom Chicka Boom* (1989), with Kristofferson, Jennings and Nelson *Highwayman 2* (1990), *The Mystery Of Life* (1991). Compilations: *Ring Of Fire (The Best Of Johnny Cash)* (1963), *Johnny Cash's Greatest Hits, Volume 1* (1967). A five-CD boxed-set, *The Man In Black, 1954-1958* (1990) includes all his Sun recordings and some Columbia ones with many outtakes and false starts, *The Best Of The Sun Years* (1992).

Further reading: *Man In Black*, Johnny Cash. *Johnny Cash: Winners Get Scars Too*, Christopher S. Wren. *Johnny Cash Discography*, John L. Smith. *Man In White*, Johnny Cash (a biography of St. Paul).

Cash, Rosanne

b. 24 May 1955, Memphis, Tennessee, USA. The daughter of Johnny Cash from his first marriage to Vivien Liberto, Cash lived with her mother in California after her parents divorced in 1966. Perhaps inevitably, she returned to Nashville, where she studied drama at Vanderbilt University, before relocating to Los Angeles to study 'method' acting at Lee Strasberg's Institute, after which she worked for three years in her father's road show. In the late 70s, she spent a year in London working for CBS, the same label as her father, and signed a record deal in Germany with Ariola resulting in her debut album, which has become a collector's item. Mainly recorded and produced in Germany with German-based musicians, it also included three tracks recorded in Nashville and was produced by Rodney Crowell. At the time, Cash was somewhat influenced by the punk ethos which she had experienced in Britain, but on her return to Nashville, she worked on demos with Crowell which gained her a deal with CBS as a neo-country act. She married Crowell in 1979, the same year her first CBS album, *Right Or Wrong,* was released. While not a huge success, the album, again produced by Crowell, included three US country hits: 'No Memories Hangin' Round' (a duet with Bobby Bare), 'Couldn't Do Nothin' Right, and 'Take Me, Take Me', while many of the backing musicians were also members of Emmylou Harris's Hot Band. 1981 brought the *Seven Year Ache*, again produced by Crowell, which went gold and reached the Top 30 of the US pop chart. It included three US country chart number 1

singles: the title track, her own composition, which reached the Top 30 of the US pop chart, 'My Baby Thinks He's A Train' (written by Leroy Preston, then of Asleep At The Wheel), and another of her own songs 'Blue Moon With Heartache'.

Somewhere In The Stars, also made the Top 100 of the US pop album charts, and included three US country chart singles, 'Ain't No Money', 'I Wonder' and 'It Hasn't Happened Yet', but overall the album was considerably less successful than its predecessor. Her next album, *Rhythm And Romance*, four US country hit singles included, two of which were overseen by Crowell: 'Never Be You', another number 1 which was written by Tom Petty and Benmont Tench, and 'Hold On'. David Malloy produced most of the album, including another country number 1 single, 'I Don't Know Why You Don't Want Me' (which Cash co-wrote with Crowell) and 'Second To No-One'. After another two years' hiatus came *King's Record Shop*, titled after, and with a sleeve picture of the store of that name in Louisville, Kentucky. This album included four US country number 1 singles: John Hiatt's 'The Way We Make A Broken Heart', her revival of her father's 1962 country hit, 'Tennessee Flat Top Box', 'If You Change Your Mind', which she co-wrote with pedal steel ace Hank DeVito, and 'Rainway Train', written by John Stewart. This album was again produced by Crowell, with whom she duetted on a fifth US country number 1 within 13 months, 'It's A Small World'. This song was included on Crowell's *Diamond And Dirt*.

Cash won a Grammy award in 1985 for Best Country Vocal Performance Female, and in 1988 won *Billboard*'s Top Single Artist Award. A wife and mother, Cash has rarely had time to work live, but this has clearly had little effect on her recording career. In 1989 came a compilation album, *Hits 1979-1989* (appropriately re-titled *Retrospective 1979-1989* for UK release), and in late 1990, *Interiors*, a hauntingly introspective album which was criticized for its apparently pessimistic outlook. Its release was later followed by the news that her marriage to Crowell had broken down. Cash was one of the pioneers of the 'New Country' movement of the late 80s, but her relative unavailability - she places her family firmly before her career - may ultimately result in others taking the glory for this forward thinking. Nevertheless, her achievements to date have ensured that the Cash family heritage in country music is far from disgraced.

Albums: *Rosanne Cash* (1978), *Right Or Wrong*

Rosanne Cash

(1979), *Seven Year Ache* (1981), *Somewhere In The Stars* (1982), *Rhythm And Romance* (1985), *King's Record Shop* (1988), *Hits 1979-1989 (UK title: Retrospective 1979-1989)* (1989), *Interiors* (1990).

Cash, Tommy

b. 5 April 1940, Dyess, Arkansas, USA. Cash is the younger brother of Johnny Cash. He originally intended to be a basketball player. In the US armed forces in Germany, he presented AFN radio's *Stickbuddy Jamboree*. Back in the USA, he worked in radio, managed his brother's music publishing company and then recorded his first single for Musicor, 'That's Where My Baby Used To Be'. He released 'Tobacco Road' and 'Jailbirds Can't Fly' on United Artists. Over at Epic in 1969, he had his biggest success in the US country charts with 'Six White Horses', a tribute to the Kennedys and Martin Luther King. Almost as successful were 'Rise And Shine' written by Carl Perkins, and 'One Song Away'. He also holds the highest placing (number 16) in the US country charts for a version of 'I Recall A Gypsy Woman'. He won a BMI award for his composition, 'You Don't Hear', a country hit for Kitty Wells. He has proved popular at UK country festivals and, in 1991, he released *The 25th Anniversary Album*, which featured guest appearances from Johnny Cash, Tom T. Hall, George Jones and Connie Smith.
Albums: *Here Comes Tommy Cash* (1968), *Your Lovin' Takes The Leavin' Out Of Me* (1969), *Six White Horses* (1970), *Rise And Shine* (1970), *The American Way Of Life* (1971), *Cash Country* (1971), *That Certain One* (1972), *Only A Stone* (1975), *The New Spirit* (1978), *The 25th Anniversary Album* (1991).

Chapman, Marshall

b. 7 January 1949, Spartanburg, North Carolina, USA. Chapman came from a wealthy family and spent time in France before moving to Nashville, Tennessee in 1973. She signed with Epic Records and toured as a rock act, but found her songs had more favour with country audiences. Her composition, 'A Woman's Heart (Is A Handy Place To Be)', was covered by Crystal Gayle and by Jessi Colter. 'Somewhere South Of Macon' was considered too outright for country radio; she also achieved notoriety with 'Don't Get Me Pregnant'.
Albums: *Me, I'm Feeling Free* (1977), *Jaded Virgin* (1978), *Marshall* (1979), *Pick Up The Tempo* (1981), *Dirty Linen* (1987).

Childre, Lew

b. 1 November 1901, Opp, Alabama, USA, d. 3 December 1961. He began his professional career at the age of 16 as a vaudeville performer and toured for years with various tent shows and played theatres throughout the southern states. He developed into an all-round entertainer, being a fine singer, comedian, dancer and instrumentalist. He was especially proficient on steel and Hawaiian guitars. He played on many top radio shows before he joined the *Grand Ole Opry* in 1945. Between then and 1948, he usually worked as a comedy act with Stringbean but then pursued a solo career. He was very popular on the *Opry* and is remembered for his comedy routines, particularly his imaginary character, Doctor Lew, who gave supposed helpful advice in answer to letters written to him. He also appeared regularly on Red Foley's network television show. Childre was a visual performer, whose full talents did not really show to their best on radio or record. He made some recordings for Gennett and ARC in the 30s but few survived and it is usually his later Starday recordings such as 'Old MacDonald's Farm' and 'Shanghai Rooster' that are heard today. He was known as that Boy From Alabama (even when he was almost 60) and his best known song was 'Alabamy Bound'. In 1980, an album taken from radio shows of 1946 was released by Old Homestead. Lew Childre died following a heart attack on 3 December 1961.
Compilations: with Cowboy Copas, Josh Graves *Old Time Get Together With Lew Childre* (1961), *On The Air 1946 Volume 1* (1980).

Clark, Guy

b. 6 November 1941, Rockport, Texas, USA. Clark has achieved considerably more fame as a songwriter than as a performer, although he is revered by his nucleus of fans internationally. Brought up in the small hamlet of Monahans, Texas, Clark worked in television during the 60s, and later as a photographer - his work appeared on albums released by the Texan-based International Artists Records. He briefly performed in folk trio with K.T.Oslin, and began writing songs for a living, moving to Los Angeles, which he eventually loathed, but which inspired one of his biggest songs, 'LA Freeway', a US Top 100 hit for Jerry Jeff Walker. Clark then wrote songs like his classic 'Desperados Waiting For A Train' which was covered by acts as diverse as Tom Rush and Mallard (the group formed by ex-members of Captain Beefheart's Magic Band) and the brilliant train song, 'Texas 1947', by Johnny Cash.

Guy Clark

His first album, *Old No. 1*, was released in 1975, and included 'Freeway', 'Desperados' and '1947', as well as several more songs of similarly high quality, like 'Let It Roll'. Despite intemperate and well deserved critical acclaim, it failed to reach the charts on either side of the Atlantic. One of the finest singer/songwriter albums of its era, it continued to sell as a reissue during the 80s. Clark's 1976 follow-up album, *Texas Cooking*, was no more successful, although it again contained classic songs like 'The Last Gunfighter Ballad' and the contagious 'Virginia's Real'. Among those who contributed to these albums simply because they enjoyed Clark's music were Emmylou Harris, Rodney Crowell, Steve Earle, Jerry Jeff Walker, Hoyt Axton and Waylon Jennings.

By 1978, Clark had moved labels to Warner Brothers, which released *Guy Clark*, which included four songs from outside writers, among them Rodney Crowell's 'Viola', 'American Dream' and Townes Van Zandt's 'Don't You Take It Too Bad', while the harmonizing friends this time included Don Everly, Gordon Payne (of the Crickets) and Kay (K.T.) Oslin. A three year gap then ensued before 1981's *The South Coast Of Texas*, which was produced by Rodney Crowell. Clark wrote two of the songs with Crowell, 'The Partner Nobody Chose' (a US country Top 40 single) and 'She's Crazy For Leavin'', while the album also included 'Heartbroke', later covered by Ricky Skaggs. 1983 brought *Better Days*, again produced by Crowell, which included vintage classics like 'The Randall Knife' and 'The Carpenter', as well as another US country chart single, 'Homegrown Tomatoes' and Van Zandt's amusing 'No Deal', but Clark was still unable to penetrate the commercial barriers which had long been predicted by critics and his fellow musicians. He began to work as a solo troubadour, after various unsuccessful attempts to perform live with backing musicians. At this point he developed the intimate show which he brought to Europe several times during the latter half of the 80s. This resulted in his return to recording with *Old Friends*, appearing on U2's label, Mother Records. The usual array of 'heavy friends' were on hand, including Harris, Crowell, Rosanne Cash and Vince Gill, but only two of the 10 tracks were solely written by Clark. Among the contributions were Joe Ely's 'The Indian Cowboy', Van Zandt's 'To Live Is To Fly' and a song co-written by Clark with his wife Susanna, and with Richard Leigh (who had written the massive hit, 'Don't It Make My Brown Eyes Blue', for Crystal Gayle). Even

with the implied patronage of U2, at the time one of the biggest acts in the world, Clark enjoyed little more success than he had previously experienced.

It would be sad if Guy Clark were to remain merely a cult figure, as he is without doubt one of the most original musical talents of the last 30 years from Texas. He has been freely acknowledged as a significant influence on the Texan performers, such as Lyle Lovett, on whose debut album Clark wrote a dedication.

Albums: *Old No. 1* (1975), *Texas Cookin'* (1976), *Guy Clark* (1978), *The South Coast Of Texas* (1981), *Better Days* (1983), *Old Friends* (1989).

Clark, Roy

b. Roy Linwood Clark, 15 April 1933, Meherrin, Virginia, USA. When he was 11-years-old the family relocated to Washington DC after his father, a competent musician who played guitar, banjo and fiddle, progressed from being a cotton picker to become a computer programmer and augmented his pay for the government job by playing at local dances. (His mother also played piano.) Clark played banjo and mandolin at an early age and was playing guitar at dances with his father by the time he was 14. He won the National Banjo Championship at the ages of 16 and 17, the latter occasion resulting in an appearance at the *Grand Ole Opry*. He considered a baseball career in his late teens but at 18 became a professional boxer. Fighting as a light-heavyweight, he won 15 fights in a row before the next fight convinced him he should look elsewhere for a living. He found work in clubs and appeared on local radio and television in such shows as the *Ozark Jubilee* and *Town And Country Time*. In 1955, he joined Jimmy Dean on his *Country Style*, Washington television show and when Dean left for New York, Clark was given the show. He played instruments, joked and sang and gradually built himself a reputation but in the early 60s, he decided to seek fame further afield and became lead guitarist and front man for Wanda Jackson. He stayed with her for about a year and played lead guitar on her hit recording of 'Let's Have A Party'. When she gave up her band, Jim Halsey took on the role of Clark's manager and soon found him a spot on one of the most popular network television shows *The Beverly Hillbillies*. Here he appeared in the dual role of Cousin Roy and (dressed as a woman) his mother Big Mama Halsey. He also signed for Capitol Records and released his first album, which contained both songs and instrumentals. In 1963, he was given the chance to play on the *Tonight Show,* owing to the fact that Jimmy Dean was hosting the programme. This led to further invitations to appear on other top television shows and his popularity rapidly grew. In later years he hosted many of the shows personally. He achieved his first chart success in 1963, when his version of Bill Anderson's 'The Tips Of My Fingers' made both the US country and pop charts. He left Capitol, joined Dot Records in 1967 and during the 60s, somewhat ironically, he had country hits with pop songs, when further double chart successes included Charles Aznavour's 'Yesterday When I Was Young' and 'September Song'. During the mid-60s, he fronted the *Swingin' Country* television series and in 1969, CBS invited him to co-host their new country comedy show *Hee Haw* with Buck Owens. This programme became one of the most popular on television, so much so that when CBS dropped it in 1971 because they felt it did not create the right impression for them, it was immediately syndicated by the show's producers and even grew in popularity. During the 70s, Clark had a great number of country chart hits, including the very humorous 'Thank God And Greyhound', 'Riders In The Sky', 'Somewhere Between Love And Tomorrow' and 'Come Live With Me', his only number 1 US country hit. He also made several popular television commercials. Clark progressed to become one of country music's biggest stars and to enable himself to keep up a punishing schedule of concert appearances, he learned to fly and piloted himself around the States. He was one of the first country artists to star in his own show on Las Vegas strip, where he still appears regularly, usually backed by an orchestra. Clark also became the first star to take his show to the Soviet Union, when in January 1976, he played to packed houses during a 21-day tour of Riga, Moscow and Leningrad. The same year, Clark also played concerts with Arthur Fiedler and the Boston Pops Orchestra. In 1977, he appeared at Carnegie Hall, New York and in 1979, he recorded an album with blues artist Clarence 'Gatemouth' Brown. Between 1979 and 1981, he recorded for MCA but during the late 80s, he was with several labels. Although he had no major hits, a version of 'Night Life' registered country hit number 50 for him in 1986. In later years, he become involved in cattle ranching, publishing, advertising and property. During his career, he has won many CMA awards including Comedian Of The Year 1970, Entertainer Of The Year 1973, Instrumental Group Of The Year (with Buck Trent) in 1975 and 1976 and was nominated as

Instrumentalist Of The Year every year from 1967 to 1980, winning in 1977, 1978 and 1980. He guested on the *Opry* many times over the years but did not become a member until 1987. He has appeared in several films and in 1986, he co-starred with Mel Tillis in a comedy western called *Uphill All The Way*, which they both also produced. Clark is a talented multi-instrumentalist and all-round entertainer, who is equally at home with various types of music. A very modest man, in spite of the many awards and achievements, he once said 'I never compare myself to anything or anyone and if anybody else does, all I can definitely say is one thing - I'm the best Roy Clark I know of'.

Albums: *The Lightning Fingers Of Roy Clark* (1962), *The Tip Of My Fingers* (1963), *Happy To Be Unhappy* (1964), *Guitar Spectacular* (1965), *Sings Lonesome Love Ballads* (1966), *Stringin' Along With The Blues* (1966), *Roy Clark* (1966), *Live* (1967), *Do You Believe This Roy Clark* (1968), *In The Mood* (1968), *Urban, Suburban* (1968), *Yesterday When I Was Young* (1969), *The Everlovin' Soul Of Roy Clark* (1969), *The Other Side Of Roy Clark* (1970), *I Never Picked Cotton* (1970), *The Magnificent Sanctuary Band* (1971), *The Incredible Roy Clark* (1971), *Roy Clark Country!* (1972), *Family Album* (1973), *Superpicker* (1973), *Come Live With Me* (1973), *Classic Clark* (1974), *Family And Friends* (1974), *The Entertainer* (1974), *Roy Clark* (1974), *Sings Gospel* (1975), with Buck Trent *A Pair Of Fives (Banjos That Is)* (1975), *So Much To Remember* (1975), *Heart To Heart* (1975), *In Concert* (1976), *Hookin' It* (1977), *My Music And Me* (1977), with Freddy Fender, Hank Thompson and Don Williams *Country Comes To Carnegie Hall* (1977), *Labour Of Love* (1978), with Trent *Banjo Bandit* (1978), with Clarence 'Gatemouth' Brown *Making Music* (1979), *My Music* (1980), *The Last Word In Jesus Is Us* (1981), *Meanwhile Back At The Country* (1981), with Grandpa Jones, Buck Owens and Kenny Price *The Hee Haw Gospel Quartet* (1981), *Live From Austin City Limits* (1982), *Turned Loose* (1982). Compilations: *The Best Of Roy Clark* (1971), *The ABC Collection* (1977), *20 Golden Pieces* (1984).

Clark, Yodelling Slim

b. Raymond LeRoy Clark, 11 December 1917, Springfield, Massachusetts, USA. Although Clark grew up listening to country music, he wanted to be a professional baseball player but an injury to his pitching arm prevented that. He was then determined to follow the style of his favourite singer, Wilf Carter (Montana Slim). (Clark's son was named Wilf Carter Clark.) He copied Carter's yodel and made his first radio broadcast in 1938. He formed the Red River Rangers, whose line-up included Kenny Roberts, who went on to solo success. Clark first recorded in 1946 and he was named the World's Champion Yodeller in 1947. He has made several albums of old-time cowboy songs and is an acknowledged authority on the subject.

Albums: *Western Songs And Dances* (1954), *Cowboy And Yodel Songs* (1962), *Cowboy Songs* (1963), *Cowboy Songs, Volume 2* (1964), *Jimmie Rodgers Songs* (1965), *Yodelling Slim Clark Sings And Yodels Favorite Montana Slim Songs Of The Mountains And Plains (Volumes 1* and *2)* (both 1966), *I Feel A Trip Coming On* (1966), *Old Chestnuts* (1967), *Wilf Carter Songs* (1967), *Yodelling Slim Clark Happens Again* (1968), *Yodelling Slim Clark Sings The Ballads Of Billy Venero* (1968), *Yodelling Slim Clark 50th Anniversary Album* (1968).

Clayton, Lee

b. 29 October 1942, Russelville, Alabama, USA. Clayton moved to Oak Ridge, Tennessee when aged four. His father encouraged his musical abilities and, when aged only 10, he played steel guitar on radio. Clayton's background is told in 'Industry', a Bruce Springsteen-styled diatribe. Between 1966 and 1969 and after a short-lived marriage, he flew jet fighters in the US Air Force, which is described in his song 'Old Number Nine'. Clayton moved to Nashville, determined to make his name as a songwriter. The 'outlaw' scene was in its infancy and Clayton's song, 'Ladies Love Outlaws', was a US country hit for Waylon Jennings and later recorded by the Everly Brothers. His 1973 *Lee Clayton*, is regarded as a classic of 'outlaw country'. Jennings and Willie Nelson have both recorded his erotic love song, 'If You Can Touch Her At All'. Clayton, however, went broke trying to establish his own band and then followed a nomadic existence. Eventually, he developed a more strident, electric sound, employing the Irish guitarist Philip Donnolly, to record dark albums full of disillusionment for Capitol Records. The melancholy 'A Little Cocaine' is about the downfall of a friend, and his own drug habits made him unreliable. In the 80s Clayton wrote two books and one stage-play, *Little Boy Blue*, all autobiographical. He returned to recording with a fine album recorded live in Oslo, *Another Night*, but the songs were familiar. Bono of U2 has said, 'There's only one country singer who has influenced me and he's an unknown feller called Lee Clayton.'

Albums: *Lee Clayton* (1973), *Border Affair* (1978), *Naked Child* (1979), *The Dream Goes On* (1981), *Another Night* (1989).

Clement, Jack

b. Jack Henderson Clement, 5 April 1931, Whitehaven, a suburb of Memphis, Tennessee, USA. Clement, the son of a dentist and choirmaster, began playing music professionally whilst in the US Marines. He moved to Washington, DC in 1952 and worked with the Stoneman Family and Roy Clark, before forming a novelty country music act, Buzz And Jack, with Buzz Busby. He worked as an Arthur Murray dance instructor in Memphis in 1954 and then formed the garage-based Fernwood Records with truck-driver Slim Wallace. They leased their first recording, 'Trouble Bound' by Billy Lee Riley, to Sam Phillips at Sun Records. As a result, Phillips employed Clement as a songwriter, session musician, engineer and producer. Clement produced Jerry Lee Lewis' 'Whole Lotta Shakin' Goin' On' as well as writing 'It'll Be Me' and 'Fools Like Me'. He also helped Johnny Cash develop his distinctive sound and wrote his US pop hits, 'Guess Things Happen That Way' and 'Ballad Of A Teenage Queen'. Clement played rhythm guitar on Cash's classic recording of 'Big River', as well as working with Roy Orbison, Charlie Rich and Conway Twitty. In 1959 Clement left Sun and formed the unsuccessful Summer Records. ('Summer hits, Summer not, Hope you like the ones we've got.') Clement then worked as an assistant to Chet Atkins at RCA Records, producing Del Wood and writing Jim Reeves' 'I Know One' and Bobby Bare's 'Miller's Cave'. On a whim, he decided that he wanted to make Beaumont, Texas the music capital of the world, but the only hit he produced there was Dickey Lee's 1962 US Top 10 hit, 'Patches'. Back in Nashville, Clement produced Johnny Cash's 1963 hit, 'Ring Of Fire', and wrote several comic songs for *Everybody Loves A Nut* including 'The One On The Right Is On The Left'. Just as Sam Phillips had been looking for 'a white boy who could sound black', Clement wanted a black country star. In 1966 he found what he wanted in Charley Pride and produced his records for many years. Pride recorded Clement's songs, 'Just Between You And Me' and 'Gone, On The Other Hand'. He also produced Tompall And The Glaser Brothers, Sheb Wooley and, surprisingly, Louis Armstrong. One of his wittiest songs is called '(If I Had) Johnny's Cash And Charley's Pride'. In 1972 Clement

formed the JMI label, signing Don Williams, but lost his money by backing a horror film set in Nashville, *Dear Dead Delilah,* with Agnes Moorehead in her last film role. He continued producing albums including *Dreaming My Dreams* (Waylon Jennings), *Our Mother The Mountain* (Townes Van Zandt) and *Two Days In November* (Doc Watson). He wrote the title track of Johnny Cash's *Gone Girl*; and Cash's hilarious liner notes indicate Clement's eccentricities. From time to time he recorded his own records including a highly-regarded single, 'Never Give A Heart A Place To Grow', and, in 1978, he finally made an album - *All I Want To Do In Life* for Elektra Records. In recent years, he has taken to performing as Cowboy Jack Clement. An example of his character and his self-confidence showed when he met Paul McCartney in Nashville. He advised the former-Beatle, 'Let's do "Yesterday" and I'll show you how to cut that sucker right'. More recently, Clement assisted the recording of five tracks in the Sun Studios which featured on U2's *Rattle And Hum*, and he continues to produce Johnny Cash regularly.
Album: *All I Want To Do In Life* (1978).

Clements, Vassar

b. 25 April 1928, Kinard, South Carolina, USA. In his youth he liked jazz and swing music as well as country, which explains his versatility as a fiddle player in later years. A friend who was a telephone operator overheard Bill Monroe say he was looking for a fiddle player, and she told Clements to contact Monroe immediately. Clements played with Monroe on the *Grand Ole Opry* in 1949 and recorded with him the following year. He also played with Jim And Jesse and Faron Young. He was featured on both volumes of the Nitty Gritty Dirt Band's influential *Will The Circle Be Unbroken*. He has played on innumerable sessions including ones with Jimmy Buffett, J.J. Cale, Steve Goodman, Emmylou Harris, Linda Ronstadt, Gene Parsons and Jerry Jeff Walker. He has played on records by the Grateful Dead and worked with their leader, Jerry Garcia, in a band called Old And In The Way. Over the years, he has performed in concert more than most session players and he has been on the road with Earl Scruggs and John Hartford. He appeared in the Robert Altman film *Nashville* (1975) and his frenzied fiddle playing is featured in several instrumental albums - *New Hillbilly Jazz* is unusual in that it also features his vocals.
Albums: *Crossing The Catskills* (1973), *Superbow*

(1975), *Vassar Clements* (1975), *Southern Country Waltzes* (1975), with Doug Jernigan, David Bromberg *Hillbilly Jazz* (1976), *Bluegrass Session* (1977), with Jernigan, Jesse McReynolds, Buddy Spicher *Nashville Jam* (1979), *Vassar* (1980), with Jernigan *More Hillbilly Jazz* (1980), *Westport Drive* (1984), *Hillbilly Jazz Rides Again* (1987), with Stéphane Grappelli *Together At Last* (1987), *New Hillbilly Jazz* (1988), with John Hartford, Dave Holland *Clements, Hartford And Holland* (1988).

Clements, Zeke

b. 6 September 1911, Warrior, near Dora, Alabama, USA. He began his professional career working as a comedian in burlesque shows but in 1928, he made his radio debut on the WLS *National Barn Dance*. He later joined the band of Otto Gray and the Oklahoma Cowboys as a guitarist and vocalist and toured for some years. In the early 30s, he joined the *Grand Ole Opry* where he changed his burlesque material to a country format. He formed his own band, the Bronco Busters, which was one of the first *Opry* bands to wear western cowboy dress and which included his brother Stanley 'Curly' Clements and featured Texas Ruby Owens as their female vocalist. After a few years, he moved to Hollywood for radio and film work and in 1938, he gained some sort of immortality by providing the voice of Bashful in Walt Disney's classic film, *Snow White And The Seven Dwarfs*. He returned to the *Opry* in 1939 and during the 40s, he became a popular performer. A talented vocalist, guitarist and fiddle player, he also wrote many songs. In 1944 and 1945, his war song 'Smoke On The Water' was a number 1 country hit for both Red Foley and Bob Wills and in 1955, Kitty Wells scored a hit with 'There's Poison In Your Heart'. He also starred on the *Louisiana Hayride* and was popular all over the south and although nicknamed the Alabama Cowboy, he was often classed as a country crooner. He later developed various business interests in Nashville. For a time, he relocated to Florida but returned to Nashville and into the late 80s, he was still making appearances on the *Opry*.

Clifton, Bill

b. William August Marburg, 5 April 1931, Riderwood, Maryland, USA. Clifton sang and played guitar, autoharp and fiddle. He became interested in the music of the Carter Family during the 40s, having been introduced to country music through visiting the tenant farmers on his father's estate. Bill subsequently made his first records for the Stinson label in 1952. By 1954 he was performing with his Dixie Mountain Boys and recording for Blue Ridge. During the 50s Clifton compiled 150 old-time folk and gospel songs and had them privately printed. He was essentially able to bridge the gap between urban folk and bluegrass, reaching both sets of audiences on an international level. In 1961, Clifton recorded 22 Carter Family songs for Starday, and later came to Britain and set up tours for Bill Monroe, the New Lost City Ramblers and the Stanley Brothers. He had been playing bluegrass and old-time country music for 11 years before arriving in England in 1963. He led a 'missionary' role, as the music was new to English ears, and by 1966 he was playing regularly and hosting a BBC radio show called *Cellar Full Of Folk*. Clifton toured throughout Europe during the 60s, and recorded a programme of old-time music for Radio Moscow in 1966. By the following year, Clifton and his family travelled to the Philippines, where he joined the Peace Corps. Later, during the 70s, he went on to New Zealand, and formed the Hamilton County Bluegrass Band. Along with Red Rector (d. 1991) and Don Stover, Clifton formed the First Generation with whom he toured the USA and Europe in 1978. Clifton has since toured Japan, the USA and Europe. He is as well known for his work arranging tours and appearances of bluegrass performers, as he is for his recordings.

Albums: with the Dixie Mountain Boys *Mountain Folk Songs* (1960), *The Bluegrass Sound Of Bill Clifton And The Dixie Mountain Boys* (1962), *Carter Family Memorial Album* (1962), with the Dixie Mountain Boys *Soldier, Sing Me A Song* (1963), with other artists *Bluegrass Spectacular* (1963), with the Dixie Mountain Boys *Fire On The Strings* (1963), with the Dixie Mountain Boys *Code Of The Mountains* (1964), with various artists *Greatest Country Fiddlers Of Our Time* (1964), with the Dixie Mountain Boys *Mountain Bluegrass Songs* (1964), *Wanderin'* (1965), with the Dixie Mountain Boys *Bluegrass In The American Tradition* (1965), *Mountain Ramblings* (1967), *Walking In My Sleep* (1969), with the Hamilton County Bluegrass Band *Two Shades Of Bluegrass* (1970), *Bill Clifton Meets The Country Gentlemen* (1971), *Happy Days* (1971), with Hedy West *Getting The Folk Out Of The Country* (1972), with the Dixie Mountain Boys *Blue Ridge Mountain Blues* (1973), with the Dixie Mountain Boys *Blue Ridge Mountain Bluegrass* (1974), *Going Back To Dixie* (1975), *Come By The Hills* (1975), with Paul Clayton, Johnny Clark and Carl Boehm *A Bluegrass Session 1952* (1975), with

Red Rector *Another Happy Day* (1976), Bill Clifton and Rector *In Europe* (1976), with Rector *Are You From Dixie?* (1977), *Clifton And Company* (1977), *The Autoharp Centennial Celebration* (1981), *Beatle Crazy* (1983), *Where The Rainbow Finds Its End* (1991).

Cline, Patsy

b. Virginia Patterson Hensley, 8 September 1932, Gore, near Winchester, Virginia, USA. Her childhood ambition was to be a *Grand Ole Opry* star. Musician/boyfriend Bill Peer changed her stage name to Patsy Hensley and then she married builder Gerald Cline. Her signing with Four-Star Records in Nashville in 1954 was a mixed blessing as its owner, Bill McCall, insisted that she would only record songs which he published. Not a songwriter herself, Patsy could only be as good as the material she was given. McCall leased her recordings to USA Decca who were looking for another female singer to promote alongside Kitty Wells. 'A Church, A Courtroom And Then Goodbye' was a morose way to launch a new artist, but another early recording, 'Come On In', became her opening number. Both Cline and Gerald had affairs and, in 1957, after their divorce, she married Charlie Dick, whose name became the butt of many jokes. She determined that their two children should not deflect her from her ambitions. Songwriter Donn Hecht gave Patsy a blues number he had written for Kay Starr, 'Walkin' After Midnight', and, after a successful appearance on Arthur Godfrey's television talent show, she went to numbers 2 and 12 in the US country and pop charts, respectively. Subsequent singles made little impact, but further success came when her Four-Star contract expired in 1957 and she could sign directly with Decca, thus enabling her to record a wide range of songs. Both Brenda Lee and Roy Drusky turned down 'I Fall to Pieces', written by two top-class Nashville songwriters Hank Cochran and Harlan Howard. Patsy took it to the top of the US country charts and number 12 in the pop charts. Her producer, Owen Bradley, bathed her throbbing voice in echo, used a vocal group, emphasized the beat and added strings ('sweetening'), thus developing country's answer to rock 'n' roll. Patsy was undecided about 'Crazy' because Willie Nelson's demo was practically a narration, but she overcame her reservations and cut a magnificent vocal in one take. Patsy discarded cowgirl outfits for staid, conventional garb and she joked about her weight problems to her audiences. Her stocky figure and unfashionable clothes made

Patsy Cline

her look older than she was but she had a wild life with her truckdrivers' language and alleged affairs including Faron Young. Her stormy marriage to Charlie Dick was played out in a huge house which became the talk of Nashville with its rug in the shape of a gold record and the gold-dust sprinkled through the marble bath. A song of teenage angst, 'She's Got You', was US country number 1 and pop Top 20 hit, and also led to her UK Top 50 debut, despite opposition from Alma Cogan's version. A pop-country version of 'Heartaches' was also a minor British hit, but, amazingly, until 1991 and a reissue of 'Crazy', Patsy Cline had never made the UK Top 20. Patsy's lover and manager, Randy Hughes, was the son-in-law of Cowboy Copas. In 1963 Randy flew Patsy to Kansas City for a benefit for the widow of a country disc jockey who had died in a car crash. The return journey was hampered by storms and poor visibility. On 5 March 1963 Patsy Cline, Cowboy Copas, Hawkshaw Hawkins and Randy Hughes were killed when their plane crashed in swamped woodlands in Camden, Tennessee, 85 miles from Nashville. Identification was difficult as only Patsy's shoulders, the back of her head and right arm were in one recognizable piece. Another country star, Jack Anglin, of the duo Johnny And Jack, was killed on the way to her funeral. Patsy's single at the time of her death was, ironically, 'Leavin' On Your Mind' and it was followed by what is arguably her best record, Don Gibson's poignant 'Sweet Dreams'. Sometimes posthumous records go to number 1, but 'Sweet Dreams' was only a moderate US hit. Tributes to Patsy Cline included 'Angels From The Opry' (Rusty Adams) and 'Missing On A Mountain' (Bonnie Owens and Tommy Dee, who was reprising his 'Three Stars' success). Patsy only recorded around 120 different songs, many of them lacklustre, but the market became saturated with different permutations of those tracks. In an effort to try something different, a duet of 'Have You Ever Been Lonely?' by two deceased performers, Patsy Cline and Jim Reeves, was skilfully compiled from separate recordings. Among the revivals of Patsy Cline's successes are 'Crazy' (Slim Dusty, Willie Nelson, Ray Price, Kenny Rogers, Linda Ronstadt), 'I Fall To Pieces' (Ralph McTell, Michael Nesmith, Linda Ronstadt) and 'Sweet Dreams' (Elvis Costello, Don Everly, Emmylou Harris, Reba McEntire). Loretta Lynn released a tribute album, I Remember Patsy in 1977. Beverly D'Angelo played Patsy Cline in the 1980 film of Loretta Lynn's life, Coal Miner's Daughter. Jessica Lange then played Patsy in Sweet Dreams,

which was based upon Ellis Nassour's well-researched, but repetitive, biography of the same name. Lange mimed to Cline's voice and, for the soundtrack, Owen Bradley gave her vocal tracks sparkling new backings, one of the few occasions on which this process has actually enhanced the original recordings. Patsy Cline was not a distinctive uptempo performer and her unique quality was that she could wring emotion out of every syllable of a tearjerker. 'Walkin' After Midnight', 'I Fall To Pieces', 'Crazy', 'She's Got You' and 'Sweet Dreams' represent less than 15 minutes of music but they form one of the greatest legacies in country music. An album, Live At The Opry, showed that she had fulfilled that childhood ambition.

Albums: Patsy Cline (1957), Showcase (1961), Sentimentally Yours (1962), Tribute To Patsy Cline (1963), Legend (1964), Portait Of Patsy Cline (1964), How A Heartache Begins (1965), Reflections (1965), Gotta Lot Of Rhythm (1965), Sweet Dreams (1985, film soundtrack), Live At The Opry (1988), Live - Volume Two (1989). Compilations: The Patsy Cline Story (1963, US Decca), Golden Hits (1966), 20 Classic Tracks (1987, Starburst), 12 Greatest Hits (1988, MCA), Dreaming (1988, Platinum Music), 20 Golden Hits (1989, Deluxe), The Patsy Cline Collection (1991), The Definitive (1992).
Further reading: Sweet Dreams, Ellis Nassour.

Clower, Jerry

b. 28 September 1926, Amite County, Mississippi, USA. During the Depression, Clower's father went to Memphis to look for work but took to drink and neglected his family. His 17-year-old mother moved back to her father's farm in Liberty, Mississippi, and when she remarried, they moved to another farm. Clower worked on the farm and served on an aircraft carrier during World War II. He married in 1947 and obtained a degree in agriculture in 1951. As a salesman in Yazoo, Mississippi, he found that he sold more fertiliser if he amused his customers. He developed a club act and, dressed in gaudy suits and with a loud voice, he became known as 'The Mouth of Mississippi'. His first album, Jerry Clower From Yazoo City was released on a small label and, when it sold by word of mouth in large quantities, he was signed to MCA. He joined the Grand Ole Opry in 1973 and established a reputation for his tales of 'coon hunts' and the antics of one Marcel Ledbetter. His material is often based on his childhood and he maintains that he tells 'stories funny' and not funny stories. He does a remarkable impression of a chainsaw but his humour is too rural to have validity outside of American country music circles. He is also a Baptist minister and an active member of the Gideon Bible Society.

Albums: *Jerry Clower From Yazoo City* (1971), *Jerry Clower - The Mouth Of The Mississippi* (1972), *Clower Power* (1973), *Country Ham* (1974), *Live In Picayune* (1975), *The Ambassador Of Goodwill* (1976), *Ain't God Good* (1977), *On The Road* (1977), *Live From The Stage Of The Grand Ole Opry* (1978), *The Ledbetter Olympics* (1980), *More Good 'Uns* (1981), *Dogs I Have Known* (1982), *Live At Cleburne, Texas* (1983), *Starke Raving* (1984), *Mississippi Talkin'* (1984), *An Officer And A Ledbetter* (1985), *Runaway Truck* (1987), *Top Gum* (1987). Compilations: *Jerry Clower's Greatest Hits* (1986).

Further reading: *Ain't God Good*, Jerry Clower. *Let The Hammer Down*, Jerry Clower. *Life Ever Laughter*, Jerry Clower.

Cochran, Hank

b. Garland Perry Cochran, 2 August 1935, Greenville, Mississippi, USA. Fellow country songwriter Glenn Martin has said, 'His life is not as pretty as his music, yet all his songs come from his life.' Cochran lost his parents whilst an infant and was placed in an orphanage. He was raised in Mississippi and, after finishing school, ran away to the oil fields of New Mexico. An uncle showed him guitar chords and he developed an interest in country music. He travelled to California and started performing regularly on a radio talent show as Hank Cochran. He gathered bookings in small clubs and he offered 16-year-old Eddie Cochran a job as lead guitarist. As 'brother duos' were popular they decided to work as the Cochran Brothers, although they were not related. They were signed to the Ekko label and their first single combined 'Mr. Fiddle' and a tribute to Hank Williams and Jimmie Rodgers, 'Two Blue Singin' Stars'. They also backed Al Dexter on his Ekko re-recording of 'Pistol Packin' Mama'. The Cochrans broadcast as part of Dallas' *Big D Jamboree*, but, hearing about Elvis Presley's dynamic appearance, they realized they would have to change. They recorded a rock 'n' roll single, 'Tired And Sleepy', and, after opening for Lefty Frizzell in Hawaii, they split up. Eddie turned to rock 'n' roll, while Hank, who was married, secured regular work on the *California Hayride*. In 1959, Hank moved to Nashville, signed with Pamper Music and befriended another of the company's writers, Harlan Howard. Together they wrote Patsy Cline's 'I Fall To Pieces', and Cochran

also wrote 'She's Got You' for her. Cochran, like Howard, had a string of successful songs: 'I'd Fight The World' (Jim Reeves), 'If The Back Door Could Talk' (Ronnie Sessions), 'It's Not Love (But It's Not Bad)' (Merle Haggard), 'I Want To Go With You' (Eddy Arnold), 'Make The World Go Away' (originally recorded by Ray Price in 1963 and then a worldwide success for Eddy Arnold in 1965), 'Tears Broke Out On Me' (Eddy Arnold), 'Which One Will It Be?' (Bobby Bare), 'Who Do I Know In Dallas?' (Gene Watson), 'Willingly' (a duet for Shirley Collie and Willie Nelson), 'You Comb Her Hair' (with Harlan Howard for George Jones). Also like Howard, he wrote country songs for Burl Ives including 'A Little Bitty Tear' and 'Funny Way Of Laughin''. Cochran's marriage was soon over and he then married Jeannie Seely, who recorded several of his songs including her US Top 10 country hit, 'Don't Touch Me', later revived by T.G. Sheppard. Hank also had his own successes including 'Sally Was A Good Old Girl' (written by Harlan Howard), 'I'd Fight The World' and 'All Of Me Belongs To You'. Despite all his productivity, he had many all-night drinking sessions and often received treatment for alcoholism. In 1978 he made a gruff-voiced album, *With A Little Help From My Friends*, with the assistance of Merle Haggard, Willie Nelson, Jack Greene and Jeannie Seely. Seely's tribute on the sleeve disguised the fact that they lived apart and they are now divorced. He recovered sufficiently to present the noted *Austin City Limits* television show when it started in 1979. His 1980 album, *Make The World Go Away*, is practically a collection of his greatest songs. Willie Nelson guests on the album and he, in turn, was featured in Nelson's film, *Honeysuckle Rose*, singing 'Make The World Go Away' with Seely. Cochran and Dean Dillon wrote George Strait's US country number 1 hits, 'The Chair' (1985) and 'Ocean Front Property' (1987).

Albums: *Hank Cochran* (1965), *Hits From The Heart* (1966), *Going In Training* (1965), *The Heart Of Cochran* (1968), *With A Little Help From My Friends* (1978), *Make The World Go Away* (1980), as the Cochran Brothers *The Young Eddie Cochran* (1983).

Coe, David Allan

b. 6 September 1939, Akron, Ohio, USA. From the age of nine, Coe was in and out of reform schools, correction centres and prisons. According to his publicity, he spent time on Death Row after killing a fellow inmate who demanded oral sex. When *Rolling Stone* magazine questioned this, Coe responded with a song, 'I'd Like To Kick The Shit Out Of You'. Whatever the truth of the matter, Coe was paroled in 1967 and took his songs about prison life to Shelby Singleton who released two albums on his SSS label. Coe wrote Tanya Tucker's 1974 US country number 1, 'Would You Lay With Me (In A Field Of Stone)?'. He took to calling himself Davey Coe - the Mysterious Rhinestone Cowboy, performing in a mask, and driving a hearse. He satirized the themes of country music with hilarious additions to Steve Goodman's 'You Never Even Called Me By My Name', but has often used the clichés himself. His defiant stance and love of motorbikes, multiple tattoos and ultra-long hair made him a natural 'Nashville outlaw', which he wrote about in the self-glorifying 'Longhaired Redneck' and 'Willie, Waylon And Me' (Willie Nelson and Waylon Jennings). In 1978 Johnny Paycheck had a US country number 1 with Coe's 'Take This Job And Shove It', which inspired a film of the same title in 1981, and Coe's own successes included the witty 'Divers Do It Deeper' (1978), 'Jack Daniels If You Please' (1979), 'Now I Lay Me Down To Cheat' (1982), 'The Ride' (1983), which conjures up a meeting between Coe and Hank Williams, and 'Mona Lisa's Lost Her Smile' (1984), which made number 2 on the US country charts, his highest position as a performer. Recordings with other performers include 'Don't Cry Darlin'' and 'This Bottle (In My Hand)' with George Jones, 'I've Already Cheated On You' with Willie Nelson, and 'Get A Little Dirt On Your Hands' with Bill Anderson. Coe's 1978 album *Human Emotions* was about his divorce - one side being 'Happy Side' and the other 'Su-i-side'. The controversial cover of *Texas Moon* shows the bare backsides of his band and crew, and he has also released two mail-order albums of explicit songs, *Nothing Sacred* and *Underground*. Coe appears incapable of separating the good from the ridiculous and his albums are erratic. At his best, he is a sensitive, intelligent writer. Similarly, his stage performances with his Tennessee Hat Band differ wildly in length and quality: sometimes it's non-stop music, sometimes it's conjuring tricks. Coe's main trick however, is to remain successful, as country music fans grow exasperated with his over-the-top publicity. He may still be an outlaw but as Waylon Jennings remarks in 'Living Legends', that only means double-parking on Music Row.

Albums: *Penitentiary Blues* (1968), *Requiem For A Harlequin* (1970), *The Mysterious Rhinestone Cowboy* (1974), *Once Upon A Rhyme* (1974), *Longhaired Redneck* (1976), *D.A.C. Rides Again* (1977), *Texas Moon* (1977), *Tattoo* (1977), *Family Album* (1978), *Human Emotions* (1978), *Nothing Sacred* (1978), *Buckstone County Prison* (1978), *Spectrum VII* (1979), *Compass Point* (1979), *Something To Say* (1980), *Invictus (Means) Unconquered* (1981), *Underground* (1981), *Tennessee Whiskey* (1981), *Rough Rider* (1982), *D.A.C.* (1982), *Castles In The Sand* (1983), *Hello In There* (1983), *Just Divorced* (1984), *Darlin' Darlin'* (1985), *Unchained* (1985), *Son Of The South* (1986), *A Matter Of Life And Death* (1987), *Crazy Daddy* (1989), *1990 Songs For Sale* (1991). Compilation: *For The Record - The First 10 Years* (1985).

Further reading: *Just For The Record*, David Allan Coe. *Ex-Convict*, David Allan Coe. *The Book Of David. Poems, Prose And Stories*, David Allan Coe.

Collins, Tommy

b. Leonard Raymond Sipes, 28 September 1930, Bethany, Oklahoma, USA. Collins reflected upon his childhood in his song about being raised on a farm, 'The Roots Of My Raising', a US country number 1 for Merle Haggard. As a young man he was an avid follower of Jimmie Rodgers and, for a while, dated singer Wanda Jackson (although, contrary to some reports, it was a lesser-known Wanda that Collins later married). On moving to Bakersfield, California, Ferlin Husky named him after a drink, Tom Collins, and, like Buck Owens, he played on his Capitol recordings of the mid-50s. Collins says he was 'singing as high as I could - Webb Pierce was in fashion' and his songs were largely light-hearted, mildly suggestive about courting such as his first records, 'You Gotta Have A License', 'You Better Not Do That' and 'I Always Get A Souvenir'. 'All Of The Monkeys Ain't In The Zoo' applied to numerous politicians and he also wrote the sensitive 'High On A Hilltop' and 'Those Old Love Letters From You'. Many songs stemmed from personal experience. Collins entered a seminary and was ordained in 1961 and, for some years, had little to do with country music.

Following a tour of Vietnam in the mid-60s, he recorded for Columbia Records, his new songs including 'If You Can't Bite, Don't Growl' and 'I Made The Prison Band'. His 20 compositions for Merle Haggard included their co-written, nostalgic 'I Wish Things Were Simpler Again'. After writing 'Hello Hag', Merle retaliated with 'Leonard', which showed his concern for Collins' drinking. Haggard needed to be persuaded to record the touching 'Carolyn' as he felt it wasn't country music, but it was the highspot of their partnership. In reality, 'Carolyn' was a coded message to Collins' wife, and he said, 'I didn't set out to mess up my life but tragedies have a habit of working for you.' Hardly recognizable as the 50s star, Collins sometimes performs rough-voiced versions of his successes around UK country clubs but newer songs like 'Tilt Me A Little Toward Tilly' still reflect his ingenuity.

Selected albums: *Words And Music Country Style* (1957), *This Is Tommy Collins!* (1959), *Songs I Love To Sing* (1961), *The Dynamic Tommy Collins* (1966), *Let's Live A Little* (1966), *Shindig* (1968), *On Tour* (1968), *Tommy Collins Callin'* (1972), *Country Souvenir* (1981), *Cowboys Get Lucky Some Of The Time* (1981), *New Patches* (1986). Compilation: *This Is Tommy Collins* (1988).

Collins Kids

A brother and sister rockabilly act, Larry Collins (b. 4 October 1944, Tulsa, Oklahoma, USA) and Lorrie Collins (b. Lawrencine Collins, 7 May 1942, Tahlequah, Oklahoma, USA) recorded numerous singles for Columbia Records in the 50s and early 60s which are revered by fans and collectors of early rock 'n' roll but which never dented the charts. The duo gained what little recognition it had through frequent television appearances. Lorrie Collins was the first of the siblings to enter show business. At the age of eight she won a singing contest and two years later the family moved to Los Angeles. Guitarist Larry joined his sister's act in 1954, after having won contests on his own for his prodigious musicianship. After the pair won a talent contest together, they were hired to perform for a television programme called *Town Hall Party* on which they soon became regulars, appearing on each programme. The Collins Kids, as they became known professionally, were signed to Columbia in 1955. As Columbia at that time was not primarily a rock 'n' roll label, poor promotion doomed the Collins Kids to failure. When Lorrie married in 1959, the act temporarily split up. They reunited briefly but with the birth of Lorrie's first child in 1961, the team was effectively terminated. Larry Collins recorded a handful of solo records, which also failed to chart, and later became a country songwriter, whose credits included co-writing the Tanya Tucker hit 'Delta Dawn' and David Frizzell and Shelly West's 'You're The Reason God Made Oklahoma'. In later life, he became a professional golfer and Lorrie retired to raise her family.

Compilations: *Collins Kids* (1983, UK release), *Rockin' Rollin' Collins Kids* (1983, German release), *Rockin' Rollin' Collins Kids, Volume 2* (1983, German release), *Hop, Skip & Jump*, boxed set (1992).

Colter, Jessi

b. Mirriam Johnson, 25 May 1943, Phoenix, Arizona, USA. Her mother became Sister Helen, an ordained Pentecostal minister, and Colter became the church pianist when only 11, hence her subsequent gospel album, *Mirriam*. She impressed Duane Eddy who produced her 1961 single, 'Lonesome Road', and married her in 1963. He wrote and recorded an instrumental, 'Mirriam', while she wrote some of his album tracks as well as 'No Sign Of The Living' for Dottie West. In 1967, Eddy and his wife recorded a duet single, 'Guitar On My Mind'. After a divorce from Eddy in 1968, she married Waylon Jennings on 26 October 1969 at her mother's church. She adopted the stage name Jessi Colter after her great-great-great uncle who was in Jesse James' notorious outlaw gang. In 1975, Jessi made number 4 in the US pop charts with the self-penned 'I'm Not Lisa', which was followed by the huge success of *Wanted: The Outlaws*. (Colter was too conscious of her appearance to ever look like an outlaw.) Her best-known duets with Waylon Jennings are 'Suspicious Minds', her soothing composition 'Storms Never Last' and 'The Union Mare And The Confederate Grey' from the concept album, *White Mansions*. In 1977 she worked with both husbands and Willie Nelson on a revival of 'You Are My Sunshine'. In recent times she has let her recording career slip, largely to nurse Jennings through his various problems, but she is still part of his stage show. Among her many compositions are 'You Hung The Moon (Didn't You, Waylon)?' and 'Jennifer (Fly My Little Baby)' about her daughter, while she turned John Lennon and Paul McCartney's 'Hey Jude' into a song for Waylon by singing 'Hey Dude'.

Albums: *A Country Star Is Born* (1970), *I'm Jessi Colter* (1975), with Waylon Jennings, Willie Nelson, Tompall Glaser *Wanted: The Outlaws* (1975), *Jessi* (1976), *Diamond In The Rough* (1976), *Mirriam* (1977), with Jennings, John Dillon, Steve Cash *White Mansions* (1978), *That's The Way A Cowboy Rock 'N' Rolls* (1978), with Jennings *Leather And Lace* (1981), *Ridin' Shotgun* (1982), with Jennings *The Pursuit Of D.B. Cooper* (1982, film soundtrack), *Rock 'N' Roll Lullaby* (1984).

Commander Cody And The Lost Planet Airmen

Although renowned for its high-energy rock, the Detroit/Ann Arbor region also formed the focal point for this entertaining country-rock band. The first of several tempestuous line-ups was formed in 1967, comprising Commander Cody (b. George Frayne IV, 19 July 1944, Boise City, Idaho, USA; piano), John Tichy (b. St. Louis, Missouri, USA; lead guitar), Steve Schwartz (guitar), Don Bolton aka the West Virginia Creeper (pedal steel), Stephen Davis (bass) and Ralph Mallory (drums). Only Frayne, Tichy and Bolton remained with the group on their move to San Francisco the following year. The line-up was completed on the Airmen's debut album, *Lost In The Ozone* by Billy C. Farlowe (b. Decatur, Alabama, USA; vocals/harp), Andy Stein (b. 31 August 1948, New York City, New York, USA; fiddle/saxophone), Billy Kirchen (b. 29 January 1948, Ann Arbor, Michigan, USA; lead guitar), 'Buffalo' Bruce Barlow (b. 3 December 1948, Oxnard, California, USA; bass) and Lance Dickerson (b. 15 October 1948, Livonia, Michigan, USA; drums). This earthy collection covered a wealth of material, including rockabilly, western swing, country and jump R&B, a pattern sustained on several subsequent releases. Despite attaining a US Top 10 single with 'Hot Rod Lincoln' (1972), the group's allure began to fade as their albums failed to capture an undoubted in-concert prowess. Although *Live From Deep In The Heart Of Texas* and *We've Got A Live One Here* redressed the balance, what once seemed so natural became increasingly laboured as individual members grew disillusioned. John Tichy's departure proved crucial and preceded an almost total desertion in 1976. The following year Cody released his first solo album, *Midnight Man*, before convening the New Commander Cody Band. Cody And Farlowe re-formed the Lost Planet Airmen in the 90s.

Albums: *Lost In The Ozone* (1971), *Hot Licks, Cold Steel And Trucker's Favourites* (1972), *Country Casanova* (1973), *Live From Deep In The Heart Of Texas* (1974), *Commander Cody And His Lost Planet Airmen* (1975), *Tales From The Ozone* (1975), *We've Got A Live One Here!* (1976), *Let's Rock* (1986), *Sleazy Roadside Stories* (1988 - live performances from 1973), *Aces High* (1992); as the Commander Cody Band *Rock 'N' Roll Again* (1977), *Flying Dreams* (1978), *Lose It Tonight* (1980). Compilations: *The Very Best Of Commander Cody And His Lost Planet Airmen* (1986), *Cody Returns From Outer Space* (1987).

Conlee, John

b. 11 August 1946, Versailles, Kentucky, USA. Conlee's early years were filled with farm chores, but he was playing the guitar on local radio before he was 10. He describes Versailles as 'a very small town with a very large barbershop chorus' in which he sang high tenor. Like soul singer Solomon Burke, he became a licensed embalmer. In the mid-70s he set about establishing himself in Nashville. He worked as a morning disc jockey, and he was signed to MCA Records. His best-known record is his debut US country hit from 1978, his own composition, 'Rose Coloured Glasses'. Ironically, it was a number 5 record, whilst seven others made number 1. Conlee had his first US country number 1 with 'Lady Lay Down', 'Backside Of Thirty', which he wrote, 'Common Man', 'I'm Only In It For The Love', 'In My Eyes', 'As Long As I'm Rockin' With You', written by 60s hitmaker Bruce Channel, and, moving to Columbia, 'Got My Heart Set On You', written by Dobie Gray. Another move, this time to the ill-fated 16th Avenue Records, effectively ended his chart career, although melodic ballads always have a market. He lives with his family on a farm outside of Nashville and he retains his parents' farm in Versailles as well as his embalmer's license.

Albums: *Rose Coloured Glasses* (1978), *Forever* (1980), *Friday Night Blues* (1980), *With Love* (1981), *Busted* (1982), *In My Eyes* (1983), *Blue Highway* (1984), *Harmony* (1987), *American Faces* (1987), *Fellow Travellers* (1989). Compilation: *Songs For The Working Man* (1986), *Doghouse* (1990).

Conley, Earl Thomas

b. 17 October 1941, Portsmouth, Ohio, USA. Conley is the son of a railway worker but he left home at 14 when his father lost his job. His influences were the *Grand Ole Opry*, followed by Elvis Presley and Jerry Lee Lewis, and then the Beatles. He originally planned to be a painter, but developed his love for country music whilst in the US Army. After his military service, Conley had a succession of manual jobs and spent his spare time either playing clubs or hawking his songs around Nashville. His first successes were as a writer - 'Smokey Mountain Memories' for Mel Street and 'This Time I've Hurt Her More (Than She Loves Me)' for Conway Twitty. He recorded for Prize, GRT and Warner Brothers with moderate success and as Earl Conley. He started using his full name in 1979 to avoid confusion with John Conlee. His single of 'Fire And Smoke' reached number 1 on

Commander Cody

the US country charts in 1979, a major achievement for the small Sunbird label. RCA Records then took over his contract, although he continued to be produced by Nelson Larkin, and scored one chart-topping country single after another. His 1982 number 1, 'Somewhere Between Right And Wrong' was issued in two formats - one for country fans, one for rock fans. In 1984, Conley became the first artist in any field to have had four number 1 hits from the same album - from *Don't Make It Easy For Me* came the title tune, which was written by Conley and his frequent partner Randy Scruggs, 'Your Love's On The Line', 'Angel In Disguise' and 'Holding Her And Loving You'. His duets include 'Too Many Times' with Anita Pointer and 'We Believe In Happy Endings' with Emmylou Harris, another country number 1 in 1988. Out of his 18 US country number 1 hits, 'Right From The Start', was as much R&B as country, and was featured in the film, *Roadhouse*. Conley's gutsy, emotional love songs found favour with US country fans, but despite a break from recording, he returned to the US country charts in 1991 with 'Brotherly Love', a recorded duet with Keith Whitley shortly before the latter's death in 1989.

Albums: *Blue Pearl* (1980), *Fire And Smoke* (1981), *Somewhere Between Right And Wrong* (1982), *Don't Make It Easy For Me* (1983), *Treadin' Water* (1984), *Too Many Times* (1986), *The Heart Of It All* (1988), *Yours Truly* (1991). Compilation: *Greatest Hits* (1985).

Cooley, Spade

b. Donnell Clyde Cooley, 22 February 1910, Grande, Oklahoma, USA, d. 23 November 1969. His grandfather and father were talented fiddlers and he was playing at dances at the age of eight. Around 1930, the family moved to Modesto, California, where Cooley played local venues. In 1934, his resemblance to Roy Rogers found him employment as a stand-in and his work with other bands soon led to him fronting his own at the Pier Ballroom, Venice. Between 1943 and 1946, he was resident at the prestigious Riverside Rancho Ballroom in Santa Monica, where he acquired the nickname of 'King Of Western Swing'. (Bill C. Malone records this as the first time the music pioneered by Bob Wills and Milton Brown had been so described.) In 1947, Cooley adapted to television and his programme on KTLA became one of the top west coast shows until 1958. Cooley, with his orchestra playing a mixture of country, jazz and dance music, became a national

star. He appeared in many films and recorded for several labels. Among his best remembered songs are 'Shame On You' (a self penned US country number 1), 'Detour' and 'Cause Cause I Love You' (with vocal by Tex Williams who worked with Cooley for some years). In the early 50s, he suffered a heart attack and although he recovered, by the end of the decade things began to go tragically wrong. A drink problem worsened and his wife left him. He hoped in vain for a reconciliation. In July 1961, in a drunken rage and in front of their young daughter, he beat his wife to death. He suffered another heart attack during his trial, which saw him receive a life sentence. A sad but model prisoner, he spent hours playing his fiddle and teaching other prisoners. With parole through good behaviour due early in 1970, he was given special release to attend a benefit concert in his honour in Oakland, where on 23 November 1969, his performance was well received by a crowd of over 3000. After he had finished playing, he stayed backstage and was talking to friends when he suddenly slumped to the floor dead - the victim of another heart attack.

Albums: *Roy Rogers Souvenir Album* (10-inch LP) (1952), *Sagebrush Swing* (10-inch LP) (1952), *Dance-O-Rama* (10-inch LP) (1955), *Fidoodlin' Spade Cooley - King Of Western Swing* (1959), *Fidoodlin'* (1961), *Spade Cooley* (1982). Club Of Spades Fan Club Album Releases: *Best Of Spade Cooley Transcribed Shows*, *King Of Western Swing Volumes 1 & 2*, *Mr Music Himself Volumes 1, 2, 3* (Television Transcriptions), *Oklahoma Stomp*, *As They Were*.

Coolidge, Rita

b. 1 May 1944, Nashville, Tennessee, USA, from mixed white and Cherokee Indian parentage. Coolidge's father was a baptist minister and she first sang radio jingles in Memphis with her sister Priscilla. Coolidge recorded briefly for local label Pepper before moving to Los Angeles in the mid-60s. There she became a highly-regarded session singer, working with Eric Clapton, Stephen Stills and many others. She had a relationship with Stills and he wrote a number of songs about her including 'Cherokee', 'The Raven' and 'Sugar Babe' In 1969-70, Coolidge toured with the Delaney And Bonnie and Leon Russell (*Mad Dogs & Englishmen*) troupes. Russell's 'Delta Lady' was supposedly inspired by Coolidge. Returning to Los Angeles, she was signed to a solo recording contract by A&M. Her debut album included the cream of LA session musicians (among them Booker T. Jones, by now her brother-in-law) and

Rita Coolidge

it was followed by almost annual releases during the 70s. Coolidge also made several albums with Kris Kristofferson to whom she was married between 1973 and 1979. The quality of her work was uneven since the purity of her natural voice was not always matched by subtlety of interpretation. Her first hit singles were a revival of the Jackie Wilson hit 'Higher And Higher' and 'We're All Alone', produced by Booker T. in 1977. The following year a version of the Temptations' 'The Way You Do The Things You Do' reached the Top 20. Coolidge was less active in the 80s although in 1983 she recorded a James Bond movie theme, 'All Time High' from *Octopussy*.

Albums: *Rita Coolidge* (1971), *Nice Feelin'* (1971), *Lady's Not For Sale* (1972), *Full Moon* (1973), *Fall Into Spring* (1974), *It's Only Love* (1975), *Anytime Anywhere* (1977), *Love Me Again* (1978), *Satisfied* (1979), *Heartbreak Radio* (1981), *Never Let You Go* (1983), *Inside The Fire* (1988).

Coon Creek Girls

History records that they were probably the first all-woman string band to make a name in country music. They played for years over WLS and the *Renfro Valley Barn Dance*. They were led by Lily Mae Ledford (b. c.1917, Powell County, Kentucky, USA; banjo/fiddle/vocals) and other members were her sister Rosie Ledford (guitar/vocals), Violet Koehler (mandolin/guitar/vocals), Daisy Lange (bass/vocals). In 1936, they became regulars on the *WLS Barn Dance*. Chicago and made higtory in 1939 when, at the request of Eleanor Roosevelt, they travelled to Washington to play before the King and Queen of England. (Around 1938, the Amburgey Sisters Bertha, Opal and Irene also played in the Coon Creek Girls. Irene later attaining country fame as Martha Carson). When Koehler and Lange left in 1939, younger sister and bassist Minnie Ledford (who was known as Black Eyed Susie) joined the group and for the next 18 years, the sisters were regulars on the *Renfro Valley Barn Dance*. They retired in 1957, although during the folk revival of the 60s, they reformed to play at some festivals. Much of their material was traditional mountain music and they became accepted experts of the genre. Many old time music lovers fondly remember their song 'You're A Flower That Is Blooming There For Me'. Rosie Ledford died of cancer at her Florida home in 24 July 1976 and was buried at Berea in Kentucky. Lily Mae died in Lexington in July 1985.

Albums: *Lily Mae, Rosie & Susie* (c.70s), *The Coon Creek Girls* (c.1982).

Cooper, Stoney, And Wilma Lee

By the time he was 12 years old, Dale T. 'Stoney' Cooper (b. 16 October 1918, near Harman, Randolph County, West Virginia, USA) could play the fiddle and guitar, and on leaving school, he joined a band called the Green Valley Boys. In 1939, he became the fiddle player with the Leary Family, a well-known gospel group, who were featured on local radio. He soon fell in love with, and married, Wilma Lee Leary (b. 7 February 1921, Valley Head, West Virginia, USA). She had started singing with her family group at the age of five and was already a fine instrumentalist, who played banjo, guitar, piano and organ. In 1938 and 1939, the Leary Family had represented the state at the National Folk Festival and made recordings in Washington for the Library of Congress. In 1940, the couple left the group and worked on local radio in Fairmont, Harrisonburg and Wheeling. Their career was slowed by the birth of their daughter Carol Lee but by the mid-40s, they began to appear on radio stations in other states. In 1947, they returned to West Virginia where, with their band the Clinch Mountain Clan, they became stars of the WWVA *Wheeling Jamboree*. In 1950, Harvard University named them the most authentic mountain singing group in America. Between 1954 and 1957, they were the featured artists of the CBS network Saturday night *Jamboree* broadcast from Wheeling's Virginia Theatre. In February 1957, their popularity saw them move to Nashville, where they became regulars on the *Grand Ole Opry*. They first recorded for Rich-R-Tone in 1947, having local success with 'The Tramp On The Street' but later for US Decca, Columbia and Hickory. They achieved Top 5 US country chart hits in 1959 with 'Come Walk With Me', 'Big Midnight Special' (co-written by Wilma Lee) and 'There's A Big Wheel'. The following year, they had Top 20 country hits with 'Johnny My Love' and Stuart Hamblen's 'This Old House' (later a 1954 US number 1 pop hit for Rosemary Clooney). Their last country chart entry came in 1961, when their version of the stark warning not to drink and drive, 'Wreck On The Highway', peaked at number 8. Between 1950 and 1970, they toured extensively in the USA as well as making overseas tours. Their *Opry* popularity also ensured that they were regularly seen on most major television programmes. In 1973, Stoney's health began to fail, he suffered a series of heart attacks and spent long periods in hospital. Finally, he suffered a heart attack on 4 February 1977, from which he died in the intensive care unit of a Nashville hospital on 22 March 1977. Wilma Lee was heartbroken and for a time she retired, but in 1979 she formed a new Clinch Mountain Clan, resumed concert and *Opry* appearances and recorded several solo albums. She even began to play the 5-string banjo again, having forsaken it years earlier for the guitar. During her career, Wilma Lee wrote many songs including 'Loving You' and 'Tomorrow I'll Be Gone' and her recordings of gospel numbers such as 'Walking My Lord Up Calvary's Hill', 'Legend Of The Dogwood Tree' and 'Thirty Pieces Of Silver' are very popular. In 1974, the Smithsonian Institution named her 'First Lady Of Bluegrass' in their series of 'Women In Country Music'. The same year, pop singer Lou Christie wrote and recorded his tribute song 'Wilma Lee and Stoney'. Wilma Lee's style and singing made her unique and writers have described her by stating 'She is not the imitator, she is the original'. Their daughter, Carol Lee Cooper, followed their musical career and from an early age regularly sang with her parents. She later formed the Carol Lee Singers, who became *Opry* regulars and who have sung backing vocals on countless recordings for many artists. She married Jimmie Rodgers Snow, the son of Hank Snow and has the distinction of playing her mother in an American filmed biography on Hank Williams.

Selected albums: *Sacred Songs* (1960), *There's A Big Wheel* (1960), *Family Favorites* (1962), *Songs Of Inspiration* (1962), *Sunny Side Of The Mountain* (1966), *Sing* (1966), *Walking My Lord Up Calvary's Hill* (c.1974), *Wilma Lee & Stoney Cooper* (1976), *Satisfied* (1976). Compilations: *Sing The Carter Family's Greatest Hits* (1977), *Early Recordings* (1978). Solo albums: Wilma Lee Cooper *A Daisy A Day* (1980), *Wilma Lee Cooper* (1982), *White Rose* (1984).

Copas, Cowboy

b. Lloyd Estel Copas, 15 July 1913, near Muskogee, Oklahoma, USA. Copas was raised on a small ranch and taught himself the fiddle and guitar before he was 10 years old. When the family moved to Ohio in 1929, Copas teamed with a fiddle-playing American Indian and worked in clubs and on radio. They parted in 1940 and, after working as a solo act, Copas replaced Eddy Arnold in Pee Wee King's Golden West Cowboys but the following year he signed for King Records, became a regular at the *Grand Ole Opry*, and formed his own band, the Oklahoma Cowboys, which at times included Hank Garland, Little Roy Wiggins, Tommy Jackson and Junior Husky. He made the US country charts first with 'Filipino Baby' in 1946 and his 10 Top 20 records between then and 1951 include 'Tennessee Waltz', 'Candy Kisses' and his own composition, 'Signed, Sealed And Delivered'. Although Copas was equally at home with ballads and honky-tonk songs, he fell victim to changing tastes and spent most of the 50s playing small clubs as a solo act. His luck changed when he signed for Starday Records in 1959. His self-penned 'Alabam' was in the US country charts for 34 weeks, 12 of them at number 1. He followed this with three more country hits, 'Flat Top', 'Sunny Tennessee' and a re-recording of 'Signed, Sealed And Delivered'. His son-in-law, Randy Hughes, also managed Patsy Cline and all three were killed, along with Hawkshaw Hawkins, in a plane crash on 5 March 1963. A few weeks later, Copas had a posthumous country hit with a record ironically entitled 'Goodbye Kisses'.

Albums: *Cowboy Copas Sings His All Time Hits* (1957), *Favorite Sacred Songs* (1957), *Sacred Songs By Cowboy Copas* (1959), *All Time Country Music Greats* (1960), *Tragic Tales Of Love And Life* (1960), *Broken Hearted Melodies* (1960), *Inspirational Songs By Cowboy Copas* (1961), *Cowboy Copas* (1961), *Mister Country Music* (1962), *Opry Star Spotlight On Cowboy Copas* (1962), *As You Remember Cowboy Copas* (1963), *Country Gentleman Of Song* (1963), *Star Of The Grand Ole Opry* (1963), *Country Music Entertainer No. 1* (1963), *Beyond The Sunset* (1963), *Unforgettable Cowboy Copas* (1963), *Cowboy Copas And His Friends* (1964), *Hymns* (1964), *The Legend Lives On* (1965), *Shake A Hand* (1967), *Tragic Romance* (1969). Compilation: *The Best Of The Cowboy Copas* (1980), *16 Greatest Hits* (1987), *Not Forgotten* (1987), *Opry Star Spotlight On Cowboy Copas* (1988), *Mister Country Music* (1988).

Cornelius, Helen

b. 6 December 1941, Hannibal, Missouri, USA. Cornelius was part of a large family raised on a farm. She sang with two sisters and their father took them to local engagements. By the 70s she had moved to Nashville and was working as a songwriter, although the records she made for Columbia had no success. Her first single for RCA, 'We Still Love Songs In Missouri' in 1975, sold well and then she was teamed with country singer Jim Ed Brown from the Browns for 'I Don't Want To Have To Marry You'. The single was banned by several radio stations but it still topped the US country charts. They had six further country Top 10 singles including 'You Don't Bring Me Flowers' and 'Saying Hello, Saying I Love You, Saying Goodbye' up to 1980. Cornelius worked as a solo performer and also teamed with Dave And Sugar in a touring version of *Annie Get Your Gun*. In 1988 she and Brown began working as a duo again.

Albums: *Helen Cornelius* (1975). With Jim Ed Brown: *I Don't Want To Have To Marry You* (1976), *Born Believer* (1977), *I'll Never Be Free* (1978), *You Don't Bring Me Flowers* (1979), *One Man One Woman* (1980).

Country Gazette

Formed in 1971, this bluegrass ensemble was rooted in several Los Angeles-based outfits. The original line-up included three ex-members of Dillard And Clark, Byron Berline (b. 6 July 1944, Cladwell, Kansas, USA; fiddle/vocals), Billy Ray Latham (banjo/vocals) and Roger Bush (bass), who were initially joined by erstwhile Dillards' guitarist Herb Pedersen (b. 27 April 1944, Berkeley, California, USA). The latter was then replaced by Alan Munde. Within months of its inception, Country Gazette was absorbed into a revue combining elements of the rapidly dissolving Flying Burrito Brothers. Wertz, Bush and Berline appeared on the unit's *Last Of The Red Hot Burritos* selection, before re-convening to complete their own group's debut, *A Traitor In Our Midst*. Although the founding trio each took sabbaticals from their creation, they, plus Munde, were its nucleus. Former Kentucky Colonels' member Roland White joined the group in 1975, and remained until its disintegration in 1981. Although not as influential as other contemporaries, Country Gazette was a superior exponent of its chosen genre.

Albums: *A Traitor In Our Midst* (1972), *Live In Amsterdam* (1972), *Don't Give Up Your Day Job* (1973), *Bluegrass Special* (1973), *Banjo Sandwich* (1974), *Live At McCabes'* (1975), *Sunny Side Of The Mountain* (1976), *Out To Lunch* (1977), *What A Way To Make A Living* (1977), *All This And Money Too* (1978), *American And Clean* (1981). Compilations: *Milestones* (1975), *From The Beginning* (1978).

Country Gentlemen

This bluegrass group were first established in Washington DC on 4 July 1957 and over the years have undergone many personnel changes. Founder members included Charlie Waller (b. 19 January 1935, Jointerville, Texas, USA; guitar/vocals), John Duffey (b. 4 March 1934, Washington DC., USA; guitar/vocals), Bill Emerson (b. 22 January 1938; banjo) and Tom Morgan. Emerson was replaced for a short time by Pete Kuykendall (a DJ and record collector who played as Pete Roberts), who, in turn, was replaced by Eddie Adcock (b. 17 June 1938, Scottsville, Virginia, USA; banjo/mandolin/vocals). Jim Cox (b. 3 April 1930, Vansant, Virginia, USA; bass/banjo/ vocals) replaced Morgan. Other members include Tom Gray, Bill Yates and Jimmy Gaudreau who replaced Duffey in 1969. Over the years, the various line-ups became popular at various major folk and bluegrass festivals. When national interest waned somewhat in bluegrass music in the late 60s, they still managed to exist and were never afraid to use material from a wide variety of writers and genres. When interest in bluegrass returned in the 70s, they were one of the first groups to appear at major venues such as Bean Blossom, Indiana. Waller, a fine vocalist, has an uncanny ability to sound like Hank Snow when he so chooses. They have toured extensively and recorded a great many albums (including one with Ricky Skaggs); since the late 60s most of their albums have been on the Rebel label. Their only US country chart hit was with 'Bringing Mary Home' in 1965.

Albums: *Country Songs Old & New* (1960), *Folk Songs & Bluegrass* (1961), *Bluegrass At Carnegie Hall* (1962), *Folk Session Inside* (1963), *On The Road* (1963), *Hootenanny* (1963), *In Concert* (1964), *Bringing Mary Home* (1965), *Folk Hits Bluegrass Style* (1966), *Sunrise Vol.2.* (1966), *Roanoke Bluegrass Festival* (1967), *The Traveler* (1968), *New Look New Sound* (1969), *Play It Like It Is* (1969), *Last Album* (1970), *New Country Gentlemen In London* (1970), *One Wide River To Cross* (1971), *Sound Off* (1971), *The Award Winning* (1972), *Going Back To The Blue Ridge Mountains* (1973), *The Country Gentlemen* (1973), *Yesterday & Today Volumes 1 & 2* (1973), *Yesterday & Today Volume 3* (1974), *Remembrances & Forecasts* (1974), *The Early Sessions* (1974), *Live In Japan* (1975), *Joe's Last Train* (1976), *Calling My Children Home* (1978), *Sit Down Young Stranger* (1980), *River Bottom* (1981), *25 Years* (double LP) (1982), *Good As Gold* (1983), *Featuring Ricky Skaggs On Fiddle* (1986), *Return Engagement* (1988), *New Horizons* (1992).

Cowboy Junkies

Toronto-based musicians, Michael Timmins (b. 21 April 1959, Montreal, Canada; guitar) and Alan Anton (b. Alan Alizojvodic, 22 June 1959,

Montreal, Canada; bass), formed a group called Hunger Project in 1979. It was not successful and, basing themselves in the UK, they formed an experimental instrumental group, Germinal. Returning to Toronto, they joined forces with Timmins' sister Margo (b. 27 June 1961, Montreal, Canada; vocal) and brother Peter (b. 29 October 1965, Montreal, Canada; drums). As the Cowboy Junkies (which was simply an attention-grabbing name), they recorded their first album, *Whites Off Earth Now!!*, in a private house. Their second album, *The Trinity Session*, was made with one microphone in the Church of Holy Trinity, Toronto for $250. The band's spartan, less-is-more sound captivated listeners and, with little publicity, the second album sold 250,000 copies in North America. The tracks included a curious reinterpretation of 'Blue Moon' called 'Blue Moon Revisited (Song For Elvis)' and the country standards, 'I'm So Lonesome I Could Cry' and 'Walking After Midnight'. Lou Reed praised their version of his song, 'Sweet Jane', and, in 1991, they contributed 'To Lay Me Down' in a tribute to the Grateful Dead, *Deadicated*. Their 1990 album, *The Caution Horses*, included several vintage country songs which, true to form, were performed in their whispered, five miles-per-hour style. The extent of the Cowboy Junkies' fast growing reputation was sufficient for them to promote the 1992 album *Black-Eyed Man* at London's Royal Albert Hall.
Albums: *Whites Off Earth Now!!* (1986), *The Trinity Session* (1988), *The Caution Horses* (1990), *Black-Eyed Man* (1992).

Craddock, Billy 'Crash'

b. William Wayne Craddock, 16 June 1939, Greensboro, North Carolina, USA. As a child, he would imitate the stars of *Grand Ole Opry* and he was performing with his brothers at talent shows from the age of 10. He played American football and he says that, to avoid being tackled, he would 'crash' through the larger players, hence his nickname. Craddock has been recording since 1957, although his first single, 'Smacky Mouth', for the Sky Castle label in Greensboro was released under the name of Billy Graddock. He then recorded 'The Millionaire' as Billy Craddock for Colonial, and went to Date for 'Ah Poor Little Baby', an underrated rock 'n' roll song which was covered for the UK market by Adam Faith. Although only 19, Craddock signed for his fourth label, but this time it was a major, Columbia. For his third single, he was billed, for the first time, as

Billy 'Crash' Craddock. The a-side, the rocking 'Boom Boom Baby', was a hit in Australia, but it was the ballad b-side, 'Don't Destroy Me', which scraped into the US Top 100. He toured Australia three times and became one of their first rock 'n' roll stars. He had no success in the UK but one of his records, 'I Want That', was covered by Johnny Kidd. After Columbia, Craddock recorded for Mercury, King and Chart and from such records as 'Anything That's Part Of You', it was evident that he was switching to country music. However, he had limited success and by the mid-60s, he had returned to his home town, married, took a day job and was singing only at weekends. In 1971 he signed for a new Nashville label, Cartwheel, and had a US Top 3 country hit with 'Knock Three Times'. He then had country hits with revivals of 'Dream Lover', 'You Better Move On', 'Ain't Nothin' Shakin'' and 'I'm Gonna Knock On Your Door'. He won awards including one from *Cashbox* as The New Find Of 1972. Moving to ABC, Craddock had several more country hits including number 1 hits with a song about suntan lotion, 'Rub It In' (also number 16 on the US pop charts), a revival of 'Ruby Baby', and 'Broken Down In Tiny Pieces', which also featured Janie Fricke. On the move yet again, he started his country hits for Capitol with 'I Cheated On A Good Woman's Love' in 1978, and continued with 'If I Could Write A Song As Beautiful As You', 'My Mama Never Heard Me Sing', 'I Just Had You On My Mind', 'Sea Cruise' and 'Love Busted'. In direct imitation of Elvis Presley, he wore a white jumpsuit and his forceful, live album shows he was still a rock 'n' roller at heart. Albums: *I'm Tore Up* (1964), *Knock Three Times* (1971), *You Better Move On* (1972), *Two Sides Of Crash Craddock* (1973), *Mr. Country Rock* (1973), *Rub It In* (1974), *Still Thinkin' 'Bout You* (1975), with Janie Frickie *Crash* (1976), *Easy As Pie* (1976), *Live* (1977), *The First Time* (1977), *Billy 'Crash' Craddock* (1978), *I Cheated On A Good Woman's Love* (1978), *Turning Up And Turning On* (1978), *Laughing And Crying, Living And Dying* (1979), *Changes* (1980), *Crash Craddock* (1981), *The New Will Never Wear Off You* (1982), *Back On Track* (1989). Compilation: *16 Favourite Hits* (1977), *The Best Of Billy 'Crash' Craddock* (1986), *Greatest Hits* (1987).

Cramer, Floyd

b. 27 October 1933, Shreveport, Louisiana, USA. The style and sound of Cramer's piano playing is arguably one of the biggest influences on post 50s'

Floyd Cramer

country music. His delicate rock 'n' roll sound is achieved by accentuating the discord in rolling from the main note to a sharp or flat, known as 'slip note'. This is perfectly highlighted in his first major hit 'Last Date' in 1960. Cramer was already a vastly experienced Nashville session player, playing on countless records during the 50s. He can be heard on many Jim Reeves and Elvis Presley records, often with his long-time friend Chet Atkins. During the early 60s he regularly made the US charts. Two notable hits were the superb 'On The Rebound', which still sounds fresh and lively more than 30 years later, and his sombre reading of Bob Wills' 'San Antonio Rose'. After dozens of albums Cramer was still making commercially successful recordings into the 80s, having a further hit in 1980 with the theme from the television soap-opera *Dallas*. With Atkins, Cramer remains Nashville's most prolific musician.

Albums: *Hello Blues* (1960), *Last Date* (1960), *On The Rebound* (1961), *America's Biggest Selling Pianist* (1961), *Floyd Cramer Get Organ-ized* (1962), *I Remember Hank Williams* (1962), *Swing Along With Floyd Cramer* (1963), *Comin' On* (1963), *Country Piano - City Strings* (1964), *Goes Honky Tonkin'* (1964), *Cramer At The Console* (1964), *Hits From The Country Hall Of Fame* (1965), *The Magic Touch Of Floyd Cramer* (1965), *Class Of '65* (1965), *The Distinctive Piano Styling Of Floyd Cramer* (1966), *The Big Ones* (1966), *Class Of '66* (1966), *Here's What's Happening* (1967), *Floyd Cramer Plays The Monkees* (1967), *Class Of '67* (1967), *Floyd Cramer Plays Country Classics* (1968), *Class Of '68* (1968), *Floyd Cramer Plays MacArthur Park* (1968), *Class Of '69* (1969), *More Country Classics* (1969), *Floyd Cramer Country* (1976), *Looking For Mr. Goodbar* (1968), *The Big Ones - Volume 2* (1970), *Floyd Cramer With The Music City Pops* (1970), *Class Of '70* (1970), *Sounds Of Sunday* (1971), *Class Of '71* (1971), *Floyd Cramer Detours* (1972), *Class Of '72* (1972), *Super Country Hits Featuring Crystal Chandelier And Battle Of New Orleans* (1973), *Class Of '73* (1973), *The Young And The Restless* (1974), *In Concert* (1974), *Class Of '74 And '75* (1975), *Floyd Cramer And The Keyboard Kick Band* (1977), *Superhits* (1979), *Dallas* (1980), *Great Country Hits* (1981), *The Best Of The West* (1981), *Originals* (1991), *Classics* (1992). Compilations: *The Best Of Floyd Cramer* (1964), *The Best Of Floyd Cramer - Volume 2* (1968), *This Is Floyd Cramer* (1970), *The Big Hits* (1973), *Best Of The Class Of* (1973), *Spotlight On Floyd Cramer* (1974), *Piano Masterpieces 1900-1975* (1975), *All My Best* (1980), *Treasury Of Favourites* (1984), *Country Classics* (1984), *Our Class Reunion* (1987), *The Best Of Floyd Cramer* (1988), *Easy Listening Favorites* (1991).

Crowell, Rodney

b. 7 August, 1950, Houston, Texas, USA. Combining careers as country songwriter, producer and artist, Crowell has become an influential figure in Nashville's new breed, along with Emmylou Harris, in whose Hot Band he worked for three years, Rosanne Cash, and fellow songwriters like Guy Clark. Crowell's introduction to playing music came before he was a teenager, when he played drums in his Kentucky-born father's bar band in Houston. He dropped out of college in the early 70s to move to Nashville, where he was briefly signed as a songwriter to Jerry Reed's publishing company, and in 1973 was appearing on local 'writer's night' with contemporaries like Clark, John Hiatt and Richard Dobson. In 1974, a demo tape of his songs was heard by Brian Ahern, who was about to produce *Pieces Of The Sky* for Emmylou Harris, and that album eventually began with Crowell's 'Bluebird Wine'. Harris's 1975 *Elite Hotel,* included Crowell's 'Till I Gain Control Again', and her 1979, *Quarter Moon In A Ten Cent Town* featured his 'I Ain't Living Long Like This' and 'Leaving Louisiana In The Broad Daylight'. During this period, Crowell also worked as a permanent member of Harris's Hot Band, playing rhythm guitar and singing harmony and duet vocals. In 1978, he also recorded his own debut album for Warner Brothers, *Ain't Living Long Like This,* using Ahern as producer and an all-star line-up of musicians including the entire Hot Band plus Ry Cooder, Jim Keltner, and Willie Nelson. Although it included two minor US country hit singles, the album was not a commercial success. In 1979, Crowell married Rosanne Cash, and has subsequently produced most of her albums, In 1980, he tried again on his own account with *But What Will The Neighbors Think*, which he co-produced with Craig Leon. It remained in the US album charts for 10 weeks, and included a US Top 40 single, 'Ashes By Now', and in 1981, he released the self-produced *Rodney Crowell,* which just failed to reach the Top 100 of the US album chart. These albums were later the basis for *The Rodney Crowell Collection,* a 1989 compilation which was virtually a 'Best Of' of his early career. In 1984, he delivered *Street Language* to Warner Brothers, who rejected it, whereupon Crowell changed four tracks and signed it to Columbia, for whom he continues to record. The album, released in 1986, included three US country chart singles,

Rodney Crowell

and established him as a country artist (although many feel that he could easily cross over to rock). *Diamond And Dirt*, co-produced by Crowell and his erstwhile Hot Band colleague, Tony Brown, was much more successful, spawning three US country number 1 singles, 'It's Such A Small World' (a duet with Rosanne Cash), 'I Couldn't Leave You If I Tried' and 'She's Crazy For Leavin''. The success of this album provoked the release of the previously mentioned compilation. In 1989, Crowell and Brown co-produced *Keys To The Highway*, which was largely recorded with his fine band, the Dixie Pearls, whose personnel includes Stewart Smith (lead guitar), Jim Hanson (bass), Vince Santoro (drums) and another erstwhile Hot Band colleague, Hank DeVito (pedal steel). Crowell's songs have been covered by Bob Seger, Waylon Jennings, George Jones and others, while he has also produced albums for Sissy Spacek, Clark and Bobby Bare. His 1992 album, *Life Is Messy*, followed soon after the revelation that his marriage to Rosanne Cash had broken down. Taken by most observers as a reply to Cash's stunning *Interiors*, the LP attempted - with some success - to marry melancholy themes to up-tempo songs.

Albums: *Ain't Living Long Like This* (1978), *But What Will The Neighbors Think* (1980), *Rodney Crowell* (1981), *Street Language* (1986), *Diamonds And Dirt* (1988), *The Rodney Crowell Collection* (1989), *Keys To The Highway* (1989), *Life Is Messy* (1992).

Curless, Dick

b. Richard Curless, 17 March 1932, Fort Fairfield, Maine, USA. Both his parents were musical and in 1948, after the family moved to Massachusetts, he was soon appearing as the Tumbleweed Kid in his own show on local radio in Ware, Massachusetts. Later he joined a band called the Trail Blazers and moved back to Maine. In 1951, he was drafted into the the army, later commenting 'They must have been hard up. I had a bad eye and heart trouble'. He was sent to Korea, purely as an entertainer, and became very popular on the AFN network as the Rice Paddy Ranger. He was discharged in 1954 and worked local clubs until ill health caused him to rest. In 1957, a win on the *Arthur Godfrey Talent Show* on network television with his version of 'Nine Pound Hammer' led to him finding work in Hollywood and Las Vegas. In the late 50s, recurring ill heath, lack of major success and personal problems led to him returning to Maine, where he bought a lorry and worked in the logging business. He returned to Hollywood in the early 60s but decided that he was not destined for success further afield and soon went back to Maine, where he worked in local clubs. In 1965, at the request of the writer, his friend Dan Fulkerson, he recorded, at his own expense, on the minor Allagash label, a song called 'A Tombstone Every Mile'. The recording attracted the attention of Capitol, who released it on their Tower label and it became a Top 5 US country hit. The song was written about a stretch of dangerous and icy road through the Maine woods and was another of the truck driving and travelling-type numbers that became popular following Dave Dudley's success two years earlier with 'Six Days On The Road'. During 1966 and 1967, he was a regular member of Buck Owens' *All American Show* and toured extensively in the States, Europe and the Far East. He sang on the soundtrack of the 1968 film *Killer's Three* but the same year was again incapacitated by ill-health. He also had to resort to wearing the eye patch, which became his trademark. He commented 'I couldn't see much at all since the right eye was interfering with the vision I had in the left'. Further hits followed though only 'Six Times A Day' attained Top 20 status. He recorded 'Big Wheel Cannonball' in 1970, which was the trucker's version of the old train song 'Wabash Cannonball', originally sung by Roy Acuff in the late 30s. He also had success with the strange-titled 'Drag 'Em Off The Interstate, Sock It To 'Em, J.P. Blues'. In 1973, 'The Last Blues Song', somewhat appropriately, provided his last country chart hit. Perhaps only Dudley was ever more popular with the truckers. Curless' style leaned more to the blues, although someone once likened his voice to an 18-wheeler revving up. In the 70s, he devoted some attention to song publishing and a talent agency but seemingly drifted into semi-retirement in his native Maine. In 1987, he attempted a comeback as a recording artist by recording an album in Norway with Norwegian musicians. He will perhaps be remembered as the first and possibly the last national country star provided by the New England State of Maine.

Albums: *Songs Of The Open Country* (1958), *Singing Just For Fun* (1959), *I Love To Tell A Story* (1960), *Hymns* (1965), *A Tombstone Every Mile* (1965), with Kay Adams *A Devil Like Me Needs An Angel Like You* (1966), *Travellin' Man* (1966), *All Of Me Belongs To You/House Of Memories* (1967), *At Home With Dick Curless* (1967), *Ramblin' Country* (1967), *The Soul Of Dick Curless* (1967), *The Long Lonesome Road* (1968), *The Wild Side Of Town* (1968),

Doggin' It (1970), *Hard Hard Travelling Man* (1970), *Comin' On Country* (1971), *Stonin' Around* (1972), with Jerry Smith *Live At The Wheeling Truck Drivers Jamboree* (1973), *The Last Blues Song* (1973), *End Of The Road* (1974), *Maine Train* (1976), *The Great Race* (1980), *Welcome To My World* (1987). Compilation: *20 Great Truck Hits* (1983).

Curtis, Sonny

b. 9 May 1937, Meadow, Texas, USA. Curtis spent his first years in extreme poverty as his family lived in a 'dugout', simply a hole in the ground with a roof on the top. Eventually the family of seven moved to a small shack, and Sonny has been singing and playing guitar since the age of eight. He befriended Buddy Holly in nearby Lubbock and he worked with him on many occasions, notably playing a fiery guitar on his own composition, 'Rock Around With Ollie Vee', in Nashville. He left Holly to work with Slim Whitman, just before he formed the Crickets, and his song, 'The Real Buddy Holly Story', emphasises the inaccuracies of the film. Curtis joined the Crickets after Holly left, and they recorded several of his songs - 'More Than I Can Say' (later a hit for Bobby Vee and Leo Sayer), 'When You Ask About Love' (Matchbox) and 'I Fought The Law' (Bobby Fuller Four, the Clash). The Crickets toured as the Everly Brothers backing group and the Everlys had a number 1 with Curtis' 'Walk Right Back'. For several years, Curtis was both a Cricket and a solo performer and he became more comfortable with ballads than out and out rock 'n' roll. He wrote the theme tune for *The Mary Tyler Moore Show*, 'Love Is All Around', while his song, 'The Straight Life', has been recorded by Glen Campbell, Bing Crosby and Val Doonican. Rosanne Cash recorded 'Where Will The Words Come From' and Keith Whitley had a US country number 1 with 'I'm No Stranger To The Rain'. Curtis is an exceptional entertainer, who often comes to the UK on acoustic tours. His songs also show his wry sense of humour - recent titles include 'I'm Too Sexy For You' and 'Why Did You Say I Do To Me (When You Still Meant To Do It With Him)?.

Albums: *Beatle Hits, Flamenco Style* (1964), *The First Of Sonny Curtis* (1968), *The Sonny Curtis Style* (1969), *Sonny Curtis* (1979), *Love Is All Around* (1980), *Rollin'* (1981), *Spectrum* (1987), *Ready, Able And Willing* (1988), *No Stranger To The Rain* (1990).

Cyrus, Billy Ray

b. 25 August 1961, Flatwoods, Kentucky, USA. Cyrus comes from a preaching family and made his singing debut in his father's gospel group. In 1983, he formed his own band, Sly Dog, but they lost their equipment in a fire in Los Angeles. He then worked as a car salesman but he kept visiting Nashville in the hope of finding musical success. In 1992, he turned the Marcy Brothers' 'Don't Tell My Heart' into the simple but immensely catchy 'Achy Breaky Heart'. Although the Cyrus virus proved infectious, the songs rhythms were close to Don Williams' 'Tulsa Time'. The video, in which the muscular, ponytailed Cyrus was mobbed by adoring women, also introduced a country music dance, the Achy Breaky. The song topped both the US pop and country charts and was easily the most successful country single released in the UK during 1992. Another star, Travis Tritt, derided Cyrus for turning country music into 'an asswiggling contest' . Cyrus' album, *Some Gave All*, also topped the US pop and country charts, while he had a further transatlantic hit 'Could've Been Me' and cut a parody of 'Achy Breaky Heart' with the Chipmunks. Whether he will continue to have success is a moot point: it is unlikely that he will find material as irresistible as 'Achy Breaky Heart' but his Mel Gibson-styled looks are very much in his favour.

Album: *Some Gave All* (1992).

D

Daffan, Ted

b. Theron Eugene Daffan, 21 September 1912, Beauregarde Parish, Louisiana. USA. He was raised in Texas and graduated from high school in Houston in 1930. Late in 1931, he began to teach himself to play the Hawaiian guitar and first appeared on KTRH Houston with the Blue Islanders in 1933. During the 30s, he was a member of both the Blue Ridge Playboys (where he played with Floyd Tillman and Moon Mullican) and the Bar X Cowboys. His keen interest in electronics led to him becoming one of the first to experiment with electronically amplifying guitars and he first recorded with an amplified steel guitar in 1939. He also developed a considerable talent for songwriting and in 1939, his song 'Truck Driver's Blues' became the first of the genre of truck-driving songs. In 1940, he formed his own band, the Texans (which he kept almost to the end of the 50s) and recording for Columbia had a hit with his song 'Worried Mind', in the face of competition from recordings by Bob Wills and Roy Acuff. In 1943, he wrote and recorded for OKeh 'No Letter Today' and his classic million-selling 'Born To Lose'. Released on the same single, they both became US country and pop hits in January 1944. The following year, he had further Top 5 country hits including 'Headin' Down The Wrong Highway'. Between 1944-46, he was resident at Venice Pier Ballroom, Los Angeles and in the late 40s, he was a regular on the popular *Town Hall Party* from Compton. He later returned to Texas with his band and played in various venues, including Houston, Dallas and Fort Worth. In 1958, he formed a publishing company with Hank Snow and in 1961, he founded his own company in Houston. Amongst his best known country songs, apart from those previously mentioned, are 'A Woman Captured Me', 'I've Got Five Dollars And It's Saturday Night', and 'Always Alone'. Over the years, his songs have also been recorded by non-country artists such as Ray Charles ('Born To Lose' and 'No Letter Today') and in 1968, pop singer, Joe Barry was credited with a million-seller for his 1961 recording of 'I'm A Fool To Care', which had previously been recorded by Les Paul and Mary Ford. Daffan was one of the first to be elected to the *Nashville Songwriters Association International Hall Of Fame*, when it was founded in 1970.

Dale, Kenny

b. 1951, Artesia, New Mexico, USA. Dale, originally a drummer, grew up in Texas and had his own band, Love Country, in Houston in early 70s. In 1977, he recorded 'Bluest Heartache Of The Year' for a small Houston label, Earthrider, but it was reissued by Capitol and reached number 11 on the US country charts. Dale had further vocal successes with 'Shame, Shame On Me', 'Red Hot Memory', 'When It's Just You And Me' and 'Moanin' The Blues', and his biggest was with a country revival of Gene Pitney's 'Only Love Can Break A Heart' (number 7, 1969). His final chart entry was with 'I'm Going Crazy' in 1986.
Albums: *Bluest Heartache Of The Year* (1977), *Red Hot Memory* (1978), *Only Love Can Break A Heart* (1979), *When It's Just You And Me* (1981).

Dalhart, Vernon

b. Marion Try Slaughter, 6 April 1883, Jefferson, Texas, USA, d. 14 September 1948. Dalhart spent his early life on a ranch but in 1902, seeking a career in music, he went to New York. He took the name of Vernon Dalhart by combining the names of two Texas towns. He sang with the Century Opera Company and, in 1913-1914, he performed in *HMS Pinafore* at the Hippodrome. He recorded for Edison's cylinders, his first release being 'Can't Yo' Heah Me Callin' Caroline?' in 1917. Dalhart made numerous records under different names with different styles, including vaudeville. In 1924 Victor Records were about to dispense with his services when he asked if he could record hillbilly music. He chose 'The Wreck Of The Old '97', which had first been recorded the previous year by Henry Whitter. It was backed by 'The Prisoner's Song', which he said was written by his cousin, Guy Massey. It became country music's first million-seller, eventually topping six million. True to character, Dalhart also recorded the song under pseudonyms for many different labels. 'The Wreck Of The Old '97' was based on fact and so Dalhart consolidated his success with several topical songs written by, and performed with, Carson Jay Robison. They included 'The Death Of Floyd Collins' and 'The John T. Scopes Trial'. In 1928, following disagreements with Robison over royalties and the choice of musicians, Dalhart pursued a solo career. The cutbacks during the Depression put paid to Dalhart's vocation although, in 1931, he recorded

'The Runaway Train' in London, which became a children's favourite. He attempted a comeback in 1939 but, despite his versatility, he could not satisfy the public. He stopped performing, although he did give singing lessons and worked as a night clerk at a hotel in Bridgeport, Connecticut. He died following a heart attack in 1948, and was elected to the Country Music Hall of Fame in 1961. As Dalhart used more than 50 pseudonyms, the full extent of his recorded career will never be known.

Albums: *Songs Of The Railroad (1924-1934)* (1972), *Old Time Songs* (1976), *Vernon Dalhart* (c.70s), *Vernon Dalhart, 1921-1927* (c.70s), *Vernon Dalhart - The First Recorded Railway Songs* (1978), *Vernon Dalhart - The First Singing Cowboy* (1978), *Ballads And Railroad Songs* (1980), *Vernon Dalhart, Volume 2* (1985), *Vernon Dalhart, Volume 3* (1985).

Dalton, Lacy J.

b. Jill Byrem, 13 October 1948, Bloomsburg, Pennsylvania, USA. Her father played guitar and mandolin, but she was originally determined to be an artist. At the age of 18 she moved to Los Angeles and then settled in Santa Cruz, where she played the clubs for 12 years. She worked as a protest singer and then became the lead singer with a psychedelic band Office under the name of Jill Croston. A demo tape impressed record producer, Billy Sherrill, who signed her to Columbia Records in Nashville in 1979. Her gravelly, bluesy voice was unusual for country singers and thus made her work distinctive. Her first album, *Lacy J. Dalton*, is regarded by many as a classic, and she is often described by the title of one of its songs, 'Hillbilly Girl With The Blues'. Her US country hits include 'Crazy Blue Eyes', 'Tennessee Waltz', 'Hard Times' and '16th Avenue'. Her *Highway Diner* album moved her into Bruce Springsteen country and she had a pop hit with 'Working Class Man'. By way of contrast, she was featured alongside Bobby Bare, George Jones and Earl Scruggs on her album, *Blue Eyed Blues*.

Album as Jill Croston *Jill Croston* (1978); as Lacy J. Dalton *Lacy J. Dalton* (1979), *Hard Times* (1980), *Takin' It Easy* (1981), *16th Avenue* (1982), *Dream Baby* (1983), *Greatest Hits* (1983), *Can't Run Away From Your Heart* (1985), *Highway Diner* (1986), *Blue Eyed Blues* (1987), *Survivor* (1989), *Lacy J.* (1990), *Crazy Love* (1991), *Chains On The Wind* (1992).

Daniels, Charlie

b. 28 October 1937, Wilmington, North Carolina, USA. Daniels, who wrote 'Carolina (I Love You)' about his youth, was the son of a lumberjack and was raised with a love of bluegrass music. He borrowed a guitar when he was 15 years old and immediately learned to play basic tunes. He then acquired skills on mandolin and fiddle, but had to modify his playing when he lost the tip of his ring finger in an accident in 1955. He formed a bluegrass band, the Misty Mountain Boys, but the group changed to the Jaguars, following a single 'Jaguar', which they recorded in 1959 (produced by Bob Johnston). Daniels says that 'for nine years we played every honky-tonk dive and low-life joint between Raleigh and Texas'. This enabled him to master a variety of musical styles, but his only national success came in 1964 when he wrote an Elvis Presley b-side, 'It Hurts Me', a tender ballad which remains one of his best compositions. In 1968, he followed Bob Johnston's suggestion to accept regular session work in Nashville. He played electric bass on Bob Dylan's *Nashville Skyline* and later appeared on his albums, *Self Portrait* and *New Morning*. He also worked with Marty Robbins, Hank Williams Jnr (on *Family Tradition*) and Ringo Starr (on *Beaucoups Of Blues*), and took Lester Flatt's place alongside Earl Scruggs. He produced an album by Jerry Corbitt, who, in turn, produced one by Daniels, both of which were released in the US by Capitol Records. The Charlie Daniels Band was formed in 1970 and they started recording for the Kama Sutra label. Although he was a multi-instrumentalist, he was a limited vocalist but was suited to the talking blues, 'Uneasy Rider', which made the US Top 10 in 1973. He followed it with his anthem for southern rock, 'The South's Gonna Do It'. In 1974, Daniels had members of the Marshall Tucker Band and the Allman Brothers Band join him on stage in Nashville. It was so successful that he decided to make his so-called *Volunteer Jam* an annual event. It has led to some unlikely mixtures of artists such as James Brown performing with Roy Acuff, and the stylistic mergers have included Crystal Gayle singing the blues with the Charlie Daniels Band. When he moved to Epic in 1976, there was a concerted effort to turn the the band into a major concert attraction, despite the fact that at 6 feet 4 inches tall and weighing 20 stone Daniels was no teenage idol: he hid his face under an oversized cowboy hat.

The albums sold well and, in 1979, when recording his *Million Miles Reflections* album, he recalled a 20s poem, 'Mountain Whippoorwill', by Stephen Vincent Benet. The band developed this into 'The Devil Went Down To Georgia', in which Johnny outplays the Devil to win a gold

Charlie Daniels

fiddle. Daniels overdubbed his fiddle seven times to create an atmospheric recording which topped the US country charts and made number 3 in the US pop charts. It was also a UK Top 20 success. In 1980 the band recorded 'In America' for the hostages in Iran; and then in 1982, 'Still In Saigon', about Vietnam. The band were featured on the soundtrack for *Urban Cowboy* and also recorded the theme for Burt Reynolds' film *Stroker Ace*, which featured Tommy Crain's banjo. (Daniels' band has been very loyal to him with Taz DiGregorio playing keyboards from the late 60s.) In 1986 Daniels appeared in the television movie, *Lone Star Kid*, and published a book of short stories, but he still continues touring and playing his southern boogie.

Albums: *Te John, Grease And Wolfman* (1970), *Charlie Daniels* (1970), *Honey In The Rock* (reissued as *Uneasy Rider*) (1973), *Way Down Yonder* (reissued as *Whiskey*) (1974), *Fire On The Mountain* (1975), *Nightrider* (1975), *Teach Yourself Rock Guitar, Volume 1* (1976 - there was no volume 2), *Saddletramp* (1976), *High Lonesome* (1976), *Volunteer Jam* (1976), *Midnight Wind* (1977), *Volunteer Jam 3 & 4* (1978), *Million Miles Reflections* (1979), *Volunteer Jam VI* (1980), *Full Moon* (1980), *Volunteer Jam VII* (1981), *Windows* (1982), *A Decade Of Hits* (1983), *Me And The Boys* (1985), *Powder Keg* (1987), *Renegade* (1991).

Darby And Tarlton

b. John James Rimbert Tarlton, 1892, Chesterfield County, South Carolina, USA. When a small child, he learned to play banjo and harmonica but at the age of eight, he changed to guitar. He soon took to playing, using a knife blade or bottle neck to fret the strings and became very efficient in the playing of negro blues and Hawaiian music, as well as the old time songs he learned from his mother. He left home in 1912 and travelled extensively from Texas and California to New York, working in cotton mills and oilfields and on occasions playing as a street musician in Chicago and New York, or touring with medicine shows. In 1923, he became friendly with Frank Ferera, who did much to popularize the Hawaiian guitar in America and from him learned the use of a steel bar, in lieu of the knife blade. He finally changed to an automobile wrist-pin in the late 20s and used it until his death. In 1926, he formed a partnership with Tom Darby, a guitarist and singer from Columbus, Georgia. Early in 1927, they auditioned for Columbia and in November that year, at their second session, they recorded 'Columbus Stockade

Blues' and 'Birmingham Jail'. When offered the choice of a flat fee or royalties for the recordings, they accepted a fee of £75, which proved an ill-chosen decision, since both songs went on to become country standards. Tarlton arranged 'Birmingham Jail' when he was actually in gaol, as a result of an involvement in illicit moonshine. Art Satherley was quoted as saying that their version of the song was the greatest hillbilly record that he ever recorded because both, as former convicts, could feel their material so deeply. Between 1927 and 1933, Tarlton recorded about 80 songs for Columbia, Victor or ARC; some were solos and others with Darby. On their duet recordings, Darby (a fine player who picked guitar in a style often described as 'black derived') mainly sang the lead vocal with Tarlton playing the steel guitar and adding harmony work, which at times included a yodel. During the early 30s, Tarlton toured in the south and in 1931, when not recording with Darby, he once worked in a cotton mill in Rockingham, South Carolina, with the Dixon Brothers. The Dixons, Dorsey and Howard, learned much from Tarlton's steel and ordinary guitar-playing ability and his influence was to show when they in turn became recording artists. Ironically, Tarlton and Darby never really got on together and in 1933, they parted and Darby returned to farming. Tarlton continued to play and worked with various bands and medicine shows until the mid-40s, when he semi-retired. Around 1963, he was persuaded to return to more active participation and played at several festivals and even recorded an album. Tarlton died in 1973 and it is believed that Darby died in the late 60s. John Morthland commented that 'If any one musician could be said to have laid the groundwork for future generations of steel players from western swing right up to today's pedal steel, it would probably be Tarlton'.

Albums: *Steel Guitar Rag* (1963), *Darby and Tarlton* (1973), *Darby & Tarlton* (1974).

Darrell, Johnny

b. 23 July 1940, Hopewell, Alabama, USA. Darrell taught himself the guitar when he was 14 years old and used his talent to entertain troops while in the US army. Darrell, who worked at a Holiday Inn in Nashville in 1964, signed with United Artists as a country performer and had several hits, mostly during the mid-60s. His successes on the US country charts include 'As Long As The Wind Blows', 'The Son Of Hickory Holler's Tramp' and a number 3, 'With Pen In Hand'. He was the first to record Kenny Rogers' hit 'Ruby, Don't Take Your Love To Town' and his version reached number 9 on the US country charts in 1967. (Strangely, Rogers' version was only to make number 39.) He subsequently recorded for Monument, Capricorn, Gusto.

Albums: *As Long As The Wind Blows* (1966), *Ruby, Don't Take Your Love To Town* (1967), *The Son Of Hickory Holler's Tramp* (1968), *The Country Sound Of Johnny Darrell* (1968), *With Pen In Hand* (1968), *Why You Been Gone So Long* (1969), *California Stop Over* (1970), *Giant Country* (1970), *More Country Gold* (1970), *Waterglass Full Of Whisky* (1974), *Greatest Hits* (1979).

Dave And Sugar

Dave Rowland (b. 26 January 1942, Anaheim, California, USA) was a pop singer and trumpeter in an army band and then became a member of the Stamps Quartet. He therefore toured with Elvis Presley and is on his records, 'My Boy' and 'Help Me'. He worked as part of the Four Guys on Charley Pride's roadshow and then formed a vocal quartet, Wild Oats. He then hit upon the concept of a group of a boy with a blonde and a brunette, and he called the group, Dave and Sugar. They joined Charley Pride's roadshow in 1975. Sugar were Vicki Hackeman (b. Louisville, Kentucky USA) and Jackie Frantz (b. Sidney, Ohio, USA). Pride co-produced their first country hits, 'Queen Of The Silver Dollar', the chart-topping 'The Door Is Always Open' and 'I'm Knee Deep In Lovin' You'. By 1979 Hackeman, who married Pride's bass guitarist, Ron Baker, and Frantz had been replaced by Melissa Dean and Sue Powell. The group topped the US country charts with 'Tear Time' and 'Golden Tears'. By 1980 the group was known as Dave Rowland and Sugar, although the group did share the lead vocals. Rowland then recorded a solo album for Warners. He released a single of his tribute to actress Natalie Wood, 'Natalie', but by 1985 he was working as Dave and Sugar again.

Albums: *Dave And Sugar* (1976), *That's The Way Love Should Be* (1977), *Tear Time* (1978), *Stay With Me/Golden Tears* (1979), *New York Wine And Tennessee Shine* (1980), *Pleasure* (1981), *Dave And Sugar - 2* (1986). Dave Rowland: *Sugar-Free* (1982).

Davies, Gail

b. 1 September 1948, Broken Bow, Oklahoma, USA. Her father was a country musician who, among other things, worked on *Louisiana Hayride* and Davies was fascinated by his jukebox filled with country music. As a performer, she went on the road with her brother Ron, whose songs have since been recorded by Helen Reddy ('Long Hard Climb') and Three Dog Night ('It Ain't Easy'). An album that they made for A&M was never released. Davies married a jazz musician and, for a while, tried to be a jazz singer. When they separated, she moved to the west coast where she worked as a session singer. As a writer, she wrote 'Bucket To The South', a US country hit for Ava Barber in 1978. Her first album, *Gail Davies*, for the Lifesong label in 1978 included her first US country hit, 'No Love Have I', alongside further successes, 'Poison Love' and 'Someone Is Looking For Someone Like You'. She moved to Warner Brothers and became a rarity - a female country performer producing her own records. She had US country hits with 'Blue Heartache', 'I'll Be There (If You Ever Want Me)' and 'Singing The Blues'. At RCA in 1984 she had further success with 'Jagged Edge Of A Broken Heart' and 'Trouble With Love'. She is not to be confused with Gail Davis, who toured with Gene Autry's roadshow and was featured in the television series, *Annie Oakley*.

Albums: *Gail Davies* (1978), *The Game* (1980), *I'll Be There* (1981), *Givin' Herself Away* (1982), *What Can I Say* (1983), *Where Is A Woman To Go* (1984), *Pretty Words* (1989), *The Other Side Of Love* (1990).

Davis, Danny, And The Nashville Brass

b. George Nowlan, 29 April 1925, Randolph, Massachusetts, USA. Davis, who calls himself a 'Yankee Irishman', bought his trumpet with his earnings from a delivery round and he played in high school bands. At the age of 14 he was performing with the Massachusetts Symphony Orchestra. From the age of 17, he was guesting with some of the best swing bands including Gene Krupa and Bob Crosby and he recorded 'Trumpet Cha Cha'. By 1958 he was working as a record producer and he produced several of Connie Francis' hit singles. He also had success with Herman's Hermits and Johnny Tillotson. In 1965, he began working with Chet Atkins at RCA and he formed the Nashville Brass, which added brass to a pop-country rhythm section: it was as though Herb Alpert was recording country music. Although some country fans were reluctant to accept them, their albums sold well and they had US country hits including 'Wabash Cannonball' and 'Columbus Stockade Blues'. For six consecutive years, Danny Davis And The Nashville

Brass were voted the Instrumental Band Of The Year at the Country Music Association's awards, and they also won a Grammy in 1969 for their *More Nashville Sounds* album. In 1980 a curious album was released in which Davis added the Nashville Brass to some existing Willie Nelson tracks. The versions of 'Night Life' and 'Funny How Time Slips Away' both made the US country charts.

Albums: *That Happy Nashville Sound* (1967), *More Nashville Sounds* (1969), *Movin' On* (1969), *You Ain't Heard Nothin' Yet* (1970), *Down Homers* (1970), *Christmas* (1970), *Hank Locklin, Danny Davis & The Nashville Brass* (1970), *Nashville Brass Turns To Gold* (1971), *Somethin' Else* (1971), *Super Country* (1971), *Live-In Person* (1972), *Turn On Some Happy* (1972), *Travelin'* (1973), *Caribbean Cruise* (1973), *In Bluegrass Country* (1974), *Latest & Greatest* (1974), *Orange Blossom Special* (1974), *Dream Country* (1975), *Country Gold* (1975), *Super Songs* (1976), *Texas* (1976), *How I Love Them Ol' Songs* (1978), *Cookin' Country* (1978), *Great Songs Of The Big Band Era* (1979), *Danny Davis, Willie Nelson & The Nashville Brass* (1980), *Cotton Eyed Joe* (1981), *Don't You Ever Get Tired Of Hurtin' Me* (1984).

Davis, Jimmie

b. James Houston Davis, 11 September 1902, on a farm at Beech Springs, near Quitman, Jackson Parish, Louisiana, USA. One of the 11 children of a sharecropping family, Davis progressed through local schools and in the early 20s, he gained a BA at Louisiana's Pineville College. Here he sang in the College Glee Club and in a group known as the Tiger Four. He returned to Beech Springs, where he became the first high school graduate to ever return to the school as a teacher. After school, he worked in the fields and busked on street corners until he had raised enough money to allow him to study for his master's degree at the State University in Baton Rouge. In the late 20s, he taught history and social science at Dodd College in Shreveport, but left to become the clerk at Shreveport Court. He also began to make regular appearances on KWKH, where he came to the attention of RCA-Victor. Between 1929 and 1933, he recorded almost 70 songs for the label. The material ranged from songs that clearly showed the influence of Jimmie Rodgers and ballads, to songs of a very risque nature which, in later years, he tended to forget that he ever recorded. (Noted author John Morthland later wrote strongly that 'Davis launched his career as a Jimmie Rodgers

imitator with the dirtiest batch of songs any one person had ever recorded in country music' and added 'Many of his early sides were *double-entendre* songs of unbridled carnality'). These included such tracks as 'Organ Grinder Blues', 'Tom Cat and Pussy Blues' and 'She's A Hum Dum Dinger (From Dingersville)'. He seemingly has the distinction of being only the second country singer (after Rodgers) to record with a coloured musician when, in 1932, he recorded with blues singer and steel guitarist Oscar Woods. In September 1934, he made his first recordings for Decca, the first number recorded being his now standard 'Nobody's Darling But Mine'. This became his first hit and led to him to record several answer versions to it. (Frank Ifield had a UK number 4 pop hit with his version of the song in 1963). A few of the old risque songs crept in at first but he soon lost these and the Rodgers' influence to concentrate on more middle of the road material. In 1938, he recorded his and Floyd Tillman's 'It Makes No Difference Now' (a major pop hit for Bing Crosby in 1941) and in 1939, he co-wrote the internationally famous 'You Are My Sunshine', with his steel guitarist Charles Mitchell. The song has been recorded by so many artists over the years that it is reputed that its copyright is the most valuable in country music. Among the artists finding success with their recordings of it, apart from Davis himself, were Bob Atcher, Gene Autry and Bing Crosby. During the 30s, Davis made a great many recordings both as a solo artist, or with others, including Brown's Musical Brownies. In 1938, Davis was made Shreveport's Commissioner Of Public Safety and in 1942, he was promoted to State Public Service Commissioner. He had Top 5 US country chart hits in the 40s with 'Is It Too Late Now', 'There's A Chill On The Hill Tonight', 'Grievin' My Heart Out Over You' and 'Bang Bang' and in 1945, he scored a country number 1 with 'There's A New Moon Over My Shoulder'. In 1944, standing as a Democrat, he was elected Governor of Louisiana, in spite of his opponents raising the subject of his early RCA recordings. During the 40s, he appeared in films, including *Strictly In The Grove* (1942) (in which he sang 'You Are My Sunshine'), *Frontier Fury* (1943) and *Louisiana* (1947). In 1948, he returned to his musical career and began to specialize more in gospel music than in straight country songs. He appeared in his last film, *Square Dance Katy*, in 1950, and during the 50s he toured, making appearances at many religious events; in 1957, he was voted the Best Male Sacred Singer. He was elected to a second term as State Governor in 1960 and again the early songs were raised by the opposition. 'Where The Old Red River Flows' gave him a Top 20 country hit in 1962 and went on to become yet another very popular and much recorded song. In 1971, he was unsuccessful in his attempt to seek a third spell as Governor and instead concentrated on his gospel music. The many songs that he had written saw him elected to the *Nashville Songwriters International Hall Of Fame* in 1971 and the following year he was inducted into the *Country Music Hall Of Fame*. In 1973, he left Decca (by then MCA) and recorded for the Canaan label, even recording a gospel version of his classic, which he called 'Christ Is My Sunshine'. During the 70s and up to the mid-80s, he continued to make recordings of gospel music and appearances at some religious venues until a heart attack in October 1987 caused him to restricted his activities. Some of his old RCA tracks were reissued in 1988 by the German Bear Family label, no doubt without Davis' blessing.

Albums: *Near The Cross* (1955), *Hymn Time* (1957), *The Door Is Always Open* (1958), *Hail Him With A Song* (1958), *You Are My Sunshine* (1959), *Someone To Care* (1960), *No One Stands Alone* (1960), *Suppertime* (1960), with Anita Kerr Singers *Sweet Hour Of Prayer* (1961), *Someone Watching Over You* (1961), *Songs Of Faith* (1962), *How Great Thou Art* (1962), *Beyond The Shadows* (1963), *Highway To Heaven* (1964), *Sings* (1964), *It's Christmas Time Again* (1964), *Still I Believe* (1965), *At The Crossing* (1965), *Gospel Hour* (1966), *My Altar* (1966), *His Marvellous Grace* (1967), *Going Home For Christmas* (1967), *Singing The Gospel* (1968), *Let Me Walk With Jesus* (1969), *In My Father's House* (1969), *Amazing Grace* (1969), *Country Side Of Jimmie Davis* (1969), *Songs Of Consolation* (1970), *Old Baptizing Creek* (1971), *What A Happy Day* (1972), *Memories Coming Home* (1972), *God's Last Altar Call* (1973), with Anita Kerr Singers *No One Stands Alone* (1973), *Souvenirs Of Yesterday* (1974), *Let Me Be There* (1974), *Christ Is My Sunshine* (1974), *Living By Faith* (1975), *Sunshine* (1975), *Live* (1976), *Golden Hits Volume 1* (1978), *Golden Hits Volume 2* (1979), *Heaven's National Anthem* (1981), *Greatest Hits Volume 1* (1981), *The Last Walk* (1985), *Sounds Like Jimmie Rodgers* (1985), *Rockin' Blues* (1988), *Barnyard Stomp* (1988).

Further reading: *You Are My Sunshine: The Jimmie Davis Story*, Gus Weill.

Davis, Mac

b. Mac Scott Davis, 21 January 1942, Lubbock,

Texas, USA. Davis grew up with a love of country music but turned to rock 'n' roll in 1955 when he saw Elvis Presley and Buddy Holly on the same show, an event referred to in his 1980 song, 'Texas In My Rear View Mirror'. Davis, who was already writing songs, learned the guitar and moved to Atlanta, Georgia where he 'majored in beer and rock 'n' roll'. Davis married when he was 20 and his son, Scotty, became the subject of several songs including 'Watching Scotty Grow', recorded by Bobby Goldsboro and Anthony Newley. In the early 60s Davis took administrative jobs with VeeJay and Liberty Records and made several unsuccessful records including a revival of the Drifters' 'Honey Love': much of this early work was collected in a 1984 compilation, inaccurately called *20 Golden Songs*. A parody of Bob Dylan, 'I Protest', was produced by Joe South. Davis wrote 'The Phantom Strikes Again', which was recorded by Sam The Sham And The Pharaohs, and, in 1967, he had his first chart success when Lou Rawls recorded 'You're Good For Me'. 'Friend, Lover, Woman, Wife' and 'Daddy's Little Man' were both recorded by O.C. Smith. Davis wrote 'Memories' and 'Nothingsville' for Elvis Presley's 1968 comeback television special, and Presley's renaissance continued with Davis' social commentary, 'In The Ghetto'. Presley also recorded 'Don't Cry, Daddy', inspired by Scotty telling Davis not to be upset by television footage of the Vietnam war, 'Clean Up Your Own Back Yard', 'Charro' and 'A Little Less Conversation'. 'Something's Burning' was a hit for Kenny Rogers And The First Edition, while Gallery made the US charts with the much-recorded 'I Believe In Music'. Davis wrote the songs for the Glen Campbell film, *Norwood*, including 'Everything A Man Could Ever Need'. Davis' second marriage was to 18-year-old Sarah Barg in 1971. His first album, named from Glen Campbell's description of him, *Song Painter*, was full of good material but his voice was limited and the album was bathed in strings. Davis topped the US charts in 1972 with the pleasant but inconsequential 'Baby, Don't Get Hooked On Me': its success ironically being due to the publicity from angry feminists. Davis says, 'The record sounded arrogant but I was really saying, 'don't get involved with me because I don't deserve it.' Davis also had US success with 'One Hell Of A Woman', 'Stop And Smell The Roses', 'Rock 'n' Roll (I Gave You The Best Years Of My Life)' and 'Forever Lovers'. *Rolling Stone*, disliking his pop-country hits, claimed that Davis had 'done more to set back the cause of popular music in the 70s than any other figure'. The curly-haired golfer often wrote of his love for his wife but in 1975 she left him for a short marriage to Glen Campbell. Davis' own career has included playing Las Vegas showrooms and the films *North Dallas 40*, *Cheaper To Keep Her* and *The Sting II*. 'You're My Bestest Friend', an obvious nod to Don Williams' success, was a US country hit in 1981 and 'I Never Made Love (Till I Made Love To You)' was on the US country charts for six months in 1985. His witty 'It's Hard To Be Humble' has become Max Bygraves' closing number. Davis' UK success has been limited but even if he has no further hits, he is assured of work in Las Vegas showrooms, and, in 1992, took over the starring role in the Broadway hit musical, *The Will Rogers Follies*.

Albums: *Song Painter* (1971), *I Believe In Music* (1972), *Baby, Don't Get Hooked On Me* (1972), *Mac Davis* (1973), *Stop And Smell The Roses* (1974), *All The Love In The World* (1974), *Burning Thing* (1975), *Forever Lovers* (1976), *Thunder In The Afternoon* (1977), *Fantasy* (1978), *It's Hard To Be Humble* (1980), *Texas In My Rear View Mirror* (1980), *Midnight Crazy* (1981), *Forty '82* (1982), *Soft Talk* (1984), *Who's Loving You?* (1984), *20 Golden Songs* (1984), *Losers* (1984), *Till I Made It With You* (1985).

Davis, Skeeter

b. Mary Frances Penick, 30 December 1931, Dry Ridge, Kentucky, USA. Skeeter was raised on a farm and as a child knew that she wanted to be a country singer. She acquired the nickname of 'Skeeter' (a local term for a mosquito) from her grandfather because he considered that she was always as active and buzzing around just like the insect. In her mid-teens, she formed a duo with school friend Betty Jack Davis (b. 3 March 1932, Corbin Kentucky, USA, d. August 1953) and together they began to sing in the Lexington area. In 1949, they appeared on local radio WLAX and later were featured on radio and television in Detroit, Cincinnati and eventually on the WWVA *Wheeling Jamboree* in West Virginia. They first recorded for Fortune in 1952 but the following year they successfully auditioned for RCA and their recording of 'I Forgot More Than You'll Ever Know' quickly became a number 1 US country and number 18 US pop hit. On 23 August 1953, the singers' car was involved in a collision with another vehicle, resulting in the death of Betty Jack and leaving Skeeter critically injured. It was over a year before Skeeter recovered physically

and mentally from the crash and it was only with great difficulty that she was persuaded to resume her career. Eventually she briefly teamed up with Betty Jack's sister, Georgia Davis and returned to singing. In 1955, she went solo and for a time worked with RCA's touring Caravan Of Stars as well as with Eddy Arnold and Elvis Presley. Her recording career, under the guidance of Chet Atkins, progressed and she gained her first solo US country chart hit in 1958 with 'Lost To A Geisha Girl', the female answer to the Hank Locklin hit, 'Geisha Girl'. The following year, her co-written song 'Set Him Free' became her first country Top 10 hit. She fulfilled one of her greatest ambitions in 1959, when she moved to Nashville and became a regular member of the *Grand Ole Opry*. During the 60s, she became one of RCA's most successful country artists, registering 26 US country hits, 12 of them achieving crossover US pop chart success. The most popular included another 'answer' song in 'I Can't Help You, I'm Falling Too', (the reply to Hank Locklin's 'Please Help Me I'm Falling') and 'My Last Date'. She co-wrote the latter with Boudleaux Bryant and pianist Floyd Cramer, whose instrumental version had been a million-seller in 1960. In 1963, she achieved a million-selling record herself with 'The End Of The World', which peaked at number 2 in both the US country and pop charts. It also gave her her only UK pop chart entry, reaching number 18 in a 13 week chart life in 1963. (The song also became a UK pop hit for Sonia in 1990). Davis also had successful recordings with Bobby Bare ('A Dear John Letter') and Don Bowman (a novelty number, 'For Loving You'). Davis toured extensively in the 60s and 70s, not only throughout the USA and Canada but also to Europe and the Far East, where she is very popular. She played all the major US television network shows, including regular appearances with Duke Ellington and also appeared on a Rolling Stones tour. Her recording career slowed down in the 70s but her hits included 'I'm A Lover (Not A Fighter)', 'Bus Fare To Kentucky' and 'One Tin Soldier'. She also made the charts with Bobby Bare on 'Your Husband, My Wife' and with George Hamilton IV on 'Let's Get Together' (a US pop hit for the Youngbloods in 1969). In 1973, she had a minor hit with the Bee Gees' 'Don't Forget To Remember' and a Top 20 country and minor pop hit with 'I Can't Believe That It's All Over'. It was to prove a slightly prophetic title, since only two more chart hits followed, the last being 'I Love Us' on Mercury in 1976 - she having left RCA two

Skeeter Davis

years earlier. She has recorded several tribute albums, including one to Buddy Holly, which featured Waylon Jennings on guitar and also one to her friend Dolly Parton. She also re-recorded 'May You Never Be Alone', a Davis' Sisters success, with NRBQ in 1985. From 1960-64, she was married to well-known WSM radio and television personality Ralph Emery, but she subsequently received heavy criticism in Emery's autobiography. She later married Joey Spampanito of NRBQ. She became something of a rebel after the break-up of her second marriage. She settled in a colonial-style mansion set in several hundred acres in Brentwood, Tennessee, and surrounded herself with dogs, Siamese cats, a dove in a gilded cage and even an ocelot named Fred. Her extreme religious beliefs saw her refusing to appear in places that sold intoxicating drinks. She even stopped growing tobacco on her farm, giving the reason for both actions: 'As a Christian, I think it's harmful to my body'. In 1973, her strong criticisms of the Nashville Police Department during her act at the *Opry* caused her to be dropped from the roster. She was later reinstated and still usually sings religious or gospel songs on her regular appearances.

Albums: *I'll Sing You A Song And Harmonize Too* (1960), *Here's The Answer* (1961), *The End Of The World* (1962), with Porter Wagoner *Duets* (1962), *Cloudy With Occasional Tears* (1963), *I Forgot More Than You'll Ever Know* (1964), *Let Me Get Close To You* (reissued as *Easy To Love*) (1964), *Authentic Southern Style Gospel* (1964), *Blueberry Hill (& Other Favorites)* (1965), *Sings Standards* (1965), *Written By The Stars* (1965), with Bobby Bare *Tunes For Two* (1965), *My Heart's In The Country* (1966), *Singing In The Summer Sun* (1966), *Hand In Hand With Jesus* (1967), *What Does It Take (To Keep A Man Like You Satisfied)* (1967), *Sings Buddy Holly* (1967), *Why So Lonely* (1968), *I Love Flatt & Scruggs* (1968), with Don Bowman *Funny Folk Flops* (1968), *The Closest Thing To Love* (1969), *Mary Frances* (1969), *A Place In The Country* (1970), *It's Hard To Be A Woman* (1970), with Bare *Your Husband, My Wife* (reissued as *More Tunes For Two*) (1970), with George Hamilton IV *Down Home In The Country* (1970), *Skeeter* (1971), *Love Takes A Lot Of My Time* (1971), *Foggy Mountain Top* (1971), *Sings Dolly* (1972), *Bring It On Home* (1972), *I Can't Believe That It's All Over* (1973), *The Hillbilly Singer* (1973), *He Wakes Me With A Kiss Every Morning* (1974), *Heartstrings* (1984), with NRBQ *She Sings, They Play* (1985). As the Davis Sisters: *Hits* (1952), *Jealous Love* (1952).

Dean, Eddie

b. Edgar Dean Glosup, 9 July 1907, Posey, Texas, USA. Dean first worked with his elder brother Jimmy on the *WLS National Barn Dance* in Chicago in the early 30s, before moving to Los Angeles in 1937. He subsequently appeared in films with Ken Maynard and Gene Autry and from 1946-48, he had his own film series for which he also wrote most of the title songs. A fine guitarist and singer, he first made the US country charts in 1948 with his song 'One Has My Name, The Other Has My Heart' but he also had a Top 10 hit, in 1955, with his cleverly compiled 'I Dreamed Of A Hillbilly Heaven', which became a pop hit for Tex Ritter in 1961.

Albums: *Greater Westerns* i (1956), *Greatest Westerns* ii (1957), *Hi-Country* (1957), *The Golden Cowboy* (50s), *Sings Country & Western* (50s), *Favorites* (1960), *Hillbilly Heaven* (1961), *Sings* (1960s), *Tribute To Hank Williams* (60s), *Sincerely Eddie Dean* (1974), *Dean Of The West* (1976), *A Cowboy Sings Country* (c.1980).

Dean, Jimmy

b. Seth Ward, 10 August 1928, near Plainview, Texas, USA. Dean's mother, who was the family's only support, ran a barber shop and as a boy, he picked cotton and worked on local farms. His mother taught him to play the piano when he was 10 years old and he taught himself guitar, accordion and harmonica as soon as he had access to the instruments. At 16, he began to study engineering but then joined the Merchant Marines for two years, after which he enlisted in the Air Force. It was during his service that Dean first became an entertainer when, with a band called the Tennessee Haymakers, he played local clubs and honkytonks near his base. He left the service in 1948 and for the next few years tried to develop his musical career. In 1952, with a new band called the Texas Wildcats, he toured US Army bases in the Caribbean, before finding work on WARL Arlington, Virginia and WTOP-TV Washington. He first recorded for Four Star the same year and early in 1953, he gained his first US country Top 10 hit with 'Bumming Around'. He had a show called *Town And Country Jamboree* on WMAL-TV Washington in 1955 and due to its popularity and some syndication, CBS offered him his own network programme. The *Jimmy Dean Show* ran from 1957 until 1958 but when it lost its sponsor and a proposed New York afternoon network series failed to materialize, Dean decided to abandon television. He continued to tour, signed

Jimmy Dean

to Columbia and in 1961, wrote and recorded a number called 'Big Bad John'. The song became a million-seller and a number 1 record in both the US country and pop charts. It also became a UK hit, reaching number 2 in the UK pop charts the same year. The song also was voted the 'Best Country and Western Recording of 1961'. Surprisingly, it was the first song that Dean had ever written. Over the years there have been several parodies of 'Big Bad John' including those by Marvin Rainwater ('Tough Top Cat'), Des O'Connor ('Thin Chow Mein') and the Country Gentlemen ('Big Bruce'). In 1962, five further US chart hits followed, including a sequel to 'Big Bad John', all achieving crossover success. Although this time not written by the artist, 'The Cajun Queen' used the same melody but Dean later admitted that he hated recording it. Released as the b-side of the sugary narration 'To A Sleeping Beauty' it gave the single double-sided chart success. His hits also included 'P.T.109', a song devoted to the wartime career of John F. Kennedy. Several other b-sides also proved popular with the record buying public including the amusing 'I Won't Go Huntin' With You, Jake' and 'Please Pass The Biscuits'. From 1963-66, he hosted a new show on the ABC-TV network and was much in demand for appearances on other major shows. He had another number 1 country hit with 'The First Thing Every Morning (And The Last Thing Every Night)' in 1965 and the following year, after moving to RCA, charted with 'Stand Beside Me'. Some further hits followed, including 'A Thing Called Love' but during the 70s, his career slowed down as he concentrated on his pork sausage manufacturing business. Notable among his later hits were a duet with Dottie West on Webb Pierce's 'Slowly' and a crossover country and pop hit narration called 'I.O.U', which he claimed was his ode of thanks to his mother. This was equally as sugary as his new version of 'To A Sleeping Beauty', both of which he made for Casino. A further recording of 'I.O.U', this time for Churchill in 1983, marked his 26th and last country chart entry. In the 80s, he still maintained some television and show appearances though it has been suggested that he preferred a string of sausages to a string of hits. Throughout his career, his easy-going, crooning style and presentation managed to bridge the gap between pop and country music more successfully than many other artists ever managed, and his television shows certainly provided a shop window for many artists as well as generating interest in country music.

Albums: *Sings His Television Favorites* (1957), *Hour Of Prayer* (1957), *Hymns* (1960), *Big Bad John (& Other Fabulous Songs & Tales)* (1961), *Favorites Of Jimmy Dean* (1961), *Portrait Of Jimmy Dean* (1962), *Everybody's Favorite* (1963), *The Songs We All Love The Best* (1964), *Jimmy Dean's Hour Of Prayer* (1964), *The First Thing Every Morning* (1965), *Jimmy Dean's Christmas Card* (1965), *Golden Favorites* (1965), with Johnny Horton *Bumming Around* (1965), *Sings The Big Ones* (1966), *Most Richly Blessed (& Other Great Inspirational Songs)* (1967), *Jimmy Dean Is Here* (1967), *Mr Country Music* (1967), *A Thing Called Love* (1968), *Speaker Of The House* (1967), *The Jimmy Dean Show* (1968), *Country's Favorite Son* (1968), *Dean's List* (1968), *Speaker Of The House* (1968), *Gotta Travel On* (1969), with Dottie West *Country Boy & Country Girl* (1970), *The Dean Of Country Music* (1970), *These Hands* (1971), *Everybody Knows* (1971), *Jimmy Dean I.O.U.* (1976), *I.O.U. (Mom, I Love You)* (1977), *Straight From The Heart* (1982).

DeHaven, Penny

b. Charlotte DeHaven, 17 May 1948, Winchester, Virginia, USA. Relocated to Berkeley Springs, West Virginia in 1956 and was appearing at local venues before she had completed high school. In 1966, using the name Penny Starr, she sang on *Jamboree USA* and gained a minor US country hit in 1967 on Band Box with 'Grain Of Salt'. In 1967, with a name change to Penny DeHaven, she became one of the first female country singers to entertain the troops in Vietnam. Between 1969 and 1974 recording for Imperial or United Artists, she registered 12 further hits including a solo version of the Beatles' 'I Feel Fine' and a Top 20 duet hit with Del Reeves with 'Land Mark Tavern'. She has appeared in several films, including *Country Music Story* and *Traveling Light*. She played a dramatic role in Clint Eastwood's *Honky Tonk Man* and also sang on the soundtrack of *Bronco Billy*. She also recorded duets with Buddy Cagle and charted in 1982 with 'We Made Memories' with Boxcar Willie. Though established on the contemporary Nashville scene, she is still looking for a major hit. Albums: *Penny DeHaven* (1972), *Penny DeHaven* (1984).

Delmore Brothers

Alton (b. 25 December 1908, Elkmont, Limestone County, Alabama, USA, d. 9 June 1964, Huntsville, USA; guitar) and Rabon (b. 3 December 1916, also Elkmont, d. 4 December 1952, Athens, Alabama, USA; fiddle/four-string tenor guitar) were two of the many children born to Charles and Mary Delmore, who, like many others of their day, struggled to make a living from a little dirt farm. The boys developed an interest in gospel music, and by 1926 they were singing harmonies and playing instruments. In 1931, they recorded for US Columbia. Two years later they secured a regular 15-minute slot on the *Grand Ole Opry* and played ragtime guitar in a style similar to Blind Boy Fuller's. Between 1933 and 1940, they recorded over 100 tracks for RCA Victor and also accompanied Arthur Smith and Uncle Dave Macon. 'Brown's Ferry Blues' from the first session was so popular that they recorded 'Brown's Ferry Blues, Part 2'. Alton sang lead to Rabon's harmony but sometimes they switched parts in mid-song. Their constant touring took its toll as both brothers drank heavily and Alton suffered from depression. They left the *Opry* in 1938 and moved to North Carolina and then Birmingham, Alabama, but they kept touring. The Delmore Brothers recorded for US Decca during 1940-41 including 'When It's Time For The Whipoorwill To Sing'. They stopped touring as a result of petrol rationing during the war, and teamed up with Grandpa Jones and Merle Travis for radio appearances and later records as the Brown's Ferry Four. In 1944 the Delmore Brothers recorded 'Prisoner's Farewell'/'Sweet Sweet Thing', both written by Jim Scott, one of Alton's pseudonyms, for the new King label, and then had major successes with 'Hillbilly Boogie', 'Freight Train Boogie' and, in particular, 'Blues Stay Away From Me'. Their lonesome sound, helped by Wayne Raney and Lonnie Glossom's harmonicas, created both a classic blues and a classic country record. The Delmore Brothers hit a stormy patch in Houston in the early 50s as Alton suffered a heart attack, lost his daughter and drank even more heavily; their father died; and Rabon's marriage fell apart. He moved to Detroit, while Alton stayed in Houston - managing a bar. In August 1952, with Rabon suffering from cancer, the Delmore Brothers made their final recordings for King in Cincinnati. Rabon died at his home in December 1952 and Alton, overcome by grief, moved to Huntsville and became a postman. He started teaching guitar and made his last record in 1956. In the early 60s, however, he worked with his son, Lionel, replacing Rabon and also wrote short stories. Alton died of liver disease in June 1964. The Delmore Brothers were elected to the Nashville Songwriters' Hall Of Fame in 1971, although, in actuality, Alton wrote 10 songs to each of Rabon's. Their close harmony work has been copied by numerous performers, notably Johnny and Dorsey Burnette and the Everly Brothers. Ray Sawyer of Dr. Hook, maintains, 'The Delmore Brothers were the first country-rockers. The licks in 'Blues Stay Away From Me' are the same as those in 'Ain't That A Shame'.'

Albums by the Delmore Brothers: *Songs By The Delmore Brothers* (1958), *The Delmore Brothers' 30th Anniversary Album* (1962), *In Memory* (1964), *In Memory, Volume 2* (1964), *24 Great Country Songs* (1966), *Best Of The Delmore Brothers* (1970), *The Delmore Brothers* (1979), *The Delmore Brothers, Volume 1* (1983), *The Delmore Brothers, Volume 2* (1984), *The Delmore Brothers, Volume 3* (1985). By the Brown's Ferry Four: *Sacred Songs* (1957), *Sacred Songs, Volume 2* (1958), *Wonderful Sacred Songs* (1965).

Further reading: *Truth Is Stranger Than Publicity*, Alton Delmore.

Denver, John

b. Henry John Deutschendorf Jnr., 31 December 1943, Roswell, New Mexico, USA. One of America's most popular performers during the 70s, Denver's rise to fame began when he was 'discovered' in a Los Angeles night club. He initially joined the Back Porch Majority, a nursery group for the renowned New Christy Minstrels but, tiring of his role there, left for the Chad Mitchell Trio where he forged a reputation as a talented songwriter.

With the departure of the last original member, the Mitchell Trio became known as Denver, Boise and Johnson, but their brief life-span ended when John embarked on a solo career in 1969. One of his compositions, 'Leaving On A Jet Plane', provided an international hit for Peter, Paul And Mary, and this evocative song was the highlight of Denver's debut album, *Rhymes And Reasons*. Subsequent releases, *Take Me To Tomorrow* and *Whose Garden Was This*, garnered some attention, but it was not until the release of *Poems, Prayers And Promises* that the singer enjoyed popular acclaim when one of its tracks, 'Take Me Home, Country Roads', broached the US Top 3 and became a UK Top 20 hit for Olivia Newton-John in 1973. The song's undemanding homeliness established a light, almost naive style, consolidated on the albums *Aerie* and *Rocky Mountain High*. 'I'd Rather Be A Cowboy' (1973) and 'Sunshine On My Shoulders' (1974) were both gold singles, while a third million-seller, 'Annie's Song', secured Denver's international status when it topped the UK charts that same year

John Denver

and subsequently became an MOR standard, as well as earning the classical flautist James Galway a UK number 3 hit in 1978. Further US chart success came in 1975 with two number 1 hits, 'Thank God I'm A Country Boy' and 'I'm Sorry'. Denver's status as an all-round entertainer was enhanced by many television spectaculars, including *Rocky Mountain Christmas*, and further gold-record awards for *An Evening With John Denver* and *Windsong*, ensuring that 1975 was the artist's most successful year to date.

He continued to enjoy a high profile throughout the rest of the decade and forged a concurrent acting career with his role in the film comedy *Oh, God* with George Burns. In 1981 his songwriting talent attracted the attention of yet another classically trained artist, when opera singer Placido Domingo duetted with Denver on 'Perhaps Love'. However, although Denver became an unofficial musical ambassador with tours to Russia and China, his recording became less prolific as increasingly he devoted time to charitable work and ecological interests. Despite the attacks by music critics, who have deemed his work as bland and saccharine, Denver's cute, simplistic approach has nonetheless achieved a mass popularity which is the envy of many artists.

Albums: *Rhymes & Reasons* (1969), *Take Me To Tomorrow* (1970), *Whose Garden Was This* (1970), *Poems, Prayers And Promises* (1971), *Aerie* (1971), *Rocky Mountain High* (1972), *Farewell Andromeda* (1973), *Back Home Again* (1974), *An Evening With John Denver* (1975), *Windsong* (1975), *Rocky Mountain Christmas* (1975), *Live In London* (1976), *Spirit* (1976), *I Want To Live* (1977), *Live At The Sydney Opera House* (1978), *John Denver* (1979), with the Muppets *A Christmas Together* (1979), *Autograph* (1980), *Some Days Are Diamonds* (1981), with Placido Domingo *Perhaps Love* (1981), *Seasons Of The Heart* (1982), *It's About Time* (1983), *Dreamland Express* (1985), *One World* (1986), *Higher Ground* (1988), *Stonehaven Sunrise* (1989), *The Flower That Shattered The Stone* (1990), *Earth Songs* (1990), *Different Directions* (1992). Compilations: *The Best Of John Denver* (1974), *The Best Of John Denver Volume 2* (1977), *The John Denver Collection* (1984), *Greatest Hits Volume 3* (1985).

Further reading: *The Man And His Music*, Leonore Fleischer. *Rocky Mountain Wonderboy*, James M. Martin.

Desert Rose Band

Formed in the mid-80s, the Desert Rose Band were akin to a mini-supergroup of country rock musicians. Lead vocalist and guitarist Chris Hillman was formerly a member of the Byrds, the Flying

Desert Rose Band

Burrito Brothers, Manassas, the Souther, Hillman, Furay Band and McGuinn, Clark & Hillman; Herb Pedersen (vocals/guitar) was one of the most famous session players on the country scene and a former member of the Dillards and Country Gazette; Bill Bryson (vocals/bass) was another Country Gazette alumnus and had also played in the Bluegrass Cardinals, as well as working on various movie soundtracks; Jay Dee Maness was one of the world's most famous pedal-steel guitarists, and among his past credentials were appearances with Gram Parsons' International Submarine Band, the Byrds and Buck Owens' Buckaroos; John Jorgenson, who played guitar, mandolin and six-string bass was the 'wunderkind' of the outfit; while Steve Duncan had drummed behind several new country artists, including Dwight Yokam. The group were eventually signed to the independent Curb Records by Dick Whitehouse, and their highly accomplished self-titled first album appeared in 1987. Among its delights was a highly effective reworking of 'Time Between', previously recorded by Hillman on the Byrds' *Younger Than Yesterday*. The follow-up *Running* was another strong work, particularly the title track, which dealt with the suicide of Hillman's father, a matter never previously mentioned in any interview. By the end of the 80s, the band were touring extensively and registering regular hits in the country charts. A third album, *Pages Of Life*, consolidated their position, and featured the memorable anti-drugs song, 'Darkness On The Playground'. In 1991, Jay Dee Maness left the group to be replaced by Tom Brumley, formerly of Rick Nelson's Stone Canyon Band.

The departure of Maness made little difference to the Desert Rose Band's sound, but John Jorgenson's decision the following year to pursue a solo career threatened the group's momentum. He was replaced by Jeff Ross (formerly with Los Angeles cow-punk band Rank & File), who brought a harsher, rock-flavoured edge to the Desert Rose Band's live show.

Albums: *The Desert Rose Band* (1987), *Running* (1988), *Pages Of Life* (1990), *True Love* (1991). Compilation: *A Dozen Roses* (1991).

Dexter, Al

b. Albert Poindexter, 4 May 1902, Jacksonville, Cherokee County, Texas, USA, d. 28 January 1984, Lewisville, Texas, USA. Multi-instrumentalist, singer and songwriter, Dexter made his first public performances at local dances and church functions. In the early 30s, he formed several bands, the first, a rarity for a white musician in Texas, consisted of all coloured musicians, when he had problems getting white musicians to play his music. This band proved very successful, but he is best remembered for his Texas Troopers; all bands played smooth western swing and honky tonk behind Dexter's vocals. He made his first recordings such as 'New Jelly Roll Blues' for Vocalion in 1935, and his 1937 'Honky Tonk Blues' is the first country song to have honky tonk in the title. Dexter gained his experience in the east Texas dancehalls, and many of his songs show the influence in their content. In 1943, his OKeh recording of the self-penned 'Pistol Packin' Mama' became a million selling number 1 song on both the US pop and country charts. (A pop version by Bing Crosby and the Andrews Sisters also became a million seller and later a rock 'n' roll version by Gene Vincent also proved successful). Based on an event that occurred when he owned a honky tonk in Turnertown, Texas, and played in polka time, the song made Dexter a wealthy man. During the next four years, recording on OKeh or Columbia Records, he had further number 1 country hits with 'Rosalita', 'So Long Pal', 'Too Late To Worry, Too Blue To Cry', 'I'm Losing My Mind Over You', 'Guitar Polka' and 'Wine, Women And Song'. These, plus eight other Top 10 hits, made him one of the most popular artists of the 40s. He opened his own Bridgeport Club in Dallas in the 50s and, apart from singing there, retired from entertaining. He eventually went into the property business and also bought a motel in Lufkin. In 1971 he was elected to the Nashville Songwriters' Association International Hall Of Fame. Dexter died in January 1984.

Albums: *Songs Of The Southwest* (1954, 10-inch album), *Pistol Packin' Mama* (1961), *Sings And Plays His Greatest Hits* (1962), *The Original Pistol Packin' Mama* (1968).

Dickens, Little Jimmy

b. James Cecil Dickens, 19 December 1920, Bolt, West Virginia, USA. Dickens has summarized his early life as the youngest of 13 children in humorous country songs such as 'A-Sleeping At The Foot Of The Bed' and 'Out Behind The Barn'. He had no intention of following his father into the coal mines, and being 4 feet 11 inches effectively ruled it out. When he was aged 17, he played guitar and sang on local radio with Johnny Bailes And His Happy Valley Boys as 'The Singing Midget' and 'Jimmy the Kid'. Dickens then worked with T. Texas Tyler but when Tyler

Little Jimmy Dickens

joined the forces, he worked in his own right, being spotted in Saginaw, Michigan by Roy Acuff. Acuff arranged a contract with US Columbia Records in 1948 and he recorded several songs including 'Country Boy' and 'Take An Old Cold Tater And Wait'. His 1950 recording, 'Hillbilly Fever', is a foretaste of rockabilly. He toured Germany with Hank Williams and he helped a young Marty Robbins to get started. In 1964, Dickens claimed to be the first country artist to circle the globe on a world tour. He achieved a crossover hit in 1965 with 'May The Bird Of Paradise Fly Up Your Nose', his only US country number 1. Dressed in colourful cowboy suits, he summarized himself in 'I'm Little But I'm Loud', and June Carter described him as 'Mighty Mouse in his pyjamas'. Despite being associated with comedy material, he also recorded quavering versions of country weepies such as 'Life Turned Her That Way', 'Just When I Needed You' and 'Shopping For Dresses', and made two religious albums. He has been a regular member of the *Grand Ole Opry* from 1949-57 and from 1975 onwards. Dickens was elected to the Country Music Hall of Fame in October 1983, and in his acceptance speech, he said, 'I want to thank Mr. Acuff for his faith in me years ago.'

Albums: *Old Country Church* (1954), *Raisin' The Dickens* (1954), *Big Songs By Little Jimmy Dickens* (1960), *Little Jimmy Dickens Sings Out Behind The Barn* (1962), *Jimmy Dickens' Best* (1964), *Handle With Care* (1965), *Alone With God* (1965), *May The Bird Of Paradise Fly Up Your Nose* (1965), *Ain't It Fun* (1967), *Big Man In Country Music* (1968), *Jimmy Dickens Comes Callin'* (1968), *Greatest Hits* (1969), *Jimmy Dickens Sings* (1969), *Hymns By The Hour* (1975), *Little Jimmy Dickens* (1984), *Country Music Hall Of Fame* (1984).

Dillard And Clark

Refugees from the Dillards and the Byrds, respectively, Doug Dillard (b. 6 March 1937) and Gene Clark (b. Harold Eugene Clark, 17 November 1941, Tipton, Missouri, USA, d. 24 May 1991) joined forces in 1968 to form one of the first country rock groups. Backed by the Expedition featuring Bernie Leadon (banjo/guitar), Don Beck (dobro/mandolin) and David Jackson (string bass), they recorded two albums for A&M Records, which confirmed their standing among the best of the early country rock exponents. *The Fantastic Expedition Of Dillard And Clark* featured several strong compositions by Clark and Leadon including 'The Radio Song', 'Out On The Side', 'Something's Wrong' and 'Train Leaves Here This Mornin''. Leadon later took the latter to his next group, the Eagles, who included the song on their debut album. By the time of their second album, Dillard and Clark displayed a stronger country influence with the induction of Flying Burrito Brothers drummer Jon Corneal, champion fiddle player Byron Berline and additional vocalist Donna Washburn. *Through The Morning, Through The Night* combined country standards with Clark originals and featured some sumptuous duets between Gene and Donna which pre-empted the work of Gram Parsons and Emmylou Harris. Although the Expedition experiment showed considerable promise, the group scattered in various directions at the end of the 60s, with Clark reverting to a solo career.

Albums: *The Fantastic Expedition Of Dillard And Clark* (1968), *Through The Morning, Through The Night* (1969).

Dillards

Brothers Rodney (b. 18 May 1942, East St. Louis, Illinois, USA; guitar/vocals) and Doug Dillard (b. 6 March 1937, East St. Louis, Illinois, USA; banjo/vocals) formed this seminal bluegrass group in Salem, Missouri, USA. Roy Dean Webb (b. 28 March 1937, Independence, Missouri, USA; mandolin/vocals) and former radio announcer Mitch Jayne (b. of May 1930, Hammond, Indiana, USA; bass) completed the original line-up which, having enjoyed popularity throughout their home state, travelled to Los Angeles in 1962 where they secured a recording deal with the renowned Elektra label. *Back Porch Bluegrass* and *The Dillards Live! Almost!* established the unit as one of America's leading traditional acts, although purists denigrated a sometimes irreverent attitude. *Pickin' & Fiddlin'*, a collaboration with violinist Byron Berline, was recorded to placate such criticism. The Dillards shared management with the Byrds and, whereas their distinctive harmonies proved influential to the latter group's development, the former act then began embracing a pop-based perspective. Dewey Martin (b. 30 September 1942, Chesterville, Ontario, Canada), later of Buffalo Springfield, added drums on a folk-rock demo which in turn led to a brace of singles recorded for the Capitol label. Doug Dillard was unhappy with this new direction and left to form a duo with ex-Byrd Gene Clark. Herb Peterson joined the Dillards in 1968 and, having resigned with Elektra,

Dillards

the reshaped quartet completed two exceptional country-rock sets, *Wheatstraw Suite* and *Copperfields*. The newcomer was in turn replaced by Billy Rae Latham for *Roots And Branches*, on which the unit's transformation to full-scale electric instruments was complete. A full-time drummer, Paul York, was now featured in the line-up, but further changes were wrought when founder member Jayne dropped out following *Tribute To The American Duck*. Rodney Dillard has since remained at the helm of a capricious act, which by the end of the 70s, returned to the traditional music circuit through the auspices of the respected Flying Fish label. He was also reunited with his prodigal brother in Dillard-Hartford-Dillard, an occasional sideline, which also featured multi-instrumentalist John Hartford.

Albums: *Back Porch Bluegrass* (1963), *The Dillards Live! Almost!* (1964), *Pickin' & Fiddlin'* (1965), *Wheatstraw Suite* (1969), *Copperfields* (1970), *Roots And Branches* (1972), *Tribute To The American Duck* (1973), *The Dillards Versus The Incredible LA Time Machine* (1977), *Mountain Rock* (1978), *Decade Waltz* (1979), *Homecoming & Family Reunion* (1979), *Let It Fly* (1991). Compilations: *Country Tracks* (1974), *I'll Fly Away* (1988).

Dillon, Dean

b. 26 March 1955, Lake City, Knoxville, Tennessee, USA. Dillon, a self-confessed victim of alcohol and substance abuse, started writing songs in the early 70s, when he appeared on a local television show. He subsequently moved to Nashville and eventually worked at Opryland Theme Park for four years as a member of the Mac McGahey quartet (McGahey had previously worked as Porter Wagoner's fiddle player for many years), with Barry Moore (bass) and Mark Barnett (banjo). This group made an obscure independent label album, *Rise And Shine*, primarily for sale at gigs. By the mid-70s, Dillon had been signed to a songwriting contract. His first big hit as a writer came in 1979 with 'Lying In Love With You', which he co-wrote with Gary Harrison and which was a Top 3 US country hit for Jim Ed Brown and Helen Cornelius. He enjoyed eight minor US country hits between 1979 and 1983, and continued to write hits for others such as 'Tennessee Whisky' for George Jones (Top 3 country, 1983) and 'Leave Them Boys Alone' for Hank Williams Jnr. (Top 10, 1983). In 1982 Dillon teamed up with singer/songwriter Gary Stewart (both were signed to RCA at the time), and the duo recorded two albums - one of which was titled

Brotherly Love - and a handful of minor hit singles - Dillon later described the partnership as 'the biggest mistake either of us could ever have made'. However, by the time the duo dissolved, Dillon had written a number of hits in partnership with other Nashville writers such as Paul Overstreet, Buzz Rabin, Randy Scraggs and especially Hank Cochran and Frank Dyeas. Many of these songs became big hits for country superstar George Strait, including such country chart-toppers as 'The Chair' (1985), 'Nobody In His Right Mind Would've Left Her' and 'It Ain't Cool To Be Crazy About You' (both 1986), 'Ocean Front Property' (1987) and 'Famous Last Words Of A Fool' (1988). These successes led to a new recording contract for Dillon with Capitol Records, which resulted in two albums produced by Randy Scruggs, *Slick Nickel* (1988) and *I've Learned To Live* (1989), which included a duet with Tanya Tucker. By 1991, he had also released another album, *Out Of Your Ever Lovin' Mind*, but he remains more successful as a songwriter than as an artist.

Albums: with Gary Stewart *Brotherly Love* (1982), *Slick Nickel* (1988), *I've Learned To Live* (1989), *Out Of Your Ever Lovin' Mind* (1991).

Dobson, Richard

b. 19 March 1942, Tyler, Texas, USA. Dobson planned to be a novelist and he only took up the guitar and started songwriting in 1963. He played in Texas folk clubs alongside Guy Clark and Townes Van Zandt, but a meeting with David Allan Coe's band outside a Nashville recording studio led to Coe immediately recording 'Piece Of Wood And Steel'. With the money he saved from working on shrimpers and oil rigs, Dobson was able to finance his highly rated debut, *In Texas Last December*. The album included 'Baby Ride Easy', which was recorded as a duet by Carlene Carter and Dave Edmunds. Dobson wrote regularly for the UK fanzine, *Omaha Rainbow*, and his novel, *Seasons And Companions*, has been published. Nanci Griffith, who recorded his song 'The Ballad Of Robin Wintersmith', calls him 'the Hemingway of country music', but he has not been able to expand his following. His best-known song is 'Old Friends', which he wrote with Guy and Susanna Clark, and which was used as the title track of Clark's 1988 album.

Albums: *In Texas Last December* (1976), *The Big Taste* (1978), *Save The World* (1982), *True West* (1986), *State Of The Heart* (1988), *Hearts And Rivers* (1989).

Dottsy

b. Dottsy Brodt, 6 April 1954, Sequin, near San Antonio, Texas, USA. In 1966, at the age of 12, she was already singing in clubs in her local area as part of a trio. She reached the finals of a major talent competition on KBER San Antonio in 1969 and appeared on television in her own show. In 1972, she began to study special education (for teaching handicapped or subnormal children) at the University of Texas, and for some time, she managed to combine her singing with her studies, even forming her own band, Meadow Muffin. While singing at a convention in San Antonio, she came to the attention of Happy Shahan, who gave her the chance to appear at major events with Johnny Rodriguez and helped her to get a contract with RCA. Her first single, 'Storms Never Last', written by Jessi Colter became a Top 20 US country chart hit in 1975 and was quickly followed by Susanna Clark's 'I'll Be Your San Antone Rose'. In the late 70s, she had further hits, including a Top 10 with '(After Sweet Memories) Play Born To Lose Again'. In 1979, Waylon Jennings played guitar and added harmony vocals to Dottsy's lead when she recorded his song, 'Trying To Satisfy You' - the result, not surprisingly, being another Top 20 hit for her. When it appeared that she would go on to major stardom, she decided to cut back on her singing and concentrate on completing her college education. She had always wanted to work with autistic and mentally retarded children, and by the early 80s was fully involved in this type of work. Her last chart entry, at the time of writing, was a 1981 minor hit on Tanglewood Records with the somewhat descriptive and suitable title 'Let The Little Bird Fly'.

Albums: *The Sweetest Thing* (1976), *Trying To Satisfy You* (1979).

Drake, Pete

b. 8 October 1932, Atlanta, Georgia, USA, d. 29 July 1988. One of the world's leading exponents of the steel guitar, Drake arrived in Nashville in the late 50s and was quickly established as one of the city's leading session musicians. His distinctive, mellow-toned style was heard on many releases, including those by Marty Robbins and Don Gibson. Pete also recorded in his own right and while billed as Pete Drake And His Talking Steel Guitar, he secured a US Top 30 hit with a 1964 single, 'Forever'. However, it was for continued studio work that Drake maintained his popularity, and he crossed over into the wider rock fraternity in the wake of his contributions to three Bob Dylan albums, *John Wesley Harding*, *Nashville Skyline* and *Self Portrait*, and to George Harrison's *All Things Must Pass*. The artist also produced Ringo Starr's C&W collection, *Beaucoups Of Blues*, and assembled the stellar cast supporting the former Beatles' drummer. During the 70s Drake appeared on albums by several 'new' country acts, including Linda Hargrove, Steve Young and Tracy Nelson, as well as completing sessions for Elvis Presley. This respected musician also inaugurated his own label, Stop Records, and opened Pete's Place, a recording studio. Drake died in July 1988 aged 55.

Albums: *Talking Steel And Singing Strings Forever* (1964), *Talking Steel Singing* (1965), *Pete Drake And His Talking Steel Guitar* (1965), *The Hits I Played On* (1969), *Pete Drake Plays All Time Country Favourites* (early 70s), *Steel Away* (1973), *The Pete Drake Show* (1973), *Fabulous Steel Guitar* (mid-70s), *Amazing* (mid-70s).

Draper, Rusty

b. Farrell Draper, Kirksville, Missouri, USA. Draper entered show business at the age of 12, singing and playing his guitar on radio in Tulsa, Oklahoma. For the next five years, he worked on various stations including Des Moines, Iowa and Quincy, Illinois. He then became the Master of Ceremonies and vocalist at the Mel Hertz Club in San Francisco. He eventually moved to Hermie King's Rumpus Room in the same city, where he stayed for the next seven years. In 1953, his recording of 'Gambler's Guitar' reached number 6 on both the US country and pop charts and gave him his first million seller. A second gold record followed in 1955 for his version of 'Shifting Whispering Sands', which reached number 3 in the pop charts but surprisingly did not even make the country chart at all. (A cover version by Eamonn Andrews made the UK Top 20). During the 50s, he had further US Top 40 pop hits with 'Seventeen' (1955), 'Are You Satisfied' (1955), 'In The Middle Of The House' (1956) and a US cover version of the UK skiffle hit 'Freight Train' (1957). He did, however, have modest UK pop chart success in 1960 with his version of 'Muleskinner Blues', which peaked at number 39. In 1962, he joined Monument Records and made the US pop charts with 'Night Life' in 1963. He did not achieve further US country chart successes until the late 60s, when he had very minor hits with 'My Elusive Dreams', 'California Sunshine' and 'Buffalo Nickel'. 'Two Little Boys' gave him another minor US hit in 1970, the last for 10 years, when 'Harbour Lights', an unlikely country song, became his last chart entry. During his career, he has also played several acting roles, including appearances in some television western series such as *Rawhide* and *Laramie,* and stage musicals including *Oklahoma* and *Annie Get Your Gun.*

Albums: *Hits That Sold A Million* (1960), *Sing Along* (c.60s), *Country Classics* (1964), *Rusty Draper Plays Guitar* (1965), *Night Life* (1966), *Something Old Something New* (1969).

Drifting Cowboys

Country star Hank Williams had been using the name, the Drifting Cowboys, since the late 30s, and he employed an existing group, the Alabama Rhythm Boys, as the Drifting Cowboys in 1943. They only acquired consistency after Hank Williams appeared at the *Grand Ole Opry* in 1949 and realized the need for a permanent band. He employed Jerry Rivers (b. 25 August 1928, Miami, Florida, USA; fiddle), Bob McNett (b. 16 October 1925, Roaring Branch, Pennsylvania, USA; guitar), Hillous Butrum (b. 21 April 1928, Lafayette, Tennessee, USA; bass) and Don Helm (b. 28 February 1927, New Brockton, Alabama, USA; steel guitar). There were no drums, as the instrument was not favoured in country circles. In 1951, McNett and Butrum were replaced by Sammy Pruett, who had been in the Alabama Rhythm Boys with Helms, and Howard Watts,

respectively. Williams used the Drifting Cowboys on his sessions, sometimes augmenting the musicians with Chet Atkins. His simply-chorded songs did not need elaborate embellishment, and the Drifting Cowboys' backings perfectly complemented the material. The group disbanded after Williams' death, and Don Helms worked with the Wilburn Brothers and formed the powerful Wil-Helm Agency. Helms and Rivers also worked in Hank Williams Jnr.'s band, the Cheatin' Hearts. Rivers wrote a biography *Hank Williams - From Life To Legend* (Denver, 1967), which was updated in 1980. In 1976 the original line-up reformed for radio shows with compere Grant Turner and comedian the Duke of Paducah. They had a minor success with 'Rag Mop' and recorded a tribute to Hank Williams, 'If The Good Lord's Willing'. Hank Williams Jnr. and Don Helms recorded a duet, 'The Ballad Of Hank Williams', which was based on 'The Battle Of New Orleans' and indicated how volatile Williams was. The Drifting Cowboys first appeared in the UK in 1979 and have always been warmly received. In 1991 they appeared at London's Wembley country music festival with Hank Williams' illegitimate daughter, Jett Williams.

Albums: *We Remember Hank Williams* (1969), with Jim Owen *A Song For Us All - A Salute To Hank Williams* (1977), *The Drifting Cowboys' Tribute To Hank Williams* (1979), *Best Of Hank Williams'*

Drifting Cowboys

Original Drifting Cowboys (1979), *Classic Instrumentals* (1981), *One More Time Around* (1982).

Driftwood, Jimmy

b. James Morris, 20 June 1907, Mountain View, Arkansas, USA. His name first came to prominence as a result of the Johnny Horton recording of Driftwood's song, 'The Battle Of New Orleans' in 1959. The single made the top of both the USA pop and country charts, but only the Top 20 in the UK. Lonnie Donegan reached number 2 in the UK with the song in the same year. Driftwood himself had recorded a version of the song the previous year for RCA Victor. With a strong musical heritage Driftwood learned to play guitar, banjo and fiddle while still young. Picking up old songs from his grandparents, and other members of his family, he later travelled about collecting and recording songs. While still performing at folk festivals, Jimmy continued to teach during the 40s. With the 50s, came the growing folk boom, and he found himself reaching a wider audience. RCA signed him to record *Newly Discovered Early American Folk Songs*, which included the aforementioned 'Battle Of New Orleans'. While the song's popularity grew, Driftwood was working for the *Grand Ole Opry*, but left in order to work on a project to establish a cultural centre at his home in Mountain View. The aim was to preserve the Ozark Mountain peoples' heritage. Having later joined the Rackensack Folklore Society, he travelled the USA, talking at universities to pass on the importance of such a project. The first Arkansas Folk Festival, held in 1963, was successful and, in 1973, the cultural centre was established. One performer at such events organized by the Rackensack Folklore Society was Glenn Ohrlin.
Selected albums: *Newly Discovered Early American Folk Songs* (1958), *The Wilderness Road* (c.60s), *A Lesson In Folk Music* (c.60s), *Songs Of Billie Yank And Johnny Reb* (1961), Compilations: *Famous Country Music Makers* (c.70s), *Americana* (1991).

Drusky, Roy

b. Roy Frank Drusky, 22 June 1930, Atlanta, Georgia, USA. Drusky showed interest only in baseball during his childhood and high school days but after attending a Cleveland Indians training camp, decided against it for a career and in 1948, joined the navy. A country band on his ship gave him an interest in music, and when next on shore leave he bought a guitar and taught himself to play. In 1950, he left the navy, enrolled at Emory University to study veterinary medicine and sought singing work to pay for the course. He formed a country band called the Southern Ranch Boys and played daily on WEAS Decatur. He later left the university and became a disc jockey on WEAS, the resident singer in a local club and appeared on WLW-A television in Atlanta. In 1953, he recorded for Starday. A year later he left his band, moved as a DJ to KEVE Minneapolis, continued with club work, but concentrated more on songwriting. In 1958, his song 'Alone With You' became a number 1 US country hit for Faron Young and led to Drusky becoming a member of the *Grand Ole Opry*, even though he had no hit recordings of his own at the time. He moved to Nashville, signed for Decca and between 1960 and 1962 had Top 5 country hits with his own recordings of 'Another', 'Anymore' (both self-penned), 'Three Hearts In A Tangle' (also a US pop chart number 35) and 'Second Hand Rose'. He moved to Mercury in 1963 and over the next decade charted several Top 10 country hits including 'Peel Me A Nanner', 'Where The Blue And Lonely Go', 'Long Long Texas Road', 'All My Hard Times' and in 1965, scored a country number 1 with 'Yes, Mr Peters', a duet recording with Priscilla Mitchell. In 1966, he had Top 20 success with the original version of 'If The Whole World Stopped Loving', a song that gave Val Doonican a big number 3 pop hit in Britain the next year. He moved to Capitol Records in 1974, having a minor hit with Elton John's 'Dixie Lily' and then to Scorpion Records in 1977, achieving his last chart entry that year with 'Betty's Song'. In the mid-60s he made three appearances in country and western films, *Forty Acre Feud, The Golden Guitar* and *White Lightning Express*. (His recording of the soundtrack title song of the last charted in 1965). From the 60s to the early 80s, he toured extensively, played the *Opry* and became involved in production and publishing work as well as hosting his own network television programmes. He is a popular artist in Britain, where he has appeared several times, both on tour and at the Wembley Festival. His relaxed singing style has led to him being referred to as the Perry Como of country music. Many felt that, had he so wished and with the right material, he may well have been the person to assume the pop/country mantle left by Jim Reeves.
Albums: *Anymore With Roy Drusky* (1961), *It's My Way* (1962), *All Time Country Hits* (1964), *The Pick Of The Country* (1964), *Songs Of The Cities* (1964), *Yesterday's Gone* (1964), *Country Music All Around*

The World (1965), *Roy Drusky* (1965), *The Great Roy Drusky Sings* (1965), with Priscilla Mitchell *Love's Eternal Triangle* (1965), with Mitchell *Together Again* (1966), *Country Song Express* (1966), *In A New Dimension* (1966), *If The Whole World Stopped Lovin'* (1966), *Now Is A Lonely Time* (1967), with Mitchell *We Belong Together* (1968), *Jody And The Kid* (1969), *My Grass Is Green* (1969), *Portrait Of Roy Drusky* (1969), *Twenty Grand Country Hits* (double album 1969), *All My Hard Times* (1970), *Country Special* (1970), *I'll Make Amends* (1970), *I Love The Way That You've Been Loving Me* (1971), *Doin' Something Right* (1972), *Good Times, Hard Times* (1973), *Peaceful Easy Feeling* (1974), *Night Flying* (1976), *This Life Of Mine* (1976), *Golden Hits* (1979), *English Gold* (1980), *Roy* (1981).

Dudley, Dave

b. David Pedruska, 3 May 1928, Spencer, Wisconsin, USA. In 1950, after an arm injury had ruined a baseball career, Dudley turned to performing country music. Following successful broadcasts in Idaho, he formed the Dave Dudley Trio in 1953. In 1960, Dudley was struck by a car while packing equipment, and spent several months in hospital. He had his first US country successes, 'Maybe I Do' and 'Under The Cover Of Night', and, also in 1961, he reluctantly recorded the up-tempo 'Six Days On The Road' to please a friend. In 1963 he released it on his own Golden Wing label and it reached number 32 in the US pop charts. The song spawned a new genre of songs about truckers, usually depicting them as hard-living, hard-loving macho men. Dudley declares 'I like my woman everywhere I go' in 'Truck Drivin' Son-Of-A-Gun'. Dudley's numerous trucking songs include 'Two Six Packs Away', 'There Ain't No Easy Run', 'One More Mile', 'The Original Travelling Man', 'Trucker's Prayer' and 'Truck Driver's Waltz', many of them being written by, and sometimes with, Tom T. Hall. In 1970, Dudley had a number 1 country hit with 'The Pool Shark' and recorded a duet with Hall, 'Day Drinkin''. He recorded for Sun Records in 1980 and had some success with 'Rolaids, Doan's Pills And Preparation H'. His comedy single, 'Where's That Truck?', with the truckers' favourite disc jockey, Charlie Douglas, did not revive his career, and it seems doubtful that he will get his trucks back on the chart highway again.
Albums: *Six Days On The Road* (1963), *Songs About The Working Man* (1964), *Travelling With Dave Dudley* (1964), *Talk Of The Town* (1964), *Rural Route No. 1* (1965), *Truck Drivin' Son-Of-A-Gun* (1965), *Free And Easy* (1966), *There's A Star Spangled Banner Waving Somewhere* (1966), *Lonelyville* (1966), *My Kind Of Love* (1967), *Dave Dudley Country* (1967), *Oh Lonesome Me/Seven Lonely Days* (1968), *Thanks For All The Miles* (1968), *One More Mile* (1969), *George And The North Woods* (1969), *It's My Lazy Day* (1969), *Pool Shark* (1970), *Will The Real Dave Dudley Please Sing?* (1971), *Listen, Betty, I'm Singing Your Song* (1971), *The Original Travelling Man* (1972), *Keep On Truckin'* (1973), *Special Delivery* (1975), *Uncommonly Good Country* (1975), *1776* (1976), *Chrome And Polish* (1978), *Interstate Gold* (1980), with Charlie Douglas *Diesel Duets* (1980), *King Of The Road* (1981).

Duncan, Johnny

b. 5 October 1938, Dublin, Texas, USA. Duncan, was born on a farm, into a music-loving family. His cousins were Dan (of England Dan And John Ford Coley) and Jimmy Seals (of Seals And Croft). Duncan thought of himself as a guitarist, and it was not until his late teens that he appreciated his singing voice. Shortly after his marriage in 1959, Duncan moved to Clovis, New Mexico and recorded demos for Norman Petty, although nothing evolved. In 1964, following a stint as a disc jockey in the southwest, he went to Nashville, working as a bricklayer while trying to break into the business. He was signed to Columbia Records and had his first US country chart entry with 'Hard Luck Joe' in 1967. Minor successes followed with 'To My Sorrow', 'You're Gonna Need Me' and 'When She Touches Me'. He also made the charts with two duets with June Stearns, 'Jackson Ain't A Very Big Town' and 'Back To Back (We're Strangers)'. He became part of Charley Pride's roadshow and wrote 'I'd Rather Lose You' for him. Chet Atkins recorded another of his compositions, 'Summer Sunday'. He had further success with 'There's Something About A Lady' and 'Baby's Smile, Woman's Kiss' and his first US country Top 10 hit with 'Sweet Country Woman' in 1973. Duncan lost interest in country music, partly caused by his marriage breaking up, and he returned to Texas. Larry Gatlin contacted him and said, 'John, apart from Ray Price and myself, you're the best singer in Texas. Why aren't you making records?' Gatlin produced Duncan on 'Jo And The Cowboy', and, on a hunch, he asked one of the Lea Jane Singers to sing a verse. Janie Frickie then became the 'mystery voice' on Duncan's following successes, finally sharing the billing on

'Come A Little Bit Closer'. Producer Billy Sherrill wanted Duncan relaxed for 'Stranger' and sent him to a bar for two hours. The bar-room song, which featured Frickie, was a number 4 country hit. Duncan's forte was plain-speaking songs about sleazy affairs such as 'Thinking Of A Rendezvous', 'It Couldn't Have Been Any Better' (both US country number 1's), 'Third Rate Romance' and 'Cheatin' In The Key Of C'. Apart from his records with Frickie, he had country hits with 'She Can Put Her Shoes Under My Bed (Anytime)', 'Hello Mexico (And Adios Baby To You)' and 'Slow Dancing'. Duncan's luck faltered with an album called *The Best Is Yet To Come*. In the 80s he remarried and settled in Texas with his new wife and family and now records for minor labels. His latest chart entry was in 1986 with 'Texas Moon'.

Albums: *Johnny One Time* (1968), with June Stearns *Back To Back* (1969), *There's Something About A Lady* (1971), *Sweet Country Woman* (1973), *Johnny Duncan* (1977), *Come A Little Bit Closer* (1977), *The Best Is Yet To Come* (1978), *See You When The Sun Goes Down* (1979), *Straight From Texas* (1979), with Janie Frickie, Millie Kirkham And the Jordanaires *In My Dreams* (1980), *You're On My Mind* (1980), with Janie Frickie *Nice 'N' Easy* (1980).

Duncan, Johnny, And The Blue Grass Boys

b. John Franklin Duncan, 7 September 1931, Oliver Springs, near Knoxville, Tennessee, USA. Duncan sang from an early age in a church choir and then, when aged 13, he joined a gospel quartet. At 16, he left Tennessee for Texas and whilst there, he formed a country group. Duncan was conscripted into the US army in 1952 and posted to England. He married an English woman, Betty, in 1953. After his demobilization, they went to the USA. Betty returned home for Christmas 1955 and, as she fell ill and needed an operation, Duncan worked in the UK for his father-in-law. He met jazz bandleader Chris Barber, who was

Johnny Duncan with Wee Willie Harris and Cliff Richard

looking to replace Lonnie Donegan. Donegan had formed his own skiffle group, a fashion he had started with Barber's band. Barber was impressed by Duncan's nasal vocal delivery and physical resemblance to Donegan and immediately recruited him, and he joined them the following night at London's Royal Festival Hall. In 1957 Duncan left the band and called his own group, the Blue Grass Boys, in homage to Bill Monroe, but they were all British - Denny Wright (guitar), Jack Fallon (bass), Danny Levan (violin), Lennie Hastings (drums). Although promoted as a skiffle artist, Duncan was a straight country performer, both in terms of arrangements and repertoire. 'Last Train To San Fernando', a Trinidad calypso he re-arranged, steamed up the UK charts but the communication cord was pulled just before it reached the top. The b-side, 'Rock-A-Billy Baby', was equally strong. Duncan was featured on BBC television's *6.5 Special* and hosted radio programmes for the BBC and Radio Luxembourg, but he only had two more Top 30 entries, 'Blue Blue Heartache' and 'Footprints In The Snow', both reaching number 27. Duncan worked as a country singer in UK clubs and encouraged local talent. In 1974 he emigrated to Melbourne, Australia where he has worked as a country singer.
Albums: *Johnny Duncan's Tennessee Songbag* (1957), *Johnny Duncan Salutes Hank Williams* (1958), *Beyond The Sunset* (1961), *Back In Town* (1970), *The World Of Country Music* (1973).

Duncan, Tommy

b. Thomas Elmer Duncan, 11 January 1911, Hillsboro, Texas, USA, d. 25 July 1967. Duncan grew up loving the music of Jimmie Rodgers and made the start of a long musical career in 1932, when he joined Bob Wills in the Light Crust Doughboys. When Wills quit in 1933 to form his own band, Duncan went with him to become one of Wills' original Texas Playboys. He stayed with Wills until 1948, when probably tired of fronting the band in Wills' absences caused mainly by his drinking, he left to form his own band the Western All Stars, taking with him several Texas Playboys. During his years with Wills they co-wrote several songs and Duncan's fine baritone vocals appeared on countless recordings including the 1940 million-selling 'New San Antone Rose'. In 1949, recording for Capitol, he registered his only solo chart hit with his version of the Jimmie Rodgers' song 'Gambling Polka Dot Blues'. In 1959, Wills and Duncan were reunited and in 1960-61, they recorded over 40 sides for Liberty. Although he made no further recordings with Wills, Duncan remained active until his death following an heart attack in July 1967. It is impossible to separate the careers of Duncan and Wills and most experts have maintained that in their solo work, they never achieved the greatness of their partnership.
(See album listing under Bob Wills). Solo album: *For The Last Time* (recorded live at Riverside Ballroom, Phoenix, Arizona) (1984).

Dunn, Holly

b. Holly Suzette Dunn, 22 August 1957, San Antonio, Texas, USA. Dunn's father was a preacher and her mother a professional artist, but they encouraged their children to sing and entertain. Dunn learned guitar and became a lead vocalist with the Freedom Folk Singers, representing Texas in the White House bi-centennial celebrations. After university, she joined her brother, Chris Waters (Chris Waters Dunn), who had moved to Nashville as a songwriter. (He wrote 'Sexy Eyes' for Dr. Hook.) Together they wrote 'Out Of Sight, Not Out Of Mind' for Cristy Lane. Amongst her other songs are 'An Old Friend' (Terri Gibbs), 'Love Someone Like Me' (New Grass Revival), 'Mixed Emotions' (Bruce Murray, brother of Anne Murray) and 'That Old Devil Moon' (Marie Osmond). Dunn sang on numerous demos in Nashville. Her self-named album for the MTM label in 1986, and her own composition 'Daddy's Hands', drew considerable attention. *Across The Rio Grande*, was a traditional yet contemporary country album featuring Vince Gill and Sam Bush and it won much acclaim. However, MTM went into liquidation and Dunn moved to Warners. Her up-tempo 'You Really Had Me Going' was a country number 1 and other country hits include 'Only When I Love', 'Strangers Again' and 'That's What Your Love Does To Me'. Her 'greatest hits' set, *Milestones*, aroused some controversy when she issued one of its tracks, the newly-recorded 'Maybe I Mean Yes', as a single. The song was accused of downplaying the trauma of date-rape, and Dunn was sufficently upset to ask radio stations not to play the record. Her career was restored to equilibrium with the low-key, but impressive *Getting It Dunn* in 1992. Dunn writes much of her own material and usually produces her albums with Chris Waters.
Albums: *Holly Dunn* (1986), *Cornerstone* (1987), *Across The Rio Grande* (1988), *The Blue Rose Of Texas* (1989), *Heart Full Of Love* (1990), *Milestones* (1991), *Getting It Dunn* (1992).

E

Eanes, Jim

b. Homer Robert Eanes Jnr, 23 December 1923, on a farm, near Martinsville, Virginia, USA. His early musical interest came from his father, a talented banjo player, who ran a local band. When only six-months-old, he suffered severe burns to his left hand that left the fingers twisted, but as a boy he developed a style of playing that, after an operation in 1937, enabled him to become a fine guitarist. He played in his father's band, appeared on local radio, where he acquired the name of Smilin' Jim Eanes (Homer seemed unsuitable) and in 1939, became the vocalist for Roy Hall's Blue Ridge Entertainers, until Hall's death in a car crash in 1943. Between 1945 and 1949, he worked with the Blue Mountain Boys on the *Tennessee Barn Dance* on WNOX Knoxville and recorded with them in New York. He briefly joined Lester Flatt and Earl Scruggs, when they formed their first Foggy Mountain Boys, before finally moving to Nashville to join Bill Monroe. He began to write songs during his time at Knoxville, the first being his now well known 'Baby Blue Eyes' and when, in 1949, he won a Capitol talent competition, it was one of the first songs he recorded. Another song, co-written at the same time with Arthur Q. Smith was 'Wedding Bells', which Eanes first sang on the *Barn Dance* in 1947. The song's ownership moved to Claude Boone, when it failed to raise interest with the listeners; he subsequently passed it on to Hank Williams, for whom it became a number 2 country hit. (Arthur Q. Smith, real name James A. Pritchett, wrote several songs which he sold to artists and Eanes assisted with some of them. Smith, who died in 1963, should not be confused with either Fiddlin' Arthur Smith or Arthur 'Guitar Boogie' Smith.) In 1951, Eanes formed his famous Shenandoah Valley Boys and recorded for Blue Ridge. He gained considerable success with the war song 'Missing In Action' (again co-written with Arthur Q. Smith), which seemingly sold in excess of 400,000 copies and led to him signing for Decca, where he recorded his popular 'I Cried Again', 'Rose Garden Waltz' and 'Little Brown Hand'. (The next year Ernest Tubb's Decca recording of 'Missing In Action' reached number 3 in the US country charts.) He moved to Starday in 1956, scoring with his own songs 'Your Old Standby' (recorded by George Jones on several occasions) and 'I Wouldn't Change You If I Could' (a number 1 US country hit for Ricky Skaggs in 1983.) He also made a recording of 'The Little Old Log Cabin In The Lane', which is rated by some as the best recorded version of this old song. Throughout the 60s and 70s, Eanes was occupied with performing, recording, songwriting and work on various radio stations including, in 1967, a spell on the *Wheeling Jamboree*. During the 70s, he was also much in demand as an MC for festivals and shows. In 1978, he suffered a severe heart attack but a year later made a European tour. (These tours were a regular occurrence and by 1990, he had completed nine and during one recorded an album with a Dutch country band.) He formed an outfit in 1984, underwent heart surgery in 1986 but as soon as possible was back entertaining and singing as always a mixture of bluegrass, gospel and country material. His fine vocals and songwriting over the years have earned Eanes the universal nickname of The Bluegrass Balladeer.

Albums: *Your Old Standby* (1967), *Jim Eanes With Red Smiley & The Bluegrass Cut-Ups* (c.1968), *Rural Rhythm Presents Jim Eanes* (c.1969), *Blue Grass Special BS2* (c.1970), *The New World Of Bluegrass* (1973), *The Shenandoah Valley Quartet With Jim Eanes* (c.1975), *Jim Eanes (Original) Shenandoah Valley Quartet* (1977), *A Statesman Of Bluegrass Music* (1977), *Where The Cool Waters Flow* (1978), *Jim Eanes & The Shenandoah Valley Boys (Early Days Of Bluegrass)* (1979), with Smoketown Strut *Ridin' The Roads* (1981), *Shenandoah Grass Yesterday And Today* (1983), *Bluegrass Ballads* (1986), *Jim Eanes, Bobby Atkins And The Countrymen* (1986), *Reminiscing* (1987), *Log Cabin In The Lane* (1988), *Let Him Lead You* (1989), *50th Anniversary Album* (1990).

Earle, Steve

b. 17 January 1955, Fort Monroe, Virginia, USA. Earle's father was an air traffic controller and the family was raised in San Antonio, Texas. Steve played an acoustic guitar from the age of ll, but he also terrorized his schoolfriends with a sawn-off shotgun. He left home many times and sang 'Help Me Make It Through The Night' and all that shit' in bars and coffee houses. He befriended Townes Van Zandt, whom he describes as a 'a real bad role model'. Earle married at the age of 19 but when his wife went with her parents to Mexico, he moved to Nashville, playing for tips and deciding to stay. He took several jobs to pay his way but they often

Steve Earle

ended in arguments and violence. Johnny Lee recorded one of Earle's songs, and Elvis Presley almost recorded 'Mustang Wine'. His second marriage was based, he says, 'on a mutual interest in drug abuse'. Earle formed a back-up band in Texas, the Dukes, and was signed to CBS, who subsequently released *Early Tracks*. Recognition came when he and the Dukes signed to MCA and made a famed 'New Country' album, *Guitar Town*, the term being the CB handle for Nashville. The title track, with its Duane Eddy-styled guitar riff, was a potent blend of country and rock 'n' roll. 'Good Ol' Boy (Gettin' Tough)' was Earle's response to President Reagan's firing of the striking air-traffic controllers, including Earle's brother. Like Bruce Springsteen, his songs often told of the restlessness of blue collar workers. 'Someday' is a cheerless example - 'There ain't a lot you can do in this town/You drive down to the lake and then you turn back around.' Earle wrote 'The Rain Came Down' for the Farm Aid II benefit, and 'Nothing But A Child' was for an organization to provide for homeless children. Waylon Jennings recorded 'The Devil's Right Hand' and Janie Frickie, 'My Old Friend The Blues'. Earle saw in the 1988 New Year in a Dallas jail for punching a policeman and during that year, he married his fifth wife and released an album with a heavy metal look, *Copperhead Road*, which included the Vietnam saga, 'Johnny Come Lately', which he recorded with the Pogues. His answering machine says, 'This is Steve. I'm out shooting heroin, chasing 13-year-old girls and beating up cops. But I'm old and I tire easily so leave a message and I'll get back to you.' Some of Earle's compositions are regarded as redneck anthems, but the views are not necessarily his own: he writes from the perspective of his creation, Bubba, the archetypal redneck. Another is The Beast - 'It's that unexplainable force that causes you to be depressed. As long as The Beast is there, I know I'll always write.' Albums: *Guitar Town* (1986), *Early Tracks* (1987), *Exit O* (1987), *Copperhead Road* (1988), *The Hard Way* (1990), *Shut Up And Die Like An Aviator* (1991), *BBC Radio 1 Live In Concert* (1992).

Edwards, Stoney

b. Frenchy Edwards, 24 December 1929, Seminole, Oklahoma, USA. Stoney grew up listening to country music, which was described in his 1973 song, 'Hank And Lefty Raised My Country Soul', and that honky tonk sound has remained with him throughout his career. He played guitar from the age of 15. He moved to California and had several manual jobs before becoming a club singer and, like Charley Pride before him, he was at first something of a novelty in Nashville - a black performer working in country music. He signed with Capitol Records in 1971 and had 15 chart singles including 'Poor Folks Stick Together', 'She's My Rock', 'Mississippi, You're On My Mind', and 'Blackbird (Hold Your Head High)'. He was dropped by Capitol in 1977 and he recorded for several smaller labels including the Music America release, 'No Way To Drown A Memory'. He lost a leg in a shooting accident and retired from the business. He returned in 1991 with an acclaimed new album, *Just For Old Times Sake*, which was produced and mostly written by Billy Joe Kirk and featured many top session musicians.
Albums: *Down Home In The Country* (1971), *Stoney Edwards, A Country Singer* (1972), *Stoney Edwards* (1973), *She's My Rock* (1973), *Mississippi, You're On My Mind* (1975), *Blackbird* (1976), *No Way To Drown A Memory* (1981), *Just For Old Time's Sake* (1991).

Elledge, Jimmy

b. 8 January 1943, Nashville, Tennessee, USA. When he was 18 years old, Jimmy Elledge sent a demo tape to famed country producer Chet Atkins, who signed him to RCA Victor Records. Elledge's debut single, the country ballad 'Funny How Time Slips Away' - produced by Atkins and written by soon-to-be country superstar Willie Nelson - reached the US Top 30 in early 1962 and earned him a gold disc for selling over a million copies. He later joined the Hickory label in the mid-60s but with no further US chart success.

Elliott, Ramblin' Jack

b. Elliott Charles Adnopoz, 1 August 1931, Brooklyn, New York, USA. The son of an eminent doctor, Elliott forsook his middle-class upbringing as a teenager to join a travelling rodeo. Embarrassed by his family name, he dubbed himself Buck Elliott, before adopting the less-mannered first name, Jack. In 1949 he met and befriended Woody Guthrie who in turn became his mentor and prime influence. Elliott travelled and sang with Guthrie whenever possible, before emerging as a talent in his own right. He spent a portion of the 50s in Europe, introducing America's folk heritage to a new and eager audience. By the early 60s he had resettled in New York where he became an inspirational figure to a new generation of performers, including Bob Dylan. *Jack Elliott Sings*

Ramblin' Jack Elliott

The Songs Of Woody Guthrie was the artist's first American album. This self-explanatory set was succeeded by *Ramblin' Jack Elliott*, in which he shook off the imitator tag by embracing a diverse selection of material, including songs drawn from the American tradition, the Scottish music-hall and Ray Charles. Further releases included *Jack Elliott*, which featured Dylan playing harmonica under the pseudonym, Tedham Porterhouse, and *Young Brigham* in 1968, which offered songs by Tim Hardin and the Rolling Stones as well as an adventurous use of dobros, autoharps, fiddles and tablas. The singer also guested on albums by Tom Rush, Phil Ochs and Johnny Cash. In 1975 Elliott was joined by Dylan during an appearance at the New York, Greenwich Village club, The Other End, and he then became a natural choice for Dylan's nostalgic, carnival tour, the Rolling Thunder Revue. Elliot later continued his erratic, but intriguing, path and an excellent 1984 release, *Kerouac's Last Dream*, shows his power undiminished.

Albums: *Jack Elliott Sings The Songs Of Woody Guthrie* (1960), *Ramblin' Jack Elliott* (1961), *Jack Elliott* (1964), *Ramblin' Cowboy* (mid-60s), *Young Brigham* (1968), *Jack Elliott Sings Guthrie And Rogers* (1976), *Kerouac's Last Dream* (1984). Compilations: *Talking Dust Bowl - The Best Of Ramblin' Jack Elliott* (1989), *Hard Travelin'* (1990)

Ely, Joe

b. 9 February, 1948, Amarillo Texas. Singer, songwriter, guitarist Ely, latterly regarded as the link between country/rock and so called new country, moved with his parents in 1958 to Lubbock, the major city of the flatlands of Texas from which such luminaries as Buddy Holly, Roy Orbison and Waylon Jennings had previously emerged. Ely formed his first band at the age of 13, playing a fusion of country and R&B, before dropping out of high school and following in the footsteps of Woody Guthrie and Jack Kerouac, hopping freight trains and working at a variety of non-musical jobs (including a spell with a circus) before finding himself stranded in New York with nothing but his guitar. He joined a theatrical company from Austin, Texas (where he now lives) and first got to travel to Europe with his theatrical employers in the early 70s before returning to Lubbock, where he teamed up with fellow singer-songwriters Jimmie Gilmore and George 'Butch' Hancock and a couple of other local musicians (including a musical saw player!) in an informal combo known as the Flatlanders. Although they were never immensely successful, the group did some recording in Nashville for Shelby Singleton's Plantation label, but only a couple of singles were released at the time. Later, when Ely was signed to MCA Records in the late 70s, the recordings by

Joe Ely

the Flatlanders, which had achieved legendary status, were anthologized on *One Road More*, an album which was first released by European label Charly Records in 1980, but did not appear in the US until the mid-80s. In 1976 Ely formed his own band, whose members included Jesse Taylor (guitar), Lloyd Maines (steel drum), Gregg Wright (bass) and Steve Keeton (drums) plus auxiliary picker Ponty Bone (accordion). This basic line-up recorded three albums for MCA *Joe Ely* (1977), *Honky Tonk Masquerade* (1978), and *Down On The Drag* (1979), before Keeton was replaced by Robert Marquam and Wright by Michael Robertson for *Musta Notta Gotta Lotta* (1981), which also featured Reese Wyhans (keyboards), among others. Although these albums were artistic successes, featuring great songs mainly written by Ely, Hancock (especially) and Gilmore, the musical tide of the times was inclined far more towards punk/new wave music than to Texan singer-songwriters.

In 1980, the Ely Band had toured extensively as opening act for the Clash, with whom Ely became very friendly, and *Live Shots* was released that year. The album featured Taylor, Marquam, Wright, Bone and Maines and was recorded on dates with the Clash, but was no more successful than the three studio albums which preceded it. In 1984 he recorded *Hi-Res*, which featured a completely new band of little known musicians, but was no more successful than the previous albums in commercial terms.

By 1987, Ely had assembled a new band which has largely remained with him to date: David Grisson (lead guitar), Jimmy Pettit (bass) and Davis McLarty (drums). This line-up recorded two artistically stunning albums for the US independent label Hightone, *Lord Of The Highway* (1987) and *Dig All Night* (1988), the latter featuring for the first time a repertoire totally composed of Ely's own songs. Both albums were licensed in the UK to Demon Records, and in the wake of this renewed interest, a tiny London label, Sunstorm Records launched by Pete O'Brien the editor of *Omaha Rainbow* fanzine, licensed two albums worth of Ely's early material. *Milkshakes And Malts*, a compilation of Ely's recordings of songs by Butch Hancock, appeared in 1988, and *Whatever Happened To Maria?*, which similarly compiled Ely's own self-penned songs, in 1989.

At this point, the band had been together for three years and had achieved an incredible on-stage empathy, especially between Ely and Grissom, whose R&B guitar work had moved the band's

music away from country. In 1990, they recorded a powerhouse live album in Austin, *Live At Liberty Lunch*, which was sufficiently impressive for Ely's old label, MCA, to re-sign him.

Among Ely's extra-curricular activities are contributions to the soundtrack of *Roadie*, a movie starring Meat Loaf, in which he can be heard playing 'Brainlock' and 'I Had My Hopes Up High', and his participation as a member of the *ad hoc* group, Buzzin Cousins, in which his colleagues are Mellencamp, John Prine, Dwight Yoakam and James McMurtry, on the soundtrack to the Mellencamp movie *Falling From Grace*. Joe Ely is one of the most completely realized artists in popular music in the 90s, especially in the live situation where he excels.

Albums: *Joe Ely* (1977), *Honky Tonk Masquerade* (1978), *Down On The Drag* (1979), *Live Shots* (1980), *One Road More* (1980), *Musta Notta Gotta Lotta* (1981), *Hi-Res* (1984), *Lord Of The Highway* (1987), *Dig All Night* (1988), *Milkshakes And Malts* (1988), *Whatever Happened To Maria* (1989), *Live At Liberty Lunch* (1990), *Love And Danger* (1992).

Emmons, Buddy

b. 27 January 1937, Mishawaka, Indiana, USA. A multi-instrumentalist and sometime singer, Emmons began playing the fiddle when he was 10 years old. Encouraged by his father, he switched to a lap-top steel guitar and then graduated to bigger models. However, he states, 'I wanted to be a boxer, but when I found out how easy it was to play and how hard it was to box, I changed my mind.' When only 18, he stepped in for Walter Haynes, steel guitarist with Little Jimmy Dickens, on a local date. As Haynes wanted to leave the band, Emmons took his place. In 1957, he and Shot Jackson built a steel guitar from scratch, the Sho-Bud, and Emmons subsequently gave his name to a steel guitar company. Emmons played with Ernest Tubb's Texas Troubadours (1957-1962) and Ray Price's Cherokee Cowboys (1962-1968), and he played on records by George Jones ('Seasons Of My Heart', 'Who Shot Sam?'), Ray Price ('Nightlife') and Faron Young ('Sweet Dreams'). He then moved to Los Angeles, played sessions for Linda Ronstadt and Henry Mancini, and became a king of the road with Roger Miller. In 1975 he returned to Nashville and established himself as a leading steel guitarist. He worked on albums by the Nashville Superpickers, and among his credits are the classic albums, *G.P.* (Gram Parsons), *John Phillips - The Wolfking Of L.A.*, *Now And Then* (the Carpenters) and *Who Knows Where*

The Time Goes? (Judy Collins). He has also worked on albums by Sandy Denny, Doug Dillard, Annette Funicello, Mickey Gilley, Arlo Guthrie, John Hartford, Albert Lee, Manhattan Transter, Rick Nelson, Willie Nelson, Mickey Newbury, Ricky Skaggs and John Stewart. Albums: with Shot Jackson *Steel Guitar And Dobro Sound* (1965), *Steel Guitar* (1975), *Buddy Emmons Sings Bob Wills* (1976), with Buddy Spicher *Buddies* (1977), with Lenny Breau *Minors Aloud* (1979), *First Flight* (1984), *Christmas Sounds Of The Steel Guitar* (1987).

England Dan And John Ford Coley

Dan Seals (b. 8 February 1950, McCamey, Texas, USA) comes from a family of performing Seals. His father played bass for many country stars (Ernest Tubb, Bob Wills) and his brother, Jimmy, was part of the Champs and then Seals And Croft. His cousins include 70s country star Johnny Duncan and songwriters Chuck Seals ('Crazy Arms') and Troy Seals. Seals formed a partnership with John Ford Coley (b. 13 October 1951) and they first worked as Southwest F.O.B., the initials representing Freight On Board. The ridiculous name did not last, but Jimmy, not wanting them to be called Seals And Coley, suggested England Dan And John Ford Coley. Their first albums for A&M sold moderately well, but they struck gold in 1976 with a move to Big Tree Records. The single, 'I'd Really Love To See You Tonight', went to number 2 in the US charts and also made the UK Top 30, although its hook owed something to James Taylor's 'Fire And Rain'. The resulting album, *Nights Are Forever*, was a big seller and the pair opted for a fuller sound which drew comparisons with the Eagles. The title track, 'Nights Are Forever Without You', was another Top 10 single. With their harmonies, acoustic-based songs and tuneful melodies, they appealed to the same market as the Eagles and, naturally, Seals And Croft. They had further US hits with 'It's Sad To Belong', 'Gone Too Far', 'We'll Never Have To Say Goodbye Again' and 'Love Is The Answer'. When the duo split, Seals, after a few setbacks, became a country star. Coley found a new partner, but their 1981 album, *Kelly Leslie And John Ford Coley*, was not a success. Albums: as Southwest F.O.B. *Smell Of Incense* (1968), *England Dan And John Ford Coley* (1971), *Fables* (1971), *I Hear The Music* (1976), *Nights Are Forever* (1976), *Dowdy Ferry Road* (1977), *Some Things Don't Come Easy* (1978), *Dr. Heckle And Mr. Jive* (1978), *Just Tell Me If You Love Me* (1980).

Everette, Leon

b. Leon Everette Baughman, 21 June 1948, South Carolina, USA. Everette was raised in New York and had no particular interest in country music as a child. In the US navy, he worked on an aircraft carrier in the Philippines. The servicemen passed the time by singing so he bought a guitar, learned by watching others and won a talent contest. Returning to South Carolina, he married, started a family and worked at the South Carolina Power and Gas Company. After an argument at work, Everette became a professional musician, working clubs in South Carolina and Georgia. He wanted success in Nashville and, in an extraordinary act of dedication, worked in the postal rooms of record companies while still playing in his home clubs. This involved commuting 500 miles a day! On top of this, he had to sleep and maintain a family life with his wife and three children. In 1977 the small True label gave Everette a chance - though not in the way he wanted. Within hours of Elvis Presley's death, Everette had recorded 'Goodbye King Of Rock And Roll'. Although True then wanted him to record some Elvis soundalikes, he was determined that he wanted to sing country and to be himself. After a small US country hit with 'I Love That Woman (Like The Devil Loves Sin)', a Florida businessman, Carroll Fulmer, formed a record label, Orlando, around him. He made the country charts with 'Giving Up Easy', 'Don't Feel like The Lone Ranger' and 'I Don't Want To Lose'. When Everette moved to RCA in 1980, he became more involved in the production of his own records. 'If I Keep On Going Crazy' with its distinctive harmonica made the USA country Top 20 and it was followed by the pile-driving 'Hurricane', which prompted him to change his band's name from Tender Loving Care to Hurricane. Everette himself is a hurricane on stage and leaps into the audience, occasionally injuring himself. At one memorable concert, he put his arm through a glass panel. Hank Williams Jnr remarked, 'No doubt about it. Leon Everette is a hard act to follow'. Among other successful singles are 'I Could'a Had You', 'Midnight Rodeo' and 'Soul Searchin''. His feelings for old-time country music are shown in 'Shadows Of My Mind' and he revived Stonewall Jackson's 'Don't Be Angry'. In a peculiar marketing exercise, RCA issued a six-track mini-album called *Doin' What I Feel* in 1983 and reissued it in 1984 with the same packaging but three different titles. He moved to Mercury and recorded, *Where's The Fire?*.
Albums: *I Don't Want To Lose* (1980), *If I Keep On*

Going Crazy (1981), *Hurricane* (1981), *Maverick* (1982), *Leon Everette* (1983), *Where's The Fire?* (1985).

Exile

Formed in Berea, Kentucky, USA in 1963 as the Exiles, the band first reached the pop charts in the late 70s before changing musical direction and becoming one of the most successful country bands of the 80s. They toured with the Dick Clark Caravan of Stars in 1965 as back-up band for artists including Brian Hyland and Tommy Roe. In the late 60s they recorded for Date Records and Columbia Records, and in the early 70s for SSS International, Date, Curb and Wooden Nickel. In 1973 they changed their name to Exile and in 1977, recording for Atco Records, they scored their first chart single. After a switch to Warner Brothers Records, Exile had a number 1 pop hit with 'Kiss You All Over', in 1978. They placed two more singles on that chart before making the switch to country. After numerous personnel changes, the group's membership in 1978, when they had their first hit, was guitarist/vocalist J.P. Pennington, keyboardist Buzz Cornelison, vocalist/guitarist Les Taylor, keyboardist/vocalist Marlon Hargis, bassist/vocalist Sonny Lemaire and drummer Steve Goetzman. Exile's second, and more lucrative career, as a country group, began in 1983 (by which time Cornelison had left). The first country chart single, 'High Cost Of Leaving', reached number 27, but was followed by four successive number 1 country singles in 1984: 'Woke Up In Love', 'I Don't Want To Be A Memory', 'Give Me One More Chance' and 'Crazy For Your Love'. There were six further number 1 country singles by 1987: 'She's A Miracle', 'Hang On To Your Heart', 'I Could Get Used To You', 'It'll Be Me', 'She's Too Good To Be True' and 'I Can't Get Close Enough'. Hargis was replaced by Lee Carroll in 1985 and Pennington left in 1989, replaced by Paul Martin. The group signed to Arista Records in 1989 with a noticeable drop in its level of commercial success.Albums: *Exile* (1973), *Mixed Emotions* (1978), *All There Is* (1979), *Don't Leave Me This Way* (1980), *Heart And Soul* (1981), *Exile* (1983), *Kentucky Hearts* (1984), *Hang On To Your Heart* (1985), *The Best Of Exile* (1985), *Keeping It Country* (1990), *Still Standing* (1990). Compilation: *Exile's Greatest Hits* (1986).

F

Fairchild, Barbara

b. 12 November 1950, Knobel, Arkansas, USA. Fairchild was raised on a farm and was entertaining at every opportunity. The family moved to St. Louis when she was 12 years old and she was soon recording for the local Norman label and working on television. In 1968 she moved to Nashville to further her career and amongst her early singles is 'Remember The Alimony' for Kapp Records. Her song, 'This Stranger (My Little Girl)', has been recorded by Loretta Lynn, Dottie West and Liz Anderson. Fairchild was signed to Columbia in 1969 and immediately achieved her first US country hit with 'Love Is A Gentle Thing', followed by various minor entries including 'A Girl Who'll Satisfy Her Man' and 'Love's Old Song'. Then, the novelty 'Teddy Bear Song', written by a St Louis policeman, topped the US country charts. She never repeated that success although she had country hits with 'Kid Stuff', 'Baby Doll', 'You've Lost That Lovin' Feelin'', 'Mississippi', 'Cheatin' Is' and 'Let Me Love You Once Before You Go'. She wrote 'Tara' for one of her daughters, and her husband and songwriting partner, steel guitarist Randy Reinhard, was part of her road band. After their divorce, she married Milton Carroll, who had recorded for RCA. In the early 80s, she became a born-again Christian and left the music business for several years. In 1986 she recorded an album with production by her old friend Don Williams, but only a single was released.
Albums: *Something Special* (1970), *Love's Old Song* (1971), *The Barbara Fairchild Way* (reissued as *Love's Old Song*) (1971), *A Sweeter Love* (1972), *Teddy Bear Song* (1972), *Kid Stuff* (1973), *Standing In Your Line* (1974), *Love Is A Gentle Thing* (1974), *Barbara Fairchild* (1975), *Free And Easy* (1977), *Mississippi* (1976), *This Is Me!* (1978), with Billy Walker *The Answer Game* (reissued as *It Takes Two*) (1979), *The Biggest Hurt* (1983).

Fargo, Donna

b. Yvonne Vaughn, 10 November 1949, Mount Airy, North Carolina, USA. Fargo is the daughter of a tobacco farmer, and she sang in church as a child. She became a schoolteacher and was discovered by her future husband, record producer Stan Silver, singing in a club in Los Angeles. She first recorded in 1969, but her success started once she had signed with Dot Records in 1971. She won gold records for her compositions, 'The Happiest Girl In The Whole USA' (number 11, US pop charts, number 1 country) and 'Funny Face' (number 5 pop, number 1 country), which was Silver's nickname for her. (She called him 'fuzzy face' because of his beard.) In 1973 she had country hits with more of her own songs - 'Superman', a tribute to her late mother 'You Were Always There', (both number 1) and 'Little Girl Gone' (number 2). In 1974 she topped the country charts again, this time with Marty Cooper's gospel song, 'You Can't Be A Beacon (If Your Light Don't Shine)'. The packaging of the USA versions of her early albums included guitar chords as well as lyrics. She moved to WEA Records and went to number 1 on the country charts with a narration, 'That Was Yesterday'. She appeared at the 1978 UK's Wembley Country Music Festival, but she came on at the end of a long evening and the spoken 'Loving You' was inappropriate. For some years she was in poor health but multiple sclerosis was not diagnosed until 1978. She has continued her career to the best of her ability and her strong beliefs led to a gospel album, *Brotherly Love*. Her duet with Billy Joe Royal, 'Members Only', was a US country hit in 1988 and she topped the US country singles chart for independent labels with a revival of the Shirelles' 'Soldier Boy', which was aimed at US forces involved in the Gulf War. Donna Fargo and her husband, Stan Silver, were declared bankrupt in 1991.
Albums: *The Happiest Girl In The Whole USA* (released in UK as *The Country Sounds Of Donna Fargo*) (1972), *My Second Album* (1973), *All About A Feeling* (1973), *Miss Donna Fargo* (1974), *Whatever I Say Means I Love You* (1975), *On The Move* (1976), *Shame On Me* (1977), *Fargo Country* (1977), *Dark Eyed Lady* (1978), *Just For You* (1979), *Fargo* (1980), *Brotherly Love* (1981), *Donna* (1983), *Winners* (1986).

Feathers, Charlie

b. Charles Arthur Feathers, 12 June 1932, Holly Springs, Mississippi, USA. The work of rockabilly legend Feathers becomes more elevated during each revival of interest in the genre. Feathers is now an enigmatic superstar, although in reality his influence totally overshadows his commercial success. His upbringing on a farm, being taught guitar by a cotton picking black bluesman and leaving home to work on an oil field gave Feathers

Charlie Feathers

a wealth of material for his compositions. In the early 50s, together with Jody Chastain and Jerry Huffman, he performed as the Musical Warriors. He was an early signing to Sam Phillips' Sun Records. He recorded his first song 'Defrost Your Heart' in 1955, and claimed to have co-written Elvis Presley's debut 'Blue Moon Of Kentucky'. He did however co-write Presley's first hit 'I Forgot To Remember To Forget'. Over the years he has continued to record for a number of labels, still unable to break through the barrier between 'cult' and 'star'. But among his early rockabilly sides was 'One Hand Loose' on King, regarded by many collectors as one of the finest examples of its kind. His highly applauded performance at London's famous Rainbow theatre in 1977 gave his career a significant boost and brought him a new audience; notably the fans who were following Dave Edmunds and his crusade for 'rockabilly'. Feather's recent recordings have suffered from the problem of being helped out by younger musicians who are merely in awe of his work and his best material is from the 50s. Influential but spartan, full of whoops and growls but irresistible country/rock, Feather's 'light comedy' style has been an 'invisible influence' over many decades, from Big Bopper in the 50s to Hank Wangford in the 80s. His 1991 release contained a reworked version of his classic 'I Forgot To Remember To Forget'. He now performs with his son and daughter on guitar and vocals respectively. His best work will endure.

Albums: *Rockabilly Kings* (1984), *Jungle Feaver* (1987), Compilations: *Rockabilly Mainman* (1978), *Honky Tonk Man* (1982), *The Legendary* 1956 *Demo Session* (1986), *The Living Legend* (1988), *Wild Wild Party* (1987), *Charlie Feathers* (1991).

Feller, Dick

b. 2 January 1943, Bronaugh, Missouri, USA. Feller grew up with a love of both country and blues music and became a proficient rock 'n' roll guitarist. In 1966, intent on becoming a professional songwriter, he moved to Nashville and found work playing sessions or going on the road with musicians including Skeeter Davis, Warner Mack and Mel Tillis. Johnny Cash had a US number 1 country hit with Feller's 'Any Old Wind That Blows' in 1972. Jerry Reed did the same in 1973 with 'Lord Mr. Ford', a song rejected by Jimmy Dean, and recorded many more of Feller's songs: 'East Bound And Down' (for the film *Smokey And The Bandit*), 'Second-Hand Satin Lady (And A Bargain Basement Boy)' and 'The

Phantom Of The Opry'. In the mid-70s Feller had his own country hits with 'Biff, The Friendly Purple Bear', 'Making The Best Of A Bad Situation', 'Uncle Hiram And His Homemade Beer' and a narrative which is even more pertinent today, 'The Credit Card Song'. His tours of UK country clubs have shown that he is not just another Feller and he can stop any show with 'Daisy Hill'.

Albums: *Dick Feller Wrote...* (1973), *No Word On Me* (1975), *Some Days Are Diamonds* (1975), *Children In Their Wishes, Ladies In Their Dreams* (1977), *Audiograph Alive* (1983).

Felts, Narvel

b. Albert Narvel Felts, 11 November 1938, Keiser, Arkansas, USA. Felts got his first guitar when aged 13 and taught himself to play. In 1956, he won a talent contest, appeared on local radio and passed an audition as a rock 'n' roll singer for Sun Records in Memphis, although his sessions were not released at the time. In 1957, his first record for Mercury Records, 'Kiss-a-me Baby', sold 20,000 copies. He made the US charts in 1959 with '3,000 Miles' and 'Honey Love', both for Pink Records. He had sporadic success for some years ('I'm Movin' On', 'Rockin' Little Angel') and then, in 1973, he had a huge country hit for the Cinnamon label with Mentor Williams' 'Drift Away', which was followed by a string of country hits - 'When Your Good Love Was Mine', 'All In The Name Of Love', 'Raindrops'. In 1975, moving to Dot Records, he had a number 2, US country hit, with 'Reconsider Me'. He recorded the most successful version of 'Funny How Time Slips Away' and mannered emotional revivals of 'Lonely Teardrops' and 'My Prayer'. In 1976, he had a US country hit with a song Conway Twitty had given him 16 years earlier, 'Lonely Kind Of Love'. He continued into the 80s, to register minor country hits, the last currently being the 1987 recording of 'When A Man Loves A Woman'. Looking like a haggard Omar Sharif, he tours with his band, the Driftaways, regularly visiting the UK and including songs from all periods of his career: his drummer is his son Narvel Felts Jnr.

Albums: *Drift Away* (1973), *Live* (1974), *When Your Good Love Was Mine* (1974), *Reconsider Me* (1975), *Narvel Felts* (1975), *Narvel The Marvel* (1976), *Doin' What I Feel* (1976), *This Time* (1976), *The Touch Of Felts* (1977), *Narvel* (1977), *Inside Love* (1978), *One Run For The Roses* (1979), *A Teen's Way* (1989), *Memphis Days* (1991), *Pink And Golden Days* (1991).

Fender, Freddy

b. Baldemar G. Huerta, 4 June 1937, San Benito, Texas, USA. Fender, a Mexican American, comes from a family of migrant workers who were based in the San Benito valley. A farm worker from the age of 10, Fender says he 'worked beets in Michigan, pickles in Ohio, baled hay and picked tomatoes in Indiana. When that was over, it was cotton-picking time in Arkansas.' Fender sang and played guitar with the blues, country and Mexican records he heard on the radio, which eventually developed into his own hybrid style. He joined the US marines in 1953, spending his time in the brig and eventually being dismissed for bad conduct. He began playing rockabilly in Texas honky-tonks in the late 50s and he recorded a Spanish version of 'Don't Be Cruel' as well as his own composition, 'Wasted Days And Wasted Nights' (1958). He recalls, 'I had a gringo manager and started recording in English. Since I was playing a Fender guitar and amplifier, I changed my name to Freddy Fender.' A fight in one club left him with a broken nose and a knife wound in his neck. Starting in 1960, Fender spent three years in Angola State Prison, Louisiana on drug offences and he recorded several tracks on a cassette recorder whilst inside, later collected on an album. Upon his release, he secured a residency at a Bourbon Street club in New Orleans. Despairing of ever finding real success, he returned to San Benito in 1969 and took regular work as a mechanic. He obtained a sociology degree with a view to helping ex-convicts. He returned to performing, however, and 'Before The Next Teardrop Falls', which he performed in English and Spanish, became a number 1 US pop hit in 1975. He had further US chart success with 'Wasted Days And Wasted Nights' (number 8 and dedicated to Doug Sahm), 'Secret Love' (number 20), 'You'll Lose A Good Thing', 'Vaya Con Dios'. Fender's overwrought vocals, which even gave something to 'How Much Is That Doggie In The Window?', were skilfully matched by Huey P. Meaux's arrangements featuring marimbas, accordion, harpsichord and steel guitar. His fuzzy hair and roly-poly body made him an unlikely pop star, but his admirers included Elvis Presley. Fender succumbed to alcohol and drugs which forced his wife, in 1985, to enter him in a clinic, which apparently cured him. Fender played a corrupted mayor in the 1987 film, *The Milagro Beanfield War*, directed by Robert Redford. In 1990, he formed an all-star Tex-Mex band, the Texas Tornados, with long-time friends Doug Sahm and Augie Meyers (from Sir Douglas

Quintet), and accordionist Flaco Jiminez. Their eponymous debut album was a critical and commercial success, but subsequent collaborations have failed to match its stylist blend of conjunto, country and R&B. Fender was signed to Warner Brothers as a soloist on the back of the group's success. *The Freddy Fender Collection*, his initial offering, was a disappointing collection of remakes of his early hits. Referring back to his military service, he says, 'It has taken me 35 years to have my discharge changed from bad conduct, and this means I am now eligible for a military funeral.'

Albums: *Before The Next Teardrop Falls* (1975), *Recorded Inside Louisiana State Prison* (1975), *Since I Met You Baby* (1975), *Are You Ready For Freddy?* (1975), *Rock n' Country* (1976), *If You're Ever In Texas* (1976), *If You Don't Love Me* (1977), *Merry Christmas - Feliz Navidad* (1977), *Swamp Gold* (1978), *The Texas Balladeer* (1979), *Tex-Mex* (1979), *Together We Drifted Apart* (1980), *El Major De Freddy Fender* (1986), *Crazy Baby* (1987), with Flaco Jiminez, Augie Meyers, Doug Sahm *Texas Tornados* (1990), with Jiminez, Meyers, Sahm *Zone Of Your Own* (1991), with Texas Tornados *The Freddie Fender Collection* (1991), *Christmas Time In The Valley* (1991).

Flatt, Lester

b. 28 June 1914, Overton County, Tennessee, USA. Versed in the old-time country music style prevalent in his rural environment, Flatt began playing guitar during the 30s. At the end of the decade he abandoned his job in a textile mill to pursue a career as a professional musician. Having made his debut on station WDBJ, Flatt became a popular entertainer throughout the south and by 1944 was a feature of the *Grand Ole Opry*. He then joined Bill Monroe's Bluegrass Boys where he later met banjoist Earl Scruggs. The two musicians left Monroe in 1948 and, as Flatt And Scruggs, redefined the modern bluegrass sound. For over 20 years the duo led various versions of their group, the Foggy Mountain Boys, which remained at the heart of America's traditional music circuit. They parted company in 1969 following which Flatt created another group, the Nashville Grass. He continued to tour and record, but his once-prolific work-rate lessened considerably following open-heart surgery in 1975.

Albums: *Lester 'N' Mac* (70s), *Flatt On Victor* (70s), *Foggy Mountain Breakdown* (1973), *On The South Bound* (1973), *Over Hills To Poor House* (1974), *Before You Go* (1974), *Flatt Gospel* (1975), *Just Flatt Gospel* (1975), *Lester Flatt* (1977), *Heaven's Bluegrass Band* (1977), *Live At The Bluegrass Festival* (1986), *Don't Get Above Your Raisin'* (1988).

Flatt And Scruggs

Lester Flatt (b. 28 June 1914, Overton County, Tennessee, USA; guitar) and Earl Scruggs (b. 1924, Cleveland County, North Carolina, USA; banjo). These influential musicians began working together in December 1945 as members of Bill Monroe's Bluegrass Boys. In February 1948 they left to form the Foggy Mountain Boys with Jim Shumate (fiddle), Howard Watts aka Cedric Rainwater (bass fiddle) - both ex-Bill Monroe - and, latterly, Mac Wiseman (tenor vocals/guitar). They became an established feature of Virginia's WCYB radio station and undertook recording sessions for the Mercury label before embarking on a prolonged tour of the south. Here they forged a more powerful, ebullient sound than was associated with their chosen genre and in November 1950 Flatt and Scruggs joined Columbia/CBS Records, with whom they remained throughout their career together. Three years later they signed a sponsorship deal with Martha White Mills which engendered a regular show on Nashville's WSM and favoured slots on their patron's television shows. Josh Graves (dobro) was then added to the line-up which in turn evolved a less frenetic sound and reduced the emphasis on Scruggs' banjo playing. Appearances on the nationally-syndicated *Folk Sound USA* brought the group's modern bluegrass sound to a much wider audience, while their stature was further enhanced by an appearance at the 1960 Newport Folk Festival. Flatt and Scruggs were then adopted by the college circuit where they were seen as antecedents to a new generation of acts, including the Kentucky Colonels, the Hillmen and the Dillards. The Foggy Mountain Boys performed the theme song, 'The Ballad Of Jed Clampett', to the popular *Beverly Hillbillies* television show in the early 60s while their enduring instrumental, 'Foggy Mountain Breakdown', was heavily featured in the film *Bonnie And Clyde*. Bluegrass students opined that this version lacked the sparkle of earlier arrangements and declared the group lacked its erstwhile vitality. By 1968 Earl Scruggs' sons, Randy and Gary, had been brought into the line-up, but the banjoist nonetheless grew dissatisfied with the constraints of a purely bluegrass setting. The partnership was dissolved the following year. While Flatt formed a new act, the Nashville Grass, his former partner added further members of his family to found the Earl Scruggs Revue.

Compilations: *Foggy Mountain Breakdown* (1975), *The Golden Era 1950-1955* (1977), *Foggy Mountain Banjo* (1978).

Fleck, Bela

b. c.1953, New York City, New York, USA. Fleck has been credited with expanding the parameters of the banjo by combining traditional bluegrass with jazz and classical music, similar to what David Grisman did with the mandolin. Inspired by the song 'Duelling Banjos' in the film *Deliverance*, Fleck took up the banjo at the age of 14. He moved to Kentucky in his early 20s to start the bluegrass group Spectrum. In 1981 he relocated to Nashville, joining the influential New Grass Revival, with whom he stayed for eight years. In 1989 he formed the Flecktones with Howard Levy (keyboards/harmonica), Victor Wooten (bass) and Roy Wooten (drumitar - a guitar wired to electric drums). The group's debut album for Warner Brothers sold over 50,000 copies and reached the Top 20 on the *Billboard* jazz charts.
Albums: *Natural Bridge, Crossing The Tracks, Inroads* (1980), with the New Grass Revival *Deviation* (1984), *Bela Fleck And The Flecktones* (1990), *Flight Of the Cosmic Hippo* (1992).

Flores, Rosie

b. San Antonio, Texas, USA. Flores's background accounts for the strong, Mexican influence in her brand of country music. When she was 12 years old, her family moved to San Diego, California and she subsequently became part of an all-girl psychedelic band, Penelope's Children. She was then backed by a punk band, the Screamers. Next came another all-girl band, the Screamin' Sirens. In 1985, she was part of a compilation album of new country artists, *A Town South Of Bakersfield*, on which she sang 'Heartbreak Train' with Albert Lee. Her first album for Reprise, *Rosie Flores*, was produced with Dwight Yoakam, but her biggest single on the US country charts, 'Crying Over You', only reached number 51. Dropped by Reprise, she re-emerged five years later on HighTone with *After The Farm*. Flores remains one of those Texas artists more popular as a cult performer in Europe than in her home country.
Albums: *Rosie Flores* (1987), *After The Farm* (1992).

Fogelberg, Dan

b. 13 August 1951, Peoria, Illinois, USA. Having learned piano from the age of 14, Fogelberg moved to guitar and songwriting. Leaving the University of Illinois in 1971 he relocated to California and started playing on the folk circuit, at one point touring with Van Morrison. A move to Nashville brought him to the attention of producer Norbert Putnam. Fogelberg released *Home Free* for Columbia shortly afterwards. This was a very relaxed album, notable for the backing musicians involved, including Roger McGuinn, Jackson Browne, Joe Walsh and Buffy Sainte-Marie. Despite the calibre of the other players, the album was not a success, and Fogelberg, having been dropped by Columbia, returned to session work. Producer Irv Azoff, who was managing Joe Walsh, signed Fogelberg and secured a deal with Epic. Putnam was involved in subsequent recordings by Fogelberg. In 1974, Fogelberg moved to Colorado, and a year later released *Souvenirs*. This was a more positive album, and Walsh's production was evident. From here on, Fogelberg played the majority of the instruments on record, enabling him to keep tight control of the recordings, but inevitably it took longer to finish the projects. Playing support to the Eagles in 1975 helped to establish Fogelberg. However, in 1977, due to appear with the Eagles at Wembley, he failed to show on-stage, and it was later claimed that he had remained at home to complete recording work on *Netherlands*. Whatever the reason, the album achieved some recognition, but Fogelberg has enjoyed better chart success in the USA than in the UK. In 1980, 'Longer' reached number 2 in the US singles charts, while in the UK it did not even reach the Top 50. Two other singles, 'Same Auld Lang Syne' and 'Leader Of The Band', both from *The Innocent Age*, achieved Top 10 places in the USA. The excellent *High Country Snows* saw a return to his bluegrass influences and was in marked contrast to the harder-edged *Exiles* which followed. From plaintive ballads to rock material, Fogelberg is a versatile writer and musician who continues to produce credible records and command a loyal cult following.
Albums: *Home Free* (1973), *Souvenirs* (1975), *Captured Angel* (1975), *Netherlands* (1977), with Tim Weisberg *Twin Sons Of Different Mothers* (1978), *Phoenix* (1980), *The Innocent Age* (1981), *Windows And Walls* (1984), *High Country Snows* (1985), *Exiles* (1987), *The Wild Places* (1990), *Dan Fogelberg Live - Greetings From The West* (1991). Compilation: *Greatest Hits* (1985).

Foley, Red

b. Clyde Julian Foley, 17 June 1910, in a log cabin between Blue Lick and Berea, Kentucky, USA. The son of a fiddle player, he learned guitar as a

Rosie Flores

child and was given parental encouragement to sing. After high school, he attended Georgetown College, Kentucky, where he was discovered by a scout for the noted WLS National Barn Dance in Chicago. In 1930, he joined John Lair's Cumberland Ridge Runners and returned to Kentucky with Lair in 1937, to help him establish the now famous Renfro Valley Barn Dance. He returned to Chicago in 1941, co-starred with Red Skelton in the network country radio show *Avalon Time* and signed with Decca. The first number he recorded was 'Old Shep', a song he had written in 1933, about a dog he had owned as a child. (Actually the dog, sadly poisoned by a neighbour, had been a German Shepherd named Hoover.) The song, later recorded by many artists including Hank Snow and Elvis Presley, has become a country classic. His first chart success came in 1944, when the patriotic wartime song 'Smoke On The Water' was a US pop chart number 7 and a 13-week occupant of the number 1 position in the country charts. On 17 January 1945, Foley had the distinction of making the first modern country records recorded in Nashville. In April 1946, Foley became a regular member of the *Grand Ole Opry*, replacing Roy Acuff as the star of NBC's prestigious *Prince Albert Show*. When he left Chicago for Nashville, he took with him a young guitar player called Chet Atkins, one of the many artists he helped. During the next eight years Foley established himself as one of the most respected and versatile performers in country music. He acted as master of ceremonies, the straight man for *Opry* comedians Rod Brasfield and Minnie Pearl and proved himself a vocalist who could handle all types of material. In 1954, he moved to KWTO Springfield, as the host of the *Ozark Jubilee*, which, in 1956, became one of the first successful network television shows. Between 1944 and 1959, Foley charted 41 solo country entries of which 38 were Top 10 hits. There were six more country number 1s, including his 1950, million-selling 'Chattanoogie Shoe Shine Boy', which also topped the pop charts. Several others achieved cross-over pop chart success. During this time he also had many major hit duets with various artists including Evelyn Knight, his daughter Betty Foley, Ernest Tubb, ('Goodnight Irene') and six with Kitty Wells, including their country number 1, 'One By One', which remained on the charts for 41 weeks. His performances of gospel numbers were so popular that recordings of 'Steal Away' (1950) (recorded by Hank Williams as 'The Funeral'), 'Just A Closer Walk With Thee' (1950) and 'Peace In

The Valley' (1951) all became million-sellers. He also recorded with the Andrews Sisters and in the late 50s even cut some rock 'n' roll recordings such as 'Crazy Little Guitar Man'. Although he continued to tour and appear on network television shows, he also moved into acting in the early 60s and co-starred with Fess Parker in the ABC-TV series *Mr. Smith Goes To Washington*. His daughter, Shirley, married one-time pop and later gospel singer Pat Boone and some ten years after Foley's death his granddaughter, Debby Boone, had both country and pop success. Foley never lost his love for country music and, unlike Eddy Arnold, never sought success as a pop artist, even though many of his recordings did attain pop chart status. His voice was mellow and had none of the raw or nasal style associated with many of his contemporaries, some have even likened it to Bing Crosby. His importance to the country music scene is often overlooked and little has been written about him but he was rightfully elected to the Country Music Hall of Fame in 1967. A great friend of Hank Williams Snr., he was ironically headlining a touring *Opry* show that included the young Hank Williams Jnr., when, after playing the matinee and evening shows, Foley suffered a heart attack and died in his sleep at Fort Wayne, Indiana, USA on 19 September 1968. This prompted Hank Jnr., seemingly the last person to speak to him, to write and record, as Luke The Drifter Jnr, the tribute narration 'I Was With Red Foley (The Night He Passed Away)', which charted for him in November 1968. In the song, Hank Jnr. relates, that after reminiscing about the problems faced by a country singer, such as himself and Hank Snr., Red's final words were 'I'm awful tired now, Hank, I've got to go to bed'.

Albums: *Red Foley Souvenir Album* (1951), *Lift Up Your Voice* (1954), with Ernest Tubb *Red & Ernie* (1956), *My Keepsake Album* (1958), *Beyond The Sunset* (1958), *He Walks With Thee* (1958), *Red Foley Souvenir Album* (1958), *Red Foley's Dickies Souvenir Album* (1958), *Let's All Sing To Him* (1959), *Let's All Sing With Red Foley* (1959), *Company's Comin'* (1961), *Golden Favorites* (1961), *Songs Of Devotion* (1961), *Kitty Wells & Red Foley's Golden Favorites* (1961), *Dear Hearts And Gentle People* (1962), *The Red Foley Show* (1963), *The Red Foley Story* (1964), *Songs Everybody Knows* (1965), *I'm Bound For The Kingdom* (1965), *Red Foley* (1966), *Songs For The Soul* (1967), with Kitty Wells *Together Again* (1967), *I Believe* (1969), *The Old Master* (1969), *Red Foley Memories* (1971), *Gospel Favorites* (1976), *Tennessee Saturday Night* (1984).

Ford, Gerry

b. 25 May 1943, Athlone, Co. Westmeath, Eire. When he was aged 16, Ford emigrated to England as an apprentice baker, and, on qualification, married and relocated to Edinburgh, where he joined the police force for 11 years. Since the late 60s he has been a country music performer, turning professional in 1976. He has recorded all his albums since 1981 in Nashville and has performed numerous times on the *Grand Ole Opry* as a guest of Opry star, Jean Shepard. He has recorded six duets with Shepard, while Boxcar Willie added train whistles to Ford's tribute, 'They Call Him Boxcar Willie'. Boxcar also wrote 'Jesus, I Need To Talk To You' for Ford's, *All Over Again*. His easy listening albums, which combine the new with the familiar, have helped to establish him as Scotland's 'Mr. Country'. In 1991, economy forced him to drop his band in favour of Nashville-made backing tapes, and they have been well received. *Thank God For The Radio* won an award as the UK country album of the year, and Ford has good cause to 'thank God for the radio' as he has presented country programmes on BBC Radio Scotland for 13 years.

Albums: *These Songs Are Just For You* (1977), *Someone To Give My Love To* (1978), *With Love* (1980), *On The Road* (1981), *Let's Hear It For The Working Man* (1982), *Memory Machine* (1984), *Thank God For The Radio* (1986), *All Over Again* (1988), *Stranger Things Have Happened* (1989), *Family Bible* (1990), *Better Man* (1991).

Ford, Tennessee Ernie

b. Ernest Jennings Ford, 13 February 1919, Bristol, Tennessee, USA, d. 17 October 1991. It is difficult to categorize a performer with so many varied achievements, but Ford can be summarized as a master interpreter of melodic songs and hymns. The fact that he was able to combine singing with his strong faith gave America's best-loved gospel singer great satisfaction. When only four years old, he was singing 'The Old Rugged Cross' at family gatherings, and from an early age, he wanted to be an entertainer. He pestered the local radio station until they made him a staff announcer in 1937, and he also took singing lessons. He subsequently worked for radio stations, WATL in Atlanta and WROL in Knoxville, where he announced the attack on Pearl Harbour. He joined the US Army Air Corps in 1942 and married a secretary, Betty Heminger, whom he met at the bombardier's school. After the war, they moved to California and he worked as an announcer and a disc jockey

of hillbilly music for KXFM in San Bernardino. He rang cowbells and added bass harmonies to the records he was playing and so developed a country yokel character, Tennessee Ernie. He continued with this on KXLA Pasadena and he became a regular on their *Hometown Jamboree*, which was hosted by bandleader Cliffie Stone. He was also known as the Tennessee Pea-Picker using the catchphrase 'Bless your pea-pickin' hearts' and appearing on stage in bib overalls and with a blacked-out tooth. Lee Gillette, an A&R for Capitol Records, heard Ford singing along with a record on air and asked Stone about him. His first record, in 1949, was 'Milk 'Em In The Morning Blues'. Ford began his chart success with 'Tennessee Border', 'Country Junction' and 'Smokey Mountain Boogie', a song he wrote with Stone. 'Mule Train' despite opposition from Frankie Laine, Gene Autry and Vaughn Monroe, was a national hit and a US country number 1. An attempt to write with Hank Williams did not lead to any completed songs, but Ford wrote 'Anticipation Blues' about his wife's pregnancy and it made the US charts in 1949. Capitol teamed him with many of their female artists including Ella Mae Morse, Molly Bee and the Dinning Sisters, and his most successful duets were 'Ain't Nobody's Business But My Own' and 'I'll Never Be Free', a double-sided single with Kay Starr. The duet just missed a gold record but he secured one, also in 1950, with his own song, 'Shotgun Boogie', which capitalized on the boogie craze and can be taken as a forerunner of rock 'n' roll. Its UK popularity enabled him to top a variety bill at the London Palladium in 1953. Ford recalls, 'When somebody told me that 'Give Me Your Word' was number 1 in your charts, I said, 'When did I record that?' because it wasn't big in America and I had forgotten about it!' Ford also had success with 'The Cry Of The Wild Goose' and the theme for the Marilyn Monroe film, *The River Of No Return*, while the superb musicians on his records included Joe 'Fingers' Carr, who was given equal billing on 'Tailor Made Woman' in 1951, Speedy West and Jimmy Bryant. Ford hosted a USA daytime television show for five days a week and, in 1955, Capitol informed him that he would be in breach of contract if he did not record again soon. He chose a song he had been performing on the show, Merle Travis' 'Sixteen Tons'. Ford says, 'The producer, Lee Gillette, asked me what tempo I would like it in. I snapped my fingers and he said, 'Leave that in.' That snapping on the record is me.' 'Sixteen Tons' topped both the US and the UK

Tennessee Ernie Ford

charts, and Ford was also one of many who recorded 'The Ballad Of Davy Crockett', the theme of a Walt Disney western starring Fess Parker, which made number 3 in the UK. His half-hour US television show, *The Ford Show* (guess the sponsor), ran from 1956-61. He closed every television show with a hymn, which led to him recording over 400 gospel songs. One album, *Hymns,* made number 2 in the US album charts and was listed for over five years. He shared his billing with the Jordanaires on several albums including *Great Gospel Songs* which won a Grammy in 1964. Ford said, 'Long before I turned pro, it was a part of my life. There are many different types of gospel music, ranging from black music to the plain old Protestant hymns. I've shown that you don't have to sing them with a black robe on.' Ford had further USA hits with 'That's All', 'In The Middle Of An Island' and 'Hicktown' but, for many years, he concentrated on gospel. In 1961 he decided to spend more time with his family and moved to a ranch in the hills of San Francisco. He recorded albums of well-known songs, be they pop or country, and he rates *Country Hits - Feelin' Blue* and *Ernie Sings And Glen Picks*, an album which showcases his deep, mellow voice with Glen Campbell's guitar, amongst his best work. Many collectors seek original copies of his albums of Civil War songs. Ford, who was elected to the Country Music Hall of Fame in 1990, remarked; 'People say to me, "Why don't you record another 'Sixteen Tons'" and I say, "There is no other 'Sixteen Tons".' He died in 1991 - appropiately enough in Bristol, Tennessee, a town which played host to some of country music's most important early recording sessions.

Albums: *This Lusty Land* (1956), *Hymns* (1956), *Spirituals* (1957), *C-H-R-I-S-T-M-A-S* (1957), *Tennessee Ernie Ford Favourites* (1957), *Ol' Rockin' 'Ern* (1957), *The Folk Album* (1958), *Nearer The Cross* (1958), *The Star Carol* (1958), with the Jordanaires *Gather 'Round* (1959), with the Jordanaires *A Friend We Have* (1960), *Sing A Hymn With Me* (1960), *Sixteen Tons* (1960), *Sing A Spiritual With Me* (1960), *Come To The Fair* (1960), *Sings Civil War Songs Of The North* (1961), *Sings Civil War Songs Of The South* (1961), *Ernie Ford Looks At Love* (1961), *Hymns At Home* (1961), *Here Comes The Tennessee Ernie Ford Mississippi Showboat* (1962), *I Love To Tell The Story* (1962), *Book Of Favourite Hymns* (1962), *Long, Long Ago* (1963), with the San Quentin Prison Choir *We Gather Together* (1963), with the Roger Wagnor Chorale *The Story Of Christmas* (1963), with the Jordanaires

Great Gospel Songs (1964), *Country Hits - Feeling Blue* (1964), *Let Me Walk With Thee* (1965), *Sing We Now Of Christmas* (1965), *My Favourite Things* (1966), *Wonderful Peace* (1966), *God Lives* (1966), *Aloha From Tennessee Ernie Ford* (1967), *Faith Of Our Fathers* (1967), with Marilyn Horne *Our Garden Of Hymns* (1967), *The World Of Pop And Country Hits* (1968), *O Come All Ye Faithful* (1968), *Songs I Like To Sing* (1969), *New Wave* (1969), *Holy Holy Holy* (1969), *America The Beautiful* (1970), *Sweet Hour Of Prayer* (1970), *Tennessee Ernie Ford Christmas Special* (1970), *Everything Is Beautiful* (1970), *Abide With Me* (1971), *Mr. Words And Music* (1972), *It's Tennessee Ernie Ford* (1972), *Country Morning* (1973), *Ernie Ford Sings About Jesus* (1973), *Precious Memories* (1975), with Glen Campbell *Ernie Sings And Glen Picks* (1975), *Tennessee Ernie Ford Sings His Great Love* (1976), *For The 83rd Time* (1976), *He Touched Me* (1977), with the Jordanaires *Swing Wide Your Golden Gate* (1978), *Tell The Old, Old Story* (1981), *Sunday's Still A Special Day* (1984).

Forester Sisters

Kathy (b. 1955), June (b. 1956), Kim (b. 1960) and Christy Forester (b. 1962) are from Lookout Mountain, Georgia, USA. Kathy and June sang in church as children, obtained their college degrees and started playing professionally: by 1982, both Kim and Christy had joined them. They formed their own band and started to explore songs and harmonies. (Kathy's husband on bass is also the group's road manager.) In 1983 they recorded some demo tapes which led to a contract with WEA Records. Their first single, '(That's What You Do) When You're In Love', made the US country Top 10. Their glossy, professional sound (and looks) appealed to country fans as they had three number 1 country hits from their first album - 'I Fell In Love Again Last Night', 'Just In Case' and 'Mama's Never Seen Those Eyes'. In 1986 they teamed up with the Bellamy Brothers for another US number 1 country single, 'Too Much Is Not Enough', and they worked together on The Brothers And Sisters Tour. In 1987 they had a further chart-topper with the title track from *You Again*.

Albums: *The Forester Sisters* (1985), *Perfume, Ribbons And Pearls* (1987), *You Again* (1987), *A Christmas Card* (1987), *Sincerely* (1988), *All I Need* (1989), *Come Hold Me* (1990), *Talkin' About Men* (1991), *I Got A Date* (1992).

Foster And Lloyd

During the early 80s, Radney Foster, from Del Rio, Texas, USA was playing in a local club when a producer suggested he moved to Nashville. The new MTM music group employed him as a staff writer and there he met Bill Lloyd. Lloyd had worked in New York and Kentucky before coming to Nashville where they wrote for Sweethearts Of The Rodeo (Foster also co-wrote with Holly Dunn her US country hit single, 'Love Someone Like Me'). Foster And Lloyd's albums feature Radney, the one with glasses, as lead singer, and, although their music has many influences, his voice keeps it country. Their US Top 10 country hits are 'Crazy Over You', 'Sure Thing' and 'What Do You Want From Me This Time'. Their album, *Version Of The Truth*, includes an instrumental, 'Whoa', which features Duane Eddy.
Albums: *Foster And Lloyd* (1987), *Version Of The Truth* (1990), *Faster And Louder* (1991).

Fox, Curly, And Texas Ruby

b. Arnim LeRoy Fox, 9 November 1910, Graysville, Tennessee, USA. At the age of 13 Fox, the son of a fiddler, was already touring with a medicine show before joining the Roane County Ramblers, with whom he made his first recordings in 1929. In the early 30s, he played with the Carolina Tarheels and in 1932 with his own band, the Tennessee Firecrackers, he was a popular performer on WSB Atlanta. In 1935, he cut some Decca recordings with the Shelton Brothers, including his noted instrumental, 'Listen To the Mocking Bird' (complete with special fiddle-made bird effects) and his vocal 'Curley's New Talking Blues'. In 1937, Fox teamed up with Texas Ruby (b. Ruby Owens, 4 June 1908, Wise County, Texas, USA, d. 29 March 1963, Nashville, Tennessee, USA). She was the sister of Tex Owens (the writer of 'Cattle Call') and had played on many radio stations, including the *Iowa Barn Dance Frolics* and appeared on the *Grand Ole Opry* in 1934 with Zeke Clements. Fox and Owens (often working with the Shelton Brothers) toured the south, where they appeared on numerous stations and where Fox won a great many fiddle contests. They were married in 1939 and became firm favourites on the *Opry*, where along with Rod Brasfield, they were stars of the Purina segment. During the 40s, they recorded for Columbia and King and between 1948 and 1955, they were regulars on a KPRC Houston television show but then returned to the *Opry* and also made further recordings for Starday. Their close partnership was ended in 1963, when Texas Ruby was tragically killed by a fire that destroyed their trailer home. Fox was shattered and effectually retired from the business and though from the mid-70s, he has, on occasions, been persuaded to make special appearances at some bluegrass festivals, he has never got over his loss. He is rated by experts to be perhaps the greatest showman of all the early day country fiddlers. Texas Ruby initially billed herself as Radio's Original Yodeling Cowgirl but she was an outstanding vocalist and once described by the internationally famous opera singer Helen Traubel as possessing the greatest singing voice she had ever heard. Equally at home with country ballads or blues songs, she was an undoubted influence on other female singers including Patsy Cline and Loretta Lynn.
Albums: *Curly Fox & Texas Ruby* (1963), *Travellin' Blues* (1963), *Favorite Songs Of Texas Ruby* (1963), *Curly Fox, Champion Fiddler Volumes 1 & 2* (1973).

Frazier, Dallas

b. 27 October 1939, Spiro, Oklahoma, USA. Frazier wrote realistically about his family's move to Bakersfield in his song 'California Cottonfields', which was recorded by Merle Haggard. In his teens, he won a talent contest sponsored by Ferlin Husky and became part of his roadshow, with Husky subsequently recording 'Timber, I'm Falling!'. However, Frazier's first success as a songwriter was with a novelty about a cartoon caveman, 'Alley-Oop'. This 1960 record by a studio band, the Hollywood Argyles, which included Frazier himself, was a US number 1 and the song was also covered by Dante And The Evergreens, the Beach Boys, Brian Poole And The Tremeloes, the Bonzo Dog Band and the Dynasores. Frazier wrote several songs in the same vein, notably 'Mohair Sam', a hit for Charlie Rich, and 'Elvira', a minor US pop hit for Frazier himself in 1966. Frazier's writing displays versatility and his songs include 'There Goes My Everything' (Jack Greene, Engelbert Humperdinck, Elvis Presley), 'Son Of Hickory Holler's Tramp' (O.C. Smith), 'Beneath Still Waters' (Emmylou Harris), 'If My Heart Had Windows' (George Jones) and 'Fourteen Carat Mind' (Gene Watson). He wrote four US country number 1 hits for Charley Pride with A.L. 'Doodle' Owens ('All I Have To Offer You (Is Me)', '(I'm So) Afraid Of Losing You Again', 'I Can't Believe That You've Stopped Loving Me', 'Then Who Am I'). Although he has a fine voice, Frazier has only had moderate success as a performer, notably with 'Everybody Ought To

Sing A Song', 'Sunshine Of My World' and 'The Birthmark Henry Thompson Talked About'. In addition to his own albums, both George Jones and Connie Smith have recorded albums of his songs. Smith's *If It Ain't Love* includes three duets with him. Although he has been involved with the ministry since 1976, many of his older songs have become successful. In 1981 the Oak Ridge Boys won a gold disc for their version of 'Elvira'.
Albums: *Elvira* (1966), *Tell It Like It Is* (1967), *Singin' My Songs* (1970), *My Baby Packed Up My Mind And Left Me* (1971).

Frickie, Janie

b. Jane Fricke, 19 December 1947, on the family farm near South Whitney, Indiana, USA. Frickie, who adopted the spelling in 1986 to avoid mispronunciations, has sung in public since the age of 10. Her father was a guitarist and her mother a piano teacher and organist. Frickie sang jingles to pay her university fees and then moved to Los Angeles to find work as a session singer. As this was not productive, she moved to Nashville and joined the Lea Jane Singers, often recording three sessions a day, five days a week. Frickie has added background vocals to thousands of records, mostly country, including ones by Crystal Gayle ('I'll Get Over You'), Ronnie Milsap ('(I'm A) Stand By My Woman Man'), Elvis Presley ('My Way'), Tanya Tucker ('Here's Some Love') and Conway Twitty ('I'd Love To Lay You Down'). Frickie's uncredited contribution on Johnny Duncan's 'Jo And The Cowboy' led to several other records with Duncan. The disc jockeys and public alike were curious about the mystery voice on his country hits, 'Stranger', 'Thinkin' Of A Rendezvous' and 'It Couldn't Have Been Any Better' and she was finally given equal billing on 'Come A Little Bit Closer'. This led to considerable interest in her first solo recordings and she had US country hits with 'What're You Doing Tonight?' and a revival of 'Please Help Me I'm Falling'. At first, she was reluctant to tour because she found herself in continuing demand as a session singer. She joined Vern Gosdin for 'Till The End' and 'Mother Country Music' and Charlie Rich for a US country number 1, 'On My Knees'. In 1982, Frickie had her first solo US country number 1 with 'Don't Worry 'Bout Me, Baby', co-written by 60s hitmaker Bruce Channel and featuring Ricky Skaggs' harmony vocals. Johnny Rodriguez' road manager, Randy Jackson, proposed to Frickie on a radio phone-in show and has since married her and become her manager. Frickie, who toured

with Alabama, had a US country number 1 with a similarly-styled high energy performance, 'He's A Heartache (Looking For A Place To Happen)' (1983). It was taken from *It Ain't Easy*, which she made with her own Heart City Band and was produced by Bob Montgomery. 'It Ain't Easy Bein' Easy' (1982) and 'Tell Me A Lie' (1983) were other US country number 1's from the same album. She joined Merle Haggard for another number 1, 'A Place To Fall Apart' (1985), which was based on a letter he had written about his ex-wife, Leona Williams, and Frickie's other duet partners include George Jones ('All I Want To Do In Life'), Ray Charles ('Who Cares?'), Tommy Cash ('The Cowboy And The Lady') and Larry Gatlin ('From Time To Time'). Her *Black And White* album was more blues-based, while *Labour Of Love* was produced by Chris Waters and included an ingenious song he had written with his sister, Holly Dunn, 'Love Is One Of Those Words' as well as Steve Earle's 'My Old Friend The Blues'. Frickie's fashions, based on her stage wear, are in many US clothes stores.
Albums: *Singer Of Songs* (1978), *Love Notes* (1979), *From The Heart* (1980), *I'll Need Someone To Hold Me When I Cry* (1981), with Johnny Duncan *Nice 'N' Easy* (1980), *Sleeping With Your Memory* (1981), *It Ain't Easy* (1982), *Love Lines* (1983), *The First Word In Memory Is Me* (1984), *Someone Else's Fire* (1985), *Black And White* (1986), *After Midnight* (1987), *Saddle The Wind* (1988), *Labor Of Love* (1989), *Janie Fricke* (1991). Compilations: *The Very Best Of Janie Fricke* (1986), *Country Store: Janie Fricke* (1988).

Friedman, Kinky

b. Richard Friedman, 31 October 1944, Palestine, Texas, USA. Friedman, a Jew in Texas, remarks, 'Cowboys and Jews have a common bond. They are the only two groups to wear their hats indoors and attach a certain importance to it.' Friedman, whose father was a university lecturer, first recorded as part of the surfing band, King Arthur And The Carrots, in 1966. One of the Carrots, Jeff Shelby, was to become Little Jewford Shelby in Friedman's band, the Texas Jewboys, the name satirising Bob Wills' Texas Playboys. Chuck Glaser of the Glaser Brothers took him to Nashville for his first album, *Sold American*. The title song combined the qualities of Ralph McTell's 'Streets Of London' with Phil Ochs' 'Chords Of Fame' and has been recorded by Glen Campbell and Tompall Glaser, the latter version being co-produced by Friedman. His Jewishness was

Kinky Friedman with John Candy and Mariel Hemingway

emphasized in songs like 'We Refuse The Right To Refuse Service To You' and 'Ride 'Em Jewboy'. Friedman's single, 'Carryin' The Torch', an offbeat look at the Statue of Liberty, was produced by Waylon Jennings. *Kinky Friedman* was a patchy mixture of blasphemy and ballads, and included a good-natured romp produced by Willie Nelson, 'They Ain't Makin' Jews Like Jesus Anymore'. A hoarse recording of 'Sold American', recorded as part of Bob Dylan's Rolling Thunder Revue, was included on *Lasso From El Paso*. Buck Owens, who published 'Okie From Muskogee', refused to allow the album to be called Asshole From El Paso. 'Ol' Ben Lucas', about nose-picking, features Eric Clapton's guitar-picking, while 'Men's Room, L.A.' is about a shortage of toilet paper and features Ringo Starr as Christ wanting to use the toilet. Friedman's own career never shone as bright as the 3D portrait of Christ he had at his home and, in 1977, he dropped his touring band and went solo. He also improved his diction so that his insults could be understood. He sang the title song of the film *Skating On Thin Ice,* and he was murdered in his acting role in *Easter Sunday,* a film starring Dorothy Malone and Ruth Buzzi. Friedman has become a perceptive writer writing on country music for *Rolling Stone* and his

novel, *Greenwich Killing Time,* is about a country singer turned detective. In 1992 a collection of his novels was published by Faber & Faber. Friedman briefly returned to performing to promote this anthology, although his live sets merely reprised his old material. Friedman says his autobiography will be printed backwards, like old Jewish texts.

Albums: *Sold American* (1973), *Kinky Friedman* (1974), *Lasso From El Paso* (1976), *Under The Double Ego* (1983), *Kinky Friedman, Live At The Lone Star* (80s).

Further reading: *Greenwich Killing Time,* Kinky Friedman. *The Kinky Friedman Crime Club,* Kinky Friedman.

Frizzell, David

b. 26 September 1941, El Dorado, Texas, USA. In the mid-50s, David hitch-hiked to California to join and tour with his older brother Lefty Frizzell. He recorded some unsuccessful country/rockabilly tracks for Columbia in 1958 and served in the US Army during the early 60s. After his discharge, he made further recordings for various labels and gained a Top 40 US country chart hit in 1970, after returning to Columbia, with 'I Just Can't Help Believing'. He worked for a time in the 70s for Buck Owens on his networked *Ranch Show* television programme, managed a nightclub and had minor hits on Cartwheel, Capitol and RSO. He first worked at the club with Shelly West (the daughter of singer Dottie West), who was at the time married to his younger brother Allen Frizzell (b.1951). Allen was for a time Dottie West's lead guitarist and front man. He had three minor country hits in the 80s, in his own right but became more involved with the business side of the industry than with performing. In 1978, the two brothers and Shelly West toured extensively. David and Shelly had a US country number 1 in 1981 with 'You're The Reason God Made Oklahoma', which featured in the Clint Eastwood film *Any Which Way You Can*. They had made a demo recording of the song some considerable time before, but it had been turned down by record companies until chosen by Eastwood for the film. Further country Top 10 hits followed including 'A Texas State Of Mind' and 'I Just Came Here To Dance'. He also had a popular solo recording, 'Lofty', a tribute to his brother, that also featured Merle Haggard. 1982 proved to be a big year for him with a US country number 1 with 'I'm Gonna Hire A Wino To Decorate Our Home', followed by a number 5 hit with 'Lost My Baby Blues'. Another duet recording with Shelly West called 'Please Surrender' was used by Eastwood in his film *Honkytonk Man*. Further solo hits include 'Where Are You Spending Your Nights These Days', 'A Million Light Beers Ago' and a further Top 20 duet with 'It's A Be Together Night'. A talented and capable singer, although by no means the equal of his legendary brother, even if at times there is a slight vocal resemblance.

Albums: *The Family's Fine But This One's All Mine* (1982), *On My Own Again* (1983), *Solo* (1984), *David Sings Lefty Frizzell* (1987); with Shelly West *Carrying On The Family Names* (1981), *David Frizzell/Shelly West Album* (1982), *Our Best To You* (1983), *In Session* (1984).

Frizzell, Lefty

b. William Orville Frizzell, 31 March 1928, Corsicana, Navarro County, Texas, USA, d. 19 July 1975. The eldest of the eight children of an itinerant oil-field worker, he was raised mainly in El Dorado, Arkansas but also lived in sundry places in Texas and Oklahoma. Greatly influenced by his parents old 78s of Jimmie Rodgers, he sang as a young boy and when aged 12, he had a regular spot on KELD El Dorado. Two years later he was performing at local dances at Greenville and further exposure on other radio stations followed as the

family moved around. At the age of 16, he was playing the honky tonks and clubs in places such as Waco and Dallas and grew into a tough character himself as he performed the music of Jimmie Rodgers plus some of his own songs.

Some accounts insist that it was then that he became known as Lefty, because of a left hook he landed in a Golden Gloves boxing match, but this appears to have been later publicity hype by Columbia. Both his father and his wife have steadfastly denied the story, stressing that Lefty never took part in any such competition and had actually got the nickname for flattening the school bully during his school days. It seems that, though he played the guitar right-handed, he adopted a southpaw stance for fighting and dropped the bully with a left hook. This story tends to be born out by the report that it was a school friend and guitarist called Gene Whitworth, who first called him Lefty. He was actually always known as Sonny to his family. Any pugilistic ability he had though was doubtless useful in some of the honky tonks that he played in his early days. In 1945, he was married and his wife, Alice, became the inspiration for several of his songs over the thirty years the marriage lasted. From time-to-time, drinking led him into trouble with the authorities and he actually got the idea for his famous song 'I Love You A Thousand Ways', while spending a night in a Texas country jail. He made his first recordings for Columbia in 1950 and had immediate success when 'If You've Got The Money, I've Got The Time' and 'I Love You A Thousand Ways', both became US country number 1 hits.

He became close friends with Hank Williams, who suggested Lefty needed to join the *Grand Ole Opry*. Frizzell replied 'Look I got the number-one song, the number-two song, the number-seven song, the number-eight song on the charts and you tell me I need to join the *Opry*'. Hank thought for a while and commented 'Darned if you ain't got a hell of an argument'. The following year he had 7 Top 10 entries, which included three more number 1 hits, 'I Want To Be With You Always' (which also made Top 30 status in the US pop charts), 'Always Late (With Your Kisses)' and 'Give Me More More More (Of Your Kisses)'. Further Top 10s followed and as Merle Haggard later sang in his song 'The Way It Was in '51', 'Hank and Lefty crowded every jukebox'. In 1952, Lefty did join the *Opry* but left after a few months saying he did not like it. In 1953, Lefty moved from Beaumont, Texas to Los Angeles, where he became a regular on *Town Hall Party*. He had by now become accepted as a national entertainer and he recorded regularly, although the hits became fewer. Problems in his own life-style were perhaps to blame and certainly he and Hank had similar troubles. Charles Wolfe quotes Lefty once saying 'All Hank thought about was writing. He did record a number he wrote because I was having trouble with my better half, called 'I'm Sorry for You, My Friend'. Sometime later Hank became annoyed with his friend, because Lefty would not give him a song called 'What Am I Gonna Do With All This Love I Have For You', which Hank wished to record. Lefty formed the opinion that if it was that good he would record it himself but for some reason he never did.

Lefty Frizzell became upset about material not being released by Columbia and in 1954, he broke up his band, stopped writing songs and tired of the way he had been exploited, he became unpredictable. He was joined in California by his brother David Frizzell and for a time they toured together. Eventually he charted again with his version of Marty Robbins 'Cigarettes And Coffee Blues' and in 1959, he gained a number 6 US country hit with 'The Long Black Veil'. The *Town Hall Party* had closed in 1960 and late in 1961, Lefty decided to move to Nashville. He played bookings where ever he could and made further recordings, gaining minor hits that included 'Don't Let Her See Me Cry'. His career received a welcome boost in 1964 when 'Saginaw, Michigan' became a country number 1 and also entered the US pop charts. This song must rate as one of country music's finest ballads and Frizzell's version has rightly become a standard and worthy of a place in any collection. Twelve more chart entries followed between 1964-72 but only 'She's Gone Gone Gone' made the Top 20.

In the late 60's, he became totally depressed that Columbia were not releasing his material. The label issued some albums but few singles that were likely chart hits. In 1968, he even recorded with June Stearns as Agnes And Orville but, bothered by the lack of promotion of his own material, his drinking worsened. In 1972, after 22 years with the label, he left Columbia and joined ABC. The change seemed to work wonders. He set about recording material for albums, resumed playing concerts all over the States and appeared on network television. He charted such songs as 'I Can't Get Over You To Change My Life', 'I Never Go Around Mirrors' and 'Railroad Lady' and his album releases proved very popular. His superb song 'That's The Way Love Goes' (his own

recording was only issued as a b-side) became a US country number 1 for Johnny Rodriguez in 1974 and Merle Haggard in 1984.

He developed high blood pressure but refused to take medication for it since he thought the medicine would interfere with his alcohol consumption. In the depths of his drinking he was never nasty, just funny, which led writer Bob Oermann to later describe him as 'a lovable, punch drunk, boozy, puddin'-headed, bear like kind of a guy who never really got along with Nashville or the *Opry*'. He spent a lot of time between concerts fishing at his home just outside Nashville and though he had recently parted from his wife, they kept in daily contact by telephone. He was 47, and looked older but the blood pressure apart, he seemed to be in reasonable health. It therefore came as a surprise to most when, on the morning of 19 July 1975, he suffered a massive stroke and though rushed to Nashville's Memorial Hospital, he died later that evening of the resulting haemorrhage. Ironically, at the time of his death, his current chart hit was called 'Falling'.

Lefty Frizzell was a great songwriter and one of the best stylists that the world of country music has ever seen. His singing was distinctive, with a style of pronunciation that made him unique and a laidback delivery and gentle vibrato that may have appeared lazy but which was really a carefully designed pattern that he alone mastered. The bending of words as emphasised in Alway-yayys Lay-yate (Always Late) and similar songs led to him being described as a genius for phrasing. John Pugh once described his singing as 'a compelling, ethereal, transcendent vocal quality that has produced some of the most hauntingly beautiful sounds ever to emanate from a pair of human vocal chords'. His influence clearly shows on later performers such as Merle Haggard, John Anderson, Stoney Edwards, Randy Travis and George Strait, who, although not perhaps intentionally trying to imitate their mentor, are readily identifiable as Frizzell clones. Since his death many artists have recorded tribute songs, while some have even recorded complete albums including Willie Nelson (*To Lefty From Willie*) and brother David Frizzell (*David Sings Lefty*). Lefty Frizzell was elected to the *Nashville Songwriters Association International Hall Of Fame* in 1972 and inducted into the *Country Music Hall Of Fame* in 1982.

Albums: *The Songs Of Jimmie Rodgers* (1951), *Listen To Lefty* (1952), shared with Carl Smith and Marty Robbins *Carl, Lefty & Marty* (1956), *The One And Only Lefty Frizzell* (1959), *Sings The Songs Of*

Jimmie Rodgers (1960), *Saginaw, Michigan* (1964), *The Sad Side Of Love* (1965), *Country Favorites* (1966), *Puttin' On* (1967), *Mom And Dad's Waltz (& Other Great Country Hits)* (1967), *Signed Sealed And Delivered* (1968), *The Legendary Lefty Frizzell* (1973), *The Classic Style Of Lefty Frizzell* (1975), *Remembering* (1975), *The ABC Collection-Lefty Frizzell* (1977), *Treasures Untold:The Early Recordings Of Lefty* (1980), *Lefty Frizzell* (1982, Columbia Historic Edition), *Lefty Frizzell In 1951* (1982), *His Last 2 Sessions* (1982), *Country Classics* (1983), *Lefty Goes To Nashville* (1983), *The Legend Lives On* (1983), Bear Family 14 album boxed set *His Life - His Music* (1984), reissued as 12 CD set *Life's Like Poetry* (1992).

Further reading: *Lefty Frizzell His Life - His Music*, Charles Wolfe, Bremen, West Germany 1984.

Froggatt, Raymond

b. Raymond William Froggatt, 13 November 1941, Birmingham, England. Froggatt had a traumatic childhood, his father dying when he was young and missing schooling through tuberculosis. Froggatt joined the Birmingham scene in the mid-60s and his group, the Monopoly, was signed to Polydor. Their first single, 'House Of Lords', was written by the Bee Gees and, at Polydor's request, he used the stage name of Steve Newman - a cross between Steve McQueen and Paul Newman - but he soon reverted back. As part of the band, the Raymond Froggatt, he recorded 'Red Balloon' and says, 'I spent some time in Paris and there's a game in which children hold balloons on strings and weave in and out of them. If you get to the end of the balloons, you marry the farmer's daughter.' Dave Clark heard Froggatt's version, covered it with the Dave Clark Five, and reached number 7 in the UK chart. Although Froggatt's 'Big Ship' was rejected for Lulu in the *Eurovision Song Contest*, it became a Top 10 hit for Cliff Richard, who recorded several more of his songs. Other compositions include 'Rachel's Comin' Home' (Joan Baez), 'Only The Memories' (Gladys Knight And The Pips) and 'Everybody's Losin'' (Leon Russell). 'Louise', a track on *Bleach*, includes a concertina solo from an 82-year-old busker.

In the mid-70s, Froggatt, with guidance from promoter Mervyn Conn, switched to country and made a popular, easy listening album, *Southern Fried Frog*, in Nashville with top producer, Larry Butler. This helped establish him as the UK's top country artist and for a time, at every live performance, fans would hold up toy frogs and sway with their 'Froggie' scarves. His rough-hewn features, shades,

white dinner jacket and torn jeans make him a distinctive figure, and he has even been accepted in Warsaw. ('I was not allowed to do 'Teach Me Pa' as the authorities thought it was subversive.') 'Don't Let Me Cry Again' was a airplay hit on BBC Radio 2 in 1983 and, more recently, he has recorded 'Maybe The Angels' for leukaemia research. Hartley Cain has long provided lead guitar for Froggatt, who says of his own playing, 'I'm worse now than I was after a few lessons. It helps with my writing because I'm not restricted to certain chord sequences. Some of my songs sound clever but really it's a total lack of knowledge.' He was also one of the few musicians to be granted the Freedom of the City of Birmingham. He remains a popular if enigmatic performer, who makes little effort to conform to audience expectations.

Albums: *The Voice And Writing Of Raymond Froggatt* (1968), *Bleach* (1972), *Rogues And Thieves* (1974), *Southern Fried Frog* (1978), *Stay With Me* (1980), *Sooner Or Later* (1982), *Why* (1984), *Raymond Froggatt* (1986), *Live At Birmingham Odeon* (1987), *Is It Rollin' Bob* (1988), *Tour '89* (1989), *Here's To Everyone* (1992), *Songs From A Minstrel* (1992). Two albums recorded in the 70s, *Handle With Care* for Bell Records, and *Let The Memphis Moon Shine On Me* for Jet, remain, to date, unissued.

Fromholz, Steven

b. 8 June 1945, Temple, Texas, USA. Fromholz's father worked for the Ford Motor Company and the family travelled around the country. At the age of 18, he met Michael Martin Murphey at North Texas State University and they formed the Dallas County Jug Band and then the Michael Murphey Trio. Fromholz became half of Frummox with Don McCrimmon, and their poor-selling 1969 album is prized by collectors. The duo split in 1971 and Fromholz and his wife ran a restaurant in Gold Hill, Colorado. Stephen Stills invited him to join Manassas on the road, but Fromholz left after six months because 'I'd had too much cocaine and was sick.' He dedicated a single he recorded for Michael Nesmith's Countryside label, 'Sweet Janey', to his wife, but the album he made for Nesmith, *How Long Is The Road To Kentucky?*, was never released. Willie Nelson had a US country hit with Fromholz's song 'I'd Have To Be Crazy' and included him on his live album, *The Sound In Your Mind*. Fromholz's Capitol album, *A Rumour In My Own Time*, featuring Nelson, Doug Dillard and John Sebastian, is a fine example of outlaw country. He was unsuited to the easy listening arrangements on *Frolicking In The Myth*, although the album contained good material. He did, however, sound fine next to Peter Fonda on the soundtrack of the film, *Outlaw Blues*. He recorded an album for Willie Nelson's Lone Star label, *Jus' Playin' Along*, and his tribute to Hondo Crouch, the eccentric owner of Luckenbach, Texas, 'Hondo's Song', featured Nelson and was, surprisingly, released as a single in the UK.

Albums: as Frummox *From Here To There* (1969), *A Rumour In My Own Time* (1976), *Frolicking In The Myth* (1977), *Jus' Playin' Along* (1978), *Fromholz - Live* (1979), *Frummox 2* (1982).

G

Gatlin, Larry, And The Gatlin Brothers Band

Larry Wayne Gatlin, b. 2 May 1948, Seminole, Texas, USA, but raised in nearby Odessa. Gatlin's brothers, Steve and Rudy, (b. 4 April 1951 and 20 August 1952 respectively, Olney, Texas, USA). Their father, an oil driller, encouraged their fledgling talent and, with their younger sister LaDonna, they sang at church functions, appeared on television and made an album. They worked together for several years until Larry enrolled at the University of Houston. In 1971, he was a temporary replacement in the Imperials gospel group, and then Dottie West recorded his songs, 'Once You Were Mine' and 'You're The Other Half Of Me', and he moved to Nashville. Johnny Cash performed 'The Last Supper' and 'Help Me' in his documentary film, *The Gospel Road*, and also sang with Kris Kristofferson on his *Jesus Was A Capricorn*. Following Kristofferson's insistence, he was signed to Monument Records, and two singles were released simultaneously - the solo 'My Mind's Gone To Memphis' and the Gatlins' 'Come On In', which featured Steve, Rudy and LaDonna. In October 1973 Gatlin had his first US country hit with 'Sweet Becky Walker', which was followed by a personal collection of beautifully-sung love songs, *The Pilgrim*, with liner notes by Johnny Cash. Further successes followed with 'Bigger They Are, The Harder They Fall' (later recorded by Elvis Presley, who also sang 'Help Me') and 'Delta Dirt'. Larry produced Johnny Duncan's 'Jo And The Cowboy' and 'Third Rate Romance', and Steve, Rudy and LaDonna joined him as part of Tammy Wynette's roadshow. (Wynette, incidentally, recorded one of the quirkiest of Gatlin's compositions, 'Brown Paper Bag'.) Wynette's autobiography recounts how her affair with Rudy created friction between him and Larry. After leaving the show, LaDonna married Tim Johnson and they work as travelling evangelists. The Gatlin brothers, with Larry singing lead, Steve bass and Rudy tenor, had a US country Top 10 hit with 'Broken Lady', which won a Grammy as the Best Country Song of 1976. Larry recalls, 'the Eagles were very hot at the time with a lot of harmony and some real pretty acoustic guitars, so I decided to write something that had our voices up front without a lot of other things going on. That was 'Broken Lady' and it set the style for the Gatlin Brothers from then on.' The Gatlin brothers had success with 'Statues Without Hearts', 'I Don't Wanna Cry' (the title line followed a chance remark to an American disc jockey), 'Love Is Just A Game' (Larry later said: 'I wrote that for Neil Diamond but then realized that he didn't need another hit record, and I did!'), and 'I Just Wish You Were Someone I Love' (his first US country number 1). Their first single for US Columbia, 'All The Gold In California', was another country number 1, but many US radio stations banned 'The Midnight Choir' as sacrilegious. Their success tailed off when Larry's songs stopped being so distinctive, and, with much reluctance, Larry agreed to perform songs by outside writers. *Houston To Denver*, is one of their best albums but, ironically, the number 1 country single, 'Houston (Means I'm One Day Closer To You)', was Larry's own song. For some years, Larry had been an embarrassment to those that knew him, even causing songwriter Roger Bowling to include a snide reference to the Gatlins in 'Coward Of The County'. For example, Larry refused to sign autographs after shows - a cardinal sin for a country performer - saying, 'It's unfair to step off a stage after I've been singing my butt off and be met with 200 people sticking pencils in my face.' From 1979 to 1984 Gatlin had spent an estimated $500,000 on cocaine, but, to the relief of his friends, he eventually underwent treatment. Once cured, he joined Nancy Reagan's 'Just Say No' anti-drug campaign. The *Smile* album included 'Indian Summer', co-written with Barry Gibb and featuring a tender-voiced Roy Orbison. Larry says, 'I think I have proven I can write great songs because those who are acknowledged as having written great songs say so.'

Albums: by the Gatlin Quartet *The Old Country Church* (1961), *The Pilgrim* (1973), *Rain-Rainbow* (1974), *Larry Gatlin With Family And Friends* (1976), *Broken Lady* (1976), *High Time* (1976), *Love Is Just A Game* (1977), *Oh! Brother* (1978), *Straight Ahead* (1979), *Help Yourself* (1980), *Not Guilty* (1981), *Sure Feels Like Love* (1982), *A Gatlin Family Christmas* (1983), *Houston To Denver* (1984), *Smile* (1986), *Partners* (1987), *Pure 'N' Simple* (1989), *Cookin' Up A Storm* (1990), *Adios* (1992). NB: The Gatlin Boys who recorded the 1980 album, *A Long Time Coming*, are a British country music band.

Gayle, Crystal

b. Brenda Gail Webb, 9 January 1951, Paintsville,

Kentucky, USA. Gayle was the last of eight children born to Ted and Clara Webb. Her sister, Loretta Lynn, had her own story told in *Coal Miner's Daughter*, but, by the time Gayle was born, her father had a lung disease. When Gayle was four, the family moved to Wabash, Indiana, where her mother worked in a nursing home. Her father died in 1959. Clara Webb, who was musical, encouraged Gayle to sing at family gatherings and church socials. Unlike Lynn, her influences came from the Beatles and Peter, Paul And Mary. In the late 60s, after graduation, she signed with her sister's recording label, USA Decca. As the label already had Brenda Lee, a change of name was needed and, when they drove past a sign for Krystal hamburgers, Lynn said, 'That's your name. Crystals are bright and shiny, like you.' At first, she was managed by Lynn's husband, Mooney, and she was part of her stage show, appearing with her at the 1971 Wembley Country Music Festival. She established herself with regular appearances on Jim Ed Brown's television show, *The Country Place*. Lynn wrote some of her first records ('Sparklin' Look Of Love', 'Mama, It's Different This Time') and therein lay the problem - Crystal Gayle sounded like Loretta Lynn. Gayle first entered the US country charts in 1970 with 'I've Cried (The Blue Right Out Of My Eyes)', which was followed by 'Everybody Oughta Cry' and 'I Hope You're Having Better Luck Than Me'. There was nothing original about the records and Gayle, wanting a say in what she did, left the label. She joined United Artists and was teamed with producer Allen Reynolds, who was having success with Don Williams. Her first records had the easy-going charm of Williams' records, but her 1974 US country hit, 'Wrong Road Again', hinted at the dynamics in her voice. Reynolds, who wrote the song, did not have enough time to devote to composing but nurtured several songwriters (including Richard Leigh and Bob McDill) who supplied Gayle with excellent songs. Gayle also had a country hit with 'Beyond You', written by herself and lawyer/manager/husband, Vassilios 'Bill' Gatzimos. Gayle entered the US country Top 10 with the title song from *Somebody Loves You*, and followed it with her first number 1 country single, 'I'll Get Over You', written by Leigh. Reynolds, when time allowed, was a fine songwriter and his 'Ready For The Times To Get Better' was featured on *Crystal*. In 1976, Gayle was voted Female Vocalist of the Year by the Academy of Country Music, but Reynolds knew there was a bigger market than country fans for her records.

He seized the opportunity when Leigh wrote the jazz-tinged ballad, 'Don't It Make My Brown Eyes Blue', although United Artists had reservations. 'They thought it was a mistake,' said Reynolds. 'It was gimmickless, straight ahead, soulful and classy, but that's all it takes.' The public found 'Don't It Make My Brown Eyes Blue' irresistible and it went to number 2 in the US pop charts and reached number 5 in the UK. 'Don't It Make My Brown Eyes Blue' won Grammy awards for the Best Female Country Vocal Performance and for the Best Country Song. The album on which it appeared, *We Must Believe In Magic*, became the first album by a female country artist to sell over a million copies. Gayle, who was Female Vocalist of the Year for both the Academy of Country Music and the Country Music Association, said, 'There is no rivalry between me and Loretta and if there is, it is on a friendly basis. I know that Loretta voted for me at the CMA awards in Nashville.' Gayle played UK dates with Kenny Rogers and appeared with great success at the Wembley Country Music Festivals of 1977 and 1979. In 1979, she became the first US country artist to perform in China. Although petite in stature, she had a mesmerizing stage act. With her back to the audience, they watched her luxurious hair sway back and forth. Gayle grows her hair to three inches off the floor. 'If it's on the ground, I find I step on it on stage. When you've hair like this, you cannot plan anything other than washing your hair and doing your concert.' Her fifth album, again produced by Reynolds, *When I Dream*, included the credit, 'Suggestions: Crystal'. It was a lavish production with 50 musicians being credited, including such established Nashville names as Hargus 'Pig' Robbins, Lloyd Green, Bob Moore and Kenny Malone. The title track, a torch ballad, brought out the best in Crystal's voice. The British writer, Roger Cook, who had settled in Nashville, gave her a soulful ballad touching on the paranoia some lovers feel, 'Talking In Your Sleep'. Released as a single, it reached number 11 in the UK and number 18 in the USA. Another popular album track/single was 'Why Have You Left The One You Left Me For?'. In 1979 Gayle released her final album for United Artists, ironically called *We Should Be Together*. It included two more country hits with the ballads, 'Your Kisses Will' and 'Your Old Cold Shoulder'. That year she joined US Columbia and quickly had a US pop hit with 'Half The Way'. She had three country number 1s among her 10 hits for the label. She recorded an excellent version of Neil Sedaka's 'The Other Side

Crystal Gayle

Of Me' and surprised many fans by reviving an early country record, Jimmie Rodgers' 'Miss The Mississippi And You'. In 1982 she moved to Elektra and worked on the soundtrack of the Francis Ford Coppola film, *One From The Heart* with Tom Waits. Gayle has had many more country chart entries, including number 1s with a revival of Johnnie Ray's 'Cry' and duets with Eddie Rabbitt ('You And I') and Gary Morris ('Making Up For Lost Time'). In 1983 she was placed in the Top 10 most attractive women in the world, and her beauty can be seen in the best-selling video which she recorded at Hamilton Palace, Canada. In 1988 Gayle appeared at the Wembley Country Music Festival and introduced her daughter Catherine to the audience. Gayle lives with her husband, son and daughter on an eight-acre ranch outside Nashville and she also owns a shop which stocks Waterford and Swedish crystal. She often plays gambling centres like Las Vegas and Atlantic City, and, also in 1988, she performed at Lake Tahoe with Lynn, the first time they had been joint headliners. She has considered recording a traditional country album with her sisters, Lynn and Peggy Sue Wright. In recent years, Gayle has joined Capitol Records and her 1990 album, *Ain't Gonna Worry*, reunited her with Reynolds. Buzz Stone produced *Three Good Reasons*, which was a heartening return to her country roots.

Selected albums: *Crystal Gayle* (1974), *Somebody Loves You* (1975), *Crystal* (1976), *We Must Believe In Magic* (1977), *When I Dream* (1978), *I've Cried The Blue Right Out Of My Eyes* (1978), *We Should Be Together* (1979), *Miss The Mississippi* (1979), *A Woman's Heart* (1980), *These Days* (1980), *Hollywood/Tennessee* (1981), *True Love* (1982), with Tom Waits *One From The Heart* (1982, film soundtrack), *Cage The Songbird* (1983), *Nobody Wants To Be Alone* (1985), *Crystal Gayle* (1986), *Straight To The Heart* (1986), with Gary Morris *What If We Fall In Love* (1987), *Nobody's Angel* (1988), *Ain't Gonna Worry* (1990), *Three Good Reasons* (1992). Compilations: *Crystal Gayle's Greatest Hits* (1983).

Gene And Debbe

Gene Thomas (b. 28 December 1938, Palestine, Texas, USA) was already a hit-maker in his own right before teaming up with Debbe Neville in 1967. Thomas had logged two chart hits: 1961's 'Sometime' and 1964's 'Baby's Gone', both country ballads. He met Neville when he was a staff songwriter for Acuff-Rose music in Nashville. Their first single, on TRX Records, 'Go With

Me', was a minor hit but 'Playboy' the following year made it to the US Top 20. After one last collaboration, 'Lovin' Season', the duo split up, Thomas returned to his writing job and Neville disappeared from the pop music scene.

Gentry, Bobbie

b. Roberta Lee Streeter, 27 July 1944, Chicasaw County, Mississippi, USA. Gentry, of Portuguese descent, was raised on a poverty-stricken farm in Greenwood, Mississippi and was interested in music from an early age. She wrote her first song at the age of seven ('My Dog Sergeant Is A Good Dog') and learnt piano - black keys only! - guitar, banjo and vibes. By her teens, she was regularly performing and she took her stage name from the film, *Ruby Gentry*. After studying both philosophy and music, she was signed to Capitol Records and recorded 'Mississippi Delta' for an a-side. To her own guitar accompaniment, Gentry recorded the b-side, 'Ode To Billie Joe', in 30 minutes. Violins and cellos were added, the song was reduced from its original seven minutes, and, because of disk jockey's reactions, it became the a-side. Despite competition from Lee Hazlewood, Gentry's version topped the US charts for four weeks and reached number 13 in the UK. Capitol's truncated version added to the song's mystery: what did Billie Joe and his girlfriend throw off the Tallahatchie Bridge and why did Billie Joe commit suicide? The song's main thrust, however, was the callousness of the girl's family to the event, and it can be twinned with Jeannie C. Riley's subsequent story of 'Harper Valley PTA'. Gentry became a regular headliner in Las Vegas and she married Bill Harrah, the manager of the Desert Inn Hotel. (Gentry's second marriage, in 1978, was to singer-songwriter Jim Stafford.) Gentry made an easy listening album with Glen Campbell, which included successful revivals of the Everly Brothers hits, 'Let It Be Me' (US Top 40) and 'All I Have To Do Is Dream' (US Top 30/UK number 3). Gentry, with good looks similar to Priscilla Presley, was given her own UK television series, *The Bobbie Gentry Show*, which helped her to top the charts in 1969 with the Burt Bacharach and Hal David song from *Promises, Promises*, 'I'll Never Fall In Love Again'. The 1976 film, *Ode To Billy Joe* (sic), starred Robby Benson and Glynnis O'Connor, and had Billy Joe throw his girlfriend's ragdoll over the bridge and commit suicide because of a homosexual affair. Gentry herself retired from performing to look after her business interests.

Albums: *Ode To Billie Joe* (1967), *Delta Sweetie*

Bobbie Gentry

(1968), *Bobbie Gentry And Glen Campbell* (1968), *Local Gentry* (1968), *Touch 'Em With Love* (1969), *I'll Never Fall In Love Again* (1970), *Fancy* (1970), *Patchwork* (1971), *Sittin' Pretty/Tobacco Road* (1971).

Gibbs, Terri

b. 15 June 1954, Augusta, Georgia, USA. Gibbs was born blind and has been playing the piano since she was three. She listened to a wide repertoire of music and, even though she is regarded as a country singer, there are many other influences, notably Ray Charles. Gibbs sang gospel in her early teens and formed her own band, Sound Dimension. Meeting Chet Atkins, she was encouraged to be a professional performer. In 1975, she started a long residency at the Augusta Steak And Ale Restaurant, playing 50 songs a night. Her appearance had impressed an MCA executive while her demo tapes had been noticed by producer/songwriter Ed Penney. Her debut single for MCA, the country soul of 'Somebody's Knockin', was reached number 13 on the US pop charts. Subsequently, she has only had country hits, which included 'Rich Man', 'Mis'ry River', 'Somedays It Rains All Day Long' and 'Anybody Else's Heart But Mine', but, despite her talent, she has not emerged as a major country star. In 1984, she recorded a duet, 'Slow Burning Fire' with George Jones and she said, 'His style and his phrasing had a big influence on my own singing.'
Albums: *Somebody's Knockin'* (1981), *I'm A Lady* (1981), *Some Days It Rains All Night* (1982), *Over Easy* (1983), *Hiding From Love* (1984), *Old Friends* (1985).

Gibson, Don

b. 3 April 1928, Shelby, North Carolina, USA. If loneliness meant world acclaim, then Gibson with his catalogue of songs about despair and heartbreak would be a superstar. Gibson learnt the guitar from an early age and started performing while still at school. He worked some years around the clubs in Knoxville and he built up a reputation via local radio. His first records were made as part of the Sons Of The Soil for Mercury in 1949. His first recorded composition was 'Why Am I So Lonely?'. Gibson recorded for RCA, Columbia and MGM (where he recorded the rockabilly 'I Ain't A-Studyin' You, Baby' in 1957), but with little chart success. However, Faron Young took his forlorn ballad, 'Sweet Dreams' to number 2 in the US country charts in 1956. It has since been associated with Patsy Cline and also recorded by Emmylou Harris, Don Everly, Roy Buchanan, Reba

McIntyre and Elvis Costello. 'I Can't Stop Loving You' was a US country hit for Kitty Wells and then, in 1960, a transatlantic number 1 for Ray Charles. In 1991, the song was revived by Van Morrison with the Chieftains. 'I Can't Stop Loving You' was also one side of the hit single (US number 7 pop, number 1 country) which marked his return to RCA in 1958. The other side, 'Oh Lonesome Me', which Gibson had originally intended for George Jones, is also a much-recorded country classic. Gibson actually sings 'Ole lonesome me' but a clerk misheard his vocal. Chet Atkins' skilful productions appealed to both pop and country fans and this single was followed by 'Blue Blue Day', reaching number 20 pop, and number 1 in the country charts, 'Give Myself A Party', 'Don't Tell Me Your Troubles', 'Just One Time' and his own version of 'Sweet Dreams'. In 1961 Gibson made his UK chart debut with 'Sea Of Heartbreak', which was followed by the similar-sounding 'Lonesome Number One'. The sadness of his songs matched Roy Orbison's, who recorded an album *Roy Orbison Sings Don Gibson* in 1967 and had a hit single with 'Too Soon To Know'. His own bleak *King Of Country Soul*, which includes some country standards, is highly regarded. Gibson lost his impetus through his alcohol and drug dependency, but he recorded successful duets with both Dottie West and Sue Thompson. He had a US country number 1 with 'Woman (Sensuous Woman)' in 1972. Gibson occasionally comes to the UK for appearances at country festivals, but strangely, his greatest composition, '(I'd Be) A Legend In My Time', a US country number 1 for Ronnie Milsap, has never been a UK hit.
Albums: *Oh Lonesome Me* (1958), *Songs By Don Gibson* (1958), *No One Stands Alone* (1959), *That Gibson Boy* (1959), *Look Who's Blue i* (1960), *Sweet Dreams* (1960), *Girls, Guitars And Gibson* (1961), *Some Favourites Of Mine* (1962), *I Wrote A Song* (1963), *God Walks These Hills* (1964), *Too Much Hurt* (1965), *Don Gibson* (1965), *The Fabulous Don Gibson* (1965), *A Million Blue Tears* (1965), *Hurtin' Inside* (1966), *Don Gibson With Spanish Guitars* (1966), *Great Country Songs* (1966), *All My Love* (1967), *The King Of Country Soul* (1968), *More Country Soul* (1968), *I Love You So Much It Hurts* (1968), *My God Is Real* (1969), with Dottie West *Dottie And Don* (1969), *Don Gibson Sings All-Time Country Gold* (1969), *Hits - The Don Gibson Way* (1970), *A Perfect Mountain* (1970), *Hank Williams As Sung By Don Gibson* (1971), *Country Green* (1972), *Woman (Sensuous Woman)* (1972), *Sample*

Don Gibson

Kisses (1972), *Am I That Easy To Forget?* (1973), with Sue Thompson *The Two Of Us Together* (1973), *Touch The Morning/That's What I'll Do* (1973), with Thompson *Warm Love* (1973), *Just Call Me Lonesome* (1973), *Snap Your Fingers* (1974), *Bring Back Your Love To Me* (1974), *Just One Time* (1974), *I'm The Loneliest Man/There She Goes I Wish Her Well* (1975), with Thompson *Oh How Love Changes* (1975), *Don't Stop Loving Me* (1975), *I'm All Wrapped Up In You* (1976), *If You Ever Get To Houston (Look Me Down)* (1977), *Starting All Over Again* (1978), *Look Who's Blue* ii (1978), *Rockin' Rollin' Gibson, Volume 1* (1982), *Rockin' Rollin' Gibson, Volume 2* (1982), *Don Gibson And Los Indios Tabajaras* (1986), *Don Gibson - The Early Days* (1986), *A Legend In My Time* (1987), *The Singer: The Songwriter, 1949-62* (1991, boxed set), *Currents* (1992).
Further reading: *Don Gibson - A Legend In His Own Time*, Richard Weize and Charles Wolfe

Gibson, Lorne

b. 1940, Edinburgh, Scotland. At the age of 17, Gibson, who was working in a cafe, found an interest in country music when a customer played him a Hank Williams EP. He said, 'The songs were simple and easy to play and sing. It was

several years before I realized how good they were.' In the early 60s, rock 'n' roll impresario, Larry Parnes, wanted to promote Gibson, who took his stage name from the make of guitar, as 'sweet rock'. Instead, Gibson signed with Tommy Sanderson, who was to manage the Hollies and Lulu. The BBC Light Programme was looking for a British country performer, so he formed the Lorne Gibson Trio, the most regular members being Steve Vaughan (guitar) and Vic Arnold (bass). His *Side By Side* series featured various musical guests including the Beatles, who had just released their first records: Lorne was then to guest on their series, *Pop Go The Beatles!* Although Gibson did not have chart hits, cover versions of Jimmy Dean's 'Little Black Book' and Freddie Hart's 'Some Do, Some Don't' for Decca sold 60,000 apiece. Gibson never made an album for Decca, saying, 'They wouldn't let me. If I'd made an album it could only have been on my own terms. They didn't want me doing country and had me listed as a calypso singer.' Gibson sang the theme of the Peter Sellers comedy film, *Heavens Above!*, and played the ghost in the pop film, *The Ghost Goes Gear*. Gibson was only filmed from one side as an accident had necessitated several stitches on the other side of his face. Over a period of months, 'Red Roses For A Blue Lady' sold a respectable 175,000, but did not make the charts. He says, 'I never expected to have a hit. I discovered early on that country music fans don't buy British records. They didn't then and, to a great extent, they still don't.' Gibson, who still performs occasionally, has maintained his repertoire - 'Devil Woman', 'Eighteen Yellow Roses', the tongue-twisting 'The Auctioneer' and an off-beat Jack Clement song, 'You've Got The Cleanest Mind In The Whole Wide World ('Cause You Change It Every Minute)'. Gibson's singles deserve to be collected onto a compilation, while an album he recorded in 1978, For The Life Of A Song, was never released. He is, however, featured on the 1974 album based on the BBC Radio 2 series Up Country.

Gill, Vince

b. Vincent Grant Gill, 5 April 1957, Norman, Oklahoma, USA. Gill's father, a lawyer who played in a part-time country band, encouraged his son to have a career in country music. While still at school, Gill joined the bluegrass group Mountain Smoke. He moved to Louisville in 1975 and joined Bluegrass Alliance with Sam Bush and Dan Crary. In 1979, he was able to demonstrate his vocal, guitar, banjo and fiddle talents with Pure Prairie League and he is present on their albums, Can't Hold Back, Firin' Up and Something In The Night. Gill then became part of Rodney Crowell's backing group, the Cherry Bombs. He began his solo recording career with a six-track mini album for RCA, Turn Me Loose. His duet with Rosanne Cash, 'If It Weren't For Him', was withdrawn due to contractual difficulties. He was among the musicians on Patty Loveless' albums, and she repaid the compliment by duetting with him on 'When I Call Your Name', which was named Single Of The Year by the Country Music Association. Gill married Janis Oliver from Sweethearts Of The Rodeo and he wrote 'Never Knew Lonely' while he was homesick in Europe. He added vocal harmonies to Dire Straits' best-selling album, On Every Street, and Mark Knopfler in turn appears on his album, Pocket Full Of Gold.
In 1991, he had Top 10 US country chart hits with 'Pocket Full Of Gold', 'Liza Jane' and 'Look At Us' and was voted the Male Vocalist Of The Year at the 1991 Country Music Association's Annual Awards Show. In 1992, he went one better when he not only picked up the Male Vocalist Of The Year award but also the award for Song Of The Year with 'Look At Us', a song he co-wrote with

Max D. Barnes. In 1992 additions to his chart successes included 'I Still Believe In You' (number 1) and 'Take Your Memory With You' (number 2). Gill later revealed he had turned down the offer to join Dire Straits for their 1992 world tour, preferring to concentrate on his own career. Among performers and public alike, Gill is now established as one of the most respected figures in country music.
Albums: Turn Me Loose (1983), The Things That Matter (1984), Vince Gill (1985), The Way Back Home (1987), When I Call Your Name (1989), Pocket Full Of Gold (1991), I Never Knew Lonely (1992), I Still Believe In You (1992).

Gilley, Mickey

b. 9 March 1936, Ferriday, Louisiana, USA. Gilley is a cousin to Jerry Lee Lewis and the evangelist, Jimmy Swaggart. Gilley's mother, a waitress, saved her money to buy him a piano when he was 12 years old and at the age of 17 he left Louisiana and started working in bars in Houston. His first record was 'Tell Me Why' for the aptly-named Minor label in 1957. He had regional success in 1959 with 'Is It Wrong?' with Kenny Rogers on bass. In 1964 he started a record label, Astro, in Houston and again did well locally with 'Lonely Wine'. The resulting album is now valued at £200. In 1968 he signed with Louisiana's Paula label and had short-lived success with 'Now I Can Live Again'. He was heard at the Des Nesadel club in Houston by local businessman, Sherwood Cryer. Cryer was impressed with Gilley's performance and invited him to his club, Shelley's, in Pasadena, Texas, with a view to a partnership. In 1971, the club re-opened as Gilley's, which, through regular exposure on television, became very popular. Gilley himself was a resident performer and, to please a jukebox operator, he recorded Harlan Howard's 'She Called Me Baby' for his Astro label. The Houston disc jockeys preferred the b-side, a revival of George Morgan's country hit, 'Room Full Of Roses'. In 1974, Playboy magazine, which had its own label, reissued it nationally and 'Room Full Of Roses' was a number 1 US country hit and also made the pop charts. Continuing with his country 'flower power', he followed it with another chart-topping revival, 'I Overlooked An Orchid'. Gilley also made the US country Top 10 with 'Overnight Sensation', a duet with Playmate-turned-country singer, Barbi Benton. His success on the US country charts was soon outstripping his cousin's as he had number 1 records with revivals ('City Lights', 'Window Up Above', 'Bring It On

Home To Me') and with new songs ('Don't The Girls All Get Prettier At Closing Time', 'She's Pulling Me Back Again'). However, most of his records were strongly influenced by Jerry Lee Lewis and were made quickly and cheaply. After Gilley signed with Epic, the producer Jim Ed Norman was determined to take him out of Lewis' shadow and have him spend more time on his records. His revival of 'True Love Ways' was a US number 1 country hit in 1980 and was followed by 'Stand By Me', which he sang in *Urban Cowboy*, a film starring John Travolta - and a mechanical bull - and set in Gilley's. Gilley's was so successful that it had been extended to take 3,500 customers and Cryer, having the patent on the mechanical bull, made a fortune by selling them to other clubs. 'Stand By Me' made number 22 on the US pop charts, and Johnny Lee, the bandleader at Gilley's, also did well with 'Lookin' For Love'. Gilley continued his run of country number one's with revivals of 'You Don't Know Me' and 'Talk To Me, Talk To Me' and also a duet with Charly McClain called 'Paradise Tonight'. In 1987 he split acrimoniously with Cryer, which resulted in the closure of Gilley's club. After a legal action, Gilley was awarded $17 million, which included considerable back royalties on T-shirts sales alone. No longer confined to the club, Gilley has toured extensively, but has not tried to build a UK following. Surprisingly, Gilley has only ever had three singles released in the UK ('Room Full Of Roses', 'Stand By Me' and 'You Don't Know Me'). Gilley mentions Jerry Lee Lewis in his stage show and includes 'Great Balls Of Fire' and is keen to record an album with his cousin. He says, 'I've always given Jerry Lee credit for being the best talent in the family. He created that piano style and it rubbed off on me.'

Albums: *Lonely Wine* (1964), *Down The Line With Mickey Gilley* (1967), *Room Full Of Roses* (1974), *City Lights* (1975), *Mickey's Movin' On* (1975), *Overnight Sensation* (1975), *Gilley's Smokin'* (1976), *First Class* (1977), *Mickey At Gilley's* (1978), *Flying High* (1978), *The Songs We Made Love To* (1979), *That's All That Matters To Me* (1980), *Down The Line* (1980), *You Really Don't Know Me* (1981), *Christmas At Gilley's* (1981), *Put Your Dreams Away* (1982), *Fool For Your Love* (1983), *You've Really Got A Hold On Me* (1983), with Charly McClain *It Takes Believers* (1984), *20 Golden Songs* (1984), *Too Good To Stop Now* (1984), *From Pasadena With Love* (1985), *I Feel Good* (1986), *Back To Basics* (1987), *Rockin' Rollin' Piano* (1987), *Chasing Rainbows* (1988).

Gilmore, Jimmie Dale

Gilmore is one of the many singer-songwriters to emerge from Lubbock. He has the three common influences for American singer-songwriters: Hank Williams, Elvis Presley and Bob Dylan. His father played in an old-time country band, and Gilmore learned fiddle, trombone and guitar. He began to perform around coffee houses in Lubbock and one of his earliest compositions was 'Treat Me Like A Saturday Night'. Joe Ely gave him a Townes Van Zandt record which changed his life: 'It was a revelation to me because I heard both worlds, folk and country, in the same place.' Gilmore, Ely and Butch Hancock worked in different combinations until all three came together in the Flatlanders, which was formed in 1971. The acoustic band also featured Steve Wesson's musical saw, and fanciful commentators have likened its sound to the Lubbock wind. The Flatlanders took their name from the landscape and they played bars around Austin and Lubbock. Gilmore's nasal whine was as flat as that landscape but it was suited to his laidback, evocative songwriting. Under the name of Jimmie Dale, they released a single of Gilmore's 'Dallas' with its oft-quoted first line, 'Did you ever see Dallas from a DC-9 at night?'. Another key song was Gilmore's 'Tonight I Think I'm Gonna Go Downtown', but the album they made in 1972 was not released until 1980. The Flatlanders was over within a year but it is fondly remembered by Ely and Hancock, who have developed solo careers. Gilmore, meanwhile, spent much of his time studying philosophy. His two albums for Hightone, *Fair And Square* and *Jimmie Dale Gilmore*, have strong country roots and include some superb Butch Hancock songs ('Red Chevrolet', 'Just A Wave, Not The Water'). In 1988 Hancock and Gilmore sang nearly 300 different songs over the course of a few nights in London. They recorded together and Gilmore became part of Elektra's American Explorer series, excelling himself on his *After Awhile* album. Gilmore may never match Ely and Hancock, but he is a significant influence on their work.

Albums: as the Flatlanders *One Road More* (1980), *Fair And Square* (1988), *Jimmie Dale Gilmore* (1989), with Butch Hancock *Two Roads - Live In Australia* (1990), *After Awhile* (1991). The albums, *Fair And Square* and *Jimmie Dale Gilmore*, were issued together on a single CD in 1989.

Gimble, Johnny

b. 30 May 1926, near Tyler, Texas, USA. The fifth of six brothers, Gimble grew up in a musical environment since all his brothers played some stringed instrument. By the age of 12, having already learned both fiddle and mandolin, he was playing with four of his brothers at local dances and made his first radio appearances while still at school. He left home when he was 17 and found work playing fiddle and banjo with the Shelton Brothers and also with Jimmie Davis on KWKH Shreveport. In 1949, he joined Bob Wills' Texas Playboys (for the first time) and moved with Wills from Oklahoma to Dallas, when he opened the Bob Wills Ranch House. Around 1951, he left full-time work with Wills but later played with him on other occasions. Gimble continued to play local venues and did session work with several artists including Marty Robbins and Lefty Frizzell but in 1955, seeking some work with security, he became a barber and moved to Waco. During the 60s, he returned to a full-time musical career. He realized that he could find a lot of work as a session musician and relocated with his family to Nashville. Here his talents were much in demand and he worked with many top artists including Merle Haggard, who used him, as an ex-Texas Playboy, on his tribute album to Bob Wills. Apart from his countless session recordings with others, he recorded in his own right and worked with the popular First Nashville Jesus Band. He moved to Austin in the late 70s but still continued with some session work in Nashville. He has toured with many artists including Willie Nelson, has been featured on the popular *Hee-Haw* and *Austin City Limits* television series and has made several appearances at the Wembley Festival in London. He is one of the finest fiddle players of all time and equally at home with western-swing, country, blues or jazz music and during his career he has won many awards.

Albums: *Fiddlin' Around* (1974), *Honky Tonk Hits* (1976), *Texas Dance Party* (1976), with the Texas Swing Pioneers *Still Swingin'* (1976), *Texas Fiddle Connection* (1981), *Honky Tonk Hurtin' Songs* (1981), *More Texas Dance Hall Favorites* (1981), *I Saw The Light* (1981), with Joe Barnhill's Nashville Sound Company *Swingin' The Standards* (1981), *My Kinda Music* (1984).

Girls Next Door

In 1982, the Nashville record producer, Tommy West, formerly of Cashman And West, asked session singer, Doris King (b. 13 February 1957, Nashville, Tennessee, USA), to find three other girls for a harmony group which could blend country with soul and big band music. King

recruited Cindy Nixon (b. 3 August 1958, Nashville, Tennessee, USA), Tammy Stephens (b. 13 April 1961, Arlington, Texas, USA) and Diane Williams (b. 9 August 1959, Hahn, AFB, Germany), and they originally called themselves Belle. Changing to The Girls Next Door, they had moderate success on the US country charts including a Top 10 entry with a revival of 'Slow Boat To China'.

Albums: *Girls Next Door* (1986), *What A Girl Next Door Can Do* (1987), *How 'Bout Us* (1990).

Girls Of The Golden West

Mildred Fern Good (b. 11 April 1913) and Dorothy Laverne Good (b. 11 December 1915, d. 12 November 1967, Hamilton, Ohio, USA), both at Mount Carmel, Illinois, USA. During the 30s, when duets were extremely popular, the Good Sisters were the most famous of the female duet singers. The Good family were of German extraction (originally being named Goad) and their father had at times been a schoolteacher, a farmer and storekeeper before moving to East St. Louis, where he worked in a factory. Their mother played guitar, taught the young Dorothy the essentials and the girls made their radio debut as Mildred and Dorothy Goad on KMOX St. Louis around 1930. They soon became Millie and Dolly Good but a smart agent dressed them in cowboy outfits with fringed skirts, announced that they came from Muleshoe, Texas and billed them somewhat imaginatively as the Girls Of The Golden West. They were to maintain the erroneous Texas connection for the whole of their career. Using only Dolly's simple guitar accompaniment and drawing heavily on western-type songs, they developed a pleasant style with Dolly singing lead vocals and Millie providing the harmony. They had both learned to yodel as children and their ability to also yodel in harmony made them almost unique in their field. Around 1931, they moved to WLS Chicago, where they joined the *National Barn Dance* and in July 1933, they made their first recordings for RCA-Victor. They made further recordings in 1934 and 1935 and in 1937 moved to WLW Cincinnati, appearing first on the *Renfro Valley Barn Dance* and then in 1939, they became stars of the *Boone County Jamboree* and *Midwestern Hayride*. They made their final Victor recordings in Chicago in 1938, which brought their recorded output to 64 tracks. During the 30s and 40s, they were a very popular act and toured extensively throughout the midwest and part of the south. They remained in Cincinnati until 1949 when, except for the odd appearance in the 50s, they nominally retired. In 1963, they recorded for Bluebonnet and Dolly did some solo work. One of their popular songs was 'Silver Moon On The Golden Gate', which they found amusing since neither had ever seen the noted bridge or even been to San Francisco.

Albums: *Girls Of The Golden West Volumes 1 - 6* (mid-60s), *The Girls Of The Golden West (Selected Recordings)* (1980), *Songs Of The West* (1981).

Goodacre, Tony

b. 3 February 1938, Leeds, England. With up to 300 shows a year, Tony Goodacre has been amongst the hardest working British country musicians. In his adolescence, Goodacre acted, sang and played piano but, realizing the advantages of being able to entertain on demand, he switched to guitar. He formed the Tigers Skiffle Group while in the Royal Air Force and conversations with American servicemen led to his passion for country music. He borrowed dozens of hard-to-obtain American country records and set about learning the songs. In September 1956, Goodacre secured his first professional engagement singing country music. He had a day job in Leeds during the late 50s and 60s but he worked clubs and pubs in the evenings. In 1969 he began working regularly with steel guitarist, Arthur Layfield, and they became the nucleus for a new group, Goodacre Country. Economics are such that Goodacre now usually works solo but he teams up with Layfield occasionally as well as several seasoned musicians, many of whom have played on his albums. Ever since 1975 when he included eight original songs on *Grandma's Feather Bed,* Goodacre has championed the cause of British country songwriters. *Written In Britain* was totally that, and amongst the songwriters he has featured are Terry McKenna, Geoff Ashford, Sammy King and Stewart Ross. George Hamilton IV, president of his fan club, encouraged Goodacre to play in Nashville, which culminated in appearances at the *Grand Ole Opry* in 1977. The following year he returned to Nashville to record *Mr Country Music,* and his tours have included the USA Australasia and Europe. In 1980, along with his wife Sylvia, Goodacre formed his own Sylvantone label, which has released albums by other British acts, some of whom received his management guidance. His albums - and videos - are sold at personal appearances where his most popular songs include 'Old Shep', 'The Country Hall Of Fame' and 'The Old Rugged Cross' as well as several of the original songs he has recorded through the years.

Albums: *Roaming 'Round In Nashville* (1974), *Grandma's Feather Bed* (1975), *Thanks To The Hanks* (1976), *Written In Britain* (1977), *Mr. Country Music* (1978), *You've Made My Life Complete* (1979), *Recorded Live In Ilkley* (1980), *25th Anniversary* (1981), *Red Roses* (1984), *The Tony Goodacre Collection* (1986), *Country Favourites* (1988), *Something Special* (1989).

Gosdin, Vern

b. 5 August 1934, Woodland, Alabama, USA. Vern's first steps in carrying out his wish to be a country singer/songwriter came in the early 50s, when as a result of singing with his two brothers in the local church they became regulars as the Gosdin Family on WVOK Birmingham. In 1953, he moved to Atlanta where he sold ice cream and in 1956 to Chicago where he ran a country music nightclub. During this time he worked hard to develop his singing, writing and also became a talented instrumentalist on guitar, banjo and mandolin. In 1960, he moved to California, where he joined his brother Rex (b. 1938), first in a bluegrass group called the Golden State Boys and then as members of Chris Hillman's bluegrass band the Hillmen. When Hillman moved on to rock as a founder member of the Byrds, Vern also worked as a session musician while continuing to perform bluegrass with Rex. He recorded for several labels with no real success and even, in 1966, recorded an album with Gene Clark, who had recently left the Byrds. In 1967, the brothers finally achieved a US country chart hit with 'Hangin' On' but lacking any follow-up success, Vern soon returned to Atlanta and opened a glass and mirror shop, singing only in his spare time. His song 'Someone To Turn To', was recorded by the Byrds at the instigation of guitarist Clarence White. In 1976, Gosdin returned to recording and charted a version of 'Hangin' On', Top 10 hits with 'Yesterday's Gone (both of which featured backing vocals by Emmylou Harris) and 'Till The End'. He left his sons to run the business and with Rex returned to touring and concerts. Between 1978 and 1988, he registered 27 more US country chart hits, including number 1s with 'I Can Tell By The Way You Dance (You're Gonna Love Me Tonight), and 'Set 'Em Up Joe'. In 1979 and 1980, his brother Rex had three minor chart entries, the biggest being a duet with Tommy Jennings on 'Just Give Me What You Think Is Fair'. Rex died on 23 May 1983 at the age of 45, some two weeks before his recording of 'That Old Time Feelin'' entered the charts. Vern continues to record and perform and is rare in that his solid country voice and heartbreaking songs are somewhat alien to much of Nashville's modern music scene. Like George Jones he appears to improve with age. Even Tammy Wynette once said 'If anybody sounded like Jones other than Jones without really trying to, it is Vern Gosdin'

Albums: with The Hillmen: *The Hillmen* (1969), *Till The End* (1977), *Never My Love* (1978), *You've Got Somebody* (1979), *Passion* (1981), *If You're Gonna Do Me Wrong, Do It Right* (1983), *Today My World Slipped Away* (1983), *Dream Lady* (1984), *There Is A Season* (1984), *If Jesus Comes Tomorrow* (1984), *Time Stood Still* (1985), *Chiseled In Stone* (1988), *Alone* (1989), *A.M.I. Sessions* (1990), *Out Of My Heart* (1991). As The Gosdin Brothers: *Gene Clark With The Gosdin Brothers* (1966), *Sounds Of Goodbye* (1968).

Grammer, Billy

b. William Wayne Grammer, 28 August 1925, Benton, Illinois, USA. Grammer was one of 13 children and a coal-miner's son. His father played the fiddle, and, by the time he was in his teens, Grammer was playing guitar, mandolin and banjo at local dances. After a spell in the forces, he started in C&W radio on WRAL in Arlington, Virginia in 1947, but established his reputation as a session guitarist in Washington. He played lead guitar for several country performers - Hawkshaw Hawkins, Grandpa Jones, T. Texas Tyler - and he worked with Jimmy Dean on his television series from 1955 to 1959. Grammer first recorded as a solo performer in 1949 but, in 1959, had a vocal success with the million-selling 'Gotta Travel On', a 19th century British melody which had previously been revived by the Weavers. Grammer's pop success was short-lived as the excellent double-sided, 'Bonaparte's Retreat'/'The Kissing Tree', barely made the US Top 50. He had a country hit with 'I Wanna Go Home' in 1963, which Bobby Bare reworked as 'Detroit City'. He joined the *Grand Ole Opry* and became a session guitarist. His first model of the Grammer Flat-Top Guitar, which he now manufactures, is in the Country Music Hall of Fame.

Albums: *Travellin' On* (1961), *Gospel Guitar* (1962), *Billy Grammer Sings Gotta Travel On* (1964), *Country Gospel Favourites* (1964), *Country Guitar* (1965), *Sunday Guitar* (1967), *Country Favourites* (1968), *Billy Grammer Plays* (1975), *Christmas Guitars* (1977).

Gray, Claude

b. 26 January 1932, Henderson, Texas, USA. During his school days, he showed more interest in music than sports and learning to play the guitar, he began to perform locally. By the late 50s, he was playing venues over a wide area, for a time he worked as a disc jockey on WDAL Meridian, Mississippi and made his first recordings for Decca. However, it was in 1960, on the 'D' label (a subsidiary of Mercury), that he gained his first US country chart hit, when his recording of Willie Nelson's 'Family Bible' peaked at number 10. This success led to him being moved to the major label and in 1961, he scored major Top 5 hits with 'I'll Just Have Another Cup Of Coffee (Then I'll Go)' and Roger Miller's song 'My Ears Should Burn (When Fools Are Talked About)'. In 1966, after further Mercury successes, he recorded for Columbia and charted with 'Mean Old Woman', before returning to Decca. He formed the Graymen, which became a very popular touring band all over the States, being especially popular on the nightclub circuit around Las Vegas. In the late 60s he had eight chart entries, including Top 20 hits with 'I Never Had The One I Wanted' and the truck-driving song 'How Fast Them Trucks Can Go'. He left Decca in 1971 but achieved a few small hits on the Million and Granny labels. In 1982 he had a minor hit with a duet recording with Norma Jean of 'Let's Go All The Way' (a 1964 solo hit for Norma Jean). Known as 'The Tall Texan' (for obvious reasons), Gray is much better as a performer, it is said, than as a recording artist. This perhaps accounted for his inability to maintain record chart hits. He is still active, his last chart entry was a minor hit with Neil Diamond's 'Sweet Caroline' in 1986.

Albums: *Songs Of Broken Love Affairs* (1962), with the Melody Singers *Country Goes To Town* (1962), *Claude Gray Sings* (1967), *Treasure Of Love* (1967), *The Easy Way Of Claude Gray* (1968), *Presenting Claude Gray* (1972).

Gray, Mark

b. 1952, Vicksburg, Mississippi, USA. Singer/songwriter Gray first played piano at the age of 12 and headed his own gospel group at 19. He joined the Oak Ridge Boys as a writer with their publishing company, also becoming the keyboard player with their road band. Later he became a member of pop-country band Exile and was lead vocalist on two of their albums, *Don't Leave Me This Way* (1980) and *Heart And Soul* (1981). In the early 80s, three of his songs were US country number 1s, 'Take Me Down' and 'The Closer You Get', both for Alabama and 'It Ain't Easy Bein' Easy' for Janie Fricke. He signed with Columbia in 1983 and between 1983 and 1988, he registered 11 US country chart successes, including solo Top 10s with 'If The Magic Is Gone' and 'Please Be Love', but his highest chart entry came with his 1985 duet recording with Tammy Wynette of 'Sometimes When We Touch'. He had two minor duet hits in 1988 with Bobbi Lace, but has not scored a solo hit since 1986.

Albums: *Magic* (1984), *This Ol' Piano* (1984), *That Feeling Inside* (1986).

Grayson, G.B.

b. Gillam Bannon Grayson, 11 November 1887, Grayson, Ashe County, Tennessee, USA, raised in Laurel Bloomery, Johnson County, d. 16 August 1930. Although blinded as a child, Grayson learned the fiddle and began singing. When the family moved to Tennessee, he took to busking. Eventually, he teamed up with Clarence 'Tom' Ashley and Doc Walsh and forged a reputation in Virginia, Tennessee and North Carolina. He met Henry Whitter, who made the original recording of 'The Wreck Of The Southern Old '97', and recorded with him in 1927. In 1929 they made the first-ever recording of 'Tom Dooley'. (Shortly after the civil war, Grayson's uncle had been involved in the capture of Tom Dula for murder.) Grayson died in a car crash near Damascus, Virginia in August 1930, leaving a wife and six children. Today he is accepted as an important pioneer of country music and also as one of the finest fiddle players of all time. He was also a superior vocalist to Whitter and even sang lead on several records using Whitter's name.

Albums: *Grayson And Whitter, 1927-1930* (1976), *Going Down The Highway* (1976).

Green, Lloyd

b. Lloyd L. Green, 4 October 1937, Mississippi, USA. Green's family moved to Mobile, Alabama when he was four years old and he was raised there. He learned Hawaiian string guitar from the age of seven and graduated to steel guitar. He was playing professionally by the time he was 10, and recalls, 'I played in clubs a couple of nights a week with a rhythm guitarist called Emmanuel Abates, who was also a yo-yo champion. He wasn't a very good guitarist and eventually he went back to his yo-yos.' Green studied psychology at the University of Southern Mississippi, but he left at 19 to make his mark in Nashville. In December 1956

he joined Faron Young's road band and stayed for 18 months. During that time, he played steel guitar on his first session, George Jones' 'Too Much Water Runs Under The Bridge'. He returned to Mobile and came back to Nashville as a shoe salesman. When he told one customer that he could not afford $75 to renew his union card, she renewed it for him. She was the widow of the publisher, Fred Rose. The first successful session on which Green played was Warner Mack's 'The Bridge Washed Out' in 1965. For the next 15 years, the steel worker averaged 400 sessions a year, which included 'It's Four In The Morning' (Faron Young), 'Easy Lovin'' (Freddie Hart) and the Byrds' seminal country-rock album, *Sweetheart Of The Rodeo*. He says, 'Bob Dylan had hinted and flirted with the steel guitar before the Byrds, but he'd only let Pete Drake colour the songs very lightly. 'You Ain't Goin' Nowhere' took a whole day to record, which was a whole new revolution for me. I was used to sessions that were highly organized and where everyone was clock-watching.' He also played on Paul McCartney's 'Sally G' but turned down a US tour because he did not want to be losing work in Nashville. He made several solo records, mostly of easy-to-listen-to country music, although his technique is skilfully demonstrated on 'I Can See Clearly Now'. He popularized the blocking technique, used by Jimmy Day in the 50s, whereby the palm of the picking hand is used to mute the strings in order to lose the ringing effect. Green, who was not a solo attraction in the USA, made successful appearances at the Wembley Country Music Festival and his 1979 three-week UK tour with Billie Jo Spears was the longest he had been away from Nashville since 1964. He also worked in the UK with his fellow session musicians Charlie McCoy and Hargus 'Pig' Robbins. He says, 'It's laughable when I read of Nashville sessionmen getting together after hours and having a jam session. We play enough music in the studio. We'd rather get drunk and have a good time.'

Albums: *Big Steel Guitar* (1964), *Day Of Decision* (1966), *The Hit Sounds* (1966), *Mr. Nashville Sound* (1968), *Cool Steel Man* (1968), *Green Country* (1969), *Moody River* (1969), with Pete Drake *The Music City Sound* (1970), *Shades Of Steel* (1975), *Steel Rides* (1976), *Lloyd Green And His Steel Guitar* (1977), *Feelings* (1976), *Ten Shades Of Green* (1976), *Lloyd's Of Nashville* (1980), *Reflections* (1991).

Greenbriar Boys

Formed in New York, USA in 1958, the

Greenbriar Boys were one of the leading exponents of urban bluegrass. The original line-up comprised John Herald (guitar/lead vocals), Bob Yellin (banjo/tenor vocals) and Eric Weissberg (banjo/mandolin/dobro/fiddle), but in 1959 the latter was replaced by Ralph Rinzler (mandolin/baritone vocals). The following year the group won the top award at the annual Union Grove Fiddler's Convention, while Yellin secured the first of several hits as a solo artist. The Greenbriar Boys completed several excellent albums for the Vanguard label and became a highly popular attraction in the club, concert and festival circuits. Individually the members appeared as session musicians for, among others, Ramblin' Jack Elliott, Joan Baez and Patrick Sky. The trio was later augmented by vocalist Dian Edmondson; this reshaped unit recorded a lone release for Elektra Records. The group then underwent a radical change. Edmondson dropped out of the line-up, while Rinzler left for an administrative post with the Newport Folk Festival committee. Herald and Yellin added Frank Wakefield (mandolin) and Jim Buchanan (fiddle), but the Greenbriars' impetus was waning and the group was officially disbanded in 1966.
Albums: *The Greenbriar Boys* (1962), *Ragged But Right* (early 60s), *Better Late Than Never* (early 60s), *Dian And The Greenbriar Boys* (1964). Compilation: *The Best Of John Herald And The Greenbriar Boys* (1972).

Greene, Jack

b. Jack Henry Greene, 7 January 1930, Maryville, Tennessee, USA. Greene took guitar lessons when he was eight years old, then added drumming to his abilities. Moving to Atlanta in the late 40s, becoming part of the Cherokee Trio with Lem Bryant and Speedy Price. He became a member of the Rhythm Ranch Boys and was a popular radio entertainer on *Georgia Jubilee* on WTJH. Greene's career was interrupted for military service in Korea, but he returned to Atlanta and joined the Peachtree Cowboys, also working as a salesperson and construction worker. In 1962 he joined Ernest Tubb And The Texas Troubadours as a drummer and occasional vocalist. He was featured on *Ernest Tubb Presents The Texas Troubadours*, and his performance on 'The Last Letter' led to solo records. Starting in 1965 with 'Ever Since My Baby Went Away', Greene had a succession of country hits, including number 1 hits with 'There Goes My Everything', 'All The Time', 'You Are My Treasure', 'Until My Dreams Come True' and

'Statue Of A Fool'. He did not leave Tubb's band until 1967, only then because Tubb tired of hearing calls for the drummer to sing. In 1969 he had a further hit with Hank Cochran's song, 'I Wish I Didn't Have To Miss You', on which he was partnered by Cochran's wife, Jeannie Seely. She became part of his roadshow and they continued to record together. To fall in line with outlaw country, they changed the name of their band from the Jolly Greene Giants to the Renegades, but they stayed with middle-of-the-road country music. His last chart entry was with 'If It's Love (Then Bet It All)' in 1984; Greene however, who joined the *Grand Ole Opry* in 1967, is still a regular performer.
Albums: *Jack Greene* (1965), *There Goes My Everything* (1966), *All The Time* (1967), *What Locks The Door* (1967), *You Are My Treasure* (1968), *I Am Not Alone* (1968), *Until My Dreams Come True* (1968), *Statue Of A Fool* (1969), *Back In The Arms Of Love* (1969), *There's A Whole Lot About A Woman A Man Don't Know* (1970), *Yours For The Taking* (1981). Albums by Jack Greene and Jeannie Seely: *I Wish I Didn't Have To Miss You* (1969), *Jack Greene And Jeannie Seely* (1970), *Two For The Show* (1971), *Live At The Grand Ole Opry* (1978).

Greenwood, Lee

b. 27 October 1942, Los Angeles, California, USA. Because of his parents' divorce, Greenwood was brought up by his grandparents in Sacramento, California, but he inherited their musical talent as his mother played piano and his father woodwind. In his teens, he played in various bands in Sacramento and Los Angeles and was even part of a dixieland jazz band at Disneyland. He played saxophone for country star Del Reeves and then formed his own band, Apollo, which found work in Las Vegas in 1962. He turned down an opportunity to join the Rascals and for many years he was arranging and playing music for bands in casinos. The environment narrowed his vocal range and he developed a husky-voiced approach to ballads similar to Kenny Rogers. In 1979 his career to a major step forward when he was heard by Larry McFadden of Mel Tillis' band, who became his manager. His first MCA single, 'It Turns Me Inside Out', was a US country hit in 1981. This was followed by several other country hits including two number 1s, 'Somebody's Gonna Love You' and 'Going, Going, Gone'. His songs were also recorded by several other performers including Kenny Rogers who found success with 'A Love Song'. In 1984 he cut an album with

Barbara Mandrell and they made the US country charts with 'You've Got A Good Love Coming To Me' and he also recorded a patriotic song he wrote, 'God Bless The USA', which won the Country Music Association's Song Of The Year. His other number 1 country singles are 'Dixie Road', 'I Don't Mind The Thorns (If You're The Rose)', 'Don't Underestimate My Love For You', 'Hearts Aren't Made To Break (They're Made To Love)', and the sensual 'Mornin' Ride'. He has won numerous country awards but is best known in the UK for the original recording of 'The Wind Beneath My Wings', which entered the UK charts in 1984.

Albums: *Inside And Out* (1982), *Somebody's Gonna Love You* (1983), *The Wind Beneath My Wings* (1984), with Barbara Mandrell *Meant For Each Other* (1984), *You've Got A Good Love Coming* (1984), *Christmas To Christmas* (1985), *Streamline* (1985), *Love Will Find It's Way To You* (1986), *If There's Any Justice* (1987), *This Is My Country* (1988), *If Only For One Night* (1989), *Holdin' A Good Hand* (1990).

Gribbin, Tom

b. 2 January 1949, Florida, USA. Gribbin trained as a lawyer but formed a band, the Saltwater Cowboys, for weekend work. They mixed country with rock and Caribbean influences. To add to their diversity, they recorded the Clash's song, 'Guns Of Brixton' but, following the Brixton riots in south London, England, the record was considered too sensitive for UK airplay. Gribbin and his band were surprisingly well-received at the Wembley Country Music Festival, which is usually a graveyard for the more radical acts. His first album, *Son Of Lightning*, was issued with two distinct covers, one for the shops and one for Wembley. For a short period, Gribbin looked as though he might be the first new wave country star to become established in the UK, but it did not happen. He returned to legal work and a weekend band.

Albums: *Son Of Lightning* (1981), *Useppa Island Rendezvous* (1984).

Griff, Ray

b. John Ray Griff, 22 April 1940, Vancouver, Canada. The family relocated to Winfield, Alberta, where he actually played drums for the Winfield Amateurs at the age of six. After learning piano and guitar, he was leading his own band on the club circuit by the time he was 18. His songwriting talent was first noted when Johnny Horton recorded 'Mr Moonlight' and in 1964, Jim Reeves after recording his song 'Where Do I Go' suggested he move to Nashville, where he worked as a writer and publisher and later formed his own publishing company. He eventually made some recordings and first made the US country charts with 'Your Lily White Hands' in 1967. Recording for several different labels throughout the 70s, he had several minor hits including his personal look back in 'The Last Of The Winfield Amateurs' and Top 20 success with 'The Morning After Baby Let Me Down', 'You Ring My Bell' and 'If I Let Her Come In'. He also had his own television series on CBC. Among his popular songs recorded by other artists are 'Canadian Pacific' (George Hamilton IV), 'It Rains Just The Same In Missouri' (Mac Wiseman), 'Better Move It On Home' (Porter Wagoner and Dolly Parton), 'Step Aside' (Faron Young), 'Baby' (Wilma Burgess) and 'Who's Gonna Play This Old Piano' (Jerry Lee Lewis). Griff, like Mel Tillis initially suffered from a stutter but like Tillis, he has overcome his problem to find success in country music.

Albums: A *Ray Of Sunshine* (1968), *Ray Griff Sings* (1972), *Songs For Everyone* (1973), *Expressions* (1974), *Ray Griff* (1976), *Last Of The Winfield Amateurs* (1976), *Raymond's Place* (1977), *Canada* (1979), *Maple Leaf* (1980), *Adam's Child* (1981).

Griffith, Nanci

b. 6 July, 1953, Seguin, Texas, USA. Singer/songwriter Griffiths straddles the boundary between folk and country music, with occasional nods to the mainstream rock audience. Her mother was an amateur actress and her father a member of a barbershop quartet. They passed on their interest in performance to Nanci, and although she majored in education at the University of Texas, she eventually chose a career in music in 1977, by which time she had been performing in public for 10 years. In 1978 her first album, *There's A Light Beyond These Woods*, was released by a local company, BF Deal Records. Recorded live in a studio in Austin, it included mainly her own compositions, along with 'Dollar Matinee', written by her erstwhile husband, Eric Taylor. The major song on the album was the title track, which Griffiths later re-recorded, concerning the dreams she shared with her childhood friend, Mary Margaret Graham, of the bigger world outside Texas. As a souvenir of her folk act of the time, this album was adequate, but it was not until 1982 that *Poet In My Window* was released by another local label, Featherbed Records. Like its

Nanci Griffith

predecessor, this album was re-released in 1986 by the nationally-distributed Philo/Rounder label. It displayed a pleasing maturity in composition, the only song included which she had not written herself being 'Tonight I Think I'm Gonna Go Downtown' penned by Jimmie Gilmore and John Reed, (once again, Eric Taylor was involved as associated producer/bass player), while the barbershop quartet in which her father, Marlin Griffiths sang provided harmony vocals on 'Wheels'.

By 1984 she had met Jim Rooney, who produced her third album, *Once In A Very Blue Moon*, released in 1985 by Philo/Rounder. This album featured such notable backing musicians as lead guitarist Phillip Donnelly, banjo wizard Bela Fleck, Lloyd Green and Mark O'Connor. It was recorded at Jack Clement's Nashville studio. As well as more of her own songs, the album included her version of Lyle Lovett's 'If I Was The Woman You Wanted', Richard Dobson's 'Ballad Of Robin Wintersmith' and the superb title track written by Pat Alger - Griffiths named the backing band she formed in 1986 the Blue Moon Orchestra. Following on the heels of this artistic triumph came 1986's *Last Of The True Believers*. Released by Philo/Rounder with a similar recipe to that which set its predecessor apart from run of the mill albums by singer/songwriters, it included two songs which would later achieve US country chart celebrity as covered by Kathy Maltea, Griffith's own 'Love At The Five And Dime' and Pat Alger's 'Goin' Gone', as well as several other songs which would become Griffith classics, including the title track, 'The Wing And The Wheel' (after which Griffiths formed her music publishing company), 'More Than A Whisper' and 'Lookin' For The Time (Working Girl)', plus the fine Tom Russell song 'St. Olav's Gate'. This album became Griffith's first to be released in the UK when it was licensed by Demon Records around the time that Griffith was signed by MCA Records. Her debut album for her new label, *Lone Star State Of Mind*, was released in 1987, and was produced by MCA's golden-fingered Tony Brown, who had been the most active A&R person in Nashville in signing new talent, including Steve Earle and Lyle Lovett as well as Griffith herself, who co-produced it. The stunning title track again involved Alger as writer, while other notable tracks included the remake of 'There's A Light Beyond These Woods' from the first album, Robert Earl Keen Jnr.'s 'Sing One For Sister' and Griffith's own 'Ford Econoline' (about the independence of 60s folk singer Rosalie

Sorrels). However, attracting most attention was Julie Gold's 'From A Distance', a song which had become a standard by the 90s as covered by Bette Midler, Cliff Richard and many others. Griffith herself published the song, and her version was the first major exposure given to the song. *Little Love Affairs*, released in 1988, was supposedly a concept album but major songs included 'Outbound Plane', which she co-wrote with Tom Russell, veteran hit writer Harlan Howard's '(My Best Pal's In Nashville) Never Mind' and John Stewart's 'Sweet Dreams Will Come', as well as a couple of collaborations with James Hooker (ex-Amazing Rhythm Aces), and keyboard player of the Blue Moon Orchestra. Later that year Griffith recorded and released a live album, *One Fair Summer Evening*, recorded at Houston's Anderson Fair Retail Restaurant. Although it only included a handful of songs which she had not previously recorded, it was at least as good as *Little Love Affairs*, and was accompanied by a live video. However, it seemed that Griffiths' talent was falling between the rock and country audiences, the latter apparently finding her voice insufficiently radio-friendly, while Kathy Mattea, who recorded many of the same song some time after Griffith, became a major star.

In 1989 came *Storms*, produced by the legendary Glyn Johns, who had worked with the Beatles, the Rolling Stones, the Eagles, Steve Miller, the Who, Joan Armatrading and many more. Johns made an album with a bias towards American radio, which became Griffiths' biggest seller at that point. The album featured as well as Hooker, Irish drummer Bran Breen (ex-Moving Hearts), Bernie Leadon (ex-Eagles), guitarist Albert Lee and Phil Everly of the Everly Brothers providing harmony vocals on 'You Made This Love A Teardrop'. Although it was a sales breakthrough for Griffiths, it failed to attract country audiences. although it reached the Top 40 of the pop albums chart in the UK, where she had regularly toured since 1987. But her major European market was Ireland, where she was regarded as virtually a superstar. 1991's *Late Night Grande Hotel* was produced by the British team of Rod Argent and Peter Van Hook, and again included a duet with Phil Everly on 'It's Just Another Morning Here', while English singer Tanita Tikaram provided a guest vocal on 'It's Too Late'. In 1991, singing 'The Wexford Carol', she was one of a number of artists who contributed tracks to the Chieftains *The Bells Of Dublin*.

In 1992, Nanci Griffiths is poised to either finally break into the big time as a Carly Simon-type figure, or to retreat to (substantial) cult status. It will be fascinating for her many European fans to discover which direction she will choose.

Albums: *There's A Light Beyond These Woods* (1978), *Poet In My Window* (1982), *Once In A Very Blue Moon* (1984), *Last Of The True Believers* (1986), *Lone Star State Of Mind* (1987), *Little Love Affairs* (1988), *One Fair Summer Evening* (1988), *Storms* (1989), *Late Night Grande Hotel* (1991).

Guitar, Bonnie

b. Bonnie Buckingham, 25 March 1923, Seattle, Washington, USA. She learned several instruments as a child, was a talented guitarist and began to write songs before she completed her education. In the early 50s she recorded for Fabor and in the mid-50s worked as a session guitarist in Los Angeles. She made her debut in the US country charts in 1957 on Dot Records with her own song 'Dark Moon'. In 1958 she formed her own Dolton label in Seattle and began to record various local acts, including a pop trio called the Fleetwoods who, in 1959 had two million selling records on her label with 'Come Softly To Me' and 'Mr Blue'. Her instrumental work, production and recording abilities with the Fleetwoods attracted the attention of Dot; wishing to concentrate on her own career, she sold Dolton and worked for Dot and ABC-Paramount, both on A&R and production and as a recording artist. In the 60s she scored Top 10 country hits with 'I'm Living In Two Worlds', '(You've Got Yourself) A Woman In Love' (her biggest hit) and 'I Believe In Love'. In 1969 she also had a minor hit with 'A Truer Love You'll Never Find', a duet recording with Buddy Killen issued as Bonnie And Buddy. She also worked with songwriter Don Robertson and recorded 'Born To Be With You' with him as the Echoes. She was a popular touring artist in the 60s and early 70s, often working with Eddy Arnold. During the 70s, she recorded for Columbia and MCA and her last chart entry was a minor hit entitled 'Honey On The Moon' in 1980, by which time she had moved to the 4 Star label. In 1986 after a long absence, she doubtless pleased her fans by releasing two albums, called *Yesterday* and *Today*.

Albums: *Moonlight & Shadows* (1957), *Whispering Hope* (1959), *Dark Moon* (1962), *Bonnie Guitar Sings* (1965), *Merry Christmas From Bonnie Guitar* (1966), *Miss Bonnie Guitar* (1966), *Two Worlds* (1966), *Favorite Lady Of Song* (c1967), *Green Green Grass Of Home* (c.1967), *Bonnie Guitar-Award Winner* (1967), *I Believe In Love* (1968), *Leaves Are The*

Tears Of Autumn (1968), *Stop The Sun/A Woman In Love* (1968), *Affair* (1969), *Night Train To Memphis* (1969), *Allegheny* (1970), *Yesterday Today* (1986). Compilation: *Dark Moon* (1992).

Guthrie, Woody

b. Woodrow Wilson Guthrie, 14 July 1912, Okemah, Oklahoma, USA, d. 3 October 1967. A major figure of America's folk heritage, Guthrie was raised in a musical environment and achieved proficiency on harmonica as a child. By the age of 16 he had begun his itinerant lifestyle, performing in a Texas-based magic show where he learned to play guitar. In 1935 Guthrie moved to California where he became a regular attraction on Los Angeles' KFVD radio station. Having befriended singer Cisco Houston and actor Will Geer, Woody established his left wing-oriented credentials with joint appearances at union meetings and migrant labour camps. Already a prolific songwriter, reactions to the poverty he witnessed inspired several of his finest compositions, notably 'Pastures Of Plenty', 'Dust Bowl Refugees', 'Vigilante Man' and 'This Land Is Your Land', regarded by many as America's 'alternative' national anthem. Guthrie was also an enthusiastic proponent of Roosevelt's 'New Deal', as demonstrated by 'Grand Coolie Dam' and 'Roll On Columbia', while his children's songs, including 'Car Car', were both simple and charming. At the end of the 30s Woody travelled to New York where he undertook a series of recordings for the folk song archive at the Library Of Congress. The 12 discs he completed were later released commercially by Elektra Records.

Guthrie continued to traverse the country and in 1940 met Pete Seeger at a folksong rally in California. Together they formed the Almanac Singers with Lee Hayes and Millard Lampell which in turn inspired the Almanac House, a co-operative apartment in New York's Greenwich Village which became the focus of the east coast folk movement. In 1942 Guthrie joined the short-lived Headline Singers with Leadbelly, Sonny Terry and Brownie McGhee, before beginning his autobiography, *Bound For Glory*, which was published the following year. He and Houston then enlisted in the merchant marines, where they remained until the end of World War II, after which Guthrie began a series of exemplary recordings for the newly-founded Folkways label. The artist eventually completed over 200 masters which provided the fledgling company with a secure foundation. Further sessions were

Woody Guthrie with Margaret 'Honey Chile' Johnson

undertaken for other outlets, while Woody retained his commitment to the union movement through columns for the *Daily Worker* and *People's World*. Guthrie's prolific output – he conscientiously composed each day – continued unabated until the end of the 40s when he succumbed to Huntington's Chorea, a hereditary, degenerative disease of the nerves. He was hospitalized in 1952, and was gradually immobilized by this wasting illness until he could barely talk or recognize friends and visitors. By the time of his death on 3 October 1967, Woody Guthrie was enshrined in America's folklore, not just because of his own achievements, but through his considerable influence on a new generation of artists. Bob Dylan, Ramblin' Jack Elliott, Roger McGuinn and Woody's son Arlo Guthrie were among his most obvious disciples, but the plethora of performers, including Judy Collins, Tom Paxton, Richie Havens and Country Joe McDonald, gathered at two subsequent tribute concerts, confirmed their debt to this pivotal figure.

Compilations: *Library Of Congress Recordings* (1964, released on CD in 1989 - 1940 recordings), *Dust Bowl Ballads* (1964, released CD issued in 1989 - 1940 recordings), *This Land Is Your Land* (1967), *Bound For Glory* (1958), *Sacco & Vanzetti* (1960), *Songs To Grow On* (1973), *Struggle* (1976), *A Legendary Performer* (1977), *Poor Boy* (1981), *Columbia River Collection* (1988), *Folkways: The Original Vision* (1989).

Further reading: *Bound For Glory*, Woody Guthrie. *Born To Win*, edited by Robert Shelton. *Woody Guthrie - A Life*, Joe Klein.

H

Haggard, Merle

b. 6 April 1937, Bakersfield, California, USA. 'Like a razor's edge, Merle Haggard sings' is how John Stewart described his voice in 'Eighteen Wheels', and that razor has been honed by his rough and rowdy ways. In the 30s Haggard's parents migrated from the Dustbowl to 'the land of milk and honey', California. Life, however, was almost as bleak there and Haggard himself was born in a converted boxcar. His father, who worked on the Santa Fe railway, died of a stroke when Haggard was nine. Many of Haggard's songs are about those early years: 'Mama's Hungry Eyes', 'California Cottonfields', 'They're Tearin' The Labour Camps Down' and 'The Way It Was In '51'. Haggard became a tearaway who, despite the efforts of his Christian mother ('Mama Tried'), spent many years in reform schools. When only 17, he married a waitress and they had four children during their ten years together. His wife showed disdain for his singing and Haggard says, 'Any listing of famous battlefields should include my marriage to Leona Hobbs'. Haggard provided for the children through manual labour and armed robbery. He was sent to San Quentin in 1957, charged with burglary; a Johnny Cash concert in January 1958 led to him joining the prison band. Songs from his prison experiences include 'Sing Me Back Home' and 'Branded Man'. Back in Bakersfield in 1960, Haggard started performing and found work accompanying Wynn Stewart. Only 200 copies were pressed of his first single, 'Singing My Heart Out', but he made the national charts with his second, Stewart's composition, 'Sing A Sad Song', for the small Tally label. Capitol took over his contract and reissued '(All My Friends Are Going To Be) Strangers' in 1965. The record's success prompted him to call his band the Strangers, its mainstays being Roy Nichols on lead guitar and Norm Hamlet on steel. When 'I'm A Lonesome Fugitive' became a country number 1 in 1966, it was clear that a country star with a prison record was a very commercial proposition. Haggard recorded an album of love songs with his second wife, Bonnie Owens, but, despite its success, they never repeated it. In 1969 a chance remark on the tour-bus led to him writing 'Okie From Muskogee', a conservative reply to draft-card burning and flower-power. President Nixon declared Haggard his favourite country singer, while Ronald Reagan, then Governor of California, gave him a full pardon. Johnny Cash refused to perform the song at the White House and Phil Ochs, a spearhead of youth culture, sang it to annoy his own fans. Some suggest that the irony in Haggard's song has been overlooked, but he has since confirmed his dislike of hippies - though several rock bands, notably the Beach Boys, performed the song as a piece of counter-culture irony. Haggard sang more specifically about anti-Vietnam demonstrators in 'The Fightin' Side Of Me', but his song about an inter-racial love affair, 'Irma Jackson', was not released at first because Capitol thought it would harm his image. Around this time, Haggard wrote and recorded several glorious singles which rank with the best of country music and illustrate his personal credo: 'I Take A Lot Of Pride In What I Am', 'Silver Wings', 'Today I Started Loving You Again' and 'If We Make It Through December'. He also sang songs by other writers, notably Tommy Collins, and recorded tributes to Jimmie Rodgers (a double-album, *Same Train, A Different Time*), Bob Wills (an album, which shows that Haggard is a fine fiddle player) and Lefty Frizzell (a song, 'Goodbye Lefty'). Another of Haggard's consuming passions is model trains and he recorded an album, *My Love Affair With Trains*. Like most successful country artists, he has also recorded Christmas and religious albums, *The Land Of Many Churches* being partly recorded at San Quentin jail. (Haggard has not recorded a full-blown prison album because he does not want to copy Johnny Cash.) Between 1973 and 1976, Haggard achieved nine consecutive number 1 records on the US country charts and his tally to date of 40 number 1 records has only been surpassed by Conway Twitty. In 1977, shortly after moving to MCA, he recorded a touching tribute album to Elvis Presley with the Jordanaires. In 1978 he divorced Bonnie Owens and married a back-up singer, Leona Williams. She wrote several songs for him and also recorded a duet album, but in 1984, they too were divorced. (Haggard divorced his fourth wife in 1991.) Haggard had often written about alcohol ('Swinging Doors', 'The Bottle Let Me Down') but his MCA albums show an increasing concern about his own consumption. Less introspective following a move to Epic in 1981, he had a major country hit with a revival of 'Poncho And Lefty' with Willie Nelson. He still writes prolifically ('I Wish Things Were Simple Again', 'Let's Chase

Merle Haggard

Each Other Around The Room') but he also revives songs of yesteryear including 'There! I've Said It Again' and 'Sea Of Heartbreak'. Coming full circle, *Amber Waves Of Grain* shows his concern for the plight of the American farmer. Haggard is pained and sad on most of his album covers but that does not detract from the quality of his work. He has refused to compromise ('My Own Kind Of Hat'). Early in 1993, Haggard was declared bankrupt, though this setback seems to have done nothing to dampen his enthusiasm for touring. Haggard wrote his autobiography in 1981.

Albums: *Strangers* (1965), *Just Between The Two Of Us* (with Bonnie Owens) (1966), *Swinging Doors And The Bottle Let Me Down* (1966), *I'm A Lonesome Fugitive* (1967), *Branded Man* (1967), *Sing Me Back Home* (1968), *The Legend Of Bonnie And Clyde* (1968), *Mama Tried* (1968), *Pride In What I Am* (1969), *Instrumental Sounds Of Merle Haggard's Strangers* (1969), *Same Train, A Different Time* (1969), *A Portrait Of Merle Haggard* (1969), *Okie From Muskogee* (1970), *Introducing My Friends, The Strangers* (1970), *Fightin' Side Of Me* (1970), *A Tribute To The Best Damn Fiddle Player In The World (Or, My Salute To Bob Wills)* (1970), *Getting To Know Merle Haggard's Strangers* (1970), *Hag* (1971), *Honky Tonkin'* (1971), *Someday We'll Look Back* (1971), with Bonnie Owens, Carter Family *The Land Of Many Churches* (1971), *Let Me Tell You About A Song* (1972), *It's Not Love, But It's Not Bad* (1972), *Totally Instrumental (With One Exception)* (1972), *I Love Dixie Blues...So I Recorded 'Live' In New Orleans* (1973), *Merle Haggard's Christmas Present* (1973), *If We Make It Through December* (1974), *Merle Haggard Presents His 30th Album* (1974), *Keep Movin' On* (1975), *It's All In The Movies* (1976), *My Love Affair With Trains* (1976), *The Roots Of My Raising* (1976), *Ramblin' Fever* (1977), *A Working Man Can't Get Nowhere Today* (1977), *My Farewell To Elvis - From Graceland To The Promised Land* (1977), *I'm Always On A Mountain When I Fall* (1978), *Serving 190 Proof* (1979), *The Way I Am* (1980), *Back To The Barrooms* (1980), *Rainbow Stew - Live* (1981), *Songs For The Mama That Tried* (1981), *Big City* (1981), *Goin' Where The Lonely Go* (1982), with George Jones *A Taste Of Yesterday's Wine* (1982), *Going Home For Christmas* (1982), with Willie Nelson *Poncho And Lefty* (1983), with Leona Williams *Heart To Heart* (1983), *That's The Way Love Goes* (1983), *The Epic Collection - Live* (1983), *It's All In The Game* (1984), *Kern River* (1985), *Amber Waves Of Grain* (1985), *Out Among The Stars* (1986), *A Friend In California* (1986), with Nelson *Seashores*

Of Old Mexico (1987), *Chill Factor* (1988), *5:01 Blues* (1989), *Blue Jungle* (1990).
Further reading: *Sing Me Back Home*, Merle Haggard with Peggy Russell.

Hall, Hillman

b. 1938, Olive Hill, Kentucky, USA, d. 1989. A younger brother of Tom T. Hall and like his brother, a songwriter of some considerable ability. Some consider that although of similar style, he was a better vocalist than Tom T., even though he failed to register any chart hits. In 1975 he recorded an album of his own songs for Warner Brothers that was produced by Marijohn Wilkin. It included a very witty look at the b-western hero in 'Celluloid Cowboy', who was 'meek as a lamb and afraid of his horse' and so small the leading lady stood in a hole for the love scenes. His 'You Can't Fool A Country Music Fan' was his personal tribute to country music. He had his brother's ability for producing strange titles as witnessed by his 'Fair To Middlin', Lower Middle Class Plain Hard Working Man', and his 'One Pitcher Is Worth A Thousand Words' surely was semi-biographical. Wilma Burgess charted his 'Parting (Is Such Sweet Sorrow)'in 1969. The album also includes his own recording of 'Pass Me By', his biggest success as a songwriter, which following hit recordings in 1973 by Johnny Rodriguez and in 1980 by Janie Frickie has become a country standard. Hillman Hall died in 1989.
Album: *One Pitcher Is Worth A Thousand Words* (1975).

Hall, Roy

b. 6 January 1907, Haywood County, North Carolina, USA, d. 16 May 1943. Hall and his brother Jay Hugh (b. 13 November 1910, Haywood County, North Carolina, USA, d. April 1974), both played guitar and in their teens, they began to entertain, while working in the local textile mills. In 1937, they appeared as the Hall Brothers on WSPA Spartanburg, South Carolina and made their first recordings for Bluebird Records. Further recordings were made in 1938, before the brothers split and Roy formed his string band, the Blue Ridge Entertainers. The band first played WSPA, before moving on to Asheville, Greensboro, Winston-Salem and finally to WDBJ Roanoke, Virginia, where it appeared twice daily. In late 1939, his Saturday evening *Blue Ridge Jamboree* attracted regular major stars including Tex Ritter and Roy Rogers. Hall was an astute business man and his show proved so popular that before long, he had to form two bands to meet all the bookings; the second band being led by his brother Jay Hugh, who had rejoined him in 1940. (Early in 1940, Jay Hugh appeared and recorded with Clyde Moody and Steve Ledford as The Happy-Go-Lucky Boys.) The bands played a mixture of old-time and modern music and undoubtedly were an influence on later bluegrass bands. Hall was one of the first bandleaders to feature the prominent use of the steel guitar. He recorded a 1938 version of 'Wabash Cannonball', which has been compared to Roy Acuff's and he also recorded 'The Orange Blossom Special' approximately seven months before the Rouse Brothers, although because of a legal argument over publishing rights, it was never released. Among the songs Hall first featured in the early 40s were 'I Wonder Where You Are Tonight' and 'Don't Let Your Sweet Love Die'. By 1945, the sales of the latter exceeded 100,000 but Hall died in a car crash on 16 May 1943 and therefore never knew. Jay Hugh Hall remained active in music until 1950 and continued to live in Roanoke until his death in April 1974. (This artist should not be confused with Roy Hall (alias Sunny David), the writer of 'Whole Lotta Shakin' Goin' On', who recorded rockabilly in the 50s.)

Album: *Roy Hall & The Blue Ridge Entertainers* (1977).

Hall, Tom T.

b. 25 May 1936, Olive Hill, Kentucky, USA. Hall was one of eight children and his father was a bricklayer and part-time minister. Hall described the family home as 'a frame house of pale-grey boards and a porch from which to view the dusty road and the promise of elsewhere beyond the hills - the birthplace of a dreamer'. Hall, who started to learn to play a schoolfriend's guitar at the age of 10, was influenced by a local musician, who died of TB when only 22 years old, hence his classic song, 'The Year That Clayton Delaney Died'. Hall's mother died of cancer when he was 13 and, two years later, his father was injured in a shooting accident, which necessitated Hall leaving school to look after the family. A neighbour, Hurley Curtis (who was later the subject of Hall's 'A Song For Uncle Curt') had a small, travelling cinema and Hall began to accompany him, playing bluegrass with other musicians. Curtis helped to get them a programme on WMOR, Morehead, Kentucky, so Hall broadcast regularly as part of the Kentucky Travellers. When the band broke up, he continued at the station as a DJ, then joined the army in 1957. Several songs ('Salute To A Switchblade', 'I

Flew Over Our House Last Night') relate to his army days. On leaving the army in 1961, he returned to WMOR and worked as both a DJ and a musician. He went to Roanoke, Virginia to study journalism; another song, 'Ode To A Half A Pound Of Ground Round' indicates how little money he had. At one stage, he stayed with an army friend ('Thank you, Connersville, Indiana') and tried to get his country songs accepted in Nashville. In 1963 his song, 'DJ For A Day' was recorded by Jimmy C. Newman. In 1964 he moved to Nashville and married Iris 'Dixie' Dean, who had emigrated from Weston-super-Mare, England, and was the editor of *Music City News*. Hall wrote several songs about Vietnam - 'Goodbye Sweetheart, Hello Vietnam' (recorded by Johnny Wright) shows support for the war, while 'Mama, Tell 'Em What We're Fightin' For' (Dave Dudley) takes another stance. 'Girls In Saigon City' is a warning to the girls back home, and 'Mama Bake A Pie (Daddy Kill A Chicken)' is about the rehabilitation of a war veteran. Margie Singleton asked Hall to write her a song like 'Ode To Billie Joe'. He came up with 'Harper Valley PTA', but it was not passed to Singleton, who was out of town. The song went to Jeannie C. Riley, who took it to number 1 in the US pop charts. The lyric related to an incident in Hall's childhood. Said Hall, 'I wrote about a lady who had criticized a teacher for spanking her child to get at her.' In 1968 Hall signed to Mercury, added a middle initial and became Tom T. Hall. His offbeat US country hits included 'Ballad Of 40 Dollars', which had been prompted by working in a graveyard, and the strummed 'Homecoming', in which a country star, who has missed his mother's funeral, returns home. He then topped the US country charts with 'A Week In The County Jail'. Hall's best songs describe people and situations ('Pinto The Wonder Horse Is Dead', 'I Miss A Lot Of Trains'), whilst his philosophizing is often crass ('The World, The Way I Want It', '100 Children'). The lighthearted 'I Can't Dance' has also been recorded by Gram Parsons with Emmylou Harris, and 'Margie's At The Lincoln Park Inn', a return to the small town hypocrisy of 'Harper Valley PTA', was a US country hit for Bobby Bare. Bare says, 'That song was written about the Capital Park Inn in Nashville, but he changed the name to protect the guilty. It's a great cheating song, one of the best'. Hall went on an expedition looking for songs and the result was his most consistent work, the album *In Search Of A Song*. Songs like 'Ramona's Revenge' and 'Tulsa Telephone Book' covered many scenes and moods, and he was backed by superlative Nashville musicians. His next album, *We All Got Together And...* was not as strong but it did include 'Pamela Brown' in which he thanks a girl for not marrying him and 'She Gave Her Heart To Jethro' to which he adds 'and her body to the whole damn world'. *The Storyteller* included his finest song, a perceptive encounter with an ageing black cleaner, 'Old Dogs, Children And Watermelon Wine'. Hall's touring band, called the Storytellers, included Johnny Rodriguez, who became a solo star. Hall recorded with Patti Page and he championed the songwriter, Billy Joe Shaver, recording his songs and writing the sleeve notes for his first album. Amongst his numerous awards and honours, Hall won a Grammy for his notes on *Tom T. Hall's Greatest Hits*. Ironically, Hall had his only substantial hit in the US pop charts (number 12 in 1974) with one of his weaker songs, 'I Love', a sentimental list of what he liked. He reworked Manfred Mann's 'Fox On The Run' for his bluegrass album, *The Magnificent Music Machine*, and he also made a highly-acclaimed, good-natured album with Earl Scruggs of *Flatt And Scruggs*. His mellow, *Songs In A Seashell*, was inspired by a fishing trip and included both original songs and standards. Although his singing range is limited, Hall can be a fine interpreter of others' material, in particular, 'P.S. I Love You' and Shel Silverstein's 'Me And Jimmie Rodgers'. In recent years, Hall has concentrated on novel-writing and children's songs. Certainly, a collection of new, adult songs is overdue.

Albums: *'The Ballad Of 40 Dollars' And Other Great Songs* (1969), *Homecoming* (1970), *I Witness Life* (1970), *100 Children* (1970), *In Search Of A Song* (1971), *We All Got Together And...* (1972), *The Storyteller* (1972), *The Rhymer And Other Five And Dimers* (1973), *For The People In The Last Hard Town* (1973), *Country Is* (1974), *Songs Of Fox Hollow* (1974), *Faster Horses* (1976), *The Magnificent Music Machine* (1976), *About Love* (1977), *New Train - Same Rider* (1978), *Places I've Done Time* (1978), *Saturday Morning Songs* (1979), *Ol' T's In Town* (1979), *Soldier Of Fortune* (1980), *The Storyteller And The Banjoman* (with Earl Scruggs) (1982), *In Concert* (1983), *World Class Country* (1983), *Everything From Jesus To Jack Daniels* (1983), *Natural Dreams* (1984), *Songs In A Seashell* (1985), *Country Songs For Kids* (1988).

Further reading: *The Songwriter's Handbook*, Tom T. Hall. *The Storyteller's Nashville*, Tom T. Hall. *The Laughing Man Of Woodmont Cove*, Tom T. Hall. *Spring Hill* (a novel), Tom T. Hall.

Hamblen, Stuart

b. Carl Stuart Hamblen, 20 October 1908, Kellyville, Texas, USA, d. 8 March 1989. The son of a travelling Methodist preacher, his childhood was spent travelling around Texas as his father's work decreed. His love of open spaces and yearning for the life of a cowboy is apparent in some of his early songs. He learned to rope and ride, and as a youngster mixed working the rodeos with his college studies to be a teacher. He passed his exams but a wish to sing and write songs led to him moving to California. He worked first with The Beverly Hill Billies, a singing group led by Zeke Manners, but soon hosted his own shows on radio and appeared at various west coast venues with his own band. He first recorded for Decca in 1934, when he cut his popular songs 'Texas Plains' and 'Ridin' Old Paint'. During the 30s and 40s, he proved a natural for Hollywood and appeared in many b-westerns, usually as the villain. At times, owing to an inability to hold his drink, he played out many of his screen roles in real life and was often jailed after shooting out street lights or brawling. He later said 'I guess I was the original juvenile delinquent'. Fortunately for him, because of his radio popularity, his sponsors usually bailed him out. He continued to write songs ,including 'My Mary' and 'Born To Be Happy' but it was not until 1949 that he registered his first US country chart entry with 'I Won't Go Huntin' With You Jake But I'll Go Chasin' Women'. Soon after, 'Remember Me, I'm The One Who Loves You' was a Top 10 country hit for himself and for Ernest Tubb. His recording of 'Black Diamond', a semi-narration, was also popular; later Hank Snow's version became a much sought-after recording. In 1949, he attended a prayer meeting in Los Angeles given by a then much lesser-known preacher named Billy Graham. He publicly announced that he was devoting his life to Christ and gave up his film and radio work but maintained his songwriting and recording. Hamblen's new-found religious fervour led to him writing 'It Is No Secret (What God Can Do)'. The generally accepted version is that Hamblen wrote the song following a conversation with his old drinking companion,film star John Wayne, who found Hamblen's zeal hard to believe, but then replied casually ,'Well it's no secret what God can do' and Hamblen, remembering these words, soon afterwards wrote the song. He first charted it himself as a Top 10 US country hit in 1951 but soon other artists had successful versions, including Red Foley with the Andrews Sisters, Jo Stafford and Bill Kenny and the

Song Spinners. A few years later Elvis Presley recorded it with the Jordanaires and it became one of his best known gospel recordings. In 1952 Hamilton decided to run for President of the USA on the tor-prohibition party ticket but as history records he lost by approximately 27 million votes. He concentrated on writing songs of a religious nature such as 'His Hands' and 'Open Up Your Heart' and, in 1954, achieved both US country and pop chart success himself with 'This Ole House'. (He wrote the song after finding the dead body of an old prospector in a tumbledown hut miles from anywhere.) Recorded by Rosemary Clooney it became a million-seller, even reaching number 1 in the British pop charts. Years later an up-tempo 1981 version by pop singer Shakin' Stevens also topped the British charts. From the late 50s, for many years, he hosted religious television shows and continued to record, though he professed to be retired. In 1971, he began his popular KLAC Sunday morning network radio programme *The Cowboy Church Of The Air*, which ran for more than a decade. He died following an operation for a brain tumour on 8 March 1989.

Albums: *It Is No Secret* (1954), *It Is No Secret* (1956), *Grand Old Hymns* (1957), *Hymns* (1957), *I Believe* (1957), *Beyond The Sun* (1959), *Remember Me* (1959), *The Spell Of The Yukon* (1961), *Of God I Sing* (1962), *In The Garden And Other Inspirational Songs* (1966), *This Old House Has Got To Go (There's A Freeway Coming Through)* (1966), *A Man And His Music* (1974), *The Cowboy Church* (1974).

Hamilton, George, IV

b. 19 July 1937, Winston-Salem, North Carolina, USA. George Hamilton IV is one of the few American country stars to have become a household name in Britain, although he is sometimes confused with the actor George Hamilton. 'George Hamilton I was a farmer in the Blue Ridge', he says,' George Hamilton II was a railroad man who loved country music and collected Jimmie Rodgers' records. My father, George Hamilton III, was the general manager of a headache powder company. I'm a city boy from a middle-class family but my parents gave me an honest love of country music. We'd listen to the *Grand Ole Opry* on a Saturday night.' In 1956, whilst at the University of North Carolina, Hamilton persuaded a local label, Colonial, to record him. He recorded one of the first teen ballads, 'A Rose And A Baby Ruth', written by his friend, John D. Loudermilk. Its regional success prompted ABC-Paramount to issue it

countrywide, Hamilton found himself at number 6 in the nation's pop chart and the single became a million-seller. The b-side, 'If You Don't Know, I Ain't Gonna Tell You', heralded the subsequent direction of his music and became a US country hit in its own right in 1962. It is also one of the few songs which Hamilton has written himself. 'There are too many great writers around to bother with mediocre music,' he says now. The title, 'A Rose And A Baby Ruth', was too obscure for UK record-buyers - a Baby Ruth was a chocolate bar - but Hamilton did make the UK Top 30 with his second American Top 10 entry, 'Why Don't They Understand?'. The song, co-written by Joe 'Mr. Piano' Henderson, was one of the first hits about the 50s generation gap. Hamilton's other US hits were 'Only One Love', 'Now And For Always' and the curio 'The Teen Commandments Of Love' with Paul Anka and Johnny Nash. He made the UK Top 30 with 'I Know Where I'm Going'. Hamilton toured on rock'n'roll package shows with Buddy Holly, Eddie Cochran and Gene Vincent, and appeared on Broadway with Louis Armstrong. His leanings towards country music were satisfied as ABC-Paramount let him record a tribute album to Hank Williams. In 1958 Hamilton married his childhood sweetheart, Adelaide ('Tinky') Peyton, and moved to Nashville where they raised a family. Hamilton started recording for RCA in 1961 and returned to the US Top 20 with John D. Loudermilk's adaptation of a western song, 'Abilene' in 1963. His other country hits include 'Break My Mind', 'Fort Worth, Dallas Or Houston' and 'She's A Little Bit Country'. Hamilton pioneered the songs of Gordon Lightfoot ('Steel Rail Blues', 'Early Mornin' Rain') which, in turn, led to a love affair with Canadian music. He recorded Joni Mitchell's 'Urge For Going' (the first artist to release one of her songs), Leonard Cohen's 'Suzanne' and Ian Tyson's 'Summer Wages', along with several albums of which *Canadian Pacific* is the best-known. He comments, 'Country music is swamped with songs about the seamy side of life - love in a honky tonk, meet me at the dark end of the street, and does your husband know? There's so much more to life than adultery and I felt that the Canadians had a different approach to songwriting. They have a long-standing love of their land and Ray Griff's 'Canadian Pacific' sums up that feeling.' Hamilton appeared at the first Wembley country music festival and he has been a regular visitor to the UK ever since. Hamilton acknowledges that he has changed the UK public's perception of country music. 'When I first came

George Hamilton IV

here, people had the idea that country music was all hicks and hillbillies, cowboys and indians. I wanted to show it was an art form, a quality music. I wore a three-piece suit which was a bit formal for the music I was playing but I wouldn't have been comfortable in jeans and a stetson.' Hamilton has championed British country music by recording home-grown songs and also by recording with the Hillsiders. In 1979, Hamilton became the first country singer to play a summer season at a seaside resort (Blackpool). Although Hamilton moved to North Carolina in 1972, he sees little of his home. He tours so often that Bob Powell, a former editor of the UK magazine, *Country Music People*, named him the International Ambassador of Country Music. In 1974 Hamilton became the first country artist to give concerts in the Soviet Union and he lectured at Moscow University. He has appeared at festivals in Czechoslovakia and recorded there. His pioneering work was recognized by *Billboard* magazine who gave him their Trendsetter award in 1975. Hamilton's best recordings were made in the late 70s when he made three albums with producer Allen Reynolds, *Fine Lace And Homespun Cloth*, *Feel Like A Million* and *Forever Young*. He nearly made the UK charts with a revival of 'I Wonder Who's Kissing Her Now' from the first album. Increasingly in recent years, Hamilton has given Christian concerts. He has been part of Billy Graham's crusades and he regularly tours British churches. Hank Wangford parodies Hamilton's sincere eyebrows, and he takes it all in good spirit as he admits, 'I have no paranoia about what the critics say about me. I accept that some folks think I'm bland, easy listening and it's pretty obvious that I'm not a great vocalist. However, I can communicate with an audience and I do try to interpret songs which say something.' Hamilton sometimes works with his son, George Hamilton V (b. 11 November 1960, Nashville, Tennessee, USA), who had a US country hit with 'She Says' and also tours the UK country clubs in his own right. Like his father, he will sign autographs until the last person has left.
Albums: *George Hamilton IV On Campus* (1958), *Sing Me A Sad Song - A Tribute To Hank Williams* (1958), *To You And Yours (From Me And Mine)* (1961), *Abilene* (1963), *George Hamilton IV's Big 15* (1963), *Fort Worth, Dallas Or Houston* (1964), *Mister Sincerity* (1965), *By George* (1966), *Steel Rail Blues* (1966), *Coast-Country* (1966), *Folk Country Classics* (1967), *Folksy* (1967), *In The Fourth Dimension* (1968), *The Gentle Sound Of George Hamilton IV* (1968), *George Hamilton IV* (1968), *Canadian Pacific*

(1969), *Back Where It's At* (1970), part with Skeeter Davis *Down Home In The Country* (1971), *North Country* (1971), with the Hillsiders *Heritage* (1971), *West Texas Highway* (1971), *Country Music Is In My Soul* (1972), *Down East Country* (1972), *Travelin' Light* (1972), *The International Ambassador Of Country Music* (1973), *Back To Down East Country* (1974), *Bluegrass Gospel* (1974), *Trendsetter* (1975), *Singing On The Mountains* (1976), *Back Home At The Opry* (1976), *Fine Lace And Homespun Cloth* (1977), *Feel Like A Million* (1978), *Forever Young* (1979), *Cuttin' Across The Country* (1981), *One Day At A Time* (1982), *George Hamilton IV With Jiri Brabec And Country Beat* (1982), *Songs For A Winter's Night* (1982), *Music Man's Dream* (1984), *Hymns Country Style* (1985), *George Hamilton IV* (1985), *Give Thanks* (1988), *A Country Christmas* (1989), with the Moody Brothers *American Country Gothic* (1989), with George Hege Hamilton V *Country Classics* (1992).

Harden, Arlene

b. 1 March 1945, England, near Pine Bluff, Arkansas, USA. Harden sang with her brother Bobby and sister Robbie as the Harden Trio on *Barnyard Frolics*, when all were teenagers in Little Rock. Later they were featured on the *Ozark Mountain Jubilee*, the *Louisiana Hayride* and in 1966, the *Grand Ole Opry*. The trio recorded for Columbia and early in 1966, they had a US country and pop hit with Bobby Harden's song 'Tippy Toeing'. Another of his songs 'Sneaking 'Cross The Border' also became a Top 20 country hit. Their last chart entry, 'Everybody Wants To Be Somebody Else', seemed to be somewhat prophetic because in 1968, they disbanded. Arlene had begun to pursue a solo career in 1967 and had minor hits that year with 'Fair Weather Love' and 'You're Easy To Love'. Between 1967 and 1978, she totalled 17 more country chart entries the most successful being 'Lovin' Man' (a female version of the Roy Orbison number 1, 'Oh Pretty Woman'). She also charted with a version of Orbison's song 'Crying' and after moving to Capitol in 1974, she recorded a country version of the Helen Reddy pop hit 'Leave Me Alone (Ruby Red Dress)', although for some reason she appears as Arleen on this release. Bobby Harden duetted with his sister in 1968 on 'Who Loves Who' and had a minor solo country chart entry in 1975 with 'One Step'. Arlene moved to Elektra in 1977, where her last chart entry was a 1978 minor hit with 'You're Not Free And I'm Not Easy'.
Albums: *What Can I Say* (1968), *Sings Roy Orbison*

(1970), *I Could Almost Say Goodbye* (1975). By Bobby Harden *Nashville Sensation* (1969). As the Harden Trio *Tippy Toeing* (1966), *Sing Me Back Home* (1968), *Great Country Hits* (1970).

Hargrove, Linda

b. 3 February 1950, Jacksonville, Florida, but was raised in Tallahassee. Hargrove learnt piano and guitar from an early age and played french horn in the school band. She was imitating Carole King's songwriting from the age of 14. She played with a local rock band and then, in 1970, she decided to try her luck in Nashville. Sandy Posey recorded her material and steel guitarist Pete Drake offered her session work and subsequently produced her records. She befriended Michael Nesmith and they wrote 'Winonah', which Nesmith recorded, and the country standard, 'I've Never Loved Anyone More', which has been recorded by Lynn Anderson, Eddy Arnold, Billie Jo Spears and Marty Robbins. An album for Michael Nesmith's Countryside label was never released, and her first (released) album for Elektra, *Music Is Your Mistress*, included a duet with Melba Montgomery, 'Don't Let It Bother You'. Her songs include 'Let It Shine' (Olivia Newton-John), 'Just Get Up And Close The Door' (Johnny Rodriguez), 'New York City Song' (Jan Howard, Tanya Tucker) and 'Something I Can Forget' (Moe Bandy), but she saved the wonderfully-titled 'Time Wounds All Heels' for herself. She had a US country hit in 1975 with 'Love Was (Once Around The Dance Floor)'. *Impressions* is an album with a Spanish flavour. She became a born-again Christian, married Charlie Bartholomew and now performs gospel concerts as Linda Bartholomew. She regards Linda Hargrove as a different person, someone who wrote secular songs and was heavily into drink and drugs.

Albums: *Music Is Your Mistress* (1973), *Blue Jean Country Queen* (1974), *Love, You're The Teacher* (1975), *Just For You* (1976), *Impressions* (1977), *A New Song* (1987)

Harris, Emmylou

b. 12 April, 1949, Birmingham, Alabama USA. Starting as a folk singer, Harris tried her luck in the late 60s in New York's Greenwich Village folk clubs, making an album for the independent Jubilee label in 1970, *Gliding Bird*, which was largely unrepresentative of her subsequent often stunning work. It included covers of songs by Bob Dylan, Fred Neil and Hank Williams, as well as somewhat ordinary originals and a title track written by her first husband, Tom Slocum. Harris then moved to Washington DC, where latter-day Flying Burrito Brother Rick Roberts heard her sing in a club, and recommended her to Gram Parsons, who was looking for a female partner. Parsons hired Harris after discovering that their voices dovetailed perfectly, and she appeared on his two studio albums, *GP* (1973) and *Grievous Angel* (1974). The latter was released after Parsons died, as was a live album recorded for a US radio station which was released as an album some years later.

Eddie Tickner, who had been involved with managing the Byrds, and who was also managing Parsons at the time of his drug-related demise, encouraged Harris to make a solo album using the same musicians who had worked with Parsons. The cream of Los Angeles session musicians, they were collectively known as the Hot Band, and among the 'pickers' who worked in the band during its 15-year life span backing Harris were guitarist James Burton (originally lead guitarist on 'Suzy Q' by Dale Hawkins, and simultaneously during his time with Emmylou, lead player with Elvis Presley's Las Vegas band), pianist Glen D. Hardin (a member of the Crickets post-Buddy Holly and also working simultaneously with both Harris and Presley), steel guitarist Hank DeVito, bass player Emory Gordy Jnr (now a highly successful Nashville-based producer), John Ware (ex-Michael Nesmith's First National Band, and a member of Linda Ronstadt's early 70s backing group) and the virtually unknown Rodney Crowell. Backed by musicians of this calibre (subsequent Hot Band members included legendary British lead guitarist Albert Lee and Ricky Skaggs, later a country star in his own right), Harris released a series of artistically excellent and often commercially successful albums starting with 1975's *Pieces Of The Sky*, and also including *Elite Hotel* (1976), *Luxury Liner* (1977) and *Quarter Moon In A Ten Cent Town* (whose title was a line in the song 'Easy From Now On', co-written by Carlene Carter and Susanna Clark, wife of singer songwriter Guy Clark). *Blue Kentucky Girl* was closer to pure country music than the country/rock that had become her trademark and speciality, and 1980's *Roses In The Snow* was her fourth album to make the Top 40 of the US pop chart. *Light Of The Stable*, a 1980 Christmas album also featuring Linda Ronstadt, Dolly Parton, Willie Nelson and Neil Young, was surprisingly far less successful. Two more albums in 1981 (*Evangeline* and *Cimmaron* - the latter featuring a cover of the Poco classic, 'Rose Of Cimmaron') were better

Emmylou Harris

sellers, but a 1982 live album, *Last Date*, was largely ignored. The following year's *White Shoes* was Harris's final album produced by Canadian Brian Ahern, her second husband, who had established a reputation for his successful work with Anne Murray, prior to producing all Emmylou's classic albums up to this point. Harris and Ahern separated both personally and professionally, marking the end of an era which had also seen her appearing on Bob Dylan's *Desire* in 1976 and *The Last Waltz,* the farewell concert/triple album/feature film by the Band from 1978.

Around this time, Harris was invited by producer Glyn Johns and British singer/songwriter Paul Kennerley to participate in a concept album written by the latter, *The Legend Of Jesse James* (Kennerley's follow-up to the similarly conceptual *White Mansions*). Harris and Kennerley later married, and together wrote and produced *The Ballad Of Sally Rose* (a concept album which by her own belated admission reflected her relationship with Gram Parsons) and the similarly excellent *13*, but never marked a return to previous chart heights. 1987 brought two albums involving Harris: *Trio*, a multi-million selling triumph which won a Grammy Award, was a collaboration between Harris, Linda Ronstadt and Dolly Parton, but Harris's own *Angel Band,* a low key acoustic

collection, became the first of Harris's not to be released in the UK, where it was felt to be too uncommercial. This fall from commercial grace occurred simultaneously with (although perhaps coincidentally) the virtual retirement of manager Eddie Tickner, who had guided and protected Harris through 15 years of mainly classic albums. 1989's *Bluebird* was a definite return to form with production by Richard Bennett and featuring a title track written by Butch Hancock, but a commercial renaissance did not occur. 1990's, *Duets*, a compilation album featuring Harris singing with Gram Parsons, Roy Orbison, George Jones, the Desert Rose Band, Don Williams, Neil Young and John Denver (among others), was artistically delightful, but appeared to be an attempt on the part of the marketing department of WEA (to whom she had been signed since *Pieces Of The Sky*) to reawaken interest in a star whom they feared might be past her commercial peak. The same year's *Brand New Dance* was not a success compared with much of her past catalogue, and in that year, the much changed Hot Band was dropped in favour of the Nash Ramblers, a bluegrass-based acoustic quintet composed of Sam Bush (ex-New Grass Revival, mandolin, fiddle and duet vocals), Al Perkins (ex-Manassas, Flying Burrito Brothers, Souther Hillman Furay dobro/banjo), *Grand Ol'*

Opry double bass player Roy Huskey Jnr, drummer Larry Atamanuik and 22-year-old new boy John Randall Stewart (acoustic guitar, harmony vocal - the Rodney Crowell replacement). In 1991, Harris and the Nash Ramblers were permitted to record a live album at the former home of the *Grand Ole Opry*, the Ryman Auditorium in Nashville. The record was poorly received in some quarters, however, and at the end of 1992, it was reported that she had been dropped by Warner Brothers, ending a 20-year association. Harris remains in the incongruous position of a legendary figure in country music who is always in demand as a guest performer in the studio, but who cannot match the record sales of those younger artists who regard her as a heroine.

Albums: *Gliding Bird* (1970), *Pieces Of The Sky* (1975), *Elite Hotel* (1976), *Luxury Liner* (1977), *Quarter Moon In A 10 Cent Town* (1978), *Blue Kentucky Girl* (1979), *Roses In The Snow* (1980), *Light Of The Stable* (1980), *Evangeline* (1981), *Cimmaron* (1981), *Last Date* (1982), *White Shoes* (1983), *The Ballad Of Sally Rose* (1985), *13* (1986), *Trio* (1987), *Angel Band* (1987), *Bluebird* (1989), *Duets* (1990), *Brand New Dance* (1990), *At The Ryman* (1992).

Hart, Freddie

b. Fred Segrest, 21 December 1926, Lochapoka, Alabama, USA. Hart was one of 10 boys and five girls born to a family of sharecroppers. He left school at 12 and started working for his parents. When he was only 15, he lied about his age - and his parents signed the papers - so that he could join the marines. He saw action at both Guam and Iwo Jima. Four years later he was back as a civilian and was teaching karate to the Los Angeles police. He acquired a black belt but, in 1951, he went into country music by joining Lefty Frizzell's band. In 1953 he was given a recording contract with Capitol but it was not until 1959 that he had his first hit - 'The Wall' with Columbia. He recorded further country hits with Monument and Kapp, including 'Hank Williams' Guitar', and, in 1969, he rejoined Capitol as a successful country performer. In 1971 Hart went to number 17 in the US pop charts with 'Easy Loving', which won the Country Music Association's Song of the Year award two years running. He explained its success as follows, 'I try to put down in my songs what every man wants to say, and what every woman wants to hear. A song like 'Easy Loving' has brought a lot of people together. Many people have told me that they have fallen in love and

gotten married because of that song.' This method of songwriting has led Hart into some obscure corners, none more so than 'The Child' in which he plays a baby in his mother's womb! His country hits include 'My Hang Up Is You', 'Bless Your Heart', 'The Pleasure's Been All Mine' and 'Why Lovers Turn To Strangers'. His compositions include 'Skid Row Joe' for Porter Wagoner and 'I Ain't Goin' Hungry Anymore' for Charlie Rich. His UK debut at the Wembley country music festival in 1978 was too overblown for some - at one stage, it looked as though he would individually thank every member of the audience. In the early 80s, he had success with 'Roses Are Red' and 'You Were There' on the small Sunbird label, but by then he was no longer fully committed to country music. With shrewd investing, Hart became wealthy and, in the 80s, he concentrated on his acres of plum trees, his trucking company and his 200 breeding bulls. He now runs a school for handicapped children in Burbank, California. In 1988, he returned with a collection of songs that he had written 'with the Lord in my heart'.

Albums: *The Spirited Freddie Hart* (1962), *Hart Of Country Music* (1965), *Straight From The Hart* (1966), *A Hurtin' Man* (1967), *Neon And The Rain* (1967), *Born A Fool* (1968), *Togetherness* (1968), *California Grapevine* (1970), *New Sounds* (1970), *Easy Loving* (1971), *My Hang Up Is You* (1972), *Bless Your Heart* (1972), *Got The All-Overs For You* (1972), *Lonesome Love* (1972), *A Trip To Heaven* (1973), *Super Kind Of Woman* (1973), *If You Can't Feel It* (1973), *You Are My World* (1973), *Hang In There Girl* (1974), *Heart 'N' Soul* (1974), *The First Time* (1975), *Freddie Hart Presents The Hartbeats* (1975), *The Best Of Freddie Hart* (1975), *That Look In Her Eyes* (1976), *People Put To Music* (1976), *The Pleasure's Been All Mine* (1977), *Only You* (1978), *My Lady* (1979), *Sure Thing* (1980), *Somebody Loves You* (1984), *I Will Never Die* (1988).

Hartford, John

b. John Harford, 30 December 1937, New York City, New York, USA. Hartford was a multi-instrumentalist country performer whose most famous composition was 'Gentle On My Mind'. He grew up in St. Louis where his early influences included bluegrass music and he became adept on banjo and fiddle as a teenager. He later mastered dobro and guitar. After working as a sign-painter, commercial artist, Mississippi riverboat deckhand and disc jockey, Hartford moved to Nashville in the early 60s. There he became a session musician before signing a solo recording deal with RCA, for which he made eight albums between 1966 and 1972. In 1967, Glen Campbell recorded the million-selling version of the lyrical 'Gentle On My Mind', which was subsequently covered by over 300 artists including Frank Sinatra, Elvis Presley and Max Bygraves. Presley's producer Felton Jarvis supervised Hartford's own recording of the song on his second album. During the late 60s, Hartford undertook selected session work, most notably on the Byrds' influential *Sweetheart Of The Rodeo.*

In 1971, he moved to Warner Brothers, where David Bromberg produced the highly-praised *Aereo Plain.* A year later, however, he left the music business to concentrate on renovating steamboats. He returned in 1976 with the Grammy-winning *Mark Twang* (on Flying Fish) which featured Hartford making all the percussion noises with his mouth. In 1977, Hartford teamed up with the Dillard brothers, Rodney and Doug, to record two country-rock flavoured albums which included quirky Hartford compositions like 'Two Hits And The Joint Turned Brown'. *Annual Waltz* was the first album under a new contract with MCA.

Albums: *Looks At Life* (1967), *Earthwords And Music* (1967), *The Love Album* (1968), *Housing Project* (1968), *John Hartford* (1969), *Iron Mountain Depot* (1970), *Aereo Plain* (1971), *Morning Bugle* (1972), *Tennessee Jubilee* (1975), *Mark Twang* (1976), *Nobody Knows What You Do* (1976), *All In The Name Of Love* (1977), *Heading Down Into The Mystery Below* (1978), *Slumbering On The Cumberland* (1979), *You And Me At Home* (1981), *Me Oh My, How Does Time Fly* (1982), *Mystery Below* (1983), *You And Me At Home* (1984), *Catalogue* (1985), *Annual Waltz* (1986), *Gum Tree Canoe* (1987), *John Hartford* (1988), *All In The Name Of Love* (1989). With Doug and Rodney Dillard *Dillard, Hartford, Dillard* (1977), *Permanent Wave* (1980).

Hawkins, Hawkshaw

b. Harold Franklin Hawkins, 22 December 1921, Huntingdon, West Virginia, USA. Hawkins started on guitar and became proficient on many instruments. Success in a talent contest in 1937 led to paid work on radio stations in Huntingdon and Charleston. In 1942, he performed on radio in Manila when stationed in the Phillipines. After his discharge, he signed with King Records and did well with 'Sunny Side Of The Mountain', which became his signature tune. He was a regular member of the WWVA's *Wheeling Jamboree* from 1946 to 1954, which he left to join the *Grand Ole Opry.* In 1948 he became one of the first country artists to appear on network television. He had US country hits with 'Pan American', 'I Love You A Thousand Ways', 'I'm Just Waiting For You' and 'Slow Poke'. The tall, handsome country singer married fellow artist Jean Shepard and they lived on a farm near Nashville where Hawkins bred horses. Their first son, Don Robin, was named after their friends, Don Gibson and Marty Robbins. In 1963 Hawkins released his best-known recording, Justin Tubb's song 'Lonesome 7-7203'. The song entered the US country charts three days before Hawkins died on 5 March 1963 in a plane crash which also claimed Patsy Cline and Cowboy Copas. 'Lonesome 7-7203' was his only number 1 record in the US country charts. Shepard was pregnant at the time and their son was named Harold Franklin Hawkins II in his memory.

Albums: *Hawkshaw Hawkins, Volume 1* (1958), *Hawkshaw Hawkins Sings Grand Ole Opry Favourites, Volume 2* (1959), *Hawkshaw Hawkins* (1959), *All New Hawkshaw Hawkins* (1963), *The Great Hawkshaw Hawkins* (1963), *Taken From Our Vaults, Volume 1* (1963), *Taken From Our Vaults, Volume 2* (1963), *Taken From Our Vaults, Volume 3* (1964), *Hawkshaw Hawkins Sings* (1964), *The Country Gentleman* (1966), *Lonesome 7-7203* (1969), *16 Greatest Hits Of Hawkshaw Hawkins* (1977), *Hawk, 1953-61* (boxed-set containing previously unissued material, 1991).

Hawkins, Ronnie

b. 10 January 1935, Huntsville, Arkansas, USA. Hawkins, who is rock 'n' roll's funniest storyteller says, 'I've been around so long, I remember when the Dead Sea was only sick'. Hawkins' father played at square dances and his cousin, Dale Hawkins, staked his own claim to rock 'n' roll history with 'Susie Q'. Hawkins, who did some stunt diving for Esther Williams' swimming revue, earned both a science and physical education degree at University of Arkansas, but his heart was in the 'chitlin' starvation circuit' in Memphis. Because the pay was poor, musicians went from one club to another using the 'Arkansas credit card' - a siphon, a rubber hose and a five gallon can. Hawkins befriended Elvis Presley - 'In 1954 Elvis couldn't even spell Memphis: by 1957 he owned it'. After Hawkins' army service, he followed Conway Twitty's recommendation by working Canadian clubs. Whilst there, he made his first recordings as the Ron Hawkins Quartet, the tracks being included on *Rrrracket Time.* In 1959 Hawkins made number 45 on the US charts with 'Forty Days', an amended version of Chuck Berry's 'Thirty Days'. He explains, 'Chuck Berry had simply put new lyrics to 'When The Saints Go Marching In'. My record company told me to add ten days. They knew Chess wouldn't sue as they wouldn't want to admit it was 'The Saints'.' Hawkins' version of Young Jessie's 'Mary Lou' then made number 26 in the US charts. With his handstands and leapfrogging, he became known as Mr. Dynamo and he pioneered a dance called the Camel Walk. In 1960 Hawkins became the first rock 'n' roller to involve himself in politics with a plea for a murderer on Death Row, 'The Ballad Of Caryl Chessman' but to no avail. The same year Hawkins with his drummer, Levon Helm, travelled to the UK for the ITV show *Boy Meets Girls*. He was so impressed by guitarist Joe Brown that he offered him a job, but, on returning home, the Hawks gradually took shape - Levon Helm, Robbie Robertson, Garth Hudson, Richard Manuel and Rick Danko. Their wild 1963 single of two Bo Diddley songs, 'Bo Diddley' and 'Who Do You Love' was psychedelia before its time. 'Bo Diddley' was a Canadian hit, and by marrying a former Miss Toronto, Hawkins made the country his home. He supported local talent and he refused, for example, to perform in clubs that did not give equal time to Canadian artists. Meanwhile, the Hawks recorded for Atlantic Records as Levon and the Hawks and were then recruited by Bob Dylan, becoming the Band. The various incarnations of the Hawks have included many fine musicians, notably the pianist Stan Szelest. Hawkins had Canadian Top 10 hits with 'Home From The Forest' and 'Bluebirds Over The Mountain', whilst his experience in buying a Rolls-Royce was recounted in Gordon Lightfoot's 'Talkin' Silver Cloud Blues'. In 1970 Hawkins befriended John Lennon and Yoko Ono, and the promotional single on which Lennon praises Hawkins' 'Down In The Alley' is a collectors' item. Kris Kristofferson wrote hilarious liner notes for Hawkins' album, *Rock And Roll Resurrection* and it was through Kristofferson that Hawkins had a role in the disastrous film, *Heaven's Gate*. Hawkins is better known for extrovert performance in the Band's film, *The Last Waltz*. The burly singer has also appeared in Bob Dylan's Rolling Thunder Revue and he has some amusing lines as 'Bob Dylan' in the film, *Renaldo And Clara*. Hawkins' segment with 'happy hooker' Xaviera Hollander includes the line, 'Abraham Lincoln said all men are created equal, but then he never saw Bo Diddley in the shower'. In 1985 Hawkins joined Joni Mitchell, Anne Murray, Neil Young and several others for the Canadian Band Aid record, 'Tears Are Not Enough' by Northern Lights. Hawkins has a regular Canadian television series, *Honky Tonk*, and he owns a 200 acre farm and has several businesses. It gives the lie to his colourful quote, '90 per cent of what I made went on women, whiskey, drugs and cars. I guess I just wasted the other 10 per cent'.

Albums: *Ronnie Hawkins* (1959), *Mr. Dynamo* (1960), *Folk Ballads Of Ronnie Hawkins* (1961), *Ronnie Hawkins Sings The Songs Of Hank Williams* (1962), *Ronnie Hawkins* (originally on Yorkville and reissued in 1976 as *The Hawk In Winter*) (1969), *Ronnie Hawkins* (album on Cotillion) (1970), *The Hawk* i (1971), *Rock And Roll Resurrection* (1972), *The Giant Of Rock And Roll* (1974), *The Hawk* ii (1979), *Rrrracket Time* (1979), *A Legend In His Spare Time* (1981), *The Hawk And Rock* (1982), *Making It Again* (1984), *Hello Again ... Mary Lou* (1991).

Hay, George D.

b. George Dewey Hay, 9 November 1895, Attica, Indiana, USA, d. 8 May 1968. On completion of his education, Hay began his working career with a company involved in property and sales. He later changed to journalism and by 1919, was working for the Memphis *Commercial Appeal*. Part of his duties were to cover court cases and as a result of what he saw and heard there, he began to write a column that he called 'Howdy Judge'. The column presented, in a humorous and inoffensive manner, the conversations between a white judge and the unfortunate blacks, who came before him on various charges. The stories, all written in dialect, quickly became extremely popular with the readers of the paper and won for their writer the nickname of 'Judge'. (In 1926, Hay published some of the stories in a book.) In 1923, the owners of the paper decided that they should try the new field of radio and founded WMC in Memphis. Hay was selected to be the newspaper's radio announcer and editor. Initially reluctant but quick to see the opportunities it offered, he began to develop a radio style. He realised from the start that immediate identification was essential and he took to using a chanting form of vocal delivery preceded by a blast from a toy wooden steamboat whistle, which he called 'Hushpuckiny'. He also gained national recognition by being the first announcer to inform the world of the death of President Harding. In 1924, his successful radio work at WMC saw him move to the Sears company to become the chief announcer on their new and more powerful WLS station in Chicago. He changed his steamboat whistle for a train whistle and soon became involved with the station's *WLS Barn Dance* (later known as the *National Barn Dance*). He began to refer to himself as the 'Solemn Old Judge' and established such a reputation that his services were much in demand. By the end of the year he had been awarded a gold cup by Readers Digest as the most popular announcer in the USA. Hay's reputation led to him being invited to Nashville to attend the dedication ceremony on 5 October 1925 of the new WSM station owned by National Life and Accident Insurance Co. Ltd. (The WSM letters stood for We Shield Millions.) While there he was offered the post of director of the station and a few weeks later having accepted, he took up his new post. He assessed the programme schedules against the actual potential audience figure and quickly decided that too much emphasis was being placed on Nashville itself and that the station could not last if it only catered for the limited audience found within the city. He knew from his experience at Chicago of the importance of the programmes having a strong rural interest. His views were not shared by all the governing body but he was given the opportunity to prove his point. Fully aware of the success of the *WLS Barn Dance*, he decided that much more should be done to include a musical content of more interest to the outlying areas, particularly those to the south. On 28 November 1925, Hay's *WSM Barn Dance* started with a programme of fiddle music played by the 77-year-old Uncle Jimmie Thompson, who was accompanied by his niece Eva Thompson Jones on piano. Hay naturally announced and it was noticed that he had once again reverted to using his steamboat whistle, which he now called Old Hickory as a mark of respect to Nashville's hero, Andrew Jackson.

After this initial performance, the show became a regular Saturday evening programme on WSM. It extended to three hours' duration and Hay featured many of the noted local artists on it. Though immensely popular in the outlying areas, the show did have its adversaries within the city. Attempts were made to have 'the hillbilly programme' stopped as it could be detrimental to the good name of Nashville. Hay successfully defended his creation and in 1927, fully aware of the fact that the station carried the NBC Grand Opera broadcasts from New York, he parodied the name by changing that of the Barn Dance to the *Grand*

Ole Opry. Hay was eventually replaced as station manager of WSM by Harry Stone in 1930 but continued with his duties on the *Opry*. His blasts on the steamboat whistle and shouts of 'Let her go, boys' became nationally known as the show opener. He also always closed with a special little verse and a final whistle blast. His instructions to musicians was always 'Keep it down to earth, boys' and he totally objected to any instrument being used that was not of the accepted acoustic variety. In the 30s and 40s, he continued to organize the *Opry*, he auditioned new talent and was responsible for the final *Opry* popularity of a great many artists, including Uncle Dave Macon (the *Opry*'s first real star), Roy Acuff and Eddy Arnold. Hay retired from active participation in the *Opry* in 1951 and moved to his daughter's home in Virginia. In 1953, his book *A Story Of The Grand Ole Opry* was published in Nashville. He was elected to the *Country Music Hall Of Fame* in 1966 for his services to the music and returned to Nashville for the occasion. It marks the esteem that he was held in by WSM to note that from his retirement in 1951 up to his death on 8 May 1968, at Virginia Beach, Virginia, he was to all intents and purposes still available for work and was paid by WSM.
Further reading: *A Story Of The Grand Ole Opry*, George D. Hay.

Hazlewood, Lee

b. Barton Lee Hazlewood, 9 July 1929, Mannford, Oklahoma, USA. Hazlewood, the son of an oil worker, served in Korea and, on his return, became a DJ in Phoenix. He set himself up as an independent record producer and wrote 'The Fool', 'Run Boy Run' and 'Son Of A Gun' for Sanford Clark. On Clark's recordings, Hazlewood was experimenting with ways of recording Al Casey's guitar, often using echo. In 1957, after 'The Fool' had become a US pop hit for the Dot label, Hazlewood formed his own Jamie label, with publisher Lester Sill and television host Dick Clark. Hazlewood created the 'twangy guitar' by slowing down Duane Eddy's notes and deepening his sound. Hazlewood and Eddy co-wrote many instrumental hits including 'Rebel Rouser', 'Cannon Ball', 'Shazam!' and, with a minimal lyric, 'Dance With The Guitar Man'. Eddy was the first major performer to include musicians' names on album sleeves and, similarly, Hazlewood was acknowledged as the producer. Eddy also backed Hazlewood on a single, 'The Girl On Death Row'/'Words Mean Nothing'. Much of Eddy's success stemmed from his regular appearances on

Dick Clark's *American Bandstand*, and Clark's payola allegations harmed Eddy's career. Hazlewood formed his LHI label and he produced the *Safe At Home* album by the International Submarine Band (including Gram Parsons). At Reprise in 1965, he wrote and produced US hits by Dean Martin ('Houston') and Dino, Desi And Billy, which included Martin's son ('I'm A Fool'). When Hazlewood was assigned to Nancy Sinatra, the daughter of the label's owner, who had made several unsuccessful singles, he promised to get her hits. Nicknaming her 'Nasty Jones', he gave her 'These Boots Are Made For Walkin'', which had been written for a man, and said, 'You gotta get a new sound and get rid of this babyness. You're not a virgin anymore so let's do one for the truck drivers. Bite the words'. Sinatra's boots stomped over the international charts, and she followed it with other Hazlewood songs including 'How Does That Grab You, Darlin'', 'Sugartown' and 'Lightning's Girl'. Their duets include the playful 'Jackson' and the mysterious 'Some Velvet Morning' and 'Lady Bird'. The partnership folded because Sinatra tired of singing Hazlewood's songs, although she has made few records since. Hazlewood, whose singing voice is as deep as Eddy's guitar, tried for the US country charts with a cover of 'Ode To Billie Joe', and he also produced Waylon Jennings' *Singer Of Sad Songs*. His own albums include *Trouble Is A Lonesome Town*, a sombre collection about the characters in a western town, and *Requiem For An Almost Lady*, a sincere tribute to a girlfriend who had died. His *Poet, Fool Or Bum* album was dismissed in one word by the *New Musical Express* - 'Bum'. One track, 'The Performer', emphasized his disillusionment and he moved to Sweden, making records for that market.

Albums: *Trouble Is A Lonesome Town* (1963), *The N.S.V.I.P.'s* (1965, soundtrack), *Lee Hazlewood Sings Friday's Child* (1966), *The Very Special World Of Lee Hazlewood* (1966), *Hazlewoodism - Its Cause And Cure* (1966), *Love And Other Crimes* (1968), with Nancy Sinatra *Nancy And Lee* (1968), *Cowboy In Sweden* (1970), with Ann-Margret *The Cowboy And The Lady* (1971), *Forty* (1971), *Requiem For An Almost Lady* (1971), with Nancy Sinatra *Did You Ever?* (1971), *13* (1972), *I'll Be Your Baby Tonight* (1973), *Poet, Fool Or Bum* (1973), *The Stockholm Kid* (1974), *A House Safe For Tigers* (1975, soundtrack), *20th Century Lee* (1976), *Movin' On* (1977), *Back On The Street Again* (1977).

Head, Roy

b. 1 September 1941, Three Rivers, Texas, USA. This respected performer first formed his group, the Traits, in 1958, after moving to San Marcos. The line-up included Jerry Gibson (drums) who later played with Sly And The Family Stone. Head recorded for several local labels, often under the supervision of famed Texas producer Huey P. Meaux, but it was not until 1965 that he scored a national hit when 'Treat Her Right' reached number 2 on both the US pop and R&B charts. This irresistible song, with its pumping horns and punchy rhythm, established the singer alongside the Righteous Brothers as that year's prime blue-eyed soul exponent. Head's later releases appeared on a variety of outlets, including Dunhill and Elektra, and embraced traces of rockabilly ('Apple Of My Eye') and psychedelia ('You're (Almost) Tuff'). However, by the 70s he had honed his style and was working as a country singer and in 1975 he earned a notable US C&W Top 20 hit with 'The Most Wanted Woman In Town'.

Albums: *Roy Head And The Traits* (1965), *Treat Me Right* (1965), *A Head Of His Time* (1968), *Same People* (1970), *Dismal Prisoner* (1972), *Head First* (1976), *Tonight's The Night* (1977), *Boogie Down* (1977), *Rock 'N' Roll My Soul* (1977), *In Our Room* (1979), *The Many Sides Of Roy Head* (1980). Compilations: *His All-Time Favourites* (1974), *Treat Her Right* (1988).

Helms, Bobby

b. Robert Lee Helms, 15 August 1933, Bloomington, Indiana, USA. Helms was something of a child prodigy, who was playing guitar and singing a mixture of pop and country on local radio at the age of 12 and from 1946-54, he regularly appeared on WWTV Bloomington. He made his debut on the *Grand Ole Opry* in 1950, having impressed WSM officials so much that they had him flown to Nashville to appear. He signed with Decca and in 1957, his recording of Lawton Williams' 'Fraulein', his first US country chart entry, was a number 1 (even reaching number 36 in the US pop charts). The song stayed in the country charts for 52 weeks, which, according to Joel Whitburn's *Record Research*, is the second longest chart tenure of all time. The same year also saw him with two further hits, 'My Special Angel' and the original version of 'Jingle Bell Rock', both of which became million sellers and made the Top 10 in the US pop charts. The former, another US country number 1, managed a Top 30 appearance in the UK charts but lost out to the Top 10 cover

Bobby Helms

version by Malcolm Vaughan. (Max Bygraves made the UK Top 10 with his version of 'Jingle Bell Rock' in 1959.) Helms had further country/pop success the following year with 'Jacqueline', from the film *The Case Against Brooklyn* (which also charted in the UK) and a US country number 10 with 'Just A Little Lonesome'. In the late 60s, he left Decca and recorded for Little Darlin' but achieved no further major chart hits. Throughout the 70s and 80s, he continued to tour, often with his wife Dori and he released an album in 1989. He is still remembered because of seasonal appearances of 'Jingle Bell Rock' but his last chart hit, 'Mary Goes Round', was on the Certron label in 1970. Interestingly, it was a cover version of Helms' recording of 'Schoolboy Crush' which became the b-side of Cliff Richard's first recording.

Selected albums: *To My Special Angel* (1957), *Country Christmas* (1958), *Best Of Bobby Helms* (1963), *Bobby Helms* (1965), *I'm The Man* (1966), *Sorry My Name Isn't Fred* (1966), *All New Just For You* (1968), *Greatest Performance* (1970), *Jingle Bell Rock* (1974), *Greatest Hits* (1975), *Pop A-Billy* (1983), *Bobby Helms Country* (1989).

Henderson, Kelvin

b. 6 August 1947, Bristol, England, and still lives in the house in which he was born. In the early 60s Henderson was influenced by Woody Guthrie, Leadbelly, Pete Seeger and, more specifically, Johnny Cash's album, *Ride This Train*. He worked in Europe, often busking on the streets, meeting his wife, Britta, and making two albums for Polydor in Sweden. Back in the UK in the mid-70s, he and his band built a reputation both in their own right and by backing such visiting American performers as Vernon Oxford, Red Sovine, Dick Feller, Jimmy Payne and Slim Whitman. His *Slow Movin' Outlaw*, for a supermarket label, Windmill, sold an estimated 100,000 copies. Those who maintain that British country music must be sub-standard should listen to *Black Magic Gun*, which easily matches American albums of that period. Although Henderson is versatile, he is at his best with deep-voiced story songs such as 'Pamela Brown', 'Saginaw, Michigan' and 'Hello In There'. His singing voice, which is far removed from his Bristol speech, combines Derroll Adams' bottom range with Waylon Jennings' cutting edge. Ironically, he recorded both 'He Went To Paris' and 'Clyde' before Jennings. His television showcase for UK country, *Country Comes West*, was hampered by a limited budget and his

syndicated radio show, *My Style Of Country*, for the BBC in the southwest is amongst the most popular regional shows. He also promotes concerts of acoustic country music and, in 1991, he toured the UK with US country singer, Joey Davis. Henderson is an excellent interpreter of modern country songs and his own compositions such as 'Big Wheel' and 'Scarlet Woman' are not dwarfed in his well-chosen company. 'I've never planned my career too closely,' he admits, 'I've been too busy playing.'

Albums: *Songs For Travellin'* (1971), *Leavin' In The Morning* (1972), *Kelvin Henderson's Country Band* (1974), *Slow Movin' Outlaw* (1975), *Black Magic Gun* (1977), *Kelvin Henderson* (1978), *Country Comes West* (1979), *Headlites* (1981), *Still On A Roll* (1985).

Highway 101

Like the Monkees, Highway 101 is a manufactured US group. Chuck Morris, the manager of the Nitty Gritty Dirt Band and Lyle Lovett, wanted to form a group which would play 'traditional country with a rock 'n' roll backbeat'. He recruited session man, Scott 'Cactus' Moser, to help him. He worked with bassist Curtis Stone, the son of Cliffie Stone, in the film, *Back To School*, and then he added session guitarist, Jack Daniels. Morris then heard some demos by Paulette Carlson (b. Minnesota, USA). She had had songs recorded by Gail Davies and Tammy Wynette and had a cameo role as a nightclub singer in the film, *Twins*. Their first single, 'Some Find Love', was not successful but, in 1987, they had their first US country hits with 'The Bed You Made For Me' (number 4), which Carlson wrote, and 'Whiskey, If You Were A Woman' (number 2). They topped the US country charts with 'Somewhere Tonight' with its songwriting credit of 'old' and 'new' country, Harlan Howard and Rodney Crowell. In 1988 they had a further chart-toppers with 'Cry, Cry, Cry' (which was a new song and not a revival of the Johnny Cash hit) and 'If You Love Me, Just Say Yes', the latter being based on the slogan of Nancy Reagan's anti-drugs campaign, 'Just say no'. Despite the quality of their work, their 1991 album, *Bing Bang Boom*, showed that the Highway may be nearing its end.

Albums: *Highway 101* (1987), *101 2* (1988), *Paint The Town* (1989), *Bing Bang Boom* (1991).

Hill, Dan

b. Daniel Hill Jnr., 3 June 1954, Toronto, Ontario, Canada. Hill achieved success when a soft ballad co-written by Hill and Barry Mann, reached number 3 in 1977, and 'Can't We Try', a duet with Vonda Sheppard, climbed to number 6 in 1987. Hill and his parents moved to Canada during the 50s and he discovered music in his teens, gravitating toward vocalists such as Frank Sinatra. Hill became a professional musician at the age of 18, playing at clubs and trying to sell his demo tapes to uninterested record labels. He gradually became popular in Canada, and signed to 20th Century Fox Records in the USA. His self-titled debut album just missed the US Top 100 in 1975 and his first chart single in the US was 'Growin' Up', in 1976. But the follow-up introduced Hill to a larger audience. It was the president of the publishing company for which he worked who teamed him with Mann, resulting in the success of 'Sometimes When We Touch'. Hill's album, *Longer Fuse*, which included that single, was also his biggest seller, reaching number 21 in 1977. The Hill-Mann collaboration was followed by a few lesser chart singles for Hill and it seemed he had disappeared from the music scene in the early 80s after recording two albums for Epic Records. In 1987, however, he collaborated with female singer Vonda Sheppard and returned to the Top 10. Hill placed one further single in the chart in early 1988 and had Top 10 hits in *Billboard*'s 'Adult' chart that year with 'Carmelia' and in 1990 with 'Unborn Heart'.

Albums: *Dan Hill* i (1975), *Longer Fuse* (1977), *Hold On* (1978), *Frozen In The Night* (1978), *If Dreams Had Wings* (1980), *Partial Surrender* (1981), *Dan Hill* ii (1987). Compilation: *The Best Of Dan Hill* (1980).

Hillman, Chris

b. 4 December 1942, Los Angeles, California, USA. Originally a mandolin player of some distinction, Hillman appeared in the Scottsville Squirrel Barkers, the Blue Diamond Boys and the Hillmen before Jim Dickson offered him the vacant bassist's role in the fledgling Byrds in late 1964. The last to join that illustrious group, he did not emerge as a real force until 1967's *Younger Than Yesterday*, which contained several of his compositions. His jazz-influenced wandering bass lines won him great respect among rock *cognoscenti* but it soon became clear that he harked back to his country roots. After introducing Gram Parsons to the Byrds, he participated in the much-acclaimed *Sweetheart Of The Rodeo* and went on to form the highly respected Flying Burrito Brothers. A line-up with Stephen Stills in Manassas and an unproductive

period in the ersatz supergroup Souther, Hillman Furay Band was followed by two mid-70s solo albums of average quality. A reunion with Roger McGuinn and Gene Clark in the late 70s proved interesting but short-lived. During the 80s, Hillman recorded two low budget traditional bluegrass albums, *Morning Sky* and *Desert Rose*, before forming the excellent and highly successful Desert Rose Band.

Albums: *Slippin' Away* (1976), *Clear Sailin'* (1977), *Morning Sky* (1982), *Desert Rose* (1984).

Hillsiders

The Hillsiders, played country when country was not cool and as the UK's leading country band, they have now introduced thousands of people to the music. The group's origins go back to 1959 when lead singer/rhythm guitarist Kenny Johnson (b. 11 December 1939, Liverpool, England) formed the Country Three. Johnson, joined by guitarist Joe Butler (b. Liverpool, England), changed the group to Sonny Webb and the Country Four, taking his stage name from the American country stars, Sonny James and Webb Pierce. In 1961, following an argument, Johnson regrouped as Sonny Webb And The Cascades. Butler played bass and they were joined by lead guitarist Frank Wan, who had been with Clinton Ford, and Brian 'Noddy' Redman, of the Fourmost and Kingsize Taylor And The Dominoes. As they were playing the beat venues frequented by Merseybeat groups, they brought their tough environment to country music and so pioneered country-rock before the Byrds. Their publicity said, 'For that country flavour and the best in pops' and their repertoire can be gauged from their recordings at the Rialto Ballroom in Liverpool for Oriole's *This Is Merseybeat* albums. The songs included George Jones' 'Who Shot Sam?', Bob Luman's 'You've Got Everything', Hank Locklin's 'Border Of The Blues' and Buck Owens' 'Excuse Me'. At Ozzie Wade's country music club in Liverpool in May 1964, Sonny Webb and the Cascades became the Hillsiders. Brian Hilton from Group One joined as lead guitarist when Frank Wan switched to steel. Wan, who tired of life on the road, was subsequently replaced by Ronnie Bennett in 1966. The Hillsiders had a residency at the Black Cat club in Liverpool but they spent time touring, working in Germany with Red Sovine and often backing visiting American artists. Bobby Bare and George Hamilton IV both made albums with the group. The Hillsiders made numerous records in their own right starting with an appearance on Decca's album, *Liverpool Goes Country*. They won numerous country awards and they became well-known through the radio programmes, *Country Meets Folk* and *Up Country*. The packaging for their album, *By Request*, features genuine requests and shows their most popular stage numbers - 'Proud Mary', 'Crying In The Rain' and 'Me And Bobby McGee'. However, they were also writing more and more of their own material, leading to their self-penned album, *Our Country*, which included the excellent 'Across The Mountain' and 'Blue Kentucky Morning', a song they had written for Patsy Powell. The promising Butler-Johnson partnership ceased when Johnson left the Hillsiders in January 1975 to be replaced by Kevin McGarry from another Liverpool band, the Westerners. As the Hillsiders sold more of their Polydor albums at shows than in the shops, they were encouraged then to set up their own label, Stile. Ronnie Bennett left the Hillsiders to develop his own steel guitar company and he was replaced by Dave Rowlands. Both the Hillsiders and Kenny Johnson with his new group, Northwind, have moved towards a more powerful-sounding country music and both of them have developed strong, original material. The Hillsiders' 'She Was My Only One' cleverly borrows a drumming rhythm from 'Cathy's Clown'. Johnson, a country disc jockey for BBC local radio in the northwest, wrote 'Today', one of the most popular songs for Merseyside weddings. Their sets too include surprises such as an instrumental 'In The Mood' from the Hillsiders or 'Halfway To Paradise' from Johnson. From time to time, Johnson and Northwind play a rockabilly set as Sonny Webb and the Cascades. Joe Butler presents country music programmes for Liverpool's Radio City and produces other acts for the Warrington-based country label, Barge. The *15 - 25* album by the Hillsiders, their 15th in 25 years, included guest appearances by Kenny Johnson and Ronnie Bennett and featured a new version of their first single, 'Diggy Liggy Lo'.

Albums by the Hillsiders: *The Hillsiders Play The Country Hits* (c.60s), *The Hillsiders* (c.60s), with Bobby Bare *The English Countryside* (1967), *Country Hits* (c.60s), *The Leaving Of Liverpool* (1969), with George Hamilton IV *Heritage* (1971), *By Request* (1972), *Our Country* (1973), *To Please You* (1975), *Goodbye Scottie Road* (1976), *On The Road* (c.70s), *A Day In The Country* (1979), *15 - 25* (1990). Albums by Kenny Johnson: *Let Me Love You Once* (1980), *The Best Of Kenny Johnson* (1982).

Hobbs, Becky

b. Rebecca A. Hobbs, 24 January 1950, Bartlesville, Oklahoma, USA. Hobbs's father loved big band music and her mother country, two influences for her later work. She was given a piano when she was nine years old. She then started playing the piano parts on rock 'n' roll records, notably those of Jerry Lee Lewis. When 15, she formed an all-girl group, the Four Faces Of Eve, and, from 1971, she worked with a bar band, Swamp Fox, in Baton Rouge. The band went to Los Angeles in 1973, but they soon broke up. Hobbs recorded what is now a highly obscure album for MCA, but Helen Reddy recorded one of the songs, 'I'll Be Your Audience'. She recorded for Tattoo and then finally had some entries on the US country charts with 'Honky Tonk Saturday Night' and 'I Can't Say Goodbye To You'. Her duet with Moe Bandy, 'Let's Get Over Them Together', was a US country hit and then came a top-selling single, 'Hottest Ex In Texas'. Her compositions include 'I Want To Know Who You Are Before We Make Love' (Alabama, Conway Twitty), 'Still On A Roll' (Moe Bandy and Joe Stampley, Kelvin Henderson), 'I'll Dance A Two Step' (Shelley West) and 'Feedin' The Fire' (Zella Lehr). Her effervescent style is well to the fore on her honky tonk album, *All Keyed Up*, which was co-produced by Richard Bennett, Steve Earle's guitarist. She has also recorded what is arguably the best of all tributes to George Jones, 'Jones On The Jukebox'.

Albums: *Becky Hobbs* (1974), *From The Heartland* (1976), *Everyday* (1977), *Becky Hobbs* (1984), *All Keyed Up* (1988).

Homer And Jethro

Homer (b. Henry D. Haynes, 27 July 1920, d. 7 August 1971, Chicago, Illinois, USA) and Jethro (b. Kenneth C. Burns, 10 March 1920, d. 4 February 1989, Evanston, Illinois, USA) were both from Knoxville, Tennessee, USA. They went to the same school and both learned to play stringed instruments as young children. In 1932, they began to work together as musicians on WNOX Knoxville, where they performed in a quartet known as the String Dusters. With Homer on guitar and Jethro on mandolin, they mainly played instrumental pop music and any vocals were usually performed as a trio. Somewhat bored with the regular format, they developed a comedy act which they used backstage. They began to present comedy versions of popular songs by maintaining the melody but changing the lyrics and before long, they were encouraged to perform them live on the radio. They were given the names of Homer and Jethro by the programme director, Lowell Blanchard. The act quickly proved a popular part of the String Dusters' routine. In 1936, they left the group to work solely as Homer and Jethro but stayed at WNOX until 1939. They then became regulars on the *Renfro Valley Barn Dance* in Kentucky but in 1941, they were both called up for military service. In 1945, they were back together as regulars on the *Midwestern Hayride* on WLW Cincinnati and between 1946 and 1948, they recorded their humorous songs for the local King label. In 1949, after a move to RCA, they had Top 10 US country chart success with a recording with June Carter of 'Baby It's Cold Outside'. In the late 1940s, they toured with their own tent show but eventually joined Red Foley on KWTO Springfield. In 1949, they toured the States as part of orchestra leader Spike Jones' show and in 1951, whilst in Chicago with Jones, they were invited to become regulars on the *National Barn Dance* on WLS, where they stayed until 1958. During the 50s and 60s, they toured extensively; their humour proving very popular in many varied venues, including Las Vegas. Their biggest country chart hit came in 1953, when 'How Much Is That Hound Dog In The Window' reached number 2. In 1959, they had a US pop Top 20 hit with 'The Battle Of Kookamonga', their take-off of Johnny Horton's hit 'Battle Of New Orleans'. Proving that no song was safe from the couple's attentions in 1964, they made their last chart entry with their version of the Beatles' 'I Want To Hold Your Hand'. They also made commercials for Kellogg's Cornflakes during the 60s, which made them household names in the USA but perhaps would have caused a drop in the company's sales had they been shown in Britain. The zany comedy tended to make people overlook the fact that the duo were fine musicians. They made instrumental albums and in 1970, they recorded with Chet Atkins (Jethro's brother-in-law) as the Nashville String Band. (It was not until the album was in the charts that RCA let it be known who the musicians were.) Atkins rated Homer as one of the best rhythm guitarists he ever knew. He was also a good enough vocalist to have pursued a singing career but had no interest in doing so. Jethro was also noted as an excellent mandolin player and one who, even in his early days, did much to make the instrument acceptable in jazz music.

The partnership came to an end after 39 years on 7 August 1971, when Homer suffered a heart attack and died. Jethro was deeply affected by Homer's death but eventually he returned to work as a musician. In the late 70s, he often worked with Steve Goodman and both toured and recorded with him. Jethro died of cancer at his home in February 1989. Homer and Jethro's parodies included such titles as 'The Ballad Of Davy Crew-Cut' and 'Hart Brake Motel' and few could match album titles like *Songs My Mother Never Sang, Ooh! That's Corny* (named after their catchphrase) or, bearing in mind they had been steadily turning out albums for 16 years, to suddenly decide to call one just *Homer & Jethro's Next Album*. They never enjoyed success in the UK but in the USA they were an institution.

Albums: *Homer & Jethro Fracture Frank Loesser* (1953), *The Worst Of Homer & Jethro* (1957), *Barefoot Ballads* (1957), *Life Can Be Miserable* (1958), *Musical Madness* (1958), *They Sure Are Corny* (1959), *At The Country Club* (1960), *Songs My Mother Never Sang* (1961), *At The Convention* (1962), *Strike Back* (1962), *Playing It Straight* (1962), *Cornier Than Corn* (1963), *Zany Songs Of The 30s* (1963), *Go West* (1963), *Ooh That's Corny* (1963), *The Humorous Side Of Country Music* (1963), *Cornfucius Say* (1964), *Fractured Folk Songs* (1964), *Sing Tenderly And Other Love Ballads* (1965), *The Old Crusty Minstrels* (1965), *Songs To Tickle Your Funny Bone* (1966), *Wanted For Murder* (1966), *Any News From Nashville* (1966), *It Ain't Necessarily Square* (1967), *Nashville Cats* (1967), *24 Great Songs* (1967), *Something Stupid* (1967), *Songs For The 'Out' Crowd* (1967), *Any News* (1968), *Cool Crazy Christmas* (1968), *There's Nothing Like An Old Hippie* (1968), *Live At Vanderbilt University* (1968), *Homer & Jethro's Next Album* (1969), *Country Comedy* (1971), *Far Out World Of Homer & Jethro* (1972), *Assault On The Rock 'N' Roll Era* (1989). With The Nashville String Band *Down Home* (1970), *Identified* (1970), *Strung Up* (1971). By Jethro Burns *Jethro Burns* (1977), *Jethro Burns Live* (1978), with Tiny Moore *Back To Back* (1980), *Tea For One* (1982), with Red Rector *Old Friends* (1983).

Horton, Johnny

b. 3 April 1925, Los Angeles, California, USA, d. 5 November 1960. Horton was raised in Tyler, Texas where his sharecropping family moved in search of work. He learned the guitar from his mother and, due to his athletic prowess, won scholarships at Baylor University and later the University of Seattle. For a time he worked in the fishing industry but began his singing career on

KXLA Pasadena in 1950 and soon acquired the nickname of 'The Singing Fisherman'. He recorded for Cormac in 1951 and then became the first artist on Fabor Robinson's Abbott label. In 1952 he moved to Mercury but was soon in conflict with the company about the choice of songs. He married Hank Williams' widow, Billie Jean, in September 1953, who encouraged him to better himself. With Tillman Franks as his manager, Horton moved to Columbia Records, and their co-written 'Honky Tonk Man' marked his debut in the US country charts. Horton recorded 'Honky Tonk Man' the day after Elvis Presley recorded 'Heartbreak Hotel' and Presley's bass player, Bill Black, was on the session. The song was successfully revived by Dwight Yoakam in 1986, while George Jones revived another song recorded that day, 'I'm A One Woman Man', in 1989. Other fine examples of Horton as a rockabilly singer are 'All Grown Up' and the hard-hitting 'Honky Tonk Hardwood Floor'. In 1959, Horton switched direction and concentrated on story songs, often with an historical basis, and had his first US country number 1 with a Tillman Franks song, 'When It's Springtime In Alaska'. This was followed by his version of Jimmie Driftwood's 'The Battle Of New Orleans', which became a number 1 pop and country hit in the USA. Lonnie Donegan's 'Battle Of New Orleans' made number 2 in the UK, but Horton's number 16 was respectable, especially as his version was banned by the BBC for referring to 'the bloody British'. Horton's next record was another historical song, 'Johnny Reb', backed with the up-tempo novelty, 'Sal's Got A Sugar Lip'. Donegan was told to cover Horton's latest record but by mistake, he covered 'Sal's Got A Sugar Lip' - and still had a hit! Horton's 'Sink The Bismarck', inspired by the film, made number 3 in the US charts, while he sang the title song of the John Wayne film, *North To Alaska* and took it to number 4 in the USA and number 23 in the UK. It also topped the US country charts for five weeks. On 5 November 1960 Horton was involved in a car collision near Milano, Texas which claimed the lives of himself and his guitarist, Tommy Tomlinson. Tillman Franks received serious injuries but eventually pulled through. Billie Jean became a country star's widow for the second time in seven years.

Albums: *Done Rovin'* (c.50s), *The Fantastic Johnny Horton* (1959), *The Spectacular Johnny Horton* (1960), *Johnny Horton Makes History* (1960), *Honky Tonk Man* (1962), *Johnny Horton* (1962), *Honky Tonk Man* (1963), *I Can't Forget You* (1965), *The Voice Of Johnny Horton* (1965), *Johnny Horton On The Louisiana Hayride* (1966), *All For The Love Of A Girl* (1968), *The Unforgettable Johnny Horton* (1968), *Johnny Horton On The Road* (1969), *The Battle Of New Orleans* (1971), *Rockin' Rollin' Johnny Horton* (1981: expanded for CD, 1991), *The Early Years* and *Johnny Horton*, 1956-60 (boxed-sets containing unissued material, 1991).

Further reading: *Johnny Horton: Your Singing Fisherman,* Michael LeVine, New York, 1982.

Houston, David

b. 9 December 1938, Bossier City, Louisiana, USA. Houston's forefathers include Sam Houston, who fought for Texas' independence from Mexico, and the Civil War general, Robert E. Lee. His parents were friends of 20s singer Gene Austin, who was his godfather and encouraged his talent. Houston made his debut on *Louisiana Hayride* when aged only 12. He continued with his studies and, encouraged by his manager, Tillman Franks, he made a one-off single for Sun Records in Memphis, 'Sherry's Lips'/'Miss Brown'. In 1963 he was signed to Epic Records, who wanted to break into the country market. His first release, 'Mountain Of Love', made number 2 in the US country charts, and was followed by further hits including 'Livin' In A House Of Love' and 'Sweet, Sweet Judy'. In 1966, a song partly written by his producer Billy Sherrill, 'Almost Persuaded', topped the US country charts and also made the Top 30. It established him as one of country music's top balladeers, and he had further country chart-toppers with 'With One Exception', 'My Elusive Dreams' (a duet with Tammy Wynette), 'You Mean The World To Me', 'Have A Little Faith', 'Already In Heaven' and 'Baby Baby (I Know You're A Lady)'. He also appeared in the 1967 country film, *Cotton-Pickin' Chicken Pluckers*. He never repeated his success with Tammy Wynette and she says in her autobiography, *Stand By Your Man*, 'If he was the last singer on earth, I'd never record with him again'. Instead, Houston has recorded several successful duets, including 'I Love You, I Love You' and 'After Closing Time', with Barbara Mandrell. His last Top 10 country success was with 'Can't You Feel It?' in 1974, and since leaving Epic, he has recorded with seven other labels. Although Houston is largely forgotten, he did have seven number 1 country records and 60 chart entries, and through some shrewd financial investments, he now only works when he wishes.

Albums: *The New Voice From Nashville* (1964),

David Houston Sings 12 Great Country Hits (1965), *Almost Persuaded* (1966), *Golden Hymns* (1967), with Tammy Wynette *My Elusive Dreams* (1967), *You Mean The World To Me* (1967), *Already It's Heaven* (1968), *David* (1969), *Baby, Baby* (1970), *The Wonders Of The Wine* (1970), *A Woman Always Knows* (1971), *Gentle On My Mind* (1972), *The Day Love Walked In* (1972), with Barbara Mandrell *A Perfect Match* (1972), *Good Things* (1973), *Old Time Religion* (1973), *What A Night* (1976), *A Man Needs Love* (1975), *David Houston '77* (1977), *From The Heart Of Houston* (1979), *From Houston To You* (1981), *David Houston Sings Texas Honky Tonk* (1982), with Mandrell *Back To Back* (1983), *The Best Of David Houston* (1985).

Howard, Harlan

b. Harlan Perry Howard, 8 September 1929, Lexington, Harlan County, Kentucky, USA. Howard was raised in Detroit and began songwriting when he was 12. After graduation, he spent four years as a paratrooper and was able to spend weekends in Nashville. His talent was recognized by Johnny Bond and Tex Ritter who published his early songs. Wynn Stewart recorded 'You Took Her Off My Hands' and Howard had his first US country hit in 1958 with 'Pick Me Up On Your Way Down' for Charlie Walker, which was followed by 'Mommy For A Day' by Kitty Wells. Many songs were recorded by Buck Owens including 'Above And Beyond', 'Excuse Me (I Think I've Got A Heartache)', 'Under The Influence Of Love', 'I've Got A Tiger By The Tail' (based on a campaign for Esso petrol) and 'Foolin' Around', most of them being co-written with Owens. In 1959 Guy Mitchell recorded Ray Price's country hit, 'Heartaches By The Number', for the pop market and went to number 1 in the US and number 5 in the UK. He married country singer Jan Howard in 1960 and they moved to Nashville, where she cut many of his demos. One of Patsy Cline's best known recordings, 'I Fall To Pieces', was written by Howard and Hank Cochran, and he also wrote her US country Top 10 single, 'When I Get Through With You (You'll Love Me Too)'. Howard wrote two of Jim Reeves' best recordings, 'I Won't Forget You' and 'The Blizzard', as well as 'The Image Of Me', a Reeves demo discovered in the 80s. Other country successes include 'Don't Call Me From A Honky Tonk' (Johnny And Jonie Mosby), 'Still In Town' (Johnny Cash), 'Three Steps To The Phone' (George Hamilton IV), 'You Comb Her Hair' (with Hank Cochran for George Jones), 'Your

Heart Turned Left (And Mine Was On The Right)' (George Jones) and 'Yours Love' (Willie Nelson). Other crossover hits were 'Too Many Rivers' (Kitty Wells and then Brenda Lee), 'Busted' (Johnny Cash and then Ray Charles) and 'The Chokin' Kind' (Waylon Jennings and then Joe Simon). He wrote numerous songs for folk singer, Burl Ives, who started recording for the country market including 'Call Me Mr. In-Between' and 'I'm The Boss'. Bob Dylan praised his song 'Ole Podner', Howard's tribute to a sick fishing buddy, producer Happy Wilson, whilst Richard Thompson has called 'Streets Of Baltimore', written by Howard and Tompall Glaser, 'a wonderfully succinct story told in three verses with every line a killer.' Howard touched a vein with his sentimental 'No Charge', which has been recorded by Melba Montgomery and Tammy Wynette and was a UK number 1 for J.J. Barrie. 'The subject is family: the raising of children, how you spoil them, and how you start bribing your children. To this day, I look at it and say, "Wow, I wrote that good".' Howard has made several albums, and although he had a US country hit with 'Sunday Morning Christian' in 1971, the albums are little more than collections of demos for other artists. In 1975 a long-forgotten Howard song, 'She Called Me Baby', was revived very successfully by Charlie Rich. In 1977 the UK division of RCA Records released a 16-track compilation album, *The Songs Of Harlan Howard*. He spends his time pitching his songs at Tree Music in Nashville and he often works with younger writers, enjoying their chord progressions. In 1984 he wrote a US country number 1 for Conway Twitty, 'I Don't Know A Thing About Love (The Moon Song)', and subsequent number 1's have been 'Why Not Me?' (with Sonny Throckmorton and Brent Maher for the Judds), 'Somebody Should Leave' (with Chick Rains for Reba McEntire) and 'Somewhere Tonight' (with Rodney Crowell for Highway 101) . Other 80s compositions include 'You're A Hard Dog To Keep Under The Porch' (with Susanna Clark for Gail Davies), 'I Don't Remember You' (with Bobby Braddock for John Conlee) and 'Never Mind' for Nanci Griffith. Howard cites 'Another Bridge To Burn' (Ray Price, Little Jimmy Dickens) as his best song: 'I can't write any better than that, and I doubt if I ever will.'
Albums: *Harlan Howard Sings Harlan Howard* (1961), *All Time Favourite Country Songwriter* (1965), *Mr. Songwriter* (1967), *Down To Earth* (1968), *To The Silent Majority, With Love* (1971), *Singer And Songwriter* (1981).

Howard, Jan

b. Lula Grace Johnson, 13 March 1930, Kansas City, Missouri, USA. Howard, with a mixture of Cherokee and Irish blood, was raised in poverty, married at 15 and had three sons in quick succession. Her husband beat her and squandered what little money they had so she divorced him in 1953. A few weeks later, she 'married' a serviceman, who was supposedly divorced, and when that relationship fell through, she moved to Los Angeles in the hope of finding work as a singer. She met and married aspiring songwriter Harlan Howard within 30 days. She sang on his demonstration records and her version of 'Mommy For A Day' (for Kitty Wells) led to her own recording contract. Her first record was a duet with Wynn Stewart, 'Yankee Go Home', which was followed by her first US country hit, 'The One You Slip Around With', in 1960. The Howards moved to Nashville and she skilfully combined the roles of housewife and country star, but often objecting to the bookings which Howard accepted. Harlan Howard wrote several of her country hits including 'Evil On Your Mind', 'What Makes A Man Wander', 'Wrong Company' and 'I Don't Mind'. In 1968 she recorded her own personal song, 'My Son', for Jimmy in Vietnam. Before the record could be released, her son had died in action. Then, her marriage broke up and a second son committed suicide. Howard worked herself out of the crisis, touring with Bill Anderson and scoring with several duets: 'I Know You're Married', 'For Loving You' (a number 1 US country hit), 'If It's All The Same To You', 'Someday We'll Be Together' and 'Dissatisfied'. She has also long spells on the road with Johnny Cash and Tammy Wynette.

Albums: with Wynn Stewart *Sweethearts Of Country Music* (1961), *Jan Howard* (1962), *Sweet And Sentimental* (1962), *Bad Seed* (1966), *Jan Howard Sings 'Evil On Your Mind'* (1966), *This Is Jan Howard Country* (1967), *Lonely Country* (1967), *Count Your Blessings, Woman* (1968), *The Real Me* (1968), with Bill Anderson *For Loving You* (1968), *Jan Howard* (1969), *For God And Country* (1970), with Bill Anderson *If It's All The Same To You* (1970), *Rock Me Back To Little Rock* (1970), *Love Is Like A Spinning Wheel* (1972), with Bill Anderson *Bill And Jan (Or Jan And Bill)* (1972), with Bill Anderson *Singing His Praise* ((1972), *Sincerely* (1976), *Tainted Love* (1984), *The Life Of A Country Girl Singer* (1984).

Further reading: *Sunshine And Shadow*, Jan Howard.

Hunley, Con

b. Conrad Logan Hunley, 9 April 1945, Luttrell, Knox County, Tennessee, USA. The Hunley family were known as a local gospel singing group and from an early age Con appeared with them. He grew up an admirer of Chet Atkins and for a time sought to emulate his idol, quickly realised the guitar was not to be his instrument and instead turned his attention to the piano. Influenced by Ray Charles and singing somewhat like Charlie Rich, he began to play in groups during his high school years and during his time in the US Air Force, played in various bands. After his discharge he returned to Knoxville, first working in a mill but soon found work in local country clubs. In 1976, he formed his own band and recorded five singles for the minor Prairie Dust label. Some were his own compositions and three of the recordings became minor hits in the US country charts and helped to build his reputation. He decided to move to Nashville in 1977 and as a result of appearances at George Jones' *Possum Holler*, he managed to get a contract with Warner Brothers. His first release on that label was Jimmy C. Newman's song 'Cry, Cry Darling' which went to number 34 in the charts. He followed this with 11 successive Top 20 hits, including 'Week End Friend', 'You've Still Got A Place In My Heart', 'I've Been Waiting For You All Of My Life' (a pop hit for Paul Anka two years later) and in 1982, 'Oh Girl', which had been a number 1 pop hit for the Chi Lites 10 years earlier. During the 80s the hits became smaller. He recorded a version of 'Satisfied Mind' that featured a guest vocal from Porter Wagoner (who had had a hit with the song in 1955) and in 1986, he charted with 'Blue Suede Shoes'. Maybe prophetically, his last successful record at the time of writing came in 1986 with a song called 'Quittin' Time' - whether it was remains to be seen.

Albums: *Con Hunley* (1979), *I Don't Want To Lose You* (1980), *Don't It Break Your Heart* (1980), *Ask Any Woman* (1981), *Oh Girl* (1982).

Husky, Ferlin

b. 3 December 1925, on a farm near Flat River, Missouri, USA. He learned to play guitar as a child and during World War II served in the US Merchant Navy. His mother wanted him to be a preacher and his father a farmer but, after discharge, he found radio work as an announcer and disc jockey but gradually turned to performing while at KXLW St. Louis. In the late 40s he moved to California, where he appeared on the Los Angeles *Hometown Jamboree* and played clubs in the Bakersfield area. Believing that Ferlin Husky, though his real name, was unsuitable he first called himself Tex Preston, then changed again to Terry Preston. He also developed an alter ego country philosopher character, Simon Crum, who he introduced into his act. (A few years later, Sheb Wooley also adopted a similar practice with his character Ben Colder, who sought to entertain with his supposed humorous parodies on popular and country songs.)

In the early 50s, he recorded for Capitol and worked with Tennessee Ernie Ford. In 1953, as Ferlin Huskey, he recorded 'A Dear John Letter' with Jean Shepard, which became a smash US country number 1, as well as reaching number 4 on the US pop charts. An answer version called 'Forgive Me John', also had success in both charts. Following success with his self-penned 'Hank's Song' (a tribute to Hank Williams), Huskey finally dropped the name of Terry Preston. In 1957, now minus the 'e' again, Husky joined the *Grand Ole Opry* and achieved another smash hit number 1 with his million selling recording of 'Gone', which, ironically, he had first recorded unsuccessfully as Preston five years earlier. In 1960, he charted a further country number 1 with the gospel/country 'Wings Of A Dove', which also became a Top 20 pop hit. He recorded 'The Drunken Driver', a tear-jerking narration about a father who runs over his son, which has been rated a classic by some and one of the worst recordings ever made by others. He became a popular entertainer on many network television shows including hosting the *Arthur Godfrey Show* and appearing as a dramatic actor on *Kraft TV Theatre*.

Whilst not always singing traditional country material, he maintained his country popularity through the character of Simon Crum. In this guise, he demonstrated a great talent for impersonating other country stars, presenting rustic comedy and even managed a number 2 country hit with 'Country Music's Here To Stay'. He recorded an album of pop songs called *Boulevard Of Broken Dreams* in 1957 and also recorded one or two rock 'n' roll singles such as 'Wang Dang Do'. Husky has appeared in several films including *Mr. Rock & Roll* and *Country Music Holiday*. From the 60s to the mid-70s, he toured extensively with his band, the Hush Puppies, and had regular country chart entries including 'Once', 'Just For You', 'True True Lovin'' and 'Freckles And Polliwog Days'. He moved to ABC Records in 1973 and on that label, achieved country chart entry number 51 (and last) in 1975 with 'An Old Memory Got In My Eye'. Husky has been married six times and has nine children, one not surprisingly being called Terry Preston. His career was slowed in 1977 by a heart operation but he recovered and continued to perform and later again recorded.

Albums: *Songs Of The Home And Heart* (1956), *Boulevard Of Broken Dreams* (1957), *Born To Lose* (1959), *Country Tunes From The Heart* (1959), *Sittin' On A Rainbow* (1959), *Favorites of Ferlin Huskey* (1959), *Gone* (1960), *Easy Livin'* (1960), *Ferlin's Favorites* (1960), *Some Of My Favorites* (1960), *Walkin' & Hummin'* (1961), *Memories Of Home* (1961), *The Heart & Soul Of Ferlin Husky* (1963), *The Unpredictable Simon Crum* (1963), *By Request* (1964), *True True Lovin'* (1965), *I Could Sing All Night* (1966), *Songs Of Music City, USA* (1966), *Christmas All Year Long* (1967), *What Am I Gonna Do Now* (1967), *Where No One Stands Alone* (1968), *White Fences And Evergreen Trees* (1968), *Just For You* (1968), *That's Why I Love You So Much* (1969), *Your Love Is Heavenly Sunshine* (1970), *Your Sweet Love Lifted Me* (1970), *One More Time* (1971), *Just Plain Lonely* (1972), *Sweet Honky Tonk* (1973), *True True Lovin'* (1973), *Champagne Ladies & Blue Ribbon Babies* (1974), *Freckles & Polliwog Days* (1974), *Mountain Of Everlasting Love* (1974), *The Foster & Rice Songbook* (1975), *Ferlin Husky* (1982), *Live* (1983).

J

Jackson, Alan

b. Newman, Georgia, USA. Jackson, the son of a motor mechanic, had a love of gospel music through church and his family. He tried several different careers but came back to country music. In 1986 he moved with his wife, Denise, to Nashville and, through a chance meeting with Glen Campbell, gained an audition with Campbell's publishing company. He wrote most of his debut album, *Here In The Real World*, which remained on the US country album chart for over a year. Jackson's hit US country singles include 'Here In The Real World' and 'Wanted'. The magazine *Country Music People* said of him, 'He's uncontroversial, stands for the flag, Mom and apple pie, looks like he washes every day and sings for middle America.' He is also one of 1990's 'hat' brigade and topped the US country charts in 1991 with 'I'd Love You All Over Again'. The release of *Don't Rock The Jukebox* that year confirmed that Jackson's initial success was no fluke. The title track was one of the years's biggest hits, while the album revealed that he had become a major songwriter, specialising in tales of working men

struggling to survive. He began to collaborate on songs with Randy Travis, co-writing the latter's number 1 hit, 'Forever Together', and further co-compositions appeared on Jackson's third album in 1992. Jackson has won a succession of industry awards in recent years, establishing him in the top rank of male country starts, immediately behind Garth Brooks.

Albums: *Here In The Real World* (1990), *Don't Rock The Jukebox* (1991), *A Lot About Livin' (And A Little 'Bout Lovin')* (1992).

Jackson, Carl

b. 1953, Louisville, Mississippi, USA. Carl Jackson started at the age of 13 by accompanying his father and his uncle on the banjo in a bluegrass band. One of his compositions, 'Banjo Man', tells how he learnt Earl Scruggs' licks by listening to his records. Jackson toured with Jim And Jesse and during that time made his first solo album, *Bluegrass Festival*. In 1972, he joined Glen Campbell's band, and Campbell produced his Capitol album, *Banjo Player*. The interplay between Campbell and Jackson, particularly on 'Duellin' Banjos', has been much admired, but staying with Campbell prevented him from developing his own musical personality. He has now branched out on his own and his fine musicianship can be heard on his album with John Starling, *Spring Training*.

Albums: *Bluegrass Festival* (1971), *Banjo Player* (1973), *Old Friends* (1978), *Banjo Man* (1981), *Song*

Alan Jackson

Of The South (1982), with John Starling and the Nash Ramblers *Spring Training* (1991).

Jackson, Stonewall

b. 6 November 1932, Tabor City, North Carolina, USA. His real name was acquired because his family tree goes back to the famous Confederate general of the American Civil War. After the death of his father, Jackson, then aged two, his mother relocated to Moultrie, Georgia, where, at the age of eight, Stonewall worked on his uncle's farm. When he was 10 he swopped his bicycle for a guitar and learned to play by watching others. He joined the army in 1948, lying about his age, but the error was soon discovered. The next year he legally joined the navy and began his singing career by entertaining his shipmates. After discharge in 1954, he spent two years working on a farm but in 1956, with no professional singing experience, he decided to try his luck in Nashville. He impressed Wesley Rose enough for him to record some demo discs of his songs; after auditioning for George D. Hay, Jackson became one of the few performers to become a member of the *Grand Ole Opry* without a recording contract. In fact, he recalled, 'I found out later it's the only time anybody's ever come and just was hired off the street'. He signed for Columbia Records in 1957 and first worked on Ernest Tubb's roadshow. He made his US country chart debut in 1958 when his recording of George Jones' prison saga 'Life To Go' reached number 2. In 1959, Jackson's recording of John D. Loudermilk's 'Waterloo' became a million selling country number 1, also reaching number 4 in the US pop charts. Between 1959 and 1963 further successes followed including 'Why, I'm Walking', 'A Wound Time Can't Erase', 'Leona' and 'Old Showboat' before he achieved another country number 1 with 'B.J. The D.J.' Throughout the mid-60s and early-70s he charted regularly, including his own songs 'Don't Be Angry' (a song he had initially recorded as a demo for Wesley Rose eight years before), 'I Washed My Face In Muddy Water' and 'Stamp Out Loneliness'. ('Don't Be Angry' was revived in 1987 by Daniel O'Donnell on his album *Don't Forget To Remember*). Jackson's style went gradually out of fashion but he did make the country Top 10 in 1971 with a country version of 'Me And You And A Dog Named Boo'. During the Vietnam War he recorded a patriotic single 'The Minute Men Are Turning In Their Graves' and even renamed his band the Minute Men to emphasize the point. *The Great Old Songs*, contains many folk ballads including arguably his best track, 'The Black Sheep'. He also has the distinction of being the first artist to record a live in-concert album at the *Opry*. He still resides in Nashville and maintains his *Opry* appearances.

Albums: *The Dynamic Stonewall Jackson* (1959), *Sadness In A Song* (1962), *I Love A Song* (1963), *Trouble And Me* (1965), *The Exciting Stonewall Jackson* (1966), *All's Fair In Love 'N' War* (1966), *Help Stamp Out Loneliness* (1967), *Stonewall Jackson Country* (1967), *The Great Old Songs* (1968), *Thoughts Of A Lonely Man* (1968), *Nothing Takes The Place Of Loving You* (1968), *I Pawned My Past Today* (1969), *The Old Country Church* (1969), *A Tribute To Hank Williams* (1969), *The Real Thing* (1970), *The Lonesome In Me* (1970), *Stonewall Jackson Recorded Live At The Grand Ole Opry* (1971), *Waterloo* (1971), *Me And You And A Dog Named Boo* (1971), *World Of Stonewall Jackson* (1972, double album), *Nashville* (1974), *Stonewall (Platinum Country)* (1979), *My Favorite Sin* (1980), *Stonewall Jackson* (1982), *Solid Stonewall* (1982), *Alive* (1984), *Up Against The Wall* (1984). Compilation: *Greatest Hits* (1982).

Jackson, Wanda

b. Wanda Jean Jackson, 20 October 1937, Maud, Oklahoma, USA. Jackson started her career as one of the rawest of female rockabilly singers before going on to successful work in both country and gospel music. Her family moved to California when she was four, settling in the city of Bakersfield, but moved back to Oklahoma when she was 12. There Jackson won a talent contest which led to her own radio programme. Country singer Hank Thompson liked her style and hired her to tour with his band. In 1954 Jackson signed to Decca Records, recording 15 country tracks; one of which, 'You Can't Have My Love', a duet with Billy Gray, made the country Top 10. The following year Jackson joined Red Foley's touring company and met Elvis Presley. He advised her to change her style to the new rock 'n' roll. When she signed with Capitol Records in 1956, she recorded a number of singles, one side of each a rocker, the other a honky-tonk country number. Only one of these rockabilly records, 'I Gotta Know', made the country charts, but her other recordings for Capitol, such as 'Honey Bop', 'Fujiyama Mama' and 'Hot Dog That Made Him Mad', are prized by collectors decades later. Only one, 'Let's Have A Party', earlier recorded by Elvis, made the US pop charts when Capitol belatedly released it in 1960. Backed by the Blue Caps, this song is delivered in raucous style and it remains an extraordinary vocal delivery. That same year Jackson chose to stay with country and recorded her own composition, 'Right Or Wrong', which has since become a hit for both Ronnie Dove and George Strait. 'Right Or Wrong' and 'In The Middle Of a Heartache' became the last of Jackson's Top 10 country songs in 1961-62, although she placed 30 singles in that chart in total. She recorded nearly two dozen albums for Capitol in the 60s. By the early 70s Jackson began recording Christian music for Capitol and later the Word and Myrrh labels, returning to rock 'n' roll for one album, *Rock 'N' Roll Away Your Blues*, in 1984.

Selected albums: *Wanda Jackson* (1958), *Rockin' With Wanda* (1960), *There's A Party Goin' On* (1961), *Right Or Wrong* (1961), *Lovin' Country Style* (1962), *Wonderful Wanda* (1962), *Love Me Forever* (1963), *Two Sides Of Wanda Jackson* (1964), *Blues In My Heart* (1964), *Wanda Jackson Sings Country Songs* (1966), *Salutes The Country Music Hall Of Fame* (1966), *Reckless Love Affair* (1967), *You'll Always Have My Love* (1967), *The Best Of Wanda Jackson* (1967), *Cream Of The Crop* (1968), *The Happy Side Of...* (1969), *Closer To Jesus* (1967), *In Person At Mr. Lucky's In Phoenix, Arizona* (1969), *Many Moods Of...* (1969), *Country!* (1970), *Woman Lives For Love* (1970), *I've Gotta Sing* (1971), *I Wouldn't Want You Any Other Way* (1972), *Praise The Lord* (1972), *When It's Time To Fall In Love Again* (1973), *Country Keepsakes* (1973), *Now I Have Everything* (1974), *Rock 'N' Roll Away Your Blues* (1984), *Her Greatest Country Hits* (1985), *Early Wanda Jackson* (1986), *Rockin' In The Country: The Best Of...* (1990).

James, Sonny

b. James Loden, 1 May 1929, Hackleburg, Alabama, USA. The Country Music Hall Of Fame includes a guitar which Sonny James' father made for him when he was three years old. James has been performing since that time and has played fiddle and guitar with the Loden's family revue. Sonny won several junior fiddle championships, although he was to play guitar on his records. He was signed by Capitol Records in 1953 and marketed as Sonny James by producer, Ken Nelson. James had his first US country hits with 'That's Me Without You', 'She Done Give Her Heart To Me' and 'For Rent', and made the UK Top 30 with a record that is now a children's favourite, 'The Cat Came Back'. He had a number 1 record on the US pop charts with 'Young Love'

in 1957, which was also a number 1 record for film star Tab Hunter. Hunter repeated his success in the UK charts, but James only reached number 11. (The original version of 'Young Love' by composer Rick Cartey is long-forgotten.) 'First Date, First Kiss, First Love' made number 25 in the US pop charts and James had 19 other records in the Hot 100. Because he was tall, quiet, respectable and good-looking, he became known as the Southern Gentleman.

He left Capitol and recorded for NRC and RCA but returned to Capitol and scored numerous country hits between 1963 and 1971 including 16 consecutive number 1's. His hits included 'You're The Only World I Know', 'Behind The Tear', 'Take Good Care Of Her', 'The Minute You're Gone', which was covered by Cliff Richard, 'A World Of Our Own' and 'I'll Never Find Another You', two of the Seekers' pop hits which he covered for the country market. He appeared in several low-budget country films - *Second Fiddle To An Old Guitar*, *Nashville Rebel*, *Las Vegas Hillbillies* (with Jayne Mansfield) and *Hillbilly In A Haunted House* (with Basil Rathbone and Lon Chaney). James has also revived pop songs for the country market including 'Only The Lonely', 'It's Just A Matter Of Time' and 'Running Bear', all three being number 1 records. His 1972 number 1, 'That's Why I Love You Like I Do', was a remade and re-titled version of the b-side of 'Young Love', 'You're The Reason (I'm In Love)'. He switched to Columbia in 1972 and continued his success with 'When The Snow Is On The Roses', 'Is It Wrong (For Loving You)?' (both making number 1), 'Little Band Of Gold' and 'Come On In'. He produced Marie Osmond's transatlantic Top 10 revival of 'Paper Roses' and made an album inside Tennessee State Prison. The 57-year-old singer recorded a new version of 'Young Love' for Dot Records, but the album, particularly the track 'You've Got Your Troubles' exposed some shaky vocals. In total, Sonny James has had 72 records in the US country charts including 23 number 1's, which puts him among the most successful country artists of all-time.

Selected albums: *Sonny* (1957), *The Southern Gentleman* (1958), *Honey* (1958), *The Sonny Side* (1959), *This Is Sonny James* (1959), *Young Love* (1962), *The Minute You're Gone* (1964), *You're The Only World I Know* (1965), *I'll Keep Holding On (Just To Your Love)* (1965), *Behind The Tear* (1965), *True Love's A Blessing* (1966), *Till The Last Leaf Shall Fall* (1966), *My Christmas Dream* (1966), *Young Love And Other Songs Of The Heart* (1967),

Sonny James

I'll Never Find Another You (1967), *Born To Be With You* (1968), *A World Of Our Own* (1968), *Heaven Says Hello* (1968), *Need You* (1968), *Close Up* (1969), *The Astrodome Presents - In Person - Sonny James* (1969), *Only The Lonely* (1969), *Traces* (1970), *It's Just A Matter Of Time* (1970), *My Love/Don't Keep Me Hanging On* (1970), *Number One (The Biggest Hits In Country Music History)* (1970), *Empty Arms* (1971), *Here Comes Honey Again* (1971), *The Sensational Sonny James* (1971), *That's Why I Love You Like I Do* (1972), *When The Snow Is On The Roses* (1972), *The Greatest Country Hits Of 1972* (1973), *The Gentleman From The South* (1973), *If She Just Helps Me Get Over You* (1973), *Sonny James* (1973), *Young Love* (1973), *Is It Wrong?* (1974), *Country Male Artist Of The Decade* (1975), *A Little Bit South Of Saskatoon* (1975), *The Guitars Of Sonny James* (1975), *200 Years Of Country Music* (1976), *When Something Is Wrong With My Baby* (1976), *A Mi Esposa Con Amor* (1977), *Sonny James In Prison - In Person* (1977), *You're Free To Go* (1977), *This Is The Love* (1978), *Favorites* (1979), *Sonny's Side Of The Street* (1979), *I'm Lookin' Over The Rainbow* (1982), *Sonny James* (1986).

Jarrell, Tommy

b. 1901, near Round Peak, Surry County, North Carolina, USA, d. 28 January 1985, Mount Airy, USA. Jarrell was an old-time fiddler, banjoist and singer, but never became a professional musician nor was heard outside his home locale until he was nearly 70 years old. The Jarrells were of Scots-Irish descent and he learned his fiddle playing and much of his vast repertoire of songs from his father Ben Jarrell, a noted old-time fiddler who played and recorded with Da-Costa Woltzs Southern Broadcasters in the late 20s. Tommy was also influenced by Fred Cockerham, another fiddler. The family moved to Mount Airy in 1921 and from 1925 to his retirement in 1966, Jarrell worked for the State Highways Department. After his wife died in 1967, he began to play the fiddle again. He became recognised as an authority on old time music and was much in demand for appearances at various folk festivals and colleges. Jarrell recorded several albums, both as a solo artist and also with Cockerham and Oscar Jenkins and to show his versatility; one 1974 album *Come And Go With Me*, featured all banjo tracks. Jarrell was invited to perform at President Reagan's inaugural ceremony but was not well enough to attend. Many of his best performances are available on record and a film, *Sprout Wings And Fly*, was made about him.

Some of his last recordings were made in June 1984, when along with Alice Gerrard, Andy Cahan and Verlen Clifton he proved that, even at the age of 83, he was still a most competent fiddle performer. Jarrell died after an heart attack at his home in 1985.

Albums: *June Apple* (1972), *Joke On The Puppy* (1972), with Oscar Jenkins, Fred Cockerham *Down At The Cider Mill* (c.1973), *Jenkins, Jarrell & Cockerham, Vol 2 (Back Home In Blue Ridge)* (c.1973), *Stay All Night* (1973), *Come And Go With Me* (1974), *Sail Away Ladies* (1976), *Pickin' On Tommy's Porch* (1983), *Rainbow Sign* (1986).

Jason And The Scorchers

This country-rock 'n' roll styled USA band was led by Jason Ringenberg (b. 22 November 1959; vocals, guitar, harmonica) who left his parents' farm in Sheffield, Illinois in 1981 to travel to Nashville. There he teamed up with Warner Hodges (b. 4 June 1959, Nashville, Tennessee, USA; guitar) and Jeff Johnson (b. Nashville, Tennessee, USA; bass). Another original member was Jack Emerson, who went on to become the band's manager. Hodges' parents provided the band's pedigree, having been country musicians who toured with Johnny Cash. The band recruited Perry Bags (b. 22 March 1962, Nashville, Tennessee, USA; drums) and became Jason And The Nashville Scorchers, with the prefix later dropped, playing fast country rock ('cow punk' was the description coined in the UK). Their first EP for the Praxis label was 1982's *Reckless Country Soul* (USA only), followed by the mini-album *Fervor* a year later. This brought them well-deserved attention in the press and was subsequently re-released in 1984 on EMI America. It was notable for the inclusion of Bob Dylan's 'Absolutely Sweet Marie', while a subsequent single tackled the Rolling Stones' '19th Nervous Breakdown'. *Lost And Found* included a cover of Hank Williams' 'Lost Highway'; the combination of these three covers gives a useful insight into the band's influences and sound.

After moving increasingly towards hard rock with *Thunder And Fire* in 1989, the Scorchers split up when that album failed to bring the expected commercial breakthrough. While guitarist Warner Hodges quit the music business in disgust, Jason Ringenberg took time to gather himself for an assault on the country market. His raunchy solo debut, *One Foot In The Honky Tonk* (credited to 'Jason'), proved to be too traditional for country radio, but he remains an irrepressible live

Jason And The Scorchers

performer.
Albums: *Fervor* (1983), *Lost And Found* (1985), *Still Standing* (1986), *Thunder And Fire* (1989).

Jennings, Tommy

b. 8 August 1938. Both his parents and his brother, Waylon Jennings, were musical but Tommy only started performing when he left the US Army. He played bass with his brother's group, the Waylors, for five years. He managed Waylon for a time and they adapted 'Delia's Gone' together. Waylon also recorded Jennings' 'Life Goes On'. Jennings has recorded spasmodically, sounding reasonably like his brother but US country chart entries tell the story - 'Make It Easy On Yourself' (number 96, 1975), 'Don't You Think It's Time' (number 71, 1978) and with Rex Gosdin 'Just Give Me What You Think Is Fair' (number 51, 1980). Jennings has no intention of copying his brother. He says, 'There's only one Waylon Jennings and there'll never be another.'
Album: *Equal Opportunity Lovin' Man* (1982).

Jennings, Waylon

b. Wayland Arnold Jennings, 15 June 1937, Littlefield, Texas, USA. Jennings' mother wanted to christen him Tommy but his father, William Alvin, insisted that the family tradition of W.A. must be maintained. His father played guitar in Texas dance halls and Jennings' childhood hero was Ernest Tubb, with whom he later recorded. When only 12 years old, he started as a radio disc jockey and then, in Lubbock, befriended an aspiring Buddy Holly. In 1958, Holly produced his debut single 'Jole Blon' and they co-wrote 'You're The One', a Holly demo which surfaced after his death. Jennings played bass on Holly's last tour, relinquishing his seat for that fatal plane journey to the Big Bopper. Jennings named his son, Buddy, after Holly and he recalled their friendship in his 1976 song, 'Old Friend'. After Holly's death, Jennings returned to radio work in Lubbock, before moving to Phoenix and forming his own group, the Waylors. They began a two-year residency at a new Phoenix club, J.D's, in 1964. The album of their stage repertoire has worn well, but less satisfying was Jennings' album for A&M, *Don't Think Twice*. 'Herb Alpert heard me as Al Martino,' says Waylon, 'and I was wanting to sound like Hank Williams'. Bobby Bare heard the A&M album and recommended Jennings to record producer Chet Atkins. Waylon started recording for RCA in 1965 and made the US country charts with his first release, 'That's The Chance I'll Have To Take'. He co-wrote his 1966 country hit, 'Anita, You're Dreaming' and developed a folk-country style with 'For Loving Me'. He and Johnny Cash shared two wild years in Nashville, so it was apt that he should star in *Nashville Rebel*, a dire, quickly-made film. Jennings continued to have country hits - 'Love Of The Common People', 'Only Daddy That'll Walk The Line' and, with the Kimberlys, 'MacArthur Park'. However, he was uncomfortable with session men, no matter how good they were, he felt the arrangements were overblown. He did his best, even with the string-saturated 'The Days Of Sand And Shovels', which was along the lines of Bobby Goldsboro's 'Honey'. When Jennings was ill with hepatitis, he considered leaving the business, but his drummer Richie Albright, who has been with him since 1964, talked him into staying on. Jennings recorded some excellent Shel Silverstein songs for the soundtrack of *Ned Kelly*, which starred Mick Jagger, and the new Waylon fell into place with his 1971 album, *Singer Of Sad Songs*, which was sympathetically produced by Lee Hazlewood. Like the album sleeve, the music was darker and tougher, and the beat was more pronounced. Such singles as 'The Taker', 'Ladies Love Outlaws' and 'Lonesome, On'ry And Mean' showed a defiant,

tough image. The cover of *Honky Tonk Heroes* showed the new Waylon and the company he was keeping. His handsome looks were overshadowed by dark clothes, a beard and long hair, which became more straggly and unkempt with each successive album.

The new pared-down, bass-driven, no frills allowed sound continued on *The Ramblin' Man* and his best album, *Dreaming My Dreams*. The title track is marvellously romantic, while the album also included 'Let's All Help The Cowboys (Sing The Blues)', an incisive look at outlaw country, 'Are You Sure Hank Done It This Way?', and a tribute to his roots, 'Bob Wills Is Still The King'. *Wanted: The Outlaws* and its hit single, 'Good Hearted Woman' transformed both Willie Nelson and Waylon Jennings' careers, making them huge media personalities in the USA. The first of the four 'Waylon And Willie' albums is the best, including the witty 'Mammas, Don't Let Your Babies Grow Up To Be Cowboys' and 'I Can Get

Waylon Jennings

Off On You'. In reality, Nelson reveals a constant habit in his autobiography, while Jennings admits to 21 years addiction in an ode bidding farewell to drugs, in his audio-biography, *A Man Called Hoss*. Jennings was tired of his mean and macho image even before it caught on with the public. He topped the US country charts for six weeks and also made the US Top 30 with a world-weary song for a small township, 'Luckenbach, Texas', which is filled with disillusionment. Further sadness followed on 'I've Always Been Crazy' and 'Don't You Think This Outlaw Bit's Done Got Out Of Hand?'. He aged quickly, acquiring a lined and lived-in face which, ironically, enhanced his image. His voice became gruffer but it was ideally suited to the stinging 'I Ain't Living Long Like This' and 'It's Only Rock & Roll'. His theme for *The Dukes Of Hazzard* made the US Top 30 but the outlaw deserved to be convicted for issuing such banal material as 'The Teddy Bear Song' and an embarrassing piece with Hank Williams Jnr., 'The Conversation'. The latter was included on *Waylon And Company*, which also featured duets with Emmylou Harris and actor James Garner. Jennings has often recorded with his wife, Jessi Colter; he and Johnny Cash had a hit with 'There Ain't No Good Chain Gang' and made an underrated album, *Heroes*. His two albums with Nelson, Cash and Kris Kristofferson as the Highwaymen were highly successful, but early 1993 it was anounced that the quartet would no longer work together. Jennings and Cash had major heart surgery at the same time and recuperated in adjoining beds. A change to MCA and to producer Jimmy Bowen in 1985 had improved the consistency of his work, including two brilliant re-workings of Los Lobos' 'Will The Wolf Survive?' and Gerry Rafferty's 'Baker Street'. His musical autobiography, *A Man Called Hoss* (Waylon refers to everyone as 'hoss'), included the wry humour of 'If Ole Hank Could Only See Us Now'. Willie and Waylon will be remembered as outlaws and certainly they did shake the Nashville establishment by assuming artistic control and heralding a new era of grittier and more honest songs. Whether they justify being called outlaws is a moot point - Jerry Lee Lewis is more rebellious than all the so-called Nashville outlaws put together.

Albums: *Waylon Jennings At J.D's* (1964), *Don't Think Twice* (1965), *Waylon Jennings - Folk/Country* (1966), *Leaving Town* (1966), *Nashville Rebel* (1966), *Waylon Sings Ol' Harlan* (1967), *The One And Only Waylon Jennings* (1967), *Love Of The Common People* (1967), *Hangin' On* (1968), *Only*

The Greatest (1968), *Jewels* (1968), *Waylon Jennings* (1969), with the Kimberlys *Country Folk* (1969), *Just To Satisfy You* (1969), *Ned Kelly* (1970, soundtrack), *Waylon* (1970), *Singer Of Sad Songs* (1970), *The Taker/Tulsa* (1971), *Cedartown, Georgia* (1971), *Good Hearted Woman* (1972), *Ladies Love Outlaws* (1972), *Lonesome, On'ry And Mean* (1973), *Honky Tonk Heroes* (1973), *This Time* (1974), *The Ramblin' Man* (1974), *Dreaming My Dreams* (1975), *MacKintosh And T.J.* (1976), with Willie Nelson, Jessi Colter, Tompall Glaser *Wanted:The Outlaws* (1976), *Are You Ready For The Country?* (1976), *Waylon 'Live'* (1976), *Ol' Waylon* (1977), with Nelson *Waylon And Willie* (1978), with Colter, John Dillon, Steve Cash *White Mansions* (1978), *I've Always Been Crazy* (1978), *The Early Years* (1979), *What Goes Around Comes Around* (1979), *Waylon Music* (1980), *Music Man* (1980), with Colter *Leather And Lace* (1981), with Nelson *WWII* (1982), with Colter *The Pursuit Of D.B. Cooper* (1982, soundtrack), *Black On Black* (1982), *It's Only Rock & Roll* (1983), *Waylon And Company* (1983), with Nelson *Take It To The Limit* (1983), *Never Could Toe The Mark* (1984), *Turn The Page* (1985), *Will The Wolf Survive?* (1985) with Nelson, Johnny Cash, Kris Kristofferson, *Highwayman* (1985), with Cash *Heroes* (1986), *Hangin' Tough* (1987), *A Man Called Hoss* (1987), *Full Circle* (1988), with Cash, Kristofferson, Nelson *Highwayman 2* (1990), *The Eagle* (1990), with Nelson *Clean Shirt* (1991), *Too Dumb For New York City - Too Ugly For L.A.* (1992). Bear Family have re-packaged Jennings' recordings in a 15-album series, *The Waylon Jennings Files*, which include many previously unissued titles.

Further reading: *Waylon Jennings*, Albert Cunniff. *Waylon - A Biography*, R. Serge Denisoff.

Jim And Jesse

The McReynolds Brothers, Jim (b. 13 February 1927) and Jesse (b. 9 July 1929, both on a farm at Coeburn, in the Clinch Mountain region of Virginia, USA), came from a musical family; their grandfather was a noted fiddle player, who had recorded for RCA Victor. The brothers learned to play several stringed instruments as children and as teenagers played at local dances. They made their radio debut in 1947 on WNVA Norton, by which time Jim usually played guitar and Jesse mandolin. Playing bluegrass/country material, they made their first recordings around 1951 for the small Kentucky label but in 1952, after moving to WVLK Lexington, they joined Capitol. Owing to the Korean War, Jesse spent two years in the Armed

Forces, one in Korea, where he worked as an entertainer with Charlie Louvin. In 1954, he rejoined his brother at WNOX Knoxville, where they first worked on the *Tennessee Barn Dance*. Later they moved on to various radio and/or television stations in Alabama, Georgia and North Florida and with their band, the Virginia Boys, they quickly established a reputation. The brothers' singing, with Jesse taking lead vocals and Jim adding high pitched tenor harmonies, was obviously influenced by other brother duos such as the Blue Sky Boys and the Louvins. Jesse's 'crosspicking' mandolin work was a prominent feature in their normal bluegrass instrumental line-up. Their touring show included the normal comedy routines and they performed a variety of material ranging from new songs to old standards and from bluegrass instrumentals to bluegrass versions of country hits.

In 1959, some of their broadcasts were sponsored by Martha White Mills, making them that company's number two advertising unit after Flatt And Scruggs. They first appeared on the *Grand Ole Opry* in 1961 and became regulars in 1964. Their style of music made them popular at many venues, including a successful appearance at the 1963 Newport Folk Festival. In 1960, they joined Columbia, having recorded for Starday during the late 50s and in 1962, the label released their work on their Epic label. Although the recordings were steady sellers, they had limited US country chart success, achieving mainly minor hits, including 'Cotton Mill Man' (1964). Their only Top 20 hit was 'Diesel On My Tail' (1967). In 1971, after moving to Capitol, they recorded an album of modern bluegrass using electrified instruments, but soon resorted back to their preferred acoustic sounds and by 1972, they were producing their own albums. They have presented their own network television shows and have easily maintained their popularity as top bluegrass performers. They have appeared at all major venues and toured extensively, both in the USA and overseas, including appearances at London's Wembley Festival. They charted in 1982 with 'North Wind' (a trio recording with Charlie Louvin) and again in 1986 with 'Oh Louisiana'.

Selected albums: *Sacred Songs* (1961), *Bluegrass Classics* (1963), *Bluegrass Special* (1963), *The Old Country Church* (1964), *Y'All Come: Bluegrass Humour* (1964), *Berry (Chuck) Pickin' In The Country* (1965), one side is Flatt And Scruggs *Stars Of The Grand Ole Opry* (1966), *Sacred Songs We Love* (1966), *Sing Unto Him A New Song* (1966),

Diesel On My Tail (1967), *All-Time Great Country Instrumentals* (1968), *Salutin' The Louvin Brothers* (1969), *Twenty Great Songs* (1970), *Wildwood Flower* (1970), *We Like Trains* (1970), *Freight Train* (1971), *The Jim & Jesse Show* (1972), *Superior Sounds Of Bluegrass* (1974), *Jesus Is The Key To The Kingdom* (1975), *Paradise* (1975), *Live In Japan* (1975), *Songs About Our Country* (1976), *Jim & Jesse* (1976), *Palace Of Songs* (1977), *Radio Shows* (1978), *Early Recordings* (1978), *Songs Of Inspiration* (1978), *Jim & Jesse Today* (1980), *The Jim & Jesse Story* (1980), *Back In Tokyo Again* (1981), *Jim & Jesse & Charlie Louvin* (1982), *Homeland Harmony* (1983), *Air Mail Special* (1985), *Somewhere My Love* (1986), *In The Tradition* (1987), *Some Old, Some New, Some Borrowed, Some Blue* (1987), *Music Among Friends* (1991). Jesse McReynolds: *Mandolin Workshop* (1972), *Me And My Fiddles* (1973), with Marion Sumner *Old Friends* (1979), *Guitar Pickin' Showcase* (1980), with Sumner *Fiddle Fantastic* (1986), *A Mandolin Christmas* (1988), *The Mandolobro* (1991).

Jiminez, Flaco

b. Leonardo Jiminez, 11 March 1939, San Antonio, Texas, USA. Jiminez' grandfather, Patricio, learned the accordion from German neighbours and played in towns in southern Texas at the turn of the century. Jiminez' father, Santiago, was a noted accordionist and played lively dance music around San Antonio. His best-known composition is the polka 'Viva Seguin', named after a small town near San Antonio. Santiago, who started recording in 1936 and made some records for RCA, played the two-button accordion and made no attempt to integrate his music with other American forms. Jiminez, nicknamed El Flaco 'the skinny one', played bajo sexto with his father and made his recording debut in 1955 on 'Los Tecolotes'. He recorded with a group, Los Caminantes and often had regional successes by considering contemporary lifestyle such as 'El Pantalon Blue Jean' and 'El Bingo'. His albums for Arhoolie gathered a following outside Texas, and his appearance alongside Bob Dylan on *Doug Sahm And Band* in 1973, brought him to the attention of rock fans. Ry Cooder began touring and recording with him, and Jiminez can be heard on Cooder's *Chicken Skin Music*, *Show Time*, *The Border* and *Get Rhythm*. Their key collaborations are the free-flowing 'He'll Have To Go' and the sombre 'Dark End Of The Street'. Jiminez's album, *Tex-Mex Breakdown*, showed that he was thinking in terms of a wider audience. He has also worked with Peter Rowan and a key track is 'Free

Mexican Airforce'. Jiminez tours in his own right and is popular at arts centres and folk venues throughout the UK. His father died in 1984 and his younger brother, Santiago Jnr, is also a professional accordionist with several albums to his name.

Selected albums: *El Principe Del Acordeon* (1977), *Flaco Jiminez Y Su Conjunto* (1978), with Santiago Jiminez *El Sonido De San Antonio* (1980), *Mis Polkas Favorites* (UK *Viva Seguin*) (1983), *Tex-Mex Breakdown* (1983), *On The Move* (1984), *San Antonio Soul* (1985), *Homenaje A Don Santiago Jiminez* (1985), with Los Paisanos, Los Hnos Barron, Los Formales *Augie Meyers Presents San Antonio Saturday Night* (1986), *Ay Te Dejo En San Antonio* (1986), with Ry Cooder, Fred Ojeda, Peter Rowan *The Accordion Strikes Back* (1987), *Flaco's Amigos* (1988), with Freddy Fender, Augie Meyers, Doug Sahm *Texas Tornados* (1990), with Fender, Meyers, Sahm *Zone Of Our Own* (1991), *Ay Te Dejo En San Antonio* (1991), *Partners* (1992).

Johnnie And Jack

This popular singing duo comprised of Johnnie Wright and Jack Anglin. They first worked together as the Dixie Early Birds on WSIX Nashville, in 1939. The following year, after forming a band, they became Johnnie And Jack And The Tennessee Hillbillies (soon changing it to the Tennessee Mountain Boys) and between 1940 and Anglin's death in March 1963, they built themselves a considerable reputation. During the early 40s, they were resident on several radio stations, including WBIG Greensboro (1940), WCHS Charleston (1941) before moving to WNOX Knoxville in 1942. When Anglin was drafted for military service, Wright's friend, Smilin' Eddie Hill, agreed to deputize. At WNOX, they played on the *Mid-Day Merry-Go-Round*, working for a time with a young fiddle player (but later guitarist) named Chet Atkins. (It was at this time that Wright's wife, Muriel Deason became Kitty Wells. During these years, she had only appeared with the band on occasions, as she was raising her first two children, Ruby and Bobby Wright. Anglin returned when the war ended and sometimes as Johnnie And Jack Featuring Kitty Wells, they continued the touring schedule of radio stations, including Raleigh, Decateur and Birmingham. In 1947, they returned to Nashville to spend a year on the *Grand Ole Opry* and made their first recordings on the Apollo label. They tended to play gospel songs and old time ballads, such as 'The Paper Boy' and 'Lord Watch O'er My

Daddy'. In 1948, they became regulars on the newly formed *Louisiana Hayride* on KWKH Shreveport, where they remained until December 1951. Late in 1948, thanks to to their friend, Chet Atkins, they joined RCA Victor and in January 1949, backed Kitty Wells on her first recordings; further recordings with her followed before she left the label. (The next year she started her highly successful Decca career.) In 1951, their repertoire began to include more modern country songs and they registered Top 5 US country chart hits of their own with 'Poison Love' and 'Crying Heart Blues'. They returned as *Opry* regulars in January 1952 and promptly registered a Top 10 hit with 'Three Ways Of Knowing'. During the 50s, working usually with Kitty Wells, they played their weekly *Opry* commitments and toured extensively, often working the same tours as Roy Acuff. In 1954, they had a country number 1 with 'I Get So Lonely' and a number 3 with 'Goodnight Sweetheart Goodnight'. Other Top 10 hits included 'Kiss Crazy Baby' and 'Stop The World (And Let Me Off)'. They are also still remembered for two songs that surprisingly did not chart for them, 'Ashes Of Love' and the rumba-rhythmed 'Down South In New Orleans'. The Tennessee Mountain Boys contained talented musicians including steel guitarist 'Shot' Jackson, fiddler Paul Warren and mandolinist Clyde Baum. Their last chart hit came in 1962, a Top 20 with 'Slow Poison'. At a time when they were one of country music's most popular and respected acts, Anglin died in a car crash on 7 March 1963, on his way to a memorial service for Patsy Cline.

Albums: *Johnnie & Jack And The Tennessee Mountain Boys* (1958), *Hits By Johnnie & Jack* (1959), *Smiles & Tears* (1962), *Poison Love & Other Country Favorites* (1963), *Sincerely* (1964), *Here's Johnnie & Jack* (1968), *Appolo Days And Others* (c.1970), with Kitty Wells *Early Country Live* (c.1970), *Johnnie & Jack & The Tennessee Mountain Boys* 6 CD set (1992).

Johnson, Michael

With a taste catholic enough to embrace both Charlie Byrd and Chuck Berry, Johnson was taught rudimentary guitar by an older brother before spending a year in Barcelona studying flamenco with Graciano Tarrago. After returning to the USA, the 22-year-old toured with the Chad Mitchell Trio (with John Denver). In 1971, his first solo album was overseen by Peter Yarrow (of Peter, Paul And Mary) and Phil Ramone but he had to wait until 1978 when 'Bluer Than Blue'

Michael Johnson

reached number 12 in the US charts. It was followed by lesser entries with 'Almost Like Being In Love' and 'This Night Won't Last Forever'. Transferring from EMI-America to RCA, Johnson next addressed himself to the C&W field, beginning well with 'I Love You By Heart', a big-selling duet with Sylvia. He was to top the country chart twice with singles from the movie *Wings* - 'Give Me Wings' (co-written by Rhonda Fleming) and Hugh Prestwick's 'The Moon Is Over My Shoulder' (featuring a galvanizing acoustic guitar solo by Don Potter). Further hits with 'Crying Shame', Randy Vanwarmer's 'I Will Whisper Your Name' and - another Prestwick opus - 'That's That' established Johnson as a star of the genre by the 90s. Illness and poor sales of his eponymous 1991 album threatened his new-found status, however.

Albums: *Michael Johnson* i (1971), *Wings* (1987), *Life's A Bitch* (1989), *Michael Johnson* ii (1991).

Jones, George

b. George Glenn Jones, 12 September 1931, Saratoga, Texas, USA. Jones is the greatest of honky tonk singers but he has also been a victim to its lifestyle. He learned guitar and, in 1947, was hired by the husband-and-wife duo, Eddie And Pearl. This developed into his own radio programme and a fellow disc jockey, noting his close-set eyes and upturned nose, nicknamed him 'The Possum'. He married at 18 but the couple separated within a year. Jones joined the marines in 1950 and, after being demobbed in November 1953, was signed by Pappy Daily to the new Starday label. He had his first country hit in 1955 with 'Why Baby Why', a pop hit for Pat Boone. He recorded some rockabilly tracks including 'Rock It' which Daily released under the name of Thumper Jones. Jones has so disassociated himself from these recordings that he is apt to destroy any copies that he sees. Daily also leased cover versions of well-known songs by Jones and other performers including Sleepy LaBeef to others for budget recordings. Jones' work, for example, was issued under the pseudonyms of Johnny Williams, Hank Davis and Glen Patterson, but collectors should bear in mind that these names were also used for other performers. In 1959 he had his first country number 1 with 'White Lightning', written by his friend, the Big Bopper. The single made number 73 on the USA Top 100 and, despite numerous country hits, it remains his biggest pop hit, perhaps because his voice is too country for pop listeners. (Jones has never reached the UK charts, although he and the Big Bopper supplied the backing vocals for Johnny Preston's 'Running Bear'.)

Jones's second US country number 1 was with the sensitive 'Tender Years' which held the top spot for seven weeks. He demonstrated his writing skills on 'The Window Up Above', which was subsequently a hit for Mickey Gilley, and 'Seasons Of My Heart', recorded by both Johnny Cash and Jerry Lee Lewis. His flat-top hairstyle and gaudy clothes may look dated to us now, but he recorded some of the most poignant country music of all-time with 'She Thinks I Still Care' and 'You Comb Her Hair' as well as the up-tempo fun of 'Who Shot Sam?'. The American public kept up with the Joneses for 'The Race Is On', but Jack Jones was the winner in the charts. George recorded prolifically for the Musicor label, although most of his numerous albums are less than 30 minutes long. He recorded successful duets with other performers; Gene Pitney ('I've Got Five Dollars And It's Saturday Night') and Melba Montgomery ('We Must Have Been Out Of Our Minds'). In 1970 he recorded the original version of 'A Good Year For The Roses', later a hit for Elvis Costello, and 'Tell Me My Lying Eyes Are Wrong', a concert favourite for Dr. Hook. His stormy marriage to Tammy Wynette (1969-75) included duet albums of lovey-dovey songs and bitter recriminations. A solo success, 'The Grand Tour', is a room by room account of what went wrong. His appalling behaviour (beating Wynette, shooting at friends, missing concerts) is largely attributed to his drinking. An album of superstar duets was hampered when he missed the sessions and had to add his voice later. His partners included Elvis Costello ('Stranger In The House'), James Taylor ('Bartender's Blues') and Willie Nelson ('I Gotta Get Drunk').

His album with Johnny Paycheck is a collection of rock 'n' roll classics. By the late 70s, his drinking and cocaine addiction had made him so unreliable that he was known as 'No Show Jones', although the song he recorded about it suggests he is proud of the name. When he did appear, he sometimes used Donald Duck's voice instead of his own. In 1979 he received medical treatment and, with support from the music industry, staged a significant comeback with *I Am What I Am*, which included his greatest single 'He Stopped Loving Her Today', and a further duet album with Wynette. Further trouble ensued when he beat up another fiancee; but a divorcee, Nancy Sepulveda, tolerated his mistreatment and married him in

1983. Jones' behaviour has improved in recent years although, as he would have it, 'If you're going to sing a country song, you've got to have lived it yourself.' In short, George Jones' major asset is his remarkable voice which can make a drama out of the most mundane lyrics. (James O'Gwynn recorded a tribute 'If I Could Sing A Country Song (Exactly Like George Jones)'.) Jones has had more records (almost 150) in the US country charts than any other performer, although his comparatively low tally of 13 number 1's is surprising. Undoubtedly, he would have had another with a duet with Dolly Parton, 'Rockin' Years', but following an announcement that he was to move to MCA, his voice was replaced by Ricky Van Shelton's. His first MCA album, *And Along Came Jones*, which included a tribute to his deceased mother, 'She Loved A Lot In Her Time', continued to show why he is regarded as the world's number 1 honky-tonk singer.

Albums: Being a George Jones completist is an exhausting task because he has had 450 albums released in the UK and USA alone. The listing concentrates only on albums of new recordings, collections of singles on albums for the first time, and compilations where previously unissued tracks have been added. In addition, in the early 70s, RCA in America reissued 15 compilations from his Musicor albums, usually with additional tracks, but they are not included below. Jones has recorded such key tracks as 'Ragged But Right' several times. Surprisingly, however, only two live albums have been issued, both in the 80s.

From Starday recordings: *Grand Ole Opry's Newest Star* (1956), *The Crown Prince Of Country Music* (1960), *The Fabulous Country Music Sound Of George Jones* (1962), *George Jones* (1966), *Long Live King George* (1966), *The George Jones Story* (1967), *Songbook And Picture Album* (1968), *Golden Country Hits* (1969), *16 Greatest Hits* (1977). From Mercury recordings: *Grand Ole Opry's New Star* (1957), *Country Church Time* (1958), *George Jones Sings White Lightning* (1959), *George Jones Salutes Hank Williams* (1960), *Greatest Hits* (1962), *George Jones Sings Country And Western Hits* (1962), *From The Heart* (1962), with Margie Singleton *Duets Country Style* (1962), *The Novelty Side Of George Jones* (1963), *The Ballad Side Of George Jones* (1963), *Blue And Lonesome* (1963), *C&W No.1 Male Singer* (1964), *Heartaches And Tears* (1964), *Singing The Blues* (1965), *Greatest Hits, Volume 2* (1965), *White Lightnin'* (1984), *The Lone Star Legend* (1985). From United Artists recordings: *The New Favourites Of George Jones* (1962), *The Hits Of His Country Cousins* (1962), *Homecoming In Heaven* (1962), *My Favourites Of Hank Williams* (1962), *George Jones Sings Bob Wills* (1962), *I Wish Tonight Would Never End* (1963), *The Best Of George Jones* (1963), with Melba Montgomery *What's In Our Heart* (1963), *More New Favourites Of George Jones* (1963), with Montgomery *Bluegrass Hootenanny* (1964) *George Jones Sings Like The Dickens* (1964), *I Get Lonely In A Hurry* (1965), *Trouble In Mind* (1965), *The Race Is On* (1965), *King Of Broken Hearts* (1965), *The Great George Jones* (1965), with Montgomery *Blue Moon Of Kentucky, Golden Hits* (1967), *The Young George Jones* (1967), *Golden Hits, Volume 2* (1967), *Golden Hits, Volume 3* (1968). From Musicor recordings: *Jones Boys' Country And Western Songbook* (instrumentals) (1964), with Gene Pitney *For The First Time* (1965), *Mr. Country And Western Music* (1965), *New Country Hits* (1965), *Old Brush Arbors* (1965) with Pitney *It's Country Time Again!* (1966), *Love Bug* (1966), *I'm A People* (1966), *We Found Heaven At 4033* (1966), with Melba Montgomery *Close Together* (1967) *Greatest Hits* (1967), *Walk Through This World With Me* (1967), *Cup Of Loneliness* (1967), with Montgomery *Let's Get Together/Party Pickin'* (1967), *Hits By George* (1967), *The Songs Of Dallas Frazier* (1968), *If My Heart Had Windows* (1968), *The George Jones Story* (1969), *My Country* (1969), *I'll Share My World With You* (1969), *Where Grass Won't Grow* (1969), *My Boys - The Jones Boys* (1969), *Will You Visit Me On Sunday?* (1970) *The Best Of George Jones* (1970), *With Love* (1971), *The Best Of Sacred Music* (1971), *The Great Songs Of Leon Payne* (1971), with Montgomery *George And Melba* (1974). From Epic recordings: with Tammy Wynette *We Go Together* (1971), *George Jones* (1972), with Wynette *Me And The First Lady* (1972), *A Picture Of Me* (1972), with Wynette *We Love To Sing About Jesus* (1972), with Wynette *Let's Build A World Together* (1973), *Nothing Ever Hurt Me* (1973), with Wynette *We're Gonna Hold On* (1973), *In A Gospel Way* (1974), *The Grand Tour* (1974), *George, Tammy And Tina* (1975), *The Best Of George Jones* (1975), *Memories Of Us* (1975), *The Battle* (1976), *Alone Again* (1976), with Wynette *Golden Ring* (1976), *All-Time Greatest Hits, Volume 1* (1977), *I Wanta Sing* (1977), *Bartender's Blues* (1978), *My Very Special Guests* (1979), with Johnny Paycheck *Double Trouble* (1980), *I Am What I Am* (1980), with Wynette *Together Again* (1980), *Still The Same Old Me* (1981), with Merle Haggard *A Taste Of Yesterday's Wine* (1982), *Shine On* (1983), *Jones Country* (1983), *You've Still Got A Place In My Heart* (1984), *By Request* (1984), *Ladies Choice* (1984) *First Time*

George Jones

Live (1985), *Who's Gonna Fill Their Shoes?* (1985), *Wine Coloured Roses* (1986), *Super Hits* (1987), *Too Wild Too Long* (1987), *One Woman Man* (1989), *Hallelujah Weekend* (1990), *You Oughta Be Here With Me* (1990), *And Along Came Jones* (1991), *Friends In High Places* (1991), *Salutes Bob Wills & Hank Williams* (1992), *Live At Dancetown USA* (1992), *Walls Can Fall* (1992).

Further reading: *Ragged But Right - The Life And Times Of George Jones*, Dolly Carlisle. *George Jones - The Saga Of An American Singer*, Bob Allen.

Jones, Grandpa

b. Louis Marshall Jones, 20 October 1913, Niagara, Henderson County, Kentucky, USA. The youngest of the 10 children of a tobacco farmer, Jones learned guitar and first appeared on radio in 1929, soon after getting his own programme on WJW Akron, where he became known as 'The Young Singer of Old Songs'. He worked on the *Lum and Abner* radio show but in 1935 joined Bradley Kincaid's touring company. Kincaid maintained that he sounded like a grumpy old man on their early morning WBZ Boston show and nicknamed him 'Grandpa', this led to Jones adopting a disguise and becoming a permanent

'Grandpa' at the tender age of twenty-two. He left Kincaid in 1937, readily finding work on many stations including WWVA Wheeling, WCHS Charleston and WMMN Fairmont before, in 1942, joining the *Boone County Jamboree* on WLW Cincinnati, where he first worked with Merle Travis, the Delmore Brothers and Ramona Riggins, (his future wife). He first recorded for the newly formed King label in 1943, recording two sides with Merle Travis that were released as the Shepherd Brothers. Further recordings were made in 1944 before he joined the Army, finally serving in the military police in Germany, where he broadcast daily on AFN radio with his band the Munich Mountaineers. After his discharge in 1946 he returned to Cincinnati but later that year moved to Nashville and became a *Grand Ole Opry* regular. Between 1947 and 1951 he recorded extensively for King and after changing his style of music from ballads to up-tempo songs and comedy numbers, produced his well-known recordings of 'Eight More Miles To Louisville', 'Mountain Dew' and 'Old Rattler', using the banjo for the first time on record on the latter. He also made some fine recordings with Merle Travis and the Delmores as the gospel group the Brown's Ferry Four. He recorded for RCA from 1952 to 1955 and later for several other labels. He entered the US country charts in 1959 with 'The All-American Boy', a pop hit for Bill Parsons and reached number 5 in 1963 with his recording of the old Jimmie Rodgers' song, 'T for Texas'. The popularity of his recordings and his *Opry* performances led to him joining the cast of the CBS network television show *Hee-Haw* in 1969, where his comedy routines with Minnie Pearl became very popular. Grandpa Jones was elected to the Country Music Hall Of Fame in 1978 and still performs regularly at the *Opry*.

Albums: *Grandpa Jones Sings His Greatest Hits* (1958), *Grandpa Jones-Strictly Country Tunes* (1959), *Grandpa Jones Makes The Rafters Ring* (1962), *Do You Remember (When Grandpa Jones Sang These Songs)* (1963), *An Evening With Grandpa Jones* (1963), *Grandpa Jones Yodeling Hits* (1963), *Rolling' Along With Grandpa Jones* (1963), *Grandpa Jones Sings Real Folk Songs* (1964), *Other Side Of Grandpa Jones (At Home/On Stage)* (1964), *Grandpa Jones Remembers The Brown's Ferry Four* (1966), *Everybody's Grandpa* (1968), *Living Legend Of Country Music* (1969), *Grandpa Jones Sings Hits From Hee-Haw* (1969), *Grandpa Jones Live* (1970), *What's For Supper?* (1974), with Ramona And the Brown's Ferry Four *The Grandpa Jones Story* (1976), with Ramona Jones *Old Time Country Music Collection* (1978), with Ramona and their four children *Grandpa Jones' Family Album* (1979, double album), *Family Gathering* (1981), with Roy Clark, Buck Owens, Kenny Price *The Hee-Haw Gospel Quartet* (1981). As a member of the Brown's Ferry Four: *Sacred Songs* (1957), *Sacred Songs Volume 2* (1958), *16 Sacred Gospel Songs* (1963), *Wonderful Sacred Songs* (1965).

Further reading: *Everybody's Grandpa (Fifty Years Behind The Mike)*, Louis M. 'Grandpa' Jones.

Judds

Freshly divorced, Naomi Judd (b. 1948) migrated with her daughters Wynonna (b. 1966) and Ashley (b. 1970) from California back to Morrill, Kentucky where she worked as a nurse in a local infirmary. Outside working and school hours, she and the children would sing anything from bluegrass to showbiz standards for their own amusement. However, when Wynonna nurtured aspirations to be a professional entertainer, her mother lent encouragement to the extent of moving the family to Nashville in 1979. Naomi's contralto subtly underlined Wynonna's tuneful drawl. While tending a hospitalized relation of

RCA record producer Brent Maher, Naomi elicited an audition in the company's boardroom. With a hick surname and a past that read like a Judith Krantz novel, the Judds - so the executives considered - would have more than an even chance in the country market. An exploratory mini-album, which contained the show-stopping 'John Deere Tractor', proved the executives correct when, peaking at number 17, 'Had A Dream' was the harbinger of 1984's 'Mama He's Crazy', the first of many country chart-toppers for the duo. The Judds would also be accorded a historical footnote as the earliest commercial manifestation of the form's 'new tradition' - a tag that implied the maintenance of respect for C&W's elder statesmen. This was shown by the Judds adding their voices to *Homecoming*, a 1985 collaboration by Jerry Lee Lewis, Roy Orbison, Johnny Cash and Carl Perkins (who would co-write Naomi and Wynonna's 1989 smash, 'Let Me Tell You About Love').

The Judds' repertoire also contained revivals of Ella Fitzgerald's 'Cow Cow Boogie', Elvis Presley's 'Don't Be Cruel' and Lee Dorsey's 'Working In A Coal Mine'. Self-composed songs included Naomi's 1989 composition, 'Change Of Heart', dedicated to her future second husband (and former Presley backing vocalist) Larry Strickland. Maher too contributed by co-penning hits such as 1984's Grammy-winning 'Why Not Me', 'Turn It Loose', 'Girls Night Out' and the title track of the Judds' second million-selling album, *Rockin' With The Rhythm Of The Rain*. The team relied mainly on songsmiths such as Jamie O'Hara ('Grandpa Tell Me About The Good Old Days'), Kenny O'Dell ('Mama He's Crazy'), Mickey Jupp, Graham Lyle and Troy Seals ('Maybe Your Baby's Got The Blues') and Paul Kennerley ('Have Mercy', 'Cry Myself To Sleep'). Most Judds records had an acoustic bias - particularly on the sultry ballads selected for *Give A Little Love*. They also have an occasional penchant for star guests that have included the Jordanaires ('Don't Be Cruel'), Emmylou Harris 'The Sweetest Gift' (*Heartland*), Mark Knopfler on his 'Water Of Love' (*River Of Time*) and Bonnie Raitt playing slide guitar on *Love Can Build A Bridge*. In 1988, the pair became the first female country act to found their own booking agency (Pro-Tours) but poor health forced Naomi to retire from the concert stage two years later. Naomi and Wynonna toured America in a series of extravagant farewell concerts, before Wynonna was free - conveniently, cynics said - to begin her long-rumoured solo career. This she did

Judds

in style, with a remarkable album that touched on gospel, soul and R&B, and confirmed her as the most distinctive and powerful female vocalist of her generation.

Selected albums: *The Judds* (1984), *Why Not Me?* (1985), *Rockin' With The Rhythm Of The Rain* (1986), *Give A Little Love* (1986 - UK only), *Heartland* (1987), *Greatest Hits* (1988), *River Of Time* (1989), *Love Can Build A Bridge* (1990), *The Judds Collection 1983 - 1990* (1991). Wynonna Judd *Wynonna* (1992).

K

Karl And Harty

Karl Davis and Hartford Connecticut Taylor, (both b. 1905, Mount Vernon, Kentucky, USA). They grew up listening to the musicians who regularly played in their town and learned many songs from their parents and from Brag Thompson, the pianist for the silent films that were shown at the local cinema. By the age of 12, Karl had learned to play the mandolin from Doc Hopkins (a noted local singer) and Harty had taught himself to play the guitar. By 1929, they were regularly appearing with Hopkins as the Kentucky Krazy Kats on WHAS Louisville. The following year, Bradley Kincaid was instrumental in them moving to WLS Chicago, where they featured on several programmes including the *National Barn Dance* and appeared with such artists as Red Foley in the Cumberland Ridge Runners. In 1933, Karl wrote 'I'm Here To Get My Baby Out Of Jail', which they recorded the following year. It proved so successful that almost every other duet group recorded it and the song went on to become a country standard. The two benefited from the new microphone and broadcasting equipment, which meant that the old mountain shouting style of singing was no longer necessary. During the 30s, their quieter style of close harmony vocal work became the form copied by other acts including the Blue Sky Boys, the Delmore Brothers and years later the Everly Brothers. They played on WLS until 1937 and then moved to *Suppertime Frolics* on Chicago WJJD and became popular over an even larger area. By the mid-40s, the changing times and the record companies' constant search for jukebox records found the pair forced to record more modern songs aimed at the honky-tonk market. They consequently recorded songs like 'Seven Beers With The Wrong Woman' and 'Don't Mix Whiskey With Women', while continuing to sing their more usual type of number such as 'Wreck On The Highway' and 'The Prisoner's Dream' on their radio programmes. They later commented that 'We were like Dr. Jekyll and Mr. Hyde and we didn't much like that either'. In the 50s, they retired from performing when live radio and country music in Chicago declined. Karl remained active as a songwriter and had songs recorded by artists including Emmylou Harris and Linda Ronstadt. There is little doubt that Karl's best known song is 'Kentucky'. He wrote it as a tribute to his home state and when it was recorded in January 1941, became very popular with US servicemen in World War II. However, it was not their own version but that of the Blue Sky Boys, in 1947, that really turned the song into a country classic. (Karl received the honour of being named a Kentucky Colonel in 1970 by a grateful state.) Harty died in 1963 and Karl in 1979.
Compilation: *Early Recordings* (1981).

Keen, Robert Earl, Jnr.

b. 11 January 1956, Houston, Texas, USA. In the mid-70s, Keen befriended Lyle Lovett at Texas A&M University, an establishment that combined academic and military activities. They often sang and played guitar together and they wrote 'This Old Porch', which appeared on Lovett's first album. Keen also formed a bluegrass band, the Front Porch Boys. In 1981, he moved to Austin and he worked as the Incredible Robert Keen and Some Other Guys Band. He financed an album on loans of $4,500, *No Kinda Dancer*, which has twice been reissued. *The Austin Chronicle* nominated him Songwriter of the Year, an honour that invariably went to Butch Hancock. On Steve Earle's advice that there were too many distractions in Austin - namely, pretty women and drugs - Keen moved to Nashville, although he returned to Texas in 1987. He was a backing singer on Nanci Griffith's 'St. Olav's Gate' and she recorded his songs, 'Sing One For Sister' and 'I Would Change My Life'. He appeared on the recording of the 1986 Kerrville Folk Festival and then recorded a live album for Sugar Hill. In 1989, he made a spirited album about Texas life, *West Textures*. His rough-hewn voice suited the bitter-sweet songs, which included a country music parody worthy of David Allan Coe, 'It's The Little Things (That Piss Me Off)'. The stand-out track, ironically, was a song he did not write, Kevin Farrell's western tale of 'Sonora's Death Row'. Although Keen is a frequent performer, he prefers to write at home. 'I'm not a very good writer on the road because I only come up with lonely hotel songs.'
Albums: *No Kinda Dancer* (1984), *The Live Album* (1988), *West Textures* (1989).

Kemp, Wayne

b. 1 June 1941, Greenwood, Arkansas, USA. His father was a motor mechanic and as a teenager Kemp drove racing cars. His interest changed to music and forming his own band, he toured the

southwest. In 1963, he gained fame as a songwriter when George Jones had a big hit with 'Love Bug'. After his own recording of 'The Image Of Me' had made little impression, Conway Twitty's version became a number 5 country hit. Twitty had further major success with Kemp's songs 'Next In Line', 'Darling You Know I Wouldn't Lie' and 'That's When She Started To Stop Loving You'. Kemp's own first hit came in 1969 with his Decca recording of 'Won't You Come Home'. Between then and 1982, also recording on MCA, United Artists and Mercury, he charted 20 more hits, the only Top 20 entrant being 'Honky Tonk Wine' (1973). In 1983, he had a minor hit on Door Knob with his song 'Don't Send Me No Angels'. (The song later being successfully recorded by both Ricky Van Shelton and George Jones.) Kemp remains active as a writer but his last chart hit was a duet with Bobby G. Rice 'Red Neck And Over Thirty' in 1986.
Albums: *Wayne Kemp* (1972), *Kentucky Sunshine* (1974).

Kendalls

Royce Kendall (b. 25 September 1934, St. Louis, Missouri, USA) and Jeannie Kendall (b. 30 November 1954, St. Louis, Missouri, USA). Royce learned guitar from the age of five and formed a duo, the Austin Brothers, with his brother, Floyce. After serving in the US Army, Royce and his wife Melba started a hairdressing business in St. Louis. Their only child, Jeannie, began harmonizing with her father on old-time country songs, and they were soon entertaining family and friends. Their first record, for a small local label, was 'Round Round Round', and their talents were recognized in Nashville by Pete Drake, although they simply recorded country versions of pop hits such as 'Leavin' On A Jet Plane', 'Proud Mary' and 'You've Lost That Lovin' Feelin''. Jeannie Kendall was among the backing singers on Ringo Starr's Nashville album, *Beaucoups Of Blues*. The family moved to Hendersonville, just outside Nashville, and the Kendalls had success with Dot Records, notably 'Two Divided By Love' and 'Everything I Own'. In the mid-70s, Ovation Records started a country division and the Kendalls, who had a contemporary sound with traditional overtones, were to test the market. When a single of 'Live And Let Live' was released, Ovation found that country disc jockeys preferred the b-side, 'Heaven's Just A Sin Away'. It topped the US country charts and became the Country Single of the Year. The father and daughter

followed the record with other 'cheating' songs, notably 'It Don't Feel Like Sinnin' To Me' and 'Pittsburg Stealers'. They had a further US country number 1 with the double-sided, 'Sweet Desire'/'Old Fashioned Love', plus further Top 10 hits with 'I'm Already Blue' and Dolly Parton's 'Put It Off Until Tomorrow'. In 1981, they moved to Mercury and continued their success with 'Teach Me How To Cheat' and 'If You're Waiting On Me (You're Backing Up)'. They had their third chart-topper in 1984 with 'Thank God For The Radio'. Jeannie, who takes most of the lead vocals, married band member, Mack Watkins. The Kendalls' success has faltered of late and the most likely scenario is that Jeannie Kendall will go solo.
Albums: *Meet The Kendalls* (1970), *Two Divided By Love* (1972), *Leavin' On A Jet Plane* (1974), *Let The Music Play* aka *Heaven's Just A Sin Away* (1977), *Old Fashioned Love* (1978), *1978 Grammy Awards Winners: Best Country Duo* (1978), *Just Like Real People* (1979), *Heart Of The Matter* (1979), *Lettin' You On A Feelin'* (1981), *Stickin' Together* (1982), *Moving Train* (1983), *Two Heart Harmony* (1985), *Fire At First Sight* (1986), *Break The Routine* (1987). Compilation: *16 Greatest Hits* (1988).

Kennedy, Jerry

b. Jerry Glenn Kennedy, 10 August 1940, Caddo Parish, Shreveport, Louisiana, USA. Kennedy has been a featured session guitarist for many top Nashville country stars and in the early 60s, he played lead guitar on some of Elvis Presley's recordings. He also worked with guitarist Charlie Tomlinson and recorded several guitar albums with him under the name of Tom And Jerry. After he became a record producer with Mercury/Phonogram, he produced the recordings of many artists including Roy Orbison, Bobby Bare, Charlie Rich, Patti Page, Roger Miller, the Statler Brothers, Reba McEntire and Becky Hobbs. He was responsible for Jerry Lee Lewis's commercial renaissance in the late 60s, when he steered the killer back towards the country market. He has also worked in several administration posts within the music industry, including that of Vice-President of A&R of the Country Division of Mercury.
Albums: *Jerry Kennedy's Dancing Guitars (Rock Elvis' Hits)* (1962), *Jerry Kennedy's Guitars & Strings Play The Golden Standards* (1963), *From Nashville To Soulville* (1965), *Jerry Kennedy Plays With All Due Respect To Kris Kristofferson* (1971), *Jerry Kennedy & Friends* (1974); as Tom And Jerry *Guitar's Greatest Hits Volume 1* (1961), *Guitar's Greatest Hits Volume*

2 (1962), *Guitars Play The Sound Of Ray Charles* (1962), *Surfin' Hootenanny* (1963).

Kentucky Colonels

Fêted as one of the finest-ever bluegrass groups, the Kentucky Colonels evolved out of a family-based ensemble, the Three Little Country Boys. The White brothers (born Le Blanc), Roland (mandolin/vocals), Clarence White (b. 6 June 1944, Lewiston, Maine, USA, d. July 1973; guitar/vocals) and Eric (bass/vocals) began performing during the mid-50s, but Billy Ray Latham (banjo) and Leroy Mack (dobro) later joined the founding trio. The unit was then renamed the Country Boys. Roger Bush replaced Eric White in 1961 after which the quintet became known as the Kentucky Colonels. Their progress was undermined following Roland White's induction into the army, although the group completed its debut album, *New Sounds Of Bluegrass America*, in his absence. The Colonels enjoyed their most prolific spell on his return. Fiddler Bobby Slone replaced Leroy Mack and the revitalized quintet recorded the classic *Appalachian Swing*. However, Clarence White grew increasingly unhappy with the music's confines and harboured ambitions for a more electric style. The group attempted an awkward compromise, offering sets both traditional and contemporary, but this forlorn balance failed to satisfy either party. A new fiddler, Scotty Stoneman, joined, but by April 1966, the Colonels had all but collapsed. Roland and Eric White did attempt to revive the group the following year, adding Dennis Morris (guitar) and Bob Warford (banjo), but although this proved short-term, numerous other reunions have taken place. Latham and Bush meanwhile joined Dillard And Clark, while Clarence White was drafted into the Byrds.

Albums: *New Sounds Of Bluegrass America* (1963), *Appalachian Swing* (1964), *Kentucky Colonels* (1974), *The White Brothers Live In Sweden* (1979). Compilations: *Livin' In The Past* (1975), *The Kentucky Colonels With Scotty Stoneman* (1975), *Kentucky Colonels 1965-1966* (1979), *Kentucky Colonels 1966* (1978), *Clarence White And The Kentucky Colonels* (1980), *On Stage* (1984), *1955-1967* (1988), *The Kentucky Colonels Featuring Clarence White* (1988).

Kentucky Headhunters

The Kentucky Headhunters come, naturally enough, from Kentucky. Ricky Lee Phelps (lead vocal) and his brother, Doug, played in various groups around Kentucky before meeting Greg Martin (lead guitar) in 1984. He introduced them

Kentucky Headhunters

to his cousins, the brothers Richard Young (rhythm guitar) and Fred Young (bass). Previously the Young brothers and Martin had been in a group, Itchy Brother, which was almost signed to Led Zeppelin's own label, Swan Song. Since then, Fred Young had played Patsy Cline's drummer in the film, *Sweet Dreams*. This time, taking their name from Muddy Waters' band, the Headchoppers, the five musicians financed their own album, *Pink* in 1988, and the tracks were subsequently released by Mercury, with additional material, in *Pickin' On Nashville*. Their first US country hit was with a revival of Bill Monroe's 'Walk Softly On This Heart Of Mine'. This was followed by their anthemic tribute to a 74-year-old marbles champion, Dumas Walker, and then by a revival of Don Gibson's 'Oh Lonesome Me'. Their boisterous stage act includes some magic from Ricky. The Kentucky Headhunters, like Lynyrd Skynyrd before them, are a controversial band who bring heavy metal influences to country music, and vice versa: on their album, *Electric Barnyard*, they thrash through 'The Ballad Of Davy Crockett'. The decision of the two Phelps brothers to quit the Headhunters in 1992 delayed the release of their third album.

Albums: *Pink* (1988), *Pickin' On Nashville* (1989), *Electric Barnyard* (1991).

Kerr, Anita

b. Anita Jean Grob, 31 October 1927, Memphis, Tennessee, USA. Kerr took piano lessons from the age of four and she was soon appearing on her mother's radio show in Memphis. By the age of 14, she was the staff pianist and was making vocal arrangements of church music for the station. In 1949, she formed the Anita Kerr Quartet (later Singers) with Gil Wright (tenor), Dorothy Ann 'Dottie' Dillard (alto) and Louis D. Nunley (baritone). They established themselves as session singers, particularly in Nashville. By the early 60s, they were featured on, it is estimated or alleged, a quarter of all the country records being made there, including records by Chet Atkins, Floyd Cramer, Jim Reeves and Hank Snow as well as pop records by Brook Benton, Perry Como, Connie Francis, Brenda Lee and Roy Orbison. Kerr also produced Skeeter Davis' 'The End Of The World'. In 1960, the quartet made the US Top 10 with 'Forever' under the name of the Little Dippers. In 1962, this time as the Anita And Th' So-And-So's, they had a minor US hit with 'Joey Baby'. From the mid-60s, the Anita Kerr Singers made several easy-listening albums and also

accompanied Rod McKuen on his best-selling poetry albums as the San Sebastian Strings And Singers.

Albums: *Voices In Hi-Fi* (1958), *Georgia On My Mind* (1965), *We Dig Mancini* (1966), *Slightly Baroque* (1967), *The Anita Kerr Singers Reflect On The Hits Of Burt Bacharach And Hal David* (1969), *Velvet Voices And Bold Brass* (1969), *The Look Of Love* (1970), *The Simon And Garfunkel Songbook* (1971), *Grow To Know Me* (1972), *Anita Kerr's Christmas Story* (1972), *Daytime, Nighttime* (1973), *Precious Memories* (1974), *Grow To Know Me* (1974), *Halleluhah Brass* (1975), *Gentle As Morning* (1975), *Halleluhah Guitarists* (1976), *Walk A Little Slower* (1976).

Kershaw, Doug

b. 24 January 1936, Tiel Ridge, Louisiana, USA. This renowned fiddle player and vocalist is a major figure in cajun, or acadian circles, the traditional music of Louisiana's French-speaking minority. He was introduced to music by 'Daddy Jack' and 'Mama Rita', who subsequently appeared in many of the artist's compositions, and joined a family-based band, the Continental Playboys, on leaving high school. When Kershaw's songwriting talent resulted in a publishing and recording deal, he formed a duo with one of his brothers, and as Rusty And Doug quickly became popular throughout the southern USA. By 1956, they were a regular attraction on *The World's Original Jamboree*, a weekly showcase for local talent, and the following year enjoyed a residency on the famed *Grand Ole Opry*. Three of Kershaw's original compositions, 'Louisiana Man', 'Joli Blon' and 'Diddy Liggy Lo', not only became cajun standards, but have been the subject of numerous cover versions by both pop and country acts. The brothers embarked on separate careers in 1964, but despite the approbation of their peers, Kershaw did not secure a larger audience until 1968, when he guested on *The Johnny Cash Show*. This appearance coincided with the release of *The Cajun Way*, the artist's debut for Warner Brothers, which affirmed his newfound popularity. Cameos on albums by Bob Dylan and John Stewart endeared Kershaw to the rock fraternity, while a series of stellar 70s recordings confirmed his talent as a flamboyant musician and gifted composer.

Albums: as Rusty and Doug *Louisiana Man* (1971), *Louisiana Man* (1976), *Cajun Country Rockers* (1979), *Cajun Country Rockers 2* (1981), *Cajun Country Rockers 3* (1984), *More Cajun Country Rock* (1984), *Jay Miller Sessions Volume 22* (1986), *Rusty,*

Doug, Wiley And Friends (1989); Doug Kershaw solo *The Cajun Way* (1969), *Spanish Moss* (1970), *Doug Kershaw* (1971), *Swamp Grass* (1972), *Devil's Elbow* (1972), *Douglas James Kershaw* (1973), *Mama Kershaw's Boy* (1974), *Alive & Kickin'* (1975), *Ragin' Cajun* (1976), *Flip Flop Fly* (1977), *Louisiana Man* (1978). Compilation: *Louisiana Cajun Country* (1979).

Kessinger Brothers

Clark Kessinger (b. 27 July 1896, South Hills, Kanawha County, West Virginia, USA, d. 4 June 1975) spent most of his life in the county either at St. Albans or South Charleston. He learned to play the banjo as a very young child and was playing the fiddle at the age of five. He made his professional debut when seven years old (earning more than his father's foundry wage), playing in the local saloons and later, as a teenager, also for country dances and on radio WOBU Charleston. He served in the US Army during World War I and on discharge started to play regularly with his nephew Luches (b. 1906, Kanawha County, West Virginia, USA, d. 1944; guitar). The record company believed that they would market better if classed as brothers and so they became known primarily as the Kessinger Brothers, but also recorded as the Wright Brothers, the Arnold Brothers and the Birmingham Entertainers. They made their first recordings for Brunswick-Vocalion in 1928 and by 1930, they were instrumental stars with some 29 single records released on Brunswick's *Songs From Dixie* series. Clark Kessinger recorded additional fiddle tunes for Vocalion releases with the material varying from old-time traditional fiddle tunes such as 'Sally Goodin' and 'Turkey In The Straw' to local tunes such as 'Kanawha March' and 'Going Up Bushy Fork'. He has been described by noted authority Ivan M. Tribe as 'an outstanding breakdown fiddler, but he was probably unexcelled in his ability to play slower and more difficult waltzes and marches with almost equal dexterity'. During the 30s, Clark met and discussed playing styles with world famous classical violinist Fritz Kreisler, when he appeared in Charleston. The Kessingers played together around the Charleston area until 1944, when Luches died. After his nephew's death, Clark continued to play at local dances and worked as a painter during the day. In 1964, he won a state fiddling contest in Virginia, which led to new successes and publicity. He played various folk festivals including Newport, the Smithsonian Folklife Society, appeared at the *Grand Ole Opry* and on network television and recorded four albums. In July 1971, he suffered a stroke soon after he had recorded an album for Rounder. He died four years later in June 1975, on his way to hospital following a further stroke.
Albums: *The Legend Of Clark Kessinger (Sweet Bunch Of Daisies)* (c.1965), *Old Time Music With Fiddle And Guitar* (1971), *The Kessinger Brothers (1928-1930 Recordings)* (1975), *The Legend Of Clark Kessinger* (c.1975), *Memorial Album* (1976), *Live At Union Grove* (1977), *Old-Time Country Music* (1970s), *Old-Time Country Music Volume 2* (1970s).

Ketchum, Hal

b. Michael Ketchum, 1952, Greenwich, New York, USA. A carpenter, he credits his early influences as Buck Owens, Merle Haggard and Marty Robbins. His early musical career included playing drums in a R&B band and guitar in a blues band. He first began to establish himself as a singer and songwriter at the Kerrville Folk Festival. In 1987, he recorded his first album which was released in cassette form only but in 1989, it was reissued in CD format by the German Sawdust label. In 1991, he joined Curb Records and his very first album produced three Top 20 US country chart singles. Ketchum tours with his band, the Alibis and promises to become one of the big artists of the future.
Albums: *Threadbare Alibi* (1989), *Past The Point Of Rescue* (1989), *Sure Love* (1992).

Kilgore, Merle

b. Merle Wyatt Kilgore, 9 August 1934, Chickasha, Oklahoma, USA. Kilgore was raised in Louisiana when the family moved to Shreveport. He learned to play guitar as a boy and started working on the radio station KENT as a disc jockey at the age of 16. By the time he was 18, he was the leading guitarist on the *Louisiana Hayride* and had also appeared on the *Grand Ole Opry* in Nashville and the *Big D Jamboree* in Dallas. Between 1952 and 1954 he was also a regular on KFAZ-TV in Monroe, Louisiana. His songwriting ability soon became apparent. In 1954, his song 'More And More' became a hit for both Webb Pierce and Guy Lombardo and in 1959, 'Johnny Reb' was a country and pop hit for Johnny Horton. Throughout the 50s, Kilgore was very active as a disc jockey, a club performer and a regular member of the *Hayride* and had his own first US country chart hits on the Starday label in 1960 with 'Dear Mama' and 'Love Has Made You Beautiful' and although it never charted, his song '42 in Chicago' is somewhat of a country standard.

In 1962, he teamed with Claude King to write 'Wolverton Mountain'. King's subsequent recording sold a million and became a US country and pop hit. It later transpired that the trigger happy old mountain man in the song, Clifton Clowers, was Kilgore's uncle. (Kilgore originally offered the song to Johnny Horton, who believed it to be the worst song Kilgore had written and when he offered it to George Jones, he told Kilgore that he hated mountain songs.) The following year, Kilgore teamed up with June Carter to write 'Ring Of Fire', which repeated the million selling success when recorded by Carter's future husband, Johnny Cash. Merle recorded for several labels but his output never proved great sellers. Through the 60s and 70s, he worked steadily including film appearances in *Country Music On Broadway*, *Nevada Smith* (for which he wrote and recorded the title song) and *Five Card Stud*. He starred in shows in Las Vegas, played Carnegie Hall, New York but gradually became more involved with music publishing, production and management. He was the opening act for Hank Williams Jnr. for 21 years and later became his manager and the vice-president of Hank Williams Jnr. Enterprises. Kilgore portrayed himself in the television movie *Living Proof: The Hank Williams Jnr. Story* in 1983.

Albums:- *There's Gold In Them Thar Hills* (1963), *Merle Kilgore, The Tall Texan* (1963), *Ring Of Fire* (1965), *Big Merle Kilgore* (1973), *Teenager's Holiday* (1991).

Kincaid, Bradley

b. 13 July 1895, near Lancaster, Garrard County, Kentucky, USA, d. 23 September 1989. Kincaid grew up strumming folk tunes, mountain ballads and vaudeville songs on an old 'hound dog' guitar, so-called because his father had swapped a hunting dog for it. He acquired a college education in Chicago and he lectured on folk music to learned societies. Kincaid described himself as a folk singer rather than a hillbilly, (a term he hated) and he became known as the Kentucky Mountain Boy. In 1926, he gained a regular spot on WLS Chicago and then became the star of its *National Barn Dance*. Kincaid began recording in 1927 and his pseudonyms included Dan Hughey, John Carpenter and Harley Stratton. His best-known records are 'Barbara Allen', 'The Fatal Derby Day', 'The Legend Of The Robin's Red Breast' and 'The Letter Edged In Black'. Like A.P. Carter of the Carter Family, he collected songs, and the individual sales of his 12 folios, *My Favourite*

Mountain Ballads And Old Time Songs, were as many as 100,000. Sears manufactured a replica of his 'hound dog' guitar. Kincaid toured extensively and, in 1936, he discovered Lewis Marshall Jones whom he renamed Grandpa Jones. Between 1944 and 1947, Kincaid was a regular on the *Grand Ole Opry* and he then bought his own radio station, WWSO Springfield. He retired in 1953, although he still performed at folk festivals. In 1963, he recorded 162 songs in four days, but only six albums from that session were ever released. He died in September 1989 in Springfield, Ohio, USA.

Albums: *American Ballads* (1950), *Bradley Kincaid Sings American Ballads And Folk Songs* (1952), *Bradley Kincaid - Mountain Ballads And Old Time Songs* (six volumes, released mid-60s) *Family Gospel Album* (1971), *Bradley Kincaid - The Kentucky Mountain Boy* (1973), *Mountain Ballads And Old Time Songs* (1976), *Favourite Old Time Songs* (1984), *Old Time Songs And Hymns* (1984), *Mountain Ballads And Old Time Songs, Volume 7* (1989).

Further reading: *Radio's Kentucky Mountain Boy - Bradley Kincaid*, Loyal Jones.

King, Claude

b. 5 February 1933, Shreveport, Louisiana, USA. King showed an early interest in music and was a proficient guitarist at the age of 12. He won a sports scholarship to the University of Idaho, intending to follow an athletic career, but changed his mind and returned to Shreveport to work on the *Louisiana Hayride*. During the 50s, he played various local venues and took to writing songs. He first recorded for Gotham in 1952, but it was in 1961, after he signed for Columbia, that he achieved his first US country and pop chart hits with 'Big River, Big Man' and 'The Comancheros'. In 1962, he teamed with Merle Kilgore to write 'Wolverton Mountain'. After the song was rejected by Johnny Horton and George Jones, King decided to record it himself and promptly found that he had a million-selling country and pop hit on his hands. During the 60s, King had an impressive list of 23 country chart hits. They included Top 10 successes with 'The Burning Of Atlanta', 'Tiger Woman' and his version of Johnny Horton's song, 'All For The Love Of A Girl'. (In 1969, King recorded a tribute album to his great friend Horton.) In the early 70s, he found things more difficult, and his only Top 20 hit came with 'Mary's Vineyard'. The total of King's country chart hits has stood at 30, the last being 'Cotton Dan' in 1977. During his career he made appearances in several films including *Swamp Girl* and in 1982, he also acted in the television mini-series, *The Blue And The Grey*.

Albums: *Meet Claude King* (1962), *Tiger Woman* (1965), *I Remember Johnny Horton* (1969), *Friend, Lover, Woman, Wife* (1970), *Chip 'N' Dales Place* (1971). Compilations: *Greatest Hits* (1977), *Claude King's Best* (1980).

King, Pee Wee

b. Julius Frank Anthony Kuczynski, 18 February 1914, Milwaukee, Wisconsin, USA. His parents, whose families had been Polish immigrants, relocated to Abrams when he was a child and he grew up in the Polish community there. His father, who played fiddle and concertina, ran a polka band and the boy was encouraged to play instruments from an early age. He first played concertina and then fiddle, but at the age of 14, he changed to accordion. He made appearances with his father's band but while still at high school and calling himself Frankie King, he formed a five-piece band that played on radio at Racine, Wisconsin. After graduating in 1932, he fronted a band he called the King's Jesters and played various radio stations and venues in Wisconsin, Michigan and Illinois. In 1934, he was given the chance to tour with Gene Autry as the accordionist with his group. In 1935, he moved to WHAS Louisville, where Autry headed a band called the Log Cabin Boys. Here he found three members of the band called Frank and being a mere 5 feet 6 inches tall, he was given the nickname of Pee Wee, which he later legalized. When Autry left for Hollywood in 1936, King took over the band and renamed it the Golden West Cowboys. In 1937, he moved to Nashville and became a member of the *Grand Ole Opry*, where he remained until 1947. His band included, at different times, such noted country music performers as Ernest Tubb, Eddy Arnold, Cowboy Copas, Redd Stewart and Clell Summey.

In 1941, he and his band with other Opry acts including Minnie Pearl toured extensively with *The Grand Ole Opry Camel Caravan*. In 1938, he made his film debut with Autry in *Goldmine In The Sky* and later appeared in other b-movie westerns, not only with Autry, but other cowboy stars including Johnny Mack Brown and Charles Starrett. In 1947-57, he had his own radio and television series on WAVE, Louisville. He recorded for RCA-Victor and in 1948, he achieved his first US country and pop chart hit with 'Tennessee Waltz'. Inspired by Bill Monroe's 'Kentucky Waltz', King and Redd Stewart merely added lyrics to Monroe's theme song the 'No Name Waltz'. King quickly followed with his other 'State' song hits 'Tennessee Tears' and 'Tennessee Polka', as well as his co-written 'Bonaparte's Retreat'. In 1951, he had a US country and pop number 1 with his song 'Slowpoke', which topped the country charts for 15 weeks and went on to sell a million. (It was also a Top 10 hit for Hawkshaw Hawkins). When released in Britain, it was for some reason called 'Slow Coach'. Other King songs to become Top 10 country hits for him were 'Silver And Gold', 'Busybody', 'Changing Partners' (a UK hit for both Kay Starr and Bing Crosby) and 'Bimbo' (later recorded successfully by Jim Reeves). It should be noted that in all cases the vocals were by Redd Stewart.

In the late 50s and early 60s, he had four television shows in different venues but in 1962, he found it a strain and gave them all up. Between 1952 and 1956, he won every award for western bands. Noted country authority Colin Escott once wrote that Bill Haley and rock 'n' roll owed a great debt to Pee Wee King, as far as instrumentation was concerned. By 1959, King found that this very genre badly affected his music and he broke up his band. For the next four years, he worked with Redd Stewart in Minnie Pearl's Roadshow. In 1963, she gave up touring but King continued to run the show until, in 1968, he once again disbanded. He later relied on local musicians to back him on his appearances. In 1969, he retired from performing to concentrate on the business side of the music industry and through the 70s spent much time on promotional work. He was one of the first members elected to the Nashville Songwriters International Hall Of Fame when it was founded in 1970 and his many varied services to the country music industry also earned him the honour of election to the Country Music Hall Of Fame in 1974. He later became a director of the Country Music Foundation in Nashville. In 1986, he appeared on the *Opry*'s 60th Anniversary Show. Albums: *Pee Wee King* (1954), *Pee Wee King* (1955), *Waltzes* (1955), *Swing West* (1955), *Swing West* (c.1958), *Back Again (With The Songs That Made Them Famous)* (1964), *Country Barn Dance* (1965), *The Legendary (Live Transcriptions)* (1967), *Golden Olde Tyme Dances* (1975), *Ballroom King* (1983), *Rompin', Stompin', Singin', Swingin'* (1984), *Hog Wild Too* (1990). Compilations: *Biggest Hits* (1966), *Best Of Pee Wee King And Redd Stewart* (1975).

Kirby, Pete

b. Beecher Kirby, c.1915, near Gatlinburg, Sevier County, Tennessee, USA. The Kirby's were a musical family with all 10 siblings playing some instrument, though not professionally. Kirby learned guitar and banjo but worked in mills and on a farm before finding work as a guitarist in an Illinois club. After hearing a dobro, he also mastered that instrument. In 1939, he became a member of Roy Acuff's, Smoky Mountain Boys, starting an association that lasted to Acuff's death in 1992. Kirby's dobro became a distinctive feature of the Acuff sound and he has become known as one of the instrument's finest exponents. He was also a fine harmony vocalist. He figured in the comedy routines that were part of Acuff's show and wearing his bib and brace overalls and frailing a banjo for his solo spots, he became known as Bashful Brother Oswald and a great favourite of the *Grand Ole Opry* audiences. He played on many of Acuff's recordings but recorded in his own right for Starday in 1962 and for Rounder in the 70s, including two fine albums with fellow Acuff band member, Charlie Collins. He was also one of the stars chosen to play on the Nitty Gritty Dirt Band's famous *1972 Will The Circle Be Unbroken* project.
Albums: *Bashful Brother Oswald* (1962), *Brother Oswald* (1972), *Banjo & Dobro* (1974), with Charlie Collins *That's Country* (1975), with Charlie Collins *Os & Charlie* (1976), *Don't Say Aloha* (c.1978).

Kirk, Eddie

b. 21 March 1919, Greeley, Colorado, USA. He actually sang and played guitar with the Beverly Hillbillies in the early 30s. He later appeared on the Compton, *Town Hall Party*, KXLA's *Hometown Jamboree*, the Gene Autry radio shows and in several b-Westerns. Kirk was an excellent yodeler and twice won the National Yodeling Championship (1935-36). In the late 40s, he recorded for Capitol and had two US country chart Top 10 hits in 1949 with 'The God's Were Angry With Me' and his version of George Morgan's 'Candy Kisses'.

Knoblock, Fred

b. Jackson, Mississippi, USA. Fred Knoblock enjoyed one brief brush with pop success before an equally brief solo run on the country charts. Knoblock had been a member of the rock band Let's Eat in the 70s. When that effort ran its course after six years, Knoblock signed as a country-rock artist to the Scotti Brothers Records label. 'Why Not Me' was the most visible result, a number 18

hit in 1980. That same year and the following he made number 10 on the US country charts with two successive singles, 'Killin' Time' (a duet with actress Susan Anton which also made number 26 pop) and a cover of Chuck Berry's 'Memphis'. One final country chart single, 'I Had It All', came in 1982, after which Knoblock teamed up with Thom Schuyler Jnr. and Paul Overstreet as the successful trio Schuyler, Knoblock And Overstreet (SKO). That outfit became SKB when Craig Bickhardt replaced Overstreet in 1987.
Album: *Why Not Me* (1980).

Knox, Buddy

b. Wayne Knox, 14 April 1933, Happy, Texas, USA. Knox was one of the first 'pop-abilly' hitmakers in the 50s. With bassist Jimmy Bowen, he formed the country band the Rhythm Orchids in 1956, adding Don Lanier (guitar) and Dave Alldred (drums). The following year Knox sang lead vocals on 'Party Doll', recorded at Norman Petty's Oklahoma studio. First issued locally on the Triple-D label, it became the first release on Roulette, formed by New York nightclub owner Maurice Levy. 'Party Doll' went to number 1 in the USA. At the same session Bowen recorded another hit, 'I'm Stickin' With You'. With his light voice skimming over the insistent rhythms, Knox was the first in a line of Texan rockers which included Buddy Holly and Roy Orbison. Both 'Rock Your Little Baby To Sleep' and the gimmicky 'Hula Love' were Top 20 hits later in 1957, when he also appeared in the film *Disc Jockey Jamboree*. Although he toured frequently with Alan Freed's package shows, 'Somebody Touched Me' (1958) was his only later hit and in 1960, Knox and Bowen moved to Los Angeles. There, Knox turned to 'teenbeat' material like 'Lovey Dovey', 'Ling Ting Tong' and 'She's Gone' (a minor UK hit in 1962) with producer Snuff Garrett. During the mid-60s he returned to country music, recording in Nashville for Reprise and had a hit with 'Gypsy Man', composed by ex-Crickets' Sonny Curtis. This led to film appearances in *Travellin' Light* (with Waylon Jennings) and *Sweet Country Music* (with Boots Randolph and Johnny Paycheck). Knox was now based in Canada, where he set up his own Sunnyhill label. He also visited Europe with rockabilly revival shows during the 70s and early 80s. Jimmy Bowen became one of Nashville's most powerful A&R men, working for Dot, MCA and latterly Capitol.
Albums: *Buddy Knox* (1957), *Buddy Knox And Jimmy Bowen* (1958), *Buddy Knox In Nashville*

Buddy Knox

(1967), *Gypsy Man* (1969), *Four Rock Legends* (1978), *Sweet Country Music* (1981), *Texas Rockabilly Man* (1987), *Travellin' Light* (1988). Compilations: *Buddy Knox's Golden Hits* (1963), *Greatest Hits* (1985), *Liberty Takes* (1986), *Party Doll And Other Hits* (1988).

Kristofferson, Kris

b. 22 June 1936, Brownsville, Texas USA. Kristofferson, a key figure in the 'New Nashville' of the 70s, began his singing career in Europe. While studying at Oxford University in 1958 he briefly performed for impresario Larry Parnes as Kris Carson while for five years he sang and played at US Army bases in Germany. As Captain Kristofferson, he left the army in 1965 to concentrate on songwriting. He worked as a cleaner at the CBS studios in Nashville, until Jerry Lee Lewis became the first to record one of his songs, 'Once More With Feeling'. Johnny Cash soon became a champion of Kristofferson's work and it was he who persuaded Roger Miller to record 'Me And Bobby McGee' (co-written with Fred Foster) in 1969. With its atmospheric opening, 'Busted flat in Baton Rouge, waiting for a train/feeling nearly faded as my jeans', the bluesy song was a country hit and became a rock standard in the melodramatic style by Janis Joplin and the Grateful Dead. Another classic among Kristofferson's early songs was 'Sunday Morning Coming Down', which Cash recorded. In 1970, Kristofferson appeared at the Isle of Wight pop festival while Sammi Smith was charting with the second of his major compositions, the passionate 'Help Me Make It Through The Night', which later crossed over to the pop and R&B audiences in Gladys Knight's version. Knight was also among the numerous artists who covered the tender 'For The Good Times', a huge country hit for Ray Price, while 'One Day At A Time' was a UK number 1 for Lena Martell in 1979. Overcoming his limited vocal range, Kristofferson's own hits began with 'Loving Her Was Easier (Than Anything I'll Ever Do Again)' and 'Why Me', a ballad which was frequently performed in concert by Elvis Presley. In 1973, Kristofferson married singer Rita Coolidge and recorded three albums with her before their divorce six years later.

Kristofferson had made his film debut in *Cisco Pike* (1971) and also appeared with Bob Dylan in *Pat Garrett And Billy The Kid*, but he achieved movie stardom when he acted opposite Barbra Streisand in a 1976 re-make of the 1937 picture *A Star Is Born*. For the next few years he concentrated on his film career but returned to country music with *The Winning Hand*, which featured duets with Brenda Lee, Dolly Parton and Willie Nelson. A further collaboration, *Highwaymen*, (with Nelson, Cash and

Kris Kristofferson

Waylon Jennings) headed the country chart in 1985. The four musicians subsequently toured as the Highwaymen and issued a second collaborative album in 1991. A campaigner for radical causes, Kristofferson starred in the post-nuclear television drama *Amerika* (1987) and came up with hard-hitting political commentaries on *Third World Warrior*.

Albums: *Kristofferson* (1970), *The Silver-Tongued Devil And I* (1971), *Me And Bobby McGee* (1971), *Border Lord* (1972), *Jesus Was A Capricorn* (1972), with Rita Coolidge *Full Moon* (1973), *Spooky Lady's Sideshow* (1974), with Coolidge *Breakaway* (1974), *Who's To Bless...And Who's To Blame* (1975), *Surreal Thing* (1976), five tracks on *A Star Is Born* (1976, film soundtrack), *Easter Island* (1977), with Coolidge *Natural Act* (1979), *The Winning Hand* (1983), with Willie Nelson *Music From Songwriter* (1984, film soundtrack), with Nelson, Johnny Cash, Waylon Jennings *Highwaymen* (1985), *Repossessed* (1986), *Third World Warrior* (1990), with Nelson, Cash, Jennings *Highwaymen II* (1991), *Live At The Philharmonic* (1992). Compilations: *Songs Of Kristofferson* (1977), *Country Store* (1988).

L

La Beef, Sleepy

b. Thomas Paulsley La Beff, 11 July 1935, Smackover, Arkansas, USA. This singing guitarist cut a popular if portly figure during a reawakening of enthusiasm for rockabilly in the late 70s. The youngest of 10 children in a watermelon farming family, his drooping eyelids earned him a nickname that became a lifelong *nom de theatre* in a musical career that began in gospel groups performing at weekends while he worked as a surveyor in Houston, Texas and then Nashville, Tennessee. In 1956, he was engaged by Starday Records to release budget-priced copies of current hits before a transfer to Columbia three years later. Though he was allowed to develop his own basso profundo hybrid of blues and C&W, the company dropped the hitless La Beef, whose discs were then issued on several smaller labels – notably Sun Records for whom he would be the sole remaining signing when it was bought out in 1969. The previous year, he made a US country chart debut with 'Every Day'. Further hits proved an entrée to many interesting projects during the 70s and 80s such as a proliferation of record releases during the rockabilly craze; a co-related part in Peter Guralnick's *Lost Highway* movie; a 1980 album on which he was backed by the cream of Nashville session players (including D.J. Fontana); the concept (*Nothin' But The Truth*) from Harper's Ferry (a club local to his home in Alston, Massachusetts), and a remarkable 1987 appearance in Hank Wangford's British television series, *The A-Z Of Country Music*.
Albums: *Black Land Farmer* (1971), *Rockabilly '77* (1977), *Downhome Rockabilly* (1978), *Western Gold* (1978), *Electricity* (1979), *It Ain't What You Eat It's The Way That You Chew It* (1980), *Ain't Got No Home* (1983), *Nothin' But The Truth* (1985). Compilation: *Early Rare And Rockin' Sides* (1980).

La Costa

b. LaCosta Tucker, 6 April 1951, Seminole, Texas, USA. The elder sister of Tanya Tucker. During the 60s, she worked briefly with her sister in a group called the Country Westerners in Phoenix, but became disenchanted with a musical career and left to work in a hospital in Toltrec, Arizona. After sister Tanya's chart hit with 'Delta Dawn' in 1972,
she returned to music and between 1974 and 1978, recording as La Costa for Capitol, she registered 12 country chart hits. These included Top 20 successes with 'Get On My Love Train', 'He Took Me For A Ride', 'This House Runs On Sunshine' and 'Western Man'. Since then, in spite of a change of label to Elektra, only two further hits (both minor) have followed, the last, 'Love Take It Easy On Me', released under her full name of LaCosta Tucker was back in 1982.
Albums: *Get On My Love Train* (1974), *With All My Love* (1975), *Lovin' Somebody* (1976), *Changing All The Time* (1980).

LaFarge, Pete

b. 1931, Fountain, Colorado, USA, d. 27 October 1964, New York City, New York, USA. The son of a Pulitzer Prize-winning author, LaFarge was a noted dramatist and painter, as well as an accomplished performer. Folksinger Cisco Houston first guided the aspiring musician's skills, which flourished in the 50s following Peter's active service in the Korean War. Of Pima-Indian heritage, LaFarge became a tireless champion of the oppressed, although his most famous composition, 'The Ballad Of Ira Hayes', a forthright indictment of the plight of the native American, achieved popularity through a sympathetic cover version by Johnny Cash. Pete also acted as a contributing editor to the radical *Broadside* magazine, and recorded for the Folkways and Columbia labels. However, he grew increasingly unhappy with his performing role and planned to abandon music in favour of writing and painting. Pete LaFarge died officially from a stroke, despite persistent rumours of suicide.
Albums: *On The Warpath* (1961), *As Long As The Grass Shall Grow* (1962), *Songs Of The Cowboys* (1964), *Iron Mountain And Other Songs* (1965).

Landsborough, Charlie

b. Charles Alexander Landsborough, 26 October 1941, Wrexham, Clywd, Wales. Landsborough's family come from Birkenhead and he has spent his life on Merseyside. After several jobs, he trained as a teacher, but music has been the mainstay of his life. He was part of a local beat group, the Top Spots, but developed his own style by writing gentle, melodic, romantic ballads, albeit influenced by the American singer-songwriter Mickey Newbury. Because of his teaching commitments and transport problems with 'unreliable cars', he is little known outside Merseyside. His main strength is as a songwriter. Foster And Allen entered the

UK charts with the astute reflections of 'I Will Love You All My Life', and Roly Daniels put 'Part Of Me' on the Irish charts. The repertoire of many Irish country artists includes 'The Green Hills Are Rolling Still', while 'Heaven Knows', which suggests that people should be colour-coded according to their deeds, has been recorded by George Hamilton IV. Landsborough does not stray from his niche of astute social or romantic observations, and, sooner or later, a big-name artist will convert one of his songs into a standard. The most likely contenders are 'No Time At All' and 'I Will Love You All My Life'.

Album: *Heaven Knows* (1989), *Songs From The Heart* (1992).

Lane, Christy

b. Eleanor Johnston, 8 January 1940, Peoria, Illinois, USA. Lane was the eighth of twelve children brought up in a economically depressed area. In 1959, she married country music fan, Lee Stoller, who encouraged her to sing country and, after many local performances, she made her first single, 'Janie Took My Place', in Nashville in 1968. She and her husband sold their Peoria nightclub, Christy's Inc., and moved to Nashville in 1972. Stoller formed LS Records, chiefly to release his wife's product. Her first entry on the US country charts was with 'Tryin' To Forget About You' in 1977. She then had Top 10 country hits with 'Let Me Down Easy', 'I'm Gonna Love You Anyway', 'Penny Arcade' and 'I Just Can't Stay Married To You'. Further country hits followed but Stoller was jailed for financial irregularities. She moved to United Artists and had a US country number 1 in 1980 with a gospel song written by Marijohn Wilkin and Kris Kristofferson, 'One Day At A Time'. Her husband, released from jail and inspired by Slim Whitman's album sales through television advertising, took over her career and started marketing her in a similar way. He did it so well that he was able to write about his success in a book, *One Day At A Time*.

Albums: *Christy Lane...Is The Name* (1977), *Love Lies* (1978), *Simple Little Words* (1979), *I Have A Dream* (1980), *Ask Me To Dance* (1980), *Fragile - Handle With Care* (1981), *Amazing Grace* (1982), *Here's To Us* (1983), *Footprints In The Sand* (1983), *Christmas Is The Man From Galilee* (1983).

Lane, Red

b. Hollis R. DeLaughter, 9 February 1939, near Bogalusa, Louisiana, USA. A singer/songwriter who learned guitar as a child. He moved to Nashville in the early 60s, where he worked with Justin Tubb and as a session musician. In 1967, he became front man for Dottie West's band and he wrote with West her 1968 hit 'Country Girl'. In the early 70s, he recorded for RCA and charted four minor hits, the biggest being 'The World Needs A Melody' and the last, 'It Was Love While It Lasted', in 1972. Since then he has remained active as a session musician and toured as a guitarist with Merle Haggard. Some of his songs have been recorded by top artists but he has failed to achieve further chart successes of his own.

Album: *The World Needs A Melody* (1971).

lang, k.d.

b. Karen Dawn Lang, 1962, Alberta, Canada. She prefers the lower case appearance of her name because 'it's generic and unlike Cherry Bomb, it's a name, not a sexuality'. This farmer's daughter had become a skilled pianist and guitarist by adolescence and, on leaving school, scratched a living in classical, *avant garde* and in the performing arts before choosing to sing country - a genre that she had once despised as the corniest in pop. However, forsaking much of its rhinestoned tackiness for a leaner, more abandoned approach on *A Truly Western Experience*, she moved from a Canadian label to Sire Records. She was known for her slightly skewered sensibility and a tough backing combo consisting in 1983 of Gordon Matthews (guitar), Ben Mink (violin/mandolin), Mike Creber (piano), John Dymond (bass) and Michel Pouliot (drums). She named them the Reclines - a genuflexion towards Patsy Cline. Overseen by Dave Edmunds, *Angel With A Lariat* was favoured by influential rock journals like *Rolling Stone* (who voted k.d. Female Vocalist of the Year) but many country radio stations refused to play it, prejudiced as they were by lang's spiky haircut and ambiguous sexuality. Nevertheless, she charted via 'Cryin'', a duet with Roy Orbison for 1987's *Hiding Out* comedy movie soundtrack. The following year, she gained a breakthrough with the lush *Shadowland* which was rendered agreeable to country consumers through a Nashville production by Owen Bradley and the presence of the Jordanaires, Brenda Lee, Loretta Lynn, Kitty Wells and other credible guest stars. Tracks such as the tearjerking 'I Wish I Didn't Love You So' and Chris Issak's 'Western Stars' exemplified what lang described as 'torch and twang' - an expression incorporated into the title of her next collection. Mostly self-composed with Mink, it set the seal on the grudging acceptance of her by bigots and, more

k.d. lang

to the point, confirmed her as a behemoth of country's New Tradition. In 1992, she became newsworthy and featured in dozens of magazines in Europe and the USA, having discovered Garth Brooks they finally picked up on the considerable talent of k.d. when the acclaimed *Ingenue* was released. This excellent release was however, far removed from country, C&W or new country, it was a sensual and deep collection firmly putting lang in sight of major honours. The same year showed k.d. as possessing a promising acting ability in her debut film role in *Salmonberries*.

Albums: *A Truly Western Experience* (1983), *Angel With A Lariat* (1987), *Shadowland* (1988), *Absolute Torch And Twang* (1989), *Ingenue* (1992).

LeDoux, Chris

b. 2 October 1948, Biloxi, Mississippi, USA. LeDoux's father was an airforce pilot who was posted to various parts of the USA. His grandfather, who had served in the US cavalry and fought against Pancho Villa, encouraged LeDoux to ride horses on his Wyoming farm. LeDoux attended high school at Cheyenne, Wyoming and, whilst still at school, he twice won the state's bareback title. In 1967, after graduating, he won a rodeo scholarship and received a national title in his third year. In 1976, he became the Professional Rodeo Cowboys Association's world champion in bareback riding.

LeDoux has been playing guitar and harmonica and writing songs since his teens, and he used his musical ability as a means of paying his way from one rodeo to another. Since 1971, he has been recording songs about 'real cowboys', although his voice would not win world championships and he has never had a substantial US country hit. His albums combine his own compositions about rodeo life with old and new cowboy songs. He describes his music as 'a combination of western soul, sagebrush blues, cowboy folk and rodeo rock 'n' roll'. For all his tough image, his music has a soft centre ('God Must Be A Cowboy At Heart' and the narration 'This Cowboy's Hat'), but one of his love songs is titled 'If You Loved Me, You'd Do It'. Charlie Daniels, Johnny Gimble and Janie Fricke are amongst the musicians on his records and Garth Brooks pays tribute to him in 'Much Too Young (To Feel This Damn Old)'. LeDoux lives with his family on a ranch in Wyoming and farms sheep. He is a popular entertainer with his band, Western Underground, particularly on the rodeo circuit. All his albums are released on his own label, American Cowboy Songs, but only *Rodeo's Singing Bronc Rider* has been released in the UK. Garth Brooks' testimony together with the success of a single, 'Ridin' For A Fall', brought him to the attention of Capitol Records, who signed LeDoux for new recordings and have reissued his earlier work.

Albums: *Songs Of Rodeo Life* (1971), *Chris LeDoux Sings His Rodeo Songs* (1972), *Rodeo Songs - Old And New* (1973), *Songs Of Rodeo And Country* (1974), *Songs Of Rodeo And Living Free* (1974), *Life As A Rodeo Man* (1975), *Songbook Of The American West* (1976), *Sing Me A Song, Mr. Rodeo Man* (1977), *Songs Of Rodeo Life* (1977, a re-recording of the 1971 album), *Western-Country (Cowboys Ain't Easy To Love)* (1978), *Paint Me Back Home In Wyoming* (1979), *Rodeo's Singing Bronc Rider* (1979), *Western Tunesmith* (1980), *Sounds Of The Western Country* (1980), *Old Cowboy Heroes* (1980), *He Rides The Wild Horses* (1981), *Used To Want To Be A Cowboy* (1982), *Thirty Dollar Cowboy* (1983), *Old Cowboy Classics* (1983), *Wild And Wooly* (1986), *Melodies And Memories* (1984), *Powder River* (1990), *Western Underground* (1991), *Whatcha Gonna Do With A Cowboy* (1992).

Further reading: *Gold Buckle, The Rodeo Life Of Chris LeDoux*, David G. Brown.

Lee, Albert

b. 21 December 1943, Leominster, Herefordshire, England. Lee is a country/rock guitarist of breathtaking ability. If a poll of polls were taken from leading guitarists in the field, Lee would be the likely winner. During the early 60s he was the guitarist of the R&B-influenced Chris Farlowe And The Thunderbirds. He departed in 1967, as by then offers of session work were pouring in. During that time he joined Country Fever, playing straight honky-tonk country music before recording as Poet And The One Man Band with Chas Hodges (later of Chas And Dave). The unit evolved into Heads Hands And Feet, a highly respected band, playing country/rock. It was during this stage in his career that Lee became a 'guitar hero'; he was able to play his Fender Telecaster at breakneck speed and emulate and outshine his American counterparts. Lee played with the Crickets in 1973-74 and spent an increasing amount of time in America, eventually moving out there. After appearing on a reunion album with Chris Farlowe in 1975, he joined Emmylou Harris's Hot Band, replacing one of his heroes, the legendary James Burton. During the late 70s and early 80s Lee performed in touring bands with Eric Clapton, Jackson Browne, Jerry

Lee Lewis and Dave Edmunds. His solo on 'Sweet Little Lisa' on Edmund's *Repeat When Necessary* is a superb example of the man's skill. Lee played a major part in the historic reunion of the Everly Brothers at London's Royal Albert Hall in 1983. He has made only two solo albums, both of which are impressive outings from one of Britain's finest guitarists.

Albums: *Hiding* (1979), *Albert Lee* (1982).

Lee, Brenda

b. Brenda Lee Tarpley, 11 December 1944, Lithonia, Georgia, USA. Even in early adolescence, she had an adult husk of a voice that could slip from anguished intimacy through sleepy insinuation to raucous lust even during 'Let's Jump The Broomstick', 'Speak To Me Pretty' and other jaunty classics that kept her in the hit parade from the mid-50s to 1965. Through local radio and, by 1956, wider exposure on Red Foley's Ozark Jubilee broadcasts, 'Little Brenda Lee' was ensured enough airplay for her first single, a revival of Hank Williams' 'Jambalaya', to crack the US country chart before her *Billboard* Hot 100 debut with 1957's 'One Step At A Time'. The novelty of her extreme youth facilitated bigger triumphs for 'Little Miss Dynamite' with the million-selling 'Rockin' Around The Christmas Tree' and later bouncy

rockers before the next decade brought a greater proportion of heartbreak ballads such as 'I'm Sorry', 'Thanks A Lot' and 'Too Many Rivers' - plus an acting role in the children's fantasy movie, *The Two Little Bears*. 1963 was another successful year - especially in the UK with the title song of *All Alone Am I*, 'Losing You' (a French translation), 'I Wonder' and 'As Usual' each entering the Top 20. While 1964 finished well with 'Is It True' and 'Christmas Will Be Just Another Lonely Day', only minor hits followed. Though she may have weathered prevailing fads, family commitments caused Brenda to cut back on touring and record only intermittently after 1966's appositely-titled *Bye Bye Blues*.

Lee resurfaced in 1971 with a huge country hit in Kris Kristofferson's 'Nobody Wins' and later recordings that established her as a star of what was then one of the squarest seams of pop. When country gained a younger audience in the mid-80s, respect for its older practitioners found her guesting with Loretta Lynn and Kitty Wells on k.d. lang's *Shadowland*. - produced in 1988 by Owen Bradley (who had also supervised many early Lee records). In Europe, Brenda Lee remained mostly a memory - albeit a pleasing one as shown by Coast To Coast's hit revival of 'Let's Jump The Broomstick', a high UK placing for 1980's *Little Miss Dynamite*

Brenda Lee

greatest hits collection and Mel Smith And Kim Wilde's 'Rockin' Around The Christmas Tree'. Lee is fortunate in having a large rock 'n' roll catalogue destined for immortality in addition to her now-high standing in the country music world. Selected albums: *Grandma, What Great Songs You Sang* (1959), *Brenda Lee* (1960), *This Is. . . Brenda* (1960), *Emotions* (1961), *All The Way* (1961), *Sincerely* (1962), *Brenda, That's All* (1962), *The Show For Christmas Seals* (1962), *All Alone Am I* (1963), *Let Me Sing* (1963), *By Request* (1964), *Merry Christmas From Brenda Lee* (1964), *Top Teen Hits* (1965), *The Versatile Brenda Lee* (1965), *Too Many Rivers* (1965), *Bye Bye Blues* (1966), *Coming On Strong* (1966), with Pete Fountain *For The First Time* (1968), *Johnny One Time* (1969), *LA Sessions* (1977), *Even Better* (1980), *Brenda Lee* (1991). Compilations: *10 Golden Years* (1966), *The Brenda Lee Story* (1974), *Little Miss Dynamite* (1980), *25th Anniversary* (1984), *The Golden Decade* (1985), *The Best Of Brenda Lee* (1986), *Love Songs* (1986).

Lee, Dickie

b. Richard Lipscombe, 21 September 1941, Memphis, Tennessee, USA. Lee was a country singer and composer whose most recorded composition was 'She Thinks I Still Care' made famous by George Jones. At high school in Memphis, he sang rock 'n' roll and recorded the Elvis Presley-influenced 'Dreamy Nights' and 'Good Lovin'' with the Collegiates for the local Sun label. When producer Jack Clement left Sun to set up his own studio in Beaumont, Texas, Lee went with him. There he concentrated on pop material, releasing an unsuccessful revival of the 1953 hit tune 'Oh Mein Papa', before recording his biggest success, the million-selling 'Patches' (1961). Produced by Clement, this lachrymose death-ballad was composed by Barry Mann and Larry Kolber. The follow-up 'I Saw Linda Yesterday', was also a hit but Lee's later teen-ballads made little impact until another song about a deceased girlfriend, 'Laurie (Strange Things Happening)', reached the US Top 20 in 1965. By now, however, Lee was based in Nashville and had established himself as a successful country songwriter following Jones' 1962 hit version of 'She Thinks I Still Care'. Among the numerous artists who later recorded the song were Elvis Presley, Michael Nesmith and Anne Murray. During the late 60s and 70s Lee himself recorded for RCA and had a country number 1 with 'Never Ending Song Of Love' in 1971. In Britain, the song was a Top 10 hit for the New Seekers. Nearly

30 more singles by Lee were US country hits over the next decade. They included 'Rocky' (1975), 'Ashes Of Love' (1976), '9,999,999 Tears' (1976) and 'It's Not Easy' (1978). Among those who successfully recorded Lee's compositions were Don Williams, Glen Campbell and Brenda Lee. Albums: *The Tale Of Patches* (1962), *Dickey Lee Sings Laurie And The Girl From Peyton Place* (1965), *Never Ending Song of Love* (1971), *Crying Over You* (1972), *Sparklin' Brown Eyes* (1973), *Rocky* (1975), *Ashes Of Love* (1976) *Angels, Roses And Rain* (1976), *Baby Bye Bye* (1977), *Dickey Lee* (1980).

Lee, Johnny

b. John Lee Ham, 3 July 1946, Texas City, Texas, USA. Lee was raised on a dairy farm in Alta Loma, Texas, but his main interest was rock 'n' roll and he led a high school band, Johnny Lee And the Roadrunners. He worked through the 60s by playing popular hits in Texas clubs and bars. In 1968, he began a ten-year working relationship with Mickey Gilley, both on the road and at his club Gilley's in Pasadena. He had moderate US country successes in the mid-70s with 'Sometimes', 'Red Sails In The Sunset' and 'Country Party', and appeared in the 1979 television movie, *The Girls In The Office*. Lee was featured in the film, *Urban Cowboy*, which was shot at Gilley's, and, in 1980, he had a US number 1 country single and US Top 5 pop hit with a song from the film, 'Lookin' For Love', which had previously been turned down by 20 different performers. Further number 1 country hits came with 'One In A Million' and 'Bet Your Heart On Me'. Another US country hit, 'Cherokee Fiddle', featured Michael Martin Murphey and Charlie Daniels. Lee married actress Charlene Tilton (who played Lucy in the television series, *Dallas*) on St. Valentine's Day 1982 in a much-publicised wedding at Tony Orlando's house, with Gilley as best man. Lee contributed a track, 'Lucy's Eyes', to an album by the stars of *Dallas*. However, their stormy marriage only lasted three years and Lee remarried in 1987. He had a further number 1 country single with a theme from a short-lived, television soap opera, *The Yellow Rose*, with actress-singer Lane Brody, who was in the country music film, *Tender Mercies*. His final solo number 1 country single was with 'You Could've Heard A Heart Break' in 1984. Lee was in the right place at the right time, but, unfortunately for him, a stringent management contract meant that he had very few financial rewards. Setting up a rival club to Gilley's, called Johnny Lee's, was not a wise career move. He reappeared in 1991 with a country version of Chris De Burgh's 'Lady in Red'.

Albums: *Here's Johnny* (1977), *For Lovers Only* (1975), *Lookin' For Love* (1980), *Bet Your Heart On Me* (1981), *Party Time* (1981), *Sounds Like Love* (1982), *Country Party* (1983), *Hey Bartender* (1983), *Till The Bars Burn Down* (1983), *Workin' For A Livin'* (1984), *Johnny Lee And Willie Nelson* (1984), *Keep Me Hangin' On* (1985), *New Directions* (1989). Further reading: *Looking For Love,* Johnny Lee with Randy Wiles.

Lewis, Bobby

b. 9 May 1946, Hodgenville, Hardin County, Kentucky, USA. Lewis, who comes from the birthplace of Abraham Lincoln, began to play the guitar at the age of 9 and made his television debut at 13. He joined *The Old Kentucky Barn Dance* on WHAS Louisville, where he also appeared on the CBS network, *Saturday Night Country Style,* before joining the WHAS-TV weekly *Hayloft Hoedown.* Being only 5 feet 4 inches tall, he found his Gibson J-200 guitar heavy and cumbersome and took to playing a lute. (He saw what he at first assumed was a strange shaped, but much lighter guitar in a music shop window. He bought it and after stringing it with steel guitar strings, he began to use it in his act. He is, in all probability, the first and maybe the only person in country music to use a lute as his main instrument). Influenced and helped by Ernest Tubb, he moved to Nashville in 1964 and recorded for United Artists. In 1966, he gained his first US country chart entry with 'How Long Has It Been?', which peaked at number 6. Further Top 20 country hits included 'Love Me And Make It All Better', 'From Heaven To Heartache' and in 1970, his version of 'Hello Mary Lou' (a pop hit for Rick Nelson in 1961). He guested on the *Grand Ole Opry*, played venues all across the States and made tours to both Europe and the Far East. After 1973, he recorded for various labels and achieved some minor chart entries, the best being 'Too Many Memories', a number 21 country hit in 1973. His last chart entry came in 1985, with a song called 'Love Is An Overload', after which he seems to have disappeared from the music scene.

Albums: *Little Man With A Big Heart* (1966), *How Long Has It Been* (1967), *A World Of Love* (1967), *An Ordinary Miracle* (1968), *From Heaven To Heartache* (1969), *Things For You And I* (1969), *Too Many Memories* (1973), *Portrait In Love* (1977), *Soul Full Of Music* (1977).

Lewis, Jerry Lee

b. 29 September 1935, Ferriday, Louisiana, USA. The 'Killer' is the personification of 50s rock 'n' roll at its best. He is rowdy, raw, rebellious and uncompromising. The outrageous piano-pounder has a voice that exudes excitement and an aura of arrogance that becomes understandable after witnessing the seething hysteria and mass excitement at his concerts. As a southern boy, Lewis was brought up listening to many musical styles in a home where religion was as important as breathing. In 1950, he attended a fundamentalist bible school in Waxahachie, Texas, but was expelled. The clash between the secular and the religious would govern Lewis's life and art for the remainder of his career. He first recorded on the *Louisiana Hayride* in 1954 and decided that Elvis Presley's label, Sun Records was where he wanted to be. His distinctive version of country star Ray Price's 'Crazy Arms' was his Sun debut, but it was his second single, a revival of Roy Hall's 'Whole Lotta Shakin' Goin' On' in 1957, that shot him to international fame. The record, which was initially banned as obscene, narrowly missed the top of the US chart, went on to hit number 1 on the R&B and country charts and introduced the fair-haired, one-man piano wrecker to a world ready for a good shaking up. He stole the show from many other stars in the film *Jamboree* in which he sang the classic 'Great Balls Of Fire', which became his biggest hit and topped the UK chart and made number 2 in the USA. He kept up the barrage of rowdy and unadulterated rock with the US/UK Top 10 single, 'Breathless' which, like its predecessor, had been written by Otis Blackwell. Problems started for the flamboyant 'god of the glissando' when he arrived in Britain for a tour in 1958, accompanied by his third wife Myra, who was also his 13-year-old second cousin. The UK media stirred up a hornet's nest and the tour had to be cancelled after only three concerts, even though the majority of the audience loved him. The furore followed Lewis home and support for him in his homeland also waned, while he never returned to the Top 20 pop chart in the UK. His last big hit of the 50s was the title song from his film *High School Confidential* which made the UK Top 20 in 1959 and number 21 in the USA. Despite a continued high standard of output, his records either only made the lower chart rungs or missed altogether. When his version of Ray Charles' 'What'd I Say' hit the UK Top 10 in 1960 (US number 30) it looked like a record revival was on the way, but it was not to be. The fickle general public may have disowned the hard-living, hell-raiser, but his hard-core fans remained loyal and his tours were sell outs during the 60s. He joined Smash Records in 1963 and although the material he recorded with the company was generally unimaginative, there were some excellent live recordings, most notably, *The Greatest Live Show On Earth* (1964).

In 1966, Lewis made an unexpected entry into rock music theatre when he was signed to play Iago in Jack Good's *Catch My Soul*, inspired by *Othello*. After a decade playing rock 'n' roll, Lewis decided to concentrate on country material in 1968. He had often featured country songs in his repertoire so his new policy was not an about-face. This changeover was an instant success - country fans welcomed back their prodigal son with open arms. Over the next 13 years Lewis was one of country's top-selling artists and was a main attraction wherever he put on his 'Greatest Show On Earth'. He first appeared at the *Grand Ole Opry* in 1973 playing an unprecedented 50-minute set. He topped the country chart with records like 'There Must Be More To Love Than This' in 1970, 'Would You Take Another Chance On Me?' in 1971 and a revival of 'Chantilly Lace' a year later. The latter also returned him briefly to the transatlantic Top 40. However, he also kept the rock 'n' roll flag flying by playing revival shows around the world and by always including his old 50s hits in his stage shows. In fact, old fans have always been well catered for as numerous compilations of top class out-takes and never previously issued tracks from the 50s have regularly been released over the last 20 years. On the personal front, his life has never been short of tragedies often compounded by his alcohol and drug problems. His family has been equally prone to tragedy. In November 1973, his 19-year-old son, Jerry Lee Jnr. was killed in a road accident following a period of drug abuse and treatment for mental illness. Lewis's own behaviour during the mid-70s was increasingly erratic. He accidentally shot his bass player in the chest - the musician survived and sued. Late in 1976, Lewis was arrested for waving a gun outside Elvis Presley's Gracelands home. Two years later, Lewis signed to Elektra Records for the appropriately titled *Rockin' My Life Away*. Unfortunately, his association with the company ended with much-publicized lawsuits. In 1981, Lewis was hospitalized and allegedly close to death from a haemorrhaged ulcer. He survived that ordeal and was soon back on the road. In 1982, his fourth wife drowned in a swimming pool. The following year, his fifth wife was found dead at his home following a methadone overdose. The deaths brought fresh scandal to Lewis's troubled life. Meanwhile, the IRS were challenging his earnings from the late 70s in another elongated dispute. A sixth marriage followed along with more bleeding ulcers and a period in the Betty Ford Clinic for the treatment of a pain-killer addiction. Remarkably, Lewis's body and spirit have remained intact, despite these harrowing experiences. During his career he has released dozens of albums, the most successful being *The Session* in 1973, his sole US Top 40 album on which many pop names of the period backed him, including Peter Frampton and Rory Gallagher. Lewis was one of the first people inducted into the 'Rock 'n' Roll Hall Of Fame' in 1986. In 1989, a bio-pic of his early career *Great Balls Of Fire*, starring Dennis Quaid, brought him briefly back into the public eye. In 1990, a much awaited UK tour had to be cancelled when Jerry and his sixth wife (who was not even born at the time of his fateful first tour) failed to show.

His cousin Mickey Gilley is an accomplished country artist, while another cousin, Jimmy Lee Swaggart, has emerged as one of America's premier television evangelists. Any understanding of the career of Jerry Lee Lewis is inextricably linked with the parallel rise and fall of Jimmy Lee. They were both excellent piano players but whereas Jerry Lee devoted his energies to the 'devil's music', Jimmy Lee damned rock 'n' roll from the pulpit and played gospel music. Jerry Lee has often described his career as a flight from God, with Jimmy Lee cast in the role of his conscience and indefatigable redeemer. The relationship, however, was more complex than that, and the spirits of these two American institutions were latterly revealed as more complementary than antithetical. When Jimmy Lee was discovered with a prostitute in a motel, the evangelist created a scandal that surpassed even his cousin's series of dramas. Tragedy, scandal and, above all, rock 'n' roll have seldom been so intrinsically a part of one musician's life.

Albums: *Jerry Lee Lewis* (1957), *Jerry Lee's Greatest* (1961), with the Nashville Teens, *Live At The Star Club, Hamburg* (1965), *The Greatest Live Show On Earth* (1965), *The Return Of Rock* (1965), *Whole Lotta Shakin' Goin' On* (1965), *Country Songs For City Folks* (1965), *By Request - More Greatest Live Show On Earth* (1967), *Breathless* (1967), *Soul My Way* (1967), *Got You On My Mind* (1968), *Another Time, Another Place* (1969), *She Still Comes Around* (1969), *I'm On Fire* (1969), with Linda Gail Lewis *Together* (1970), *She Even Woke Me Up To Say*

Jerry Lee Lewis

Goodbye (1970), *A Taste Of Country* (1971), *There Must Be More To Love Than This* (1971), *Rockin' Rhythm And Blues* (1971), *Johnny Cash And Jerry Lee Lewis Sing Hank Williams* (1971), *Monster* (1971), *Would You Take Another Chance On Me* (1972), *The Killer Rocks On* (1972), *Old Tyme Country Music* (1972), with Johnny Cash *Sunday Down South* (1972), *The Session* (1973), *Live At The International, Las Vegas* (1973), *Great Balls of Fire* (1973), *Southern Roots* (1974), *Rockin' Up A Storm* (1974), *Rockin' And Free* (1974), *I'm A Rocker* (1975), *Live At The Star Club, Hamburg* (1980), *When Two Worlds Collide* (1980), *My Fingers Do The Talking* (1983), *I Am What I Am* (1984), *Keep Your Hands Off It* (1987), *Don't Drop It* (1988), *Great Balls Of Fire!* (1989, film soundtrack), *Rocket* (1990). Compilations: *Golden Hits* (1974), *Country Music Hall Of Fame Hits Vol. 1* (1969), *Country Music Hall Of Fame Hits. Vol. 2* (1969), *The Best Of Jerry Lee Lewis* (1970), *Original Golden Hits Vol. 1* (1970), *Original Golden Hits Vol. 2* (1971), *Rockin' With Jerry Lee Lewis* (1972), *Original Golden Hits Vol. 3* (1973), *Fan Club Choice* (1974), *Whole Lotta Shakin' Goin' On* (1974), *Good Rockin' Tonight* (1975), *Jerry Lee Lewis And His Pumping Piano* (1975), *Rare Jerry Lee Lewis Vol. 1* (1975), *Rare Jerry Lee Lewis Vol. 2* (1975), *I'm A Rocker* (1975), *The Jerry Lee Lewis Collection* (1976), *Golden Hits* (1976), *The Original Jerry Lee Lewis* (1976), *Nuggets* (1977), *Nuggets Vol. 2* (1977), *The Essential Jerry Lee Lewis* (1976), *Shakin' Jerry Lee* (1978), *Back To Back* (1978), *Duets* (1979), *Jerry Lee Lewis* (1979), *Good Golly Miss Molly* (1980), *Trio Plus* (1980), *Jerry Lee's Greatest* (1981), *Killer Country* (1981), *Jerry Lee Lewis* (1982), *The Collection* (1986), *The Pumpin' Piano Cat* (1986), *The Great Ball Of Fire* (1986), *The Wild One* (1986), *At The Country Store* (1987), *The Very Best Of Jerry Lee Lewis* (1987), *The Classic Jerry Lee Lewis* (1989), *Killer's Birthday Cake* (1989), *Killer's Rhythm And Blues* (1989), *The EP Collection* (1990), *Pretty Much Country* (1992).

Light Crust Doughboys

A western swing group that originally featured Bob Wills (fiddle), Herman Arnspiger (guitar) and Milton Brown (vocals) who were then performing as the Aladdin Laddies, (sponsored by the Aladdin Mantle Lamp Company) on WBAP Fort Worth, Texas. When Burrus Mill and Elevator Company, the makers of Light Crust flour, sponsored a show on KFJZ in 1931, their general manager Wilbert Lee O'Daniel decided to use them for his show. During their first broadcast for the new sponsors, after originally being named the Fort Worth

Doughboys, the station announcer referred to them as the Light Crust Doughboys. The public wrote in for more although the group did not get paid. O'Daniel actually sacked them two weeks later claiming to dislike 'their hillbilly music'. The station continued to use them without a sponsor and O'Daniel relented, later appearing on the programme himself. Arnspiger had left (being replaced by Sleepy Johnson) and Brown's brother Durwood had joined, when the group made their first recordings for Victor on 9 February 1932. In 1932, Milton Brown left to follow a very successful career with his own swing band, the Musical Brownies until his untimely death in a car crash in 1936. In 1933, Wills, after an acrimonious association with O'Daniel, left to form his famed Texas Playboys. The Doughboys although undergoing many changes of personnel remained with Burrus Mills until 1942 and made many popular recordings. After a short spell as the Coffee Grinders (due to sponsorship by the Duncan Coffee) and without Burrus Mill's sponsorship, they once again became the Light Crust Doughboys. Throughout the 50s and 60s, they worked on radio and television, played live shows and recorded for several labels but never managed to recapture their original popularity.
Selected albums: *The Light Crust Doughboys* (1959), *String Band Swing Volumes 1 & 2* (1981), *We're The Light Crust Doughboys From Burrus Mills*, *The Light Crust Doughboys Original Hit Songs*, *The Light Crust Doughboys 1936-1939*.

Lilly Brothers

Mitchell B. Lilly (b. 15 December 1921) and Charles Everett Lilly (b. 1 July 1923) were both born at Clear Creek, near Beckley, West Virginia, USA. Always known as Everett and Bea, the two brothers began performing in the mid-30s, being especially influenced by Bill Monroe and the Blue Sky Boys. In the late 30s, using mandolin and guitar to back their high harmony vocals, they began their professional career. In 1939, they played the *Old Farm Hour*, at the radio station WCHS Charleston, as the Lonesome Holler Boys. They sometimes played three radio shows a day as well as evening dances and in late 1939 and 1940, they were a very popular act on WJLS Beckley. When America became involved in World War II, Everett joined the armed forces. In 1945, they played with Molly O'Day at Beckley and also at KRLD Dallas and WNOX Knoxville. They next formed the Smiling Mountain Boys, which included Paul Taylor, Burk Barbour (fiddle) and

Lonnie Glosson (harmonica), but surprisingly, they refused the opportunity to record for the King label. Between 1948-50, they were a featured duet with Red Belcher And His Kentucky Ridge Runners and played WWVA Wheeling with him. The brothers split up in 1950 when Everett joined Lester Flatt and Earl Scruggs, playing mandolin and taking tenor vocals. In 1951, he appeared on the classic Flatt and Scruggs Columbia recordings of such numbers as 'Somehow Tonight', ''Tis Sweet To Be Remembered' and 'Over The Hills To The Poorhouse'. (He is the only sideman of their band to actually receive a billing on a record label.) Late in 1952, the brothers reunited and relocated to Boston, where with Don Stover (banjo) and Tex Logan (fiddle), and initially calling themselves the Confederate Mountaineers, they played local radio, television and clubs for several years until for a short time in 1958. Everett again joined Flatt and Scruggs. In 1959, the Lillys and Stover began to play at Boston's Hillbilly Ranch, where they stayed for approximately 16 years. In 1960, they were recorded live at this venue by Robert Tainaka and a tape of their act gained album release in Japan, with the result that the Lilly Brothers became the most popular act of its kind in that country. Everett Lilly retired back to West Virginia, heartbroken, following the death in a car crash of his son, Giles, in 1970. Bea stayed in Boston and Stover went on to form his own band. In 1973, the brothers and Stover were persuaded to re-form and not only recorded an album for the County label but actually made two tours of Japan. Their success was described as 'nothing less than phenomenal' and the live recording of one concert resulted in the release of three albums. Everett later worked for a Japanese company and arranged further tours for American bluegrass groups to tour Japan. They continued to play their mountain, folk and old-time music on occasions at folk festivals and colleges. In 1979, they featured as the subjects of an educational film, True Facts In A Country Song. There were many brother harmony acts in West Virginia but it seems that only the Lillys, along with the Bailes Brothers, really gained a reputation of any size outside their own state.

Albums: with Don Stover Live At Hillbilly Ranch (1960), with Don Stover Folk Songs Of The Southern Mountains (1961), Bluegrass Breakdown (1963), Country Songs Of The Lilly Brothers (1964), with Don Stover Early Recordings (1971), What Will I Leave Behind (1973), Holiday In Japan (Volumes 1-3) (1973).

Lindsey, LaWanda

b. 12 January 1953, Tampa, Florida, USA. LaWanda's family moved to Savannah, Georgia soon after her birth. Lindsey's father was the manager of a local country music radio station and he played on air with his group, the Dixie Showboys. From the age of five, Lindsey was featured with the band. Conway Twitty was impressed by her talent and, through his help, she signed with Chart Records in 1967. Her first singles included 'Beggars Can't Be Choosers', 'Wave Bye Bye To The Man' and two duets with Kenny Vernon, 'Eye To Eye' and 'Pickin' Wild Mountain Berries', which was her biggest-selling record. In 1970, she had a solo hit on the US country charts with 'Partly Bill'. Although she continued to record and has had several minor successes, she has not manage to establish herself as an adult country artist.

Albums: Swingin' And Singin' My Songs (1969), We'll Sing In The Sunshine (1970), with Kenny Vernon Pickin' Wild Mountain Berries (1970), This Is LaWanda Lindsey (1974).

Locklin, Hank

b. Lawrence Hankins Locklin, 15 February 1918, McLellan, Florida, USA. A farm boy, Locklin worked in the cottonfields as a child and on the roads during the Depression of the 30s. He learned to play the guitar at the age of 10 and soon after performed on local radio and at dances. His professional career started in 1938 and after an interruption for military service, he worked various local radio stations, including WALA Mobile and KLEE Houston. In 1949, he joined the Louisiana Hayride on KWKH Shreveport and achieved his first country chart entry with his Four Star recording of his self-penned 'The Same Sweet One'. In 1953, 'Let Me Be The One' became his first country number 1. After moving to RCA in the mid-50s, he had Top 10 US country hits with 'Geisha Girl', his own 'Send Me The Pillow You Dream On', both also making the US pop charts, and 'It's A Little More Like Heaven'. His biggest chart success came in 1960, when his million-selling recording of 'Please Help Me I'm Falling' topped the US country charts for 14 successive weeks and also reached number 8 in the pop charts. It also became one of the first modern country songs to make the British pop charts, peaking at number 9 in a 19-week chart stay. (An answer version by Skeeter Davis called '(I Can't Help You) I'm Falling Too' also became a US country and pop hit the same year.) Locklin

Hank Locklin

became a member of the *Grand Ole Opry* in 1960 and during the next decade, his fine tenor voice and ability to handle country material saw him become one of the most popular country artists. He registered over 20 US chart entries including 'We're Gonna Go Fishing' and a number 8 hit with the now country standard 'The Country Hall Of Fame' in 1967. He hosted his own television series in Houston and Dallas in the 1970s and during his career has toured extensively in the States, Canada and in Europe. He is particularly popular in Ireland, where he has toured many times and, in 1964, recorded an album of Irish songs. Although a popular artist in Nashville, he always resisted settling there. In the early 60s, he returned to his native Florida and built his home, the Singing L, on the actual cottonfield where he had once worked as a boy. After becoming interested in local affairs, his popularity saw him elected mayor of his home town of McLellan. Although Locklin's last chart success was a minor hit in 1971, he remains a firm favourite with the fans and still regularly appears on the *Opry*.

Albums: *Foreign Love* (1958), *Please Help Me I'm Falling* (1960), *Encores* (1961), *Hank Locklin* (1962), *Happy Journey* (1962), *10 Songs* (1962), *This Song Is Just For You* (1962), *A Tribute To Roy Acuff* (1962), *The Ways Of Life* (1963), *Irish Songs, Country Style* (1964), *Sings Hank Williams* (1964), *Born To Ramble* (1965), *My Kind Of Country Music* (1965), *Down Texas Way* (1965), *Sings Eddy Arnold* (1965), *The Girls Get Prettier* (1966), *The Gloryland Way* (1966), *Bummin' Around* (1967), *Send Me The Pillow You Dream On* (1967), *Sings Hank Locklin* (1967), *Nashville Women* (1967), *Wabash Cannonball* (1968), *Country Hall Of Fame* (1968), *Queen Of Hearts* (1968), *My Love Song For You* (1968), *Softly - Hank Locklin* (1969), *Best Of Today's Country Hits* (1969), *Lookin' Back* (1969), *That's How Much I Love You* (1969), *Candy Kisses* (1970), *Bless Her Heart - I Love Her* (1970), *Hank Locklin & Danny Davis & The Nashville Brass* (1970), *The First Fifteen Years* (1971), *The Mayor Of McLellan, Florida* (1972), *Hank Locklin* (1975), *The Golden Hits* (1977), *There Never Was A Time* (1977), with various artists *Carol Channing & Her Country Friends* (1977), *All Kinds Of Everything* (1979), *Please Help Me I'm Falling* (1986). Compilation: *20 Of The Best* (1982).

Loudermilk, John D.

b. 31 March 1934, Durham, North Carolina, USA. Loudermilk's first musical experience was banging a drum for the Salvation Army and he played various instruments as a child and appeared regularly on the radio from the age of 11. In 1956, George Hamilton IV recorded his song, 'A Rose And A Baby Ruth', which went from the local to the national charts, reaching number 6. A few months later Eddie Cochran made his debut in the US Top 20 with 'Sittin' In The Balcony', another Loudermilk song which he had recorded himself under the pseudonym, Johnny D.

When Loudermilk moved to Nashville, a stream of hits followed, the UK chart successes being 'Waterloo' (Stonewall Jackson, 1959); 'Angela Jones' (Michael Cox, 1960); 'Tobacco Road' (Nashville Teens, 1964); 'Google Eye' (which was a catfish, Nashville Teens, 1964); 'This Little Bird' (Marianne Faithfull, 1965, and subsequently parodied by the Barron Knights); 'Then You Can Tell Me Goodbye' (Casinos, 1967, and a US country number 1 for Eddy Arnold); 'It's My Time' (the Everly Brothers, 1968); 'Indian Reservation (The Lament Of The Cherokee Reservation Indian)' (Don Fardon, 1970 and a US number 1 for the Raiders, 1971) and 'Sunglasses' (a revival of a Skeeter Davis record by Tracey Ullman, 1984). His controversial 'death' song, 'Ebony Eyes', was the b-side of the Everly Brothers' 1961 number 1, 'Walk Right Back'. Other successful b-sides include 'Weep No More My Baby' (Brenda Lee's 'Sweet Nuthins'); 'Stayin' In' (Bobby Vee's 'More Than I Can Say'); 'Heaven Fell Last Night' (the Browns' 'The Three Bells') and 'In A Matter Of Moments' (Louise Cordet's 'I'm Just A Baby'). Near misses include 'All Of This For Sally' (Mark Dinning), 'The Guitar Player (Him And Her)' for Jimmy Justice and 'To Hell With Love' for Adam Faith. He arranged an old song, 'Abilene', for George Hamilton IV, and it made the US charts in 1963 and became a country standard. His other country music successes include 'Talk Back Trembling Lips' (Ernest Ashworth and Johnny Tillotson); 'Bad News' (Johnny Cash and Boxcar Willie); 'Break My Mind' (George Hamilton IV, Gram Parsons and the Hillsiders); 'You're Ruinin' My Life' (Hank Williams Jnr.) and 'Half-Breed' (Marvin Rainwater). He wrote clever novelty songs for Bob Luman ('The Great Snowman' and 'The File') and for Sue Thompson ('Sad Movies (Make Me Cry)', 'Norman', 'James (Hold The Ladder Steady)' and 'Paper Tiger', all US Top 30 hits).

Loudermilk had his own hit with 'The Language Of Love', which made number 13 in the UK in 1962. He made several albums of his own material and they have been collected onto two Bear Family compilations, *Blue Train* and *It's My Time*,

John D. Loudermilk with disc jockey Mike Read

which contain two previously unreleased tracks in 'The Little Wind Up Doll' and 'Giving You All My Love'. He has often worked in the UK and performs his songs in a similar manner to Burl Ives. He produced Pete Sayers' best album, *Bogalusa Gumbo*, in 1979 but an album which he recorded at the same sessions has not been released.

Albums: *The Language Of Love* (1962), *Twelve Sides Of Loudermilk* (1962), *John D. Loudermilk Sings A Bizarre Collection Of Unusual Songs* (1965), *Suburban Attitudes In Country Verse* (1967), *Country Love Songs* (1968), *The Open Mind Of John D. Loudermilk* (1969), *Elloree* (70s), *Just Passing Through* (1977). Compilations: *Blue Train* (1989), *It's My Time* (1989).

Louvin Brothers

Brothers Lonnie Ira Loudermilk (b. 21 April 1924) and Charlie Elzer Loudermilk (b. 7 July 1927, both Rainesville, Alabama, USA). They were raised on a forty-acre farm in Henegar, Alabama, but only half of it could be cultivated. Despite their poverty, their parents sang gospel songs and encouraged their sons' musical talents. Ira took up the mandolin and Charlie the guitar and they created perfect harmonies for country and gospel music,

inspired, in particular, by the Blue Sky Boys. In 1943, after winning a talent contest in Chattanooga, they began broadcasting regularly, leading to three shows a day for WMPS in Memphis. They recorded for Decca, MGM and Capitol but they found it hard to make ends meet and worked night shifts in the Post Office. Some radio broadcasts to promote a songbook, *Songs That Tell A Story*, have been released and show the Louvin Brothers at their best, with no additional instruments. Their career was also interrupted by Charlie's military service in Korea. (Their 'Weapon Of Prayer' is an emotional plea for peace.) They performed as the Louvin Brothers because the family name was considered too long for stage work, although their cousin, John D. Loudermilk, was to have no such qualms. Capitol Records re-signed the brothers as gospel artists but a tobacco company sponsoring a portion of the *Grand Ole Opry* told them to sing secular songs as 'you can't sell tobacco with gospel music'. They crossed over to the country market with their own composition 'When I Stop Dreaming', which is now a standard. Their secular US country hits included 'I Don't Believe You've Met My Baby' (their only number 1), 'Hoping That You're Hoping', 'You're

Running Wild' and 'My Baby's Gone', but Charlie says, 'I don't think we ever did a show without some gospel music. Our mother would have thrashed us if we hadn't done that!'

By the late 50s, their sound was old-fashioned and their songs too melodramatic for the rock 'n' roll era. The Everly Brothers, who acknowledged their debt to the Louvins, may also have contributed unwittingly to their downfall. Charlie says, 'Ken Nelson told Ira, in 1958, that the mandolin was hindering the sales of our music, so my brother lost total interest in the mandolin and never picked another note on it on a record. He had put 25 years of his life into mastering that instrument, and it messed his head to hear a good friend whose opinion he respected say, 'You're the problem, you've got to throw that thing away.' Ira's drink problem worsened, their own relationship deteriorated and their last success together was, ironically, 'Must You Throw Dirt In My Face?'. Charlie broke up the partnership on 18 August 1963. '*He* had said a lot of times he was going to quit, but it was the first time *I* had ever said it.' Charlie went on to have solo hits with 'I Don't Love You Anymore' and 'See The Big Man Cry, Mama'. Ira started his solo career with 'Yodel Sweet Molly' but he was shot and badly injured by his wife, Faye, whom he then divorced. He then married Florence, who sang on his shows as Anne Young, but soon afterwards they both perished in a car crash in Jefferson City, Missouri, USA on 20 June 1965. Ira and Bill Monroe had pledged that whoever lived the longest would sing at the other's funeral, and Monroe sang 'Where No One Stands Alone'.

Gram Parsons introduced their songs to a new audience, recording 'The Christian Life' with the Byrds, and 'Cash On The Barrelhead' and 'The Angels Rejoiced In Heaven Last Night' with Emmylou Harris. After Parsons' death, Harris continued recording their songs: 'If I Could Only Win Your Love', 'When I Stop Dreaming', 'You're Learning' and, with Don Everly, 'Everytime You Leave'. Charlie Louvin had a country hit with 'You're My Wife, She's My Woman' and made two successful albums with Melba Montgomery. A single, 'Love Don't Care' with Emmylou Harris, made the US country charts.

Albums: by the Louvin Brothers *Tragic Songs Of Life* (1956), *Nearer My God To Thee* (1957), *The Louvin Brothers* (1957, MGM recordings), *Ira And Charlie* (1958), *The Family Who Prays* (1958), *Country Love Ballads* (1959), *Satan Is Real* (1960), *Those Louvin Brothers Sing The Songs Of The Delmores* (1960), *My Baby's Gone* (1960), *Encore* (1961), *Country Christmas With The Louvin Brothers* (1961), *Weapon Of Prayer* (1962), *Keep Your Eyes On Jesus* (1963), *The Louvin Brothers Sing And Play Their Current Hits* (1964), *Thank God For My Christian Home* (1965), *Two Different Worlds* (1966), *The Louvin Brothers Sing The Great Roy Acuff Songs* (1967), *Country Heart And Soul* (1968), *The Great Gospel Singing Of The Louvin Brothers* (1973), *Songs That Tell A Story* (1981), *Radio Favourites* (1987), *Live At The New River Ranch* (1989), *Running Wild* (1992); by Charlie Louvin *Charlie Louvin* (1965), *Less And Less/I Don't Love You Anymore* (1965), *The Many Moods Of Charlie Louvin* (1966), *Lonesome Is Me* (1966), *I'll Remember Always* (1967, a tribute to Ira Louvin), *I Forgot To Cry* (1967), *Will You Visit Me On Sundays?* (1968), *Here's A Toast To Mama* (1969), *Hey Daddy* (1969), *The Kind Of Man I Am* (1969), *Ten Times Charlie* (1970), with Melba Montgomery *Something To Brag About* (1971), with Montgomery *Baby, You've Got What It Takes* (1971), *It Almost Felt Like Love* (1974), *Country Souvenirs* (1981), *Charlie Louvin* (1982), *Jim And Jesse And Charlie Louvin* (1982), *Charlie Louvin* (1989), *Then, Now And Forever* (1990), *50 Years Of Making Music* (1991); by Ira Louvin *The Unforgettable Ira Louvin* (1965).

Lovett, Lyle

b. 1 November 1957, Houston, Texas, USA. Singer/songwriter Lovett grew up 25 miles north of Houston in the rural Klein community (an area largely populated by farmers of German extraction) which was named after his grandfather, Adam Klein. During his teenage years, as Houston's borders expanded, Lovett was exposed to more urban influences, and attended Texas A&M University where he studied journalism and then German. During this period (late 70s), he began writing songs, his early heroes included Guy Clark (who later wrote a dedication on the sleeve of Lovett's first album), Jerry Jeff Walker and Townes Van Zandt. Having visited Europe (to improve his German) in the late 70s, he met a local country musician named Buffalo Wayne (who apparently took his name from his favourite western heroes), and remained in touch after returning to Texas - when Wayne was organizing an event in Luxembourg in 1983, he booked Lovett, and also on the bill was an American band from Phoenix whose members included Matt Rollings (keyboards) and Ray Herndon (guitar) who were later involved with Lovett's albums.

Lyle Lovett

Lovett worked the same Texas music circuit as Nanci Griffith, singing on two of her early albums, *Once In A Very Blue Moon* (1984, which included one of his songs, 'If I Were The Woman You Wanted') and *Last Of The True Believers* (1985), on which he is pictured on the front of the sleeve. When Guy Clark heard a demo tape by Lovett in 1984, he passed it onto Tony Brown of MCA Records, and by 1986, Lovett had signed to MCA/Curb. His self-titled debut album was idiosyncratic, to say the least, including both the song covered by Griffith and 'Closing Time', which was covered by Lacy J. Dalton, as well as a fine song he co-wrote with fellow singer/songwriter Robert Earl Keen Jnr., 'This Old Porch'. However, his acceptance was slow in US country music circles, and Lovett first received substantial critical acclaim when the album was eventually released in Europe. 1987 brought a follow-up, *Pontiac*, after Lovett had successfully toured Europe backed only by 'cellist John Hagen. The album made it clear that Lovett was rather more than a folk or country artist, with such songs as the surreal 'If I Had A Boat' and 'She's Hot To Go', while guests on the album included Emmylou Harris. By this time, Lovett was talking about both recording and touring with what he called His Large Band, with several saxophone players and a female backing singer, Francine Reed, as well as a regular rhythm section, and his third album, released in 1989, was indeed titled *Lyle And His Large Band*. Including an insidiously straight cover of the Tammy Wynette standard 'Stand By Your Man', and a version of the R&B oldie, 'The Glory Of Love', this again delighted critics by its very humour and eclecticism, but further confused record buyers, especially in the USA, who were unsure whether this was a country record or jazz or something quite different.

At this point Lovett moved away from Nashville, where he was regarded as too weird, and as a result, his fourth album, produced by Los Angeles heavyweight George Massenburg, was not released until early 1992. Its title *Joshua Judges Ruth* (three consecutive books in the Old Testament, but meaning something very difference if read as a phrase) was symptomatic of Lovett's intelligence, but perhaps equally so of his idiosyncratic approach. As usual, critics loved it, although it included hardly any traces of country music, and seemed to portray him as a Tom Waits-like figure - ultra sophisticated, but somewhat off the wall. In 1992, Lovett was chosen as the opening act for many of the dates on the first world tour during the 90s by Dire Straits. This exposed him to a huge international audience, but seems to have done little to extend his cult following.

Albums: *Lyle Lovett* (1986), *Pontiac* (1987), *Lyle Lovett And His Large Band* (1989), *Joshua Judges Ruth* (1992).

Lulu Belle And Scotty

Lulu Belle (b. Myrtle Eleanor Cooper, 24 December 1913, Boone, North Carolina, USA) and Scott Wiseman (b. 8 November 1909, Spruce Pine, near Ingalls, North Carolina, USA, d. 31 January 1981). Lulu Belle learned to play the guitar and sing mountain songs as a child but after the family relocated to Evanston, Illinois in 1929, she first worked as a clerk. In 1932, she successfully auditioned at WLS television company Chicago and was given a spot on the *National Barn Dance* programme, where as Lulu Belle, she initially worked with Red Foley. Wiseman grew up on the family farm and developed his first musical skills by learning to play a home-made banjo. He became interested in a musical career after seeing Bradley Kincaid perform and by working in his school holidays, he bought himself a guitar. In 1927, he made his radio debut, singing and playing in a manner that showed a distinct Kincaid influence, on WRVA Richmond. Initially doubtful that he could make his living by music, he decided to study for a teaching career. From 1929-32, he attended the Teachers College at Fairmont, West Virginia and obtained a degree. During these years, he wrote songs and, appearing as Skyland Scotty, was regularly featured on WMMN Fairmont. In 1933, he joined the *National Barn Dance*, where he began to work with Lulu Belle. He made his first recordings (solo) in December 1933, when playing his guitar for one of the few times on record, he cut four songs for RCA-Victor. One of the songs was 'Home Coming Time In Happy Valley', which soon became a popular song for the duo. They were married on 13 December 1934, by which time they had become a very popular act. On stage, Scotty wore plain, casual attire and played banjo, while Lulu Belle dressed in old gingham styled dresses, pantalettes and usually wore pigtails. Their simple harmony singing, interspersed with comedy and novelty songs, endeared them to the network audience and gained them the nickname of the Sweethearts of Country Music.

In 1936, Lulu Belle was voted the most popular woman on American radio and between 1938 and 1944, their national popularity saw them appear in seven films including *Shine On Harvest Moon*. They remained stars of the WLS *National Barn Dance* from 1933-58 but also had a spell on the *Boone County Jamboree* (later the *Midwestern Hayride*) on WLW Cincinnati as well as playing on the *Grand Ole Opry* and the *Ozark Jubilee*. They were also regulars on WNNBQ-TV Chicago from 1949-57. Over the years, they recorded for various labels including Conqueror, Vocalion, and Bluebird. They popularized many songs including 'Mountain Dew' (written by Scotty with Bascombe Lunsford), 'Remember Me', 'My Heart Cries For You', 'Tying The Leaves' and 'Does Your Spearmint Lose Its Flavour On The Bed Post Overnight?'. (A UK pop hit for Lonnie Donegan with 'Chewing Gum' substituted for 'Spearmint' in 1959.) Perhaps their best-known song is one that originated at a time when Scotty was hospitalized with appendix trouble. During a visit Lulu Belle said 'Have I told you lately that I love you' and it inspired him to write a song. Gene Autry recorded it in November 1945 and in 1946, it was a Top 5 US country hit for Autry, Tex Ritter, Red Foley and Foy Willing. It went on to become a country standard and has been recorded over the years by many artists, including Bing Crosby with the Andrews Sisters, Jim Reeves, Van Morrison and Elvis Presley. In 1958, after Scotty had obtained an MA Teaching degree at Northwestern University at Evanston, they semi-retired from the entertainment business. They moved back to Spruce Pine, where Scotty taught people with speech problems at the college. They also bought a cattle farm but still made a few concert appearances and recorded for the Starday label in the 60s. At one time, they presented their *Breakfast In The Blue Ridge* radio show, supposedly live from their home but, in reality, taped in Chicago. They appeared at the 1975 *Fan Fair* in Nashville and on the *Opry* but generally, during the 70s, Scotty continued to teach and they restricted themselves to local appearances. In 1971, his many songs saw him elected to the Nashville Songwriters International Hall of Fame. Lulu Belle became interested in politics and in 1974, she was elected to the North Carolina House of Representatives. Scotty died following a heart attack, when driving home from Gainsville, Florida. Lulu Belle remarried in 1983 (Ernest Stamey, an old family friend) and in 1986, she recorded a solo album for the Old Homestead label.

Albums: *Lulu Belle & Scotty* (1963), *The Sweethearts Of Country Music* (1963), *Down Memory Lane* (1964), *Lulu Belle & Scotty (Sweethearts Still)* (1965), *Just A Closer Walk With Thee* (60s), *Have I Told You Lately That I Love You* (1974), *Early And Great Volume 1* (1985), *Country & Western Memories, Volume 3 Lulu Belle & Scotty* (c.1986), *Tender Memories Recalled Volumes 1 & 2* (1989), *Tender Memories Recalled Volumes 2 & 3* (1991). Solo album: Lulu Belle *Snickers & Tender Memories* (1986).

Luman, Bob

b. Robert Glynn Luman, 15 April 1937, Blackjack, near Nacogdoches, Texas, USA, d. 27 December 1978. Luman's father, Joe, a school caretaker, bus driver and gifted musician, taught his son country music, but Luman's first love was baseball, which he played on a semi-professional basis until 1959. He was influenced by seeing Elvis Presley in concert, later saying, 'That was the last time I tried to sing like Webb Pierce or Lefty Frizzell'. His band then won a talent contest sponsored by the Texas Future Farmers of America and judged by Johnny Horton. In 1955, Luman recorded the original version of 'Red Cadillac And A Black Moustache' and also a scorching 'Red Hot' for Imperial Records. He joined *Louisiana Hayride* as replacement for Johnny Cash and came into contact with guitarist James Burton and bass player James Kirkland, whom he recruited for his band. Unfortunately for Luman, Ricky Nelson was so impressed by Luman's musicians that he made them a better offer. After a brief, unsuccessful period with Capitol Records, Luman moved to Warner Brothers, who released 'Class Of '59' and 'Dreamy Doll', both featuring Roy Buchanan. He had a transatlantic hit with Boudleaux Bryant's satire on 'death discs' like 'El Paso' and 'One Of Us (Will Weep Tonight)' in 'Let's Think About Living'. 'If we keep losing our singers like this,' he concluded, 'I'll be the only one you can buy.' He failed to repeat his success, despite such clever novelties as 'The Great Snowman' and 'Private Eye'. After spending part of the early 60s in the army due to the draft laws, he became a member of the *Grand Ole Opry* in 1964 and made many country records for the Hickory label, including John D. Loudermilk's witty 'The File'. He became a big-selling US country artist via his Epic recordings, 'When You Say Love', 'Lonely Women Make Good Lovers' and 'Neither One Of Us Wants To Be The First To Say Goodbye', subsequently a pop hit for Gladys Knight And The Pips. In 1976, he underwent major surgery and then, prompted and produced by Johnny Cash, he recorded *Alive And Well*. Despite the title, he collapsed and died shortly after an appearance at

Judy Lynn

the *Grand Ole Opry*. In recent years, Luman's work has been reassessed with retrospectives and, like Johnny Burnette, it is his early, rockabilly work that most interests collectors. To quote one of his country hits, 'Good Things Stem From Rock 'n' Roll.'

Albums: *Let's Think About Living* (1960), *Livin' Lovin' Sounds* (1965), *Ain't Got Time* (1968), *Come On Home And Sing The Blues To Daddy* (1969), *Getting Back To Norman* (1970), *Is It Any Wonder That I Love You?* (1971), *A Chain Don't Talk To Me* (1971), *When You Say Love* (1972), *Lonely Women Make Good Lovers* (1972), *Neither One Of Us* (1973), *Red Cadillac And A Black Moustache* (1974), *Still Loving You* (1974), *A Satisfied Mind* (1976), *Alive And Well* (1977), *Bob Luman* (1978), *The Pay Phone* (1978), *Try Me* (1988). Compilations: *The Rocker* (1984), *More Of That Rocker* (1984), *Still Rockin'* (1984), *Carnival Rock* (1988), *Wild-Eyed Woman* (1988).

Lynn, Judy

b. Judy Voiten, 12 April 1936, Boise, Idaho, USA. The daughter of bandleader Joe Voiten (he once worked with Bing Crosby) she grew up to be a teenage rodeo rider. She also became a yodelling champion and in 1955, she represented her State in the Miss America contest. Later the same year, when the touring *Grand Ole Opry* show played Boise, she deputised for indisposed Jean Shepard, which resulted in her joining the show. In 1957, she co-hosted with Ernest Tubb the first national television showing of the *Opry*. This led to appearances on many major television shows and after leaving the touring *Opry* show, in 1960, she formed her own band and started her own television series. 'Footsteps Of A Fool' became her first and only US country Top 10 hit, when it charted in 1962. Noted for her beauty and elegance, her colourful western-style Nudie costumes and with a repertoire that ran from big ballads to yodels, she became very popular. She was one of the first country singers to appear in Las Vegas and was actually a featured artist around the Nevada casino circuit for over twenty years, being a frequent performer at such major venues as the Golden Nugget Club and Caesar's Palace. She recorded for several labels including ABC, United Artists, Musicor and Columbia Records and her last country chart hit was 'Padre' in 1975. She retired from the music industry in 1980 to become a church minister. (She is not related to country star Loretta Lynn.)

Albums: with the Sunshine Boys *Sings At The Golden Nugget* (1962), *Here Is Our Girl Judy Lynn* (1963), *The Judy Lynn Show* (1964), *The Judy Lynn Show Act 2* (1965), *The Judy Lynn Show Plays Again* (1966), *Number One Most Promising New Country And Western Girl Singer* (1964), *Honey Stuff* (1966), *Judy Lynn In Las Vegas* (1967), *Golden Nuggets* (1967), *Sings At Caesar's Palace* (1969), *Parts Of Love* (1971), *Naturally* (1973).

Lynn, Loretta

b. Loretta Webb, 14 April 1935, Butcher Hollow, Kentucky, USA. Lynn is a coal miner's daughter, being the second of the eight children of Ted and Clara Webb. She is one-quarter Cherokee and her name came from her mother's fondness for film star, Loretta Young. She was raised in a small shack during the Depression and was attracted to country music as an 11-year-old, when the family acquired a radio and she heard the singing of Molly O'Day. Her autobiography tells of her makeshift wardrobe and how, at the age of 13, she married a serviceman, Oliver Vanetta Lynn, known to his friends as Doolittle or Mooney, which was short for Moonshine. He took her to Custer, Washington, and she had four children and several miscarriages by the time she was 18. They had six children and Lynn was a grandmother at the age of 29. 'Mooney', recognizing her talent, encouraged her to sing in local clubs and her band, the Trailblazers, included her brother, Jay Lee Webb, on guitar. Her talent was recognized by Don Grashey of Zero Records, who took her to Los Angeles in February 1960 where she recorded four of her own songs. Zero had no money for promotion so she and Mooney promoted 'I'm A Honky Tonk Girl' themselves, the song taking its style from Kitty Wells's 'It Wasn't God Who Made Honky Tonk Angels'. Mooney said that 'they drove 80,000 miles to sell 50,000 copies' but it reached number 14 in the US country charts and enabled her to appear regularly on *Grand Ole Opry*. Many female singers were jealous of her success, but Patsy Cline sprang to her defence and they became close friends. (Lynn released a tribute album to her in 1977.)

When they moved to Nashville, she became a regular on a weekly television show with the Wilburn Brothers, who also managed her. Kitty Wells and Patsy Cline were two of her major influences and she was pleased to be assigned to their producer, Owen Bradley, by USA Decca Records. 'Success', her second country hit, peaked at number 6 in 1962, and she had further hits with 'Before I'm Over You' and 'Blue Kentucky Girl'.

Loretta Lynn

She then developed a hard-hitting persona as the wife who stood no nonsense from her rivals ('You Ain't Woman Enough', 'Fist City') or her husband (her first country number 1 'Don't Come Home A Drinkin' (With Lovin' On Your Mind)' from 1966, 'Your Squaw Is On The Warpath'). Her best-known record, the autobiographical 'Coal Miner's Daughter', was a US country number 1 in 1970. Shel Silverstein, ironically a *Playboy* cartoonist, wrote 'One's On The Way' in which she was harassed by her children and an insensitive husband. She answered Tammy Wynette's 'Stand By Your Man' in 1975 with the double standards of 'The Pill', which was banned by several USA radio stations. By way of contrast, she subsequently had a country hit with a song called 'Pregnant Again'.

Although her first duets were with Ernest Tubb, she formed a regular team with Conway Twitty and the combination of the two distinctive voices worked well, especially in 'After The Fire Is Gone', 'As Soon As I Hang Up The Phone', 'The Letter' and the amusingly-titled 'You're The Reason Our Kids Are Ugly'. When she fell out with the Wilburn Brothers, she formed United Talent Inc. with Twitty. As the brothers still owned her publishing, she was reluctant to record her own material, although subsequently she was elected to the Nashville Songwriters International Hall of Fame. In 1972, Lynn was the first woman to become the Country Music Association's Entertainer of the Year and she also shared the Vocal Duo of the Year award with Twitty. In 1973, she made the cover of *Newsweek* and was the first woman in country music to become a millionaire. However, she met with little UK success and some of her UK releases sold less than 200 copies. Her best-selling autobiography, *Coal Miner's Daughter*, showed how the human spirit could combat poverty and sickness, but also illustrated that the problems of endless touring could be as traumatic. Lynn's musicians call her 'Mom' and share their problems with her. Sissy Spacek won an Oscar for her portrayal of Lynn, which included reproducing her singing, in the 1980 film *Coal Miner's Daughter*, and the film also featured Tommy Lee Jones as her husband and Levon Helm of the Band as her father. Her country music success includes 16 number 1 singles, 60 other hits, 15 number 1 albums and numerous awards, but she has never sought pop success. She owns a huge ranch, 70 miles outside of Nashville, which has the whole town of Hurricane Mills in its grounds. Another part of the property, the Loretta Lynn Dude Ranch, is a tourist attraction with camping facilities. Despite her prolific output in the 60s and 70s, she has not recorded much recently but she is considering an album of traditional country music with her sisters, Crystal Gayle and Peggy Sue Wright. To quote Roy Acuff, 'A song delivered from Loretta is from the deepest part of her heart.'

Albums: *Loretta Lynn Sings* (1963), *Before I'm Over You* (1964), *Songs From My Heart* (1965), *Blue Kentucky Girl* (1965), *Hymns* (1965), *I Like 'Em Country* (1966), *Country Christmas* (1966), *You Ain't Woman Enough* (1966), *Don't Come Home A-Drinkin'* (1967), *Singin' With Feelin'* (1967), *Who Says God Is Dead* (1968), *Fist City* (1968), *Your Squaw Is On The Warpath* (1969), *Woman Of The World/To Make A Man* (1969), *Here's Loretta Singing 'Wings Upon Your Horns'* (1969), *Loretta Writes 'Em And Sings 'Em* (1970), *Coal Miner's Daughter* (1971), *I Want To Be Free* (1971), *You're Lookin' At Country* (1971), *One's On The Way* (1971), *God Bless America Again* (1972), *Alone With You* (1972), *Here I Am Again* (1972), *Entertainer Of The Year* (1973), *Love Is The Foundation* (1973), *They Don't Make 'Em Like My Daddy* (1974), *Back To The Country* (1975), *Home* (1975), *When The Tingle Becomes A Chill* (1976), *Somebody Somewhere* (1976), *On The Road With Loretta And The Coal Miners* (1976), *I Remember Patsy* (1977), *Out Of My Head And Back In My Bed* (1978), *We've Come A Long Way Baby* (1979), *Loretta* (1980), *Lookin' Good* (1980), *Making Love From Memory* (1982), *I Lie* (1982), *Lyin', Cheatin', Woman Chasin', Honky Tonkin', Whiskey Drinkin' You* (1983), *Just A Woman* (1985). Compilations: *Great Country Hits* (1985), *Golden Greats* (1986), *The Very Best Of Loretta Lynn* (1988), *20 Greatest Hits* (1989). With Ernest Tubb: *Mr. And Mrs. Used To Be* (1965), *Singin' Again* (1967), *If We Put Our Heads Together* (1969). Albums with Conway Twitty: *We Only Make Believe* (1971), *Lead Me On* (1971), *Louisiana Woman, Mississippi Man* (1973), *Country Partners* (1974), *Feelins'* (1975), *United Talent* (1976), *Dynamic Duo* (1977), *Country Partners* (1974), *Honky Tonk Heroes* (1978), *Diamond Duets* (1979), *Two's A Party* (1981), *Making Believe* (1988).

Further reading: *Coal Miner's Daughter*, Loretta Lynn with George Vecsey.

M

McAuliffe, Leon

b. William Leon McAuliffe, 1 March 1917, Houston, Texas, USA, d. 20 August 1988, Tulsa, Oklahoma, USA. McAuliffe learned both guitar and steel guitar while at school, and when aged 16 joined the Light Crust Doughboys. In March 1935, he joined Bob Wills' Texas Playboys as steel guitarist, remaining with him until December 1942, when military service intervened. Wills' entreaties of 'Take It Away Leon' became an expected shout, both on live and recorded performances. He formed his own band, the Western Swing Band, in 1946, but after becoming the owner of the Cimarron Ballroom, Tulsa, in the early 50s, changed the band's name to the Cimarron Boys. He recorded for Majestic, Columbia, Dot and Starday finding success with such numbers as 'Steel Guitar Rag' and 'Panhandle Rag', and played regularly on KVOO and KRMG, Tulsa. In the late 50s and for most of the 60s, McAuliffe and his band toured extensively in the USA, appeared on many television shows and even visited Europe. He formed Cimarron Records in 1961, and the next year had US country chart success with his version of 'Faded Love', before moving to Capitol in 1964. He retired in the late 60s, but in 1973, he played on the famous last recordings made by Wills and soon afterwards was persuaded to front a line-up of ex-Texas Playboys. This band played successfully during the 70s and early 80s, and recorded for Capitol and Delta. He died in August 1988, and is remembered as one of the all-time great steel guitarists.
Albums: *Take Off* (1958), *The Swinging Western Strings Of Leon McAuliffe* (1960), *Cozy Inn* (1961), *Mister Western Swing* (1962), *The Swinging West With Leon McAuliffe & His Cimarron Boys* (1964), *The Dancin'est Band Around* (1964), *Everybody Dance, Everybody Swing* (1964), *The Swinging Western Strings Of Leon McAuliffe* (1960), *Golden Country Hits* (1966), *Take It Away, Leon* (1973), *For The Last Time* (1975), *Steel Guitar Rag* (1982), *Leon McAuliffe & His Western Swing Band* (1984).

McCall, C.W.

b. William Fries, 15 November 1928, Audubon, Iowa, USA. Fries loved country music as a child, but had a successful career in advertising in Omaha, culminating in a 1973 campaign for the Metz bread company which involved a truckdriver called C.W. McCall. 'It was just a name that came out of thin air,' says Fries. He had done the voice-over himself and developed the character on record. McCall had a US country hit with 'The Old Home Filler-Up And Keep On A-Truckin' Cafe', and then made the pop chart with a tale of brake failure on 'Wolf Creek Pass'. President Nixon had imposed a 55-mph speed limit during an oil shortage; CB radio, which had been confined to farmers and radio hams, was in demand so that motorists could warn each other of radar traps. McCall told the story of 'Convoy' in CB jargon and the accompanying press release enabled DJs to explain the song to their listeners. 'Convoy' took the hammer down and soared to number 1 on both the US pop and country charts, also making number 2 in the UK. A parody 'Convoy G.B.' by Laurie Lingo And The Dipsticks (in actuality, BBC Radio 1 disc jockeys Dave Lee Travis and Paul Burnett) made number 4. McCall's record was the inspiration for a film of the same name, directed by Sam Peckinpah and starring Kris Kristofferson. The soundtrack featured 'Convoy' and previously released material by other artists. McCall went to number 2 on the US country charts with the narration, 'Roses For Mama', and scored a minor US pop hit with 'There Won't Be No Country Music (There Won't Be No Rock'n'Roll)', but he soon returned to advertising. In 1982, he moved to Ouray, Colorado and was elected mayor in 1986.
Albums: *Wolf Creek Pass* (1975), *Black Bear Road* (1975), *Wilderness* (1976), *Rubber Duck* (1976), *Roses For Mama* (1977), *C.W. McCall And Co.* (1978).

McCarters

Jennifer and twins Lisa and Teresa were born in the late 60s, in Dolly Parton's home town of Sevierville, Sevier County, Tennessee, USA. Their father, a factory foreman, played banjo in local bands, and their mother was a gospel singer. When Jennifer was 11 years old and her siblings were nine, they were performing clog dancing routines they had learned from watching the groups on the *Grand Ole Opry*. Three years later, realizing that they would not make a living by that occupation, Jennifer learned to play the guitar and sing, and soon the twins were adding harmony vocals. Around 1984, they made their debut on a Knoxville television station and gained further experience working with *Opry* stars Stu Philips and Archie Campbell, as well as busking on the streets of their home town. In 1986, after some persistent and persuasive telephoning by Jennifer, the girls managed to get an audition with Kyle Lehning, Randy Travis' record producer, which led to them signing for Warner Brothers. They made their US country chart debut in January 1988, with Top 10 hits named 'Timeless And True Love' and 'The Gift', the title track of their first album. Soon after, they became part of the Randy Travis show and toured extensively in the USA and Europe. They have also appeared on many top US network television shows. Their close-harmony singing is similar to the 'Trio' recordings of Dolly Parton, Linda Ronstadt and Emmylou Harris. Jennifer also showed a talent for songwriting and with Carl Jackson co-wrote their beautifully descriptive ballad 'Letter From Home'. By the time their second album appeared in 1990, they had become known as Jennifer McCarter And The McCarters. Albums: *The Gift* (1988), *Better Be Home Soon* (1990).

McClain, Charly

b. Charlotte Denise McClain, 26 March 1956, Jackson, Tennessee, USA. McClain began her musical career when only nine years old with her brother in a band called Charlotte And The Volunteers. For six years they worked locally and also had television appearances. She then started modelling swimsuits, changed her name to Charly and was signed to Epic in 1976. She had US country hits with 'Lay Down', 'Make The World Go Away', 'Surround Me With Love' and a duet with Johnny Rodriguez, 'I Hate The Way I Love It'. McClain had her first US country number 1 with the soap opera saga of 'Who's Cheatin' Who'. This was followed by 'Sleepin' With The Radio On' and two duets with Mickey Gilley, 'Paradise Tonight' (a number 1) and 'Candy Man'. In 1983, she married Wayne Massey, a star of the television soap *One Life To Live*, and they scored with the duets 'With Just One Look In Your Eyes' and 'You Are My Music, You Are My Song'. Massey encouraged her to record 'Radio Heart', also a US country number 1, and he became her record producer when she switched from Epic to Mercury Records. McClain has appeared in the television series, *Hart To Hart* and *Fantasy Island*, and has been featured in numerous commercials. Albums: *Here's Charly McClain* (1977), *Let Me Be Your Baby* (1978), *Alone Too Long* (1979), *Women Get Lonely* (1980), *Who's Cheatin' Who* (1981), *Encore* (1981), *Surround Me With Love* (1981), *Too Good To Hurry* (1982), *Paradise* (1983), *The Woman In Me* (1983), with Mickey Gilley *It Takes Believers* (1984), *Charly* (1984), *Radio Heart* (1985), *Still I Stay* (1987), *Charly McClain* (1988).

McClinton, O.B.

b. Obie Burnett McClinton, 25 April 1940, Senatobia, Mississippi, USA, d. 23 September 1987. The son of a Baptist preacher, McClinton was dissuaded from listening to R&B, but took solace in country music. Having worked for a time as a disc jockey at radio-station WDIA in Memphis, he forged a career as a songwriter, penning country-soul ballads for Otis Redding ('Keep Your Arms Around Me'), before finding the ideal foil in James Carr. Two of McClinton's compositions, 'You've Got My Mind Messed Up' (1966) and 'A Man Needs A Woman' (1968), stand among this singer's finest work. McClinton then became a staff writer at the Stax label and, in January 1971, began recording as a C&W artist on the company's Enterprise subsidiary. His four albums there offered varied material, including versions of Wilson Pickett's 'Don't Let The Green Grass Fool You' (1972) - his most successful country chart single - and Merle Haggard's 'Okie From Muskogee'. McClinton briefly moved to Mercury in 1976, where he had a hit with 'Black Speck', before moving to Epic, where he scored a half-dozen minor C&W hits. One of the few successful black country singers, McClinton died of abdominal cancer in September 1987. Albums: *O.B. Clinton Country* (1972), *Obie From Senatobie* (1973), *O.B. McClinton Live At Randy's Rodeo* (1973), *Chocolate Cowboy* (1981).

McCoy, Charlie

b. 28 March 1941, Oak Hill, West Virginia, USA. When McCoy was eight years old, he ordered a harmonica for 50 cents and a box-top, but he was more interested in the guitar. He played in rock 'n' roll bands in Miami, where Mel Tillis heard him and suggested that he came to Nashville to work as a singer. This did not work out, but he played drums for US hitmakers Johnny Ferguson and Stonewall Jackson. In 1961, McCoy recorded as a singer for US Cadence Records and entered the charts with 'Cherry Berry Wine'. He then formed a rock 'n' roll band, Charlie McCoy And The Escorts, which played in Nashville clubs for several years. McCoy played harmonica on Ann-Margret's 'I Just Don't Understand' and Roy Orbison's 'Candy Man', and the success of the two records led to offers of session work. McCoy became the top harmonica player in Nashville playing up to

400 sessions a year. He worked with Bob Dylan, playing harmonica on 'Obviously Five Believers', trumpet on 'Rainy Day Women, Nos. 12 And 35', and bass on several other tracks. The success of Dylan and other rock musicians in Nashville prompted McCoy and other sessionmen to form Area Code 615. McCoy had a US chart hit in 1972 with a revival of 'Today I Started Loving You Again', but, considering his love of blues harmonica player Little Walter, his records are unadventurous and middle-of-the-road. Nevertheless, he often made the US country charts with instrumental interpretations of over-worked country songs. McCoy joined Barefoot Jerry and was featured on the group's 1974 US country hit, 'Boogie Woogie'. He now limits his session appearances, largely because he is musical director of the television series, *Hee-Haw*. McCoy frequently visits the UK and has played the Wembley Country Festival with other Nashville musicians.

Albums: *The Real McCoy* (1969), *Charlie McCoy* (1972), *Goodtime Charlie* (1973), *Fastest Harp In The South* (1973), *The Nashville Hit Man* (1974), *Christmas Album* (1974), *Harpin' The Blues* (1975), *Charlie My Boy* (1975), *Play It Again, Charlie* (1976), *Country Cookin'* (1977), *Appalachian Fever* (1979), *One For The Road* (1986), *Charlie McCoy's 13th* (1988), *Beam Me Up, Charlie* (1989).

McDaniel, Mel

b. 6 September 1942, Checotah, Oklahoma, USA. McDaniel began working in bands around Tulsa - first on trumpet, then on guitar - and J.J. Cale wrote and produced his first single, 'Lazy Me'. He moved to Nashville in 1969, and, after two years of banging on doors, his brother found him steady work at a club in Anchorage, Alaska. In the mid-70s, he began recording demos for a Nashville publisher and his singing talents were then recognised. In 1976 he entered the US country charts with 'Have A Dream On Me' and he had a considerable success with 'Gentle To Your Senses'. A record about a synthetic lover, 'Plastic Girl', was banned by radio stations. He recorded many songs by Bob McDill including 'Louisiana Saturday Night', 'Right In The Palm Of Your Hand', 'I Call It Love' and his US country number 1, 'Baby's Got Her Blue Jeans On'. He wrote Conway Twitty's tribute to the *Grand Ole Opry*, 'The Grandest Lady Of Them All', while his hippie anthem 'Roll Your Own', has been recorded by Hoyt Axton, Arlo Guthrie and Commander Cody.

Albums: *Gentle To Your Senses* (1977), *Mello* (1978), *The Farm* (1978), *Countrified* (1981), *Take Me To The Country* (1982), *Naturally Country* (1983), *Mel McDaniel & Oklahoma Wind* (1984), *Let It Roll* (1985), *Stand Up* (1985), *Just Can't Sit Down Music* (1986), *Now You're Talkin'* (1988), *Rockabilly Boy* (1989), *Country Pride* (1991).

McDowell, Ronnie

b. Fountain Head, Tennessee, USA. McDowell initially built his career on his ability to imitate the voice of Elvis Presley, a talent he was called upon often to utilize in films and television programmes. He also recorded his own music, however, and, by the 80s, was a major star in his own right in the country field. McDowell began trying out his Presley imitation while in the US Navy in 1968. Upon his discharge, he worked as a sign painter in Nashville while trying to sell his songs. Among the country artists who recorded his compositions were Roy Drusky and Billy Walker. He recorded for minor record labels such as Chart and Scorpion during the mid-70s, with no success, and released a cover version of Roy Orbison's 'Only The Lonely' in 1976, which also did not chart. McDowell's first single to chart was 'The King Is Gone', his tribute to his departed hero, which he wrote (with Lee Morgan) and recorded on Scorpion two months after Presley's death. It reached number 13 on both the country and pop charts. His real breakthrough came later that year, with 'I Love You, I Love You, I Love You', which reached number 5 on the country chart (it was also his last single to cross over to pop, although it placed near the bottom of that chart). McDowell continued to place singles on the country charts through 1980, having switched to Epic Records in 1979. That same year he supplied the voice of Presley for the soundtrack of the film *Elvis*.

At the start of 1981, he began a long string of country Top 10 singles with 'Wandering Eyes', which was followed by the number 1 'Older Women' and 10 other Top 10 country hits. By the middle of the 80s, he was able to release music with little remaining of the Elvis sound, and could finally claim to have succeeded on the merits of his own voice. Later, he returned to his early vocation as the voice of Elvis in the short-lived 1989 television series titled *Elvis*. McDowell switched labels to MCA Records' Curb division in 1986. One of his biggest hits of the late 80s was a remake of the old Conway Twitty hit 'It's Only Make Believe', with the originator supplying a guest vocal.

Albums: *The King Is Gone* (1977), *Live At The Fox* (1978), *Tribute To The King* (1979), *I Love You, I Love You, I Love You* (1978), *Elvis* (1979, film soundtrack), *Rockin' You Easy, Lovin' You Slow* (1979), *Love So Many Ways* (1980), *Going, Going...Gone* (1980), *Good Time Lovin' Man* (1981), *Greatest Hits* (1982), *Love To Burn* (1982), *Personally* (1985), *Country Boy's Heart* (1983), *Willing* (1984), *In A New York Minute* (1985), *All Tied Up In Love* (1986), *Older Women And Other Greatest Hits* (1987), *Best Of Ronnie McDowell* (1990), *Unchained Melody* (1991).

McEntire, Pake

b. Dale Stanley McEntire, 1952, Chockie, Oklahoma, USA. Brother of Reba McEntire, Pake sang at rodeos with her and their other sister Susie as the Singing McEntires in the early 70s. He has competed professionally in roping events for many years. McEntire had his first US country success with 'Every Night' in 1986; 'Savin' My Love For You' went to number 3. Reba sang harmony on his 1987 entry, 'Heart Vs. Heart'.
Albums: *Too Old To Grow Up Now* (1986), *My Whole World* (1988).

McEntire, Reba

b. Reba Nell McEntire, 28 March 1955, Chockie, Oklahoma, USA. One of four children, McEntire recorded 'The Ballad Of John McEntire', which was about her grandfather. The family owned a 7,000 acre ranch and participated in rodeos; hence McEntire's song 'Daddy'. She sang with her sister Susie and brother Pake McEntire as the Singing McEntires and, in 1972, they recorded for the small Boss label. In 1974, she was asked to sing 'The Star-Spangled Banner' at the National Rodeo Finals in Oklahoma City. Honky-tonk singer Red Steagall heard her, which led to a recording contract with Mercury. Her first single, 'I Don't Want To Be A One Night Stand', made the US country charts in 1976, the year in which she married rodeo rider Charlie Battles. It was followed by several minor successes, including a revival of 'Sweet Dreams' and two duets with Jacky Ward ('Three Sheets To The Wind', 'That Makes Two Of Us'). She made the US country Top 10 with '(You Lift Me) Up To Heaven', the Top 5 with 'Today All Over Again' and, in 1982, number 1 with 'Can't Even Get The Blues'. She often recorded country waltzes and had another chart-topper in 1983 with 'You're The First Time I've Thought About Leaving'. She then left Mercury for MCA, although the label was to release an

album of outtakes, *Reba Nell McEntire*, in 1986. She continued her country hits with 'Just A Little Love', 'He Broke Your Memory Last Night', 'Have I Got A New Deal For You', and the number 1 hits, 'How Blue' and 'Somebody Should Leave'. Her best-known single and title track of a best-selling album was 'Whoever's In New England'. McEntire's own battles with Battles ended in their divorce in 1987, and she married her bandleader, Narvel Blackstock in 1989. Several of her successes, although they were not written for her ('I Know How He Feels' and 'New Fool At An Old Game'), have overtones from her own life. She has won numerous country music awards, but her 1988 album, *Reba*, although very successful, irritated traditionalists who questioned her revival of a pop hit, 'Sunday Kind Of Love', and her version of Otis Redding's 'Respect'. McEntire was adamant: 'I can sing any kind of song, but whatever I sing, it'll come out country.' She appeared, killing graboids with an elephant gun, in the well-reviewed horror film *Tremors*. In March 1991, tragedy struck when seven of the nine members of McEntire's band died in a plane crash shortly after taking off from San Diego.
The following year, McEntire herself was involved in a forced landing at Nashville airport, evoking memories of the earlier tragedy. She dedicated her next album, *For My Broken Heart*, to her friends and colleagues. It proved to be one of her most successful projects, and the title track was a major hit single.
Albums: *Reba McEntire* (1977), *Out Of A Dream* (1979), *Feel The Fire* (1980), *Heart To Heart* (1981), *Unlimited* (1982), *Behind The Scenes* (1983), *Just A Little Love* (1984), *Have I Got A Deal For You* (1985), *My Kind Of Country* (1986), *Whoever's In New England* (1986), *Reba Nell McEntire* (1986), *What Am I Gonna Do About You* (1986), *The Last One To Know* (1987), *So So So Long* (1988), *Merry Christmas To You* (1988), *Reba* (1988), *Sweet Sixteen* (1989), *Live* (1989), *Rumour Has It* (1990), *For My Broken Heart* (1991), *It's Your Call* (1992).

McGee, Sam And Kirk

Samuel Fleming McGee (b. 1 May 1894, d. 21 August 1975) and David Kirkland McGee (b. 4 November 1899, d. 24 October 1983) were both born and raised on the family farm near Franklin, Williamson County, Tennessee, USA. Their father was a noted fiddle player, and the brothers learned to play the banjo as children but changed their style in their teens. Sam worked as a blacksmith, but

Reba McEntire

around 1910, he became interested in the guitar and learned to play from black street musicians. During his career he became so proficient that he has been a major influence on many musicians and was most likely the first white musician to use the guitar as a solo instrument, instead of a mere accompaniment for vocals or fiddle music. Kirk concentrated on the banjo, although he later played guitar, mandolin and fiddle, and also developed into a fine vocalist. In 1925, Sam first met and played with Uncle Dave Macon and, the following year, made his first appearance with Macon on the *Grand Ole Opry*. Soon after, they were joined by Kirk and both played with Macon, as well as performing as a duo. In 1927, together with fiddler Mazy Todd, they went to New York with Macon and recorded as Uncle Dave Macon And His Fruit Jar Drinkers. They recorded with Macon until the mid-30s, as well as recording as a duo, including their noted 1934 recording of 'Brown's Ferry Blues'. They were among the first members of the *Opry* ever to record, which later led to Sam stating, 'They recorded us because we were outstanding in the field and that's where they found us - outstanding in the field'. In 1930, they also teamed up with Fiddlin' Arthur Smith and both toured and played the *Opry* with him as the Dixieliners. They worked with Smith until 1938, when he left for Hollywood. Strangely, though recognized as one of the *Opry*'s most influential bands, they never actually recorded with Smith until years later in the 60s, when they were reunited by Mike Seeger. During the 40s, they toured with Bill Monroe, appeared occasionally with Macon and still played the *Opry*. It seems likely that Sam was the first member to play an electric guitar on the *Opry*. It was only the use of an amplified Spanish guitar and an early electric lap steel, but the action soon incurred the wrath of George D. Hay, who quickly told Sam to 'Keep it down to earth'. In the 50s and 60s, the folk revival found them touring and still on the *Opry*. In later years, Kirk went into the property business and Sam continued to work the farm until he died in a tractor accident in 1975, at the age of 82. After Sam's death, Kirk played the *Opry* as a member of the *Opry*'s own Fruit Jar Drinkers String Band, frequently playing fiddle rather than banjo. He died after a heart attack at his home in Franklin in 1983, having appeared on the *Opry* only a few days previously. It is interesting to note that, in 1924, Sam had learned to play the guitar-banjo, and his recordings using it, made with Macon in 1926 and 1927, are probably the only known examples ever made by a white musician with this difficult instrument. The brothers contribution to the history of country music, with their gospel, blues instrumentals and old folk ballads, is considerable and, although they made many recordings during their long careers, few are now available.

Albums: one side each act *Opry Old Timers Sam & Kirk McGee And The Crook Brothers* (1962), *Fiddlin' Arthur Smith & His Dixieliners* (1962), *Rare Old Fiddle Tunes (Fiddlin' Arthur Smith & His Dixieliners)* (1962), *Old Timers Of The Grand Ole Opry* (1964), with Arthur Smith *Milk 'Em In The Evening Blues* (1965), *Opry Old Time Songs And Guitar Tunes, Volume One* (1985). By Sam McGee: *The Grandad Of The Country Guitar Pickers* (1963). Kirk McGee: *Mister Kirk* (1980). They also appear on several album releases of Uncle Dave Macon material and sundry individual tracks appear on various artists albums of old time music.

McGhee, Wes

b. 26 October, 1948, Lutterworth, Leicestershire, England. One of the very few British performers whose Texas-inspired country music is regarded as creditable in the USA. McGhee has suffered more than most from the British refusal to accept homegrown country music as genuine. He has worked with noted Texan artists including Ponty Bone and Freddie Kre (for both of whom he produced albums in the 80s), Butch Hancock, Jimmie Dale Gilmore and Kimmie Rhodes. As a promising teenage guitarist, McGhee was involved with the celebrated Reg Calvert, (who worked as patron for a number of emergent musicians in the 60s from a large country house where several groups, none of which became famous, lived communally). During the late 60s, McGhee worked in Hamburg as one of many musicians following the Merseybeat trail - his first wife was German. During the early 70s, he fronted an early pub/rock combo known as McGhee, but management problems, among other things, conspired to sabotage the recording contract which he was promised. By the mid-70s, McGhee had become friendly with Arthur Anderson, a musician he had met on the gig circuit, and they joined forces to record an album of McGhee's original material, with Anderson engineering and producing. The result, *Long Nights And Banjo Music*, was released on their own label, Terrapin Records, in 1978, with McGhee as lead vocalist and lead guitarist, plus assistance from, among others, Bob Loveday (violin, later with the Penguin Cafe Orchestra and the post Boomtown

Wes McGhee

Rats Bob Geldof band) and Rick Lloyd (later a member of the chart-topping Flying Pickets). The achievement of completing the album was of far greater significance than much of the self-conscious country/rock it contained, and McGhee and Anderson scraped together enough finance - by renting out their homemade studio and by McGhee writing and recording radio commercials - to release a second album in 1980, *Airmail*, which gave notice that he was a considerable songwriting talent.

Before *Landing Lights* was released in 1983, Anderson had left the partnership, although he worked on part of the album, some of which was recorded in Texas with local musicians like Kre (ex-Jerry Jeff Walker), Bone and Lloyd Maines (ex-Joe Ely), Gilmore and Rhodes. Probably McGhee's best original studio album to date in terms of original songs, it was released on his own TRP label, as was 1985's *Thanks For The Chicken*, a live double album made in Texas with a mixed British/Texan band including Kre, Bone, Rhodes and Texan fiddler Alvin Crow, plus McGhee's long-time backing vocalist, Ian Bartholomew (primarily an actor), Patti Vetta, and Irish multi-instrumentalist Dermot O'Conner. As well as numerous fine McGhee originals, the album included covers of Richard Thompson's 'Tear Stained Letter', Joe 'King' Carrasco's 'Mexcal Road' and the sublime 'Contrabandistas', written by record producer and Rhodes's husband, Joe Gracey, and his partner, Bobby Earl Smith. The album even included a song sung in Mexican - McGhee had developed a cult following in Mexico owing to his semi-successful attempts to cater for the Hispanic audience.

Although he remained virtually unknown in Britain, his talent was recognized by pioneering American music publisher Bug Music, which signed him during the second half of the 80s, as his fifth album *Zacatecas*, was released in 1986. A much more measured collection, it was his first studio album made without cost-cutting, and included a remarkable epic titled 'Monterey', plus a cover of the 60s hit by Troy Shondell, 'This Time'. As usual, there was little commercial interest in Britain, although McGhee began working frequently in Texas, both on his own account and as lead guitarist with Kimmie Rhodes, who had duetted with him on a track from *Thanks For The Chicken*, and with whom he played on several of her albums. Finally, in 1991, a UK label, Minidoka, was interested enough in McGhee to release a compilation of remixed tracks from his

previous studio albums titled *Neon And Dust*, although at the time of writing, this again has not achieved the success its quality no doubt deserves.
Albums: *Long Nights And Banjo Music* (1978), *Airmail* (1980), *Landing Lights* (1983), *Thanks For The Chicken* (1985) *Zacatecas* (1986), *Neon And Dust* (1991).

McKinlay, Bob

b. 13 May 1942, Ashton-in-Makerfield, near Wigan, Lancashire, England. Like many others, McKinlay learned guitar from Bert Weedon's *Play In A Day*. He was a member of the northwest beat group, The Long And The Short, which made the UK Top 30 in 1964 with 'The Letter', featuring session musician Jimmy Page on lead guitar. They appeared in the film, *Gonks Go Beat*, and then McKinlay was offered a place in the Mojos. He soon, however, returned to Wigan and a job in a printing works. He became a mature student and gained a degree in sociology and a teaching diploma. He visited Nashville in 1977 and, on his return, formed a country group. He decided to become a full-time professional and toured the UK country clubs with American singer-songwriter, Steve Young. McKinley is enormously popular around country clubs and he manages to support a band. His songs include his personal credo, 'English Born - Dixie Fried', and this Wigan peer has made several cassettes to sell at his shows. He has emulated Bert Weedon by issuing his own guitar tutor.
Albums: *English Born - Dixie Fried* (1979), *Country Good And Rollin'* (1982), *My Songbird* (1984), *Country Tapestry* (1985), *Roots And Offshoots* (1987), *Once More* (1989), *Singer-Songwriter* (1990).

Mack, Warner

b. Warner McPherson, 2 April 1938, Nashville, Tennessee, USA. Warner Mack is one of the few country musicians to be born in Nashville, although at the age of seven he moved to Jackson, Tennessee, and at nine, to Vicksburg, Mississippi. Mack, whose father was a minister, tells his story in the song 'Tennessee Born, Mississippi Raised'. He played at various school functions and started performing on the radio show *Louisiana Hayride*. In 1957, he wrote and recorded 'Is It Wrong (For Loving You)?', which was later a number 1 country hit for Sonny James. In 1964 Mack had success with a Jim Glaser song, 'Sitting In An All Night Cafe', but while it was climbing the country charts, he suffered serious injuries in a car accident. Mack, whose stage name came about through a mistake on a record label, had a US country number 1 with his own composition, 'The Bridge Washed Out', and had further success with 'Talking To The Walls' and 'How Long Will It Take?'. He was the first country artist to record a national commercial for Coca-Cola. His last US country chart entry was 'These Crazy Thoughts' in 1977. Mack has completed successful tours of UK country clubs, always closing with an emotional version of 'He Touched Me'.

Albums: *Warner Mack's Golden Country Hits, Vol. 1* (1961), *Warner Mack's Golden Country Hits, Vol. 2* (1962), *Great Country And Western Hits* (1964), *The Bridge Washed Out* (1965), *The Country Touch* (1966), *Everybody's Country Favourites* (1966), *Drifting Apart* (1967), *The Many Moods Of Warner Mack* (1968), *The Country Beat Of Warner Mack* (1969), with his sister Dean *Songs We Sang In Church And Home* (1969), *I'll Still Be Missing You* (1969), *Love Hungry* (1970), *You Make Me Feel Like A Man* (1971), *Great Country* (1973), *The Best Of The Best Of Warner Mack* (1978), *The Prince Of Country Blues* (1983), *At Your Service* (1984), *Warner Mack - The England Tour* (1984).

Macon, Uncle Dave

b. David Harrison Macon, 7 October 1870, Smart Station, Warren County, Tennessee, USA, d. 22 March 1952. Macon's family moved to Nashville when his father, a Confederate captain in the Civil War, bought the city's Broadway Hotel. Macon learned to play the banjo and acquired songs from the vaudeville artists who stayed at the hotel. He married in 1889 and started the Macon Midway Mule And Wagon Transportation Company, which was later described in the song 'From Here To Heaven'. His mule-drawn wagons carried goods between Murfreesboro and Woodbury. Macon performed at venues along the way. However, the business collapsed following the advent of a motorized competitor in 1920. Although he had worked as a jovial entertainer for many years, he never thought of turning professional until a pompous farmer asked him to play at a wedding. Macon demanded $15 in the sure knowledge he would be turned down: it was accepted and became his first professional booking. At the age of 52, when Uncle Dave Macon launched his professional career, his songs and humour proved so popular that he was soon known all over the south. He became the first star of the *Grand Ole Opry* when it was launched in 1925 with material covering folk tunes, vaudeville, blues, country and gospel music. In 1927, Macon formed the Fruit Jar Drinkers with Sam And Kirk McGee and Mazy Todd - their tracks among the finest produced by old-time string bands. In 1931 he was the main attraction of the *Opry*'s first touring show, working with his son, Dorris, and the Delmore Brothers. Between 1924 and 1938, he recorded over 170 songs, which makes him among the most recorded of the early-day country stars. Despite the age of the recordings, his whooping and hollering brings them to life, and notable successes included 'Arkansas Traveller' and 'Soldier's Joy'. 'Hill Billie Blues' is possibly the first recorded song ever to use hillbilly in its title. His 1927 recording of 'Sail Away Ladies' was converted into the 50s skiffle hit, 'Don't You Rock Me, Daddy-O'. Macon appeared with Roy Acuff in the 1939 film, *Grand Ole Opry*, which showed that, even at an advanced age, he was a fine showman. Macon stopped touring in 1950 and he made his last appearance at the *Opry* on 1 March 1952. After his death at Murfreesboro in 1952, a monument was erected near Woodbury by his fellow *Opry* associates and he was elected to the Country Music Hall Of Fame in 1966.

Albums: *Uncle Dave Macon - First Featured Star Of The Grand Ole Opry* (1966), *Uncle Dave Macon - Early Recordings, 1925-1935* (1971), *Go Long Mule* (1972), *The Gayest Old Dude In Town* (1974), *Dixie Dewdrop* (1975), *Uncle Dave Macon At Home - His Last Recordings* (1976), *Keep My Skillet Good And Greasy* (1979), *Laugh Your Blues Away* (1979).

Maddox, Rose

b. Roselea Arbana Maddox, 15 December 1926, near Boaz, Alabama, USA. In the Depression days of 1933, Charlie and Lula Madox took their five young children (Cal, Henry, Fred, Don and Rose), whose ages ranged from 7 to 16, illegally boarded freight trains and headed for California, eventually settling near Bakersfield. They followed the various harvests, working as 'fruit tramps', and were soon joined by eldest son, Cliff. All were musical, and to help their income, they began to play for local dances with the 12-year-old Rose providing the vocals, even in noisy honky tonks. They first appeared on radio on KTRB Modesto in 1937, but by 1941, when they disbanded owing to Cal, Fred, and Don being drafted, they had become a popular act, due initially to appearances on the powerful KFBK Sacramento station. In 1946, they reformed as the Maddox Brothers And Rose and became popular over a wide area. Their bright and garish stage costumes earned them the title: 'the most colourful hillbilly band in America'. Cliff died in

1948, and his place was taken by Henry. By the early 50s, with an act that included comedy as well as songs, they were regulars on the *Louisiana Hayride*, played concerts and also appeared on the *Grand Ole Opry*. In 1947, they recorded for Four Star before moving to Columbia in 1951. Their successes included Rose's stirring recordings of 'The Philadelphia Lawyer' and 'The Tramp On The Street'. Rose also recorded with her sister-in-law, Loretta, as Rosie And Rita. By the mid-50s, Rose was beginning to look to a solo career. In 1957, she signed for Capitol and about that time the Maddox Brothers nominally disbanded. Rose soon established herself as a solo singer and, during the 60s, had several chart hits including 'Gambler's Love', 'Conscience I'm Guilty' and her biggest hit 'Sing A Little Song Of Heartache'. She also had four very successful duet recordings with Buck Owens, namely 'Mental Cruelty', 'Loose Talk', 'We're The Talk Of The Town' and 'Sweethearts In Heaven'. In the late 60s, she suffered the first of several heart attacks which have affected her career, but by 1969 she had recovered and made the first of her visits to Britain. She continued to work when health permitted throughout the 70s, but had no chart success. After leaving Capitol in 1967, she recorded for several labels including Starday, Decca and King. In the 80s, she recorded two albums for Arhoolie Records and her famous Varrick album *Queen Of The West*, on which she was helped by Merle Haggard and the Strangers and Emmylou Harris. Her son, Donnie, died in 1982 and she sang gospel songs with the Vern Williams band at his funeral. She frequently appeared with Williams, a popular west coast bluegrass musician who also provided the backing on some of her 80s recordings. In 1987, Maddox suffered a further major heart attack which left her in a critical condition for some time. Her situation was aggravated by the fact that she had no health insurance but benefit concerts were held to raise the funds. Rose Maddox possessed a powerful, emotive voice and was gifted with the ability to sing music of all types. Her recordings range from early hillbilly songs and gospel tunes through to rockabilly numbers that have endeared her to followers of that genre. Later she worked with long-time friend and rockabilly artist Glen Glenn, recording the album *Rockabilly Reunion* with him at the Camden Workers Club, London in March 1987. Many experts rate the album *Rose Maddox Sings Bluegrass* as her finest recorded work. On it she is backed by great bluegrass musicians such as Don Reno, Red Smiley and Bill Monroe.

Albums: *Precious Memories* (1958), *Glorybound Train* (1960), *The One Rose* (1960), *A Big Bouquet Of Roses* (1961), with Bill Monroe *Rose Maddox Sings Bluegrass* (1962), *Rosie* (1970), *Alone With You* (1963), *Reckless Love & Bold Adventure* (1977), *This Is Rose Maddox* (1980), *A Beautiful Bouquet* (1983), with Merle Haggard & The Strangers, Emmylou Harris *Queen Of The West* (1983), with Glen Glenn *Live In London - Rockabilly Reunion* (1988). As The Maddox Brothers & Rose: *A Collection Of Standard Sacred Country Songs* (1956), *I'll Write Your Name In The Sand* (1961), *The Maddox Brothers & Rose* (1961), *The Maddox Brothers & Rose* (1962), *The Maddox Brothers & Rose 1946-1951 Vols. 1 & 2* (1964), *The Maddox Brothers & Rose Go Honky Tonkin'* (1965), *Family Folks* (1982), *Rockin' Rollin'* (1982), *The Maddox Brothers & Rose On The Air Vol. 1* (1985), *The Maddox Brothers & Rose On The Air Vol. 2* (1982), *The Maddox Brothers & Rose* (1986), *Rose Of The West Coast Country* (1991).

Mainer, J.E.

b. Joseph Emmett Mainer, 20 July 1898, in a one room log house in Buncombe County, North Carolina, USA, d. 12 June 1971. Mainer played banjo at the age of nine but later became an accomplished fiddle player. He worked in textile mills from the age of 12 but began playing locally with other musicians in the 20s. He eventually formed Mainer's Mountaineers which consisted of his banjo playing brother Wade Mainer and guitarists Daddy John Love and Claude 'Zeke' Morris. In 1932, Mainer played regularly on radio in Gastonia but in 1934, sponsored by Crazy Water Crystals, and performing as the Crazy Mountaineers, they became regulars on WBT Charlotte. They later moved to WPTF Raleigh but also played in New Orleans and on the Mexican border stations. Over the years there were various changes of personnel including Steve Ledford, Snuffy Jenkins and Morris's brothers Wiley and George. They first recorded as J.E. Mainer's Mountaineers for Bluebird in 1935 and are still remembered for their recordings of 'Johnsons's Old Grey Mule', 'Take Me In The Lifeboat' and 'Maple On The Hill'. By the end of the 40s, Mainer's RCA recordings exceeded 200 but he later recorded for King and during the 60s, made recordings for the folk music archives of the Library of Congress and a whole series of albums for Rural Rhythm. Mainer's Mountaineers were one of the most important of all the early day string bands and greatly influenced later bands and musicians. Mainer remained active and regularly appeared at bluegrass and folk festivals until his death from a heart attack.

Albums: *Good Ole Mountain Music* (1960), *Variety Album* (1961), *Legendary Family From The Blue Ridge Mountains* (1963), *J.E. Mainer's Crazy Mountaineers.Volumes 1 & 2* (1963), *The Legendary J.E. Mainer Volumes 1-20* (1966-71), *70th Happy Birthday* (1968), *J.E. Mainer* (1968), *At Home With Family And Friends Volumes 1 & 2* (c.1981).

Mainer, Wade

b. 21 April 1907, near Weaverville, North Carolina, USA. The younger brother of J.E. Mainer and a fine singer and talented banjoist who developed a clever two-fingered style that made his playing readily identifiable. In 1937, after initially playing with his brother's Mountaineers, he formed his own Sons of The Mountaineers, which at times included Wade Morris, Jay Hugh Hall, Steve Ledford and Clyde Moody. He recorded for Bluebird until 1941, being especially remembered for his 1939 recording of 'Sparkling Blue Eyes'. He later made some recordings for King before moving in the 50s to work for Chevrolet in Flint, Michigan. After retirement from that in the 70s, he returned to recording with the Old Homestead label.

Albums: *Soulful Sacred Songs* (1961), *Early Radio* (c.1971), *Wade Mainer & The Mainer Mountaineers* (1971), *Sacred Songs Of Mother And Home* (1972), *Rock Of My Soul* (1972), *Mountain Sacred Songs* (1972), *From The Maple On The Hill* (c.1973), *Wade Mainer & The Sons Of The Mountaineers* (1979), *Old Time Songs* (1982), *Early And Great Volumes 1 & 2* (1983), *Wade & Julia Mainer* (1985).

Mandrell, Barbara

b. 25 December 1948, Houston, Texas, USA, but raised in Oceanside, near Los Angeles, California. Mandrell comes from a musical family: her father, Irby, sang and played guitar and her mother, Mary, played piano and taught music. At the age of 12, Mandrell demonstrated the steel guitar at a national convention and then worked in Las Vegas with Joe Maphis and Tex Ritter. By her teens, she also played saxophone, guitar, banjo and bass. Her parents formed the Mandrells with herself and two boys, one of whom, drummer Ken Dudney, became her husband in 1967. Their extensive touring schedule included forces bases in Vietnam. Mandrell first recorded in 1966 for the small Mosrite label, and her sobbing 'Queen For A Day', with Glen Campbell on guitar, was reissued with a revised accompaniment in 1984. Mandrell signed with Columbia in 1969, and, for a time, she concentrated on country versions of soul hits - 'I've Been Lovin' You Too Long', 'Treat Him Right', 'Show Me' and 'Do Right Woman - Do Right Man'. Despite her glossy Las Vegas look, she joined the *Grand Ole Opry* in 1972, switched to ABC-Dot in 1975 and had her first Top 5 country single with 'Standing Room Only'. In 1977 she had her first US country number 1 with 'Sleepin' Single In A Double Bed', which was written by Kye Fleming and Dennis Morgan, who also wrote further number 1 hits, including 'Years' and 'I Was Country When Country Wasn't Cool', which was released during *Urban Cowboy*'s popularity and featured George Jones. Her version of the soul hit, '(If Loving You Is Wrong) I Don't Want To Be Right', was another country number 1 and also a US pop hit, leading her to name her band, the Do-Rites. Mandrell also covered Poacher's 'Darlin'' for the US country market. Her television series, *Barbara Mandrell And The Mandrell Sisters*, ran from 1980-82 and was screened in the UK. There was good-humoured interplay between Mandrell and her sisters, Irene (b. Ellen Irlene Mandrell, 29 January 1956, California, USA) and Louise Mandrell, and the diminutive Barbara had the same vivacious appeal as Dolly Parton. She had further US country number 1 singles, 'Til You're Gone' and 'One Of A Kind Pair Of Fools', and also fared well with 'To Me', a duet with Lee Greenwood. In 1984 she and her two children were badly injured when her car was hit head-on. She was unable to work for a year, although she had another child, and lost much credibility when she sued, on her insurer's advice, the late driver's family for $10 million. Her Capitol recordings have not seen much chart success, but she maintains that the accident has strengthened her faith.

Albums: *Treat Him Right* (1971), with David Houston *A Perfect Match* (1972), *The Midnight Oil* (1973), *This Time I Almost Made It* (1974), *This Is Barbara Mandrell* (1976), *Midnight Angel* (1976), *Lovers, Friends And Strangers* (1977), *Love's Ups And Downs* (1978), *Moods* (1978), *Just For The Record* (1979), *Love Is Fair* (1980), *Looking Back* (1981), *Live* (1981), *In Black And White* (1982), *He Set My Life To Music* (1982), *Spun Gold* (1983), with Houston *Back To Back* (1983), *Clean Cut* (1984), with Lee Greenwood *Meant For Each Other* (1984), *Christmas At Our House* (1984), *Get To The Heart* (1985), *Moments* (1986), *Sure Feels Good* (1987), *I'll Be Your Jukebox Tonight* (1988), *Morning Sun* (1990), *No Nonsense* (1991), *Key's In The Mailbox* (1991).

Barbara Mandrell

Further reading: *Get To The Heart: My Story*, Barbara Mandrell with George Vecsey. *The Barbara Mandrell Story*, Charles Paul Conn.

Mandrell, Louise

b. Thelma Louise Mandrell, 13 July 1954, Corpus Christi, Texas, USA. Mandrell began playing guitar, banjo and fiddle as a child and joined her sister, Barbara Mandrell, in the latter's band on bass in 1969. She had a short-lived marriage with Ronny Shaw, who opened for Barbara Mandrell, and her second marriage also failed. She was a featured singer with Merle Haggard's roadshow in the mid-70s. She signed to Epic and had US country hits with 'Put It On Me', 'Everlasting Love' and 'Reunited' (which was a duet with her third husband, R.C. Bannon). She had further success with RCA and was the butt of her sister's jokes on the television series, *Barbara Mandrell And The Mandrell Sisters*. In 1983, she had solo country hits with 'Save Me' and 'Too Hot To Sleep', which led to her own television series. Her 1988 single with Eric Carmen, 'As Long As We Got Each Other', made the US country charts despite only promotional copies being issued.
Albums: with R.C. Bannon *Inseparable* (1979), with Bannon *Love Won't Let Us Go* (1980), *Louise Mandrell* (1981), with Bannon *Me And My R.C.* (1982), with Bannon *(You're My) Superwoman, (You're My) Incredible Man* (1982), *Close Up* (1983), *Too Hot To Sleep* (1983), *Maybe My Baby* (1985), *I'm Not Through Loving You Yet* (1984).

Manifold, Keith

b. Keith Cyril Manifold, 2 April 1947, Biggin By Hartington, near Buxton, Derbyshire, England. Manifold learned to play guitar and after completing his education, he sought a singing career. He was influenced by such artists as Jimmie Rodgers and Hank Williams. He was also greatly inspired by the recordings and particularly the yodels of Wilf Carter (Montana Slim) and quickly became one of the few British artists to become completely proficient in the art of yodelling. He made his professional debut at a local club in Derbyshire in June 1965. In 1974, he became the first UK country artist to benefit from appearances on television's *Opportunity Knocks*, eventually finishing second to the series' overall winner Lena Zavaroni. He made his first recordings for the Westwood label in 1974. In 1975, he performed the winning song, 'Who's Gonna Bring Me Laughter', in the 1975 *Opportunity Knocks* Songwriters Competition, which led him to record

for a major label, and he was also voted the *Billboard* Best British Solo Artist at London's Wembley Festival. In 1977, he recorded for DJM and in September 1978, he became the first British country artist to be sponsored and taken to the USA to record an album in Nashville, using Nashville musicians. In 1986, he varied his style to record a gospel album, whereon he was backed by the Pilling Brass Ensemble. Manifold has maintained his popularity over the years, still tours extensively in the British Isles and has also regularly played in several European venues. Occasionally he is joined on stage by his two daughters. He also owns an entertainments agency and is involved with promotional work and a recording studio.
Albums: *Casting My Lasso* (1974), *Let's Sit Down* (1974), *Yodelling Just For You* (1975), *Danny Boy* (1975), *Inheritance* (1977), *In Nashville* (1978), *Remembering* (1979), *Old Folks Home* (1983), *Time* (1985), *Keith Manifold & White Line Fever* (1986), *Old Rugged Cross* (1986), *She's Mine* (1989), *I Dreamed About Mama Last Night* (1989), *Love Hurts* (1991).

Maphis, Joe, And Rose Lee

b. Otis W. ('Joe') Maphis, 12 May 1921, near Suffolk, Virginia, USA, d. 27 June 1986, Nashville, Tennessee, USA. His father taught him to play the fiddle as a child and he was performing at local dances by the age of 10. At 16, Maphis was a featured musician on WBRA Richmond, by which time he also played guitar, mandolin and bass. During the 40s, he starred on several top country shows, including *Boone County Jamboree* (later the *Midwestern Hayride*) (WLW Cincinnati), *National Barn Dance* (WLS Chicago) and *Old Dominion Barn Dance* (WRVA Richmond), where he first met his future wife Rose Lee (b. 29 December 1922, Baltimore, Maryland, USA). She was singing and playing the guitar before she reached her teens and at the age of 15, as Rose Of The Mountains, she had her own show on radio in Hagerstown, Maryland. In 1948, she met Joe and they were soon married. They moved to Los Angeles in 1951, where they became regulars on Cliffie Stone's *Hometown Jamboree* and later stars of the televised *Town Hall Party* from KFI Compton. Joe also worked with Merle Travis on occasion and they recorded two duet albums together. In the 50s, apart from their own recordings they worked as session musicians. Joe, with his super-fast picking on his unusual double-necked guitar, was much in demand by both country and pop artists and he recorded with rockabilly singers such as Wanda

Jackson and Ricky Nelson, with whom he also toured. Maphis appeared with many of the major country stars, including Jimmy Dean and Jerry Lee Lewis on network television shows. From the 50s, for almost 30 years, he and Rose Lee toured with their own show, joined later by their three children Jody, Dale and Lorrie. During this time they not only played in every state but also in Europe and the Far East. They made their home in Nashville in the 60s, where Joe's multi-instrumental skills were much in demand for session work. He played the background music on several films and television series, including *Thunder Road*, *Have Gun Will Travel*, *The Virginian* and *The FBI Story*. Their abilities won them the nickname of Mr & Mrs Country Music. Over the years, they recorded in their own right for several labels, including Capitol, Starday and CMH. In 1960, Joe gave 11-year-old Barbara Mandrell her first big break in country music when he included her on his show at the Showboat Hotel and Casino, Las Vegas. (Contrary to many reference books, although Barbara referred to him as Uncle Joe, he was not her real uncle) Joe Maphis, who was Bert Weedon's favourite picker, became known as the King Of The Strings and ranks with Merle Travis and Chet Atkins as one of the finest guitarists of all time. He died in June 1986.

Albums: by Joe Maphis *Fire On The Strings* (1957), *Hi-Fi Holiday For Banjo* (1959), with Merle Travis *Two Guitar Greats* (1964), *Hootenanny Star* (1964), *Golden Gospel Guitar* (1965), *The Amazing Joe Maphis* (1965), *Country Guitar Goes To The Jimmy Dean Show* (1966), *New Sound Of Joe Maphis* (1967), *Gospel Guitar* (1970), *Gospel Guitar Vol.2* (1971), with Jody Maphis *Guitaration Gap* (1971), *Grass 'N' Jazz* (1977), with Merle Travis *Country Guitar Giants* (1979, double album), *Flat Picking Spectacular* (1982, double album); by Joe and Rose Lee Maphis: *Rose Lee Maphis* (1961), *Rose Lee & Joe Maphis with the Blue Ridge Mountain Boys* (1962), *Mr & Mrs Country Music* (1964), with Dale Maphis *Dim Lights, Thick Smoke* (1978), *Boogie Woogie Flat Top Guitar Pickin' Man* (1979), *Honky Tonk Cowboy* (1980).

Martell, Linda

b. Leesville, South Carolina, USA. Initially a R&B singer who included some country material in her repertoire. In 1969, while working the clubs and military bases in her home State, she attracted the attention of Shelby Singleton, who signed her to his Plantation label. In 1969 and 1970, she registered three Billboard country hits namely 'Color Him Father', her version of the Freddy Fender hit, 'Before The Next Teardrops Falls' and 'Bad Case Of The Blues'. Further chart success eluded her but she is credited with being the first black female country singer to appear on the *Grand Ole Opry* after her appearance there in August 1969.

Album: *Color Me Country* (1970).

Martin, Benny

b. 8 May 1928, Sparta, Tennessee, USA. Martin grew up in a musical family (his father and two sisters played as the Martin Family) and he was taught to play the guitar, mandolin and fiddle as a child - receiving tuition on the latter from Lester Flatt's father. After making his radio debut on WHUB Cookeville around 1939, he became a member of Big Jeff And The Radio Playboys on the *Mid-Day Merry-Go-Round* at WNOX Knoxville, and in 1942, moved with them to WLAC Nashville. They relocated to Chattanooga, playing WDOD and WAPO, and toured with Bisby's Comedians tent show, where they worked with Rod Brasfield. In 1946, they returned to WLAC and Martin left the band and joined WSM. He worked briefly as a member of the Musical Millers on the *Martha White Show* before his musical talents as a fiddle player and vocalist found him in demand. During the late 40s and 50s, he played with many famous acts, including Bill Monroe, Roy Acuff, Lester Flatt and Earl Scruggs (he also played on their Columbia recordings made between November 1952 and August 1953) and Johnny And Jack. He toured extensively, particularly during his time with Roy Acuff with whom he visited Germany in 1949. He made some solo vocal recordings for Mercury Records in the early 50s, and from 1953-60, he was a member of the *Grand Ole Opry*. He had minor US country hits in the 60s, with 'Rosebuds And You' and a duet with bluegrass musician Don Reno on the patriotic offering 'Soldier's Prayer in Viet Nam'. Martin, always a popular entertainer, continued to play with various acts throughout the 70s and 80s and has recorded albums with several other top instrumentalists, as well as appearing as a guest on other artists' albums. The *Tennessee Jubilee* album, made with John Hartford and Lester Flatt, includes his tribute to the early days of bluegrass, 'Lester, Bill And Me'. It is interesting to remember that, during the 50s, he worked on perfecting an unusual eight-string fiddle, which he often used on the *Opry*. He originally got the idea after playfully using his fiddle bow on Bill Monroe's mandolin.

Albums: *Country Music's Sensational Entertainer* (1961), *Old Time Fiddlin' & Singin'* (1964), *Benny Martin with Bobby Sykes* (1965), with Don Reno *Bluegrass Gospel Favorites* (1967), with John Hartford, Lester Flatt *Tennessee Jubilee* (1975), *The Fiddle Collection* (1976, double album), *Turkey In The Grass* (1977), *Big Daddy Of The Fiddle And Bow* (1979, double album), *Southern Bluegrass Fiddle* (1980), with Buddy Spicer *Great American Fiddle Collection* (1980), with Reno *Gospel Songs From Cabin Creek* (1990).

Martin, Grady

b. Thomas Grady Martin, 17 January 1929, Chapel Hill, Marshall County, Tennessee, USA. As a boy, Martin was obsessed by both the fiddle and guitar, and he attended all the shows he could to watch and learn. When aged only 15, he was taken to Nashville to play with the Bailes Brothers on the *Grand Ole Opry*. He and his friend, Jabbo Arrington, travelled to Chicago to play on 1946 recordings by fiddler Curly Fox and his wife, Texas Ruby. He became a resident musician on the *Grand Ole Opry* but, in 1949, he and Arrington joined a band formed by Little Jimmy Dickens. Their twin guitars can be heard on Dickens' country hits, 'A-Sleepin' At The Foot Of The Bed' and 'Hillbilly Fever'. Martin formed a group of session musicians, the Slewfoot Five, who recorded in their own right and were credited on hit records by Bing Crosby ('Till The End Of The World') and Burl Ives ('The Wild Side Of Life'). Martin played on sessions for Red Foley, Bobby Helms, Webb Pierce and Marty Robbins ('El Paso'). He also played on Buddy Holly's Nashville sessions, including 'Love Me' and 'Modern Don Juan', and the distinctive introduction to Johnny Horton's 'Battle Of New Orleans'. A failure in electrical equipment led to him 'inventing' feedback on Marty Robbins' US hit, 'Don't Worry'. Martin and Chet Atkins are the only musicians to have accompanied both Hank Williams and Elvis Presley. Martin played on Presley's recording sessions from 1962-65, and he became a mainstay of the so-called Nashville sound. He also worked with Joan Baez, J.J. Cale, Kris Kristofferson ('Why Me Lord'), Roy Orbison ('Oh Pretty Woman') and Leon Russell. Martin has also toured with Jerry Reed and latterly with Willie Nelson, and can be seen in his film, *Honeysuckle Rose*. Nelson says, 'Grady Martin has been my hero forever. There's nobody to have in the studio than Grady Martin, because not only does he play great guitar, he knows what everybody else is supposed to be doing too.'

Albums: *Dance-O-Rama* (1955), *Powerhouse Dance Party* (1955), *Jukebox Jamboree* (1956), *The Roaring Twenties* (1957), *Hot Time Tonight* (1959), *Big City Lights* (1960), *Swinging Down The River* (1962), *Songs Everybody Knows* (1964), *Instrumentally Yours* (1965), *A Touch Of Country* (1967), *Cowboy Classics* (1967).

Martin, Jimmy

b. James Henry Martin, 10 August 1927, on a farm near Sneedville, Tennessee, USA. He learned to play the guitar as a boy and first appeared on radio in Morristown in 1948. He joined Bill Monroe in 1949 and remained with him (except for a short break) until 1954. Many rate Martin to be the finest lead singer and guitarist ever to work with Monroe. He played on some of Monroe's best recordings and sang notable duets with him including 'Memories Of Mother And Dad'. In the mid-50s, he worked with the Osborne Brothers, with whom he recorded '20-20 Vision', before eventually forming his own Sunny Mountain Boys. Martin went on to become a legend of bluegrass music, he played the WJR Detroit *Barn Dance*, *Louisiana Hayride* and all major venues. Over the years his band has contained some of the greatest bluegrass musicians including J.D. Crowe, Doyle Lawson and Alan Munde. He recorded for Decca and had some chart successes including 'Rock Hearts' (1958) and 'Widow Maker' (1964). He also achieved acclaim for his work on the Nitty Gritty Dirt Band's legendary 1972 album, *Will The Circle Be Unbroken*. Many experts believe that Martin has never been afforded full credit for his contributions over the years. It may be that his frankness and the perfection that he expects from his musicians has at times gone against him.

Albums: *Good 'N' Country* (1960), *Country Music Time* (1962), *This World Is Not My Home* (1963), *Widow Maker* (1964), *Sunny Side Of The Mountain* (1965), *Mr. Good 'N' Country Music* (1966), *Big And Country Instrumentals* (1967), *Tennessee* (1968), *Free Born Man* (1969), *All Day Singing* (1970), *I'd Like To Be Sixteen Again* (1972), *Moonshine Hollow* (1973), *Jimmy Martin & The Sunny Mountain Boys* (1973), *Fly Me To Frisco* (1974), *Me 'N' Old Pete* (1978), *Greatest Bluegrass Hits* (1978), *To Mother At Christmas* (1980), with Ralph Stanley *First Time Together* (1980), *Will The Circle Be Unbroken* (1980), *One Woman Man* (1983), *With The Osborne Brothers* (1983), *Big Jam Session* (1984), *Stormy Waters* (1985), *Hit Parade Of Love* (1987).

Martin, Mac, And The Dixie Travelers

b. William D. Colleran, 26 April 1925, Pittsburg, Pennsylvania, USA. Colleran began his career as a teenager singing with Ed Brozi in a touring medicine show, and was influenced by acts such as the Monroe Brothers and the Blue Sky Boys. After World War II, he became interested in bluegrass music. In 1949, he and his band played regularly on WHJB Greensburg, Pennsylvania, and since there were three members of the band called Bill, he decided he would become Mac Martin. In the early 50s, he was noted for his banjo playing and fine vocal work, and in 1953, was playing with a band on WHOD Homestead, Pennsylvania, which was likened to that of Lester Flatt and Earl Scruggs. In 1957, he and his band took a residency at Walsh's Lounge in Pittsburg where they played weekly for the next 15 years. In 1963, the Travelers recorded two albums for Gateway records, although only one was released. A few years later, they recorded four albums for Rural Rhythm. Noted mandolin specialist Bob Artis (b. 26 July 1946, Santa Monica, California, USA) joined the band and when Mac Martin left for a time in 1972, Artis took over. In 1974, when the band recorded for County, Martin had returned. Apart from his playing Artis wrote many articles for publications such as *Bluegrass Unlimited* and *Muleskinner News* and his book *Bluegrass* was published in 1975.

Albums: *Folk And Bluegrass Favorites* (1966), *Traveling Blues* (1968), *Goin' Down The Country* (1968), *Just Like Old Times* (1970), *Back Trackin'* (1971), *Dixie Bound* (1974), *Travelin' On* (1978), *Basic Bluegrass* (1987), *Traveler's Portrait* (1989). Further reading: *Bluegrass*, Bob Artis.

Mathis, Country Johnny

b. 28 September 1933, Maud, Texas, USA. Not to be confused with his more successful namesake, this Johnny Mathis is a country singer/songwriter. He appeared on the *Big D Jamboree*, Dallas but moved to Shreveport and made his debut on the *Louisiana Hayride* in 1953. In 1954, he and Jimmy Lee Fautheree recorded as Jimmy And Johnny and gained a number 3 US country chart hit with his song 'If You Don't Somebody Else Will'. During his days at Shreveport, Mathis worked with Johnny Horton and co-wrote some songs with him including 'I'll Do It Everytime'. Horton also recorded some of Mathis' songs. Although Mathis appeared on the *Grand Ole Opry,* He had no solo chart hits after 'Please Talk To My Heart' in 1963. The following year that song became a Top 10 hit

for Ray Price and, 16 years later, charted again for Freddy Fender. His songs have been recorded by many stars, including George Jones, Faron Young, Charley Pride and Engelbert Humperdinck. Mathis recorded both country and gospel material for Little Darlin' and Hilltop Gospel during the 60s and 70s, but despite being around the country music scene for three decades, he remains basically an unknown.

Albums: *Great Country Hits* (1964), *Country Johnny Mathis* (1965), *He Keeps Me Singing* (1967), *Come Home To My Heart* (1970), *The Best Of My Country* (1973), *Heartfelt* (1981).

Mattea, Kathy

b. 21 June 1959, Cross Lane, West Virginia, USA. During her teens, Mattea began playing with her guitar at church functions and, when she attended university, she joined a bluegrass group, Pennsboro. She decided to go with the bandleader to Nashville and, amongst several jobs, she worked as a tour guide at the Country Music Hall Of Fame. Despite the competition, her vocal talents were appreciated and she was soon recording demos, jingles and commercials. In 1982, she became part of Bobby Goldsboro's road show. She signed with Mercury and worked with Don Williams' producer, Allen Reynolds. Her first single, 'Street Talk', made the US country charts, and then, after some minor successes, her version of Nanci Griffith's 'Love At The Five And Dime' reached number 3. She topped the US country charts with 'Goin' Gone', written by the delightfully eccentric Fred Koller, and had further chart-toppers with '18 Wheels And A Dozen Roses', 'Life As We Knew It', 'Come From The Heart' and 'Burnin' Old Memories'. Mattea is married to Jon Vezner, who won awards for the best country song of the year with Mattea's 'Where've You Been', written about his grandparents' love. Her 1991 album, *Time Passes By*, includes her version of 'From A Distance' which she recorded in Scotland with her friend, folksinger Dougie MacLean. Her song, 'Leaving West Virginia', is used by the West Virginia Department of Tourism. Mattea overcame persistent throat problems to record *Lonesome Standard Time* in 1992.

Albums: *Kathy Mattea* (1984), *From My Heart* (1985), *Walk The Way The Wind Blows* (1986), *Untasted Honey* (1987), *Willow In The Wind* (1989), *Time Passes By* (1991), *Lonesome Standard Time* (1992). Compilation: *A Collection Of Hits* (1990).

Kathy Mattea

Maynard, Ken

b. 21 July 1895, Vevay, Indiana, USA, d. 23 March 1973, California, USA. Maynard, who could play guitar, banjo and fiddle, worked in rodeos until he broke into films as a stunt man. He became the first motion picture singing cowboy, when he sang in *The Wagon Master* in 1929. In this part-talkie (it was 40% silent), he sang 'The Lone Star Trail' and 'The Cowboy's Lament'. He recorded eight cowboy songs for Columbia in 1930. A cowboy song was used for a film title for the first time in Maynard's 1930 film *The Strawberry Roan*. His career as a singing cowboy basically ended with the film debut of Gene Autry in Maynard's 1934 film, *In Old Sante Fe*. His singing, which has been described as rustic, was not comparable to that of Autry, Roy Rogers or later singing cowboys but he continued for some years as a noted cowboy actor. (His brother Kermit Maynard (1898-1971) was also a cowboy actor).

Miki And Griff

Miki (b. Barbara MacDonald Salisbury, 20 June 1920, Ayrshire, Scotland, d. 20 April 1989) was raised on Rothesay on the Isle of Bute. When she joined the George Mitchell Choir, she met Griff (b. Emyr Morus Griffith, 9 May 1923, Holywell, Wales). They learned vocal discipline and stagecraft there. They married in 1950, and leaving Mitchell, developed a comedy act with props and novelty numbers such as 'Spooks' and 'Ol' McDonald's Farm'. Griff's moustache became a recognizable trademark. In 1958, they fell in love with the Everly Brothers' album of traditional country ballads, *Songs Our Daddy Taught Us*, as well as country albums by the Louvin Brothers, and they would sing their songs for the own amusement in dressing-rooms. Lonnie Donegan heard them and invited them to perform those songs on his television series. He arranged a contract with Pye Records and produced their first records. In 1959, 'Hold Back Tomorrow' made the UK Top 30, and they made very successful EPs, *Rockin' Alone (In An Old Rockin' Chair)* and *This Is Miki - This Is Griff*, which topped the EP charts. They appeared on several of Donegan's own records, including 'Virgin Mary' and 'Michael Row The Boat'. Miki recorded a tender version of 'I Never Will Marry' with only Donegan's whistling and acoustic guitar for accompaniment, and they were to work with him until 1964. In 1962, Miki And Griff's only UK Top 20 hit came when they covered Burl Ives' 'A Little Bitty Tear', and the following year they made the Top 30 with a cover of Steve Lawrence

and Eydie Gorme's US hit, 'I Want To Stay Here'. Lesser-known records such as 'This Time I Would Know', 'Oh, So Many Years' and Harlan Howard's humorous 'Automation' were just as good. Although they often covered songs by other performers, their records were always instantly recognizable. Record producer Tony Hatch used to say, 'Miki can create a better harmony than I can ever write for her.' Visiting the USA, they received a standing ovation on Roy Acuff's portion of the *Grand Ole Opry* in 1964. Miki And Griff are easily the most-recorded UK country act, with most of their recordings being for Pye. They did, however, record two albums for Major-Minor and included the weepie 'Two Little Orphans'. In later years, they performed as a duo to the accompaniment of Miki's piano. Griff's humour was always evident, and his emotion-charged version of 'These Hands' was always a showstopper. Miki developed into a fine songwriter - in particular, 'God Was Here (But I Think He Left Early)'. They always had time for their fans, but Miki, who disguised her illness on stage for some months, died of cancer in April 1989. Understandably, Griff has not returned to performing since and, instead, cheers up the patients in the hospital where he visited Miki. The duo are fondly remembered by many listeners for introducing them to country music, and they were a fine, middle-of-the-road act in their own right.

Albums: *Miki And Griff* (1961), *The Country Style Of Miki And Griff* (1962), *I Want To Stay Here* (1963), *Those Rocking Chair People* (1969), *Two Little Orphans* (1970), *Tennessee Waltz* (1970), *Lonesome* (1970), *The Country Side Of Miki And Griff* (1972), *Let The Rest Of The World Go By* (1973), *Country Is* (1974), *Two's Company* (1975), *This Is Miki - This Is Griff* (1976), *Etchings* (1977), *Country* (1978), *At Home With Miki And Griff* (1987). Compilation: *The Best Of Miki And Griff* (1983).

Miller, Jody

b. 29 November 1941, Phoenix, Arizona, USA, but raised in Blanchard, Oklahoma. Miller's father loved country music and played fiddle, and all her four sisters were singers. She led a folk trio while still at school and, after graduation, moved to California to pursue a singing career, but a severe car accident forced her to return home. She established herself locally, after appearing on Tom Paxton's television show, and she gained a reputation as a folk singer. Actor Dale Robertson introduced her to Capitol Records, and her first album, *Wednesday's Child*, was a blend of folk and pop music. Her first US chart success was with 'He Walks Like A Man' and then she went to number 12 with the answer to Roger Miller's 'King Of The Road', 'Queen Of The House'. As a result, she won a Grammy for the best female country performance. She recorded a dramatic teen anthem about being misunderstood, 'Home Of The Brave', which was more significant than its chart placings imply (US 25/UK49). This, however, was a one-off as she then recorded more conventional country hits, having some success with 'Long Black Limousine'. In 1968, she left the business to raise a daughter, but returned to work with producer Billy Sherrill in Nashville in 1970. Her first success was with a Tony Hatch song, 'Look At Mine'. She then scored with country versions of pop hits, 'He's So Fine', 'Baby I'm Yours' and 'Be My Baby'. A duet with Johnny Paycheck, 'Let's All Go Down The River', also fared well. She made little attempt to change with the times and in the early 80s, she retired to breed quarter horses on a 1,000 acre ranch in Blanchard, Oklahoma.

Albums: *Wednesday's Child Is Full Of Woe* (1963), *Jody Miller* (1965), *Home Of The Brave* (1965), *Queen Of The House* (1965), *Jody Miller Sings The Great Hits Of Buck Owens* (1966), *The Nashville Sound Of Jody Miller* (1969), *Look At Mine* (1970), *There's A Party Goin' On* (1972), *He's So Fine* (1972), *Good News* (1973), *House Of The Rising Sun* (1974), *Country Girl* (1975), *Will You Love Me Tomorrow?* (1976), *Here's Jody Miller* (1977).

Miller, Ned

b. Henry Ned Miller, 12 April 1925, Raines, Utah, USA. When Miller was a small child, the family moved to Salt Lake City, Utah where, after completing his education, he worked as a pipe fitter. He became interested in songwriting and country music, learned to play the guitar, but had no real inclination to be a performer. In the mid-50s, he married and moved to California, where he hoped to sell some of his songs and joined the Fabor label as a writer and/or performer. Early in 1957, a deal between Fabor and Dot Records, which gave the latter label first choice of all Fabor masters, saw two of his songs, 'Dark Moon' and 'A Fallen Star', both become US country and pop hits for Bonnie Guitar and Jimmy C. Newman respectively. Miller himself played guitar on the former recording, which also was a number 4 US pop hit for Gale Storm. The song became a UK Top 20 pop hit for Tony Brent and was also recorded by the Kaye Sisters and Joe Loss And His Orchestra. In July 1957, Miller's most famous song appeared when, as a result of a game of patience, he wrote 'From A Jack To A King'. Both his own version and a pop one by Jim Lowe were released by Dot, but created no major impression. From the start, Miller had little interest in a career as a singer and detested touring, he suffered constantly with stage fright and shyness, and was always a most reluctant performer. Stories are told of him on occasions actually sending a friend to perform as Ned Miller in his place. Although he made some further recordings, including 'Lights In The Street' and 'Turn Back', he achieved no chart success and concentrated on his writing. Between 1959 and 1961, he recorded briefly for Jackpot and Capitol.

In 1962, he persuaded Fabor Robison to reissue his recording of 'From A Jack To A King' and this time, despite Miller's reluctance to tour and publicise the song, it became a number 2 country and number 6 pop hit. Released in the UK on the London label, it also soon reached number 2 in the UK pop charts. 'From A Jack To A King', an old-fashioned, traditional sounding country song, was hardly a record that was ahead of its time, but it became an extraordinary success in Britain, where, in April 1963, it held the number 2 position for four weeks - in spite of the fact that there was no promotion from either the artist or label, and it went against the grain of songs that were hits at the time. It obviously says much for the quality of the song. Further Fabor recordings followed and Miller had Top 20 US country and pop hits with 'Invisible Tears' (1964) and 'Do What You Do Do Well' (1965). (The latter number also made a brief appearance in the British pop charts.) He returned to Capitol in 1965, and had five minor hits before being dropped by the label, again due to his unwillingness to tour. He moved to Republic where, in 1970, he achieved his last chart entry with 'The Lover's Song'. He then gave up recording and after moving to Prescott, Arizona, finally wrote his last song in the mid-70s. After eight years at Prescott, he settled in Las Vegas where he completely withdrew from all public appearances and gave up songwriting. In 1991, the German Bear Family label released a 31 track CD of his work, which included some previously unissued material.

Albums: *From A Jack To A King* i (1963), *Ned Miller (Sings The Songs Of Ned Miller)* (1965), *Teardrop Lane* (1967), *In The Name Of Love* (1968), *Ned Miller's Back* (1970), *From A Jack To A King* ii (1981), *From A Jack To A King* iii (1991).

Miller, Roger

b. 2 January 1936, Fort Worth, Texas, USA, d. 25 October 1992, Los Angeles, California, USA. Miller was brought up in Erick, Oklahoma, and, during the late 50s, moved to Nashville, where he worked as a songwriter. His 'Invitation To The Blues' was a minor success for Ray Price, as was '(In The Summertime) You Don't Want Love' for Andy Williams. Miller himself enjoyed a hit on the country charts, with the portentously titled 'When Two Worlds Collide'. In 1962, he joined Faron Young's band as a drummer and also wrote 'Swiss Maid', a major hit for Del Shannon. By 1964, Miller was signed to Mercury's Smash label, and secured a US Top 10 hit with 'Dang Me'. The colloquial title was reinforced by some humorous, macabre lyrics ('They ought to take a rope and hang me'). The song brought Miller several Grammy awards, and the following year, he enjoyed an international Top 10 hit with 'King Of The Road'. This stoical celebration of the hobo life, with its jazz-influenced undertones, became his best-known song. The relaxed 'Engine Engine No. 9' was another US Top 10 hit during 1965, and at the end of the year, Miller once more turned his attention to the UK market with 'England Swings'. This affectionate, slightly bemused tribute to swinging London at its zenith neatly summed up the tourist brochure view of the city ('bobbies on bicycles two by two . . . the rosy red cheeks of the little children'). Another international hit, the song was forever associated with Miller. The singer's chart fortunes declined the following year, and a questionable cover of Elvis Presley's 'Heartbreak Hotel' barely reached the US Top 100. In 1968, Miller secured his last major hit with a poignant reading of Bobby Russell's 'Little Green Apples', which perfectly suited his understated vocal style. Thereafter, Miller moved increasingly towards the country market and continued performing regularly throughout America. In 1982, he appeared on the album *Old Friends* with Ray Price and Willie Nelson. Miller's vocals were featured in the Walt Disney cartoon *Robin Hood*, and in the mid-80s he wrote a Broadway musical, *Big River*, based on Mark Twain's *The Adventures Of Huckleberry Finn*.

Roger Miller finally lost his battle with cancer when, with his wife Mary and son Roger Jnr. at his bedside, he died on 25 October 1992. A most popular man with his fellow artists, he was also a great humorist and his general outlook was adequetly summed up when he once told the backing band on the *Grand Ole Opry*, 'I do this in the key of B natural, which is my philosophy in life.'

Albums: *Roger And Out* (1964), *The Return Of Roger Miller* (1965), *The 3rd Time* (1965), *Words*

Roger Miller

And Music (1966), *Walkin' In The Sunshine* (1967), *A Tender Look At Love* (1968), *Roger Miller* (1969). *Roger Miller* (1970), *Off The Wall* (1978), *Making A Name For Myself* (1980), *Motive Series* (1981), *Old Friends* (1982), *Roger Miller* (1987), *The Big Industry* (1988), Compilation: *Little Green Apples* (1976), *Best Of Roger Miller* (1978), *Greatest Hits* (1985).

Milsap, Ronnie

b. Ronnie Lee Millsaps, 16 January 1943, Robbinsville, North Carolina, USA. Milsap's mother had experienced a stillborn birth and the prospect of raising a blind child made her mentally unstable. Milsap's father took him to live with his grandparents and divorced his mother. What little vision young Ronnie had was lost after receiving a vicious punch from a schoolmaster; both eyes have now been removed. He studied piano, violin and guitar at the State School for the Blind in Raleigh, and although he had the ability to study law, he chose instead to be a professional musician. After some workouts with J.J. Cale and a 1963 single, 'Total Disaster', for the small Princess label, he toured *Playboy* clubs with his own band from 1965. Among his recordings for Scepter were early compositions by Ashford And Simpson, including the memorable 'Let's Go Get Stoned', relegated to a b-side. A few months later it was a million-selling single for another blind pianist, Ray Charles. Following a residency at TJ's club in Memphis, Milsap performed at the 1969 New Year's Eve party for Elvis Presley. Presley invited him to sing harmony on his sessions for 'Don't Cry Daddy' and 'Kentucky Rain', ironically the only time he has been part of a UK chart hit. After several recordings with smaller labels, Milsap made *Ronnie Milsap*, for Warner Brothers, with top soul and country musicians. He worked throughout 1972 at Roger Miller's King Of The Road club in Nashville, and then signed with RCA. *Where The Heart Is* was a tuneful, country collection including the US country hits, 'I Hate You' and 'The Girl Who Waits On Tables'. 'Pure Love' is among the most uplifting country singles of all time, while Don Gibson's 'I'd Be A Legend In My Time' was even more successful. In 1975, Milsap came to the UK as Glen Campbell's opening act, and the strength of his concert performances can be gauged from RCA's *In Concert* double-album, hosted by Charley Pride, in which he duets 'Rollin' In My Sweet Baby's Arms' with Dolly Parton and tackles a wild rock 'n' roll medley. His live album from the *Grand Old Opry*, shows a great sense of humour - 'You don't think I'm gonna fall off this stage, do you? I got 20 more feet before the edge. That's what the band told me.' He had a crossover hit - number 16 on the US pop charts - with Hal David's, 'It Was Almost Like A Song'. Milsap bought a studio from Roy Orbison, GroundStar, and continued to record prolifically. In 1979, RCA sent an unmarked, pre-release single to disc jockeys, inviting them to guess the performer. The funky seven-minute disco workout of 'Hi-Heel Sneakers' was by Milsap, but, more often than not, he was moving towards the Barry Manilow market. Milsap also helped with the country music score for Clint Eastwood's film, *Bronco Billy,* and he recorded a flamboyant tribute album to Jim Reeves, *Out Where The Bright Lights Are Glowing.* A revival of Chuck Jackson's 'Any Day Now (My Wild Beautiful Bird)' reached number 14 on the US pop charts and also became *Billboard*'s Adult Contemporary Song Of The Year. His *Lost In The Fifties Tonight* album had doo-wop touches, but the album should have remained completely in that mould. Milsap also recorded a duet with Kenny Rogers, 'Make No Mistake, She's Mine'. He moved away from synthesizers and sounded more country than ever on 'Stranger Things Have Happened'. Enjoying his 35th US country number 1 with a Hank Cochran song, 'Don't You Ever Get Tired (Of Hurtin' Me)', Milsap remains a formidable force in US country music, and only Conway Twitty and Merle Haggard have had more chart-toppers. It shows remarkable consistency by an artist with little traditional country to his name.

Albums: *Ronnie Milsap* (1971), *Where The Heart Is* (1973), *Pure Love* (1974), *A Legend In My Time* (1975), *Night Things* (1975), *A Rose By Any Other Name* (1975), *20-20 Vision* (1976), *Mr. Mailman* (1976), *Ronnie Milsap Live* (1976), *Kentucky Woman* (1976), *It Was Almost Like A Song* (1977), *Only One Love In My Life* (1978), *Images* (1979), *Milsap Magic* (1980), *Out Where The Bright Lights Are Glowing* (1981), *There's No Gettin' Over Me* (1980), *Inside* (1982), *Keyed Up* (1983), *One More Try For Love* (1984), *Lost In The Fifties Tonight* (1986), *Christmas With Ronnie Milsap* (1986), *Heart And Soul* (1987), *Stranger Things Have Happened* (1989), *Back To The Grindstone* (1991).

Further reading: *Almost Like A Song*, Ronnie Milsap with Tom Carter.

Mize, Billy

b. 29 April 1929, Kansas City, Kansas, USA. Raised in the San Joaquin Valley of California, Mize first learned to play guitar as a child, but converted to steel guitar when he received one for his 18th birthday. Originally, he was influenced by the music of Bob Wills and when he moved to Bakersfield, he formed his own band and played residences and local venues. He also worked as a disc jockey on KPMC. In 1953, he appeared on *The Cousin Herb Trading Post Show* on KERO-TV Bakersfield, and became affectionately known as Billy The Kid. He was a regular with the show for 13 years, including hosting it at one stage. Mize still played his other appearances, and in 1955, began to appear on the *Hank Penny Show* on Los Angeles television. In 1957, his popularity grew to the extent that, for several years, he managed to appear on seven Los Angeles television stations weekly, including *Town Hall Party*, and still maintained his Bakersfield commitments. He naturally developed into a television personality and, in 1966 and 1967, he became host/singer of Gene Autry's *Melody Ranch* network show on KTLA. He also commenced his own syndicated *Billy Mize Show* from Bakersfield. He first recorded for Decca in the 50s, and later for Challenge and Liberty, before making the US country charts in 1966 with his Columbia recording of 'You Can't Stop Me'. Between 1966 and 1977, he totalled 11 US chart entries, including his own composition 'Make It Rain'. Some of his songs were hits for other artists, such as 'Who Will Buy The Wine' (Charlie Walker), 'My Baby Walks All Over Me' (Johnny Sea) and 'Don't Let The Blues Make You Bad' (Dean Martin). He maintained rigorous schedules throughout the 60s and 70s, and appeared in the television series *RFD Hollywood*. He later became a television producer with his own production company. He has also worked as a musician on numerous recording sessions, including playing steel and rhythm guitar on many of Merle Haggard recordings. His brother Buddy (b. 5 August 1936, Wichita, Kansas, USA.) is a noted country songwriter, record producer and radio personality. He also relocated to Bakersfield, and his songs have been recorded by Buck Owens, Johnny Cash, Marty Robbins, Hank Snow and many others. In the early 80s, Buddy and Billy worked together on various television projects. Billy currently heads Billy Mize Productions, making television spectaculars with Merle Haggard. Albums: *This Time And Place* (1969), *You're Alright With Me* (1971), *Love'N'Stuff* (1976).

Moffatt, Hugh

b. 10 November 1948, Fort Worth, Texas, USA. Unlike most country performers, Moffatt played trumpet in his high school band and had a fondness for big band jazz. He obtained a degree in English from Rice University in Houston and learned to play the guitar. Moffatt played acoustic sets in Austin and Washington and then, in 1973, moved to Nashville. He says, 'I was interested in Nashville purely because of Kris Kristofferson. He proved that you can take the folk and the literary tradition, and you can be in Nashville, too.' In 1974, Ronnie Milsap recorded Moffatt's 'Just In Case'. Moffatt recorded two singles for Mercury - a cover of 'The Gambler' and his own 'Love And Only Love' - but the contract then terminated. In the early 80s he formed the band Ratz, which included Moffatt's wife, Pebe Sebert, and released a five-track EP, *Putting On The Ratz*. In 1987, his superb album *Loving You* was released, and included a song written with Sebert, 'Old Flames (Can't Hold A Candle To You)'. He admits, 'That title and the ideas were Pebe's. We wrote it three months after we were married. We spent three months writing it, as we wanted it to be right. Everybody knew it would be a hit.' The song has been successfully recorded by Joe Sun, Dolly Parton and Foster And Allen. The only other song they wrote together was 'Wild Turkey', which was recorded by Lacy J. Dalton. Other Moffatt songs include 'Love Games' (Jerry Lee Lewis), 'Praise The Lord And Pass Me The Money' (Bobby Bare), 'Why Should I Cry Over You?' (George Hamilton IV) and 'Words At Twenty Paces' (Alabama). His sister, Katy, is also a recording artist, at home on both acoustic and hard-rocking material. Her albums are *Walking On The Moon* (1988) and *Child Bride* (1989). They have released a duet of 'Rose Of My Heart', which has also been recorded by Johnny Rodriguez and Nicolette Larson.
Albums: *Loving You* (1987), *Troubadour* (1989), *Live And Alone* (1991), with Katy Moffatt *Dance Me Outside* (1992).

Monroe, Bill

b. William Smith Monroe, 13 September 1911, on a farm near Rosine, Ohio County, Kentucky, USA. The Monroes were a musical family; his father, known affectionately as Buck, was a noted step-dancer, his mother played fiddle, accordion and harmonica, and was respected locally as a singer of old time songs. Among the siblings, elder brothers Harry and Birch both played fiddle, and brother Charlie and sister Bertha, guitar. They were all influenced by their uncle, Pendleton Vanderver, who was a fiddler of considerable talent, and noted for his playing at local events.

Hugh Moffatt

Bill Monroe

(Monroe later immortalized him in one of his best-known numbers, 'Uncle Pen', with tribute lines such as 'Late in the evening about sundown; high on the hill above the town, Uncle Pen played the fiddle, oh, how it would ring. You can hear it talk, you can hear it sing'). At the age of nine, Monroe began to concentrate on the mandolin; his first choice had been the guitar or fiddle, but his brothers pointed out that no family member played mandolin, and as the baby, he was given little choice, although he still kept up his guitar playing. His mother died when he was 10, followed soon after by his father. He moved in to live with Uncle Pen and they were soon playing guitar together at local dances. Bill also played with a black blues musician, Arnold Schultz, who was to become a major influence on the future Monroe music. After the death of his father, most of the family moved away in their search for work. Birch and Charlie headed north, working for a time in the car industry in Detroit, before moving to Whiting and East Chicago, Indiana, where they were employed in the oil refineries. When he was 18, Bill joined them, and for four years, worked at the Sinclair refinery. At one time, in the Depression, Bill was the only one with work, and the three began to play for local dances to raise money to live on. In 1932, the three Monroe brothers and their girlfriends became part of a team of dancers and toured with a show organised by WLS Chicago, the radio station responsible for the *National Barn Dance* programme. They also played on local radio stations, including WAE Hammond and WJKS Gary, Indiana. In 1934, Bill, finding the touring conflicted with his work, decided to become a full time musician. Soon after, they received an offer to tour for Texas Crystals (the makers of a patent purgative medicine), which sponsored radio programmes in several states. Birch, back in employment at Sinclair and also looking after a sister, decided against a musical career. Bill married in 1935, and between then and 1936, he and Charlie (appearing as the Monroe Brothers) had stays at various stations, including Shenandoah, Columbia, Greenville and Charlotte. In 1936, they moved to the rival and much larger Crazy Water Crystals and, until 1938, they worked on the noted *Crazy Barn Dance* at WBT Charlotte for that company. They became a very popular act and sang mainly traditional material, often with a blues influence. Charlie always provided the lead vocal, and Bill added tenor harmonies.

In February 1936, they made their first recordings on the Bluebird label of RCA-Victor, which proved popular. Further sessions followed, and in total they cut some 60 tracks for the label. Early in 1938, the brothers decided that they should follow their own careers. Charlie kept the RCA recording contract and formed his own band, the Kentucky Pardners. Since he had always handled all lead vocals, he found things easier and soon established himself in his own right. Prior to the split, Bill had never recorded an instrumental or a vocal solo, but he had ideas that he wished to put into practice. He moved to KARK Little Rock, where he formed his first band, the Kentuckians. This failed to satisfy him, and he soon moved to Atlanta, where he worked on the noted *Crossroad Follies,* at this time, he formed the first of the bands he would call the BlueGrass Boys. In 1939, he made his first appearance on the *Grand Ole Opry,* singing his version of 'New Muleskinner Blues', after which George D. Hay (the Solemn Old Judge) told him, 'Bill, if you ever leave the Opry, it'll be because you fire yourself'. (Over 50 years later, he was still there.)

During the early 40s, Monroe's band was similar to other string bands such as Mainer's Mountaineers, but by the mid-40s, the leading influence of Monroe's driving mandolin and his high (some would say shrill) tenor singing became the dominant factor, which set the Blue Grass Boys of Bill Monroe apart from the other bands. This period gave birth to a new genre of music, and led to Bill Monroe becoming known affectionately as the Father of Bluegrass Music. He began to tour with the *Opry* road shows, and his weekly network WSM radio work soon made him a national name. In 1940 and 1941, he recorded a variety of material for RCA-Victor, including gospel songs, old-time numbers and instrumentals such as the 'Orange Blossom Special' (the second known recording of the number). War-time restrictions prevented him from recording between 1941 and early 1945, but later that year, he recorded for Columbia. In 1946, he gained his first country chart hits when his own song, 'Kentucky Waltz', reached number 3, and his now-immortal recording of 'Footprints In The Snow' reached number 5 in the US country charts. By 1945, several fiddle players had made their impact on the band's overall sound, including Chubby Wise, Art Wooten, Tommy Magness, Howdy Forrester and in 1945, guitarist/vocalist Lester Flatt and banjo player Earl Scruggs joined. David 'Stringbean' Akeman had provided the comedy and the banjo playing since 1942, although it was generally reckoned later that his playing contributed little to the overall sound that Monroe sought. Scruggs' style of playing was very different, and it quickly became responsible for not only establishing his own name as one of the greatest exponents of the instrument, but also for making bluegrass music an internationally identifiable sound. It was while Flatt and Scruggs were with the band that Monroe first recorded his now-immortal song 'Blue Moon Of Kentucky'.

By 1948, other bands such as the Stanley Brothers were beginning to show the influence of Monroe, and bluegrass music was firmly established. During the 40s, Monroe toured with his tent show, which included his famous baseball team (the reason for Stringbean's first connections with Monroe), which played against local teams as an attraction before the musical show began. In 1951, he bought some land at Bean Blossom, Brown County, Indiana, and established a country park, which became the home for bluegrass music shows. He was involved in a very serious car accident in January 1953, and was unable to perform for several months. In 1954, Elvis Presley recorded Monroe's 'Blue Moon Of Kentucky' in a 4/4 rock tempo and sang it at his solitary appearance on the *Opry*. A dejected Presley found the performance made no impact with the *Opry* audience, but the song became a hit. It also led to Monroe re-recording it in a style that, like the original, started as a waltz but after a verse and chorus featuring three fiddles, it changed to 4/4 tempo: Monroe repeated the vocal in the new style. (Paul McCartney's 1991 album, *Unplugged,* contains a version in both styles). Monroe toured extensively throughout the 50s, and had chart success in 1958 with his own instrumental number, 'Scotland'. He used the twin fiddles of Kenny Baker and Bobby Hicks to produce the sound of bagpipes behind his own mandolin - no doubt his tribute to his family's Scottish ancestry. By the end of the decade, the impact of rock 'n' roll was affecting his record sales and music generally. By this time, (the long departed) Flatt and Scruggs were firmly established with their own band and finding success on television and at folk festivals. Monroe was a strong-willed person and it was not always easy for those who worked with him, or for him, to achieve the perfect arrangement. He had stubborn ideas and, in 1959, he refused to play a major concert in Carnegie Hall, because he believed that Alan Lomax, the organiser, was a communist. He was also suspicious of the Press and rarely, if ever, gave interviews. In 1962, however, he became friendly with Ralph Rinzler, a writer and member of the Greenbriar Boys, who became his manager.

In 1963, Monroe played his first folk festival at the University of Chicago. He soon created a great interest among students generally and, with Rinzler's planning, he was soon busily connected with festivals solely devoted to bluegrass music. In 1965, he was involved with the major Roanoke, Virginia, festival and in 1967, he started his own at Bean Blossom. During the 60s, many young musicians benefitted from their time as a member of Monroe's band, including Bill Keith, Peter Rowan, Byron Berline, Roland White and Del McCoury. In 1969, he was made an honorary Kentucky Colonel, and in 1970, was elected to the *Country Music Hall Of Fame* in Nashville. The plaque stated 'The Father of Bluegrass Music. Bill Monroe developed and perfected this music form and taught it to a great many names in the industry'. Monroe has written many songs, including 'Memories Of Mother And Dad', 'When The Golden Leaves Begin To Fall', 'My Little Georgia Rose' and 'Blue Moon Of Kentucky' (the latter a much-recorded country standard) and countless others. Many have been written using pseudonyms such as Albert Price, James B. Smith and James W. Smith. In 1971, his talent as a songwriter saw him elected to the Nashville Songwriters Association International Hall Of Fame. He kept up a hectic touring schedule throughout the 70s, but in 1981, he suffered with cancer. He survived after treatment and, during the 80s, maintained a schedule that would have daunted much younger men. In 1984, he recorded the album *Bill Monroe And Friends,* which contains some of his songs sung as duets with other artists, including the Oak Ridge Boys ('Blue Moon Of Kentucky'), Emmylou Harris ('Kentucky Waltz'), Barbara Mandrell ('My Rose Of Old Kentucky'), Ricky Skaggs ('My Sweet Darling') and Willie Nelson ('The Sunset Trail'). Johnny Cash, who also appears on the album, presumably did not know any Monroe songs because they sang Cash's own 'I Still Miss Someone'.

Over the years since Monroe first formed his bluegrass band, some of the biggest names in country music have played as members before progressing to their own careers. These include Clyde Moody, Flatt And Scruggs, Jim Eanes, Carter Stanley, Mac Wiseman, Jimmy Martin, Sonny Osborne, Vassar Clements, Kenny Baker and son James Monroe. Amazingly, bearing in mind his popularity, Monroe's last chart entry was 'Gotta Travel On', a Top 20 country hit in March 1959. However, his records are still collected and the German Bear Family label has released boxed sets on compact disc of his Decca recordings. (Between 1950, when he first recorded for Decca and 1969, he made almost 250 recordings for the label) He continued to play the *Opry* and, in 1989, he celebrated his 50th year as a member, the occasion being marked by MCA (by then the owners of Decca) recording a live concert from the *Opry* stage, which became his first-ever release on CD format. He first visited the UK in 1966, did an extended tour in 1975, and has always been a very popular personality on the several occasions he has played the UK's Wembley Festival. He underwent surgery for a double coronary bypass on 9 August 1991, but by October, he was back performing and once again hosting his normal *Opry* show.

Albums: *Knee Deep In Bluegrass* (1958), *I Saw The Light* (1959), *Mr. Bluegrass* (1960), *The Great Bill Monroe & The BlueGrass Boys* (1961), *Bluegrass Ramble* (1962), *The Father Of Bluegrass Music* (1962), *My All-Time Country Favorites* (1962), *Early Bluegrass Music* (1963), *Bluegrass Special* (1963), *Sings Country Songs* (1964), *I'll Meet You In Church Sunday Morning* (1964), *Original Bluegrass Sound* (1965), *Bluegrass Instrumentals* (1965), *The High Lonesome Sound* (1966), *Bluegrass Time* (1967), *A Voice From On High* (1969), *Bill Monroe & His Blue GrassBoys (16 Hits)* (1970), *Bluegrass Style* (1970), *Kentucky Bluegrass* (1970), *Country Music Hall Of Fame* (1971), *Uncle Pen* (1972), *Bean Blossom* (1973, double album), *The Road Of Life* (1974), *Weary Traveller* (1976), *Bill Monroe & His Bluegrass Boys 1950-1972* (c1976), *Sings Bluegrass, Body And Soul* (1977), *Bluegrass Memories* (1977), *Bill Monroe With Lester Flatt & Earl Scruggs:The Original Bluegrass Band* (1978), *Bean Blossom 1979* (1980), *Bluegrass Classic (Radio Shows 1946-1948)* (1980), *The Classic Bluegrass Recordings Volume 1* (1980), *The Classic Bluegrass Recordings Volume 2* (1980), *Orange Blossom Special (Recorded Live At Melody Ranch)* (1981), *Master Of Bluegrass* (1981), *Live Radio* (1982), *MCA Singles Collection Volumes 1, 2 & 3* (1983), *Bill Monroe & Friends* (1984), *Bluegrass '87* (1987), *Southern Flavor* (1988), *Muleskinner Blues* (1991). Bear Family CD Boxed Sets: *Bill Monroe BlueGrass 1950-1958* (1989), *Bill Monroe BlueGrass 1959-1969* (1991). As The Monroe Brothers *Early Bluegrass Music* (1963), *The Monroe Brothers, Bill & Charlie* (1969), *Feast Here Tonight* (1975). With Birch Monroe *Brother Birch Monroe Plays Old-Time Fiddle Favorites* (1975). With James Monroe *Father And Son* (1973), *Together Again* (1978). With Kenny Baker *Kenny Baker Plays Bill Monroe* (1976). With Lester Flatt *Bill Monroe And Lester Flatt* (1967). With Rose Maddox *Rose Maddox Sings Bluegrass* (1962). With Doc Watson *Bill & Doc Sing Country Songs* (1975).

Monroe, Birch

b. 1901, on a farm near Rosine, Ohio County, Kentucky, USA, d. 15 May 1982. Birch was the fiddle-playing elder brother of Bill Monroe who, after the death of his parents, moved to Detroit with brother Charlie Monroe. Here, they worked for a time in the motor industry, before moving to work in the oil refineries at Whiting and East Chicago, Indiana. In 1929, they were joined by brother Bill, and during the Depression, the three began to play at local venues; eventually Bill and Charlie worked professionally together as the Monroe Brothers. From the mid-to late 40s, he worked with brother Bill's band, playing bass and taking bass vocals, as well as acting as their manager and booking agent. He remained connected with his brother's business enterprises, and from 1951 to the end of the 70s, he managed the country park at Bean Blossom, Indiana, which featured the weekly *Brown County Jamboree*. His recording career was limited to those made with his brother's band, except in the mid-70s, when accompanied by the BlueGrass Boys and under the production of Bill, he recorded an album of fiddle music. Birch Monroe died in 1982, and is buried in the Monroe family plot on Jerusalem Ridge, Rosine, Kentucky. Album: *Brother Birch Monroe Plays Old-Time Fiddle Favorites* (1975).

Monroe, Charlie

b. 4 July 1903, on a farm near Rosine, Ohio County, Kentucky, USA, d. 27 September 1975. Charlie was the elder brother of Bill Monroe who, after the death of his parents, moved to Detroit with fiddle-playing brother Birch Monroe. Here they worked for a time in the motor industry, before moving to work in the oil refineries at Whiting and East Chicago, Indiana. In 1929, they were joined by brother Bill and during the Depression, the three began to play at local venues; eventually Bill and Charlie worked professionally together as the Monroe Brothers. In 1938, they decided to pursue their own careers. At the time of the split, they had a contract with RCA-Victor, for whom they had recorded 60 songs; Charlie, who had always taken the lead vocals (though Bill had written many of their songs), kept this contract. Throughout the 40s, he toured and recorded for RCA-Victor, and at times his band, the Kentucky Pardners, which became one of North Carolina's most popular hillbilly bands, included notable musicians such as guitarist Lester Flatt and mandolin players Red Rector, Ira Louvin and Curly Sechler. He differed from his brother in that his band played a mixture of country and bluegrass, and Charlie, a highly respected guitarist, frequently used an electric guitar. He made many fine recordings, and though he never achieved a chart hit, Monroe is remembered for his versions of numbers such as 'Down In The Willow Garden' (an old folk song) and his own compositions 'Rubber Neck Blues', 'It's Only A Phonograph Record' and 'Who's Calling You Sweetheart Tonight?'. He joined Decca around 1950, but although they made some concert appearances together, further recordings with brother Bill never materialized. In the early 50s, tired of the touring, he broke up his band and semi-retired to his Kentucky farm. In 1957, he supposedly retired to manage a coal mine and yard near Rosine, but made some special appearances and, during the early 60s, recorded two albums on the Rem label. His wife became ill with cancer, and to meet the medical expenses, Monroe left Kentucky and worked in Indiana for a lift company until his wife died. He remarried in 1969, when he moved to Tennessee, and in 1972, he was persuaded to appear with Jimmy Martin at a Gettysburg bluegrass festival, which led him to make some further appearances at similar events. He relocated to Reidsville, North Carolina, and in late 1974, he, too, was diagnosed as suffering from cancer. He made his last public performance in his old home area of Rosine, Kentucky, around early August, and died at his home in Reidsville in September 1975, but is buried in the Monroe family plot on Jerusalem Ridge, Rosine, Kentucky. Although his work was not as important as that of brother Bill, he nevertheless made a significant contribution to the formation of what is now known as bluegrass music.

Albums: *Bluegrass Sound* (1963), *Lord Build Me A Cabin* (1965), *Charlie Monroe Sings Again* (1966), *Who's Calling You Sweetheart Tonight?* (1969), *Noon-Day Jamboree (Radio Shows 1944)* (1970), *Songs Of Charlie Monroe & the Kentucky Pardners (Vintage Radio Recordings)* (1970), *Live At Lake Norman Music Hall* (1975), *Tally Ho* (1975), *Charlie Monroe & His Kentucky Pardners* (c.70s), one side of second album by Phipps Family *Memories Of Charlie Monroe* (1975, double album), *Charlie Monroe's Boys:The Early Years* (1982), *Vintage Radio 1944* (1990). As The Monroe Brothers: *Early Bluegrass Music* (1963), *The Monroe Brothers, Bill & Charlie* (1969), *Feast Here Tonight* (1975).

Monroe, James

b. James William Monroe, 1941. Son of Bill Monroe. James began his musical career in 1964, playing upright bass with his father's BlueGrass Boys. In 1969, he became the band's guitarist and also began to take lead vocals. He left the Bluegrass Boys in 1972, and formed his own bluegrass band, the Midnight Ramblers, but later recorded two albums with his father. In the mid-70s, he recorded several albums for Atteiram, including a tribute to his uncle, Charlie Monroe, on which his father also appeared. Soon afterwards he drastically reduced his performing to help with the running of his father's business affairs.

Albums: with Bill Monroe *Father And Son* (1973), *Sings Songs of 'Memory Lane' Of His Uncle Charlie Monroe* (1976), *Together Again* (1978). With the Midnight Ramblers *Something New! Something Different! Something Good!* (1974), *Midnight Blues* (1976), *Satisfied Mind* (1984).

Monroe, Melissa

b. Melissa Katherine Monroe, 1936, d. December 1990. Daughter of Bill Monroe. A singer and instrumentalist, Monroe toured with her father's road show during the 40s and 50s. She made some solo recordings for Columbia in the early 50s, but did not achieve any chart success.

Montana, Patsy

b. Rubye Blevins, 30 October 1912, Hot Springs, Arkansas, USA. Montana was the 11th child, and first daughter, of a farmer and in her childhood she learned organ, guitar, violin and yodelling. In 1928 she worked on radio in California as Rubye Blevins, the Yodelling Cowgirl from San Antone. In 1931 she joined Stuart Hamblen's show, appearing on radio and at rodeos as part of the Montana Cowgirls. Hamblen renamed her Patsy as it was 'a good Irish name'. In 1933 she joined the Kentucky Ramblers who, because of their western image, became the Prairie Ramblers. In 1935 Montana recorded her self-penned 'I Want To Be A Cowboy's Sweetheart', the first million-seller by a female country singer. She recorded many other western songs including 'Old Nevada Moon' and 'Back On The Montana Plains' - several of her songs had Montana in the title. She appeared in several films including *Colorado Sunset* with Gene Autry. During the war, she recorded with the Sons Of The Pioneers and the Lightcrust Doughboys; her 'Goodnight Soldier' was very popular. She continued with her cowgirl image after the war but retired in 1952 and moved to California. She returned to touring in the 60s, often with her daughter Judy Rose, and recorded for Starday with Waylon Jennings on lead guitar. She won popularity in the UK with her appearances in country clubs. Montana, who presented a picture of independence through her cowgirl image, has inspired many yodelling singers including Rosalie Allen, Texas Ruby and Bonnie Lou.

Albums: *New Sounds Of Patsy Montana At The Matador Room* (1964), *Precious Memories* (1977), *Patsy Montana And Judy Rose - Mum And Me* (1977), *I Want To Be A Cowboy's Sweetheart* (1977), *Patsy Montana Sings Her Original Hits* (1980), *Early Country Favourites* (1983), *Patsy Montana And The Prairie Ramblers* (1984), *The Cowboy's Sweetheart* (1988).

Montgomery, Melba

b. 14 October 1938, Iron City, Tennessee, USA. Born into a musical family, Montgomery's father ran a church choir and both her brothers, Carl and Earl, became country songwriters, often supplying her with material. In 1958 she and her brothers were finalists in a nationwide talent contest sponsored by Pet Milk - another finalist was Johnny Tillotson. Her success led to an appearance on the *Grand Ole Opry* where she impressed Roy Acuff. He added her to his roadshow and she spent four years covering the USA and its military bases abroad. In 1962 she recorded two singles, 'Happy You, Lonely Me' and 'Just Another Fool Along The Way', for Lonzo and Oscar's Nugget label. She recorded prolifically for United Artists and Musicor, although she made the US country charts with 'Hall Of Shame' and 'The Greatest One Of All', Melba is better known for her duets with George Jones ('We Must Have Been Out Of Her Minds', which she wrote) and Gene Pitney ('Baby, Ain't That Fine'). Substantial successes eluded her at Capitol, although she recorded duets with Charlie Louvin, notably 'Something To Brag About'. She gave Elektra a number 1 country single with 'No Charge', written by Harlan Howard, although it was covered for the UK market by J.J. Barrie. She has spent the past decade raising her family.

Albums: with George Jones *What's In Our Heart* (1963), *Melba Montgomery - America's Number One Country And Western Girl Singer* (1964), *Down Home* (1964), with Jones *Bluegrass Hootenanny* (1964), *I Can't Get Used To Being Lonely* (1965), with Jones *Blue Moon Of Kentucky* (1966), *Country Girl* (1966), *Hallelujah Road* (1966), with Gene Pitney *Being Together* (1966), with Jones *Close Together* (1966), *The Mood I'm In* (1967), *Melba Toast* (1967), *Don't Keep Me Lonely Too Long* (1967), *I'm Just Living* (1967), with Jones *Let's Get Together/Party Pickin'* (1967), with Jones *Great Country Duets Of All Time* (1969), *The Big Country World Of Melba Montgomery* (1969), with Charlie Louvin *Somethin' To Brag About* (1971), with Louvin *Baby, You've Got What It Takes* (1971), *Melba Montgomery - No Charge* (1973), *No Charge* (1974), *Aching Breaking Heart* (1975), *Don't Let The Good Times Fool You* (1975), *The Greatest Gift Of All* (1975), *Melba* (1976), *Melba Montgomery* (1978), *Melba Montgomery* (1982).

Moody, Clyde

b. 19 September 1915, Cherokee, North Carolina, USA, d. 7 April 1989, Nashville, Tennessee, USA. Raised in Marion, North Carolina, Moody had learned the guitar by the age of eight and soon after became a professional musician. He left home when he was 14. He first worked with Jay Hugh Hall, initially as Bill And Joe on WSPA Spartanburg, South Carolina in 1929 but later with Steve Ledford, they became the Happy-Go-Lucky Boys. (He also played some semi-professional baseball with Asheville, South Carolina). Between 1937 and 1940, while continuing to appear as a duo, they also played with Wade Mainer's Sons Of The Mountaineers and recorded for Bluebird, both as a duo and with the group. They performed on many Carolina radio stations until they left Wade Mainer and joined his brother, J.E. Mainer, in Alabama. In 1941 Moody had a disagreement with both Hall and Mainer, and left to join Bill Monroe back in North Carolina. During his time with Monroe, Moody appeared on various recordings including the classic version of his own song 'Six White Horses', which was coupled with 'Mule Skinner Blues' as Monroe's Blue Grass Boys' first Bluebird single release. Moody soon left, and hiring Lester Flatt as his partner, he worked WHBB Burlington as the Happy-Go-Lucky Boys; however, in 1942, he rejoined Monroe and stayed with him until 1945. When he finally left, his place was taken by Flatt. Moody worked with Roy Acuff for a short time but soon went solo and made his first solo recordings that year. He played the *Grand Ole Opry* during the late 40s but left to work on early television in Washington DC. His 1947 recording of 'Shenandoah Waltz' (co-written with Chubby Wise) is reputed to be the top selling record for the King label, having had sales in excess of three million. The song is now a bluegrass standard, although most experts would say the

Moody's original version is more that of a country ballad singer, such as Red Foley, than that of a bluegrass artist. He began to specialize in waltz ●●●●●● ●●● ●●●●●● ●●●● ●●●●●● ●●●● ●● ●●●●●●● the nickname of The Hillbilly Waltz King. In 1948, he had Top 20 US country chart hits with 'Carolina Waltz' and 'Red Roses Tied In Blue' and in 1950, his recording of 'I Love You Because' reached number 8. He left King in 1951 and recorded for Decca but from 1957 to the early 60s, he was less active on the music scene. He returned to North Carolina, where he developed business interests in mobile homes and for a long time hosted his own daily television show *Carolina In The Morning* in Raleigh. During the 60s, he recorded for Starday, Wango and Little Darlin'. He returned to Nashville in 1971 and once more became involved with the music scene. He guested on the *Opry*, played various bluegrass festivals, toured extensively with his friend Rambling Tommy Scott's Medicine Show and recorded for Old Homestead. During the mid-70s, his health began to suffer but he continued to perform whenever he was able, until he died in Nashville on 7 April 1989.
Albums: *The Best Of Clyde Moody* (1964), *All Time Country & Western Waltzes* (1969), *Moody's Blues* (1972), *A Country Tribute To Fred Rose* (1976), with Tommy Scott *We've Played Every Place More Than Once* (1978), with Scott *Early Country Favorites* (1980).

Morgan, George

b. 28 June 1924, Waverley, Tennessee, USA, d. 7 July 1975. Morgan was raised in Barberton, Ohio and by the time he was nine, he was performing his own songs on guitar. He enlisted in the US Army during the War but was discharged three months later on medical grounds. He formed a band and found work on a radio station in Wooster, Ohio, and wrote 'Candy Kisses' after a broken romance. RCA showed an interest in Morgan, who performed 'Candy Kisses' on the *Grand Ole Opry* to great acclaim, but their tardiness led to US Columbia signing him instead. 'Candy Kisses' was a US country Number 1 in 1949 despite competition from cover versions from Elton Britt, Red Foley and Eddie Kirk. However, there was friction between Morgan and Hank Williams, who regarded 'Candy Kisses' as 'stupid' and its singer 'a cross-eyed crooner'. Morgan, a crooner in the vein of Eddy Arnold, called his band the Candy Kids and he consolidated his reputation with 'Please Don't Let Me Love You', 'Room Full Of Roses', 'Almost', 'You're The Only Good Thing' and 'Mr.

Ting-A-Ling (Steel Guitar Man)'. In 1953 Morgan became the first country performer to record with a symphony orchestra. In 1964 Morgan's duet of 'Slippin' Around' with Marion Worth was very successful, but by then Morgan was finding hits hard to come by. In 1967 he moved to Starday and then Nashville, Stop, US Decca and 4 Star, all with only minor successes. Morgan, a CB buff, suffered a heart attack whilst helping a friend install an aerial on his roof. Later that year, he celebrated his birthday at the *Opry* with the debut of his daughter, Lorrie. Within a few days he was undergoing open heart surgery but died on 7 July 1975. In 1979, a duet with Lorrie, 'I'm Completely Satisfied With You', made the US country charts. Lorrie Morgan married Keith Whitley and has been following a highly successful solo career since his death in May 1989.
Albums: *Morgan, By George* (1957), *Golden Memories* (1961), *Tender Lovin' Care* (1964), with Marion Worth *Slippin' Around* (1964), *Red Roses For A Blue Lady* (1965), *A Room Full Of Roses* (1967), *Candy Kisses* (1967), *Country Hits By Candlelight* (1968), *Steal Away* (1968), *Barbara* (1968), *Sounds Of Goodbye* (1969), *Misty Blue* (1969), *George Morgan Sings Like A Bird* (1969), *The Real George* (1969), *A Room Full Of Roses* (1971), *Red Roses From The Blue Side Of Town* (1974), *A Candy Mountain Melody* (1974), *George Morgan - From This Moment On* (1975), *Red Rose From The Blue Side Of Town* (1977), *George Morgan - Country Souvenirs Of The 1950s* (1990).

Morris Brothers

Wiley (mandolin/guitar/vocals) and Claude 'Zeke' Morris (guitar/vocals) are one of the many brother acts remembered for their fine harmony singing. At different times both worked with other bands including those of J.E. Mainer, Wade Mainer and Charley Monroe. They made their first recordings (accompanied by fiddler Homer Sherrill) for Bluebird in January 1938 and their next session (in September) yielded their noted version of 'Let Me Be Your Salty Dog'. They retired in the late 40s but did make some rare appearances later including at the 1964 Newport Folk Festival and on a special television programme with Earl Scruggs. They were actually the first musicians ever to employ noted banjoists Earl Scruggs and Don Reno in their band. A third brother George Morris also played with them on occasions.
Album: with Homer Sherrill *Wiley, Zeke & Homer* (c.1973).

Morris, Gary

b. 7 December 1948, Fort Worth, Texas, USA. Morris sang in a church choir and learned guitar, playing along to the Beatles' records. When he and two friends auditioned for a club owner in Denver, they were told they were 'on in 15 minutes . . . providing they played country music'. They stayed at the club for five years and then Morris returned to Texas. He started campaigning for Jimmy Carter and in 1978, after Carter's election, Morris performed on a country show at the White House. As a result, he was signed to MCA but when the singles did not sell, he moved to Colorado and formed a band, Breakaway. Producer Norro Wilson, who had been at the White House, signed him to Warners, but when Wilson moved to RCA, Morris found himself in limbo. Eventually, he had US country hits with 'Headed For A Heartache', 'Dreams Die Hard', 'Don't Look Back' and 'Velvet Chains'. In 1983, he became the first artist to put 'The Wind Beneath My Wings' on the US country charts and also scored hits with 'The Love She Found In Me', 'Why Lady Why?' and a duet with Lynn Anderson, 'You're Welcome To Tonight'. He first appeared on the *Grand Ole Opry* in 1984, the same year he appeared on Broadway in *La Bohème* (alongside Linda Ronstadt). Morris had his first US country number 1 in 1985 with 'Baby Bye Bye' and he has had further US number 1 records with 'I'll Never Stop Loving You', 'Making Up For Lost Time' (a duet with Crystal Gayle), '100% Chance Of Rain' and 'Leave Me Lonely'. He returned to Broadway in 1987 for the main role in *Les Misérables* and was also featured on the 1988 symphonic recording. He moved from opera to soap opera by playing the blind country singer, Wayne Masterson, in *The Colbys*. Morris has the vocal and the acting ability to take his career in any number of directions, although his commercial standing had dropped substantially by the early 90s.
Albums: *Gary Morris* (1982), *Why Lady Why* (1983), *Faded Blue* (1984), *Anything Goes...* (1985), *Second Hand Heart* (1986), *Plain Brown Wrapper* (1986), with Crystal Gayle *What If We Fall In Love* (1987), *Stones* (1989), *Full Moon, Empty Heart* (1991).

Morton, Tex

b. Robert William Lane, 8 August 1916, Nelson, New Zealand, d. 23 July 1983, Sydney, Australia. A Maori neighbour taught Morton his first guitar chords and he became so obsessed with music that, at the age of 15, he ran away from home and busked on the streets of Waihi. When asked one day by the town's policemen if his name was Bobby Lane, he noticed a nearby garage sign that gave the name of 'Morton' and quickly informed the officer that his name was Bob Morton and that he was a street singer and entertainer. He worked on various jobs, including one with a travelling troupe known as the Gaieties Of 1932. He made some aluminium disc recordings in Wellington (never commercially released), which proved very popular on local radio and may well be the first country music records made outside the USA. In 1932, he moved to Australia and worked with travelling shows, where apart from singing, he worked as a magician, a boxing booth fighter, with wild animals, as the stooge for others and even rode as a Wall Of Death rider. In 1934, with a repertoire of Australian bush ballads as well as the early country songs that he had heard on record, he moved to Sydney. He undertook whatever jobs he could find, including going to sea as a stoker and electrician, and once worked as a labourer for the firm responsible for installing the lighting on Sydney Harbour Bridge. After eventually winning a major talent show, he made his first recordings for Regal Zonophone in February 1936 when, among the four tracks recorded, two, 'Happy Yodeller' and 'Swiss Sweetheart', were his own compositions. The records sold well, further sessions soon followed and by 1937, Tex Morton the Yodelling Boundary Rider was a nationally known star. When he played his first concert in Brisbane, the crowd totalled 50,000. He continued to record throughout the late 30s, the material ranging from known country songs and his own numbers to recitations of the works of famous Australian poets Henry Lawson and Banjo Patterson. He published his Tex Morton songbook and a newspaper even ran a comic strip of his adventures. In 1939, a major star, he had established his own travelling circus/rodeo, where apart from singing, he entertained with trick shooting, fancy riding, a memory act and magic. World War II forced him to close his show and he invested heavily in a dude ranch, losing all his money when the project failed. After the war, he reformed his rodeo, linked it with another major touring zoo and circus and toured all over Australia. In 1949, he decided to move to the USA and, having by then learned an act using hypnotism as well as his other talents, he moved to Los Angeles. After spending two years working as a singer and acting on radio and in some films, he began to appear as The Great Doctor Robert

Morton - the World's Greatest Hypnotist. In 1951, he toured the USA and Canada with his one-man show on which he sang, did recitations, trick shooting, mind reading and hypnotism. He proved so popular that he set attendance records in many cities, including St. Louis, Boston and Vancouver and in Toronto his show outran *South Pacific*. Ever the showman, he used many gimmicks to attract the crowd, including stunts such as walking blindfold on the parapet of the tallest building in the town. In the early 60s, with many similar acts now performing, he gave up the hypnotism and, for a time, he worked on the stage and in films as Robert Morton. He returned to Australia in 1965, where he briefly and unsuccessfully resurrected The Great Morton. He toured for a while with a small rodeo show but soon found that television had made such entertainment no longer viable. He continued to record and in 1973, he scored a major Australian hit with his song 'The Goodiwindi Grey' (a tribute to a famous racehorse), recorded at what turned out to be his last recording session. Throughout the 70s, he appeared on television and in Australian films and although he often tried to leave out the old hillbilly and yodelling songs, the public would not let him. It is estimated that during his long career he recorded over 1000 songs and had many major national hits with numbers such as 'Beautiful Queensland', 'The Black Sheep' (his best selling song) and 'Good Old Droving Days'. Tex Morton died from pneumonia in July 1983. He was without doubt a most unusual person who had easily fulfilled his boyhood ambition to be an entertainer.

Selected albums: *The Tex Morton Story* (1959), *Tex Morton Looks Back* (1961), *Songs Of The Outback* (1961), *The Versatile Tex Morton* (1962), *Sing, Smile And Sigh* (c.1964), *Encores* (c.60s), *Hallelujah I'm A Bum* (c.60s, double album), *The Travelling Showman* (c.60s), *Tex Morton Today* (c.1970), *Tex Morton's Australia* (1973), Early tracks some with sister Dorrie *Red River Valley* (1975).

Mosby, Johnny And Jonie

b. 26 April c.30s, Ft. Smith, Arkansas, USA. Mosby moved to Los Angeles when a child and during the 50s built a reputation around the local country circuit, soon fronting his own band. He first met Jonie (b. Janice Irene Shields, 10 August 1940, Van Nuys, Los Angeles, California, USA) when she successfully auditioned for the post of female vocalist with his band early in 1958; and that same year they married. They made their first recordings for a minor label in 1959 and had local

chart success with 'Just Before Dawn'. They were later signed to Columbia Records and achieved their first US country chart entry in 1963 with a Harlan Howard song called 'Don't Call Me From A Honky Tonk'. They left Columbia and joined Capitol in 1964 and by 1973 had 16 further hits to their credit. These included 'Trouble In My Arms', 'Keep Those Cards And Letters Coming In' and 'Just Hold My Hand'. They also showed a penchant for recording, with minor success, country versions of songs that were pop hits, such as 'Hold Me, Thrill Me, Kiss Me' (Mel Carter), 'I'm Leaving It Up To You' (Dale And Grace) and 'My Happiness' (Connie Francis). Jonie and Johnny limited their touring in favour of raising their family but appeared on various television shows and for several years had their own *Country Music Time* on Los Angeles television. They moved to Nashville in the 70s but achieved no chart hits after 1973.

Albums: *The New Sweethearts Of Country Music* (1965), *Mr & Mrs Country Music* (1965), *Make A Left And Then A Right* (1968), *Hold Me* (1969), *I'll Never Be Free* (1969), *Just Hold My Hand* (1969), *My Happiness* (1970), *Oh, Love Of Mine* (1970).

Mullican, Moon

b. Aubrey Mullican, 29 March 1909, Corrigan, Polk County, Texas, USA, d. 1 January 1967. Mullican was raised on a farm which was manned by black workers. One sharecropper, Joe Jones, taught Mullican how to play blues guitar. His father bought an old pump organ so that the family could practice hymn-singing, but the Aubrey preferred to pound out boogie-woogie and the blues. When Mullican was 14 years old, he went into a cafe in nearby Lufkin and sat at the piano; he came out two hours later with $40 in tips. When aged 16, and after an argument with his father, he moved to Houston and started playing the piano in brothels and honky tonks. He would work all night and sleep all day, hence his nickname 'Moon'. In the late 30s Mullican made his first recordings for US Decca as part of Cliff Bruner's Texas Wanderers, taking the lead vocal for 'Truck Driver Blues', arguably the first trucking song. He also recorded as part of Leon Selph's Blue Ridge Playboys. He helped musician Jimmie Davis became the State Governor of Louisiana and later joined his staff. In 1944 he invested his savings in 10 large jukeboxes but they were confiscated by the authorities because he refused to pay the appropriate tax. In 1946 he was signed by Sid Nathan to the new King label and 'New Pretty

Blonde', a parody in pigeon French of 'Jole Blon', became a million-seller. He won another gold disc with 'I'll Sail My Ship Alone', and also found success with a tribute to mothers, 'Sweeter Than The Flowers', the double-sided 'Mona Lisa'/'Goodnight Irene' and 'Cherokee Boogie', which was one of a succession of boogie records.

In 1949 he wrote 'Jambalaya' with Hank Williams, although he was not given a credit. This is probably unjust because the style of the song - and the subject matter of food! - were more in keeping with Mullican's other work than Williams'. In the mid-50s, Mullican delighted in the advent of rock 'n' roll as he said he had been doing that all along. Backed by the hit-making Boyd Bennett And His Rockets, he recorded 'Seven Nights To Rock'. However, he was too portly and bald for teenage record buyers. Jerry Lee Lewis acknowledges Mullican as a major influence - in particular, Mullican's playing of the melody with just two fingers on his right hand - and has recorded 'I'll Sail My Ship Alone'. He recorded for Coral and Starday but alcohol and too much jambalaya got the better of him. When asked why he chose the piano, Mullican replied, 'Because the beer kept sliding off my fiddle.' In 1962, the 19-stone Mullican collapsed on stage in Kansas City. He stopped drinking and returned to performing, making an album for Kapp, *The Moon Mullican Showcase*, produced by Jack Clement. He recorded the novelty, 'I Ain't No Beatle (But I Want To Hold Your Hand)' for Spar. On New Year's Eve, 1966, he resolved to cut down on pork chops but died the following day. Governor Jimmie Davis sang at his funeral.

Albums: *Moon Over Mullican* (1958), *Moon Mullican Sings His All-Time Greatest Hits* (1958), *The Old Texan Sings And Plays 16 Of His Favorite Tunes* (1959), *The Many Moods Of Moon Mullican* (1960), *Instrumentals* (1962), *Mr. Piano Man* (1964), *Moon Mullican Sings 24 Of His Favorite Tunes* (1965), *Moon Mullican's Unforgettable Great Hits* (1967), *The Moon Mullican Showcase* (1969), *Seven Nights To Rock* (1983), *Just To Be With You* (1984), *Sweet Rockin' Music* (1984).

Murphey, Michael Martin

b. c.1946, Dallas, Texas, USA. Having been influenced by gospel music at an early age, Murphey aspired to become a Baptist minister. From 1965-70, as a staff songwriter for Screen Gems, Murphey was writing theme tunes and soundtrack material for television. He grew disillusioned with the poor financial rewards, and left. For a short while he was a member of the Lewis And Clark Expedition, which he formed, before going solo. *Geronimo's Cadillac* was produced in Nashville by Bob Johnston, who had originally got Murphey signed to A&M Records. The title track was released as a single, and achieved a Top 40 place in the USA. As well as folk, country and blues, Murphey's early gospel leanings are evident in the overall sound of what is an excellent album. He signed to Epic in 1973, after releasing *Cosmic Cowboy Souvenir* which continued the urban cowboy theme of his earlier work. His albums followed a more middle-of-the-road format after this, with occasional glimpses of his better work, as in *Peaks, Valleys, Honky-Tonks And Alleys*. However, he did reach number 3 in the US singles charts, achieving a gold disc, in 1975, with 'Wildfire'. Apart from *Blue Sky, Night Thunder* also achieved gold status. Murphey has never had the degree of commercial success his writing would indicate that he is capable of. However, as a writer, Murphey has had songs covered by John Denver, Cher, Claire Hamill, Hoyt Axton, Bobby Gentry and the Monkees, for whom he wrote 'What Am I Doin' Hangin' 'Round'.

He also wrote songs for Michael Nesmith after the latter's exit from the Monkees, including 'The Oklahoma Backroom Dance'. Murphey later played at Ronnie Scott's club in London, for a press presentation, and was supported on the occasion by J.D. Souther, Don Henley, Dave Jackson and Gary Nurm. *Geronimo's Cadillac* is probably his best remembered work. *Michael Martin Murphey* included a number of songs Murphey had co-written with Michael D'Abo. Murphey was featured in the film *Urban Cowboy* which included his song 'Cherokee Fiddle'. Much of the film was shot at Mickey Gilley's Bar. Murphey has continued recording easy listening country and, in 1987, had a number 1 country single with a wedding song, 'A Long Line Of Love'. He had US country hits with 'A Face In The Crowd', a duet with Holly Dunn, and 'Talkin' To The Wrong Man', which featured his son, Ryan. His 1990 album, *Cowboy Songs*, saw him return to his roots.

Albums: with the Lewis And Clark Expedition *I Feel Good, I Feel Bad*, *Geronimo's Cadillac* (1972), *Cosmic Cowboy Souvenir* (1973), *Michael Murphey* (1973), *Blue Sky Night Thunder* (1975), *Swans Against The Sun* (1976), *Flowing Free Forever* (1976), *Lone Wolf* (1977), *Peaks, Valleys, Honky-Tonks And Alleys* (1979), *Michael Martin Murphey* (1982), *The Heart Never Lies* (1983), *Tonight We Ride* (1986),

Americana (1987), *River Of Time* (1988), *Land Of Enchantment* (1989), *Cowboy Songs* (1990), *Cowboy Christmas - Cowboy Songs II* (1991). Compilation: *The Best Of Michael Martin Murphey* (1982)

Murray, Anne

b. 20 June 1946, Springhill, Nova Scotia, Canada. This doctor's daughter enjoyed local celebrity for her trained singing, which was accompanied by her own piano accompaniment. Nevertheless, she regarded music as a pastime when she graduated to New Brunswick University prior to a post as a physical training instructor at a Prince Edward Island school. In 1964 she was persuaded to audition for *Sing Along Jubilee*, a regional television show, but was selected instead for the same network's *Let's Go*, hosted by Bill Langstroth (her future husband). Income from a residency on the programme and solo concerts was sufficient for Murray to begin entertaining professionally in a vaguely folk/country rock style, though she could also acquit herself admirably with both R&B and mainstream pop material. Like Linda Ronstadt - seen by some as her US opposite number - she was mainly an interpreter of songs written by others. Issued by Arc Records, 1968's *What About Me*, created sufficient impact to interest Capitol Records, who signed her to a long term contract.

From *This Was My Way*, an arrangement of Gene MacLellan's remarkable 'Snowbird', soared into *Billboard*'s Top 10 (and was also her biggest UK hit). Despite regular appearances on Glen Campbell's *Goodtime Hour* television series, subsequent releases - including the title track to *Talk It Over In The Morning* - sold only moderately until 1973 when she scored another smash hit with 'Danny's Song', composed by Kenny Loggins (with whom she duetted 11 years later on 'Nobody Loves Me Like You Do', a country chart-topper). Although finishing 1976 as *Billboard*'s second most successful female artist, family commitments necessitated a brief period of domesticity before 1978's 'You Needed Me' won her a Grammy award. While revivals of Bobby Darin's 'Things' and the Monkees' 'Daydream Believer' were aimed directly at the pop market, it was with the country audience that she proved most popular. 'He Thinks I Still Care' (originally a b-side) became her first country number 1. However, between 'Just Another Woman In Love', 'Could I Have This Dance' (from the film *Urban Cowboy*), 1983's bold 'A Little Good News' and other country hits, she had also recorded a collection of children's ditties (*Hippo In My Tub*), commensurate with her

executive involvement with Canada's Save The Children Fund. In 1989 Springhill's Anne Murray Center was opened in recognition for her tireless work for the charity.

Albums: *What About Me* (1968), *This Was My Way* (1970), *Snowbird* (1970), *Anne Murray* (1971), *Talk It Over In The Morning* (1971), *Annie* (1972), *Anne Murray And Glen Campbell* (1972), *Danny's Song* (1973), *Love Song* (1974), *Country* (1974), *Highly Prized Possession* (1974), *Together* (1975), *Love Song* (1975), *Keeping In Touch* (1976), *Let's Keep It That Way* (1977), *Hippo In My Tub* (1979), *I'll Always Love You* (1980), *Somebody's Waiting* (1980), *Where Do You Go To When You Dream* (1981), *Christmas Wishes* (1981), *The Hottest Night Of The Year* (1982), *A Little Good News* (1983), *Heart Over Mind* (1985), *Something To Talk About* (1986), *Harmony* (1989). Compilations: *A Country Collection* (1980), *Greatest Hits* (1980), *The Very Best Of Anne Murray* (1981).

N

Naylor, Jerry

b. Jerry Naylor Jackson, 6 March 1939, Stephenville, Texas, USA. Naylor sang country music from an early age; when aged only 14, he appeared on *Louisiana Hayride*. Whilst in the US Army, he broke his back, an injury that has continued to plague him since then. He befriended Glen Campbell in Albuquerque, New Mexico and in 1961 moved with him to Hollywood. He found work as a disc jockey and a single, 'You're Thirteen', was released in the UK. He and Campbell joined the Crickets in 1962 and is featured on 'Don't Ever Change', 'My Little Girl' and 'Teardrops Fall Like Rain'. In 1964 he had a heart attack brought about, he says, 'by the stress of being Buddy Holly's replacement'. He played the leading role in a concept album, a country opera entitled *The Legend Of Johnny Brown* in 1966. He returned to the Crickets for their 1971 album, *Rockin' 50s Rock And Roll*, but mostly he has followed a solo career, making numerous singles for US labels including Motown's country division. His best-known record is 'Is That All There Is To A Honky Tonk?' in 1975. He now works as a disc jockey in Angoura, California and he is known to Buddy Holly fans for his outrageous claims such as being a Cricket throughout their hitmaking years.
Albums: *Happy Birthday USA* (1976), *Love Away Her Memory* (1977), *Once Again* (1978).

Nelson, Rick

b. Eric Hilliard Nelson, 8 May 1940, Teaneck, New Jersey, USA, d. 31 December 1985, De Kalb, Texas, USA. Nelson came from a showbusiness family and his parents had sung in bands during the 30s and 40s. They had their own US radio show, *The Adventures Of Ozzie And Harriet,* soon transferred to television, in which Ricky and his brother David appeared. By 1957 Nelson embarked on a recording career, with the million selling, double-sided 'I'm Walkin''/'A Teenager's Romance'. A third hit soon followed with 'You're My One And Only Love'. A switch from the label Verve to Imperial saw Nelson enjoy further success with the rockabilly 'Be-Bop Baby'. In 1958 Nelson formed a full-time group for live work and recordings, which included James Burton (guitar), James Kirkland (later replaced by Joe Osborn) (bass), Gene Garf (piano) and Richie Frost (drums). Early that year Nelson enjoyed his first transatlantic hit with 'Stood Up' and registered his first US chart topper with 'Poor Little Fool'. His early broadcasting experience was put to useful effect when he starred in the Howard Hawks movie western, *Rio Bravo* (1959), alongside John Wayne and Dean Martin. Nelson's singles continued to chart regularly and it says much for the quality of his work that the b-sides were often as well known as the a-sides. Songs such as 'Believe What You Say', 'Never Be Anyone Else But You', 'It's Late', 'Sweeter Than You', 'Just A Little Too Much' and 'I Wanna Be Loved' showed that Nelson was equally adept at singing ballads and uptempo material. One of his greatest moments as a pop singer occurred in the spring of 1961 when he issued the million-selling 'Travelin' Man' backed with the exuberant Gene Pitney composition 'Hello Mary Lou'. Shortly after the single topped the US charts, Nelson celebrated his 21st birthday and announced that he was changing his performing name from Ricky to Rick.

Several more pop hits followed, most notably 'Young World', 'Teenage Idol', 'It's Up To You', 'String Along' (his first for his new label, Decca), 'Fools Rush In' and 'For You'. With the emergence of the beat boom, Nelson's clean-cut pop was less in demand and in 1966 he switched to country music. His early albums in this vein featured compositions from such artists as Willie Nelson, Glen Campbell, Tim Hardin, Harry Nilsson and Randy Newman.

In 1969 Nelson formed a new outfit the Stone Canyon Band featuring former Poco member Randy Meisner (bass), Allen Kemp (guitar), Tom Brumley (steel guitar) and Pat Shanahan (drums). A version of Bob Dylan's 'She Belongs To Me' brought Nelson back into the US charts and a series of strong, often underrated albums followed. A performance at Madison Square Garden in late 1971 underlined Nelson's difficulties at the time. Although he had recently issued the accomplished *Rick Sings Nelson*, on which he wrote every track, the audience were clearly more interested in hearing his early 60s hits. Nelson responded by composing the sarcastic 'Garden Party', which reaffirmed his determination to go his own way. The single, ironically, went on to sell a million and was his last hit record. After parting with the Stone Canyon Band in 1974, Nelson's recorded output declined, but he continued to tour extensively. On 31 December 1985, a chartered plane carrying him to a concert date in Dallas caught fire and crashed

Rick Nelson

near De Kalb, Texas. Nelson's work deserves a place in rock history as he was one of the few 'good looking kids' from the late 500s who had a strong voice which, coupled with exemplary material, remains durable.

Albums: *Teen Time* (1957), *Ricky* (1957), *Ricky Nelson* (1958), *Ricky Sings Again* (1959), *Songs By Ricky* (1959), *More Songs By Ricky* (1960), *Rick Is 21* (1961), *Album Seven By Rick* (1962), *A Long Vacation* (1963), *For Your Sweet Love* (1963), *Ricky Sings For You* (1964), *The Very Thought Of You* (1964), *Spotlight On Rick* (1965), *Best Always* (1965), *Love And Kisses* (1966), *Bright Lights And Country Music* (1966), *Country Fever* (1967), *On The Flip-Side* (1967, film soundtrack), *Another Side Of Rick* (1969), *In Concert* (1970), *Rick Sings Nelson* (1970), *Rudy The Fifth* (1971), *Garden Party* (1972), *Windfall* (1974), *Intakes* (1977), *Playing To Win* (1981). Compilations: *It's Up To You* (1963), *Million Sellers* (1964), *The Very Best Of Rick Nelson* (1970), *Legendary Masters* (1972), *The Singles Album 1963-1976* (1977), *The Singles Album 1957-63* (1979), *Rockin' With Ricky* (1984), *String Along With Rick* (1984), *The Best Of Ricky Nelson* (1985), *All The Best* (1986).

Further reading: *Ricky Nelson*, Joel Selvin.

Nelson, Tracy

b. 27 December 1944, Madison, Wisconsin, USA. Tutored on both piano and guitar as a child, Nelson began a singing career while studying at Wisconsin University. She was a member of two bands, including the Imitations, prior to recording her solo debut, *Deep Are The Roots*, in 1965. Charlie Musselwhite (harmonica) and Peter Wolfe (guitar) added support to a set drawing much of its inspiration from blues singers Ma Rainey and Bessie Smith. In 1966 Nelson became a founder member of Mother Earth, an excellent country/blues attraction which she later came to dominate as original members pursued other projects. By 1973, when they were recording regularly in Nashville, the group had become known as Tracy Nelson/Mother Earth, and that year's *Poor Man's Paradise* was, effectively, a solo album. The singer's independent career was officially launched the following year with *Tracy Nelson*, which included a powerful version of Bob Dylan's 'It Takes A Lot To Laugh It Takes A Train To Cry'. Ensuing recordings revealed a mature, self-confident vocalist working in an eclectic style redolent of Bonnie Raitt. Recording opportunities decreased during the 80s, although Nelson continues to perform live; in 1990 she completed

several live dates in the UK.

Albums: *Deep Are The Roots* (1965), *Tracy Nelson* (1974), *Sweet Soul Music* (1975), *Time Is On My Side* (1976), *Home Made Songs* (1978), *Doin' It My Way* (1980), *Come See About Me* (1980).

Nelson, Willie

b. Willie Hugh Nelson, 30 April 1933, Abbott, Texas, USA. Following their mother's desertion and the death of their father, Nelson and his sister Bobbie were raised by their grandparents. Bobbie was encouraged to play the piano and Willie the guitar. By the age of 7 he was writing cheating-heart-style songs. 'Maybe I got 'em from soap operas on the radio,' he said, 'but I've always seemed to see the sad side of things.' Bobbie married the fiddle player Bud Fletcher, and they both played in his band. When Fletcher booked western swing star Bob Wills, the 13-year-old Willie Nelson joined him for a duet. After graduation he enlisted in the US Air Force, but was invalided out with a bad back, which has continued to plague his career to the present day. In 1953 Nelson began a traumatic marriage in Waco, Texas. 'Martha was a full-blooded Cherokee Indian,' says Nelson, 'and every night was like Custer's last stand.' When they moved to Fort Worth, Texas, Nelson was criticized for playing beer-joints and inappropriately evangelising – he fortunately gave up the latter. A Salvation Army drummer, Paul English, has been his drummer ever since, and is referred to in 'Me And Paul' and 'Devil In A Sleepin' Bag'. Nelson's first record, 'Lumberjack', was recorded in Vancouver, Washington in 1956 and written by Leon Payne. Payne, then a radio disc jockey, advertised the records for sale on the air. For $1, a listener received the record and an autographed 8 x 10 photo of Nelson. 3,000 copies were sold by this method. In Houston he sold 'Family Bible' to a guitar scholar for $50 and when it became a country hit for Claude Gray in 1960, Nelson's name was not on the label. He also sold 'Night Life' for $150 to the director of the same school: Ray Price made it a country hit and there have now been over 70 other recordings. Nelson moved to Nashville where his off-beat, nasal phrasing and dislike of rhinestone trimmings made him radically different from other country musicians. He recorded demos in 1961, which he later rescued from a fire. The demos were spread over three collections, *Face Of A Fighter*, *Diamonds In The Rough* and *Slow Down Old World*, but they are often repackaged in an attempt to pass off old material as new. These one-paced collections are not meant to encourage new fans as the songs are bleak, very bleak or unbearably bleak. From time to time Nelson has re-recorded one of these songs for another album.

In 1961 three of Nelson's country songs crossed over to the US pop charts: Patsy Cline's 'Crazy', Faron Young's 'Hello Walls' and Jimmy Elledge's 'Funny How Time Slips Away'. Ray Price employed Nelson playing bass with his band, the Cherokee Cowboys, not knowing that he had never played the instrument. Nelson bought a bass, practised all night and showed up the next day as a bass player. Touring put further pressures on his marriage and he was divorced in 1962. The following year Nelson had his first country hits as a performer, first in a duet with Shirley Collie, 'Willingly' and then on his own with 'Touch Me'. His 40 tracks recorded for Liberty Records were top-heavy on strings, but they included the poignant 'Half A Man' and the whimsical 'River Boy'. He also wrote a witty single for Joe Carson, 'I Gotta Get Drunk (And I Sure Do Dread It)'. When Liberty dropped their country performers, Nelson moved to Monument. He gave Roy Orbison 'Pretty Paper', which made the UK Top 10 in 1964 and became Nelson's most successful composition in the UK. Some Monument tracks were revamped for The Winning Hand, which gave the misleading impression that Nelson had joined forces with Kris Kristofferson, Brenda Lee and Dolly Parton for a double-album. In 1965 Nelson married Shirley Collie and took up pig-farming in Ridgetop, Tennessee. During the same year Ray Price refused to record any more of Nelson's songs after an accident when Nelson shot his fighting rooster. They eventually joined forces for an album. Chet Atkins produced some fine albums for Nelson on RCA, including a tribute to his home state, Texas In My Soul.

However, he was only allowed to record with his own musicians on the live Country Music Concert album, which included an emotional 'Yesterday' and a jazzy 'I Never Cared For You'. He recorded around 200 tracks for the label, including well-known songs of the day like 'Both Sides Now', 'Help Me Make It Through The Night' and, bizarrely, the UK comedy team, Morecambe And Wise's theme song, 'Bring Me Sunshine'. Yesterday's Wine remains his finest RCA album, although it begins rather embarrassingly with Nelson talking to God. Nelson wrote seven of the songs in one night, but he was unstable as he drank heavily and used drugs. 'What Can You Do To Me Now?' indicated his anguish.

During 1970 his show-business lawyer, Neil Rushen, thought Nelson should record for Atlantic Records in New York. The singer used his own band, supplemented by Doug Sahm and Larry Gatlin. Atlantic did not feel that The Troublemaker was right for the label and it only surfaced after he had moved to Columbia. Shotgun Willie was closer to rock music and included Leon Russell's 'A Song For You' and the reflective 'Sad Songs And Waltzes'. Phases And Stages (1974), made in Muscle Shoals, Alabama, looked at the break-up of a marriage from both sides - the woman's ('Washing The Dishes') and the man's ('It's Not Supposed To Be That Way'). Nelson also recorded a successful duet with Tracy Nelson (no relation) of 'After The Fire Is Gone'. He toured extensively and his bookings at a rock venue, the Armadillo World Headquarters in Austin, showed that he might attract a new audience. Furthermore, Waylon Jennings' hit with 'Ladies Love Outlaws' indicated a market for 'outlaw country' music. The term separated them from more conventional country artists, and, with a pigtail and a straggly beard, Nelson no longer looked like a country performer. Ironically, they were emphasizing the very thing from which country music was trying to escape - the cowboy image. In 1975 Nelson signed with Columbia and wanted to record a lengthy, old ballad, 'Red Headed Stranger'. His wife suggested that he split the song into sections and fit other songs around it. This led to an album about an old-time preacher and his love for an unfaithful woman. The album consisted of Willie's voice and guitar and Bobbie's piano. Columbia thought it was too low-key, too religious and needed strings. They were eventually persuaded to release it as it was and Red Headed Stranger (1975) has since become a country classic. Nelson's gentle performance of the country standard, 'Blue Eyes Crying In The Rain', was a number 1 country hit and also made number 21 on the US pop charts in 1975.

With brilliant marketing, RCA then compiled Wanted: The Outlaws with Jennings, Nelson, Jessi Colter and Tompall Glaser. It became the first country album to go platinum and it included a hit single, 'Good Hearted Woman', in which Jennings' thumping beat and Nelson's sensitivity were combined beautifully. The first Waylon And Willie (1978) album included Ed Bruce's witty look at outlaw country, 'Mammas, Don't Let Your Babies Grow Up To Be Cowboys' and two beautifully restrained Nelson performances, 'If You Can

Willie Nelson

Touch Her At All' and 'A Couple More Years'. Their two subsequent albums contained unsuitable or weak material and perfunctory arrangements, although the humorous *Clean Shirt* (1991) was a welcome return to form. Since then, they have added Johnny Cash and Kris Kristofferson for tours and albums as the Highwaymen. Nelson has also recorded two albums with Merle Haggard, including the highly successful 'Poncho And Lefty', as well as several albums with country stars of the 50s and 60s. His numerous guest appearances include 'Seven Spanish Angels' (Ray Charles), 'The Last Cowboy Song' (Ed Bruce), 'Are There Any More Real Cowboys?' (Neil Young), 'One Paper Kid' (Emmylou Harris), 'I Gotta Get Drunk' (George Jones), 'Waltz Across Texas' (Ernest Tubb), 'They All Went To Mexico' (Carlos Santana) and 'Something To Brag About' (Mary Kay Place). Utilizing modern technology, he sang with Hank Williams on 'I Told A Lie To My Heart'. He invited Julio Iglesias to join him at the Country Music Awards and their duet of Albert Hammond's 'To All The Girls I've Known Before' was an international success.

Nelson has recorded numerous country songs, including a tribute album to Lefty Frizzell, but, more significant has been his love of standards. He had always recorded songs like 'Am I Blue?' and 'That Lucky Old Sun', but *Stardust* (1978), which was produced by Booker T. Jones of the MGs, took country fans by surprise. The weather-beaten, top-hatted character on the sleeve *was* Willie Nelson but the contents resembled a Bing Crosby album. Nelson sang ten standards, mostly slowly, to a small rhythm section and strings. The effect was devastating as he breathed new life into 'Georgia On My Mind' and 'Someone To Watch Over Me', and the album remained on the US country charts for nearly 10 years. Nelson recorded 103 songs in a week with Leon Russell but their performance of standards falls far short of *Stardust*. Nelson tried to recapture the magic of *Stardust* on the lethargic *Without A Song*, which contained the first Nelson/Julio Iglesias duet, 'As Time Goes By'. In both performance and arrangement, his Christmas album, *Pretty Paper* (1979), sounds like a mediocre act at a social club, but the jaunty *Somewhere Over The Rainbow* (the Arlen/Harburg classic) is much better. In 1982 Johnny Christopher showed Nelson a song he had written, 'Always On My Mind'. Nelson wanted to record the song with Merle Haggard, but Haggard did not care for it, so Nelson recorded an emotional and convincing version on his own, which went to Number 5 in the US charts. It was some time before Nelson learnt that Elvis Presley had previously recorded the song. The resulting album, which included 'Let It Be Me' and 'A Whiter Shade Of Pale', showed his mastery of the popular song. Other modern songs to which he has added his magic include 'City Of New Orleans', 'Wind Beneath My Wings' and 'Please Come To Boston'. He sang another Presley hit, 'Love Me Tender', on the soundtrack of *Porky's Revenge*. When Robert Redford met Nelson at a party, he invited him to join the cast of *The Electric Horseman*. Willie had an entertaining role as Redford's manager, and he made a major contribution to the soundtrack with 'My Heroes Have Always Been Cowboys'. Redford wanted to star in the film of *Red Headed Stranger* (1987) but it was cast eventually with Nelson in the title role. His other films include *Barbarosa* (in which he played an old gunfighter), a re-make of *Stagecoach* with his outlaw friends, and the cliche-ridden *Songwriter* with Kris Kristofferson. He is more suited to cameo roles and has the makings of a latter-day Gabby Hayes.

Nelson's record label, Lone Star, which he started in 1978 with Steven Fromholz and the Geezinslaw Brothers, was not a commercial success, but he later developed his own recording studio and golf course at Pedernales, Texas. He often adds the passing vocal and he produced *Timi Yuro - Today* there in 1982. He took over the Dripping Springs Festival and turned it into a festival of contemporary country music: Willie Nelson's Fourth of July Picnic. He has organized several Farm Aid benefits, and he and Kenny Rogers represented country music on the number 1 USA For Africa single, 'We Are The World'. With all this activity, it is hardly surprising that his songwriting has suffered and he rarely records new compositions now. He wrote 'On The Road Again' for the country music film in which he starred, *Honeysuckle Rose*, and he also wrote a suite of songs about the old west and reincarnation, *Tougher Than Leather*, when he was in hospital with a collapsed lung.

Among the many songs which have been written *about* Willie Nelson are 'Willy The Wandering Gypsy And Me' (Billy Joe Shaver), 'Willie, Won't You Sing A Song With Me' (George Burns), 'Crazy Old Soldier' (Lacy J. Dalton), 'Willon And Waylee' (Don Bowman), 'The Willie And Waylon Machine' (Marvin Rainwater), 'Willie' (Hank Cochran and Merle Haggard) and 'It's Our Turn To Sing With Ol' Willie' (Carlton Moody And The Moody Brothers). Nelson's touring band, Family, is a very tight unit featuring musicians who have been with him for many years. Audiences love his image as an old salt, looking rough and playing a battered guitar, and his headbands have become souvenirs in the same way as Elvis' scarves. His greatest testimony comes from President Jimmy Carter, who joined him onstage and said, 'I, my wife, my daughter, my sons and my mother all think he's the greatest'. Unfortunately, the USA's Inland Revenue Service took a different view and, in an effort to obtain $16 million in back taxes, they had Nelson make an acoustic album, which was sold by mail order. His collaboration with artists like Bob Dylan and Paul Simon on *Across The Borderline* brought him back into the commercial mainstream for the first time in several years. In 1991 Nelson married Annie D'Angelo and they now have a young family. Nelson is a true outlaw and arguably the greatest legend and performer in country music since Hank Williams.

Albums: *...And Then I Wrote* (1962), *Here's Willie Nelson* (1963), *Country Willie - His Own Songs* (1965), *Country Favorites - Willie Nelson Style* (1966), *Country Music Concert (Live At Panther Hall)* (1966), *Make Way For Willie Nelson* (1967), *The Party's Over* (1967), *Texas In My Soul* (1968), *Good Times* (1968), *My Own Peculiar Way* (1969), *Both Sides Now* (1970), *Laying My Burdens Down* (1970), *Willie Nelson And Family* (1971), *Yesterday's Wine* (1971), *The Words Don't Fit The Picture* (1972), *The Willie Way* (1972), *Shotgun Willie* (1973), *Phases And Stages* (1974), *Red Headed Stranger* (1975), with Waylon Jennings, Jessi Colter and Tompall Glaser *Wanted: The Outlaws* (1976), *The Sound In Your Mind* (1976), *Willie Nelson - Live* (1976), *The Troublemaker* (1976), *To Lefty From Willie* (1977), *Stardust* (1978), *Face Of A Fighter* (1978), *Willie And Family Live* (1978), with Jennings *Waylon And Willie* (1978), *The Electric Horseman* (1979), *Willie Nelson Sings Kristofferson* (1979), *Pretty Paper* (1979), *Danny Davis And Willie Nelson With The Nashville Brass* (1980), with Leon Russell *One For The Road* (1980), with Ray Price *San Antonio Rose* (1980), *Honeysuckle Rose* (1980), *Family Bible* (1980), *Somewhere Over The Rainbow* (1981), with Roger Miller *Old Friends* (1982), *Diamonds In The Rough* (1982), with Merle Haggard *Poncho And Lefty* (1982), with Johnny Bush *Together Again* (1982), *Always On My Mind* (1982), with Jennings *WWII* (1982), with Webb Pierce *In The Jailhouse Now* (1982), with Kris Kristofferson, Brenda Lee and Dolly Parton *The Winning Hand* (1982), *Without A Song* (1983), *Tougher Than Leather* (1983), with Jennings *Take It To The Limit* (1983), with Jackie King *Angel Eyes* (1984), *Slow Down Old World* (1984), *City Of New Orleans* (1984), with

Kristofferson *Songwriter* (1984), with Johnny Cash, Jennings and Kristofferson *Highwayman* (1985), with Faron Young *Funny How Time Slips Away* (1985), with Hank Snow *Brand On My Heart* (1985), *Me And Paul* (1985), *Half Nelson* (1985), *The Promiseland* (1986), *Partners* (1986), with Haggard *Seashores Of Old Mexico* (1987), *Island In The Sea* (1987), with J.R. Chatwell *Jammin' With J.R. And Friends* (1988), *What A Wonderful World* (1988), *A Horse Called Music* (1989), with Cash, Jennings and Kristofferson *Highwayman 2* (1990), *Born For Trouble* (1990), with Jennings *Clean Shirt* (1991), *Who'll Buy My Memories - The IRS Tapes* (1991), *Across The Borderline* (1993). Compilations: *Willie Nelson's Greatest Hits (And Some That Will Be)* (1981), *Country Willie* (1987), *The Collection* (1988), *Across The Tracks - The Best Of Willie Nelson* (1988), *20 Of The Best* (1991).

Further reading: *Willie Nelson Family Album*, Lana Nelson Fowler. *Willie Nelson - Country Outlaw*, Lola Socbey. *Willie*, Michael Bane. *I Didn't Come Here And I Ain't Leavin'*, Willie Nelson with Bud Shrake. *Heartworn Memories - A Daughter's Personal Biography Of Willie Nelson*, Susie Nelson.

Neon Philharmonic

Neon Philharmonic was essentially the work of two musicians, the Nashville, Tennessee-based singer-songwriter Don Gant (b. 1942) and arranger/conductor/composer Tuppy Saussy. Gant's career included writing songs with Roy Orbison and singing solo and background for country artists such as Don Gibson and John D. Loudermilk. He produced records for many artists, including Bobby 'Blue' Bland, Jimmy Buffett and Lefty Frizzell. Gant also ran ABC-Dunhill Records and was president of the Nashville branch of the National Academy of Recording Arts and Sciences (NARAS). Gant teamed with Saussy in 1969 and recorded the latter's 'Morning Girl' for Warner Brothers Records with a chamber group comprised of members of the Nashville Symphony Orchestra. The record made the US Top 20 and one follow-up single also reached the charts. The 'group' released two albums and five further singles but the novelty had diminished. Gant died on the 6th March, 1987.

Albums: *Moth Confesses* (1969), *Neon Philharmonic* (1969).

Nesmith, Michael

b. Robert Michael Nesmith, 30 December 1942, Houston, Texas, USA. Although best-known as a member of the Monkees, Nesmith enjoyed a

prolific career in music prior to this group's inception. During the mid-60s folk boom he performed with bassist John London as Mike and John, but later pursed work as a solo act. Two singles, credited to Michael Blessing, were completed under the aegis of New Christy Minstrels' mastermind Randy Sparks, while Nesmith's compositions, 'Different Drum' and 'Mary Mary' were recorded, respectively, by the Stone Poneys and Paul Butterfield. Such experience gave the artist confidence to demand the right to determine the Monkees' musical policy and his sterling country-rock performances were the highlight of the group's varied catalogue. In 1968 he recorded *The Witchita Train Whistle Sings*, an instrumental set, but his independent aspirations did not fully flourish until 1970 when he formed the First National Band. Former colleague London joined Orville 'Red' Rhodes (pedal steel) and John Ware (drums) in a group completing three exceptional albums which initially combined Nashville-styled country with the leader's acerbic pop, (*Magnetic South*), but later grew to encompass a grander, even eccentric interpretation of the genre (*Nevada Fighter*). The band disintegrated during the latter's recording and a Second National Band, on which Nesmith and Rhodes were accompanied by Johnny Meeks (bass; ex-Gene Vincent and Merle Haggard) and Jack Panelli (drums), completed the less impressive *Tantamount To Treason*. The group was disbanded entirely for the sarcastically-entitled *And The Hits Just Keep On Comin'*, a haunting, largely acoustic, set regarded by many as the artist's finest work. In 1972 he founded the Countryside label under the aegis of Elektra Records, but despite critically-acclaimed sets by Iain Matthews, Garland Frady and the ever-present Rhodes, the project was axed in the wake of boardroom politics. The excellent *Pretty Much Your Standard Ranch Stash* ended the artist's tenure with RCA, following which he founded a second label, Pacific Arts. *The Prison*, an allegorical narrative which came replete with a book, was highly criticized upon release, although recent opinion has lauded its ambition. Nesmith reasserted his commercial status in 1977 when 'Rio', culled from *From A Radio Engine To The Photon Wing*, reached the UK Top 30. The attendant video signalled a growing interest in the visual arts which flourished following *Infinite Rider On The Big Dogma*, his biggest selling US release. In 1982 *Elephant Parts* won the first ever Grammy for a video, while considerable acclaim was engendered by a subsequent series, *Michael Nesmith In Television*

Parts, and the film Repo Man, which the artist financed. Having refused entreaties to join the Monkees' 20th Anniversary Tour, this articulate entrepreneur continues to pursue his various diverse interests including a highly successful video production company (Pacific Arts), while rumours of new recordings continue to proliferate.

Albums: The Wichita Train Whistle Sings (1968), Magnetic South (1970), Loose Salute (1971), Nevada Fighter (1971), Tantamount To Treason (1972), And The Hits Just Keep On Comin' (1972), Pretty Much Your Standard Ranch Stash (1973), The Prison (1975), From A Radio Engine To The Photon Wing (1977), Live At The Palais (1978), Infinite Rider On The Big Dogma (1979). Compilations: The Best Of Mike Nesmith (1977), The Newer Stuff (1989).

New Grass Revival

The New Grass Revival evolved around the fiddle talents of Sam Bush, who also plays guitar, mandolin and sings. Another longstanding member is bas player, John Cowan, who, somewhat surprisingly, contributed soaring R&B-styled vocals to an acoustic band. The four-piece group had some success with the Leon Russell song, 'Prince Of Peace'. They toured with Russell and cut a live album and video together at Perkins' Palace in Pasadena. In 1984 the band moved to Sugar Hill Records and their albums, whilst essentially bluegrass, also include jazz, reggae and soul. Amongst the later members of the Revival is the highly respected banjo player, Bela Flack. In 1991 Emmylou Harris formed an acoustic band, the Nash Ramblers, to accompany her, the leader of the group being Sam Bush. The New Grass Revival are the most significant acoustic country band in the USA, but Bush's involvement with Harris may limit their future activities.

Albums: Arrival Of The New Grass Revival (1973), Fly Through The Country (1975), Commonwealth (1976), When The Storm Is Over (1977), Too Late To Turn Back Now (1978), Barren Country (1980), Leon Russell And The New Grass Revival (1981), On The Boulevard (1984), New Grass Revival (1986), Hold On To A Dream (1987), Friday Night In America (1989).

Newbury, Mickey

b. Milton J. Newbury Jnr., 19 May 1940, Houston, Texas, USA. Newbury began by singing tenor in a harmony group, the Embers, who recorded for Mercury Records. He worked as an air traffic controller in the US Air Force and was stationed in England. He later wrote 'Swiss Cottage Place', which was recorded by Roger Miller. In 1963 he worked on shrimp boats in Galveston, Texas and started song writing in earnest. In 1964 he was signed to Acuff-Rose Music in Nashville. Among his early compositions are 'Here Comes The Rain, Baby' (Eddy Arnold and Roy Orbison), 'Funny Familiar Forgotten Feelings' (Don Gibson and Tom Jones), 'How I Love Them Old Songs' (Carl Smith) and 'Sweet Memories' (Willie Nelson). In 1968 Kenny Rogers And The First Edition had a US pop hit with the psychedelic 'Just Dropped In (To See What Condition My Condition Was In)'. Newbury recorded low-key albums of his own but his voice was so mournful that even his happier songs sounded sad. After two albums for RCA, he moved to Mercury and wrote and recorded such sombre songs as 'She Even Woke Me Up To Say Goodbye' (later recorded by Jerry Lee Lewis), 'San Francisco Mabel Joy' (recorded by John Denver, Joan Baez, David Allan Coe and Kenny Rogers) and 'I Don't Think About Her (Him) No More', which has been recorded by Don Williams and Tammy Wynette, and also by Bobby Bare, under the title of 'Poison Red Berries'. Newbury, who by now lived on a houseboat, was intrigued by the way his wind chimes mingled with the rain, thus leading to the sound effects he used to link tracks with. This gave his albums of similar material a concept. His gentle and evocative 'American Trilogy' - in actuality a medley of three Civil War songs ('Dixie', 'The Battle Hymn Of The Republic' and 'All My Trials') - was a hit in a full-blooded version by Elvis Presley in 1972. Says Newbury, 'It was more a detriment than a help because it was not indicative of what I could do.' Nevertheless, his Rusty Tracks also features reworkings of American folk songs. Amongst his successful compositions are 'Makes Me Wonder If I Ever Said Goodbye' (Johnny Rodriguez) and 'Blue Sky Shinin'' (Marie Osmond). He has scarcely made a mark as a performer in the US country charts (his highest position is number 53 for 'Sunshine') but he was elected to the Nashville Songwriters International Hall of Fame in 1980. Ironically, he has released few new songs since and his 'new age' album in 1988 featured re-recordings of old material. Although he performs USA dates with violinist Marie Rhines, he makes a habit of cancelling UK tours.

Albums: Harlequin Melodies (1968), Mickey Newbury Sings His Own (1968), Looks Like Rain (1969), 'Frisco Mabel Joy (1971), Heaven Help The Child (1973), Live At Montezuma (1973, also issued as a double-album with *Looks Like Rain*), *I Came To Hear The Music* (1974), *Lovers* (1975), *Rusty Tracks* (1977), *His Eye Is On The Sparrow* (1978), *The Sailor* (1979), *After All These Years* (1981), *In A New Age* (1988). Compilation: *Sweet Memories* (1988).

Newman, Jimmy C.

b. Jimmy Yves Newman, 27 August 1927, Big Mamou, Louisiana, USA. Since he was of half French origin, spoke both English and French and grew up in the heart of the cajun area of the State, it is no surprise that he went on to become one of the main artists to bring that genre of music into the field of country music. He left school prematurely when his father died to help support his eight siblings. Newman first became interested in country music through hearing his brother Walter play guitar and sing Jimmie Rodgers' songs. In the mid-40s he played in a local cajun band and made his first recording in French in 1946. Later, he formed his own band, played local radio and small venues around the State, and eventually got his own programme on KPLC-TV in Lake Charles, where his mixture of cajun and country music soon proved popular. In 1949 he recorded the original version of the Webb Pierce hit 'Wondering'. The release failed to chart but, determined to find a hit song, he wrote and recorded 'Cry Cry Darling'. Listeners to his early recordings will note a prominent hiss on his pronunciation of the letter 'S', caused by a badly fitted gold tooth. Fred Rose tried to eliminate the problem by changing lyrics, such as in 'Cry Cry Darling', where 'sunshine' became 'moonlight'. (A little later a partial denture replaced the offending tooth and permanently cured the problem). Also through the auspices of Fred Rose, Newman joined Dot Records. In 1954 a new recording of 'Cry Cry Darling' reached number 4 on the US country charts and led him to join the *Louisiana Hayride*. Between 1955 and 1957 he had five more Top 10 country hits, the biggest being his recording of Ned Miller's 'A Fallen Star', which became a number 2 country and number 23 pop hit. Newman acquired the 'C' to his name when the drummer on the recording of the song, T. Tommy Cutrer, labelled him Jimmy 'Cajun' Newman and the initial stuck. He did not like rockabilly or novelty songs, but did record 'Bop-A-Hula' and the Jim Reeves song 'Step Aside Shallow Waters'.

In 1958 he moved to MGM, where Top 10 country hits included 'You're Making A Fool Out Of Me' and 'A Lovely Work Of Art'. In 1961 he left MGM because he felt he was losing his cajun roots. He joined Decca and in the next nine years charted 16 country hits including such popular recordings as 'DJ For A Day' and 'Artificial Rose' and cajun numbers including 'Alligator Man', 'Bayou Talk' and 'Louisiana Saturday Night'. His last chart hit came in 1970 with a song called 'I'm Holding Your Memory'. He later recorded for several minor labels including Plantation. From the mid-50s through the 70s he toured extensively throughout the States, played some overseas concerts and has also appeared on all major network radio and television shows. He became a member of the *Grand Ole Opry* in 1956 and still maintains his regular appearances, often hosting one of the show's segments. Newman's plaintive tenor vocals and traditional fiddle and steel guitar backing were ideally suited to the country music of the 50s and 60s and at times, except for his cajun numbers, he was comparable in vocal work to Webb Pierce. He has always proved a great favourite with UK audiences on the occasions when he has appeared at the Wembley Festival and continues to tour with veteran cajun musicians like fiddle player Rufus Thibodeaux.

Albums: *This Is Jimmy Newman* (1959), *Jimmy Newman* (1962), *Songs By Jimmy Newman* (1962), *Folk Songs Of The Bayou Country* (1963), *Artificial Rose* (1966), *Country Crossroads* (1966), *A Fallen Star* (1966), *Sings Country Songs* (1966), *The World Of Country Music* (1977), *Born To Love You* (1968), *The Jimmy Newman Way* (1968), *The Jimmy Newman Style* (1969), *Country Time* (1970), *Progressive C.C* (1977), with Hank Locklin and Rita Remington *Carol Channing & Her Country Friends* (1977), *The Cajun Cowboy* (1978), *The Happy Cajun* (1979, *Cajun Country* (1982), *Wild 'N' Cajun* (1984), *Cajun & Country Too* (1987), *Lache Pas La Patate* (1987), *Bop A Hula* (1990), *The Alligator Man* (1991). Compilation: *Greatest Hits Volume 1* (1981), *Jimmy Newman & Al Terry - Earliest Recordings 1949-1952* (1981).

Newton, Juice

b. Judy Kaye Cohen, 18 February 1952, Lakehurst, New Jersey, USA. This singing daughter from a military family spent most of her childhood in Virginia. While completing a formal education in California, she fronted Dixie Peach, a country-rock combo that was re-named Silver Spur for three RCA albums in the mid-70s. Despite assistance from top Los Angeles session musicians, immediate solo success was dogged by Bonnie Tyler's version of 'It's A Heartache' eclipsing Newton's own,

though she gained a US country hit by proxy when the Carpenters covered her self-composed 'Sweet Sweet Smile' in 1978. Two years later, she arrived in Billboard's Top 5 with a revival of Chip Taylor's 'Angel Of The Morning' (her only UK hit) and then 'Queen Of Hearts' (also a hit for Dave Edmunds), while the *Juice* album containing both peaked at number 22. She enjoyed more hits in the pop charts with 'Love's Been A Little Hard On Me', *Quiet Lies* and a 1983 overhaul of the Zombies' 'Tell Her No', but it was the country market that came to provide the bulk of her success. After encouraging response when she performed 'The Sweetest Thing I've Ever Known' at 1981's annual Country Radio Seminar, this old Silver Spur track was re-mixed for a single to become a country number 1 the following year. Other genre successes included a reworking of Brenda Lee's 'Break It To Me Gently', Dave Loggins' 'You Make Me Want To Make You Mine', 'Hurt' and a duet with Eddie Rabbitt, 'Born To Each Other'. She later married polo star Tom Goodspeed.
Albums: *Juice Newton And Silver Spur* (1975), *After The Dust Settles* (1977), *Come To Me* (1977), *Well Kept Secret* (1978), *Take A Heart* (1979), *Juice* (1981), *Quiet Lies* (1982), *Dirty Looks* (1983), *Can't Wait All Night* (1984), *Old Flame* (1986), *Friends And Lovers* (1986). Compilation: *Collection* (1983), *Greatest Hits* (1984).

Nielsen-Chapman, Beth

Nielsen-Chapman sang harmony on Tanya Tucker's 1988 US number 1 country single, 'Strong Enough To Bend', which she wrote with Don Schlitz. She also sang harmony and wrote Willie Nelson's 1989 US country number 1, 'Nothing I Can Do It About It Now'. Her debut album for Warners failed to secure her role as a singer, however.
Album: *Beth Nielsen-Chapman* (1990).

Nitty Gritty Dirt Band

Formed in Long Beach, California in 1965, this enduring attraction evolved from the region's traditional circuit. Founder members Jeff Hanna (guitar/vocals) and Bruce Kunkel (guitar/vocals) had worked together as the New Coast Two, prior to joining the Illegitimate Jug Band. Glen Grosclose (drums), Dave Hanna (guitar/vocals), Ralph Barr (guitar) and Les Thompson (bass/vocals) completed the embryonic Dirt Band line-up, although Groslcose and Dave Hanna quickly made way for Jimmie Fadden (drums/guitar) and Jackson Browne (guitar/vocals). Although the last musician only remained for a matter of months - he was replaced by John McEuen his songs remained in the group's repertoire throughout their early career. *Nitty Gritty Dirt Band* comprised of jugband, vaudeville and pop material, ranging from the quirky 'Candy Man' to the orchestrated folk/pop 'Buy For Me The Rain', a minor US hit. *Ricochet* maintained this balance, following which Chris Darrow, formerly of Kaleidoscope (US), replaced Kunkel. The Dirt Band completed two further albums, and enjoyed a brief role in the film *Paint Your Wagon*, before disbanding in 1969. The group reconvened the following year around Jeff Hanna, John McEuen, Jimmie Fadden, Les Thompson and newcomer Jim Ibbotson. Having abandoned the jokey elements of their earlier incarnation, they pursued a career as purveyors of superior country-rock. The acclaimed *Uncle Charlie And His Dog Teddy* included excellent versions of Mike Nesmith's 'Some Of Shelly's Blues', Kenny Loggins' 'House At Pooh Corner' and Jerry Jeff Walker's 'Mr. Bojangles', a US Top 10 hit in 1970. *Will The Circle Be Unbroken*, recorded in Nashville, was an expansive collaboration between the group and traditional music mentors Doc Watson, Roy Acuff, Merle Travis and Earl Scruggs. Its charming informality inspired several stellar performances and the set played an important role in breaking down mistrust between country's establishment and the emergent 'long hair' practitioners. Les Thompson left the line-up following the album's completion, but the remaining quartet, buoyed by an enhanced reputation, continued their eclectic ambitions on *Stars And Stripes Forever* and *Dreams*. In 1976 the group dropped its 'Nitty Gritty' prefix and, as the Dirt Band, undertook a pioneering USSR tour the following year. Both Hanna and Ibbotson enjoyed brief sabbaticals, during which time supplementary musicians were introduced. By 1982 the prodigals had rejoined Fadden, McEuen and newcomer Bob Carpenter (keyboards) for *Let's Go*. The Dirt Band were, by then, an American institution with an enduring international popularity. 'Long Hard Road (Sharecropper Dreams)' and 'Modern Day Romance' topped the country charts in 1984 and 1985, respectively, but the following year a now-weary McEuen retired from the line-up. Former Eagles guitarist Bernie Leadon augmented the group for *Working Band*, but left again on its completion. He was, however, featured on *Will The Circle Be Unbroken Volume Two*, on which the Dirt Band rekindled the style of their greatest

Nitty Gritty Dirt Band

artistic triumph with the aid of several starring names, including Emmylou Harris, Chet Atkins, Johnny Cash, Ricky Skaggs, Roger McGuinn and Chris Hillman. The set deservedly drew plaudits for a group about to enter the 90s with its enthusiasm still intact.

Albums: *The Nitty Gritty Dirt Band* (1967), *Ricochet* (1967), *Rare Junk* (1968), *Alive* (1968), *Uncle Charlie And His Dog Teddy* (1970), *All The Good Times* (1971), *Will The Circle Be Unbroken* (1972), *Live* (1973), *Stars And Stripes Forever* (1974), *Dreams* (1975), *Dirt Band vs The Hollywood Time Machine* (1976), *Dirt Band* (1978), *An American Dream* (1979), *Make A Little Magic* (1980), *Jealousy* (1981), *Let's Go* (1982), *Plain Dirt Fashion* (1984), *Partners, Brothers And Friends* (1985), *Hold On* (1987), *Workin' Band* (1988), *Will The Circle Be Unbroken Volume II* (1989), *Rest Of The Dream* (1991), *Not Fade Away* (1992). Compilations: *Pure Dirt* (1968), *Dead And Alive* (1969), *Dirt, Silver And Gold* (1976), *Gold From Dirt* (1980), *Early Dirt 1967-1970* (1986), *Twenty Years Of Dirt* (1986), *Country Store: The Nitty Gritty Dirt Band* (1987), *The Best Of The Nitty Gritty Dirt Band* (1988), *More Great Dirt: The Best Of The Nitty Gritty Dirt Band, Volume 2* (1989).

Noack, Eddie

b. De Armand A. Noack Jnr., 29 April 1930, Houston, Texas, USA, d. 5 February 1978. Noack who gained degrees in English and Journalism at University of Houston made his radio debut in 1947 and first recorded for Goldstar in 1949. In 1951, he cut several songs for Four Star including 'Too Hot To Handle'. Leased to the TNT label, it drew attention to his songwriting and was recorded by several artists. He joined Starday in 1953 (beginning a long association with 'Pappy' Daily), where his immediate success came as a writer when several of his songs were recorded by top artists including Hank Snow who scored a major hit with 'These Hands' in 1956. Noack moved with Daily to his D label where in 1958, after recording rockabilly tracks as Tommy Wood, he had a country hit with 'Have Blues Will Travel'. During the 60s, Noack quit recording to concentrate on songwriting and publishing and had many of his songs including 'Flowers For Mama', 'Barbara Joy', 'The Poor Chinee', 'A Day In The Life Of A Fool' and 'No Blues Is Good News' successfully recorded by George Jones Noack did make some further recordings in the 70s, including arguably some of his best for his fine tribute album to Jimmie Rodgers. He moved to Nashville and in

1976, recorded an album that found release in Britain (where he had toured that year) on the Look label. He worked in publishing for Daily and in an executive role for the Nashville Songwriters Association until his death from cirrhosis in 1978. A fine performer somewhat in the style of Hank Williams, he is perhaps more appreciated today as a singer than he was in his own time.

Albums: *Remembering Jimmie Rodgers* (1972), *Eddie Noack i* (1976), *Eddie Noack ii* (1980), *Gentlemen Prefer Blondes* (c.1981).

Norma Jean

b. Norma Jean Beasley, 31 January 1938, near Wellston, Oklahoma, USA. Norma Jean showed an early interest in singing and after the family relocated to Oklahoma City, when she was five years old, she was given guitar tuition by an aunt. At the age of 13 she had her own thrice-weekly show on KLPR and in 1958, after working with several other artists including Leon McAuliffe, she became a regular on Red Foley's *Ozark Jubilee* television show, where she first dropped her surname and where her melodic singing soon attracted nationwide attention. In 1960 she moved to Nashville and became the featured vocalist with Porter Wagoner on both his network television show and on the *Grand Ole Opry*. She recorded for Columbia in the early 60s but did not gain her first US country chart success, 'Let's Go All The Way', until 1964, by which time she had joined RCA. (The Columbia material is contained on her only Columbia album, *Country's Favorite*; released in 1966 on their Harmony subsidiary, it is now highly sought after by collectors.) Further hits followed, including country Top 10's with 'Go Cat Go' and 'I Wouldn't Buy A Used Car From Him' and a Top 5 recording of 'The Game Of Triangles' with Bobby Bare and Liz Anderson. Equally at home with up-tempo songs such as 'Truck Driving Woman', country monologues like 'Old Doc Brown' or a weepy on the lines of 'There Won't Be Any Patches In Heaven', she built up a considerable reputation. She married in 1967 and left Wagoner's show and though she continued to record regularly into the early 70s, she cut out most of her public appearances to concentrate on her home - a 1000 acre farm near Oklahoma City. (Wagoner filled the vacancy with a young girl called Dolly Parton). Norma Jean recorded in the 80s and had a minor chart entry in 1982 with Claude Gray of her first hit 'Let's Go All The Way'.

Albums: *The Porter Wagoner Show (with Norma Jean)*

(1963), *Porter Wagoner In Person (with Norma Jean)* (1964), *Let's Go All The Way* (1964), *Pretty Miss Norma Jean* (1965), *Country's Favorite* (1966), with Wagoner *Live On The Road* (1966), *A Tribute To Kitty Wells* (1966), *Please Don't Hurt Me* (1966), *Sings Porter Wagoner* (1967), *Jackson Ain't A Very Big Town* (1967), with Bobby Bare and Liz Anderson *The Game Of Triangles* (1967), *The Body And Mind* (1968), *Heaven Help The Working Girl* (1968), *Heaven's Just A Prayer Away* (1968), *Love's A Woman's Job* (1968), *Country Giants* (1969), *It's Time For Norma Jean* (1970), *Another Man Loved Me Last Night* (1970), *Norma Jean* (1971), *Sings Hank Cochran Songs* (1971), *It Wasn't God Who Made Honky Tonk Angels* (1971), *I Guess That Comes From Being Poor* (1972), *Thank You For Loving Me* (1972), *The Only Way To Hold Your Man* (1973), *Norma Jean* (1978).

Oak Ridge Boys

Originally called the Country Cut-Ups, the Oak Ridge Boys were formed in 1942 in Knoxville, Tennessee. They often performed at the atomic energy plant in Oak Ridge where, in the midst of a war, their optimistic gospel songs were welcomed, and so they were renamed the Oak Ridge Quartet. They recorded their first records in 1947 and there were many changes in personnel, although Wally Fowler remained its leader. The group disbanded in 1956, only to emerge as the New Oak Ridge Quartet with a new leader, Smitty Gatlin. Handled by Wally Fowler, they recorded their first records in 1947, moving their base to Nashville, but disbanded in 1956. A year later, they reformed in a revised line-up by an original member, Smitty Gatlin. They became full-time professionals in 1961 and the album on which they changed from the Oak Ridge Quartet to the Oak Ridge Boys included strings and horns, an unusual move for a gospel group. William Lee Golden (b. 12 January 1939, near Brewton, Alabama, USA), who had admired the group since he saw them as an adolescent, became their baritone in 1964. When Gatlin decided to become a full-time minister, Golden recommended Duane David Allen (b. 29 April 1943, Taylortown, USA) who became the group's lead vocalist in 1966. They established themselves as the best-loved white gospel group in the USA and they won numerous awards and Grammys. Further changes came in 1972 with bass singer, Richard Anthony Sterban (b. 24 April 1943, Camden, New Jersey, USA) and in 1973 with tenor Joseph Sloan Bonsall (b. 18 May 1948, Philadelphia, Pennsylvania, USA) becoming part of the group. Although most gospel fans enjoyed their high-energy, criss-crossing performances, they were criticized for adding a rock 'n' roll drummer to their band. They recorded a single, 'Praise The Lord And Pass The Soup', with Johnny Cash and the Carter Family in 1973. In 1975, they switched to country music but their first secular single, 'Family Reunion', only reached number 83 in the US country charts. Their total income fell to $75,000 in 1975 and they made a loss in 1976. Columbia Records dropped them, ironically at the same time as they were accompanying their labelmate, Paul Simon, on 'Slip Slidin' Away',

which had sentiments diametrically opposite to gospel music. They opened for Johnny Cash in Las Vagas, played the USSR with Roy Clark, and had a major country hit with 'Y'All Come Back Saloon'. They topped the US country charts with 'I'll Be True To You' (a death disc), the classic 'Leavin' Louisiana In The Broad Daylight' and 'Trying To Love Two Women'. In 1981 they made number 5 on the US pop charts with 'Elvira' and followed it with 'Bobbie Sue' (number 12). Ronald Reagan, in a presidential address, said: 'If the Oak Ridge Boys win any more gold, they'll have more gold in their records than we have in Fort Knox.' Further country hits followed with 'American Made', 'Love Song', 'I Guess It Never Hurts To Hurt Sometime' (written by Randy Vanwarmer), 'Make My Life With You' and 'Come On In (You Did The Best You Could)'. In award ceremonies, they ousted the Statler Brothers as the top country vocal group, and their band has won awards in its own right. Golden, who stopped cutting his hair in 1979, became a mountain man, going bear hunting and sleeping in a teepee. When he was dismissed in 1986 for 'continuing musical and personal differences', he filed a $40m. suit, which was settled out of court. He released a solo album, *American Vagabond*, also in 1986, and has since formed a family group called the Goldens. His replacement was their rhythm guitarist, Steve Sanders (b. 17 September 1941, Richmond, Georgia, USA), formerly a child gospel performer and Faye Dunaway's son in the film *Hurry Sundown*. The Oak Ridge Boys continue with their philosophy to 'Keep it happy, keep it exciting' and do nothing which will tarnish their image. They turn down beer commercials and only sing positive songs. To quote Joe Bonsall, 'We're just an old gospel group with a rock 'n' roll band playing country music.'

Albums: *The Oak Ridge Boys Quartet* (1959), *Wall Fowler's All Nite Singing Gospel Concert Featuring The Oak Ridge Quartet* (1960), *The Oak Ridge Boys With The Sounds Of Nashville* (1962), *Folk Minded Spirituals For Spiritual Minded Folk* (1962), *Sing For You* (1964), *I Wouldn't Take Nothing For My Journey Now* (1965), *The Sensational Oak Ridge Boys From Nashville, Tennessee* (1965), *Sing And Shout* (1966), *At Their Best* (1966), *Solid Gospel Sound Of The Oak Ridge Quartet* (1966), *Together* (1966), *Sings River Of Love* (1967), as Wally Fowler And The Oak Ridge Quartet *Gospel Song Festival* (1970), *International* (1971), *Light* (1972), *Hymns* (1973), *Street Gospel* (1973), *Gospel Gold Heartwarming* (1974), *Oak Ridge Boys* (1974), *Super Gospel - Four*

Oak Ridge Boys

Sides Of Gospel Excitement Heartwarming (1974), *Sky High* (1975), *Old Fashioned, Down Home, Handclappin' Footstompin', Southern Style, Gospel Quartet Music* (1976), *Y'all Come Back Saloon* (1977), *Live 1977*, *Room Service* (1978), *The Oak Ridge Boys Have Arrived* (1979), *Together* (1980), *Fancy Free* (1981), *Bobbie Sue* (1982), *Christmas* (1982), *American Made* (1983), *The Oak Ridge Boys Deliver* (1983), *Friendship* (1983), *Seasons* (1985), *Step On Out* (1985), *Where The Fast Lane Ends* (1986), *Christmas Again* (1986), *Monongahela* (1987), *New Horizons* (1988), *American Dreams* (1989), *Unstoppable* (1991), *The Long Haul* (1992). Further reading: *The Oak Ridge Boys - Our Story*, with Ellis Winder and Walter Carter.

O'Connor, Mark

b. 4 August 1962, Seattle, Washington, USA. A naturally gifted instrumentalist, who first began to play the guitar at the age of six and won a University of Washington classical/flamenco guitar contest when he was aged 10. A year later, tiring of just the guitar, he turned to the fiddle and within weeks was playing it at square dances. Influenced by noted Texas fiddler Benny Thomasson, he played at festivals and contests. By the age of 14, he had already won two National Fiddle Championships, a Grand Masters Fiddle Championship, the National Guitar Flatpicking Championship and had also produced two albums. After graduation in 1979, he toured extensively on the festival circuits, where he worked with several noted bluegrass musicians. After touring Japan with Dan Crary, he became the guitarist with David Grisman's quintet, where he also worked on a tour with the jazz violinist Stéphane Grappelli. In 1981, while O'Connor was recovering from a broken arm sustained in a skiing accident, Grisman reduced to a quartet and O'Connor became the fiddle player with the Dixie Dregs. He left in 1983 and began to work with many artists including John McKuen, Peter Rowan, Chris Hillman and the legendary Doc Watson. His multi-instrumental ability has seen him much in demand and he has played on countless recordings as a session musician. By the late 80s, his music mixed various genres including bluegrass, rock, jazz and classical. In 1990, he began to follow a more independent career and writing much of his own material, he began to concentrate more on his own recordings. His collaboration with the cream of country sessionmen on *New Nashville Cats* won him much critical acclaim, and his revival of Carl Perkins' 'Restless', with vocals by Ricky Skaggs, Steve Wariner and Vince Gill, won several CMA Awards. O'Connor then began work on a record of duets with famous violinists from the classical as well as country fields. His flatpicking guitar work has been compared to Doc Watson and many now rate him Nashville's top fiddle player. He is also an accomplished banjoist and in 1983, he won a World Mandolin Championship.
Albums: *Mark O'Connor Four-Time National Junior Fiddle Champion* (1975), *Pickin' In The Wind* (1976) *Texas Jam Session* (1977), *In Concert* (1977), *Markology* (1980), *On The Rampage* (1980), with Fred Carpenter *Cuttin' Loose* (1980), with David Grisman Quintet *Quintet '80* (1980), *Soppin' The Gravy* (1981), *False Dawn* (c.80s), with Doc and Merle Watson *Guitar Album* (1983), *Meanings Of* (1986), *Stones From Which The Arch Was Made* (1987), *Elysian Forest* (1988), *The Championship Years* (1990), *New Nashville Cats* (1991).

O'Day, Molly

b. LaVerne Lois Williamson, 9 July 1923, McVeigh, Pike County, Kentucky, USA, d. 5 December 1987. O'Day learned several instruments and first sang with her brother Cecil 'Skeets' Williamson on WCHS Charleston in 1939; initially using the name Mountain Fern but soon changing to Dixie Lee. In 1940, she joined the Forty Niners, a group led by singer/guitarist Leonard (Lynn) Davis, (b. 15 December 1914, Paintsville, Kentucky, USA) who she married in April 1941. In 1942, she changed her stage name to Molly O'Day and together with Davis, worked on a variety of radio stations, including WHAS Louisville and WNOX Knoxville. Between 1946 and 1951, with their band the Cumberland Mountain Folks, they recorded almost 40 sides for Columbia. These included such heart rending numbers as 'The Drunken Driver' and 'Don't Sell Daddy Any More Whiskey'. She was the first artist to record Hank Williams' songs, ('When God Comes To Gather His Jewels' and 'Six More Miles') after hearing Hank in 1942 singing 'Tramp On The Street', which also became one her most requested numbers. In the early 50s, she and her husband turned to religious work (Davis later becoming an evangelist) but her singing was slowed by tuberculosis, which led to the removal of part of a lung, although they later recorded some religious material for Rem and GRS. Throughout the 60s and 70s, they did limited radio work centred around their home in Huntington, West Virginia. O'Day is rated by many to be the greatest woman country singer of all time; her individual emotional style causing some to call her 'the female Hank Williams or Roy Acuff'. She died of cancer in 1987.

Albums: *Hymns For The Country Folks* (1960), *Molly O'Day Sings Again* (1961), *The Unforgettable* (1963), *The Living Legend Of Country Music* (1966), *A Sacred Selection* (c.1975), *Skeets Williamson & Molly O'Day* (c.1975), *Molly O'Day Radio Favorites* (1981), *The Soul Of Molly O'Day Volume 1* (1983), *The Soul Of Molly O'Day Volume 2* (1984), *In Memory* (1990), *Molly O'Day The Cumberland Mountain Folks* (2 CD) (1992).

O'Dell, Kenny

b. Kenneth Gist, Jnr., c.early 40s, Oklahoma, USA. O'Dell began writing songs in his early teens and after completing his education, he formed his own Mar-Kay record label in California. In the early 60s, he recorded his own 'Old Time Love' but it failed to chart. After working for a time with Duane Eddy, he formed a group, Guys And Dolls, with which he toured for some five years. In 1966, he wrote and recorded 'Beautiful People', which became a smash hit in Atlanta. Liberty Records told Bobby Vee he could record a better version and have a national hit. Vee later said he should never have listened to them but in spite of split sales both versions made the US Top 40. After further unsuccessful attempts for chart successes, he moved to Nashville in 1969, where he managed Bobby Goldsboro's publishing company. He continued with his songwriting, sometimes with Larry Henley and in 1972, after producer Billy Sherrill had heard O'Dell's own recording, Sandy Posey charted with their song 'Why Don't We Go Somewhere And Love'. Sherrill became interested in O'Dell's songs and had Charlie Rich record 'I Take It On Home'. In 1973, Rich had a smash country and pop hit with 'Behind Closed Doors', which won O'Dell the CMA's *Song Of The Year* award. (He actually played guitar on Rich's recording). In the latter half of the 70s, he tried to relaunch his singing career with Capricorn. He had a Top 10 country hit with 'Let's Shake Hands And Come Out Lovin'' in 1978 but 'Medicine Woman' in 1979 has proved so far to be his last country hit. He was infinitely more successful and will always be remembered for his writing rather than his singing. Many artists have benefited by recording his songs including Anthony Armstrong Jones ('I've Got Mine'), Tanya Tucker ('Lizzie And The Rainman'), both Billie Jo Spears (1977) and the Bellamy Brothers & Forrester Sisters (1986) ('Too Much Is Not Enough'), Dottie West ('When It's

Just You And Me'), the Judds ('Mama He's Crazy') and many others.

Albums: *Beautiful People* (1968), *Kenny O'Dell* (1974), *Let's Shake Hands And Come Out Lovin'* (1978).

O'Donnell, Daniel

b. 12 December, 1961, Kincasslagh, Co. Donegal, Eire. O'Donnell is without doubt the biggest selling act ever in the musical genre known as 'Country 'n' Irish'. He is a clean-cut and gimmick-free vocalist with leanings towards sentimental MOR material. He first emerged in Britain in 1985, although he was already popular in Ireland. His first attempts at singing came when he worked as backing vocalist in the band which backed his sister, folk/country singer Margo O'Donnell, during the early 80s, and his popularity among the female audiences increased at high speed. After a handful of early recordings, (later released after he came to fame as 'The Boy From Donegal') he signed to Michael Clerkin's Ritz Records, an Irish label based in London, and *Two Sides Of Daniel O'Donnell* was released in 1985. It was promoted by the first in a continuing series of nationwide UK tours which attracted capacity audiences (largely composed of fans of artists like the late Jim Reeves. O'Donnell usually features in his stage show a medley of songs connected with Reeves). 1986 brought a second O'Donnell release, *I Need You*, which was his first to reach the UK country album charts (which it did in March 1987). That year's album *Don't Forget To Remember* (featuring a cover of the hit by the Bee Gees as its title track), was O'Donnell's first to enter the UK country chart at number 1, which has also occurred with his five subsequent original albums, although the next one to be released in chronological terms, *The Boy From Donegal*, consisted mainly of material recorded in 1984 before he signed to Ritz, and was released in the UK by Prism Leisure.

In 1988, Ritz licensed O'Donnell's next release, *From The Heart*, to Telstar Records, a television marketing company, and as well as entering the UK country chart at number 1, the album also reached the UK pop album chart in the autumn of that year, while a video, *Daniel O'Donnell Live In Concert*, was released. 1989 brought *Thoughts Of Home*, an album and video which were both advertised on television by Telstar - the album made the Top 40 of the pop chart and the video became O'Donnell's first to reach the UK Music Video chart; once again, all subsequent videos have featured in the latter chart, which the original *Live*

Daniel O'Donnell

In Concert also entered in the wake of *Thoughts From Home*. By 1990, O'Donnell was back with an album, *Favourites*, (and a companion video, *TV Show Favourites*), which was composed of material filmed for a hugely successful Irish television series. However, of far greater interest in 1990 was the news that he was making an album with noted producer Allen Reynolds (who had enjoyed major success with Don Williams, Crystal Gayle, Kathy Mattea and latterly, Garth Brooks) in Nashville - the first since O'Donnell's breakthrough that he had recorded with his original producer John Ryan. Released in late 1990, *The Last Waltz* was somewhat closer to genuine country music than its predecessors, and once again entered the UK country album charts at the top and charted strongly in the UK pop equivalent, while another video, *An Evening With Daniel O'Donnell*, had been in the Top 20 of the UK Music Video chart for 18 months at the time of writing.

During 1991, it was decided that nearly all of O'Donnell's album catalogue was MOR rather than country, and at a stroke, a UK country album chart - in which O'Donnell occupied the majority of the Top 10 - hardly featured his albums at all. This produced an avalanche of complaints (including one from a nun) and public demonstrations urging that the decision be reversed

and his albums reinstated in the country list, which eventually occurred in late 1991. Another release, *The Very Best Of Daniel O'Donnell*, a compilation composed partly of previously released items along with some newly recorded material, continued O'Donnell's remarkable success story. In musical terms, what O'Donnell records is unadventurous, yet his immense popularity in the UK and Eire makes it clear that his output has been brilliantly targeted. As yet, he has not released an album in the USA, although imported albums have been sold prodigiously in areas with population composed of large numbers of people of Irish extraction, and several concert appearance, including one at New York's Carnegie Hall in 1991, have been commercial triumphs.

Albums: *Two Sides Of Daniel O'Donnell* (1985), *I Need You* (1986), *Don't Forget To Remember* (1987), *The Boy From Donegal* (1987), *From The Heart* (1988), *Thoughts Of Home* (1989), *Favourites* (1990), *The Last Waltz* (1990), *Follow Your Dream* (1992). Compilation: *The Very Best Of Daniel O'Donnell* (1991).

O'Kanes

Jamie O'Hara (b. Toledo, Ohio, USA) planned to be a professional American footballer until knee injuries forced him to change his mind. He says,

O'Kanes

'My father gave me a guitar as a gift. Two years later, I was in Nashville. That either shows a lot of confidence, a lot of arrogance or a lot of stupidity.' He wrote 'Grandpa (Tell Me 'Bout The Good Old Days)' for the Judds and befriended another songwriter, Keiran Kane. Kane (b. Queens, New York, USA) had worked amongst rock acts in Los Angeles in the early 70s and then moved to Nashville. He wrote 'Gonna Have A Party' for Alabama. O'Hara and Kane became friendly, sharing their frustration at not getting songs recorded, and they began collaborating on material. They recorded demos in Kane's attic studio. Columbia thought they were good enough to release on their own account. The acoustic recordings (two guitars, bass, fiddle, mandolin, accordion, drums) made a stunning album debut in 1987. Their harmonies were reminiscent of a mellow version of the Louvin Brothers. They made the US country Top 10 with their first single, 'Oh Darlin' (Why Don't You Care For Me No More)' and then topped the chart with 'Can't Stop My Heart From Loving You'. Although their album was quiet and low-key, their rousing shows won them further acclaim. They were among the 'new traditionalists' in country music, but they stopped performing when Columbia failed to renew their recording contract. Their final chart entry was 'Rocky Road'.
Albums: *O'Kanes* (1987), *Tired Of The Runnin'* (1988), *Imagine That* (1990).

Osborne Brothers

Bobby Van (b. 7 December 1931; mandolin/vocals) and Sonny (b. 29 October 1937; banjo/vocals) both at Hyden, Kentucky, USA. A talented bluegrass duo, Bobby played with the Lonesome Pine Fiddlers in 1949 and in 1951, they recorded with Jimmy Martin. During Bobby's military service in 1952, Sonny, though barely 15 years old, was playing and appearing on the *Grand Ole Opry* with Bill Monroe. They were reunited in 1953, appeared on WROL Knoxville and made further recordings with Martin. From 1956-59, they played the WWVA *Wheeling Jamboree* and recording with Red Allen, they had a 1958 hit on MGM with 'Once More'. In 1963. they joined the *Opry* and after changing to the Decca label had several country chart successes including 'Rocky Top'. Never afraid to modernise their bluegrass, (Sonny actually once stated that he did not care too much for the genre), they added other musicians and used electrified instruments including a steelguitar, piano and drums, which caused some

traditionalists to criticise their work. In spite of the instrumental innovations, their unique harmonies saw them readily accepted and they survived the competition of rock and pop music much better than some of the other bluegrass groups. They toured with major stars including Conway Twitty and Merle Haggard and also played non-country venues such as night clubs and even a concert at the White House. In the mid-70s. they began recording for the new CMH label and later recorded ceveral albums including one with Mac Wiseman with whom they charted 'Shackles And Chains' in 1979.
Albums: with Red Allen *Country Pickin' & Hillside Singin'* (1959), *Bluegrass Music* (1961), *Bluegrass Instrumentals* (1962), *Cuttin' Grass* (1963), *Voices In Bluegrass* (1965), *Up This Hill And Down* (1966), *Modern Sounds Of Bluegrass* (1967), *Yesterday, Today & The Osborne Brothers* (1968), *Favorite Hymns* (1969), *Up To Date & Down To Earth* (1969), *The Osborne Brothers* (1970), *Ru-Beeee* (1970), *Country Roads* (1971), *The Osborne Brothers* (1971), *Georgia Pinewoods* (1971), *Bobby & Sonny* (1972), *Bluegrass Express* (1973), *Midnight Flyer* (1973), *Fastest Grass Alive* (1974), *Pickin' Grass And Singin' Country* (1975), *Number One* (1976), *The Osborne Brothers & Red Allen* (1977), *From Rocky Top To Muddy Bottom* (2LP) (1977), *Bluegrass Collection* (2LP) (1978), with Buddy Spicher *Bluegrass Concerto* (1979), with Mac Wiseman *The Essential Bluegrass Album* (1979), *I Can Hear Kentucky Calling Me* (1980), *Bluegrass Spectacular* (1982), *Bluegrass Gold* (1982), *Some Things I Want To Sing About* (1984), *Once More* (1986), *Favorite Memories* (1987), *Singing, Shouting Praises* (1988). By Bobby Osborne: *Bobby Osborne & His Mandolin* (1981). By Sonny Osborne: *Early Recordings Volumes 1, 2,.3* (1979), *Sonny Osborne & His Sunny Mountain Boys* (c.70s), *Songs Of Bluegrass, Five String In Hi-Fi*.

Oslin, K.T.

b. Kay Toinette Oslin, 1943, Crossitt, Arkansas, USA. Oslin was raised in Mobile, Alabama and then in Houston. She loved Hank Williams and the Carter Family, but hated early 60s country music because 'it was middle-aged men singing about drinking whiskey and cheating on their wives'. She attended drama school and worked in Houston as a folk trio with Guy Clark and radio producer David Jones. A live album she made with Texas singer Frank Davis was never released. She was in the chorus for the Broadway production of *Hello, Dolly!* starring Betty Grable. For many years, she played bit parts, did session work and sang

K.T. Oslin

commercials. She sang harmony on the 1978 album, *Guy Clark*, but her 1981 Elektra singles of 'Clean Your Own Tables' and 'Younger Men (Are Startin' To Catch My Eye)', released as Kay T. Oslin, did not sell. In 1982 Gail Davies recorded her song, 'Round The Clock Lovin'', which prompted her to borrow $7,000 from an aunt to form a band for a Nashville showcase. The Judds recorded her song, 'Old Pictures', whilst her own piano-based ballad, '80's Ladies', was a Top 10 country single and an anthem for older, single women. (Oslin herself is unmarried.) An album of songs from the female perspective, also called *80's Ladies*, was a top-selling country album that crossed over to the pop market. Tom T. Hall described her as 'everybody's screwed-up sister'. Her number 1 country singles are 'Do Ya' (she stopped a faster take being released when she realized it worked much better at half-tempo), 'I'll Always Come Back' and the partly-narrated 'Hold Me'. Although it is unique for a woman of this age to first make her mark in country music, it is doubtful if she can maintain the momentum, particularly as she seems to have exhausted her original flow of songs. Certainly the long silence since she released the patchy, but still impressive, *Love In A Small Town*, and its number 1 single 'Come Next Monday', appears ominous.

Albums: *80's Ladies* (1987), *This Woman* (1988), *Love In A Small Town* (1990).

Overstreet, Tommy

b. Thomas Cary Overstreet, 10 September 1937, Oklahoma City, Oklahoma, USA. He grew up in Houston, the home town of his uncle, the 30s pop singer Gene Austin, and learned to play the guitar at the age of 14. Here he first appeared on KTHT radio and in a local production of *Hit The Road* but after completing high school, he moved to Abilene. During 1956-57, he studied radio and television production at the University of Texas and also featured on Slim Willett's local television show, at one time appearing as Terry Dean from Abilene. Between 1957 and 1964 (military service excepted), he toured with Gene Austin, after which he worked for a time as a songwriter with Pat Boone's Cooga Music in Los Angeles. He recorded, without success, for Dunhill and eventually returned to Texas. In 1967, he moved to Nashville, where his University training saw him become manager of Dot Records' office. He also recorded for the label and after two minor hits, he scored a Top 5 US country and minor pop hit with 'Gwen (Congratulations)'. This launched his

career and, during the 70s, he registered 27 *Billboard* country chart hits. Although he never achieved a number 1, he did have Top 5 hits with 'Ann (Don't Go Runnin')', 'Heaven Is My Woman's Love' and '(Jeannie Marie) You Were A Lady'. He was never solely a country performer and with his band Nashville Express, he toured extensively both in the USA and to Europe. (He played at the Wembley Festival in London in 1977). He was at one time especially popular in Germany, where a recording of 'Heaven Is My Woman's Love', sung in German, was a hit. He appeared on most of the top US television programmes and made guest appearances on the *Grand Ole Opry* and *Hee-Haw*. He left Dot in 1979 and had six minor hits on Elektra, including 'What More Could A Man Need', but by the early 80s he was recording for minor labels. By this time, he had become a polished cabaret style entertainer, far removed from any country roots. Many may perhaps doubt that any really ever existed. He had a minor hit with 'Next To You' in 1986, which would seem to be his last chart entry at the time of writing.

Albums: *Gwen (Congratulations)* (1971), *This Is Tommy Overstreet* (1972), *Heaven Is My Woman's Love* (1972), *My Friends Call Me T.O.* (1973), *Woman Your Name Is My Song* (1974), *I'm A Believer* (1975), *Live From The Silver Slipper* (1975), *Turn On To Tommy Overstreet* (1976), *Vintage '77* (1977), *Hangin' Around* (1977), *A Better Me (10th Anniversary Album)* (1978), *There'll Never Be Another First Time* (1978), *The Real Tommy Overstreet* (1979), *I'll Never Let You Down* (1979), *I Can Hear Kentucky Calling* (1980), *Tommy Overstreet* (1982), *Dream Maker* (1983).

Owens, Bonnie

b. Bonnie Campbell, 1 October 1932, Blanchard, Oklahoma, USA. Bonnie was a yodelling country singer, who married Buck Owens in 1947. Their son, Alvis Alan Owens (b. 22 May 1948), became the singer, Buddy Alan. Buck and Bonnie Owens toured together and had a radio series in Arizona. They divorced in 1953 but both moved to Bakersfield in the early 60s, where she made her first records, 'Dear John Letter', 'Why Daddy Don't Live Here Anymore' and 'Don't Take Advantage Of Me'. After a relationship with Merle Haggard's manager, Fuzzy Owen, she married Haggard in 1965, becoming part of his stage-show and recording a successful duet album with him. Their marriage was unusual in that Owens tolerated Haggard's affairs - 'I don't care what you do so long as you don't flaunt it in my face', she is reputed to have said. In 1970 they co-wrote 'Today I Started Loving You Again'. She stopped performing in 1975 to look after their family and business interests. They divorced in 1978 but she is now an integral part of his road show.

Albums: *Don't Take Advantage Of Me* (1965), with Merle Haggard *Just Between The Two Of Us* (1966), *Your Tender Loving Care* (1967), *All Of Me Belongs To You* (1967), *Somewhere Between* (1968), *Hi-Fi To Cry By* (1969), *Lead Me On* (1969), *Mother's Favourite Hymns* (1971).

Owens, Buck

b. Alvis Edgar Owens Jnr., 12 August 1929, Sherman, Texas, USA. Buck Owens became one of the leading country music stars of the 60s and 70s, along with Merle Haggard, the leading exponent of the 'west coast sound'. Owens gave himself the nickname Buck at the age of three, after a favourite horse. When he was 10, his family moved to Mesa, Arizona, where Owens picked cotton and 13 years of age began playing the mandolin. He soon learned guitar, horns and drums as well. Owens performed music professionally at the age of 16, starring, along with partner Ray Britten, in his own radio programme. He also worked with the group Mac's Skillet Lickers, and at 17 married their singer, Bonnie Campbell, who later launched her own career as Bonnie Owens. The couple bore a son, who also had a country music career as Buddy Alan. In 1951 Owens and his family moved to Bakersfield, California, at the suggestion of an uncle who said work was plentiful for good musicians. Owens joined the Orange Blossom Playboys, with which he both sang and played guitar for the first time, and then formed his own band, the Schoolhouse Playboys. Owens made ends meet by taking on work as session guitarist in Los Angeles, appearing on recordings by Sonny James, Wanda Jackson, Tommy Sands and Gene Vincent. When the Playboys disbanded in the mid-50s Owens joined country artist Tommy Collins as singer and guitarist, recording a few tracks with him. In 1955-56 Owens recorded his first singles under his own name, for Pep Records, using the name Corky Jones for rockabilly and his own name for country recordings. Owens signed to Capitol Records in March 1957. It was not until his fourth release, 'Second Fiddle', that he made any mark, reaching number 24 on *Billboard*'s country chart. His next, 'Under Your Spell Again', made number 4, paving the way for over 75 country hits, more

than 40 of which made that chart's Top 10. Among the biggest and best were 'Act Naturally' (1963), later covered by the Beatles, 'Love's Gonna Live Here' (1963), 'My Heart Skips A Beat' (1964), 'Together Again' (1964), 'I've Got A Tiger By The Tail' (1965), 'Before You Go' (1965), 'Waitin' In Your Welfare Line' (1966), 'Think Of Me' (1966), 'Open Up Your Heart' (1966) and a cover of Chuck Berry's 'Johnny B. Goode' (1969), all of which were number 1 country singles. Owens recorded a number of duets, with singer Susan Raye, and also his son Buddy Alan. He also released more than 100 albums during his career. In addition, his compositions were hits by other artists, notably Emmylou Harris ('Together Again') and Ray Charles ('Crying Time'). Owens' band, the Buckaroos (guitarist Don Rich, bassist Doyle Holly, steel guitarist Tom Brumley and drummer Willie Cantu), was also highly regarded. Their down-to-basics, honky-tonk instrumental style helped define the Bakersfield sound - Owens' recordings never relied on strings or commercialized, sweetened pop arrangements. The Buckaroos also released several albums on their own. In 1969, Owens joined as co-host the country music television variety programme *Hee Haw*, which combined comedy sketches and live performances by country stars. He stayed with the show until the mid-80s, long after his Capitol contract expired, and he had signed with Warner Brothers Records (1976). Although Owens continued to place singles in the country charts with Warners, his reign as a top country artist had faltered in the mid-70s and he retired from recording and performing to run a number of business interests, including a radio station and recording studio, in Bakersfield. In 1988, country newcomer Dwight Yoakam convinced Owens to join him in recording a remake of Owens' song 'Streets Of Bakersfield'. It reached number 1 in the country chart and shed new light on Owens. He signed with Capitol again late in 1988 and recorded a new album, *Hot Dog*, featuring re-recordings of old Owens songs and cover songs of material by Chuck Berry, Eddie Cochran and others. Although Owens had not recaptured his earlier status by the early 90s, he had become active again, recording and touring, including one tour as a guest of Yoakam.

Selected albums: *Buck Owens Sings Harlan Howard* (1961), *Under Your Spell Again* (1961), *Together Again/My Heart Skips A Beat* (1964), *The Instrumental Hits Of Buck Owens And The Buckaroos* (1965), *I've Got A Tiger By The Tail* (1965),

Buck Owens

Carnegie Hall Concert (1966), Buck Owens In London (1969), Big In Vegas (1970), with Susan Raye We're Gonna Get Together (1970), I Wouldn't Live In New York City (1971), The Songs Of Merle Haggard (1972), Hot Dog (1988), Act Naturally (1989). Compilation: The Best Of Buck Owens (1964), The Best Of Buck Owens, Volume 2 (1968).

Oxford, Vernon

b. 8 June 1941, Benton County, Arkansas, USA. Oxford comes from a musical, church-going family, and his father passed his fiddle-playing talent onto his son. He was given a guitar when he was 13-years-old and has been singing country and country/gospel ever since. In 1964 he moved to Nashville with his wife, Loretta, and, after being turned down by several companies, RCA Records signed him, releasing a single and an album, both called 'Woman, Let Me Sing You A Song'. Oxford's recordings are a throwback to the rural honky tonk sound of Hank Williams with a voice to match, but he claims, 'I am being me. I sing a lot of Hank's songs but I never set out intentionally to imitate him. I guess we're both country boys and we both sing from the heart.' RCA dropped Oxford when his records didn't sell, but a contingent of British fans lobbied RCA so hard that they reversed the decision. RCA released a UK double-album in its Famous Country Music Makers series, although Oxford was anything but famous at the time. Oxford won more British fans with UK appearances, particularly at Wembley Country Music Festivals. He made the US country charts with 'The Shadows Of My Mind' and then, in 1976, with his controversial 'Redneck! (The Redneck National Anthem)', written by Mitchell Torok, and, in the same vein, 'Redneck Roots' and 'A Good Old Fashioned Saturday Night Honky Tonk Barroom Brawl'. He also recorded a humorous duet with Jim Ed Brown called 'Mowing The Lawn'. He claims he just dreamed the words and music of his own songs, 'She's Always There' and 'Better Way Of Life'. Since 1977, Oxford has not had chart success in the USA, but that is not one of his objectives. He says, 'Going to church doesn't make you a Christian, and, in 1978, I was born again, even though I was a Baptist already'. However, Oxford, the subject of a BBC-television documentary, says, 'I do cheating songs but now I do them to represent what sin is: I use them to make a point about Jesus Christ. 'Redneck!' shows what I used to be before I was saved. I sing gospel songs at the end of every show and tell them about the Truth. Sometimes I combine singing with preaching. When I called a girl out of the audience once, the power of God knocked her down and she slithered like a snake across the floor. I have found peace and happiness and I would like to help others to find it too.'
Albums: Woman, Let Me Sing You A Song (1966), Famous Country Music Makers (1973), By Public Demand (1975), America's Unknown Superstar (1976), I Just Want To Be A Country Singer (1976), Tribute To Hank Williams (1978), Nobody's Child (1978), If I Had My Wife To Love Over (1979), Keepin' It Country (1979), I Love To Sing (1980), His And Hers (1980), A Better Way Of Life (1981), Pure Country (1982), The Tradition Continues (1983), Power In The Blood (1989), 100% Country (1990).

Ozark Mountain Daredevils

One of country-rock's more inventive exponents, the Ozark Mountain Daredevils featured the songwriting team of John Dillon (b. 6 February 1947, Stuttgart, Arkansas, USA; guitar, fiddle, vocals) and Steve Cash (b. 5 May 1946, Springfield, Missouri, USA; harmonica, vocals) with Randle Chowning (guitar, vocals), Buddy Brayfield (keyboards), Michael 'Supe' Granda (b. 24 December 1950, St. Louis, Missouri, USA; bass) and Larry Lee (b. 5 January 1947, Springfield, Missouri, USA; drums). The group were originally based in Springfield, Missouri. Their acclaimed debut album, recorded in London under the aegis of producer Glyn Johns, contained the US Top 30 single, 'If You Want To Get To Heaven', while a second success, 'Jackie Blue' which reached number 3, came from the group's follow-up collection, It'll Shine When It Shines. Recorded at Chowning's ranch, this excellent set showcased the Ozarks' strong harmonies and intuitive musicianship, factors maintained on subsequent releases, The Car Over The Lake Album and Men From Earth. A 1978 release, It's Alive, fulfilled the group's obligation to A&M Records and two years later they made their debut on CBS. Paradoxically the Ozarks' subsequent work lacked the purpose of those early releases although the unit continues to enjoy a cult popularity. The group was reactivated in the late-80s by Dillon and Cash with Granda, Steve Canaday (b. 12 September 1944, Springfield, Missouri, USA; drums) and D. Clinton Thompson (guitar) and the resulting album, Modern History, released on the UK independent Conifer label, found the Ozarks with a new lease of life.
Albums: Ozark Mountain Daredevils (1973), It'll Shine When It Shines (1974), The Car Over The Lake

Album (1975), *Men From Earth* (1976), *Don't Look Down* (1978), *It's Alive* (1978), *Ozark Mountain Daredevils* (1980), *Modern History* (1989). Compilation: *The Best Of The Ozark Mountain Daredevils* (1983).

P

Page, Patti

b. Clara Ann Fowler, 8 November 1927, Tulsa, Oklahoma, USA. A popular singer, who allegedly sold more records during the 50s than any other female artist; her total sales (singles and albums), are claimed to be in excess of 60 million. One of eight girls, in a family of 11, Fowler started her career singing country songs on radio station KTUL in Tulsa, and played weekend gigs with Art Klauser And His Oklahomans. She successfully auditioned for KTUL's *Meet Patti Page* show, sponsored by the Page Milk Company, and took the name with her when she left. Jack Rael, who was road manager and played baritone saxophone for the Jimmy Joy band, heard her on the radio and engaged her to sing with them; he later became her manager for over 40 years. In 1948, Page appeared on the top rated *Breakfast Club* on Chicago radio, and sang with the Benny Goodman Septet. In the same year she had her first hit record, 'Confess', on which, in the cause of economy, she overdubbed her own voice to create the effect of a vocal group. In 1949, she used that revolutionary technique again on her first million-seller, 'With My Eyes Wide Open I'm Dreaming'. The song was re-released 10 years later with a more modern orchestral backing. Throughout the 50s, the hits continued to flow: 'I Don't Care If The Sun Don't Shine', 'All My Love' (US number 1), 'The Tennessee Waltz' (said to be the first real 'crossover' hit from country music to pop, and one of the biggest record hits of all time), 'Would I Love You (Love You, Love You)', 'Mockin' Bird Hill' (a cover version of the record made by Les Paul and Mary Ford, who took multi-tracking to the extreme in the 50s), 'Mister And Mississippi', 'Detour' (recorded for her first country music album), 'I Went To Your Wedding', 'Once In Awhile', 'You Belong To Me', 'Why Don't You Believe Me', '(How Much Is) That Doggie In The Window', written by novelty song specialist, Bob Merrill, and recorded by Page for a children's album; 'Changing Partners', 'Cross Over The Bridge', 'Steam Heat', 'Let Me Go, Lover', 'Go On With The Wedding', 'Allegheny Moon', 'Old Cape Cod', 'Mama From The Train' (sang in a Pennsylvanian Dutch dialect), 'Left Right Out Of Your Heart', and many more. Her records continued to sell well into the 60s, and she had her last US Top 10 entry in 1965 with the title song from the Bette Davis-Olivia De Havilland movie, *Hush, Hush, Sweet Charlotte*. Page also appeared extensively on US television during the 50s, on shows such as the *Scott Music Hall*, the *Big Record* variety show, and her own shows for NBC and CBS. She also appeared in films, including *Elmer Gantry* (1960), *Dondi* (1961, a comedy-drama, in which she co-starred with David Janssen) and *Boys Night Out* (1962). In the 70s, she recorded mainly country material, and in the 80s, after many successful years with Mercury and Columbia Records, signed for the Nashville-based company Plantation Records, a move which reunited her with top record producer Shelby Singleton. In 1988, Page gained excellent reviews when she played the Ballroom in New York, her first appearance in that city for nearly 20 years.

Albums: *Let's Get Away From It All* (1955), *I've Heard That Song Before* (1955), *Patti Page On Camera* (1955), *Three Little Words* (1955), *The Waltz Queen* (1955), *Indiscretion* (1955), *Romance On The Range* (1955), *I'll Remember April* (1956), *Page I* (1956), *Page II* (1956), *Page III* (1956), *You Go To My Head* (1956), *In The Land Of Hi Fi* (1956), *Music For Two In Love* (1956), *The Voices Of Patti Page* (1956), *Page IV* (1956), *My Song* (1956), *The East Side* (1956), *Manhattan Tower* (1956), *Just A Closer Walk With Thee* (1957), *Sings And Stars In 'Elmer Gantry'* (1960), *Country And Western Golden Hits* (1961), *Go On Home* (1962), *Golden Hit Of The Boys* (1962), *Patti Page On Stage* (1963), *Say Wonderful Things* (1963), *Blue Dream Street* (1964), *The Nearness Of You* (1964), *Hush, Hush, Sweet Charlotte* (1965), *Gentle On My Mind* (1968), *Patti Page With Lou Stein's Music, 1949* (1988) Compilations: *Patti Page's Greatest Hits* (1961), *Patti Page's Golden Hits, Volume 2* (1963), *The Best Of Patti Page* (1984).

Page, Stu

b. 12 May 1954, Leeds, Yorkshire, England. Page, who has been playing the guitar since he was 10 years old, began his career by session work around Leeds. In 1973, after helping out an American bluegrass band, the Warren Wikeson Band, he was invited to join them in Boston for a year. When he returned to the UK, he took various day jobs, but played in several semi-pro bands. In 1984 he formed Stu Page And Remuda, and says, 'It's a word for a spare horse and that's what we were. We only got the gigs when someone had let the organizer down.' Besides being a talented guitarist,

Patti Page

Page has a powerful voice which belies his small stature, and his band includes Terry Clayton (bass), Andy Whelan (guitar), Pat McPartling (drums) and Tim Howard (pedal steel). They have recorded several cassettes for sale at shows, together with the excellent album, *The Stu Page Band*, which was produced by Joe Butler of the Hillsiders for Barge Records. Page's major influence is Merle Haggard and the band's singles include 'He Made The Whole World Sing', 'Are You Still In Love With Me?' and the double a-side, 'Florida Feelin''/'Honeysuckle Dreamin''.

Albums: *Radio Nights* (1984), *Front Page News* (1985), *The Stu Page Band* (1989), *Fresh Pages* (1990).

Parsons, Gram

b. Cecil Ingram Connor, 5 November 1946, Winter Haven, Florida, USA, d. 19 September 1973. Parsons' brief but influential career began in high-school as a member of the Pacers. This rock 'n' roll act later gave way to the Legends which, at various points, featured country singer Jim Stafford as well as Kent Lavoie, later known as Lobo. By 1963 Gram had joined the Shilos, a popular campus attraction modelled on clean-cut folk attraction the Journeymen. The quartet - Parsons, George Wrigley, Paul Surratt and Joe Kelly - later moved to New York's Greenwich Village, but Gram left the line-up in 1965 upon enrolling at Harvard College. His studies ended almost immediately and, inspired by the concurrent folk-rock boom, founded the International Submarine Band with John Nuese (guitar), Ian Dunlop (bass) and Mickey Gauvin (drums). Two excellent singles followed, but having relocated to Los Angeles, Parsons' vision of a contemporary country music found little favour amid the prevalent psychedelic trend. The group was nonetheless signed by producer Lee Hazelwood, but with Dunlop and Gauvin now absent from the line-up, Bob Buchanan (guitar) and Jon Corneal (drums) joined Gram and Nuese for *Safe At Home*. This excellent set is now rightly viewed as a landmark in the development of country-rock, blending standards with several excellent Parsons' originals, notably 'Luxury Liner'. However, by the time of its release (April 1968), the quartet had not only folded, but Gram had accepted an offer to join the Byrds. His induction resulted in *Sweetheart Of The Rodeo* on which the newcomer determined the group's musical direction. This synthesis of country and traditional styles followed the mould of *Safe At Home*, but was buoyed by the act's excellent harmony work. Although Parsons' role as vocalist was later diminished by Hazelwood's court injunction - the producer claimed it breached their early contract - his influence was undeniable, as exemplified on the stellar 'Hickory Wind'. However, within months Gram had left the Byrds in protest over a South African tour and instead spent several months within the Rolling Stones' circle. The following year he formed the Flying Burrito Brothers with another ex-Byrd, Chris Hillman, 'Sneaky' Pete Kleinow (pedal steel guitar) and bassist Chris Ethridge (bass). *The Gilded Palace Of Sin* drew inspiration from southern soul and urban country music and included one of Parsons' most poignant compositions, 'Hot Burrito #1'. *Burrito Deluxe* failed to scale the same heights as internal problems undermined the unit's potential. Gram's growing drug dependency exacerbated this estrangement and he was fired from the group in April 1970. Initial solo recordings with producer Terry Melcher were inconclusive, but in 1972 Parsons was introduced to singer Emmylou Harris and together they completed *G.P.* with the assistance of Elvis Presley's regular back-up band. An attendant tour leading the Fallen Angels - Jock Bartley (guitar), Neil Flanz (pedal steel), Kyle Tullis (bass) and N.D. Smart II (drums) - followed, but Parsons' appetite for self-destruction remained intact. Parsons lived the life of a true 'honky tonk hero' with all the excesses of Hank Williams, even down to his immaculate embroidered Nudie tailored suits. Sessions for a second album blended established favourites with original songs, many of which had been written years beforehand. Despite its piecemeal content, the resultant set, *Grievious Angel*, was a triumph, in which plaintive duets ('Love Hurts', 'Hearts On Fire') underscored the quality of the Parsons/Harris partnership, while 'Brass Buttons' and 'In My Hour Of Darkness' revealed a gift for touching lyricism. Gram's death in 1973 as a result of 'drug toxicity' emphasized its air of poignancy, and the mysterious theft of his body after the funeral, whereupon his road manager, Philip Kaufman cremated the body in the desert, carrying out Gram's wishes, added to the singer's legend. Although his records were not a commercial success during his lifetime, Parsons' influence on a generation of performers, from the Eagles to Elvis Costello, is a fitting testament to his talent. Emmylou Harris adopted his mantle with a series of superior of country-rock releases while an excellent concept album, *Ballad Of Sally Rose* (1985), undoubtedly drew on her brief relationship with this star-struck singer. Parson's catalogue is painfully small compared to his enormous importance in contemporary country/rock, and his work is destined to stand alongside that of his hero Hank Williams.

Albums; G.P. (1972), Grievous Angel (1973), Sleepless Nights (1976), Gram Parsons And The Fallen Angels - Live 1973 (1981). Compilation: Gram Parsons (1982), The Early Years (1984).

Further reading: Gram Parsons: A Music Biography, Sid Griffin. Hickory Wind: The Life And Times Of Gram Parsons, Ben Fong-Torres

Parton, Dolly

b. 19 January 1946, Locust Ridge, Tennessee, USA, Dolly Rebecca Parton's poor farming parents paid the doctor in corn meal for attending the birth of the fourth of their 12 offspring. After her appearances as a singing guitarist on local radio as a child, including the Grand Ole Opry in Nashville, Parton left school in 1964. Her recorded output had included a raucous rockabilly song called 'Puppy Love' for a small label as early as 1958, but a signing to Monument in 1966 - the time of her marriage to the reclusive Carl Dean - yielded a C&W hit with 'Dumb Blonde' as well as enlistment in the prestigious Porter Wagoner Show as its stetsoned leader's voluptuous female foil in duets and comedy sketches. While this post adulterated her more serious artistic worth, she notched up further country smashes, among them 'Joshua', the autobiographical 'Coat Of Many Colours' and, with Wagoner, 'Last Thing On My Mind' (the Tom Paxton folk standard), 'Better Move It On Home' and 1974's 'Please Don't Stop Loving Me'.

On the crest of another solo hit with 'Jolene' on RCA that same year, she resigned from the show to strike out on her own - though she continued to record periodically with Wagoner. Encompassing a generous portion of her own compositions, her post-1974 repertoire was less overtly country, even later embracing a lucrative stab at disco in 1979's 'Baby I'm Burning' and non-originals ranging from 'House Of The Rising Sun' to Jackie Wilson's 'Higher And Higher'. 'Jolene' became a 'sleeper' UK Top 10 entry in 1976 and she continued her run in the US country chart with such as 'Bargain Store' (banned from some radio stations for 'suggestive' lyrics), 'All I Can Do' and 'Light Of A Clear Blue Morning' (1977). That same year, 'Here You Come Again' crossed into the US pop Hot 100, and her siblings basked in reflected glory - mainly Randy who played bass in her backing band before landing an RCA contract himself, and Stella Parton who had already harried the country

list with 1975's 'Ode To Olivia' and 'I Want To Hold You With My Dreams Tonight'.

Their famous sister next ventured into film acting, starring with Lily Tomlin and Jane Fonda in 1981's 9 To 5 (for which she provided the title theme), and with Burt Reynolds in the musical Best Little Whorehouse In Texas. Less impressive were Rhinestone and 1990's Steel Magnolias. She also hosted a 1987 television variety series which lost a ratings war. Nevertheless, her success as a recording artist, songwriter and big-breasted 'personality' remained unstoppable. As well as ploughing back royalties for 70s covers of Parton numbers by Emmylou Harris, Linda Ronstadt and Maria Muldaur into her Dollywood entertainment complex, she teamed up with Kenny Rogers in 1983 to reach the UK Top 10 with a Bee Gees composition, 'Islands In The Stream'. With Rogers too, she managed another US country number 1 two years later with 'Real Love'. Although other 80s singles such as 'I Will Always Love You' and 'Tennessee Homesick Blues' did make the pop charts, they became as well-known as many that did. Trio with Ronstadt and Harris won a Grammy for best country album in 1987. Her CBS debut, Rainbow, represented her deepest plunge into mainstream pop - though 1989's White Limozeen (produced by Ricky Skaggs) retained the loyalty of her multi-national grassroots following. In 1992, Whitney Houston had the biggest selling single of the year in the UK with Parton's composition, 'I Will Always Love You', which she sang in the film, The Bodyguard. Her celebration of international womanhood, 'Eagle When She Flies', confirmed her return to the country market in 1991.

Selected albums: Hello, I'm Dolly (1967), Dolly Parton And George Jones (1968), Just Because I'm A Woman (1968), with Porter Wagoner Just The Two Of Us (1969), with Wagoner Always, Always (1969), My Blue Ridge Mountain Boy (1969), with Wagoner Porter Wayne And Dolly Rebecca (1970), A Real Live Dolly (1970), with Wagoner Once More (1970), with Wagoner Two Of A Kind (1971), Joshua (1971), with Wagoner We Found It (1973), Jolene (1974), Bargain Store (1975), Dolly (1976), All I Can Do (1976), New Harvest . . . First Gathering (1977), Here You Come Again (1977), Heartbreaker (1978), Dolly Parton And Friends At Goldband (1979), Great Balls Of Fire (1979), Dolly Dolly Dolly (1980), 9 To 5 And Odd Jobs (1980), Heartbreak Express (1982), Burlap And Satin (1983), The Great Pretender (1984), Rhinestone (1984, film soundtrack), Once Upon A Christmas (1984), with Linda

Dolly Parton with Willie Nelson

Ronstadt, Emmylou Harris *Trio* (1987), *Rainbow* (1988), *White Limozeen* (1989), *Eagle When She Flies* (1991), *Straight Talk* (1992 film soundtrack). Compilations: *The Best Of Porter Wagoner And Dolly Parton* (1974), *The Dolly Parton Collection* (1980), *Greatest Hits* (1982).

Parton, Stella

b. 4 May 1949, Locust Ridge, near Sevier County, Tennessee, USA. Parton, the sixth of 12 children, made her radio debut with her sister, Dolly Parton, in 1955. She sang in local clubs and arrived in Nashville in 1972. She recorded, without success, for the small Royal American and Music City labels and toured with a gospel group. She returned to country music in 1975 with a defence of Olivia Newton-John's awards from the Country Music Association called 'Ode To Olivia'. She spent 18 weeks in the US country charts with 'I Want To Hold You In My Dreams Tonight' for the Country Soul label before switching to Elektra. She then made the US country Top 20 with 'Danger Of A Stranger', 'Standard Lie Number 1' and 'Four Little Letters'. Parton is a slim blonde but the cover of her 1978 album, *Stella Parton*, was airbrushed to give her the same assets as her famous sister! On that album, ten of the Parton family join her on 'Down To Earth', while she is also featured on the soundtrack of her sister's film, *Rhinestone*. She has also played in a stage version of the film *The Best Little Whorehouse In Texas*, taking the role Dolly originally played in the film.
Albums: *I Want To Hold You In My Arms Tonight* (1975), *Country Sweet* (1977), *Stella Parton* (1978), *Love Ya* (1979), *So Far . . . So Good* (1982).

Paycheck, Johnny

b. Donald Eugene Lytle, 31 May 1941, Greenfield, Ohio, USA. The title of Paycheck's 1977 country hit, 'I'm The Only Hell (Mama Ever Raised)', is apt as he has been in trouble throughout his life: the wild eyes on his album sleeves give the picture. Although only 5 feet 5 inches, he is tougher than most and he served two years for assaulting an officer whilst in the US Navy. He moved to Nashville and played bass and sometimes steel guitar for Porter Wagoner, Faron Young, Ray Price and chiefly, George Jones. He made several records with Jones, singing tenor on *I'm A People* and the hit singles, 'Love Bug' and 'The Race Is On'. At first, he recorded rockabilly as Donny Young in 1959 ('Shaking The Blues', written by Jones) and then sang country on Mercury Records ('On Second Thoughts'). Most people think the

name Johnny Paycheck was a parody of Johnny Cash, but it came from a heavyweight boxer who was KO'd by Joe Louis in two rounds in 1940 and was close to Paycheck's own Polish family name. By now, he had developed Jones' mannerisms and he had country hits with 'A-11' and 'Heartbreak, Tennessee'. He wrote Tammy Wynette's first hit, 'Apartment No. 9' and Ray Price's 'Touch My Heart'. He formed his own Little Darlin' Records in 1966 and had country hits with 'The Lovin' Machine', Bobby Bare's composition 'Motel Time Again' and 'Don't Monkey With Another Monkey's Monkey'. His supposedly live album from Carnegie Hall was recorded in a studio on April Fool's Day, 1966. Paycheck became an alcoholic, the label went bankrupt and he was arrested for burglary. He moved to Los Angeles, living hand to mouth, spending what little money he had on drink and drugs. Record producer Billy Sherrill straightened him out and he had a massive country hit with 'Don't Take Her, She's All I Got' in 1971. This was followed by 'Someone To Give My Love To', 'Mr. Lovemaker' and 'Song And Dance Man'. Paycheck also had success on the US country charts with a gospel-flavoured duet with Jody Miller, 'Let's All Go Down To The River'. Further troubles led to bankruptcy and a paternity suit in 1976. In 1977, at the height of outlaw country, he had his biggest country hit with David Allan Coe's anthem to working people, 'Take This Job And Shove It', and its b-side 'Colorado Cool-Aid' was successful in its own right. He is well known in country circles in the UK for his narration, 'The Outlaw's Prayer' from *Armed And Crazy*. His lifestyle is reflected in 'Me And The I.R.S.', 'D.O.A. (Drunk On Arrival)', and '11 Months And 29 Days', which was his sentence of passing a dud cheque at a Holiday Inn - a case of Johnny Badcheck. A law suit with his manager followed and his friends, George Jones and Merle Haggard, made albums with him. In 1981, after he went back to a woman's house after a concert, he was arrested for allegedly raping her 12-year-old daughter. The charges were reduced - he was fined and given probation - but he was dropped by Epic Records, although he maintained, 'I dropped them. I couldn't stand the back-stabbing stench there anymore'. Then, in 1985, he got into a bar-room argument with a stranger - and shot him. While awaiting trial, he recorded with the 'de-frocked' evangelist, John Wesley Fletcher. Paycheck served a nine-year sentence and said, 'This will probably be my last time around. The fans have taken me back every time, but you only stay young for so long'. He was released in 1991 and resumed his career. Whatever happens, his extraordinary life story is a bankable tale. It may be the only way he can resolve his problems with the IRS.

Albums: *Johnny Paycheck At Carnegie Hall* (1966), *The Lovin' Machine* (1966), *Gospeltime In My Fashion* (1967), *Jukebox Charlie* (1967), *Country Soul* (1967), *Wherever You Are* (1969), *Johnny Paycheck Again* (1970), *She's All I Got* (1971), *Heartbreak, Tennessee* (1972), *Mr. Lovemaker* (1972), *Song And Dance Man* (1972), *Somebody Love Me* (1973), *Slide Off Your Satin Sheets* (1977), *Take This Job And Shove It* (1978), *Armed And Crazy* (1978), *11 Months And 29 Days* (1979), with George Jones *Double Trouble* (1980), *Everybody's Got A Family - Meet Mine* (1980), *New York Town* (1980), with Merle Haggard *Mr. Hag Told My Story* (1981), *Lovers And Losers* (1982), *Back On The Job* (1984), *I Don't Need To Know That Right Now* (1984), *Apartment No. 9* (1985), *Modern Times* (1987), *Honky Tonk And Slow Music* (1988), *Outlaw At The Cross* (1989). Compilations: *Biggest Hits* (1983), *16 Greatest Hits* (1988).

Payne, Jimmy

b. 12 April 1936, Leachville, Arkansas, USA. The family moved to Gideon, Missouri in 1944 and Jimmy enjoyed country music and singing in church. He had a gospel programme on the radio on Saturdays and was picking cotton during the week. In 1957, he moved to St. Louis to work as a professional country singer. He met Chuck Glaser whilst in the US Army and he played guitar with the Glaser Brothers band. Chuck Glaser took over his management when he formed his band, the Payne Gang. He made several singles including 'Ladder To The Sky', 'What Does It Take (To Keep A Woman Like You Satisfied)' and 'My Most Requested Song'. He first appeared on the *Grand Ole Opry* in 1966. He cut several singles including his own composition, 'Woman, Woman', which had national success in 1967 when it was recorded by Gary Puckett And The Union Gap. He continued to have only minor success as a solo artist - 'L.A. Angels', 'Rambling Man' and 'Turning My Love On' - but he wrote Charley Pride's US number 1 country single, 'My Eyes Can Only See As Far As You'. He wrote the popular title track of his gospel album, *Walk With Me The Rest Of The Way*, with Jim Glaser. In 1986 he recorded a duet, 'Ugly Women And Pickup Trucks', with Tompall Glaser.

Album: *Woman, Woman, What Does It Take* (1968),

Live At Broadmoor (1976), *Walk With Me The Rest Of The Way* (1978), *The Best That Love Can Give* (1980), *The Album Version* (1986).

Payne, Leon

b. Leon Roger Payne, 15 June 1917, Alba, Texas, USA. Payne became blind as a young child following the application of the wrong medication for an eye complaint. Between 1924 and 1935, he attended the Texas School for the Blind in Austin, where he studied music and learnt to play guitar, banjo, organ, piano, trombone and drums. After graduating, he worked briefly as a one man band. In 1935, he appeared as a vocalist on KWET Palestine and during the 30s, he worked with several bands including, in 1938, that of Bob Wills. In spite of his blindness, he travelled extensively (often hitchhiking to venues) and appeared on many Texas stations as well as the *Louisiana Hayride*. In 1948, he played with Jack Rhodes Rhythm Boys but in 1949, he formed his own band, the Lone Star Buddies, and played the *Grand Ole Opry*. Although a fine vocalist, he is best remembered for his songwriting and from the late 40s, his songs were regularly hits for other artists. These included 'Cry Baby Heart' (George Morgan), 'Lost Highway' and 'They'll Never Take Her Love From Me' (Hank Williams), 'For Now And Always' and 'There Wasn't An Organ At Our Wedding' (Hank Snow), 'You Can't Pick A Rose In December' (Ernest Ashworth) and 'Blue Side Of Lonesome' (Jim Reeves and George Jones). There is little doubt that the song for which he will always be remembered is 'I Love You Because'. Written in 1949, for his wife Myrtie, it has been recorded by countless artists including Ernest Tubb, Carl Smith, Johnny Cash and Elvis Presley. In the UK, it is always associated with Jim Reeves, whose recording was a number 5 UK pop hit in 1964. The fact is often overlooked that, in 1949, Payne's own recording was a US country number 1; the only version to actually top the charts. In 1956, he recorded a cover version of Presley's 'My Baby Left Me', under the pseudonym of Rock Rogers. He refused to use his own name for rock 'n' roll, in case it upset country music fans. During his career, Payne recorded for various labels including MGM, Bluebird, Bullet, Capitol, Decca and Starday. One album made for the latter label featured songs appertaining to events of the Old West. In 1965, he suffered a heart attack and retired to San Antonio, where he died following a further heart attack on 11 September 1969. He was one of the first members elected to the Nashville

Songwriters International Hall Of Fame, when it was founded in 1970. Two radically different performers have paid tribute to his work - Elvis Costello with a recording of Payne's most famous song, the mass-murder saga 'Psycho', and George Jones with an album devoted to Payne's compositions.

Albums: *Americana* (1963), *A Living Legend Of Country Music* (1963), *Gone But Not Forgotten* (1988).

Pearl, Minnie

b. Sarah Ophelia Colley, 25 October 1912, Centerville, Tennessee, USA. The daughter of a prominent businessman, she, unlike many country artists, grew up in relative luxury though under the strict supervision of her mother, who played the local church organ. She developed an interest in the stage as a small child and later, when permitted, watched vaudeville shows at a Nashville theatre, being very impressed by the act of comedienne Elviry Weaver. After graduating from high school, she attended Nashville's Ward-Belmont College, a fashionable finishing school for young ladies, where, in 1932, she acquired a degree in speech and drama. She worked as a teacher in her home town for two years, before finding work with a company that toured the south producing amateur plays in rural areas. In 1936, after meeting what was later described as 'an amusing old mountain woman' when touring in Alabama, she began to develop her *alter ego*. Colley worked hard over the next few years, gradually building her act and it was not until November 1940, that she first auditioned for the *Grand Ole Opry*. Although the *Opry* management had some misgivings that she would be accepted as a country character, because of her known upper-class education, she was permitted to appear on the late evening show. Roy Acuff was impressed and a few weeks later signed her to his road show. The audience on the night were amused and Minnie Pearl was on the *Opry* to stay and destined to become one of its most popular stars. Minnie Pearl, dressed in her cheap frilly cotton dress and wearing a wide-brimmed hat with the price label still attached, became an *Opry* legend. After an opening catchphrase of 'How-dee, I'm just so proud to be here', she chattered incessantly about the community of Grinder's Switch (an actual small railway switching point near Centerville), told appallingly corny jokes, recited comic monologues, sang (badly), included a little dance and related how one day she would catch her boy friend, Hezzie.

Since 1940, Minnie Pearl has worked with most major country stars and once featured in popular routines with *Opry* comedian Rod Brasfield. In 1947, she appeared on the first country show to play Carnegie Hall, New York (she returned with a second show in 1961) and also married Henry Cannon, a commercial pilot, who became her manager. She later joked 'I married my transportation'. She has toured extensively with *Opry* and other shows in America and Canada and appeared in Europe, including a 1949-1950 tour with her friends Hank Williams, Red Foley and Rod Brasfield. Over the years she has appeared on all major network radio and television shows. She has recorded for several labels but not being a recognized vocalist failed to find chart success to match that of her stage act. Her only country chart entry came in 1966 with a Top 10 hit in 'Giddyup Go - Answer', the woman's reply to Red Sovine's country number 1. During her long career she has received many awards, the most important being her election to the Country Music Hall of Fame in 1975. The plaque reads 'Humor is the least recorded but certainly one of the most important aspects of live country music'. Although somewhat of a legend in the USA, especially in Nashville, where there is now a Minnie Pearl Museum in the Opryland complex, her appallingly unfunny jokes and distinctly rural humour, coupled with a distinct lack of exposure outside of her homeland, have never quite established her to anywhere near the same status in Britain. She suffered a severe stroke in 1991, and was forced into semi-retirement: scores of country stars contributed to a television tribute to her while she was in hospital, testifying to the respect in which she is held within the industry.

Albums: *Howdee (Cousin Gal From Grinder's Switch At The Party)* (1963), *Laugh-A-Long* (1964), *America's Beloved Minnie Pearl* (1965), with various artists, narration by Minnie Pearl *The Country Music Story* (1966), *Howdy!* (1967), *Looking For A Feller* (1970), with Grandpa Jones *Grand Old Opry Stars* (1975).

Penny, Hank

b. Herbert Clayton Penny, 18 August 1918, Birmingham, Alabama, USA. His father, who became a hypnotist, learned to play the guitar and wrote poetry, after being disabled in a mine accident, gave him his first guitar tuition and the interest in entertaining. At the age of 15, he joined the act of Hal Burns on WAPI, playing banjo and learning comedy routines. In 1936, he moved to

Minnie Pearl

New Orleans where he worked with Lew Childre on WWL. He disliked the *Grand Ole Opry's* hillbilly music and became somewhat obsessed by what he termed Texas fiddle music, being the Western-Swing music of Bob Wills and Milton Brown. He returned to Birmingham, formed his band the Radio Cowboys and began to present his swing music, first on WAPI and WKBC Birmingham and then at WDOD Chattanooga. Penny made his first recordings for ARC (with Art Satherley) in 1938, recording such uptempo swing-jazz-country tunes as 'Hesitation Blues'. In 1939, he moved to WSB Atlanta and joined the *Crossroads Follies*. Here, Boudleaux Bryant and steel guitarist Noel Boggs joined the band. In July 1939, he recorded 'Won't You Ride In My Little Red Wagon', which became his signature tune. The group disbanded in 1940 and for a time Penny worked solo on WSB but recorded with a 'pickup' band in 1941. In 1942, he moved to WLW Cincinnati, appeared regularly on the *Boone County Jamboree* and *Mid-Western Hayride* and worked with Merle Travis and Grandpa Jones. He toured with various shows and also fronted a group called the Plantation Boys, with whom he recorded for King Records in 1944.

He moved to Hollywood in 1945, re-formed his band and played the ballroom circuits of California. Later that year, he took over the band of Deuce Spriggins, played a residency at the famed *Riverside Rancho* and had his own show on KXLA and KGIL. He made further recordings for King and also appeared in four Charles Starrett b-movie westerns. He registered his first US country chart hits in 1946 with 'Steel Guitar Stomp' and 'Get Yourself A Redhead' (both reaching number 4). In 1947, apart from his band work, he played on ABC's network *'Roundup Time* as a comedian. He had a further number 4 country hit in 1950, with 'Bloodshot Eyes', which also was a hit for R&B artist Wynonie Harris. Penny also joined his friend Spade Cooley's network television show as a comedian but still maintained a rigorous schedule of playing dance halls with his band now known as the Penny Serenaders. He recorded for RCA-Victor in 1950, using an enlarged band that recorded as Hank Penny And His California Cowhands. In 1951, he left Spade Cooley and became the comedian with the Dude Martin stage and television show and he was also one of the founders of the Palomino Club in North Hollywood. He married country singer Sue Thompson in 1953, for a time hosted his own show on KHJ-TV and also moved from RCA to

Decca. In the late 50s, the effects of rock music saw him move to Las Vegas and begin to include pop music in his repertoire. He divorced in 1963 but married his vocalist Shari Bayne in 1966. (During the 70s, Sue Thompson had chart successes with solo hits as well as duet hits with Don Gibson for Hickory records.) Penny quit Las Vegas in 1968 and after a spell back in California, he moved to Nashville in 1970. Disliking the city and its music, he worked as a DJ on KFRM Wichita and with his wife, he played the local club circuit. In 1976, he returned to California, where he remained active, played in a few films and organized reunion concerts of some of the television and western-swing music celebrities of the 50s, including Cliffie Stone. He ranks as one of the most important exponents of western-swing music, although he rarely receives the publicity afforded to the likes of Wills, Brown and Cooley. There are several country musicians who benefited from their experience as a member of Hank Penny's band, including Herb Remington, Curly Chalker and Roy Clark.

Selected albums: *Tobacco State Swing* (1981), *Rompin', Stompin', Singin', Swingin'* (1983), *Country And Western Memories* (1986).

Perkins, Carl

b. Carl Lee Perkins, 9 April 1932, Ridgely, Tennessee, USA (his birth certificate misspelled the last name as Perkings). Carl Perkins was one of the most renowned rockabilly artists recording for Sun Records in the 50s and the author of the classic song 'Blue Suede Shoes'. As a guitarist, he influenced many of the next generation of rock 'n' rollers, most prominently George Harrison and Dave Edmunds. His parents, Fonie 'Buck' and Louise Brantley Perkins, were share-croppers during the 30s Depression and the family was thus very poor. As a child Perkins listened to the *Grand Ole Opry* on the radio, exposing him to C&W (or hillbilly) music, and he listened to the blues being sung by a black sharecropper named John Westbrook across the field from where he worked. After World War II the Perkins family relocated to Bemis, Tennessee, where he and his brothers picked cotton; by that time his father was unable to work due to a lung illness. Having taught himself rudimentary guitar from listening to such players as Butterball Page and Arthur Smith, Perkins bought an electric guitar and learned to play it more competently. In 1953 Carl, his brothers Jay (rhythm guitar) and Clayton (upright bass), and drummer W.S. 'Fluke' Holland formed a band that

Carl Perkins

worked up a repertoire of hillbilly songs performing at local honky-tonks, primarily in the Jackson, Tennessee area, where Carl moved with his recent wife Valda Crider in 1954.

Borrowing some of his technique from the black musicians he had studied set Carl Perkins apart from the many other country guitarists in that region at that time; his style of playing lead guitar fills around his own vocals was similar to that used in the blues. Encouraged by his wife, and by hearing a record by Elvis Presley on the radio, Perkins decided in 1954 to pursue a musical career. That October the Perkins brothers travelled to Memphis to audition for Sam Phillips at Sun Records. Phillips was not overly impressed, but agreed the group had potential. In February 1955 he issued two songs from that first Perkins session, 'Movie Magg' and 'Turn Around', on his new Flip label. Pure country in nature, these did not make a dent in the market. Perkins' next single was issued in August, this time on Sun itself. One track, 'Let The Jukebox Keep On Playing', was again country, but the other song, 'Gone! Gone! Gone!' was pure rockabilly. Again, it was not a hit. That November, after Phillips sold Presley's Sun contract to RCA Records, Phillips decided to push

the next Perkins single, an original called 'Blue Suede Shoes'. The song had its origins when Johnny Cash, another Sun artist, suggested to Perkins that he write a song based on the phrase 'Don't step on my blue suede shoes'. It was recorded at Sun on 19 December 1955, along with three other songs, among them the b-side 'Honey Don't', later to be covered by the Beatles. 'Blue Suede Shoes' entered the US *Billboard* chart on 3 March 1956 (the same day Presley's first single entered the chart), by which time several cover versions had been recorded, by a range of artists from Presley to Lawrence Welk. Perkins' version quickly became a huge hit and was also the first country record to appear on both the R&B chart and the pop chart, in addition to the country chart. Just as Perkins was beginning to enjoy the fruits of his labour, the car in which he and his band were driving to New York was involved in a severe accident near Dover, Delaware, when their manager, Stuart Pinkham, fell asleep at the wheel. Perkins and his brother Clayton suffered broken bones; brother Jay suffered a fractured neck; and the driver of the truck they hit, Thomas Phillips, was killed. 'Blue Suede Shoes' ultimately reached number 2 on the pop chart, a number 1 country

Carl Perkins

hit and an R&B number 2. Owing to the accident, Perkins was unable to promote the record, the momentum was lost, and none of his four future chart singles would climb nearly as high. In the UK, 'Blue Suede Shoes' became Perkins' only chart single, and was upstaged commercially by the Presley cover. Perkins continued to record for Sun until mid-1958, but the label's newcomers, Johnny Cash and Jerry Lee Lewis, occupied most of Sam Phillips' attention. Perkins' follow-up to 'Blue Suede Shoes', 'Boppin' The Blues', only reached number 70, and 'Your True Love' number 67. While still at Sun, Perkins did record numerous tracks that would later be revered by rockabilly fans, among them 'Everybody's Trying To Be My Baby' and 'Matchbox', both of which were also covered by the Beatles. On 4 December 1956, Perkins was joined by Lewis and a visiting Presley at Sun in an impromptu jam session which was recorded and released two decades later under the title 'The Million Dollar Quartet'. (Johnny Cash, despite having his photograph taken with Presley, Lewis and Carl, did not take part in the 'million dollar session' - he went shopping instead.) One of Perkins' last acts while at Sun was to appear in the film *Jamboree*, singing a song called 'Glad All Over'. In January 1958, Perkins signed with Columbia Records, where Cash would soon follow. Although some of the songs he recorded for that label were very good, only two, 'Pink Pedal Pushers' and 'Pointed Toe Shoes', both obvious attempts to recapture the success of his first footwear-oriented hit, had a minor impression on the charts. Later that year Jay Perkins died of a brain tumour, causing Carl to become an alcoholic, an affliction from which he would not recover until the late 60s.

In 1963 Perkins signed with Decca Records, for which there would be no successful releases. He also toured outside of the USA in 1963-64; while in Britain he met the Beatles, and watched as they recorded his songs. Perkins, who, ironically, was becoming something of a legend in Europe (as were many early rockers), returned to England for a second tour in October 1964. By 1966 he had left Decca for the small Dollie Records, a country label. In 1967 he joined Johnny Cash's band as guitarist and was allotted a guest singing spot during each of Cash's concerts and television shows. In 1969, Cash recorded Perkins' song 'Daddy Sang Bass', a minor hit in the USA. By 1970, Perkins was back on Columbia, this time recording an album together with new rock revival group NRBQ. In 1974 he signed with Mercury

Records. Late that year his brother Clayton committed suicide and their father died. Perkins left Cash in 1976 and went on the road with a band consisting of Perkins' two sons, with whom he was still performing in the 90s. A tribute single to the late Presley, 'The EP Express', came in 1977 and a new album, now for the Jet label, was released in 1978. By the 80s Perkins' reputation as one of rock's pioneers had grown. He recorded an album with Cash and Lewis, *The Survivors* (another similar project, with Cash, Lewis and Roy Orbison, *The Class Of '55*, followed in 1986). Perkins spent much of the 80s touring and working with younger musicians who were influenced by him, among them Paul McCartney and the Stray Cats. In 1985 he starred in a television special to mark the 30th anniversary of 'Blue Suede Shoes'. It co-starred Harrison, Ringo Starr, Dave Edmunds, two members of the Stray Cats, Rosanne Cash and Eric Clapton. In 1987 Perkins was elected to the Rock And Roll Hall of Fame. He signed to the Universal label in 1989 and released a new album, *Born To Rock*. His early work has been anthologized many times in several countries. During 1991 and 1992, he underwent treatment for throat cancer.

Selected albums: *The Dance Album Of Carl Perkins* (1957), *Whole Lotta Shakin'* (1958), *Teen Beat/The Best Of Carl Perkins* (1961), *Country Boy Dreams* (1968), *Blue Suede Shoes* (1969), *On Top* (1969), with the NRBQ *Boppin' The Blues* (1970), *My Kind Of Country* (1974), *Carl Perkins Show* (1976), *From Jackson, Tennessee* (1977), *Ol' Blue Suede's Back* (1978), with Jerry Lee Lewis and Johnny Cash *The Survivors* (1982), *The Class Of '55* (1986), *The Heart And Soul Of Carl Perkins* (1987), *Honky Tonk Gal: Rare And Unissued Sun Masters* (1989), *Born To Rock* (1990), *Friends, Family & Legends* (1992). Compilations: *Greatest Hits* (1969), *The Sun Years* (1982), *Up Through The Years, 1954-1957* (1986), *Original Sun Greatest Hits* (1986), *The Classic Carl Perkins* (1990, box-set).

Pierce, Webb

b. 8 August 1921, near West Monroe, Louisiana, USA, d. 24 February 1991, Nashville, Tennessee, USA. Pierce's father died when he was three months old, his mother remarried and he was raised on a farm seven miles from Monroe. Although no one in the family performed music, his mother had a collection of country records which, together with watching Gene Autry films, were his first country music influences. He learned to play guitar and when he was 15 was given his own weekly radio show on KMLB Monroe. During World War II he served in the Army, married Betty Jane Lewis in 1942 and after his discharge they relocated from Monroe to Shreveport where, in 1945, he found employment in the men's department of the Sears Roebuck store. In 1947, he and his wife appeared on an early morning KTBS show as 'Webb Pierce with Betty Jane, the Singing Sweetheart'. He also sang at many local venues and developed the style that became so readily identifiable and was later described as 'a wailing whiskey-voiced tenor that rang out every drop of emotion'. He recorded for 4-Star in 1949 and soon afterwards moved to KWKH, where he became a member of the *Louisiana Hayride* on its inception that year.

In 1950, he and Betty Jane were divorced and Pierce began building his solo career. He founded Pacemaker Records and a publishing company with Horace Logan, the director of the *Hayride*. His recording of 'Drifting Texas Sands', labelled as 'Tillman Franks and the Rainbow Valley Boys', due to Pierce still being under contract to 4-Star, created attention. His growing popularity attracted US Decca and in March 1951 he made his first recordings for that label. His third Decca release, 'Wondering', a song from the 30s by Joe Werner and the Riverside Ramblers, began his phenomenal success as a recording artist when, in March 1952, it spent four weeks at number 1 in the US country charts and gave Pierce his nickname of 'The Wondering Boy'. Two more number 1s 'That Heart Belongs To Me' (a self-penned song) and 'Back Street Affair' followed - all three remaining charted in excess of 20 weeks. (The latter song also led to Kitty Wells' second chart hit with the 'answer' version 'Paying For That Back Street Affair' early in 1953). In November 1952 he married again, this time to Audrey Grisham and finally gave up his job at Sears Roebuck. He left the *Hayride* and replaced Hank Williams on the *Grand Ole Opry*. During his days at Shreveport his band included such future stars as Goldie Hill, Floyd Cramer, Jimmy Day, the Wilburn Brothers and Faron Young. He remained a member of the *Opry* roster until 1955, leaving because of his heavy touring commitments but rejoined briefly in 1956 before a disagreement with the management caused him to once again leave. The problem concerned the fact that Pierce was having to give up lucrative Saturday concerts elsewhere to return to Nashville to meet his Opry commitments for which he received only the standard Opry fee. Pierce's chart successes during

the 50s and 60s totalled 88 country hits. Further number 1 singles included 'It's Been So Long', 'Even Tho'', 'More And More', 'I Don't Care', 'Love Love Love' and a duet with Red Sovine of George Jones' song 'Why Baby Why'.

Arguably his best remembered number 1 hits are his version of the old Jimmie Rodgers' song 'In The Jailhouse Now', which held the top spot for 21 weeks and his co-written, 'Slowly', which remained there for 17, both songs charting for more than 35 weeks. The recording of 'Slowly' is unique because of Bud Isaacs' electric pedal steel guitar, which created a style that was copied by most other country bands. He also had nine US pop chart hits, the biggest being 'More And More', which reached number 22 in 1954. Pierce recorded rockabilly and rock 'n' roll numbers having Top 10 country chart success with the first recorded version of 'Teenage Boogie' and with the Everly Brothers 'Bye Bye Love' but his vocal version of 'Raunchy' failed to chart. In the mid-50s Pierce and the Opry manager, Jim Denny, formed Cedarwood Music, which handled other artists songs as well as Pierce's own and also bought three radio stations. When Denny died in 1963, Pierce retained the radio stations and left the publishing company to his late partner's family. (He later acquired two more stations but eventually sold all five for a sum reputed to be almost $3 million.) He toured extensively and appeared in the films *Buffalo Guns* (his co-stars being Marty Robbins and Carl Smith), *Music City USA, Second Fiddle To A Steel Guitar* and *Road To Nashville* and during his career, dressed in rhinestone studded suits, he became known as one of the most flamboyant, even by country standard, of the singers of his era. During the 60s he had two Pontiac cars fancily studded with silver dollars, large cattle horns mounted as a decoration on the radiator, ornamental pistols and rifles and even leather seats that resembled saddles. Later his expensive Oak Hill, Nashville home with its guitar-shaped swimming pool brought so many tourist buses around the normally quiet area that he had problems with his neighbours, particularly Ray Stevens. Pierce totally ignored suggestions that he was bringing country music into disrepute, maintaining that the fans had paid for his pool and were therefore entitled to see it. After heated court proceedings he was forced to erect a sign warning fans to stay away. His comment on Stevens, who had been the organizer of the objectors, was 'That's what he gets for livin' across the street from a star'. Johnny Cash in his song 'Let There Be

Webb Pierce

Country' mentions the event when he sings 'Pierce invites the tourists in and Ray keeps them away'.

After 'Honky Tonk Song' in 1957, he never gained another number 1 record but he did add eight further country hits during the 70s on either Decca or Plantation. When the Columbia duet version of 'In The Jailhouse Now', that he recorded with Willie Nelson, charted in 1982 to register his 97th and last country hit, it gave him the distinction of having charted records in four decades. In the early 1980s he sold his Oak Hill home and retired to the Brentwood area of Nashville. He retired from touring but made special appearances when it pleased him and reflecting on his career said 'I've been blessed with so much. I guess it turned out the way I wanted it'. In 1985 he made a good-time album concentrating on Pierce's songs, with his friends Jerry Lee Lewis, Mel Tillis and Faron Young, but contractual problems led to it being withdrawn shortly after issue. Asked about recording again in 1986 he commented 'Hell, I might get a hit and then everybody would be botherin' me again'. Late in the 80s his health began to fail, he survived open heart surgery but early in 1990 it was diagnosed that he was suffering with cancer. He underwent several operations but finally died in Nashville on 24 February 1991. He had been nominated for membership of the Country Music Hall of Fame in August 1990: most authorities expected that he would be elected but it was not to be. The honour may be bestowed before long but sadly it will come too late for him to know. Pierce was, without any doubt, one of country music's most successful and popular honky-tonk singers.

Albums: *Webb Pierce* (1955), *The Wondering Boy* (1956), *Just Imagination* (1957), *Bow Thy Head* (1958), *Webb* (1959), *Bound For The Kingdom* (1959), *The One & Only Webb Pierce* (1959), *Walking The Streets* (1960), *Webb With A Beat* (1960), *Fallen Angel* (1961), *Cross Country* (1962), *Hideaway Heart* (1962), *Bow Thy Head* (1963), *I've Got A New Heartache* (1963), *Sands Of Gold* (1964), *Country Music Time* (1965), *Just Webb Pierce* (1965), *Memory Number One* (1965), *Sweet Memories* (1966), *Webb Pierce* (1966), *Webb's Choice* (1966), *Where'd Ya Stay Last Night* (1967), *Fool, Fool, Fool* (1968), *Country Songs* (1969), *Saturday Night* (1969), *Webb Pierce Sings This Thing* (1969), *Love Ain't Never Gonna Be No Better* (1970), *Merry Go Round World* (1970), *Country Favorites* (1970), *Webb Pierce Road Show* (1971), *I'm Gonna Be A Swinger* (1972), *Without You* (1973), *Carol Channing & Webb Pierce-Country & Western* (1976), *Faith, Hope And Love* (1977), with Willie Nelson *In The Jailhouse Now* (1982), with Jerry Lee Lewis, Mel Tillis and Faron Young *Four Legends* (1985). Compilations: *Golden Favorites* (1961), *The Webb Pierce Story* (1964), *The Living Legend Of Webb Pierce* (1977), *Golden Hits Volume 1* (1977), *Golden Hits Volume 2* (1977), *Webb 'The Wondering Boy' Pierce 1951-1958* (1990).

Pillow, Ray

b. 4 July 1937, Lynchburg, Virginia, USA. A singer, guitarist and songwriter, who had no initial thoughts of a singing career. He dropped out of high school in the eleventh grade and enlisted in the US Navy, where he actually completed his high school diploma. In 1958, he was discharged and entered college and one day for a dare, he deputized for the singer in the college rock band. He found he enjoyed singing and also learned to play the guitar but still had no immediate ideas of a singing career. In 1961, he travelled to Nashville and competed in the National Pet Milk Talent Contest. He did not win but the WSM radio judges placed him in second place. He returned to Lynchburg and after completing his college degree, he found work with a trucking company. However, he found that now he wanted to be an entertainer and returned to Nashville. He played small clubs, honky tonks and local radio stations and gradually built enough of a reputation that in 1964, he was given a recording contract by Capitol. His first charted in 1965 with 'Take Your Hands Off My Heart' and followed it with a Top 20 hit in 1966 with 'Thank You Ma'am'. Capitol also paired him with Jean Shepard and the duo had major successes with 'I'll Take The Dog', 'Mr Do It Yourself' and 'Heart We Did All We Could'. Pillow joined the *Grand Ole Opry* in 1966 and for a time toured with the *Martha White Show*. Although he never achieved any further major hits, he continued to record for various labels including ABC, Mega and MCA having minor hits with such songs as 'Gone With The Wine', 'Wonderful Day', 'Countryfied' and 'Living In The Sunshine Of Your Love'. His last chart entry, 'One Too Many Memories', came in 1981 on First Generation. A fine singer with a pleasant style of delivery, Pillow continues to appear on the *Opry* and make personal appearances.

Albums: *Presenting Ray Pillow* (1965), with Jean Shepard *I'll Take The Dog* (1966), *Even When It's Bad It's Good* (1967), *Wonderful Day* (1968), *Ray Pillow Sings* (1969), *People Music* (1970), *Slippin' Around With Ray Pillow* (1972), *Countryfied* (1974),

Ray Pillow (1982), *One Too Many Memories* (1984).

Poacher

This UK group was formed in Warrington, Cheshire in 1977 by guitar and singer Tim Flaherty (b. 1950). 'I'd played in local bands but I'd always wanted to be in one that had a pedal steel and a banjo.' The original line-up featured Flaherty (vocals), Adrian Hart (lead guitar), Allan Crookes (bass), Pete Allen (steel guitar), Pete Longbottom (banjo) and Stan Bennett (drums). Within months of being formed, Poacher won a heat on ITV television's *New Faces* and then the all-winners final with a new British country song, 'Silver Dollar Hero'. Their first single, 'Darling', made a minor impact on the UK charts and a few months later the song was a hit for Frankie Miller. Other versions come from Tom Jones and Barbara Mandrell, but Poacher's original made number 86 in the US country charts, no mean achievement for a British group. Despite several singles ('Star Love', 'You Are No Angel'), Poacher have not reached the UK charts, although they are a very popular cabaret and country club act. Flaherty's own song, the excellent 'I Want To Hear It From You', was scheduled for a 1990 release and then withdrawn. Flaherty and Crookes remain from the original line-up, and vocalist/guitarist Peter John Frampton is a talented addition. Frampton has written the first country song about Warrington, 'Buttermarket'. The contents of their albums are more adventurous than their titles.
Albums: *Poacher* (1978), *Alive And Gigging* (1981), *Along The Way* (1989).

Poole, Charlie

b. 22 March 1892, Alamance County, North Carolina, USA, d. 21 May 1931. A talented five-string banjo player who because of a childhood hand injury played in a thumb and three fingered picking style that was later further developed by Earl Scruggs. In 1917, Poole teamed up with fiddle player Posey Rorer (b. 22 September 1891, Franklin County, Virginia, USA, d. March 1935) and the two played throughout West Virginia and North Carolina. In 1922, they added a guitarist, initially Clarence Foust but when they made their first Columbia recordings on 27 July 1925, the regular guitarist was Norman Woodlieff. Perhaps due to their itinerant life style, they adopted the name of North Carolina Ramblers in 1923 and as such they became one of the most influential of the early string bands. They are still remembered for their recording of 'Don't Let Your Deal Go

Down'. In 1926, Roy Harvey (b. 24 March 1892, Monroe County, West Virginia, USA) replaced Woodlieff and in 1928, following a disagreement, Poole replaced Rorer with Lonnie Austin. Working with other musicians, including his son Charlie Jnr. (b. James Clay Poole, 1913). Poole continued to play but made his last recordings on 9 September 1930. (Woodlieff and Rorer made further recordings with other musicians and Harvey also recorded with his own North Carolina Ramblers band.) Poole was in real life very much a rambler, a trait which saw an early end to his 1911 marriage. He was also a heavy drinker and met a premature death from a heart attack in 1931, while celebrating an offer to play music for a Hollywood Western. Posey Rorer died in 1935 and was buried near Poole.
Albums: *Charlie Poole & The North Carolina Ramblers 1925-1930, Volumes 1 - 4* (1965-71), *Charlie Poole & Ihe Highlanders, Charlie Poole 1926-1930* (1975).

Prairie Ramblers

The group was originally formed as the Kentucky Ramblers by Charles 'Chick' Hurt (b. 1901, d. 1967; mandolin) and 'Happy' Jack Taylor (b. c.1900, d. 1962; tenor banjo). Both men were born in the Summershade area, near Glasgow, Kentucky, USA. Hurt moved to Kewanne, Illinois, when a young man and there organized his first band, but a few years later was reunited with Taylor, his childhood friend. They joined forces with Shelby David 'Tex' Atchison (b. 1912; fiddle/lead vocals) and Floyd 'Salty' Holmes (guitar/harmonica/jug player), both being born near Rosine, Ohio County, Kentucky, USA. (Atchison was actually born on the farm adjoining that of Bill Monroe's father). In 1932, they made their radio debut on WOC Davenport, Iowa and later the same year, they moved to WLS Chicago, first working on the *Merry-Go-Round* and then the *National Barn Dance*. In June 1933, they joined forces with Patsy Montana, who recorded with them when they made their first recordings for RCA-Victor's Bluebird label in December that year. By this time, with the growing interest in cowboy songs and music, the band had become the Prairie Ramblers. In 1934, they spent six months at WOR New York and returned to WLS specializing more in pop-styled cowboy songs and swing music. They emphasized the cowboy image, appeared at venues on horseback and western dress, even using the Gene Autry song, 'Ridin' Down The Canyon', as their signature tune.

They joined ARC records and by the end of 1936, they had recorded over 100 sides for that label. Their repertoire covered a wide variety of songs including gospel numbers like 'How Beautiful Heaven Must Be' but in 1935, they were persuaded to record some numbers that were somewhat *risqué*. Hurt was not keen and to change their overall sound, they added the clarinet and vocals of Bill Thawl and recorded them under the name of the Sweet Violet Boys, although it was an open secret whom the band really were. Some of the songs were written by Bob Miller (he also played piano on many of the Ramblers' recordings), who sought anonymity by copywriting them under the rather poorly camouflaged pseudonym of Trebor Rellim. Amongst the songs were numbers such as 'There's A Man Who Comes To Our House Every Single Day (Poppa Comes Home And The Man Goes Away)', 'Jim's Windy Mule' and 'I Love My Fruit' - a song that has been suggested as being the first gay hillbilly song. (It seems that they made the young Patsy Montana leave the studio when this material was being recorded.) Atchison and Holmes left in 1938 and were replaced by fiddler Alan Crockett and guitarist/vocalist Kenneth Houchens. In the early 1940s, they added the accordion of Augie Kline and electric guitarist George Barnes. Patsy Montana left around 1941 to pursue her solo career. The Ramblers appeared in various films, some with Gene Autry and also later recorded with Rex Allen. They made their final recordings for Mercury Records in December 1947, by which time their material was no longer of any specific type. At the time when they left WLS and disbanded in 1948, one of their songs was 'You Ain't Got No Hillbilly Anymore' - a fact many people agreed with. Hurt and Taylor continued to work around the Chicago area as a duo for a time until they eventually retired.

Compilations: *Tex's Dance* (1982), *Patsy Montana And The Prairie Ramblers* (1984), *Sing It Fast And Hot* (1989).

Price, Kenny

b. 27 May 1931, Florence, Kentucky, USA, d. 4 August 1987, Florence, Kentucky, USA. Price was raised on a farm in Boone County, Kentucky and he was given a guitar when he was five years old. He played guitar as a teenager on a radio station in Cincinnati and then entertained troups when he was in the forces. His break came in 1957 when he was invited to appear on Arthur Godfrey's television show in what was the first colour transmission in the US - perhaps they were attracted to his highly-coloured Nudie suits! He moved to Nashville in the early 60s and, after signing with the new Boone label in 1965, he had several US country hits - 'Walkin' On New Grass', 'Happy Tracks', 'Pretty Girl, Pretty Clothes, Pretty Sad', 'Grass Won't Grow On A Busy Street' and 'My Goal For Today'. He was a comedian and because he was 20 stone, he was known as 'The Round Mound Of Sound'. He became a regular member of *Hee Haw* television show. He moved to RCA and had US Top 10 country singles with 'Northeast Arkansas Mississippi County Bootlegger', 'Biloxi' and 'The Sheriff Of Boone County'. In 1973 Craig Baguley, the owner of *Country Music People*, wrote a tribute to him, 'Kenny Price' which was recorded by the Johnny Young Four. His final chart entries included 'Afraid You'd Come Back', 'Well Rounded Travellin' Man' and, ironically, 'She's Leavin' (And I'm Almost Gone)'. Price later died of a heart attack in 1987.

Albums: *One Hit Follows Another* (1967), *Southern Bound* (1967), *Walkin' On New Grass* (1969), *Happy Tracks* (1969), *Heavyweight* (1970), *Northeast Arkansas Mississippi County Bootlegger* (1970), *The Sheriff Of Boone County* (1971), *The Red Foley Songbook* (1971), *Charlotte Fever* (1971), *Super Sideman* (1972), *You Almost Slipped My Mind* (1972), *Sea Of Heartbreak And Other Don Gibson Tunes* (1973), *30 California Women* (1973), *Turn On Your Lovelight And Let It Shine* (1974), *Best Of Both* (1980), with Roy Clark, Grandpa Jones, Buck Owens *Hee-Haw Gospel Quartet* (1981), *A Pocket Full Of Tunes* (1982).

Price, Ray

b. Ray Noble Price, 12 January 1926, on a farm near Perryville, Cherokee County, Texas, USA. Price grew up on a farm and by the time he left high school, was already singing and playing guitar locally. In 1942, while studying veterinary medicine at Abilene's North Texas Agricultural College, he was drafted into the Marines. He returned to his studies in 1946, also began performing at local clubs and as the Cherokee Cowboy, he appeared on KRBC. He still had thoughts of a career as a rancher but in 1949, the opportunity to join the *Big D Jamboree,* in Dallas, finally convinced him that his future lay in country music. He first recorded for a minor label, Bullet, and had some success in Texas with 'Jealous Lies' but in 1952, he joined Columbia and had immediate US country Top 10 hits with 'Talk To

Ray Price

Your Heart' and 'Don't Let The Stars Get In Your Eyes'. Price moved to Nashville, where he became a member of the *Grand Ole Opry*. He was also befriended by Hank Williams, with whom he lived for a time and on occasions worked with the Drifting Cowboys on shows that Hank missed. When he later formed his own band, the Cherokee Cowboys, quite apart from appearances by members of the old Hank Williams band, it was occasionally to include Willie Nelson, Johnny Paycheck, Johnny Bush, Buddy Emmons and Roger Miller. Price's vocals and the excellence of the Cherokee Cowboys represented some of the finest honky tonk country music of all time. The immense popularity Price gained may be judged by his chart successes. In the 20 years between 1954 and 1974 he amassed a total of 64 US country chart hits, only 11 of which failed to make the Top 20 and 13 also crossed over to the pop charts. He registered 7 country number 1 hits including 'Crazy Arms' (his first million-seller), 'My Shoes Keep Walking Back To You', 'City Lights' (his second million-seller, which also launched Bill Anderson's songwriting career) and 'For The Good Times', a third million-seller which first introduced the songwriting talent of a young Nashville janitor called Kris Kristofferson. He also recorded what is probably the most popular country version of 'Release Me', a song that 13 years later became a UK pop chart number 1 for Engelbert Humperdinck. In 1967, Price varied from honky-tonk music to a more pop-oriented approach. His backings began to feature strong orchestral accompaniment, far removed from the traditional fiddle and steel guitar influence of his mentor, Hank Williams. Price maintained that most of his songs were ballads and that the strings provided the soul. In concert, he often used up to ten violins in his backing but for his records there were often many more, in fact, when he recorded his version of 'Danny Boy', the backing was by an orchestra that consisted of forty-seven musicians. He also dispensed with any western-style dress and took to appearing in smart evening suits; the Cherokee Cowboy was dead. He toured extensively and appeared on all major network radio and television shows.

By 1973, Price had grown rather tired of the touring and semi-retired to his ranch near Dallas to breed horses. Five years later, he found that he missed it all and once more was to be found back on the circuit. From the mid-70s, through to the late 80s, he recorded for Myrrh, ABC, Monument, Dimension, Warner Brothers, Viva and Step One and although there were few Top 20 hits after 1974, he continued regularly to register country charts entries. In 1980, in an effort to boost his somewhat flagging chart successes, he asked Willie Nelson to record an album with him. Willie obliged his old boss and their duet of 'Faded Love', from the album *San Antonio Rose*, charted at number 3. A feud had existed for many years between Price and Nelson dating back to when they were neighbours. Willie had shot and eaten one of Price's fighting roosters for killing some of his hens and Price swore he would never record another Nelson song. (The reason why Price kept fighting roosters is open to conjecture.) He eventually got over it, but Willie had no real reason to agree to the request to record the album since Price had not in fact recorded any of his songs for a long time. Price appeared in the Clint Eastwood film *Honkytonk Man*. From the mid-80s, some of his recordings were of dubious country content such as his versions of the Frank Sinatra pop hit 'All The Way' and the 1931 Gene Austin hit 'Please Don't Talk About Me When I'm Gone' but on others he tended to revert more to the simple country backings of his early days. When 'I'd Do It All Over Again' charted in December 1988, it took his tally of country hits to 108 and in the statistics produced by Joel Whitburn for his *Record Research*, based on country music chart success 1944-88, Price stands at number 6 in the Top 200 country artists of all time.

Albums: *Heart Songs* (1957), *Talk To Your Heart* (1958), with orchestra and chorus *Faith* (1960), *Sings San Antonio Rose (A Tribute To The Great Bob Wills)* (1962), *Night Life* (1963), *Love Life* (1964), *Burning Memories* (1965), *Western Strings* (1965), *The Other Woman* (1965), *Another Bridge To Burn* (1966), *Ray Price - Collector's Choice* (1966), *Touch My Heart* (1967), *Born To Lose* (1967), *Danny Boy* (1967), *She Wears My Ring* (1968), *Take Me As I Am* (1968), *I Fall To Pieces* (1969), *Christmas Album* (1969), *Sweetheart Of The Year* (1969), *For The Good Times* (1970), *The World Of Ray Price* (1970), *You Wouldn't Know Love* (1970), *Make The World Go Away* (1970), *I Won't Mention It Again* (1971), *Release Me* (1971), *The Lonesomest Lonesome* (1972), *She's Got To Be A Saint* (1973), *Like Old Times Again* (1974), *This Time Lord* (1974), *You're The Best Thing That Ever Happened To Me* (1974), *If You Ever Change Your Mind* (1975), *Say I Do* (1975), *Hank 'N' Me* (1976), *Rainbows And Tears* (1976), *Help Me* (1977), *How Great Thou Art* (1977), *Reunited - Ray Price And The Cherokee Cowboys* (1977), *Precious Memories* (1977), *There's Always Me*

(1979), with Willie Nelson *San Antonio Rose* (1980), *Ray Price* (1981), *Town And Country* (1981), *Tribute To Willie & Kris* (1981), *Diamonds In The Stars* (1981), *Loving You* (1982), *Somewhere In Texas* (1982), *Master Of The Art* (1983), *Portrait Of A Singer* (1985), *Welcome To The Country* (1985), *A Revival Of Old Time Singing* (1987), *The Heart Of Country Music* (1987), *A Christmas Gift For You* (1987), *Just Enough Love* (1988), *By Request Greatest Hits Volume 4* (1988), *Hall Of Fame Series* (1992), *Sometimes A Rose* (1992), with Faron Young *Memories That Last* (1992). Compilations: *Welcome To My World* (1971), *Ray Price's All-Time Greatest Hits* (1972), *Greatest Hits, Volume 1, 2 & 3* (1986), *By Request - Greatest Hits, Volume 4* (1988).

Pride, Charley

b. 18 March 1938, Sledge, Mississippi, USA. Charley Pride was born on a cotton farm, which, as a result of his success, he was later able to purchase. Pride says, 'My dad named me Charl Frank Pride, but I was born in the country and the midwife wrote it down as Charley'. Harold Dorman, who wrote and recorded 'Mountain of Love', also hails from Sledge and wrote 'Mississippi Cotton Pickin' Delta Town' about the area, for Pride. As an adolescent, Pride followed what he heard on the radio with a cheap guitar, breaking with stereotypes by preferring country music to the blues. He played baseball professionally but he reverted to music when the Los Angeles Angels told him that he didn't have a 'major league arm'. In 1965 producer Jack Clement brought Pride to Chet Atkins at RCA Records. They considered not disclosing that he was black until the records were established, but Atkins decided that it was unfair to all concerned. 'The Snakes Crawl at Night' sold on its own merit and it was followed by 'Just Between You And Me' which won a Grammy for the best country record by a male performer. On 7 January 1967 Ernest Tubb introduced him at the *Grand Ole Opry*, 42 years after the first black performer - DeFord Bailey - to appear there, in 1925. Prejudice ran high but the quality of Pride's music, particularly the atmospheric live album from Panther Hall, meant that he was accepted by the red-neck community. At one momentous concert, Willie Nelson kissed him on stage. Pride has had 29 number 1 records on the US country charts including six consecutive chart-toppers between 1969 and 1971.

His most significant recordings include 'Is Anybody Goin' to San Antone?', which he learnt and recorded in 15 minutes, and 'Crystal Chandelier',

Charley Pride

which he took from a Carl Belew record and is still the most-requested song in UK country clubs. Strangely enough, 'Crystal Chandelier' was not a US hit, where his biggest single is 'Kiss An Angel Good Mornin''. Unfortunately, Pride fell into the same trap as Elvis Presley by recording songs that he published, so he did not always record the best material around. Nevertheless, over the years, Charley Pride has encouraged such new talents as Kris Kristofferson, Ronnie Milsap, Dave And Sugar (who were his back-up singers) and Gary Stewart (who was his opening act). In 1975 Pride hosted a live double-album from the *Opry*, *In Person*, which also featured Atkins, Milsap, Dolly Parton, Jerry Reed and Stewart. By the mid-80s, Pride was disappointed at the way RCA was promoting 'New Country' in preference to established performers so he left the label. He then recorded what is arguably his most interesting project, a tribute album to Brook Benton. Sadly, it was not released as he signed with 16th Avenue Records, who preferred new material. Records like 'I'm Gonna Love Her On The Radio' and 'Amy's Eyes' continue his brand of easy-listening country, but he has yet to recapture his sales of the late 60s. Pride has had a long and contented family life and his son, Dion, plays in his band. ('We took the name from Dion And The Belmonts. We just liked it.'). Seeing him perform in concert underlines what a magnificent voice he has. Sadly, he doesn't test it in other, more demanding musical forms, although he argues that 'the most powerful songs are the simple ones.'

Albums: *Country Charley Pride* (1966), *Pride Of Country Music* (1967), *The Country Way* (1967), *Make Mine Country* (1968), *Songs Of Pride . . . Charley, That Is* (1968). *Charley Pride - In Person* (1969), *The Sensational Charley Pride* (1969), *Just Plain Charley* (1970), *Charley Pride's Tenth Album* (1970), *Christmas In My Home Town* (1970), *From Me To You (To All My Wonderful Fans)* (1971), *Did You Think To Pray?* (1971), *I'm Just Me* (1971), *Charley Pride Sings Heart Songs* (1971), *A Sunshine Day With Charley Pride* (1972), *Songs Of Love By Charley Pride* (1973), *Sweet Country* (1973), *Amazing Love* (1973), *Country Feelin'* (1974), *Pride Of America* (1974), *Charley* (1975), *The Happiness Of Having You* (1975), *Sunday Morning With Charley Pride* (1976), *She's Just An Old Love Turned Memory* (1977), *Someone Loves You Honey* (1978), *Burgers And Fries* (1978), *You're My Jamaica* (1979), *There's A Little Bit Of Hank In Me* (1980), *Roll On Mississippi* (1981), *Charley Sings Everybody's Choice* (1982), *Live* (1982), *Night Games* (1983), *The Power*

Of Love (1984), *After All This Time* (1987), *I'm Gonna Love Her On The Radio* (1988), *Moody Woman* (1989), *Amy's Eyes* (1990), *Classics With Pride* (1991). Compilations: *The Best Of Charley Pride* (1969), *The Best Of Charley Pride, Volume 2* (1972), *The Imcomparable Charley Pride* (1973), *The Best Of Charley Pride, Volume 3* (1977), *Greatest Hits* (1981).

Prophet, Ronnie

b. 26 December 1937, Calumet, Quebec, Canada. Prophet, whose second cousin is Canadian country singer, Orvel Prophet, was raised on a farm but spent his adolescence playing clubs in Montreal. In the late 60s Ronnie, deciding that this Prophet needed more than honour in his own country, established himself at the Carousel Club in Nashville. With his comedy and impressions, he stood apart from other country performers. Chet Atkins called him 'the greatest one-man show I've seen' and Prophet himself comments, 'I believe that if an audience goes to a live show, then they should get a *live* show. I'm irritated by artists who are walking jukeboxes.' In truth, Prophet has not had enough country hits to be a walking jukebox, and he has only had five minor successes on the US country charts - 'Sanctuary' (number 26), 'Shine On' (number 36). His serious records resemble Conway Twitty at his most mannered. In 1978, Prophet was a major success in the UK at the Wembley Country Music Festival, which led to further appearances, UK tours and his own television programmes. Although he is an excellent MC, Prophet has not sustained his popularity, possibly because 'Harry The Horny Toad' and 'The Phantom Of The Opry' wear thin.

Albums: *Ronnie Prophet Country* (1976), *Ronnie Prophet* (1977), *Just For You* (1978), *Faces And Phrases* (1980), *Audiograph Alive* (1982), *I'm Gonna Love Him Out Of You* (1983), *Ronnie Prophet And Glory-Anne* (c.80s), *Ronnie Prophet* (1987).

Pruett, Jeanne

b. Norma Jean Bowman, 30 January 1937, Pell City, Oklahoma, USA. Pruett, one of 10 children, used to listen to the *Grand Ole Opry* with her parents and she harmonized with her brothers and sisters. She married Jack Pruett and, in 1956, they settled in Nashville where he became Marty Robbins' long-standing lead guitarist. She wrote several songs for Robbins, and 'Count Me Out' was a US country hit in 1966. After some unsuccessful records for RCA, she made the US country charts with 'Hold On To My Unchanging

Love' for Decca in 1971. It was followed by a country number 1 in 1973, 'Satin Sheets', which was also a US pop hit. Another Top 10 country single, 'I'm Your Woman', was on the charts at the same time as a Robbins' single she had written, 'Love Me'. (After Robbins' death, a duet version of the same song was also a country hit.) Although she did not repeat the success of 'Satin Sheets', she generated interest in 1979 with 'Please Sing Satin Sheets For Me'. Although she regularly appears at *Grand Ole Opry*, Pruett has never been fully committed to her career as she values her home life and is a prize cook and gardener.

Albums: *Love Me* (1972), *Satin Sheets* (1973), *Welcome To The Sunshine* (1974), *Honey On His Hands* (1975), *Encore* (1980), *Country* (1982), *Star Studded Nights* (1982), *Audiograph Alive* (1983), *Stand By Your Man* (1984), *Jeanne Pruett* (1985).

Puckett, Riley

b. George Riley Puckett, 7 May 1894, near Alpharetta, Georgia, USA, d. 13 July 1946. Due to the accidental use of overly strong medication to treat a minor eye infection, he was blinded as a baby. In 1912, after graduating from the Georgia Academy for the Blind in Macon, where he first learned to play the banjo and piano, he sought the life of a musician and moved to Atlanta. He appeared at the Georgia Old Time Fiddler's Convention in 1916, drawing good reviews as 'the blind banjoist'. (He made further appearances at the conventions, the last being in 1934, when he won the banjo contest.) He also took to playing the guitar and singing and worked local dances and busked on the streets. In 1922, he made his radio debut on WSB as a special guest with the Hometown Band - a local band led by fiddler Clayton McMichen. The programmes of the powerful WSB could be heard over most of the United States and Puckett's performance attracted attention. He was a fine singer and listeners were also greatly impressed by his excellent yodelling. In 1923, he, McMichen and Gid Tanner began to play together as the Skillet Lickers. Puckett made his first recordings in New York in March 1924, when he and Tanner became the first hillbilly artists to appear on the Columbia label. He recorded such solo numbers as 'Little Old Log Cabin In The Lane' and 'Rock All My Babies To Sleep'. By yodelling on the latter, he probably became the first hillbilly singer to yodel on record - preceding the blue yodels of Jimmie Rodgers by three years. (It has never been established just where he first learned this art.) He was badly injured in a car crash in 1925 and subsequently married his nurse. (They had one daughter, Blanche but later parted.)

His recordings proved so popular that, by the end of the year, only the recordings of Vernon Dalhart received more orders among Columbia artists. The Skillet Lickers, who underwent various changes in line-up during their existence, made their first recordings in 1926 and proved very successful. Their 1927 recording of 'A Corn Licker Still In Georgia' very quickly sold a quarter of a million copies. During the years that Puckett played with the Skillet Lickers, he still made solo concert and recording appearances. When, because of the Depression, the Skillet Lickers disbanded in 1931, he was still much in demand as a solo artist. They re-formed briefly in 1934, when he and Tanner recorded together for the last time. (Tanner tired of the music business and returned to chicken farming.) During the 30s and early 40s, Puckett travelled extensively making personal appearances and for some time he also had his own very popular tent show, which toured the mid-west, Texas, Oklahoma and the southern states. He was featured on various radio stations and at times ran his own bands. In 1945, he was a regular member of the *Tennessee Barn Dance* on WNOX Knoxville, where he appeared with the Delmore Brothers, Chet Atkins and Sam And Kirk McGee. After leaving Columbia in 1934, he made recordings for RCA Victor and Decca. His final recordings were made for RCA in 1941, in a session that included the pop oriented 'Where The Shy Little Violets Grow' and Carson Jay Robison's 'Railroad Boomer'. The undoubted secret of Puckett's success, quite apart from his instrumental abilities, was his large repertoire. He could sing (and play) equally well any songs ranging from old time folk ballads like 'Old Black Joe' and 'John Henry' (his 1924 version is in all probability the first time the song was recorded) through to vaudeville numbers such as 'Wait Till The Sun Shines Nellie' and 'Red Sails In The Sunset'. His fine banjo playing included standards such as 'Cripple Creek' and 'Oh Susanna' and his unique guitar style, with its very fast thumb played bass string runs, has been equalled by very, very few other guitarists: one exception being another blind musician, Doc Watson. Prior to his untimely death in 1946, he was appearing regularly on WACA Atlanta, with a band called the Stone Mountain Boys. A boil on his neck caused blood poisoning and though he was rushed to hospital, it was too late and he died on 13 July. One of the pallbearers at his funeral was his old associate, Gid Tanner. It seems ironic that, as with his blindness, the correct treatment at the appropriate time could no doubt have effected a proper cure. Puckett is one of country music's most interesting and talented but, unfortunately, now overlooked characters.

Compilations: with Gid Tanner And The Skillet Lickers *Gid Tanner And His Skillet Lickers* (1973), *The Skillet Lickers* (1973), *Gid Tanner And His Skillet Lickers, Volume 2* (1975), *Kickapoo Medicine Show* (1977), *A Day A The County Fair* (1981), *A Corn Licker Still In Georgia* (80s). Solo compilations: *Waitin' For The Evening Train* (1977), *Old Time Greats, Volume 1* (1978), *Old Time Greats, Volume 2* (1986), *Red Sails In The Sunset* (1988).

Further reading: *Riley Puckett (1894-1946)*, Charles K.Wolfe, with *Discography* by John Larson, Tony Russell, Richard Weize.

Pure Prairie League

Formed in 1971, this US country rock group comprised Craig Lee Fuller (vocals/guitar), George Powell (vocals/guitar), John Call (pedal steel guitar), Jim Lanham (bass) and Jim Caughlin (drums). Their self-titled debut album was a strong effort, which included the excellent 'Tears', 'You're Between Me' (a tribute to McKendree Spring) and 'It's All On Me'. The work also featured some novel sleeve artwork, using Norman Rockwell's portrait of an ageing cowboy as a symbol of the Old West. On *Pure Prairie League*, the figure was seen wistfully clutching a record titled 'Dreams Of Long Ago'. For successive albums, the cowboy would be portrayed being ejected from a saloon, stranded in a desert and struggling with a pair of boots. The image effectively gave Pure Prairie League a brand name, but by the time of their *Bustin' Out*, Fuller and Powell were left to run the group using session musicians. This album proved their masterwork, one of the best and most underrated records produced in country rock. Its originality lay in the use of string arrangements, for which they recruited the services of former David Bowie acolyte Mick Ronson. His work was particularly effective on the expansive 'Boulder Skies' and 'Call Me Tell Me'. A single from the album, 'Amie', was a US hit and prompted the return of John Call, but when Fuller left in 1975 to form American Flyer, the group lost its major writing talent and inspiration. Powell continued with bassist Mike Reilly, lead guitarist Larry Goshorn and pianist Michael Connor. Several minor albums followed and the group achieved a surprise US Top 10 hit in 1980 with 'Let Me Love You Tonight'. Fuller is now with Little Feat, while latter-day guitarist Vince Gill, who joined Pure Prairie League in 1979, has become a superstar in the country market in the 90s.

Albums: *Pure Prairie League* (1972), *Bustin' Out* (1972), *Two Lane Highway* (1975), *If The Shoe Fits* (1976), *Dance* (1976), *Live!! Takin' The Stage* (1977), *Just Fly* (1978), *Can't Hold Back* (1979), *Firin' Up* (1980), *Something In The Night* (1981). Compilation: *Pure Prairie Collection* (1981).

R

Rabbitt, Eddie

b. Edward Thomas Rabbitt, 27 November 1944, Brooklyn, New York City, USA. Rabbitt, whose name is Gaelic, was raised in East Orange, New Jersey. His father, Thomas Rabbitt, a refrigeration engineer, played fiddle and accordion and is featured alongside his son on the 1978 track, 'Song Of Ireland'. On a scouting holiday, Rabbitt was introduced to country music and he soon became immersed in the history of its performers. Rabbitt's first single was 'Six Nights And Seven Days' on 20th Century Fox in 1964, and he had further singles for Columbia, 'Bottles' and 'I Just Don't Care No More'. Rabbitt, who found he could make no headway singing country music in New York, decided to move to Nashville in 1968. Sitting in a bath in a cheap hotel, he had the idea for 'Working My Way Up From The Bottom', which was recorded by Roy Drusky. At first, he had difficulty in placing other songs although George Morgan recorded 'The Sounds Of Goodbye' and Bobby Lewis 'Love Me And Make It All Better'. He secured a recording contract and at the same time gave Lamar Fike a tape of songs for Elvis Presley. Presley chose the one he was planning to do himself, 'Kentucky Rain', and took it to number 16 in the US country charts and number 21 in th UK. Presley also recorded 'Patch It Up' and 'Inherit The Wind'. In 1974 Ronnie Milsap topped the US country charts with 'Pure Love', which Rabbitt had written for his future wife, Janine, the references in the song being to commercials for Ivory soap ('99 44/100th per cent') and 'Cap'n Crunch'. Rabbitt also recorded 'Sweet Janine' on his first album. He had his first US country success as a performer with 'You Get To Me' in 1974, and, two years later, topped the US country charts with 'Drinkin' My Baby (Off My Mind)', a good time drinking song he had written with Even Stevens.

He often wrote with Stevens and also with his producer, David Molloy. Rabbitt followed his success with the traditional-sounding 'Rocky Mountain Music' and two more drinking songs, 'Two Dollars In The Jukebox (Five In A Bottle)' and 'Pour Me Another Tequila'. Rabbitt was criticized by the Women's Christian Temperance Union for damaging their cause. Further number 1s came with 'I Just Want To Love You', which he had written during the session, 'Suspicions' and the theme for the Clint Eastwood film, *Every Which Way But Loose*, which also made number 41 in the UK. Rabbitt harmonized with himself on the 1980 country number 1, 'Gone Too Far'. Inspired by the rhythm of Bob Dylan's 'Subterranean Homesick Blues', he wrote 'Drivin' My Life Away', a US Top 5 pop hit as well as a number 1 country hit, for the 1980 film *Roadie*. A fragment of a song he had written 12 years earlier gave him the concept for 'I Love A Rainy Night', which topped both the US pop and country charts. He had further number 1 country hits with 'Step By Step' (US pop 5) and the Eagles-styled 'Someone Could Lose A Heart Tonight' (US pop 15). He also had chart-topping country duets with Crystal Gayle ('You And I') and Juice Newton ('Both To Each Other (Friends And Lovers)'), the latter being the theme for the television soap opera, *Days Of Our Lives*. Rabbitt's son, Timmy, was born with a rare disease in 1983 and Rabbitt cut back on his commitments until Timmy's death in 1985. Another son, Tommy, was born in good health in 1986. Rabbitt topped the US country charts by reviving a pure rock 'n' roll song from his youth in New York, Dion's 'The Wanderer'. During his son's illness, he had found songwriting difficult but wrote his 1988 US country number 1, 'I Wanna Dance With You'. His ambition is to write 'a classic, one of those songs that will support me for the rest of my life'.

Albums: *Eddie Rabbitt* (1975), *Rocky Mountain Music* (1976), *Variations* (1978), *Loveline* (1979), *Horizon* (1980), *Step By Step* (1981), *Radio Romance* (1982), *Rabbitt Trax* (1986), *I Wanna Dance With You* (1988), *Jersey Boy* (1990), *Ten Rounds* (1991).

Rainwater, Marvin

b. Marvin Karlton Percy, 2 July 1925, Wichita, Kansas, USA. A big-voiced, rockabilly singer-songwriter, who is a quarter Cherokee Indian (using his mother's maiden name on stage). He became a regular on Red Foley's *Ozark Mountain Jubilee* in the early 50s and after being spotted on Arthur Godfrey's Talent Scouts television show in the mid-50s was signed to Coral. The first of his two singles for them 'I Gotta Go Get My Baby' became a hit for the label when their top act Teresa Brewer covered his record. Rainwater then joined MGM and his second release, the self-composed 'Gonna Find Me A Bluebird', in 1957 gave him his only US Top 40 hit. Later that year a duet with Connie Francis (before her string of

Marvin Rainwater

hits), 'Majesty Of Love', graced the US Top 100. In 1958 another of his songs 'Whole Lotta Woman', which only reached number 60 in his homeland, topped the UK chart and his UK recorded follow-up 'I Dig You Baby' also entered the British Top 20. He later recorded without success for Warwick, Warner Brothers, United Artists, Wesco, his own label Brave, as well as UK labels Philips, Sonet and Westwood. In subsequent years, the man who performed in full American Indian regalia, has played the rockabilly and country circuit on both sides of the Atlantic.
Albums: *Marvin Rainwater Sings* (1958), *Marvin Rainwater* (1962). Compilation: *Classic Recordings* (1992).

Raney, Wayne

b. 17 August 1921, Wolf Bayou, near Batesville, Arkansas, USA. He became interested in music at an early age, due to the fact that a crippled foot prevented him playing games. He learned to play the harmonica and listened intently to the playing of Lonnie Glosson on Border radio station XEPN. In 1934, at the age of 13, he hitchhiked to the station's studios in Eagle Pass and recorded some transcription records. He returned home but when

he was 17, he teamed up with Glosson and in 1938, the pair became favourites on KARK Little Rock and continued to play together on many occasions throughout the 40s. In 1941, Raney had his own show on WCKY in Cincinnati and sold a great many 'talking harmonicas' by mail order through the programme. In the late 40s, he became friendly with the Delmore Brothers and between 1946 and 1952, made many King recordings with them as the Delmore Brothers, the Brown's Ferry Four or under his own name. (Some recordings also included Glosson.) One of his most popular was the 1946 recording of 'Harmonica Blues'. He obtained two Top 20 US country chart hits in 1948 with 'Lost John Boogie' and 'Jack And Jill Boogie'. In 1949, his recording of 'Why Don't You Haul Off And Love Me', which he co-wrote with Glosson, became a country number 1 and also made number 22 in the US pop charts. In the mid-50s, he left the King label and spent some time as a member of the *Grand Ole Opry* and toured with its shows. He recorded contributions to rock 'n' roll in 1957, such as his Decca version of 'Shake Baby Shake'. He left WCKY in 1961 and moved back to his native Arkansas, where he relocated to Concord, opened his own Rimrock recording studio and became involved with promotion work. Albums: *Songs From The Hills* (1958), *Wayne Raney And The Raney Family* (1960), *Don't Try To Be What You Ain't* (1964), *Gathering In The Sky* (c.60s), *We Need A Lot More Of Jesus* (c.60s), *Early Country Favorites* (1983).

Rattlesnake Annie

b. Rosanne Gallimore, 26 December 1941, Puryear, Tennessee, USA. Rattlesnake Annie, of Cherokee heritage, was born into a poor family of tobacco farmers. They had no electricity or modern conveniences, apart from a radio, on which Gallimore would hear country music from Nashville. Many of her songs ('Cotton Mama', 'Bulger Wilson', 'Good Ole Country Music') are about those years. As part of the Gallimore sisters, she appeared on the *Junior Grand Ole Opry* in 1954 but when she married Max McGowan, her ambitions were put on hold while she raised a family. David Allan Coe recorded her song, 'Texas Lullaby' and she became Rattlesnake Annie by wearing a rattlesnake's tail on her right ear. Her first album, although self-financed, featured top Nashville musicians and established her as both a performer and a songwriter. Because she shares the same love of traditional country music as Boxcar Willie, she has been accepted in the UK and even more so in Czechoslovakia where her album with local country star, Michal Tuny, was a best-seller. She recorded 'Long Black Limousine' with Willie Nelson, a performer who favours the same casual approach to stage wear.
Albums: *Rattlesnakes And Rusty Water* (1980), with Michal Tuny *Rattlesnake Annie And The Last Cowboy* (1983), *Country Livin'* (1985), *Rattlesnake Annie* (1987), *Indian Dreams* (1991), *Crossroads* (1990), *Rattlesnake Annie Sings Hank Williams* (1991).

Raven, Eddy

b. Edward Garvin Futch, 19 August 1944, Lafayette, Louisiana, USA. Eddy, one of 11 children, was raised in bayou country. His father, a truck driver and blues guitarist, would take him to honky tonks. He was given a guitar, and by the time he was 13 years old, he was playing in a rock 'n' roll band. When the family moved to Georgia in 1960, he worked for a radio station and recorded his own song, 'Once A Fool', as Eddy Raven for the small Cosmo label. They returned to Lafayette in 1963 and Eddy worked in La Louisianne record store and also made singles for the owner's label. In 1969 he recorded *That Crazy Cajun Sound*, which impressed Jimmy C. Newman, who secured Raven a songwriting contract in Nashville with Acuff-Rose. He also worked as lead singer for Jimmie Davis' band and toured with him during an election campaign for Governor of Louisiana. In 1971 Don Gibson had a Top 5 US country hit with Raven's 'Country Green', which was followed by Jeannie C. Riley's 'Good Morning, Country Rain'. He also wrote 'Back In The Country' (Roy Acuff), 'Sometimes I Talk In My Sleep' (Randy Cornor) and 'Touch The Morning' (Don Gibson). He had his first US country chart entry with 'The Last Of The Sunshine Cowboys' in 1974 for ABC and then recorded for Monument ('You're A Dancer') and Dimension ('Sweet Mother Texas', 'Dealin' With The Devil'). He had four country hits from his Elektra album, *Desperate Dreams*, including 'Who Do You Know In California?' and 'She's Playing Hard To Forget'. A second album for Elektra was never released and Raven spent two years resolving management problems. He wrote a Top 5 country record for the Oak Ridge Boys, 'Thank God For Kids'. He came back on RCA in 1984 with the escapist theme of 'I Got Mexico', a style he returned to in 1988 for 'Joe Knows How To Live'. He followed it with other hits, including 'I Could Use Another You', 'Shine Shine Shine' and 'You're Never Too Old For Young Love'. He went to number 1 with a bluesy song written by Dennis Linde and first recorded by Billy Swan, 'I'm Gonna Get You'. Linde also wrote his 1989 number 1, 'In A Letter To You', for the new Universal label. That year he also returned to the cajun sounds of his youth for 'Bayou Boys' in a mixture he describes as 'electric cajun'. In 1991 he moved to the ninth label of his career, Capitol.
Albums: *That Cajun Country Sound* (1969), *This Is Eddy Raven* (1976), *Eyes* (1980), *Desperate Dreams* (1981), *I Could Use Another You* (1984), *Love And Other Hard Times* (1985), *Right Hand Man* (1987), *Temporary Sanity* (1989), *Right For The Flight* (1991).

Raye, Collin

b. 1960, Arkansas, USA. Raye was raised in Texas, where his mother often opened shows for visiting star performers. For many years he and his brother Scott worked in Oregon and then in casinos in Las Vegas and Reno, but their contract to record for Warner Brothers as the Wray Brothers led nowhere. The brothers split and Collin was signed as a solo act to Epic by producer Bob Montgomery. A collection of romantic songs, *All I*

Can Be, was a best-selling country album in the USA and 'Love Me' topped the US country chart as well as being featured on BBC Radio 2's playlist. Albums: *In This Life* (c.80s), *All I Can Be* (1991).

Raye, Susan

b. 8 October 1944, Eugene, Oregon, USA. In 1961, with no personal thoughts of being a country singer, she found her mother had entered her in a talent show. She won and was soon singing and working as a disc jockey on local radio. By the mid-60s, she was a regular on the Portland television show *Hoedown*, where she was seen by Buck Owens' manager. Between 1968 and 1976, she worked with Owens, became a Capitol recording artist in her own right and was a regular performer on the top television show *Hee Haw*, which Owens co-hosted. Between 1970 and 1977, she registered 21 solo country hits, including 'I've Got A Happy Heart' and her version of Kay Starr's pop hit 'Wheel Of Fortune'. During this time she also recorded duets with Owens, six of which charted including a Top 10 with 'The Great White Horse'. She retired for a time but reappeared in the country charts in 1986 with 'I Just Can't Take The Leaving Anymore'.

Albums: *One Night Stand* (1970), *Willy Jones* (1971), *Pitty Pitty Patter* (1971), *I've Got A Happy Heart* (1972), *Wheel Of Fortune/L.A International Airport* (1972), *My Heart Has A Mind Of It's Own* (1972), *Plastic Trains, Paper Planes* (1973), *Singing Susan Raye* (1974), *Love Sure Feels Good In My Heart* (1973), *Hymns By Susan Raye* (1973), *The Cheating Game* (1973), *Whatcha Gonna Do With A Dog Like That* (1975), *Honey Toast And Sunshine* (1976), *Susan Raye* (1977), *There And Back* (1985), *Then And Now* (1986). With Buck Owens: *The Great White Horse* (1970), *We're Gonna Get Together* (1970), *Merry Christmas From Buck Owens & Susan Raye* (1971), *The Best Of Buck & Susan* (1972), *The Good Old Days Are Here Again* (1973).

Red River Dave

b. David McEnery, 15 December 1914, San Antonio, Texas, USA, close to the Alamo. Being a Texan, McEnery naturally became interested in things appertaining to the western life and as a boy at school, took to playing the guitar and singing cowboy songs. His fondness for 'Red River Valley' led to his nickname when he started his professional career. He played on local radio in the early 30s, but during the decade he also played many stations in various places, including New York State where the northern audiences were taken with the singing cowboy and his strange saga songs. He developed a penchant for writing songs of historic events such as 'The Battle Of The Alamo' and 'Pony Express' and his first real break came in 1937, with his saga song 'Amelia Earhart's Last Flight'. Following this, he moved to Chicago for a time and in 1939, was invited to New York to sing his song of the lost aviator and others on the first commercial television broadcast at the World's Fair. In the early 40s, he returned to San Antonio, Texas and began regular appearances on Border Radio station XERF where, billing himself as 'your favourite Texas Farmboy', he sang his songs and sold his sets of six songbooks, which he classed as 'a complete library of cowboy, hillbilly and sacred songs'. He also appeared on local US stations and during the 40s and 50s, recorded for several labels. He wrote many songs including 'I'm A Convict With Old Glory In My Heart' (about the man who wanted to fight but was in jail) and as the war ended, he tugged at his listeners heartstrings' with such maudlin numbers as 'The Blind Boy's Dog' (later recorded with success by Hank Snow). He has never been short on gimmicks. In 1936, he claimed to be the first (and probably the last) singing cowboy to broadcast from an airship when high above Miami, he sang 'Way Out There', over the airwaves of CBS, from the Goodyear blimp. In 1946, he was handcuffed to a piano for 12 hours and wrote songs from titles that people selected from magazines. By the end, he claimed a total of 52 completed songs.

In the 40s, he appeared in several films, including *Swing In The Saddle, Hidden Valley* and *Echo Ranch* but had made some appearances in earlier films in the 30s. Although he was a singer of cowboy songs for many years and is an expert on them, he is probably now best remembered for his saga songs. After the success of the Amelia Earhart song, he continued over the years to turn out such numbers of news interest including 'Ballad Of Emmett Till', 'The Flight Of Gary Powers', 'The Flight Of Apollo Eleven' and 'The Ballad Of Patty Hearst'. He has appeared on countless radio and television programmes and built the reputation of being something of a character, as well as becoming an ordained Pentecostal minister. Many of the major stars have recorded his songs and amongst his many tribute songs, he once recorded a dedication to his friend, Bob Wills, called 'Somewhere I Hear Angels Singing The San Antone Rose'. He moved to Nashville in the mid 70s, where he became noted for his flamboyant western dress with gold boots, his long white hair and goatee beard, all of which made him look a most distinctive resident somewhat like a modern Buffalo Bill Cody. He later returned to his native Texas, where he dispensed with the white locks and beard and reverted to more normal attire but still maintained his regular public appearances at folk festivals and similar events in many parts of the USA.

Albums: with the Texas Tophands *Songs Of The Rodeo* (1961), *Red River Dave Sings* (1962), *Red River Dave Volumes 1* and *2* (mid-60s), *Days Of The Yodeling Cowboys* (80s), *More Days Of Yodeling Cowboys Volume 2* (80s), *Yodelin' Cowboy Memories* (80s).

Reed, Jerry

b. Jerry Hubbard, 20 March 1937, Atlanta, Georgia, USA. Reed has had three distinct careers: as a respected country guitarist, as a composer and singer of clever pop/country hits and as a genial, jokey television personality and film actor. A cotton mill worker, he was one of many youths brought up on country music who played rockabilly in the mid-50s. His own records for Capitol were unsuccessful but Reed's songs were taken up by Gene Vincent ('Crazy Legs') and Brenda Lee. After army service, Reed moved to Nashville working as a session guitarist and scoring minor hits with 'Hully Gully Guitars' and the traditional 'Goodnight Irene'. He also wrote songs for Porter Wagoner ('Misery Loves Company') and Johnny Cash ('A Thing Called Love') Reed's skill at the finger-picking guitar style was showcased on two duet albums with Chet Atkins in the 70s. Atkins also produced Reed's albums and singles. Reed's career gathered momentum after he signed a recording contract with RCA in 1965. Two years later he recorded the boastful 'Guitar Man' and 'U.S. Male' both of which were covered successfully by Elvis Presley in 1968. Reed had two big US pop hits in 1971 with the swamp-rock styled 'Amos Moses' and 'When You're Hot, You're Hot' (based on his television catch-phrase), but his continuing popularity was with country audiences; the latter was a US country chart number one for five weeks. Another country number 1 followed with 'Lord Mr Ford' in 1973, a humorous attack on the cost of running a car in the 70s. During the late 70s he was less successful but he returned to prominence with the recording of the Tim DuBois song 'She Got The Goldmine (I Got The Shaft)' for RCA in 1982. Produced by Rick Hall, it was a country number 1. Reed became well known to television viewers with appearances on Glen Campbell's show in the early 70s. This led to cameo roles in several Burt Reynolds movies including *W.W. And the Dixie Dance Kings* (1975), *Gator* (1976) and *Smokey And The Bandit* (1977).

Albums: *Tupelo Mississippi Flash* (1967), *Alabama Wild Man* (1969), *Cookin'* (1970), *Georgia Sunshine* (1971), *When You're Hot You're Hot* (1971), *Ko Ko Joe* (1972), *Jerry Reed* (1972), *Hot A Mighty* (1973), *Lord Mr Ford* (1973), *Half And Half* (1974), *Live At Exit Inn - Hot Stuff* (1974) *Red Hot Picker* (1975), *Uptown Poker Club* (1975), *Smell The Flowers* (1975), *Me And Chet* (1976), *Sweet Love Feelings A Good Woman's Love* (1977), *Sings Jim Croce* (1977), *Eastbound And Down* (1977), *Both Barrels* (1978), *In Concert* (1980), with Chet Atkins *Sneakin' Around* (1992). Compilations: *The Best Of Jerry Reed* (1972), *20 Of The Best* (1982).

Reed, Ola Belle

b. 1915, in the mountains of western North Carolina, USA. Reed learned the clawhammer-style of banjo playing as a child and grew up singing the old time songs of her local area. She played with the North Carolina Ridge Runners in the 30s and after World War II, with their band the New River Boys And Girls, she and her brother played at many North Carolina events. She featured on numerous radio stations and became an acknowledged authority on Appalachian tunes, as well as her old time gospel, bluegrass and folk music. Later she appeared with her husband Bud and son David, with whom she established the New River Ranch country park at Oxford, Pennsylvania. This venue attracted a great many lovers of her music from the New England area. In the late 70s, she recorded an album that ensured she would be correctly remembered, although she perhaps tempted fate somewhat prematurely by calling it *My Epitaph*.

Albums: *Ola Belle Reed* (1975), *Ola Belle & Bud Reed, All In One Evening* (c.1976), *My Epitaph* (1977), *Ola Belle Red & Family* (1978).

Reeves, Del

b. Franklin Delano Reeves, 14 July 1933, Sparta, North Carolina, USA. A singer, songwriter and multi-instrumentalist who had his own radio show at the age of 12. Reeves moved to California, where by the late 50s, he had his own television show. He first charted in 1961 with 'Be Quiet Mind' on Decca, but in 1965, he registered a US country number 1 with 'Girl On A Billboard' after moving to United Artists, with whom he stayed until 1980. A number 4 hit with 'The Belles Of

Jerry Reed

Southern Bell' followed and he moved to Nashville. He became a regular on the *Grand Ole Opry* (having first guested on it 1958) and remained on the roster through to the 80s. Between 1966 and 1986, he registered almost 50 country chart hits, including 'Looking At The World Through A Windshield', 'Good Time Charlies' and 'The Philadelphia Phillies'. He also achieved chart success with duet recordings with Bobby Goldsboro, Penny DeHaven and Billie Jo Spears. Reeves has appeared in several films including *Second Fiddle To An Old Guitar*, as well as hosting many television shows. He has toured extensively and with his wife written many popular country songs. A fine entertainer who also is noted for his comedy and impressions of other artists, his casual manner has led to him being called The Dean Martin Of Country Music. He later moved into management and in 1992, he discovered Billy Ray Cyrus.

Albums: *Girl On The Billboard* (1965), *Doodle-OO-Doo-Doo* (1965), *Getting Any Feed For Your Chickens* (1966), *Sings Jim Reeves* (1966), *Mr Country Music* (1966), *Special Delivery* (1966), *Santa's Boy* (1966), *Struttin' My Stuff* (1967), *Six Of One, Half A Dozen Of The Other* (1967), *Little Church In The Dell* (1967), with Bobby Goldsboro *Our Way Of Life* (1967), *Looking At The World Through A Windshield* (1968), *Running Wild* (1968), *Down At Good Time Charlie's* (1969), *Wonderful World Of Country Music* (1969), *Big Daddy Del* (1970), *Country Concert - Live* (1970), *Out In The Country* (1970), *Del Reeves Album* (1971), *Friends & Neighbours* (1971), *Before Goodbye* (1972), *Trucker's Paradise* (1973), *Live At The Palomino Club* (1974), *With Strings And Things* (1975), *Tenth Anniversary* (1976), with Billie Jo Spears *By Request* (1976), *Del Reeves* (1979), *Baby I Love You* (1988), with Liz Lyndell *Let's Go To Heaven Tonight* (1980).

Reeves, Jim

b. James Travis Reeves, 20 August 1923, Galloway, Texas, USA, d. 31 July 1964. (Reeves' plaque in the Country Music Hall Of Fame mistakenly gives his date of birth as 1924.) Reeves' father died when he was 10 months old and his mother was left to raise nine children on the family farm. Although only aged five, Reeves was entranced when a brother brought home a gramophone and a Jimmie Rodgers record, 'Blue Yodel No. 5'. When aged nine, he traded stolen pears for an old guitar he saw in a neighbour's yard. A cook for an oil company showed him the basic chords and when aged 12, he appeared on a radio show in Shreveport, Louisiana. Because of his athletic abilities, he won a scholarship to the University of Texas. However, he was shy, largely because of a stammer, which he managed to correct while at university. (Reeves' records are known for perfect diction and delivery.) His first singing work was with Moon Mullican's band in Beaumont, Texas and he worked as an announcer and singing disc jockey at KGRI in Henderson for several years. (Reeves bought the station in 1959.) He recorded two singles for a chain store's label in 1949. In November 1952 Reeves moved to KWKH in Shreveport, where his duties included hosting the *Louisiana Hayride*. He stood in as a performer when Hank Williams failed to show and was signed immediately to Abbott Records. In 1953, Reeves received gold discs for two high-voiced, country novelties, 'Mexican Joe' and 'Bimbo'. In 1955 he joined the *Grand Ole Opry* and started recording for RCA in Nashville, having his first hit with a song based on the 'railroad, steamboat' game, 'Yonder Comes A Sucker'. Chet Atkins considered 'Four Walls' a 'girl's song', but Reeves persisted and used the song to change his approach to singing. He pitched his voice lower and sang close to the microphone, thus creating a warm ballad style which was far removed from his hillbilly recordings. 'Four Walls' became an enormous US success in 1957, crossing over to the pop market and becoming a template for his future work. From then on, Atkins recorded Reeves as a mellow balladeer, giving him some pop standards and replacing fiddles and steel guitar by piano and strings. (Exceptions include an album of narrations, *Tall Tales And Short Tempers*.)

Reeves had already swapped his western outfit for a suit and tie, and, in keeping with his hit 'Blue Boy', his group, the Wagonmasters, became the Blue Boys. He always included a religious section in his stage show and also sang 'Danny Boy' to acknowledge his Irish ancestry. 'He'll Have To Go', topped the US country charts for 14 weeks and made number 2 in the US pop charts. In this memorable song Reeves conveyed an implausible lyric with conviction, and it has now become a country standard. A gooey novelty, 'But You Love Me Daddy', recorded at the same session with Steve, the nine-year-old son of bass player Bob Moore, was a UK Top 20 hit 10 years later. Having established a commercial format, 'Gentleman Jim' had success with 'You're The Only Good Thing', 'Adios Amigo', 'Welcome To My World' (UK number 6) and 'Guilty', which features French horns and oboes. His records often

Jim Reeves

had exceptional longevity; 'I Love You Because' (number 5) and 'I Won't Forget You' (number 3) were on the UK charts for 39 and 25 weeks, respectively. He became enormously popular in South Africa, recording in Afrikaans, and making a light-hearted film there, *Kimberley Jim*, which became a local success. Reeves did not like flying but after being a passenger in a South African plane which developed engine trouble, he obtained his own daytime pilot's license. On 31 July 1964 pilot Reeves and his pianist/manager, Dean Manuel, died when their single-engine plane ran into difficulties during a storm and crashed into dense woods outside Nashville. The bodies were not found until 2 August despite 500 people, including fellow country singers, being involved in the search. Reeves was buried in a specially-landscaped area by the side of Highway 79 in Texas, and his collie, Cheyenne, was buried at his feet in 1967. Reeves continued to have hits with such ironic titles as 'This World Is Not My Home' and the self-penned 'Is It Really Over?'. Although Reeves had not recorded 'Distant Drums' officially - the song had gone to Roy Orbison - he had made a demo for songwriter Cindy Walker. Accompaniment was added and, in 1966, 'Distant

Drums' became Reeves' first UK number 1. He had around 80 unreleased tracks and his widow followed a brilliant, if uncharitable, marketing policy whereby unheard material would be placed alongside previously issued tracks to make a new album. Sometimes existing tracks were remastered and duets were constructed with Deborah Allen and the late Patsy Cline. Reeves became a best-selling album artist to such an extent that *40 Golden Greats* topped the album charts in 1975. Both the Blue Boys and his nephew John Rex Reeves have toured with tribute concerts. Although much of Jim Reeves' catalogue is available, surprisingly there is still no biography of Reeves, who was the first crossover star. Reeves' relaxed style has influenced Don Williams and Daniel O'Donnell but the combination of pop balladry and country music is more demanding than it appears, and Reeves remains its father figure.

Albums: *Jim Reeves Sings* (1956), *Singing Down The Lane* (1956), *Bimbo* (1957), *Jim Reeves* (1957), *Girls I Have Known* (1958), *God Be With You* (1958), *Songs To Warm The Heart* (1959), *He'll Have To Go* (1960), *According To My Heart* (1960), *The Intimate Jim Reeves* (1960), *Talking To Your Heart* (1961), *Tall Tales And Short Tempers* (1961), *The Country*

Side Of Jim Reeves (1962), *A Touch Of Velvet* (1962), *We Thank Thee* (1962), *Good 'N' Country* (1963), *Gentleman Jim* (1963), *The International Jim Reeves* (1963), *Twelve Songs Of Christmas* (1963), *Have I Told You Lately That I Love You?* (1964), *Moonlight And Roses* (1964), *Kimberley Jim* (1964), *The Jim Reeves Way* (1965), *Distant Drums* (1966), *Yours Sincerely* (1966), *Blue Side Of Lonesome* (1967), *My Cathedral* (1967), *A Touch of Sadness* (1968), *Jim Reeves On Stage* (1968), *Jim Reeves - And Some Friends* (1969), *Jim Reeves Writes You A Record* (1971), *Young And Country* (1971), *My Friend* (1972), *Missing You* (1972), with Deborah Allen *Don't Let Me Cross Over* (1979), *Abbott Recordings, Volume 1* (1982), *Abbott Recordings, Volume 2* (1982), *Live At The Opry* (1987), *The Definitive Jim Reeves* (1992), *Dear Hearts & Gentle People* (1992). Compilations are always available and the Bear Family boxed-set *Gentleman Jim, 1955-59* includes previously unreleased material.

Reno, Don

b. 21 February 1927, Spartanburg, South Carolina, USA, d. 16 October 1984. Reno who began his career on local radio at the age of 12 and was playing professionally with the Morris Brothers at 14, went on to become one of the world's greatest five-string banjo players. A fine tenor vocalist, he also played mandolin, guitar and harmonica. In 1941, he worked with Arthur Smith but between 1944 and 1946, his career was interrupted by army service. He and Earl Scruggs, (who he replaced in Bill Monroe's band in 1948) popularized the three finger roll technique of playing initially introduced by Snuffy Jenkins in the late 30s. In 1949, Reno left Monroe to start his own band, the Tennessee Cut-Ups. Soon after guitarist Red Smiley (b. Arthur Lee Smiley, Asheville, North Carolina, USA, d. 2 January 1972) joined him and the two recorded and worked together at various major venues including the *Wheeling Jamboree* and the *Old Dominion Barn Dance*. Although still recording together, they semi-disbanded in the early 50s when Reno, wishing to expand the market for his playing, again worked with Arthur (Guitar Boogie) Smith until May 1955. In 1955, with Smith playing a tenor banjo, they recorded the definitive version of 'Feuding Banjoes'. The tune was later used (without their consent) under the title of 'Duelin' Banjoes' as the soundtrack of the film, *Deliverance*. Smith and Reno sued the film company and won. Reno and Smiley resumed their touring in 1955 and it lasted until 1964, when the worsening effects of wounds received during

war-time service forced Smiley to give up the travelling. He continued to appear on a Roanoke television show and still recorded and made some special appearances with Reno. In 1966, Reno began working with bluegrass singer/guitarist Bill Harrell. In 1969, Smiley returned to more full time work with Reno until his death in 1972. They are remembered for their fine version of Reno's song 'I'm Using My Bible For A Road Map' and in 1961, they achieved a Top 20 US country hit with 'Don't Let Your Sweet Love Die' and also charted the novelty number, 'Jimmy Caught The Dickens (Pushing Ernest In The Tubb)', under the pseudonym of Chick & His Hot Rods. After Smiley's death, Reno continued to work with Harrell until 1976 and made further recordings for CMH. He moved to Lynchburg, Virginia to semi-retirement but still worked on occasions with his three sons until his death in 1984. Reno wrote many country songs including the standard 'I Know You're Married But I Love You Still', (a chart hit for both Bill Anderson and Jan Howard and Red Sovine).

Solo albums: *Mr 5-String Plays Bluegrass* (1965), *A Song For Everyone* (1966), with Benny Martin *Bluegrass Gospel Favorites* (1967), *Fastest Five String Alive* (1969), with Eddie Adcock *Bluegrass Super Session* (1970), *Mr 5-String Banjo* (1973), *Magnificent Bluegrass Band* (1978), *30th Anniversary Album* (1979), *Arthur Smith & Don Reno Feudin' Again* (1979), *Still Cutting Up* (1983), with Bobby Thompson *Banjo Bonanza* (1983), *The Final Chapter* (1986), *Family & Friends* (1989). With Red Smiley: *Instrumentals* (1958), *Folk Ballads & Instrumentals* (1958), *Good Ole Country Ballads* (1959), *Someone Will Love Me In Heaven* (1959), *A Variety Of Country Songs* (1959), *Hymns & Sacred Songs* (1960), *New & Original Folk Songs Of The Civil War* (1961), *Wanted* (1961), *Country Songs* (1961), *Banjo Special* (1962), *Another Day* (1962), *Country Folk Sing & Instrumentals* (1962), *World's 15 Greatest Hymns* (1963), *World's Best 5-String Banjo* (1963), *Bluegrass Hits* (1963), *Sweet Ballads Of The West* (1963), *True Meaning Of Christmas* (1963), *Tribute To Cowboy Copas* (1964), *On The Road* (1964), *Variety Show* (1966), *24 Country Songs* (1967), *Emotions* (1969), *I Know You're Married But I Love You Still* (1969), *Together Again* (1971), *Last Time Together* (1973), *Songs For My Many* (1976), *Live At The Lone Star Festival* (1977), *16 Greatest Hits* (1977), *16 Gospel Greats* (1978), *A Day In The Country* (1989). With Red Smiley & Bill Harrell: *Letter Edged In Black* (1971). With Bill Harrell: *Bluegrass Favorites* (1967), *Reno & Harrell* (1967),

Yellow Pages (1967), All The Way To Reno (1968), Most Requested Songs (1968), A Variety Of Sacred Songs (1968), I'm Using My Bible For A Road Map (1970), Bluegrass On My Mind (1971), Dixie Roads (1974), Tally Ho (1974), Spice Of Life (1975), Bi-Centennial Bluegrass (1975), Dear Old Dixie (1976), The Don Reno Story (1976), Home In The Mountains (1977).

Reno, Jack

b. 30 November 1930, near Bloomfield, Iowa, USA. Reno, a singer/guitarist, first worked on radio at the age of 16 and, from 1955, was a regular member of the Ozark Jubilee. He continued working on radio, both in and out of the forces, and had his first record success in the US country charts with 'Repeat After Me' on the JAB label. His best-known single was 'I Want One' for Dot Records, but he also charted with country versions of pop hits, 'Hitchin' A Ride', 'Do You Want To Dance?', 'Beautiful Sunday' and 'Let The Four Winds Blow', with his last chart entry 'Jukebox' in 1974. His awards include the Country Music Association's Disc Jockey Of The Year in 1978, but his career was curtailed by Hodgkin's disease. He recovered but, apart from duets with his daughter Sheila in 1986, he has become more involved in management and production.
Albums: Meet Jack Reno (1968), I Want One (1968), I'm A Good Man In A Bad Frame Of Mind (1969), Hitchin' A Ride (1970), Interstate 7 (1978), The Best Of Jack Reno (1990), Hitchin' A Ride To The Country (1990).

Reynolds, Allen

In the USA during the late 50s, Reynolds started his professional career as a record producer when he worked with his friend, country singer, Dickey Lee, and they had a regional hit with 'Dream Boy'. He then worked at Sun Records in Memphis, becoming friends with producer Jack Clement, who recorded him singing 'Through The Eyes Of Love' for RCA in 1960. Reynolds was drafted and began a banking career, but he then wrote a pop hit, 'Five O'Clock World', for the Vogues. He was soon an established country star and Reynolds produced Crystal Gayle ('Don't It Make My Brown Eyes Blue' and 'When I Dream'). Because of his production commitments, Reynolds has never been prolific as a songwriter but his small output is of a high standard and includes, 'Dreaming My Dreams' (Waylon Jennings, Don Williams), 'I Recall A Gypsy Woman' (Waylon Jennings, Don Williams), 'Somebody Loves You' (Crystal Gayle) and 'We Should Be Together' (Don Williams). Crystal Gayle is associated with 'Wrong Road Again', but Reynolds' own version made the US country charts, albeit number 95, in 1978. Some of his songs are written with Bob McDill, whose work is frequently performed by Reynolds' artists. In the late 80s, he established Kathy Mattea with his productions of 'Love At The Five And Dime' and 'Walk The Way The Wind Blows'. He had the biggest successes of his career with Garth Brook

Rice, Bobby G.

b. Robert Gene Rice, 11 July 1944, on a farm at Boscobel, Wisconsin, USA. The Rice Family were musical and all six siblings were taught an instrument as children. After first playing for local parties, the family progressed to running the local Circle D Ballroom. Rice, who plays guitar and banjo, made his first appearances there with the family at the age of five. From the mid-50s, for almost seven years, the family also presented their own show on WRCO Richmond, Wisconsin, on which Bobby became the featured vocalist. In 1962, after graduation and after the family group disbanded, Bobby pursued a musical career. He formed the Rock-A-Teens band, which played rock 'n' roll locally and on its own programme on WIST-TV. After two years, missing country music, he began to sing as a duo with his sister Lorraine. They proved popular in their area, hosted their own television show and sang backing harmonies on others. After Lorraine retired, he formed his own band, began songwriting and played what he termed modern country, which included country arrangements of pop songs. He moved to Nashville in the late 60s and recorded for Royal American. In the early 70s, his first five chart entries were all minor hits with songs that had been pop hits of the early 60s, including 'Sugar Shack' and 'Hey Baby'. Further hits followed, including Top 10s with 'You Lay So Easy On My Mind' (self-penned; a UK pop hit for Andy Williams in 1975), 'You Give Me You' and 'Freda Comes, Freda Goes'. Between 1976 and 1988, he charted 19 hits but only 'The Softest Touch In Town' made the Top 30; the last being 'Clean Livin' Folk' - a duet with Perry LaPointe in 1988. He recorded albums for several different labels but has seemingly failed to maintain the popularity he established in the 70s.
Albums: Hit After Hit (1972), You Lay So Easy On My Mind (1973), She Sure Laid The Lonelies On Me (1974), Write Me A Letter (1975), Instant Rice

(1976), *Bobby G. Rice* (1982). Compilation: *Greatest Hits* (1980).

Rich, Charlie

b. 14 December 1932, Colt, Arkansas, USA. One of Charlie Rich's country hits is 'Life Has Its Little Ups And Downs', and the ups and downs of his own life have been dramatic. Rich's parents were cotton farmers and he heard the blues from the pickers and gospel music from his parents as his father sang in a choir and his mother played organ. Rich himself developed a passion for Stan Kenton's music, so much so that his friends nicknamed him 'Charlie Kenton'. He played piano and saxophone and studied music at the University of Arkansas. While in the US Air Force, he formed a small group in the vein of the Four Freshmen, the Velvetones, with his wife-to-be, Margaret Ann. After the forces, they bought a farm but following bad weather, he opted for playing in Memphis clubs for $10 a night. At first, Sam Phillips felt that Rich was too jazz-orientated for his Sun label, but arranger Bill Justis gave him some Jerry Lee Lewis records and told him to return 'when he could get that bad'. Soon Rich was working on sessions at Sun including some for Lewis ('I'll Sail My Ship Alone'), Bill Justis and Carl Mann. He wrote 'The Ways Of A Woman In Love', 'Thanks A Lot' (both recorded by Johnny Cash), 'Break Up' (Ray Smith and Lewis), 'I'm Comin' Home' (Mann and then covered by Elvis Presley) and the continuation of 'Don't Take Your Guns To Town', 'The Ballad Of Billy Joe' (Lewis and Rich himself). His first single, 'Whirlwind', was issued in the USA in August 1958 on the Sun subsidiary, Phillips International. His first US hit came in 1960 when 'Lonely Weekends', a bright, echoey rock 'n' roll song which he had intended for Jerry Lee Lewis, made number 22 in the US charts. Time has shown it to be a fine rock 'n' roll standard but Rich's original recording was marred by heavy-handed chorus work from the Gene Lowery Singers.

Rich recorded 80 songs at Sun although only 10 singles and one album were released at the time. Many of the tracks have been issued since, some even being doctored to include an Elvis soundalike. Rich was not able to consolidate the success of 'Lonely Weekends' but some of his songs from that period, 'Who Will The Next Fool Be?', an R&B success for Bobby 'Blue' Bland and later Jerry Lee Lewis, 'Sittin' And Thinkin'' and 'Midnight Blues', have remained in his act. Rich's heavy drinking caused his wife to leave with the children, but he convinced her that he would change. In 1962 Rich, like Elvis before him, went from Sun to RCA, albeit to their subsidiary, Groove. From then on, Rich recorded in Nashville although Groove were grooming him as a performer of jazz-slanted standards ('I've Got You Under My Skin', 'Ol' Man River', 'Nice 'N' Easy'). He had no hits at the time but his reflective ballad, 'There Won't Be Anymore', was a US Top 20 hit 10 years later; similarly, 'I Don't See Me In Your Eyes Anymore' and 'Tomorrow Night' were to become US country number 1s. Many regard Rich's period with producer Jerry Kennedy at Smash as his most creative, particularly as Margaret Ann was writing such excellent material as 'A Field Of Yellow Daisies'. He almost made the US Top 20 with Dallas Frazier's Coasters-styled novelty about a hippie, 'Mohair Sam', but he says, 'One hit like 'Mohair Sam' wasn't much use. What I needed was a string of singles that would sell albums. I was also unlucky in that I put 'I Washed My Hands In Muddy Water' on the b-side. Johnny Rivers heard it, copied my arrangement and sold a million records.' His next label, Hi, adopted another approach by putting Rich with familiar country songs, but the album's sales were poor and he seemed destined to play small bars forever, although salvation was at hand. Billy Sherrill, who had worked as a recording engineer with Rich at Sun, signed him to Epic in 1967. He knew Rich's versatility but was determined to make him a successful country singer. Choosing strong ballads, often about working-class marriage in the over-30s, and classy middle-of-the-road arrangements, he built up Rich's success in the US country charts, although it was a slow process. In 1968 his chart entries were with 'Set Me Free' (number 44) and 'Raggedly Ann (number 45) and even Margaret Ann's cleverly written but thinly-veiled comment on their own marriage, 'Life Has Its Little Ups And Downs', only reached number 41. His first substantial US country hit was with 'I Take It On Home' in 1972. In view of the material, Rich's lined face and grey hair became assets and he was dubbed 'The Silver Fox'. Although Rich's piano was often relegated to a supporting role, it complements his voice on Kenny O'Dell's ballad, 'Behind Closed Doors'. The 1973 song gave Rich a number 1 country and Top 20 pop hit and became the Country Song of the Year. Rich's recording was used to amusing effect for Clyde's love affair in the Clint Eastwood film, *Every Which Way But Loose*. The follow-up, 'The Most Beautiful Girl', partly written by

Charlie Rich

Sherrill, was a US Number 1, and the b-side 'Feel Like Goin' Home' was almost as strong. (Rich had chosen the title after being the subject of the opening essay in Peter Guralnick's study of blues and rock 'n' roll, *Feel Like Going Home*.) In the UK, 'The Most Beautiful Girl' made number 2 and was quickly followed by a Top 20 placing for 'Behind Closed Doors'. His *Behind Closed Doors* which contained both hits and songs written by himself, his wife and son Allan, was a smash and he topped the US country charts with 'There Won't Be Anymore' (number 18, pop), 'A Very Special Love Song' (number 11), 'I Don't See Me In Your Eyes Anymore', 'I Love My Friend' (number 24) and 'She Called Me Baby'. Also, 'Everytime You Touch Me (I Get High)' was number 3, country and 19 in the pop chart. Allan Rich, a member of his father's road band, recorded his father's 'Break Up', while Rich's evocative composition 'Peace On You' was also the title song of a Roger McGuinn album.

In 1974 Rich was voted the Entertainer of the Year by the Country Music Association of America. The next year, instead of announcing the winner (John Denver) on a live television show, he burnt the envelope. He says, 'I was ill and I should

never have been there' but country fans were not so sympathetic and Rich lost much support. His records too were starting to sound stale as Sherrill had difficulty in finding good material and put too much emphasis on the strings. Nevertheless, there were gems including 'Rollin' With The Flow', which returned Rich to the top of the US country charts, and a duet with Janie Fricke, 'On My Knees', also a country number 1. Rich made a gospel album, *Silver Linings*, with Billy Sherrill and says, 'We had a similar background of gospel music. His father was a Baptist preacher and he used to preach on horseback. That's him in the left-hand corner of the cover. I regard 'Milky White Way' as one of my best recordings.' In 1978 Rich moved to United Artists where Larry Butler continued in the same vein. Occasionally the material was right - 'Puttin' In Overtime At Home', 'I Still Believe In Love' and the bluesy 'Nobody But You' - but, by and large, the records found Rich on automatic pilot. In 1980 he moved to Elektra where he recorded a fine version of Eric Clapton's 'Wonderful Tonight' and had a country hit with 'I'll Wake You Up When You Get Home'. There followed a long decade or more of silence from Rich, amid rumours that his occasionally self-destructive lifestyle had taken its toll. But he returned triumphantly in 1992 with *Pictures And Paintings*, an album overseen by his long-time champion, journalist Peter Guralnick. Mixing jazzy originals with reinterpretations of songs from his past, the album proved to be Rich's most satisfying work since *The Fabulous Charlie Rich* 22 years earlier.

Albums: *Lonely Weekends With Charlie Rich* (1960), *That's Rich* (1965), *The Many New Sides Of Charlie Rich* (1965), *The Best Years* (1966), *Charlie Rich Sings Country And Western* (1967), *Set Me Free* (1968), *The Fabulous Charlie Rich* (1970), *Boss Man* (1970), *Behind Closed Doors* (1973), *Very Special Love Songs* (1974), *The Silver Fox* (1974), *Everytime You Touch Me (I Get High)* (1975), *Silver Linings* (1976), *Take Me* (1977), *Rollin' With The Flow* (1977), *I Still Believe In Love* (1978), *The Fool Strikes Again* (1979), *Nobody But You* (1979), *Once A Drifter* (1980), *Pictures And Paintings* (1992). Compilations are available.

Riley, Jeannie C.

b. Jeannie Carolyn Stephenson, 19 October 1944, Anson, Texas, USA. Riley wanted to be a country singer, and, after marrying her childhood sweetheart, Mickey Riley, she persuaded him to move to Nashville. He worked in a filling station while she became a secretary on Music Row for music publisher, Jerry Chesnut. She also recorded demo records for his writers and her voice appealed to record producer, Shelby Singleton, who felt that Alice Joy's voice was too smooth on the demo for Tom T. Hall's song of small town hypocrisy, 'Harper Valley PTA', which owed much to Bobbie Gentry's 'Ode To Billie Joe', and was more suited to a female singer than Hall himself. Riley recorded the song in one take and then rang her mother to tell her she had recorded a million seller. It was an understatement as 'Harper Valley PTA' topped the USA charts and sold over six million. It was a UK hit but only made number 12. With her mini-skirts and knee-length boots, Riley acted out the central character of 'Harper Valley PTA' and she recorded a concept album about others in Harper Valley. Her singles include 'The Girl Most Likely To', 'There Never Was A Time' and 'The Back Side Of Dallas', but she had no other substantial hits. She started drinking and her marriage ended in 1970. By 1976, she was a born-again Christian and she and Mickey had remarried. A successful film based on the song was produced in 1978 and led to a television series, both starring Barbara Eden. Riley will not work in clubs which serve alcohol and although she has made Christian albums, everyone remembers the day she 'socked it to the PTA', hence her record, 'Return To Harper Valley' in 1987.

Albums: *Harper Valley PTA* (1968), *Sock Soul* (1968), *Yearbooks And Yesterdays* (1968), *The Songs Of Jeannie C. Riley* (1969), *Things Go Better With Love* (1969), *Country Girl* (1970), *The Generation Gap* (1970), *Jeannie* (1972), *Down To Earth* (1972), *Give Myself A Party* (1972), *When Love Has Gone Away* (1973), *Just Jeannie* (1974), *Sunday After Church* (1975), *Fancy Friends* (1977), *Wings To Fly* (1979), *From Harper Valley To The Mountain Top* (1981), *On The Road* (1982), *Pure Country* (1982), *Total Woman* (1987).

Further reading: *From Harper Valley To The Mountain Top*, Jeannie C. Riley with Jamie Buckingham.

Ritter, Tex

b. Woodward Maurice Ritter, 12 January 1905, Murvaul, Texas, USA, d. 2 January 1974. While studying political science at the University of Texas and during a later spell at law school, Ritter developed interests in the folklore and music of the southwestern states. He began singing folk songs and was soon a popular radio entertainer. He also appeared in concert and other stage performances, including a Broadway show in 1930. In the mid-30s he went to Hollywood, where he became one of the most popular singing cowboys in films, simultaneously making numerous recordings. Amongst his films were *Sing Cowboy Sing* (1937), *Song Over The Buckaroo* (1939), *Rainbow Over The Range* (1940) *Deep In The Heart Of Texas* (1942) and *Frontier Bullets* (1945). By the late 40s the type of film in which Ritter appeared had had its day, and he subsequently toured extensively with his own stage show and also sang at the Grand Ole Opry. He continued to make records and in 1952 he had his biggest hit with the song 'High Noon (Do Not Forsake Me)', which he sang in the film *High Noon*. In the mid-50s and early 60s he made a handful of film appearances, mostly cameo roles. In the late 60s Ritter returned to his early interest in politics and tried unsuccessfully to gain nomination for the US Senate. He died in 1974.

Compilations: all various dates *The Streets Of Laredo, High Noon, Lady Killin' Cowboy, Singin' In The Saddle, Songs From The Western Screen, Collectors Series*.

Robbins, Marty

b. Martin David Robinson, with twin sister,

Jeannie C. Riley

Mamie, 26 September 1925, near Glendale, Arizona, USA, d. 8 December 1982. He later maintained that his father hated him and that his early childhood was unhappy. Reports indicate that John Robinson (originally a Polish immigrant named Mazinski) suffered from a drink problem that led to him abusing his family before eventually leaving his wife, Emma, to cope alone with their seven children plus the two from her previous marriage. At one time they lived in a tent in the desert, but in 1937 his parents divorced and Emma and the children moved to a shack in Glendale, where she took in laundry to support the family. In his early teens, Marty spent some time with an elder brother breaking wild horses on a ranch near Phoenix. Consequently his education suffered; he attended high school in Glendale but never graduated, and by the early 40s he was becoming involved in a life of petty crime. He left home to live the life of a hobo until he joined the US Navy in May 1943. It was during his three years in the service, where he saw action in the Pacific, that he learned to play the guitar and first started songwriting and singing. He also acquired a love of Hawaiian music which would show several times during his career. After discharge in February 1946, he returned to Glendale, where he tried many jobs before starting to sing around the clubs and on local radio under the names of either Martin or Jack Robinson. (His mother strongly disapproved of him singing in clubs and he used the name 'Jack' to try to prevent her finding out.) By 1950, he had built a local reputation and was regularly appearing on KTYL Mesa and on both radio and in his own television show *Western Caravan* on KPHO Phoenix. He married Marizona Baldwin on 27 September 1948; a marriage that lasted until Marty's death. A son, Ronald Carson Robinson, was born in 1949 and 10 years later their daughter Janet. (Ronald eventually became a singer, performing both as Ronnie Robbins and as Marty Robbins Jnr.)

Through the assistance of Little Jimmy Dickens, and by now known as Marty Robbins, he was signed by Columbia, for whom he first recorded in November 1951. In December 1952, 'I'll Go On Alone' became his first US country hit. It charted for 18 weeks, two of which were spent at number 1. (Marty wrote the song because initially his wife disliked his showbusiness life.) He moved to Nashville in January 1953 and became a member of the *Grand Ole Opry*. Early in his career, he acquired the nickname of 'Mr Teardrop' and later wrote and recorded a song with that title. In 1955,

his career, which by the end of 1954 appeared somewhat becalmed, received a welcome boost by the success of his recordings of rockabilly numbers, 'That's All Right' (originally written and recorded by Arthur 'Big Boy' Crudup in 1947 but more recently a hit for Elvis Presley) and 'Maybelline' both became Top 10 country hits. He had always realised that it would be advantageous to record in differing styles and accordingly his recordings varied from country to pop, from Hawaiian, to gospel and even some with his own guitar providing the sole accompaniment. In 1956, he achieved another country number 1 with his version of Melvin Endsley's 'Singing The Blues'. The song also made number 17 in the US pop charts, where Guy Mitchell's version was number 1. The following year, Marty turned Endsley's song 'Knee Deep In The Blues' into a number 3 country hit but again lost out in the pop charts to Mitchell, who had immediately covered Robbins' recording. Somewhat frustrated Robbins made his next recordings in New York with Ray Conniff and his orchestra and during 1957-58, with what may be best termed teenage love songs, he registered three more country number 1s with his own song, 'A White Sports Coat (And A Pink Carnation)' (a million-seller), the Hal David-Burt Bacharach song, 'The Story Of My Life' and 'Stairway Of Love'. The first two were also major US pop hits for him. (In the UK, the former was a hit for the King Brothers and Terry Dene, while Michael Holliday had Top 3 successes with the latter two.)

During the late 50s, he formed a talent and booking agency and launched his own record label. Robbins had always had a love of the old west. He always rated the cowboy state of Arizona as his home (his maternal grandfather had once been a Texas Ranger), and in the late 50s he appeared in three b-westerns, *Raiders Of Old California*, *Badge Of Marshal Brennan* and *Buffalo Gun*. The first two were straight acting roles but the latter co-starred Webb Pierce and Carl Smith and included several songs. It was also at this time that he began to record the material that would see release on albums such as his now legendary *Gunfighter Ballads And Trail Songs*. (He actually recorded the whole album in one day.) In 1959, he wrote and charted the title track of the film *The Hanging Tree*, which starred Gary Cooper, before his classic 'El Paso' became a number 1 country and pop hit. It gave him a second million-seller and was also the first country music song to be awarded a Grammy. The success of this song established Marty once and for

Tex Ritter

all and songs such as 'Big Iron' and 'Running Gun' became firm favourites with audiences the world over.

During the 60s, he registered 31 country hits, 18 of which also found success in the pop charts. The country number 1s included 'Don't Worry', (which has the distinction of being the first song to include the 'fuzz' sound on the recording. Unknown to all at the time, a fuse had blown in the control room channel carrying Grady Martin's lead guitar with the result that it came out fuzzy. Robbins liked the effect and left it in), 'Devil Woman' (a UK Top 5 pop hit for him), 'Ruby Ann', 'Ribbon Of Darkness', 'Tonight Carmen' and 'I Walk Alone'. In 1964, Robbins supported Barry Goldwater in his bid for President and also wrote, 'Ain't I Right' and 'My Own Native Land', two protest songs against Communism and anti-American war protesters. He felt the first would be a hit but Columbia, fearing racial repercussions, would not let him release them. However, his guitarist and backing vocalist, Bobby Sykes's recordings of the songs were released on the Sims label. He used the pseudonym Johnny Freedom, but sounded so much like his boss that for years many people have believed the recordings were by Robbins himself. (Marty's own recordings were later released by Bear Family on the album *Pieces Of Your Heart*.)

In 1969, Frankie Laine scored a pop hit with Robbins' semi-autobiographical song 'You Gave Me A Mountain', while Johnny Bush had the country version. Surprisingly Marty's own recording was never released as a single. He also had a great interest in stock-car racing and during the 60s he began driving at the Nashville Speedway, an occupation that later saw him fortunate to survive several serious crashes. Also during the 60s, he filmed a television series called *The Drifter*, appeared in eight films, including *Hell On Wheels*, *The Nashville Story*, *Ballad Of A Gunfighter*, *Road To Nashville* and *From Nashville With Music*, and wrote a Western novel *The Small Man*. In August 1969, he suffered a heart attack on his tour bus near Cleveland and in January 1970 he underwent bypass surgery. He soon returned to his punishing schedules and in April he was starring in Las Vegas. The same year his moving ballad 'My Woman, My Woman, My Wife' became his second Grammy winner and the *Academy Of Country Music* voted him The Man of the Decade. (Originally it had been intended that Frankie Laine should have the song but Robbins' wife told him to keep it for himself.) He left Columbia for Decca

in 1972 but returned in December 1975 and immediately registered two number 1 country hits with 'El Paso City' (a look back at his previous hit) and the old pop ballad 'Among My Souvenirs'. He had previously returned to El Paso with the nine-minute long 'Feleena (From El Paso)'. During the 70s, he had further 30 country hits, made film appearances in *Country Music*, *Guns Of A Stranger*, *Country Hits* and *Atoka* as well as starring in his network television series *Marty Robbins Spotlight*.

His songwriting talents saw him elected to the Nashville Songwriters International Hall Of Fame in 1975. His extensive touring schedules included crowd pleasing appearances at the 1975 and 1976 Wembley Festivals in London. He continued with these punishing schedules into the 80s but was again hospitalized following a second heart attack in January 1981. He returned to London for the April 1982 Festival, before making a tour in Canada. 'Some Memories Just Won't Die' became his biggest hit since 1978 and on 11 October 1982 he was inducted into the Country Music Hall Of Fame in Nashville. He toured on the west coast but in Cincinnati, on 1 December 1982, he played what turned out to be his last concert. The following day he suffered his third heart attack. He underwent major surgery but died of cardiac arrest on 8 December and was buried in Nashville three days later. A few days after his funeral his recording of 'Honky Tonk Man', the title track of a Clint Eastwood film in which he had made a cameo appearance, entered the charts, eventually peaking at number 10. A quiet and withdrawn man offstage, Robbins possessed an on-stage ability to communicate with and hold his audience and his clever use of in-jokes, asides and sheer personality made him one of the finest entertainers to grace any genre of music. His tally of 94 *Billboard* country chart hits places him in eighth position in the list of most-charted country artists. He actually charted at least one song every year from 1952 (when he first recorded) to 1983 and during this period he also registered 31 pop hits.

Albums: *Rock 'N' Rollin' Robbins* (1956), *Song Of Robbins* (1957), *Song Of The Islands* (1957), *Marty Robbins* (1958), *Gunfighter Ballads And Trail Songs* (1959), *Marty's Greatest Hits* (1959), *More Gunfighter Ballads And Trail Songs* (1960), *More Greatest Hits* (1961), *Just A Little Sentimental* (1961), *Devil Woman* (1962), *Marty After Midnight* (1962), *Portrait Of Marty* (1962), *Hawaii's Calling Me* (1963), *Return Of The Gunfighter* (1963), *R.F.D. Marty Robbins* (1964), *Island Woman* (1964), *Turn The Lights Down Low* (1965), *What God Has Done* (1965), *Saddle*

Marty Robbins

Tramp (1966), *The Drifter* (1966), *Christmas With Marty Robbins* (1967), *My Kind Of Country* (1967), *Tonight Carmen* (1967), *By The Time I Get To Phoenix* (1968), *Bend In The River* (1968), *I Walk Alone* (1968), *Heart Of Marty Robbins* (1969), *It's A Sin* (1969), *Singing The Blues* (1969), *My Woman, My Woman, My Wife* (1970), *The Story Of My Life* (1970), *From The Heart* (1971), *Today* (1971), *Marty Robbins Favorites* (1972), *Song Of The Islands* (1972), *I've Got A Woman's Love* (1972), with his Friends *Joy Of Christmas* (1972), *This Much A Man* (1972), *Bound For Old Mexico* (1973), *Marty Robbins* (1973), *Good 'N' Country* (1974), *Have I Told You Lately That I Love You* (1974), *No Sign Of Loneliness Here* (1976), *El Paso City* (1976), *Two Gun Daddy* (1976), *Adios Amigo* (1977), *Don't Let Me Touch You* (1977), *All Around Cowboy* (1979), *The Performer* (1979), *With Love* (1980), *Encore* (1981), *Everything I've Always Wanted* (1981), *The Legend* (1981), *Come Back To Me* (1982), *Some Memories Just Won't Die* (1982), *Sincerely* (1983), *Forever Yours* (1983), *Twentieth Century Drifter* (1983), *Just Me And My Guitar* (1983), *Rockin' Rollin' Robbins Volumes 1, 2, 3* (1983-85), *Hawaii's Calling Me* (1983), *Marty Robbins Files Volumes 1-5* (1983-85), *In The Wild West Parts 2, 4, 5* (1984-85), *Pieces Of Your Heart* (1985), Bear Family 5 CD Boxed Set: *Marty Robbins Country 1951-58* (1991).
Further reading: *Marty Robbins: Fast Cars And Country Music*, Barbara J. Pruett.

Roberts, Kenny

b. 14 October 1927, Lenoir City, Tennessee, USA. After Roberts' mother died when he was a child, the family relocated to a farm near Athol, Massachusetts. He learned guitar, harmonica and fiddle and grew up listening to the music of the singing cowboys and the yodelling of Elton Britt. He won a talent competition when he was 13 years old and first played with the Red River Rangers on WHAI Greenfield in 1942. He moved to WKNE Keene, New Hampshire the following year, where he became a member of the Down Homers. In 1946, the group moved to Fort Wayne, Indiana, where they regularly played the Barn Dance programme known as the *Hoosier Hop*. When the group relocated to Connecticut, Roberts decided it was time to launch his solo career. He had first recorded as a member of the group, but in early 1947 he recorded some solo tracks for Vita-Coustic. When these were not released, he moved to Coral. He worked regularly on stations in Fort Wayne and also KMOF St Louis, before moving to WLW Cincinnati in 1948.

He acquired many nicknames during his career not least of which was the title of The Jumping Cowboy, which he got for a strange ability to jump several feet in the air while singing. He performed this feat regularly on his WLW children's television programme. He was an outstanding yodeller and naturally many of his recordings demonstrate this talent with such fine examples as 'She Taught Me How To Yodel' and 'Yodel Polka'.

Experts in the art rate that his speciality 'galloping yodel' made him the world's fastest yodeller. In 1949, he achieved his greatest hit when his recording of 'I Never See Maggie Alone' became a million seller. It was a Top 10 hit in both US pop and country charts and also has the distinction of possibly being the first British composition to make the Top 10 in the US country charts. (It dated from 1926 and was written by Harry Tilsley (words) and Everett Lynton (music).) In 1949 1950, he had further US country chart hits with 'Wedding Bells', 'Jealous Heart' and 'Choc'late Ice Cream Cone'. During the 50s and mid-60s, he recorded for various labels, though few releases appeared but in the late 60s, he recorded four complete albums for Starday. In the 70s, he recorded a tribute album to his idol Elton Britt and was asked to take Britt's place on a concert in 1972 in New Jersey on the night that Britt died. He semi-retired for a time in the late 50s but soon returned and has maintained an active participation ever since. He has fronted his own shows on radio and television on many stations and has appeared at all the major venues, including the *Wheeling Jamboree* and the *Grand Ole Opry*. With his wife Bettyanne (who writes some of his songs), he has toured in Australia, the Far East and throughout Europe. He is especially popular in the British country clubs, where he is still rated by his best-known nickname of King Of The Yodelers.

Albums: *Indian Love Call (Kenny Roberts, America's King Of The Yodelers)* (1965), *Yodelin' Kenny Roberts Sings Country Songs* (1966), *Country Music Singing Sensation* (1969), *Jealous Heart* (1970), *I Never See Maggie Alone* (1971), *Yodelin' With Kenny Roberts* (1971), *Tribute To Elton Britt* (1972), *Feelings Of Love* (1978), *Just Call Me Country* (1988), *You're My Kind Of People* (1991).

Robison, Carson Jay

b. 4 August 1890, Oswego, near Chetopa, Labette County, Kansas, USA, d. 24 March 1957. Robison's father was a champion fiddle player and his mother a pianist and singer, and, by the age of

14, Robison was competent enough to play the guitar professionally. Robison left home and worked with various dance bands and radio stations developing into a multi-instrumentalist. Victor Records were impressed when he made his first recording as a backing musician for Wendell Hall and employed him on a regular basis. They particularly liked his two-tone whistle which was used to good effect on Felix Arnolt's piano novelty, 'Nola'. Between 1924 and 1928, Robison was associated with Vernon Dalhart, singing tenor harmony and playing guitar. They recorded 'The Wreck Of The Number 9', 'Little Green Valley', 'My Blue Ridge Mountain Home', 'Golden Slippers' and many topical songs. Robison recorded with Frank Luther (b. Francis Luther Crow, 4 August 1905, Kansas, USA) as Bud and Joe Billings and released 'Will The Angels Play Their Harps For Me?' and 'The Wanderer's Warning', both of which became popular in Britain in 1929, and 'Barnacle Bill'. In 1932 Carson Robison and the Buckeroos became the first country band to tour the UK. They made records here, entertained royalty and played London's Berkeley Hotel for 13 weeks. Proud of his success, Robison changed his band's name to the Pioneers and, following a commercial series on Radio Luxembourg, they became Carson Robison and the Oxydol Pioneers. Robison also toured the UK in 1936 and 1939 and also played in Australasia. During World War II, Robison maintained his popularity by writing topical songs which ridiculed Hitler, Mussolini and Hirohito such as 'We're Gonna Have To Slap That Dirty Little Jap (And Uncle Sam's The Man That Can Do It)'. 'Turkey In the Straw' was rated the most popular song of 1942, and his songbooks included 'The Runaway Train', 'Carry Me Back To The Lone Prairie', 'Take Me Back To My Boots And Saddle' and 'Empty Saddles'. In 1947, Robison recorded his narration, 'Life Gets Tee-Jus, Don't It', which was also successful for Peter Lind Hayes. Robison recorded square dance music for MGM in the 50s as well as bringing himself up to date with 'Rockin' And Rollin' With Granmaw'. He died in New York on 24 March 1957. Vernon Dalhart was elected to the Country Music Hall Of Fame in 1981 and although Robison played a crucial part in his success, he has yet to be elected himself.
Albums: *Square Dance* (1955), *Life Gets Tee-Jus, Don't It* (1958), *The Immortal Carson Robison* (1978), *Just A Melody* (1980), *Carson J. Robison, The Kansas Jayhawk* (1987).

Rodgers, Jimmie

b. James Charles Rodgers, 8 September 1897, Meridian, Mississippi, USA, d. 26 May 1933, New York, USA. 'The Singing Brakeman' was, deservedly and unanimously, the first to be elected to Nashville's Country Music Hall Of Fame as virtually every C&W trend that has emerged since his death in 1933 has been traceable to his influence. Like his father, Rodgers was a blue-collar worker for the Mobile and Ohio Railroad but an inherited bronchial complaint (worsened by a bout of pneumonia in 1920) obliged him to seek a less strenuous livelihood. As he had entertained fellow employees by singing to his own banjo or guitar backing, a musical career seemed a viable option. With a wife and infant daughter to feed, he toured as a 'nigger minstrel' in a tent show before fronting his own trio for a North Carolina radio station residency in which he included a majority of his own compositions. Mostly incorporating his trademark 'blue yodel', 'Muleskinner Blues', 'T For Texas' and much of his repertoire was couched in rural phrasing and imagery that owed as much to the blues as cowboy ballads.
Rodgers' national popularity was to grow largely from performances on *Barn Dance*, an in-concert programme broadcast from Nashville and renamed *Grand Ole Opry* in 1927. In response to a feature in a Tennessee newspaper that same year, Rodgers auditioned for RCA talent scout Ralph Peer. A 'field' taping, 'The Soldier's Sweetheart'/'Sleep Baby Sleep' was an immediate commercial success as was the less crudely-recorded follow-up, 'The Sailor's Plea'. Next came the million-selling 'Blue Yodel', 'Brakeman's Blues' and 1929's 'Yodelling Cowboy'. In 1931, a session with the Carter Family produced mostly humorous items and 'The Wonderful City', the only sacred piece among the songs he committed to vinyl. His final 12 songs were completed in a New York studio two days before a tubercular haemorrhage killed him.
Selected albums: *20 Of The Best* (1984), *Train Whistle Blues* (1986), *Never No Mo' Blues* (1987), *My Old Pal* (1989), *The Singing Brakeman* 6 CD set (1992).

Rodriguez, Johnny

b. Juan Raul Davis Rodriguez, 10 December 1951, Sabinal, Texas, USA. Rodriguez grew up with a large family living in a shanty town 90 miles from the Mexican border. He was given a guitar when he was seven and, as a teenager, he sang with a beat group. His troubles with the law included goat rustling (he barbecued the goats). A Texas ranger,

The Singing Brakeman

Jimmie Rodgers

Kenny Rogers

who heard him singing in his cell, found him a job at the Alamo village and he drove stagecoaches, rode horses and entertained tourists. Tom T. Hall recognized his talent and employed him as lead guitarist with his road band, the Storytellers. He was signed to Mercury Records who particularly liked the way he could switch from English to Spanish. Rodriguez went to number 9 in the US country chart with his first release, 'Pass Me By' in 1972 and he then had three consecutive number 1 records, 'You Always Come Back (To Hurting Me)', 'Riding My Thumb To Mexico' and 'That's The Way Love Goes'. He wrote many of his songs and occasionally wrote with Hall. In 1975 he had further number 1 country records with 'I Just Can't Get Her Out Of My Mind', 'Just Get Up And Close The Door' and 'Love Put A Song In My Heart'. In 1977, he had a Top 10 country hit with a revival of the Eagles' 'Desperado'. He moved to Epic Records in 1979 and scored by singing 'I Hate The Way I Love It' with newcomer Charly McClain. However, his drug addiction made him more erratic. He started to take less care over his records and, in 1983, he sacked his band. He realised he could only obtain a new one if he adopted a more responsible attitude. He moved to Capitol in 1988 and had a country hit with a classy ballad, 'I Didn't (Every Chance I Had)'.

Albums: *Introducing Johnny Rodriguez* (1973), *All I Ever Meant To Do Was Sing* (1973), *My Third Album* (1974), *Songs About Ladies In Love* (1974), *Just Get Up And Close The Door* (1975), *Love Put A Song In My Heart* (1975), *Reflecting* (1976) *Practice Makes Perfect* (1977), *Just For You* (1977), *Love Me With All Your Heart* (1978), *Rodriguez Was Here* (1979), *Rodriguez* (1979), *Sketches* (1979), *Gypsy* (1980), *Through My Eyes* (1980), *After The Rain* (1981), *For Every Rose* (1983), *Fooling With Fire* (1984), *Full Circle* (1986), *Gracias* (1988).

Rogers, David

b. 27 March 1936, Atlanta, Georgia, USA. From 1952, (military service excepted), his ambition to entertain saw him playing local venues, including almost six years at the Egyptian Ballroom until 1967, when he joined the *Wheeling Jamboree* on WWVA. Rogers made his US country chart debut on Columbia in 1968 with 'I'd Be Your Fool Again' and soon moved to Nashville. In 1972, his recording of 'Need You' reached number 9, a position equalled in 1974 by 'Loving You Has Changed My Life', after he became the first country artist on the Atlantic label. During the late 70s, he registered 13 minor hits on Republic but in the early 80s, he recorded for several minor labels. 'I'm A Country Song', a minor hit on Hal Kat in 1984, was his thirty-seventh and currently his last chart hit. Rogers is perhaps best remembered for his excellent 1973 album recalling the *Grand Old Opry's* years at the Ryman Auditorium.

Albums: *The World Called You* (1970), *She Don't Make Me Cry* (1971), *Need You* (1972), *Just Thank Me* (1973), *Farewell To The Ryman* (1973), *Hey There Girl* (1974), *Country* (1984).

Rogers, Kenny

b. Kenneth David Rogers, 21 August 1938, Houston, Texas, USA. Rogers was the fourth of eight children, born in a poor area, where his father worked in a shipyard and his mother in a hospital. By sheer perseverance, he became the first member of his family to graduate. By 1955 Rogers was part of a doo-wop group, the Scholars, who recorded 'Poor Little Doggie', 'Spin The Wheel' and 'Kangewah', which was written by gossip columnist, Louella Parsons. At 19, he recorded 'That Crazy Feeling' as Kenneth Rogers for a small Houston label. Rogers' brother, Lelan, who had worked for US Decca, promoted the record and its limited success prompted the brothers to form their own label, Ken-Lee, although Rogers' single 'Jole Blon' was unsuccessful. Rogers also recorded 'For You Alone' for the Carlton label as Kenny Rogers The First. When Lelan managed Mickey Gilley, Rogers played bass on his 1960 single, 'Is It Wrong?' and he played stand-up bass with the Bobby Doyle Three and appears on their 1962 album of standards, *In A Most Unusual Way*. After recording solo for Mercury, Rogers joined the New Christy Minstrels and he appears on their 1967 album of pop hits, *New Kicks!*, while forming a splinter group with other Minstrels - Mike Settle, Thelma Camacho and Terry Williams. They took their name, the First Edition, from the flyleaf of a book and developed a newsprint motif, dressing in black and white and appearing on black and white sets. They signed with Reprise and Rogers sang lead on their first major hit, Mickey Newbury's song about the alleged pleasures of LSD, 'Just Dropped In (To See What Condition My Condition Was In)'. *The First Edition* was in the mould of the Association and Fifth Dimension, but they had developed their own style by *The First Edition's 2nd*. The album did not produce a hit single and was not released in the UK, but the First Edition returned to the US charts with Mike Settle's ballad, 'But You Know I Love You', which was also recorded by Buddy Knox and

Nancy Sinatra.

The First Edition had heard Roger Miller's low-key arrangement of 'Ruby, Don't Take Your Love To Town' and they enhanced it with an urgent drumbeat. Mel Tillis' song was based on an incident following the Korean war but it had implications for Vietnam. The record, credited to Kenny Rogers And The First Edition, reached number 6 in the US charts and number 2 in the UK. Its follow-up, 'Reuben James', about a coloured man who was blamed for everything, was only moderately successful, but they bounced back with Mac Davis' sexually explicit 'Something's Burning' (US number 11, UK number 8). The b-side, Rogers' own 'Momma's Waitin'', incorporates the major themes of country music - mother, prison, death, God and coming home - in a single song. The group had further US success with 'Tell It All Brother' and 'Heed The Call', performed the music for the Jason Robards film, *Fools*, and hosted a popular television series. In 1972 all stops were pulled out for the beautifully-packaged double album, *The Ballad Of Calico*, written by Michael Murphey and dealing with life in a silver mining town. After leaving Reprise, Rogers formed his own Jolly Rogers label which he has since described as 'a lesson in futility', and, when the group broke up in 1974, he owed $65,000. In 1975 Rogers signed with United Artists and his producer, Larry Butler, envisaged how he could satisfy both pop and country markets. Impotence was an extraordinary subject for a hit record, but 'Lucille' (US number 5, UK number 1) established Rogers as a country star. He wrote and recorded 'Sweet Music Man' but the song is more appropriate for female singers and has been recorded by Billie Jo Spears, Anne Murray, Tammy Wynette, Dolly Parton and Millie Jackson. Rogers, who had a second solo hit with 'Daytime Friends', toured the UK with Crystal Gayle, and, although plans to record with her did not materialize, he formed a successful partnership with Dottie West. Don Schlitz' story-song, 'The Gambler', was ideal for Rogers and inspired the television movies, *The Gambler*, *The Gambler II* and *The Gambler Returns* which featured Rogers. His love for poignant ballads about life on the road, such as 'She Believes In Me' (US number 5), is explained by his own life.

Rogers had the first of four marriages in 1958 and blames constant touring for the failure of his relationships. His fourth marriage was to Marianne Gorden, a presenter of the USA television series *Hee-Haw* and an actress who appeared in *Rosemary's Baby*. His stage show then promoted his happy, family life and included home movies of their child, Christopher Cody. (Rogers says the worst aspect of touring is being bombarded with grey-bearded lookalikes!) 'You Decorated My Life' was another US hit and then came 'Coward Of The County' (US number 3, UK number 1). This song too became a successful television movie and the album *Kenny*, sold five million copies. Rogers also made the documentary *Kenny Rogers And The American Cowboy*, and a concept album about a modern-day Texas cowboy, *Gideon*, led to a successful duet with one of its writers Kim Carnes, 'Don't Fall In Love With A Dreamer' (US number 4). Rogers' also had success with 'Love The World Away' from the soundtrack of the film, *Urban Cowboy*, and 'Love Will Turn You Around' from *Six Pack*, a lighthearted television movie in which he starred. Rogers' voice was ideal for Lionel Richie's slow-paced love songs and 'Lady' topped the US charts for six weeks. This was followed by 'I Don't Need You' (US number 3) from the album Richie produced for Rogers, *Share Your Love*. Rogers and Sheena Easton revived the Bob Seger song, 'We've Got Tonight' (US number 6). Having sold 35 million albums for United Artists, Rogers moved to RCA and *Eyes That See In The Dark,* was produced by Barry Gibb and featured the Bee Gees. It included 'Islands In The Stream' (US number 1, UK number 7) with Dolly Parton, which was helped by her playful approach on the video. Further US hits include 'What About Me?' with James Ingram and Kim Carnes and 'Make No Mistake, She's Mine' with Ronnie Milsap. Surprisingly, Rogers has not recorded with his close friend Glen Campbell, although he took the cover photograph for his album, *Southern Nights*. Rogers was also featured on the most successful single ever made, USA For Africa's 'We Are The World'. George Martin was an inspired choice of producer for *The Heart Of The Matter* album, which led to two singles which topped the US country charts, 'Morning Desire' and 'Tomb Of The Unknown Love'. The title track from *They Don't Make Them Like They Used To* was the theme song for the Kirk Douglas and Burt Lancaster film, *Tough Guys*, but overall, Rogers' success on RCA may have disappointed its management who had spent $20 million to secure his services. Rogers returned to Reprise but the opening track of his first album, 'Planet Texas', sounded like a joke. His son, Kenny Rogers Jnr, sang background vocals on his father's records and launched his own career in 1989 with the single, 'Take Another Step Closer'.

Roy Rogers, Trigger and Dale Evans

Now, Rogers breeds Arabian horses and cattle on his 1,200-acre farm in Georgia and has homes in Malibu, Bel Air and Beverly Hills. He owns ꞏꞏꞏꞏꞏꞏꞏꞏꞏꞏ and recording studios and has 200 employees. This is impressive for someone who was described by *Rolling Stone* as an 'overweight lightweight'. He says, 'I've never taken my talent that seriously. At one time I had a three-and-a-half octave range and sang the high parts in a jazz group. Now I don't use it because I don't have to. If Muhammad Ali can beat anyone without training, why train?'

Albums: by the First Edition *The First Edition* (1967), *The First Edition's 2nd* (1968), *The First Edition '69* (1969), *Ruby, Don't Take Your Love To Town* (1969), *Something's Burning* (1970), *Fools* (1970, soundtrack), *Tell It All Brother* (1971), *Transition* (1971), *The Ballad Of Calico* (1972), *Backroads* (1972), *Monumental* (1973), *Rollin'* (1974). By Kenny Rogers *Love Lifted Me* (1976), *Kenny Rogers* (1976), *Daytime Friends* (1977), with Dottie West *Every Time Two Fools Collide* (1978), *Love Or Something Like It* (1978), *The Gambler* (1978), *Ten Years Of Gold* (1979), with West *Classics* (1979), *Kenny* (1979), *Gideon* (1980), *Share Your Love* (1981), *Christmas* (1981), *Love Will Turn You Around* (1982), *We've Got Tonight* (1983), *Eyes That See In The Dark* (1983), *What About Me?* (1984), with Dolly Parton *Once Upon A Christmas* (1984), *The Heart Of The Matter* (1985), *Short Stories* (1986), *They Don't Make Them Like They Used To* (1986), *I Prefer The Moonlight* (1987), *Something Inside So Strong* (1989), *Christmas In America* (1989), *The Very Best Of Kenny Rogers* (1991), *You're My Kind Of People* (1991), *Some Prisons Don't Have Walls* (1991), *Back Home Again* (1992). Several compilations of Rogers' best-known tracks are available.

Further reading: *Making It In Music*, Kenny Rogers and Len Epand. *Kenny Rogers - Gambler, Dreamer, Lover*, Martha Hume.

Rogers, Roy

b. Leonard Franklin Slye, 5 November 1911, Cincinnati, Ohio, USA. Rogers worked on the west coast picking fruit and, after several singing jobs, he formed the Sons Of The Pioneers in 1933. They performed in many western films, and, as a result of Republic's dispute with Gene Autry, Rogers received his first starring role, playing a singing congressman in the 1938 film, *Under Western Skies*. When he and John Wayne jumped off a cliff in *Dark Command*, Hollywood's treatment of horses was severely questioned, which led to the formation of the Society for Prevention of Cruelty to Animals. In 1946 his wife died shortly after giving birth to their son, Roy Jnr. On 31 December 1947 he married an actress from his film, *The Cowboy And The Senorita*, Dale Evans. His films include *King Of The Cowboys*, *Son Of Paleface* with Bob Hope and Jane Russell, and *Hollywood Canteen*, in which he sang 'Don't Fence Me In'. Rogers' four-legged friend, Trigger ('the smartest horse in the movies') had been ridden by Olivia de Havilland in *The Adventures Of Robin Hood* and cost Rogers $2,500. His films and television series (100 shows between 1951 and 1957) also featured a lovable, toothless and fearless old-timer George 'Gabby' Hayes. They contained no sex and little violence (he'd wing the baddies in black hats), and his wholesome image found favour when he toured UK theatres in the 50s. High prices are now paid for Roy Rogers memorabilia, be it cut-out dolls, thermos flasks or holster sets. Rogers' records include 'Blue Shadows On The Trail', 'These Are The Good Old Days', a tribute to the past, 'Hoppy, Gene And Me' and 'Ride, Concrete Cowboy, Ride' from the film *Smokey And The Bandit 2*. His palomino Trigger died in 1965 at the age of 33 and was stuffed and mounted, as is referred to in Jimmy Webb's song 'P.F. Sloan'. Rogers became a successful businessman with a chain of restaurants, and he and Evans confined their appearances to religious ones. He made his first film in 16 years in 1975, *Mackintosh And T.J.*, while his son, Roy Rogers Jnr., made an album *Dusty* in 1983. Don McLean recorded Rogers' famous signature tune 'Happy Trails' and Rogers revived it with Randy Travis in 1990. San Francisco rock band the Quicksilver Messenger Service used Rogers' *Happy Trails* as the title of their album in 1968 as well as recording the song as the closing track. He returned to the US country chart with his album, *Tribute*, in 1991, which included guest appearances from contemporary country performers. Clint Black helped to revitalize his career, the first time Rogers had accepted help from a man in a black hat.

Albums: *Souvenir Album* (1952), with Spade Cooley *Skip To My Lou And Other Square Dances* (1952), *Roy Rogers Roundup* (1952), with Dale Evans *Hymns Of Faith* (1954), with Evans *Sweet Hour Of Prayer* (1957), with Evans *Jesus Loves Me* (1959), with Evans *The Bible Tells Me So* (1962), with The Sons Of The Pioneers *Pacos Bill* (1964), *Lore Of The West* (1966), with Evans *Christmas Is Always* (1967), *The Country Side Of Roy Rogers* (1970), *A Man From Duck Run* (1971), *Take A Little Love And*

Linda Ronstadt

Pass It On (1972), with Evans *In The Sweet Bye And Bye* (1973), *Happy Trails To You* (1975), with Evans *The Good Life* (1977), with The Sons Of The Pioneers *King Of The Cowboys* (1983), *Roy Rogers* (1984), with Evans, Roy Rogers Jnr. *Many Happy Trails* (1984), *The Republic Years* (1985), *Roll On Texas Moon* (1986), *Tribute*, (1991).

Ronstadt, Linda

b. Linda Maria Ronstadt, 15 July 1946, Tucson, Arizona, USA. The daughter of a professional musician, Ronstadt's first singing experience was gained with her sisters in the Three Ronstadts. She met guitarist Bob Kimmel at Arizona's State University and together the two aspirants moved to Los Angeles where they were joined by songwriter Kenny Edwards. Taking the name the Stone Poneys, the trio became popular among the city's folk fraternity and scored a US Top 20 hit with 'Different Drum'. Ronstadt embarked on a solo career in 1968. Her early solo albums, *Hand Sown, Home Grown* and *Silk Purse* signalled a move towards country-flavoured material, albeit of a more conservative nature. The singer's third album marked a major turning point and featured a core of excellent musicians, including Don Henley, Glen Frey, Bernie Leadon and Randy Meisner who subsequently formed the Eagles. The content emphasized a contemporary approach with songs by Neil Young, Jackson Browne and Eric Anderson, and the set established Ronstadt as a force in Californian rock. The artist's subsequent two albums showed the dichotomy prevalent in her music. *Don't Cry Now* was largely undistinguished, chiefly because the material was weaker, while *Heart Like A Wheel*, paradoxically given to Linda's former label to complete contractual obligations, was excellent.

This platinum-selling set included 'You're No Good', a US number 1 pop hit, and a dramatic version of Hank Williams' 'I Can't Help It', which won Ronstadt a Grammy award for best female country vocal. This highly successful release set the pattern for the singer's work throughout the rest of the decade. Her albums were now carefully constructed to appease both the rock and country audiences, mixing traditional material, singer/songwriter angst and a handful of rock 'n' roll/soul classics, be they from Tamla/Motown ('Heatwave'), Roy Orbison ('Blue Bayou') or Buddy Holly ('That'll Be The Day'). Despite effusive praise from the establishment media and a consistent popularity, this predictable approach resulted in lethargy, and although *Mad Love* showed a desire to break the mould, Ronstadt was increasingly trapped in an artistic cocoon.

The singer's work during the 80s has proved more divergent. Her performance in Joseph Papp's production of *Pirates Of Penzance* drew favourable reviews, although her subsequent role in the more demanding *La Boheme* was less impressive. Ronstadt also undertook a series of releases with veteran arranger/conductor Nelson Riddle, which resulted in three albums - *What's New, Lush Life* and *For Sentimental Reasons* - consisting of popular standards. In 1987 a duet with James Ingram, produced 'Somewhere Out There', the title track to the film *An American Tail*, this gave her a number 2 US hit (UK Top 10) hit, while that same year her collaboration with Dolly Parton and Emmylou Harris, *Trio* and a selection of mariachi songs, *Canciones De Mi Padre*, showed an artist determined to challenge preconceptions. Her 1989 set, *Cry Like A Rainstorm*, revealed a crafted approach to mainstream recording and included 'Don't Know Much', a haunting duet with Aaron Neville, which gave Linda Ronstadt another number 2 hit in the USA (and the UK). Ronstadt, while hugely popular and successful, has never been truly recognised by the *cognoscenti*. Her change in styles may have been a contributing factor. She has courted (with great success), country/rock, country, rock 'n' roll, latin, standards, opera, light opera, AOR and white soul.

Albums: *Hand Sown, Home Grown* (1969), *Silk Purse* (1970), *Linda Ronstadt* (1971), *Don't Cry Now* (1973), *Heart Like A Wheel* (1974), *Prisoner In Disguise* (1975), *Hasten Down The Wind* (1976), *Simple Dreams* (1977), *Living In The USA* (1978), *Mad Love* (1980), with Kevin Kline, Estelle Parsons, Rex Smith *Pirates Of Penzance* (1981), *Get Closer* (1982), *What's New* (1983), *Lush Life* (1984), *For Sentimental Reasons* (1986), with Emmylou Harris, Dolly Parton *Trio* (1987), *Canciones De Mi Padre* (1987), *Cry Like A Rainstorm - Howl Like The Wind* (1989). Compilations: includes five Stone Poney tracks *Different Drum* (1974), *Greatest Hits: Linda Ronstadt* (1976), *Retrospective* (1977), *Greatest Hits: Linda Ronstadt Volume 2* (1980).

Royal, Billy Joe

b. 3 April 1942, Valdosta, Georgia, USA. Raised in Marietta, Georgia, Royal's father owned a truck-driving company and the family moved to Atlanta when Royal was aged 10. At school he entertained in school concerts, and after graduation, worked for two years in a nightclub in Savannah, Georgia. Starting in 1962, Royal made several unsuccessful

Billy Joe Royal

singles, but then teamed with a local songwriter/producer, Joe South. In 1965 they made the US Top 20 with 'Down In The Boondocks' and 'I Knew You When', which in theme and vocal delivery was similar to Gene Pitney's hits. Royal's subsequent records were not so successful but he failed to appreciate the potential of 'Rose Garden' as it later became a hit for Lynn Anderson. In 1969, he returned to the US Top 20 with 'Cherry Hill Park' and worked for several years in Las Vegas. Royal, whose early influences came from country musicians, turned to country music and his 1987 *Looking Ahead* spent a year on the US country albums chart. His US country hits include: 'Burned Like A Rocket', 'I'll Pin A Note On Your Pillow', 'I Miss You Already' and a duet with Donna Fargo, 'Members Only'. He has also revived Aaron Neville's 'Tell It Like It Is' and Johnny Tillotson's 'It Keeps Right On A-Hurtin''. Despite his return to the US charts, Royal has yet to improve in the UK on his Number 38 position for 'Down In The Boondocks'.

Albums: *Down In The Boondocks* (1965), *Billy Joe Royal* (1965), *Hush* (1967), *Cherry Hill Park* (1969), *Looking Ahead* (1987), *The Royal Treatment* (1987), *Tell It Like It Is* (1989), *Out Of The Shadows* (1990).

Russell, Johnny

b. John Bright Russell, 23 January 1940, Sunflower County, Mississippi, USA. Russell's family moved to Fresno, California when he was 12 years old and his ambitions were centred around country music. He wrote his own songs and performed as a singer/guitarist. Jim Reeves heard his first record, 'In A Mansion Stands My Love' (for Radio Records when he was 18) and recorded the song as the b-side of 'He'll Have To Go'. Other early Russell compositions include Loretta Lynn's 'Two Mules Pull This Wagon' and the Wilburn Brothers' 'Hurt Her Once For Me'. Russell was working on a song about Hollywood but a chance remark, 'They're gonna put me in the movies', enabled him to complete it as 'Act Naturally'. Russell's co-writer, Vonnie Morrison, placed the song with Buck Owens and it became a number 1 US country hit. 'Act Naturally' was recorded by the Beatles with Ringo Starr on lead vocals for their *Help!* album and was also the b-side of their US number 1, 'Yesterday'. Russell, who had recorded as a sideline for MGM and ABC-Paramount, took his own career seriously when he signed with Chet Atkins for RCA in 1971. He had US country hits with 'Catfish John', 'The Baptism Of Jesse Taylor', 'She's In Love With A Rodeo Man' and, most significantly, 'Rednecks, White Socks And Blue Ribbon Beer', which became an anthem in the south. 'I was appearing on Charley Pride's road show,' says Russell, 'and he wouldn't let me sing the song 'cause he thought it was racial.' Strangely, Russell did not write his biggest RCA singles. He explains, 'I like singing people songs and as I tend to write hurting love songs, I never wrote the kind of songs that were right for me.' Russell's 1977 single 'Obscene Phone Call' was banned by several USA radio stations. In 1978 he moved to Mercury and his singles included 'While The Choir Sang The Hymn, I Thought Of Her', 'You'll Be Back Every Night In My Dreams' and 'Song Of The South'. Russell married his second wife, Beverly Heckel, in 1977 when she was 17. She had her own chart success with 'Bluer Than Blue' and she joined his stage show. George Strait had a US country number 1 in 1984 with Russell's 'Let's Fall To Pieces Together' and Gene Watson did well with 'I Got No Reason Now For Going Home'. Although Johnny Russell's name was known only to die-hard fans in the UK, he was a showstopper at the 1985 Wembley country music festival with his Burl Ives-styled personality and humour. (Ives did, in fact, record a Russell song, 'Mean Mean Man'.) Russell weighs 25 stone and his opening remark, 'Can you all see me at the back?', was a winner and a successful UK tour with Boxcar Willie followed. A heart attack put Russell out of action for sometime but he is now back on the road and still remains one of Nashville's leading songwriters. As he says, 'I carry a lot of weight in this town.'

Albums: *Mr. And Mrs. Untrue* (1971), *Catfish John/Chained* (1972), *Rednecks, White Socks And Blue-Ribbon Beer* (1973), *She's In Love With A Rodeo Man* (1974), *Here Comes Johnny Russell* (1975), *Something Old Something New* (1991).

Sahm, Doug

b. 6 November 1941, San Antonio, Texas, USA. Born of Lebanese-American extraction, Sahm is highly knowledgeable and a superbly competent performer of Texas musical styles, whether they be blues, country, rock 'n' roll, western swing, cajun or polkas. He made his recording debut in 1955 with 'A Real American Joe', under the name of Little Doug Sahm and within three years was fronting the Pharoahs, the first of several rough-hewn backing groups. Sahm recorded a succession of singles for local labels, including his Little Richard pastiche 'Crazy Daisy' (1959), plus 'Sapphire' (1961) and 'If You Ever Need Me' (1964). For several years, Sahm had been pestering producer, Huey P. Meaux, to record him. Meaux, having success with Barbara Lynn and Dale And Grace, was not interested. However, the producer found himself without a market when Beatlemania hit America, and shut himself away in a hotel with the Beatles' records, determined to discover what made them sell. He then called Sahm, told him to grow his hair, form a group and write a tune with a Cajun two-step beat. Accordingly, Sahm assembled his friends, Augie Meyers (keyboards), Frank Morin (saxophone), Harvey Kagan (bass) and Johnny Perez (drums). Meaux gave them an English-sounding name, the Sir Douglas Quintet and subsequently scored an international hit in 1965 with the catchy 'She's About A Mover'. The group also had success in the US charts with 'The Rains Came', but, after being arrested for possession of drugs, the group disbanded and Sahm moved to California to avoid a heavy fine. He formed the Honkey Blues Band, but had difficulty in getting it on the road. He then gathered the rest of the Quintet in California for another classic single, 'Mendocino', its spoken introduction being indicative of the hippie-era. The album, also called Mendocino, is a forerunner of country-rock. The Sir Douglas Quintet toured Europe and made the successful Together After Five, while Sahm made an excellent country single under the name of Wayne Douglas, 'Be Real'. He moved to Prunedale in northern California and befriended a Chicano band, Louie And The Lovers, producing their Rise. Sahm, having resolved his problems with the authorities, went back to Texas and released The Return Of Doug Saldaña, the name reflecting his affection for Chicanos. The album, co-produced with Meaux, included an affectionate tribute to Freddy Fender, 'Wasted Days And Wasted Nights', which prompted Meaux to resurrect Fender's career and turn him into a country superstar. Sahm appeared with Kris Kristofferson in the film, Cisco Pike, and told his record company that the song he performed, 'Michoacan', was about a state in Mexico. Disc jockeys, however, realized that he was actually praising marijuana and airplay was restricted. Atlantic Records' key producer, Jerry Wexler, decided that progressive country was becoming fashionable and signed both Willie Nelson and Doug Sahm. Sahm's high-spirited Doug Sahm And Band, was made in New York with Bob Dylan, Dr. John and accordionist Flaco Jiminez, and Sahm achieved minor success with 'Is Anybody Going To San Antone?'. The Sir Douglas Quintet were resurrected intermittently which resulted in two fine live albums, Wanted Very Much Alive and Back To The 'Dillo. Although it might seem strange that the band should tour with the new wave band the Pretenders, Sahm's voice and style were arguably an influence on Elvis Costello. Sahm himself says, 'I'm a part of Willie Nelson's world and at the same time I'm a part of the Grateful Dead's. I don't ever stay in one bag'. Among Sahm's finest albums are Hell Of A Spell, a blues album dedicated to Guitar Slim, and The Return Of The Formerly Brothers, with guitarist Amos Garrett and pianist Gene Taylor. In 1990, Doug re-used the name, the Texas Tornadoes, for an album with Meyers, Jiminez and Fender. The album, which included Sahm's witty 'Who Were You Thinkin' Of?' and Butch Hancock's 'She Never Spoke Spanish To Me', showed that he has lost none of his powers. In the UK, the Sir Douglas Quintet may be regarded as one-hit-wonders, but in reality Sahm has recorded a remarkable catalogue of Texas music.

Albums: Doug Sahm And Band (1973), Texas Tornado (1973), Groovers Paradise (1974), Texas Rock For Country Rollers (1976), Live Love (1977), Hell Of A Spell (1980), Texas Road Runner (1986), Live Doug Sahm (1987), Back To The 'Dillo (1988), Juke Box Music (1989), The Texas Tornadoes (1990), as Texas Tornados Zone Of Our Own (1991), Hangin' On By A Thread (1992). Compilations: Sir Douglas - Way Back When He Was Just Doug Sahm (1979), Sir Douglas - His First Recordings (1981), Sir Doug's Recording Trip (1989), The Best Of Doug Sahm And The Sir Douglas Quintet (1991).

Sainte-Marie, Buffy

b. 20 February 1941, Piapot Reserve, Saskatchewan, Canada. An honours graduate from the University of Massachusetts, Buffy eschewed a teaching career in favour of a folksinger. She was signed to the Vanguard label in 1964, following her successful performances at Gerde's Folk City. Her debut *It's My Way*, introduced a remarkable compositional and performing talent. Sainte-Marie's impassioned plea for Indian rights, 'Now That The Buffalo's Gone', reflected her native-American parentage and was one of several standout tracks, along with 'Cod'ine' and 'The Universal Soldier'. The latter was recorded, successfully, by Donovan, which helped introduce Buffy to a wider audience. Her second selection included 'Until It's Time For You To Go', a haunting love song which was later recorded by Elvis Presley. However, Sainte-Marie was also a capable interpreter of other writer's material, as her versions of songs by Bukka White, Joni Mitchell and Leonard Cohen showed. Her versatility was also apparent on a superb C&W collection, *I'm Gonna Be A Country Girl Again*, and on *Illuminations*, which featured an electronic score on several tracks. A campaigner for Indian rights, Sainte-Marie secured an international hit in 1971 with the theme song to the film, *Soldier Blue*, but subsequent releases failed to capitalize on this success. Temporarily bereft of direction, Buffy returned to the Indian theme with *Sweet America*, but with the collapse of the ABC labels, she retired to raise her family and concentrate on her work for children's foundations. She composed the 1982 Joe Cocker/Jennifer Warnes' hit, 'Up Where We Belong' which featured in the film *An Officer And A Gentleman*. Her welcome return in 1991, following her signing with Chrysalis Records, produced the warmly-received *Coincidence And Likely Stories*, which displayed her current interest in computer technology.

Albums: *It's My Way* (1964), *Many A Mile* (1965), *Little Wheel Spin And Spin* (1966), *Fire, Fleet And Candlelight* (1967), *I'm Gonna Be A Country Girl Again* (1968), *Illuminations* (1970), *She Used To Wanna Be A Ballerina* (1971), *Moonshot* (1972), *Quiet Places* (1973), *Buffy* (1974), *Changing Woman* (1975), *Sweet America* (1976), *Coincidence And Likely Stories* (1992). Compilations: *The Best Of Buffy Sainte-Marie* (1970), *Native North American Child: An Odyssey* (1974), *The Best Of Buffy Sainte-Marie, Volume 2* (1974).

Satherley, Art

b. Arthur Edward Satherley, 19 October 1889, Bristol, England. Known as 'Uncle Art', Satherley was a pioneer in the US recording industry during the 20s and 30s. As a talent scout, producer and A&R person, he was credited with providing the American Recording Company with one of the strongest country music catalogues in the USA. After travelling to America in 1913, he worked for the Wisconsin Chair Company which also made phonograph cabinets. He soon moved into the recording business, promoting blues artists, such as Ma Rainey, Blind Blake and Blind Lemon Jefferson for the Paramount label. In 1929, he joined the newly formed ARC, and toured the US in search of new talent in the areas of country, hillbilly, blues and 'race' music, and was at the forefront in promoting new markets. During the 30s he recorded artists such as Hank Penny, Roy Acuff, Bob Wills, Big Bill Broonzy, Bill and Cliff Carlisle, Blind Boy Fuller and Gene Autry. The latter had enormous hits with 'Silver Haired Mother Of Mine', 'Yellow Rose Of Texas' and 'Tumbling Tumbleweeds'.

When ARC became Columbia in 1938, Satherley stayed with the company as an A&R executive until his retirement in 1952. Among the artists whose careers he guided and influenced were Marty Robbins, Lefty Frizzell, Bill Monroe, Carl Smith, Spade Cooley, Al Dexter and Little Jimmy Dickens. Satherley's assistant for many years, David Law, eventually became a leading producer, and was responsible for the early recordings of David Frizzell, younger brother of the legendary Lefty. Satherley was elected to the Country Music Hall Of Fame in 1971 for his pioneering work in the genre.

Sawyer Brown

The members of the band Sawyer Brown come from different parts of the USA: Mark Miller (b. Dayton, Ohio, USA vocals) and Gregg Hubbard (keyboards) were schoolfriends in Apopka, Florida: Bobby Randall (b. Midland, Michigan, USA, guitar) and Jim Scholten (b. Michigan, USA; bass) and Joe Smyth (drums) were part of the Maine Symphony Orchestra. They all came to Nashville around 1980 and took varying roles in singer Don King's band. In 1983 they decided to work together, without King, first as Savanna and then as Sawyer Brown, taking their name from a street in Nashville. In 1983, they took part in a US television talent show, *Star Search*. They won the first prize of $100,000 and a recording contract.

Buffy Sainte-Marie

Their first single, 'Leona', was a US country hit and they toured with Kenny Rogers and Dolly Parton. Miller wrote their second single, a country number 1 hit, 'Step That Step' (1985), about the perseverance needed in the music business. They established themselves as a goodtime country band and had further country hits with 'Used To Blue', 'Betty's Bein' Bad', 'This Missin' You Heart Of Mine' and a remake of George Jones' 'The Race Is On'. 'My Baby's Gone' made number 11 on the country charts in 1988, but they have since lost much of their impetus.

Albums: *Sawyer Brown* (1985), *Shakin'* (1986), *Out Goin' Cattin'* (1986), *Somewhere In The Night* (1987), *The Boys Are Back* (1989), *Dirt Road* (1992).

Schneider, John

b. 8 April 1954, Mount Kisco, Westchester County, New York, USA. Schneider, a gifted musician and actor, has appeared in musicals from the age of 14. He played Bo Duke in the long-running US television series about a disaster-prone, hillbilly family, *The Dukes Of Hazzard* from 1979-85. He is featured on the 1982 cast album of the same name. In 1981 he had his first US hit (pop chart number 14, country number 4) with a revival of Elvis Presley's 'It's Now Or Never', and proved himself to be one television star who could sing. However, despite other successes on the US country chart, he was not accepted as a bona fide artist by country disc jockeys. In 1984, the disc jockeys were given unmarked copies of 'I've Been Around Enough To Know', and many of them played the record believing it to be by George Strait. Schneider's identity was revealed and the single topped the US country chart. He had further number 1's with 'Country Girls', 'What's A Memory Like You (Doing In A Love Like This)?' and 'You're The Last Thing I Needed Tonight'. Schneider, though, unlike most country stars, did not care for touring and his final US Top 10 country hit was in 1987 with 'Love, You Ain't Seen The Last Of Me', at a time when he was planning to do just that. He returned to acting and was in a successful series, *Grand Slam*, in 1990.

Albums: *Now Or Never* (1981), *Dukes Of Hazzard* (1982, television cast), *White Christmas* (1981), *Quiet Man* (1982), with Jill Michaels *If You Believe* (1983), *Too Good To Stop Now* (1984), *Trying To Outrun The Wind* (1985), *A Memory Like You* (1986), *Take The Long Way Home* (1986), *You Ain't Seen The Last Of Me* (1987).

Scruggs, Earl

b. 6 January 1924, Cleveland County, North Carolina, USA. Scruggs was raised in the Appalachian Mountains, and learned to play banjo from the age of five. In 1944, he joined Bill Monroe's Bluegrass Boys, where he perfected his three-finger banjo technique. He later left with fellow member Lester Flatt, to form the Foggy Mountain Boys in 1948. They enjoyed a long career spanning 20 years, and were reportedly only outsold during the 60s, on CBS Records, by Johnny Cash. The duo became synonymous with their recordings of 'Foggy Mountain Breakdown', which was used in the film *Bonnie And Clyde* and 'The Ballad Of Jed Clampett', which was the theme tune for the television series *The Beverly Hillbillies*. In 1969, after Flatt and Scruggs parted company, the Earl Scruggs Revue was formed featuring Earl (banjo/vocals), and his sons, Randy (lead guitar/slide guitar/bass/vocals), Gary (bass/harmonica/vocals), Steve (guitar), plus Josh Graves (dobro/guitar/vocals) and Jody Maphis (drums/vocals). The Earl Scruggs Revue performed to great acclaim at the Wembley International Festival of Country Music in 1972. *His Family And Friends*, which comes from a 1971 National Educational Television Soundtrack, included guest appearances by Bob Dylan, Joan Baez and the Byrds. *Anniversary Special, Volume 1*, included a veritable who's who of the music scene, including Roger McGuinn and Dan Fogelberg. Graves left the group during the mid-70s to pursue a solo career. Scruggs' innovation in taking traditional fiddle tunes and transposing them for playing on banjo helped push back the boundaries of bluegrass, and paved the way for the later 'Newgrass' revival.

Albums: *Nashville's Rock* (c.1970), *Earl Scruggs Performing With His Family And Friends* (1972), *I Saw The Light With Some Help From My Friends* (1972), *Live At Kansas State* (1972), *Duelling Banjos* (1973), *The Earl Scruggs Revue* (1973), *Where Lillies Bloom* (c1970), *Rocking Across The Country* (1973), *Anniversary Special, Volume 1* (1975), *The Earl Scruggs Revue, Volume 2* (1976), *Family Portrait* (1976), *Earl Scruggs, 5-String Instructional Album* (1976), *Live From Austin City Limits* (1977), *Strike Anywhere* (1977), *Bold And New* (1978), *Today And Forever* (1979), *Rockin' 'Cross The Country* (1974), *Top Of The World* (1983).

Further reading: *Earl Scruggs And The 5-String Banjo*, Earl Scruggs.

Earl Scruggs Revue

Seals, Dan

b. 8 February 1950, McCamey, Texas, USA. Leaving successful pop duo England Dan And John Ford Coley was, at first, a disastrous career move for Dan Seals. His management left him with unpaid tax bills and mounting debts and he lost his house, his van and his money. He says, 'I was bankrupt, separated and living at friends' places. My kids were with friends. It was a real bad time'. Furthermore, the two albums that he made for Atlantic Records as a solo artist, *Stones* and *Harbinger*, meant little. However, Kyle Lehning, who produced his hits with England Dan And John Ford Coley, never lost faith and helped to establish him on the US country charts with 'Everybody's Dream Girl' in 1983. Further country hits followed and he had a US number 1 hit with 'Meet Me In Montana', a duet with Marie Osmond, in 1985. Seals then had an extraordinary run of eight consecutive US number 1 country singles: the dancing 'Bop', the rodeo story 'Everything That Glitters (Is Not Gold)', 'You Still Move Me', 'I Will Be There', 'Three Time Loser', the wedding song 'One Friend', 'Addicted' and 'Big Wheels In The Moonlight', many of which he wrote himself. *Won't Be Blue Anymore*, sold half a million copies in the USA, while another big-selling record, *On The Front Line*, included an exquisite duet with Emmylou Harris, 'Lullaby'. A switch of labels from Capitol to Warners in 1992 altered his style little.
Albums: *Stones* (1980), *Harbinger* (1982), *Rebel Heart* (1983), *San Antone* (1984), *Won't Be Blue Anymore* (1985), *On The Front Line* (1986), *Rage On* (1988), *On Arrival* (1990), *Walking The Wire* (1992). Compilation: *The Best Of Dan Seals* (1987).

Seals, Troy

b. 16 November 1938, Big Hill, Kentucky, USA. Seals, a cousin to Dan Seals, began playing guitar in his teens and formed his own rock 'n' roll band. In 1960, he was working in a club in Ohio with Lonnie Mack and Denny Rice, where he befriended a visiting performer, Conway Twitty. Twitty introduced him to Jo Ann Campbell, who had had a few successes on the US pop charts. Seals married Campbell and they worked as a duo, making the US R&B charts with 'I Found A Love, Oh What A Love' in 1964. After some time working as a construction worker, Seals moved to Nashville to sell his songs. 'There's A Honky Tonk Angel (Who'll Take Me Back In)', written by Seals and Rice, was a US country number 1 for Conway Twitty, while Cliff Richard's version for the UK market was withdrawn when he discovered what honky tonk angels were (!). Elvis Presley also recorded the song, along with Seals' 'Pieces Of My Life'. Seals' most recorded song is 'We Had It All', written with Donnie Fritts, which has been recorded by Rita Coolidge, Waylon Jennings, Brenda Lee, Stu Stevens and Scott Walker. His songwriting partners include Don Goodman and Will Jennings, a university professor in English literature, and together they all wrote 'Feelins'', a US country number 1 for Conway Twitty and Loretta Lynn; with Mentor Williams 'When We Make Love', a US country number 1 for Alabama; with Max D. Barnes 'Don't Take It Away' (another US country number 1 for Conway Twitty) and 'Storms Of Life' (Randy Travis). One of his best songs is the mysterious 'Seven Spanish Angels', written with Eddie Setser, a US country number 1 for Willie Nelson and Ray Charles. Seals has done much session work as a guitarist and has had a few minor country hits himself.
Albums: *Now Presenting Troy Seals* (1973), *Troy Seals* (1976).

Seely, Jeannie

b. Marilyn Jeanne Seeely, 6 July 1940, Titusville, Pennsylvania, USA. Seely had studied banking but she had been singing in public from 11 years old. She gained valuable experience by working as a secretary in Los Angeles for Liberty Records. In 1965 with encouragement from the man she later married, Hank Cochran, she came to Nashville. She worked for Ernest Tubb and then for Porter Wagoner. In 1966, she went to number 2 on the US country charts with Cochran's 'Don't Touch Me', and won a Grammy as the Best Country Female Vocalist. She had success with more of Cochran's songs, notably 'I'll Love You More', 'Welcome Home To Nothing' and 'Just Enough To Start Me Dreaming', and dedicated an album to him, *Thanks, Hank*. Being a small blonde in a miniskirt, she was a distinctive partner for the six-foot Jack Greene and they had a succession of US country hits, including a number 2, 'I Wish I Didn't Have To Miss You'. Seely wrote 'It Just Takes Practice' (Dottie West), 'Senses' (Willie Nelson and Connie Smith) and 'Leavin' And Sayin' Goodbye' (Jack Greene, Faron Young and Norma Jean). In 1973 she had success with 'Can I Sleep In Your Arms Tonight, Mister?', a parody by Hank Cochran of the old-time 'May I Sleep In Your Barn Tonight, Mister?'. She also made a bid for the outlaw country market with a song addressed to Jessi Colter, 'We're Still Hangin' In

There, Ain't We, Jessi?'.

Albums: *Thanks, Hank* (1967), *I Love You More* (1968), *Little Things* (1968), *Jeannie Seely* (1969), *Please Be My New Love* (1970), *Make The World Go Away* (1972), *Can I Sleep In Your Arms?* (1973), *Seely Style* (1976); with Jack Greene *I Wish I Didn't Have To Miss You* (1969), *Jack Greene And Jeannie Seely* (1970), *Two For The Show* (1971), *Live At The Grand Ole Opry* (1978).

Sessions, Ronnie

b. 7 December 1948, Henrietta, Oklahoma, USA. Sessions grew up in Bakersfield, California. His first record, in 1957, was a novelty version of Little Richard's 'Keep A-Knockin'' made with Richard's band. Through a schoolboy friend he knew the host, Herb Henson, of a television series, *Trading Post*, and he became a regular performer. He studied to be a vet but he also recorded for local labels and, joining Gene Autry's Republic label in 1968, he had regional hits with 'The Life Of Riley' and 'More Than Satisfied'. He moved to Nashville and his songwriting talent was recognized by Hank Cochran. However, his first country hits were with revivals of pop songs, 'Never Been To Spain' and 'Tossin' And Turnin''. Over at MCA, he had major country hits in 1977 with 'Wiggle, Wiggle' and Bobby Goldsboro's 'Me And Millie (Stompin' Grapes And Gettin' Silly). He failed to consolidate his success and, after being dropped by MCA in 1980, he has hardly recorded since. His last US country chart entry was in 1986 with 'I Bought The Shoes That Just Walked Out On Me'.

Album: *Ronnie Sessions* (1977).

Shaver, Billy Joe

b. 15 September 1941, Corsicana, Texas, USA. Shaver was raised in Waco, Texas and lost two fingers in a saw-mill accident. In typically contradictory fashion, he took up bronc-busting as a safer job and started to learn guitar. An early song, 'Two Bits Worth Of Nothing', was written about his wife - a lady he has both married and divorced three times! Shaver spent some years in Nashville before Bobby Bare discovered him. He and Bare co-wrote his first single, 'Chicken On The Ground', for Mercury Records in 1970. Bare hit the US country charts with the simple, gutsy philosophy of 'Ride Me Down Easy' in 1973. Johnny Rodriguez did well with 'I Couldn't Be Me Without You', while Tom T. Hall favoured 'Old Five And Dimers' and a song about Willie Nelson, 'Willy The Wandering Gypsy And Me'. Waylon Jennings' important album *Honky Tonk*

Heroes contained nine Shaver songs including their co-written 'You Ask Me To', which was subsequently recorded by Elvis Presley. Shaver's first album, produced by Kris Kristofferson, contained his gruff-voiced versions of many excellent songs including his first country hit, 'I Been To Georgia On A Fast Train'. His Texan influences (blues, jazz, Mexican) and his themes (life on the road, brief encounters, how it used to be) fitted in with outlaw country music. His best song, 'Black Rose', tells of his love for a black girl and contains the dubious line, 'The Devil made me do it the first time, The second time I done it on my own.' Shaver hated live performances and he fell prey to ulcers, alcoholism and drug-addiction, so much so that an album for MGM Records was never made. Other songwriters wrote about him, including Kris Kristofferson's 'The Fighter' and Tom T. Hall's 'Joe, Don't Let The Music Kill You'. In 1976, Shaver released his second album and followed it with a glittering line-up (Willie Nelson, Ricky Skaggs, Emmylou Harris) for 'Gypsy Boy'. He turned to religion and 'I'm Just An Old Chunk Of Coal (But I'm Gonna Be A Diamond Someday)' was recorded by both Johnny Cash and John Anderson. Perhaps there were too many outlaw singers and Shaver, with his lack of product, was overlooked. His output of six studio albums in 17 years, with several songs repeated, is astonishingly low, particularly for a country singer.

Albums: *Old Five And Dimers Like Me* (1973), *When I Get My Wings* (1976), *Gypsy Boy* (1977), *I'm Just An Old Chunk Of Coal* (1981), *Billy Joe Shaver* (1982), *Salt Of The Earth* (1987), *Live In Australia* (1989).

Shelton, Ricky Van

b. 1952, Grit, near Lynchburg, Virginia, USA. Shelton was raised in a church-going family and he learned to love gospel music. His brother worked as a musician and through travelling with him, he also acquired a taste for country music. He worked as a pipefitter but his soon-to-be wife, Bettye, realized his singing potential and, in 1984, suggested that they went to Nashville where she had secured a personnel job. In 1986 he impressed producer Steve Buckingham during a club performance, and his first recording session yielded a US Top 30 country hit in 'Wild-Eyed Dream'. He then made the country Top 10 with one of his best records, the dramatic story-song, 'Crimes Of Passion'. In 1987 he had a US country number 1 by reviving a song from a Conway Twitty album, 'Somebody Lied'. In 1988 he had another number

Billy Joe Shaver

l by reviving Harlan Howard's song, 'Life Turned Her That Way', which, unlike Merle Tillis, he performed in its original 4/4 tempo. His revival of an obscure Roger Miller song, 'Don't We All Have The Right', also went to number l, thus giving him five country hits from his first album. Since then, he has had US country number l's with revivals of 'I'll Leave This World Loving You', 'From A Jack To A King' and a new song, 'Living Proof'. Although Shelton has much in common with his hard-nosed contemporaries, he succumbed to a middle-of-the-road album of familiar Christmas songs. He recorded a duet of 'Sweet Memories' with Brenda Lee, whilst 'Rockin' Years' with Dolly Parton was a number l country single in 1991. To help his career, Shelton's wife has been studying law, whilst he knows that he must conquer his fear of flying. In 1992, Shelton recorded an album of semi-spiritual material, *Don't Overlook Salvation*, as a gift to his parents, before scoring more hits with the new recordings included on *Greatest Hits Plus*.

Albums: *Wild-Eyed Dream* (1987), *Loving Proof* (1988), *Ricky Van Shelton Sings Christmas* (1989), *Ricky Van Shelton III* (1990), *Backroads* (1991), *Don't Overlook Salvation* (1992), *Greatest Hits Plus* (1992).

Shepard, Jean

b. Imogene Shepard, 21 November 1933, Pauls Valley, Oklahoma, USA. Shepard was one of 11 children in a family, which moved to Visalia, California in 1946. Shepard learned to sing by listening to Jimmie Rodgers' records on a wind-up Victrola. She joined the Melody Ranch Girls, in which she played string bass and sang, and recorded for Capitol while still at school. The record was not successful but she subsequently played on the same bill as Hank Thompson, who reminded Capitol of her talent. In 1953 a single for the Korean war, 'Dear John Letter', with a narration from Ferlin Husky, topped the US country charts for 23 weeks. Because she was under 21, she could not legally leave the State on her own and the problem was making Husky her guardian. Shepard followed 'Dear John' with 'Forgive Me, John' while the original was satirized by Stan Freberg. Shepard had further country hits with 'Satisfied Mind' and 'Beautiful Lies' and she has been a regular member of the *Grand Ole Opry* since 1955. She worked with Red Foley from 1955-57 on his television show, *Ozark Jubilee*. Her 1956 *Songs Of A Love Affair* was a concept album, one side from the single woman's view, the other from the wife's. She was married to Hawkshaw Hawkins, who was killed in 1963 in the plane crash which also took

Jean Shepard

the lives of Patsy Cline and Cowboy Copas. At the time Shepard was eight months pregnant with their second child. She returned to country music in 1969 with 'I'll Fiddle To An Old Guitar' and she named her road band, The Second Fiddles. She also had success with 'Happy Hangovers To You', 'If Teardrops Were Silver', and two duets with Ray Pillow, 'I'll Take The Dog' and 'Mr. Do-It-Yourself'. Shepard was one of the first artists to be produced by crossover producer Larry Butler. In the 70s, she did well on the US country charts with Bill Anderson's songs, 'Slippin' Away', 'At The Time', 'The Tips Of My Fingers' and 'Mercy' and recorded an album of his songs, *Poor Sweet Baby*. In 1975 she recorded a tribute to Hawkshaw Hawkins, 'Two Little Boys', which was written by their sons. Shepard was opposed to Olivia Newton-John's award from the Country Music Association and she helped to found the Association Of Country Music Entertainers to 'keep it country'. To the public, it looked like sour grapes, especially as she had recorded 'Let Me Be There' and several pop hits. In recent years Shepard has recorded duets with Gerry Ford, and often plays UK country clubs, accompanied by her guitarist/husband, Benny Birchfield.

Albums: *Songs Of A Love Affair* (1956), *Lonesome Love* (1959), *This Is Jean Shepard* (1959), *Got You On My Mind* (1961), *Heartaches And Tears* (1962), *Lighthearted And Blue* (1964), *It's A Man Everytime* (1965), with Ray Pillow *I'll Take The Dog* (1966), *Many Happy Hangovers* (1966), *Hello Old Broken Heart* (1967), *Heart, We Did All That We Could* (1967), *Your Forevers Don't Last Very Long* (1967), *A Real Good Woman* (1968), *Heart To Heart* (1968), *Seven Lonely Days* (1969), *I'll Fly Away* (1969), *A Woman's Hand* (1970), *Declassified Jean Shepard* (1971), *Just As Soon As I Get Over Loving You* (1972), *Just Like Walking In The Sunshine* (1972), *Here And Now* (1971), *Slippin' Away* (1973), *Poor Sweet Baby* (1975), *For The Good Times* (1975), *I'm A Believer* (1975), *The Best Of Jean Shepard* (1975), *Mercy, Ain't Love Good* (1976), *I'll Do Anything It Takes* (1978), *Slippin' Away* (1982).

Sheppard, T.G.

b. William Browder, 20 July 1944, Humboldt, Tennessee, USA. Sheppard is a nephew of old-time country performer, Rod Brasfield, and his mother was a piano teacher who gave him lessons. Sheppard began his professional musical career in Memphis in the early 60s working as a backup vocalist for Travis Wammack and then performing as Brian Stacey, having a regional hit with 'High School Days'. After his marriage in 1965, Sheppard became a record promoter for Stax and RCA. In 1974, he was signed by Motown's country arm, Melodyland, and had two number 1 country records with 'The Devil In The Bottle' and 'Trying To Beat The Morning Home'. He took his name from The German Shepherd dogs but many have thought his name represents The Good Shepherd. Sheppard merged his Memphis soul background with country music, which included revivals of the Four Tops' 'I Can't Help Myself' and Neil Diamond's 'Solitary Man'. Over at Warners, Sheppard had a US country number 1 with 'Last Cheater's Waltz' and followed it with another 10. In 1981 Sheppard made the US Top 40 with 'I Loved 'Em Every One'. His duets include 'Faking Love' with Karen Brooks, 'Home Again' with Judy Collins and 'Make My Day' with Clint Eastwood.

Albums: *T.G.Sheppard* (1975), *Motels And Memories* (1976), *Solitary Man* (1976), *T.G.* (1978), *Daylight* (1978), *Three-Quarters Lonely* (1979), *Smooth Sailin'* (1980), *I Love 'Em All* (1981), *Finally* (1982), *Perfect Stranger* (1982), *Slow Burn* (1983), *One Owner Heart* (1984), *Livin' On The Edge* (1985), *It Still Rains In Memphis* (1986), *One For The Money* (1987), *Crossroads* (1988).

Sherrill, Billy

b. Philip Campbell, 5 November 1936, Winston, Alabama, USA. Sherrill's father was a travelling evangelist - he is shown on horseback on the cover of Charlie Rich's album *Silver Linings* - and Sherrill played piano at his meetings. He also played saxophone in a local rock'n'roll band, Benny Cagle and the Rhythm Swingsters. In 1956 he left to work with Rick Hall in the R&B-styled Fairlanes. His 1958 Mercury single, 'Like Making Love', was covered for the UK market by Marty Wilde, and he had some success in Alabama with an instrumental, 'Tipsy', in 1960. He worked for Sun Records' new Nashville studios from 1961 to 1964; in particular, he brought out Charlie Rich's talent as a blues singer. He and Rick Hall then established the Fame studios in Nashville. In 1964 he started working for Columbia Records and he produced R&B records by Ted Taylor and the Staple Singers as well as an album by Elvis Presley's guitarist, Scotty Moore, *The Guitar That Changed The World*. He co-wrote and produced David Houston's US number 1 country hit, 'Almost Persuaded', and his subsequent hits with Houston include a duet with Tammy Wynette, 'My Elusive Dreams'. It was Sherrill who discovered Wynette and in 1968 they wrote 'Stand By Your Man' in half an hour and recorded it immediately. Although Sherrill's records crossed over to the pop market, he did not avoid country music instruments such as the steel guitar, although he did favour lavish orchestrations. He also discovered Tanya Tucker, Janie Frickie and Lacy J. Dalton, and has made successful records with Charlie Rich ('Behind Closed Doors', 'The Most Beautiful Girl'), George Jones, Marty Robbins and Barbara Mandrell. He became a freelance producer in 1980 but he continued to work with many of the same artists. He has produced over 10 albums apiece for David Allan Coe, George Jones and Tammy Wynette; other credits include *The Baron* for Johnny Cash and the soundtrack for the film, *Take This Job And Shove It*. His best works include two all-star country albums, *My Very Special Guests* with George Jones, and *Friendship* with Ray Charles. The friction between him and Elvis Costello whilst making the album, *Almost Blue*, was shown on a UK television documentary, but the album did very well and yielded a Top 10 hit, 'A Good Year For The Roses'.

Album: *Classical Country* (1967).

Silverstein, Shel

b. Shelby Silverstein, 1932, Chicago, Illinois, USA. A former artist with *Stars And Stripes* magazine, Silverstein joined the staff of *Playboy* at its inception during the early 50s and for almost two decades his cartoons were a regular feature of the publication. He later became a successful illustrator and author of children's books, including *Uncle Shelby's ABZ Book*, *Uncle Shelby's Zoo* and *Giraffe And A Half*. Silverstein was also drawn to the folk scene emanating from Chicago's Gate Of Horn and New York's Bitter End, latterly becoming a respected composer and performer of the genre. Early 60s collaborations with Bob Gibson were particularly memorable and in 1961 Silverstein completed *Inside Folk Songs* which included the original versions of 'The Unicorn' and '25 Minutes To Go', later popularized, respectively, by the Irish Rovers and Brothers Four. Silverstein provided 'novelty' hits for Johnny Cash ('A Boy Named Sue') and Loretta Lynn, ('One's On The Way'), but an association with Dr. Hook proved to be the most fruitful. A series of successful singles ensued, notably 'Sylvia's Mother' and 'The Cover Of *Rolling Stone*', and a grateful group reciprocated by supplying the backing on *Freakin' At The Freaker's Ball*. This ribald set included many of Silverstein's best-known compositions from this period,

including 'Polly In A Porny', 'I Got Stoned And I Missed It' and 'Don't Give A Dose To The One You Love Most', the last-named of which was adopted in several anti-venereal disease campaigns. *The Great Conch Robbery*, released on the traditional music outlet Flying Fish, was less scatological in tone, since which Silverstein has adopted a less-public profile.

Albums: *Hairy Jazz* (1959), *Inside Folk Songs* (1961), *I'm So Good I Don't Have To Brag* (1965), *Drain My Brain* (1966), *A Boy Named Sue* (1968), *Freakin' At The Freaker's Ball* (1969), *Songs And Stories* (1972), *The Great Conch Train Robbery* (1979).

Sizemore, Asher, And Little Jimmy

Asher Sizemore (b. 6 June 1906, Manchester, Kentucky, USA, d. c.1973) and his eldest son Jimmy (b. 29 January 1928, Paintsville, Kentucky, USA). Sizemore initially worked as a bookkeeper for a mining company in Pike County but longed to be a singer. In 1931, Singing old time and cowboy songs, he first appeared on radio in Huntington, West Virginia, before moving to WCKY Cincinnati and then WHAS Louisville, where he was first joined on air by his five-year-old son. In 1933, the duo were hired by the *Grand Ole Opry*, where they remained a popular act for about 10 years. Jimmy, at the age of five, allegedly had a repertoire of over 200 songs and understandably because of his extreme youth, his *Opry* and radio performances gained him a considerable following. He sang duets with his father but is remembered for his youthful renditions of such numbers as 'Chewing Gum' and 'The Booger Bear'. In 1934, he achieved recording success with a maudlin rendition of 'Little Jimmy's Goodbye To Jimmie Rodgers'. The Sizemores toured regularly but to augment their income, Asher established a very successful mail order service for their annual books of *Health & Home Songs* and they also made transcription disc recordings that Asher syndicated to stations throughout the south and mid-west. By the late 30s, the act also included Jimmy's younger brother Buddy. Drawing mainly on sentimental numbers that contained regular references to mother, home, death, heaven and righteousness, with some interruption for part of World War II, they maintained a successful career throughout the 40s, mainly in the mid-west. In 1950, now joined by daughter Nancy Louise, Asher returned to WKLO Louisville. Jimmy and Buddy both served in the US Forces in Korea, Buddy being killed in action in November 1950. Asher and Jimmy later moved to Arkansas where they both worked on radio. Asher Sizemore died in the 70s but Jimmy was still working in radio in an executive capacity into the 80s.

Albums: *Mountain Ballads & Old Hymns* (1966), *Songs Of The Soil* (1984).

Skaggs, Ricky

b. Ricky Lee Skaggs, 18 July 1954, Brushey Creek, near Cordell, Kentucky, USA. His father, Hobert, was a welder, who enjoyed playing the guitar and singing gospel songs with Skaggs' mother, Dorothy. Skaggs was to record one of her songs, 'All I Ever Loved Was You'. Hobert came back from a welding job in Ohio with a mandolin for the five-year-old Skaggs, but had to return before he could show him how to play it. Within two weeks, Skaggs had figured it out for himself. In 1959 he was taken on stage during one of Bill Monroe's concerts and played 'Ruby' on Monroe's mandolin to rapturous applause. At the age of seven, he played mandolin on Flatt And Scruggs' television show, and then learnt guitar and fiddle. Whilst working at a square dance with his father, he met Keith Whitley and they were to form a trio with Whitley's banjo-playing brother, Dwight, recording bluegrass and gospel shows for local radio. In 1970 they opened for Ralph Stanley, formerly of the Stanley Brothers, who was so impressed that he invited them to join his band, the Clinch Mountain Boys. They both made their recording debuts on Stanley's *Cry From The Cross*. The youngsters made two albums together, but Skaggs soon left in 1972, discouraged by the long hours and low pay.

Skaggs married Stanley's cousin and worked in a boiler room in Washington DC. However, he returned to music by joining the Country Gentlemen, principally on fiddle. Then, from 1974 to 1975, he played in the modern bluegrass band, J.D. Crowe And The New South. He later recorded a duet album with another member of the band, Tony Rice. Skaggs' first solo *That's It*, includes contributions from his own parents. He formed his own band, Boone Creek, and recorded bluegrass albums, although they also touched on western swing and honky tonk. He was then offered a job in Emmylou Harris' Hot Band. 'Emmy tried to get me to join three times before I went. I wanted to stay in bluegrass and learn as much about the music as I could, but when Rodney Crowell left, I had an incentive to join her because I knew I'd be able to sing a lot.' From 1977 to 1980, Skaggs was to encourage Harris' forays into traditional country music via her *Blue Kentucky Girl, Light Of The Stable* and, especially, *Roses In The Snow*. Although Skaggs had rarely been a lead vocalist, his clear, high tenor was featured on an acoustic-based solo album, *Sweet Temptation*, for the North Carolina label, Sugar Hill. Emmylou Harris and Albert Lee were amongst the guest musicians. While he was working on another Sugar Hill album, *Don't Cheat In Our Hometown*, Epic Records took an interest in him. He switched to Epic and made his debut on the US country charts with a revival of Flatt And Scruggs' 'Don't Get Above Your Raising', which he later re-recorded in concert with Elvis Costello. *Rolling Stone* likened Skaggs' first Epic release, *Waitin' For The Sun To Shine*, to Gram Parsons' *Grievous Angel* as they both represented turning-points in country music.

Skaggs was putting the country back into country music by making fresh-sounding records which related to the music's heritage. As if to prove the point, he had US number 1 country hits by reviving Flatt and Scrugg's 'Crying My Heart Out Over You' and Webb Pierce's 'I Don't Care'. He was the Country Music Association Male Vocalist of the Year for 1982, and became the 61st - and youngest - member of the *Grand Old Opry*. Despite the old-time feeling, he appealed to rock fans in a sell-out concert at London's Dominion Theatre, which was released on a live album. Skaggs had played on Guy Clark's original version of 'Heartbroken' and his own recording of the song gave him another country chart-topper. He also completed his *Don't Cheat In Our Hometown*, which was released, after much negotiation, by Epic. Skaggs is a principled performer who leaves drinking or cheating songs to others, but he justified the title track, originally recorded by The Stanley Brothers, by calling it a 'don't cheat' song. Skaggs played on Albert Lee's first-class solo *Hiding*, and he had another number 1 with his own version of Lee's 'Country Boy', although the whimsical lyric must have baffled American listeners. With a revival of Bill Monroe's 'Uncle Pen', Skaggs is credited as being the first performer to top the country charts with a bluegrass song since Flatt And Scruggs in 1963, although he says, ''Uncle Pen' would not be a bluegrass single according to law of Monroe because there are drums and electric instruments on it.' Skaggs won a Grammy for the best country instrumental, 'Wheel Hoss', which was used as the theme music for his BBC Radio 2 series, *Hit It, Boys*. In 1981 Skaggs,

Ricky Skaggs

now divorced, married Sharon White of the Whites. They won the Vocal Duo of the Year award for their 1987 duet, 'Love Can't Ever Get Better Than This'. He also recorded a playful duet of 'Friendship' with Ray Charles, and says, 'The people who call me Picky Ricky can't have met Ray Charles. He irons out every wrinkle. I would sing my lead part and he'd say, "Aw, honey, that's good but convince me now: sing to your ol' daddy." Skaggs has worked on albums by the Bellamy Brothers, Rodney Crowell, Exile and Jesse Winchester. Johnny Cash had never previously used a fiddle player until Skaggs worked on *Silver*. Skaggs' busy career suffered a setback when his son, Andrew, was shot in the mouth by a drug-crazed truckdriver, but returned in 1989 with two fine albums in the traditional mould: *White Limozeen*, which he produced for Dolly Parton, and his own *Kentucky Thunder*. *My Father's Son* in 1991 was his most consistent album in years, but its poor sales led Columbia to drop him from their roster in 1992. Skaggs is modest about his achievements, feeling that he is simply God's instrument. He has rekindled an interest in country music's heritage, and many musicians have followed his lead. He remains one of the best performers in country music today.

Albums: with Keith Whitley *Tribute To The Stanley Brothers* (1971), with Keith Whitley *Second Generation Bluegrass* (1972), *That's It* (1975), as Boone Creek *Boone Creek* (1977), as Boone Creek *One Way Track* (1978), with Tony Rice *Take Me Home Tonight In A Song* (1978), *Sweet Temptation* (1979), with Tony Rice *Skaggs And Rice* (1980), *Waitin' For The Sun To Shine* (1981), *Family And Friends* (1982), *Highways And Heartaches* (1982), *Don't Cheat In Our Hometown* (1983), *Country Boy* (1984), *Live In London* (1985), *Love's Gonna Get Ya!* (1986), *Comin' Home To Stay* (1988), *Kentucky Thunder* (1989), *My Father's Son* (1991).

Skillet Lickers

One of the most popular of string bands of early country music. The original members were James Gideon Tanner (b. 6 June 1885, near Monroe, Georgia, USA, d. 1962, Winder, Georgia, USA; fiddle, vocals), Riley Puckett, Clayton McMichen (b. 26 January 1900, Allatoona, Georgia, USA, d. 3 January 1970, Battletown, Kentucky, USA; fiddle/vocals) and Fate Norris (banjo, harmonica, vocals). The members had been performing in various combinations around Atlanta before 1924 but it was in that year that Tanner (a fiddle playing chicken farmer) and the blind guitarist Puckett

recorded to become Columbia's first hillbilly talent. In 1926, with McMichen and Norris they recorded for the first time as Gid Tanner And The Skillet Lickers. Over the years there were line-up variations and other important members included Lowe Stokes, Bert Layne (both outstanding fiddlers), Hoke Rice (guitar), Gid's brother Arthur (banjo/guitar) and teenage son Gordon (fiddle). By 1931, in some combination or other, they had cut 88 sides for Columbia - all but six being released. Their material included fiddle tunes, traditional ballads and pop songs plus little comedy skits such as their noted 'A Corn Licker Still In Georgia'. In 1934, Gid Tanner And The Skillet Lickers were credited with a million-selling record for their recording of 'Down Yonder' (Gordon Tanner was the featured fiddler on the recording). (In 1959 pianist Del Wood also sold a million with her version of this tune.) After the Skillet Lickers disbanded in the 30s, Tanner returned to chicken farming until his death in 1962. McMichen went on to a successful career with his own band the Georgia Wildcats (which at one time included Puckett) and held the title of National Fiddling Champion from 1934-49. Gordon Tanner who later led the Junior Skillet-Lickers, died following a heart attack on 26 July 1982. Bill C. Malone suggests that 'much of the band's popularity can be attributed to the energetic personality and showmanship of Tanner who whooped, sang in falsetto and in general played the part of the rustic fool'. McMichen is reputed to have suggested that 'Tanner's fiddle playing was just as unrestricted and tended to detract from the overall quality of the band'. In the 80s, Tanner's grandson, Phil, led a band known as the Skillet Lickers II.

Albums: *Gid Tanner* (70s), *Gid Tanner & His Skillet Lickers* (1973), *Gid Tanner & His Skillet Lickers, Volume 2* (1975), *Kickapoo Medicine Show* (1977), *A Day At The County Fair* (1981), *A Corn Licker Still In Georgia* (80s).

Skinner, Jimmie

b. 29 April 1909, Blue Lick, near Berea, Kentucky, USA, d. 27 October 1979. He relocated with the family to Hamilton, near Cincinnati, Ohio in 1926, where he found work in a factory. In 1928, he heard recordings by Jimmie Rodgers that so impressed him that he bought a guitar and set out to be a singer. He first broadcast on WCKY Covington and in the early 30s with his brother Esmer, he recorded two instrumentals for Gennett, though neither was released. Skinner began to write songs and continued to perform in his local area. In 1941, he was signed by RCA but again due to war-time material shortages he had no releases. During the next few years, he played regularly on several stations including WHPD Mt.Orab, Ohio and WHTN Huntingdon, West Virginia. He finally had record releases after recording for Red Barn Records although he had to handle distribution himself. His recording of 'Will You Be Satisfied That Way' was popular enough in Knoxville to get him a regular spot on WROL. In the late 40s, he and a partner took over the Cincinnati Radio Artist label and he issued several of his recordings including 'Don't Give Your Heart To A Rambler' (revived by Travis Tritt in 1991) and 'Doin' My Time'. The same year Ernest Tubb had major US country chart success with his song 'Let's Say Goodbye Like We Said Hello'.

In 1949, Skinner achieved his first chart hit with 'Tennessee Border'. In 1951, he was working both as a disc jockey on WNOP Covington and as an entertainer. He decided that there should be a special shop for the wants of country music followers and accordingly, with Lou Epstein, he opened *The Jimmie Skinner Music Center* in Cincinnati. The shop, which sold records, instruction manuals, song books and magazines by mail order, proved a tremendous success. He publicized the shop in trade publications and even presented live radio programmes from it. Other artists quickly realised the value and contributed adverts for their own records. He also later formed his own Vetco record label. The resultant publicity saw Skinner become a nationally known artist, although he had no major chart success during several years with Capitol and Decca. He joined Mercury in 1956 and the following year had a Top 10 country hit with 'I Found My Girl In The U.S.A.'. He had written the song as his answer to the Bobby Helms hit 'Fraulein'. Skinner then wrote an answer called 'I'm The Girl In The U.S.A', which was recorded by fellow Mercury artist, Connie Hill. Between 1958 and 1960, he had 8 further country hits including 'What Makes A Man Wander', 'Dark Hollow' and 'Reasons To Live'. Skinner never became a major star but he was always busily connected with the industry through his music store and his radio and touring work. In 1974, he decided to move to Nashville; he thought it more suited to his songwriting ideas but he still continued to tour his beloved Kentucky and Ohio. It was on such an occasion that, following a show near Louisville, he complained of pains in his arm and immediately headed for his

Henderson, Nashville home, where he died on 27 October 1979, presumably as the result of an heart attack. Noted writer John Morthland described his style as 'Unusually eloquent. He was probably the most underrated of those who sought to follow in the footsteps of Jimmie Rodgers and always less maudlin than most white country blues singers'.

Albums: *Songs That Make The Jukebox Play* (1957), *Country Singer* (1961), *Sings Jimmie Rodgers* (1962), *Jimmy Skinner (The Kentucky Colonel)* (1963), *Country Blues* (1964), *Jimmie Skinner's Number One Bluegrass* (1966), *Sings Bluegrass* (1968), *Have You Said Hello To Jesus Today* (c.1969), *Sings The Blues* (1975), *Bluegrass Volume 2* (1976), with Joe Clark *Old Joe Clark* (1976), *Jimmie Skinner And His Country Music Friends* (1976), *Number 1 Bluegrass* (1977), *Requestfully Yours* (c.1977), *Another Saturday Night* (1988).

S-K-O

This US group comprised three songwriters, Thom Schuyler, Fred Knobloch and Paul Overstreet, who decided to work together as an occasional band. Schuyler (b. 1952, Bethlehem, Pennsylvania, USA) was, by trade, a carpenter, whose songwriting abilities were discovered by Eddie Rabbitt when he was making alterations to the latter's studio. Schuyler wrote '16th Avenue', 'Hurricane' and 'I Don't Know Where To Start' and had *Blue Heart*, released by Capitol Records, which led to some entries on the US country chart. With Paul Overstreet, he wrote 'I Fell In Love Again Last Night' (the Forester Sisters), and 'A Long Line Of Love' (Michael Martin Murphey), both US country number 1 hits. Knobloch, pronounced 'no-block', (b. Jackson, Mississippi, USA) worked in Atlanta, Georgia and Los Angeles, California, before moving to Nashville, Tennessee in 1983. He wrote 'The Whole World's In Love When You're Lonely' and 'Julianne' (the Everly Brothers). As Fred Knoblock (sic), he had a US pop hit with 'Why Not Me' and country hits with 'Memphis' and, with Susan Allanson, 'Killin' Time'. Overstreet (b. VanCleave, Mississippi, USA), a more traditional country songwriter, wrote both 'On The Other Hand' and 'Forever And Ever, Amen' with Don Schlitz (both US country number 1 hits for Randy Travis); 'Diggin' Up Bones' with Al Gore (also a number 1 for Travis); and 'You're Still New To Me' with Paul Davis (a US country number 1 for Marie Osmond and Paul Davis). Fred was briefly married to Dolly Parton's sister, Freida. The first S-K-O release, 'You Can't Stop Love', made the US country Top

10. Their second single, 'Baby's Got A New Baby', topped the US country chart in 1987. At that time, Overstreet opted for a solo career and he had a further US country number 1 with Tanya Tucker and Paul Davis with a song he wrote with Don Schlitz, 'I Won't Take Less Than Your Love'. He also wrote 'You Again' (the Forester Sisters), 'When You Say Nothing At All' (Keith Whitley) and 'Deeper Than The Holler' (Randy Travis), all with Don Schlitz and all US country number 1 hits. His place was taken by songwriter, Craig Bickhardt (b. Pennsylvania, USA), thus making the group S-K-B. Bickhardt had a band, Wire And Wood, which opened for many well-known acts in the early 70s. He wrote or co-wrote 'Finally Found A Reason' (Art Garfunkel), 'I'm Falling In Love Tonight' (the Judds), 'Never Been In Love' (Randy Meisner), 'You're The Power' (Kathy Mattea), 'Give A Little Love To Me' (the Judds), 'I Know Where I'm Going' (the Judds), and songs for the film, *Tender Mercies*. S-K-B finally had a US Top 10 country single with 'Givers And Takers' before disbanding in 1989.
Albums: with Schuyler, Knobloch, Overstreet *S-K-O* (1987), with Schuyler, Knobloch, Bickhardt *No Easy Horses* (1987).

Sledd, Patsy

b. Patsy Randolph, 29 January 1944, Falcon, Missouri, USA. One of ten children, she began to play the guitar and sing at the age of 10. She entertained locally when 15, performing as the Randolph Sisters with one of her sisters but soon followed a solo career. She was featured on the *Ozark Opry* and worked with a band on Austin's *Nashville Opry* before moving to Nashville in 1965. She joined Roy Acuff and toured with him all over the States, to the Caribbean and to Vietnam. Her performances led to solo spots on *Hee-Haw* and the *Mid-Western Hayride*. In 1961, she recorded for United Artists and in 1971 for Epic but failed to chart on either label. She moved to Mega in 1972 and gained her first US country chart hit with 'Nothing Can Stop My Loving You'. Her biggest chart hit 'Chip Chip' came in 1974, the year she made her British debut at London's Wembley Festival as a support member of the George Jones-Tammy Wynette Show. When Jones' mother died suddenly and the two stars returned to the States without appearing at the Festival, she found herself more the star than the support and gained respect from the crowd for her fine performance with the Jones Boys. Surprisingly very little seems to have been heard of her since that time. After a minor hit with 'The Cowboy And The Lady' in 1976, her name was missing from the charts until 1987 when, recording on Showtime Records, she briefly charted with 'Don't Stay If You Don't Love Me'. It rather seems to have been her that didn't stay.
Albums: *Yours Sincerely* (1973), *Chip Chip* (1974).

Smith, Arthur

b. 1 April 1921, Clinton, South Carolina, USA. After the family moved to Kershaw when he was four years old, his father ran the town band and his son played trumpet with it. A few years later, by now playing guitar, mandolin and banjo, he formed a country band with two of his brothers. He graduated with honours in the late 30s but turned down lucrative employment, deciding instead to form a Dixieland Jazz Band, the Crackerjacks, which played on WSPA Spartanburg. After his brothers were drafted, he worked on WBT Charlotte, until joining the Navy in 1944. He played in the Navy band, wrote songs and on his return to civilian life organised variety shows featuring country and gospel music on WBT and WBT-TV and in 1947, also gave bible classes. In 1948, he achieved Top 10 US country chart success with his MGM recordings of 'Guitar Boogie' and 'Banjo Boogie', with the former crossing over to the US pop chart and introducing many people to the potential of the electric guitar. (*Billboard* initially seemed unsure in which chart to place the recording.) Fender began to produce his 'Broadcaster' model, soon changing the name to 'Telecaster', the start of that instrument's popularity. The following year 'Boomerang', another guitar instrumental became a country hit. (In 1959, 'Guitar Boogie' was a US and UK pop hit for the Virtues and the same year became British guitarist Bert Weedon's first UK pop hit, although both recorded it as 'Guitar Boogie Shuffle'.) *The Arthur Smith Show* on television started in the 50s and became so popular that by the mid-70s, it was still networked to most of the States and artists from all fields were eager guests. Smith and the Crackerjacks (no longer a jazz band) recorded regularly over the years for various labels with gospel music always prominent. Smith later became a deacon in a Baptist church.
By the 70s, he had also extended his business interests to include record, show and commercial productions and was also a director of a large insurance company. For a time in the mid-70s, he even ran a chain of supermarkets and formed the Arthur Smith Inns Corporation. In 1973, he and banjoist Don Reno instigated legal action against

Warner Brothers over the use of 'Duellin' Banjos' as the theme music for the film *Deliverance*. They claimed that the music was based on a tune called 'Feudin' Banjos', written by Smith and recorded by them in 1955. After approximately two years of legal wrangling they won the case, received damages and legal rulings about future royalties. 'Duellin' Banjos' was named 'Best Country Music Song Of The Year' in 1973. The following year George Hamilton IV recorded his Bluegrass Gospel album at Smith's recording studio in Charlotte, North Carolina. Smith has copyrighted more than 500 songs, only one of which, 'Our Pilot Knows The Sea', is co-authored. In 1991, he published his first book, *Apply It To Life*. It includes the words and music to 10 of his best-known hymns, which have also been released as an album with vocals by Johnny Cash, George Beverly Shea, George Hamilton IV and Smith himself with the Crossroads Quartet. This artist should not be confused with Fiddlin' Arthur Smith or with Arthur Q. Smith (real name James A. Pritchett), a Knoxville songwriter, who sometimes co-wrote songs with Jim Eanes.

Albums: *Foolish Questions* (1955), *Specials* (1955), *Fingers On Fire* (1955), *Fingers On Fire* (1958), *Mr Guitar* (1962), *Arthur Smith And The Crossroads Quartet* (1962), *Arthur 'Guitar Boogie' Smith Goes To Town* (1963), *In Person* (1963), *Arthur 'Guitar' Smith And Voices* (1963), *The Arthur Smith Show* (1964), *Original Guitar Boogie* (1964), *Down Home With Arthur 'Guitar Boogie' Smith* (1964), *Great Country & Western Hits* (1965), *Arthur Smith & Son* (1966), *Presents A Tribute To Jim Reeves* (1966), *Guitar Boogie* (1968), *The Guitars Of Arthur 'Guitar Boogie' Smith* (1968), *Arthur Smith* (1970), *Battling Banjos* (1973), with George Hamilton IV *Singing On The Mountain* (1973), *Guitars Galore* (1975), *Feudin' Again* with Don Reno (1979), *Jumpin' Guitar* (1987), with Johnny Cash, George Beverly Shea and George Hamilton IV *Apply It To Life* (1991). Further reading: *Apply It To Life*, Arthur Smith.

Smith, Arthur 'Fiddlin'

b. 1898, Bold Springs, Humphreys County, Tennessee, USA. One of the 14 children of an old-time fiddle player, he started to play the fiddle at the age of four and began playing locally in his teens but seriously thought of a musical career around 1925, when he worked as a lineman for the railroad. Several of his siblings also played instruments and around 1929, he first played on the *Grand Ole Opry* with his guitar playing brother, Homer. In 1930, he teamed with brothers Sam and Kirk McGee and played the *Opry* as The Dixieliners, soon after giving up his railroad work and becoming a full-time professional musician. His excellent playing, coupled with the McGees' guitar and banjo, soon made the Dixieliners one of the most influential of the *Opry* bands, who even through the Depression were in great demand. Surprisingly they did not record together until reunited in the 60s. Smith recorded under his own name and was accompanied by the Delmores, probably because the record company initially thought that their name would attract even more attention.

He first recorded fiddle tunes for Bluebird Records in 1935, including his now famous 'Mocking Bird'. At the time they were not successful and to keep his contract, his next recordings featured vocals, with 'More Pretty Girls Than One' being very successful. He left both the *Opry* and the McGees in 1938 and relocated to Hollywood, where he appeared in b-westerns and toured with Jimmy Wakely and the Sons Of The Pioneers, played all over the States and wrote songs. In the early 50s 'Beautiful Brown Eyes', co-written by Smith and Alton Delmore, was a US country and pop hit for Jimmy Wakely and also for pop singer Rosemary Clooney. He eventually returned to Nashville in the late 50s, where he rejoined his old friends the McGees. This time they did record together and played numerous folk festivals and other concert appearances. Smith, who also played banjo died in 1973. Noted authority Charles K. Wolfe in *The Grand Ole Opry, The Early Years 1925-35* comments that 'Arthur Smith's fiddling style was more influential in the South than that of any other fiddler except possibly, Clayton McMichen'. This artist should not be confused with Arthur 'Guitar Boogie' Smith or Arthur Q. Smith (real name James A. Pritchett), a Knoxville songwriter, who sometimes co-wrote songs with Jim Eanes.

Albums: with Sam & Kirk McGee *Fiddlin'* (early 60s) *Arthur Smith & His Dixieliners* (1962), *Rare Old Fiddle Tunes (Fiddlin' Arthur Smith & His Dixieliners)* (1962), with Sam & Kirk McGee *Old Timers Of The Grand Ole Opry* (1964), McGee Brothers and Arthur Smith *Milk 'Em In The Evening Blues* (1965), *Fiddlin' Arthur Smith, Volume 1 & 2* (1978).

Smith, Cal

b. Calvin Grant Shofner, 7 April 1932, Gans, Oklahoma, USA. The family moved to California, where he met the rodeo-rider Todd Mason, becoming his stooge for knife and bullwhip tricks. Mason taught him how to play the guitar and at the age of 15 he was a vocalist with the San Francisco country band, Kitty Dibble And Her Dude Ranch Wranglers. After military service, he played bass for Bill Drake, whose brother Jack was a prominent member of Ernest Tubb's Texas Troubadours. This led to him becoming master of ceremonies under the name of Grant Shofner, for Ernest Tubb and the Texas Troubadours from 1962-68. His first appearance on one of Tubb's recordings was 'The Great Speckled Bird' in 1963. Tubb arranged a record contract with Kapp and Smith's first record on the US country charts was 'The Only Thing I Want' in 1967. Two years with Decca followed and he finally broke through with 'I've Found Someone Of My Own' and a chart-topping Bill Anderson song, 'The Lord Knows I'm Drinking'. He joined MCA in 1973 and had further chart-toppers with the Don Wayne songs, 'Country Bumpkin' and 'It's Time To Pay The Fiddler'. A 1974 hit, also written by Bill Anderson, was called 'Between Lust And Watching TV' and he recorded a popular 'mother' song, 'Mama's Face'. His last Top 20 hit on the US country charts was 'I Just Came Home To Count The Memories' in 1977. Although Smith has a good voice, he was often landed with mediocre material he subsequently left the business for several years. He joined Ernest Tubb on his double-album *The Legend And The Legacy* although it's bizarre to hear two men singing 'Our Baby's Book'.

Albums: *All The World Is Lonely Now* (1966), *Goin' To Cal's Place* (1967), *Travellin' Man* (1968), *At Home With Cal* (1968), *It Takes Me All Night Long* (1969), *Drinking Champagne* (1969), *Country Hit Parade* (1970), *I've Found Someone Of My Own* (1972), *Swinging Doors* (1973), *Country Bumpkin* (1974), *It's Time To Pay The Fiddler* (1975), *My Kind Of Country* (1975), *Jason's Farm* (1976), *I Just Came Home To Count The Memories* (1977), *Stories Of Life* (1986).

Smith, Carl

b. 15 March 1927, Maynardsville, Tennessee, USA. The legendary Roy Acuff also came from Maynardsville and was Smith's hero. Smith sold seeds to pay for his first guitar and then cut grass to pay for lessons. He became a regular on a Knoxville country radio station, served in the navy in World War II, and was discovered by the 40s country singer, Molly O'Day, which led to a recording contract with Columbia Records. In 1951 he made his US country chart debut with 'Let's Live A Little', had a double-sided success with 'If Teardrops Were Pennies'/'Mr. Moon' and followed it with a number 1, 'Let Old Mother Nature Have Her Way'. His impressive tally of 41 chart records during the 50s included four more chart-toppers, 'Don't Just Stand There', 'Are You

Carl Smith

Teasing Me?' (both 1952), 'Hey, Joe' (1953) and 'Loose Talk' (1955) as well as having success with 'This Orchid Means Goodbye', 'Cut Across Shorty' and 'Ten Thousand Drums'. Smith was a ballad singer with a rich, mature voice and, as he preferred steel guitars and fiddles to modern instrumentation, he did not cross over to the pop market. Known as the Tall Gentleman, he was a natural for television and for several years he hosted a very successful country series in Canada, *Carl Smith's Country Music Hall*. He also appeared in the westerns, *The Badge Of Marshal Brennan* (1957) and *Buffalo Gun* (1961), the latter with Webb Pierce and Marty Robbins. Smith had a tempestuous marriage to June Carter from the Carter Family and their daughter, Carlene Carter, is also a recording artist. After their divorce and in 1957, Smith married Goldie Hill, who had had her own number 1 country single with 'I Let The Stars Get In My Eyes' (1953). Although Smith rarely made the US country Top 10 after the 50s, he had hits until well into the 70s and his total of 93 has rarely been passed. In the 80s, Carl re-recorded his hits for new albums, but it was only a half-hearted comeback. His main interest is in his prize-winning quarter-horses, which he raises on a 500-acre ranch outside Nashville.

Albums: *Carl Smith* (1956), *Softly And Tenderly* (with the Carter Sisters) (1956), *Sentimental Songs* (1957), *Smith's The Name* (1957), *Sunday Down South* (1957), *Let's Live A Little* (1958), *The Carl Smith Touch* (1960), *Easy To Please* (1962), *Tall, Tall Gentleman* (1963), *There Stands The Glass* (1964), *I Want To Live And Love* (1965), *Kisses Don't Lie* (1965), *Man With A Plan* (1966), *Satisfaction Guaranteed* (1967), *Country Gentleman* (1967), *The Country Gentleman Sings His Favourites* (1967), *Country On My Mind* (1968), *Deep Water* (1968), *Gentleman In Love* (1968), *Take It Like A Man* (1969), *A Tribute To Roy Acuff* (1969), *Faded Love And Winter Roses* (1969), *Carl Smith And The Tunesmiths* (1970), *Anniversary Album* (1970), *I Love You Because* (1970), *Knee Deep In The Blues* (1971), *Carl Smith Sings Bluegrass* (1971), *Don't Say You're Mine* (1972), *The Great Speckled Bird* (1972), *If This Is Goodbye* (1972), *The Girl I Love* (1975), *The Way I Lose My Mind* (1975), *This Lady Loving Me* (1977), *Silver Tongued Cowboy* (1978), *Greatest Hits, Volume 1* (1980), *Legendary* (1981), *Old Lonesome Times* (1988).

Smith, Connie

b. Constance June Meadows, 14 August 1941, Elkhart, Indiana, USA but was raised in West Virginia and Ohio. One of 14 children, she longed to be a country singer and taught herself to play the guitar whilst in hospital recovering from a leg injury, caused by an accident with a lawn mower. She sang at local events as a teenager and appeared on several radio and television shows. She married and for a time settled to the life of a housewife but after the birth of her first child, again, took to singing. Her break came in 1963, when she was booked to sing at the Frontier Ranch, a park near Columbus. Headlining the show was Bill Anderson, who was so impressed with her performance that he invited her to Nashville to appear on the *Ernest Tubb Record Shop* live show. Two months later, she returned to make demo recordings, which won her an RCA contract. In 1964, her recording of Anderson's song 'Once A Day' became her first hit, spending 8 weeks at number 1 and 28 weeks in the US country charts. She became an overnight success and in the next five years added more Top 10 hits including 'If I Talk To Him', 'The Hurtin's All Over', 'Cincinnati, Ohio' and 'Baby's Back Again'. She later recorded an album of Anderson's songs, although she did not work with him. She became a member of the *Grand Ole Opry* in 1965, was much in demand for tours and concert appearances and appeared in such films as *Road To Nashville, Las Vegas Hillbillies* and *Second Fiddle To An Old Guitar*. In the early 70s, further Top 10 hits included 'I Never Once Stopped Loving You', 'Just One Time' and 'Just For What I Am' and tours included Europe, Australia and the Far East. She moved to Columbia in 1973, where her first hit came with a recording of her own song 'You've Got Me Right Where You Want Me' and in 1977 to Monument, where her biggest hit was a country version of 'I Just Want To Be Your Everything' (a pop number 1 for Andy Gibb). From 1979-85, she was absent from the charts as she retired from active participation in music, apart from some *Opry* appearances, as she devoted her time to raising her family. A born-again Christian (her eldest son Darren is a missionary), she has performed gospel music on the *Opry* and recorded an album of Hank Williams' gospel songs. She regularly plays the *Opry*, network radio and television shows and delighted her British fans by her appearance in Britain in 1990.

Albums: *Cute 'N' Country* (1965), *The Other Side Of Connie Smith* (1965), *Born To Sing* (1966), *Miss Smith Goes To Nashville* (1966), *Sings Great Sacred Songs* (1966), *Connie In The Country* (1967), *Downtown Country* (1967), *Sings Bill Anderson*

Connie Smith

(1967), *I Love Charley Brown* (1968), *Sunshine And Rain* (1968), *Soul Of Country Music* (1968), *Back In Baby's Arms* (1969), *Connie's Country* (1969), with Nat Stuckey *Young Love* (1969), *I Never Once Stopped Loving You* (1970), *Sunday Morning* (1970), *Come Along And Walk With Me* (1971), *My Heart Has A Mind Of Its Own* (1971), *Just One Time* (1971), *Where Is My Castle* (1971), *If It Ain't Love (And Other Great Dallas Frazier Songs)* (1972), *Ain't We Havin' Us A Good Time'* (1972), *City Lights-Country Favorites* (1972), *A Lady Named Smith* (1973), *Love Is The Look You're Looking For* (1973), *Dream Painter* (1973), *God Is Abundant* (1973), with Nat Stuckey *Even The Bad Times Are Good* (1973), *Collections* (1974), *Connie Smith Now* (1974), *That's The Way Love Goes* (1974), *I Never Knew (What That Song Meant Before)* (1974), *Joy To The World* (1975), *Sings Hank Williams Gospel* (1975), *I Got A Lot Of Hurtin' Done Today* (1975), *I Don't Want To Talk It Over Anymore* (1976), *The Song We Fell In Love To* (1976), *Pure Connie Smith* (1977), *New Horizons* (1978).

Smith, Margo

b. Betty Lou Miller, 9 April 1942, Dayton, Ohio, USA. Smith began her singing career while still at school as a member of the Apple Sisters vocal group. She trained as a teacher but also had hopes of a singing career. She wrote songs in her spare time and eventually made some unsuccessful recordings for Chart Records. In 1975, after changing labels to 20th Century, she made her US country chart debut with her own song, 'There I've Said It' and quit her job as a teacher. She moved to Warner the following year and immediately had two Top 10 country hits with 'Save Your Kisses For Me' and 'Take My Breath Away'. By 1981, she had 20 chart entries including two number 1s, 'Don't Break The Heart That Loves You' and 'It Only Hurts For A Little While'. Several others such as 'If I Give My Heart To You' and 'My Guy' were versions of songs that had already had pop chart success for other singers. She duetted with Norro Wilson ('So Close Again') and Rex Allen Jnr. ('Cup Of Tea'). She was dropped by Warner in 1981 but managed a few minor hits on indie labels (the last being 'Echo Me' on Playback in 1988), but recorded an album for Dot/MCA in 1986. Traditionalists would rate much of her work as country-pop but she is a brilliant yodeler and usually features this now unusual talent for lady vocalists in her stage show.
Albums: *Margo Smith* (1975), *Song Bird* (1976), *Happiness* (1977), *Don't Break The Heart That Loves You* (1978), *Just Margo* (1979), *A Woman* (1979), *Diamonds And Chills* (1980), *Margo Smith* (1986), *The Best Yet* (1988).

Smith, Sammi

b. 5 August 1943, Orange, California, USA. As her father was a serviceman, the family moved around, and when aged only 11, she was singing pop standards in night clubs. She was discovered in 1967 by Johnny Cash's bass player, Marshall Grant. Minor US country hits followed with 'So Long, Charlie Brown' and 'Brownsville Lumberyard'. She toured with Waylon Jennings and befriended a janitor at Columbia Records, Kris Kristofferson. Her warm, husky version of his song, 'Help Me Make It Through The Night', sold two million copies and was voted the Country Music Association's Single of the Year for 1971. Ironically, her record label, Mega, had been formed as a tax write-off and the last thing the owner wanted was a hit record. Smith had further country hits with 'Then You Walk In', 'For The Kids', 'I've Got To Have You', 'The Rainbow In Daddy's Eyes' and 'Today I Started Loving You Again', but she never topped 'Help Me Make It Through The Night' because, as she says, 'It was like following a Rembrandt with a kindergarten sketch'. Smith wrote 'Sand-Covered Angels', recorded by Conway Twitty, and 'Cedartown, Georgia' by Waylon Jennings. At Elektra, she recorded 'As Long As There's A Sunday' and 'Loving Arms' but in the 80s she only had limited US country chart success. Smith's former husband is Willie Nelson's guitarist Jody Payne and, being part Apache herself, she has adopted two Apache children and has an all American Indian band, Apache Spirit. In 1978 she set up the Sammi Smith Scholarship for Apache Advance Education, the aim being to increase the number of Apache lawyers and doctors.
Albums: *He's Everywhere* (1970), *The World Of Sammi Smith* (1971), *Lonesome* (1971), *Something Old, Something New, Something Blue* (1972), *The Toast Of '45* (1973), *The Best Of Sammi Smith* (1974), *Rainbow In Daddy's Eyes* (1974), *Sunshine* (1975), *Today I Started Loving You Again* (1975), *The Very Best Of Sammi Smith* (1975), *As Long As There's A Sunday* (1976), *Help Me Make It Through The Night* (1976), *Her Way* (1976), *New Winds, All Quadrants* (1978), *Mixed Emotions* (1979), *Girl Hero* (1979), *Better Than Ever* (1986), *Here Comes That Rainbow Again* (1990).

382

Snow, Hank

b. Clarence Eugene Snow, 9 May 1914, Brooklyn, near Liverpool, Nova Scotia, Canada. After his parents divorced when he was eight years old, Snow spent four unhappy years with his grandmother, finally running away to re-join his mother when she re-married. His already miserable childhood worsened when he was cruelly ill-treated by his stepfather, which led him to abscond again. This time, though only 12-years-old, it was to sea and he spent the next four years working on fishing boats in the Atlantic where, on several occasions, he almost lost his life. An early interest in music, gained from his mother who had been a pianist for silent films before he was born, led him to sing for fellow crew members. He left the sea and returned home, working wherever he could but seeking a singing career. He gained great inspiration listening to his mother's recordings of Jimmie Rodgers, and acquiring a cheap guitar, practiced the Rodgers' blue yodel, guitar playing and delivery and set out to emulate his idol. He began to sing locally, eventually, through the help of Cecil Landry the station announcer and chief engineer, obtained a weekly unpaid spot on CHNS Halifax on a programme called Down On The Farm, where he became known as 'Clarence Snow and his Guitar' and 'The Cowboy Blue Yodeller'. It was Landry who, in 1934, first suggested the name of Hank, since he reckoned the boy needed a good western name. Snow became a talented guitarist and in the following years always played lead guitar for his own recordings. He met and married his wife, Minnie, in 1936 and for a long time the couple struggled to earn enough money to live on. Eventually through sponsorship, he was given a programme on the network Canadian Farm Hour.

In October 1936, by now known as 'Hank the Yodelling Ranger', he persuaded Hugh Joseph of RCA-Victor, Montreal, to allow him to record two of his own songs - 'Lonesome Blue Yodel' and 'The Prisoned Cowboy'. This marked the start of a recording career destined to set the record of being the longest one that any country artist ever spent with the same record company. Jimmie Rodgers' influence remained with him and when their only son was born in 1937, he was named Jimmie Rodgers Snow. In 1944, after further recordings and regular work in Canada, and having become 'Hank The Singing Ranger', due to the fact that as his voice deepened he found he could no longer yodel, he extended his career to the USA. He played various venues, including the Wheeling Jamboree and in Hollywood, usually appearing with his performing horse, Shawnee. The anticipated breakthrough did not materialize and during the late 40s, he struggled to achieve success. RCA, New York, guardedly informed him that they could not record him until he was known in America but eventually they relented and in 1949 his recording of 'Brand On My Heart' gained him success in Texas. In December 1949, he achieved his first minor country chart hit with 'Marriage Vow'. At the recommendation of fellow Jimmie Rodgers' devotee, Ernest Tubb, he made his debut on the Grand Ole Opry in January 1950, without making a great impression and seriously considered abandoning thoughts of a career in the USA. This idea was forgotten when his self-penned million-seller, 'I'm Moving On', established him for all-time. It spent 44 weeks in the US country charts, 21 at number 1 and even reached number 27 on the US pop charts. In the late 40s, Snow worked on tours with Hank Williams later stating 'I found Hank to be a fine person but the stories about him have been blown completely out of proportion. Take it from me, Hank Williams was okay'. Williams can actually be heard introducing Snow on the 1977 A Tribute To Hank Williams.

Snow formed a booking agency with Colonel Tom Parker and in 1954, they were responsible for Elvis Presley's only Opry performance. Presley sang 'Blue Moon Of Kentucky' but failed to make any impression with the audience that night. Parker, to Snow's chagrin, took over Presley's management, but Presley recorded material associated with Snow including 'A Fool Such As I', 'Old Shep' and later 'I'm Movin' On'. 'I don't mean to brag but Elvis was a big fan of mine and he was always sitting around singing my songs', says Snow. After his initial breakthrough, Snow became an internationally famous star whose records sold in their millions and between 1950-80, he amassed 85 country chart hits. Further number 1 records were 'The Golden Rocket', 'I Don't Hurt Anymore', 'Let Me Go, Lover', 'Hello Love' and the tongue twisting 'I've Been Everywhere'. The latter, which gave him his second million-seller, was an Australian song originally naming Australian towns but Snow reckoned it would not mean much to Americans and requested the writer to change it to suit. He was later proud to state he recorded it on the sixth take, in spite of the fact that there were 93 place names to memorize. Hank Snow's penchant for wearing a toupee, that does not always appear to fit correctly, has at times caused mirth and many people believe he deliberately emphasizes it. Legend has it that, humorously for

Hank Snow

the audience, one night his fiddler player removed it with his bow on stage and understandably received instant dismissal from his boss. Some album sleeves clearly indicate the tragedy; album such as *My Nova Scotia Home* are most beautiful designs, while the noose on *Songs Of Tragedy* easily makes it one of the most remembered.

It is generally assumed that the character played by Henry Gibson in Robert Altman's controversial 1975 film *Nashville* was modelled on Snow. Over the years his melodic voice, perfect diction and distinctive guitar playing make his recordings immediately identifiable and his band, the Rainbow Ranch Boys, has always contained some of country music's finest musicians. His songwriting gained him election to the *Nashville Songwriters International Hall Of Fame* in 1978 and the following year he was inducted to the *Country Music Hall Of Fame*, the plaque rightly proclaiming him as one of country music's most influential entertainers. In 1981, after a 45-year association, he parted company from RCA stating it was 'because I would not record the type of things that are going today'. Snow has not recorded since, feeling that 'I have done everything in the recording line that was possible'. He resisted over-commercializing country music during his long career and says of the modern scene, that '80% of today's would be country music is a joke and not fit to listen to - suggestive material and a lot of it you can't even understand the words, just a lot of loud music'. Snow has played in many countries all over the world, being a particular favourite in the UK. An ability to handle all types of material has led to him being classed among the most versatile country artists of all time. Remembering his own unhappy childhood he set up a foundation in Nashville to help abused children. He rarely tours now but maintains his regular *Opry* appearances and still is readily recognized by his flamboyant stage costumes, which have been his hallmark over the years.

Albums: *Hank Snow Sings* (1952), *Country Classics* (1952), *Salutes Jimmie Rodgers* (1953), *Country Guitar* (1954), *Just Keep A-Moving* (1955), *Old Doc Brown & Other Narrations* (1955), *Country & Western Jamboree* (1957), *Sacred Songs* (1958), *The Hank Snow E-Z Method of Spanish Guitar* (c.1958), *When Tragedy Struck* (1959), *Sings Jimmie Rodgers Songs* (1959), *The Singing Ranger* (1959), *Souvenirs* (1961), *Big Country Hits (Songs I Hadn't Recorded Till Now)* (1961), *Southern Cannonball* (1962), *One & Only Hank Snow* (1962), with Anita Carter *Together Again* (1962), *Railroad Man* (1963), *I've Been Everywhere* (1963), *The Last Ride* (1963), *More Hank Snow Souvenirs* (1964), *Old & Great Songs by Hank Snow* (1964), *Songs of Tragedy* (1964), with Chet Atkins *Reminiscing* (1964), *Gloryland March* (1965), *Heartbreak Trail* (1965), *Highest Bidder And Other Favorites* (1965), *Your Favorite Country Hits* (1965), *Gospel Train* (1966), *This Is My Story* (1966), *The Guitar Stylings of Hank Snow* (1966), *Gospel Stylings* (1966), *Travelin' Blues* (1966), *Spanish Fireball* (1967), *My Early Country Favorites* (1967), *Snow In Hawaii* (1967), *Christmas With Hank Snow* (1967), *My Nova Scotia Home* (1967), *My Nova Scotia Home* (different to last) (1968), *Lonely And Heartsick* (1968), *Somewhere Along Life's Highway* (1968), *Tales of The Yukon* (1968), *I Went To Your Wedding* (1969), *Snow In All Seasons* (1969), *Hits Covered By Snow* (1969), *Cure For The Blues* (1970), *In Memory of Jimmie Rodgers* (1970), *Memories Are Made Of This* (1970), with Chet Atkins *C.B. Atkins & C.E. Snow By Special Request* (1970), *Wreck Of The Old 97* (1971), *Award Winners* (1971), *Tracks & Trains* (1971), *Lonesome Whistle* (1972), *The Jimmie Rodgers Story* (1972), *Legend Of Old Doc Brown* (1972), *Snowbird* (1973), *When My Blue Moon Turns To Gold Again* (1973), *Grand Ole Opry Favorites* (1973), *Hello Love* (1974), *I'm Moving On* (1974), *Now Is The Hour - For Me To Sing To My Friends In New Zealand* (1974), *That's You And Me* (1974), *You're Easy To Love* (1975), *All About Trains* (1975, one side Jimmie Rodgers), with Rodgers *Live From Evangel Temple* (1976), *#104 - Still Movin' On* (1977), *Living Legend* (1978), *Mysterious Lady* (1979), *Instrumentally Yours* (1979), with Kelly Foxton *Lovingly Yours* (1980), *By Request* (1981), with Kelly Foxton *Win Some, Lose Some, Lonesome* (1981), with Willie Nelson *Brand On My Heart* (1985), Compilations: *Hits, Hits & More Hits* (1968), *Hank Snow, The Singing Ranger Volume 1 (1949-1953)* (1989), *Hank Snow, The Singing Ranger Volume 2 (1953-1958)* (1990), *Hank Snow, The Thesaurus Transcriptions (1950-1956)* (1991), *Hank Snow, The Singing Ranger Volume 3 (1958-1969)* 12 CD set (1992).

Sonnier, Jo-el

b. 2 October 1946, Rayne, Louisiana, USA. The son of sharecroppers, Sonnier (pronounced Sawn-ya) was working in cottonfields from the age of five. He began singing and playing accordion, worked on local radio and recorded his first single, 'Tes Yeaux Bleus' (Your Blue Eyes) when aged 13. He recorded his 'white roots cajun music' for the Swallow and Goldband labels, and when 26 years old, moved to California and then to Nashville in search of national success. In 1976 he recorded Lefty Frizzell's 'Always Late (With Your Kisses)' for Mercury and then formed a band called Friends, which included Albert Lee, David Lindley and Garth Hudson. His session work has included 'Cajun Born' for Johnny Cash and 'America Without Tears' for Elvis Costello. In 1987 Sonnier was signed to RCA and Steve Winwood guested on 'Rainin' In My Heart', a track on *Come On Joe*. He had a country hit with a frenzied version of Richard Thompson's 'Tear-Stained Letter'. He has toured the USA with Alabama and the Charlie Daniel's Band and, by all accounts, his UK debut at the Mean Fiddler in 1989 was electrifying. He was once known as the 'Cajun Valentino'.

Albums: *Cajun Life* (1980), *Come On Joe* (1988), *Have A Little Faith* (1989), *Tears Of Joy* (1991), *The Complete Mercury Sessions* (1992).

Sons Of The Pioneers

The Sons Of The Pioneers was founded in 1933 by Leonard Slye (aka Roy Rogers), when he recruited two friends - Bob Nolan (b. Robert Clarence Nobles, 1 April 1908, New Brunswick, Canada) and Tim Spencer (b. Vernon Spencer, 13 July 1908, Webb City, Missouri, USA) - to reform a singing trio, known originally as the O-Bar-O Cowboys, and to undergo a name change to the Pioneer Trio. When they found regular radio work in Los Angeles, they added fiddle player Hugh Farr (b. 6 December 1903, Llano, Texas, USA). Someone suggested that they looked too young to be pioneers so they became the Sons Of The Pioneers. They were signed to US Decca Records in 1935, and Hugh's brother, Karl (b. Karl Marx Farr, 25 April 1909, Rochelle, Texas, USA) joined as a guitarist. The Sons Of The Pioneers sang in numerous western films and when Rogers was groomed as a singing cowboy in 1937, he was replaced as lead singer by Lloyd Perryman (b. Lloyd Wilson Perryman, 29 January 1917, Ruth, Arkansas, USA). Their best-selling records include 'Cool Water' and 'Tumbling Tumbleweeds', both written by Nolan. Spencer wrote the country standards, 'Cigarettes, Whisky And Wild, Wild Woman' and 'Room Full Of Roses'. Due to throat problems, Tim Spencer retired from performing in 1949 but managed the group for some years. He died on 26 April 1974. Lloyd Perryman, who became the leader of the group when Spencer and Nolan left in 1949, died on 31 May 1977. On 20 September 1961, Karl Farr collapsed and died on stage after being irritated when a guitar-string broke, while his brother survived until 17 April 1980. Nolan died on 16 June 1980, requesting that his ashes be scattered across the Nevada desert. Other members of The Sons Of The Pioneers include Pat Brady, Ken Carson, Ken Curtis, Tommy Doss and Shug Fisher. Many critics rate the Perryman, Curtis and Doss recordings, which include the 1949 versions of 'Riders In The Sky' and 'Room Full Of Roses', as the best. Despite personnel changes, The Sons Of The Pioneers' recordings reflect a love of God, the hard-working life of a cowboy, and an admiration for 'home on the range'. The legacy of the Hollywood cowboys is still with us in the work of Ian Tyson but his songs paint a less romantic picture.

Albums: *Cowboy Hymns And Spirituals* (1952), *Western Classics* (1953), *25 Favourite Cowboy Songs* (1955), *How Great Thou Art* (1957), *One Man's Songs* (1957), *Wagons West* (1958), *Cool Water (And 17 Timeless Favourites)* (1959), *Room Full Of Roses* (1960), *Lure Of The West* (1961), *Westward Ho!* (1961), *Tumbleweed Trail* (1962), *Good Old Country Music* (1963), *Trail Dust* (1963), *Country Fare* (1964), *Down Memory Lane* (1964), *Legends Of The West* (1965), *The Sons Of The Pioneers Sing The Songs Of Bob Nolan* (1966), *The Sons Of The Pioneers Sing Campfire Favourites* (1967), *San Antonio Rose And Other Country Favourites* (1968), *South Of The Border* (1968), *The Sons Of The Pioneers Visit The South Seas* (1969), *Riders In The Sky* (1973), *A Country And Western Songbook* (1977), *Sons Of The Pioneers - Volumes 1 & 2* (previously unissued radio transcriptions) (1980), *Let's Go West Again* (1981). Compilations: *The Sons Of The Pioneers - Columbia Historic Edition* (1982), *20 Of The Best* (1985), *Radio Transcriptions, Volumes 1-4* (1987), *Cool Water, Vol. 1 (1945-46)* (1987), *Teardrops In My Heart, Vol. 2 (1946-47)* (1987), *A Hundred And Sixty Acres, Vol. 3 (1946-47)* (1987), *Riders In The Sky, Vol. 4 (1947-49)* (1987), *Land Beyond The Sun, Vol. 5 (1949-50)* (1987).

Further reading: *Hear My Song: The Story Of The Celebrated Sons Of The Pioneers*.

South, Joe

b. Joe Souter, 28 February 1940, Atlanta, Georgia, USA. South was obsessed with technology and, as a child, he developed his own radio station with a transmission area of a mile. A novelty song, 'The Purple People Eater Meets The Witch Doctor', sold well in 1958, and he became a session guitarist in both Nashville and Muscle Shoals. South backed Eddy Arnold, Aretha Franklin, Wilson Pickett, Marty Robbins and, in particular, Bob Dylan (*Blonde On Blonde*) and Simon And Garfunkel (most of *The Sounds Of Silence* LP). His 1962 single, 'Masquerade', was released in the UK, but his first writing/producing successes came with the Tams' 'Untie Me' and various Billy Joe Royal singles including 'Down In The Boondocks' and 'I Knew You When'. In 1968, he sang and played several instruments on Royal's *Introspect*. One track, 'Games People Play', made number 12 in the US charts and number 6 in the UK, and he also played guitar and sang harmony on Boots Randolph's cover version. The song's title was taken from Eric Berne's best selling book about the psychology of human relationships. Another song title, '(I Never Promised You A) Rose Garden' came from a novel by Hannah Green, and was a transatlantic hit for country singer, Lynn Anderson. 'These Are Not My People' was a US country hit for Freddy Weller, 'Birds Of A Feather' was made popular by Paul Revere And The Raiders, but, more significantly, 'Hush' became Deep Purple's first US Top 10 hit in 1968. South himself made number 12 in the US with 'Walk A Mile In My Shoes', which was also featured by Elvis Presley in concert, but his own career was not helped by a drugs bust, a pretentious single 'I'm A Star', and a poor stage presence. He told one audience to 'start dancing around the hall, then when you come in front of the stage, each one of you can kiss my ass.' South's songs reflect southern life but they also reflect his own insecurities and it is not surprising that he stopped performing. He had heeded his own words, 'Don't It Make You Want To Go Home'.

Albums: *Introspect* (1968 - released in the UK as *Games People Play*), *Don't It Make You Want To Go Home* (1969), *Walkin' Shoes* (1970), *So The Seeds Are Growing* (1971), *Midnight Rainbows* (1975), *Joe South, You're The Reason, To Have, To Hold And To Let Go* (1976), *Look Inside* (1976). Compilations: *Joe South's Greatest Hits* (1970), *The Joe South Story* (1971).

Sovine, Red

b. Woodrow Wilson Sovine, 17 July 1918, Charleston, West Virginia, USA, d. 4 April 1980. Sovine was taught the guitar by his mother and was working professionally by the time he was 17 on WCHS Charleston with Johnny Bailes and then as part of Jim Pike And His Carolina Tarheels. In 1948 Sovine formed his own band, The Echo Valley Boys, and became a regular on *Louisiana Hayride*. Sovine acquired the nickname of 'The Old Syrup Sopper' following the sponsorship by Johnny Fair Syrup of some radio shows, and the title is apt for such narrations as 'Daddy's Girl'.

Sovine recorded for US Decca Records and first made the country charts with 'Are You Mine?', a duet with Goldie Hill. Later that year, a further duet, this time with Webb Pierce, 'Why Baby Why', made number 1 on the US country charts. They followed this with the tear-jerking narration, 'Little Rosa', which became a mainstay of Sovine's act. From 1954 Sovine was a regular at *Grand Ole Opry* and, in all, he had 31 US country chart entries. He particularly scored with maudlin narrations about truckdrivers and his successes include 'Giddyup Go' (a US country number 1 about a truckdriver being reunited with his son), 'Phantom 309' (a truck-driving ghost story!) and his million-selling saga of a crippled boy and his CB radio, 'Teddy Bear' (1976). Sequels and parodies of 'Teddy Bear' abound, Sovine refused to record 'Teddy Bear's Last Ride', which became a US country hit for Diana Williams. He retaliated with 'Little Joe' to indicate that Teddy Bear was not dead after all. Among his own compositions are 'I Didn't Jump The Fence' and 'Missing You', which was a UK hit for Jim Reeves. Sovine recorded 'The Hero' as a tribute to John Wayne and his son, Roger Wayne Sovine, was named in his honour. The young Sovine was briefly a country singer, making the lower end of the US country charts with 'Culman, Alabam' and 'Little Bitty Nitty Gritty Dirt Town'. Sovine's country music owed nothing to contemporary trends but his sentimentality was popular in UK clubs. He had no big-time image and, whilst touring the UK, he made a point of visiting specialist country music shops. In 1980 Sovine died of a heart attack at the wheel of his car in Nashville. The following year, as CB radio hit the UK, a reissue of 'Teddy Bear' reached number 5, his first UK chart entry.

Albums: *Red Sovine* (1957), *Country Music Time* (1957), *The One And Only Red Sovine* (1961), *Golden Country Ballads Of The 60's* (1962), *Red Sovine* (1964), *Red Sovine - Fine* (1964), *Little Rosa* (1965), *Town And Country Action* (1965), *Country Music Time* (1966), *Giddyup Go* (1966), *I Didn't Jump The Fence* (1967), *Farewell So Long Goodbye* (1967), *Phantom 309* (1967), *The Nashville Sound Of Red Sovine* (1967), *Sunday With Sovine* (1968), *Tell Maude I Slipped* (1968), *The Country Way* (1968), *Classic Narrations* (1969), *Closing Time 'Til Dawn* (1969), *Who Am I?* (1969), *I Know You're Married* (1970), *Ruby, Don't Take Your Love To Town* (1970), *The Greatest Grand Ole Opry* (1972), *It'll Come Back* (1974), *Teddy Bear* (1976), *Woodrow Wilson Sovine* (1977), *16 New Gospel Songs* (1980).

Spears, Billie Jo

b. 14 January 1937, Beaumont, Texas, USA. Discovered by songwriter Jack Rhodes, Billie Jo's first record, as Billie Jo Moore, 'Too Old For Toys, Too Young For Boys', earned her $4,200 at the age of 15. Despite appearances on *Louisiana Hayride*, she did not record regularly until she signed with United Artists in 1964. Following her producer, Kelso Herston, to Capitol Records, she had country hits with 'He's Got More Love In His Little Finger' and 'Mr. Walker, It's All Over'. After time off, following the removal of a nodule on her vocal cords, she recorded briefly for Brite Star and Cutlass. In 1974, Spears returned to United Artists where producer Larry Butler was developing a successful country roster. Her trans-Atlantic smash, 'Blanket on the Ground', was controversial in America. 'It sounded like a cheating song,' says Spears 'and the public don't think girls should sing cheating songs!' In actuality, it was about adding romance to a marriage and its success prompted other records with a similar theme and tempo - 'What I've Got In Mind' (which had originally been a rhumba) and ''57 Chevrolet'. The traditional 'Sing Me An Old-Fashioned Song' sold well in the UK, whilst her cover of Dorothy Moore's ballad 'Misty Blue' was successful in the USA. She is also known for her cover of Gloria Gaynor's 'I Will Survive'. She maintains, 'It is still a country record. I am country. I could never go pop with my mouthful of firecrackers.' A duet album with Del Reeves *By Request* and a tribute to her producer *Larry Butler And Friends* with Crystal Gayle and Dottie West were not released in the UK. A single of her blues-soaked cover of 'Heartbreak Hotel' was cancelled in 1977 because she did not want to exploit Elvis Presley's death. Billie Jo Spears has performed prolifically including over 300 concerts in the UK and her ambition is to make a live album at the Pavillion, Glasgow. Among her UK recordings are a duet with Carey Duncan of 'I Can Hear Kentucky Calling Me' and an album *B.J. - Billie Jo Spears Today* with her stage band, Owlkatraz. Of late, she has recorded husky-voiced versions of familiar songs for mass-marketed albums. A true ambassador of country music, she signs autographs and talks to fans after every appearance. She buys all her stage clothes in the UK and refuses to wear anything casual. 'If I didn't wear gowns,' she says, 'they'd throw rotten tomatoes.'

Albums: *The Voice Of Billie Jo Spears* (1968), *Mr. Walker, It's All Over* (1969), *Miss Sincerity* (1969), *With Love* (1970), *Country Girl* (1970), *Just Singin'* (1972), *Blanket On The Ground* (1974), *Billie Jo* (1975), *What I've Got In Mind* (1976), with Del

Billie Jo Spears

Reeves *By Request* (1976), *If You Want Me* (1977), *Everytime I Sing A Love Song* (1977), *Lonely Hearts Club* (1978), *Love Ain't Gonna Wait For Us* (1978), *I Will Survive* (1979), *Standing Tall* (1980), *Special Songs* (1981), with Reeves *Del And Billie Jo* (1982), *B.J. - Billie Jo Spears Today* (1983), *We Just Came Apart At The Dreams* (1984), *Unmistakably* (1992). Compilation: *Singles - Billie Jo Spears* (1979), *17 Golden Pieces Of Billie Jo Spears* (1983), *20 Country Greats* (1988).

Sprague, Carl T.

b. 1895, near Houston, Texas, USA, d. 1978. Sprague, possibly the first of the singing cowboys, was born on a ranch where he learned western songs around the camp fire. Although he attended college to study ranching, he accepted a coaching post in the college's athletic department. In 1925, impressed by Vernon Dalhart's success, he wrote to Victor Records and suggested that they record his cowboy songs. 'When The Work's All Done This Fall', a story of a cowboy killed in a night stampede, sold nearly a million copies. Despite its success, he was unwilling to give up his college post but he continued to make records, sometimes accompanied by two fiddle players from the college band. Amongst his records are 'Following The Cow Trail', 'The Girl I Loved In Sunny Tennessee', 'Rounded Up In Glory' and 'Roll On Little Dogies' as well as such familiar cowboy songs as 'Home On The Range' and 'Red River Valley'. In 1937 he left his coaching post and ran a general store before being recalled to the army. During World War II, he was involved with recruitment in the Houston and Dallas areas and became a Major. After selling insurance and various other jobs, he retired to Bryan, Texas but during the 60s, he donned a working cowboy's clothes for television appearances and university lectures. Between 1972-74, he recorded 29 tracks, which have been released by Bear Family. Sprague died in Bryan in 1978 - his singing was a hobby but his knowledge has been a guideline for students of western music.
Albums: *The First Popular Singing Cowboy* (1975), *Cowboy Songs From Texas* (1978).

Stampley, Joe

b. 6 June 1943, Springhill, Louisiana, USA. Stampley met Hank Williams when he was 7 years old, who gave him the advice to 'just be yourself and act like yourself and maybe later on it will pay off for you'. He became friends with local disc jockey, Merle Kilgore, when he was 15 and they began to write songs together. In 1958, Kilgore obtained for him the chance to record for Imperial. This led to the release of a single, 'Glenda', which sold well in his own locale but failed elsewhere. In 1961, a further recording on Chess Records, 'Teenage Picnic', also failed. He later recorded a tribute to his labelmate Chuck Berry, 'The Sheik Of Chicago'. Stampley, influenced in his early days by artists such as Jerry Lee Lewis, chose the piano as his instrument and in his high school years turned his interests to rock music. In the mid-60s, he was the lead singer of a rock group, the Cut-Ups, who soon became the Uniques. In 1966, they had minor local successes with 'Not Too Long Ago' (a Kilgore/Stampley song), 'Will You Love Me Tomorrow' and 'All These Things' but in 1969, the Uniques disbanded. In the early 70s, he decided to return to country music and moved to Nashville, where initially he worked as a staff writer for Gallico Music. He signed for Dot Records and achieved minor chart success in 1971 with 'Take Time To Know Her'. The following year he gained his first US country number 1 with his own 'Soul Song'. (It also became his only US pop chart success peaking at number 37). This proved the start of a very successful period for him as a recording artist. By 1979, he had taken his total of country chart entries to 32 including two more number 1 hits with 'Roll On Big Mama' (1975) and a solo version of the song that he had recorded ten years previously in the rock band, 'All These Things' (1976). Other Top 5 hits included 'I'm Still Loving You', 'Take Me Home To Somewhere' and 'Do You Ever Fool Around'.
He moved to Epic in 1975, working with Norro Wilson as his producer until 1978, when Billy Sherrill took over. It was during 1979, as a result of touring together in Europe, that Stampley joined forces with Moe Bandy and a single release of 'Just Good Ole Boys' became a number 1 country hit and led to a continuation of the partnership over the following years. The idea of Moe and Joe came to them in the Hard Rock Cafe, London during their appearance at the Wembley Festival. It was perhaps not too surprising that they proved a successful double act; they sounded a little alike when they sang and on stage they looked alike. Between 1979-85, their further hits were to include 'Holding The Bag', 'Tell Ole I Ain't Here', 'Hey Joe (Hey Moe)' and in 1984, they ran into copyright problems with their parody about pop singer Boy George called 'Where's The Dress', when they used the intro of Culture Club's hit 'Karma Chameleon'. Quite apart from their single

successes they recorded several albums together. During the 80s, Stampley continued to make solo *Billboard* chart entries but many critics, perhaps unfairly, suggested they came because of the publicity achieved by his association with Bandy. Recordings with Bandy apart, his only Top 10 hits in the 80s were 'I'm Gonna Love You Back To Loving Me Again' and 'Double Shot Of My Baby's Love'. He also had a minor hit with a duet recording with Jessica Boucher of 'Memory Lane'. His overall total of 57 US *Billboard* country chart entries is impressive but few traditional country fans would be too enthusiastic with some of his recordings. Perhaps his contributions were accurately summed up by the critic who wrote 'Joe Stampley and Billy 'Crash' Craddock led a field of country rockers, who in the 70s, injected a 50s flavour into their songs'. During his career Stampley claims to have played every state in the union and a lot of other countries as well. He played the *Grand Ole Opry* in the 70s, in the days when it was centred at the Ryman Auditorium but has never been a regular member. He once stated his regret was that he had never had a million selling record.

Albums: *If You Touch Me* (1972), *Soul Song* (1973), *Take Me Home To Somewhere* (1974), *I'm Still Loving You* (1974), *Joe Stampley* (1975), *Billy, Get Me A Woman* (1975), *All These Things* (1976), *Ten Songs About Her* (1976), *The Shiek Of Chicago (Chuck Berry)* (1976), *Saturday Nite Dance* (1977), *Red Wine And Blue Memories* (1978), *I Don't Lie* (1979), with Moe Bandy *Just Good Ole Boys* (1979), *After Hours* (1980), *I'm Gonna Love You Back To Loving Me Again* (1981), with Moe Bandy *Hey Moe, Hey Joe* (1981), *Encores* (1981), *Backslidin'* (1982), *I'm Goin' Hurtin'* (1982), *Memory Lane* (1983), with Bandy *The Good Ole Boys Alive And Well* (1984), with Bandy *Live From Bad Bob's In Memphis* (1985), *I'll Still Be Loving You* (1985).

Stanley Brothers

Carter Glen Stanley (b. 27 August 1925, McClure, Dickenson County, Virginia, USA) and his brother Ralph Edmond Stanley (b. 25 February 1927, Big Spraddle Creek, near Stratton, Dickenson County, Virginia, USA). Their father Lee Stanley was a noted singer and their mother played banjo. They learned many old time songs as children and soon began to sing at church and family functions. In 1941, with two school friends, they formed the Lazy Ramblers and played some local venues. In 1942, with Carter playing guitar and Ralph the banjo, they appeared as a duo on WJHL Johnson City, Tennessee. After graduation, Ralph spent eighteen months in the Army, mainly serving in Germany. In 1946, after a brief spell with Roy Sykes' Blue Ridge Mountain Boys, they formed their own Clinch Mountain Boys and began playing on WNVA Norton. Soon after they moved to WCYB Bristol, Tennessee, to appear regularly on *Farm And Fun Time*. Their intricate harmony vocal work (Carter sang lead to Ralph's tenor harmony) and their variety of music, with styles varying from the old-time to including some bluegrass, then being popularized by Bill Monroe, proved a great success. In 1947, they made their first recordings for the Rich-R-Tone label and later moved to WPTF Raleigh, North Carolina. With their standard five instrument line-up, they became one of the most renowned bluegrass bands and were much in demand for concert appearances.

Between 1949-52, they made some recordings for Columbia which are now rated as classic bluegrass. These included many of Carter's own compositions such as 'The White Dove', 'Too Late To Cry', 'We'll Be Sweethearts In Heaven' and 'The Fields Have Turned Brown'. They disbanded for a short time in 1951. Ralph briefly played banjo with Bill Monroe before being injured in a car crash. During this time, Carter played guitar and recorded with Bill Monroe. However, they soon reformed their band and returned to *Farm And Fun Time* on WCYB. After leaving Columbia, they first recorded a great many sides for Mercury. The material included more self-penned numbers, honky-tonk songs, instrumentals and quite a lot of of gospel songs recorded with quartet vocal harmonies. Ralph Stanley has always maintained that this period produced their best recordings and experts have rated the mid-50s as the Stanley Brothers' 'Golden Era'. Later recordings were issued on Starday, King, Wango, Rimrock and Cabin Creek. (Over the years Copper Creek records have released a series taken from radio shows, which at the time of writing already totals 10 albums.) Their only US country chart success came in 1960; a Top 20 hit for the novelty number 'How Far To Little Rock'.

Through the 50s and up to the mid-60s, they played at venues and festivals all over the States and made overseas tours. It was during a European tour in March 1966, that they appeared in concert in London. The hectic schedules caused Carter to develop a drink problem; his health was badly affected and he died in hospital in Bristol, Virginia, on 1 December 1966. After his brother's death,

Ralph Stanley reformed the Clinch Mountain Boys and continued to play and recorded bluegrass music. In 1970, he started the annual Bluegrass Festival (named after his brother), an event which attracted large numbers of musicians and bluegrass fans. Over the years, his style of banjo playing has been copied by many young musicians and he has become respected (like Monroe) as one of the most important artists for popularizing bluegrass music. During the 70s and 80s, the Clinch Mountain Boys have included within their ranks such country artists as Ricky Skaggs, Keith Whitley and Larry Sparks and others including John Conlee and Emmylou Harris have recorded Stanley Brothers songs. British bluegrass followers were delighted to see Ralph Stanley live at the 1991 Edale Festival.

Albums: by the Stanley Brothers *Country Pickin' & Singin'* (1958), *The Stanley Brothers* (1959), *Everybody's Country Favorites* (1959), *Mountain Song Favorites* (1959), *Hymns & Sacred Songs* (1959), *Sacred Songs From The Hills* (1960), *For The Good People* (1960), *Old Time Camp Meeting* (1961), *Sing Everybody's Country Favorites* (1961), *The Stanley Brothers* (1961), *In Person* (1961), *Sing The Songs They Like The Best* (1961), *Live At Antioch College-1960* (1961), *Award Winners At The Folk Song Festival* (1962), *The Mountain Music Sound* (1962), *Good Old Camp Meeting Songs* (1962), *Five String Banjo Hootenanny* (1963), *The World's Finest Five String Banjo* (1963), *Just Because (Folk Concert)* (1963), *Hard Times* (1963), *Country-Folk Music Spotlight* (1963), *Old Country Church* (1963), *Bluegrass Songs For You* (1964), *Hymns Of The Cross* (1964), *Bluegrass Songs For You* (1965), *The Stanley Brothers - Their Original Recordings* (1965), *The Angels Are Singing* (1966), *Jacob's Vision* (1966), *Bluegrass Gospel Favorites* (1966), *The Greatest Country & Western Show On Earth* (1966), *A Collection Of Original Gospel & Sacred Songs* (1966), *The Stanley Brothers Go To Europe* (1966), *An Empty Mansion* (1967), *Memorial Album* (1967), *The Best Loved Songs Of The Carter Stanley* (1967), *The Legendary Stanley Brothers Recorded Live, Volume 1* (1968), *The Legendary Stanley Brothers Recorded Live, Volume 2* (1969), *On Stage* (1969), *How Far To Little Rock* (1969), *Deluxe Album* (1970), *Together For The Last Time* (1971), *Rank Strangers* (1973), *The Stanley Brothers* (1974), *The Stanley Brothers On The Air* (1976), *A Beautiful Life* (1978), *I Saw The Light* (1980), *The Columbia Sessions, Volume 1* (1981), *Shadows Of The Past* (1981), *The Columbia Sessions, Volume 2* (1982), *The Stanley Brothers* (1983, 6-album set), *Stanley Brothers On Radio, Volume 1* (1984), *Stanley Brothers On Radio, Volume 2* (1984), *The Starday Sessions* (1984), *The Stanley Series* (80s, 10-album set), *On WCYB Bristol Farm & Fun Time* (1988), *Gospel Songs From Cabin Creek* (1990).

Albums By Ralph Stanley: *The Bluegrass Sound* (1968), *Brand New Country Songs By* (1968), *Over The Sunset Hill* (1968), *Old Time Music* (c.1969), *Hills Of Home* (1970), *Cry From The Cross* (1971), *Ralph Stanley Live In Japan* (1971), *Sings Michegan Bluegrass* (1971), *Something Old Something New* (1972), *Plays Requests* (1973), *Old Country Church* (1973), *I Want To Preach The Gospel* (1973), *The Stanley Sound Around The World* (1973), *Gospel Echoes Of The Stanley Brothers* (1973), *A Man And His Music* (1975), *Let Me Rest On A Peaceful Mountain* (1975), *Live at McClure* (1976), *Old Home Place* (1977), *Clinch Mountain Gospel* (1978), *Down Where The River Bends* (1979), *I'll Wear A White Robe* (1980), *Hymn Time* (1980), with Jimmy Martin *First Time Together* (1980), *The Stanley Sound Today* (1981), *The Memory Of Your Smile* (1982), *Child Of The King* (1983), *Bluegrass* (1983), *Sings Traditional Bluegrass And Gospel* (1983), *Live At The Old Home Place* (1983), *Snow Covered Mound* (1984), *Singing Sixteen Years* (c.1984), *Shadows Of The Past* (c.1984), *I Can Tell You The Time* (1985), *Live In Japan* (1986), *Lonesome & Blue* (1986), *I'll Answer The Call* (1988), *Ralph Stanley & Raymond Fairchild* (1989), *(Clawhammer) The Way My Mama Taught Me* (1990), *Like Father Like Son* (1990), *Pray For The Boys* (1991).

Albums issued on Wango in early 60s as John's Gospel Quartet: *John's Gospel Quartet* (reissued 1973 as *The Stanley Brothers of Virginia Volume.1*), *John's Country Quartet* (reissued 1973 as *The Long Journey Home*), *John's Gospel Quartet Volume 2* (reissued 1973 as *The Stanley Brothers Volume 4*), *John's Gospel Quartet Songs Of Mother & Home* (reissued 1973 as *The Little Old Country Church House*).

Starcher, Buddy

b. Oby Edgar Starcher, 16 March 1906, Kentuck, Jackson County, West Virginia, USA. He first learned to play banjo but later became an outstanding guitarist. In 1928, he was probably the first hillbilly artist to appear on radio in the Baltimore area. Between 1930 and 1960, he continually moved around, not only playing venues in his home State, Virginia and Kentucky (especially Charleston and Fairmont), but further afield to Miami, Iowa and Philadelphia. In 1946, he recorded in Chicago for Four Star, including his best-known song 'I'll Still Write Your Name In

The Sand'. Now a much recorded bluegrass standard, it reached number 8 in the country charts. Later he recorded for other labels including Columbia, Starday, Decca, Bluebonnet and Bear Family. In 1960, his television show in Charleston had higher local ratings than NBC's *Today*. In 1966, he had a number 2 country and number 39 pop hit with 'History Repeats Itself' - his cleverly written narration detailing the many similarities between the assassinations of Presidents Lincoln and Kennedy. In the late 60s, he returned to radio and for some years managed radio stations, being usually brought in as a troubleshooter to pick up ailing stations - once they were running successfully, he moved on to the next challenge. He has written many fine songs including 'Song Of The Water Wheel' (a hit for Slim Whitman) and also some prose. In the late 30s, he married fellow artist, Mary Ann (Vasas) who in 1941, took over from Patsy Montana on WLS Chicago.

Albums: *Buddy Starcher & His Mountain Guitar* (1962), *History Repeats Itself* i (1966), *History Repeats Itself* ii (1966), *Buddy Starcher Volume 1* (1967), *Country Soul & Inspiration* (c.60s), *Country Love Songs* (1978), *The Boy From Down Home* (1984), *Pride Of The West Virginia Hills* (1984), *Me And My Guitar* (1986).

Further reading: *Buddy Starcher - Biography*, Robert H. Cagle.

Starr, Kenny

b. Kenneth Trebbe, 21 September 1953, Topeka, Kansas, USA. Starr grew up in Burlingame, Kansas and, according to publicity, was fronting his own band, the Rockin' Rebels, from the age of nine. As a teenager, he played clubs as part of a pop act, Kenny and the Imperials. Starr switched to country music in 1969 and won a talent contest in Wichita. A promoter invited him to appear on a forthcoming show with Loretta Lynn and Conway Twitty, where he won a standing ovation. Lynn suggested he moved to Nashville and gave him a job with her roadshow. With her support, he recorded for MCA from 1973-78 and had a US country Top 10 hit with 'The Blind Man In The Bleachers'. He had further success with 'Tonight I Face The Man Who Made It Happen', 'Hold Tight', 'Slow Drivin'' and 'Me And The Elephant', but he was soon forgotten.

Album: *The Blind Man In The Bleachers* (1975).

Statler Brothers

The Statler Brothers hail from Staunton, a town on the edge of Shenandoah Valley, Virginia, USA. In 1955 Harold W. Reid (bass, b. 21 August 1939, Augusta County, Virginia, USA), Philip E. Balsley (baritone, b. 8 August 1939, Augusta County, Virginia, USA), Lew C. DeWitt (tenor, b. 8 March 1939, Roanoke County, Virginia, USA) and Joe McDorman formed a gospel quartet. Although McDorman never became a Statler, he has worked with them occasionally. In 1960 he was replaced by Harold's brother, Donald S. Reid (b. 5 June 1945, Staunton, Virginia, USA), who is now the group's lead singer. Originally the quartet was called The Kingsmen, but they changed it to avoid confusion with a US pop group. The Statler Brothers was chosen from the manufacturer's name on a box of tissues, and the group point out that they might have been the Kleenex Brothers. In 1963, they auditioned for Johnny Cash, who invited them to be part of his road show. He also secured a record contract with Columbia, but the label was disappointed with the poor sales of their first records. Having been refused further studio time, they recorded Lew DeWitt's song, 'Flowers On The Wall', during a break in one of Johnny Cash's sessions. The infectious novelty made number 4 on the US pop charts (number 2, country) and, despite the American references, also entered the UK Top 40. The Statler Brothers continued with Cash's roadshow and recorded both with him ('Daddy Sang Bass') and on their own ('Ruthless', 'You Can't Have Your Kate And Edith Too'). Dissatisfied by the promotion of their records and by the lukewarm material they were given, they switched to Mercury Records in 1970 and their records have been produced by Jerry Kennedy since then.

With such US country hits as 'Bed Of Roses', 'Do You Remember These?', 'I'll Go To My Grave Loving You' and the number 1 'Do You Know You Are My Sunshine?', they established themselves as the number 1 country vocal group. They left Cash's roadshow in 1972, but they recorded a tribute to him, 'We Got Paid By Cash', as well as tributes to their favourite gospel group ('The Blackwood Brothers By The Statler Brothers') and their favourite guitarist ('Chet Atkins' Hand'). DeWitt was incapacitated through Crohn's disease and left in 1982. He released the solo *On My Own*, in 1985, but he died in Waynesboro, Virginia, on 15 August 1990. Many of their songs relate to their love of the cinema - 'The Movies', 'Whatever Happened To Randolph Scott?' and 'Elizabeth', a country number 1 written, inspired by watching Giant, by Jimmy Fortune, who replaced DeWitt. Fortune also wrote two other number 1 US country records for them, 'My Only Love' and 'Too Much On My Heart'. They also had considerable success with a spirited revival of 'Hello Mary Lou', which was praised by its composer, Gene Pitney. Their stage act includes the homespun humour of their alter egos, Lester 'Roadhog' Moran And The Cadillac Cowboys, and they gave themselves a plywood disc when the first 1,250 of the resulting album were sold. On the other hand, The Statler Brothers' Old-Fashioned Fourth Of July Celebration in Staunton attracts 70,000 a year. The Statler Brothers are managed from office buildings, which used to be a school which Dewitt and The Reids attended.

Albums: *Flowers On The Wall* (1966), *Big Hits* (1967), *Oh Happy Day* (1969), *Bed Of Roses* (1971), *Pictures Of Moments To Remember* (1971), *Interview* (1972), *Country Music Then And Now* (1972), *Symphonies In E Major* (1973), *Thank You World* (1974), *Alive At Johnny Mack Brown High School* (as by Lester 'Roadhog' Moran And His Cadillac Cowboys) (1973), *Carry Me Back* (1973), *Sons Of The Motherland* (1975), *The Holy Bible - Old Testament* (1975), *The Holy Bible - New Testament* (1975), *Harold, Lew, Phil And Don* (1976), *The Country America Loves* (1977), *Short Stories* (1977), *Entertainers, On And Off The Record* (1978), *The Originals* (1979), *Christmas Card* (1979), *Tenth Anniversary* (1980), *Years Ago* (1981), *The Legend Goes On* (1982), *Country Gospel* (1982), *Today* (1983), *Atlanta Blue* (1984), *Partners In Rhyme* (1985), *Christmas Present* (1985), *Four For The Show* (1986), *Radio Gospel Favourites* (1986), *Maple Street Memories* (1987), *Live* (1990), *Music, Memories And You* (1990), *All American Cowboy* (1991), *Words And Music* (1992).

Steagall, Red

b. Russell Steagall, 22 December 1937, Gainesville, Texas, USA. In 1954, he contacted polio, which badly affected the use of his left hand and arm. Realising his hoped for football career was no longer a possibility, he turned his attention to music. During his convalescence, as part of the therapeutic treatment, he first began to play the mandolin and then, as his fingers strengthened, the guitar. By playing local dances and clubs, he financed his course at West Texas State University, where he got a degree in Agriculture and Animal Science and then for five years worked for Sand Mark Oil as a soil analyst. He moved to California in 1965, sang locally and for a year worked as a salesman of industrial chemicals. Working first with his friend, Don Lanier, he began to develop his

songwriting and in 1966, Ray Charles recorded their song 'Here We Go Again'. He concentrated on his writing, later claiming that by 1969 sixty of his songs had been recorded by other artists. In 1969, Ray Sanders had a hit with his song 'Beer Drinkin' Music' and Steagall himself made his first recordings on Dot. In 1971, Del Reeves had a hit with 'A Dozen Pairs Of Boots' and the following year, having moved to Nashville and joined Capitol, Steagall gained his own first country chart hit with 'Party Dolls And Wine'.

During the 70s, later recording for ABC/Dot and Elektra and with his continued strong leaning towards Western-Swing and honky tonk songs, Steagall charted a steady succession of country chart entries, though none made the Top 10. His biggest came with 'Lone Star Beer And Bob Wills Music' - a number 11 in 1976. His love for Bob Wills' music saw him also chart a tribute song 'Bob's Got A Swing Band In Heaven'. For years, with his band the Coleman County Cowboys, he played dance halls and rodeos, all over the West. Steagall became a genuine singing cowboy with his own Texas ranch and his keen interest in things Western saw him become one of the top entertainers on the US rodeo circuit, playing some 250 dates a year for many years. In 1974, he was instrumental in Reba McEntire becoming a star, after hearing her sing the national anthem at the National Rodeo Finals. In the 80s, he cut down touring drastically but remained active in various ventures, including his publishing house. He also cut out most of his songwriting to concentrate on writing poetry about the West and breeding quarter horse on his ranch. In 1987, he made his debut as an actor in a children's film called *Benji, The Hunted* - a dog story with the animal perhaps getting the best lines. Somewhat surprisingly, his last chart entry was 'Hard Hat Days And Honky Tonk Nights' back in 1980.

Albums: *Party Dolls And Wine* (1972), *Somewhere My Love* (1972), *If You've Got The Time I've Got The Song* (1973), *Finer Things In Life* (1975), *Lonestar Beer And Bob Wills Music* (1976), *Texas Red* (1976), *For All Our Cowboy Friends* (1977), *Hang On Feelin'* (1978), *It's Our Life* (c.1980), *Cowboy Favorites* (1985), *Red Steagall* (1986).

Stevens, Ray

b. Ray Ragsdale, 24 January 1941, Clarksdale, Georgia USA. A prolific country-pop writer and performer, Stevens' novelty hits of the 70s and 80s form a history of the fads and crazes of the era. He became a disc jockey on a local station at 15 and the following year recorded 'Five More Steps' on the Prep label. Stevens' first nonsense song, 'Chickie Chickie Wah Wah' was written in 1958 but it was not until 1961, with Mercury Records that he had a Top 40 hit with the tongue-twisting 'Jeremiah Peabody's Poly Unsaturated Quick Dissolving Fast Acting Pleasant Tasting Green And Purple Pills'. This was followed by 'Ahab The Arab' (1962) and 'Harry The Hairy Ape' (1963). Stevens also had a penchant for social comment which came through in songs like 'Mr Businessman' (1968), 'America Communicate With Me' and the first recording of Kris Kristofferson's 'Sunday Morning Coming Down'. However, the zany songs were the most successful and in 1969 he sold a million copies of 'Gitarzan' and followed with a version of Leiber And Stoller's Coasters' hit 'Along Came Jones' and 'Bridget The Midget (The Queen Of The Blues). His first number 1 was the simple melodic ballad 'Everything Is Beautiful' in 1970. All of these, however, were outsold by 'The Streak' which topped the charts on both sides of the Atlantic in 1974. Stevens' softer side was evident in his version of Erroll Garner's 'Misty' which won a Grammy in 1976 for its bluegrass-styled arrangement. Later novelty efforts, aimed principally at country audiences included 'Shriner's Convention' (1980), 'It's Me Again Margaret' (1985), 'I Saw Elvis In A UFO' (1989) and 'Power Tools'.

Albums: *1,837 Seconds Of Humor* (1962), *Ahab The Arab* (1962), *This Is Ray Stevens* (1963), *Gitarzan* (1969), *Unreal!!!* (1970), *Everything Is Beautiful* (1970), *Turn Your Radio On* (1972), *Boogity Boogity* (1974), *Misty* (1975), *Just For The Record* (1975), *Feel The Music* (1976), *Shriner's Convention* (1980), *Don't Laugh Now* (1982), *Me* (1983), *He Thinks He's Ray Stevens* (1985), *Surely You Joust* (1988), *I Have Returned* (1988), *Beside Myself* (1989). Compilations: *Ray Stevens' Greatest Hits* (1971), *The Very Best Of Ray Stevens* (1975), *Both Sides Of Ray Stevens* (1986), *Greatest Hits* (1987).

Stevens, Stu

b. Wilfrid Pierce, 25 September c.1937, Annesley Woodhouse, Kirkby-In-Ashfield, Nottinghamshire, England. He drove tractors on the farm at the age of eight, but his ambition to be a farmer was never fully realised. When he was about 13-years-old, his father, a miner, died so Wilfrid left school to work down the mines to keep the family. His first singing experience came after his brother entered him in a local talent show around 1965. He won and his powerful deep voice

found him a regular paid singing spot at the club. It seemed to him much easier than farming so he bought himself a guitar (later learned piano) and began to put together a repertoire of songs. In the late 60s, as Stuart Stevens, he made his first recordings for EMI, including the release of a single ('Soft Is The Night'/'Tender Hearted'). He also appeared on the Lonnie Donegan television show. In March 1970, he was booked to entertain at a reception for the American country stars of the Wembley Festival. Performing as Willard Pierce, he created such an impression that it led to him appearing on the Festival itself the following day - seemingly the first British artist to do so. He made a noteworthy appearance on *Opportunity Knocks* in 1972 (unfortunately falling foul of the 'never work with children or animals' adage and lost by three votes to a child drummer). He recorded for the Youngblood label in 1972, with the subsequent album, *Stories In Song*, selling some 12,000 copies. In 1973, he performed at a disc jockey Convention in Nashville, subsequently appearing at many major venues, including the *Grand Ole Opry* and on network television. He was signed by Cliffie Stone to the US Granite label in 1974, who released his Youngblood album in the USA and in Europe. His recording of 'My Woman My Woman My Wife' became popular on both sides of the Atlantic, even drawing praise from the song's writer Marty Robbins.

Further trips to the States followed until, sadly for him, both Granite and Youngblood ceased record production, leaving him without a label in either country. He had continued to play the British clubs, first with his band Silver Mist, then with Pat and Roger Johns, before eventually appearing with his two sons Stuart (bass guitar) and Steven (keyboards). He also opened his own recording studios and worked on production with other artists. He formed his own Major Oak, Eagle and Ash labels and released albums, which proved popular with his British fans. Twelve out of 28 unissued Youngblood tracks later appeared on his album *The Loner*. In 1979, he almost made the British Top 40 with 'The Man From Outer Space' which, after initially being released on his own Eagle label, was picked up by MCA Records and received air-play and jocularity from Terry Wogan on BBC radio. Further singles followed, including 'If I Heard You Call My Name', 'One Red Rose' and 'Hello Pretty Lady', which sold well for country records, but not well enough for a major label seeking pop record sales. This resulted in him parting company with MCA.

Stu's national popularity increased and he regularly played the theatre and concert hall circuit, always doing it his way and always refusing to perform anything he did not wish to sing. Many think, no doubt correctly, that had he become a 'yes' man and allowed himself to be type-cast, he would undoubtedly have become a major star. In 1984, Stu and his wife were devastated by the death, from a rare heart disease, of their youngest son. Steven (19), a keyboard player of very outstanding abilities, who had appeared on stage from the age of seven. Although Stu played out his immediate special bookings, he soon tended to withdraw from active participation in the music scene. In recent years, he has made infrequent appearances but in the main 'The Voice', as he was affectionately known to his fans, has been silent - a great, if understandable, loss to British country music.
Albums: *Stories In Song* (1973), *Command Performance* (1976), *Together Again* (1977), *Stu Stevens - Country Music Volume 7* (1977, cassette only), *Stories In Song Volume 2 - The Loner* (1978), *The Man From Outer Space* (1979), *Stu* (1979), *Emma And I* (1980), *Old Rugged Cross* (1981, cassette only), *Songs That Made Stu Stevens* (1981), *The Voice - Live* (1982, cassette only), *In Memory Of Steven (Live)* (1986, cassette only), *The Man And His Music* (1986, cassette only).

Stewart, Gary

b. 28 May 1945, Jenkins, Kentucky, USA. Stewart's family moved to Florida when he was 12, and he made his first record for the local Cory label and played in a beat group called the Amps. Teaming up with a policeman, Bill Eldridge, he wrote Stonewall Jackson's 1965 US country hit, 'Poor Red Georgia Dirt'. Several songwriting successes followed including chart entries for Billy Walker ('She Goes Walking Through My Mind', 'When A Man Loves A Woman (The Way I Love You)', 'Traces Of A Woman', 'It's Time To Love Her'), Cal Smith ('You Can't Housebreak A Tomcat', 'It Takes Me All Night Long') and Nat Stuckey ('Sweet Thang And Cisco'). Gary recorded an album for Kapp, *You're Not The Woman You Used To Be*, and then moved to RCA. He had his first US country hit with a country version of the Allman Brothers' 'Ramblin' Man' and then made the Top 10 with 'Drinkin' Thing'. For some years, Stewart worked as the pianist in Charley Pride's roadband and he can be heard on Pride's *In Concert* double-album. He established himself as a hard driving, honky-tonk performer with *Out Of Hand* and a US country number 1,

'She's Actin' Single (I'm Drinkin' Doubles)', although his vibrato annoyed some. His 1977 *Your Place Or Mine*, included guest appearances from Nicolette Larson, Emmylou Harris and Rodney Crowell. His two albums with songwriter Dean Dillon were not commercial successes, and Stewart returned to working in honky-tonk clubs. However, drug addiction got the better of him and his life collapsed when his wife left him and his son committed suicide. In the late 80s, he returned to performing, carrying on in the same musical style as before.
Albums: *You're Not The Woman You Used To Be* (1973), *Out Of Hand* (1975), *Steppin' Out* (1976), *Your Place Or Mine* (1977), *Little Junior* (1978), *Gary* (1979), *Cactus And Rose* (1980), with Dean Dillon *Brotherly Love* (1982), with Dean Dillon *Those Were The Days* (1983), *Brand New* (1988), *Battleground* (1990).

Stewart, Redd

b. Henry Redd Stewart, 21 May 1921, Ashland City, Tennessee, USA. After the family relocated to Kentucky, Stewart while still at school learned piano, fiddle and guitar and by the mid-30s, was performing in the Louisville area. He joined Pee Wee King's Golden West Cowboys on WHAS in 1937, first as a musician but also became featured vocalist when Eddy Arnold left to pursue his solo career. Stewart moved with King to the *Grand Ole Opry* until he was called up for military service during which he wrote 'A Soldier's Last Letter', which became a hit for Ernest Tubb. He rejoined King after the war and from 1947-57, they appeared on a popular weekly radio and television show on WAUE Louisville and toured extensively. The two were to enjoy some 30 years of successful songwriting collaboration. Their successes included 'Tennessee Waltz' (Stewart added lyrics to King's signature tune the 'No Name Waltz'), the song becoming a hit for both King and Cowboy Copas in 1948, a million-seller for Patti Page in 1950 and charted again by Lacy J. Dalton in 1980. Other million-sellers were 'Slowpoke', a 1951 hit for King, and 'You Belong To Me' for Jo Stafford in 1952. Stewart also wrote the Jim Reeves winner 'That's A Sad Affair'. He sang on all of King's hits but never charted with his solo recordings, although he recorded for several labels. After King retired in 1969, Stewart continued to be active in the music world.
Solo albums: *Sings Favorite Old Time Songs* (1959), *I Remember* (1974). (See also album listing for Pee Wee King).

Stewart, Wynn

b. Wynnford Lindsey Stewart, 7 June 1934, on a farm near Morrisville, Missouri, USA, d. 17 July 1985, Hendersonville, Tennessee, USA. Stewart's uncle was a major league pitcher, which gave him thoughts of a baseball career, until told that he would never be big enough. He became interested in songwriting, learned to play the guitar and, at the age of 13, appeared regularly on KWTO Springfield. A year later the family moved to California, where Stewart became friendly and for a time ran a band, with Ralph Mooney, the now legendary steel guitarist. Stewart first recorded for Intro in 1954 and local success with his own song 'Strolling' led to him signing for Capitol. In 1956, his recording of 'Waltz Of The Angels' became his first hit, further minor ones followed but it was not until 1959, after he moved to the Challenge label, that he achieved major success with 'Wishful Thinking' and also recorded with Jan Howard. In the late 50s, he moved to Las Vegas, where he opened the Nashville Nevada Club and hosted his own television series on KTOO. In 1959, Miki And Griff had a UK pop chart hit with Stewart's song 'Hold Back Tomorrow'. Competition for places in his band was fierce and in 1962, Stewart gave Merle Haggard the job of playing bass and singing the odd song during his own breaks. A year later he provided Haggard with 'Sing A Sad Song', which became his first chart hit. He returned to California in the mid-60s, toured with his band the Tourists and also rejoined Capitol, where between 1965-71 he had 17 country chart hits including 'It's Such A Pretty World Today', his only number 1. He moved to RCA in 1972, but achieved his next Top 20 hits in 1976 with 'After The Storm' and his own version of 'Sing A Sad Song', after moving to Playboy Records. Stewart's reputation became somewhat marred by problems, his private life suffered (he was married three times) and at times drinking caused him to miss bookings. He eventually moved to Nashville, where he believed he could achieve another breakthrough with a special come-back tour. At 6 pm on 17 July 1985, the evening the tour was due to start, he suffered a heart attack and died. A fine singer, who should have been a bigger star, for, as John Morthland later wrote, 'He may not have been as consistent as Haggard or Buck Owens but at his best, he was their equal as a writer'.

Albums: with Jan Howard *Sweethearts Of Country Music* (1961), *Wynn Stewart* (1962), *Songs Of Wynn Stewart* (1965), *Above And Beyond* (1967), *It's Such A Pretty World Today* (1967), *Wynn Stewart And Jan Howard Sing Their Hits* (1968), *In Love* (1968), *Love's Gonna Happen To Me* (1968), *Something Pretty* (1968), *Let The Whole World Sing With Me* (1969), *Yours Forever* (1969), *You Don't Care What Happens To Me* (1970), *It's A Beautiful Day* (1970), *Baby It's Yours* (1971), *After The Storm* (1976), *Wishful Thinking (The Challenge Years 1958-1963)* (1988).

Stone, Cliffie

b. Clifford Gilpin Snyder, 1 March 1917, Burbank, California, USA, d. 17 June 1985. In the early 30s Stone played bass and trombone in dance bands before becoming a country music compere and disc jockey in 1935. During the 40s he was bandleader and host of the CBS network *Hollywood Barn Dance* and from 1943 to 1947 he compered almost thirty other country radio shows weekly. He joined Capitol in 1946, working on production as well as recording and had chart hits in 1947-48, including 'Peepin' Through The Keyhole' and 'When My Blue Moon Turns To Gold Again'. In 1949, he hosted the famed *Hometown Jamboree* and, from 1953 to its closure in 1960, the radio and television show *Town Hall Party*. These shows did much to popularize country music over a wide area and many artists benefited from their appearances on them. One prominent regular on *Hometown Jamboree* was Stone's father, a banjo playing comedian who performed as Herman the Hermit. Stone discovered Tennessee Ernie Ford in 1949 and was his manager for many years; he also worked with many other artists including Spade Cooley, Lefty Frizzell, Hank Thompson and Molly Bee. During the 60s he cut back on his own performing, concentrating on management, a booking agency and several music publishing firms including Central Songs, which he sold to Capitol in 1969. Throughout the 60s-70s he was involved in production, formed Granite records, did committee work for the Country Music Association and ATV Music before retiring in the late 70s. Over the years he wrote many songs and worked with Merle Travis on such classics as 'Divorce Me C.O.D', 'So Round So Firm So Fully Packed' and 'No Vacancy'. During his career Stone rarely left his native California, he died at Burbank following a heart attack in June 1985 and was elected to the Country Music Hall Of Fame in 1989 for his services to the music in the non-performer category.

Albums: *The Party's On Me* (1958), *Cool Cowboy* (1959), *Square Dance Promenade* (1960), *Original Cowboy Sing-a-long* (1961), *Together Again* (1967).

Stone, Doug

b. 1956, Newnan, Georgia, USA. Stone, the product of a broken home, was encouraged to become a musician by his mother. Stone, who can sing and play guitar, keyboards, fiddle and drums, worked as part of a trio around Georgia for several years without finding commercial success. He then auditioned for the producer Bob Montgomery who immediately signed him to Epic Records. In 1990, Stone had his first US country hit with 'I'd Be Better Off In A Pine Box'. Like many other 'new country' singers, he was a throwback to the honky tonk tradition of George Jones and Merle Haggard. His other successes have included 'I Thought It Was You', 'A Jukebox With A Country Song' and one of the slickest country songs of recent years, 'Warning Labels'.
Albums: *Doug Stone* (1990), *I Thought It Was You* (1991), *From The Heart* (1992).

Stoneman Family

The Stoneman Family originated with Ernest V. 'Pop' Stoneman (b. 14 May 1893, in a log cabin near Monarat, Carroll County, Virginia, USA), who learned to play guitar, autoharp, banjo and harmonica and showed a talent to quickly learn songs that he either heard or read in early song books. He worked in cotton mills, coal mines and as a carpenter in various parts of the area. It was while working as the latter at Bluefield, West Virginia, that he heard the first recordings of fellow Virginian, Henry Whitter. Ernest was unimpressed by Whitter's singing and like others, believed that he could do better. He travelled to New York where, providing his own autoharp and harmonica backings, he auditioned for Columbia and OKeh. The former showed no interest, but he made his first recordings for OKeh in September 1924, including his million seller, 'The Sinking Of The Titanic'. It proved to be one of the biggest hits of the 20s and has since been recorded by many artists, including Roy Acuff. The records sold well enough and further sessions soon followed; on one he was accompanied by Emmett Lundy, a noted Virginian fiddler and on occasions, he recorded with his fiddle playing wife, Hattie Stoneman (b.1900).
In 1926, he recorded for RCA-Victor with his first band the Dixie Mountaineers and later with the Blue Ridge Cornshuckers. In the following years many recordings were made, which saw release on various labels, some under pseudonyms such as Slim Harris, Ernest Johnson, Uncle Ben Hawkins and Jim Seaney. In July 1927, he recorded at the noted sessions at Bristol, Tennessee, where Ralph Peer also recorded the Carter Family and Jimmie Rodgers. Due to the Depression, he did not record between 1929-33, but even so he had proved so popular that, between 1925-34, he had still recorded over two hundred songs. Some recordings were with other musicians, including his banjoist cousin George Stoneman (1883-1966), fiddlers Alex 'Uncle Eck' Dunford (c.1978-1953) and Kahle Brewer (b.1904) and on his last pre-World War II session in 1934, he was accompanied by his eldest son Eddie (b.1920), who played banjo and took some vocals. In 1931, financially insecure, in spite of the earnings from record sales, he moved to Washington, DC where, to support his family (he and his wife had 23 children in all), he worked as a carpenter in a naval gun factory. Some of the children learned to play some instrument during childhood and when, after the War, he gradually began to return to entertaining, his band was made up of his wife and their own children.
A winning appearance on a television quiz show in 1956 led to him to reactivate his career. With his wife and five of his children, he recorded again (on Folkways) in 1957. After adding some contemporary country and bluegrass music to the old time and folk songs that he had always performed, the Stoneman Family became a popular touring act. They played on the *Grand Ole Opry* in 1962 and even appeared at *Fillmore West* in San Francisco, America's first psychedelic ballroom. In 1964, they moved their home to California, where they became active on the west coast folk scene and appeared at the prestigious Monterey Folk Festival. They also played on various network television shows in the 60s, including that of Jimmy Dean and between 1966-68, they hosted their own series. At this time, the group consisted of Pop (autoharp/guitar), Calvin 'Scotty' Scott (fiddle), Van Hayden (guitar), Donna (mandolin), Roni (Veronica) (banjo) and Jim (bass). They had five minor hits with recordings on MGM in the late 60s but later recorded for other labels including Starday and RCA. In 1967, the CMA voted the Stoneman Family the Vocal Group Of The Year. Ernest Stoneman made his last recordings on 11 April 1968, and continued to perform with the group almost up to his death, in Nashville, on 14 June 1968.
He was in all probability the first person ever to record using an autoharp and he is well remembered by exponents for his ability to play the melody line, instead of merely playing chords, the standard method of playing the instrument,

even by its inventor. (This ability is demonstrated on some of his recordings, including 'Stoney's Waltz'.) He is also accepted as being the only country musician to record on both Edison cylinders and modern stereo albums and he was also the leading performer of string-band music in the Galax area of Virginia. After 'Pop' Stoneman's death, Patti (autoharp) gave up her solo career to join with Donna, Roni, Van and Jim and as the Stoneman Family, they continued to play his music and toured all over the States and in Europe. In 1972, they recorded a live album, *Meet The Stonemans,* at London's Wembley Festival. Scotty Stoneman who also worked with the Blue Grass Champs and the Kentucky Colonels, won many fiddle competitions, including the National on several occasions and at the time of his death, in 1973, he was rated one of the world's finest bluegrass fiddle players. Hattie Stoneman, who first recorded in 1925, died in hospital in Murfreesboro, Tennessee on 22 July 1976, aged 75. In later years, Donna left to concentrate on gospel music, Roni became a featured star of the television show *Hee-Haw.* Patti, Jim and Van continued to play as the Stoneman Family. Twin brothers Gene and Dean (b.1931) performed for a time in the Maryland area as the Stoneman Brothers, until Dean formed his Vintage Bluegrass band. In 1981, several members of the family reunited to record a special album. Dean Stoneman died of a lung complaint in Lanham, Maryland on 28 February 1989.

Albums by Ernest V. Stoneman: *Cool Cowboy* (1958), *Ernest V.Stoneman & His Dixie Mountaineers (1927-1928)* (1968), *Pop Stoneman Memorial Album* (1969), *Ernest V.Stoneman & the Blue Ridge Corn Shuckers* (c.1975), *Ernest V.Stoneman Volume 1* (1986), *Ernest V.Stoneman Volume 2* (1986).

Albums by the Stoneman Family: *Banjo Tunes & Songs* (1957), *Old Time Tunes Of The South* (1957), *Bluegrass Champs* (1963), *Big Ball In Monterey* (1964), *White Lightning* (1965), *Those Singin', Swingin', Stompin', Sensational Stonemans* (1966), with the Tracy Schwarz Band *Down Home* (c.1966), with the Tracy Schwarz Band *The Stoneman Family* (c.1966), *All In The Family* (1967), *Stoneman's Country* (1967), *The Great Stonemans* (1968), *A Stoneman Christmas* (1968), *The Stoneman Family Live* (1968), *Tribute To Pop Stoneman* (1969), *In All Honesty* (1970), *Dawn Of The Stoneman's Age* (1970), *The Stonemans* (1970), *California Blues* (1971), *Meet The Stonemans* (1972), *Cuttin' The Grass* (1976), *On The Road* (1977), *Country Hospitality* (1977), *First Family Of Country Music* (1981), *Family Bible* (1988).

Solo albums: Scotty Stoneman *Mr Country Fiddler* (1967), Scotty Stoneman with the Kentucky Colonels *1965 Live In L.A.* (1978).

Story, Carl

b. 29 May 1916, Lenoir, Caldwell County, North Carolina, USA. Story followed his musical father by playing the fiddle and he was fronting his own band when only 19 years old. He played fiddle with Bill Monroe in 1942-43, but was then enlisted for the War. After demobilisation, he turned to guitar and reformed his own band, the Rambling Mountaineers, becoming popular on several radio stations. His records for Mercury are a mixture of mainstream country and bluegrass, and his many excellent musicians include Clarence 'Tater' Tate (fiddle), Bobby Thompson (banjo) and the brothers Bud and Willie Brewster (mandolin and banjo, respectively). Story's own bass-baritone was not the most natural voice for bluegrass music but he developed a countertenor which was ideally suited to the music. He co-wrote 'I Overlooked An Orchid', later a country hit for Mickey Gilley, as well as many gospel songs - 'Lights At The River', 'My Lord Keeps A Record' and 'Are You Afraid To Die?'. Many of Story's early recordings have been reissued by the German Cattle label.

Albums: *Gospel Quartet Favourites* (1958), *America's Favourite Country Gospel Artist* (1959), *Preachin', Prayin', Shoutin' and Singin'* (1959), *Everybody Will Be Happy* (1961), *Get Religion* (1961), *Gospel Revival* (1961), *Mighty Close To Heaven* (1963), *All Day Singing With Dinner On The Ground* (1964), *Good Ole Mountain Gospel Music* (1964), *There's Nothing On Earth That Heaven Can't Cure* (1965), *Sacred Songs Of Life* (1965), *Glory Hallelujah* (1966), *Songs Of Our Saviour* (1966), *From The Altar To Vietnam* (1966), *Carl Story Sings The Gospel Songs You Asked For* (1966), *The Best Of Country Music* (1967), *My Lord Keeps A Record* (1968), *Daddy Sang Bass* (1969), *Precious Memories* (1969), *'Neath The Tree Of Life* (1971), *Precious Memories* (1971), *Light At The River* (1974), *Mother's Last Word* (1975), *Mountain Music* (1976), *The Bluegrass Gospel Collection* (1976), *Live At Bill Grant's Bluegrass Festival* (1977), with the Brewster Brothers *Just A Rose Will Do* (1977), *Lonesome Wail From The Hills* (1977), *Songs From The Blue Ridge Mountains* (1979), *Bluegrass Sound In Stereo* (1980), *The Early Days* (1980), *It's A Mighty Hard Road To Travel* (1980), *Bluegrass Time* (1980), *A Beautiful City* (1982), *Country And Bluegrass Classics* (1983).

Strait, George

b. 18 May 1952, Poteet, Texas, USA. Strait, the second son of a school teacher, was raised in Pearsall, Texas. When his father took over the family ranch, he developed an interest in farming. Strait heard country music throughout his youth but the record which cemented his love was Merle Haggard's *A Tribute To The Best Damn Fiddle Player In The World (Or, My Salute To Bob Wills)*. Strait dropped out of college to elope with his girlfriend, Norma, and then enlisted in the US Army. Whilst there, he began playing country music. Then, at university studying agriculture, he founded the Ace In The Hole band, a name he has used to this day. (His 1989 US country number 1, 'Ace In The Hole', was not about his band, nor did it feature them.) In 1976, he briefly recorded for Pappy Daily's D Records in Houston, one title being 'That Don't Change The Way I Feel About You'. Starting in 1977, Strait made trips to Nashville, but he was too shy to do himself justice. Disillusioned, he was considering a return to Texas but his wife told him to keep trying. A club owner he had worked for, Erv Woolsey, was working for MCA Records: he signed him to the label and then became his manager.

In 1981, Strait's first single, 'Unwound', made number 6 in the US country charts. After two further hits, 'Fool Hearted Memory', from the film in which he had a cameo role, *The Soldier*, went to number 1. Strait was unsure about the recitation on 'You Look So Good In Love', but it was another chart-topper and led to him calling a racehorse, Looks Good In Love. Strait's run of 18 US country number 1 hits also included 'Does Fort Worth Ever Cross Your Mind?' (1985), 'Nobody In His Right Mind Would've Left Her' (1986), 'Am I Blue' (1987), 'Famous Last Words Of A Fool' (1988) and 'Baby's Gotten Good At Goodbye' (1989). Strait was a throwback to the 50s honkytonk sound of country music. He used twin fiddles and steel guitar and his strong, warm delivery was similar to Haggard and Lefty Frizzell. He made no secret of it as he recorded a fine tribute to Frizzell, 'Lefty's Gone'. Strait suffered a personal tragedy when his daughter, Jennifer, died in a car accident in 1986. Managing to compose himself, *Ocean Front Property*, became the first album to enter *Billboard*'s country music chart at number 1, and it included another classic single, 'All My Ex's Live In Texas', which also demonstrated his love of western swing. The white-stetsoned Strait, who also manages to run a large farm, became one of the USA's top concert attractions, winning many awards from the Country Music Association, but it was only in 1989 that he became their Entertainer of the Year. After *Chill Of An Early Fall*, his most impressive album to date, Strait scored a major commercial success with a starring role in the film *Pure Country*, though his soundtrack album was a disappointment.

Albums: *Strait Country* (1981), *Strait From Your Heart* (1982), *Right Or Wrong* (1983), *Does Fort Worth Ever Cross Your Mind?* (1984), *Something Special* (1985), *Merry Christmas Strait To You* (1986), *No. 7* (1987), *Ocean Front Property* (1987), *If You Ain't Lovin' (You Ain't Livin')* (1988), *Beyond The Blue Neon* (1989), *Livin' It Up* (1990), *Chill Of An Early Fall* (1991), *Holding My Own* (1992), *Pure Country* (1992). Compilations: *Greatest Hits* (1986), *Greatest Hits, Volume 2* (1987).

Street, Mel

b. King Malachi Street, 21 October 1933, near Grundy, West Virginia, USA, d. 12 October 1978. Street began performing on local radio in the 50s and then he moved to Niagara Falls and New York, making his living on building sites. He later wrote and recorded the song, 'The High Line Man', about working on radio station masts. He returned to West Virginia and worked in car repairs. He also played clubs and honky tonks, and he recorded his song, 'Borrowed Angel', for a small label in 1970. Two years later it was reissued and became a US country hit. He had further hits with 'Lovin' On Back Streets' and 'I Met A Friend Of Yours Today'. Street became an alcoholic and, beset by personal problems, he shot himself on his 45th birthday in Hendersonville, Tennessee. His US single at the time was 'Just Hangin' On'. George Jones sang 'Amazing Grace' at his funeral. Since his death, he has had country hits with 'The One Thing My Lady Never Puts In Words' and, a duet with Sandy Powell, 'Slip Away'. In 1981, his television-advertised, *Mel Street's Greatest Hits*, sold 400,000 copies.

Albums: *Borrowed Time* (1972), *Mel Street* (1973), *Two Way Street* (1974), *Smokey Mountain Memories* (1975), *Country Colours* (1976), *Mel Street* (1977, Polydor release), *Mel Street* (1978, Mercury release), *Country Soul* (1978). Compilations: *Greatest Hits* (1976), *The Very Best Of Mel Street* (1980), *The Many Moods Of Mel Street* (1980).

Stringbean

b. David Akeman, 17 June 1914, Annville, Jackson County, Kentucky, USA, d. 10 November 1973.

George Strait

Akeman was raised on a farm and received his first banjo by trading a pair of his prized bantams. Between 1935 and 1939 he worked with several bands including that of local celebrity Asa Martin, who, because of his gangling appearance, gave him the nickname of String Beans. Akeman's baseball pitching attracted the attention of Bill Monroe, who signed him for his private team, not knowing that he was also a banjo player. During his time with Monroe, Akeman also worked with Willie Egbert Westbrooks as String Beans And Cousin Wilbur. In 1945 he left Monroe, being replaced by Earl Scruggs and for three years worked with Lew Childre, the two becoming a popular *Grand Ole Opry* act. Akemen, now known as Stringbean, also adopted the strange stage attire, probably based on one worn by old time comedian Slim Miller, which gave the effect of a tall man with very short legs. He married Estelle Stanfill in 1945, who shared his love of the outdoor life and acted as his chauffeur, as Akemen had never learned to drive. In 1946, he formed a lasting friendship with Grandpa Jones and by 1950 was an established solo star of the *Opry*, which he remained to his death. Akeman recorded for Starday in the 60s, achieving success with songs such as 'Chewing Gum', 'I Wonder Where Wanda Went' and 'I'm Going To The Grand Ole Opry And Make Myself A Name'. In 1969, along with Jones, he also became a regular on the network television show *Hee-Haw*. His love of the quiet country life and distrust of banks had fatal consequences when, on returning to their farm at Goodlettsville after his *Opry* performance on 10 November 1973, the Akemans surprised two intruders. Stringbean was shot on entering the house and his wife, then parking the car, was pursued and shot down on the lawn. The killers fled with $250 leaving the bodies to be discovered early next morning by Grandpa Jones. John and Douglas Brown were arrested, charged with murder and in spite of the public outcry for the death penalty, were sentenced to life imprisonment.

Albums: *Old Time Pickin' & Singin' With Stringbean* (1961), *Stringbean* (1962), *Kentucky Wonder* (1962), *A Salute To Uncle Dave Macon* (1963), *Old Time Banjo Picking And Singing* (1964), *Way Back In The Hills Of Old Kentucky* (1964), *Hee-Haw Cornshucker* (1971), *Me & Old Crow (Got A Good Thing Goin')* (1972), *Stringbean Goin' To The Grand Ole Opry* (1977).

Strunk, Jud

b. Justin Strunk, Jnr., 11 June 1936, Jamestown, New York, USA. Strunk was a story-telling banjo player who was popular in both the country and pop markets at the time he died in a plane crash on 15 October 1981. He was raised in Farmington, Maine and was entertaining locals even as a child. He performed as a one-man show for the US Armed Forces and appeared in an off-Broadway musical production titled *Beautiful Dreamer*. He relocated to California in the early 70s and appeared on television with his story-songs. In 1973 he signed to MGM Records and released 'Daisy A Day', a song that appeared on both the pop and country charts. He returned to the country charts three more times, with other humorous tales such as 'Next Door Neighbor's Kid' and 'The Biggest Parakeets In Town'.

Albums: *Jud Strunk's Downeast Viewpoint* (1970), *Daisy A Day* (1973).

Stuart, Marty

b. 1958, Philadelphia, Mississippi, USA. Stuart learned the mandolin and played with the Sullivan Family Gospel Singers, and went on the road with Lester Flatt when only 13 years old. After Flatt's death in 1979, Stuart became part of Johnny Cash's band. He married Cash's daughter, Cindy, although they were soon divorced. Cash was among the guests on his *Busy Bee Cafe*. Stuart had a US country hit with 'Arlene' in 1985. When his first album for US Columbia, *Marty Stuart*, did not sell they shelved plans to release a second, *Let There Be Country*, which featured Emmylou Harris and Mark O'Connor. He has appeared on many albums, including all-star gatherings such as *Will The Circle Be Unbroken, Vol.2, Class Of '55* and *Highwaymen*. In 1988 he returned to playing mandolin for Jerry Sullivan's gospel group and he subsequently produced their highly acclaimed album, *A Joyful Noise*. He revitalized his own career with a powerful mixture of country and rockabilly called *Hillbilly Rock* for MCA. His duet with Travis Tritt, 'The Whiskey Ain't Workin'', was a US country hit and they worked together on the 'No Hats' tour. He was part of Mark O'Connor's influential 1991 album, *The Nashville Cats*. Stuart collects rhinestone suits, owns one of Hank Williams' guitars, tours in Ernest Tubb's bus and follows his dictum of 'Hillbilly rules, OK?'

Albums: *Marty* (1979), *Busy Bee Cafe* (1982), *Marty Stuart* (1985), *Hillbilly Rock* (1989), *Tempted* (1991).

Stuckey, Nat

b. Nathan Wright Stuckey II, 17 December c.mid-30s, Cass County, Texas, USA (his actual date of birth has been variously given as 1933, 1934, 1937 or 1938), d. 24 August 1988. After studying for and obtaining a degree in radio and television, he worked as a disc jockey, first on KALT Atlanta, Texas and then moving to KWKH Shreveport, Louisiana. He began to entertain and between 1958 and 1959, fronting his own band the Cornhuskers, he played the local clubs until his performances won him a spot on KWKH's *Louisiana Hayride*, which he played from 1962-66. After first recording for Sim, he joined the Paula label and in 1966, 'Sweet Thang', which reached number 4, gave him his first US country chart entry. He named his band after the song and during the late 60s, he registered further hits on Paula, before moving in 1968 to RCA, when he also relocated to Nashville. His Top 20s included 'Oh Woman', 'My Can Do Can't Keep Up With My Want To', 'Plastic Saddle', 'Joe And Mabel's 12th Street Bar And Grill', 'Cut Across Shorty', 'Sweet Thang And Cisco' and a duet with Connie Smith of the Sonny James' 1957 country and the pop number 1 'Young Love'. (Gary Stewart played piano in Stuckey's band for some time). He recorded three albums with Connie Smith, including in 1970, an all gospel album with one track, 'If God Is Dead (Who's That Living In My Soul)', making the *Billboard* charts. During the 60s, he also had success as a songwriter with his songs becoming hits for other artists such as 'Waitin' In Your Welfare Line' (a country number 1 for Buck Owens) and 'Pop A Top' (a country number 3 for Jim Ed Brown). His name continued to appear in the charts in the 70s and he had major success with 'She Wakes Me With A Kiss Every Morning' and 'I Used It All On You'. In 1976, he moved to MCA but by the end of the decade his career had begun to fade and his name had disappeared from the charts; the last entry being 'The Days Of Sand And Shovels' in 1978. He continued to tour but could not maintain his earlier successes and he was reduced to mainly playing minor venues. In his latter years, he was even working as a jingle singer and doing commercials. In 1985, he made a final trip to Europe (he had toured several times previously), when he appeared in London at the Wembley Festival. He formed his own publishing company in Nashville but died of lung cancer in August 1988.

Albums: *Nat Stuckey Really Sings* (1966), *All My Tomorrows* (1967), *Country Favorites* (1967), *Nat Stuckey Sings* (1968), *Keep 'Em Country* (1969), *New Country Roads* (1969), with Connie Smith *Young Love* (1969), *Old Man Willis* (1970), *Sunday Morning With Nat Stuckey And Connie Smith* (1970), *Country Fever* (1970), *Only A Woman Like You* (1971), *She Wakes Me With A Kiss Every Morning* (1971), *Forgive Me For Calling You Darling* (1972), *Is It Any Wonder That I Love You* (1972), *Take Time To Love Her* (1973), *Nat Stuckey* (1973), with Connie Smith *Even The Bad Times Are Good* (1973), *In The Ghetto* (1974), *Independence* (1976).

Sun, Joe

b. James J. Paulson, 25 September 1943, Rochester, Minnesota, USA. Sun says, 'I grew up on a farm and, like almost everyone else in the middle of nowhere, listened to the radio.' Sun listened to country and blues stations, hence the strong blues edge to his country music. In the early 70s, he moved to Chicago for a job in computers but he attended folk clubs along Wells Street and was further influenced by John Prine and Steve Goodman. He built up the confidence to become a performer himself, first working as Jack Daniels and then with a group, the Branded Men. During a stint as a disc jockey in Minneapolis, he was mesmerised by Mickey Newbury's 'Are My Thoughts With You?' and decided to move to Nashville. He arrived in 1972 and formed his own graphics company, The Sun Shop, and then used his disc jockey experience to become a record-plugger. He helped to re-establish Bill Black's Combo. In 1977 he worked for the newly-formed country division of Ovation Records, defiantly promoting a b-side the Kendalls' 'Heaven's Just A Sin Away', which went to number 1 in the US country chart. Ovation invited him to record some records and he quickly went to number 14 in the US country charts with Hugh Moffatt's song, 'Old Flames (Can't Hold A Candle To You)'. He had further hits with 'High And Dry', 'I Came On Business For The King' and, with Sheila Andrews, 'What I Had With You'. 'Shotgun Rider' also made the US pop charts, while his cover of 'The Long Black Veil' includes an introduction from its writer, Danny Dill and Marijohn Wilkin. After Ovation went bankrupt, he moved to Elektra but his hard-rocking country style was poorly promoted. With his group, the Solar System, he took to touring Europe two or three times a year. His album, *Hank Bogart Still Lives*, is a tribute to his heroes. His favourite of his own compositions is 'The Sun Never Sets': 'I don't think I'll do much better than that.'

Albums: *Old Flames (Can't Hold A Candle To You)* (1978), *Out Of Your Mind* (1979), *Livin' On Honky Tonk Time* (1980), *Storms Of Life* (1981), *I Ain't*

Honky Tonkin' No More (1982), *The Sun Never Sets* (1984), *Twilight Zone* (1987), *Hank Bogart Still Lives* (1989), *Dixie And Me* (1992).

Swan, Billy

b. Billy Lance Swan, 12 May 1942, in Cape Giradeau, Missouri, USA. Swan grew up listening to country stars like Hank Williams and Lefty Frizzell and then fell under the spell of 50s rock 'n' rollers. At the age of 16, he wrote 'Lover Please', which was recorded by a local plumber who also had an early morning television show (!), *Mirt Mirley And The Rhythm Steppers*. Elvis Presley's bass player, Bill Black, approved and recorded it with his Combo in 1960 before passing it to Clyde McPhatter. McPhatter's version went to number 7 on the US charts, but was overshadowed in the UK by the Vernons Girls, whose version made number 16. Swan, who had insurance money as a result of losing an eye in an accident, moved to Memphis, primarily to write for Bill Black's Combo. He befriended Elvis Presley's uncle, Travis Smith, who was a gate guard at Graceland. Soon, Swan was also minding the gate and attending Elvis' late night visits to cinemas and funfairs. Swan decided that he would be more likely to find work as a musician in Nashville, but the only employment he found was as a janitor at Columbia's studios. He quit while Bob Dylan was recording *Blonde On Blonde*, offering his job to Kris Kristofferson who had entered the building looking for work. Billy swanned around for some time, mainly working as a roadie for Mel Tillis, before meeting Tony Joe White and producing demos of his 'swamp rock'. Swan was invited to produce White officially and their work included *Black And White* with its million-selling single, 'Polk Salad Annie'.

By now Kristofferson had his own record contract and he invited Swan to play bass with his band. They appeared at the Isle of Wight Festival in 1970 where Kristofferson's song 'Blame It On The Stones' was taken at face value. While Kristofferson was being jeered, Swan leaned over and said, 'They love you, Kris.' Billy then joined Kinky Friedman in his band, the Texas Jewboys: he appears on his albums and Friedman recorded 'Lover Please'. Kristofferson invited him to join his band again and producer Chip Young, noticing that Swan's voice was similar to Ringo Starr's, invited him to record for Monument. The first single was a revival of Hank Williams' 'Wedding Bells'. Swan was given an electric organ as a wedding present by Kristofferson and Rita Coolidge. He was fooling

around and the chords to 'I Can Help' appeared. Within a few minutes, he also had the lyrics. On the record, Chip Young's guitar effectively balanced Billy's swirling organ and, with its heavy echo, the production was very 50s. The tune was so infectious that it topped the US charts for two weeks and made number 6 in the UK.

The subsequent album was a cheerful, good-time affair, almost as though Sun Records had decided to modernize their sound. Billy had a similar song prepared for the follow-up single, 'Everything's The Same (Ain't Nothin' Changed)' but Monument preferred to take something from the album to promote its sales. 'I'm Her Fool' with its humorous barking ending was released but it was banned by several radio stations because of the line, 'She pets me when I bury my bone'. A slow version of 'Don't Be Cruel' made number 42 in the UK. Elvis Presley recorded a full-blooded version of 'I Can Help' in 1975, which became a UK Top 30 hit in 1983. Apparently, Presley was amused by the line, 'If your child needs a daddy, I can help', and he sent Swan the socks he wore on the session as a souvenir. Elvis died before he could record Swan's 'No Way Around It (It's Love)'. One of the many asides on Jerry Lee Lewis' version of 'I Can Help' is 'Think about it, Elvis'. Billy Swan released three more albums for Monument and then one each for A&M and Epic, but he failed to recapture the overall quality of his first. Amongst his guest musicians were Carl Perkins, who joined him on remakes of 'Blue Suede Shoes' and 'Your True Love' and an unreleased 'Matchbox', Scotty Moore and Otis Blackwell. The Kristoffersons recorded 'Lover Please' and also a song by Billy and his wife, Marlu, 'Number One'. Swan and Kristofferson co-wrote 'Nobody Loves Anybody Anymore' on Kristofferson's *To The Bone*. Swan has also played on albums by Barefoot Jerry, Harry Chapin, Fred Frith and Dennis Linde. He has worked with T-Bone Burnett on several of his albums and they co-wrote 'Drivin' Wheel' (later recorded by Emmylou Harris), 'The Bird That I Held In My Hand'. Swan briefly worked with Randy Meisner of the Eagles in a country-rock band, Black Tie, who released *When The Night Falls* in 1986. The album includes a tribute to rock 'n' roll's wildman, 'Jerry Lee', as well as familiar songs like 'If You Gotta Make a Fool of Somebody' and 'Chain Gang'. Since then, Swan has preferred the security of touring with Kris Kristofferson.

Albums: *I Can Help* (1975), *Billy Swan* (1975), *Rock 'N' Roll Moon* (1976), *Billy Swan - Four* (1977),

You're OK, I'm OK (1978), *I'm Into Lovin' You* (1981), *When The Night Falls* (as part of Black Tie) (1986).

Albums: *Drifter* (1981), *Just Sylvia* (1982), *Snapshot* (1983), *Surprise* (1984), *One Step Closer* (1985).

Sweethearts Of The Rodeo

Sisters Janis and Kristine Oliver grew up in California and spent much time harmonising. In 1973 they started working as an acoustic duo, taking their name from a Byrds album. Although they mostly performed contemporary country-rock songs, they also had some traditional country leanings. They both were married, becoming Janis Gill and Kristine Arnold. Janis went to Nashville with her husband, Vince Gill, who became one of the first of the 'new country' singers. Janis invited her sister to Nashville, where they won a major talent contest. In 1986, they recorded their first album, *Sweethearts Of The Rodeo*, which yielded five US country singles including 'Hey Doll Baby'. By and large, Kristine is the lead singer and Janis the songwriter, although their wide repertoire includes 'I Feel Fine' and 'So Sad (To Watch Good Love Go Bad)'. The long delay before Columbia released *Sisters* led to rumours that the duo's time at the label was drawing to a close.

Albums: *Sweethearts Of The Rodeo* (1986), *One Time One Night* (1988), *Buffalo Zone* (1990), *Sisters* (1992).

Sylvia

b. Sylvia Kirby Allen, 9 December 1956, Kokomo, Indiana, USA. Sylvia was singing in a church choir from a young age and always wanted to be a professional singer. She took a secretarial job for producer Tom Collins in Nashville in 1976 and he was soon using her on songwriting demos. She worked as a backing vocalist on sessions for Ronnie Milsap and Barbara Mandrell and went on the road with Janie Frickie. She was signed to RCA and worked as an opening act for Charley Pride. She had US country hits with 'Tumbleweed', 'Drifter' (a number 1), 'The Matador' and 'Heart On The Mend', which all came from her first album. In 1982 she had her second US country number 1 and a Top 20 pop hit with 'Nobody', which had only been completed hours before the session. She did not develop her style of merging country music with a disco beat as, in 1985, she took time out to write more personal material. Her duet with Michael Johnson, 'I Love You By Heart', was on the US country chart for 25 weeks, but her most unusual success was with James Galway on a revival of 'The Wayward Wind'.

T

Taylor, Eric

b. c.1947, USA. Taylor wrote stories as a child and later put his talent into narrative songs. He served in Vietnam, experiencing drug and alcohol problems, and then he befriended singer-songwriters, Guy Clark and Townes Van Zandt, in Houston, Texas in 1969. He and his ex-wife Nanci Griffith recorded albums for the small Featherbed label, *Shameless Love* and *Poet In My Window*, respectively. Each was featured on the other's album and Taylor's 'Only Lovers' is about their relationship. Despite his talents as a performer, Taylor decided to qualify as a psychologist and devote his time to helping addicts in Houston. He sang background vocals on Griffith's 1988 live album, *One Fair Summer Evening*, which included his song about the death of Crazy Horse, 'Deadwood, South Dakota', described by Griffith as 'one of the best pieces of writing I've ever heard'.
Album: *Shameless Love* (1981).

Tenneva Ramblers

Formed in 1924, they comprised Claude Grant (b. 1906, d. 1976; guitar/vocals), his brother Jack (b. 1903, d. 1968, mandolin), both from Bristol, Tennessee, USA and Jack Pierce (b. 1908; fiddle) of Smyth County, Virginia, USA, but were sometimes joined by Smokey Davis (a blackface comedian) and on recordings by Claude Slagle (banjo). In 1927, Jimmie Rodgers offered them work as his backing group. After initially refusing, they changed their name to the Jimmie Rodgers Entertainers and made some appearances with him. They were scheduled to back Rodgers on his first recordings but just prior to the session, they left him and reverted to their old name to pursue a recording career of their own. They remained active on various radio stations until 1954, sometimes being known as the Grant Brothers. They are remembered for their recording of 'The Longest Train'.
Album: *The Tenneva Ramblers* (c.70s).

Texas Tornados

Following the success of the Highwaymen (Johnny Cash, Waylon Jennings, Kris Kristofferson, Willie Nelson), four lesser-known Tex-Mex musicians formed the Texas Tornados and secured a contract with a major label, Reprise/WEA. Doug Sahm and organist Augie Meyers, who had been part of the Sir Douglas Quintet and had frequently worked together were joined by accordionist Flaco Jiminez and one-time country star, Freddy Fender. Their enthusiastic debut, *Texas Tornados*, was both a commercial success and a Grammy winner. In actuality, Fender and Jiminez were missing from several tracks and the album, with its mixture of country, blues and Mexican music, was similar to what Sahm and Meyers had been playing for years. Subsequent albums also sound like the Sir Douglas Quintet with friends: their excellent music has included an English/Spanish version of Bob Dylan's 'To Ramona', Butch Hancock's 'She Never Spoke Spanish To Me' and Sahm's standards, 'Who Were You Thinkin' Of' and 'Is Anybody Goin' To San Antone?'.
Albums: *Texas Tornados* (1990), *Zone Of Our Own* (1991), *Hangin' On By A Thread* (1992).

Thomas, B.J.

b. Billy Joe Thomas, 7 August 1942, Hugo, Oklahoma, USA. B.J. Thomas maintained a sturdy career in the USA in both the pop and country fields from the mid-60s into the late 80s. After getting experience by singing in church during his youth, Thomas joined the Triumphs in Houston, Texas, who released a number of unsuccessful singles on small labels. Collaborating with songwriter Mark Charron, a member of the Triumphs, the group recorded an original song, 'Billy And Sue', and released it on the Bragg label without national success. (It was re-released on Warner Brothers Records in 1964 but again failed to take off.) Thomas then recorded a cover of Hank Williams' 'I'm So Lonesome I Could Cry' for Texas producer Huey P. Meaux. It was released on Scepter Records, a New York company and vaulted to number 8 on the national singles chart in the USA. Thomas enjoyed further Top 40 hits with 'Mama' (also recorded successfully by Dave Berry), 'Billy And Sue' and 'The Eyes Of A Woman'. In 1968, Thomas returned to the US Top 10 with the soft-rock 'Hooked On A Feeling', written by Mark James, who also penned 'Suspicious Minds' and 'Always On My Mind' for Elvis Presley. In late 1969, Thomas reached number 1 in the US with 'Raindrops Keep Falling On My Head', a song by Burt Bacharach and Hal David which was featured in the hit film *Butch Cassidy And The Sundance Kid*. 1970 ended with another Top 10 success, 'I Just Can't Help

Believing', written by Barry Mann and Cynthia Weil. Thomas's last significant single for Scepter was 1972's 'Rock And Roll Lullaby', another Mann and Weil composition, which reached number 15 and featured Duane Eddy on guitar and the Blossoms on backing vocals. After that, the company folded, and it was not until 1975, now signed to ABC Records (after a brief, unproductive stint at Paramount), that Thomas enjoyed another hit. '(Hey Won't You Play) Another Somebody Done Somebody Wrong Song' provided his second number 1 and also topped the country charts. That record provided a second career for Thomas as a country star. Although he switched record company affiliations often, moving from ABC to MCA in 1978, to Cleveland International in 1983, and to Columbia Records in 1985, Thomas maintained his status in that field until the late 80s. Featuring gospel material in his act as well as straight country, he drew a new audience and continued to sell records. Thomas enjoyed a particularly strong string of country singles in 1983-84, beginning with two number 1 records, 'Whatever Happened To Old Fashioned Love' and 'New Looks From An Old Lover'. 'Two Car Garage' and 'The Whole World's In Love When You're Lonely' also made the Top 10, while a duet with Ray Charles, 'Rock And Roll Shoes', reached number 15. Simultaneous with his country career, Thomas recorded a number of gospel-inspired albums for the Myrrh label.
Selected albums: *I'm So Lonesome I Could Cry* (1966), *Tomorrow Never Comes* (1966), *Songs For Lovers And Losers* (1967), *On My Way* (1968), *Young And In Love* (1969), *Raindrops Keep Fallin' On My Head* (1969), *Everybody's Out Of Town* (1970), *Most Of All* (1970), *Billy Joe Thomas* (1972), *B.J. Thomas Country* (1972), *Songs* (1973), *Longhorn And London Bridges* (1974), *Reunion* (1975), *Help Me Make It To My Rockin' Chair* (1975), *B.J. Thomas* (1977), *Home Where I Belong* (1977), *B.J. Thomas* (1977), *Everybody Loves* (1978), *Happy Man* (1979), *New Looks* (1983), *Throwin' Rocks At The Moon* (1985). Compilations: *Greatest Hits, Vol. 1* (1969), *Greatest Hits, Vol. 2* (1971), *ABC Collection* (1976).

Thompson, Hank

b. Henry William Thompson, 3 September 1925, Waco, Texas, USA. Thompson, as a young boy, was fond of records by Jimmie Rodgers and the Carter Family. He first learned the harmonica and then his parents gave him a guitar for his tenth birthday. He also played Hawaiian guitar, learned

conjuring tricks and had a ventriloquist's doll. With his range of talents, he was a popular performer at Saturday morning stage shows in Waco. In 1942, he began his own local radio series, *Hank - The Hired Hand*. From 1943 Thompson served three years in the US navy. He worked as an electrical engineer and, in his spare time, he entertained his shipmates. He says, 'The navy enhanced my career as it gave the opportunity to perform all the time. When I was overseas, I knew the guys were getting tired of hearing the same songs and so I started writing.' In 1946, he returned to Waco, formed the Brazos Valley Boys (named after the river running through Waco), and began performing at dances throughout Texas. His own song, 'Whoa Sailor', was a regional hit on Globe Records. It was followed by 'A Lonely Heart Knows' on Bluebonnet. Country star Tex Ritter heard Thompson and recommended him to his label, Capitol. Almost immediately, Thompson had a number 2 country hit with '(I've Got A) Humpty Dumpty Heart'. In 1949 he had another country hit with a re-recorded 'Whoa Sailor'. Thompson was a tall, upright performer with a resonant voice not unlike Ritter's, who dressed himself and his band in expensive Nudie suits. Applying his engineering knowledge, he gave the band a powerful live sound and lighting, and soon he had the most successful western swing band in the USA.
In 1951 Thompson began a 13-year partnership with the Hollywood record producer Ken Nelson and recorded his most successful single, 'The Wild Side Of Life', in one take. (Ironically 'Crying In The Deep Blue Sea' was the original a-side). 'The Wild Side Of Life' stayed at the top of the US country charts for 15 weeks and won Thompson a gold record. Kitty Wells recorded an answer version, 'It Wasn't God Who Made Honky Tonk Angels', while Thompson himself answered 'Goodnight, Irene' with 'Wake Up, Irene'. Defying conventions, Thompson was permitted to repeat its snare drum sound on the *Grand Ole Opry*. Thompson had further country hits with 'Waiting In The Lobby Of Your Heart', 'Rub-A-Dub-Dub', 'Breakin' The Rules', 'Honky Tonk Girl', 'The Blackboard Of My Heart', and 'Breakin' In Another Heart', which was co-written with his wife Dorothy. In 1957 Thompson parodied rock 'n' roll in 'Rockin' In The Congo' and became a successful performer in Las Vegas. He heard 'Squaws Along The Yukon' on a hunting trip in Alaska with Merle Travis and together they arranged and updated the song. In 1959 became

Hank Thompson

the first country artist to record in stereo via the best-selling *Songs For Rounders*, and the first to record an 'in concert' album, *Live At The Golden Nugget*. He heard a band in a club in Holbrook, Arizona and was most impressed with their original song, 'A Six Pack To Go'. He turned the song into a country standard, later reviving it in duet with George Strait, and had further country hits with 'She's Just A Whole Lot Like You' and 'Oklahoma Hills'. Since Thompson left Capitol in 1964, he has recorded for several labels and his country hits have included 'Smokey The Bar', 'Where Is The Circus?', 'The Older The Violin, The Sweeter The Music' and, appropriately, 'Mr. Honky Tonk, The King Of Western Swing'. He has recorded tribute albums to the Mills Brothers (*Cab Driver*) and Nat 'King' Cole. In 1973 Thompson opened a school of country music in Claremore, Oklahoma, where he taught. He was elected to the *Country Music Hall Of Fame* in 1989, and still tours throughout the world, wearing his sequinned jackets: 'The public is entitled to something that is colourful and flashy. We're in show business and there's nothing colourful about a T-shirt and ragged jeans.'

Albums: *Songs Of The Brazos Valley* (1953), *North Of The Rio Grande* (1955), *New Recordings Of All Time Hits* (1956), *Favourite Waltzes* (1956), *Hank Thompson Favourites* (1957), *Hank!* (1957), *Dance Ranch* (1958), *Songs For Rounders* (1959), *Most Of All* (1960), *This Broken Heart Of Mine* (1960), *An Old Love Affair* (1961), *At The Golden Nugget* (1961), *A Six Pack To Go* (1961), *No. 1 Country And Western Band* (1962), *Live At The Cherokee Frontier Days Rodeo In Wyoming* (1962), *Live At The State Fair Of Texas* (1963), *It's Christmas Time With Hank* (1964), *Breakin' In Another Heart* (1965), *Breakin' The Rules* (1966), *The Countrypolitan Sound Of Hank Thompson's Brazos Valley Boys* (1967), *Just An Old Flame* (1967), *Country Blues* (1968), *Hank Thompson Sings The Gold Standards* (1968), *On Tap, In The Can Or In The Bottle* (1968), *Smokey The Bar* (1969), *Salutes Oklahoma* (1969), *The Instrumental Sound Of Hank Thompson's Brazos Valley Boys* (1970), *Next Time I Fall In Love (I Won't)* (1971), *Cab Driver - A Salute To The Mills Brothers* (1972), *1000 And One Nighters* (1973), *Kindly Keep It Country* (1973), *Movin' On* (1974), *Hank Thompson Sings The Hits Of Nat 'King' Cole* (1975), *Back In The Swing Of Things* (1976), *The Thompson Touch* (1977), with Roy Clark, Freddy Fender and Don Williams *Country Comes To Carnegie Hall* (1977), *Doin' My Thing* (1977), *Brand New Hank* (1978), *Take Me Back To Texas* (1980), *Hank Thompson* (1986), *Here's To Country Music* (1988).

Compilations: *Where Is The Circus (And Other Heart Breakin' Hits)* (1966), *A Gold Standard Collection* (1967), *25th Anniversary Album* (1972), *Best Of The Best Of Hank Thompson* (1980), *Greatest Hits, Volumes 1 & 2* (1987).

Thompson, Sue

b. Eva Sue McKee, 19 July 1926, Nevada, Missouri, USA. Sue's earliest ambition was to be a singing cowgirl, and she sang at many local functions. She continued performing when the family moved to California and she appeared regularly on a Dude Martin's country television show in San Francisco. A single with Martin, 'If You Want Some Lovin'', led to a solo contract with Mercury Records. In 1960, she sang on Red Foley's portion of the *Grand Ole Opry* and she signed with the country label, Hickory. John D. Loudermilk wrote 'Sad Movies (Make Me Cry)' and 'Norman', which went to numbers 5 and 3 respectively on the US pop charts and both became million sellers. Boudleaux and Felice Bryant wrote another US hit, 'Have A Good Time', and Loudermilk returned with the novelties, 'James (Hold The Ladder Steady)' and 'Paper Tiger'. Despite her American success, Thompson only had two minor Top 50 entries in the UK, but she was unlucky as Carol Deene covered all three Loudermilk songs. Through her novelty songs she became known as 'the girl with the itty bitty voice', so she turned to more mature material. In the 70s she was teamed with Don Gibson, the two registering nine US country successes including 'The Two Of Us Together' and 'Oh How Love Changes'. Her last significant country success was with 'Big Mabel Murphy' in 1975. She married singer Hank Penny.

Albums: *Meet Sue Thompson* (1962), *Two Of A Kind* (1962), *Paper Tiger* (1962), *With Strings Attached* (1966), *Country Side Of Sue Thompson* (1966), *This Is Sue Thompson* (1969), *And Love Me* (1974), *Sweet Memories* (1974), *Big Mabel Murphy* (1975). With Don Gibson: *The 2 Of Us Together* (1973), *Warm Love* (1974), *Oh How Love Changes* (1975).

Thompson, Uncle Jimmie

b. James Donald Thompson, 1848, near Baxter, Smith County, Tennessee, USA. Little is known of his early life except that the family moved to Texas just before the Civil War, and by 1860 Thompson was already a capable fiddle player using a style described as the long bow technique, common to the state. He learned tunes from Civil War veterans and other sources and though generally described as a farmer, he travelled extensively. He returned to Smith County, Tennessee probably in the early 1880s, where he married a local girl. Around 1902 Thompson and his family returned to Texas. By this time he was playing more public performances and in 1907 he won an eight-day fiddling contest in Dallas. It was probably 1912, when he once more returned to Tennessee and bought a farm near Henderson. His wife died soon afterwards but in 1916 he remarried and moved to Laguardo, Wilson County. He acquired an old truck, which he adapted as a mobile caravan and began to tour the state playing his fiddle at fairs or wherever he could make a dollar. He was always a hard drinking man and stubborn in his ways. About 1923 he drove all the way back to Texas just to take part in a fiddling contest. At the age of 77 his wish to broadcast came true when George D. Hay made him the first artist on his new *WSM Barn Dance* programme that was to become the *Grand Ole Opry*. He boasted that he could play a thousand tunes and was deeply upset when he found that his niece Eva made him have his trousers pressed for the occasion. His comment was 'Hey, thar, who ironed them damn wrinkles im my britches? I like my britches smooth and round to fit my kneecaps.' Following his broadcast, Uncle Jimmie became somewhat of a celebrity, with his eccentricity endearing him to many people. Some of his habits did not endear him to George D. Hay, particularly his likeness for a jug of local moonshine 'just to lubricate his arm' nor his seeming inability to play to his allotted time without considerably overrunning.

By 1927, with the emergence of many new artists, his *Opry* appearances were very limited. He first recorded in Atlanta for Columbia in 1926 and later in 1930 recorded in Knoxville for Brunswick/Vocalion. Experts comment that he was still a player of great ability when he made his last recordings. He died from pneumonia at his home in Laguardo, Tennessee on 17 February 1931. Eva Thompson Jones was the only member of the *Opry* cast to attend his funeral. He once stayed at Eva's house in Nashville and when later asked how he liked it he replied, 'I wouldn't have it, there ain't nowhere for to spit when I chew my tobacco'. Examples of his recorded work may be found on various compilation albums of early string band and country music.

Further reading: *The Grand Ole Opry (The Early Years 1925-35)*, Charles K. Wolfe.

Tillis, Mel

b. Lonnie Melvin Tillis, 8 August 1932, Tampa, Florida, USA. The family relocated to Dover, 18 miles east of Tampa, when he was only eight months old. He contracted malaria when aged only three, and was left with a permanent stutter. During his school days, various treatments failed to cure this speech problem and though originally embarrassed by it, he managed in later years to turn it into a trademark. He learned to play guitar (and later the fiddle) during his early teens and at high school was a football player and also played drums in a band. In the early 50s, devoid of any real career ideas, he enlisted in the Air Force. He was discharged in 1955 when for a short time he attended the University of Florida. Bored, he dropped out and worked at various tasks including strawberry picking and truck driving. In 1956 he wrote a song called 'I'm Tired', which was recorded by and became a big hit for Webb Pierce. This enabled Tillis, as he said later, 'to get the hell out of the strawberry patch in a hurry'. He found that the stutter never appeared when he sang and gradually his confidence grew and he moved to Nashville. During 1956 and 1957 he began to perform and made his first recording, only to be told he needed original material, which prompted him to concentrate more on writing. He signed with Columbia and had his first US country chart success with his co-written song 'The Violet And The Rose' in 1958. In the next few years several of his songs proved hits for other artists including Webb Pierce ('Tupelo County Jail' and 'I Ain't Never'), Johnny And Jack ('Lonely Island Pearl'), Ray Price ('Heart Over Mind') and Carl Smith ('Ten Thousand Drums'). His status received a further boost in 1963 when Bobby Bare had major country and pop hits with 'Detroit City', which he had co-written with Danny Dill. Three years later 'The Snakes Crawl At Night' launched the recording career of Charley Pride.

In the mid-60s Tillis moved to Kapp Records, and in 1967 received his biggest hit up to that time with the Harlan Howard song 'Life Turned Her That Way', which made both pop and country charts. (The song later became a standard and a US country number 1 in 1988 for Ricky Van Shelton). In 1967 Johnny Darrell had a number 9 US country hit with 'Ruby, Don't Take Your Love To Town', a song that two years later became a million selling US pop hit for Kenny Rogers And The First Edition. (It also reached number 2 in the UK pop charts the same year). By the late 60s Tillis had established a reputation as both a writer and a performer and with his band the Statesiders, named after his 1966 hit 'Stateside', he toured extensively.The same pattern continued throughout the 70s, when he averaged 250 concerts annually and was also much in demand for appearances on network television shows. He achieved his first country Top 10 hit in 1969 with 'These Lonely Hands Of Mine'. During the 70s, recording for MGM and MCA, he had 33 country hits of which 24 were Top 10 records, including 5 number 1s with 'I Ain't Never', 'Good Woman Blues', 'Heart Healer', 'I Believe In You' and 'Coca Cola Cowboy'. (The last, like his number 2 hit 'Send Me Down To Tucson', featured in the Clint Eastwood film *Every Which Way But Loose*). In 1970 he recorded an album with Bob Wills and during the 70s he also made several hit recordings with Sherry Bryce, including 'Take My Hand', which achieved crossover success. He recorded for Elektra in the early 80s, charting seven successive Top 10 hits, including a further number 1 with 'Southern Rains'. In 1983, he returned to MCA and the next year made number 10 with his recording of Tommy Collins 'New Patches'. He later recorded for RCA and Mercury. Duet recordings in the 80s were with Glen Campbell and Nancy Sinatra.

In the 80s, his daughter Pam Tillis began to forge a flourishing career as a songwriter, graduating to a very successful recording career in the 90s.

He has appeared in several films including *W.W. And The Dixie Dance Kings*, *Smokey And The Bandit 2*, *Murder In Music City* and in 1986 he co-starred with Roy Clark in a comedy western called *Uphill All The Way*, which they both also produced. He became a very successful businessman and at one time owned several publishing companies including Sawgrass and Cedarwood. His recordings have generally balanced out between honky tonk and the accepted Nashville Sound. Around 1980, he went to play what he thought was a limousine convention in Tulsa. It turned out to be a limousine, which is an exotic breed of cattle. He developed an interest by buying a 2,200 pound bull which he named 'Stutterin' Boy'. It was only one of 50 such bulls in the USA and he had a party to introduce it to the media! Tillis has been buying adjacent smallholdings outside Nashville and he himself owns a 400-acre farm. He said, 'A lot of people invest their money in tax shelters, but I feel I am doing something to benefit the country...this bull is going to breed more and better cattle, and that's no b-b-b-bull.' During his career, he has won many awards, including being named as CMA

Entertainer Of The Year in 1976 and as one of country music's most prolific songwriters, he was inducted into the Nashville Songwriters International Hall Of Fame the same year. The stutter still exists when he speaks but he always jokes and uses it to his advantage, regularly opening his show with comments such as 'I'm here to d-d-dispel those rumours going round that M-M-Mel T-Tillis has quit st-st-st-stuttering. That's not true I'm still st-st-stuttering and making a pretty good living at it t-t-too'.

Albums: *Heart Over Mind* (1961), *Stateside* (1966), *The Great Mel Tillis* (1966), *Life Turned Her That Way* (1966), *Mr Mel* (1967), *Let Me Talk To You* (1968), *Something Special* (1969), *Sings Ole Faithful* (1969), *Who's Julie* (1969), *Mel Tillis/Bob Wills* (1970), *One More Time* (1970), *Big 'N' Country* (1970), *She'll Be Hanging 'Round Somewhere* (1970), *The Arms Of A Fool/Commercial Affection* (1971), *Live At The Sam Houston Coliseum* (1971), with Sherry Bryce *Living & Learning/Take My Hand* (1971), *Would You Want The World To End* (1972), *I Ain't Never/Neon Rose* (1972), *Mel Tillis* (1972), *Walking On New Grass* (1972), *Mel Tillis & The Statesiders On Stage Live In Birmingham* (1973), *Sawmill* (1973), with Bryce *Let's Go All The Way Tonight* (1973), *Midnight, Me And The Blues/Stomp Them Grapes* (1974), *Mel Tillis & The Statesiders* (1974), *M-M-Mel And The Statesiders* (1975), *Welcome To Mel Tillis Country* (1976), *Love Revival* (1976), *Love's Troubled Waters* (1977), *Heart Healer* (1977), *I Believe In You* (1978), *Are You Sincere* (1979), *The Entertainer* (1979), *Me And Pepper* (1979), *The Great Mel Tillis* (1979), *M-M-Mel Live* (1980), *Your Body Is An Outlaw* (1980), *Southern Rain* (1980), with Nancy Sinatra *Mel And Nancy* (1981), *It's A Long Way To Daytona* (1982), *After All This Time* (1983), *New Patches* (1984), with Jerry Lee Lewis, Webb Pierce and Faron Young *Four Legends* (1985), *California Road* (1985).

Further reading: *Stutterin' Boy, The Autobiography Of Mel Tillis*, Mel Tillis with Walter Wager.

Tillman, Floyd

b. 8 December 1914, Ryan, Oklahoma, USA. Tillman was the youngest of 11 children of a sharecropping family who moved to Post, Texas when he was a few months old. He first learned to play mandolin and banjo but later changed to guitar, performing with Adolph Hofner's band, even singing a few songs, though later admitting he wished to be a songwriter since he could not sing. He changed to Mack Clark's dance band in Houston, leaving to join the Blue Ridge Playboys of Leon Selph, when Clark's band professed his song 'It Makes No Difference Now' was too hillbilly. (The song later became a hit for both Gene Autry and Bing Crosby and established Tillman as a songwriter, in spite of the fact that he once sold it to Jimmie Davis for $200 but managed to obtain joint ownership in 1966, when the copyright came up for renewal.) The Blue Ridge Playboys, who included Moon Mullican, Bob Dunn and Cliff Brunner, became noted as specialists of honky tonk music. During World War II he served in the Army Air Corps but returned to songwriting and playing with his band around the honky tonks of the Houston area on his discharge. He first recorded for Decca in 1939 but scored his own solo chart successes in the 40s. He had a number 1 US country hit with 'They Took The Stars Out Of Heaven' in 1944 and followed with other Top 10 hits including 'G.I. Blues'. 'Drivin' Nails In My Coffin', 'I Love You So Much It Hurts', 'I Gotta Have My Baby Back', 'Slippin' Around' and the follow-up 'I'll Never Slip Around Again'. (The last two songs have led to comment that Tillman was one of the first artists to write and record songs of cheating or infidelity). His songs proved even more successful when recorded by other artists. In 1949 'Slippin Around' was a million-selling number 1 US country and pop hit for Margaret Whiting and Jimmy Wakely and a country number 1 and pop number 17 for Ernest Tubb. The song has charted for others since, including Texas Jim Robertson (1950), Marion Worth and George Morgan (1964), Roy Drusky and Priscilla Mitchell (1965) and Mack Abernathy (1988). (The Whiting and Wakely combination also registered Top 10 country and pop chart success with the follow-up song later the same year.) In the early 50s, Tillman gave up his band and inclined towards semi-retirement by being more selective on when and where he would perform. The last track he recorded with the band, 'I Don't Care Anymore', possibly summed up his feelings. He gained his last chart entry in 1960 with 'It Just Tears Me Up' but he made further recordings on minor labels, including an album of his songs with various friends such as Merle Haggard and Willie Nelson, both of whom were influenced by his style. Tillman was one of the first to champion the use of the electric guitar in country music and also one of the first country artists to travel by aeroplane to get to his bookings. At times his growling raucous vocals, certainly an acquired taste, made Ernest Tubb seem gentle and completely in tune, but his songwriting alone

gained him admission to the *Nashville Songwriters Association International Hall Of Fame* in 1970 and saw him inducted into the *Country Music Hall Of Fame* in 1984.
Selected albums: *Let's Make Memories* (1962), *Country* (1967), *Dream On* (1968), *I'll Still Be Loving You* (1969), *Floyd Tillman & Friends* (1982). Compilations: *Floyd Tillman's Greatest* (1958), *Floyd Tillman's Best* (1964), *Sings His Greatest Hits Of Lovin'* (1965), *Dream On* (1968), *Portraits Of Floyd Tillman* (1971), *Golden Hits* (1975), *Country Music Hall Of Fame Series* (1991).

Tillotson, Johnny

b. 20 April 1939, Jacksonville, Florida, USA. Tillotson's father was a country music disc jockey and Tillotson himself was appearing on local radio from the age of nine. His parents encouraged his talent by giving him first a ukelele and then a guitar, and he was influenced by the singing cowboys (Gene Autry, Roy Rogers) and country singer, Hank Williams. He appeared regularly on Tom Dowdy's television show, from which he was recommended to Archie Bleyer, the owner of Cadence Records. His first single in 1958 combined the teen ballad, 'Dreamy Eyes' with the up-tempo 'Well, I'm Your Man'. Although his roots were in country music, he was encouraged to revive the R&B ballads, 'Never Let Me Go', 'Pledging My Love' and 'Earth Angel'. In 1960 he released the classic teen-ballad, 'Poetry In Motion', which went to number 2 in the USA and number 1 in the UK. The b-side, 'Princess, Princess', was popular in its own right and the equal of many of his later hits. Tillotson's follow-up, 'Jimmy's Girl', was less successful but he went to number 3 in the USA with 'It Keeps Right On A-Hurtin'', a self-penned country ballad. The song has been recorded by over 100 performers including Elvis Presley. Tillotson's baby-face and slight frame made him an ideal teen-idol for the early 60s, but his musical preference was country music. He had further success by reviving the country songs, 'Send Me The Pillow That You Dream On' and 'I Can't Help It (If I'm Still In Love With You)'. In the film *Just For Fun* he sang 'Judy, Judy, Judy', which he wrote with Doc Pomus and Mort Shuman. His ballad, 'You Can Never Stop Me Loving You' was a US Top 20 hit, but Kenny Lynch's version was preferred by UK record-buyers. A spell in the US army prevented Tillotson from capitalizing on his success, but when he signed with MGM he was determined to become a country performer. 'Talk Back Trembling Lips'

Johnny Tillotson

was a US Top 10 hit, but his subsequent records – 'Worried Guy', 'I Rise, I Fall', 'She Understands Me', 'Heartaches By The Number' – only reached the Top 40. He also appeared in Las Vegas, hence a single of 'Cabaret'. Tillotson is popular on US army bases in Europe and he has several of his hits in Japanese, following successful appearances in Japan. The 30-track compilation, *All The Early Hits - And More!!!*, which was released in the UK by Ace Records in 1990, is the best introduction to his work and includes an early version of 'Poetry In Motion'.

Albums: *Tillotson's Best* (1962), *It Keeps Right On A-Hurtin'* (1962), *Judy, Judy, Judy* (1963), *Alone With You* (1963), *Johnny Tillotson* (1964), *The Tillotson Touch* (1964), *She Understands Me* (1964), *That's My Style* (1965), *Our World* (1966), *Tillotson Sings Tillotson, Volume 1* (1966), *No Love At All* (1966), *Here I Am* (1967), *Tears On My Pillow* (1970), *Johnny Tillotson* (1971), *Johnny Tillotson* (1977). Compilation: *All The Hits* (1987).

Tippin, Aaron

b. 1959, South Carolina, USA. Tippin wrote all of his debut album, *You've Got To Stand For Something Else*, which he recorded with a crack studio band including Mark O'Connor, Larrie Londin, and Emory Gordy Jnr., who also produced. The album was both modern and a throwback to the country music of the 40s, and its title track was a favourite of American soldiers during the Gulf War. The muscular country singer has numerous female fans and his macho stance is evident from song titles like 'I Wouldn't Have It Any Other Way'.

Albums: *You've Got To Stand For Something* (1990), *Read Between The Lines* (1992).

Tompall And The Glaser Brothers

The three youngest of the six children of Louis and Marie Glaser, namely, Tompall (b.Thomas Paul Glaser, 3 September 1933), Chuck (b. Charles Vernon Glaser, 27 February 1936) and Jim (b. James Wilson Glaser, 16 December 1937), were born in Spalding, Nebraska, USA. They were raised in a farming community and, from the time Tompall was 14, he was singing in a trio with Chuck and Jim. Their break into professional show-business came in 1957 when they won *Arthur Godfrey's Talent Show* on television. Other on-screen appearances followed and they joined Marty Robbins' roadshow and moved to Nashville in 1958. Their first singles included a cover of The Coasters' 'Yakety Yak', and in 1959, they were signed to US Decca Records, primarily as folksingers but soon switched to country. They sang on several of Robbins' records including 'She Was Only Seventeen' and 'El Paso' and Jim and Tompall wrote 'Running Gun'. They also toured with Johnny Cash and can be heard on his 1962 *The Sound Of Johnny Cash* as well as his transatlantic success, 'Ring Of Fire'. Among their sessions are Roy Orbison's 'Leah' and Claude King's 'The Comancheros' and others for Patsy Cline, George Jones and Hank Snow, who also recorded Chuck's song, 'Where Has All The Love Gone?'. Jim wrote a transatlantic pop hit for Gary Puckett And The Union Gap, 'Woman Woman', whilst Tompall (with Harlan Howard) wrote an archetypal country song in 'Streets Of Baltimore', recorded by Bobby Bare, Charley Pride and Gram Parsons. In 1965 they recorded a folk EP as the Charleston Trio for Bravo Records. In 1966 the brothers moved to MGM and created some of the best harmony singing in country music. Amongst their successes on the US country charts were 'Rings', 'Gone, On The Other Hand', 'The Moods Of Mary' and 'Faded Love'. In 1971 they launched the Glaser Sound Studios in Nashville and they continued to work there after disbanding in 1973.

Tompall found success as a solo artist after being part of the highly successful *Wanted: The Outlaws* project with Waylon Jennings and Willie Nelson. Many Nashville outlaws hung out and recorded at the studios, notably Kinky Friedman. In 1975 Chuck Glaser, who had discovered John Hartford and Dick Feller, had a stroke which paralysed his vocal chords, but with enormous resilience he regained his abilities. He produced Hank Snow's *The Mysterious Lady* and the story-album of *Christopher The Christmas Tree*. Jim Glaser's solo career floundered when he failed to have solo hits and could no longer support a band. In 1979 the brothers reformed and, with Tompall gruffer than ever, had success with 'Lovin' Her Was Easier' and 'Weight Of My Chains'. In 1983 Jim was replaced by Sherrill Nielsen (also known as Shaun Nielsen), who had sung alongside Elvis Presley's narration of 'Softly, As I Leave You' and released the improbably titled *The Songs I Sang For Elvis*. Jim had US country hits with 'The Man In The Mirror', 'When You're Not A Lady', 'You Got Me Running' and 'You're Gettin' To Me Again', a US country number 1. His song, 'Who Were You Thinking Of (When We Were Making Love Last Night)?', was a US pop hit for Dandy and the Doolittle Band. Tompall has also worked as a solo artist and his albums include love ballads from

World War II. An album tribute to Bob Wills remains unreleased. He recorded 'Ugly Women And Pick-Up Trucks' with Jimmy Payne and he produced the 1986 *Mac Wiseman*, and Ethel And The Shameless Hussies' *Born To Burn*.

Albums: by Tompall And The Glaser Brothers *This Land* (1960), *Country Folks* (1962), *Tompall And The Glaser Brothers* (1967), *Through The Eyes Of Love* (1968), *The Wonderful World Of Tompall And The Glaser Brothers* (1968), *Now Country* (1969), *Tick Tick Tick* (1970), *The Award Winners* (1971), *Rings And Things* (1972), *Tompall And The Glaser Brothers Sing Great Hits From Two Decades* (1973), *Busted* (1981), *Lovin' Her Was Easier* (1981), *After All These Years* (1982).

Albums: by Jim Glaser *Just Looking For A Home* (as Jim Glaser and the Americana Folk Trio) (1961), *The Man In The Mirror* (1984), *Past The Point Of No Return* (1985), *Everyone Knows I'm Yours* (1986).

Albums: by Tompall Glaser *Tompall Glaser Sings The Ballad Of Namu The Killer Whale And Other Ballads Of Adventure* (1966), *Charlie* (1973), *Take The Singer With The Song* (1974), *Tompall Sings The Songs Of Shel Silverstein* (1974), *The Great Tompall And His Outlaw Band* (1976), *Tompall And His Outlaw Band* (1977), *The Wonder Of It All* (1977), *Nights On The Borderline* (1986), *A Collection Of Love Ballads From World War II* (1987), *The Rogue* (1992).

Travis, Merle

b. Merle Robert Travis, 29 November 1917, Rosewood, Kentucky, USA, d. 20 October 1983, Tahlequah, Oklahoma, USA. He was the son of a tobacco farmer but by the time Travis was four-years-old the family had moved to Ebenezer, Kentucky, and his father was working down the mines. Travis's father often remarked, 'Another day older and deeper in debt', a phrase his son used in 'Sixteen Tons'. His father played the banjo, but Travis preferred the guitar. He befriended two coal-miners, Mose Reger and Ike Everly, the father of the Everly Brothers, who demonstrated how to use the thumb for the bass strings while playing the melody on treble strings. Travis hitched around the country, busking where he could, and in 1935, he joined the Tennessee Tomcats and from there to a better-known country group, Clayton McMichen's Georgia Wildcats. In 1937 he became a member of the Drifting Pioneers, who performed on WLW Cincinnati. In 1943 he recorded for the local King label, recording a solo as Bob McCarthy and a duet with Grandpa Jones as the Shepherd Brothers. He and Jones did many radio shows together and many years later, re-created that atmosphere for an album. Travis, Jones and the Delmore Brothers also worked as a gospel quartet, the Browns Ferry Four. After war service in the marines, he settled in California and worked with artists such as Tex Ritter. Travis' arrangement of 'Muskrat' for Ritter was later developed into a hit single for the Everly Brothers.

He played with several bands, becoming one of the first to appreciate that a guitar could be a lead instrument, and he had success as a solo artist for the newly-formed Capitol Records with 'Cincinnati Lou', 'No Vacancy', 'Divorce Me C.O.D.', 'Missouri' and a US country number 1, 'So Round, So Firm, So Fully Packed'. He co-wrote Capitol's first million-seller, 'Smoke, Smoke, Smoke That Cigarette' with Tex Williams, who recorded it. Burl Ives and Josh White were spearheading a craze for folk music, so Capitol producer, Lee Gillette, asked Travis for a 78 rpm album set of Kentucky folk songs. 'I don't know any' said Travis. 'Then write some' was the reply. His eight-song *Folk Songs Of Our Hills*, included 'Nine Pound Hammer' (a rewritten folk song), 'Dark As A Dungeon' and 'Sixteen Tons' with spoken introductions about the coal-mining locale. Although Travis maintained that 'Sixteen Tons' was a 'fun song', it dealt with the exploitation of miners in the company store. It won a gold record for Tennessee Ernie Ford in 1955 and was parodied by Spike Jones as 'Sixteen Tacos' and by Max Bygraves as 'Seventeen Tons'. Travis himself was also enjoying a country hit with a revival of 'Wildwood Flower' with Hank Thompson, and he won acclaim for his portrayal of a young GI in the 1954 film *From Here To Eternity*, in which he sang 'Re-enlistment Blues'. Travis's *Walkin' The Strings* is a highly-regarded album of acoustic guitar solos. His style influenced Doc Watson, who called his son after him, and Chet Atkins, who did the same with his daughter.

In 1948 he devised a solid-body electric guitar, which was built for him by Paul Bigsby and developed by Leo Fender. 'I got the idea from a steel guitar' he said, 'I wanted the same sustainability of notes, and I came up with a solid-body electric guitar with the keys all on one side.' Travis had an entertaining stage act in which he would mimic animals on his guitars. He was a good cartoonist and he worked as a scriptwriter on Johnny Cash's television shows. He took part in the Nitty Gritty Dirt Band's tribute to country music, *Will The Circle Be Unbroken?*, and was one of the Texas Playboys in the Clint Eastwood film,

Honkytonk Man. Travis was elected to the Country Music Hall Of Fame in 1977 but his drug addiction and alcoholism made him unreliable and wrecked his private life. Says Tennessee Ernie Ford, 'Merle Travis was one of the most talented men I ever met. He could write songs that would knock your hat off, but he was a chronic alcoholic and when those binges would come, there was nothing we could do about it.' Travis died in October 1983. A posthumous album of blues songs played on 12-string guitar, *Rough, Rowdy And Blue*, included a tune from his mentor, Mose Reger, 'Merry Christmas, Pretty Baby'. His friend and fellow guitarist, Joe Maphis, wrote a tribute 'Me And Ol' Merle', which concluded, 'We liked good whiskey and we loved the pretty girls, And we loved them guitars - Me and Ol' Merle.'

Albums: *Folk Songs Of The Hills* (1946), *The Merle Travis Guitar* (1956), *Back Home* (1957), *Walkin' The Strings* (1960), *Travis!* (1962), *Songs Of The Coal Miners* (1963), with Joe Maphis *Two Guitar Greats* (1964), with Johnny Bond *Great Songs Of The Delmore Brothers* (1969), *Strictly Guitar* (1969), with Chet Atkins *The Atkins-Travis Travelling Show* (1974), with Joe Maphis *Country Guitar Giants* (1979), *The Merle Travis Story* (1979), *Light Singin' And Heavy Pickin'* (1980), *Guitar Standards* (1980), *Travis Pickin'* (1981), with Mac Wiseman *The Clayton McMichen Story* (1982), with Grandpa Jones *Merle And Grandpa's Farm And Home Hour* (1985), *Rough, Rowdy And Blue* (1986).

Further reading: *In Search Of My Father*, Pat Travis Eatherly.

Travis, Randy

b. Randy Bruce Traywick, 4 May 1959, Marshville, North Carolina, USA. The second of the six children of Harold and Bobbie Rose Traywick, this singer/songwriter shows in his style and delivery a heavy influence of Lefty Frizzell and Merle Haggard. His father, a builder, was a country music fanatic who even built a music room complete with stage on to the Travis' house just so that the family could perform for friends. Although not a working musician, he played guitar, wrote songs, on occasions performed in public and had once recorded two of his songs 'A Lonely Shadow' and 'The Reason I Came'. He is also reputed to have had problems with drink and later acquired a reputation for his drinking, fighting, shooting and frightening people around the Marshville area. In 1982, he lost his home and everything else, after a venture into turkey raising went wrong. (He managed to get it back in 1985). Through his father's insistence, Randy learned guitar and began performing publicly with his elder brother Ricky, a more accomplished guitarist, when he was 9. The two were later joined by bass playing brother David and with their father arranging the bookings, they played local clubs over a wide area.

Over the years they were frequently in trouble with the law for varying offences such as drunkenness, theft, drugs and driving offences, including being clocked by the police at 135 miles an hour. While on probation in 1977, Travis appeared at the *Country City USA*, a Charlotte nightclub managed and co-owned by Lib Hatcher (Mary Elizabeth Robertson). Impressed by his vocals, she found him regular work at the club and also provided him with a home, although the association soon saw her divorced from husband Frank Hatcher. Under her guidance (in spite of objections from his father who she eventually banned from the club) and with variations made to his probation orders, Travis began to develop his musical career. She financed his first recordings (as Randy Traywick) made on the Paula label under Joe Stampley's production in Nashville, which resulted in 'She's My Woman' making a brief US country chart appearance in 1979. In 1981 Travis and Hatcher moved to Nashville. The following year she became manager of the *Nashville Palace* nightclub and hired Travis, (under the name of Randy Ray), as the resident singer, who also assisted as a dishwasher and cook.

In November 1982, he recorded his first album *Randy Ray Live At The Nashville Palace* and gradually, through Hatcher's shrewd management, he began to establish himself around Nashville. Late in 1984, he came to the attention of Martha Sharp, an A&R director of Warner Brothers, who was looking for a young and preferably sexy looking singer to record following the successes at CBS by Ricky Skaggs and at MCA by George Strait. With another name change, this time to Randy Travis (at the suggestion of Sharp) and under the production of Kyle Lehning, he cut four tracks on 30 January 1985. 'Prairie Rose' was used on the soundtrack album for the Patrick Wayne (son of John) film *Rustler's Rhapsody*. 'On The Other Hand' made number 67 on the US country charts. Two weeks later Travis officially signed a contract with Warner Brothers. Soon after, he scored his first Top 10 with '1982'. The year 1986 was a big one for him with a reissue of 'On The Other Hand' and 'Diggin' Up Bones' both making number 1 and 'No Place Like Home' peaking at number 2. His first Warner album, *Storms Of Life*,

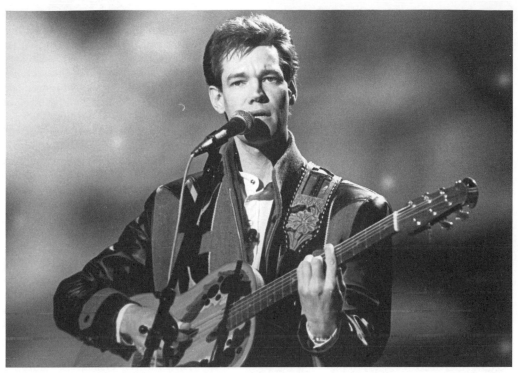

Randy Travis

became the first country debut album to sell a million within a year of issue, he won a Grammy as Best Country Newcomer and he joined the *Grand Ole Opry*. In 1987-88, he registered six more successive number 1s with 'Forever And Ever, Amen', 'I Won't Need You Anymore (Always And Forever)', 'Too Gone Too Long', 'I Told You So' (a self-penned song), 'Honky Tonk Moon' and 'Deeper Than The Holler'. The majority of the songs were composed by noted songwriters, including Don Schlitz, Paul Overstreet, Troy Seals and Max D. Barnes. By 1988, Travis was a superstar and had collected a great many awards along the way, including that of Male Vocalist of the Year by the Country Music Association. In 1989, he survived a car crash and registered further number 1s with 'Is It Still Over' and 'It's Just A Matter Of Time'. The latter song co-written by Brook Benton being cut under the production of famed producer Richard Perry, who actually used the recording as the only country number on his noted *Rock Rhythm And Blues* compilation album. The attempt at something different with 'Promises', cut with only an acoustic guitar, failed by his standards when it peaked at number 17. In 1990, *Heroes And Friends* drew glowing reviews and found him duetting with a number of stars including Merle Haggard, George Jones, Loretta Lynn, Dolly Parton, Tammy Wyunette and non-country notables such as B.B. King and Clint Eastwood. Perhaps the most nostalgia came for the version of 'Happy Trails' recorded with singing cowboy legend Roy Rogers. The going got tougher in 1990-91, with strong competition from Ricky Van Shelton, Clint Black and Garth Brooks but he registered further number 1 hits with 'Hard Rock Bottom Of Your Heart' and 'Forever Together'.

In 1991, it was revealed that he had married Lib Hatcher, putting an end to a long period of speculation about his private life and the nature of their relationship. Pundits reckoned the affair would harm his career, but the simultaneous release of two greatest hits collections in 1992 confirmed his continued popularity, and produced another number 1 hit, 'Look Heart, No Hands'.

Albums: *Randy Ray Live At The Nashville Palace* (1982), *Storms Of Life* (1986), *Always And Forever* (1987), *Old 8 x 10* (1988), *An Old Time Christmas* (1989), *No Holdin' Back* (1989), *Heroes And Friends* (1990), *High Lonesome* (1991), *Greatest Hits Volume One*, (1992), *Greatest Hits Volume Two* (1992).

Further reading: *Randy Travis; The King Of The New Country Traditionalists*, Don Cusic.

Tritt, Travis

b. c.1962, Marietta, Georgia, USA. He started writing songs and playing honky tonks and beer joints when he was about 14 years old. One of Tritt's songs is called, 'Son Of The New South', and his US country hit, 'Put Some Drive Into Your Country' includes the lines, 'I made myself a promise when I was just a kid/I'd mix Southern rock and country and that's just what I did.' In other words, Tritt is where Merle Haggard meets Lynyrd Skynyrd. Although the title track of his debut album presented him as a honky tonk revivalist, Tritt's music reflects his childhood love for the classic country of George Jones and the southern rock of the Allman Brothers. He reached superstar status in 1991 with the first single from *It's All About To Change* - a wonderful bar-room ballad of love betrayed, 'Here's A Quarter (Call Someone Who Cares)'. The follow-up, 'Anymore', proved his credentials as a balladeer, while his acting in the award-winning video clip for the song won him several offers of film work. After two magnificent albums, *T-R-O-U-B-L-E* was something of a holding operation, though it contained at least one classic, the traditional-sounding 'Lord Have Mercy On The Working Man'. Tritt further extended the boundaries of modern country with a nine-minute workout on Buddy Guy's blues standard, 'Leave My Woman Alone'. He combined with Marty Stuart for two hit singles and a series of concerts playfully titled The No-Hats Tour in honour of the duo's full heads of hair. Only some outspoken criticism of Billy Ray Cyrus in the summer of 1992, and the desicion to issue a sentimental album of Christmas favourites later in the year, threatened his relentless progress to the top. An accomplished songwriter and performer, with one of the most distinctive voices in country music, he is potentially a major talent.

Albums: *Country Club* (1990), *It's All About To Change* (1991), *T-R-O-U-B-L-E* (1992), *A Travis Tritt Christmas - Loving Time Of The Year* (1992).

Tubb, Ernest

b. Ernest Dale Tubb, 9 February 1914, near Crisp, Ellis County, Texas, USA, d. 6 September 1984, Nashville, Tennessee, USA. The youngest of the five children of Calvin Tubb, the foreman of a 300-acre cotton farm, and his wife Sarah. In 1920 the family relocated across Texas to Benjamin and in 1925 they moved again this time to Kemp. The following year, his parents divorced and initially he stayed with his mother, when she moved to her brother's farm near Lively. His mother, a very religious woman who was one-quarter Cherokee, could play the piano and organ and sang hymns around the farms and at the local church. Obviously his education suffered and he later related that he only went to school when he could not find work. In 1928 Tubb heard a recording of Jimmie Rodgers singing one of his blue yodels. He was immediately fascinated by the man's music and quickly decided he wanted to be a singer; consequently he began to learn Rodgers' songs and whenever he had the money, he bought his records. In 1930 after his mother remarried, he travelled around working on various tasks and living at different times with married siblings or his remarried father.

Early in 1933, while working on the roads near Benjamin, he became friendly with a young guitarist called Merwyn 'Buff' Buffington, who liked Tubb's singing but suggested he should learn to play guitar. He bought his first guitar from a pawnshop in Abilene and Buffington taught him his first chords. In May 1933 Tubb was greatly distressed by the death of Jimmie Rodgers, although the event actually strengthened his resolve to be like his idol. He moved to San Antonio, where he lived with his brother, Calvin Jnr. He also renewed his acquaintance with Buffington, who at the time was playing guitar with the Castleman Brothers (Joe and Jim) on Radio KONO. He persuaded Tubb to make some appearances as guest vocalist with them, which led to him getting his own twice-weekly early morning show. On 26 May 1934 he married Lois Elaine Cook. Still very much the Rodgers' imitator, he decided to check the telephone directory for a Mrs Jimmie Rodgers. He found one and his call led to a meeting with Jimmie's widow. Mrs Carrie Rodgers was impressed and not only gave him a picture but also showed him many of her late husband's possessions and agreed to listen to his radio show. She had had many requests for help since Rodgers' death but Tubb's singing impressed her and some months later, she offered to help him with his career.

In 1936 she loaned him one of Jimmie's C.F. Martin guitars and in October that year, mainly due to her influence with her late husband's label, he made his first recordings for RCA. (She later gave him the guitar which, after using it for many years, Tubb donated to the *Country Music Hall Of Fame Museum*). The first two of the six songs recorded were tribute songs written by Elsie McWilliams, Rodgers' sister-in-law; the others

Ernest Tubb

were self-penned numbers. RCA released the first two but sales were poor. A further session in March 1937 saw another single released but again sales were poor. It is now accepted that these two singles are so scarce that they represent the most collectable recordings of Tubb's entire career. (The other RCA tracks were not released until 1942, by which time Tubb was a known artist). He played countless small venues and appeared on various radio stations as he struggled to keep his family, which by now comprised Justin (b. 1935) and Violet Elaine (b. 1939). (Roger Dale (b. 1938) died in a car crash when only seven weeks old.) In spite of Mrs Rodgers' help, it was not until April 1940 that Tubb recorded again. This time, again probably as a favour to Mrs Rodgers, it was for Decca. By now his style and sound had changed, due to the fact that late in 1939 his tonsils had been removed, taking with them his ability to yodel. This effectively stopped him being a Rodgers' clone and he began to develop his own identity. (In later years, he recalled the event with his awfully titled song 'He Took 50 Dollars And My Yodel, When He Took My Tonsils Out'). Decca were impressed enough to record further sessions. He was sponsored by a flour company and began touring and appearing on KGKO Fort Worth, as the Gold Chain Troubadour.

He continued to write songs and in April 1941, this time using a backing that included the electric guitar of KGKO's staff guitarist Fay 'Smitty Smith', he recorded six more numbers. (On 'Our Baby's Book', Smith played a steel guitar, the first time the instrument appeared on a Tubb recording). After some argument with Decca over which song to release first, Tubb's choice of 'Walking The Floor Over You' was accepted. In the first year it sold 400,000 copies and went on to become a million selling record and Tubb's greatest hit. In 1941 he sang it and three more songs in the Charles Starrett film, *Fighting Buckeroos*, and in 1942 he appeared with Starrett again in *Ridin' West*. That same year, his popularity gained him a release from his Gold Chain contract and he moved to Nashville. By January 1943 the *Grand Ole Opry* had a new honky-tonk singer who dared to use an electric lead guitar on such a sacred stage. When a union strike stopped recordings in 1942 and 1943, he toured extensively on various shows, including tours with Pee Wee King but he was soon fronting his own band, the Texas Troubadours. In 1944 he appeared in the film *Jamboree* and the same year, making his first recordings with his own band, he gained his first US country chart number 1 and a

pop chart number 16 with 'Soldier's Last Letter'. In February 1946 he was most probably the second modern country artist ever to record in Nashville; Decca having recorded Red Foley the previous year.

In 1947, he opened the now world famous Ernest Tubb Record Shop in Nashville and started his *Midnight Jamboree,* initially on the *Opry,* but before long the show was being broadcast direct from the actual record shop itself. He also headlined the first ever country music show held in New York's Carnegie Hall, telling the audience 'This place could sure hold a lot of hay'. He continued to tour and record and by the end of 1948 he had amassed 16 country Top 5's, including two more number 1s with 'It's Been So Long Darling' and 'Rainbow At Midnight' and four songs had made the pop charts. His popularity was increased even further in 1949, when he tallied 12 chart entries (11 Top 10 hits) including number 1 hits with 'Slippin' Around' and 'Blue Christmas'. He also had number 2 hits with duet recordings with Red Foley ('Tennessee Border #2') and with the Andrews Sisters ('I'm Biting My Fingernails And Thinkin' Of You'). Bing Crosby even asked to record with him but the session never materialized. (However, Bing did record 'I'm Walking The Floor Over You' and in 1960 it also became a UK pop hit for Pat Boone). 1948 also saw Tubb's first marriage end in divorce but in June 1949, he married Olene Adams Carter. (This marriage lasted 26 years and produced five children). Tubb was always ready to give a helping hand and in 1950 he helped fellow Rodgers' admirer Hank Snow to get on the *Opry.* He had befriended Hank Williams when he first broke into country music and in 1953, he sang 'Beyond The Sunset' at Hank's funeral. During the 50s he maintained a rigorous touring and recording schedule. By the end of the decade, although only achieving one number 1, with his duet with Red Foley of 'Goodnight Irene', he totalled 34 hits, the majority being Top 10's. Major hits included 'I Love You Because', 'Driftwood On The River' and 'Missing In Action'. In 1953 he and Hank Snow, Danny Dill and Lew Childre were the first country acts to tour a live war zone when they played about 40 shows in Korea, many in the open air and within range of the enemy guns. Tubb had been advised not to go and on his return his health had suffered and for a time he was unable to perform. By the mid-50s, eldest son Justin Tubb, then establishing himself as an artist and songwriter, became involved with some of the business organization. The hits slowed in the 60s but the popularity did not and in spite of his health problems, he kept up a rigorous touring schedule and hosted his network television show. His hits included 'Thanks A Lot', 'Pass The Booze', his nostalgic 'Waltz Across Texas' and a duet with Loretta Lynn titled 'Mr & Mrs Used To Be'. In 1965 as a reward for his important contributions to the music, he became the sixth member of the *Country Music Hall Of Fame*. The many songs that he had written and successfully recorded also led to him being one of the first writers elected to the *Nashville Songwriters International Hall Of Fame* when it was founded in 1970. During the 70s he played the *Opry*, hosted the *Midnight Jamboree* and in spite of the worsening effects of the emphysema that had first developed in 1965, he still kept up a touring schedule that would have taxed younger men.

He finally parted company with Decca and in 1979, to mark his 65th birthday, Pete Drake masterminded a tribute on First Generation Records called *The Legend And The Legacy*, on which various stars overdubbed vocal contributions on Tubb's recordings. (Tubb was not informed until the project was completed). The album became a best seller and singles of a Tubb and Willie Nelson duet of 'Waltz Across Texas' and a joint Merle Haggard, Chet Atkins, Charlie Daniels and Tubb version of 'Walking The Floor Over You' both charted. It was initially released as a double-album but ran foul of various claims of conflicting contractual details or unauthorized performances. It was subsequently withdrawn and copies supposedly destroyed. Record One of the original issue soon reappeared as a single album on Cachet, minus only a single track - the Nelson/Tubb duet. By 1982 his failing health forced him to retire. In the last year of touring, he had to rest on his bed in his customized touring bus and take oxygen between and during shows. (This shows an ironic similarity to the latter days of the career of his idol, Jimmie Rodgers, almost 50 years before). He made one of his last recordings in 1982, when he spoke a line on the Waylon Jennings and Hank Williams Jnr. song 'Leave Them Boys Alone'.

Ernest Tubb died in September 1984 of emphysema and related complications in Nashville's Baptist Hospital. He was buried on 10 September in Nashville's Hermitage Memorial Gardens. Over the years the Texas Troubadours included some of country music's finest musicians, such as Jimmie Short, Leon Rhodes, Billy Byrd, Jerry Byrd and Red Herron. Two others, Jack Greene and Cal Smith, went on to successful solo careers. Ernest Tubb registered in all 91 country chart hits of which only 17 failed to made the Top 20. His distinctive growling vocals, in a voice that deepened but softened as the years went by, may not endear themselves to exponents of perfect pitch. He usually started his songs somewhat off-key and by some means that only he possessed, he managed to use his flatness as an emphasis to put across the songs, be they happy or sad. After starting out as a blatant imitator, no one could deny that he became a completely original and unique artist.

Albums: *Favorites* (1951), *Jimmie Rodgers Songs* (1951), *Old Rugged Cross* (1951), *Sing A Song Of Christmas* (1952), *The Daddy Of 'Em All* (1956), *Favourites* (1956), *The Ernest Tubb Story* (1958), *The Importance Of Being Ernest* (1959), *Ernest Tubb & His Texas Troubadours* (1960), *Ernest Tubb Record Shop* (1960), with guests *Midnight Jamboree* (1960), *All Time Hits* (1961), *Golden Favorites* (1961), *On Tour* (1962), *The Family Bible* (1963), *Presents The Texas Troubadours* (1964), *Just Call Me Lonesome* (1964), *Blue Christmas* (1964), *Thanks A Lot* (1964), *My Pick Of The Hits* (1965), *Country Dance Time* (1965), *Hittin' The Road* (1965), with Loretta Lynn *Mr & Mrs Used To Be* (1965), *Stand By Me* (1966), *Ernest Tubb And His Texas Troubadours* (1966), *By Request* (1966), *Country Hits Old & New* (1966), *Another Story* (1967), with Lynn *Singin' Again* (1967), *The Terrific Texas Troubadours* (1968), *Country Hit Time* (1968), *Sings Hank Williams* (1968), *Great Country* (1969), with Lynn *If We Put Our Heads Together* (1969), *Let's Turn Back The Years* (1969), *Saturday Satan, Sunday Saint* (1969), *A Good Year For The Wine* (1970), *One Sweet Hello* (1971), *Baby, It's So Hard To Be Good* (1972), *Say Something Nice To Sarah* (1972), *I've Got All The Heartaches I Can Handle* (1973), *Greatest Hits Volume 1* (1973), *Greatest Hits Volume II* (1974), *Ernest Tubb* (1975), *Living Legend* (1977), with various artists *The Legend & The Legacy* (1979), *Ernest Tubb & His Texas Troubadours* (1983), *Honky Tonk Classics* (1983), *Rare Recordings* (1983), *Live, 1965* (1989), with various artists *The Ernest Tubb Collection Parts 1 & 2* (1990).

Further reading: *Ernest Tubb:The Original E.T.*, Norma Barthel.

Tubb, Justin

b. Justin Wayne Tubb, 20 August 1935, San Antonio, Texas, USA. The eldest son of country music legend Ernest Tubb. He attended Castle Heights Military School, Lebanon, from 1944-48.

He was naturally attracted to his father's music and when school holidays permitted, he toured with his father and regularly appeared on his WSM radio programme. He made his debut on the *Grand Ole Opry* at the age of nine. He hung around backstage and later described himself as 'a little stage rat'. He began to write songs and by the time he left Brackenridge High School, San Antonio, he was an accomplished guitarist and singer. In 1952, tiring of being told he was going to be just like his father, he entered the University of Texas at Austin with thoughts of a career in journalism. The following year he wrote a tribute song to Hank Williams which his father recorded. He quit the University, the journalism forgotten, when he was offered the job of a disc jockey on WHIN Gallatin. This gave him the chance to sing some of his own songs to his listeners and also led to a Decca contract. He gained his first US country chart hit in 1954 when 'Looking Back To See', a duet with Goldie Hill, reached number 4. In 1955 he became the youngest ever regular member of the *Opry*. He always resisted any attempt to capitalize on his father's name and for some time he deliberately avoided appearing on the same shows. In the 60s when Ernest's health began to cause him trouble, he did begin to combine his career with assisting his father in his business ventures and later became manager of the *Ernest Tubb Midnight Jamboree* radio show and record shops, as well as forming his own publishing company. He had solo Top 10's with 'I Gotta Go Get My Baby' and 'Take A Letter Miss Gray' and further duet successes with Lorene Mann with 'Hurry, Mr Peters' (the answer song to the Roy Drusky-Priscilla Mitchell hit 'Yes, Mr Peters') and 'We've Gone Too Far Again'. Many of his songs became hits for others including 'Keeping Up With The Joneses' (Faron Young-Margie Singleton), 'Love Is No Excuse' (Jim Reeves-Dottie West) and 'Lonesome 7-7203' (Hawkshaw Hawkins). Over the years, he has recorded for several labels, including Starday, Challenge and RCA. He has toured all over the USA, Canada, Europe, even to Vietnam, and he has also appeared on all major US television shows. Like his father, Tubb is a strict traditionalist, and during the 70s his career faltered. He registered his personal feelings about attempts to change country music in his song 'What's Wrong With The Way That We're Doing It Now', which won him five standing ovations for encores on the first occasion that he sang it on the *Opry*. He still makes *Opry* appearances and is regularly expected to sing that song and his tribute to his late father 'Thanks Troubadour, Thanks'.

Albums: *Country Boy In Love* (1957), *Modern Country Sound Of Justin Tubb* (1962), *Star Of The Grand Ole Opry* (1962), *Justin Tubb* (1965), *Where You're Concerned* (1965), with Lorene Mann *Together And Alone* (1966), *That Country Style* (1967), *Things I Still Remember* (1969), *New Country Heard From* (1974), *Justin Tubb* (1979).

Tucker, Tanya

b. Tanya Denise Tucker, 10 October 1958, Seminole, Texas, USA. Her father, Beau, a construction worker, and her mother, Juanita, encouraged her fledgling musical talents. Her early years were spent in Wilcox, Arizona, and by the time the family got to Phoenix, it was 1967. Her father booked her to perform with visting country stars on stage at local fairs Never one to consider that some songs might be too old for her, she was singing 'You Ain't Woman Enough To Take My Man' before she was 13. The family moved to St. George, Utah, and her mother impressed the producer of the Robert Redford film, *Jeremiah Johnson*, which led to Tucker (and her horse!) being featured. To further their daughter's career, they moved to Las Vegas, where Beau financed a demo tape. In 1972 Tucker was signed to Columbia Records in Nashville by producer Billy Sherrill, although she disliked his choice of song - 'The Happiest Girl In The Whole USA', later a hit for Donna Fargo. Subsequently, she made the US country Top 10 with Alex Harvey's 'Delta Dawn', and did equally well with the double-sided 'Jamestown Ferry'/'Love's The Answer', and then had a US country number 1 with 'What's Your Mama's Name?', a story song with a twist in its last line. 'Blood Red And Goin' Down', the title referring to a Georgia sunset, was about a daughter watching her father kill her cheating mother, while 'Would You Lay With Me (In A Field Of Stone)?' was an adult love song, written by David Allen Coe for his brother's wedding. The young Tucker became a country star, was featured on the cover of *Rolling Stone*, and, through 200 appearances a year, devoloped a powerful, if precocious, stage presence. Moving to MCA on her 16th birthday, she was determined to make records that were in keeping with the sophisticated country-rock of The Eagles, and she topped the country charts with 'Lizzie And The Rainman' (also US Top 40), which was based on the Burt Lancaster film, *The Rainmaker*, 'San Antonio Stroll' and 'Here's Some Love'. In 1978 she wrote and recorded 'Save Me', an ecologically inspired single about seal culls on Canada's Magdalen Islands. Depending on your view, the provocative cover picture of *TNT* was either tacky or sensual, but it was certainly a different approach for a country star. She was booed on the *Grand Ole Opry* for performing raucous rock 'n' roll. *Tear Me Apart* was made with producer Mike Chapman, and included a hoarse segue of 'San Francisco' with 'I Left My Heart In San Francisco'. Neither album sold as well as expected, but Tucker found herself in gossip columns via her stormy relationship with Glen Campbell. She commented: 'Men are supposed to slow down after 40, but it's the opposite with Glen', and their duets included a revival of Bobby Darin's 'Dream Lover'. The dream was over when Campbell knocked out her front teeth. Hardly surprisingly, she kept her mouth shut for the glum cover of her next album, *Changes*. As fate would have it, they were to find themselves on the same label, Capitol, and Tucker's career has revitalised with *Girls Like Me*, an album which spawned four Top 10 country singles. In 1988 she had three number 1 country singles - 'I Won't Take Less Than Your Love' (with Paul Davis and Paul Overstreet), 'If It Don't Come Easy' and 'Strong Enough To Bend' - but it was also the year in which she entered the Betty Ford clinic for cocaine and alcohol addiction. Tucker has only written sparodically, but she co-wrote Hank Williams Jnr's 'Leave Them Boys Alone'.

After many years in country music her contributions were finally rewarded by the Country Music Association when they voted her Female Vocalist Of The Year in 1991, although she had to miss attending the event, having just had her second child. Her country chart successes included two number 2s with 'Down To My Last Teardrop' and '(Without You) What Do I Do About Me'. In 1992 further hits included 'Some Kind Of Trouble', but more awards were not forthcoming although she did receive a nomination for *What Do I Do About Me* as Album Of The Year.

Albums: *Delta Dawn* (1972), *What's Your Mama's Name?* (1973), *Would You Lay With Me* (1974), *Lovin' And Learnin'* (1975), *Tanya Tucker* (1975), *Here's Some Love* (1976), *You Are So Beautiful* (1977), *Ridin' Rainbows* (1977), *TNT* (1978), *Tear Me Apart* (1979), *Dreamlovers* (1980), *Should I Do It?* (1981), *Live* (1982), *Changes* (1982), *Love Me Like You Used To* (1987), *Strong Enough To Bend* (1988), *Tennessee Woman* (1990), *Greatest Hits Encore* (1990), *What Do I Do With Me* (1991), *Lizzie And The Rainman* (1992), *Hits* (1992), *Can't Run From Yourself* (1992).

Twitty, Conway

b. Harold Lloyd Jenkins, 1 September 1933, Friars Point, Mississippi, USA. His father, a riverboat pilot, named him after a silent film comedian and gave him a guitar when he was five years old. The boat travelled between Mississippi and Arkansas, and the family moved to Helena, Arkansas. Twitty's schoolboy friends - Jack Nance, Joe E. Lewis and John Hughey - have played in his professional bands. In 1946, he recorded a demo, 'Cry Baby Heart', at a local radio station, although he was convinced that his real calling was to be a preacher. He was drafted into the US army in 1954 and worked the Far East service bases with a country band, the Cimarrons. He hoped for a baseball career, but when he returned to the USA in 1956 and heard Elvis Presley's 'Mystery Train', he opted for a career in music. Like Presley, he was signed by Sam Phillips to Sun Records, although his only significant contribution was writing 'Rockhouse', a minor US hit for Roy Orbison. His various Sun demos are included, along with later recordings for Mercury and MGM, in the eight-album, Bear Family set, *Conway Twitty - The Rock 'n' Roll Years*.

In 1957, whilst touring with a rockabilly package, he and his manager stuck pins in a map and the combination of a town in Arkansas with another in Texas led to Conway Twitty, a name as memorable as Elvis Presley. Twitty then moved to Mercury where 'I Need Your Lovin'' made number 93 in the USA pop charts. He had written 'It's Only Make Believe' with his drummer Jack Nance in-between sets at the Flamingo Lounge, Toronto, and he recorded it for MGM with the Jordanaires, a croaky vocal and a huge crescendo. The record became a transatlantic number 1, and subsequent UK Top 10 versions of 'It's Only Make Believe' are by Billy Fury (1964), Glen Campbell (1970) and Child (1978). Twitty's record sounded like an Elvis Presley parody so it was ironic that Peter Sellers should lampoon him as Twit Conway and that he became the model for Conrad Birdie in the musical, *Bye Bye Birdie*. Twitty, unwisely but understandably, followed 'It's Only Make Believe' with more of the same in 'The Story Of My Love', while the b-side, the harsh and sexy 'Make Me Know You're Mine', remains one of the 'great unknowns'. His debut, *Conway Twitty Sings*, includes a beat treatment of 'You'll Never Walk Alone', which was undoubtedly heard by Gerry And The Pacemakers.

Twitty came to the UK for ITV television's pioneering *Oh Boy!* and his presence eased his rock

Conway Twitty

'n' roll version of Nat 'King' Cole's 'Mona Lisa' into the Top 10. His US Top 10 recording of a song, 'Lonely Blue Boy', which had been left out of Elvis Presley's film *King Creole*, led to him naming his band the Lonely Blue Boys, although they subsequently became the Twitty Birds. Another US hit, 'Danny Boy' could not be released in the UK because the lyric was still in copyright, this did not apply to its melody, 'The Londonderry Air', so Twitty recorded a revised version, 'Rosaleena'. Whilst at MGM, he appeared in such unremarkable movies as *Platinum High School* and *Sex Kittens Go To College*, which also featured Brigitte Bardot's sister. Twitty continued croaking his way through 'What Am I Living For?' and 'Is A Bluebird Blue?', but was also recording such country favourites as 'Faded Love' and 'You Win Again'. After being dropped by MGM and a brief spell with ABC-Paramount, Twitty concentrated on placing his country songs with other artists including 'Walk Me To The Door' for Ray Price. He began recording his own country records for producer Owen Bradley and USA Decca Records in Nashville, saying, 'After nine years in rock 'n' roll, I had been cheated and hurt enough to sing country and mean it.' In March 1966 Twitty appeared in the US country charts for the first time with 'Guess My Eyes Were Bigger Than My Heart'. His first US country number 1 was with 'Next In Line' in 1968 and this was followed by 'I Love You More Today' and 'To See An Angel Cry'.

He became the most consistent country chartmaker of all-time, although none of his country records made the UK charts. His most successful country record on the US pop charts is 'You've Never Been This Far Before', which made number 22 in 1973. 'Hello Darlin'' was heard around the world when he recorded a Russian version for the astronauts on a USA-USSR space venture in 1975. His records, often middle-of-the-road ballads, include 'I See The Want To In Your Eyes', 'I'll Never Make It Home Tonight', 'I Can't Believe She Gives It All To Me', 'I'd Love To Lay You Down' and 'You Were Named Co-Respondent'. He has recorded several successful duet albums with Loretta Lynn, and also with Dean Martin and his own daughter, Joni Lee ('Don't Cry, Joni'). His son, who began recording as Conway Twitty Jnr., changed to Mike Twitty, while another daughter, Kathy Twitty, had minor country hits both as herself ('Green Eyes') and as Jesseca James ('Johnny One Time'). Through the 70s, Twitty was expanding into property, banking and fast food, although his Twittyburgers came to a greasy end. His wife Mickey, whom he has married and divorced twice, published *What's Cooking At Twitty City?*, in 1985. His tacky museum and theme park, Twitty City, is up for sale. By the end of 1988, Twitty's total of number 1 country hits totalled 40. Despite his new successes, the focal point of his stage act is still 'It's Only Make Believe' and he says, 'I still get goosebumps when I perform 'It's Only Make Believe'. I get wrapped up in the song and lose track of everything except making it better than the last time I did it.'

Albums: *Conway Twitty Sings* (1958), *Saturday Night With Conway Twitty* (1959), *Lonely Blue Boy* (1960), *The Rock 'N' Roll Story* (1961), *The Conway Twitty Touch* (1961), *'Portrait Of A Fool' And Others* (1962), *R&B '63* (1963), *Hit The Road* (1964), *Look Into My Teardrops* (1966), *Country* (1967), *Here's Conway Twitty* (1968), *Next In Line* (1968), *I Love You More Today* (1969), *You Can't Take The Country Out Of Conway* (1969), *Darling, You Know I Wouldn't Lie* (1969), *Hello Darling* (1970), *Fifteen Years Ago* (1970), *To See My Angel Cry* (1970), *How Much More Can She Stand?* (1971), *Conway Twitty* (1972), *I Wonder What She'll Think About Me Leaving* (1971), *Conway Twitty Sings The Blues* (1972), *Shake It Up* (1972), *I Can't Stop Loving You* (1973), *You've Never Been This Far Before* (1973), *I Can't See Me Without You* (1972), *She Needs Someone To Hold Her* (1973), *Clinging To A Saving Hand* (1973), *Honky Tonk Angel* (1974), *I'm Not Through Loving You Yet* (1974), *Linda On My Mind* (1975), *The High Priest Of Country Music* (1975), *Twitty* (1975), *Now And Then* (1976), *Play Guitar Play* (1977), *I've Already Loved You In My Mind* (1977), *Georgia Keeps Pulling On My Ring* (1978), *Conway* (1978), *Cross Winds* (1979), *Country-Rock* (1979), *Boogie Grass Band* (1979), *Rest Your Love* (1980), *Heart And Soul* (1980), *Rest Your Love On Me* (1980), *Mr. T.* (1981), *Southern Comfort* (1982), *Dream Maker* (1982), *Merry Twismas* (1983), *Lost In The Feeling* (1983), *By Heart* (1984), *Chasing Rainbows* (1985), *Live At Castaway Lounge* (1987), *Borderline* (1987), *House On The Old Lonesome Road* (1989), *Crazy In Love* (1990), *Even Now* (1991); with Loretta Lynn *We Only Make Believe* (1971), *Lead Me On* (1971), *Louisiana Woman, Mississippi Man* (1973), *Feelin's* (1975), *United Talent* (1976), *Dynamic Duo* (1977), *Country Partners* (1974), *Honky Tonk Heroes* (1978), *Diamond Duets* (1979), *Two's A Party* (1981), *Making Believe* (1988).

Further reading: *The Conway Twitty Story - An Authorised Biography*, Wilbur Cross and Michael Kosser.

Tyler, T. Texas

b. David Luke Myrick, 20 June 1916, Mena, Arkansas, USA, d. 28 January 1972, Springfield, Missouri, USA. Tyler spent his early boyhood in Texas but was educated in Philadelphia. He learned guitar in his teens and was heard on local radio in the early 30s. He worked with Slim Clere as Slim And Tex in Charleston between 1939-42, before adopting a solo career at Shreveport, Fairmont and Indianapolis. He saw military service from 1944-46 and then moved to Los Angeles where he formed his own band, and his television series *Range Round Up* gained an award as Best Country Music Show of 1950. In 1946 he recorded for 4 Star Records, having initial success with 'Filipino Baby' but he established himself in 1948 when his recitation 'Deck Of Cards' made number 2 in the US country and number 21 in the US pop charts. A version by Tex Ritter also became a Top 10 US country chart hit the same year. (The narration later became a million seller for Wink Martindale in 1959 and a UK pop hit in 1973 for comedian Max Bygraves.) The number may be medieval and it was certainly used as a church sermon long before Tyler was born. Over the years it has appeared in many different forms and it is possible that it was a version entitled 'The Gentleman Soldier's Prayer Book' that Tyler first read in the late 30s. He may well also have known a poem about Wild Bill Hickok's card playing written by Captain Jack Crawford, the 'Poet Scout'.

Tyler had further Top 10 successes with the tearjerking narration 'Dad Gave My Dog Away', 'Memories Of France', 'My Bucket's Got A Hole in It', 'Bumming Around' and finally in 1954 with 'Courtin' In The Rain'. He also recorded for Starday and Capitol, appeared in several western films and was one of the first country stars to appear at Carnegie Hall. He perhaps favoured western swing, but performed all types of country music in a growl. His many *Grand Ole Opry* and touring appearances and theme song 'Remember Me' won him the nickname of 'The Man With A Million Friends'. In 1957, after some alcohol problems, Tyler became an ordained church minister and gospel singer at Springfield, Missouri, where he died of cancer in January 1972.

Albums: *Deck Of Cards* (1958), *T. Texas Tyler* (1959), *The Great Texan* (1960), *Songs Along The Way* (1961), *Salvation* (1962), *T.Texas Tyler* (1962), *10 Songs He Made Famous* (1962), *Hits Of T.Texas Tyler* (1965), *The Man With A Million Friends* (1966).

Tyson, Ian And Sylvia

Ian Dawson Tyson, b. 25 September 1933, British Columbia, Canada. His father came to Canada in 1906 with dreams of being a cowboy and passed his love to his son who worked on a farm, entered amateur rodeos and worked as a lumberjack. He says, 'I'm always grateful for my logging and rodeo days because that's where the songs come from.' While recovering from a rodeo injury, Ian taught himself guitar and then played 'rockabilly in the chop-suey bars of Vancouver'. He says, 'I couldn't play very well as I only knew A, D and E. That's when I wrote 'Summer Wages'.' In 1959, he met Sylvia Fricker, (b. September 1940, Chatham, Ontario, Canada), the daughter of a music teacher. They formed a folk duo, Ian and Sylvia, and were married in 1964. They moved to Greenwich Village and were signed by Bob Dylan's manager, Albert Grossman. Ian says, 'I could never match Dylan's output. For every good song I wrote, he wrote eight.' They recorded folk-based albums and made popular the songs of fellow Canadian Gordon Lightfoot including 'Early Morning Rain' and 'For Lovin' Me'. Ian wrote about migrant workers in 'Four Strong Winds', later recorded by Neil Young, and about a rodeo from a girl's point of view in 'Someday Soon', beautifully recorded by Judy Collins. Fricker wrote 'You Were On My Mind', a US hit for We Five and a UK one for Crispian St Peters. By the end of the 60s, they went electric and formed a folk/rock group, the Great Speckled Bird, and the album of the same name was produced by Todd Rundgren. They then veered towards country music, and Sylvia wrote Crystal Gayle's US country hit, 'River Road'. They split up professionally in 1974 and were divorced in 1975, although Ian produced Sylvia's *Woman's World*. Sylvia was featured on the Canadian Live Aid single, 'Tears Are Not Enough' by Northern Lights. Ian bought a 160-acre ranch in Longview, Alberta, Canada and reared cutting horses with his second wife, Twylla. His tributes to working cowboys, *Old Corrals And Sagebrush* and *Ian Tyson*, were made with the simplicity of albums by the Sons Of The Pioneers. The more high-tech *Cowboyography* sold 50,000 copies in Canada alone and Tyson had a hit with a song he wrote with his protege Tom Russell, 'Navajo Rug', since recorded by Jerry Jeff Walker. His songs show compassion and understanding for the cowboy's life and, when he has not written them himself, they have been immaculately chosen, for example, 'Night Rider's Lament' and 'Gallo De Cielo'. He comments, 'As the song says, my heroes have always been cowboys and still are it seems.'

Albums: by Ian And Sylvia: *Ian And Sylvia* (1962), *Four Strong Winds* (1964), *Northern Journey* (1964), *Early Morning Rain* (1965), *Play One More* (1966), *So Much For Dreaming* (1967), *Lovin' Sound* (1967), *Nashville* (1968), *Full Circle* (1968), *Great Speckled Bird* (1969), *Ian And Sylvia* (1971), *You Were On My Mind* (1972); by Ian Tyson *Ol' Eon* (1974), *One Jump Ahead Of The Devil* (1978), *Old Corrals And Sagebrush* (1983), *Ian Tyson* (1984), *Cowboyography* (1987), *I Outgrew The Wagon* (1989); by Sylvia Tyson *Woman's World* (1975), *Big Spotlight* (1986), *You Were On My Mind* (1990).

V

Vagabonds

A vocal harmony trio of minister's sons comprising of Dean Upson (who had first formed a trio at WLS Chicago in 1925), Curt Poulton (who joined Upson in 1928) and Herald Goodman, who joined them on KMOX St. Louis in 1930. All were trained musicians (though only Poulton played guitar) who read and arranged music. In 1931, their performances attracted the attention of Harry Stone, who signed them to the *Grand Ole Opry* in Nashville. Their appointment represented a turning point for the *Opry* and Stone's action was against *Opry* founder George D. Hay's usual policy of using only what he termed 'down home folk' and his preference for string bands. The Vagabonds were the first really true professional entertainers to play the *Opry* and proved so popular that they also appeared regularly on WSM's other shows. They made many recordings and are reputed to have formed Nashville's first country music publishing house Old Cabin Music on their arrival in 1931. Equally accomplished with gospel, pop or country music, they are remembered for their reflective ballad 'When It's Lamp Lighting Time In The Valley', which they recorded in 1933 and which has been recorded by many artists since including Tex Ritter and Hylo Brown. They remained a popular act for many years although there were naturally some personnel changes. In the late 30s, Goodman left to front his own band, Upson eventually worked for WSM and later became the commercial manager at KWKH Shreveport. Poulton became involved with promotional work. (They should not be confused with Dunn's Vagabonds, a Houston based band of the late 30s).

Van Dyke, Leroy

b. Leroy Frank Van Dyke, 4 October 1929, Spring Fork, Missouri, USA. Besides working on the family farm, he learnt the guitar and sang country songs. He obtained a degree in agriculture from the University of Missouri. He then worked as a farm reporter and also trained as an auctioneer. He worked for army intelligence during the Korean war and because he entertained the troops so successfully, he was determined to be a professional entertainer. He wrote a tongue-twisting song based on his experience as an auctioneer, and, following

television appearances, 'The Auctioneer' made the US Top 20 in 1956 and remains one of the classic novelty records. Although he had no further hits with Dot Records, 'Honky Tonk Song', 'Heartbreak Cannonball' and 'Leather Jacket' are highly rated by rockabilly fans, and they include Al Casey and Joe Maphis among the studio musicians. Moving to Mercury, he recorded a sophisticated cheating song, 'Walk On By', which topped the US country charts and was also a transatlantic pop hit (UK 5, US 5). He followed it with 'If A Woman Answers (Hang Up the Phone)', 'Black Cloud', and his only other UK success, 'Big Man In A Big House'. Two of his best records, 'I Sat Back And Let It Happen' and a cover of Bob Dylan's 'It's All Over Now, Baby Blue', have been overlooked, and his last US country hit of any significance was 'Texas Tea' in 1977. He also put his auctioneering skills to advantage in the 1967 film, *What Am I Bid* but despite looking like James Garner, he never became a movie star.

Albums: At *The Trade Winds* (1962), *Walk On By* (1962), *Movin' Van Dyke* (1963), *Songs For Mom & Dad* (1964), *Out Of Love* (1965), *The Leroy Van Dyke Show* (1965), *Country Hits* (1966), *Lonesome Is* (1968), *I've Never Been Loved* (1969), *Just A Closer Walk With Thee* (1969), *Greatest Hits* (1972), *World's Most Famous Auctioneer* (1974), *Gospel Greats* (1977), *Rock Relics* (1979), *Leroy Van Dyke* (1982), *The Auctioneer* (1984).

Van Zandt, Townes

A country and folk-blues singer and guitarist, Van Zandt is a native Texan and great grandson of one of the original settlers who founded Fort Worth in the mid-19th Century. The son of a prominent oil family, Townes turned his back on financial security to pursue the beatnik life in Houston. First thumbing his way through cover versions, his acoustic sets later graced the Jester Lounge and other venues where his 'bawdy bar-room ballads' were first performed. Although little-known outside of a cult country rock following, many of his songs are better publicized by the covers afforded them by Merle Haggard, Emmylou Harris, Don Gibson and Willie Nelson. This gave songs such as 'Pancho And Lefty' and 'If I Needed You' the chance to rise to the top of the country charts. Much of Van Zandt's material was not released in the UK until the late 70s, though his recording career actually began with *For The Sake Of A Song*, released in the US in 1968. His media awareness belies the debt many artists, including the Cowboy Junkies and Go-Betweens, profess to owing him. Steve Earle went further: 'Townes Van Zandt is the best songwriter in the whole world, and I'll stand on Bob Dylan's coffee table in my cowboy boots and say that'. Interest is still alive as the recent re-issue of the *Live And Obscure* (albeit re-titled *Pancho And Lefty*) on Edsel proves. Van Zandt continues to live a reclusive life in a cabin in Tennessee, recording occasionally purely for the chance to 'get the songs down for posterity'.

Albums: *For The Sake Of A Song* (1968), *Our Mother The Mountain* (1969), *Townes Van Zandt* (1969), *Delta Momma Blues* (1971), *High And Low And In Between* (1972), *The Late Great Townes Van Zandt* (1972), *Live At The Old Quarter* (1977), *Flyin' Shoes* (1978), *At My Window* (1987), *Live And Obscure* (1987), *Rain On A Conga Drum* (1991) *Pancho And Lefty* (1992).

Vanwarmer, Randy

b. Randall Van Wormer, 30 March 1955, Indian Hills, Colorado, USA. Randy Vanwarmer is best remembered for his 1979 US Top 5/UK Top 10 single 'Just When I Needed You Most'. Vanwarmer and his mother moved to England when Randy was 12, following the death of his father in an automobile accident. He began singing and making demo-tapes and in 1979 moved back to the US, settling in Woodstock, New York. He signed with Bearsville Records, based in Woodstock, and recorded his own composition, 'Just When I Need You Most', that same year. The easy-listening hit was followed by two more minor chart singles and a low-charting album, *Warmer*, also in 1979. Vanwarmer never returned to the pop scene but in 1988 he made the country charts with two singles, 'I Will Hold You' and 'Where The Rocky Mountains Touch The Morning Sun' on 16th Ave. Records. He also cut an album for that company, *I Am*, which was not a success.

Albums: *Warmer* (1979), *Terraform* (1980), *Beat Of Love* (1981), *Thing That You Dream* (1983), *I Am* (1988).

Virginia Squires

This modern US bluegrass group comprised Rickie Simpkins (fiddle/mandolin/vocals), Ronnie Simpkins (bass/vocals), Sammy Shelor (guitar/banjo/vocals) and Mark Newton (guitar/vocals). The Simpkins Brothers originate from a musical family from the hills just southwest of Roanoke, Virginia. They played together in a family group but eventually formed Upland Express, a bluegrass band that had an album release on Leather Records in the 70s. They separated in

the early 80s, when Rickie worked with the McPeak Brothers and Ronnie became a member of the Bluegrass Cardinals. In 1982 they reunited in Richmond, in a band called the Heights Of Grass, but early in 1983, with Mark Newton (previously a member of Knoxville Grass) and Sammy Shelor (one time member of the Country Boys) they became the Virginia Squires. Playing a variety of bluegrass, rock, old time and country, they became a very popular band in their native state and recorded for the Rebel label.

Albums: *Bluegrass With A Touch Of Class* (1984), *Mountains And Memories* (1985), *I'm Working My Way* (1986), *Hard Times And Heartaches* (1987), *Variations* (1988).

Vokes, Howard

b. 13 June 1931, Clearwater, Pennsylvania, USA. One of the 13 children of a coal miner, Vokes got his first guitar at the age of eight. At 15, influenced by the recordings he heard of Roy Acuff and Jimmie Rodgers and radio broadcasts of the *Grand Ole Opry*, he played in some tough spots in nearby mining towns and on local radio. Two years later, he was shot in the ankle in an hunting accident and during his long convalescence, he took to writing songs. His recovery complete he formed, the Country Boys and toured with and managed other artists including Hank King and Denver Duke and Jeffrey Null. (The latter duo found success with two Hank Williams' tribute songs that Vokes had written.) His first recording success came with his version of Doc Williams, 'Willie Roy, The Crippled Boy'. Roy Acuff recorded his songs 'Mountain Guitar' and 'A Plastic Heart' and Wanda Jackson had success with 'Tears At The Grand Ole Opry'. Vokes visited Nashville and recorded an album of sad songs for Starday. Apart from his own appearances, Vokes, a staunch traditionalist whose own recordings have been released in many countries, has worked tirelessly over the years promoting traditional country music and working to help young artists in his native State. His name is respected by the fact that after starting his career with a nickname of Cowboy, he is now known internationally as Pennsylvania's King Of Country Music.

Albums: *Tragedy & Disaster In Country Songs* (1963), *Sings The Songs Of Broken Love Affairs* (1977), *Tears At The Grand Ole Opry* (1979).

W

Wagoner, Porter

b. 12 August 1930, on a farm near West Plains, Missouri, USA. Wagoner grew up listening to country music on the radio, especially the weekly *Grand Ole Opry* broadcasts. He learned to play the guitar at the age of 10 and owing to his father's illness, had his education was curtailed in order that he could help with the farm work. He made his first singing performances, at the age of 17, in the grocery store where he also worked to help the family budget. The store owner was so impressed that he sponsored an early morning show on the local radio in West Plains. In 1951, his singing attracted the attention of the programme director of KWTO Springfield, who offered him work on that station. Soon afterwards Red Foley, who was then organizing his new television series the *Ozark Jubilee,* heard him and promptly added him to the cast. Although he was relatively unknown, the television and radio exposure gained him a recording contract with RCA Records and he made his debut in the US country charts in 1954 with 'Company's Comin''. The following year 'A Satisfied Mind' gave him his first major country chart hit, spending 4 of the 33 weeks that it was charted at number 1. This marked the start of a recording career that, between 1955 and 1983, scarcely saw a year when his name did not appear at least once in the country charts.

He began to write songs and also adopted the Nudie Cohen suits and coloured boots that were to remain his trademark. Wagoner's glittering and twinkling outfits and blonde hair in the D.A. style, once led someone to remark that it was the first time they were aware that a Christmas tree could sing. (He and Hank Snow were two of the few artists to keep to this type of dress, when most others were adopting more conservative styles, although it should be said that Snow had more dress sense). When RCA suggested he record some rock 'n' roll tracks to keep abreast of the current trend, he refused, stating, 'It just didn't suit my personality. I couldn't sing the songs'. Following further Top 10 country hits with 'Eat Drink And Be Merry' and the semi-narration 'What Would You Do (If Jesus Came To Your House)?', he became a regular member of the *Opry* in 1957. He also turned down the opportunity to record 'Bye

Bye Love', which became a country and pop hit for both the Everly Brothers and Webb Pierce that year. In 1960, Wagoner was given a television series sponsored by the Chattanooga Medicine Company. Whatever their reason for choosing the lanky Wagoner (he had become known as the Thin Man From West Plains) to host the show is not clear but it was certainly a wise choice. Initially carried by 18 stations, it became so popular that by the end of the 60s, it was networked to 86 and soon after to over 100. The show, which featured Wagoner and his band The Wagonmasters, also acted as a shop window for new and established stars. His musicians included Buck Trent (who first used his electric banjo on the show), fiddler Mack Magaha and bass playing comedian Speck Rhodes, who was one of the last of the rustic country comedians. Norma Jean was the show's female singer for several years until she retired to get married in 1967 and was replaced by a young newcomer called Dolly Parton.

Between 1957 and 1964, Wagoner had further Top 10 country hits with 'Your Old Love Letters', 'I've Enjoyed As Much Of This As I Can Stand' and 'Sorrow On The Rocks', plus another number 1 with 'Misery Loves Company'. In 1965, he had a major hit in the USA with the original version of 'Green Green Grass Of Home'. The following year Tom Jones' recording became a UK pop number 1 and in 1975, Elvis Presley also achieved minor UK pop success with the song. The late 60s, also saw Wagoner have number 2 US country hits with 'The Cold Hard Facts Of Life' and 'The Carroll County Accident', the latter even attaining US pop chart status; both songs have now become country standards. In 1967, Wagoner began his association with Dolly Parton, which during the next seven years produced a great many Top 10 country hits such as 'The Last Thing On My Mind', 'Just Someone I Used To Know', 'Daddy Was An Old Time Preacher Man', 'If Teardrops Were Pennies' and 'Please Don't Stop Loving Me' (their only number 1). Together they won many awards, including the CMA Vocal Group of the Year in 1968 and Vocal Duo of the Year in both 1970 and 1971.

The partnership ended acrimoniously in 1974, when Dolly Parton left to pursue her solo career. Most authorities believe that, having already become a star in her own right, she should have moved on earlier. Wagoner was naturally upset to lose so obvious an asset, lawsuits followed and it was to be several years before they again became friends. After the split with Parton, his career began

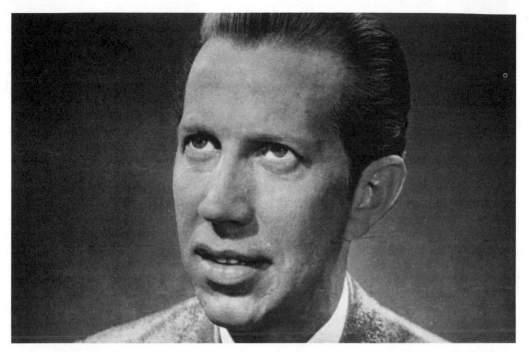

Porter Wagoner

to slow down and before the late 70s, he was classed as 'the last of the hillbillies' by the modern producers, he was in semi-retirement as a performer. However, during the 70s, when many of RCA's main artists were recording material of a crossover nature, Wagoner continued rigidly with his strict country music. He still managed some chart solo hits, albeit of a more minor nature, such as the wistful 'Charlie's Picture' (also a minor US pop hit), 'Carolina Moonshiner' (penned by Dolly Parton) and 'Ole Slew Foot'. In 1981, RCA dropped his records from their catalogue and he left the label. He joined Warner Brothers and had minor hits with 'Turn The Pencil Over', a beautiful country ballad that he sang on the soundtrack of the Clint Eastwood film *Honkytonk Man* and 'This Cowboy's Hat'. When the latter charted in 1983, it took his country chart hits to 81. He also re-recorded some of his earlier hits on *Viva*, naturally including 'Green Green Grass Of Home', and demonstrated that he was still very much a solid country artist. Over the years he became a wealthy man and in recent times has devoted more time to various business interests, as well as working in record production, but he is still active as a performer, at one time appearing regularly with his All-Girls Band and still wearing his rhinestones. During his career he kept up a punishing schedule of touring, playing over 200 concerts a year, whilst still maintaining his network television show and *Opry* appearances. The quality of his duets with Dolly Parton are arguably the finest by any other duo in country music and his own solo vocal abilities ranged from toe-tapping material and country ballads to being, most likely, the next best exponent to Hank Williams, in performing monologues such as 'Men With Broken Hearts', in a convincing manner without them sounding trite. He will, no doubt, one day be deservedly inducted into the *Country Music Hall Of Fame* as an artist who has made a major contribution to country music.

Albums: *A Satisfied Mind* (1956), *Porter Wagoner And Skeeter Davis Sing Duets* (1962), *A Slice Of Life - Songs Happy And Sad* (1962), with Norma Jean and Curly Harris *The Porter Wagoner Show* (1963), *Y'All Come* (1963), with Norma Jean *In Person* (1964), *The Bluegrass Story* (1965), *Old Log Cabin For Sale* (1965), *The Thin Man From West Plains* (1965), with the Blackwood Brothers *Grand Old Gospel* (1966), with Norma Jean *Live - On The Road* (1966), *Confessions Of A Broken Man* (1966), *I'm Day Dreamin' Tonight* (1966), *Your Old Love Letters* (1966), with the Blackwood Brothers *More Grand Gospel* (1967), *Soul Of A Convict And Other Great Prison Songs* (1967), *Sings Ballads Of Heart & Soul* (1967), *The Cold Hard Facts Of Life* (1967), *Green Green Grass Of Home* (1968), with Dolly Parton *Just Between You And Me* (1968), *Gospel Country* (1968), *The Bottom Of The Bottle* (1968),

Country Feeling (1969), The Carroll County Accident (1969), with Parton Just The Two Of Us (1969), with Parton Always, Always (1969), Me And My Boys (1969), Skid Row Joe/Down In The Alley (1970), with Parton Porter Wayne And Dolly Rebecca (1970), You Got-ta Have A License (1970), with Parton Once More (1970), Howdy Neighbor Howdy (1970), Sings His Own (1971), with Parton Two Of A Kind (1971), Porter Wagoner Country (1971), Simple As I Am (1971), Blue Moon Of Kentucky (1971), with Parton The Right Combination/Burning The Midnight Oil (1972), What Ain't To Be Just Might Happen (1972), with Parton Together Always (1972), Experience (1972), Ballads Of Love (1972), with Parton Love And Music (1973), The Farmer (1973), The Silent Kind (1973), with Parton We Found It (1973), I'll Keep On Loving You (1973), Highway Headed South (1974), with Parton Porter 'N' Dolly (1974), Tore Down (1974), Sings Some Love Songs (1975), with Parton Say Forever You'll Be Mine (1975), Porter (1977), Today (1979), Porter Wagoner & Dolly Parton (1980), Down Home Country (1982), Natural Wonder (1982), Viva (1983), One For The Road (1983), Country Memories (1985, cassette only), Porter Wagoner (1986). Compilations: The Best Of Porter Wagoner (1966), The Best Of Porter Wagoner And Dolly Parton (1974), 20 Of The Best (1982), The Thin Man From West Plains (1989), The Bluegrass Story (1989).

Wainwright, Loudon, III

b. 5 September 1946, Chapel Hill, North Carolina, USA. Loudon Wainwright I was in insurance while his son, Loudon Wainwright II, became a journalist for Life magazine. Wainwright's parents settled in Westchester Country, 60 miles outside of New York City although he went to a boarding school in Delaware ('School Days') and he was friends with an adolescent Liza Minnelli ('Liza'). He studied acting in Pittsburgh where singer George Gerdes encouraged his songwriting. By 1968, after a brief spell in an Oklahoma jail for a marijuana offence, Wainwright was playing folk clubs in New York and Boston and was signed to Atlantic Records. His first albums featured his high-pitched voice and guitar with few additions, and his intense, sardonic songs, described by him as 'reality with exaggeration', were about himself. He was hailed as the 'new Bob Dylan' for such songs as 'Glad To See You've Got Religion', 'Motel Blues' and 'Be Careful, There's A Baby In The House'. He later said: 'I wasn't the new anyone. Media people call you the new-something because it's the only way they know to describe what you

do'. His UK debut, opening for the Everly Brothers, was disastrous as Teddy Boys barracked him, but he found his métier at the 1972 Cambridge Folk Festival.

Wainwright's third album, for Columbia Records, included a surprise US Top 20 pop hit in 'Dead Skunk'. 'I had run over a skunk that had been run over a few times already. It took 15 minutes to write. I remember being bowled over at how much people liked it when I had put so little into it. It's about a dead skunk but people thought it was about Nixon and that's all right by me.' Wainwright wrote 'A.M. World' about his success and, almost defiantly, he followed it with Attempted Moustache, that had indistinct vocals and was uncommercial even by his standards, although it did include the whimsical 'Swimming Song'. Unrequited, partly recorded live, was a return to form and included the hilarious, but controversial, 'Rufus Is A Tit Man' (which Wainwright described as 'a love song, not a dirty song'), one of many songs he was to record about his children ('Pretty Little Martha' and 'Five Years Old') His marriage to Kate McGarrigle (see Kate And Annie McGarrigle) ended in 1977 and Loudon then had a child with Suzzy Roche of the Roches. His album, A Live One, actually recorded in 1976 demonstrates his wit but this gawky, lanky, square-jawed singer with enormous tongue, grimaces and contortions needs to be seen in person to be fully appreciated.

Wainwright has appeared in a few episodes of the television series M*A*S*H, appeared on stage in The Birthday Party and Pump Boys And Dinettes, and he is most recently best known in the UK for his topical songs on the Jasper Carrott television series. His wit and neuroses surfaced in such songs as 'Fear Of Flying' and 'Watch Me Rock, I'm Over 30' (both from T-Shirt), but he reached top form on three albums for Demon - Fame And Wealth, I'm Alright and More Love Songs. The albums, sometimes co-produced with Richard Thompson, have included 'I Don't Think Your Wife Likes Me', 'Hard Day On The Planet' (written while watching Live Aid), 'Unhappy Anniversary', 'Not John' (a tribute to John Lennon) and 'This Song Don't Have A Video'. Many of his later compositions are about the music industry of which he later claimed, 'I wanna be in showbiz one way or another until I die, so it's a mixed blessing not to be a huge success. I've been successful on my own terms - by failing'.

Albums: Loudon Wainwright III (1969), Album II (1971), Album III (1972), Attempted Moustache (1974), Unrequited (1975), T-Shirt (1976), Final

Exam (1978), *A Live One* (1979), *Fame And Wealth* (1983), *I'm Alright* (1984), *More Love Songs* (1986), *Therapy* (1989).

Wakely, Jimmy

b. Clarence Wakely, 16 February 1914, near Mineola, Arkansas, USA, d. 25 September 1982, Mission Hills, California, USA. Wakely's family relocated to Oklahoma when he was child, moving several times as they struggled to make a living usually by sharecropping. He gave himself the name of Jimmy, attended High School at Cowden, Oklahoma, learned to play the guitar and piano and worked on various projects, until after winning a local radio talent contest, he became a musician. In 1937, he married and moved to Oklahoma City, where he first worked as the pianist with a local band and appeared in a medicine show, before he was given a spot on WKY with Jack Cheney and Scotty Harrel as the Bell Boys. (Cheney was soon replaced by Johnny Bond). In 1940, as the Jimmy Wakely Trio, they were hired by Gene Autry to appear on his CBS *Melody Ranch* radio show in Hollywood. He worked with Autry for two years, at one time being known as the Melody Kid, before leaving to form his own band, which at times included Merle Travis, Cliffie Stone and Spade Cooley. Wakely made his film debut in 1939, in the Roy Rogers b-movie western *Saga Of Death Valley* and went on to appear in support roles (sometimes with his trio) in many films and with many other cowboy stars. In 1944, he starred in *Song Of The Range* and between then and 1949, when he made *Lawless Code*, he starred in almost 30 Monogram films. He became so popular as a cowboy actor that, in 1948, he was voted the number 4 cowboy star after Rogers, Autry and Charles Starrett. He made his first appearance in the US country charts in 1944 with his Decca recording of 'I'm Sending You Red Roses'. In 1948, recording for Capitol, he charted two country number 1 hits - 'One Has My Name, The Other Has My Heart' (which held the top spot for 11 weeks and remained in the country charts for 32, as well as being a national US Top 10 hit) and 'I Love You So Much It Hurts'.

In 1949, he had even more success with solo hits including 'I Wish I Had A Nickel' and 'Someday You'll Call My Name', plus several duet hits with Margaret Whiting, including their million-selling recording of Floyd Tillman's song 'Slipping Around', which was a country and pop number 1. At this time, Wakely's popularity was such that, in *Billboard*'s nationwide poll, he was voted America's third most popular singer behind Perry Como and Frankie Laine - edging Bing Crosby into fourth place. Wakely and Whiting followed it with several more Top 10 country and pop hits including 'I'll Never Slip Around Again' and 'A Bushel And A Peck'. Strangely, after his 1951 solo Top 10 hits 'My Heart Cries For You' (a UK pop hit for Guy Mitchell), 'Beautiful Brown Eyes' and a further duet with Margaret Whiting, entitled 'I Don't Want To Be Free', Wakely never made the country charts again. During the late 40s and the 50s, he toured extensively throughout the USA, the Pacific, the Far East, Korea and Alaska, sometimes appearing with Bob Hope. Musical tastes changed with the coming of Hank Williams and other country singers and the cowboy song and image lost much of its appeal. Wakely, however, hosted his own network radio show from 1952-58 and in 1961 he co-hosted a network television series with another silver screen cowboy Tex Ritter. During the 60s and throughout much of the 70s, he was still a popular entertainer, mainly performing on the west coast (he made his home in Los Angeles) or playing the club circuits of Las Vegas and Reno with his family show, which featured his children Johnny and Linda. He had formed his own Shasta label in the late 50s and in the 70s, he subsequently recorded a great deal of material on that label. In 1971, he was elected to the Nashville Songwriters Association International Hall Of Fame. Jimmy Wakely died, after a prolonged illness, in 1982.

Albums: *Christmas On The Range* (1954), *Songs Of The West* (1954), *Santa Fe Trail* (1956), *Enter And Rest And Pray* (1957), *Country Million Sellers* (1959), *Merry Christmas* (1959), *Sings* (1960), *Christmas With Jimmy Wakely* (1966), *Slipping Around* (1966), with Margaret Whiting *I'll Never Slip Around Again* (1967), *Show Me The Way* (1968), *Heartaches* (1969), *Here's Jimmy Wakely* (1969), *Lonesome Guitar Man* (60s), *Now And Then* (1970), *Big Country Songs* (1970), *Jimmy Wakely Country* (1971), *Blue Shadows* (1973), *Family Show* (1973), *The Wakely Way With Country Hits* (1974), *Jimmy Wakely* (1974), *On Stage Volume 1* (1974), *Western Swing And Pretty Things* (1975), *The Gentle Touch* (1975), *The Jimmy Wakely CBS Radio Show* (1975), *Jimmy Wakely Country* (1975), *Singing Cowboy* (1975), *An Old Fashioned Christmas* (1976), *A Tribute To Bob Wills* (1976), *Precious Memories* (1976), *Moments To Remember* (1977), *Reflections* (1977).

Walker, Billy

b. Billy Marvin Walker, 14 January 1929, Rails, Texas, USA. Walker was born on a farm but was raised in an orphanage after his mother's death. He returned to live with his father, when he was 11-years old, who had re-married. Walker learned the guitar from his father and, after seeing a Gene Autry film, he was determined to become a singer. He appeared on radio in Clovis when aged 15 and then, when 17, appeared 'The Travelling Texan' on the Big D Jamboree radio show on KRLD Dallas. Walker recorded for Capitol Records from 1949-51 but he did not make the US country charts until he recorded 'Thank You For Calling' for Columbia in 1954. He dispensed with his mask and joined both *Louisiana Hayride* and *Ozark Jubilee*. Since 1960, Walker has been a regular performer at the *Grand Ole Opry*. Walker was the first to record Willie Nelson's 'Funny How Time Slips Away' and he passed another of another Nelson's songs, 'Crazy', to Patsy Cline. In 1962 Walker had his first US country number 1 with 'Charlie's Shoes' and subsequent successes included 'Cross The Brazos At Waco', 'A Million To One' and 'Sundown Mary' and 'She Goes Walking Through My Mind' and 'Sing Me A Love Song To Baby', followed by a succession of minor chart successes for a variety of companies, including his own Tall Texan label. By the end of 1988, he had had 65 records in the US country charts, including duets with Barbara Fairchild, 'The Answer Game' and 'Let Me Be The One'. Among his own songs is a tribute to Marty Robbins, 'He Sang The Songs About El Paso'. Walker, who is a born-again Christian, has built up a UK following, with appearances at Wembley festivals and country clubs. In 1986, Walker said, 'Current crossover trends are like mixing chocolate, strawberry and vanilla in the same bowl. Not only is it an ugly colour but it leaves a bad taste in one's mouth.'

Albums: *Everybody's Hits But Mine* (1961), *Thank You For Calling* (1964), *Anything Your Heart Desires* (1964), *The Gun, The Gold And The Girl* (1965), *A Million And One* (1966), *The Walker Way* (1967), *I Taught Her Everything She Knows* (1967), *Billy Walker Salutes The Hall Of Fame* (1968), *How Big Is God* (1969), *Portrait Of Billy* (1969), *Country Christmas* (1969), *Charlie's Shoes* (1970), *Darling Days* (1970), *When A Man Loves A Woman* (1970), *I'm Gonna Keep On Lovin' You* (1971), *Billy Walker Live* (1972), *There May Be No Tomorrow* (1972), *The Billy Walker Show* (1972), *The Hand Of Love* (1973), *Too Many Memories* (1973), *Fine As Wine* (1974), *Lovin' And Losin'* (1975), *Alone Again* (1976), *The Tall Texan Sings His Songs* (1978), *Star Of The Grand Ole Opry* (1979), *Lovin' Things* (1979), with Barbara Fairchild *The Answer Game* (1979), with Fairchild *It Takes Two* (1980), *Soap And Water* (1980), *Don't Ever Leave Me In Texas* (1980), *Circumstances* (1980), *Waking Up To Sunshine* (1980), *How Great Thou Art* (1981), *Are You Sincere?* (1982), *Life Is A Song* (1983), *The Tall Texan* (1985), *Precious Memories* (1985), *Billy Walker* (1986), *For My Friends* (1987), *Wild Texas Rose* (1988). Compilations: *Billy Walker's Greatest Hits* (1963), *Big Country Hits* (1967), *All Time Greatest Hits* (1973), *Best Of The Best Of Billy Walker* (1988).

Walker, Charlie

b. 2 November 1926, Copeville, Collins County, Texas, USA. A talented musician, Walker joined Bill Boyd's Cowboy Ramblers in 1943 and worked as a disc jockey for the Armed Forces Radio Network during World War II. By the early 50s, he was voted one of country music's Top 10 DJ's and his vocal talent saw him join Decca. His first chart hit was 'Only You, Only You' but after moving to Columbia in 1958, he scored a major number 2 hit with Harlan Howard's song 'Pick Me Up On Your Way Down', which established him as a major artist. Between 1960 and 1974, Walker achieved 23 more country hits having Top 10 success with 'Wild As A Wild Cat' and 'Don't Squeeze My Sharmon'. He later recorded for Epic, RCA, Capitol and Plantation. Many of his most popular recordings are honky tonk songs such as 'Close All The Honky Tonks', 'Honky Tonk Season' and 'Honky Tonk Women' (a number 1 British pop hit for the Rolling Stones). He joined the *Grand Ole Opry* in 1967 (having first guested in 1954) and still makes appearances. Walker is also noted for his ability as a compere and in that capacity, he has appeared at such prestigious venues as Las Vegas' *Golden Nugget*. A fine golfer, he also regularly broadcasts on major golfing events. He appeared in the film *Country Music* and is still active, although mainly as a broadcaster. His last chart hit was 'Odds And Ends (Bits And Pieces)'.

Albums: *Greatest Hits* (1961), *Close All The Honky Tonks* (1965), *Born To Lose* (1965), *Wine Women And Walker* (1966), *Country Style* (1967), *Don't Squeeze My Sharmon* (1967), *Golden Hits* (1967), *Greatest Hits* (1968), *He Is My Everything* (1968), *Live In Dallas* (1969), *Honky Tonkin'* (1971), *Charlie Walker* (1972), *Break Out The Bottle (Bring On The Music)* (1973), *Golden Hits* (1978), *Texas Gold* (1979), *Greatest Hits* (1981).

Walker, Jerry Jeff

b. 16 March 1942, Oneonta, New York, USA. Although he initially pursued a career as a folk singer in New York's Greenwich Village, Walker first forged his reputation as a member of Circus Maximus. He left this promising group following their debut album when a jazz-based initiative proved incompatible with his own ambitions. Having moved to Key West in Florida, Walker resumed work as a solo artist with *Drifting Way Of Life*, before signing with the Atco label when his former outlet showed little interest in his country/folk material. He enjoyed a minor hit with 'Mr. Bojangles', a tale of a street dancer Walker reputedly met in a drunk tank. Although the singer's own rendition stalled in the chart's lower reaches, it became a US Top 10 entry by the Nitty Gritty Dirt Band and has since been the subject of numerous cover versions including a lethargic one by Bob Dylan. By the early 70s Walker was based in Austin, Texas where he became a kindred spirit to the city's 'outlaw' fraternity, including Willie Nelson and Waylon Jennings. He also built one of the region's most accomplished backing groups, later to follow its own career as the Lost Gonzo Band. A low-key approach denied the artist the same commercial success, but Jerry Jeff has enjoyed the approbation of colleagues and a committed cult following. His wry humour is often blunted by sentimentality, yet he is capable of turning trite into simple eloquence. Albums: *Mr. Bojangles* (1968), *Drifting Way Of Life* (1969), *Jerry Jeff Walker* (1969), *Five Years Gone* (1969), *Bein' Free* (1970), *Jerry Jeff Walker* (1972), *Viva Terlingua!* (1973), *Walker's Collectables* (1974), *Ridin' High* (1975), *It's A Good Night For Singin'* (1976), *A Man Must Carry On* (1977), *Contrary To Ordinary* (1978), *Jerry Jeff* (1978), *Too Old To Change* (1979), *Reunion* (1981), *Cowjazz* (1982), *Gypsy Songman* (1988), *Live At Guene Hall* (1989), *Navajo Rug* (1991), *Hill Country Rain* (1992). Compilations: *The Best Of Jerry Jeff Walker* (1980).

Wallace, Jerry

b. 15 December 1928, Guildford, Missouri, USA. A pop-country singer/guitarist who made his initial recordings for Allied in 1951, but achieved his first chart success when his 1958 Challenge recording of 'How The Time Flies' reached number 11 in the US pop charts. After further pop successes, including his recording of film star Audie Murphy's song 'Shutters And Boards', he first appeared in the country charts with his 1965 Mercury recording of 'Life's Gone And Slipped Away'. Between then and 1979, he went on to register 32 more country hits, including a number 1 with 'If You Leave Me Tonight I'll Cry' (also a minor pop hit) and a number 2 with 'Do You Know What It's Like To Be Lonesome'. His later recordings were on many different labels including Liberty and MCA and his last chart entry was 'If I Could Set My Love To Music' on the Door Knob label in 1980. A talented actor and narrator, he has done voice-overs for commercials and appeared in many top television plays and shows such as *Night Gallery* and *Hec Ramsey*.
Albums: *Just Jerry* (1959), *There She Goes* (1961), *Shutters And Boards* (1962), *In The Misty Moonlight* (1964), *Another Time, Another Place, Another World* (1968), *This One's On The House* (1968), *Sweet Child Of Sunshine* (1968), *Bitter Sweet* (1969), *Greatest Hits* (1969), *This Is Jerry Wallace* (1971), *Jerry Wallace* (2LP) (1972), *Do You Know What It's Like To Be Lonesome* (1973), *Primrose Lane* (1973), *To Get To You* (1973), *I Wonder Whose Baby/Make Hay While The Sun Shines* (1974), *Coming Home To You* (1975), *Jerry Wallace* (1975), *All I Want Is You* (1975), *I Miss You Already* (1977).

Walters, Hank

b. William Ralph Walters, 2 August 1933, Liverpool, England. Walters had acquired the name 'Hank' whilst working on the Liverpool docks because of his love of country music. As a schoolboy, Walters learned accordion and acquired a passion for Jimmie Rodgers and Hank Williams' music. In 1946 he formed Spike Walters And His Hillbillies, one of the UK's first country groups. Conscripted in 1951, he and some other soldiers were billed as, the Dusty Road Ramblers for a show in Khartoum, Sudan. Back home, Walters used the name for his own country group and they appeared regularly at the Cavern as well as having a residency at the Black Cat Club. Most of the early Merseybeat groups saw him perform and Walters recalls, 'John Lennon said to me, "I don't go much on your music, but give us your hat." I told him that I didn't think his group would get anywhere unless they got with it and played country.' By 1962 the Cavern's policy had switched to beat groups, but Walters was still able to get bookings with his country music and Scouse humour. He turned down an offer from Polydor to record a cover version of 'Twenty Four Hours From Tulsa', but he was featured on the Decca album, *Liverpool Goes Country*. Hank Walters and the Dusty Road Ramblers continue as one of the most popular acts on Merseyside and he also fronts the Hank Walters

Family. The hillbilly docker has performed well at national country music festivals, but the group has been reluctant to travel because of day jobs, although Walters has now retired from the doctor. 'Progress', 'Sweet Liverpool', 'Rollin' Home' and 'The Dosser' are well-known in the city. The mainstays of his repertoire are 'I Could Never Be Ashamed Of You', 'Are You Teasing Me?', 'Close To The Edge', 'I Saw The Light' and, surprisingly, 'The Ugly Bug Ball'. He says, 'New country is just young voices singing old songs. I've been doing them for years.'

Albums: *Hank Walters* (1973), *Progress* (1979).

Wangford, Hank

b. Samuel Hutt, 15 November 1940, Wangford, Suffolk, England. Wangford's father, Allen Hutt, was chief sub-editor of the communist newspaper *The Daily Worker* and president of the National Union of Journalists. His mother taught English to Russian students. Wangford studied medicine at Cambridge University and later became a doctor. He was converted to country music by Gram Parsons who attended for treatment in 1971. After a period in the USA, Wangford became gradually more involved in country music and, despite the demands of his professional work, yearned to be a performer. When his girlfriend married his best friend, he consoled himself in a pub near the Wangford bypass in Suffolk. Here he devised the character of Hank Wangford, who would sing songs from the Wangford Hall of Pain. He says, 'Hank Wangford was a good name for the classic country star. He sings about pain, he sings about heartache, and that was good because Sam could go on living and being normal.' Starting in 1976, Wangford built a reputation on the London pub-rock circuit. His persona was both a glorification of country music and an affectionate parody of its excesses.

He formed Sincere Management (motto: 'It's in the post.') and Sincere Products ('Brought to you with no regard to quality'). Wangford generated publicity as a gynaecologist-cum-country singer, often being photographed with a Harley Street sign. His media image however, has proved more sustainable than the lightweight music which, in fairness, is highly successful in the pub/club environment. 'Chicken Rhythm' is derived from Ray Stevens' quirky 'In The Mood', and 'Cowboys Stay On Longer' is a close cousin to David Allan Coe's 'Divers Do It Deeper'. Wangford has always been able to surround himself with talented band members, notably Andy Roberts (Brad Breath) and Melanie Harrold (Irma Cetas), who have more musical talent. His fiddler and co-singer, former member of the Fabulous Poodles and Gram Parsons lookalike, Bobby Valentino, later embarked on a solo career. Wangford, with his ponytail, stubble and gap-toothed features is an engaging entertainer, creating a stage show 'Radio Wang' and presenting two country music series for Channel 4 television. He also works as the senior medical officer at a family planning clinic in London, and he says, 'I have had letters of referral from doctors which start 'Dear Dr. Wangford', so the transmogrification is complete.'

Albums: *Live: Hank Wangford* (1982), *Hank Wangford* (1985), *Rodeo Radio* (1985), *Stormy Horizons* (1990).

Further reading: *Hank Wangford, Vol.III The Middle Years*, Sam Hutt, London, 1989.

Wariner, Steve

b. 25 December 1954, Noblesville, Indiana, USA. Wariner was playing in his father's country group from the age of 10. One night he had a residency at a club near Indianapolis and the starring attraction, Dottie West, came on stage early to harmonize with him. He then played bass for West and after that, for Bob Luman. Luman recorded several of Wariner's songs, whilst Wariner was to revive Luman's success, 'Lonely Women Make Good Lovers'. He played for Chet Atkins, who took him to RCA Records as a solo performer. Wariner was offered, and rejected, 'You Needed Me', but in 1978 he had a minor US country hit with his own song, 'I'm Already Taken', which was subsequently recorded by Conway Twitty. After several other chart records, he had his first country number 1 in 1981 with 'All Roads Lead To You' but his follow-ups, 'Kansas City Lights', 'Midnight Fire' and 'What I Didn't Do', were only moderately successful. Wanting to make records with a stronger country element, he moved to MCA Records in 1985 and had country number 1 hits with 'Some Fools Never Learn', 'You Can Dream On Me' (which he wrote with John Hall of Orleans), 'Love's Highway', 'Small Town Girl', 'Lynda' (a tribute to actress Lynda Carter who played 'Wonder Woman') and 'The Weekend'. He has recorded duets with Nicolette Larson ('That's How You Know When Love's Right') and Glen Campbell ('The Hand That Rocks The Cradle'), the latter is one of the strongest influences on his work. After winning a CMA Vocal Event award for his contribution to Mark O'Connor's 'Restless'

Hank Wangford

in 1991, Wariner adopted a tougher image and sound for the highly successful *I Am Ready*.

Albums: *Steve Wariner* (1982), *Midnight Fire* (1983), *One Good Night Deserves Another* (1985), *Life's Highway* (1985), *Down In Tennessee* (1986), *It's A Crazy World* (1987), *I Should Be With You* (1988), *I Got Dreams* (1989), *I Am Ready* (1991).

Watson, Doc

b. Arthel Watson, 2 March 1923, Deep Gap, North Carolina, USA. This blind acoustic folk-guitarist's work found great success in the 60s and was rediscovered by country-rock fans following his appearance on the Nitty Gritty Dirt Band's *Will The Circle Be Unbroken* in 1972. He played harmonica and banjo as a child, later progressing to guitar. In the 50s he played pop and commercial country in local clubs. After being spotted on a traditional music bill alongside his neighbour Clarence Ashley, Watson was booked for the famous Gerde's Folk City in New York in 1960. Recordings followed, for premier folk labels Folkways and Vanguard, and his reputation was enhanced by a notable Newport Folk Festival appearance in 1963. Two years later, he began to work with his son Merle, another excellent flat-picking guitarist who, in later years, inspired his father to diversify from the folk ballads and blues which were his wont. They won Grammys for *Then & Now* and *Two Days In November*; by the late 70s, Doc had become a revered figure, receiving rapturous receptions wherever he played and guesting on records by Flatt And Scruggs and Chet Atkins. Watson went into semi-retirement following the tragic death of his son in a farming accident in 1985, but remains well represented on record, via latter-day recordings for the Flying Fish and Sugar Hill labels.

Albums: *Doc Watson And Family* (1963), *Doc Watson* (1964), with Merle Watson *Doc Watson And Son* (1965), *Southbound* (1966), *Home Again* (1966), *Good Deal* (1968), *The Elementary Doc Watson* (1972), *Then & Now* (1973), *Two Days In November* (1974), with Merle *Memories* (1975), *In The Pines* (1984), *Riding The Midnight Train* (1984), *On Praying Ground* (1990). Compilations: *The Essential Doc Watson* (1974, double set), *A Folk And Country Legend* (1982), *Portrait* (1988), *The Essential Doc Watson, Volume 1* (1989). with Merle *Remembering Merle* (1992)

Watson, Gene

b. Gary Gene Watson, 11 October 1943, Palestine, Texas, USA. Raised in Paris, Texas, in a musical family, he first worked as a professional at the age of 13. In 1963, he moved to Houston, where he found daytime employment in car engine and bodywork repairs. During the evenings, his vocal style, with its slight nasal sound in best country tradition, made him a very popular honky-tonk singer around the local clubs such as the Dynasty, where he was resident for several years. He recorded for several labels including Reeder, (whose owner Russ Reeder went on to become his manager and producer) Wide World and Stoneway before gaining his first country chart entry with 'Bad Water' on the Resco label in 1975. The same year, he moved to Capitol Records and had a US Top 10 country hit with the suggestive 'Love In The Hot Afternoon'. Further Top 10 hits followed, including 'Paper Rosie', 'One Sided Conversation', 'Farewell Party', 'Should I Come Home?' and 'Nothing Sure Looked Good On You'. In 1981, after moving to MCA Records, his recording of 'Fourteen Carat Mind' gave him his first US country number 1. He moved to Epic in 1985, gaining a number 5 hit with 'Memories To Burn' but changed to Warner Brothers Records in 1988, where he immediately repeated the success with 'Don't Waste It On The Blues'. Although he charted regularly throughout the 80s, he failed to find another number 1. In 1987, he recorded 'Tempted' with Tammy Wynette, which appears on her *Higher Ground* album. Generally favouring sad ballads and backed up by his band the Farewell Party, he has become a favourite not only in the USA but also with British audiences. It may be that lack of publicity has prevented him becoming the major star his undoubted vocal talent merits. The decision by Lib Hatcher, Randy Travis's manager, to handle Watson's career in the late 80s sparked hopes of a commercial renaissance, but the liaison ended in rancour and talk of litigation.

Albums: *Gene Watson* (1971), *Love In The Hot Afternoon* (1975), *Because You Believed In Me* (1976), *Paper Rosie* (1977), *Beautiful Country* (1977), *Reflections* (1978), *Should I Come Home (Or Should I Go Crazy)* (1979), *No One Will Ever Know* (1980), *Between This Time And Next Time* (1981), *Old Loves Never Die* (1981), *This Dreams On Me* (1982), *Sometimes I Get Lucky* (1983), *Little By Little* (1984), *Heartaches, Love And Stuff* (1985), *Memories To Burn* (1985), *Starting New Memories* (1986), *Texas Saturday Night* (1986), *Honky Tonk Crazy* (1987), *Back In The Fire* (1989), *At Last* (1991), *In Other Words* (1992). Compilation: *Greatest Hits* (1986).

Weatherly, Jim

b. 17 March 1943, Pontotoc, Mississippi, USA.
Weatherly has been a professional songwriter since
1971. His composition 'Neither One Of Us
(Wants To Be The First To Say Goodbye)' was a
US country hit for Bob Luman and then a pop hit
for Gladys Knight And The Pips. Ray Price, who
has recorded over 50 Weatherly songs, had a
number 1 country hit with 'Best Thing That Ever
Happened To Me', which was again covered for
the pop market by Gladys Knight And The Pips.
Weatherly recorded his own 'Midnight Plane To
Houston' for Jimmy Bowen's Amos label. Cissy
Houston had originally wanted to record a soul
version, but felt 'Midnight Train To Houston' by
Cissy Houston did not sound right and, with
Weatherly's permission, changed it to 'Midnight
Train To Georgia'. Gladys Knight And The Pips
had their biggest hit when they covered it and they
also recorded Weatherly's 'Where Peaceful Waters
Flow' and 'The Going Ups And The Coming
Downs'. The 600 different versions of Weatherly's
songs cover a wide range of artists and emotions
but he concentrates mainly on dreamy love songs
for his own albums. His singles include 'It Must
Have Been The Rain' and his credo 'The Need
To Be', but the only one to make any commercial
impact was 'I'll Still Love You', a US Top 10
country hit in 1975. He says, 'Every song I
compose is a personal statement. My music tells
how I feel, what I believe, and what I see. I try to
tell all of it in an intimate, subtle way.'
Albums: *A Gentler Time* (1973), *Weatherly* (1973),
The Songs Of Jim Weatherly (1974) *Magnolias And
Misfits* (1975) *The People Some People Choose To
Love* (1976) *Pictures And Rhymes* (1977).

Weller, Freddy

b. 9 September 1947, Atlanta, Georgia, USA.
Weller played guitar and sang at school and was in
a group, the Believers, with Joe South. One of his
first sessions was for Billy Joe Royal's hit single,
'Down In The Boondocks'. Weller replaced the
lead guitarist in the successful 60s pop band, Paul
Revere And The Raiders. He wrote several songs
with Tommy Roe including his transatlantic
number 1, 'Dizzy'. His opportunity to go solo
came when a recording session for the Raiders was
cancelled and producer Mark Lindsay offered to
record Weller on his own. They cut 'Games
People Play', which became a US number 2
country hit. Weller had further country hits with
'These Are Not My People', 'Down In The
Boondocks' and 'The Promised Land', eventually

leaving the Raiders in 1971. His sensual songs were
sometimes seen as controversial, notably his song
for Bob Luman, 'Lonely Women Make Good
Lovers'. Does his last country hit, a minor one in
1980 called, 'Lost In Austin', explain his absence
from the charts?.
Albums: *Games People Play / These Are Not My
People* (1969), *Listen To The Young Folks* (1970),
The Promised Land (1971), *Country Collection*
(1972), *Roadmaster* (1972), *Too Much Monkey
Business* (1973), *Sexy Lady* (1974), *Freddy Weller*
(1975), *Liquor, Love And Life* (1976), *One Man
Show* (1977), *Love Got In The Way* (1978), *Go For
The Night* (1980), *Ramblin' Man* (1982),

Wells, Houston, And The Marksmen

b. Andrew Smith, 1938, Northumberland,
England. Wells left school at 14 years old and
worked in a timber mill. He then became a tree-
feller for the Forestry Commission and, after a spell
in the merchant navy, worked in a pulp mill in
Vancouver, Canada. On returning to the England,
he and his family moved to Wickford, Essex. In
nearby Southend, Pete Willsher (lead guitar/lap
steel guitar) had formed a country band, the
Coasters they comprised Brian Gill (bass), Norman
Hull (guitar) and Peter Nye (drums). When Wells
joined them in 1959, they became Andy Smith
And The Coasters. Because of the American group
of the same name, the Coasters changed to the
Marksmen, while Parlophone Records decided
that Smith was too plain and renamed him
Houston Wells. Record producer Joe Meek was
impressed with their sound and their first two
singles were 'This Song Is Just For You' and
'Shutters And Boards', which was backed by
Meek's 'North Wind'. Their third single, 'Only
The Heartaches', made the UK Top 30 in August
1963. They recorded further singles, an EP,
Ramona, and *Western Style*, for Meek. They were
particularly popular in Ireland where 'Only The
Heartaches' made the Top 10. However, the
Marksmen felt that they were being exploited by
Wells and his management and, on a trip to
Ireland, they tore up Wells's return ticket home in
his presence. Wells continued to record, using
another group, the Outlaws, as the Marksmen.
Meek was fascinated by dead performers and so his
resident songwriter, Geoff Goddard, wrote a
tribute to Jim Reeves, 'We'll Remember You', for
Wells. However, Goddard and Meek became
embroiled in an argument regarding the credits for
'Have I The Right?' and the song remained
unreleased until 1964 when the Honeycombs took

the song to the UK number 1 spot and the US Top 5. Wells continued with his Irish success and had a number 6 single in 1966 with 'Above And Beyond' and he also revived 'Hello Mary Lou'. Of the Marksmen, Pete Willsher has become one of the UK's top country steel guitarists. The 28 released tracks which Houston Wells recorded with Joe Meek have never been reissued, largely because of problems with Meek's estate. Once this is resolved, listeners will be able to hear one of the UK's first professional country bands. As it stands, their records are more collectable than many of their American counterparts.

Album: *Western Style* (1963).

Wells, Kitty

b. Muriel Ellen Deason, 30 August 1919, Nashville, Tennessee, USA. The family relocated to Humphries County but returned to Nashville in 1928, where Muriel's father, who played guitar and sang for local dances, worked as a brakeman for the Tennessee Central Railroad. She grew up singing in the church choir, learned to play guitar and in 1934, she dropped out of school to work in a local shirt factory. The following year, she teamed with her sisters Mabel and Willie Mae and their cousin, Bessie Choate, to form the singing Deason Sisters. In 1936, they appeared on WSIX Nashville singing 'Jealous Hearted Me' and were cut off in mid-song by the station, who for some reason believed the song to be too *risqué* for their listeners. The audience disagreed and the girls were given a regular early morning programme. In 1937, Muriel met aspiring country singer Johnnie Wright and on 30 October that year, the two were married. Soon after, the newly weds and Wright's sister, Louise, began appearing on radio station WSIX as Johnnie Wright And The Harmony Girls. In 1939, Wright and Muriel teamed up with Jack Anglin (their future brother-in-law) first appearing as Johnnie Wright And The Happy Roving Cowboys with Jack Anglin, later becoming Johnnie And Jack And The Tennessee Hillbillies then the Tennessee Mountain Boys. In 1943, Muriel first became known as Kitty Wells. Wright chose the name from an old song popularized on the *Grand Ole Opry* by the Pickard Family and the Vagabonds. Over these years, Kitty did not always sing on a regular basis with Wright, due to the fact that, by this time, she had two children Ruby Wright and Bobby Wright to look after; a second daughter Carol Sue Wright followed.

Kitty made her first solo recordings for RCA-Victor in 1949, one song being 'Gathering Flowers For The Master's Bouquet', now generally rated to be the first recording, on a major label, of the song that has become a country gospel standard. A further session the next year failed to produce a hit and she left the label. In December 1951, she moved back to Nashville and with Johnnie And Jack becoming members of the *Opry* in January 1952, she decided to retire. However, basically for the session fee, she had been persuaded by Wright and Paul Cohen of Decca to record a demo of a female answer song to Hank Thompson's then current US country number 1, 'The Wild Side Of Life'. On 3 May 1952, under the production of Owen Bradley, she recorded 'It Wasn't God Who Made Honky Tonk Angels'. Two months later, unaware that it had been released, Kitty Wells found she had recorded a future million seller. By 8 August, it was beginning a six-week stay at number 1 in the country charts and had become a Top 30 pop hit. The publishers of 'Wild Side Of Life' sued on the grounds that their song's melody had been used. Since both songs had used the tune of the old song 'I'm Thinking Tonight Of My Blue Eyes' and 'The Great Speckled Bird', the case was thrown out of court. The song was the first real woman's song in country music and the recording made Kitty Wells country music's first female singing star in her own right and gave her the distinction of becoming the first female country singer to have a number 1 record. (Initially the *Opry* management felt the lyrics were unsuitable, but an intervention by the influential Roy Acuff saw them relent). Obviously Kitty Wells's retirement was shelved and by the end of the 50s, she had registered 35 successive Top 20 country hits, 24 making the Top 10. There were further answer songs in 'Paying For That Back Street Affair', 'Hey Joe' and 'I'll Always Be Your Fraulein' and a less successful one called 'My Cold Cold Heart Is Melted Now'. During this time, as one of several duet hits with Red Foley, 'One By One', became a country number 1 in 1954. She also had Top 10 duets with Webb Pierce, including 'Oh, So Many Years' and 'Finally'. She also recorded with Roy Acuff.

In 1959, Decca took the unusual step of signing her to a lifetime contract. During the 60s, her list of chart hits extended to almost seventy and though only 'Heartbreak USA' (1961) made number 1, there were 11 more that made the Top 10. These included 'Left To Right' and 'Unloved Unwanted'. The hits slowed down during the 70s, the last two coming in 1979 and taking her total to 81 in all. From the 50s through to the end of the 70s, she toured extensively, making personal appearances not only in the USA and Canada but all over the world. After Jack Anglin's death in 1963, Johnny Wright toured with his wife and family as the Kitty Wells And Johnny Wright Family Show. In 1969, they hosted a syndicated television show that ran for many years. In the early 70s, she did sever her connections with Decca (by then MCA Records) and signed with Capricorn where, backed by some of the Allman Brothers Band, she recorded *Forever Young*. (The title track was a Bob Dylan song - a daring thing for a traditional country singer at the time).

She made her first appearance in Britain at the 1974 Wembley Festival. She also continued to record for several minor labels including in 1989, two albums for Step One with Owen Bradley, a man who had produced her million-seller at Decca, thirty-seven years previously. Over the years she has won many awards, including being voted *Billboard*'s, Female Country Artiste from 1953 to 1965 but her greatest award came in 1976, when she was elected to the *Country Music Hall Of Fame* in Nashville. The plaque noted that 'In true country tradition her sincere vocal stylings convey the real feeling of the songs, be they happy or sad'. Many of her hits were country weepies such as 'Mommy For A Day', 'I Gave My Wedding Dress Away', 'This White Circle On My Finger' and 'I Hope My Divorce Is Never Granted'. There is little doubt that because of her successes, later female singers have perhaps found that they were more accepted in the business. In 1952, Kitty Wells was named the Queen Of Country Music by Fred Rose and in the opinions of country traditionalists, she still holds her title with dignity and sincerity. She has, as country historian Bill C. Malone noted, 'preserved an image of wholesomeness and domesticity that was far removed from the world she often sang about'.

Albums: *Country Hit Parade* (1956), *Winner Of Your Heart* (1956), *Lonely Street* (1958), *Dust On The Bible* (1959), *After Dark* (1959), *Seasons Of My Heart* (1960), *Kitty's Choice* (1960), *Heartbreak USA* (1961), *Golden Favorites* (1961), with Red Foley *Golden Favorites* (1961), *Queen Of Country Music* (1962), *Singing On Sunday* (1962), *Queen Of Country Music* (1962), *Christmas With Kitty Wells* (1962), *Especially For You* (1964), *Country Music Time* (1964), *Burning Memories* (1965), *Kitty Wells Family Gospel Sing* (1965), *Lonesome, Sad & Blue* (1965), *Guilty Street* (1966), *Kitty Wells* (1966), *Country All The Way* (1966), *The Kitty Wells' Show* (1966), *Songs Made Famous By Jim Reeves* (1966), *Love Makes The World Go Round* (1967), *Queen Of*

Honky Tonk Street (1967), with Foley *Together Again* (1967), *Kitty Wells' Showcase* (1968), with Johnnie Wright *We'll Stick Together* (1969), *Country Heart* (1969), *Singing 'Em Country* (1970), *Your Love Is The Way* (1970), *Pledging My Love* (1971), *They're Stepping All Over My Heart* (1971), *I've Got Yesterday* (1972), *Sincerely* (1972), with Wright *Heartwarming Gospel Songs* (1972), *Yours Truly* (1973), *Forever Young* (1974), *Kitty Wells & Roy Drusky* (1987). Compilations: *Kitty Wells' Golden Favourites* (1961), *The Kitty Wells Story* (1963), *Cream Of Country Hits* (1968), *Bouquet Of Hits* (1969), *Hall Of Fame, Volume 1* (1979), *Early Classics* (1981), *Greatest Hits Volume 1* (1989), *Greatest Hits Volume 2* (1989), *The Golden Years 1949-1957* (1987, five album box set).

Further reading: *Queen Of Country Music, The Life Story Of Kitty Wells*, A.C.Dunkleberger. *Kitty Wells, The Golden Years*, Bob Pinson, Richard Weize, Charles Wolfe.

West, Dottie

b. Dorothy Marie Marsh, 11 October 1932, McMinnville, Tennessee, USA, d. 4 September 1991. The eldest of ten children, she worked the cotton and sugar cane crops on the family farm as well as looking after her younger siblings. Country music was popular with her parents and she first learned to play guitar from her father. She completed a college education and graduated with a music degree. During her college days she sang at various events and met and married Bill West, an electronics engineer student, who later became a noted country steel guitarist and her manager. (The marriage produced four children, including country singer Shelly West, and lasted until 1969.) They moved to Cleveland in the mid-50s, where they both appeared regularly on the *Landmark Jubilee* television show. They moved to Nashville in 1959, where Dottie was befriended by Patsy Cline and briefly joined Starday and Atlantic Records.

In 1962, at the recommendation of Jim Reeves, Chet Atkins signed her to RCA Records. Her first US country chart hit 'Let Me Off At The Corner' was in 1963, the same year that the first song she wrote, 'Is This Me', became a number 3 country hit for Jim Reeves. The following year a duet, 'Love Is No Excuse', with Reeves was a country Top 10 hit as well as a minor pop chart entry. A country Top 10 solo hit of her own song 'Here Comes My Baby' followed, which so successfully launched her career that between 1964-84, she charted a further 60 US country hits. The following year the song made her the first female country singer to win a Grammy. In the late-60s, she had country hits with 'Would You Hold It Against Me', 'Paper Mansions', 'Country Girl' (which became a successful Coca-Cola advert), 'Reno' and duet recordings with Don Gibson, including a number 2 country hit with 'Rings Of Gold'. Her ability to sing country tear-jerkers was adequately shown with such numbers as 'Mommy, Can I Still Call Him Daddy' (which even featured her four-year-old son Dale). She recorded with Jimmy Dean in the early 70s, and in 1973 she had further major success with commercials for Coca-Cola, which featured her own award-winning song 'Country Sunshine' and led to her nickname of the 'Country Sunshine Girl'.

She left RCA in 1976 and in 1980 she had number 1 country hits with 'A Lesson In Leavin'' and 'Are You Happy?' on the United Artists label. In the mid-70s, she married her band's drummer Byron Metcalf, but they later divorced in 1980. Between 1979-81 she registered three country number 1 duet recordings alongside Kenny Rogers with 'Every Time Two Fools Collide', 'All I Ever Need Is You' and 'What Are We Doin' In Love?'. She has won many solo awards and in 1978 and 1979 she and Rogers were voted the Country Music Association Vocal Duo of the Year. She appeared in two films Second Fiddle To An Old Guitar and There's A Still On The Hill, and has played the Grand Ole Opry regularly since first becoming a member in 1964. Between 1981-85, she registered some minor hits on Liberty and Permian but only 'It's High Time' and 'Together Again' (another duet with Kenny Rogers) made the US country Top 20. In 1991, she was declared bankrupt and many of her possessions were auctioned off to pay an Inland Revenue Service debt of almost $1 million. On Friday 30 August 1991, due to problems with her own car, she asked an 81-year-old neighbour to drive her to the Opry for her scheduled appearance. His car crashed at speed when it left the ramp to the Opry car park, vaulted in the air and hit the central division. Both occupants were rushed to the Vanderbilt Medical Centre in a critical condition. Dottie West suffered a severe rupture of the liver and, in spite of several operations, surgeons could not control the bleeding. Although fully aware of the extent of her injuries, she was unable to speak and sadly died a few days later on 4 September. During her career she toured extensively, played all the major network television shows and was popular in Britain where she appeared on several occasions.

Albums: *Country Girl Singing Sensation* (1964), *Here Comes My Baby* (1965), shared with Melba Montgomery *Queens Of Country Music* (1965), *Dottie West Sings* (1966), *Suffer Time* (1966), *I'll Help You Forget Her* (1967), *Sings Sacred Ballads* (1967), *The Sound Of Country Music* (1967), *With All My Heart And Soul* (1967), *Country Girl* (1968), *What I'm Cut Out To Be* (1968), *I Fall To Pieces* (1969), *Sings Eddy Arnold* (1969), with Don Gibson *Dottie & Don* (1969), *Feminine Fancy* (1969), *Making Memories* (1970), *Making Believe* (1970), *Forever Yours* (1970), *Country And West* (1970), with Jimmy Dean *Country Boy And Country Girl* (1970), *A Legend In My Time* (1971), *Have You Heard* (1971), *Careless Hands* (1971), *I'm Only A Woman* (1972), *Country Sunshine* (1973), *Would You Hold It Against Me* (1973), *Dottie* (1973), *Dottie West* (1973), *House Of Love* (1974), *If It's All Right With You/Just What I've Been Looking For* (1974), *Loving You* (1974), *Carolina Cousins* (1975), *When It's Just You And Me* (1977), with Kenny Rogers *Every Time Two Fools Collide* (1978), with Rogers *Classics* (1979), *Special Delivery* (1979), *Go For The Night* (1980), *Wild West* (1981), *Once You Were Mine* (1981), *High Times* (1981), *Full Circle* (1982), *New Horizons* (1983), *Just Dottie* (1984). Compilations: *The Best Of Dottie West* (1973), *Twenty Of The Best* (1986).

West, Shelly

b. 23 May 1958, Cleveland, Ohio, but raised in Nashville, Tennessee, USA. The daughter of country singer Dottie West, it seemed natural that she should follow her mother into showbusiness. After completing her high school education in 1975, she sang backing harmonies for her mother. In 1977, she married Allen Frizzell (Lefty and David Frizzell's youngest brother), who was her mother's bandleader. They moved to California, where they joined David Frizzell and played the club circuits over several states. She began to sing with David and in 1981 charted a US country number 1 with 'You're The Reason God Made Oklahoma', which featured in the Clint Eastwood film *Any Which Way You Can*. Further country Top 10 hits followed, including 'A Texas State Of Mind' and 'I Just Came Here To Dance'. In 1982, their duet 'Please Surrender', was used by Eastwood in his film *Honky Tonk Man*. In 1983, she had a solo US country number 1 with 'Jose Cuervo' and further solo hits with 'Flight 309 To Tennessee' and 'Another Motel Memory'. A further Top 20 duet hit, 'It's A Be Together Night' with David Frizzell, followed in 1984. She was

Shelly West with David Frizzell

divorced in 1985 and currently her career seems to have slowed down, with no chart hits since 1986.
Albums: solo *Red Hot* (1983), *West By West* (1983), *Don't Make Me Wait On The Moon* (1985); with David Frizzell *Carrying On The Family Names* (1981), *David Frizzell/Shelly West Album* (1982), *Our Best To You* (1983), *In Session* (1984).

Wheeler, Billy Edd

b. 9 December 1932, Whitesville, West Virginia, USA. He grew up in coal-mining camps and his song, 'Coal Tattoo', which was recorded by Judy Collins, is based on what he saw around him. He collected folk songs himself and elements of both folk and country music can be heard in his songwriting. He performed with his guitar at school and college events, was in the US navy from 1957-58 and then became a schoolteacher. In 1958 a rock 'n' roll version of 'The Boll Weevil Song', which he called 'Rock Boll Weevil', was recorded by Pat Boone. He performed folk songs with the Lexington Symphony Orchestra in 1961. He then became a full-time professional performer. 'Rev. Mr Black', a narrative song about a travelling preacher, made the US Top 10 for the Kingston Trio in 1963, and they followed it with the story of 'Desert Pete'. Wheeler himself had a solo US hit with a song about an outside toilet, 'Ode To The

Little Brown Shack Out Back'. His 1967 composition, 'Jackson', was successful for the duos, Johnny Cash and June Carter, and Nancy Sinatra and Lee Hazlewood. Other compositions include 'Blistered' (Johnny Cash), 'Blue Roses' and 'The Man Who Robbed The Bank At Santa Fe' (both Hank Snow). His *Nashville Zodiac* album was made with Doug Kershaw and includes three Kershaw's compositions. Wheeler continues to perform and says, 'I can't bear to think how empty my life would have been without my guitar.'
Albums: *Billy Edd: USA* (1961), with the Bluegrass Singers and the Berea Three *Billy Edd And Bluegrass Too* (1962), *Memories Of America* (1963), *The Wheeler Man* (1965), *Goin' Town And Country* (1966), *Paper Birds* (1967), *I Ain't The Worrying Kind* (1968), *Nashville Zodiac* (1969), with Shelly Manne *Young Billy Young* (1969, soundtrack), *Billy Edd Wheeler - Love* (1971), *The Music Of Billy Edd Wheeler* (1973), *Wild Mountain Flowers* (1979).

Wheeler, Onie

b. Onie Daniel Wheeler, 10 November 1921, Senath, Missouri, USA, d. 26 May 1984. Wheeler was a country singer whose career lasted for nearly 40 years, although only one single charted in the USA. Wheeler won a talent contest while serving in the Armed Forces during World War II and, upon leaving the service in 1945, he chose to pursue a singing career. He performed on a number of southern radio stations in Missouri, Arkansas and Kentucky, and moved to Michigan in 1948, where he made his first recordings for the tiny Agana label. Wheeler and his singing partner and wife Betty Jean went back to Missouri in 1952 and performed a stint on radio station KSIM in addition to performing in clubs. Continuing to move from one location to another, Wheeler was finally signed to OKeh Records in 1953 and released numerous singles for that label and then its parent, Columbia Records, fusing honky-tonk country and gospel styles. Although he did not quite perform in the rockabilly style, his up-tempo bop found him sharing billings with artists such as Elvis Presley and Jerry Lee Lewis. At the end of his Columbia contract in 1957, Wheeler recorded a number of tracks at the Sun Records studios in Memphis, which were not released for another two years. Further moves saw him relocate to California and back to St. Louis, Missouri, where he recorded for small labels into the early 60s. A 1962 session for Epic Records featured a duet between Wheeler and his daughter Karen. Working as a member of George Jones's road show, Wheeler recorded for United Artists Records and Musicor Records in 1964-65, after which he left Jones to join Roy Acuff's show. Wheeler scored his only placement on the country charts, 'John's Been Shucking My Corn', in 1971, on Royal American Records. After that, the recordings dwindled and Wheeler repaired guitars at home, although he continued to tour sporadically in Europe and Asia. He was operated on for an aneurysm in January 1984 and died onstage at the *Grand Ole Opry* house in May 1984.

Albums: *John's Been Shucking My Corn* (1971), *Something New And Something Old* (70s). Compilation: *Onie's Bop* (1991).

White, Clarence

b. 7 June 1944, Lewiston, Maine, USA, d. 14 July 1973. White started playing acoustic guitar and singing in a bluegrass group with his brothers when only 10 years old, and the group materialized into the Kentucky Colonels in 1961. After leaving the Kentucky Colonels, he switched to electric guitar and became a session musician, playing on albums by Randy Newman and Linda Ronstadt. He joined Nashville West in 1968, and then the Byrds, whose line-up was Roger McGuinn, Gene Parsons, and John York, who was subsequently replaced by Skip Battin. White is very prominent

on the *untitled* album including the hit single, 'Chestnut Mare'. He still worked on sessions, including the Everly Brothers' superb 'I'm On My Way Home Again'. The Byrds flew the coop in 1973 and White reformed the Kentucky Colonels to play Los Angeles clubs and also to tour Europe. He worked on albums by Maria Muldaur and Gene Parsons and also began his solo album, although only four tracks were recorded. He was knocked down and killed while loading equipment after a show on 14 July 1973. What there is of his solo album was included on the compilation on Sierra Briar Records, Silver Meteor.

White, Tony Joe

b. 23 July 1943, Oak Grove, Louisiana, USA. A country singer and songwriter, White was also tagged with the label 'swamp rock', a musical genre he helped to create. Originally he was a member of Tony And The Mojos before defecting to Texas to start Tony And The Twilights. He started recording in 1968 and many people presumed he was black after hearing his layered vocals. He scored his first hit on Monument with 'Polk Salad Annie' in 1969, later covered by Elvis Presley. Also contained on his debut *Black And White* was 'Willie And Laura Mae Jones', which was covered by Dusty Springfield. After hitting once more with 'Groupie Girl' he wrote 'Rainy Night In Georgia' which would became a standard. His first three albums were produced by Billy Swan, and Cozy Powell drummed for him at the 1970 Isle Of Wight festival. He moved to Warner Brothers Records in 1971 and had a hit in 1979 with 'Mamas Don't Let Your Cowboys Grow Up To Be Babies', an answer record to Ed Bruce's country chart-topper of the previous year, 'Mamas Don't Let Your Babies Grow Up To Be Cowboys'.

Albums: *Black And White* (1968), *Continued* (1969), *Tony Joe* (1970), *Tony Joe White* (1971), *The Train I'm On* (1972), *Home Made Ice Cream* (1973), *Eyes* (1977), *Real Thing* (1980), *Dangerous* (1983), *Roosevelt And Ira Lee* (1984), *Live!* (1990), *Closer To The Truth* (1992). Compilation: *The Best Of Tony Joe White* (1973).

Whites

b. 13 December 1930, Oklahoma, USA. H.C. White grew up in Wichita Falls, Texas. He named himself Buck because of his love of the cowboy film star, Buck Jones. He had roots in western swing music and played piano on the original recording of Slim Willet's 'Don't Let The Stars Get

In Your Eyes' in 1952. He played piano in various western swing bands and as a sideman to visiting country stars in the Wichita Falls area, where his daughters, Sharon (b. 17 December 1953) and Cheryl (b. 27 January 1955), were born. In 1962 the family settled in Greenwood, Arkansas and Buck became involved in bluegrass music for the first time, forming the Down Home Folks with his wife and their friends, Arnold and Peggy Johnston. The children of the two families worked together as the Down Home Kids.

In 1967, working as Buck White And The Down Home Folks, the family group consisted of Buck, his wife Pat and their daughters, Cheryl and Sharon. Following a successful, impromptu performance at Bill Monroe's Beanblossom Festival in 1971, they moved to Nashville to further their career. Pat retired from the group in 1973 and they developed a clean-cut sound around Cheryl and Sharon's distinctive harmonies, Buck's mandolin playing and Jerry Douglas's dobro. A short-lived contract with Capitol Records in 1982 led to a single on US country charts as the Whites, 'Send Me The Pillow That You Dream On', and they had their first US country Top 10 entry with 'You Put The Blue In Me'. Emmylou Harris invited them to be the opening act for the tour to support *Blue Kentucky Girl*, which featured Cheryl and Sharon's harmonies. Ricky Skaggs, who married Sharon in 1981, produced *Whole New World*, and Buck White played piano on Skaggs's number 1 country hit, 'Crying My Heart Out Over You'. The Whites have appeared on numerous sessions, but their own US country hits include 'Hangin' Around', 'I Wonder Who's Holding My Baby Tonight', 'Pins And Needles', 'If It Ain't Love (Let's Leave It Alone)' and 'Hometown Gossip'.

Albums: *Buck White And The Down Home Folks* (1972), *Live At The Old Time Pickin' Parlour* (1977) *That Down Home Feeling* (1977), *Poor Folks Pleasure* (1978), *More Pretty Girls Than One* (1979), *Old Familiar Feeling* (1983), *Forever You* (1984), *Whole New World* (1985). *Greatest Hits* (1987).

Whitley, Keith

b. 1 July 1955, Sandy Hook, Kentucky, USA, d. 8 May 1989, Goodlettsville, Tennessee, USA. Whitley, who grew up in a musical family, learned to play the guitar from the age of six and was on the radio with Buddy Starcher in Charleston, West Virginia when eight. He joined Ralph Stanley And His Clinch Mountain Boys when he was 15 and both he, and his friend Ricky Skaggs, made their recording debut on the same record, *Cry From The*

Cross. At the age of 17, he survived a 120 mph car crash which killed a friend, and at 19, he drove a car off a cliff into a river. Whitley joined J.D. Crowe And The New South and his lead vocals on *Somewhere Between*, were appreciated in Nashville. In 1983 he signed with RCA Records, recorded a mini-album, *A Hard Act To Follow* and had his first US country success with 'Turn Me To Love' in 1984. He had further successes with 'I've Got The Heart For You' and 'Miami, My Amy'. Whitley's excessive drinking made him unreliable, but it did give him a hardened, honky-tonk voice, and he then only needed the right song. He was unlucky in that his version of 'Does Fort Worth Ever Cross Your Mind?' was never released and 'On The Other Hand' was only an album track.

He found what he needed in 'Don't Close Your Eyes', which was a number 1 US country single in 1988 with the resulting album selling over half-a-million copies. The song was inspired by the film, *California Suite*. Whitley had another country number 1 with 'When You Say Nothing At All', and his version of Lefty Frizzell's 'I Never Go Around Mirrors' includes an additional verse by its co-writer, Whitey Shaffer, and harmonies from Frizzell's brother, Allen. In 1986 he married Lorrie Morgan, the daughter of country singer, George Morgan, and a performer in her own right. Whitley recovered from his alcoholism and the couple started a family. In 1989 he had a US country number 1 with a Sonny Curtis song, 'I'm No Stranger To The Rain', but he subsequently returned to drinking, which resulted in him dying at his home in Goodlettsville, Tennessee in 1989. He had a posthumous number 1 with 'I Wonder Do You Think Of Me?'. *Kentucky Bluebird* collected together out-takes and broadcast material from throughout his career and spawned a posthumous hit single, 'Brotherly Love', a duet with Earl Thoams Conley.

Albums: with Ricky Skaggs *Tribute To The Stanley Brothers* (1971), with Skaggs *Second Generation Bluegrass* (1972), *A Hard Act To Follow* (1984), *L.A. To Miami* (1986), *Don't Close Your Eyes* (1988), *I Wonder Do You Think Of Me?* (1989), *Greatest Hits* (1990), *Kentucky Bluebird* (1992).

Whitley, Ray

b. Raymond Otis Whitley, 5 December 1901, Atlanta, Georgia, USA, but grew up in Alabama, d. 21 February 1979. He began his singing and acting career in New York in 1930, when, while working on the building of the Empire State Building, he formed his Range Ramblers and began to broadcast on WMCA. In 1932, he worked and travelled with the World Championship Rodeo organisation, renaming his band, the Six Bar Cowboys. By 1938, he was with RKO Pictures. Following answering an early morning call from the studio on the actual day of recording that an extra song was required for the film *Border G-Man*, he returned to his bedroom to dress and to tell his wife, saying 'I'm back in the saddle again'. She suggested that was a good title for a song and sitting on the edge of his bed, he wrote the first verse of 'Back In The Saddle Again'. Later that day he sang it for the film and on 26 October 1938, he recorded it for Decca. In 1939, he and his friend Gene Autry revised the song and Autry sang it in his film *Rovin' Tumbleweeds*, later adopting it as his theme song for his CBS *Melody Ranch* show. Between 1936 and 1954, Whitley appeared in 54 films and recorded for several other labels including Okeh and Apollo. He also co-wrote several songs with Fred Rose and later in his career he managed both the Sons Of The Pioneers and Jimmy Wakely. He also worked with Gibson on the production of their J-200 guitar, which has been used by many country singers. In the late 70s, he was a popular figure at Western festivals where he entertained with songs and his talent to use a heavy bull whip. Whitley died while on a fishing trip to Mexico in 1979.

Whitman, Slim

b. Otis Dewey Whitman Jnr, 20 January 1924, Tampa, Florida, USA. Whitman was unhappy because his stutter was ridiculed by other children and consequently he left school as soon as he could. Even though his stutter is now cured, he has never cared for public speaking and says little during his stage act. Several members of his family were musical and he became interested in Jimmie Rodgers' recordings when he discovered that he too could also yodel. After leaving school, he worked in a meat-packing plant where he lost part of a finger, which, several years later led to him turning a guitar tutor upside down and learning to play left-handed. He later remarked, 'Paul McCartney saw me in Liverpool and realized that he too could play the guitar left-handed.' Whitman sang at his family's local church, the Church of the Brethren, and it was here, in 1938, that he met the new minister's daughter, Geraldine Crisp. After borrowing $10 from his mother for the license, he married her in 1941. Whitman regards his long-standing marriage as a major ingredient in his success, and he wrote and dedicated a song to her,

'Jerry'. During World War II, he worked as a fitter in a shipyard and then saw action in the US Navy. Whilst on board, he realized his talents for entertaining his fellow crew but in his first concert, he foolishly chose to sing 'When I'm Gone You'll Soon Forget Me'! No matter, his singing became so popular that the captain blocked his transfer to another ship - fortunately for Whitman, as the other ship was sunk with all hands lost.

After his discharge, he had some success in baseball, but he preferred singing, choosing the name Slim Whitman as a tribute to Wilf Carter (Montana Slim), and often working on radio. He first recorded for RCA-Victor, at the suggestion of Tom Parker, in 1949. After moderate successes with 'I'm Casting My Lasso Towards The Sky' and 'Birmingham Jail', he moved to Shreveport, Louisiana so that he could appear each week on the radio show, *Louisiana Hayride*. His wife embroidered black shirts for Whitman and the band which has led him to claim he was the original 'Man In Black'. His steel player, Hoot Rains, developed an identifiable sound, but it came about by accident: when Rains overshot a note on 'Love Song Of The Waterfall', Whitman decided to retain it as a trademark. Whitman maintained a level-headed attitude towards his career and was working as a postman whilst his first single for Imperial Records, 'Love Song Of The Waterfall', was selling half-a-million copies. 'You don't quit on one record,' he says, 'Then I had 'Indian Love Call' and I decided to go. I was told that if I ever wanted my job back, I could have it'. 'Indian Love Call' came from Rudolf Friml's operetta, *Rose Marie*, and, in 1955, its title song gave Slim Whitman 11 consecutive weeks at the top of the UK charts, an achievement which was only beaten in 1992 by Bryan Adams' 'Everything I Do'. 'All I did was throw in a few yodels for good measure,' says Slim, 'and the folks seemed to go for it.' The b-side of 'Indian Love Call', 'China Doll', was a UK hit in its own right, and his other chart records include 'Cattle Call', 'Tumbling Tumbleweeds', 'Serenade' and 'I'll Take You Home Again, Kathleen', although, astonishingly, he has never topped the US country charts. He says, 'A lot of people think of me as a cowboy because I've sung 'Cattle Call' and one or two others. The truth is, I've never been on a horse in my life.' In 1955, Whitman moved back to Florida, which restricted his appearances on the *Grand Ole Opry* because he found the trips too time-consuming. In 1956 Whitman became the first country star to top a bill at the London Palladium. Despite being a light-

Slim Whitman

voiced country balladeer, he was featured in the 1957 rock 'n' roll film, *Disc Jockey Jamboree*. He has always taken a moral stance on what he records, perhaps because he is married to a preacher's daughter, refusing, for example, to record 'Almost Persuaded'. He says, 'I'm not a saint. It's just that I've no interest in singing songs about cheating or the boozer'. His popularity in Britain was such that his *25th Anniversary Concert* album was recorded at the Empire Theatre, Liverpool in March 1973. He had a UK hit in 1974 with 'Happy Anniversary', but United Artists executive, Alan Warner, decided that his US country albums were wrong for the UK market and that he should record albums of pop standards which could be marketed on television. His 1976 album, *The Very Best Of Slim Whitman*, entered the UK album charts at number 1, and was followed by *Red River Valley* (number 1) and *Home On The Range* (number 2). Whitman then repeated his role as a purveyor of love songs for the middle-aged in the US. Since 1977, Whitman has toured with his son, Byron (b. 1957), whom he says is matching him 'yodel for yodel', and they have pioneered the double yodel. Of his continued success, constantly playing to full houses, he says, 'I don't know the secret. I guess it's the songs I sing and my friendly attitude. When I say hello, I mean it'.

Albums: *Slim Whitman Sings And Yodels* (1954), *America's Favorite Folk Artist* (1954), *Slim Whitman Favorites* (1956), *Slim Whitman Sings* (1957), *Slim Whitman Sings* (1958), *Slim Whitman* (1958), *Slim Whitman Sings* (1959), *I'll Walk With God* (1960), *Slim Whitman Sings Annie Laurie* (1961), *Just Call Me Lonesome* (1961), *Once In A Lifetime* (1961), *Slim Whitman Sings* (1961), *Heart Songs And Love Songs* (1963), *Irish Songs - The Slim Whitman Way* (1963), *I'm A Lonely Wanderer* (1963), *Yodeling* (1963), *Love Song Of The Waterfall* (1964), *Reminiscing* (1964), *More Than Yesterday* (1965), *Forever* (1966), *God's Hand In Mine* (1966), *A Time For Love* (1966), *A Travellin' Man* (1966), *A Lonesome Heart* (1967), *Country Memories* (1967), *In Love, The Whitman Way* (1968), *Unchain Your Heart* (1968), *Happy Street* (1969), *Slim!* (1969), *Slim Whitman* (1969), *The Slim Whitman Christmas Album* (1969), *Ramblin' Rose* (1970), *Tomorrow Never Comes* (1970), *It's A Sin To Tell A Lie* (1971), *Guess Who* aka *Snowbird* (1971), *I'll See You When* (1973), *25th Anniversary Concert* (1973), *Happy Anniversary* (1974), *Everything Leads Back To You* (1975), *Home On The Range* (1977), *Red River Valley* (1977), *Ghost Riders In The Sky* (1978), *Just For You* (1980), *Songs I Love To Sing* (1980),

Christmas With Slim Whitman (1980), *Mr. Songman* (1981), *Till We Meet Again* (1981), *I'll Be Home For Christmas* (1981), *Country Songs, City Hits* (1982), *Angeline* (1984), *A Dream Come True - The Rarities Album* (1987), with Byron Whitman *Magic Moments* (1990), *Cow Poke* (1992). Compilations: *All Time Favourites* (1964), *Fifteenth Anniversary* (1967), *The Very Best Of Slim Whitman* (1976), *All My Best* (1979), *Slim Whitman's 20 Greatest Love Songs* (1979), *20 Golden Greats* (1992).

Further reading: *Mr. Songman - The Slim Whitman Story*, Kenneth L. Gibble.

Whitstein Brothers

Robert (Bob) and Charles Whitstein were both born in the mid-40s, on the family farm at Colfax, Louisiana, USA. The eldest two of the nine children of R.C. Whitstein, who apart from farming, was a skilled guitarist, fiddler and vocalist, and who presented a weekly programme of country music on the local radio station. Under their father's guidance, the boys first appeared in their pre-teens on a local television talent show. Their close harmony singing to their own accompaniment, Bob playing guitar and Charles on mandolin, soon attracted attention and they made their debut recording for a small Texas label, J-Bo. Around 1963, they moved to Hopkinsville, Kentucky and while working as part-time carpenters and bricklayers, they began to play and sing around Nashville. They appeared on the *Grand Ole Opry* and toured with Faron Young as the Whitt Brothers. They were both drafted for military service, with Robert serving in Vietnam. In the early 70s, finding no success in Nashville, they settled in Louisiana, only performing locally while following other occupations. In 1984, after making some demo recordings and receiving some assistance from Tillman Franks and Jesse McReynolds (of Jim And Jesse), they recorded their first album for Rounder Records. Their biggest influence of all the earlier brother harmony acts were the Louvin Brothers and Charlie Louvin states that the Whitsteins are the nearest that he has ever heard to the sound of the Louvins. Neither Whitstein is a full-time musician and in 1988, when Robert was unable to take time off work to tour the UK, his place was actually taken by Charlie Louvin. The brothers toured in the UK in 1990 and are a popular act, particularly at bluegrass festivals both in Europe and in the states.

Albums: *Rose Of My Heart* (1984), *Trouble Ain't Nothing But The Blues'* (1987), *Old Time Duets* (1990).

Whitter, Henry

b. William Henry Whitter, 6 April 1892, near Fries, Grayson County, Virginia, USA, d. 10 November 1941, Morganton, North Carolina, USA. Whitter first entertained fellow workers at a cotton mill in Fries but, in March 1923, bored with the work, he travelled to New York. Using his own guitar and harmonica, he auditioned for OKeh Records. OKeh was unsure about his raw, nasal singing but the increasing interest in hillbilly records encouraged them to release a song about the crash of a mail train, 'The Wreck Of The Old '97'. Vernon Dalhart realized the song's potential and recorded a better version, which became a millionseller. In 1924 Whitter formed a successful string band, the Virginia Breakdowners, with James Sutpin (fiddle) and John Rector (banjo). In 1927 Whitter started performing with a blind fiddler, G.B. Grayson. Their work included the first recorded version of 'Tom Dooley'. After Grayson died in a car crash in 1930, Whitter lost interest in his music and made few recordings. He died of complications from diabetes in 1941.
Albums: *Grayson And Whitter, 1927-1930* (1976), *Going Down Lee Highway* (1976).

Wilburn Brothers

Brothers Virgil Doyle Wilburn (b. 7 July 1930, Hardy, Arkansas, USA, d. 16 October 1982) and Thurman Theodore 'Teddy' Wilburn (b. 30 November 1931, Hardy, Arkansas, USA). They started their careers as children singing with their siblings as the Wilburn Family. This featured two elder brothers, Lester (b. 19 May 1924), Leslie (b. 13 October 1925) and sister Vinita Geraldine (b. 5 June 1927), all born in Hardy, Arkansas. Their father, Benjamin Wilburn, a disabled World War I veteran, whose ill-health prevented him doing normal work, thought that perhaps his children becoming entertainers would help the family budget. He bought a mandolin, guitar and fiddle from the Sears, Roebuck catalogue and in 1937, after his tuition, the Family were singing on the streets of Thayer, eighteen miles over the State line in Missouri. They went on to play local radio stations and in 1940, after a reference from Roy Acuff, who saw them singing at Birmingham, Alabama, they were invited to join the Grand Ole Opry. They immediately became very popular and attracted large amounts of mail but after six months, tired of problems concerning child labour laws, the Opry management asked them to leave. They returned home and continued to entertain, although the onset of World War II affected their careers. Between 1948 and 1951, the Wilburn Family worked on KWKH Shreveport, where the four brothers regularly appeared on the *Louisiana Hayride*. (Geraldine left the group in 1948 to marry.) In 1951, because of the Korean War, both Teddy and Doyle were drafted for US Army service.

In 1953, after discharge, they began to work as a duo, toured and worked with several major acts, including Webb Pierce, Faron Young and Ernest Tubb and played on the *Opry*, becoming full cast members in 1956. They recorded for Decca, first charting in 1955 with 'I Wanna Wanna Wanna' but the following year they had Top 10 country hits with 'I'm So In Love With You' and 'Go Away With Me'. Further chart successes followed, including two Top 10 duets with Ernest Tubb ('Mister Love' and 'Hey, Mr Bluebird'). In the late 50s, they joined with Leslie and Lester to found the publishing company Sure-Fire Music, which handled their own and other artists' songs. During the 60s, they toured extensively and frequently made the country charts with their recordings. Their Top 5 hits included 'Trouble's Back In Town' (1962), 'Roll Muddy River' (1963), 'It's Another World' (1965) and 'Hurt Her Once For Me' (1967). They hosted their own network television show, on which they featured the young Loretta Lynn (they also obtained a Decca recording contract for her), and also appeared in a series on Australian television. They extended their business interests to include Wil-Helm Talent, which became one of Nashville's top booking agencies and handled many of the major stars. Although they had no chart successes after 'Arkansas' in 1972, they maintained their popularity and still appeared on the *Opry* throughout the 70s. Doyle Wilburn died in Nashville in 1982, as the result of cancer. Teddy maintained the family tradition and continued to appear on the *Opry*, often accompanied by brothers Lester and Leslie.
Albums: *The Wilburn Brothers* (1957), *Side By Side* (1958), *Living In God's Country* (1959), *Ernest Tubb & The Wilburn Brothers* (1959), *The Big Heartbreak* (1960), *City Limits* (1961), *The Wilburn Brothers Sing* (1961), *The Wonderful Wilburn Brothers* (1961), *Folk Songs* (1962), *Carefree Moments* (1962), *Trouble's Back In Town* (1963), *Take Up Thy Cross* (1964), *Never Alone* (1964), *I'm Gonna Tie One On Tonight* (1965), with Ernest Tubb and Loretta Lynn *The Wilburn Brothers Show* (1966), *Let's Go Country* (1966), *Two For The Show* (1967), *Cool Country* (1967), *I Walk The Line* (1968), *Its Another World* (1968), *It Looks Like The Sun's Gonna Shine* (1969),

We Need A Lot More Happiness (1969), *Little Johnny From Down The Street* (1970), *Sing Your Heart Out Country Boy* (1970), *That Country Feeling* (1970), *That She's Leaving Feeling* (1971), *A Portrait* (1975), *Sing Hinson And Gaither* (1978), *Stars Of The Grand Ole Opry* (1979). Compilation: *Country Gold* (1965, reissued 1985).

Williams, Doc

b. Andrew J. Smik Jnr., 26 June 1914, Cleveland, Ohio, USA. A noted traditionalist who except for short spells at Memphis (1939) and Frederick (1945) was associated with the *Wheeling Jamboree* at WWVA Wheeling, West Virginia for over 40 years, after first appearing with his band the Border Riders in 1937. He married Chickie (b. Jessie Wanda Crupe, 13 February 1919, Bethany, West Virginia, USA) in 1939 and she sang regularly with the band. (In later years they were sometimes joined by their three daughters Barbara, Madeline and Karen.) Their family show also featured brother Cy Williams (fiddle) and Marion Martin (chordovox). Doc regularly played hundreds of shows a year in the northeastern States, the New England area and in eastern Canada. He has also made several trips to Britain, where he always proved immensely popular around the country clubs. He has made many recordings for his own Wheeling label and though he never achieved any chart entries, he is always associated with such songs as 'Wheeling Back To Wheeling', 'My Old Brown Coat And Me' and the tearjerkers 'Daddy's Little Angel' and 'He Said He Had A Friend'. It has also been claimed that Chickie cut the original version of 'Beyond The Sunset'.
Albums: *Sings Country & Western, 25th Anniversary Album, Wheeling Back To Wheeling, Williams Family Sacred Album, Doc Williams Show, Collector's Series Volumes 1 & 2, Daddy's Little Angel, From Out Of The Beautiful Hills Of West Virginia, Doc & Chickie Together, Favorites Old And New, Reminiscing*, with Karen Williams *The Three Of Us, We've Come A Long Way Together* (c.50s-c.70s).

Williams, Don

b. 27 May 1939, Floydada, Texas, USA. Williams' father was a mechanic whose job took him to other regions and much of Williams' childhood was spent in Corpus Christi, Texas. Williams' mother played guitar and he grew up listening to country music. He and Lofton Kline formed a semi-professional folk group called the Strangers Two, and then, with the addition of Susan Taylor, they became the Pozo-Seco Singers, the phrase being a geological one to denote a dry well. Handled by Bob Dylan's manager Albert Grossman, they has US pop hits with 'Time', 'I Can Make It With You' and 'Look What You've Done'. Following Lofton Kline's departure, they had several replacements resulting in a group lacking direction and were as likely to record 'Green Green Grass Of Home' as 'Strawberry Fields Forever'. After Williams had failed to switch the trio to country music, they disbanded in 1971. He then worked for his father-in-law but also wrote for Susan Taylor's solo album via Jack Clement's music publishing company. Clement asked Williams to record albums of his company's best songs, mainly with a view to attracting other performers. In 1973 Don Williams, Volume 1 was released on the fledgling JMI label and included such memorable songs as Bob McDill's apologia for growing old 'Amanda' and Williams' own 'The Shelter Of Your Eyes'. Both became US country hits and JMI could hardly complain when Tommy Cash and then Waylon Jennings released 'I Recall A Gypsy Woman', thus depriving Williams of a certain winner. (In the UK, Williams' version made number 13, his biggest success.) Williams' work was reissued by ABC/Dot and Don Williams, Volume 2 included 'Atta Way To Go' and 'We Should Be Together'. Williams then had a country number 1 with Wayland Holyfield's 'You're My Best Friend', which has become a standard and is the perennial singalong anthem at his concerts. By now, the Williams style had developed: gently-paced love songs with straightforward arrangements, lyrics and sentiments. Williams was mining the same vein as Jim Reeves but he eschewed Reeves' smartness by dressing like a ranch-hand. At concerts, he'd put his hand to his battered stetson and say, 'You want me to remove my what?'.
Besides having a huge contingent of female fans, Williams counted Eric Clapton and Pete Townshend amongst his admirers. Clapton recorded his country hit, 'Tulsa Time', written by Danny Flowers from Williams' Scratch Band. The Scratch Band released their own album, produced by Williams, in 1982. Williams played a band member himself in the Burt Reynolds film *W.W. And The Dixie Dancekings* and also appeared in *Smokey And The Bandit 2*. Williams' other successes include 'Till The Rivers All Run Dry', 'Some Broken Hearts Never Mend', 'Lay Down Beside Me' and his only US Top 30 pop hit 'I Believe In You'. Unlike most established country artistes, he has not sought duet partners although he and

Emmylou Harris scored with an easy-paced version of Townes Van Zandt's 'If I Needed You'. Williams' best record is with Bob McDill's homage to his southern roots, 'Good Ol' Boys Like Me'. Moving to Capitol Records in the mid-80s such singles as 'Heartbeat In the Darkness' and 'Senorita', but the material was not as impressive. He took a sabbatical in 1988 and his recent RCA recordings, which include 'I've Been Loved By The Best', show that nothing has changed. Williams continues to be a major concert attraction maintaining his stress-free style. When interviewed, Williams gives the impression of being a contented man who takes life as he finds it. He is a rare being - a country star who is free of controversy.

Albums: with the Pozo-Seco Singers *Time* (1966), *I Can Make It With You* (1967), *Shades Of Time* (1968); Don Williams solo *Don Williams, Volume 1* (1973), *Don Williams, Volume 2* (1974), *Don Williams, Volume 3* (1974), *You're My Best Friend* (1975), *Harmony* (1976), *Visions* (1977), *Country Boy* (1977), *Expressions* (1978), *Portrait* (1979), *I Believe In You* (1980), *Especially For You* (1981), *Listen To The Radio* (1982), *Yellow Moon* (1983), *Cafe Carolina* (1984), *New Moves* (1986), *Traces* (1987), *One Good Well* (1989), *As Long As I Have You* (1989), *True Love* (1990), *Currents* (1992). Compilations: *Very Best Of Don Williams* (1980), *Golden Greats* (1985), *Best Of Don Williams, Volumes 2, 3 & 4* (1988), *Currents* (1992).

Williams, Hank

b. Hiram (misspelt on birth certificate as Hiriam) Williams, 17 September 1923, Georgiana, Alabama, USA, d. 1 January 1953, Virginia, USA. Mis-spelling notwithstanding, Williams disliked the name and took to calling himself Hank. He was born with a spine defect which troubled him throughout his life, and was further aggravated after being thrown from a horse when he was 17-years-old. Initially, his parents, Lon and Lilly, ran a general store, but Lon later entered a veterans hospital following a delayed reaction to the horrors he had experienced during World War I. The young Williams was raised by his imposing, resourceful mother, who gave him a cheap guitar when he was seven. He learned chords from an elderly black musician, Teetot (Rufe Payne). Williams later said, 'All the musical training I ever had came from him.' It also explains the strong blues thread which runs through his work. In 1937, Lilly opened a boarding-house in Montgomery, Alabama. Williams won a talent contest and formed his own band, the Drifting Cowboys. As clubs were tough, Hank hired a wrestler, Cannonball Nichols as a bass player, more for protection than musical ability, but he could not be protected from his mother, who handled his bookings and earnings. (In truth, Williams was disinterested in the money he made.) While working for a medicine show, he met Audrey Sheppard and married her in December 1944. Lilly and Audrey were rivals but both would thump the pale, lanky singer for his lack of co-operation.

Williams was a local celebrity but, on 14 September 1946, Hank and Audrey went to Nashville and impressed Fred Rose and his son Wesley at the relatively new Acuff-Rose publishing. On 11 December 1946 Williams made his first recordings for the small Sterling label. They included 'Callin' You' and 'When God Comes And Gathers His Jewels'. Fred Rose secured a contract with the more prestigious MGM Records, and he acted as his manager, record producer and, occasionally, co-writer ('Mansion On The Hill', 'Kaw-liga'). Williams' first MGM release, 'Move It On Over', sold several thousand copies. If you imagine the fiddle on that track and 'Rootie Tootie' being replaced by drums and it's easy to see why Don Everly referred to Williams as 'the first rock 'n' roll singer'. Williams joined the prestigious radio show, *Louisiana Hayride*, in 1948 and was featured on its concert tours. Fred Rose opposed him reviving 'Lovesick Blues', originally recorded by Emmett Miller in 1925 and later a success for Rex Griffin in 1939. Nevertheless, he recorded the song, following Miller and Griffin with their playful yodels. 'Lovesick Blues' topped the US country charts for 16 weeks and remained in the listings for almost a year. The *Grand Ole Opry*, although wary of his hard-drinking reputation, invited him to perform 'Lovesick Blues', which led to an unprecedented six encores. He and the Drifting Cowboys became regulars and the publicity enabled them to command $1,000 for concert appearances. One night, comedian and film star Bob Hope could only follow Williams by wearing a cowboy hat and declaring 'Hello folks, this is Hank Hope'. 'Wedding Bells' made number 2 as did a contender for the greatest country single ever released, the poignant 'I'm So Lonesome I Could Cry', backed with the old blues song, 'My Bucket's Got A Hole In It': the Opry sponsors, disapproving of the word 'beer' in the latter song, had Williams sing 'milk' instead. In 1950, he had three country number 1 hits, 'Long Gone Lonesome Blues', 'Why Don't You Love Me?' and 'Moanin' The Blues'. The following year, he had

Hank Williams

two further chart-toppers with 'Cold, Cold Heart' and 'Hey, Good Lookin''. Another superb double-sided hit, 'Howlin' At The Moon'/'I Can't Help It (If I'm Still In Love With You)', made number 2.

In 1952, Hank went to number 1 by praising cajun food in 'Jambalaya', while 'Half As Much' made number 2. Another well-balanced double-sided hit 'Settin' The Woods On Fire'/'You Win Again' made number 2. Williams was a showman, often wearing a flashy suit embroidered with sequins and decorated with musical notes. Although MGM studios thought about making films with him, nothing materialised. It's arguable that, with his thinning hair, he looked too old or maybe he was just too awkward. His lifestyle was akin to the later spirit of rock 'n' roll. He drank too much, took drugs (admittedly, excessive numbers of painkillers for his back), played with guns, destroyed hotel rooms, threw money out of windows and permanently lived in conflict. His son, Hank Williams Jnr., said, 'I get sick of hearing people tell me how much they loved my daddy. They hated him in Nashville.'

Williams' songs articulated the lives and loves of his listeners and he went a stage further by recording melodramatic monologues as Luke The Drifter. They included 'Beyond The Sunset', 'Pictures From Life's Other Side', 'Too Many Parties And Too Many Pals' and 'Men With Broken Hearts'. Although Luke the Drifter's appeal was limited, Fred Rose saw how Williams' other songs could have wide appeal. Country songs had been recorded by pop performers before Williams but Rose aggressively sought cover versions. Soon Tony Bennett ('Cold, Cold Heart'), Jo Stafford ('Jambalaya') and Joni James ('Your Cheatin' Heart') had gold records. Williams' wife, 'Miss Audrey', also made solo records but Hank knew her talent was limited. She was frustrated by her lack of success and many of Hank's songs stem from their quarrels. They were divorced on 29 May 1952 and, as Williams regarded possessions as unimportant, she was awarded their house and one-half of all his future royalties. He did, however, hate losing custody of his son.

Like any professional show, the *Opry* preferred sober nondescripts to drunk superstars and on 11 August 1952, Hank was fired and told that he could return when he was sober. Williams did not recognize his problem. He joked about missed shows and falling off stage. He lost Fred Rose's support, the Drifting Cowboys turned to Ray Price, and, although the *Louisiana Hayride* tolerated his wayward lifestyle, his earnings fell and he was reduced to playing small clubs with pick-up bands. Williams met the 19-year-old daughter of a policeman, Billie Jean Jones, and said, 'If you ain't married, ol' Hank's gonna marry you.' On 19 October 1952 he did just that - three times. First, before a Justice of the Peace in Minden, Louisiana, and then at two concerts at the New Orleans Municipal Auditorium before several thousand paying guests. The newly-weds spent Christmas with relations in Georgiana, Alabama. His biggest booking for some time was on New Year's Day, 1953 with Hawkshaw Hawkins and Homer And Jethro in Canton, Ohio, but, because of a blizzard, Williams' plane was cancelled. An 18-year-old taxi driver, Charles Carr, was hired to drive Williams' Cadillac. They set off with Hank having a bottle of whiskey for company. He sank into a deep sleep. A policeman who stopped the car for ignoring speed restrictions remarked, 'That guy looks dead'. Five hours later, Cook discovered that his passenger was indeed dead. Death was officially due to 'severe heart attack with haemorrhage' but alcohol and pills played their part. At the concert that night, the performers sang Williams' 'I Saw The Light' in tribute. An atmospheric stage play *Hank Williams: The Show He Never Gave* by Maynard Collins, filmed with Sneezy Waters in the title role, showed what might have happened had Williams arrived that night.

Some commentators took Williams' current number 1, 'I'll Never Get Out Of This World Alive', as an indication that he knew he was going. Chet Atkins, who played 'dead string rhythm' on the record, disagreed, 'All young men of 28 or 29 feel immortal and although he wrote a lot about death, he thought it was something that would happen when he got old.' 20,000 saw Williams' body as it lay in state in an embroidered Nudie suit (designed by Miss Audrey) at the Montgomery Municipal Auditorium. His shrine in Montgomery Oakwood Cemetery is the subject of Steve Young's song, 'Montgomery In The Rain'.

1953 was a remarkable year for his records. 'Kaw-Liga', inspired by a visit to South Alabama and backed by 'Your Cheatin' Heart', went to the top of the chart, and his third consecutive posthumous number 1 was with Hy Heath and Fred Rose's 'Take These Chains From My Heart'. MGM, desperate for fresh material, overdubbed a backing onto demos for 'Weary Blues From Waitin'' and 'Roly Poly'. Hank Williams was the first deceased star to have his recordings altered. Albums of Hank Williams with strings and duets with his son followed. In 1969, Hank Jnr. completed some of his father's scribblings for an album, 'Songs My Father Left Me', the most successful being 'Cajun Baby'. In recent years, Williams and Willie Nelson proved a popular duo with 'I Told A Lie To My Heart', whilst a battered demo of 'There's A Tear In My Beer', which had been given by Hank to Big Bill Lister to perform, was magically restored with the addition of Hank Williams Jnr.'s voice and, accompanied by an even more ingenious video, sold 250,000 copies.

Hank Williams recorded 166 different songs between 1946-52, and there are over 200 tribute records. The first was 'The Death Of Hank Williams' by disc jockey Jack Cardwell. Other contemporary ones included 'Hank, It Will Never Be The Same Without You' by Ernest Tubb, 'Hank Williams Will Live Forever' by Johnnie And Jack, 'The Life Of Hank Williams' by Hawkshaw Hawkins and 'Hank Williams Meets Jimmie Rodgers' by Virginia Rounders. Most tributes lack inspiration, are too morbid and too reverent, and are recorded by artists who would normally never see a recording studio. The most pertinent tributes are Moe Bandy's reflective 'Hank Williams, You Wrote My Life', Johnny Cash's jaunty 'The Night Hank Williams Came To Town', Tim Hardin's plaintive 'Tribute To Hank Williams', Kris Kristofferson's rousing 'If You Don't Like Hank Williams' and Emmylou Harris' isolated 'Rollin' And Ramblin''. Hank Williams *is* the Phantom of the Opry. His influence on Moe Bandy, George Jones, Vernon Oxford and Boxcar Willie is especially marked. They have recorded albums of his songs as have Roy Acuff, Glen Campbell, Floyd Cramer, Don Gibson, Ronnie Hawkins, Roy Orbison, Charley Pride, Jack Scott, Del Shannon and Ernest Tubb. Also, Johnny Cash, Jerry Lee Lewis, Little Richard, Elvis Presley, Linda Ronstadt and Richard Thompson have also appropriated his repertoire. Major UK chart hits include 'Lovesick Blues' by Frank Ifield, 'Take These Chains From My Heart' by Ray Charles, and 'Jambalaya' by the Carpenters. Before Hank was laid to rest, Lilly, Audrey and Billie Jean were squabbling for the rights to Williams's estate. Audrey's name is on his tombstone through writing the inscription, and the inaccurate 1964 bio-pic *Your Cheatin' Heart*, which starred George Hamilton as Hank Williams miming to Hank Williams Jnr.'s recordings, did not even mention Billie Jean. Both wives performed as Mrs. Hank Williams, and Billie Jean was widowed a second time when Johnny Horton died in 1960.

A more recent development has been the claims of Jett Williams, the illegitimate daughter of Williams and country singer Bobbie Jett, who was born three days after his death. Emotion does not come out of thin air and there seems to be an equation linking suffering with art. The pressures shaped and fed his awareness and heightened his creative powers. His compact, aching songs flow seamlessly and few have improved upon his own emotional performances. Hank Williams was arguably the greatest country singer and songwriter who ever lived. His plaque in the Country Music Hall Of Fame states that 'The simple beautiful melodies and straightforward plaintive stories in his lyrics of life as he knew it will never die.'

Albums: *Hank Williams Sings* (1952), *Moanin' The Blues* (1952), *Hank Williams Memorial Album* (1953), *Hank Williams As Luke The Drifter* (1953), *Honky Tonkin'* (1954), *I Saw The Light* (1954), *Ramblin' Man* (1954), *On Stage* (1962), *On Stage, Volume 2* (1963), *Mr. And Mrs. Hank Williams* (1969), *Live At The Grand Ole Opry* (1976), *Just Me And My Guitar* (1985), *The First Recordings* (1986), *There's Nothing As Sweet As My Baby* (1990), *Rare Demos - First To Last* (1990). Compilations: *Hank Williams - 40 Greatest Hits* (1978, CD release 1989), *I Ain't Got Nothing But Time* (1986), *Lost Highway 1948-49* (1986), *Long Gone Lonesome Blues 1949-50* (1987), *Hey Good Lookin' 1950-51* (1987), *Rare Takes And Radio Cuts* (1988), *The Original Singles Collection* (1992, triple CD - 83 tracks).
Further reading: *Sing A Sad Song: The Life Of Hank Williams*, Roger Williams. *Your Cheatin' Heart*, Chet Flippo. *Hank Williams: A Bio-Bibliography*, George William Koon.

Williams, Hank, Jnr.

b. Randall Hank Williams Jnr., 26 May 1949, Shreveport, Louisiana, USA. The son of Hank Williams, he was nicknamed Bocephus after a puppet on the *Grand Ole Opry*. Being the son of a country legend has brought financial security, but it was difficult for him to firmly establish his own individuality. His mother, Audrey, was determined that he would follow in his father's footsteps. When only eight-years-old, he was touring, performing with his father's songs and even appeared on the *Grand Ole Opry*. He also had a high school band, Rockin' Randall And The Rockets. He signed for the same label as his father, MGM Records, as soon as his voice broke. In the 60s, Williams had country hits with 'Long Gone Lonesome Blues', 'Cajun Baby', a revival of 'Endless Sleep', and the only version of 'Nobody's

Child' to ever make the country charts. He also recorded an embarrassing narration about his relationship with his father, 'Standing In The Shadows'. Even worse was his maudlin dialogue as Luke the Drifter Jnr., 'I Was With Red Foley (The Night He Passed Away)'. He copied his father's style for the soundtrack of the film biography of his father, *Your Cheatin' Heart* (1964), and starred in the inferior *A Time To Sing*. He was just 15-years-old and Connie Francis was 26 when they released a duet about adultery 'Walk On By'.

In 1974, Williams Jnr. moved to Alabama where he recorded a hard-hitting album *Hank Williams Jnr. And Friends* with Charlie Daniels and other top-class southern country rockers. Like his father, he has had arguments with Audrey, gone through an unhappy marriage and over-indulged in alcohol and drugs. 'Getting Over You' relates to his life, and in another song, he explains that it's the 'Family Tradition'. On 8 August 1975, Hank Williams Jnr. fell 500 feet down a Montana mountain face. Although close to death, he made a remarkable recovery, needing extensive medical and cosmetic surgery. Half of his face was reconstructed and he had to learn to speak, (and sing), all over again. It was two years until he could perform once more. Since 1977, Williams Jnr., who is managed by his opening act Merle Kilgore, has been associated with the 'outlaw country music' genre. Waylon Jennings, for example, wrote Hank Jnr.'s country hit, 'Are You Sure Hank Done It This Way?' and produced his album, *The New South*. In 1983, he had eight albums on the US country charts simultaneously, yet was not chosen as Entertainer of the Year in the Country Music Awards. In 1985, Williams released his fiftieth album, 'Five-O'. Williams' songs often lack distinctive melodies, while the lyrics concentrate on his macho, defiant persona. His best compositions include 'Montana Cafe', 'OD'd In Denver', the jazzy 'Women I've Never Had' and his visit to a gay disco, 'Dinosaur'. 'If The South Woulda Won' was criticised for being racist but, possibly, he was being sardonic. However, there was no mistaking of his tone to Saddam Hussein in 'Don't Give Us A Reason'. Among his other successes are 'I Fought The Law', 'Tennessee Stud', 'Ain't Misbehavin'' and his *cri de coeur*, 'If Heaven Ain't A Lot Like Dixie'. Although Williams has shown determination to move away from his father's shadow, he still sings about him. Many tribute songs by others - 'If You Don't Like Hank Williams' and 'Are You Sure Hank Done It This Way?' - have an added dimension through his interpretations. Williams himself was the subject of a tribute from David Allan Coe, who insisted that a man of six feet four inches and 15 stone should not be called 'Jnr.'.

Williams' rowdy image did not fit in well with the clean-cut 'hat acts' of the early 90s, and his record sales and airplay faltered. He remains a sell-out concert draw, although a well-publicized incident during 1992 where he arrived onstage drunk, and spent most of the 20-minute performance insulting his audience, did little for his status in the Nashville community.

Selected albums: *Hank Williams Jnr. Sings The Songs Of Hank Williams* (1963), *Connie Francis And Hank Williams Jnr. Sing Great Country Favorites* (1964), *Your Cheatin' Heart* (1964, film soundtrack), *Father And Son - Hank Williams Sr And Hank Williams Jnr.* (1964), *Ballad Of The Hills And Plains* (1965), *Father And Son - Hank Williams Sr And Hank Williams Jnr. Again* (1966), *Blue's My Name* (1966), *Country Shadows* (1966), *My Own Way* (1967), *My Songs* (1968), *A Time To Sing* (1968, film soundtrack), *Luke The Drifter Jnr.* (1969), *Songs My Father Left Me* (1969), *Live At Cobo Hall, Detroit* (1969), *Luke The Drifter Jnr., Volume 2* (1969), *Sunday Morning* (1970), *Singing My Songs* (1970), *Luke The Drifter Jnr., Volume 3* (1970), with Louis Johnson *Removing The Shadow* (1970), *All For The Love Of Sunshine* (1970), *I've Got A Right To Cry/They All Used To Belong To Me* (1971) *Sweet Dreams* (1971), *Eleven Roses* (1972), with Johnson *Send Me Some Lovin'/Whole Lotta Lovin'* (1972), *After You/Pride's Not Hard To Swallow* (1973), *Hank Williams: The Legend In Story And Song* (1973, a double album in which Hank Jnr. narrates his father's life), *Just Pickin' - No Singing* (1973), *The Last Love Song* (1973), *Living Proof* (1974), *Bocephus* (1975), *Hank Williams Jnr. And Friends* (1975), *One Night Stands* (1977), *The New South* (1977), *Family Tradition* (1979), *Whiskey Bent And Hell Bound* (1979), *Habits Old And New* (1980), *Rowdy* (1980), *The Pressure Is On* (1981), *High Notes* (1982), *Strong Stuff* (1983), *Man Of Steel* (1983), *Major Moves* (1984), *Five-O* (1985), *Montana Cafe* (1986), *Live* (1987), *Born To Boogie* (1987), *Wild Streak* (1988), *Lone Wolf* (1990), *America - The Way I See It* (1990), *Pure Hank* (1992), *Maverick* (1992). Compilations: *Hank Williams Jnr.'s Greatest Hits* (1982), *The Magic Guitar Of Hank Williams Jnr.* (1986), *Country Store* (1988).

Further reading: *Living Proof*, Hank Williams Jnr., with Michael Bane.

Williams, Leona

b. Leona Belle Helton, 7 January 1943, Vienna, Missouri, USA. One of the 12 children of musical parents (all played instruments), Leona worked with the family group as a child. In 1958, she had her own show on KWOS Jefferson City. She married drummer Ron Williams in 1959 and with Leona playing bass, both worked with Loretta Lynn. In 1968, she signed for Hickory with whom she achieved three minor hits, including 'Once More', before moving to MCA. In 1975, she joined Merle Haggard's show, initially as a backing vocalist. However, when Haggard divorced Bonnie Owens, she not only became the featured vocalist but on 7 October 1978, she also became the third Mrs Haggard. They combined to write several songs and recorded an album together but the marriage soon proved turbulent. In 1978, they had a number 8 US country hit with 'The Bull And The Beaver' but in 1983, when the marriage ended, they appeared in the charts with the appropriately named 'We're Strangers Again'. She later married songwriter and guitarist Dave Kirby. She also made solo recordings for Electra and Mercury and her songs have been recorded by other stars including Tammy Wynette but she has so far failed to score a big solo hit. Williams does hold the distinction of being the first female country singer to record a live album in a prison.
Albums: *That Williams Girl* (1970), *San Quentin's First Lady* (1976), *A Woman Walked Away* (1977), with Merle Haggard *Heart To Heart* (1983), *Someday When Things Are Good* (1984).

Williams, Tex

b. Sollie Paul Williams, 23 August 1917, Ramsey, Fayette County, Illinois, USA, d. 11 October 1985, Newhall, California, USA. His father was a keen fiddler and, by the time he was 13-years-old, Williams had a local radio programme as a one-boy band. He toured with the Reno Racketeers but he soon turned to Hollywood. In 1940 he appeared alongside Tex Ritter in Rollin' Home To Texas and then made a long chain of westerns, many of them Saturday morning serials. He managed to overcome his limp, a legacy of childhood polio, and he became known as 'Tex', as presumably Illinois Williams did not have the same ring. Williams also played bass and sang with Spade Cooley's western swing band, establishing himself as a vocalist on Cooley's 1945 country hit, 'Shame On You'. In 1947, Capitol Records had their first million-selling record with Williams' fast-talking, deep-voiced monologue, 'Smoke! Smoke! Smoke!', which he wrote with Merle Travis. As his songs often praised smoking, he became known as 'The Man Who Sings Tobacco Best', but this was before the link between cigarettes and cancer was known.

In 1948, Williams had success with another narration, 'Life Gits Tee-jus, Don't It?', but the composer Carson J. Robison had the main honours. Williams' other successes included 'That's What I Like About The West', 'Never Trust A Woman', 'Don't Telephone, Don't Telegraph, Tell A Woman', 'Suspicion' and 'Talking Boogie'. He and his band played dance halls all over the USA and he promoted Nudie's stage suits, helping Nudie become the tailor to country stars. His 1963 album, *Tex Williams In Las Vegas*, was recorded at the Mint Club in 1963, featuring Glen Campbell and produced by one of the Crickets, Tommy Allsup. His subsequent singles included 'Too Many Tigers', 'Bottom Of The Mountain', 'The Night Miss Nancy Ann's Hotel For Single Girls Burned Down' and 'Smoke! Smoke! Smoke! '68' with Merle Travis. The smoke, smoke, smoke caught up with him and he died of lung cancer in 1985 at his home in Newhall, California.
Albums: *Dance-O-Rama-Tex Williams* (1955), *Tex Williams Best* (1958), *Smoke! Smoke! Smoke!* (1960), *Country Music Time* (1962), *Tex Williams In Las Vegas* (1963), *Tex Williams* (1966), *Two Sides Of Tex Williams* (1966), *The Voice Of Authority* (1966), *A Man Called Tex* (1971), *Those Lazy, Hazy Days* (1974), *Tex Williams And California Express* (1981). Compilation: *14 All-Time Country Hits* (1978).

Willing, Foy

b. Foy Willingham, 1915, Bosque County, Texas, USA, d. 24 June 1978. After first singing on local radio while still at school, he moved to New York where he appeared on radio for Crazy Water Crystals in 1933. He returned to radio work in Texas in 1935 but two years later, he moved to California, where he formed the Riders Of the Purple Sage. Initially it comprised himself, Jimmy Dean and Al Sloey but over the years there were many others including Scotty Herrell, Billy Leibert, Paul Sellers and Johnny Paul. Using an instrumental line-up that included accordion, fiddle and guitar and closely resembling the Sons Of The Pioneers, they became very popular on several radio shows including the *Hollywood Barn Dance*. They also appeared in numerous Republic pictures with either Roy Rogers or Monte Hale. Their popularity saw them record for several labels and are best remembered for their recordings of 'Ghost

Tex Williams

Riders In The Sky' (Capitol) and 'No One To Cry To' (Majestic). They formally disbanded in 1952 but later made nostalgic appearances at festivals, some further recordings and in 1959, they toured with Gene Autry. Foy Willing continued to appear at Western events until his death in 1978. (This group should not be confused with the New Riders Of The Purple Sage, a country-rock band of the 70s).

Albums: *Cowboy* (1958), *New Sound Of American Folk* (1962).

Willis Brothers

Guy (b. James, 5 July 1915, Alex, Arkansas, USA, d. 13 April 1981, Nashville, Tennessee, USA; guitar/vocals), Skeeter (b. Charles, 20 December 1917, Coalton, Oklahoma, USA, d. March 1976; fiddle/vocals) and Vic (b. Richard, 31 May 1922, Schulter, Oklahoma, USA; accordion/piano/vocals). Using clever combinations that saw any brother able to sing lead or harmony, they first appeared on KGEF Shawnee in 1932 as the Oklahoma Wranglers. In 1942, they moved to the Brush Creek Follies on KMBC Kansas City, Missouri but their careers were interrupted by military service. In 1946, they backed Hank Williams when he made his first Sterling recordings in December that year. They also joined the *Grand Ole Opry* and began a long association with Eddy Arnold. They left the *Opry* in 1949 and during the 50s, were popular on various shows including the *Ozark Jubilee* and the *Midwestern Hayride*. They rejoined the *Opry* in 1960 and during the decade found country chart success on Starday including a Top 10 hit with 'Give Me Forty Acres'. During their career they recorded for several other labels, even worked as session musicians and toured extensively including overseas trips. They appeared in several films including *Feudin' Rhythm* and *Hoe Down* and also hold the distinction of being the first country act to perform at the Constitution Hall in Washington. Guy retired after Skeeter died of cancer in 1976 and Vic formed the Vic Willis Trio and continued to perform.

Albums: *In Action* (1962), *Code Of The West* (1963), *Let's Hit The Road* (1965), *Sensational* (1965), *Give Me Forty Acres* (1965), *Road Stop-Jukebox Hits* (1965), *Wild Side Of Life* (1966), *Goin' To Town* (1966), *Bob* (1967), *Hey, Mister Truck Driver* (1968), *Bummin' Around* (1969), *For The Good Times* (1971), *Travellin' & Truck Driver Hits* (c.1971), *Y'All/A Satisfied Mind* (c.1972).

Wills, Billy Jack

b. 1926, on a farm near Memphis, Hall County, Texas, USA. Billy Jack was the youngest brother of Bob Wills and the ninth of the Wills' family children. He naturally grew up influenced by his brother Bob's music and joined the Texas Playboys in 1945. He initially played bass but, after 1949 he usually played drums and also took some vocals. He added the lyrics to the old fiddle tune called 'Faded Love', that had been written by Bob and his father John Wills. He shared the vocal when it was first recorded in 1950 and the song reached number 8 in the US country charts. It went on to become a country standard and was later a hit for Patsy Cline (1963), Leon McAuliffe (1963), Tompall And The Glaser Brothers (1971) and Willie Nelson and Ray Price (1980). In the mid-50s, he formed his own band and recorded for Four Star.

Albums: *Billy Jack Wills & His Western Swing Band* (c.1983), *Crazy Man Crazy* (c.1885).

Wills, Bob

b. James Robert Wills, 6 March 1905, on a farm near Kosse, Limestone County, Texas, USA, d. 13 May 1975, Fort Worth, Texas, USA. The eldest of the ten children of John Thompkins Wills and Emmaline (Foley): Bob was a sickly child and there were fears that he would not survive his early years. His father, known locally as Uncle John, was a fiddler (reckoned by many to be the best in all the Brazos River area), and later taught his son, Bob to play the mandolin so that he could accompany his father's playing, but initially the child showed no great interest in music. In 1913, the Wills family relocated to Memphis, Texas. Bob rode his pet donkey behind the family wagon and the five-hundred mile journey took over two months. John and Bob played for farm dances along the way to raise money for food and it was at one of these dances that Bob first became interested in music played by Negro families, featuring trumpet and guitar. When he was 10-years-old, much to his father's relief, he took up the fiddle and made his first solo public appearance. His father failed to appear on time at a dance and in spite of only knowing six fiddle tunes for dancing, he kept playing alone. (His father eventually arrived at 2 am, too drunk to play.)

John Wills was fairly successful as a farmer and by 1921, he had moved to a 600 acre ranch/farm near Oxbow Crossing, which remained their home until 1931. The family continued to play for local functions. In fact, it was suggested that the Wills family, which by 1926 had 9 children, produced more music than cotton. Bob realised the farm could not keep them all and in 1924, he moved to Amarillo where, by working on building sites and as a shoeshine boy, he made enough money to buy himself a fiddle. He then found work playing for dances on Saturday nights and made his first radio broadcasts on Amarillo's two radio stations, KGRS and WDAG. A year later, he returned home driving a Model T Ford, which enabled him to appear as a fiddler over a wider area. In 1926, he married for the first time and leased a farm, but after a crop failure in 1927, he and his wife moved to Amarillo and he gave up farming for good.

He moved to Fort Worth where, sometimes in blackface, he found work in a Medicine Show. Here he met guitarist Herman Arnspiger and the two men began to appear as the Wills Family Band. They played for dances, did comedy routines and in November 1929, they recorded for Brunswick, in Dallas, although the two songs were not released. In 1930, the duo became a quartet when Milton Brown and his brother Durwood joined as vocalist and guitarist respectively, although Durwood was at the time still at school. (Milton Brown later became famous with his own band, the Musical Brownies.) They found regular work playing for dances, at times adding banjoist, Frank Barnes and played on KTAT and KFJZ where the assistant programme director of the latter station, Alton Strickland, would five years later became Wills' pianist. In 1930, Wills' band were sponsored on WBAP by the Aladdin Lamp Company (they appeared as the Aladdin Laddies), and also gained a residency at the Crystal Springs dance hall in Fort Worth. In January 1931, through the sponsorship of the Burrus Mill and Elevator Company and billed as the Light Crust Doughboys, he and the band began to advertise Light Crust Flour on KFJZ. After two weeks, in spite of their popularity with the listeners, the President of Burrus Mill, Mr. Wilbert Lee O'Daniel (later a US Senator and Governor of Texas) sacked them, because he considered their music was too hillbilly. KFJZ kept them on air without a sponsor and Wills succeeded in getting O'Daniel to resume sponsorship and pay the band as well, although for a time all members had to work a 40-hour week in the mill.

Their popularity grew and soon the programme was being heard over all the southwest, even reaching as far as Oklahoma City. The band recorded for RCA-Victor in 1932, the only recordings made by Wills with the Light Crust Doughboys. The same year, vocalist Thomas Elmer Duncan replaced Milton Brown. In 1933, after differences of opinion and an odd drinking spree that saw him miss shows, Wills was sacked by O'Daniel. He moved to Waco, assembled a band that included his brother, Johnnie Lee Wills and Duncan and for the first time, he called his band the Playboys: he also added 'formerly the Light Crust Doughboys'. (He found himself in law-suits from O'Daniel for using the name but eventually the Tenth Court Of Civil Appeals found in his favour.) He then moved to Oklahoma City, where he began to call his band the Texas Playboys, but O'Daniel stopped his programme by promising the radio station he would put on the *Burrus Mill Show* there in Oklahoma if they did not broadcast Wills's band. Mills moved to KVOO Tulsa, where in February 1934, Bob Wills And The Texas Playboys finally began to broadcast and this time O'Daniel's attempts to stop them failed.

In 1935, the group made their first historic studio recordings. The band consisted of twelve musicians namely Bob Wills (fiddle), Tommy Duncan (vocals/piano), Johnnie Lee Wills (tenor banjo), Son Lansford (bass), Herman Arnspiger (guitar), Sleepy Johnson (guitar), Jesse Ashlock (fiddle), Art Baines (fiddle/trombone), Smokey Dacus (drums), Robert McNally (saxophone), Al Stricklin (piano) and Leon McAuliffe (steel guitar). Wills stayed in Tulsa and during the late 30s, he continued to shape his band and changes in personnel saw the arrival of guitarist Eldon Shamblin and saxophonist Joe Ferguson. In 1936, Leon McAuliffe first recorded his 'Steel Guitar Rag'. Wills made further recording sessions in Chicago (1936) and Dallas (1937 and 1938). When he recorded in Saginaw, Texas in April 1940, his band numbered 18 musicians - more than the big bands of the period such as Glenn Miller, Benny Goodman and the Dorseys were using. It was at this session that he recorded his million-selling version of 'New San Antonio Rose', the (Tommy Duncan) vocal version of his 1935 fiddle tune, previously known as 'Spanish Two Step'. This version differed from his original fiddle one, in that it featured only reeds and brass and was played in the swing style as used by the big bands of the time. (Over the years the song has usually been referred to as simply 'San Antonio Rose'.)

Wills was by this time one of the top-selling recording artists in the States. In 1939, the demand was such that Wills decided for the first time to run a second band, which was led by his brother Johnnie Lee and also included his younger brother

Luke Wills. Although successful with his music, Bob Wills was far from successful in marriage. He had troubles at times with excessive drinking and a fondness for the ladies. He was divorced in 1935 and married and divorced a second time in 1936. In 1938, he married again but once more was divorced within the year and though he persuaded this wife to re-marry him, they were divorced for the second time in 1939. He married again in July 1939, only to be divorced (yet again!) in June 1941.

In 1940, he appeared with Tex Ritter in the film *Take Me Back To Oklahoma*, even duetting with Ritter on the title track and the following year, with his full band, he featured in the film *Go West Young Man*. In 1942, Duncan left for military service (he rejoined on discharge) but Wills maintained a band containing 15 instruments although only four were stringed. He recorded in Hollywood and made eight b-movie westerns with Russell Hayden. He was also married that year to Betty Anderson, a girl 18 years his junior and this time in spite of his drinking, the marriage would last until his death. After the filming was completed, more band members left for the US Army and Wills moved to Tulsa, finally disbanding in December 1942. He enlisted himself but was discharged in July 1943. He moved to California, reformed a band and returned to the film studios. Wills never liked Hollywood but he loved the cowboy image. He spent lavishly on horses, harness and dress for himself and was a popular figure on his favourite stallion, Punkin, around the California rodeo circuit. He bought a ranch in the San Joaquin Valley and stocked it with horses and a dairy herd 'just to keep my father busy'.

At one stage in 1944, his band consisted of 22 instruments and 2 vocalists but he never recorded with this unit. Duncan left in 1947 to form his own band, probably because he had tired of having to take responsibility for fronting the band, when Wills failed to appear through a drinking spree. During 1944-45, Wills had US country and pop chart hits with 'New San Antonio Rose', 'We Might As Well Forget It' and 'You're From Texas'. He also had country number 1 hits with such war songs as 'Smoke On The Water', 'Stars And Stripes At Iwo Jima', 'Silver Dew On The Blue Grass Tonight' and 'White Cross At Okinawa'. In 1946, his 'New Spanish Two-Step' topped the country charts for 16 weeks as well as having Top 20 pop success. Wills left Columbia in 1947 to record for MGM Records and in 1950, he recorded his classic 'Faded Love' - a composition

that he and his father wrote with some words added by brother Billy Jack Wills. He toured extensively and relocated to Dallas, where he invested heavily in a dancehall that he called Bob Wills Ranch House. Due to dishonesty by people employed to run his affairs, he soon found himself heavily in debt. Faced with jail, he sold his Bob Wills Music Company and accidentally with it the ownership of 'San Antonio Rose'.

For two years, he struggled to raise funds; he ran two bands - one played at the Ranch House and he toured with the other. In January 1952, he finally sold the Ranch House to a Jack Ruby - a name then unknown outside Dallas, but later internationally known following the assassination of President John F. Kennedy. Throughout the 50s, he recorded and toured extensively and several times moved his base of operations. Wills continued to experiment but the influence of television began to affect the dancehalls, tastes had changed and he never recaptured the earlier successes. He recorded in Nashville for the first time in 1955 and again in 1956, but most of his recordings were made in California. In 1959, he appeared at the Golden Nugget in Las Vegas but still missed a few shows through his drinking. He was reunited with Tommy Duncan, and during the period of 1960-1961 they recorded over forty sides for Liberty Records. In 1962, he suffered a heart attack but in 1963, he was back even though he sold his band to Carl Johnson. He suffered a further heart attack in 1964 and when he recovered sufficiently to work again, he always acted as a front man for other bands. Between 1963-69, he recorded almost an hundred sides for either Liberty, Longhorn or Kapp Records. He was elected to the Country Music Hall Of Fame in 1968.

After an appearance on 30 May 1969, he suffered a stroke and was rushed to hospital where he underwent two major operations. The stroke left him paralysed on the right side and hospitalized for months.

In 1970, he moved to Tulsa and in 1971 underwent surgery for a kidney complaint, but suffered a stroke on the left side a few hours after the operation. Months later, he recovered sufficiently to talk and to use his left arm, even telling people that he would play again. Country star Merle Haggard admired Wills and was influenced by his music and in 1970, he recorded his album *Tribute To The Best Damn Fiddle Player In The World (Or My Salute To Bob Wills)*, which actually featured some of the Texas Playboys. Wills was unable to attend the recordings but in 1971, he was reunited with ten of his old Texas Playboys at Haggard's house, near Bakersfield and watched and listened as recordings were made. In 1973, he made a few appearances, at one even holding his fiddle while Hoyle Nix used the bow. He travelled to Dallas to attend a recording session of the Texas Playboys and on 3 December even included a few of his famous yells and 'hollers' as the band recorded some of his hits. During the night, he suffered a further stroke and remained unconscious for almost eighteen months until his death from pneumonia on 13 May 1975.

He was buried in Memorial Park, Tulsa, a city that saw much of the glory days of Bob Wills' western swing music. It could never be said that he copied any other style - he devised his own, as the words of his song said 'Deep within my heart lies a melody'. His long-time friend and steel guitarist Leon McAuliffe, who, though 12-years-younger than Wills, had retired from the music scene, summed things up when he said 'My desire wore out before my body, Bob never did wear out at this. His body wore out before his desire did'. There have been other bands that played the music but none that ever matched the instrumental integration or the wide variation in the styles and music of Bob Wills. His habit of uttering spasmodic high pitched shouts during the playing of numbers, such as his famed 'Ah haaa', originated from the days when, as a young boy, he performed with his father at ranch dances in Texas. His father (and the cowboys) used similar loud cries at points when the music or the whiskey moved them to feel that something was special. His other habit of talking to his musicians such as his noted, 'Take it away, Leon', was picked up from his association as a youth with black musicians, who always talked to each other while they were playing. He believed it was the best way of getting the best out of musicians or even having a joke at their expense. He may even have had more fans without his continued 'hollers' or interjections, particularly over Duncan's vocals but as Waylon Jennings sang 'When you're down in Austin, Bob Wills is still the King'.

Albums: *Ranch House Favourites* (1951), *Old Time Favorites By Bob Wills & His Texas Playboys 1* (1953), *Texas Playboys 2* (1953), *Bob Wills Round Up* (1954), *Dance-O-Rama No: 2* (1955), *Ranch House Favorites* (1956), *Bob Wills Special* (1957), *Bob Wills & His Texas Playboys* (1957), *Western Swing In Hi-Fi* (1957), *Together Again - Bob Wills & Tommy Duncan* (1960), *Bob Wills & Tommy Duncan* (1961),

Living Legend - Bob Wills & His Texas Playboys (1961), *Mr Words & Mr Music* (1961), *Sings And Plays* (1963), *Best Of Bob Wills & His Texas Playboys - Original Recordings* (1963), *Keepsake Album #1* (1965), *The Great Bob Wills* (1965), *San Antonio Rose/Steel Guitar Rag* (1965), *Western Swing Along* (1965), with Leon Rausch *From The Heart Of Texas* (1966), *King Of Western Swing* (1967), *Bob Wills* (1967), *Here's That Man Again* (1968), *Plays The Greatest String Band Hits* (1969), *A Country Walk* (1969), *Time Changes Everything* (1969), *The Living Legend* (1969), *The Bob Wills Story* (1970), *In Person* (1970), *Legendary Masters - Bob Wills & Tommy Duncan* (1971), *A Tribute To Bob Wills* (1971), *San Antonio Rose* (1971), *The History Of Bob Wills & The Texas Playboys* (1973), *The Bob Wills Anthology* (1973), *For The Last Time* (1974), *The Legendary Bob Wills* (1975), *Bob Wills & His Texas Playboys In Concert* (1976), *I Love People* (1976), *The Tiffany Transcriptions* (1977), *The Tiffany Transcriptions 1945-1948* (1978), *Lonestar Rag* (1979), *Faded Love* (1981), *The Rare Presto Transcriptions Volumes 1 - 5* (1981-1985, German releases), *31st Street Blues* (1981), *Columbia Historic Edition* (1982), *The San Antonio Rose Story* (1982), *Texas Fiddle & Milk Cow Blues* (1982), *Heaven, Hell Or Houston* (1983), *The Tiffany Transcriptions Volumes 1 to 8* (1983-1988), *The Golden Era* (1987). Further reading: *San Antonio Rose, The Life and Music of Bob Wills*, Charles R.Townsend. *The Life of Bob Wills, The King Of Western Swing*, Jimmy Latham. *My Years With Bob Wills*, Al Stricklin. *Hubbin' It, The Life Of Bob Wills*, Ruth Sheldon.

Wills, Johnnie Lee

b. 2 September 1912, on a farm near Kosse, Limestone County, Texas, USA. d. 25 October 1984. Younger brother of Bob Wills and the fourth of the Wills' family children. He learned to play the guitar as a child but later played tenor banjo and fiddle. He made his musical debut in 1933, when he became one of brother Bob's second band, working as Johnnie Lee Wills and His Rhythmaires. He appeared with Bob in the 1940 Tex Ritter film, *Take Me Back To Oklahoma*. In early 1941, he recorded for Decca having success with 'Milk Cow Blues'. Throughout the 40s and 50s, he led western swing bands, working in conjunction with brother Bob. He played the Southwest dance circuits but was mainly centred at Oklahoma City or Tulsa where, until 1964, he played a residency at *Cain's Dancing Academy*. In 1950, recording on Bullet, he achieved Top 10 US country and pop charts success with 'Rag Mop' (a

number he co-wrote with Deacon Anderson that
was also a pop hit for the Ames Brothers) and a
country number 7 with 'Peter Cottontail'. He also
made further recordings for Decca, Imperial and
RCA-Victor, as well as over 200 fifteen minute
transcription discs for use on KVOO Tulsa and
other stations. In 1964, he left Cain's, ran his
western wear store in Tulsa and organized the
Tulsa Annual Stampede rodeo. He returned to
leading a band in the 70s and with some of the old
Playboys, he recorded for the Flying Fish and Delta
labels. In 1971, he played banjo on the Bob Wills'
tribute recordings made at Merle Haggard's home
in Bakersfield and later made some appearances at
Playboy Reunion Shows but did not appear on the
1973 recording session in Dallas, Texas. He most
modestly never rated himself as a good enough solo
banjo or fiddle player for people to listen to but he
was highly respected as a band leader. He died in
Tulsa in October 1984.
Albums: *Best Of Johnnie Lee Wills* (c.60s), *Where
There's A Wills There's A Way* (1962), *At The Tulsa
Stampede* (1963), *Reunion* (1978), *Tulsa Swing*
(1978), *Dance All Night* (1980), *Rompin' Stompin'
Singin' Swingin'* (1983).

Wills, Luke

b. Luther J Wills, 10 September 1920, on a farm
near Memphis, Hall County, Texas, USA.
Younger brother of Bob Wills and the seventh of
the Wills' family children. He was rated so
differently from the rest of the family that it was a
family joke that his mother had picked up the
wrong baby, after one of the many social dances
held in the area. He learned to play stand-up bass as
a child and made his musical debut in 1939 in the
second Wills' band, led by elder brother Johnnie
Lee Wills, called the Rhythmaires. He appeared in
b-movie westerns in the early 40s with Bob but in
1943, he joined the US Navy. After service, he led
Bob's second band and covered the dance circuit of
northern and central California, appearing first as
Luke Wills And the Texas Playboys Number 2 but
to avoid confusion this soon became Luke Wills'
Rhythm Busters. He recorded for King and RCA-
Victor, adopting a similar style of comments and
interjections as Bob though not in a high pitched
voice.
In 1948, the Rhythm Busters were disbanded and
he worked with Bob until 1950, when he
reformed his own band and took over in
Oklahoma City, when Bob returned to Texas to
his new dancehall. He rejoined Bob in 1952 and
played and sang with the Playboys, often fronting

the band in Bob's absence, until they disbanded in
1964. He then worked outside of the music
industry in Las Vegas. In 1971, he played bass on
the Bob Wills' tribute recordings made at Merle
Haggard's home in Bakersfield and later made
some appearances at Playboy Reunion Shows but
did not appear on the 1973 recording session in
Dallas. Although contributing in no small way to
his eldest brother's legend, he was not elected to
the Country Music Hall Of Fame. In the late 70s,
he left the music business and retired to Las Vegas.
Album: *Luke Wills' Rhythm Busters - High Voltage
Gal* (1988).

Wiseman, Mac

b. Malcolm B. Wiseman, 23 May 1925, Crimora,
Virginia, USA. Wiseman attended the
Conservatory of Music at Dayton, Virginia and
developed a great knowledge of the folk music of
his native Shenandoah Valley. He first worked as a
disc jockey on WSVA Harrisburg but was soon
playing such shows as the *Tennessee Barn Dance* on
WLOX Knoxville, where he also worked with
Molly O'Day. During the 40s, his talent with
bluegrass music saw him play and record with the
bands of Bill Monroe and Flatt And Scruggs. He
made his first solo recordings for Dot in 1951 and
from 1957-61, he was the label's A&R man. After
recording for Capitol, he returned to Dot but in
the early 70s, he later recorded with Lester Flatt for
RCA. Over the years Wiseman has worked on a
variety of radio stations, played all the major US
country venues and travelled extensively including
several tours to Britain, where he is always a
popular artist. A prolific recording artist on various
labels, his most popular recordings include such
songs as 'Tis Sweet To Be Remembered'. His few
actual chart hits include Top 10 successes with
'The Ballad Of Davy Crockett' and 'Jimmy Brown
The Newsboy' and a minor hit with his humorous
'Johnny's Cash And Charley's Pride'. In 1979, he
even charted with 'My Blue Heaven' as Mac
Wiseman & Friend (the friend being Woody
Herman).
Albums: *I Hear You Knocking* (1955), *Songs From
The Hills* (1956), *Tis Sweet To Be Remembered*
(1957), *Beside The Still Waters* (1959), *Great Folk
Ballads* (1959), *Keep On The Sunny Side* (1960), *12
Great Hits* (1960), *Fireball Mail* (1961), *Best Loved
Gospel Hymns* (1961), *Bluegrass Favorites* (1962),
Sincerely (1964), with Osborne Brothers *Bluegrass*
(1966), *A Master At Work* (1966), *This Is Mac
Wiseman* (1966), *Songs Of The Good Old Days*
(1966), *Old Time Country Favorites* (1966), *Mac*

Wiseman (1967), *Golden Hits* (1968), *Sings Johnny's Cash & Charley's Pride* (1970), with Lester Flatt *Lester 'N' Mac* (1971), with Lester Flatt *On The Southbound* (1972), with Lester Flatt *Over The Hills To The Poorhouse* (1973), *Concert Favorites* (1973), *16 Great Performances* (1974), *The Mac Wiseman Story* (double LP) (1976), *Country Music Memories* (1977), *New Traditions Volume 2* (1976), *New Traditions Volume 2* (1977), *Sings Gordon Lightfoot* (1977), *Mac Wiseman* (1977), *Golden Classics* (1979), with Osborne Brothers *Essential Bluegrass* (1979), *Songs That Made The Jukebox Play* (double LP) (1980), *Bluegrass Gold* (1982), *Live In Concert* (1982), *Greatest Bluegrass Hits* (1983), *If Teardrops Were Pennies* (1984), *Early Dot Recordings Volume 1* (1985), *Mac Wiseman* (1986), *Early Dot Recordings Volume 2* (1988), *Grassroots To Bluegrass* (1990).

Withers, Tex

No one knows when and where Tex Withers was born, his real name or his parents. The deformed baby was abandoned in the USA, and his rise in British country music showed remarkable resilience because he was four feet tall and a hunchback with a painful history of severe spinal problems and tuberculosis. Withers wore western dress throughout the day as he longed to be an American Indian - his wife, known as White Fawn, dressed as his squaw and smoked a clay pipe. A good-natured man who laughed at his handicaps, Withers was the long-standing compere at West London's Nashville Room and won several awards as the Top UK country singer, his show-stoppers being 'These Hands' and a narration about a Red Indian's difficulties in coming to terms with society, 'The Ballad Of Ira Hayes'. *Tex Withers Sings Country Style* sold 135,000 copies, whilst his 1973 album, *The Grand Ole Opry's Newest Star* was recorded mainly in Nashville, Tennessee. He was championed by Hank Snow, but his professional career was cut short by throat illness. Withers became bankrupt and his illiteracy made work difficult. His last years were spent as a cleaner at Gatwick Airport and Haywards Heath railway station. He found his happy hunting-ground on 29 December 1986, probably aged 53, and merited an obituary in *The Times*.
Albums: *Tex Withers Sings Country Style* (1970), *The Grand Ole Opry's Newest Star* (1973), *Tex Withers* (1976). Compilation: *Blue Ribbon Country* (1984).

Wolf, Kate

b. 27 January 1942, Sonoma County, San Francisco, California, USA, d. 10 December 1986. Wolf was a songwriter-singer-guitarist who worked her home area and organized the Santa Rosa folk festivals. Her first albums, *Back Roads* and *Lines On Paper*, were recorded independently and released on her own Owl label. Those albums were made with a band named after a country song, Wildwood Flower, and although country and bluegrass feature in her work, Wolf is a contemporary folk artist. In 1979 she recorded *Safe At Anchor* for the Kaleidoscope label, which many claim to be her finest set. Wolf wrote and sang beautifully, clearly and perceptively about the preciousness of life and the precariousness of relationships. She was also a fine interpreter of others' material such as the slow version of Jack Tempchin's 'Peaceful Easy Feeling'(recorded by the Eagles), and John Stewart's 'Some Kind Of Love' on the live double-album *Give Yourself To Love*. In November 1985 she recorded a memorable television concert for *Austin City Limits*, which became *An Evening In Austin*. It was her last happy moment: she developed leukaemia and although she was not fit to record, she compiled the retrospective *Gold In California*. The title track of *The Wind Blows Wild* was recorded at her hospital bedside and she died in 1986. She had had no hits and her songs were largely unknown, but, gradually, the quality of her work has surfaced. Her husband, Terry Fowler - the subject of 'Green Eyes' - keeps her name alive. Her songs ironically include such titles as 'Love Still Remains' and 'Unfinished Life'.
Albums: *Back Roads* (1976), *Lines On Paper* (1977), *Safe At Anchor* (1979), *Close To You* (1981), *Give Yourself To Love* (1983), *Poet's Heart* (1985), *The Wind Blows Wild* (1988), *An Evening In Austin* (1988). Compilation: *Gold In California* (1986).

Wood, Del

b. Adelaide Hazlewood, 22 February 1920, Nashville, Tennessee, USA, d. 3 October 1989. Wood's parents gave her a piano for her fifth birthday with the hope that she would become a classical pianist. She had different ideas and aimed for a career at the *Grand Ole Opry*. She developed a thumping ragtime style that, in 1951, saw her record her version of 'Down Yonder', a tune that had proved a million-seller for Gid Tanner and the Skillet Lickers in 1934. Wood's version on the Tennessee label reached number 5 in the US country charts and also became a million-seller. After guesting on the *Opry* in 1952 and refusing the chance of playing with Bob Crosby, she joined the roster in 1953. Her playing proved so popular that she toured with *Opry* shows, even to Japan. She recorded for several labels making popular versions of such numbers as 'Johnson Rag' and 'Piano Roll Blues'. She had no more chart entries, but she won herself the nickname of 'Queen Of The Ragtime Pianists'. She remained a member of the *Opry* until her death in the Baptist Hospital, Nashville, on 3 October 1989, following a stroke on 22 September, the day she was scheduled to appear on the *Legendary Ladies Of Country Music Show*. It has been written that after Mother Maybelle Carter, Del Woods is recognized as being the most successful female country solo instrumentalist.

Albums: *Down Yonder* (1955), *Hot Happy & Honky* (1957), *Mississippi Showboat* (1959), *Buggies, Bustles & Barrellhouse* (1960), *Flivvers, Flappers & Fox Trots* (1960), *Ragtime Goes International* (1961), *Ragtime Goes South Of The Border* (1962), *Honky Tonk Piano* (1962), *Piano Roll Blues* (1963), *It's Honky Tonk Time* (1964), *Roll Out The Piano* (1964), *Uptight, Lowdown & Honky Tonk* (1966), *There's A Tavern In The Town* (c.60s), *Del Wood Favorites, Encore-Del Wood, Ragtime Favorites, Plays Berlin & Cohen Volumes, Ragtime Glory Special* (all c.70s).

Wooley, Sheb

b. Shelby F. Wooley, 10 April 1921, near Erick, Oklahoma, USA. Wooley, who is part Cherokee Indian, grew up on the family farm, learned to ride as a child and rode in rodeos as a teenager. His father swopped a shotgun to get him his first guitar and while still at high school, he formed a country band that played at dances and on local radio. After leaving school, he found work in an oil-field as a welder, but soon tired of this work and moved to Nashville. He appeared on the WLAC and WSM radio stations and recorded for the Bullet label. In 1946, he relocated to Fort Worth, where until 1949, he became the front man for a major show on WBAP, sponsored by Calumet Baking Powder. He then moved to Los Angeles, where he signed with MGM Records and with thoughts of a film career as well, he also attended the Jack Koslyn School of Acting. In 1949, he got his first screen role (as a heavy) in the Errol Flynn film *Rocky Mountain*. In 1952, he made a memorable appearance as Ben Miller, the killer plotting to gun down Gary Cooper in the classic western *High Noon*. During the 50s, he appeared in several other films including *Little Big Horn* (1951), *Distant Drums* (1951), *Man Without A Star* (1955), *Giant* (1956) and *Rio Bravo* (1959). He is also well remembered for his performances as Pete Nolan in the television series *Rawhide*, which ran from 1958-65. (He also wrote some scripts for the series.) During his career, he has appeared in over 40 films. Other artists began to record songs he had written and in 1953, Hank Snow had a big hit with 'When Mexican Joe Met Jole Blon' - a parody of two hit songs. In 1958, his novelty number, 'Purple People Eater', became a million-seller and even reached number 12 in the UK pop charts. He based the song on a schoolboy joke that he had heard from Don Robertson's son and initially, MGM did not consider it to be worth releasing. Further US pop successes included 'Sweet Chile'. He first appeared in the US country charts in 1962, when another novelty number, 'That's My Pa', became a number 1. It was intended that Wooley should record 'Don't Go Near The Indians' but due to film commitments Rex Allen's version was released before he could record it. Wooley jokingly told MGM that he would write a sequel and came up with the comedy parody 'Don't Go Near The Eskimos'. He developed an alter-ego drunken character, whom he called Ben Colder and in this guise, he recorded and charted it and other humorous parodies of pop/country hits including 'Almost Persuaded No. 2', 'Harper Valley PTA (Later That Same Day)' and 'Fifteen Beers (Years) Ago'. (The name Ben Colder was the selection made by MGM from the three alternatives that Wooley offered. The other two were Ben Freezin and Klon Dyke.) He had some further minor hits with serious recordings, including 'Blue Guitar' and 'Tie A Tiger Down'. In 1969, he joined the CBS network *Hee Haw* country show, remained with it for several years and also wrote the theme music. Throughout the 60s and 70s, he maintained a busy touring schedule appearing all over the States and overseas. In 1968, Ben Colder was voted Comedian of the Year by the Country Music Association. He cut back during the 80s and although he has remained a popular entertainer, he has had no chart entries since 1971. Over the years, the parodies by the drunken Ben Colder have proved more popular than his serious recordings and have certainly accounted for the majority of his record sales.

Albums: as Sheb Wooley *Sheb Wooley* (1956), *Songs From The Days Of Rawhide* (1961), *That's My Pa & That's My Ma* (1962), *Tales Of How The West Was Won* (1963), *It's A Big Land* (1965), *Warm & Wooley* (1969), *Blue Guitar* (1985). Compilation: *Country Boogie Wild And Wooley (1948-55)* (1984); as Ben Colder *Ben Colder* (1961), *Spoofing The Big*

Sheb Wooley

Ones (1963), *Ben Colder Strikes Again* (1966), *Wine Women & Song* (1967), *Harper Valley PTA & Other Parodies Of Top Ten Hits* (1968), *Have One On Ben Colder* (1969), *Big Ben Colder Wild Again* (1970), *Ben Colder* (1970), *Live & Loaded At Sam Houston Coliseum* (1971), *Wacky World Of Ben Colder* (1973). Compilation: *Golden Hits* (1980).

Wright, Bobby

b. 30 March 1942, Charleston, West Virginia, USA. The son of Kitty Wells and Johnnie Wright. He appeared with his parents on the *Louisiana Hayride* at the age of eight, and three years later made his first recordings. After the family relocated to Nashville, he learned to play guitar but initially he had more interest in sports and drama. In 1962, he went to California and successfully auditioned for the role of a young guitar playing southern boy in a proposed drama. The show did not materialize, but his performance won him the role of Willie, the radio operator, in a new comedy television series called *McHale's Navy*. He stayed as a regular until the series ended in 1966. He recorded for Decca (his parent's label) and in 1967, he scored his first US country chart hit with 'Lay Some Happiness On Me'. A few more minor hits followed and after further acting roles, his dislike of Hollywood saw him return to Nashville, where he began to appear with his parents. He had by this time also learned to play bass, trumpet and drums and he soon became an important part of the family show. In the early 70s, he appeared on their syndicated television series and toured extensively with them. Over the years, he has also been a popular artist on other syndicated television shows. In 1971, he had a Top 15 country hit with 'Here I Go Again'. He recorded country covers of some pop hits and in 1974, he had Top 30 country success with his ABC recording of Terry Jacks' pop number 1, 'Seasons In The Sun'. He later recorded for United Artists, registering his last solo success, 'I'm Turning You Loose', on that label in 1979. He appeared in the UK with his parents at the 1974 Wembley Festival and more recently received praise for his performance with the family at the 1988 Peterborough Festival. A talented all-round entertainer, he continues to be an important part of the family show and has not made any further attempts to pursue a solo career.

Albums: *Here I Go Again* (1971), *Seasons Of Love* (1974).

Wright, Carol Sue

b. 1945, Nashville, Tennessee, USA. The youngest of the three children of Kitty Wells and Johnnie Wright, she began to sing with her parents from an early age. In December 1955, standing on a chair to reach the microphone, Wright duetted with her mother when she recorded their well-known version of 'How Far Is Heaven?'. In the late 50s, she sang with her sister, Ruby Wright, as the Wright Sisters, recording under the production of Chet Atkins for the Cadence label, who saw them as the female version of the label's popular Everly Brothers. She toured for a time with the family show but eventually, with no desire to pursue a singing career, she restricted her appearances and settled to raising her own family. In the 80s, she and sister Ruby ran the family Museum and Tourist attraction in Nashville.

Wright, Johnnie

b. John Robert Wright, 13 May 1914, on a farm near Mt. Juliet, Wilson County, Tennessee, USA. His grandfather was a champion old-time fiddler, his father a banjo player and while still at school, Wright learned to play these instruments, as well as the guitar and began to sing locally. He relocated to Nashville in 1933, where he worked daily as a cabinet maker and entertained at local venues. In 1936, he began to appear on radio WSIX Nashville and the following year, he met Kitty Wells who, as Muriel Deason, was then appearing on the station as part of the singing Deason Sisters. On 30 October 1937, they were married and with Wright's sister, Louise, the trio began to play WSIX as Johnnie Wright And The Harmony Girls. In 1939, they teamed up with their brother-in-law Jack Anglin, first appearing as Johnny Wright and the Happy Roving Cowboys with Jack Anglin but by 1940, Wright and Anglin had become Johnnie And Jack. After Anglin's untimely death in 1963, Wright re-organised their band, the Tennessee Mountain Boys and recorded for Decca as a solo artist. He made his US country chart debut in 1964 with the strangely titled 'Walkin', Talkin', Cryin', Barely Beatin' Broken Heart'. In 1965, he scored a number 1 country hit with Tom T. Hall's song 'Hello Vietnam'. He followed with further minor hits including 'I'm Doing This For Daddy', 'Mama's Little Jewel' and 'American Power'. During this time, he toured and worked in conjunction with Kitty Wells and in 1968, they charted with their duet, 'We'll Stick Together'. After this, their careers fully merged and with their children Ruby, Bobby and Carol Sue Wright, they become the Kitty Wells-Johnny Wright Family Show.

Johnnie Wright

Albums: *Hello Vietnam* (1965), *Country Music Special* (1966), *Country The Wright Way* (1967), *Sings Country Favorites* (1968).

Wright, Ruby

b. 27 October 1939, Nashville, Tennessee, USA. The eldest of the three children of Kitty Wells and Johnnie Wright, she sang with her parents from an early age. At the age of 13, she was signed by RCA Records and under the production of Chet Atkins, she had single releases as Ruby Wells. (There was a pop singer called Ruby Wright, but no doubt RCA believed it would help to use her mother's stage name). In the mid-50s, she was a member of a close harmony female singing trio, Nita, Rita and Ruby. (Nita was Anita Carter and Rita was Rita Robbins, the sister of Marty Robbins' guitarist and yodeler, Don Winters). Working with Atkins, they leaned heavily to a pop presentation but were backed by country studio musicians and had minor success with numbers like 'Rock Love' and 'Hi De Ank Tum'. They were basically only a recording act since family touring made live appearances difficult for Nita and Ruby. Rita also never conquered stage fright; the trio broke up and she retired. Ruby began to sing with her sister, Carol Sue Wright, as the Wright Sisters, recording (again with Atkins) for Cadence, who saw them as a female version of the label's popular Everly Brothers. In 1964, she had a Top 15 solo US country and minor pop hit with 'Dern Ya', a female answer song to Roger Miller's 'Dang Me'. In the late 60s, she made the country chart with her Epic label recordings of 'A New Place To Hang Your Hat' and 'A Better Deal Than This'. During the 1970's, she recorded for several small labels including Plantation and Scorpion and had some success with 'Yester-me, Yester-you, Yesterday'. She continued to appear with her parents' show but in the 1980's, along with her sister Carol Sue, took to running the family Museum and Tourist attraction in Nashville.
Albums: *Dern Ya* (1966), as Nita, Rita & Ruby *Rock Love* (1985).

Wynette, Tammy

b. Virginia Wynette Pugh, 5 May 1942, Itawamba County, near Tupelo, Mississippi, USA. Wynette is primarily known for two songs, 'Stand By Your Man' and 'D.I.V.O.R.C.E.', but her huge catalogue includes 20 US country number 1 hits, mostly about standing by your man or getting divorced. After her father died when she was 10-months-old, she was raised by her mother and

grandparents and she picked cotton from an early age. When 17-years-old, she married construction worker, Euple Byrd, and trained as a hairdresser. She subsequently made an album with their third child, Tina - *George, Tammy And Tina* in 1975. Byrd did not share her ambition of being a country singer, so she left and moved to Nashville. She impressed producer Billy Sherrill and had her first success in 1966 with a Johnny Paycheck song, 'Apartment No. 9'. She almost topped the US country charts with 'I Don't Want To Play House', in which a child shuns his friends' game because he senses his parents' unhappiness. It was the template for numerous songs including 'Bedtime Story' in which Wynette attempts to explain divorce to a three-year-old and 'D.I.V.O.R.C.E.' in which she does not.
Her own marriage to guitarist Don Chapel disintegrated after he traded nude photographs of her and, after witnessing an argument, country star George Jones eloped with her. Not knowing the turmoil of her own life, American feminists in 1968 condemned Wynette for supporting her husband, right or wrong, in 'Stand By Your Man', but she maintains, 'Sherrill and I didn't have women's lib in mind. All we wanted to do was to write a pretty love song'. The way Wynette chokes on 'After all, he's just a man' indicates pity rather than than support. Having previously recorded a country chart-topper with David Houston ('My Elusive Dreams'), an artistic collaboration with George Jones was inevitable. Their albums scaled new heights in over-the-top romantic duets, particularly 'The Ceremony', which narrates the marriage vows set to music. In an effort to separate Jones from alcohol, she confiscated his car-keys, only to find him riding their electric lawn-mower to the nearest bar. 'The Bottle' was aimed at George as accurately as the real thing. 'Stand By Your Man' was used to good effect in *Five Easy Pieces* (which starred Jack Nicholson), and the record became a UK number 1 on its sixth reissue in 1975. It was followed by a UK Top 20 placing for 'D.I.V.O.R.C.E.', but it was Billy Connolly's cover-parody about his D.O.G. that went to the UK number 1 slot.
Wynette also had two best-selling compilations in the UK album charts. By now her marriage to Jones was over and 'Dear Daughters' explains the position to them. Jones, in more dramatic fashion, retaliated with 'The Battle'. Even more difficult to explain to her daughters is her 44-day marriage to estate agent, Michael Tomlin. After torrid affairs with Rudy Gatlin (of Larry Gatlin And The Gatlin

Tammy Wynette

Brothers) and Burt Reynolds (she saved the actor's life when he passed out in the bath), she married record producer, George Richey, whose own stormy marriage had just ended. In 1978, she was kidnapped outside a Nashville car-park and was subjected to a brutal beating. She has also experienced many health problems including several stomach operations. Throughout the traumas, she continued to record songs about married life, 'That's The Way It Could Have Been', 'Til I Can Make It On My Own', '(You Make Me Want To Be) A Mother' and 'Love Doesn't Always Come (On The Night That It's Needed)'. None of these songs have found acceptance outside the country market, but 'Stand By Your Man' has become a standard with versions ranging from Loretta Lynn (who also took an opposing view in 'The Pill'), Billie Jo Spears and Tina Turner, to two male performers, David Allan Coe and Lyle Lovett.

Her autobiography was made into a television movie in 1981. In 1986, Wynette entered the Betty Ford clinic for drug dependency and, true to form, followed it with a single, 'Alive And Well'. She played in a daytime soap, *Capital*, in 1987, although its drama was light-relief when compared to her own life. Her stage show includes a lengthy walkabout to sing 'Stand By Your Man' to individual members of the audience. Her standing in the rock world increased when she was co-opted with the KLF on 'Justified And Ancient' which became a Top 3 UK hit in 1991. Her duet album, *Higher Ground* is more imaginatively produced than her other recent albums and, although she undoubtedly has many more dramas to come, she says, 'All I really want to do is stay country and keep going 'til I'm older than Roy Acuff.'

Albums: *Your Good Girl's Gonna Go Bad* (1967), *Take Me To Your World* (1967), *D.I.V.O.R.C.E.*

(1967), *Stand By Your Man* (1968), *Inspiration* (1969), *The Ways To Love A Man* (1969), *Run Angel Run* (1969), *Tammy's Touch* (1970), *The First Lady* (1970), *Christmas With Tammy Wynette* (1970), *We Sure Can Love Each Other* (1971), with George Jones *We Go Together* (1971), *Bedtime Story* (1972), with Jones *Me And The First Lady* (1972), *My Man* (1972), with Jones *We Love To Sing About Jesus* (1972), *Kids Say The Darndest Things* (1973), with Jones *Let's Build A World Together* (1973), with Jones *We're Gonna Hold On* (1973), *Another Lonely Song* (1974), *Woman To Woman* (1974), *George, Tammy And Tina* (1975), *I Still Believe In Fairy Tales* (1975), *Til I Can Make It On My Own* (1976), with Jones *Golden Ring* (1976), *You And Me* (1976), *Let's Get Together* (1977), *One Of A Kind* (1977), *Womanhood* (1978), *Just Tammy* (1979), *Only Lonely Sometimes* (1980), with Jones *Together Again* (1980), *You Brought Me Back* (1981), *Good Love And Heartbreak* (1982), *Soft Touch* (1982), *Even The Strong Get Lonely* (1983), *Sometimes When We Touch* (1985), *Higher Ground* (1987), *Next To You* (1989), *Heart Over Mind* (1990). Compilations: *Tammy's Greatest Hits* (1969), *Tammy's Greatest Hits, Volume II* (1971), *Best Of Tammy Wynette* (1975), *Classic Collection* (1982), *Biggest Hits* (1983), *Anniversary: 20 Years Of Hits* (1987), *Tears Of Fire - The 25th Anniversary Collection* (1992, 3CD set).

Further reading: *Stand By Your Man*, Tammy Wynette with Joan Dew.

Y

Yearwood, Trisha

b. Georgia, USA. In 1985, Yearwood started working as a session singer in Nashville. She was discovered by Garth Brooks and sang backing vocals on his album, *No Fences*. She was the opening act on his 1991 tour and became the first female singer to top the US country charts with her debut single, 'She's In Love With The Boy'. Further singles like 'The Woman Before Me' and 'Wrong Side Of Memphis' have not done so well, but her albums, which combine quality songs with star guests, have a long shelf life.
Albums: *Trisha Yearwood* (1991), *Hearts In Armor* (1992).

Yoakam, Dwight

b. 23 October 1956, Pikesville, Kentucky, USA. A singer/songwriter with an early love of the country honky-tonk music of Buck Owens and Lefty Frizzell who has always shown a distinct hatred of the Nashville pop/country scene. He briefly sought Nashville success in the mid-70s but his music was rated too country even for the *Grand Ole Opry*. He relocated to Los Angeles in 1978 and worked the clubs, playing with various bands including Los Lobos but for several years, he worked as a truck driver to earn his living. In 1984, the release of a mini album on the Enigma label led to him signing for Warner Brothers. In 1986, he registered Top 5 US country chart hits with Johnny Horton's 'Honky Tonk Man' and his own 'Guitars, Cadillacs'. His driving honky-tonk music made him a popular visitor to Britain and gave him some success in the USA but his outspoken views probably prevented greater fame. In 1987, he scored with his version of the old Elvis Presley pop hit 'Little Sister'. He followed it in 1988 with a number 9 hit with his idol Lefty Frizzell's classic 'Always Late (With Your Kisses)' and a number 1 with his self-penned 'I Sang Dixie'. He also had a duet number 1 of 'The Streets Of Bakersfield' with veteran 60s superstar Buck Owens, with whom he played live concerts, after being partly instrumental in persuading Owens to come out of retirement and again record for Capitol. Like Don Williams and others, he seems permanently attached to his stetson, while the graphic designers of his album sleeves would seem to suggest that his long jean-clad legs and backside are his main selling features. There seems little doubt that Yoakam's songwriting talents and singing style will ensure further major success and some of his honky- tonk music has done much to attract the rock audiences, much in the way that Garth Brooks has done. His straight country style is what attracts rock audiences, however: his attempt to cross over into the mainstream rock market with the ill-conceived *La Croix D'Amour* was little short of a disaster.
Albums: *Guitars, Cadillacs* (1986), *Hillbilly DeLuxe* (1987), *Buenas Noches From A Lonely Room* (1988), *Just Lookin' For A Hit* (1989), *If There Was A Way* (1991), *La Croix D'Amour* (1992).

Young, Faron

b. 25 February 1932, Shreveport, Louisiana, USA. Young was raised on the farm his father bought just outside Shreveport and learned to play the guitar and sing country songs as a boy. Greatly influenced by Hank Williams (in his early days he was something of a sound-alike) and while still at school, he formed a country band and began to establish a local reputation as an entertainer. In 1950, he gave up his college studies to accept an offer of a professional career and joined radio station KWKH, where he soon became a member of the prestigious *Louisiana Hayride* show and found other work in the nightclubs and honky tonks. He became friends with Webb Pierce and for a time toured with him as a vocalist with Pierce's band. In 1951, he made his first recordings for the Gotham label with Tillman Franks and his band and achieved minor success with 'Have I Waited Too Long' and 'Tattle Tale Eyes' before he joined Capitol Records. In the summer of 1952, Faron was dating a girl called Billie Jean Jones, when she attracted the attention of Hank Williams. He persuaded Faron to arrange a double date, which resulted in Hank threatening him with a pistol and claiming Jones for his own. Young backed off and Billie Jean became the second Mrs Hank Williams. In 1953, Young formed his own band, moved to Nashville, where he became a member of the *Grand Ole Opry* and gained his first US country chart hit with a self-penned song called 'Goin' Steady' . His career was interrupted when, because of the Korean War, he was drafted into the army. Although interrupted by this, his career certainly benefited from the exposure he received after winning an army talent competition. This led to him touring the world entertaining US forces, as well as appearing on recruiting shows that were networked to hundreds of radio stations. Young

Dwight Yoakam

returned to Nashville in November 1954 and resumed his career, gaining his first US country number 1 the following year with 'Live Fast, Love Hard, Die Young' .

This established him beyond any doubt as a major recording star and between 1955 and 1969 he amassed a total of 63 US country chart hits of which 46 made the Top 20. He developed the knack of picking the best material by other writers and had a number 2 hit with Don Gibson's 'Sweet Dreams' and further number 1s with Roy Drusky's songs 'Alone With You' and 'Country Girl'. In 1961, he recorded 'Hello Walls' thus making the song one of the first Willie Nelson compositions to be recorded by a major artist. It reached number 1 in the US country charts, also became a Top 20 US pop hit and was Young's first million seller. In 1956, his popularity as a singer earned him a role in the film *Hidden Guns*. This led to his own nickname of The Young Sheriff and his band being called the Country Deputies. (At one time Roger Miller was a member of the band). In later years he became the Singing Sheriff before, as he once suggested, someone queried his age and started asking 'What's he trying to prove?'. After the initial success with this easily forgettable b-western, he made further film appearances over the years including *Daniel Boone, Stampede, Raiders Of Old California, Country Music Holiday, A Gun And A Gavel, Road To Nashville* and *That's Country*. He left Capitol for Mercury in 1962, immediately charting with 'The Yellow Bandanna', 'You' ll Drive Me Back' and a fine duet recording with Margie Singleton of 'Keeping Up With The Joneses'.

In 1965, he had a US country Top 10 hit with 'Walk Tall', a song which had been a UK pop hit for Val Doonican the previous year. Young quit the *Opry* in the mid-60s, finding, like several other artists, that it was not only difficult keeping up the expected number of Saturday night appearances but also that he lost a lot of lucrative bookings. After the success of 'Hello Walls', he perhaps unintentionally tended to look for further pop chart hits and in consequence his recordings, at times, became less country in their arrangements but he soon returned to his country roots, usually choosing his favourite twin fiddle backings. Young easily kept his popularity throughout the 60s and 70s and toured extensively in the USA and made several visits to Europe, where he performed in the UK, France and Germany. He appeared on all the major network television shows but seemed to have little interest in having his own regular series.

At times he has not endeared himself to some of his fellow performers with his imitations of their acts. The 70s found him still a major star with a series of Top 10 hits including 'Step Aside', 'Leavin' And Saying Goodbye', 'This Little Girl Of Mine' and 'Just What I Had In Mind' . 'It's Four In The Morning', another country number 1, had crossover success and also gave him a second million-seller. It also became his only UK pop chart success, peaking at number 3 during a 23 week chart run. He left Mercury in 1979 and briefly joined MCA. In 1988, he joined Step One and 'Stop And Take The Time', a minor hit, became country chart entry number 85. Over the years he has become involved in several business interests and apart from losing heavily in the 60s, in respect of investments to convert an old baseball stadium into a stock car racing track in Nashville, he has been very successful. Young became involved in publishing companies, a recording studio, a booking agency plus co-ownership of *Music City News* newspaper. He has always been noted for very plain speaking and has incurred the wrath of the establishment on several occasions for his outspoken views. A suggested association with Patsy Cline led to various stories of his dalliances and whether correct or not, it may well be that he has revelled in the publicity they caused.

In September 1972, he gained unwanted publicity by his reaction to an incident at a show. At a time when 'This Little Girl Of Mine' was a hit for him, he invited six-year-old Nora Jo Catlett to join him on stage in Clarksville, West Virginia. She refused, whereupon Young swore at the audience, stormed off stage, grabbed the child and spanked her repeatedly. (The child collected autographs and had been told by her mother not to approach the stage but to wait near the front until Young finished his act.) The child's father swore out a warrant for his arrest and after pleading guilty to a charge of assault, he was fined $35. The following year a civil action claiming $200,000 was filed. In his defence, Young claimed the child spat in his face. Eventually, almost two years later, the Catlett family were awarded only $3400. He has been involved in various actions, once stating 'I am not an alcoholic, I'm a drunk' and on one occasion, he shot out the light fittings of a Nashville bar. He is reputed to have had affairs with many women while remaining supposedly happily married. In 1987, after 34 years of marriage, his wife finally obtained a divorce on the grounds of physical abuse. She claimed that he had also threatened her and their 16-year-old daughter with a gun and often shot holes in the kitchen ceiling. It may perhaps be more accurate to describe him as the singing outlaw rather than the singing sheriff! Perhaps a fair summing up would be to quote the heading from an article written in 1980 by Bob Allen, who parodied Young's hit song by writing 'Live Fast, Love Hard And Keep On Cussin'. He is now semi-retired but still makes concert performances as well as guest appearances on the *Opry*.

Albums: *Sweethearts Or Strangers* (1957), *The Object Of My Affection* (1958), *My Garden Of Prayer* (1959), *This Is Faron Young* (1959), *Talk About Hits* (1959), *Sings The Best Of Faron Young* (1960), *Hello Walls* (1961), *The Young Approach* (1961), *All-Time Great Hits* (1963), *This Is Faron* (1963), *Aims At The West* (1963), *Memory Lane* (1964), *Country Dance Favorites* (1964), *Songs For Country Folks* (1964), *Story Songs Of Mountains And Valleys* (1964), *Falling In Love* (1965), *Pen And Paper* (1965), *Faron Young* (1966), *Sings The Best Of Jim Reeves* (1966), *If You Ain' t Lovin', You Ain't Livin'* (1966), *It's A Great Life* (1966), *Unmitigated Gall* (1967), *Here's Faron Young* (1968), *I' ll Be Yours* (1968), *This Is Faron Young* (1968), *Just Out Of Reach* (1968), *The World Of Faron Young* (1968), *I' ve Got Precious Memories* (1969), *Wine Me Up* (1969), *20 Hits Over The Years* (1969), *Occasional Wife/If I Ever Fall In Love With A Honky Tonk Girl* (1970), *Leavin' And Sayin' Goodbye* (1971), *Step Aside* (1971), *It's Four In The Morning* (1972), *This Little Girl Of Mine* (1972), *This Time The Hurtin's On Me* (1973), *Just What I Had In Mind* (1973), *Some Kind Of Woman* (1974), *A Man And His Music* (1975), *I' d Just Be Fool Enough* (1976), *That Young Feelin'* (1977), *Chapter Two* (1979), *Free And Easy* (1980), *The Young Sheriff (1955-1956 Radio Broadcasts)* (1981), *The Sheriff* (1984), with Jerry Lee Lewis, Webb Pierce, Mel Tillis *Four Legends* (1985), *Here's To You* (1988), *Country Christmas* (1990), *The Classic Years* 5 CD set (1992), with Ray Price *Memories That Last* (1992). Compilations: *Greatest Hits Volumes 1, 2 & 3* (1988), *The Classic Years 1952 - 1962* (1992).

Young, Steve

b. 12 July 1942, Noonan, Georgia, USA. Young has claimed to be the reincarnation of a cavalry officer in the American Civil War and one of his songs about reincarnation is 'In The Ways Of The Indian'. He was raised in Alabama and his superb 'Montgomery In The Rain' is about congregating around Hank Williams' grave. Young played folk music in New York and various southern towns before moving to Los Angeles. In 1968 he recorded as part of the group Stone Country for

Steve Young

RCA. Then in 1969, he made his first album, *Rock, Salt And Nails*, for A&M Records with sessionmen including James Burton, Gene Clark and Gram Parsons. It included a song written while he was homesick, the pastoral and mystical 'Seven Bridges Road', which has been recorded by Rita Coolidge and Joan Baez and, with commercial success, by the Eagles. Young's albums often repeat songs but sometimes for good reason: 'I originally did 'Lonesome, On'ry And Mean' as a bluesy bluegrass song in 3/4, but Waylon Jennings turned it into a rocker in 4/4. I got intrigued by that and so I did it that way too.' He dedicated the autobiographical 'Renegade Picker' to Jerry Lee Lewis because 'he refuses to play it safe'. *No Place To Fall*, was delayed because RCA were too busy pressing Elvis Presley albums following his death and Young's career lost momentum. He also had to combat drug and alcohol addiction. 'Every waking moment I was drinking and I just didn't care. I don't do drink or drugs anymore, but I am into Zen meditation, which certainly helps my creativity.' Although Young is better known as a songwriter, his only US country success is with Willie Nelson's 'It's Not Supposed To Be That Way'. He has made several engaging UK appearances, often in country clubs and with a sense of humour which belies his grim material. 'I don't think of myself as a country singer or a folk singer. What I do comes from Southern roots, American roots, and I just let it go where it goes.'

Albums: *Rock, Salt And Nails* (1969), *Seven Bridges Road* (1972), *Honky Tonk Man* (1975), *Renegade Picker* (1976), *No Place To Fall* (1977), *To Satisfy You* (1981), *Look Homeward Angel* (1986), *Long Time Rider* (1990), *Solo, Live* (1991).

The Guinness Encyclopedia of Popular Music

Compiled and Edited by Colin Larkin

' A landmark work. As much as the history of popular music deserves. ★★★★★' *Q Magazine*

'This is an absolutely invaluable addition to any musicologist's shelf.' *Vox*

The most comprehensive and authoritative guide to popular music that has ever been published, *The Guinness Encyclopedia of Popular Music* covers every important artist, band, genre, group, event, instrument, publisher, promoter, record company and musical style from the world of popular music in four 832-page volumes in a slipcase.

The product of over four years of intensive labour by an international group of more than 100 skilled writers, musicologists and advisors, its scope is truly global. Compiled in an A-Z format, it covers all forms of popular music from 1900 to 1992 and contains almost 10,000 entries varying in length from 100 to 5,000 words.

A bibliography of over 4,000 entries is included along with a full index of artists' names.

For further details of this essential reference work, please write to:
Section D,
The Marketing Department,
Guinness Publishing,
33 London Road,
Enfield,
Middlesex EN2 6DJ,
England.

Proposed Titles for Inclusion in the

'Guinness Who's Who of Popular Music Series'

The Guinness Who's Who of 50s Music
The Guinness Who's Who of 60s Music★
The Guinness Who's Who of 70s Music★
The Guinness Who's Who of 80s Music
The Guinness Who's Who of Indie and New Wave Music★
The Guinness Who's Who of Blues Music★
The Guinness Who's Who of Folk Music
The Guinness Who's Who of Reggae
The Guinness Who's Who of Soul Music
The Guinness Who's Who of Country Music★
The Guinness Who's Who of Jazz★
The Guinness Who's Who of Heavy Metal Music★
The Guinness Who's Who of Gospel Music
The Guinness Who's Who of UK Rock and Pop
The Guinness Who's Who of USA Rock and Pop
The Guinness Who's Who of Danceband Pop
The Guinness Who's Who of World Music
The Guinness Who's Who of Stage Musicals

★ Already published

For further information on any of these titles please write to:
Section D,
The Marketing Department,
Guinness Publishing,
33 London Road,
Enfield,
Middlesex EN2 6DJ,
England

The Guinness Who's Who of Jazz

General Editor: Colin Larkin

The history of jazz is a long and varied one, from its beginnings in the whorehouses and bars of the turn of the century, to the top concert halls of today. Encapsulating the embryonic forms of New Orleans, trad, boogie-woogie, and the ragtime of Louis Armstrong, Jelly Roll Morton, Scott Joplin and Fats Waller, The Guinness Who's Who of Jazz, follows the progress of jazz through the big bands and jive artists such as Paul Whitman, Bix Biederbeck, Duke Ellington, Count Basie, Glenn Miller, Cab Calloway and Louis Jordan on to the present day, via the innovative bop sounds of the 50s and 60s with Miles Davis, John Coltrane, Coleman Hawkins, Dave Brubeck, Dizzy Gillespie and the modern sounds of Andy Shepard, John Surman, Wynton Marsalis, Elton Dean and Courtney Pine. Special consideration is given to the talent of the past decade, making this book instantly more accessible than all its rivals.

The Guinness Who's Who of Jazz also contains entries on the various noted orchestra and band sidemen, the composers, arrangers and label owners. With hundreds of entries it will become an indispensable book for aficionados of the music and will act as an introduction to its many newcomers.

This book is available from all good bookshops and selected record stores. For information on this or on forthcoming titles in the series, please write to:

Section D,
The Marketing Department,
Guinness Publishing,
33 London Road,
Enfield,
Middlesex EN2 6DJ,
England

The Guinness Who's Who of Sixties Music

General Editor: Colin Larkin

From the publishers of *The Guinness Encyclopedia of Popular Music* comes the definitive guide to the groups and artists who created the music of the 60s. From the early years of Del Shannon, Bobby Darin, Ricky Nelson, and Cliff Richard; the Beach Boys, Jan and Dean and the Shangri-Las to the beat-boom with the Beatles and the Rolling Stones; the 'swinging London' era of the Who and the Kinks, and the explosion of sound from California's west coast with the Byrds, Doors, Jefferson Airplane and Grateful Dead. Folk protest, the blues boom, psychedelia, soul, jazz, ska, Merseybeat, pirate radio plus the impact on a whole generation by Bob Dylan - it's all told here with information on the musicians, songwriters and personalities.

From those who survived to those lost in the mists of time, everything you'd ever want to know is included in this complete and accurate record of the music and major artists of the decade. With hundreds of entries written by some of today's leading rock writers, this is the definative guide to the movers and shakers of 60s music.

This book is available from all good bookshops and from selected record stores. For information on this or on forthcoming titles in the series, please write to:

Section D,
The Marketing Department,
Guinnesss Publishing,
33 London Road,
Enfield,
Middlesex EN2 6DJ,
England

The Guinness Who's Who of Indie and New Wave Music

General Editor: Colin Larkin

From the publishers of *The Guinness Encyclopedia of Popular Music* comes the definitive guide to the groups and artists who have moulded the shape of popular music in the 70s 80s and 90s. From the beginnings of punk in the late-70s with the Sex Pistols, Clash, Damned, X-Ray Spex and the Buzzcocks in the UK, and Television, Talking Heads, Blondie and the Ramones in the US, modern popular music was shaken to its foundations. These bands paved the way in the ensuing years for many new and varied forms of exciting music including Siouxsie And The Banshees, Joy Division/New Order, the Cure, Smiths, Cocteau Twins, Birthday Party, Jesus And Mary Chain, Happy Mondays, Stone Roses, James and R.E.M.

This book contains entries on all these bands plus many others on groups and artists who are usually, and unjustifiably, ignored in lesser encyclopedias. In all, there are hundreds of entries including contributions by some of the leading pop and indie writers today plus an introduction by Johnny Rogan.

This book is available from all good bookshops and from selected record stores. For information on this or on forthcoming titles in the series, please write to:

Section D,
The Marketing Department,
Guinness Publishing,
33 London Road,
Enfield,
Middlesex,
EN2 6DJ,
England.

The Guinness Who's Who of Blues

General Editor: Colin Larkin

From the publishers of *The Guinness Encyclopedia of Popular Music* comes the definitive guide to the Blues. The return of Eric Clapton and Gary Moore to their blues roots has coincided with the rise of musicians such as Robert Cray and Jeff Healey. This, together with the phenominal revival of John Lee Hooker's career with *The Healer* and *Boom Boom* puts us in the midst of the biggest blues boom since the 60s. Collected in this volume are the artists who shaped the blues, which in turn greatly influenced the development of popular music in the 20th century. Included are, Elmore James, Robert Johnson, Muddy Waters, B.B. King, Lightnin' Hopkins, Leadbelly, Buddy Guy and Albert Collins; the great singers Bessie Smith, Victoria Spivey, Billie Holiday, Big Joe Turner and Koko Taylor and the legion of white musician's who have popularized the blues since the 60s, such as Alexis Korner, Paul Butterfield, Mike Bloomfield, Roy Buchanan, John Mayall, Johnny Winter, Peter Green and Stevie Ray Vaughan.

This book is available from all good bookshops and from selected record stores. For information on this or on forthcoming titles in the series, please write to:

Section D,
The Marketing Department,
Guinness Publishing,
33 London Road,
Enfield,
Middlesex,
EN2 6DJ,
England.